CASES AND NOTES ON LAND LAW

Cases and Notes on Land Law

The Honourable Bora Laskin
A Justice of Appeal in the Supreme Court of Ontario
Formerly Professor of Law in the Faculty
of Law, University of Toronto

UNIVERSITY OF TORONTO PRESS

Reprinted in 2018

Reprinted, 1959
Revised Edition, 1964
Reprinted in the U.S.A. 1966, 1969

ISBN 8020 2031 3

ISBN 978-1-4875-7706-3 (paper)

PREFACE

THIS COLLECTION OF CASES, notes and statutes, leavened here and there by text (some borrowed and some contributed by me), is an attempt to bring together in an orderly fashion material on land law with a Canadian emphasis which might be useful as a teaching aid in any Canadian common law school. I entertain some hope that the practising lawyer may also find the collection useful as a source of selective authorities on the matters covered, as well as providing him with some analytical and critical approaches to problems falling within the limits of my treatment of the subject of land law.

The scope and arrangement of the materials included in the book reflect the distribution of property teaching in the University of Toronto Faculty of Law, a distribution which shows a compulsory first year course in personal property and land law, a compulsory second year course in real estate transactions, an optional third year course in community planning law, and a compulsory third year course in wills and trusts (administration of estates) which emphasizes also estate planning. This is, by no means, the only accepted or possible distribution for Canadian purposes, and I am aware that my collection straddles several courses in other Canadian common law schools given in different years.

While my scheme of organization exhibits what I believe is a necessary concession to history in this subject, I have, with this limitation, pointed my selection of materials to the contemporary understanding and use of the principles and institutions of land law as seen through Canadian case law and legislation. There is little room for pride here in originality either by our judges (for whom, however, there was the extenuation of *stare decisis*) or by our legislators. Landlord and tenant law, which takes up a relatively generous portion of this casebook, is a good illustration of a rather indiscriminate adherence to English doctrines without much effort to examine the different roles played by the lease here and in England. From time to time, in the notes to the cases reproduced in full or in part, I have suggested alternative or connected lines of inquiry designed to shake out some of the inevitability in which land law is often shrouded. It is not intended by this to make a fetish of uncertainty or to confuse, but simply to induce students (and lawyers too) to sharpen their critical faculties and powers of analysis and to use them in land law as they do in such subjects as contracts and torts.

While England has gone much farther in statutory reform of land law than we have in Canada, it is of interest to note a recent call there for a more contemporary approach to the subject. Professor Hargreaves in a review article on the seventh edition of Cheshire's standard text, The Modern Law of Real Property, had this to say about English land law: "Not since Littleton has there been a serious attempt to isolate its principles from their historic origin, to examine them as living contributions to contemporary thought, and to apply them in the construction of a systematic analysis of the whole field which would satisfy the demands of scientific jurisprudence and prove worthy of the greatest system of property law that the world has ever known" (Modern Real Property, (1956) 19 Mod. L. Rev. 14). The United States has been much more alive to this kind of call, as witness works like the American Law Institute's Restatement of Property, Professor Powell's treatise on Real Property and the seven-volume work entitled American Law of Property. There has been nothing in Canada comparable to the English texts, let alone those in the United States (where there is a proliferation of general casebooks and specialized treatises as well). We have to go back to Armour's second edition of Real Property, 1916, to find any general treatment of the subject, and this is a work which, basically, is founded on Blackstone. We will get no farther than Armour unless it be by the efforts of the law teachers, to whom Professor Hargreaves feels England too will have to look for any systematic study of basic land law problems.

There are three particular professional acknowledgments which I most happily make in addition to the general acknowledgment of help that one accepts as of course from earlier and older toilers in the field. Professor R. R. Powell of Columbia University School of Law and his publishers, Matthew Bender and Company Inc., Albany, New York, have kindly given me permission to reproduce verbatim sections 17 to 28 inclusive of volume 1 of Professor Powell's admirable treatise on Real Property. Similarly, West Publishing Co., Saint Paul, Minnesota, have allowed me to reproduce the following portions of the late Professor Bigelow's Introduction to the Law of Real Property: chapter 1, section 6; chapter 2, sections 7 and 8; and the first third of chapter 5. The third professional acknowledgment is to the American Law Institute for its permission, readily given, to quote in full the following materials from the Restatement of Property: sections 9, 18, 19 (and comment), 20 (and comment a), 21 (and comment a), 22, 457, 458, 459, and comment to section 450(e), comment a to section 453, and comment c to section 483.

I am under obligation also to the Incorporated Council of Law Reporting for England and Wales for its permission to reproduce cases and attendant fact statements in the law reports published under its auspices.

The toil and tedium associated with the preparation of a casebook such as this were shared with me by Mrs. David Fuller and Miss Margaret McKellar who typed my manuscript, and I am glad to record my appreciation of their assistance. Miss Jean Houston of the University of Toronto Press provided valuable help in her supervision of the technical side of the printing and publication of this volume.

BORA LASKIN

Faculty of Law
University of Toronto

I have seized upon the occasion of a reprinting of this book to make a few minor revisions and to bring the statutory references, particularly for British Columbia and Ontario, up to date.

September 1, 1964 B.L.

CONTENTS

TABLE OF CASES

[A page number in italics indicates a case that is reproduced in full or in some material part. The other page numbers indicate cases that are abstracted or referred to in connection with a problem or as illustrative of the text.]

CASES AND NOTES ON LAND LAW

INTRODUCTION

A PERSON embarking on legal studies is bound to be impressed by two features of the land law of Canada's common law provinces: first, its long history and consequent early emergence (compared with other branches of law) as a relatively well-formed and compact body of law; and secondly, its terminology. Land law as treated here is only part, albeit a significant part, of the more embracive law of property. As a basic institution of society, property has been variously analyzed, justified and explained by philosophers, political scientists, sociologists, economists and lawyers; and as a concept, it has undergone constant evolution, from being regarded as, largely, a mere tangible to a more refined appreciation that it is a cluster of values related to, or an expression of, the kind of society that recognizes them and the kind of legal system that protects them. The central place that land occupied in early thinking and legal concern with property needs no elaboration. As an object or thing that gave rise to a system of relations governing its acquisition, use and disposition, it also threw off "values" that had no tangible character and some of which were defined as "incorporeal" in contrast to its own corporeality. The easy confusion between a thing and the legally protected interests in it showed the need for a more exact terminology (especially when those interests began to multiply), lest analysis and evaluation should bog down in a semantic swamp: see, for example, the attempt at an exact vocabulary in the *Restatement of Property*, vol. 1, chaps. 1 and 2.

Because our land law in Canada (excluding Quebec) is still marked by its English origins—even more so than the present English law—and because much of it is intelligible only in the light of its history, it will be useful to begin study of the subject by summarizing its historical foundations. A brief explanation may be made at this point of the scope of the expression "land law". It is intended to cover not only what is usually subsumed under the title "real property" law but also "landlord and tenant" law. In the inherited English development, the forms of action determined the classification of interests in land, and real property was distinguished from personalty according to whether an action was or was not available for specific recovery of the subject matter of the litigation. On this basis, leasehold interests were classified as personal property, although even before the end of the fifteenth century the remedy of specific recovery became available for such interests. Additionally, the leasehold was used for investment purposes, to some extent to escape the church's prohibition of usury; and the essentially contractual relationship of landlord and tenant distinguished this system of landholding from the feudal real property system. English law thus rejected the civil law distinction between immovables and movables. Important consequences ensued from the division of real and personal property. Before the modern enactments on intestate succession, real property descended to the heir (under the primogeniture principle of the common law) and personalty descended to the intestate's personal representative, i.e., the administrator appointed by the court, who was, of course, obliged to deal with it according to the law of succession. In testate devolution a leasehold as personalty could be bequeathed at a time when a will of real property was still prohibited. Even today, where a testator in merely general terms leaves his real property to one beneficiary and his personalty to another, any leaseholds he held will go to the beneficiary of the personalty. Modern legislation, as, for example, in Ontario, now provides that upon a person's death, whether testate or intestate, all his real and personal property shall go to his personal representative (executor or administrator) in trust for the persons by law beneficially entitled thereto: see Devolution of Estates Act, R.S.O. 1960, c. 106, section 2; see for a similar provision Devolution of Real Property Act, R.S.A. 1955 c. 83, sections 3 and 4; Devolution of Estates Act, R.S.M. 1954, c. 63, section 17; Devolution of Estates Act, R.S.N.B. 1952, c. 62, section 3; Devolution of Real Property Act, R.S.S. 1953, c. 118, sections 4 and 5. These provisions are related to the administration of estates and leave the dichotomy of realty and personalty unaffected in substance; see, for example, the problem raised in *Re Gauthier*, [1944] O.R. 401, [1944] 3 D.L.R. 401, on whether a mortgagee's estate in mortgaged land is, on his death, personalty or realty and whether the right to the mortgage money is personalty; and see Annotation by Dr. J. D. Falconbridge, [1944] 3 D.L.R. 405. The distinction between realty and personalty exists not only on the level of estates in land but also in respect of interests such as an easement which is realty or personalty according to the nature of the dominant tenement to which it is appurtenant. Moreover, interests such as easements and profits à prendre may be created either as descendible interests or for a term of years only.

[On the institution of property, which has a vast literature, see *Cohen*, Property and Sovereignty, (1927) 13 Cornell L. Quarterly 8; 1 *Powell*, Real Property, chap. 2.]

CHAPTER I

HISTORICAL BACKGROUND

1. THE FEUDAL SYSTEM

A CONVENIENT STARTING POINT for examination of the foundations of land law is the Norman Conquest in 1066 which gave England a distinctive feudalism, as elaborated below. For a general discussion, see *Stenton*, English Feudalism; 1 *Pollock and Maitland*, History of English Law, 2nd ed., pp. 64-73, 229-406; *Plucknett*, Concise History of the Common Law (1956, 5th ed.), pp. 506-545.

1 POWELL, REAL PROPERTY (1949)

§ 17. The Conquest as the point of beginning.

It is said above that at the time of the Conquest two great river systems of the past joined forces. The cultural inheritances grouped together in the forces of the invading William came to live, and eventually, to mingle, with the ways of life which had grown in the preceding centuries on the island of Great Britain.

The Britons, Celtic in ancestry and occupying all of Great Britain down to the fifth century A.D., remained largely unaltered by Roman influence during the four and a half centuries of Roman military occupation (55 B.C. to 407 A.D.). The invading hordes from Jutland, from the Danish islands, and from the northern central parts of modern Germany were not as tolerant as the Romans had been. They came in waves. The earliest were Jutes (449). Then followed wave on wave of Angles and of Saxons over a period of three hundred fifty years (450-800). Two more centuries of victorious Danish immigration occurred. As a result the Britons were gradually pushed back into the rugged areas of Wales, across protecting waters into Ireland and, to a lesser degree, into the fortresses of Scotland. The Britain of modern times had become the land of the Angles, Saxons, Jutes and Danes.

The law of these new peoples was one derived from northern central Europe with almost no Celtic or Roman ingredients. The importance in this law of the concept of the "folk" has been well stressed by Jolliffe. "As tribalism is more or less clearly seen to be the age when kindred and the blood-tie govern society, as feudalism is that when land-right determines privilege, duty and status, so this is the era of the folk, an era in which the nations have ceased to wander and settled life begins to enforce the lesson that society has other ties than common blood, yet before agriculture and its gains begin to breed the conviction that a man's social and political virtue is drawn from the land he holds." Looseness and impermanence of grouping and diversity of law from place to place were characteristic of the Anglo-Saxon society. Herein one finds the amazing power of rules derived from local customs to survive the centuries of feudalism and to persist even in our present law. Three modes of land holding appear to have had considerable recognition. Land held by "bookright" had its qualities fixed by the written charter or "book", given usually by the king to some church order or dignitary. Land of private persons, held on terms fixed by the customs of a community, was spoken of as "folkright". The church and some of the most land-wealthy persons loaned out land for periods often measured by lives, in return for agreed services. Such land was designated as "laen-land". These types of land interests affected only a small percentage of those constituting the Anglo-Saxon society. Concerning the law operating as to the masses we know too little to make statements of present significance. As Jolliffe has said: "One thing only is clear, that the English peasantry moved across the line of the Conquest in every state of dependence and independence, status and relation to the state....

"We cannot guess the future of the society had it been left to work out its own fate. On the eve of the Conquest its bent was not fully decided. It was territorialized, but not feudalized. It had lordship but not tenure; its nobles by blood had died out and its official notables had yet to be recognized as a nobility. If ever it had reached the phase of feudalism it would have done so but slowly in the absence of foreign intervention. It is possible that, since it had already made the transition from the tribal to the territorial state and developed a stable local administration, a strong succession of native kings might have guided it to become a kingdom of the Scandinavian type, but with greater stability, a more closely knit community, and a more complex government. If the successors of Harold had failed in leadership the kingdom of England could hardly have survived, and the Humber and Thames might again have become national boundaries; normal ability in its kings would probably have kept the united kingdoms one. Thus the groundwork of a nation state had been laid, perhaps more truly than in any Continental kingdom. It remained for the Normans to engraft into the community the endurance of the fees and honours, ultimately strengthening the fabric of society though perhaps at some sacrifice of variety and energy, and to elaborate the court and household of the king into a judicial and fiscal machine which made a new chapter in the history of government. And with this we enter upon a third and well-defined phase of English history."

William brought with him from the Continent a relatively small group. This group, however, included persons of substantially different backgrounds. Stenton in his book on English Feudalism, 1066-1166, describes their diversities thus: "The Normans brought with them a tradition of centralization which, however often it might be broken by individuals, determined the general character of English feudalism. But the Normans formed only one of the elements from which English feudal society arose. In 1086, men bearing names derived from places outside the Norman border appear in every part of England. It is not always realized how greatly their presence must have complicated King William's essential task of bringing all his followers into the same general scheme of feudal relationships....

"The lands to the east of Normandy had supplied many knights to the army of the Conquest, and lords from Flanders, Picardy, and the Boulonnais can easily be traced in Domesday Book. Their settlement had begun early.... But in the eleventh century, Flanders like Normandy was a highly developed feudal state, and there can have been little in Norman custom which would seem strange to the average Flemish knight. The settlement which really complicated the first phase of English feudalism came from Brittany. There had been a large Breton contingent in the army of Hastings. The Bretons formed one of the three divisions in which it advanced against the English position, and many Breton lords received land in England....

"Little can be said in definite terms of the society which had been familiar to the Breton followers of the duke of Normandy. Contemporary records are few, and those which have survived are rarely as explicit as we could wish. Nevertheless, enough material has been preserved to show a fundamental difference between Breton and Norman feudalism at this date. The whole history of Brittany shows that the duke's authority was small when measured by Norman standards.... But the differences between Breton and Normandy society lie deeper. In the eleventh century, Breton knighthood was essentially a personal distinction, a mark of social status rather than a qualification for military service. Feudalism itself was an exotic institution in Brittany, imposed upon a society which in 1066 was still Celtic in character and in much of its organization. The evidence which comes from this time shows a most curious blending of Celtic and feudal ideas."

So the date of the Conquest provides a time at which two diverse lines of history met for mixing. It gives us, therefore, a convenient moment of time at which to begin this brief review of the evolution of the law of land tenure.

§ 18. Factors influencing consequences of the Conquest.

It is always difficult to project one's present experience back into a society so superficially different as that of the eleventh century. Yet men have not greatly changed in the intervening period. Desires and motivations are largely identical now with those which existed then. Thus it is important to realize that the Norman expedition into England was substantially an eleventh century counterpart of several movements which have been happening in recent decades. During the past seventy-five years many American corporations have expanded the areas contributing to their profits so as to cover the whole of continental United States and many areas beyond these confines. These corporations have often been the product of the initiative and push of one man, as for example, John D. Rockefeller or George Eastman. The spread of such an enterprise has been typically marked by the absorption or extinction of competitors, a growing domination of the sources of needed materials and a control of the channels of distribution of the finished product. The ambitious, somewhat ruthless seeker of power in the eleventh century became a William the Conqueror. His modern human equivalent sometimes sought an outlet for his energy as the organizer of some tremendous business enterprise. Another analogy which helps toward an understanding of William's problems and conduct is the modern political boss. William had to have the support of many persons to organize and to execute the invasion of England. With Hastings won, he needed the continued undivided loyalty of these henchmen—and of many more. The modern political boss who has won one election but hopes to win more, and who distributes the available patronage as a reward for past service and as insurance of future support is merely a modern counterpart of William after his military success at Hastings. Further close analogies are obviously found in the activities of Germany during the first two or three years of World War II. Thus the consequences of the Conquest were dictated in no small degree by the underlying ever modern seeking of power through the ruthless using of what is available to attain what is desired.

Other factors which played important roles in determining the consequences of the Conquest were the small number of William's army and the difficulties of transport from the vicinity of Hastings into the interior of England. Caution, slowness of penetration, replacements only of top Anglo-Saxons by Normans, so that the mass of the population were largely unaffected by—or even perhaps unaware of the change of masters, became the necessary and the adopted modes of procedure.

§ 19. Land as the medium of life.

As William exploited the gains of his military victory, substantial quantities of land came within his power of disposition. The Saxon king and many of the important Saxon land holders died at Hastings. Successive efforts at "rebellion" against the spreading lava flow of Norman power resulted in further Saxon deaths. The lands formerly dominated by the Saxon king and by his henchmen became "forfeited" and William (with his group) could designate good Normans to step into the vacated positions of land control. Furthermore, as Norman power entered more deeply into England's interior, the process of "commendation" became a new source of land control. Anglo-Saxon persons of importance, recognizing the irresistible approach of the alien foe, sought to salvage something from the wreckage. This was done by seeking out the Normans and agreeing to accept some Norman as "overlord", under whom the Saxon would retain what he had had, less, of course, what he had to pay as tribute to his new overlord for protection. Thus by the continuing processes of forfeiture and commendation, disposition of land domination became the wherewithal—the wealth—with which William and his followers must obtain the satisfaction of their needs for subsistence and of their desires for a richer life.

§ 20. Norman needs as moulders of the land tenures.

An examination of the known facts as to the circumstances in which William and his followers found themselves in the period immediately after 1066 reveals that they must have been keenly aware of four basic necessities. Their military manpower needed to be substantially increased. Fighting was to be expected and the surest route to speedy domination of all England was in an overwhelming number of soldiers. Their stomachs neened recurrent fillings and their backs required clothing and equipment. As their retainers increased in number these needs would grow greater. Their lives were anomalous combinations of acceptance and belief in God and of daily lives which included murder, robbery, rapine and other mortal sins. They felt deeply and seriously the need for safeguarding their ultimate destinies by securing the intercession of the Church on their behalfs. Lastly they were a small group seeking to dominate a much more numerous native populace. They must have realized (as the later English did in India) the psychological effectiveness of maintaining establishments and personal entourages which spoke of strength. Incidentally the rigors of current life would be considerably lessened by such contributions to relative luxury. So perhaps we can designate the four fundamental needs of the Norman groups as safety, subsistence, salvation and splendor.

The four types of land grants, utilized by William and his group in consolidating their position in England, correspond exactly to these four needs. Military tenure provided the armed forces. Socage tenure provided the agricultural products essential to the continuance of life. Frankalmoign tenure made certain the intercession of the Church for the welfare of the giver's soul. Serjeanty tenure provided the serviential retinue of ostentatious living. Our modern law of land has grown chiefly from the socage root but some aspects of the other tenures deserve attention because of the illumination so derivable as to the processes in the evolution of law.

§ 21. The general structure of tenure.

In the distribution of the available land spoils the King graciously recognized the past loyalty and helpfulness of his important followers by allocating to each control over substantial areas of the land acquired from Saxons by forfeiture or commendation. These men, in turn, parcelled out the large tracts so acquired, into smaller tracts which were given as rewards to their personal followers. The process was repeated in a descending scale until the actual user of the land was reached. Each such grant created a relationship of lord and tenant, in which the lord agreed to protect the tenant and to safeguard his land holding in return for an agreed service to be rendered by the tenant to the lord. Each such relationship included recurrent incidents which gave economic returns from time to time to the lord.

Systematized by 1100, or shortly thereafter, the system of tenure resembled roughly a pyramid with the King at the apex. Immediately beneath him were the "tenants in capite" who were almost exclusively Normans. Beneath these, in turn, were the "mesne" or intermediate, tenants who became less Norman and more Saxon as the rungs of the ladder down from the King became more numerous. At the bottom of the land owning class was the tenant paravail. This last character was described as "seised in demesne" while intermediate and top tenants were said to be "seised in service".

§ 22. Military tenure—Origin of incidents.

Grants of land in return for the furnishing of some military service were common both in the Germanic background of the Anglo-Saxons and also in the continental background of William's followers. In these preludes to feudalism, chieftain and man had a relation characterized by intimacy and mutual good will. Subordination existed more for the common good and general defense than for the aggrandizement of the chief. In that early atmosphere of close personal loyalty one must look for the beginnings of those aspects of English military tenure which became known as its "incidents". The incidents of military tenure which found their roots in this relationship of personal loyalty—in addition to the core of military service—were the aids, the control of wardship and marriage, the fines on alienation and the requirements of attornment, the lord's duties of warranty and defense and the ceremonial practices of homage and fealty. When a tenant died he ceased to be able to provide his strong right arm for the battles of his lord. Just as wages or salary cease with death today, so the grant of land made in consideration of military service ended on the tenant's death in the early years of feudalism. If some son or other relative of the deceased tenant succeeded in convincing the lord that he would be a good substitute for the deceased, he might receive from the lord a regrant of the land previously had by the deceased. The regrant on death was a favor given if, but only if, the lord chose to select the new person as his tenant. From this background originated the payment of relief, a sum paid by the new person to the lord to help the lord's judgment to incline in favor of the claimant. Also out of the same matrix came the primer seisin payment for the same purpose required of a tenant in capite. Obviously, if the deceased left no close relative to claim the privilege of a regrant the land became the lord's to do with as he chose, that is, it escheated.

Thus the details of military tenure all trace back to two ideas or facts in the backgrounds of our English ancestors. They arose either out of the original relationship of intimacy and personal loyalty between chief and follower or from the regrant on death being thought of as a favor which the lord had the power to grant or to refuse.

§ 23. Military tenure—Factors affecting evolution of incidents.

Three pairs of conflicting interests provided the media for the development of land law out of tenurial grants. The lord would naturally seek to get as much as possible from the tenant in return for the land given him and the tenant would seek to part with as little as was necessary, so that he would have the more left for himself. In this struggle of self-interests between lord and tenant there gradually emerged a defined scope of current and recurrent duties and benefits. As has been indicated above when a tenant died, the lord wished to be wholly free in his further dealings with this land, so that he could make as advantageous a new deal for himself as might be possible. But children and relatives of the deceased wished to retain whatever advantages had been connected with the tenancy of this land. Thus the adverse interests of lord and heir of the tenant reached a compromise known to modern law as the law of inheritance of land. The third pair of opposed interests were those of tenant and his heir. The tenant might well desire to have full power of disposition of his tenancy. If, however, the tenant had, and exercised this power nothing would remain for the heir to inherit. So the extent of the freedom of alienation represents the final adjustment reached in the opposed interests of tenant and his heir.

Thus the law of land has come to us largely as a composite of the ultimate adjustment of the struggle between lord and tenant as to current duties, between lord and tenant's heir as to the right of inheritance and between tenant and tenant's heir as to the extent of freedom of alienation.

A second factor affecting the evolution of the incidents of military tenure is one which affects the evolution of all law. A relationship which starts in a voluntary response to a seen need gradually crystallizes into a detail of more or less clearly defined duties and obligations. As parties to the relationship are either niggardly in their doing or ruthless in their demanding, lines are drawn to which parties must conform. Thus the decades following 1066 illustrate this common emergence of folkways into rules of increasing definiteness.

A third factor which had particular importance in this particular branch of the law was the economic decrease in the purchasing power of money. To whatever extent the processes causing the crystallization of duties as between parties to a land tenure, caused those duties to be commuted into money payments of so many shillings (or other money units), the duties so commuted were destined to diminishing significance as the purchasing power of money decreased with the growth of trade. To whatever extent these duties became defined in terms of units which altered along with the changes in the purchasing power of money, these duties were likely to continue to be important aspects of land law.

§ 24. Military tenure—Some of its characteristics.

This book has no place for a detailed discussion of the evolution of all the incidents of military tenure. It must suffice to trace some only of these evolutive processes, thereby finding some beginnings of present law and some outstanding instances of the processes by which law changes.

The basic duty in military tenure was to render military service. But for how long? and where? within England? on the Continent? To the extent that the duration of this service became accepted as forty days, the army so recruited was of little value for a campaign across the Channel where most of the battles had to be waged. So it can perhaps, be said with fair accuracy that for the first century (1066-1166) military tenure really was accompanied by the rendition of military service by tenants to lords but there was little or no *law* defining the scope or character of the service thus requirable. During the next century the practice developed of substituting a money payment—called scutage—for the service, computed, in many instances, on the basis of eight pence a day for forty days a year. So, during this second century (1166-1266) the scutage payments provided military service by providing funds sufficient for the hiring of mercenary professional troops. But, by the middle of the thirteenth century, the decrease in the purchasing power of 320 pence had set in and after 1266 this aspect of military tenure provided neither soldiers nor the money wherewith to hire soldiers. The basic duty of military tenure was on the road to complete unimportance. This meant that the relationship of military tenure thenceforth depended for its advantages and disadvantages to both lord and tenant upon its other incidents.

The aids consisted of contributions made, as Blackstone says, originally as "mere benevolences, granted by the tenant to his lord, in times of difficulty and distress". "Difficulty and distress" are broad terms which were doubtless construed differently by grasping lords and penurious tenants. Magna Carta marks the efforts of tenants to confine the duty to pay aids to three situations only, namely the ransoming of the lord's body, the knighting of the lord's oldest son and the first marrying of the lord's eldest daughter. The omission of this restriction from the Henry III reissue of Magna Carta (1217) was followed by some exactions of other aids until 1297. The Statute of Westminster I fixed the amount of the two aids which could be taken by inferior lords in connection with the knighting of the son and the marriage of the daughter at twenty shillings per knight's fee, and a similar restriction was imposed on tenants in capite in 1351. When thus fixed in amount each aid constituted about five per cent of the usual annual income of a knight's fee, but, since fixed as to amount in terms of money units, these aids were on the road to unimportance because of the impending decrease in the purchasing power of money.

After the right of inheritance became established, the death of a tenant survived only by infant children raised special problems. The lord could reasonably expect continuously available service from the land in question. This was assured by the right of wardship which the lord had if the male heir was under twenty-one or the female heir was under fourteen. Wardship consisted of custody of the body and possession of the lands of the infant male heir until he became twenty-one or of an infant female heir (under fourteen at the death of the ancestor) until she became sixteen, and thus presumably able to provide a husband able to discharge the duties connected with the tenancy. While the lord had this wardship he could operate the affected lands without any duty to account. This right was capable of grave abuse and this possibility was too frequently realized. It will be noted that the decreasing purchasing power of money exerted no influence on the economic value of this right to a lord. When the deceased tenant held two or more parcels under different lords there were rules of priority which settled which of the lords could exercise this valuable right. In these we have no present interest. Keen rivalries existed between lords holding land in England. It was vitally important to the welfare of Lord A that no hostile element be admitted to his inner circle. So a lord had a perfectly rational basis for concern as to the person married by the infant heir to a portion of the lands granted by this lord. Thence, came the "right of marriage", under which the lord could control the marriage of his former tenant's progeny. Out of this right grave abuses developed under which lords prostituted the right by using it as a source of profit rather than as a legitimate method of protection. Wardship and marriage became the most burdensome and the most objectionable features of military tenure.

Thinking back to the time when lord and tenant had a close relation of personal loyalty, it is not difficult to see why each felt a special stake in the personality of the other. Just as a sentry in modern warfare has no privilege to substitute a buddy on his post, so a tenant could not substitute someone else as tenant without the lord's approval. Thence came the fines on alienation, a money payment made by a tenant to his lord to procure the lord's acceptance of the new tenant. Similarly, in early times a tenant's consent to a change in overlords was necessary. Out of this came attornment, which was the tenant's acceptance of the new person as lord.

Corollaries of the situations which gave rise to military tenures were the lord's agreement to defend his tenant against wrongdoing third persons and to give to the tenant other lands of equal value if he were ousted from the lands handed over. This latter was the "warranty" of feudalism. In a period of somewhat formalistic law, the tenant's swearing of homage and fealty were fitting ceremonial recognitions of the creation of the relationship of lord and man.

In examining the consequences of the idea that a regrant on death of a tenant was a favor for which the lord could exact a money payment, one is struck with the similarity between this "relief" of the feudal system and the modern death tax on inheritance or succession. In each, the owner of the ultimate property (lord in feudalism, the state today) permits an heir to take if, but only if, the owner of the ultimate property receives a percentage of the value of the asset inherited. Historically land grants in return for military service began in the forests of Germany at will. In time they became annual, then later for life. Then on the death of the tenant the lord selected a new tenant who might be, but need not be, the former tenant's son. The increase in certainty that the successor would be a relative of the deceased tenant, marked the beginning of the right of inheritance. The exclusion of all children but the eldest son (when there was a son) became a peculiarity found only in English law. It developed in connection with military tenures. The "relief" amounted to one hundred shillings for a knight's fee. When thus crystalized as to amount the payment represented about twenty-five per cent of the annual return of a normal knight's fee. Since, however, the relief became fixed in terms of money units, its importance was certain to diminish with the already begun decrease in the purchasing power of money. The comparable exaction from a tenant in capite was designated "primer seisin". Identical in theory with the relief applicable to lesser tenants it differed in one vital particular. Instead of being expressed in money units, roughly equal to a quater of the land's annual produce, it consisted of the full use by the lords of the land for one year subsequent to the death of the tenant. Such use had a value which kept pace with any change in the purchasing power of money. Hence primer seisin as to tenants in capite became a burdensome and objectionable feature of tenancies in capite while relief sank into relative unobjectionability as to lesser tenancies. In this fact rests one of the seeds of the legislation of 1660 eliminating all tenancies in capite.

Escheat, of course, became constantly more firmly entrenched. Whenever a tenant died either without heirs or under such circumstances that his heirs were treated as unworthy to inherit, the land became free from further claim and the lord's ultimate right became an unchallenged right to exclusive possession and redisposition.

In reviewing the characteristics of military tenure herein considered we have seen how the law of land has been shaped by the circumstances of its formulation and evolution. Scutage, the aids, fines on alienation and relief, all crystalized into sums measured by money units, were doomed to later insignificance by the economic factors decreasing the purchasing power of money. On the contrary, wardship, marriage and escheat were the characteristics which persisted into the fifteenth, sixteenth and seventeenth centuries and hence are the aspects of military tenure most important in our study of the developing land law. Objectionable and burdensome as these rights became they furnished good reasons for the Commonwealth's determination to reform the law of tenures as a part of their sweeping reforms in English law. This movement for abolition was, of course, greatly aided by the gradual disappearance of the desire for a type of tenure which originated in the assumed necessity of local armies for local dignitaries.

§ 25. Manorial organization.

The agricultural activities in England are very old, stretching back of the Conquest into and beyond the haze of the beginnings of history. Vinogradoff, in the late twenties, wrote a book on Villeinage in England which argues persuasively that communal ownership of land accompanied by individual working of changing areas characterized the early centuries of the Angles and Saxons in England. Vinogradoff thus relates this background to the manor of early Norman days:

"The question has been asked whether we ought not to regard these communal arrangements as derived from the exclusive right of ownership, and the power of coercion vested in the lord of the soil. I think that many features in the constitution of the thirteenth century manor show its gradual growth and comparatively recent origin. The so-called manorial system consists, in truth, in the peculiar connexion between two agrarian bodies, the settlement of villagers cultivating their own fields, and the home-estate of the lord tacked on to this settlement and dependent on the work supplied by it. I take only the agrarian side, of course, and do not mention the political protection which stands more or less as an equivalent for the profits received by the lord from the peasantry. And as for the agrarian arrangement, we ought to keep it quite distinct from forms which are sometimes confused with it through loose terminology. A community paying taxes, farmers leasing land for rent, labourers without independent husbandry of their own, may be all subjected to some lord, but their subjection is manorial. Two elements are necessary to constitute the manorial arrangement, the peasant village and the home farm worked by its help."

Doubtless these "home-estates" of lords worked by the help of the adjacent "peasant village" had existed before the coming of the Normans, but the Normans regularized, absorbed and systematized what they found so that it provided the much needed wherewithal of life to the invading host. The Norman who became lord of the manor assumed control of his whole neighborhood. The typical manor contained three types of land, the "demesne" or retained land which was the immediate source of support for the inhabitants of the manor house, the large adjacent areas granted to subtenants of importance, sometimes in military tenure, sometimes in socage tenure, and the land left available for common use for grazing, the cutting of wood and other similar purposes.

The lord of the manor held the whole manor from some overlord. The basis of that holding was sometimes military tenure, sometimes socage tenure. Thus socage tenure might simultaneously be the basis on which a whole manor was held and the basis of the relation between the lord of a manor and one or more of his subordinate tenants.

Many aspects of the manorial organization other than its socage tenure, had importance in the development of the land law. The demesne land of the lord was typically worked by persons who came to be known as "copyholders". In return for the privilege of working ten, twenty, thirty acres of his own, these farm laborers rendered agreed quantities of manual labor on the lord's lands. The manager of the manor kept books in which he recorded what each worker had to do and what he was entitled to receive therefor. The rights of the tenant depended on a "copy" of this record plus the customary rights of the workers in that manor. Copyholders became an important class of the agrarian population. Their local "customs" became an important source of land law. One channel for this latter influence was the large ingredient of English copyholders in the early settlers of the New World. The common lands of the manor required an adjustment of the conflicting claims of many persons trying simultaneously to derive benefit from the same land. This process set in motion much of what is now known as the law of easements, including rights to enter on land of another and to remove trees or peat or stone found thereon. The manor was frequently a largely self-contained unit. This meant that controversies between its inhabitants had to be settled by judicial agencies within itself. In this localization of the judicial process under the general supervision of the lord of the manor is found the means whereby customary law evolved and grew strong.

§ 26. Socage tenure—Service and incidents.

The basic service, in return for which land was granted in socage was agricultural or monetary in character. Sometimes it consisted of enumerated defined work. More often it consisted of a definite quantity of some product of the land or of a money payment periodically payable. Definiteness was, from the earliest known time, its outstanding characteristic. Many of its incidents were like those owed by a tenant in military tenure. The tenant owed to his lord the aids. On a tenant's death the lord had the right to escheat and to either primer seisin or relief, according to whether the deceased was a tenant in capite or a lesser lord. The incidents of "wardship" and "marriage" were absent. In this fact lay one of the most important reasons for the preference for, and the survival of, this type of land tenure. If a socage tenant died survived only by infant heirs, the upbringing of this child and the management of his land went to the "nearest of those relations who could have no hope of inheriting the land. Thus, in the common case, when the dead tenant in socage left a son and a widow, the widow would have the wardship of her son and of his land; she would be 'guardian in socage', for she never could be his heir. To state the main upshot of the rule—maternal kinsfolk have the wardship of a paternal inheritance, paternal kinsfolk of a maternal inheritance. When the heir attained his fifteenth year, guardianship in socage came to an end. If the dead man held one tenement by knight's service, another by socage, the wardship of the one would belong to its lord, that of the other to a kinsman of the heir; as to the wardship of the heir's body, this and his marriage would belong to the lord of whom he held by military tenure."

In this "guardianship in socage"—and not in the wardship of military tenure is found the beginning of the present law of guardian and ward. Such a guardian had the duty to account for all his expenditures and receipts. In this aspect of the relationship is found one of the earliest types of fiduciary accountablitity. In the ascertainment of the persons taking a socage tenancy by inheritance another important difference from military tenure existed. While a large part of the socage tenures were governed by the rule of primogeniture, local customs persisted as to some localities. In some towns the tenants held from their lords by a species of socage tenure called "burgage" or "borough English". Such land descended to the deceased tenant's youngest son, instead of either to the oldest son or to all of the sons equally. The reason for, or origin of, this custom is not known. It has been suggested by Littleton that its explanation lies in the fact that the youngest son, may, least of all his brethren, help himself. A more colorful explanation has been that the overlord's often asserted right to the "first night" with his tenant's bride made the youngest child the one most certain to be a child of the tenant. These burgage tenures had no persistent influence on American land law. The local custom of gavelkind which prevailed in the County of Kent, is suggestive of modern equal inheritance by the children of a deceased landowner. As the custom then existed lands descended to all sons equally, could be disposed of by the tenant after he became fifteen years of age and by will and did not escheat on attainder of the tenant for felony.

Tenure in socage came to include not only well to do farmers but also all others who held at a rent, whether the rent was heavy or negligible. It thus included many of the great landowners of the kingdom, especially those who held a whole manor in this type of land ownership, or who became grantees of large parcels of land from some church. "It was the least encumbered of all the tenures with obsolete and oppressive incidents.... It was because it fitted in best with the newer ideas which regarded land-holding simply as a form of property, that it finally superseded all other free tenures."

§ 27. Frankalmoign tenure.

This type of land holding once applied to between a third and a half of all England. Its prototypes antedated the Conquest but the period during which a substantial part of these tenures was created was from 1100 to 1290. It is suggested above (§ 20) that the great frequency of land grants to the church sprang from the conflict between the beliefs and the type of life characteristic of Normans in the period which followed the Conquest. Generally speaking, there were no feudal incidents due from the Church to the conveyor of land in frankalmoign.

Thus land so conveyed constituted, in effect, outright gifts to the church. The atmosphere of such grants is illustrated in an eleventh century charter of confirmation given by Roger de Valognes to Binham Priory. The great extent of land thus controlled by the Church became a considerable challenge to the secular power of the King. The Church courts urged that since God was a party conveyee in each of these land grants, God was interested in the outcome of litigation affecting any such land and hence, the Ecclesiastical Courts should have jurisdiction of all controversies affecting land held in frankalmoign. Ecclesiastical success in this claim would have greatly lessened the rapidly growing power of the King's Courts. The King graciously conceded that *if* God were interested the Church courts should handle these cases, but subtly insisted that in each controversy a jury be summoned in the King's Court to decide whether God had the requisite interest. The outcome of these preliminary inquires sufficiently safeguarded the King's Courts. Finally, the Statute Quia Emptores, in 1290, records the King's position of sufficient strength to prohibit further grants of this type unless sanctioned by the King. No present consequences in American land law are attributable to the frankalmoign tenures.

§ 28. Serjeanty tenure.

The conveyances of land in serjeanty were made to procure for large households, the needed services of stewards, marshals, chamberlains, cooks, falconers, dog-keepers and the like. Such grants had less certainty than those made in return for either military service or agricultural products. Sometimes they had the incidents of military tenure, sometimes these incidents differed in burdensomeness from those found in the military tenures. Gradually serjeanties were differentiated into "grand serjeanty" and "petit serjeanty" and the former of these became assimilated to military tenure while the latter became a form of socage tenure. This process of assimilation was aided, in both its branches, by the practice, common in the thirteenth century, of substituting a money payment for the several specific services theretofore required of a tenant.

[The foregoing is reproduced by the kind permission of the author and publishers.]

BIGELOW, INTRODUCTION TO THE LAW OF REAL PROPERTY

[Chap. 1] Section 6. Statutory Changes in the Feudal System.

The earlier history of the growth of the law with respect to the power of the tenant to alien his lands is a matter with respect to which considerable doubt exists. It is by no means certain whether for the first two hundred years after the Norman Conquest the growth was toward a restriction of the power of alienation, or toward a development of freedom in the power of alienation. It seems reasonably certain that by the time of Henry II the power of the tenant to alien his lands, subject to the payment of the ordinary fines, was definitely established.

Land may be alienated in one of two ways: For example, if A is the lord and B is the tenant, B may alienate his complete interest to C. This may be called alienation by substitution. Since the services were regarded as being due from the land, an alienation of this sort would not deprive A, as overlord, of any of his feudal dues. At the same time, however, he might be prejudiced, as regards the personality of the tenant by the change from one favorably disposed to him to one not so favorably disposed. More than this, if B alienated his land to several different persons, instead of to one person, there would be more difficulty on the part of A in collecting his feudal dues.

In comparison with the case just above put, B, the feudal tenant of A, instead of conveying to C all his possible interests in the land, and thereby substituting C in his place, might convey a part of the land to C in perpetuity, but at the same time reserve to himself from C certain obligations with respect to the land conveyed; B thereby interposing himself as a mesne lord between A and C, so that C would hold his lands from, and be in a tenure relation to, not A, but B. This is known as alienation by subinfeudation. It would not affect the personal relations between A and B, nor would it cut off the feudal obligations owed to A by the land. A could distrain upon chattels on any part of the land to enforce his right to the services owed by B. But it nevertheless might seriously prejudice A in the most valuable of his feudal rights, viz., the incidents of tenure. Suppose, for example, that B should convey a part of the land to C, subject only to the obligation to pay one penny yearly. If, now, B should die, leaving only a minor heir, A would have his right of wardship. But, instead of being entitled under it to take possession of all the land that B had originally held as his tenant and get what he could from it, all he would be entitled to, with respect to the part subinfeudated to C, would be the one penny per annum. So, again, if B died without heirs, so that his interest would escheat to A, the only subject-matter of the escheat as regards the part subinfeudated to C would be the reservation of one penny per annum.

The first legislation that seems to have been passed directed against this state of affairs is found in Magna Carta as affirmed in 1217, which provides (section xxxix): "No freeman from henceforth shall give or sell any more of his land, but so that of the residue of the lands the lord of the fee may have the services due to him which belong to the fee."

Apparently this provision was not regarded as an adequate settlement of the matter. The subject was definitely settled by legislation in the reign of Edward I. In the year 1290 was passed the statute of Quia Emptores. The ordinary translation is as follows:

"Forasmuch as purchasers of lands and tenements of the fees of great men and other lords have many times heretofore entered into their fees, to the prejudice of the lords, to whom the freeholders of such great men have sold their lands and tenements to be holden in fee of their feoffors and not of the chief lords of the fees, whereby the same chief lords have many times lost their escheats, marriages, and wardships of lands and tenements belonging to their fees, which thing seems very hard and extreme unto those lords and other great men, and moreover in this case manifest disheritance, our lord the king in his parliament at Westminster after Easter the eighteenth year of his reign, that is to wit in the quinzine of Saint John Baptist, at the instance of the great men of the realm granted, provided, and ordained, that from henceforth it should be lawful to every freeman to sell at his own pleasure his lands and tenements or part of them, so that the feoffee shall hold the same lands or tenements of the chief lord of the same fee, by such service and customs as his feoffor held before.

"c. 2. And if he sell any part of such lands or tenements to any, the feoffee shall immediately hold it of the chief lord, and shall be forthwith charged with the services for so much as pertaineth or ought to pertain to the said chief lord, for the same parcel, according to the quantity of the land or tenement so sold; and so in this case the same part of the service shall remain to the lord, to be taken by the hands of the feoffee, for the which he ought to be attendant and answerable to the same chief lord according to the quantity of the land or tenement sold for the parcel of the service so due.

"c. 3. And it is to be understood that by the said sales or purchases of lands or tenements, or any parcel of them, such lands or tenements shall in no wise come into mortmain, either in part or in whole, neither by policy ne craft, contrary to the form of the statute made thereupon of late. And it is to wit that this statute extendeth but only to lands holden in fee simple, and that it extendeth to the time coming. And it shall begin to take effect at the Feast of Saint Andrew the Apostle next coming."

The effects of this statute may be briefly summarized as follows:

1. It allowed complete alienation by way of substitution upon the payment of a fine, even though the lands were thereby divided.

2. It abolished subinfeudation in the case of a conveyance of the fee simple in the way illustrated in the third paragraph of this section and made the feoffee hold of the feoffor's overlord upon the same terms as those upon which the feoffor had held of the feoffor's overlord. It did not forbid subinfeudation of estates less than a fee simple, e.g. estates in fee tail and for life.

3. It did not affect the rights of the king against the tenants in capite, because of the general principle that the rights of the king are not affected by a statute unless he is specially named therein.

4. It applied only to conveyances in fee simple.

So long as English society continued on what might fairly be called a military basis, so long as protection to property and life through legal process was not very direct and adequate, and the need for protection and assistance between the lord and the tenant was immediate and close, the feudal organization of society, with its onerous incidents, might nevertheless be regarded as a not unfair working arrangement. In the course of time, however, the feudal element in English economic life ceased to have any real value, the agricultural element became more pronounced, and then gradually a commercial aspect developed. The king's courts asserted their jurisdiction over all the country, and life and property became secure. With this growth of society the justification for the feudal incidents disappeared. They became a mere source of profit upon the part of the lord, with no corresponding benefit to the tenant. An element that operated to make this burden all the more heavy was the fact that, with the breaking down of the feudal system, the relation of lord and tenant was no longer kept sharply in mind, and the doctrine gradually arose that every tenant was presumed to be a tenant in capite, unless it appeared that he was a mesne tenant. It has already been pointed out that the feudal burdens of the tenants in capite were distinctly more onerous than those of the mesne tenants. The effect of Quia Emptores was also to work the holding of any given tenant toward the top of the feudal pyramid. When feudalism was definitely terminated as a real factor in English economic organization by the War of the Roses, and the establishment of the Tudors, the objection to these burdensome incidents became constantly stronger. Blackstone [Commentaries, vol. 2, p. 75] thus describes the situation.

"For the present I have only to observe, that by the degenerating of knight service, or personal military duty, in escuage, or pecuniary assessments, all the advantages (either promised or real) of the feudal constitution were destroyed, and nothing but the hardships remained. Instead of forming a national militia composed of barons, knights, and gentlemen, bound by their interest, their honor, and their oaths, to defend their king and country, the whole of this system of tenures now tended to nothing else but a wretched means of raising money to pay an army of occasional mercenaries. In the meantime the families of all our nobility and gentry groaned under the intolerable burthens, which (in consequence of the fiction adopted after the Conquest) were introduced and laid upon them by the subtlety and finesse of the Norman lawyers. For, besides the scutages to which they were liable in defect of personal attendance, which however were assessed by themselves in parliament, they might be called upon by the king or lord paramount for aids, whenever his eldest son was to be knighted, or his eldest daughter married; not to forget the ransom of his own person. The heir on the death of his ancestor, if of full age, was plundered of his first emoluments arising from his inheritance, by way of relief and primer seisin; and if under age, of whole of his estate during his infancy. And then, as Sir Thomas Smith very feelingly complains, 'when he came to his own, after he was out of wardship, his woods decayed, houses fallen down, stock wasted and gone, lands let forth and ploughed to be a barren', to reduce him still further, he was yet to pay half a year's profits as a fine for suing out his livery; and also the price or value of his marriage, if he refused such a wife as his lord and guardian had bartered for, and imposed upon him; or twice that value if he married another woman. Add to this, untimely and expensive honor of knighthood, to make his poverty more completely splendid. And when by these deductions his fortune was so shattered and ruined, that perhaps he was obliged to sell his patrimony, he had not even that poor privilege allowed him without paying an exorbitant fine for a license of alienation."

In the reign of James I a proposal was made to abolish all these incidents, but this proposal was defeated. On the overthrow of Charles I, steps were taken to do away with these feudal obligations, and a statute to that effect was enacted in 1656. On the restoration of Charles II, in 1660, the statute was re-enacted in order to put its validity beyond question. The statute provides as follows:...

[Here the author reproduced the terms of the Statute of Tenures, 1660, 12 Car. II, c. 24. He then continued as follows:]

The result of this statute, although the language of it is confusing, and the statute is poorly drawn, is clear. It abolished military tenure. It turned all tenure into free and common socage and discharged most of even the slight burdens incident to that tenure.

It is to be noticed that neither Quia Emptores nor the statute abolishing the court of wards and liveries purported to do away with the idea that land was "held" of some one, either the king or some one lower down in the order of holding. The recent important legislation in England, known as the Law of Property Act, (1925 (Imp.), c. 20) also leaves this idea untouched. As has already been pointed out, almost all the feudal incidents that were the important elements in the relation of lord and tenant have as such disappeared. Save in very exceptional cases, the only one that has any practical importance today is escheat.

In this concept of "holding" land rather than "owning" it, the theory of the law of England is today what it was eight hundred years ago, namely, that the owner, even when he has the largest possible rights in his land that the law recognizes, is not the owner of his land in the same sense that he is, for example, the owner of his watch. He holds his land in tenure under the sovereign.

[The foregoing is reproduced by the kind permission of the publishers.]

[1 *Powell*, Real Property, at p. 65, comments on the legislation of 1660 as follows:

"The surviving aspects of the earlier tenurial system were chiefly three, escheat, relief as a form of succession tax and the basic idea that all land is 'held' rather than owned.

"This legislation of 1660 completed the economic task begun by the Statute Quia Emptores 370 years before, namely the shift, in the selling of fee interests in land, from stress on benefits derivable in the future from recurrent or occasional payments to be made by the tenant to a stress on the lump sum to be obtained if ever at the time of sale as the capital equivalent of the asset then conveyed."

A manor created in 1203 by a charter of John was held *in capite ut de corona* and by knight service until the Statute of Tenures, 1660, turned military tenures into free and common socage. In 1837 the lord of the manor granted a section of some thirteen acres to one Atkinson and his heirs "to be holden of the lord or lords, lady or ladies, of the said manor in free and common socage". Atkinson's successor in title was one Holliday, a bastard, who died in 1910, a bachelor and intestate. The lord of the manor took possession by escheat but the Crown disputed his rights, and an inquisition of escheat was held in 1921 which decided that the land in question escheated to the Crown. The lord had in the meantime sold the land to the petitioner who sought to traverse the inquisition on the ground that the lord of the manor in 1837, being a tenant *in capite ut de corona*, was entitled to make the subinfeudation of 1837 to Atkinson to hold of himself the lord. Should the petitioner succeed? See *In re Holliday*, [1922] 2 Ch. 698.]

A.-G. OF ALBERTA v. HUGGARD ASSETS LTD. AND A.-G. OF CANADA. Privy Council. [1953] A.C. 420; [1953] 3 D.L.R. 225; 8 W.W.R. (N.S.) 561

Appeal by defendants from a judgment of the Supreme Court of Canada, [1951] S.C.R. 427, [1951] 2 D.L.R. 305, affirming a judgment of the Alberta Supreme Court, Appellate Division, [1950] 1 D.L.R. 823, [1950] 1 W.W.R. 69, which affirmed on equal division a judgment of Boyd McBride J., [1949] 4 D.L.R. 211, [1949] 2 W.W.R. 370, declaring that no royalty could be exacted in respect of petroleum and natural gas on certain land.

The judgment of their Lordships was delivered by LORD ASQUITH OF BISHOPSTONE:

The issue raised on this appeal is shortly whether the Crown in right of the Province of Alberta is entitled to levy certain royalties from Huggard Assets Ltd. respondents in the appeal and plaintiffs in the action, on petroleum and natural gas derived by them from a certain area in that Province.

The facts leading up to this litigation, which will have to be unfolded in more detail later, can with advantage be stated in brief outline at the outset. The plaintiffs claim an interest in these minerals as successors of a company called the Northern Alberta Exploration Co. Ltd., the original grantees of the area under a grant in the form of a patent dated August 25, 1913 (ex. 8 of the Appendix of Exhibits). The grantor was the Crown in the right of the Dominion.

The Crown in right of Alberta succeeded, under the Transfer Agreements Acts of 1930, to any right which the Crown in right of the Dominion had theretofore owned in Crown lands, mines and minerals situate in Alberta, and royalties derived therefrom; together with the right to enforce "any power or right, which, by any contract, lease or other arrangement, or by any Act of the Parliament of Canada relating to any of the lands, mines, minerals or royalties hereby transferred or by any regulation made under any such Act, is reserved" to the Crown in right of the Dominion. These provisions have been described as constituting a "statutory novation", the Province stepping into the shoes of the Dominion, and succeeding to its rights. The main issue in the case is whether the Dominion, at the time of the grant in 1913, was entitled to the right to exact royalties, which are now in dispute. The determination of that issue depends on the answer to the two further questions:

(1) What, on its true construction, does the grant of 1913 in its reddendum purport to provide in respect of royalties payable by the grantee?

(2) Whatever on its true construction that provision means, is it legally valid and enforceable?

It may be convenient to set out the habendum and reddendum of the grant at this stage: "To have and to hold the same unto the grantee in fee simple. Yielding and paying unto US and OUR SUCCESSORS such royalty upon the said petroleum and natural gas, if any, from time to time prescribed by regulations of OUR GOVERNOR in COUNCIL it being hereby declared that this grant is subject in all respects to the provisions of any such regulations with respect to royalty upon the said petroleum and natural gas or any of them; and to such Regulations governing petroleum and natural gas as were in force on 1st September, 1909": and there follow provisions for forfeiture on failure to pay such royalty.

At the time of the grant there were Regulations in existence affecting the terms on which the Dominion could dispose of Crown lands, mines and minerals in Alberta, but none of these Regulations prescribed a specific rate of royalty chargeable in respect of petroleum or natural gas derived from these sources.

(1) The first question which their Lordships have to decide is whether in these circumstances, having regard to the terms of the grant, and in particular to the words "from time to time", the reddendum purported to entitle the Crown, as grantor—then in right of the Dominion—to levy royalties "prescribed" by a Regulation, or a succession of Regulations, made after the date of the grant. Their Lordships have considered this question and are clearly of opinion that the answer must be in the affirmative. The grant does purport to confer such a right on the grantor. This was the unanimous opinion of the Supreme Court of Canada. Any other answer would render the words "from time to time" meaningless. It is true that in the case of *Majestic Mines Ltd.* v. *A.-G. Alta.*, [1941] 2 W.W.R. 353 [aff'd [1942] 1 D.L.R. 474, [1942] 1 W.W.R. 321, aff'd [1942] S.C.R. 402, [1942] 4 D.L.R. 593], a different conclusion was reached but the crucial words "from time to time" were absent, and clearly the decision might have been the other way if they had been present. (Their Lordships may point out, as some argument was based on the words "if any" as used in the reddendum in the present case, that in their view these words plainly qualify the word "royalty" and not "petroleum or natural gas", or "natural gas" only.)

(2) This answer, however, merely disposes of the problem what it was that the grant purported to provide. A more difficult question remains, viz.: Whether the grant could validly contain such a provision. This question emerged when, some time after the 1930 Transfer

Agreement had vested Crown lands, mines and minerals (situate in Alberta) and rights and powers in respect of royalties on such lands, etc., in the Crown in right of that Province, the Province, by various Orders in Council made between 1941 and 1948 (ref.: S/C p. 3, para. 6) purported to impose a royalty on any petroleum and natural gas derived from lands, etc., vested in the Province by the 1930 Act. As the result of this imposition the plaintiffs brought the present action and claimed in the prayer to their statement of claim the following relief:

"1. A declaration that the Lieutenant-Governor in Council (of Alberta) was not entitled to exact any royalty with respect to petroleum and natural gas produced from the lands.

"2. An order rectifying the patent by striking out all references to royalties."

Four points of varying importance may conveniently be noted here:

(a) No facts are alleged or were proved which would possibly support a plea of rectification. There was no preceding contract representing the real bargain to which the terms of the grant failed to give effect. This disposes of the second branch of the prayer.

(b) The plaintiffs at no stage contended—nor did the defendants—that the grant was wholly invalid. The plaintiffs impugned only the provision as to royalties, wishing this to be deleted and the rest to stand.

(c) No point was taken in the statement of claim, or at any stage of the argument till the case was heard before this Board, to the effect that a grant in terms of this reddendum or a royalty levied in accordance therewith could only be authorized by a Regulation as opposed to an Order in Council. At every stage until the ultimate appeal an Order in Council was assumed to be as good as a Regulation for these purposes. Nevertheless much of the Board's time was occupied with this argument and with a number of other contentions not raised below.

(d) No point was taken by counsel prior to the hearing before this Board, that the English Statute of Tenures, 1660, c. 24, extended to this region of Canada and invalidated any grant of minerals in fee simple on terms which permitted the Crown as grantor to levy a royalty the existence or quantum of which could be determined from time to time by its own caprice or whim. This last point was however raised *proprio motu* by the Supreme Court of Canada, which by a majority of 4 to 3, decided the appeal before them largely on it.

It is now time to indicate the course which the proceedings below followed. The Supreme Court of Alberta, Trial Division (Boyd McBride J.) decided for the plaintiffs. It considered that only point (1)—the construction of the reddendum of the grant—was in issue. The learned Judge decided—erroneously in their Lordships' view—that the reddendum did not on its true construction purport to entitle the Crown as grantor to impose royalties on petroleum and natural gas by Regulations to be made in future, none having been imposed thereon by any Regulation in force when the grant was made. He did not consider what might be the validity of a provision which did purport to give the Crown such a right: but decided for the plaintiffs on the ground that the Crown did not in the grant even stipulate for the power it claimed later to exercise.

The defendants appealed to the Appellate Division of the Supreme Court which, the four learned Judges being equally divided, dismissed the appeal.

There was then a further appeal to the Supreme Court of Canada. The learned Judges (7 in all) were unanimously of opinion that the learned trial Judge and the Appellate Division were in error in supposing that the reddendum of the grant did not purport to have a prospective operation. They all thought that according to its tenor it empowered the Crown to prescribe royalties in respect of petroleum and natural gas by a Regulation posterior to the date of the grant, albeit none were prescribed by any Regulation anterior to that date. In this view their Lordships have recorded their concurrence. The Supreme Court, though favourable to the appellant defendants on this point, dismissed the appeal by a majority of 4 to 3, for a different reason: one which, their Lordships were imformed, was not raised before them by counsel, and which had certainly been raised by no one in the trial or Appellate Divisions.

The main reason for this decision was that owing to the supposed application of Charles II's Statute of Tenures, 1660, a royalty in the form contended for by the Crown was contrary to law, bad for uncertainty, and void, and that no competent legislation had validated it. They further held that the condition for payment of royalties being bad, the forfeiture clause conditioned on its breach was bad also, and that the grant was valid minus the provision as to royalties.

Such is a bare summary of the three Canadian decisions upon which the appeal came before this Board.

The ratio on which the Supreme Court of Canada reached its conclusions, albeit by a bare majority, must be most carefully weighed, and a more precise account of it given; for so far it has only been adumbrated.

But before doing so their Lordships observe that it may prove convenient to describe a royalty which the grantor claims to be entitled to impose for the first time after the contract or grant, at any figure he chooses, or to vary from time to time at his uncontrolled discretion, as a "variable royalty". It will also make for brevity to refer to the areas which came to be called after 1670 "Prince Rupert's Land" and the "North West Territories", simply as "Rupert's Land".

The argument in support of the proposition that the grant could not validly provide for a "variable royalty" in this sense of the term may be summarized under the following heads:

(1) A royalty is akin to rent if not a species of it. A rent must be "certain": and a rent variable at the whim of the lessor is uncertain. So, therefore, is a royalty similarly variable: and unenforceable independently of any argument founded on the Statute of King Charles II.

(2) The *Statute of Tenures*, 1660 applies to Canada or that part of it called Rupert's Land, which was vested in the Dominion in 1870 and from which in 1905 Alberta (including the mineral lands in question) was carved out. This statute by ss. 2 and 4 abolishes grants in fee of land on tenures (such as the old English tenure by knight service) for which the consideration consisted at one time of uncertain services, or of payments by way of composition for such services which reflected in their quantum or in the method of their determination the uncertainty of the services themselves. Section 4 provided that "all Tenures hereafter to be created by the King's Majesty... upon any ... grants ... of any Estate of Inheritance at the Common Law ... shall be in free and common Socage, and shall be adjudged to be in free and common Socage only, and not by Knights-Service ... and shall be discharged of all Wardship, Value and Forfeiture of Marriage, Livery, Primer Seisin, *Ousterlemain*", and certain other burdens incident to tenure by knights-service. Section 4 relates to estates to be created "hereafter". Sections 1 and 2 abolish knights-service tenure and its characteristic burdens (which in those sections were described as including "escuage") in respect of existing estates, and convert them also into tenure by free and common socage, free from those burdens for the future. The hall-mark, it was said, in Littleton, Coke on Littleton, and Blackstone, of tenure by "free and common socage" was and is that any services, or cash composition in lieu thereof, must be "certain": and, so the argument continued, since a "variable royalty" could not be described as "certain" in any sense of the word, *ergo* "a variable royalty" was prohibited by the statute.

(3) It was further contended that whether or not the Act of 1660 applied to Rupert's Land with the results described in (2) above, in any case the Charter, by which in 1670 Charles II granted Rupert's Land to the Hudson's Bay Co. expressly included a term providing for the prevalence of free and common socage as the standard basis of tenure of land therein. The same result, it was suggested, could be reached if Rupert's Land was a "settled" colony (as it has been since held to be in *Walker* v. *Walker*, 48 D.L.R. 1, [1919] A.C. 947; *Board* v.

Board, 48 D.L.R. 13, [1919] A.C. 956): even if there were no such provision in the Charter, for it is well established that settlers import into a settled Colony the common and statute law of their country as they existed at the time of settlement and so far as applicable to the settled territory. But the terms of the Charter would seem to make resort to this rule superfluous so far as the establishment of socage tenure is concerned.

All these three arguments, even if otherwise sound, are liable to be met by two answers: (i) that a "variable" royalty *is* consistent with "free and common socage", or (ii) that if it is not, Dominion legislation has displaced the requirement of such socage tenure and validated a form or forms of tenure which are inconsistent with it. The second of the three arguments—that based on the 1660 Act—may, in addition to these possible objections, be exposed to a third: namely that the Statute of Charles II never applied to Canada; or to the material part of Canada, namely "Rupert's Land".

Their Lordships proceed to consider each of these three arguments in turn: in the first instance in abstraction from the possible effect of any "validating" legislation.

(1) They do not consider that the first of the arguments in question is established. There may well be an analogy between royalties in respect of a grant, and rent in respect of a lease and it may well be that rents must be in some sense of the word "certain". But what does "certain" mean in this connection? What is an "uncertain" rent? A rent, payable in year 1, the amount of which is to depend on events which cannot happen till year 3, would seem to be in any sense of the word, "uncertain" and bad. The tenant could never tell till year 3 how much rent he was liable to pay in year 1; consequently neither he nor his lessor could know for how much, if anything, the latter could in year 1 distrain. This is an extreme case. Short of it, it is clear that a fluctuating rent is not as such necessarily "uncertain"—certainly not if it is mathematically calculable, so as to attract the operation of the maxim *certum est quod certum reddi potest*. The only decided case cited to the Board in which a rent was held "uncertain" is the old case of *Parker* v. *Harris* (1702) 1 Salk, 262, 91 E.R. 230, the report of which is both laconic and obscure. It would seem that what was "uncertain" there was not the quantum of the rent but the times at which it was to be payable. It is said in the present case that the royalty is "uncertain" because its amount depends on the whim, from time to time, of the grantor. It seems doubtful whether this quality is fatal. In this very case, the Charter of 1670 provided for a royalty which in some sense depends on the whim of the grantor, the King. He is to receive two elks and two black beavers every time he visits the territories in question. No one can tell whether he will visit the territory at all; nor if he does, how often: yet his unpredictable election to visit it never; seldom; or repeatedly, determines the number of elks and beavers to be "yielded up". In these circumstances their Lordships are not satisfied that this contention is made out. But whether sound or unsound, it would still (like the other two) fall to the ground if adequate "validating legislation" were proved.

(2) The majority of the Supreme Court, as has been stated, based their decision, in the main, on the *Statute of Tenures*, 1660. Their reasoning assumes that this statute applied to Canada, or at least to "Rupert's Land".

The Act has no express "extent" clause. An Act of the Imperial Parliament today, unless it provides otherwise, applies to the whole of the United Kingdom and to nothing outside the United Kingdom: not even to the Channel Islands or the Isle of Man, let alone to a remote overseas colony or possession. In 1660 there was, of course, no United Kingdom. The Acts of Union of 1706 (with Scotland) and of 1800 (with Ireland) were still in the womb of time. True, it happened that since the accession to the English throne of James I—already then King of Scotland—the same person was the Sovereign of both England and Scotland, just as later, the same person was to occupy the British and the Hanoverian thrones. But that coincidence of sovereignties is beside the present purpose.

Their Lordships are unaware that there was, in 1660, any technical rule of draftsmanship governing the geographical area to which an English Act of Parliament was presumed to apply where its terms were silent on that point. The question whether such an Act applied outside England (which since 1536 has by Act of Parliament included Wales) must depend in such circumstances on the intention of its framers: to be deduced from the nature of its subject matter and substantive provisions. It would presumably have no such external application if its subject-matter were beyond question of merely insular and domestic import.

Their Lordships, if it were necessary to decide the point, would incline to the view that the Act of 1660 was of purely local application: that it applied to England only. Its main objects were two (i) to abolish certain oppressive incidents of feudal military tenure, "wardships", "marriages", "primer seisin", "ousterlemain" and the like. To effect this it was necessary to abolish the military or knights-service tenures themselves,—the soil from which those incidents sprang. Their sacrifice must involve the King in financial loss, for which he was to be compensated under the terms of the Act (ss. 15 to 27) by certain duties on strong liquors, for instance beer, cider, perry and *aqua vitae*; some home produced, some imported. It seems to their Lordships strained to suppose that such an Act, recording a compromise between the King of England and his people, the main object of which was the abolition of certain peculiarities of our insular medieval land tenure, was intended to apply to a vast tract of country thousands of miles away which was only inhabited at the time by a few Indians and half-castes: people who had never smarted under wardships, marriage and primer seisin, and had almost certainly never heard of them. It seems to their Lordships that these and the other provisions of the Act—notwithstanding that it provides that "free and common socage" should prevail in future, and abolishes tenure by "escuage"—were not intended to apply outside England and Wales; to which, along with Berwick-on-Tweed, the machinery for collecting the compensatory duties is expressly confined (s. 47).

Their Lordships have dwelt on this point somewhat at length because the judgments of the majority of the Supreme Court of Canada are so largely founded on it. Having regard however to the conclusions they have reached on other points, it is almost academic, because apart from the Rule governing settled colonies the Charter of 1670 under which the Hudson's Bay Company was granted Rupert's Land provides expressly for tenure of that land in "free and common socage and not *in capite* or by Knightes-service". That being so, two questions remain:

A. Were the terms of the grant which is in question in this case—a grant subject to a "variable royalty"—inconsistent with and in breach of the requirements of tenure in "free and common socage"?

B. If yes, were those requirements still valid when the grant was made in 1913, or had legislation, Regulations or Orders passed in the meantime so far modified them as to validate the grant?

A. The first of these questions is open to doubt; for as their Lordships have observed, in the Charter itself the consideration moving from the tenant—the royalty—is as to its amount largely at the discretion of the grantor, the King of England. If he chooses never to visit the area, no royalty is payable at all: and this would seem to argue that a considerable degree of "uncertainty" in the consideration moving from the tenant is compatible with "free and common socage", notwithstanding the *dicta* of Littleton, Coke and Blackstone, to the contrary. One instance given by Littleton (Coke on Littleton 96A) of a tenure on "certain" services is where the tenure depends on the tenant shearing all sheep on the grantor's land: a service which can clearly be made more or less burdensome according as the grantor chooses to have upon his land few or many sheep. Littleton himself describes this as a "certainty in uncertainty".

Rather than plunge into the jungle of learned disagreement which surrounds what is or is not involved in free and common socage, their Lordships will assume, without deciding, that it is inconsistent with the terms of the 1913 grant.

B. Upon that assumption, the residual question is whether competent legislation has validated the grant. Their Lordships have come to the conclusion that it *has* done so.

There can be no question that the Dominion Parliament was competent at all material times, after 1870, by clear enactment to repeal or vary any law as to land tenure prevailing in Rupert's Land before that region was in that year vested in the Dominion: even if this meant introducing forms of tenure unknown in the past to English law, or forbidden by it. The question is not whether the Dominion possessed the necessary power but whether in fact it exercised it.

The Legislature of a new country with a small population and vast possibilities of development might well favour an elastic policy in its efforts to attract settlers, and be the less inclined to submit indefinitely to the fetters of English feudal tradition in such matters as land tenure.

By a complex of legislation between 1868-1870, into the details of which their Lordships do not think it necessary to enter, the Hudson's Bay Co. surrendered its grant of Rupert's Land for £ 300,000 and on 23rd June, 1870, that region was admitted to the Dominion. The Charter of 1670 under which it had been granted to the Hudson's Bay Company expressly provided, as has been seen, that tenure should be in "free and common socage". Interim legislation (e.g., the Act of 1869 (Can.), c. 3) provided that all laws in force in Rupert's Land at the time of its admission should (unless contrary to the B.N.A. Act, 1867) remain in force till altered. An Imperial Act of 1871, c. 28, "to remove doubts", confirmed all Dominion statutes relating to this transaction and gave power to the Dominion inter alia to make provision for the "peace, order, and good government of any territory not for the time being included in any Province". (Which would aptly describe that part of Rupert's Land which later became Alberta). Subsequent Dominion Acts followed containing similar provisions, e.g., R.S.C. 1906, c. 62 (which itself reproduced similar provisions in an Act of 1886 and even earlier legislation), and by s. 12 enacted as follows: "Subject to the provisions of this Act, the laws of England relating to civil and criminal matters, as the same existed on the fifteenth day of July, in the year one thousand eight hundred and seventy, shall be in force in the Territories, in so far as the same are applicable to the Territories, and in so far as the same have not been, or are not hereafter, as regards to the Territories, repealed, altered, varied, modified, or affected by any Act of the Parliament of the United Kingdom or of the Parliament of Canada, applicable to the Territories, or by any ordinance of the Territories."

This provision was in force at the time of the disputed grant of 1913.

It can hardly be said that tenure by socage was in 1870 a part of the "Laws of England" *inapplicable* to Rupert's Land, since this tenure had been in force in that tract under the terms of its Charter, for exactly two centuries before its transfer to the Dominion. Nevertheless, the question remains whether by competent legislation subsequent to the transfer, this part of the "Laws of England" had been "repealed, altered, varied or modified" in such a way as to validate the present grant. Such validating provisions, if they exist, must be sought mainly, if not entirely, in the successive Dominion Lands Acts and Regulations or Orders made thereunder....

[The learned Lord here reviewed federal legislation, and regulations and orders thereunder and then continued as follows:]

.... Under s. 76 (k) of the 1908 Act the Crown in right of the Dominion had in their Lordships' opinion power to deal with a case such as this by applying to it certain of the terms (those as to royalties) of a superseded Regulation. This was a special case. Oil and gas had not been discovered in paying quantities but research and expenditure, attended with much benefit to the public, had been carried out and incurred by the prospectors, the predecessors in title of the respondent company. Hence they were allowed to acquire the land and rights in question without complying with any Regulation (assuming one to exist) but were compelled to submit to liability in future to a royalty not prescribed by any Regulation in force at the time of the grant.

Their Lordships do not consider that in dealing with such special or hard cases under s. 76 (k) it was intended that the discretion of the Crown should be fettered or controlled by incidents of English feudal land tenure. It had been expressly enacted that the Dominion Parliament could repeal, vary or modify any English law prevailing before 1870 in Territories such as Rupert's Land, and Territories like Alberta which might be carved out of it. In providing as it did in s. 76 (k) of the 1908 Act for a discretionary power to deal with hard or anomalous cases the Legislature was, as it seems to their Lordships, arrogating to itself the right to infringe the requirements of "free and common socage", so far as the end in view required. Where the justice of the individual case required it, it seems to their Lordships unreasonable (unless the language of the material enactments forces them to such a conclusion) to hold that the Crown's liberty to deal with such cases was intended to be exercised only within the limits set by a rigid respect for the (obscure and debated) frontiers of historical socage tenure.

If this conclusion is justified, it follows that the grant of 1913 was valid not only in other respects but in respect of the variable and prospective royalties reserved to the Crown in right of the Dominion. Those rights have now been transferred to Alberta. In 1930 the *Transfer Agreement Acts* were passed in identical terms by the Legislatures of Alberta (1930, c. 21), of the Dominion (1930, c. 3), and of the Imperial Parliament (1930, c. 26)...

Section 3 [of the Schedule to the Alberta Act] is as follows: "Any power or right, which, by any such contract, lease or other arrangements, or by any Act of the Parliament of Canada relating to any of the lands, mines, minerals or royalties hereby transferred or by any regulation made under any such Act, is reserved to the Governor in Council or to the Minister of the Interior or any other officer of the Government of Canada, may be exercised by such officer of the Government of the Province as may be specified by the Legislature thereof from time to time, and until otherwise directed, may be exercised by the Provincial Secretary of the Province."

The right to levy a "variable" royalty on these lands was a "right" which within s. 3 by "contract ... or other arrangements ... relating to ... lands, mines, minerals or royalties" was originally reserved to the Crown in right of the Dominion and by ss. 1 and 3 was in 1930 transferred from the Crown in right of the Dominion to the Crown in right of the Province of Alberta: which accordingly was justified through its Lieutenant-Governor in Council, in levying by the various Orders in Council of 1941-1948 (set out in para. 6 of the statement of claim) the royalties complained of by the plaintiffs-respondents in the present case.

Appeal allowed.

[Copyhold tenure as well as local customs affecting freeholds were abolished in England by the Law of Property Act, 1922 (Imp.), c. 16, s. 128. See, generally, *Megarry and Wade*, Law of Real Property (1959, 2d ed.), c. 2.]

[In *Lunenburg* v. *Lunenburg*, [1932] 1 D.L.R. 386, 4 M.P.R. 181, Ross J. speaking for the Supreme Court of Nova Scotia, *en banc*, said:

"In this case we are primarily called on to construe an Act of the Legislature and not to discuss abstruse questions of real property law. I think it is safe to say, that the Legislature never intended to inflict on the parties the Chinese puzzle that would result from a declaration such as the plaintiff seeks in this action. The Legislature enacted that on the payment of a certain amount of money the defendant should have 'the use forever' of certain portions of the building for court room, Judges' room, etc. I am not concerned about giving the defendant's interest any special technical name; all I am concerned with is that the right was created by the statute and I adopt the opinion of Jessel, M.R., in the case of *Sevenoaks Maidstone &*

Turnbridge R. Co. v. *London Chatham & Dover R. Co.* (1879), 11 Ch. D. 625, that interests unknown to the common law may be created by statute. Even if there is no such thing at common law as a lease in perpetuity I do not see why Parliament cannot create an estate equivalent to such lease. I think this reasoning finds support in the case of *Manchester Ship Canada Co.* v. *Manchester Racecourse Co.*, [1900] 2 Ch. 352, at p. 360.

"If the Legislature has declared that the defendant is to get the 'use forever' of the premises I do not see how the Court can say that it got someting else. It might be different if it could be successfully urged that the Legislature obviously intended to confer a fee simple, but that is exactly what in my judgment the Legislature never intended to do. The plaintiff was and still is the owner in fee simple of the property in question, subject to the statutory rights of the defendant.

"The Act (1893, c. 115, s. 5) provides that:—'The county shall keep the rooms and offices above mentioned in good repair, and shall pay for any insurance that the municipality of Lunenburg may insure upon the same, and shall pay any expenses of heating such portion of said building to such extent and as needed for county purposes.'

"If the defendant acquired a title in fee simple the argument is of course that it would be liable for all repairs, exterior as well as interior.

"I think the only liability on the defendant for repairs is found in the Act of 1893 and that is to keep the offices and rooms in good repair. I would construe that to mean only the interior of the portions occupied by the defendant and I think that would be the meaning given to similar words if found in a lease of the premises in question."]

2. LAND LAW AND TENURE IN CANADA

"IT HAS BEEN SAID", remarked Riddell J. in *Miller* v. *Tipling* (1918), 43 O.L.R. 88, at p. 96, 43 D.L.R. 469, at p. 477, "that the law of land in countries under the common law of England is a 'rubbish-heap which has been accumulating for hundreds of years, and ... is ... based upon feudal doctrines which no one (except professors in law schools) understands'—and rather with the implication that even the professors do not thoroughly understand them or all understand them the same way." Readers and students will have to determine for themselves how far this estimate is correct on either or both counts.

It is a fact that free and common socage has been and is the only freehold tenure operative in the common law provinces. The Constitutional Act, 1791 (Imp.) c. 3, under which Upper Canada and Lower Canada were created provided in section 43 as follows: "... all lands which shall be hereafter granted within the said Province of Upper Canada shall be granted in free and common soccage, in like manner as lands are now holden in free and common soccage in that part of Great Britain called England; and that in every case where lands shall be hereafter granted within the said Province of Lower Canada, and where the grantee thereof shall desire the same to be granted in free and common soccage, the same shall be so granted; but subject nevertheless to such alterations with respect to the nature and consequences of such tenure of free and common soccage, as may be established by any law or laws which may be made by his Majesty, his heirs or successors, by and with the advice and consent of the Legislative Council and Assembly of the Province."

Moreover, so far as Ontario is concerned, the first statute of the newly-created province of Upper Canada, 1792, c. 1, stipulated that "from and after the passing of this Act [i.e. from and after October 15, 1792] in all matters of controversy relative to property and civil rights resort shall be had to the laws of England as the rule for the decision of the same". This provision is now included in section 1 of the Property and Civil Rights Act, R.S.O. 1960,

c. 310. In addition, there is specific Ontario legislation re-enacting such landmark statutes as De Donis Conditionalibus and Quia Emptores (see An Act respecting Real Property, R.S.O. 1897, c. 330, which is still in force and reproduced in R.S.O. 1960, vol. 5, appendix A) and the Statute of Uses (see Statute of Uses, R.S.O. 1897, c. 331, likewise in force and reproduced in R.S.O. 1960, vol. 5, Appendix A).

It will have been noticed that free and common socage is a permissible tenure in Quebec. There too the land law system had its feudal characteristics as evidenced by the seigniory system. Feudal and seigniorial duties and charges were abolished, however, in 1854 and replaced by "constituted rents" payable to the seignior in lieu of the feudal burdens. These rents were redeemable by a capital payment. At the same time the seigniory holdings were changed to holdings in *franc-alleu roturier*. (See the Seigniories' Act, R.S.Q. 1941, c. 321.) While it may be said that the present land law system in Quebec is, generally speaking, no longer based on tenurial relationships, there are comparable institutions like the emphyteutic lease and life rents (see Quebec Civil Code, arts, 567 ff. and 1901 ff.). In dealing with land held in Quebec in free and common socage, the Privy Council summed up the position thereon as follows in *St. Francis Hydro Electric Co.* v. *The King*, [1937] 2 D.L.R. 353, at p. 362:

"... It is undeniable that the decisions in Quebec including the decisions on appeal to His Majesty in Council have uniformly regarded lands granted in free and common soccage as subject to the French law except as regards tenure. (See for example *Leamy* v. *The King*, 54 S.C.R. 143, at pp. 147-8, 33 D.L.R., at pp. 238-9.) The position may be summarized as follows:—The original law was the old French law. After the Treaty of Paris in 1763, the English common law was introduced by Murray's Ordinance of September 17, 1764, and the Courts were directed to determine cases agreeably 'to equity, having regard nevertheless to the laws of England, as far as the circumstances and present situation of things will admit, until such time as proper Ordinances ... can be established by the Governor and Council, agreeable to the laws of England.' This introduction of the English law was repealed by the Quebec Act of 1774, with an exception, however, as to lands granted in free and common socage. The Constitutional Act of 1791, s. 43, provided that in Lower Canada lands should be thereafter granted in free and common socage when the grantee should so desire, but 'subject nevertheless to such alterations with respect to the nature and consequences of such tenure of free and common soccage, as may be established by any law or laws which may be made by His Majesty, His heirs or successors, by and with the advice and consent of the Legislative Council and Assembly of the Province.' At this date there might well have been doubts as to the legal position but in the Act, 1857, c. 45 of the Legislature of the United Canadas, a declaration is to be found in the following terms:

"'5. The Laws which have governed lands held in Free and Common Soccage in Lower Canada, in matters other than alienation, descent and rights depending upon marriage, are hereby declared to have always been the same with those which governed lands held in *franc alleu roturier*, except in so far only as it may have been otherwise provided by any Act of the Legislature of Lower Canada, or of this Province....'"

In the Pacific and Western provinces there is governing legislation establishing an "in force" date for English law, so far as not inapplicable by reason of local circumstances, or, so far as applicable, and subject, of course, to local legislation. In the result, the situation is not unlike that in Ontario: the only freehold tenure is free and common socage and statutes like Quia Emptores and the Statute of Uses are in force. In British Columbia, the relevant date is November 19, 1858 (see English Law Act, R.S.B.C. 1960, c. 129); in Alberta and in Saskatchewan, the relevant date is July 15, 1870 (as established by the North-West Territories Act, 1886 (Can.), c. 25, s. 3 and carried forward on the creation of those provinces in 1905 by the Alberta Act, 1905 (Can.), c. 3, s. 16, and by the Saskatchewan Act, 1905 (Can.), c. 42, s. 16, respectively); and in Manitoba the relevant date is likewise July 15, 1870. The history of the application of English land law in the last mentioned province deserves some elaboration which has a bearing on the position in Alberta and Saskatchewan as well. The history goes back to the grants of land to the Hudson's Bay Company in 1670 in free and common socage, land which "was treated as extending to what became known later as Rupert's Land and the North-Western Territory" (per Lord Haldane in *Walker* v. *Walker* [1919] A.C. 947, at p. 950 where there is a discussion of the history). When this land became part of Canada by order-in-council of June 23, 1870, issued by virtue of s. 146 of the B.N.A. Act and the Rupert's Land Act, 1868 (Imp.), c. 105, the law there was the English law in 1670 as brought in by the settlers so far as applicable; any applicable Imperial legislation enacted thereafter; and laws promulgated by the Hudson's Bay Company under its charter powers. The Company had passed an ordinance in 1851 making applicable to the District of Assiniboia (later Manitoba), then part of Rupert's Land, the law of England not as of 1670 but as at the date of Queen Victoria's accession; and in 1864 this was replaced by a provision embracing "all such laws of England of subsequent date as may be applicable". In 1869 the Dominion, anticipating the incorporation of the Hudson's Bay Company territory into Canada enacted legislation (1869, c. 3) providing for the continuance in force, so far as consistent with the B.N.A. Act, of all laws, until properly altered. By the Manitoba Act 1870 (Can.), c. 3, confirmed by 1871 (Imp.), c. 28, the province of Manitoba was established and, subject thereto, the 1869 Act of the Dominion was temporarily continued in force. By a statute of 1874, c. 12, the new province made applicable English law as of July 15, 1870 "so far as the same can be made applicable to matters relating to property and civil rights in this province". This, of course, could not bring into force any law in relation to matters within federal authority under the B.N.A. Act, and in 1888, a Dominion statute, c. 51, introduced into Manitoba as of July 15, 1870, English law, so far as applicable, dealing with matters within federal legislative authority. This problem did not arise in the case of British Columbia because in 1871 the legislature there introduced English law as of November 19, 1858, before that colony became a province, and thus at a time when it was not bound by the distribution of legislative power under the B.N.A. Act. For additional discussion of the historical situation see *Sinclair* v. *Mulligan* (1888), 5 Man. R. 17, aff'g 3 Man. R. 481; *Trusts and Guarantee Co.* v. *The King* (1916), 54 S.C.R. 107, at pp. 124 ff.

In the Northwest Territories, the applicable English law is that as of July 15, 1870, save as subsequently varied (Northwest Territories Act, R.S.C. 1952, c. 331, s. 17, amended 1960, c. 20, s. 2) and in the Yukon the legal inheritance is the laws and ordinances in force in the Northwest Territories on June 13, 1898 (being the date on which the Yukon was established as a separate territory), so far as applicable and so far as not altered (Yukon Act, 1952-53 (Can.), c. 53, s. 22, amended 1960, c. 24, s. 5).

The Maritime Provinces are regarded as having been colonies by settlement to which, broadly speaking, English law was brought by settlers so far as reasonably applicable and subject, of course, to change by competent legislation: see *Uniacke* v. *Dickson* (1848), 2 N.S.R. 287; *Doe d. Hanington* v. *McFadden* (1836), 2 N.B.R. 260; *Doe d. Evans* v. *Doyle* (1860), 4 Nfld. L. R. 432. (As to the law of Newfoundland consequent upon its union with Canada, see Schedule to 1949 (Can.), c. 1, Terms of Union of Newfoundland with Canada, section 18.) There is no doubt of the applicability to those provinces of enactments like Quia Emptores and the Statute of Uses, and of the reception of the common law rules on seisin and conveyancing. On the other hand, some doctrines of the common law and some statutes were deemed inapplicable, e.g. primogeniture in Newfoundland (see *Doe d. Evans* v. *Doyle*, *supra*) and the Statute of Enrolments in Nova Scotia (see *Berry* v. *Berry* (1882), 16 N.S.R. 66).

[For some interesting history on the introduction of English law into Nova Scotiâ, see Whence Came the Common Law into Canada, (1920) 56 Can. L. J. (N.S.) 281.]

[See *Hogg*, The Effect of Tenure on Real Property Law, (1909) 25 L.Q. Rev. 178. Is the proposition "cujus est solum ejus est a centro usque ad coelum" a necessary consequence of tenure? To what extent, if at all, may a person assert any possessory or proprietary interest in the air space over land? See *Clifton* v. *Bury* (1887), 4 T.L.R. 8 (Q.B.); *U.S.* v. *Causby* (1946), 328 U.S. 256; *Note*, (1947) 45 Mich. L. Rev. 875. In *Lacroix* v. *The Queen*, [1954] Ex. C.R. 69, [1954] 4 D.L.R. 470 it was held that "air and space are not susceptible of ownership and fall in the category of *res omnium communis*", but this does not prevent the surface owner from use and enjoyment, as by putting up buildings. However, he had no right to expropriation compensation merely because the air space over his land was used as a flightway by aircraft taking off and landing at an adjacent airport. On the other hand, it was held in *Kelsen* v. *Imperial Tobacco Co.*, [1957] 2 Q.B. 334, [1957] 2 All E.R. 343 that the rule that, *prima facie*, the air column above a building passes with a transfer of the property, was not displaced in the case of a lease of a one-storey building; and consequently the lessee was entitled to a mandatory injunction for the removal of a sign which protruded in the air space from an adjacent three-storey building. The action sounded in trespass and not in nuisance, and relief was proper although there was no interference with enjoyment of the leasehold. See *Wright*, Cases on the Law of Torts (1963, 3rd ed.), pp. 57 ff.; *Richardson*, Private Property Rights in the Air Space at Common Law, (1953) 31 Can. Bar Rev. 117; *Note*, Ownership and Control of Air-space, (1953) 37 Marquette L. Rev. 176; *Note*, Evolution of Federal Jurisdiction over Air-space, (1954) 29 N.Y.U.L. Rev. 169.

A person may enjoy a freehold interest in an upper floor or room of a building: see *Iredale* v. *Loudon* (1908), 40 S.C.R. 313. Similarly, subsurface freehold interests in land may be created by horizontal severance: see *Algoma Ore Properties Ltd.* v. *Smith*, [1953] 2 D.L.R. 543 (Ont.) (rev'd on other grounds [1953] O.R. 634, [1953] 3 D.L.R. 343 (C.A.)), where Judson J. said (at p. 545): "The point of the case is that this devise is one of all the mines and minerals. In a similar case as far back as 1808 Mansfield C.J. said: 'The grant of the stratum must be taken to be a grant in fee simple': *Stoughton* v. *Leigh* (1808), 1 Taunt. 402 at p. 409, 127 E.R. 889. The principle is that there may be a severance of the mines and minerals from ownership of the surface and that the mines and minerals so severed are a separate tenement capable of being held for the same estates as other hereditaments: 22 Hals., 2nd ed., p. 535; Armour on Real Property, 2nd ed., p. 47. The right to sever and create separate fees simple in the surface and the mines and minerals has been recognized in *Ex p. Jackson*, [1925] 1 D.L.R. 701, 21 A.L.R. 168; *Bucke* v. *Macrae Mining Co.*, [1927] 3 D.L.R. 1, S.C.R. 403, and *Cavana* v. *Tisdale*, [1942] 1 D.L.R. 465, O.R. 31; affd [1942] 4 D.L.R. 65, S.C.R. 384." There is often a construction problem in such situations on whether the interest is merely a profit à prendre or a freehold. A similar construction problem may arise in respect of a grant dealing with standing timber, because it is clear that a person may enjoy a freehold interest in standing timber apart from a freehold interest in the surrounding soil: see *Eastern Construction Co. Ltd.* v. *National Trust Co.*, [1914] A.C. 197, 15 D.L.R. 755 (P.C.); *Smith* v. *Daly and Booth Lumber Ltd.*, [1949] O.R. 601, [1949] 4 D.L.R. 45.

[The Courts have been wont to say that decisions on land law, especially if they have lain unchallenged for some time, should not ordinarily be unsettled even if it be the fact that they are not entirely satisfactory: see *Doe d. Evans* v. *Doyle* (1860), 4 Nfld. L.R. 432; *Re Hazell*, 57 O.L.R. 290, [1925] 3 D.L.R. 661.]

THE ESCHEATS ACT, R.S.O. 1960, c. 123

1. In this Act,
   (a) "heir" means a person beneficially entitled to property of an intestate;
   (b) "property" means real property or personal property.

2. (1) Where any property has become the property of the Crown by reason of the person last seised thereof or entitled thereto having died intestate and without lawful heirs, or has become forfeited for any cause to the Crown, the Public Trustee may cause possession thereof to be taken in the name of the Crown, or if possession is withheld may cause an action to be brought for the recovery thereof, without an inquisition being first made.

(2) The proceedings in the action may be in all respects similar to those in other actions for the recovery of property.

3. Notwithstanding section 2, where mining lands as defined by *The Mining Act* have become forfeited to the Crown, such mining lands shall be dealt with and disposed of as Crown lands in the manner provided in *The Mining Act*.

4. The Lieutenant-Governor in Council may grant any property which has become the property of or has become forfeited to the Crown as mentioned in section 2, or any it to a person having a legal or moral claim upon the person to whom it had belonged, or of carrying into effect any disposition of it which such person may have contemplated, or of rewarding a person making discovery of the escheat or forfeiture, as to the Lieutenant-Governor in Council seems proper.

5. Any such grant may be made without actual entry or taking possession of such property or inquisition being first made, and, if possession of the property is withheld, the person to whom the grant is made may institute proceedings for the recovery thereof in a court of competent jurisdiction.

6. Where any such forfeiture takes place, the Lieutenant-Governor in Council may waive or release any right to which the Crown may thereby have become entitled so as to vest the property, either absolutely or otherwise, in the person who would have been entitled thereto but for the forfeiture, and the waiver or release may be either for valuable consideration or otherwise and may be upon such terms and conditions as to the Lieutenant-Governor in Council seems proper.

7. (1) Where possession of any real estate or interest therein has been taken by the Public Trustee under the provisions of this Act, the Lieutenant-Governor in Council may direct the sale of such real estate at such price and upon such terms as is determined and the Public Trustee shall thereupon be authorized to sell, in accordance with the directions of the Order in Council, the whole or any part of such real estate or any interest therein and to convey it to the purchaser.

(2) Where possession of any personal estate has been taken by the Public Trustee under this Act, the Public Trustee may sell such personal estate at such price and upon such terms as to him seem proper.

[For comparable legislation, see Ultimate Heir Act. R.S.A. 1955, c. 348; Escheats Act, R.S.B.C. 1960, c. 132; Escheats Act, R.S.M. 1954, c. 74; Escheats and Forfeitures Act, R. S. N. B. 1952, c. 73; Escheats Act, R.S.N.S. 1954, c. 86; Escheats Act, R.S.P.E.I. 1951, c. 51; Quebec Civil Code, art. 401; Escheat and Confiscation Act, R. S. Q. 1941, c. 102, amended 1949, c. 38; Escheats Act. R.S.S. 1953, c. 81. In Newfoundland, The Abandoned Lands Act, R.S. Nfld. 1952, c. 186, provides that certain lands (e.g. those granted under the Crown Lands Act) which remain unused and unoccupied for 40 years may, on an application to the Supreme Court, be declared to revert to the Crown. By section 23, nothing in the Act is to prevent application of the general law relating to escheat of lands to the Crown.

Where escheat takes place in respect of land within the territorial limits of any Province it is to the Crown in right of the Province and not to the Crown in right of Canada: see *A.-G. of Ontario v. Mercer* (1883), 8 App. Cas. 767. If the Crown takes land by escheat, does it take subject to deceased's debts? See *Re Androws* (1957), 10 D.L.R. 2d 731 (Man.

Surr. Ct.); *Re Hole*, [1948] 4 D.L.R. 419, [1948] 2 W.W.R. 754, 56 Man. R. 295; *Note*, (1949) 27 Can. Bar Rev. 592.

In *Jones* v. *McClean*, 39 Man. R. 321, [1931] 2 D.L.R. 244 [1931] 1 W.W.R. 315 (C.A.), Fullerton J.A. said: "I know of no principle of English law under which real estate can pass from one to another by 'abandonment'. One man cannot abandon his property to another. The term is not applicable to the transfer of property. A man may sell or give away his property to another but he clearly cannot 'abandon' it to another."]

CHAPTER II

POSSESSORY ESTATES

1. DOCTRINE OF ESTATES

THE TENURIAL FEATURES of the feudal system emphasized that a person "holds" land but does not "own" it. True, after *Quia Emptores*, the "holding" would come, more and more, to be only of the Crown, but the concept has remained to this day. The holder's interest under one of the feudal tenures was an "estate" (derived from "status"), because a relationship was established between the type of tenure interest and a man's position or status. A person holding by one of the free tenures (military service, socage, frankalmoign or serjeanty) was a freeholder and his estate was a freehold in quality. (Tenure by villeinage or copyhold was the unfree tenure.) Moreover, in time it was recognized that estates could be measured quantitatively (in terms of duration rather than area) and that, quantum-wise, freehold estates were of uncertain duration, as contrasted with an interest lasting for a defined period, e.g. a leasehold interest. Freehold estates thus came to be classified and valued according to the potential length of time they might last. The final shape of the classification depended on the settlement of three sets of conflicts which were thrown up by the personal and land-holding features of the feudal system: (1) the conflict between the lord and his tenant; (2) the conflict between the lord and the presumptive heir of the tenant; and (3) the conflict between the tenant and his presumptive heir. (The development of primogeniture made it possible to speak of "heir" rather than "heirs".) While the first conflict had its main effect on the evolution of tenures and their incidents, the latter two were more closely related to the development of estates because out of the second came the principle of inheritability, and out of the third, the principle of alienability. The personal aspect of the relation of lord and man meant that on the termination of that relationship by the death of the tenant his estate would also terminate. The recognition of a right of inheritance against the lord modified the strictly personal character of feudalism and made it possible to mark off inheritable estates from others which might end with the death of the holder. Alienability as a feature of estate holding between lord and tenant is represented in the struggle leading to Quia Emptores, 1290; but even before this, the tenant established a power of alienation against the claim of the presumptive heir of his inheritable estates.

D'ARUNDEL'S CASE, Brac. N.B. 1054 (1225)

Radulf the son of Roger sought against William of Arundel five acres of land in Trelley, three acres in Treberned, two acres in Tredeiset and one acre in Hendrie and their appurtenances of which Roger his father was seized in law and in feudal services in the time of Lord Henry the King, and which descended from Roger by the law of the land to this same Radulf as his son and heir.

And William came and defended his right, and said that the same Roger, the father, conveyed with quiet enjoyment all the land and its appurtenances to William, the father of William, in the King's Court all his right and inheritance therein; to William and his heirs solely and free from himself and his heirs forever, and offered a deed of Roger by which these things were attested.

And Radulf came and admitted the deed of his father and covenant of quiet enjoyment, but asked judgement whether his father could convey all the land which he held by military tenure, retaining no service to himself and his heirs.

And since Radulf admitted his father's deed and it was attested by the deed that his father Roger conveyed all his land and warranted quiet enjoyment from his heirs, it was adjudged that William should go in peace and Radulf be in mercy.

[1 *Restatement of Property* (1936), section 9: "The word 'estate', as it is used in this Restatement, means an interest in land which (a) is or may become possessory; and (b) is ownership measured in terms of duration."]

2. SEISIN AND POSSESSION

"SEISIN" has been aptly described as the quality of the possession of a freehold estate or the root of proprietary interest in a freehold: see *Maitland.* The Mystery of Seisin, (1886) 2 Law. Q. Rev. 481; 2 *Pollock and Maitland,* History of English Law, 2nd ed., p. 29; *Bordwell,* Seisin and Disseisin, (1920-21) 34 Harv. L. Rev. 592, 717.

BIGELOW, INTRODUCTION TO THE LAW OF REAL PROPERTY

[Chap. 2] Section 7. Seisin and Possession.

The distinction that the law makes between freehold and nonfreehold estates, which has already been referred to, is of importance in another regard, namely, in the distinction between seisin and possession. The word "seisin" is a very old one in the English law. In the first one or two centuries after the Conquest, it was used merely to indicate possession, either of land or of chattels. Thus the old writers speak indifferently of a man being seised of land or of a horse. Gradually, however, the term "seisin" began to take on a more technical meaning, and to be distinguished from the word "possession".

In discussing the origin of the nonfreehold estates it has been pointed out that the estate for years was in the beginning regarded as giving the lessee for years only a contract right against his lessor, that his occupation of the land was more in the nature of a chattel interest therein than of a holding within the feudal organization. Consequently for the purposes of determining feudal relations and obligations the freehold lessor of the tenant for years was the only one looked to by the overlord. Gradually the term "seisin" was applied only to denote the possession of a tenant holding a freehold estate, and the occupancy of a tenant holding a nonfreehold estate was designated as possession, and this difference in the terms is now definitely established. Consequently, if A, owning in fee simple, leases to B for years, B has the possession, but A still retains the seisin, even though, of course, the de facto occupant of the land is B.

The next step in the development of the doctrine of seisin may be illustrated by the following case: Suppose A, the owner in fee, grants to B for life. B. now having a freehold estate, has the seisin. B, however, owes A the feudal obligations of homage, fealty, and the like. Consequently the feudal lawyers said that A also was seised in respect of these rights. They distinguished between the two by saying that B was seised in his demesne and that A was seised in his services. This idea of a seisin that was not in fact accompanied by an actual possession was applied in another type of case. Thus, if A had a right to rent from B's land,

and A's estate in the rent was a freehold (i.e., in fee or for life), A was said to be seised of the rent to which he is thus entitled; and if A was deprived of the rent by the tortious act of B or of a third person, A was said to be disseised of the rent, and he could bring an action to recover the rent that was almost identical with the action that he would bring to recover the seisin of land from which he had been tortiously ousted. It is not necessary to follow further these interesting questions of the somewhat refined doctrines of seisin. Our concern at present is only with the seisin of the demesne; that is, with the actual possession of the land under a freehold title. In connection with the idea of seisin in this most elementary sense one other aspect of the doctrine, of extreme importance in the law of conveyances of interests in land and of the creation of future estates in land which are next to be considered, requires to be specifically stated. The purpose of the feudal organization of society and the whole theory upon which it was constructed were that all land should always be in the possession of some tenant having a freehold interest therein—that is, a seisin—who should be responsible for the performance of the feudal obligations. From this principle follows the doctrine that the seisin of land can never be in abeyance, or, to state the same thing in a different form, that some one must always be seised of any given piece of land. There were a few minor exceptions to this rule, but they are of so slight importance as not to require further mention.

[Chap. 5.] Disseisin and the Remedies Therefor.

The importance of the seisin of the land, the freehold possession of it, in the earlier law, has already been referred to. This doctrine of seisin remains to be considered from still another point of view, viz., as to the effect produced upon the rights of persons having an interest in land by a wrongful ouster or disseisin therefrom.

Suppose that A is seised of land in fee simple, and that B wrongfully enters upon him and puts him out. The effect of this act by B, technically called a disseisin, is to divest A of the seisin of the land and to vest a tortious seisin in B. Or, again, suppose that A has a reversion in fee, subject to a life estate in B, and B wrongfully enfeoffs X in fee. This also operates as a disseisin of A. The same result follows if the tenant for life should enfeoff X in tail. This would give X a tortious seisin in tail, with a tortious reversion in fee in B, the tenant for life. The effect of a disseisin, if committed against a tenant in fee, was necessarily to deprive him of all his interest in the land and to vest a tortious seisin in the disseisor, which might be divided into smaller tortious estates in the manner above indicated. A's interest was no longer an estate; after the disseisin, all he possessed was a right of entry or a right of action. These rights were peculiarly personal to himself. They could descend to his heir, but they could not be alienated.

A's remedies after a disseisin of the sort above indicated were three: He had, first, the right of self-help. If within a short time after his disseisin (under the older law, apparently five days) he made a re-entry upon the disseisor, he might thereby successfully re-establish himself in the seisin of the land. At a later date this period was probably somewhat lengthened, but it was always brief, and by the Statute 3 Rich. II, ch. 8, it was provided that no entry should be made, even by the disseisee, if it involved a breach of the peace. If the circumstances were such that A could not safely make this re-entry upon the land, he could keep alive his right of entry by making once a year as near the land as possible a definite assertion of his right thereto and a demand for the repossession thereof. This was known as keeping alive the right of entry by continual claim. Even under these circumstances, however, the right of entry was lost if the disseisor died in the wrongful seisin of the land, so that the wrongful seisin thereof descended to his heirs. In this case the right of entry was said to be tolled by descent cast.

If the disseisee, for one reason or another, lost his right of entry, he was then driven to bring his action. Actions for the assertion of rights in land were of two sorts: droitural and possessory. The purpose of the droitural action, as the name indicates, was to determine, as between the plaintiff and the defendant, who had the right to the land. The droitural actions, however, were very slow, very expensive, and gave a great advantage to the defendant, because of the mere fact that he was in the possession of the land with respect to which the action was being brought. Consequently in the reign of Henry II (1154-1189) the so-called possessory actions first made their appearance. The purpose of these actions was to determine, not the question of the ultimate right to the land, but who was entitled to the immediate possession thereof. That is to say, in the hypothetical case under discussion, if A had lost his right of entry, his next step would be to bring a possessory action based upon the fact that he had been in possession of the land. In this action neither A nor B would be allowed to raise the question of the ultimate ownership of the land; the only question that would be decided would be whether A had been in the seisin of the land and B had put him out without any judgment justifying B in so doing. If so, A would have judgment for a restoration to possession and for damages. After A had been thus revested with the seisin of the land, B might, as plaintiff, litigate the question of who was really entitled to the land. The purpose and limited scope of this possessory action made it necessary that it should be brought within a short time after the disseisin complained of. The form of possessory action first devised was the novel disseisin; later other forms were invented to meet varying situations.

If the plaintiff, A, delayed too long in the bringing of his possessory action, so that this method of procedure was no longer open to him, or if he was defeated in his possessory action through some technical reason, he would still be able to bring his droitural action. He would no longer be able to rely upon his right to immediate possession, but despite the fact that the defendant would have the benefit of the actual seisin of the land, the plaintiff would still have it open to him to show that he nevertheless had a better right to the land than did the defendant, and if he ultimately succeeded in obtaining a judgment in the droitural action, he would then be restored to the land from which he had been disseised.

By the beginning of the 17th century both the writs of entry and writs of right had become practically obsolete, and the action of ejectment, of which mention has been made in the discussion of leasehold estates, had become the almost universal method of settling the right to both possession and title of land. The use of fictions by which this action was enlarged from its original narrow purpose is characteristic of the method by which the common-law judges accomplished desirable results by the adoption of means that were originally intended for no such purpose.

[Reproduced by the kind permission of the publishers.]

[See *Cheshire*, Modern Law of Real Property (7th ed. 1954), at pp. 29-30:

"If A., the tenant of land, is ejected by B. at the present day, his proprietary rights are still exercisable, while B. has nothing that can properly be called ownership until he has been in possession long enough to acquire a title under the Limitation Act. But the position was far otherwise in early days. The former rights of the disseisee, A., were reduced in the eyes of the law to a right of entry, a reduction that entailed certain grave consequences. Thus, he lost the power of alienation, for a right of entry could neither be devised until 1837, nor conveyed *inter vivos* until 1845; if he died intestate, he left nothing to be inherited by his heirs, for until the Inheritance Act, 1833, the principle was *seisina fecit stipitem*; if he failed to recover seisin, his widow had no right to dower; if he died heirless, the land did not in all cases escheat to his lord; if he died leaving an infant heir, his lord was not entitled to wardship.

"In short, to be disseised was to lose all beneficial rights over the land until seisin was regained as the result of successful proceedings.

"On the other hand, the disseisor enjoyed all such rights. Thus, in the sphere of alienation, he could make a feoffment, *i.e.* a conveyance, in fee simple to X., the effect of which was to divest the estate of the disseisee, A., and to vest a fee simple in X. Such a feoffment was called a tortious feoffment, but the estate conveyed to X., though it took effect by wrong, was an effective fee simple until displaced by a successful action.

"Again, after the power of testamentary disposition had been extended to realty by the Wills Act, 1540, the disseisor could devise the land; he was succeeded by his heir if he died intestate; and it was his wife, not the wife of the disseisee, who was dowable out of the land."]

3 BLACKSTONE, COMMENTARIES (Lewis edition), chap. X, pp. 1161 ff.

Outster of the *freehold* is effected by one of the following methods:—1. Abatement; 2. Intrusion; 3. Disseisin; 4. Discontinuance; 5. Deforcement.

An *abatement* is where a person dies seised of an inheritance and before the heir or devisee enters, a stranger who has no right makes entry and gets possession of the freehold. This entry of him is called an abatement, and he himself is denominated an abator.

The second species of injury by ouster, or amotion of possession from the freehold, is by *intrusion* which is the entry of a stranger, after a particular estate of freehold is determined, before him in remainder or reversion. And it happens where a tenant for term of life dieth seised of certain lands and tenements, and a stranger entereth thereon, after such death of the tenant, and before any entry of him in remainder or reversion. This entry and interposition of the stranger differ from an abatement in this; that an abatement is always to the prejudice of the heir or immediate devisee; an intrusion is always to the prejudice of him in remainder or reversion.

Desseisin is a wrongful putting out of him that is seised of the freehold. The two former species of injury were by a wrongful entry where the possession was vacant; but this is an attack upon him who is in actual possession, and turning him out of it. Those were an ouster from a freehold in law; this is an ouster from a freehold in deed. Disseisin may be effected either in corporeal inheritances, or incorporeal. Disseisin of things corporeal, as of houses, lands, etc., must be by entry and actual dispossession of the freehold; as if a man enters either by force or fraud into the house of another, and turns, or at least keeps, him or his servants out of possession. Disseisin of incorporeal hereditaments cannot be an actual dispossession: for the subject itself is neither capable of actual bodily possession, or dispossession; but it depends on their respective natures, and various kinds; being in general nothing more than a disturbance of the owner in the means of coming at or enjoying them.

The injury of *discontinuance* happens when he who hath an estate-tail maketh a larger estate of the land than by law he is entitled to do: in which case the estate is good, so far as his power extends who made it, but no further. As if tenant in tail makes a feoffment in fee-simple, or for the life of the feoffee, or in tail; all which are beyond his power to make, for that by the common law extends no further than to make a lease for his own life; in such case the entry of the feoffee is lawful during the life of the feoffor; but if he retains the possession after the death of the feoffor, it is an injury, which is termed a discontinuance: the ancient legal estate, which ought to have survived to the heir in tail, being gone, or at least suspended, and for a while discontinued.

The fifth and last species of injuries by ouster or privation of the freehold, where the entry of the present tenant or possessor was originally lawful, but his detainer is now become unlawful, is that by *deforcement*. This, in its most extensive sense, is *nomen generalissimum;* a much larger and more comprehensive expression than any of the former: it then signifying the holding of any lands or tenements to which another person hath a right. So that this includes as well an abatement, an intrusion, a disseisin, or a discontinuance, as any other species of wrong whatsoever, whereby he that hath right to the freehold is kept out of possession. But, as contradistinguished from the former, it is only such a detainer of the freehold from him that hath the right of property, but never had any possession under that right, as falls within none of the injuries which we have before explained.

[The Limitations Act, R.S.O. 1960, c. 214, section 9 reads: "No continual or other claim upon or near any land shall preserve any right of making an entry or distress or of bringing an action"; section 10: "No descent cast, discontinuance or warranty, which has happened or been made since the 1st day of July, 1834, or which may hereafter happen or be made, shall toll or defeat any right of entry or action for the recovery of land."

The right of entry upon a disseisin was not devisable by will in England until the Wills Act, 1837 (Imp.) c. 26, nor was it disposable by deed until the Real Property Act, 1845 (Imp.), c. 106, s. 6 (now replaced by s. 4 (2) of the Law of Property Act, 1925 (Imp.), c. 20). For similar legislation see Wills Act, R.S.O. 1960, c. 433, s. 1 (a); Conveyancing and Law of Property Act, R.S.O. 1960, c. 66, s. 10; Property Act, R.S.N.B. 1952, c. 177, s. 14; Real Property Act, R.S.N.S. 1954, c. 244, s. 26; Real Property Act, R.S.P.E.I. 1951, c. 138, s. 9.]

3. SEISIN AND CONVEYANCING

BIGELOW, INTRODUCTION TO THE LAW OF REAL PROPERTY

[Chap. 2] Section 8. Transfer of Seisin and Possession.

The most natural and obvious way of transferring rights in any tangible object is by delivering that object to the person to whom it is desired to transfer the rights in it. Indeed, if the rights are conceived of as inhering in the object, this would seem to be almost the only way by which the rights could be transferred. One of the oldest and the most commonly used methods of conveying estates in land was based upon this conception. To be sure, the land could not be physically picked up like a book and handed to the grantee. But the nearest approximation to that would be equally satisfactory, namely, to put the grantee physically into the possession of the land, under such circumstances as would make it manifest that the intent was thereby to transfer to him a freehold interest in the land. This was in fact, as has already been said, the most common way of transferring seisin of land under the early English law. It was technically called livery of seisin, or feoffment. It was done by A, the feoffor, taking B, the feoffee, to the land in question and there handing him a branch or a piece of turf as a symbolical delivery of the land. No deed was required; the physical act of delivery was the operative act to transfer the title. The act of giving or receiving livery could be performed by an agent. As a matter of security this always took place in the presence of witnesses, and, if the transaction was of any importance, a formal document was ordinarily drawn up, stating the fact of the livery, and what land was given, and for what estates. This document was called the charter of feoffment. From the nature of livery of seisin it follows that it was a present act—that is, the seisin could be passed out of the feoffor only by an act of present delivery; an attempt to make a livery of seisin to take effect at some future date was a nullity. This doctrine appears to have been qualified somewhat by the so-called livery in law. Under this latter doctrine the feoffor could take the feoffee to the neighborhood of the land, point it out to him, and declare to him that he thereby gave him livery. This was effectual if the feoffee entered into the land during the life of the feoffor.

The method adopted for the transfer or creation of nonfreehold interests was analogous to livery of seisin. Of course, since the tenant for years had only a possession, and not seisin, the transaction was not technically a livery of seisin. But the same fundamental idea of a physical installation on the land prevailed. It was a less ceremonious affair, partly, doubtless, for the reason that the estate created was of not so long a duration. There was one important difference between the creation of a freehold estate and a nonfreehold estate. Since the nonfreehold estate was in its origin a contract rather than a property right, the doctrine that the estate could not be created to begin in futuro had no application. Consequently, A could make a lease to B of Blackacre to begin at a specified future date. On that date it was merely necessary for B to enter into possession. He was not regarded as having a leasehold interest in the interval, but he was regarded as having a right to the lease, and this right was technically called an interesse termini.

If A, the owner in fee, wished to convey his land to B in fee, subject to a contemporaneous three-year lease in favor of C, this required a combination of livery of seisin and possession; the seisin clearly could not be delivered directly to B, for that would mean putting him into the land to the exclusion of C's leasehold interest. On the other hand, C could not take a livery of seisin to himself, since he had a nonfreehold interest. The creation of these estates was accomplished by putting C into the possession of the land and delivering seisin to him for B, who was thus considered as having been vested with the seisin subject to C's three-year possessory interest.

These methods of creating freehold and nonfreehold estates continued in England unchanged by statute until the latter part of the 17th century. In the Statute of Frauds it was provided, among other things that "all leases, estates, interests of freehold, or terms of years, or any uncertain interest of, in, to or out of any messuages, manors, lands, tenements or hereditaments made or created by livery and seisin only, or by parol, and not put in writing and signed by the parties so making or creating the same, or their agents thereunto lawfully authorized by writing, shall have the effect of leases or estates at will only, and shall not, either in law or equity be deemed or taken to have any other or greater force or effect; *** except nevertheless all leases not exceeding the term of three years from the making thereof." ***

The law as thus outlined continued substantially unchanged until the 19th century, at which time, after various pieces of legislation, it was finally provided in 1845 (8 & 9 Vict. c. 106, s. 2) that after October 1, 1845, all corporeal tenements and hereditaments should, as regards the conveyance of the immediate freehold thereof, be deemed to lie in grant as well as in livery.

[Reproduced by the kind permission of the publishers.]

[See *Thorne*, Livery of Seisin, (1936) 52 Law Q. Rev. 345, pointing out that the "stress laid upon livery of seisin as the essential element of the conveyance has been due to an incomplete distinction between seisin in the sense of possession and seisin in the sense of ownership."

At common law, non-possessory freehold interests (for example, a seigniory, a reversion or a remainder) were transferable by deed of grant. In the case of a seigniory, attornment was necessary to perfect the transfer; and it was equally necessary in the conveyance of land held under a lease. The requirement of attornment was abolished by 4 and 5 Anne, c. 16, s. 9 (now replaced by s. 151 of the Law of Property Act, 1925 (Imp.), c. 20). For similar legislation, see Landlord and Tenant Act, R.S.O. 1960, c. 206, ss. 60 and 61.]

CONVEYANCING AND LAW OF PROPERTY ACT, R.S.O. 1960, c. 66

2. All corporeal tenements and hereditaments shall, as regards the conveyance of the immediate freehold thereof, lie in grant as well as in livery.

3. A feoffment, otherwise than by deed, shall be void and no feoffment shall have any tortious operation.

[For similar legislation, see Property Act, R.S.N.B. 1952, c. 177, ss. 9 (2), 10; Conveyancing Act, 1956 (N.S.), c. 3, s. 3; Real Property Act, R.S.P.E.I. 1951, c. 138, ss. 5, 6, 7. Cf. Land Registry Act, R.S.B.C. 1960, c. 208, ss. 20, 53, 54.]

4. COMMON LAW CONSEQUENCES

THE NECESSITY at common law of a present livery of seisin to effect a transfer of a possessory freehold interest in land left its imprint in two principles which have survived despite the statutory abolition of the requirement of livery of seisin. These are: (1) There can never be an abeyance of seisin of a freehold estate; and (2) no freehold estate can be given or transferred to begin in the future. The matter is succinctly put as follows by *Williams*, Real Property (23rd ed. 1920), at pp. 391-2: "If on the occasion of any feoffment such feudal possession [seisin] was not at once parted with, it remained for ever with the grantor. Thus a feoffment or any other conveyance of a freehold made today to A to hold from tomorrow would be absolutely void as involving a contradiction. For if A is not to have the seisin until tomorrow it must not be given him till then."

As will be seen later, the requirement of present livery of seisin was not incompatible with the possibility of successive estates in the same land. Once it was established that estates were to be classified in terms of duration, it could be seen that interests might arise successively, and that, moreover, interests of more or less finite duration might be carved out of interests of indefinite or potentially infinite duration. It is this understanding that gave us a law of future interests. However, this development took place within a fairly closed system which recognized only certain kinds of estates. As stated by 1 *Simes and Smith*, Law of Future Interests (2nd ed. 1956), p. 39, "it is conceivable that in a system of property law a person could limit new interests according to his own whim, and that the variety of possibilities would be only limited by his imagination and desires. But no such idea was even remotely connected with the common law of this period [the 17th and 18th centuries]. Estates were either freehold or nonfreehold. Of the freehold estates there was the fee simple, the fee tail and the life estate. Of the nonfreehold interests, there was the estate for years and the tenancy at will. When an interest was created, it was forced into one of these categories like sardines in a tin, and made to fit". Of course, interests in land could be created and were developed which were not estates (as, for example, easements and restrictive covenants) but even here there was a tendency to limit them not only in class but also in kind. This is a matter which will be treated further on in this casebook.

CHAPTER III

ESTATE IN FEE SIMPLE

1. CHARACTERISTICS AND MODE OF CREATION

THE LARGEST OR HIGHEST of the freehold estates is the fee simple which (to paraphrase *Plucknett*, Concise History of the Common Law (5th ed. 1956), at p. 558) was inheritable by primogeniture from about 1200 A.D. on, was alienable without consent of presumptive heirs from about the same time and became freely alienable without the lord's consent after the Statute of Quia Emptores of 1290. It still retains the characteristics of inheritability (subject now to particular rules of intestate succession) and alienability and, in addition, is also devisable by will. The holder of an estate in fee simple absolute is, to all intents and purposes, an absolute owner although technically he is a mere tenant of the Crown.

At common law, an estate in fee simple could be created or transferred *inter vivos* only by a conveyance to the "grantee and his heirs". If A wished to convey a fee simple estate in certain land to B, he would fail if he purported to make the feoffment to "B in fee simple", or to "B forever", or to "B and his assigns" or to "B and his successors"; all he would have accomplished would be to give B an estate for life.

This strict rule of common law conveyancing did not obtain in the case of wills since feudal doctrines were inapt and the testator's intention, as expressed in the language used, was the governing consideration. Nor did it obtain in the case of a grant to a corporation, whether a corporation aggregate (e.g. a limited company) or a corporation sole. In the case of the former, no words of limitation were necessary to convey a fee simple; in the case of the latter, it was sufficient to mak the grant to the corporation sole "and his successors".

Words of Purchase and Words of Limitation

In a grant to "A and his heirs", the words "and his heirs" are properly described as words of limitation; that is, words which define or characterize the nature of the interest given to A. It is immaterial that A is legally or otherwise incapable of having heirs; it is immaterial both so far as the nature of A's interest is concerned and so far as the interest of a transferee from A is concerned. In the latter case, if such transferee has been given a fee simple by A, the fact that A's line of heirs (lineal and collateral) dies out will not affect the duration of the estate now held by the transferee. The words "to A" in the grant are words of purchase, that is words designating the person to whom an interest is given, whether it be by grant or devise, and whether it be by way of gift in the strict sense or for consideration. Hence, to take by "purchase" is to be distinguished from taking by "descent". If A's "heirs" ever succeed to his interest it will not be by "purchase" from A's grantor but by "descent" from A if he fails to dispose of his interest in his lifetime or to devise it by will.

[For an explanation of the magic common law formula of "and his heirs", see *Megarry and Wade*, Law of Real Property (1959, 2nd ed.), at pp. 50 ff.

In *In re Davison's Settlement*, [1913] 2 Ch. 498, at p. 502, Warrington J. said:

"I think, therefore, I am quite right in saying that the real question is, Is a grant by deed to A. and his heir-at-law sufficient to create an estate in fee simple? It is an extraordinary thing that such a question should arise at the present day, and that there should be so little distinct authority upon it as there is.

"Now the authorities, such as there are in the case, seem to be against the contention. In the first place, the definition of a fee simple by Littleton (Co. Litt. la) is in these terms: 'Tenant in fee simple is he which hath lands or tenements to hold to him and his heires for ever.' Lord Coke's comment on that is (Co. Litt. 8b): 'And it is to be observed, that every word of Littleton is worthy of observation. First (Heires) in the plural number; for if a man give land to a man and his heire in the singular number, he hath but an estate for life, for his heire cannot take a fee simple by descent, because he is but one, and therefore in that case his heire shall take nothing.' Now if there were nothing else, that would be absolutely plain, and there would be no room for any further argument, but in Mr. Hargrave's note to this passage in Coke on Littleton there is this statement: 'According to many authorities, *heir* may be nomen collectivum, as well in a deed as a will, and operate in both in the same manner as *heirs* in the *plural* number.' Then he cites amongst others a case in Cro. Eliz., and some passages in Rolle's Abridgment. Now the case in Cro. Eliz. is reported as *Clerk* v. *Day* (Cro. Eliz. 313). It was a case decided before Lord Coke wrote his commentary on Littleton, at the time when he himself was Solicitor-General. The case as stated in the report is this: 'The case upon special verdict was, Joan Marsh devised—it was therefore the case of a will—certain land to Rose her daughter for life; and, "if she marry after my death, and have *heir* of her body, then I will that *the heir*, after my daughter's death, shall have the land, and to the heirs of their body begotten; and if my daughter die without issue of her body begotten, then Philip Taylor shall have it to him and his heirs." Joan Marsh died. Rose married Silly, and had issue. The question was, If Rose had an estate in tail, or for life only? First, it was agreed by all the justices, that a devise to one and the heir of his body, is an estate tail, and shall go to all the heirs of her body; for "heir" is nomen collectivum, and one can have but one heir at one time, and this shall go from heir to heir; but Gawdy and Fenner held, that Rose had but an estate for life, for so it is limited by express words, that she shall have for life, then her heir shall take as a purchaser, and it shall not execute in Rose. Popham, *Chief Justice*, *contra*, for the estate is limited to the ancester, and after limited to the heir, and shall execute in the ancester, especially the words being, "if she hath any heirs", and therefore intended that any heir shall have it.' There is a note at the foot of the case, which note is taken from Parker C.B.'s manuscript: 'Lord Raymond inspected the roll of this case (the true name of which is *Cheat* v. *Day*. See 2 Stra. 804) and that the devise was: "If she marry after my death, and have any heir of her body then lawfully begotten, I will that that heir after my daughter's death shall have the land, &c."' Now I think that is certainly an authority, and there are plenty of others, that in the case of a will, as Mr. Hargrave says, 'heir' may be nomen collectivum, and may operate in the same manner as 'heirs', in the plural number; but it is not an authority for the statement that it may so operate in a deed as in a will."]

CONVEYANCING AND LAW OF PROPERTY ACT, R.S.O. 1960, c. 66

4. A limitation in a conveyance or will that before the 27th day of May, 1956, would have created an estate tail shall be construed as an estate in fee simple or the greatest estate that the grantor or testator had in the land.

5. (1) In a conveyance it is not necessary, in the limitation of an estate in fee simple, to use the words "heirs."

(2) For the purpose of such limitation it is sufficient in a conveyance to use the words "in fee simple," or any other words sufficiently indicating the limitation intended.

(3) Where no words of limitation are used, the conveyance passes all the estate, right, title, interest, claim and demand that the conveying parties have in, to, or on the property conveyed, or expressed or intended so to be, or that they have power to convey in, to, or on the same.

(4) Subsection 3 applies only if and as far as a contrary intention does not appear from the conveyance, and has effect subject to the terms of the conveyance and to the provisions therein contained.

THE WILLS ACT, R.S.O. 1960, c. 433

30. Where any real estate is devised to any person without any words of limitation such devise shall, subject to *The Devolution of Estates Act*, be construed to pass the fee simple, or other the whole estate or interest, that the testator had power to dispose of by will, unless a contrary intention appears by the will.

33. Where any real estate is devised to a trustee or executor such devise shall be construed to pass the fee simple, or other the whole estate or interest that the testator had power to dispose of by will in such real estate, unless a definite term of years absolute or determinable, or an estate of freehold is thereby given to him expressly or by implication.

[For similar legislation, see Transfer and Descent of Land Act, R.S.A. 1955, c. 342, s. 8; Land Registry Act, R.S.B.C. 1960, c. 208, s. 22 (2) (3); Law of Property Act, R.S.M. 1954, c. 138, s. 4; Real Property Act, R.S.M. 1954, c. 220, s. 91; Property Act, R.S.N.B. 1952, c. 177, s. 11 (3); Conveyancing Act, 1956 (N.S.), c. 3, ss. 3 (2), 6.]

Consider the effect today of a grant or devise

(1) to A: see *Re Airey* (1921), 21 O.W.N. 190.

(2) to A in fee: see *Millard* v. *Gregoire* (1913), 47 N.S.R. 78, 11 D.L.R. 539 (C.A.); *Re Taylor* (1916), 36 O.L.R. 116, 28 D.L.R. 488 (C.A.).

(3) to A all rents and profits: see *Moore* v. *Power* (1858), 8 U.C.C.P. 109; *Re Vair and Doyle* (1922), 23 O.W.N. 407; *McKenzie* v. *McKenzie*, 56 O.L.R. 247, [1925] 1 D.L.R. 373.

(4) to A for his sole use: see Re *Grafton* (1924), 25 O.W.N. 666, varied 26 O.W.N. 262 (C.A.).

(5) to A or his heirs: see *Re Wright and Fowler* (1916), 10 O.W.N. 299.

(6) to A and his heirs male.

[*Williams*, The Doctrine of Repugnancy, (1943) 59 Law Q. Rev. 343, refers on p. 354 to a "general rule that it is impossible for a settlor by the terms of his grant to meddle with the law of intestate succession"; and he continues as follows: "For example, it has long been settled law that on a conveyance 'to A and his heirs male' A gets a fee simple, the limitation as it stands being 'unknown to the law'. The rule is applied not only to attempts to change the intestacy rules *in perpetuum* for the property settled (to which there are abvious objections) but also to attempts to change them merely on the death of the first donee. Thus on a gift to A absolutely, but if he die intestate then to B, the condition is struck out and the absolute gift stands. Similarly on a gift to A absolutely subject to a gift of 'what remains at his death' to B, the gift to B is struck out. Most of the cases offer no better reason for the rule than the doctrine of repugnancy, which saves the trouble of thinking out a better reason. Sometimes, by an almost imperceptible transition, the Court changes from saying that the gift to B is repugnant to the absolute gift to A, to saying that the gift to B is repugnant *to the law*—thus converting the concealed tautology into an avowed one. In *Shaw* v. *Ford*

(1877), 7 Ch. D. 669 at 674, Fry J. repeated the formula but with obvious lack of relish; the 'reason alleged' for the rule, he said, was 'the contradiction or contrariety between the principle of law which regulates the devolution of the estate and the executory devise which is to take effect only at the moment of devolution, and to alter its course'. He added that he was 'not bound to inquire into the logical sufficiency of the reason given', because the rule was well established. A slightly stronger attempt at explanation was made in *Holmes* v. *Godson* (1856), 8 De G.M. & G. 152 at 159-60, 165, where it was said that interferences with the intestacy rules were 'against the policy of the law'. In the absence of fuller explanation why they are against the policy of the law, this can hardly be regarded as a reason. If a testator is allowed to interfere with the intestacy rules that would otherwise apply to his own estate (as he is), why is he not allowed to interfere with the intestacy rules that would otherwise apply to the estate of his legatee or devisee, so far as regards property that he bequeathes or devises?"]

2. THE RULE OF "NO REMAINDER AFTER A FEE SIMPLE"

A HOLDER of an estate in fee simple who grants a lesser estate has something left; but once he disposes of his fee simple interest it is obvious that since Quia Emptores, he cannot remain in a tenurial relationship with his grantee. It also followed that if in a grant or devise, the holder of a fee simple disposed of it he could not purport to limit or control the grantee's or the devisee's title or power of further disposition. Here we face a constructional problem because the proposition just stated is true only if it is found that what the grantor or testator gave was an estate in fee simple absolute, and not some lesser or other interest. Illustrations of this problem follow. By and large the question arises under wills and is usually treated in a wills course, but some acquaintance with it is desirable here.

The rule of "no remainder after a fee simple" was of signal importance in the common law of future interests because it meant that once a fee simple was given, a future estate could not be limited to take effect upon the termination of the fee simple, whether on the occurrence of a stated contingency or otherwise. Such a limitation became possible only with the development of uses and under wills.

RE HORNELL. Ontario Court of Appeal. [1945] O.R. 58, [1945] 1 D.L.R. 440

This was an appeal from a judgment of Kelly J., [1944] 4 D.L.R. 572, [1944] O.W.N. 664, on a motion for construction of a home-drawn will containing the following provision: "I give and bequeath to my wife Margaret Hornell all my personal property, monies, real estate and mortgages, to have and to hold after she pays all legal claims against my estate. On the death of my wife what remains of my estate is to go to my daughter Jean Winnifred Hornell."

LAIDLAW J. A., dissenting:... I come to the irresistible conclusion that the testator intended by the words used in his will to benefit both his wife and his daughter Jean Winnifred. He meant that his widow should have an estate in his property for her use and enjoyment during her lifetime and that after that life estate the part of his property then unused by his widow should go to his daughter Jean Winnifred. That is the meaning from the natural, logical and common sense point of view.

I agree that if one reads only the first sentence of the paragraph quoted it is capable of meaning that Margaret Hornell took in fee simple. But such a course is contrary to the proper principle that the will as a whole must be considered.... The respondent's contention entirely ignores the gift over or attempts to get rid of it by calling it repugnant. The Court cannot properly disregard a word in a will if meaning can be given to it, and "if that meaning is not contrary to some intention plainly expressed in other parts of the will" quoting from Halsbury, Laws of England (2nd ed.), vol. 34, p. 198. Much less has the Court any right in such a case to disregard all of a specific provision.

Upon argument of this appeal the Court was referred to a great many cases which I have read with interest. But it has been made plain, and is fully appreciated by the Court and counsel that the proper use of them is limited. They constitute authority as to rules of construction and rules of law but the construction put by a Court on words in one will is not authority binding the Court to adopt the same or similar construction on words of another will. Two minds may fairly differ on the interpretation to be placed on language which appears to be similar or identical. I am bound, however, to follow established principles of law, whenever they are properly applicable to the facts and circumstances of a particular case. The construction I put on the words of the will under consideration does not give rise to the application of any rule of law, and accomplishes a result which does justice. Any other construction, I think, defeats or impairs the real intention of the testator by the application of technical rules unknown and unsuspected by him or the author of the will. Thus, as mentioned above, consequences are produced contrary to that intention and injustice is done.

Respondent's counsel refers in particular to *Re Walker* (1925), 56 O.L.R. 517. It was held there that from the words used in the will the testator intended his wife to have all the rights incident to ownership of property and a gift over at her death was an attempt by the testator to do that which is impossible. It was made plain that the attempted gift over was, in the opinion of the Court, repugnant to the prior gift to the testator's wife and consequently was void. The language used in the will showed a testamentary intention in favour of the wife which prevailed over the subordinate intention indicated by the words used in making the gift over. The subordinate intention being repugnant to the dominant intention was necessarily rejected. It is, of course, well settled that a gift absolute makes any subsequent attempt by the donor to deal with the subject of the gift of no effect whatever. But in my opinion the words used in the will of David Hornell to express his intention show that the gift to his wife is fixed in character by the subsequent words making provision out of the same property for his daughter. The intention as found in the words used in the latter clause dominates the intention disclosed in the words of gift to the testator's wife in the first clause. I think that the gift over prevails and the gift in favour of the wife is subordinate to it. This view does not in any way conflict with the decision in *Re Walker*, but applies the principles therein discussed to the language of the will now before the Court.

I do not discuss any of the other numerous cases referred to in argument. It is sufficient to say that my decision is in accord with the principles I have discussed and depends, as it ought to, on the authority of the particular words used in the will in question.

My conclusion is that the appeal ought to be allowed and the declaration in the judgment of the Court below set aside. In lieu thereof it ought to be declared that Margaret Hornell took a life estate with power for the purpose of her maintenance, to encroach on the capital of the property of the late David Hornell and upon her death Jean Winnifred Hornell took an estate in fee simple in the part of the property then remaining.

McRUER J. A.: ... My view is that the intention of the testator gathered from the language used, is that he wished his wife Margeret Hornell to have all his property absolutely, but if anything remained of the property given to her at the time of her death, it should go to his daughter Jean Winnifred Hornell.

In *Re Walker*, 56 O.L.R. 517 at p. 522, Middleton J. A. states: "When a testator gives property to one, intending him to have all the rights incident to ownership, and adds to this a gift over of that which remains in specie at his death or at the death of that person, he is endeavouring to do that which is impossible. His intention is plain but it cannot be given effect to. The Court has then to endeavour to give such effect to the wishes of the testator as is legally possible, by ascertaining which part of the testamentary intention predominates and by giving effect to it, rejecting the subordinate intention as being repugnant to the dominant intention."

After carefully considering the arguments advanced by counsel for the appellants, I feel that I am bound to hold, on the authorities, that the words used by the testator showed a dominant intention in favour of Margaret Hornell, and that the last sentence of the clause is inoperative to cut down the absolute nature of the gift to Margaret Hornell.

Counsel for the appellant argued that the words "to have and to hold after she pays all legal claims against my estate", when read with the words "On the death of my wife, what remains of my estate", indicated an intention to restrict the gift to a life estate, and quoted many cases in support of his argument.

I am of the opinion that if the Court restricted the interest of the wife in this case to a life estate, it would have to read into the will a limitation on the estate of the wife that is not warranted by the language used.

Counsel also argued that "to hold" meant to hold without spending. Similar words were not so interpreted in *Re Scott*, [1926] 1 D.L.R. 151, 58 O.L.R. 138.

The appeal should be dismissed.

HENDERSON J. A. agreed with McRUER J. A.

Appeal dismissed.

[See *Kennedy*, Gift by Will to W: At Her Death "What Remains" to the Children, (1950) 28 Can. Bar Rev. 839. For decisions comparable to *Re Hornell*, see *Yarmie* v. *Panchyshyn*, [1952] 3 D.L.R. 693, 6 W.W.R. (N.S.) 173 (Sask. C.A.); *Bartrop* v. *Blackstock* (1957), 10 D.L.R. 2d 192, 21 W.W.R. (N.S.) 241 (Sask. C.A.); and cf. *Re Gouk*, *Allen* v. *Allen*, [1957] 1 All E.R. 469, [1957] 1 W.L.R. 493 (Ch.).]

3. INHERITABILITY OF AN ESTATE IN FEE SIMPLE

IT HAS ALREADY been pointed out that at common law, land (or, more accurately, interests in land) descended to the "heir", under a principle of primogeniture. Moreover, descent was traced from the person who was last actually seised—*seisina fecit stipitem*—and not from the person last entitled. This situation prevailed until changed by legislation in the nineteenth century (see Inheritance Act, 1833 (Imp.), c. 106); and with the assimilation in many of the provinces of Canada of real to personal property for purpose of intestate administration and the enactment of statutory rules of distribution, the principle referred to became meaningless. In the developed common law, inheritance of interests in land was by lineal descendants and, failing any, then by collaterals; lineal ascendants were excluded. Precedence among lineal descendants was determined under the following rules (as set out in 2 *Pollock and Maitland*, History of English Law, 2nd ed., p. 260): (1) a living descendant excludes his or her own descendants; (2) a dead descendant is represented by his or her own descendants; (3) males exclude females of equal degree; (4) among males of equal degree only the eldest inherits; (5) females of equal degree inherit together as co-heiresses; and (6) the rule that a dead descendant is represented by his or her descendants overrides the preference for males, so that a granddaughter by a dead eldest son will exclude a younger son.

If there were no lineal descendants, collaterals took on a parentelic basis and under a rule that the collaterals must be of the blood of the first purchaser, i.e. of him who first acquired the estate to the family otherwise than by descent. A person's *parentela* is the total of those who trace their blood from him; and inheritance on this system was based on the order of proximity of a parentelic line to the deceased. Moreover, in collateral inheritance, the male stocks were preferred to the female unless the land in question descended from a female, i.e. unless a female was the "first purchaser", and further, the rule of representation also applied among collaterals. Thus, to take an ordinary case, the nearest parentela to a deceased was his father's; the next would be his grandfather's, then his great grandfather's and so on. So long as the nearest line had any representative, he or she would take to the exclusion of anyone in a remoter line, and, of course, to the exclusion of anyone "remoter" in his or her own line. It should also be noted that the common law excluded persons of the half-blood from any inheritable right. While posthumous children could inherit, illegitimate children, aliens and felons could not. It has already been pointed out that ancestors in any degree were excluded. Again, neither husband nor wife as such was an heir or heiress of the other nor within the rules of collateral inheritance. For them the law provided curtesy or dower, interests which are considered in a later chapter.

A word may be said about the system of inheritance of personalty which was largely administered by the ecclesiastical courts in England until the nineteenth century. It is commonly referred to as the "gradualistic" system (in its determination of collateral inheritance) and was influenced by Roman law. For some time in early English law, there was a tripartite division of a deceased's personalty, one-third going to the wife, one-third to the children and one-third (the "dead's part") going to the church. (If no wife or children survived, then the other would get one-half and the "dead's part" would be also one-half.) However, testaments of chattels were common, apparently because they were made as part of the last rites administered by the church. When the Statute of Distributions was enacted by 1670 (Imp.), c. 10 to strengthen the jurisdiction of the ecclesiastical courts over administrators of intestates' goods, there was included in it a set of rules respecting the determination of distributive shares of personalty, being the theretofore prevailing rules with some modifications. Under these rules (as amended by the Statute of Frauds, 1677 (Imp.), c. 3 and the Statute of Distributions, 1685 (Imp.), c. 17), an intestate's personalty after payment of debts went to his surviving spouse and children or next of kin. The spouse took one-third and the children two-thirds; if there was no spouse, the children took all; if there was a spouse but no children, the spouse took one-half and the next of kin took the other half. If the surviving spouse was the husband he took his wife's personalty absolutely. If there were neither spouse nor children (nor representatives of deceased children), the next of kin took everything. Where children took they shared equally, and the rule of representation (succession *per stirpes*) applied. There was no preference of males over females. If any advancement had been made to a child in the intestate's lifetime, it was deducted from his share to ensure equality of distribution (the hotchpot rule), but only where the intestate was a father.

In the determination of collateral inheritance that collateral who was of the nearest degree to the intestate or propositus (person from whom descent is traced) took to the exclusion of others. The degree of relationship was ascertained by reference to the common ancestor of propositus and respective claimants. If claimants were of equal degree they shared equally. By counting from the deceased to the common ancestor and then down to the claimant (taking each generation as one degree) one would arrive at the degree of kinship to the propositus. Thus an uncle would be three degrees removed, and so too would a nephew. A grandnephew would be four degrees removed and so too would be a first cousin. The result of the Statute of Distributions, as amended, was that subject to claims of a surviving spouse, if there were no issue, the intestate's father took. If the father was dead, the intestate's mother, brothers and sisters shared equally. Representation was allowed to brothers' and sisters' children so that they claimed in their parents' right if they were competing with another claimant, as, for example, a surviving brother or the mother. However, if there were only brothers' and sisters' children to consider, they took not *per stirpes* but *per capita.* No distinction or preference was made between next of kin of the whole blood and those of the half-blood. Finally, if an intestate died without lineal or collateral claimants, his or her personalty went to the Crown as *bona vacantia.*

The result of the different rules for descent of realty and personalty may be illustrated as follows. An uncle would take personalty ahead of a grandnephew but he would share with a nephew where the latter was not in a position to claim as representative of the intestate's deceased brother or sister. So far as realty was concerned, an uncle was in the parentela of the intestate's grandparents while a nephew or grandnephew was in the closer parentela of the intestate's parents.

[The rules of descent of realty in Upper Canada were those of the common law until 1834 when they were varied by legislation based on English legislation of the previous year; and further variation was made by legislation in 1852: see *Armour*, Real Property (2nd ed. 1916), chap. 19, for a review of these changes. In 1886, descent of realty was assimilated to that of personalty by the Devolution of Estates Act, 1886 (Ont.), c. 22.]

DEVOLUTION OF ESTATES ACT, R.S.O. 1960, c. 106, amended 1960-61, c. 22; 1961-62, c. 34

4. Subject to the other provisions of this Act, in the administration of the assets of a deceased person, his real property shall be administered in the same manner, subject to the same liability for debts, costs and expenses and with the same incidents as if it were personal property, but nothing in this section alters or affects as respects real or personal property of which the deceased has made a testamentary disposition the order in which real and personal assets are now applicable to the payment of funeral and testamentary expenses, the costs and expenses of administration, debts or legacies, or the liability of real property to be charged with the payment of legacies.

27. (1) Subject to subsections 2 and 3, an illegitimate child or relative shall not share under any of the provisions of this Act.

(2) Where the mother of an illegitimate child dies intestate as respects all or any of her real or personal property and does not leave any legitimate issue surviving her, the illegitimate child, or, if he is dead, his issue, is entitled to take any interest therein to which he or such issue would have been entitled if he had been born legitimate.

(3) Where an illegitimate child dies intestate in respect of all or any of his real or personal property, his mother, if surviving, is entitled to take any interest therein to which she would have been entitled if the child had been born legitimate and she had been the only surviving parent.

29. (1) Subject to section 12, the real and personal property, whether separate or otherwise, of a married woman in respect of which she dies intestate, shall be distributed as follows: one-third to her husband if she leaves issue, and one-half if she leaves no issue, and subject thereto shall devolve as if her husband had predeceased her.

(2) A husband who, if this Act had not been passed, would be entitled to an interest as tenant by the curtesy in real property of his wife, may, by deed or instrument in writing executed, and attested by at least one witness, and delivered to the personal representative,

if any, or if there is none, deposited in the office of the Registrar of the Supreme Court at Osgoode Hall, within six months after his wife's death, elect to take such interest in the real and personal property of his wife as he would have taken if this Act had not been passed, in which case the husband's interest therein shall be ascertained in all respects as if this Act had not been passed, and he shall be entitled to no further interest thereunder.

30. Subject to subsection 2 of section 6 of *The Legitimation Act* and except as otherwise provided in this Act, the personal property of a person dying intestate shall be distributed as follows: one-third to the wife of the intestate and all the residue by equal portions among the children of the intestate and such persons as legally represent the children in case any of them have died in his lifetime, and if there are no children or any legal representatives of them then two-thirds of the personal property shall be allotted to the wife, and the residue thereof shall be distributed equally to every of the next of kindred of the intestate who are of equal degree and those who legally represent them, and for the purpose of this section the father and the mother and the brothers and sisters of the intestate shall be deemed of equal degree; but there shall be no representations admitted among collaterals after brothers' and sisters' children, and if there is no wife then all such personal property shall be distributed equally among the children, and if there is no child then to the next of kindred in equal degree of or unto the intestate and their legal representatives and in no other manner; provided that if there is only one child or legal representatives of only one child the personal property of a person dying intestate shall be distributed as follows: one-half to the wife of the intestate and the other half to the child or the legal representatives of the child.

31. If, after the death of a father, any of his children die intestate without wife or children in the lifetime of the mother, every brother and sister and the representatives of them shall have an equal share with her, anything in section 30 to the contrary notwithstanding.

CHILD WELFARE ACT. R.S.O. 1960, c. 53, amended 1961-62, c. 14; 1962-63, c. 12

76. (1) For all purposes the adopted child, upon the adoption order being made, becomes the child of the adopting parent and the adopting parent becomes the parent of the adopted child as if the adopted child had been born in lawful wedlock to the adopting parent.

(2) For all purposes the adopted child, upon the adoption order being made, ceases to be the child of the person who was his parent before the adoption order was made and that person ceases to be the parent of the adopted child.

(3) The relationship to one another of all persons, whether the adopted child, the adopting parent, the kindred of the adopting parent, the parent before the making of the adoption order and the kindred of that parent or any other person, shall be determined in accordance with subsections 1 and 2.

(4) Subsections 2 and 3 do not apply for the purposes of the laws relating to incest and the prohibited degrees of marriage to remove any person from a relationship in consanguinity, which, but for this section, would have existed.

77. Every person heretofore adopted under the laws of Ontario and every person adopted under the laws of any other province or territory of Canada or under the laws of any other country shall for all purposes in Ontario be governed by this Part.

[For comparable legislation, see Intestate Succession Act, R.S.A. 1955, c. 161; Administration Act, R.S.B.C. 1960, c. 3, amended 1963, c. 1; Devolution of Estates Act, R.S.M. 1954, c. 63; Devolution of Estates Act, R.S.N.B. 1952, c. 62, amended 1956, c. 33; Descent of Property Act, R.S.N.S. 1954, c. 69; Intestate Succession Act, R.S. Nfld. 1952, c. 153; Probate Act, R.S.P.E.I. 1951, c. 124; Quebec Civil Code, articles 597, 598, and 606 ff.; Intestate Succession Act, R.S.S. 1953, c. 119.

Adoption legislation in Canada is set out, and the effect of adoption on intestate succession is discussed, in *Kennedy*, The Legal Effects of Adoption, (1955) 33 Can. Bar Rev. 751, at pp. 763 ff. and 813 ff.]

Illustrative cases of competing claims on intestate succession:

1. Son and widow of deceased son: *Re MacKenzie*, 61 O.L.R. 230, [1927] 4 D.L.R. 825.

2. Widow and nephew and children of deceased niece: *Crowther* v. *Cawthra* (1882), 1 O.R. 128.

3. Uncle and first cousin: *Bowers* v. *Littlewood* (1719), 1 P. Wms. 594, 24 E.R. 531 (Ch.); *Re Dunn* (1929), 37 O.W.N. 169; *In re Kroesing Estate*, [1928] 1 D.L.R. 643, [1928] 1 W.W.R. 224 (Alta.); *Re Wilson, MacKay and Wortman* v. *Bulmer*, [1949] 3 D.L.R. 408 (N.B.); *Re Weaver*, [1950] O.R. 537, [1950] 4 D.L.R. 357; *Re Shaw*, [1955] 4 D.L.R. 268, [1955] O.W.N. 353.

4. Grandfather and brother: *Evelyn* v. *Evelyn* (1754) 3 Atk. 762, 26 E.R. 1237 (Ch.).

5. Grandfather and uncle: *Re Dixon Estates*, [1948] 2 W.W.R. 108 (Man.).

6. Grandfather and children of deceased brother: see *Evelyn* v. *Evelyn*, *supra*.

7. Father, mother, brothers and sisters: *Walker* v. *Allen* (1897), 24 O.A.R. 336; *Lewin* v. *Lewin* (1904), 36 N.B.R. 365 (CA.); *Hansard* v. *Hansard* (1938), 12 M.P.R. 576 (N.B.).

8. Brothers and sisters of the half-blood and children of deceased brothers and sisters: *Re Greenshields Estate* (1914), 6 O.W.N. 303.

9. Brothers and sisters of the whole blood and children of deceased sister of the half-blood: *Re Kishen Singh, Cox* v. *Kaur* (1957), 8 D.L.R. 2d 575, 22 W.W.R. (N.S.) 95 (B.C.).

10. Brothers and sisters, children of deceased sister and grandchildren of deceased sister: *Phillips* v. *Gillis* (1898), 6 E.L.R. 575 (P.E.I. C.A.); *In re Budd Estate, Harmon* v. *Furber*, 42 Man. R. 152, [1934] 3 D.L.R. 587, [1934] 2 W.W.R. 182 (C.A.); *Carter* v. *Patrick*, 49 B.C.R. 411, [1935] 2 D.L.R. 811, [1935] 1 W.W.R. 383; *Re Drain, Nixon* v. *Drain*, [1948] 2 D.L.R. 617, [1948] 1 W.W.R. 280 (B.C.); *Re McLea*, [1948] 2 W.W.R. 12 (Man.); *Re McMahon, Day* v. *McMahon*, [1948] 1 D.L.R. 80, 20 M.P.R. 413 (N.B.C.A.).

11. Grandniece and cousin: *Lee* v. *Branscombe* (1925), 52 N.B.R. 239.

12. Nephew and grandnephew: *Re Beaulieu*, [1951] 4 D.L.R. 687 (B.C.); *Re McIver Estate*, 57 B.C.R. 139, [1941] 3 W.W.R. 849.

13. Niece and aunt: *Re Bailey*, [1948] O.R. 127, [1948] 2 D.L.R. 367; *Re Hunter*, [1954] O.R. 809, [1954] 4 D.L.R. 796.

14. Brother and widow and children of deceased brother: *Re Forgie*, 56 Man. R. 56, [1948] 3 D.L.R. 329, [1948] 1 W.W.R. 793.

15. Cousins and children of deceased cousins: *Re Haggart*, [1947] 2 D.L.R. 72, [1947] 1 W.W.R. 79 (Alta.).

16. Cousins and half cousins: *Re Adams* (1903), 6 O.L.R. 697.

17. Stepson: *Re White Estate*, [1945] 2 D.L.R. 803, [1945] 1 W.W.R. 78 (Alta.).

18. Posthumous children: *Wallis* v. *Hodson* (1740), 2 Atk. 114, 26 E.R. 472 (Ch.).

[On descent from or through illegitimate or adopted persons, see *Re W*, [1925] 2 D.L.R. 1177, 56 O.L.R. 611; *In re Stone Estate*, [1924] S.C.R. 682, [1925] 1 D.L.R. 60; *Re Hamilton* (1951), 28 M.P.R. 53 (N.B.); *Re Miller Estate* (1957), 22 W.W.R. (N.S.) 571 (Man.); *Re Carlson* (1957), 11 D.L.R. 2d 485 (Sask. C.A.).

On descent to illegitimate or adopted persons, see *Re Walker*, [1954] O.W.N. 653; *Re Miller*, [1955] 3 D.L.R. 404, [1954] O.W.N. 897; *Re Niven*, 58 B.C.R. 176, [1942] 4 D.L.R. 285, [1942] 3 W.W.R. 692; *Re Ogal Estate*, [1940] 2 D.L.R. 345, [1940] 1 W.W.R. 665 (Alta.).

Can a right of inheritance be founded on an adoption agreement? See *Re Rice* (1957), 8 D.L.R. 2d 775 (Ont.).

Where under family maintenance or dependants' relief legislation a statutory right is given to a designated class of persons to seek the aid of the Court in interfering with a testator's will, there have been conflicting views (which, of course, could easily be cured by explicit terms in the legislation) on whether this statutory right to share in the estate devolves on the death of a claimant. The prevailing view is that it does not: see *Wetzel* v. *National Trust Co.* (1956), 4 D.L.R. 2d 171, 18 W.W.R. (N.S.) 556 (Sask. C.A.): *Re McMaster* (1957), 10 D.L.R. 2d 436 (Alta.); *Re Kerby*, [1949] O.W.N. 187. But see *Barker* v. *Westminster Trust Co.*, [1941] 4 D.L.R. 514, [1941] 3 W.W.R. 473, 57 B.C.R. 21 (C.A.); *Re McCaffery*, [1931] O.R. 512, [1931] 4 D.L.R. 930 (App. Div.).

Statutory provision for allowance to intestate's concubine: see *Re Administration Act, Re Rosse* (1952), 4 W.W.R. (N.S.) 218 (B.C.).

If a "wife" obtains a foreign divorce decree which would not be recognized by the Courts of the husband's domicile, may she share in his estate on his intestacy? See *Plummer* v. *Sloan*, [1942] 1 D.L.R. 34, [1941] 3 W.W.R. 788 (Alta. C.A.).

The rule of policy against allowing a criminal to profit from his crime applies to exclude a murderer from any distributive share on his victim's intestacy: *Re Medaini*, [1927] 4 D.L.R. 1137 (B.C.); *In re Sigsworth*, [1935] Ch. 89; *Nordstrom* v. *Baumann*, [1962] S.C.R. 147, 31 D.L.R. 2d 255.

May a person contract out of his or her distributive share on another's intestacy? See *Re Rist Estate*, [1939] 2 D.L.R. 644, [1939] 1 W.W.R. 18, aff'g [1938] 4 D.L.R. 410, [1938] 3 W.W.R. 101 (Alta. C.A.); *Jones* v. *Kline* [1938] 4 D.L.R. 391 (Alta.); *Henderson* v. *Northern Trusts Co.*, [1953] 1 D.L.R. 108, 6 W.W.R. (N.S.) 337 (Sask.); *Re Schop, Cliff* v. *Schop*, [1948] O.W.N. 338. Cf. *Re Winter*, [1955] 1 D.L.R. 134 (Ont.); *Re Draper* (1956), 1 D.L.R. 2d 366 (Ont.).]

4. PROTECTION

Remedies of self-help, of the possessory assizes, writs of entry and of right, and of the action of ejectment, are now part of the history of land law, but their impact has by no means been completely erased; for example, self-help is still permitted within limits: see *Hemmings* v. *Stoke Poges Golf Club Ltd.*, [1920] 1 K.B. 720, 36 T.L.R. 77 (C.A.). Cf. *Aglionby* v. *Cohen*, [1955] 1 All E.R. 785 (Q.B.). See Cr. Code (Can.), ss. 42, 73. Simple actions for possession and for an injunction against trespass or for damages are the ordinary remedies available to protect possessory or non-possessory estates in land, as the case may be; as to trespass actions to protect non-possessory interests, see *Hiltz* v. *Langille and Langille* (1956), 4 D.L.R. 2d 624 (N.S.).

Settlement of conflicting title claims may also be pursued through actions for possession or trespass but they are of limited value for title purposes. Generally, however, there are now statutory procedures available to quiet title (e.g. Quieting Titles Act, R.S.O. 1960, c. 340). Title questions arising under vendor and purchaser transactions, and under registry and land titles systems are beyond the scope of this casebook.

Note on Disclaimer

Just as a trustee may disclaim (e.g. *Mallott* v. *Wilson*, [1903] 2 Ch. 494) and as a donee of a power of appointment may disclaim (e.g. Conveyancing and Law of Property Act, R.S.O. 1950, c. 68, s. 25) may the holder of an estate or other beneficial interest disclaim, and if so what happens to the estate or interest? See Real Property Act, R.S.M. 1954, c. 220, s. 73. See *Re Hatfield*, [1957] 2 All E.R. 261 (Ch.). Cf. *Re Schar, Midland Bank Executor and Trustee Co.* v. *Damer*, [1950] 2 All E.R. 1069 (Ch.), holding that a disclaimer (as contrasted with a release) cannot be made by one only of several joint tenants, but that in the particular circumstances there was a release by one joint tenant to his co-tenants.

5. DEFEASIBLE ESTATES IN FEE SIMPLE

WITH THE STATUTE OF QUIA EMPTORES, tenure could no longer exist between the grantor and grantee of an estate in fee simple. This did not, however, prevent the creation of defeasible estates in fee simple by which the holder of a fee simple conveyed it subject to a condition subsequent or (to use an alternative expression) subject to a power of termination. Nor, apparently, did it prevent (certainly not in the United States) the recognition of another type of defeasible fee simple, the estate in fee simple subject to a conditional limitation or the estate in fee simple with a special or collateral limitation (using the terminology of Gray) or the qualified fee (to use Blackstone's expression) or, simply, the determinable fee simple (to use the terminology of the Restatement of Property). The estate in fee simple subject to a condition subsequent left the grantor or his heirs with a right of re-entry on breach of the condition, but until entry was made or action taken to enforce it, the estate subsisted in the grantee or his assignees. The fee simple determinable left the grantor or his heirs or assigns with a possibility of reverter. On the happening of the stated event the fee simple determinable terminated automatically and the person with the possibility of reverter regained the fee simple absolute. The right of re-entry (or power of termination) on breach of condition subsequent and the possibility of reverter are common law future interests and reference will be made to them in more detail in chapter VIII below.

Mention may appropriately be made here of a third type of defeasible fee simple which became possible with the development of uses as an equitable interest, and, after the Statute of Uses, 1536, could be created as a legal interest. This is the estate in fee simple subject to an executory limitation (Gray referred to it as a fee simple subject to a conditional limitation); and the reason why such an estate was impossible at common law was because it violated the common law rule that seisin in the holder of an estate could not be cut short by limiting an estate in favour of a third person (i.e. other than the grantor) upon the occurrence of a stated event. As it has been put alternatively, the common law did not permit the creation of an estate in derogation of a prior one arising under the same deed. Further, at common law the benefit of a condition could be given only to a grantor or his heirs and not to a third person.

The following limitations are illustrative of the interests above-mentioned:

1. A grants to B and his heirs but if B ceases to farm the land A and his heirs may re-enter and terminate the estate.
2. A grants to B and his heirs on condition that (or, provided that) the land is used for a public school and, if not, right of re-entry.

3. A grants to B and his heirs on condition that B pay an annual rent of $ 1,000 and if not right of re-entry.
4. A grants to B and his heirs so long as the land is farmed.
5. A grants to B and his heirs while B (a widower) remains unmarried.
6. A grants to B and his heirs until B assigns for the benefit of creditors or becomes bankrupt. (Contrast the following: A grants to B and his heirs so long as C lives.)
7. A grants to B and his heirs but if B dies without children him surviving then to C and his heirs.
8. A grants to B and his heirs but if B ceases to farm the land then to C and his heirs.

[The right of entry and possibility of reverter may fail of effect because of uncertainty of the condition or stated event or contingency. What would be the consequence in each case? In England and Canada the rule against perpetuities applies to rights of entry on condition subsequent, and, in England, apparently, also to possibilities of reverter. The situation in the United States is different; the rule does not apply in either case.]

HOPPER v. CORPORATION OF LIVERPOOL. Chancery of Lancaster. 1944. 88 Sol. J. 213

By a lease dated May 7, 1787, Liverpool Corporation demised to one S a piece of land for three specified lives and a further term of 21 years at a rent of one penny and a further rent therein mentioned. By an assignment of June 17, 1801, S assigned to members of a committee of the Liverpool Library part of the land which had been demised to him to hold it on trust for the residue of the term for all existing subscribers to the institution and all others who might thereafter become subscribers or become interested therein, as tenants in common, subject to all existing or future rules of the institution. By a conveyance of February 23, 1805, Liverpool Corporation, after reciting the lease and the fact that a building had been erected on the land demised to members of the Liverpool Library (the building being known as the Lyceum and the land as the Lyceum land), in consideration of the sum of 20s. paid to the Corporation by some of the proprietors of the Liverpool Library granted the reversion of the Lyceum land to such proprietors, their heirs and assigns to hold it to their use "during such time and so long as the said building called the Lyceum or any other building to be from time to time erected on the site thereof shall be used and enjoyed for the uses and purposes of the said institution called the Lyceum agreeably to the original articles of its establishment", and in trust for the present subscribers to or proprietors of the said institution as tenants in common. The lease of 1787 ultimately expired, and the successors to the grantees under the 1805 conveyance, as trustees, continued in possession of the Lyceum land. The Lyceum and library (which had been maintained in the building as part of a scheme which lead to the assignment of 1801 and the conveyance of 1805) were continued until 1941 when the library was discontinued and the books offered to the Liverpool Corporation whose library had been destroyed by enemy action. The Lyceum trustees considered letting part of the premises for commercial purposes and because this raised an issue as to the effect of the limitation in the 1805 conveyance, they sued for a declaration that they were entitled as trustees for the Lyceum, and the latter was beneficially entitled to the Lyceum land and buildings for an estate in fee simple absolute. The Corporation of Liverpool pleaded that the conveyance of 1805 had created merely a fee simple determinable with a right of reverter to it when the buildings on the land should cease to be used and enjoyed for the purposes stated in the conveyance.

SIR JOHN BENNETT, VICE-CHANCELLOR (after dealing with the documents in the case): The first point raised by Mr. Roxburgh was whether a fee simple determinable has existed at all since the Statute Quia Emptores. This statute is set out in "Halsbury's Statutes," vol. 15, at p. 48. The statute put an end to subinfeudation, so that if B, being feudal tenant of A, granted the land or part of the land of which he was feudal tenant, to C, C became feudal tenant not of B, but of A. Mr. Gray, in his book "On Perpetuities," 4th ed., at p. 26, says that the right or possibility of reverter of an estate in fee simple limited to determine on the happening of an event which might or might not happen, implied tenure, i.e., feudal tenure, and that since the Statute Quia Emptores there can be no such fee. Sanders in his book on "Uses and Trusts," 5th ed., vol. I, at p. 209, says the same thing, and also says the right of reversion was in the nature of an escheat. I find it difficult to follow Mr. Gray's reasoning as to why, after the Statute Quia Emptores, there could be no "fee determinable." If the reversion was a right in the nature of an escheat, an incident of feudal tenure, then the Statute Quia Emptores would not make such a right impossible, as it did not end such tenure but substituted the grantor's overlord for the grantor. It may well be that after the statute this kind of limitation became practically obsolete, until the time when such limitations could be followed by limitations taking effect as executory limitations.

At p. 712 of his book, Mr. Gray quotes the opinon of Sir Howard Elphinstone that Mr. Gray's "reasoning against the possibility of reserving a right of reverter to the grantor is conclusive," but that the truth is "that when the limitation comes to an end the lands will fall into the hands of the lord of the fee by a right somewhat in the nature of an escheat," and Sir Frederick Pollock in his book on "Land Laws," 3rd ed., p. 226, prefers this view, though he is not definite on the question. The same point is mentioned in "Halsbury's Laws of England," 2nd ed., vol. 27, p. 668, note (c), where it is stated that "it was generally assumed that the determination was in favour of the grantor and his heirs," and the view of Sir Howard Elphinstone that the reversion was to the overlord is also mentioned. On several occasions, in giving judgments on other matters, judges have expressly left open the question whether estates in fee determinable can exist, and in *Collier* v. *Walters*, 17 Equity, at p. 26, Sir George Jessel, M.R., says: "In fact there is not any authority to be found for any such determinable fee," but it is not clear that he meant to say that a "fee determinable" could not exist at all. Joyce, J., in *Re Leach* [1912] 2 Ch., at p. 427, took the view that such limitations could be made, "notwithstanding what may have been said in any book as to the effect of the Statute Quia Emptores upon the creation of estates in fee simple determinable or qualified." In this case the determinable fee admitted of an executory limitation to take effect on its determination, the executory limitation necessarily taking effect, if at all, within the time allowed by the rule against perpetuities, a possibility which is mentioned by Mr. Challis in his book, 3rd ed., at p. 254. Mr. Challis does not agree with Mr. Gray that such estates cannot exist since the Statute Quia Emptores, and quotes the opinion of many authorities of great weight to support his view, and he takes the view that the reversion was in the grantor. "Fees determinable" are mentioned and provided for both in the Law of Property Act, 1925 (see First Schedule to that Act) and in the Settled Land Act, 1925. After considering these authorities, I am of opinion that such fees can exist. It has been suggested that possibly on such limitations nowadays the reversion is in the Crown as overlord, and any decision I come to in this case is without prejudice to any claim of such a right by the Crown, as the Attorney-General is not a party to these proceedings. The Liverpool Corporation can only have an interest if the reversion is in the grantor, as it cannot claim any rights as feudal overlord. My judgment in this case is therefore upon the assumption that the reversion belongs to the grantor.

The second question which was raised and argued was whether the possibility of reverter on a "fee determinable" is subject to the rule against perpetuities. Gray, at p. 107, says: "the point that reversionary interests which may never take effect might be subject to the rule against perpetuities has not been raised in any reported case," but I think that must have been written before the decision of Byrne, J., in *Re Trustees of Hollis's Hospital and Hagues Contract* [1899] 2 Ch. 540, and *Attorney-General* v. *Cummins* [1906] 1 I.R. 406. When I consider the judgment of Palles, C.B., in the last-mentioned case and the opinions of some of the eminent legal writers on this subject to which I have been referred, I have considerable doubt whether at common law any clear distinction was drawn between estates in fee determinable and estates in fee subject to a condition. I doubt if at common law at one time a distinction would have been drawn between a grant in fee simple until the happening of an event, which might or might not happen, and a grant in fee simple with a condition that it was to terminate when the same event happened. Challis, at p. 253, when speaking of "determinable fees," says: "Littleton styles such limitations conditions in law." Palles, C.B., in his judgment above referred to says: "There has been some argument as to the nature of the estate granted by the Letters Patent. In my opinion, that estate is that which is sometimes called a base or qualified fee, and sometimes a fee determinable. The grant passed the quit rents in fee subject to a condition determining that fee upon the payment by the Crown at any time of the sum of £5,000. Under such a grant the grantee, until the happening of the determining event has the whole estate in him, and the old common law doctrine was undoubtedly that a possibility of reverter, a possibility coupled with an interest, remained in the grantor, and that the fee of the rents would, upon the performance of the condition, revert to the Crown." In both cases there is only a possibility of reverter. Challis, at p. 82, says: "Reverter and reversion are synonymous terms, denoting an estate vested in interest though not in possession: but the word reverter is sometimes loosely used to denote what is properly styled possibility of reverter. Possibility of reverter denotes no estate, but, as the name implies, only a possibility to have an estate at a future time. Of such possibilities there are several kinds; of which two are usually denoted by the term now under consideration: (1) the possibility that a common law fee may return to the grantor by breach of a condition subject to which it was granted, and (2) the possibility that a common law fee, other than a fee simple"—I think there he means a fee simple absolute—"may revert to the grantor by the natural determination of the fee". Both Mr. Gray, in section B of his book, and Mr. Challis, at p. 76, agree that a possibility of this kind was not alienable. It follows that the grantor had no vested estate which he could dispose of at any time. It is said in "Halsbury's Laws of England," vol. 27, at p. 722: "The grant of a fee simple, notwithstanding that it was determinable, was in law considered as the grant of the whole fee. Hence, there was no remnant of the fee left for the grantor to grant as a remainder, nor was there any reversion in himself, but, in case of conditional or determinable fees, he had an interest which was called a 'possibility of reverter.'" In the *Buckhurst Peerage* case, 2 A.C., at p. 26, Lord Cairns, L.C., says: "The common law did understand one mode of putting an end to an estate which, in the first instance, appeared to be granted absolutely, that is to say, it understood the mode of terminating an estate by means of the annexation of a condition. If a condition was annexed to an estate, which otherwise would have been absolute, then on the happening of the condition the estate was defeated. But then, my lords, it was not defeated for the benefit of a remainder-man, nor could a remainder have been annexed to the condition; it was defeated or defeasible by and for the donor, who was entitled to enter for the condition broken. My lords, that was the state of things by common law. At the time that that was the state of things at common law, it was found to be so inconvenient for the purposes of families, and in dealing with land, that there were introduced what were called 'Uses,' which, at the time of their introduction, were analogous to what now are trusts in the Court of Chancery."

Speaking of determinable fees, it is said in "Halsbury's Laws of England," vol. 27, at p. 667: "It is no objection that the future event may happen at a time beyond the limit allowed by the rule against perpetuities"—and this is explained in a note, when it is said: "The principle is either that possibilities of reverter are older than the rule against perpetuities and are subject only to the common law, or that the collateral limitation determines but does not originate, an estate. The latter is probably the better reason." The first reason, that such possibilities of reverter date back beyond the Statute of Uses and are older than the rule against perpetuities, is the reason relied on by Mr. Challis to explain why they are not subject to the rule against perpetuities, and also in *Attorney-General* v. *Cummins*, above mentioned, Palles, C.B., says: "Thus, the only real question is whether the estate of the Crown is defeated by the rule against perpetuities. The grant in question operated at common law. It did not take effect under the Statute of Uses, and the modern rule against perpetuities never applied to common law conveyances. It is impossible that it could have applied, as it had its origin in the Statute of Uses, as is matter of elementary knowledge; and the subject-matter of that statute did not include conveyances other than those to uses." Then he goes on to deal with the question of possibility. I do not think I need read more of that judgment. With regard to the second reason given in the note of Halsbury, it appears that a grantor is in of his old estate when he re-enters for non-payment of a rent or on the determination of an estate on the happening of a condition. Mr. Gray, at p. 309, says: "On re-entry on non-payment of a rent the grantor is in of his old estate"; and Mr. Challis, at p. 219, says of a fee simple subject to a condition: "If an entry be made, the estate to which the condition is annexed is destroyed; whereby the fee reverts to the grantor or his heirs in the same manner in all respects as before the grant of the estate subject to the condition." It is to be observed that when it is said that a grantor is in of his old estate it is not the same thing as a resulting trust, which is an equitable right, and cases on resulting trusts in favour of a grantor or testator do not appear to me to have any application to such a case as the present one. It appears, therefore, that the only reasons given why the rule against perpetuities does not apply to "fees determinable" are equally applicable in the case of "fees subject to a condition."

But, in the case of *Re Trustees of Hollis's Hospital and Hagues Contract* [1899] 2 Ch. 540, Byrne, J., decided that the rule against perpetuities does apply in the case of reverter in fees subject to a condition. In that case: "The property contracted to be sold formed part of certain property which had been conveyed by H to trustees upon trusts for the hospital by deeds of lease and release, dated May 17 and 18, 1726. The release contained a proviso that if at any time thereafter the premises thereby conveyed or any part thereof, or the rents, issues, and profits of the same or of any part thereof, should be employed or converted to or for any other uses, intents or purposes than those thereinbefore mentioned, then and from thenceforth all and every the premises thereinbefore conveyed should revert to the right heirs of H party thereto." Byrne, J., said: "It is contended on behalf of the purchaser that a good title cannot be made by reason of the clause in the deed of 18th May, 1726, providing for the reverter to the right heirs of Thomas Hollis, senior, inasmuch as the sale will be a breach of the condition and, alternatively, that the title shown is not one which ought to be forced upon a purchaser. It is contended on behalf of the vendors—that is, the trustees other than W. H. Anthony—that the condition is void as tending to a perpetuity, and that whether the clause in question be construed as operating by way of shifting use, as they say it should be, or by way of condition subsequent. The effect of the method of conveyance adopted was as follows: the lease for a year operated and the bargainee, John Williams, was in possession by the Statute of Uses. The release operated by enlarging the estate or possession of the bargainee to a fee—this was at the common law—and the use being declared in favour of persons other than the bargainee the statute intervened and annexed or transferred the possession of the releasee to the use of the trustees to whom the use was declared. I think the clause about which the contest arises is in terms and form a true common law condition subsequent, being aptly worded and being in favour of the heirs of Thomas Hollis, senior. It is true that words of an express condition may in certain cases be intended as a limitation, but the rule is that it shall not ordinarily be so construed, and there does not appear to be any reason in the present case why it should be construed as a limitation rather than as a condition. It was conceded in argument that if the clause in question ought to be construed as a limitation or as creating a shifting use it would be void as infringing the rule against perpetuities, and it was argued that the clause ought to be construed as one intended to shift the use which was vested by virtue of the release in the trustees, upon the happening of the contemplated event, into the heirs of the original bargainor, and that it was not possible for it to operate otherwise, having regard to the fact that the estate to be defeated was one existing only by virtue of the statute. I do not think that this argument can prevail." Then he went on to deal with *Rudhall's* case, and he said, on p. 551: "The next question is whether or not the condition, being an express common law condition subsequent, is void for perpetuity. I have not been referred to any case deciding the question, nor have I since the argument, after a considerable search, been able to find any authority in the reports enabling me to say that the point has been judicially decided. For the exposition of our very complicated real property law, it is proper in the absence of judicial authority to resort to text-books which have been recognised by the courts as representing the views and practice of conveyancers of repute. Except in the comparatively recent although most valuable book of the late Mr. Challis (whose loss we all regret), to which I shall have to refer more fully later on, I cannot find any definite statement of opinion adverse to the views expressed by Mr. Sanders and Mr. Lewis in their well-known treatises, and I will first refer to 'Sanders on Uses and Trusts.'" Then he said, giving the reference: "I find in 'Lewis on Perpetuity' the opinion of the author expressed in clear and unambiguous language. Amongst quite modern text writers I find a similar expression of opinion. See the work of the learned American author, Mr. Gray, who has written on the law of perpetuity, at p. 215, where he states his view, in spite of the fact there are American authorities tending the other way, the point not having been taken or argued in such authorities; see also 'Marsden on Perpetuities,' p. 4. I have purposely avoided referring to certain dicta in recent cases until I come to examine Mr. Challis' argument, which was in fact the basis of the argument put forward on the part of the purchaser in the present case. That argument and the learned author's expression of opinion are to be found in Challis's 'Law of Real Property,' 2nd ed., pp. 174-177. Pausing at the introductory paragraphs, I do not propose to embark on a consideration of the origin and development of the rule or rules against perpetuities, about which there have been and will continue to be grave differences of opinion amongst real property lawyers. I find a clear and well-recognised rule certainly applicable to all ordinary methods of disposition in vogue since the Statute of Uses, and what I have to do is to see whether or not that rule is applied to prevent the effectuating by means of a common law condition what is forbidden by the law in the case of all other methods of disposition of property. Mr. Challis is right, of course, when he says that 'when any part of the common law is found to require amendment, the Legislature alone is competent to apply the remedy.' But the courts have first to find what is the common law—that is, the principle embodied in what is called the common law—and to apply it to new and ever-varying sets of fact and circumstances. The common law is to be sought in the expositions and declarations of it in the decisions of the courts and in the writing of lawyers. New statutes and the course of social development give rise to new aspects and conditions which have to be regarded in applying the old principles. The policy of the law against the creation of perpetuities was certainly asserted at a very early date, as was also the policy of discountenancing unrestricted restraints upon alienation." Then he said at the bottom of p. 553: "I think some of Mr. Challis' criticism of the dicta of Jessel, M. R., in the case of *In re Macleay*, L.R. 20 Eq. 186, are not quite reasonable." Then he discusses Mr. Challis' views and goes on: "The decision of North, J. in *Dunn* v. *Flood*, 25 Ch. D. 629, as to the remoteness of the power of re-entry in that case was *obiter*, in the same sense that it was unnecessary for the purposes of the decision to determine it, although it was a question raised and argued; but I think that Mr. Challis, in saying that nothing was said on appeal to support the *obiter dictum*, appears to have overlooked the observation of Baggallay, L. J., where he says: 'This right of re-entry was held by Mr. Justice North to be void for remoteness. We have not heard the counsel for the defendant, but, as at present advised, I concur with Mr. Justice North that this right could not be enforced being void under the rule against perpetuities.'" Then he goes on to say:" The result appears to be that there are expressions of opinions by Jessel, M. R., North, J., and Baggallay, L. J., and the opinion of two great real property lawyers, in favour of the invalidity of such a condition as the one in question; besides the opinions of modern text writers; while on the other side there is nothing definite except the opinion and reasoning of the late Mr. Challis in his work of real property. It is to be noticed that Mr. Challis put forward the surmise that at the present day the courts would not acquiesce in the conclusion he draws without great reluctance; and in reference to his appeal to arguments to be derived from history, I may refer to his own observations." This decision was followed by Eve, J., in *Re Da Costa* [1912] 1 Ch. 337. Mr. Justice Byrne in his judgment rejected the arguments of Mr. Challis, and I cannot reconcile his judgment with that of Chief Baron Palles above quoted, in which he follows the same reasoning as did Mr. Challis. Whatever my own view might have been, I am bound by the decision of Byrne, J., followed by that of Eve, J. I cannot but think that if the rule against perpetuities applies to the possibility of reverter on a fee subject to a condition which may or may not happen, it must equally apply to the possibility of reverter on a fee limited to determine on an event which may or may not happen. I am therefore of opinion that the rule against perpetuities does apply in this case, and that any possibility of a reverter to the Liverpool Corporation is defeated by that rule. Having come to this conclusion, it is unnecessary for me to decide whether, if the rule against perpetuities did not previously apply, the position has now been altered owing to the provisions of the Law of Property Act, 1925, or the Settled Land Act, 1925.

The third question argued in this case was whether the event in which the fee simple determined did not make it inalienable, and was in consequence repugnant, or was void by reason of the provisions of the Statute Quia Emptores. I will consider this question on the basis that the limitation of the fee simple determinable was in other respects valid. It has been conceded on behalf of the corporation in the course of the argument that the estate of the Lyceum would not be terminated by reason of the lettings mentioned in para. 7 of the Statement of Claim, or, now that the library has been discontinued, by the letting of that portion of the building which was occupied by the library. If this is so, then I do not think it would be impossible to sell the building, but the fact that part, possibly a substantial part, would have to be used for a certain purpose, and the estate might be lost entirely if it was not so used, would no doubt considerably reduce the value. In the same way a restrictive covenant as to user might reduce the value, but would not be void for that reason, and the danger of the estate coming to an end is not unlike the position in the case of *In re Chardon* [1928] 1 Ch. 464, where there was a gift of the interest on the sum of £200 so long as a grave was maintained. In my opinion the limitation is not void on this ground.

The fourth question argued was whether the event which determines the fee simple estate of the Lyceum is void for uncertainty. This ought perhaps to have been the first question in order of priority. However, it was argued as the last question, and I have taken it in the same order. The words to be considered are: "so long as the said building called the Lyceum or any other building to be from time to time erected on the site thereof... shall be used and enjoyed for the uses and purposes of the said institution called the Lyceum agreeably to the original articles for its establishment as the same articles are recited or expressed in the Enrolment of the said Indenture of Bargain and Sale of the 17th June, 1801." This last-mentioned indenture recites certain proposals for erecting a news-room and coffee-room with a library in one building and recites that certain named gentlemen on behalf of themselves and all others the subscribers to the said institution had contracted for the purchase of the piece of land thereinafter more particularly described for the sum of £1,344 for the purpose of erecting and building thereon the said new intended erection or building to be made use of as a news-room and library pursuant to the proposals published as aforesaid. Now it is to be gathered from the recited proposals that there were to be a news-room and a coffee-room and a library, but that the members of the library need not be members of the news-room and coffee-room, and it was admitted on behalf of both parties to this action that the library and the news-room and coffee-room must be regarded as separate institutions, and Mr. Gray, on behalf of the corporation, submitted that on the true construction of the clause I am considering the original building or a new building might be used and enjoyed by anyone, not necessarily the Lyceum Institution, for the uses and purposes of the said institution as mentioned. I think it is relevant to bear in mind that this case arose from the fact that the Lyceum trustees, after the library had been discontinued, were uncertain whether they could let the part of the building previously occupied by the library, and in my opinion they have quite good grounds for being uncertain. The corporation have now conceded that the lettings of the rooms mentioned in para. 7 of the Statement of Claim and the letting of the part of the building formerly occupied by the library would not determine the fee simple estate of the trustees. It follows that it is not necessary that the whole building should be "used and enjoyed" for the uses and purposes mentioned in the conveyance of 1805.

The question naturally follows as to what part or proportion of the building must be so used and enjoyed, and if a new building is built how are these questions to be answered? For instance, could the site be sold for the purpose of having a large new hotel built on it, if the hotel provided accommodation for a news-room and coffee-room for the members of the Lyceum, and if so, what accommodation would be sufficient? It appears to me that if the estate of the Lyceum trustees determines, when the present building, or a new building in place of the present building, ceases to be used and enjoyed for the uses and purposes mentioned, the event which causes the determination must be construed as a condition subsequent. Conditions subsequent which cause a forfeiture must, in order to be valid, be so framed that the persons affected (or the court if they seek its guidance) can from the outset know with certainty the exact event on the happening of which their interests are to be divested. See judgment of Lord Russell in *Clayton* v. *Ramsden* [1943] A.C. at p. 326, and *Clavering* v. *Ellison*, 7 H.L. Cas. 707. In *Sifton* v. *Sifton* [1938] A.C. 656, a testator directed certain yearly payments to his daughter, and then said: "the payments to my said daughter to continue only so long as she shall reside in Canada." This was held by the House of Lords to be a condition subsequent, which was void for uncertainty. In the case of *In re Viscount Exmouth*, 23 Ch. D. 158, at p. 164, Fry, J., said: "... The condition must be clear and certain. That, in my opinion, includes not only certainty of expression in the creation of the limitation, but also certainty in its operation. It must be such a limitation that, at any given moment of time it is ascertainable whether the limitation has or has not taken effect." In this present case I think there is uncertainty of expression in the creation of the limitation and uncertainty in its operation. It seems to me impossible to say beforehand exactly what circumstances would terminate this estate of the Lyceum trustees. In my opinion the condition subsequent which is to determine the estate of the Lyceum trustees is void for uncertainty. Having come to these conclusions, I shall make a declaration in the terms of para. 1 of the claim in the statement of claim leaving out the words "absolute and," so the declaration will read: "A declaration that the plaintiffs as trustees for the Lyceum and the Lyceum beneficially through the plaintiffs as such trustees are entitled to the Lyceum land conveyed by the conveyance and the buildings thereon for an estate in fee simple free from any right of reverter right of re-entry or other legal equitable right interest trust or claim vested in the Liverpool Corporation." Having so decided, it follows the defendants will pay the costs of the action.

Judgment accordingly.

[See *Powell*, Determinable Fees (1923), 23 Col. L. Rev. 207; 1 *Restatement of Property*, chap. 4, pp. 117 ff.; *Farrer*, Reverter to Donor on a Determinable Fee (1934), 50 Law Q. Rev. 33.

In *Moser* v. *Barss*, [1947] 4 D.L.R. 313 (N.S.), land was conveyed to trustees of a church "forever to be used only for the purpose of a church or school but for no other purpose whatsoever". On a question being propounded to the Court whether the grantor or his heirs, or persons claiming through or under him, have any interest in the land, Sir Joseph Chisholm C. J. stated that "he [the grantor] completely divested himself of all interest therein by his demise", and he went on to indicate that the gift was a charitable one. Do you agree? Cf. *Re Cooper's Conveyance Trusts, Crewdson* v. *Bagot*, [1956] 3 All E.R. 28, [1956] 1 W.L.R. 1096 (Ch.).

In *Re Hunter*, [1947] O.W.N. 342, a testator had devised land to A "until it is sold". What interest does A have in the land? A determinable fee simple? A determinable life estate? A fee simple with an executory limitation over? A fee simple with a power of appointment in the testator's executors?]

CHAPTER IV

THE RISE AND FALL OF THE ESTATE IN FEE TAIL

1. DEVELOPMENT OF THE ESTATE: ALIENABILITY AND THE "LANDED" TRADITION

As WE HAVE SEEN, in the thirteenth century a tenant in fee simple established his power to transfer his interest without the concurrence of his presumptive heir. Later, as a result of *Quia Emptores* this power was established as against the tenant's overlord. In the meantime, attempts were made to fashion limitations which would ensure lineal descent of estates in land as part of a marriage settlement or as part of a family settlement and, in either case, as a means of identifying a family with an estate symbolizing status and wealth. Such a limitation was perfected by a feoffment to "A and the heirs of his body". Pressure for alienability resulted, however, in a construction of this limitation as follows: (1) if A had heirs of the body, the condition of the limitation was satisfied and he could thereafter alienate as for a fee simple free of any claim of his lineal descendants and free of any reversionary claim by the feoffor; (2) if A had no heirs of the body, his interest was merely for life with a reversion to the feoffor; and (3) if A had heirs of the body but did not alienate, the estate descended according to the terms of the limitation. This type of estate was the fee simple conditional, and it may be noted that the same technicality in the use of the term "heirs" was required as in the case of the creation of an estate in fee simple. Some variation was open, e.g., to A and the heirs male of his body; to A and the heirs of his body by his wife Mary; to A and the heirs female from him proceeding. But having regard to the construction put upon all such limitations, the feoffor's or donor's intention to maintain an inheritable estate inalienable against lineal descendants of the feoffee or donee, and with a reversion on the failure of the lineal descendants, could in certain events be defeated.

A statute of 1285, De Donis Conditionalibus, sought to retrieve the situation by providing "it is ordained that the will of the giver, according to the form in the deed of gift manifestly expressed, shall be from henceforth observed; so that they to whom the land was given under such condition, shall have no power to alien the land so given, but that it shall remain unto the issue of them to whom it was given after their death, or shall revert unto the giver or his heirs, if issue fail, either by reason that there is no issue at all, or if any issue be, and fail by death, or heir of the body of such issue failing."

Remedies were given to protect the interests of issue (formedon in the descender) and reversioners (formedon in the reverter). Formedon in the remainder was developed at common law to protect remainder interests. (Formedon is from *forma doni*, form of the gift.)

De Donis thus superseded the fee simple conditional and brought into being a new estate, the fee tail (from the French "tailler", meaning to cut or shape) which exhibited the following varieties: (1) fee tail general; (2) fee tail general male; (3) fee tail general female; (4) fee tail special; (5) fee tail special male; (6) fee tail special female. If a feoffment was made to A and the heirs of his body by his wife Mary (a fee tail special) and Mary died without having children, A was a tenant in tail after possibility of issue extinct, or in other words, in the position of a mere life tenant.

It followed from the nature of a fee tail that (1) the tenant for the time being could alienate only his own interest; and (2) it was not devisable by will. The common law, moreover, did not permit a fee tail to be destroyed by merger as where the tenant in fee tail acquired the reversion or remainder in fee simple; to allow this would have defeated the declared purpose of *De Donis.*

As in the case of a fee simple, the technicality of form for creation of an estate tail at common law (i.e., necessary use of "heirs" followed by words of procreation) did not obtain in case of wills, and, subject to the finding of a contrary intention, devises to "A and his issue", to "A and his descendants" and to "A but if he dies without heirs of the body then to B" sufficed to give A a fee tail.

[What estate was created by a devise "to A but if he die without leaving an heir then to B"? See *Re Thompson,* [1936] O.R. 8, [1936] 1 D.L.R. 39 (C.A.).

In *In re Haig* (1925), 57 O.L.R. 129, (App. Div.), land was devised to N (an infant) for life, and at his death to his sons and daughters but in the event that N had no sons or daughters the land was to go to others at N's death. *Held,* N's interest was an estate in fee tail. Why? See *Wild's Case* (1599), 6 Co. Rep. 17a; *Grant* v. *Fuller* (1902), 33 S.C.R. 34.]

Descent in a fee tail was traced from the last *purchaser,* i.e. from the original donee in tail, and not from a person taking by operation of law, e.g., by descent. Primogeniture applied and males were preferred to females. Representation was allowed so that lineal descendants, however remote, of a deceased represented their ancestor.

The fee tail had advantages for the tenant in tail and his family because creditors of a tenant could go against his interest only; his issue in tail were not bound by any sale or lease that he made (subject to later statutes); and forfeiture for treason or other cause was also limited to his interest. "Thus all members of the community except perhaps the great landowners themselves were interested in obtaining a relaxation of the practice of strictly entailing lands which had grown up under the provisions of the Statute of Westminster II." (*Digby,* History of the Law of Real Property (5th ed., 1897), pp. 252-3.) The estate tail, being an interest on the terminination of which a reversion or remainder would take effect, restricted the marketability of land so long as there was no failure of issue, and thus represented an about-face on freedom of alienation. By the end of the fifteenth century the Courts lent their assistance to a method of "disentailing" which involved contrived litigation and fiction. It was indicated in *Taltarum's Case* (1472), Y.B. 12 Edw. IV, 19, and in its developed form the right to "suffer a common recovery" (as this disentailing method was called) was regarded by the Courts as so bound up with a fee tail that any attempt in a limitation to deprive a tenant in tail of this right was void: see *Mary Portington's Case* (1613), 10 Co. Rep. 35b, 77 E.R. 976.

It was first established that if a tenant in tail purported to convey a fee simple and left his issue lands of equal value they could not challenge the conveyance. Later, it was sufficient if the tenant in tail left them a judgment for lands of equal value. On this basis, and by resorting to the writ of right the following procedure was worked out: (1) the proposed grantee of a fee simple in the entailed lands would issue a writ of right against the tenant in tail in possession, claiming the lands in fee simple; (2) a judgment against the defendant would not itself prevent the issue from asserting their rights, and hence the defendant would vouch over to warranty some third person, his alleged grantor, and thus call on him to defend the action; (3) the vouchee to warranty would default, judgment would go for plaintiff and a judgment for lands of equal value would be given to the tenant in tail against the vouchee to warranty (the vouchee was a man of straw who swore falsely that he had warranted the title of the tenant in tail; in time the Court crier played the role of common vouchee); and (4) recovery of the lands in fee simple was if necessary enforced by the sheriff. The effect of the judgment was to bar both the issue and any reversioner or remainderman. It was not unusual for the successful plaintiff to convey the lands in fee simple to the tenant in tail, and hence that plaintiff might also be merely a chosen instrument to effect a disentailment.

Since the common recovery was available only against a person seised, a difficulty could arise where the estate in fee tail was preceded by a life estate. (The life tenant was the "protector of the settlement".) In such case the protector's consent was necessary to an effective recovery. It may be noted that by a statute, 14 Eliz., c. 8, a tenant in tail after possibility of issue extinct could only bar issue by a common recovery and not any estate expectant on the termination of the fee tail.

Another method of disentailing was by the "fine", which involved a compromised law suit ending in a "final concord" between the parties, entered as a judgment after approval by the Court. Although *De Donis* expressly declared that a fine would be void, subsequent legislation in 1489 and 1540 (Statutes of Fines) made the fine available again but because it operated only to bar issue and not reversioners or remaindermen it was not as effective as a common recovery. Its result was a "base" fee, lasting as long as there was no failure of issue. If the fine had any advantage, it was that it did not need the participation of the person seised. In form, it involved a suit against a tenant in tail for recovery of the land and the compromise would be an agreement that the plaintiff should have the land. Fines and recoveries were abolished by the Fines and Recoveries Act, 1833 (Imp.), c. 74, which substituted a simple method of disentailing through the execution and recording of a disentailing assurance. (For legislation modelled on the English Act, see Estates Tail Act, R.S.O. 1950, c. 117, repealed by 1956 (Ont.), c. 19)

[On recoveries and fines generally, see *Williams and Eastwood*, Principles of the Law of Real Property (1933), pp. 144 ff.; *Megarry and Wade*, Law of Real Property (1959, 2d ed.), pp. 87 ff.; *Plucknett*, Concise History of the Common Law (1956, 5th ed.), pp. 617-623.]

RE CARR AND SMITH. Ontario High Court. [1950] O.R. 26, [1950] 1 D.L.R. 746.

LEBEL J.: This is a motion under the *Vendors and Purchasers Act*, R. S. O. 1937, c. 168.

Until March 17, 1924, John G. Carr was the owner in fee simple of farm lands comprising some fifty acres in the Township of Romney, in the County of Kent. On that date, by deed, he granted them to his son Ernest L. Carr "and the heirs of his body lawfully begotten and in default of such heirs to Margaret Alice Teskey, Annabelle Charlton, Hulda May Collard, Percy LeRoy Carr, William Edison Carr and their heirs and assigns to and for their sole and only use forever". The habendum in the deed is in the same language. There was thus created an estate tail in favour of Ernest L. Carr and his issue with remainder in fee simple to the five persons named who were his brothers and sisters. I shall hereinafter refer to John G. Carr as "the father", to Ernest L. Carr as "the son" and to the latter's brothers and sisters as "the remaindermen".

The creation by the father of that kind of estate which is now of very infrequent occurrence, was expressed in the conveyance to be "in consideration of a Life Lease to be given by the Grantee to the Grantor and of Natural Love and Affection". And by a lease bearing the same date as the conveyance, the son leased the lands to his father "for and during the term of the natural life of the Lessee"; the consideration being "the sum of One ($ 1.) dollar and the covenants and agreements hereinafter reserved and contained on the part of the said Lessee". By the covenants and agreements contained in the lease the father was required to pay taxes but no rent.

On April 26, 1924, the son purported to convey the lands to Olive Fern Carr, his wife, in fee simple, in consideration of natural love and affection and the sum of one dollar. This instrument contains these, among other recitals:

"AND WHEREAS by deed bearing date the 17th day of March, 1924, the said John G. Carr granted the hereinafter described lands to the Grantor herein in fee tail, subject however to a life lease given by the Grantor herein to the said John G. Carr, which said life lease is dated the 17th of March, 1924;

"AND WHEREAS the Grantor is now desirous of barring the entail and conveying the lands to the Grantee herein."

On January 30, 1946, the son as mortgagor, his wife joining therein to bar her dower, mortgaged the lands to Delbert Coatsworth to secure the sum of $ 3,000, the instrument being expressed to be drawn in pursuance of the *Short Forms of Mortgages Act.*

The father died on or about March 9, 1934, and the son died, without issue, on or about December 15, 1947.

On March 26, 1949, Olive Fern Carr, the administratrix of the estate of Ernest L. Carr, as vendor, agreed to sell the lands for $ 10,000. The solicitors for the proposed purchaser objected to title; they required proof that the deed from Ernest L. Carr to his wife "was sufficient to bar the entail and also to bar any interest in reversion" of the five remaindermen....

... Counsel for the vendor contended that the entail was barred, and with it the remaindermen's estate in fee simple, by the deed to Olive Fern Carr, or, in the alternative, by the mortgage to Coatsworth.

Counsel for the purchaser took a neutral position; he intimated that his client was anxious to acquire the lands.

Section 3 of the *Estates Tail Act*, R.S.O. 1937, c. 156, provides: "Every actual tenant in tail, whether in possession, remainder, contingency or otherwise, may dispose of, for an estate in fee simple absolute... the land entailed as against all persons... including His Majesty, whose estates are to take effect after the determination, or in defeasance of such estate tail; saving always the rights of all persons in respect of estates prior to the estate tail in respect of which such disposition is made, and the rights of all other persons except those against whom such disposition is, by this Act, authorized to be made."

By this section it is therefore clear that the remaindermen are persons "against whom such disposition is, by this Act, authorized to be made", and that a tenant in tail may make a disposition of the lands entailed for an estate in fee simple absolute as against the remaindermen "saving always the rights of all persons in respect of estates prior to the estate tail in respect of which such disposition is made". But counsel for the remaindermen, conceding that the son could legally have barred his own issue, if he had had any, assert that he could not during his father's lifetime defeat their clients' estate in remainder without the concurrence of his father. The contention is that the deed to the son and the life lease to the father must be read together, and that together they comprise a settlement of the land so as to make ss. 8 and 18 of the Act applicable.

Section 8 provides: "If at the time there is a tenant in tail of land under a settlement, and there is subsisting in the same land... under the same settlement, an estate for years, determinable on the dropping of a life or lives, or any greater estate, not being an estate for years, *prior to the estate tail*, then the person who is the owner of the prior estate... shall be the protector of the settlement so far as regards the land in which such prior estate is subsisting, and shall... be deemed the owner of such prior estate... and an estate by way of resulting use or trust to or for the settlor shall be deemed an estate under the same settlement within the meaning of this section."

It is sufficient to say for the purpose of this motion that by s. 18 of the Act a tenant in tail may not dispose of the lands entailed so as to defeat the estate of the remaindermen in fee simple without the consent of the protector of the settlement, and counsel for the remaindermen argue that the late John G. Carr, by force of the deed and the concurrent lease, was the protector of the settlement, and that his consent was necessary for the effective determination of the remaindermen's estate. Counsel for the vendor take the opposite view.

There can, of course, be no doubt that the father intended his lands to go to his other sons and daughters in the event that the son to whom he granted the lands in tail should die without issue, as he did, and it remains to be decided whether that son could, and did in fact, defeat his father's intention. The problem must be resolved according to the strict legal rights of the parties and these depend upon the meaning and effect to be given to the two documents which are said to comprise the settlement.

In *Birdsill* v. *Birdsill* (1919), 50 D.L.R. 708, 46 O.L.R. 345 at p. 347, Riddell J. (as he then was) said: "I am unable to see that the actual object of the grantor was important; he must take the effect in law of his conveyances: *Lawlor* v. *Lawlor* (1881), 6 A.R. (Ont.) 312; (1882), 10 Can. S.C.R. 194; *Culbertson* v. *McCullough* (1900), 27 A.R. (Ont.) 459, and cases cited"; and I subscribe to the observation made by Martin L. J. A. in *Ostrom* v. *The "Miyako"*, [1924] 2 D.L.R. 200 at p. 202, Ex. C.R. 86, 34 B.C.R. 4: "This result may seem a hardship, but the longer I sit upon this Bench the more I am convinced that the only real justice is strict justice for all concerned."

Although the universal practice in olden times seems to have been to put a settlement of land in one document, I am prepared to assume that the deed and the lease comprise a settlement in this instance. The question then, put bluntly, is—Did the two documents read together have the effect of reserving or creating a life lease in favour of the father *which was prior to the son's estate tail?* If not, giving the saving provision of s. 3 and the language of s. 8 their ordinary meaning, the father was not the protector of the settlement at the date of the deed from the son to his wife. I think he was not, for the following reasons.

The father did not, by any words expressed in either of the two documents, reserve a life lease in his own favour, and it is not permissible, in my opinion, to imply that he did in view of the precise language used. The most that can be said in the remaindermen's favour is that the two documents were contemporaneous, but it is to be observed as to their effect that the consideration for the deed to the son is expressed to be "a Life Lease *to be given* by the Grantee to the Grantor and... Natural Love and Affection". Thus, the lease was to be given back to the father as part consideration for the grant, and the son could not give the lease to the father until he had acquired title to the lands. Furthermore, the consideration for the grant to the son is expressly different from the consideration for the lease back to the father, since the latter document makes no mention of the grant to the son.

It is true that one of the recitals in the deed from the son to his wife states that his deed from his father was subject to a life lease in his father's favour, but the words "subject however to" do not mean necessarily that the father's life lease was prior, or was to be considered prior, to the deed to the son. If the recital could be said to mean that, in my opinion, it would be an incorrect statement of the legal effect of the two concurrent documents.

It was argued by Mr. Steele that if it were held that the life lease did not constitute a prior estate the father could have been dispossessed by the remaindermen had the son predeceased him without barring the entail. That is no doubt true on the authority of *Doe d. Graham* v. *Newton* (1847), 3 U.C.Q.B. 249, but it in no way alters the situation in my view.

It was not argued, nor have I been able to find in the two documents any language which might lead me to conclude, that their combined effect was to create an estate by way of a resulting use or trust in favour of the father, so as to make him the protector of the settlement under the concluding words of s. 8. The express language used in the documents is contrary to any such implication, in my opinion.

Having reached the conclusion that the life lease was not an estate prior to the son's estate tail and hence that the father was not the protector of the settlement at the time his son conveyed the lands to his wife, the question as to the legal effect of the mortgage given by the son on January 30, 1946, need not be answered. However, in view of the able and exhaustive argument of counsel for the remaindermen, I think I should answer it as a matter of courtesy.

To begin with it cannot be assumed that when the son gave the mortgage he did not know what he was about. To do so would be to conclude that his name instead of his wife's as mortgagor was inserted in error. There is nothing to suggest that such was the case.

It is argued on behalf of the vendor, upon the authority of *Re Hazell*, [1925] 3 D.L.R. 661, 57 O.L.R. 290, that whatever might be the effect of the deed to the wife, the subsequent mortgage barred the entail, including the estate in remainder. It was said that if the father had been the protector of the settlement he had ceased to be such upon his decease in 1934, that his prior life estate, if it could be held to be such, had died with him and that there was thus no one whose consent was required at the time the mortgage was given. Counsel for the remaindermen sought to counter this argument by saying that the son's deed to his wife had the effect of converting the estate tail into a base fee, and that by reason of the conveyance to her the son had parted with the base fee and could not afterwards validly mortgage the lands. It was argued that but for his conveyance to his wife, the son could have barred the entail and the interest of the remaindermen by giving a mortgage at any time between the date of his father's death and the date of his own decease, but that since the son had conveyed his interest to his wife she, as owner of the base fee, was the only person who could have afterwards so barred the interest of the remaindermen. The position thus taken was that if the son's wife had been the mortgagor instead of the son at the time the mortgage to Coatsworth was given, the remaindermen's interest would have been barred effectively.

I do not think the argument on behalf of the remaindermen is well founded because, with great respect, it seems to proceed upon a misconception of the nature of all the incidents of an estate tail.

By s. 1 (1) (*b*) of the Act: "'Base fee' shall mean exclusively that estate in fee simple into which an estate tail is converted where the issue in tail are barred, but persons claiming estates by way of remainder or otherwise are not barred."

By s. 1 (1) (*g*) of the Act: "'Tenant in tail' shall include a person who, where an estate tail has been barred and converted into a base fee, would have been tenant of such estate tail if the same had not been barred."

Section 5 of the Act provides: "Where an estate tail has been barred and converted into a base fee the person who, if such estate tail had not been barred, would have been actual tenant in tail of land may dispose of such land as against all persons, including His Majesty, whose estates are to take effect after the determination, or in defeasance of the base fee into which the estate tail has been converted, so as to enlarge the base fee into a fee simple absolute; saving always the right of all persons, in respect of estates prior to the estate tail which has been converted into a base fee, and the rights of all other persons except those against whom such disposition is by this Act authorized to be made."

The saving provision in the section lastly quoted is of no assistance to the remaindermen here for it is with "estates prior to the estate tail which has been converted into a base fee", that the provision has to do. In any case at the time of the mortgage the father was deceased and there was at that time no estate of any kind prior to the son's estate tail.

The first five lines of s. 7 of the Act read: "If a tenant in tail makes a disposition of the land under this Act, by way of mortgage, or for any other limited purpose, such disposition shall, to the extent of the estate thereby created, be an absolute bar to all persons as against whom such disposition is by this Act authorized to be made."

It is unnecessary to quote further from this section because it was fully considered by Middleton J. A. in *Re Hazell*, [1925] 3 D.L.R. at p. 669, 57 O.L.R. at p. 295, where that great Judge had this to say (s. 7 was then s. 8): "By virtue of the Act now found as the Estates Tail Act, R.S.O. 1914, c. 113, s. 8, if a tenant-in-tail makes a mortgage, this, to the extent of the estate thereby created, is an absolute bar of the estate tail and conveys to the mortgagee the fee simple in the land, or such lesser estate as may be specified by the mortgage. Upon the discharge of the mortgage, the effect of the provision of the Registry Act now found as R.S.O. 1914, c. 124, s. 67, was held to be the vesting in the mortgagor, not his original estate tail, but the fee simple in the land barred of the entail."

Thus when the son mortgaged the lands to Delbert Coatsworth the mortgage was an absolute bar of the estate tail and conveyed the fee simple in the land to the latter. When it is discharged, the vendor, or any person taking under her, will acquire, not the son's original estate tail, or the base fee into which it was created, but the fee simple in the land barred of the entail.

If this is the result one may ask what was the effect of the son's earlier conveyance to his wife if it did not bar the entail and the interest of the remaindermen as I have held that it did in the circumstances. In my opinion she was then, as owner of the base fee, entitled, subject to the life lease, to the use and enjoyment of the lands as against her husband during his lifetime, or at least until he raised the base fee into an estate in fee simple by a subsequent disposition in her favour or in favour of some third person.

I find no authority whatever for the proposition that the son's wife, as owner of the base fee, could ever have barred the entail and the interest of the remaindermen. The argument that a tenant in tail cannot bar the entail after parting with the base fee is answered by the language of s. 1 (1) (*g*) of the Act. See also Armour on Real Property, 2nd. ed., p. 538, and *Bankes* v. *Small* (1887), 36 Ch. D. 716 at pp. 721, 727.

The motion succeeds and there will be an order declaring that the purchaser's requisitions on title have been satisfactorily answered.

Motion granted.

[Why is it not arguable, in view of s. 5 of the Estates Tail Act, referred to in *Re Carr and Smith*, that the only power left in the tenant in tail after he has created a base fee is to enlarge it (after the death of the protector of the settlement) into a fee simple in favour of the holder of the base fee? Would not such holder be entitled to insist, in view of the usual covenant by a grantor for further assurances, that the tenant in tail enlarge the base fee into a fee simple after the protector's death?

In *Lawlor* v. *Lawlor* (1882), 10 S.C.R. 194, referred to in the above case, it was held that where an estate tail is mortgaged and the mortgage is subsequently discharged through a statutory form of discharge (see now Registry Act, R.S.O. 1960, c. 348, s. 70) which is registered, the mortgagor or his successors obtain not the original estate in fee tail but a fee simple by virtue of the Estates Tail Act. Cf. *Plomley* v. *Felton* (1888), 14 App. Cas. 61 (P.C.); *Falconbridge*, Law of Mortgages of Land (1942, 3rd ed.), pp. 343-345.]

2. ABOLITION OF THE FEE TAIL

STATUTES abolishing the fee tail have been enacted in Alberta (Transfer and Descent of Land Act, R.S.A. 1955, c. 342, s. 10); British Columbia (Land Registry Act, R.S.B.C. 1948, c. 171, s. 23); New Brunswick (Property Act, R.S.N.B. 1952, c. 177, s. 18); Nova Scotia (Real Property Act. R.S.N.S. 1954, c. 244, s. 5); Ontario (Conveyancing and Law of Property Act, R.S.O. 1960, c. 66, s. 4); and Saskatchewan (Land Titles Act, 1960 (Sask.), c. 65, ss. 236 and 237).

In general, the statutes provide that a limitation which theretofore would have created an estate tail shall be construed to give to the grantee or devisee a fee simple or the greatest estate that the grantor or testator had. The abolition of the fee tail (as, for example, the recent Ontario legislation) in no way relieves a solicitor or title examiner from the duty of understanding the old law governing estates tail because he may be faced with constructional or other problems posed by the estate tail, in the course of passing on the marketability of a title.

The New Brunswick provision abolishing estates tail is the only one of those above-mentioned which adverts specifically to interests expectant on the ordinary termination of an estate tail. It reads as follows: "Estates tail are abolished and every estate which would hitherto have been adjudged a fee tail shall be adjudged a fee simple; and if no valid remainder is limited thereon, shall be a fee simple absolute, and may be conveyed or devised by the tenant in tail, or otherwise shall descend to his heirs as a fee simple." What is the effect of the enactment where there is a valid remainder limited after a fee tail? Note that the original Nova Scotia enactment abolishing estates tail (1851, 1st ser., chap. 112) was in the very terms just quoted. In *Ernst* v. *Zwicker* (1897), 27 S.C.R. 594, a majority of the Supreme Court was content to adopt an earlier Nova Scotia decision, *Re Simpson* (1863), 5 N.S.R. 317 (C.A.), which, in effect, ignored the statutory qualification of the limitation of a valid remainder upon a fee tail. In *Re Simpson*, the Court pointed to the similarity of the Nova Scotia and New Brunswick provisions and indicated that they must have been borrowed from a New York enactment but without taking over the whole of it, so that what was in fact borrowed left difficulties of construction.

The New York statute (New York Consolidated Laws, chap. 50, s. 32) is in somewhat the same terms as the New Brunswick provision but it continues as follows: "Where a remainder in fee shall be limited on an estate which would be a fee tail... such remainder shall be valid as a contingent limitation on a fee, and shall vest in possession on the death of the first taker without issue living at the time of such death."

In Manitoba and in Prince Edward Island, the estate tail as such survives but is subject to conversion into a fee simple by registration of disentailing assurances: see Law of Property Act, R.S.M. 1954, c. 138, s. 31; Real Property Act, R.S.P.E.I. 1951, c. 138, ss. 15 and 16.

In England, the fee tail as a legal interest has been abolished by the Law of Property Act, 1925 (Imp.), c. 20, ss. 1 (3), 130, and entailed interests exist only in equity (e.g. under a trust) but may be so created in either real or personal property. Moreover by s. 176, a tenant in tail in possession (other than a tenant in tail after possibility of issue extinct) may by will dispose of the land so as to give a fee simple; for an application of this provision see *Re Manor Farm, Kytes Hardwick, Acheson* v. *Russell*, [1950] 2 All E.R. 572 (Ch.). In addition, of course, disentailing assurances may still be executed but they need no longer be enrolled. On the situation in the United States and on the fee tail in general, see 1 *Restatement of Property*, chap. 5, especially Introductory Note; 2 *Powell*, Real Property (1950), pp. 59-83.

CHAPTER V

LIFE ESTATES: HUSBAND AND WIFE

1. CREATION AND TYPES OF LIFE ESTATES

THE LIFE ESTATE is a freehold, of finite albeit uncertain duration; and, the common law recognized various types, some arising conventionally and others by operation of law. Conventional estates for life may be created by deed or will, either for the life of the grantee or devisee or for the life (or, indeed, lives) of a third person (or persons). The latter type is an estate *pur autre vie*. Of the life estates arising by operation of law, the most important were or are curtesy and dower, and the modern "homestead" interest provided under statute; these will be discussed later in this chapter.

The creation of an estate for life at common law did not involve any special form of words; indeed, the failure to use the proper formula to create a freehold of inheritance might result in the creation of a life estate only. Of course, under modern legislation a conveyance by A to B will not necessarily create a life estate (as it would at common law) but will give B all that A had to convey, subject to any contrary intention. The life estate is a lesser or smaller estate of freehold than an inheritable freehold, and the holder of a fee simple absolute who grants a life estate has a reversion left or may limit a remainder on the life estate. Indeed, he may limit successive life estates followed by an ultimate remainder in fee simple. It is thus clear that "ownership of land" where a life tenant and reversioner, or a life tenant and remainderman, are involved is "segmented ownership" which necessarily requires consideration of the range of uses to which a life tenant (having only a limited interest) may put the land or the extent to which he may "waste" it, and his powers of disposition or leasing. Such divided ownership may raise difficulties as to proper maintenance, or as to sale or mortgaging of the land as a whole, and hence it may be preferable to put the title in a trustee to administer it for the benefit of a life tenant and remainderman. This is not uncommon under wills.

It is paradoxical today that a life estate as a freehold is a higher type of estate than a leasehold, even one for 99 or 999 years. Consider what, if any, consequences flow now from this scale of valuation; see chapter VII, *infra*.

The estate *pur autre vie* created a difficulty for the common law where the grantee died before the end of the measuring life or lives. Thus, if A conveyed to B for the life of C, and B died before C (the cestui que vie), a dilemma was presented. B had nothing to dispose of by will; his personal representatives could not take realty but only personalty; and his heir could not take because B did not have an estate of inheritance. The grantor could not take either until C's death. In such case the first person who entered after B's death took as *general occupant*. By a later development, if the conveyance was by A to B and his heirs for the life of C (or if C, a life tenant, conveyed to B and his heirs), then on B's death his heir took as *special occupant* during C's lifetime. Since he did not take by descent (but rather by "purchase" in a sense) he was not liable for B's debts. The Statute of Frauds, 1677 (Imp.), c. 3, s. 12, made such estates *pur autre vie* devisable and descendible saving the position of a special occupant who was made liable to the extent thereof for the deceased's debts. At the present time, this kind of life interest is devisable and inheritable in the same way as any other inheritable interest: see, for example, Wills Act, R.S.O. 1960, c. 433, s. 8; Devolution of Estates Act, R.S.O. 1960, c. 106, s. 2 (1).

The estate tail after possibility of issue extinct is, of course, a mere life estate.

At common law, any attempt by a tenant for life to convey in fee simple or in fee tail gave rise to a liability to forfeiture because the tortious conveyance was a denial of a superior title in the life tenant's overlord, or, a denial of the tenure between them. However, the tortious feoffment endured until the forfeiture was effected, e.g. by exercise of right of entry; and moreover, it had the effect of destroying contingent remainders limited after the life estate. By statute now, feoffments or conveyances have no "tortious" operation.

Ordinarily the measuring life in a life estate is that of the grantee but constructional problems may arise in particular circumstances; see the elaborate discussion in 1 *Restatement of Property*, ss. 107 ff; and see also 2 *Powell*, Real Property, chap. 15.

[Is it possible to create an estate for life in an unborn person? Suppose A grants to the first son of B for life, B being then unmarried? Or, A grants to B for life then to B's first son for life, B being then unmarried?]

[Questions of construction as to whether a life interest or larger interest is created have already been noted in chapter III, section 2. For other illustrations, see *Re Lane's Estate*, [1946] 1 All E. R. 735 (Ch.) (legacy "for life use, to revert to estate is she does not remarry"; legatee remarries); *Re Plant*, [1946] O.R. 521 (C.A.) ("my bonds and money... I wish put in my mother's name... mother to have a drawing account up to $ 30 per month; at the death of my mother... all money and bonds left to go to X.")

Defeasible estates for life may be created, either as determinable interests or as interests subject to a condition subsequent. What is the effect of a grant *inter vivos* "to B for life provided he pays $ 100 per year and if not to C"? Or "to B for life on condition he pays $ 100 per year, remainder to C"?

Property is left to A for life or during widowhood, remainder to B in fee simple. A remarries but a few years later the marriage is annulled. What is A's position with respect to the property? See *Re Dewhirst*, *Flowers* v. *Dewhirst*, [1948] 1 All E. R. 147 (Ch.).]

[1 *Restatement of Property*, s. 18, defines a life estate as follows:

"An estate for life is an estate which is not an estate of inheritance, and

"(a) is an estate which is specifically described as to duration in terms of the life or lives of one or more human beings, and is not terminable at any fixed or computable period of time; or

"(b) though not so specifically described as is required under the rule stated in Clause (a), is an estate which cannot last longer than the life or lives of one or more human beings, and is not terminable at any fixed or computable period of time or at the will of the transferor."]

IN RE AMOS, CARRIER v. PRICE. Chancery. [1891] 3 Ch. 159

NORTH J.: By his will the testator appointed two persons to be his executors, but he made no devise or bequest to them, although, of course, the personal estate would vest in them for the purpose of their performing their duty as executors. Then comes this gift, "I give, devise, and bequeath unto *Thomas Price* the property known as 27, *Bath Terrace*, the conditions to be as follows:—that the property be left to him for his life and for the life of his heir, after which it becomes the property of the *Boiler Makers and Iron Ship Builders Society.*" Then two other houses are given to two other persons in substantially identical words, the only difference being that the first house is leasehold and the other two houses are freehold. The conditions in each case are exactly the same as those which I have read....

...The only remaining question is, what interest do the tenants for life take? I confess I do not understand what the testator had in his mind; and I can only construe his language as I find it. In my opinion, the property is given to each devisee or legatee for a limited interest, which is described as "for his life and for the life of his heir." For the devisee's own life the gift is clearly good. The question is, whether the interest which he takes comes to an end upon his death, the interest for the life of his heir being too vague to be recognized. I do not see any reason in point of law which prevents the gift from being good. There is no hiatus of any kind; the gift to the devisee for his life would necessarily come to an end at his death. But at the very moment of his death the person who is his heir is ascertained, and there is nothing discontinuous in the limitation which prevents it from being good. I see no ground for saying that the heir takes beneficially. In my opinion, it is a limitation to a tenant for two lives, the lives being his own and that of his heir in each case. I think that is the meaning of the testator's words, and I can see nothing in law to prevent their taking effect.

2. HUSBAND AND WIFE: THE COMMON LAW

THE "PROPERTY" RELATIONS of husband and wife at common law exhibited the disabilities of the married woman found in other branches of the law, most of which have now been remedied by legislation and to some extent also by judicial decision. Upon marriage, a husband acquired an estate *jure uxoris* in his wife's freeholds of which she was seised, becoming entitled to their use and to rents and profits. She could no longer dispose of them during their joint lives without his concurrence but he alone could dispose of them although only to the extent of his own interest which lapsed if he predeceased his wife and which, if he survived her, could last only for his own life as an estate by the curtesy on fulfilment of the preconditions of that estate. Leaseholds of the wife were, however, subject to the husband's disposition during their joint lives but if he did not dispose of them and predeceased his wife, they belonged to her; he could not dispose of them by will. Conversely, they were his if he survived her. Personalty of the wife (other than leaseholds) went to the husband absolutely upon the marriage in so far as it was personalty reduced to possession, and such assets passed under the husband's will or on intestacy from him. The same was true of choses in action of the wife which the husband realized during coverture. (See 3 *Holdsworth*, History of English Law (4th ed., 1935), pp. 525 ff.; *Lamb* v. *Cleveland* (1891), 19 S.C.R. 78, per Gwynne J. at p. 88.)

Some mitigation of the wife's disabilities was achieved in equity by the recognition of a power in her to deal with property given either to trustees or to her husband for her separate use. But her independence in control of her assets awaited the enactment of married women's property legislation, modelled in the Canadian provinces upon the Married Women's Property Act, 1882 (Imp.), c. 75.

[See *Haskins*, Estate by the Marital Right (1948), 97 Univ. of Pa. L. Rev. 344. For situations in the law based apparently on survival of the notion of legal unity of husband and wife, see *Williams*, Legal Unity of Husband and Wife (1947), 10 Mod. L. Rev. 16. See also *Kahn-Freund*, Inconsistencies and Injustices in the Law of Husband and Wife (1952), 15 Mod. L. Rev. 133; (1953), 16 Mod. L. Rev. 33, 148.

In *Edwards* v. *A.-G. of Canada*, [1930] A.C. 124, [1930] 1 D.L.R. 98, [1929] 3 W.W.R. 479 (P.C.), it was held that a woman (including a married woman) was a "person" within s. 24 of the British North America Act, 1867 (respecting appointment to the Senate), and this notwithstanding the common law disabilities of married women operative at the time of the passing of the Act.

In *Kowbel* v. *The Queen*, [1954] S.C.R. 498, [1954] 4 D.L.R. 337, 110 Can. C. C. 47, 18

C. R. 380, rev'g [1953] O.R. 761, [1953] 3. DL.R. 809, 106 Can. C. C. 65, 17 C. R. 69, it was held that the common law rule that a husband and wife by reason of conjugal unity are legally incapable of conspiring with each other survived by reason of s. 16 of the Cr. Code, R.S.C. 1927, c. 36; this provision is now s. 7 (2) of the new Cr. Code.]

3. CURTESY

IF ISSUE were born alive during the life of the wife and capable of inheriting her freeholds of inheritance of which she became actually seised and which became possessory interests during coverture, the husband's estate *jure uxoris* became an estate by the curtesy initiate; and if he survived her his estate became curtesy consummate. The husband's estate by the curtesy was thus a life estate, measured by his own life and operable in respect of all the wife's inheritable freeholds as to which the above mentioned conditions were satisfied: see 1 *American Law of Property* (1952), s. 5.58. Curtesy could exist in the wife's equitable estates of inheritance as well as in her legal estates despite the want of seisin in a strict sense.

Curtesy was lost by divorce or by judicial separation (as to property acquired while the separation existed) but an old line of English cases held that it was not affected by the husband's desertion or adultery. In these latter respects, there have been decisions in the United States to the contrary, based, however, on modern statutes: see 2 *Powell*, Real Property, pp. 152 ff.

Curtesy has, practically speaking, been abolished in England: see *Cheshire*, Modern Law of Real Property (7th ed., 1954), p. 173; Administration of Estates Act, 1925 (Imp.), c. 23, ss. 45 (1) (b), 51 (2); Law of Property Act, 1925 (Imp.), c. 20, s. 130 (4). In Canada, it has been abolished in Alberta (Transfer and Descent of Land Act, R.S.A. 1955, c. 342, s. 5); in British Columbia (Administration Act, R.S.B.C. 1960, c. 3, s. 112); in Manitoba (Law of Property Act, R.S.M. 1954, c. 138, s. 10); in New Brunswick (Married Woman's Property Act, R.S.N.B. 1952, c. 140, s. 8; Devolution of Estates Act, R.S.N.B. 1952, c. 62, s. 32); in Saskatchewan (Devolution of Real Property Act, R.S.S. 1953, c. 118, s. 18); and in the Northwest Territories and the Yukon Territory (see Land Titles Act, R.S.C. 1952, c. 162, s. 13).

In the provinces where it survives, the following provisions may be noted:

(*a*) In Nova Scotia, s. 27 of the Married Women's Property Act, R.S.N.S. 1954, c. 168, provides in general that any interest to which a husband is entitled by virtue of his marriage in the realty of his wife shall not during her life or the life of any of her children who survive her be subject to her husband's debts. By s. 7 (a) of the Descent of Property Act, R.S.N.S. 1954, c. 69, where a married woman dies intestate, her husband, if she leaves issue, is entitled, in addition to his tenancy by the curtesy, to take one-third of her personalty, and subject to such tenancy by the curtesy the remaining interests in her realty and personalty go to her children. If she leaves no issue one-half of all realty and personalty go to the husband. Is this provision affected by or subject to, s. 16 of the Act which provides that "nothing in this Act shall affect the title of a husband as a tenant by the curtesy"?

(*b*) In Ontario, s. 29 of the Conveyancing and Law of Property Act, R.S.O. 1960, c. 66, reads as follows: "Where a husband has issue born alive and capable of inheriting land to which his wife is entitled in fee simple, and the husband survives his wife, whether such issue live or not, the husband is, subject to *The Married Women's Property Act*, entitled to an estate for his natural life in such land as may not have been disposed of by her deed or will; but if he has no such issue by his wife he is not entitled to any further or other estate or interest in such land in the event of surviving his wife, except such as is devised to him by her will, or such as he becomes entitled to under *The Devolution of Estates Act*."

Further it is provided by s. 29 of the Devolution of Estates Act, R.S.O. 1960, c. 106, that:

"(1) Subject to section 12, the real and personal property, whether separate or otherwise, of a married woman in respect of which she dies intestate, shall be distributed as follows: one-third to her husband if she leaves issue, and one-half if she leaves no issue, and subject thereto shall devolve as if her husband had predeceased her.

"(2) A husband who, if this Act had not been passed, would be entitled to an interest as tenant by the curtesy in real property of his wife, may, by deed or instrument in writing executed, and attested by at least one witness, and delivered to the personal representative, if any, or if there is none, deposited in the office of the Registrar of the Supreme Court at Osgoode Hall, within six months after his wife's death, elect to take such interest in the real and personal property of his wife as he would have taken if this Act had not been passed, in which case the husband's interest therein shall be ascertained in all respects as if this Act had not been passed, and he is entitled to no further interest thereunder."

If a husband elects under Ontario law to take his curtesy (see *Chevalier* v. *Trepannier* (1902), 1 O.W.R. 847), does he also become entitled to his common law rights in his wife's personalty? Is this subject to his wife's debts? See Married Women's Property Act, R.S.O. 1960, c. 229, s. 9; and cf. *In re Lambert's Estate*, *Stanton* v. *Lambert* (1888), 39 Ch. D. 626; *Dorsey* v. *Dorsey* (1898), 29 O.R. 475, aff'd 30 O.R. 183 (C.A.).

By s. 10 of the Devolution of Estates Act, R.S.O. 1960, c. 106, the Court may order a sale of land free from curtesy and in such order provide for satisfaction of the claim to curtesy out of the purchase money.

(*c*) In Prince Edward Island, s. 109 of the Probate Act, R.S.P.E.I. 1951, c. 124, reads as follows: "Nothing in this Part shall be construed to affect any right of dower or estate by the curtesy which would arise but for the operation of this Part. But the value of any dower or estate by the curtesy shall be considered as a portion of the share inherited by the wife or husband to whom it passes and shall be deducted from the total of such share in computation of the balance thereof. Provided, however, that the wife or husband may elect to waive such dower or estate by the curtesy and thereupon shall be entitled to receive her or his full share of the distributable estate."

In fine, where curtesy does survive, it arises only upon the intestacy of the wife survived by her husband, and hence may be defeated by an *inter vivos* or testamentary disposition. In Prince Edward Island, s. 114 (2) of the Probate Act stipulates that "if a husband has left his wife and is living in adultery at the time of her death, he shall take no part of his wife's estate".

In view of provisions for a husband on his wife's intestacy and for sfatutory relief against terms of her will (family maintenance or dependants' relief legislation), is there any justification for retaining curtesy?

4. DOWER

AT COMMON LAW, whenever a husband became seised (otherwise than as a joint tenant) of an estate of inheritance during coverture which issue of the marriage, if any, could inherit, the wife obtained an inchoate right of dower therein which became consummate on the husband's death survived by his wife. The dower right was a life interest in one-third of such freeholds of inheritance and constituted a clog on the husband's title even in his lifetime. True enough, the wife had no present right which she could assert (see *Fries* v. *Fries*, [1951] 1 D.L.R. 293, [1950] O.W.N. 661), but a purchaser from the husband would find his title affected by dower if the wife survived her husband, unless dower was barred by the wife or otherwise lost, as by divorce or adulterous desertion: see *Whimbey* v. *Hyde*, [1927] 3 D.L.R. 237, 60 O.L.R. 399 (C.A.); *Re Kempson*, [1950] 3 D.L.R. 792, [1950] O.W.N. 586.

Modern provisions for a distributive share to a surviving wife in her husband's estate and for statutory relief against the terms of his will (family maintenance or dependants' relief legislation), as well as family homestead legislation, have made the survival of common law dower an anachronism. It has been abolished in Alberta (Transfer and Descent of Land Act, R.S.A. 1955, c. 342, s. 4); in British Columbia (Administration Act, R.S.B.C. 1960, c. 3, s. 112); in Manitoba (Law of Property Act, R.S.M. 1954, c. 138, s. 9); and in Saskatchewan (Devolution of Real Property Act, R.S.S. 1953, c. 118, s. 18). It has been replaced in these provinces by homestead legislation, considered in the succeeding section of this Chapter. It has been abolished too in the Northwest Territories and in the Yukon Territory (Land Titles Act, R.S.C. 1952, c. 162, s. 12).

Dower has also been abolished in England by the Administration of Estates Act, 1925 (Imp.), c. 23, ss. 45 and 56. Even as early as 1833 under the Dower Act of that year (1833 (Imp.), c. 105) dower could be avoided on a disposition of realty by the husband by deed or by will or by a declaration in a deed or will against dower, and this without the concurrence of the wife.

In those provinces which retain common law dower, it has come under statutory regulation: see Dower Act, R.S.N.B. 1952, c. 64; Dower Act, R.S.N.S. 1954, c. 75; Dower Procedure Act, R.S.N.S. 1954, c. 76; Dower Act, R.S.O. 1960, c. 113; Dower Act, R.S.P.E.I. 1951, c. 46. Its still not inconsiderable importance in Canada makes it proper to deal in some detail with its application and impact.

Magna Carta gave the widow a 40 day right of quarantine in her deceased husband's main house pending assignment to her of her dower, and this right is still enshrined in Ontario's Dower Act, s. 1. Unlike the case with curtesy, the Court of Chancery did not recognize dower in equitable estates but this was done in England by legislation (Dower Act, 1833, s. 2)' which was copied in New Brunswick (s. 1), in Nova Scotia (s. 2), in Ontario (s. 3), and in Prince Edward Island (s. 4). Similarly, a provision of the English Act (s. 3) giving dower in lands in which the husband had only a right of entry was copied in New Brunswick (s. 2), Nova Scotia (s. 3), Ontario (s. 4) and in Prince Edward Island (s. 5). Relevant provisions of the Ontario Dower Act are set out below as a basis for consideration of the problems raised by the continued existence of dower.

THE DOWER ACT, R.S.O. 1960, c. 113

1. A widow, on the death of her husband, may tarry in his chief house for 40 days after his death, within which time her dower shall be assigned her, if it has not been assigned her before, and in the meantime she shall have her reasonable maintenance, and for her dower shall be assigned to her the third part of all the lands of her husband whereof he was seized at any time during coverture, except such thereof as he was so seized of in trust for another.

3. Where a husband dies beneficially entitled to any land for an interest which does not entitle his widow to dower at common law, and such interest, whether wholly equitable or partly legal and partly equitable, is or is equal to an estate of inheritance in possession, other than an estate in joint tenancy, his widow is entitled to dower out of such land.

4. Where a husband has been entitled to a right of entry or action in any land, and his widow would be entitled to dower out of the land if he had recovered possession of it, she is entitled to dower out of it, although her husband did not recover possession of it, but such dower shall be sued for or obtained within the period during which such right of entry or action might be enforced.

5. Dower is recoverable out of any separate and distinct lot, tract or parcel of land that, at the time of the alienation by the husband or at the time of his death, if he died seized

thereof, was in a state of nature and unimproved by clearing, fencing or otherwise for the purposes of cultivation or occupation; but this does not restrict or diminish the right to have woodland assigned to the dowress under section 29, from which it is lawful for her to take firewood necessary for her own use, and timber for fencing the other portions of the same lot, tract or parcel assigned to her.

6. No dower is recoverable out of any land which has been heretofore or is hereafter granted by the Crown as mining land in case such land is, on or after the 31st day of December, 1897, granted or conveyed to the husband of the person claiming dower and he does not die entitled thereto.

7. Land dedicated by the owner thereof for a street or public highway is not subject to any claim for dower by the wife of the person by whom it was dedicated.

8. Where a wife willingly leaves her husband and goes away, and continues with her adulterer, she is barred forever of her action to demand her dower that she ought to have of her husband's land, unless her husband willingly and without coercion is reconciled to her and suffers her to dwell with him; in which case she is restored to her action.

9. (1) No bar of dower contained in a mortgage or other instrument intended to have the effect of a mortgage or other security upon land operates to bar such dower to any greater extent than is necessary to give full effect to the rights of the mortgagee or grantee under such instrument.

(2) Where land comprised in such mortgage or other instrument is sold under a power of sale contained therein or under any legal process, the wife of the mortgagor or grantor who has so barred her dower in such land is entitled to dower in any surplus of the purchase money arising from such sale that remains after satisfaction of the claim of the mortgagee which such surplus purchase money was derived had it not been sold and, except where the mortgage or other instrument is for the purchase money of the land, the amount to which she is entitled shall be calculated on the basis of the amount realized from the sale of the land and not upon the amount realized from the sale over and above the amount of the mortgage only.

10. (1) A mortgagee or other person holding any money out of which a married woman is dowable under section 9 may pay it into the Supreme Court to the credit of such married woman and the other persons interested therein.

(2) The court may, on a summary application, make such order as is deemed just for securing the right of dower of a married woman in any money out of which she is dowable.

11. A widow is not entitled to take her interest in money under section 9, and, in addition thereto, a share of the money as personal estate.

12. (1) A person whose wife is of unsound mind and is confined in an institution under *The Mental Hospitals Act* at the time he becomes the owner of any land, may at any time while his wife is so confined sell and convey or mortgage such land, freed and discharged of any claim of his wife for dower therein.

(2) A person whose wife has not lived in Ontario since their marriage may sell and convey or mortgage any land freed and discharged of any claim of his wife for dower therein.

13. (1) An owner of land, who is married and wishes to sell or mortgage the land free from dower, may in any case where,

(a) he and his wife are living apart; or
(b) the whereabouts of his wife is unknown; or
(c) his wife is of unsound mind and is confined as such in a hospital for mentally ill, mentally defective or epileptic persons,

apply to a judge of the Supreme Court or to a judge of the county or district court of the county or district in which the owner resides or the land is situate for an order dispensing with the concurrence of his wife for the purpose of barring her dower.

(2) The judge may, by order made in a summary way, upon such evidence as to him seems proper and upon notice to be served personally, dispense with the concurrence of the wife for the purpose of barring her dower.

(3) Where the judge is satisfied that for any reason notice cannot be served personally, the order may be made after notice has been served upon the Public Trustee and in such other manner as the judge directs.

(4) The judge may make the order without imposing any conditions or he may, unless the wife has been living apart from the husband under such circumstances as disentitle her to dower, ascertain and state in the order the value of the dower and by the order direct that the amount thereof shall be paid into court or shall remain a charge upon the land or be secured otherwise for the benefit of the wife or be paid or applied for her benefit as he deems best.

(5) After the making of the order a conveyance or mortgage by the owner, expressed to be free from his wife's dower, is, subject to the terms and conditions mentioned in the order, sufficient to bar her right thereto.

(6) This section extends to any case in which an agreement for sale has been made, or a conveyance executed by the husband, and part of the purchase money retained by the purchaser on account of dower or an indemnity given against such dower, and in any such case the application may be made by any person interested in the land, the purchase money retained or the indemnity.

14. [Like order authorized where wife is mentally ill but not confined in a hospital.]

15. Where a judge makes an order under section 13 or 14 with reference to a parcel of land, he may afterwards make orders in respect of other sales or mortgages by the husband on the evidence adduced on the first application and on such further evidence as satisfies him that the circumstances under which he made the original order still exist.

16. Where the owner of land has become bankrupt and it is sought to sell such land in order to wind up his estate, and the wife of such owner will not release her dower, the trustee or assignee in bankruptcy may apply to a judge of the Supreme Court or to a judge of the county or district court of the county or district in which the land is situate, for an order enabling him to convey the land free from the dower of the wife, and the order may be made subject to the like conditions and upon the like proceedings as are provided for in section 13.

17. (1) Where an owner of land, being at the time married, sells and conveys or has sold and conveyed, or mortgages or has mortgaged the land, his wife not having joined in the conveyance or mortgage and the purchaser or mortgagee not having had notice that the grantor or mortgagor had a wife living at the time, the purchaser or mortgagee may, if any of the circumstances set out in clauses *a* to *c* of subsection 1 of section 13 existed at the time of the conveyance or mortgage, apply during the lifetime of the grantor or mortgagor to a judge of the Supreme Court or to a judge of the county or district court of the county or district in which he resides or the land is situate, for an order enabling him to convey or mortgage the land free from the dower of the wife, and the order may be obtained subject to the like conditions and by the like proceedings as are provided by section 13.

(2) A person claiming under the grantee or mortgagee is entitled to apply in like manner and obtain like relief founded on the right which such grantee or mortgagee had, or on the applicant's own interest having been acquired by purchase for value in good faith without notice that such owner had a wife at the time of the conveyance or mortgage.

19. Where a wife has joined or hereafter joins in a conveyance or mortgage purporting to convey or mortgage land, or has signed or signs, otherwise than as a witness, a conveyance or mortgage by which her husband conveys or mortgages or purports to convey or mortgage land, but the conveyance or mortgage contains no words purporting to release her dower or

other estate or interest in the land, the conveyance or mortgage has the same effect as if it contained a bar of dower by the wife and she thereby barred her dower in the land.

20. A married woman under 21 years of age and of sound mind may bar her dower in any land by joining with her husband in a deed or conveyance thereof to a purchaser for value or to a mortgagee, or in a transfer or charge under *The Land Titles Act* in which deed, conveyance, transfer or charge, a release or bar of her dower is contained, and she may in like manner release her dower to any person to whom such land has been previously conveyed.

[As to dower in land which is under The Land Titles Act, see ss. 123 to 126 of the Act, R.S.O. 1960, c. 204. Elaborate provisions for assignment of dower are contained in ss. 21-34 of the Ontario Dower Act. See also Ontario Rule 624.]

FREEDMAN v. MASON. Ontario High Court. [1956] O.R. 849, 4 D.L.R. 2d 576

Action for specific performance of a contract of sale of land to which the defence was inability to make title by reason of the refusal of the vendor's wife to bar dower.

McRUER C. J. H. C. (after dealing with the facts and certain terms of the contract of sale): What the purchaser demanded on the date fixed for closing was that he get a conveyance free from any dower-interest of Mrs. Mason, and by his amendment he asks the vendor to take something less than the purchase-price because of the dower-interest, or that by some process of the Court a conveyance can be made free from Mrs. Mason's dower interest.

In order to decide whether there is any power in the Court to enforce the contract under the conditions asked for by the plaintiff, it is of first importance to decide what the nature of Mrs. Mason's interest is. The origin of dower in English law is not certain, but unquestionably its purpose was, and still is, to give a wife a measure of security for her support after her husband's death.

Deans says in the Students Legal History, 2nd ed., p. 6, that it was a Saxon institution. In its early history it depended on express gift. At the time of Glanville (Henry II) it still depended on express gift and a husband could alienate his wife's dower. It is said that a wife probably obtained the right to dower independently of her husband's endowment in the time of Henry III. At first the right attached to the lands of which the husband was seized at the time of the marriage. However, Magna Carta, c. 7, provides: "For her dower shall be assigned unto her the third part of all the lands of her husband which were his during coverture, except she were endowed of less at the church-door."

Originally, there were five classes of dower: (1) dower by the common law; (2) dower *ad ostium ecclesiae*; (3) dower *ex assensu patris*; (4) dower by the custom; and (5) dower *de la plus belle*. However, in Canada there is but one class of dower, that is, dower at common law. Holdsworth, History of English Law, 3rd ed., vol. 3, p. 193, speaking of dower at common law, says: "But at the end of the thirteenth century it was settled that the husband's alienation could not affect the right; and that the wife's consent to be valid must be given by means of a fine, during the levying of which she was separately examined by the court as to the reality of her consent."

Cameron, The Law of Dower, 1882, defines dower at common law at p. 4 as follows: "Dower at Common Law, may be defined to be an estate for life to which a wife is entitled after the decease of her husband in the third part of every estate of inheritance of which her husband was solely seized, either in deed or in law, at any time during the coverture, to have and to hold to her in severalty by metes and bounds, for the term of her natural life, whether she has had issue by her husband or not, and provided she be past the age of nine years at the time of her husband's death." At p. 389 the learned author states: "Eventually it became established, that the title of dower, though inchoate until the death of the husband, yet being an interest attached on the lands from the instant of the concurrence of marriage and seisin, might be extinguished."

The right to dower is an inchoate right during the husband's lifetime, but it is not an estate in the land until properly assigned to her after her husband's death, when she may claim possession in priority to leases created by her husband without her consent: *Allan* v. *Rever* (1902), 4 O.L.R. 309.

In *Allen* v. *Edinburgh Life Ass'ce Co.* (1877), 25 Gr. 306, Proudfoot V.-C., in an exhaustive judgment decided that since the passing of the Ontario statute, 40 Vict., c. 8, the right of a woman to dower, as well during the life of her husband as after his death, is such an interest in lands as can be sold under a *fi. fa.* at law. The learned Vice-Chancellor's conclusion was that dower until assigned was a possibility coupled with an interest in land and the interest was the same before the death of the husband as it was after his death, but before assignment. This was followed by Ferguson J. in *Devereux* v. *Kearns* (1886), 11 P.R. (Ont.) 452, and in *Douglas* v. *Hutchinson* (1884), 6 O.R. 581, and approved in *Robertson* v. *Larocque* (1889) 18 O.R. 469.

In *Gamble* v. *Gummerson* (1862), 9 Gr. 193 at p. 196, Esten V.-C. referred to a dower interest in this way: "When the estate appears to be subject to a title of dower... the master is bound to report against the title."

In *Robertson* v. *Robertson* (1878), 25 Gr. 486, Spragge C. said: "As an incident to that title, the wife had an inchoate right to dower, which also was a legal right,—an interest recognized by the law, and over which the husband could by law exercise no control. The interest of the wife, while of a different nature, was co-extensive with that of the husband, i.e., embracing the whole of the land, and could not be affected without her formal consent, by anything done or suffered by the husband."

In *Morrison* v. *Morrison* (1917), 34 D.L.R. 677, 39 O.L.R. 163, it was held that a dower interest was not an "interest in land" within the meaning of the *Partition Act*. Meredith C. J. C. P. stated that a widow's right was to have her one-third assigned to her and that a right to possession then arose.

In *Ungerman* v. *Maroni*, (1956), my learned brother Kelly in an unreported judgment refused specific performance in a case where the vendor could not obtain a bar of dower from his wife who was living apart from him, and could not obtain the discharge of a mortgage because he was unable to locate the mortgagee. Although at the time of the trial the wife was divorced from the husband, the case was decided as of the date that the contract was to be completed. This judgment was sustained in the Court of Appeal: [1956] O.W.N. 650. The judgment of Roach J. A., after pointing out that the purchaser argued that the undischarged mortgage and the dower-interest were matters of conveyancing, and not matters of title, said (p. 652): "Counsel referred to cases that at a first glance might seem to indicate that his submission is sound. On analysis, however, I think that they do not support that submission." The appeal was accordingly dismissed.

From these authorities it would seem clear that during the lifetime of her husband a wife has an interest in all his real property, and that this interest cannot be alienated or interfered with by the husband without the wife's consent. A wife has a right to elect to take her dower in preference to any benefit she may receive under the *Devolution of Estates Act*, R.S.O. 1950, c. 103, s. 8 (1), and unless it appears by express statement or clear inference, she takes her dower in addition to any provisions made for her in her husband's will: Per Middleton J. in *Re Wadsworth* (1911), 2 O.W.N. 999. It is also clear that a vendor of the fee simple in real property whose wife is still living and will not release her dower-interest, cannot force a purchaser to take the title with abatement or with provision for setting aside a sum to protect the purchaser against loss by reason of the right arising in the wife to have her dower assigned. "When the agreement itself provides for what is to happen upon certain events, then it alone is to be resorted to, and there cannot be any recourse either to law or equity for any other remedy": Per Middleton J. in *Bowes* v. *Vaux* (1918), 43 O.L.R. 521 at p. 527.

That being so, was the contract in question null and void because Mrs. Mason, acting on the independent advice of her personal solicitor, refused to sign the deed? I think it was. The day before the transaction was to be closed the plaintiff stated in writing that he would require a deed "with the necessary Bar Dower by the wife". This the defendant could not give. He offered all he could give and the plantiff's solicitor refused to accept it, stating that his instructions were not to proceed with the transaction if he could not secure a bar of dower. As I have said, he made no suggestion that he would accept a deed with abatement of the purchase-price or that a portion of the purchase-money be set aside to provide for the wife's claim for dower. He insisted on his right to have a clear title, which the defendant could not give, and on the day fixed for closing, time being of the essence of the contract, I think all contractual rights came to an end and the contract cannot be revived by an application made at the trial to amend the pleadings by claiming specific performance with an amount set aside as requested in the amended prayer.

Dealing with the amendment, however, it seems to me, as the case was argued at the trial, that what the plaintiff really wants is an order for specific performance with an amount set aside to answer any claim Mrs. Mason may have for dower and that the Court make some kind of order barring Mrs. Mason's dower in the land. This the Court cannot do. Whatever the precise nature of a dower-interest in lands, there is no power in the Court to expropriate it and it would be unconscionable to do so in an action to which the wife is not a party. No matter what order the Court might now make, Mrs. Mason could in the event of her husband's death apply to have one-third of the property in question set aside for her enjoyment for life, and no provision in her husband's will could deny that to her.

Action dismissed.

[See also *Re Rowe*, [1957] O.R. 9, 10 D.L.R. 2d 215.

On appeal in *Freedman* v. *Mason*, the judgment of McRuer C.J.H.C., *supra*, was reversed by the Court of Appeal, [1957] O.R. 441, 9 D.L.R. 2d 262, and the reversal was affirmed by the Supreme Court of Canada, [1958] S.C.R. 483, 14 D.L.R. 2d 529. These courts took the view that the purchaser's insistence on a deed with bar of dower did not preclude him from subsequently seeking specific performance. He could take such title as the vendor had, one encumbered by inchoate dower, and require the vendor to pay into Court, out of the purchase price, a sum not exceeding one-third thereof as security against any future claim to dower. *Re Woods and Arthur* (1921), 49 O.L.R. 279, 58 D.L.R. 620 was followed. But see *Shuter* v. *Patten* (1921), 51 O.L.R. 528, 67 D.L.R. 577 (App. Div.); *Note* (1945), 29 Minn. L. Rev. 280.]

Does a wife have dower in lands which her husband contracted to sell before marriage but the contract remained unexecuted until after the marriage? See *Gordon* v. *Gordon* (1864), 10 Gr. 466 (Ch.).

A purchases land from B through mortgage financing and his mortgage to B is registered before he receives or registers a deed from B. If he sells the land subject to the mortgage does his wife have dower on his death? See *Whyte* v. *Davey*, [1933] O.W.N. 147.

Suppose A buys land subject to a mortgage which he proposes to refinance. The new mortgage is executed and registered before discharge of the old one is registered. A now sells the land to B subject to the new mortgage. Is his wife entitled to dower if (1) she did not bar dower in the new mortgage; (2) she did bar dower therein? See *Re Tierney*, [1927] 3 D.L.R. 943, 60 O.L.R. 652.

A husband in purchasing land may take title in the name of a trustee to prevent common law dower from attaching (the wife of a trustee has no dower claim) and there is no "fraud" on marital rights involved in so doing: see *Gillis* v. *Sewell*, [1942] 4 D.L.R. 582 (Ont.). Another device, not uncommon in Ontario, is to take title by a deed to uses; the problems in this connection are indicated in the following case.

RE WALSH AND SOVIS. Ontario High Court. [1956] O.R. 202, 2 D.L.R. 2d 356

WELLS J.: This is an application under the provisions of the *Vendors and Purchasers Act*, R.S.O. 1950, c. 407, in respect of a point of title. As originally made, the question was whether two deeds which purported to be drawn to uses were capable of conveying the fee to a grantee free of the inchoate right to dower vested in the wife of each grantor. The history of the title seems to be, briefly, as follows:

By instrument No. 120519 for the Township of North York, there was a grant from a company called Wrentham Estates Ltd. to one James Walsh. The deed was dated September 13, 1951, and in the premises it granted the lands in question to the grantee in fee simple. There then followed a description of the lands and certain very elaborate building restrictions, and in the *habendum* clause which followed these words were used: "TO HAVE AND TO HOLD unto the Grantee to such uses as he, the Grantee, may from time to time by deed, will, mortgage or other instrument in writing, appoint, and until and in default of appointment and insofar as such appointment may not extend, unto the use of the Grantee in fee simple."

This was followed by a deed registered as Instrument No. 165188 for the Township of North York, and by this deed James Walsh purported to convey to the present vendor, F. Norman Walsh, the lands in question, and in the premises did grant and appoint unto the grantee in fee simple. This, again, is followed by a *habendum* clause in the precise words used in the deed from Wrentham Estates Ltd. to James Walsh.

The question as originally raised by the purchaser is whether the conveyance from James Walsh to F. Norman Walsh, and the proposed conveyance from F. Norman Walsh to Stephen Sovis, the purchaser, in which it is proposed to use the words in the premises that "the Grantor doth grant and appoint unto the Grantee in fee simple", are sufficient to convey the fee in the lands to the purchaser free of the dower of the wives of James Walsh and F. Norman Walsh respectively. On the matter coming before me, I deemed it proper to direct that the wives of both of these gentlemen should be added, pursuant to R. 602, so that the question could be determined once and for all between these gentlemen and their respective wives.

On the return of the motion before me, counsel advised that in so far as the deed from James Walsh was concerned, the question was no longer of practical importance, as the lady to whom James Walsh was married at the time he gave the deed has granted him a power of attorney to bar her claim to dower. The question remains, however, as to whether the proposed conveyance from F. Norman Walsh to Stephen Sovis, in the form I have indicated, is sufficient to convey the fee to Sovis free of the inchoate claim to dower vested in Mrs. Wilda Walsh, the wife of F. Norman Walsh. She was duly served with notice of the application and appears before me now through her counsel.

The objection taken by the solicitor for Sovis is set out in his requisition on title, in which he says this: "Unfortunately, the granting clause conveys in fee simple without mention of uses and the uses are then set out in the Habendum. We think you will agree with us that the attempt to cut down the fee simple by the Habendum is not possible in law and the result is that the wife of James Walsh would have dower rights and we would, therefore, require a release of dower from her or evidence that he is unmarried. James Walsh reconveyed to F. Norman Walsh on the 19th day of January, 1954, and in this deed the same thing happened so that we will also require release of dower from the wife, if any, of F. Norman Walsh."

A fee simple is, of course, the largest estate that any subject can acquire in land and, as has been stated by some authorities, it is not possible to mount a limitation on it which would, in effect, cut down the very full and ample estate granted by the fee simple.

Cheshire, in his Modern Law of Real Property, 7th ed., p. 243, after pointing out that no remainder can be limited after an estate in fee simple, says: "Since a fee simple estate is the largest interest that can be enjoyed in land, it was a rule of the common law that a future estate could not be limited to take effect as a remainder expectant upon the determination of a preceding fee simple. A fee could not be mounted on a fee. Thus if a grant had been made in fee simple with a proviso that it should determine upon the payment of a certain sum or upon failure of the grantee to do a certain act, and go over to a stranger, the gift over was void."

Norton on Deeds, 2nd ed. puts the matter this way, at p. 317: "If words of limitation are added to the grantee's name both in the premises and in the habendum, the limitation in the habendum will, if possible, be considered as explanatory of that in the premises; but if the limitations are repugnant, the estate given by the premises cannot be abridged by the habendum."

In the deed under consideration the question is whether the creation of the use in the habendum is effective, or is repugnant to the grant in fee simple in the premises. The situation has been considered in a number of Ontario cases and was dealt with by Middleton J., as he then was, in *Re Osborne & Campbell* (1918), 55 D.L.R. 258, 15 O.W.N. 48. There, as in the case at bar, the land in question was conveyed to M "in fee simple", "to have and to hold unto the said M, his heirs and assigns forever, to such uses as he shall by deed or deeds in writing or by his last will and testament appoint and in default of appointment to the use of him and his heirs absolutely". M died on April 22, 1915, and by his will gave all his property to his executors in trust to convert and divide the proceeds. In that case, as in the case at bar, notice under R. 602 was served on the wife, but in that case she did not appear to assert any claim. The vendor's contention was that under the *Wills Act* the will operated as a due execution of the power, and the estate passed by virtue of the exercise of the power. With this, Middleton J. agreed, relying on *Re Greaves' Settlement Trusts* (1883), 23 Ch. D. 313, as an authority.

He said: "In the absence of any claim on the part of the wife, the difficult question as to the true construction and effect of this deed, suggested in Armour's note (Real Property, 2nd ed., p. 114), should not be considered. See, per Draper, C.J., in *Lyster* v. *Kirkpatrick* (1866), 26 U.C.R. 217, 228: 'It appears to have been settled ever since *Sir Edward Clere's* case (6 Co. 18a) that a power over the inheritance may co-exist with a fee in the same person; as where A. seised in fee made a feoffment to the use of such person and of such estate as he should limit and appoint by his last will, and died, making a will... the devise was upheld as a valid execution of the power.' See also *Maundrell* v. *Maundrell* (1805) 10 Ves. 246, 254 and 255, 32 E.R. 839."

A declaration was made in that case that the wife was not entitled to dower, and the objection was not well taken.

That decision is chiefly useful for what it suggests, rather than for what it decides, as the facts were somewhat different from the case at bar in that the question was whether the exercise of the power of appointment by the will was sufficient. It is, I think, chiefly valuable for what it suggests and the authorities that were relied on.

Following this decision, a most interesting annotation was contributed to the Dominion

Law Reports by the late Mr. E. D. Armour, K.C., which may be found in 55 D.L.R. 259. Questioning the judgment, he confined his criticism to the finding that the will operated as an exercise of the power, but some of his comments, I think, shed light on the situation which I am now considering, and are quite illuminating.

At p. 260 he had this to say: "Assuming, however, that according to his Lordship's dictum the power was well exercised by the will, it does not follow, in the writer's opinion, that dower was defeated. The effect of a conveyance to a grantee in fee simple to such uses as he may appoint, is to vest in him an estate in fee simple by common law, the conveyance so operating: *Savill Brothers Ltd.* v. *Bethell*, [1902] 2 Ch. 523 at 541: The limitation in fee vests the estate in him, and he is in by the common law; and the addition of a declaration of uses does not add anything to his estate. The utmost that can be said of it is that it may afford an alternative mode of conveyance to the simple grant."

And then, after a very careful analysis of the authorities on which Middleton J.'s judgment was based, he concluded at p. 261: "It is therefore submitted with deference, that M. had all the legal and beneficial interest in the land in fee simple, by the limitations in the conveyance, *and in default of appointment*, and having died seised his widow was entitled to dower." I have italicized the words "and in default of appointment" because in the case at bar it is proposed that there should be no default in respect of the exercise of the power of appointment, and, of course, in *Re Osborne & Campbell*, *supra*, there was no exercise of such power during M's lifetime.

The matter subsequently came before Orde J. in *Re Cooper & Knowler* (1920), 19 O.W.N. 27. In that case the grant was similar in form to that in *Re Osborne & Campbell*, and Orde J. refused to decide the matter because, as he said, there was so much doubt in view of Mr. Armour's opinion, as expressed in his Real Property, 2nd ed., p. 114, that he did not think he should force the title on an unwilling purchaser. It is significant, I think, that in that case the wife was not before the Court. It is also significant, I think, that the decision in *Re Osborne & Campbell* was not brought to his attention during the argument, but when it was brought to his attention he made a further note pointing out that he had not changed his view as to the doubts which existed in his mind.

In the annotation to which I have referred [55 D.L.R. 259], Mr. Armour also commented on this decision, and at p. 261 he said this: "The previous paragraph may be a fitting introduction to a consideration of *Re Cooper and Knowler*. Though the death of the grantee does not affect the interpretation of the deed, it does affect the right to dower; and in that way the cases are not exactly similar, and *Re Osborne* affords no assistance in determining what should have been the decision in the later case. The point presented in that case for determination was squarely put, viz., whether, on a grant to A. or his heirs to such uses as he should by deed or will appoint, and in default of appointment, to A. his heirs and assigns, A. could by exercising the power of appointment by deed defeat his wife's right to dower. His Lordship declined to decide this in the wife's absence, and, as there is a doubt about it, refused to force the title on the purchaser. As a matter of law, the wife was at the moment entitled to dower, for the husband was seised of an inheritance in fee simple; and the question put was whether a conveyance made under the power would divest her of her right. The question whether he can do so under the limitations in that case must therefore still remain in doubt. And meanwhile it is wise in drawing conveyances to uses to defeat dower to introduce a grantee to uses who is not also the *cestui que use*. Then the terms of the statute will be fulfilled, for there will be a person seised to the use of some other person, who may exercise the power over the use."

Subsequently, Rose J., as he then was, in *Re Strauss & Fierstein* (1924), 26 O.W.N. 304, expressed the same view as Orde J. He made the following observation: "In Sugden on Powers, 8th ed., p. 479, the question whether dower attaches is treated as determined finally and adversely to the widow by *Ray* v. *Pung* (1882), 5 B & Ald. 561; but there is so much weight in the opposed view of the authorities in Armour on Real Property, 2nd ed., pp. 114, 115, note (j), that it must be considered that such title as the vendor can make is too doubtful to be forced upon an unwilling purchaser. If the wife, if any, of the vendor could be brought in under Rule 602, it would be proper to decide the point; but, unless she can be bound, a single Judge would act unjustly toward the purchaser in attempting to decide it."

Orde J.A., as he had then become, in *Re Morris & Chertkoff*, [1925] 2 D.L.R. at p. 1116, 56 O.L.R. at p. 666, again refused to reach a decision in the absence of the wife, who had not been served under R. 602.

It was because of these decisions that I felt it proper that notice of this application and an order joining the grantors' wives should be made pursuant to R. 602, and it was pursuant to this that Mrs. Wilda Walsh was added as a party to this motion.

The next case in which the matter was very thoroughly canvassed was *Re Hazell*, [1925] 3 D.L.R. 661, 57 O.L.R. 290, var'g 57 O.L.R. 166. This was heard originally by Logie J. and went to the Court of Appeal, where the judgment was delivered by Middleton J.A., as he had then become. It appears from the decision at first instance in that case that the owner of the land had taken a grant containing the words "unto the said grantee to and for the uses hereinafter declared", and a *habendum* clause followed in these words: "To have and to hold unto the grantee to and for such uses as he shall by deed mortgage will or other instrument in writing appoint and in default of and until such appointment or in so far as such appointment shall not extend unto the use of the grantee his heirs and assigns forever." It is to be observed that the words in the deed under consideration in that case were very different from the words used in the deed presently under consideration, but the decision is chiefly important for the clarifying of the effect of the judgment in *Ray* v. *Pung* (1822), 5 B. & Ald. 561, 106 E.R. 1296, and the establishing, in my opinion beyond any question, of the fact that a use and a fee may coexist in one person at one time.

To continue with the narration of the facts in the *Hazell* case, the grantee in the deed which I have just cited then conveyed to one B., and this conveyance took the form of another deed to uses in which the grantor did "grant, limit and appoint unto the said grantee, in fee simple, to and upon the uses hereinafter contained", which words of grant were followed by an *habendum* clause similar to the one which I have already quoted. In essence, of course, this second deed is very much closer to the deed under consideration than is the first one. Subsequently, B. conveyed to one H. by an ordinary form of deed in which the words used were: "The grantor doth grant, limit and appoint unto the grantee, in fee simple." B.'s wife did not join in this conveyance. At pp. 665-6 D.L.R., p. 291 O.L.R., Middleton J.A. said:

"The second question raised is, whether Marshall, by the execution of the conveyance to Brown in exercise of the power, defeated any right to dower that might exist in Marshall's wife. This question is based upon the difficulty that was at one time supposed to exist by reason of the grantee to uses holding in fee until he exercised the power of appointment, it being suggested that the estate and the power could not co-exist in the same individual.

"At one time this question was greatly debated and an extraordinary diversity of opinion existed, but all doubt was put at rest by the decision of the Judges in the case of *Ray* v. *Pung*, 5 B. & Ald. 561. This case arose in Chancery, where after a very full argument Leach, V.-C. 5 Madd., at p. 320, thought that the conflicting authorities created too much doubt to make it fit that the Court of Chancery should bind the purchasers without the further opinion of a Court of Law, and accordingly the opinion of the K.B. Judges was taken; in the result a certificate was given by all the Judges to the effect that under the circumstances the wife was not dowable out of the lands in question in case of her surviving her husband. 5 B. & Ald. at pp. 568-9. From that time on, no doubt was expressed as to the law until a note appeared in Armour on Real Property, p. 114, in which reference is made to the great authorities acquainted with the mediaeval learning necessary to appreciate fully the difficulties surrounding the whole situation whose opinions were in conflict, and the opinion expressed by the Justices of the King's Bench is disposed of by the brief words: 'see also *Ray* v. *Pung*.'

"Since then, a quite unnecessary unrest seems to have developed in certain quarters, as evidenced by the numerous applications under the Vendors and Purchasers Act, R.S.O. 1914, referred to in the judgment in review.

"It was suggested upon the argument that the case of *Ray* v. *Pung* did not really determine the question, because in that case the property was conveyed to an intermediary and not to the husband. I am quite unable to see that this really makes any difference. Counsel arguing that case evidently did not regard the point as of importance, for Barber, representing the wife (5 B. & Ald. at p. 566) claimed dower because, although the trustee intervened, the fee had become vested in the husband, and, this being so, the dower attached. He also contended [p. 567] that the power of appointment was nugatory, being nothing distinct or different from the fee. To this Mr. Preston, for the other side, answered (p. 563) that when the settlor made the appointment the qualified and determinable fee came to an end, and the wife's dower, being merely incidental to it, came to an end with it. Upon the exercise of the appointment, the appointee took his estate in the same manner as if it had been inserted in the original deed creating the power and had stood in the place of the power. He did not claim title under the husband but under the grantor to the husband. He also relied (p. 565) upon the language of Eldon, L. C., in *Maundrell* v. *Maundrell*, 10 Ves. at p. 255, as shewing that a power and the fee may well subsist distinctly in the same person; and that the power is not merged in the fee—the case of *Goodill* v. *Brigham*, 1 B. & P. 192, suggesting a different doctrine, being out of harmony with the general course of the law. The difficulty arises from the fact that no reasons for the opinion of the Court were given, the Judges merely signing a certificate to the Court of Chancery that the wife was not entitled to dower."

And after discussing the authorities at very considerable length, the learned Judge observed at p. 668 D.L.R., p. 294 O.L.R.:

"This is the view entertained more than a century ago. Recent text-writers of the highest standing give no uncertain sound. For example, Farwell, L. J., on Powers, 3rd ed., p. 45 quotes, as his 11th proposition, 'A power may co-exist with the fee,' amplifying thus: 'If a man limits his estate to such uses as he shall appoint, and in the meantime and until such appointment to the use of himself and his heirs, the fee simple continues to reside in the settlor, subject to be divested by an exercise of his power of appointment...'

"In 24 Halsbury, p. 192, note (m), it is said: 'if land is limited to such uses as the husband shall appoint, and in default of appointment to himself in fee, dower attaches at once, because he is seised until the execution of the power... but upon the execution of the power the right to dower is defeated.' For this *Ray* v. *Pung*, 5 Madd. 310, is cited.

"'When the husband's fee, by virtue of which the wife claims dower, is liable to be defeated by the exercise of a power vested in the husband, such an exercise of the power will defeat the wife's right to dower:' Challis' Law of Real Property, 3rd ed., p. 347; *Ray* v. *Pung* being given as the sole authority.

"In Tudor's Leading Cases on Real Property, 4th ed., p. 114, the statement is repeated in almost the same words.

"I have made this somewhat tedious review of the authorities for the purpose of shewing that the doubt which once existed was removed more than a century ago. It is a well-established principle of real property law that questions such as this, once placed at rest, should not be again agitated, even if it should be shewn that the earlier decisions are not in all respects satisfactory. Here, however, the great weight of reason, as well as of authority, is in favour of the conclusion arrived at."

He added to this observation an approval of the manner in which Logie J. had dealt with the second conveyance to uses.

In the report of the case at first instance, Logie J. said at pp. 663-4 D.L.R., p. 169 O.L.R.:

"Marshall, by the execution of the deed to Brown, exercised his power of appointment; and, although until the exercise of that power he was seised of an inheritance in fee in possession, upon his execution of the power Brown came in as if named in the conveyance from Cooper, and so Brown's right is paramount to any inchoate right of dower in Marshall's wife. See the judgment of Eldon, L. C., in *Maundrell* v. *Maundrell,* 10 Ves. at p. 263, adopted by Draper, C. J., in our own Court in *Lyster* v. *Kirkpatrick* (1866), 26 U.C.Q.B. 217, at p. 228; Leith's Blackstone, 2nd ed., p. 153.

"The inchoate right of dower in Brown's wife depends upon the nature of the estate which he acquired.

"It is argued that, by executing a deed to Brown to such uses as Brown might by deed, will, or mortgage appoint, Marshall engrafted a use upon a use which the Statute of Uses would not execute; and so Brown was a trustee for the person to whom he appointed; and, not dying beneficially entitled, his wife has no dower: the Dower Act, R.S.O. 1914, c. 70, s. 4.

"This contention takes no account of the peculiar qualities inherent in powers and how these are affected by the Statute of Uses, 27 Hen. VIII., c. 10. Marshall and Brown both took under the statute (*Savill Bros. Ltd.* v. *Bethell,* [1902] 2 Ch. 523), being seised to the use of another.

"If A., seised in fee simple, conveyed to B. in fee to the use of C. in fee to the use of D. in fee, the privity or confidence existed in the first instance between B. and C. and then between C. and D., but on account of the intervention of C. there was not any direct use, trust, or confidence between B. and D., and B. could not be said to be seised to the use of D.

"In other words, the statute only executed one use or supplied one conveyance. A. could not give any legal ownership to D., because C. did not take any seisin but only a use, and could not acquire seisin save by the statute, which was deemed *functus* when it divested the seisin from B. to C.

"'So in order to pass the legal ownership thus acquired by C. from him to D., there must have been required a *new conveyance*' by C. to D. (Jones' Law of Uses, pp. 24-5), and it would make no difference if the uses were granted by one or more instruments. But, where an estate is limited to such uses as A. shall appoint, an appointment by A. to such uses as B. shall appoint is valid and effectual (where there is a general power equivalent to absolute ownership) to pass the legal estate to B.'s appointee.

"The statute does not operate with effect till the last power is exercised. The seisin originally created waits until estates are raised by B.'s power, and when this last power is exercised the statute transfers the legal estate: Farwell, 3rd ed., p. 505; Sugden, p. 196.

"Here the estate is limited to such uses as Marshall shall appoint. He, by virtue of his power, appointed to Brown to such uses or as Brown should appoint.

"When Brown appointed in fee to Hazell, the original seisin was attracted, and the statute transferred the legal estate to Hazell, and the right to dower of Brown's wife is defeated, because the necessary element of seisin in Brown is absent."

After this decision the matter appeared to rest until an application was made in *Re Armstrong & Brown,* [1952] O.W.N. 55. This was an appeal from my brother Aylen. His reasons for judgment are reported in [1951] O.W.N. 877. He came to the conclusion that dower attached. In that case the words of grant were "to grant and appoint unto the said Grantee to the uses hereinafter declared in fee simple," and the habendum clause set out and defined the uses. The matter came on by way of appeal, and Hope J. A., giving the oral judgment of the Court of Appeal, said:

"We are all of the opinion that this appeal should be allowed. While the granting clause in the deed to Stewart did unfortunately contain the words 'in fee simple', which are not normally contained in the granting clause of a deed to uses to defeat dower, nevertheless it also contained the words 'and appoint... to the uses hereinafter declared', which are not consonant with an estate in fee simple but directly refer to and incorporate in the granting clause the words of the habendum, which are those customarily employed in a deed to uses. It is well established that a power of appointment to uses and an estate in fee simple may exist simultaneously in a grantee: see *Re Hazell* (1925), 57 O.L.R. 166, varied 57 O.L.R. 290, [1925] 3 D.L.R. 661.

"The judgment below will be set aside and an order will issue declaring that the requisition on title has been satisfactorily answered. As the appellant's counsel waives any claim thereto, there will be no order as to costs."

As I read this judgment, it was the view of the Court of Appeal that where an estate in fee simple and a power of appointment to uses coexisted, the exercise of the power was sufficient to convey the fee free of dower. It is quite true that while Armstrong was seised of an estate in fee simple, his wife had an inchoate claim to dower, but upon the exercise of the power the Statute of Uses operated to transfer the fee to the object of the appointment free of the wife's claim in that respect. With respect, that must be, I think, the meaning of this judgment, and indeed it seems to follow very logically from the principles implicit in the decision in *Re Hazell* which I have discussed above.

It would seem to me that the same considerations must apply to the case at bar. I am somewhat supported in this view by consideration of a very excellent discussion of the whole matter to be found in Norton on Deeds, *op. cit.*, p. 314. In discussing generally the effect of habendum in a deed, the learned editor says: "Where a person is mentioned as grantee in the premises, a person mentioned in the habendum, but not in the premises, cannot take an immediate estate in the land granted, but can take an estate in remainder: Co. Litt. 231 a; but any person, though not named in the premises or in the habendum, can take any estate, either immediate or in remainder, by way of use declared on the estate limited in the habendum: *Sammes Case* (1609), 13 Rep. 54."

Following this statement there is a very useful discussion on the point raised in this case, which may be found from the bottom of p. 317 to part-way down p. 319. The matter is, I think, fairly summed up in the quotation which the learned editors make from Blackstone's Commentaries, the reference being to 2 Bl. Com. 298. What is there said is this: "The office of the habendum is properly to determine what estate or interest is granted by the deed, though this may be performed, and sometimes is performed, in the premises. In which case the habendum may lessen, enlarge, explain, or qualify, but not totally contradict or be repugnant to the estate granted in the premises. As if a grant be 'to A and the heirs of his body' in the premises, habendum 'to him and his heirs for ever,' or *vice versa*, here A has an estate tail, and a fee simple expectant thereon. But had it been in the premises 'to him and his heirs,' habendum 'to him for life,' the habendum would be utterly void; for an estate of inheritance is vested in him before the habendum comes, and shall not afterwards be taken away or divested by it."

I think it is quite clear that in the case at bar the defining of the uses in the *habendum* does not take away from the estate in fee simple enjoyed by the grantee, nor is it repugnant thereto, and it continues in him until he, by his own act of appointment, divests himself of the fee. And the learned editors of Norton quote as follows from Challis on Real Property, 3rd ed., p. 413:

"'But a modification introduced by the habendum is permitted to take effect if it is so far consistent with the language of the premises that its admission does not make any part of the language simply void or nugatory. In such cases there is not, properly speaking, a repugnancy between them.'" I think these observations apply to the case under consideration.

Sammes' Case (1609), 13 Co. Rep. 54, 77 E.R. 1464 referred to in the first of these quotations, arose in the Court of King's Bench, and was referred to the Judges in the reign of James I. It was resolved in the words of the report that it was a case that "should be sent to the Judges, assistants to this Court for their resolution thereon." The Court which heard it was a strong Court indeed, and included Sir Edward Coke, who was then Lord Chief Justice of the Common Pleas. Norton summarizes this decision at p. 401 of the edition I have quoted, and I think does it more successfully than the English Reports, and I use the quotation which is made by him, based on the original report, as I think the matter in question is there more adequately set out. He says: "Release by freeholder to a copyholder 'unto the said J S, habendum unto J S and G S , their heirs and assigns, to the use of J S and G S, their heirs and assigns for ever.' *Held*, that though, as G S was not named in the premises, he could take nothing in the habendum, yet the use limited to J S and G S and their heirs is good: *Sammes' Case* (1609), 13 Rep. 54; Ley, 11. And it was said, *ibid.*, at p. 56, 'if a man maketh a feoffment in fee to one, to the use of him and the heirs of his body; in this case, for the benefit of the issue, the Statute according to the limitation of the uses, divests the estate vested in him by the common law, and executes the same in himself by force of the Statute, and yet the same is out of the words of the Statute of 27 Hen. 8, which are, where any person, etc., stand or be seised, etc., to the use of any other person; and here he is seised to the use of himself; and the other clause is, where divers and many persons, etc., be jointly seised, etc., to the use of any of them, etc.; and in this case A is sole seised: but the Statute of 27 Hen. 8 hath been always beneficially expounded, to satisfy the intention of the parties, which is the direction of the use according to the rule of the law. So if a man, seised of lands in fee simple, by deed covenants with another, that he and his heirs will stand seised of the same land, to the use of himself and the heirs of his body, or unto the use of himself for life, the remainder over in fee; in that case, by the operation of the Statute, the estate which he hath at the common law is divested, and a new estate vested in himself, according to the limitation of the use."

As I have perhaps already indicated, the coexistence of a fee and a use in one person is something that is allowed by law and, in my view, one is in no way repugnant to the other. As Mr. Armour suggested, it simply provides by reason of the operation of the statute of 27 Hen. VIII (1535), c. 10 (the *Statute of Uses*), which is in force in this Province, an alternative method of conveyance which can be exercised by the holder of a fee, who also has a power of appointment if he so desires. The vendor here, in the deed which he proposes to give to the purchaser, is doing just that. As I see it, the deed is sufficient to convey, when it is delivered by the execution of the use, the fee in the land in question free from the dower of Wilda Walsh, his wife.

There will accordingly be an order that the requisition has been validly answered and that it does not constitute a valid objection to the title. . . .

[See also *Burt* v. *Owen*, [1943] 3 D.L.R. 640 (P.E.I.); *Re Rowe*, [1957] O.R. 9, 10 D.L.R. 2d 215.

Dower may be barred by a wife either during coverture (e.g. on the occasion of a conveyance by the husband) or by ante-nuptial settlement under which she accepts other provision made for her in lieu of dower in present or after-acquired freeholds of inheritance. Formerly, ante-nuptial settlements were effected through "jointures" operating under the Statute of Uses, 1536: see 2 *Blackstone*, Commentaries (Lewis ed.), p. 137.]

Dower in Mortgaged Land

The history of this subject in Ontario is fully treated by *Falconbridge*, Law of Mortgages of Land (3rd ed., 1942), chap. 18.

RE LESPERANCE. Ontario High Court in Chambers. 61 O.L.R. 94, [1927] 4 D.L.R. 391

ROSE, J.: This is a motion for the payment out of court of moneys paid in under sec. 11

of the Dower Act (R.S.O. 1914, ch. 70) by a second mortgagee, who sold under the power of sale contained in his mortgage and realised more than enough to satisfy the claim of the first mortgagee....

The case that has to be considered may therefore be stated thus: The owner of the legal estate mortgages it (his wife barring her dower); he then mortgages the equity of redemption (his wife again barring her dower); the first mortgage is discharged, and what was at first a mortgage of the equity of redemption becomes a mortgage of the land; then the equity of redemption is mortgaged, i.e., a second mortgage is made (the mortgagor's wife barring her dower); and finally the mortgagee of the equity of redemption sells under his power of sale and realises more than the amounts of the two mortgages. And the question is: Is the wife entitled to dower in the surplus; and, if so, upon what basis is the amount to which she is entitled to be calculated?

Counsel for the execution creditors point out that sec. 4 of the Dower Act, which confers dower in equitable estates, applies only when the husband dies beneficially entitled; and they contend that sec. 10 (2) of the Act, which applies when "land" comprised in a mortgage is sold under a power of sale, has no application where what has been mortgaged, and what is sold, is an equity of redemption; and they say, therefore, that the wife has no right of dower. This contention does not seem to me to be sound. Before the original of sec. 10 (1) was passed in 1879, if a mortgage's wife joined in the mortgage to bar her dower, she was not entitled to dower in the equitable estate which remained in her husband after the mortgage, unless he died beneficially entitled thereto; and the husband might defeat the claim to dower in the equitable estate by a transfer in his lifetime. But the effect of the section is that a married woman is entitled to dower out of an equity of redemption in land, whether or not her husband dies seised of it, where such equity has arisen by his having executed a mortgage of the legal estate in which she has joined to bar her dower (I adopt the statement made by Mr. Falconbridge in his Law of Mortgages of Real Estate, p. 284). The equity of redemption which the husband has in the land of which before the execution of the mortgage he was the owner is the equitable estate out of which dower is given by sec. 10: *Re Luckhardt* (1898), 29 O.R. 111. Now, as stated, the present case is to be dealt with on the assumption that Lesperance was the owner of the legal estate. Therefore when he made his first mortgage, his wife joining to bar her dower, he retained an equitable estate out of which by the statute his wife was entitled to dower whether or not he died possessed; and when, upon the mortgaging of that equitable estate, the wife joined to bar her dower, the bar of dower was, I think, such a bar as is referred to in sec. 10 (1). Certainly, it was "a bar of dower contained in a mortgage," and certainly, although what was mortgaged was less than the legal estate, the instrument was intended to give the mortgagee security upon the land; therefore, I think that the bar of dower was a "bar of dower contained in a mortgage or other instrument intended to have the effect of a mortgage or other security upon land" within the meaning of the statute and that it did not operate to any greater extent than was "necessary to give full effect to the rights of the mortgagee." And so when what had been a second mortgage became a first mortgage and a new second mortgage was made, the interest last mortgaged was an equitable interest of the husband in which the wife had a dower right which was not dependent upon the husband's dying beneficially entitled, and a bar of dower was just as essential in the case of the last of the mortgages (the mortgage containing the power under which the sale was made) as it had been in the case of the mortgage to the Huron and Erie Mortgage Corporation; and, as the bar is not to operate "to any greater extent than shall be necessary to give full effect to the rights of the mortgagee," I think it is clear that the wife is entitled to dower out of the moneys in court.

When a surplus arises from a sale made under a power contained in a first mortgage there is no difficulty as to the basis upon which the amount payable to the wife is to be ascertained;

for by sec. 10 (2) it is enacted that (except where the mortgage is for the purchase-money of the land) the basis of calculation shall be the amount realised from the sale of the land, and not merely the surplus of such amount over the sum secured by the mortgage. But counsel contend that there is no way of applying sec. 10 (2) in the case of a sale under the power contained in a mortgage of the equity of redemption except by treating the equity of redemption as the "land comprised in" the second mortgage, and basing the calculation upon the amount realised from the sale of the equity of redemption (i.e. upon the excess of the purchase-price over the amount secured by the first mortgage). I am, however, unable to agree that the case depends entirely upon sec. 10 (2). By sec. 11 (2) the duty of the Court is to "make such order as may be deemed just for securing the right of dower of a married woman in any money out of which she shall be dowable." If sec. 10 (2) specifies the basis upon which the amount to which the woman is entitled shall be ascertained, that basis must be taken; but, if the right is clear and the basis is not laid down in sec. 10 (2), then the Court must proceed to ascertain the basis that will secure such right as the woman is by the Act declared to have. Now before the legal estate was mortgaged the wife had her common-law dower, and when she joined in the first mortgage to bar her dower, the bar, by the statute, operated only to such extent as should be necessary to give full effect to the rights of the mortgagee; there was no reason why, for the benefit of her husband or his creditors, she should agree, and she did not agree, that in case she survived her husband she should have for life any less than one-third of his land; and, applying the principle established by sec. 10 (1), sec. 10 (2) enacts that upon a sale of the land by the mortgagee the basis of calculation of the dower shall be the amount realised from the sale of the land, and not the surplus only. Similarly, when on the making of the second mortgage the wife barred her dower in the equitable estate, she did so, as the statute declared, only to the extent necessary to give full effect to the rights of the second mortgagee; and I think that a holding that the bar contained in the second mortgage had the effect of benefiting the husband's creditors by reducing the wife's right from a right to one-third of the land (subject to the rights of the mortgagees) to a right to one-third of the equity of redemption would be a holding that the bar had an effect which the statute denies to it. Therefore, whether sec. 10 (2) can or cannot be invoked, I think that the wife's right in the present case is to have her dower calculated on the full amount realised from the sale under the power contained in the mortgage to Cleary.

The amount realised from the sale of the land was $ 10,700. Lesperance and his wife are said to be each about 46 years of age. According to the table "H" printed in Cameron on Dower, p. 598, which seems to be the table generally used, the present value of the wife's right is therefore $ 3.96 per $ 100, or $ 423.72. I suppose that the proper order will be one for payment out of court of that sum to Mrs. Lesperance and for the payment of the balance to the Sheriff of the County of Essex to be dealt with according to the statute; but the form of order may be discussed with me if the parties differ about it....

[In *Re Robinson*, [1938] 4 D.L.R. 771, [1938] O.W.N. 361, where mortgaged land was sold by a widow as executrix (she having in her husband's lifetime joined in the mortgage to bar dower) it was held that her dower was calculable on the full sale price of the land. Why?

Dower is effectively extinguished by foreclosure of a mortgage in which the wife has barred dower but the wife is a person entitled to intervene in the proceedings and to redeem: see *Falconbridge, op. cit.*, at pp. 432-33. Cf. the position of a wife under homestead legislation. Does she have an estate or interest entitling her to redeem a homestead sold for taxes where the statutory provision for redemption applies in favour of "a person who has an interest in or charge upon" the land? See *Mennig* v. *St. Andrews* (1952), 4 W.W.R. (N.S.) 427, 60 Man. R. 24.

A and B buy land as joint tenants and give back a mortgage to secure part of the purchase price. On A's death, B (a married man) as surviving joint tenant enters into a contract to sell the land free from encumbrance and to accept a mortgage to secure part of the purchase price. B thereupon pays off the existing mortgage and a certificate of discharge is registered. Is the purchaser from B entitled to insist on a bar of dower by B's wife in order to have a good title? See *Re Bing and May*, [1946] O.W.N. 247.]

RE SMITH. Ontario Court of Appeal. [1952] O.R. 135, [1952] 2 D.L.R. 104

Appeal from a judgment of LeBel J., on an application for advice in the administration of an estate.

The judgment of the Court was delivered by HOGG J. A.: This is an appeal from a judgment pronounced by LeBel J. on December 8, 1951, after the hearing of a motion brought by the executor of the estate of the late William T. C. Smith, for the advice of the Court with respect to the dower to which the testator's widow would be entitled out of the proceeds of the sale of certain property which comprised the only asset of the said estate.

The first question which the Court was requested to answer is as follows:

"Is the widow entitled to have her dower interest in the real property known as 85 Old Mill Road calculated on the full sale price of the property regardless of encumbrances?"

The issue before the Court depends both upon the facts and upon the construction and interpretation of s. 9 of the *Dower Act*, now R.S.O. 1950, c. 109. The facts, in brief, are the following:

Mr. Smith, who died on May 27, 1950, was at the time of his death the owner, registered under the provisions of the *Land Titles Act*, of the real property in question. It had been purchased by the late Mr. Smith from a Mrs. Frances Armstrong in her capacity as executrix under the will of her deceased husband William Allan Armstrong. At the time of the closing of the sale the deceased gave a mortgage of the said lands, in which his wife joined to bar her dower, to the Prudential Insurance Company of America to secure a loan of $ 11,000. The proceeds of the loan secured by this mortgage were paid in cash as part of the purchase-price of the property. At the same time, the deceased also gave a mortgage of the lands to Mrs. Armstrong in her personal capacity to secure the sum of $ 3,000, in which Mrs. Smith joined to bar her dower. The proceeds of this mortgage were also paid to the vendor as part of the purchase-price. Both mortgages were filed in the Land Titles Office subsequent to the deed of conveyance or transfer.

After Mr. Smith's death the Guaranty Trust Co. of Canada, in its capacity as trustee under his will sold the property to one T. W. Martin for the sum of $ 21,500 and Mrs. Smith executed the deed of conveyance to bar her dower for the purpose of the sale and, by agreement with the trustee, reserved her right to dower payable out of the proceeds of the sale. The basis upon which the amount of dower is to be calculated is the subject of the application for the advice of the Court.

LeBel J. came to the conclusion that the amount of dower was to be calculated on the proceeds of the sale after deducting the amount remaining due upon the two above-mentioned mortgages. It was his opinion that the mortgages were given "to secure unpaid purchase-money" or "for the purchase-money of the land". The learned Judge, in a carefully considered judgment, discussed the leading case of *Re Auger* (1912), 5 D.L.R. 680, 26 O.L.R. 402, and the earlier cases to which reference is therein made and based his decision upon his interpretation of those judgments. The material facts in the *Auger* case were that land had been purchased for the sum of $ 3,000 and conveyed to the purchaser by a deed of conveyance which recited that it had been agreed between the parties to the transaction that $ 2,800 of the purchase-price should remain a lien upon the land to be collaterally secured by a mortgage.

The grantor released to the purchaser all his claims upon the land "excepting the said lien for unpaid purchase money and mortgage to be given therefor". The mortgage for the above-mentioned amount was executed on the same date as the conveyance and the purchaser's wife joined in it to bar her dower. After the death of the purchaser the property was sold, and it was held as the result of an application to the Court to determine the rights of the widow respecting her dower in the land, that dower was to be calculated on the proceeds of the sale of the land after deducting the amount remaining due upon the mortgage at the time of the husband's death. Meredith C. J. delivered the judgment and considered the effect of the judgment in *Campbell* v. *Royal Canadian Bank.* (1872), 19 Gr. 334, upon the matter in issue. The learned Chief Justice said at p. 683 D.L.R., p. 405 O.L.R.:

"Before any legislation on the subject, it had been held, in *Campbell* v. *Royal Canadian Bank*, 19 Gr. 334, that where a wife joins with her husband to bar dower in mortgage to secure the purchase-money of mortgaged lands, and the husband dies, and the mortgaged land is sold to satisfy the mortgage, she is entitled to dower in the proceeds after satisfying the mortgage debt, but no more."

He then referred to a further passage from the judgment of Spragge C. in the *Campbell* case and said that the observations made by the Chancellor did not appear to be limited to cases in which, as in the one he was dealing with, the mortgage was for unpaid purchase-money. Meredith C. J. then said: "However, in the subsequent case of *Doan* v. *Davis*, 23 Gr. 207, where the mortgage was not given to secure unpaid purchase-money, the same learned Judge held that the widow was entitled to dower out of the whole value of the mortgaged premises, and not only out of their value beyond the mortgage-debt."

In further reference to the *Campbell* case, Meredith C. J. said [p. 684] that it decided that where a wife joins in a mortgage by her husband "to secure unpaid purchase-money" she is not entitled to dower in the full value of the land. He held that the subsequent legislation on the subject did not substantially change the view taken by the Court of Chancery as to the effect of a bar of dower.

It is to be noted that in *Campbell* v. *Royal Canadian Bk.* the mortgages were given by the husband to the vendor for the whole amount of the purchase-money paid for the property out of which his widow subsequently claimed dower, and in the *Auger* case the mortgage was given to the vendor to secure part of the purchase-price.

Section 9 (1) of the *Dower Act* is to the effect that no bar of dower contained in any mortgage or other security upon land shall operate to bar dower to any greater extent than shall be necessary to give full effect to the rights of the mortgagee. Subsection (2) of s. 9 relates only to cases in which the mortgaged land has been sold under a power of sale in the mortgage or under legal process, but I think it will assist in an understanding of the *Auger* case to set it out in full. It reads: "Where land comprised in such mortgage or other instrument is sold under any power of sale contained therein or under any legal process, the wife of the mortgagor or grantor who has so barred her dower in such land shall be entitled to dower in any surplus of the purchase money arising from such sale which may remain after satisfaction of the claim of the mortgagee or grantee, to the same extent as she would have been entitled to dower in the land from which such surplus purchase money was derived had the same not been sold and, except where the mortgage or other instrument is for the purchase money of the land, the amount to which she is entitled shall be calculated on the basis of the amount realized from the sale of the land and not upon the amount realized from the sale over and above the amount of the mortgage only."

This subsection is the same as s. 3, of the Act of 1895 (Ont.), c. 25, which was quoted by Meredith C. J. in the *Auger* case. He stated that it applied only where there was a sale under power of sale or under any legal process and that the basis of calculating the amount of dower to which a widow was entitled where the mortgage was given to secure unpaid purchase-price remained the same under s. 3 as where the land was not sold under power of sale or other legal process. He held that the aforesaid s. 3 of the 1895 Act did not alter the basis of calculation.

It is apparent that the words "for the unpaid purchase money" were regarded in the *Auger* case as having the same effect and import as the words "to secure unpaid purchase money." The words "to secure" mean to guarantee or make safe against loss, and are not a synonym for the words "to obtain" or "to procure". I think that the effect of the judgment in the *Auger* case is that the mortgage, in order to be held to have been given for unpaid purchase-money, must have been given to the mortgagee to secure the amount owing to him as vendor, for the whole purchase-price or part of the purchase-price due by the mortgagor for the lands which were being acquired, and not given by the purchaser of the land to a third party to obtain money which was then paid to the vendor of the property in satisfaction in cash of the purchase-price or part of it.

The facts present in the appeal now before this Court are not that the two mortgages executed by William Smith were given as security for a debt owed by him to the vendor of the property being purchased by him. These mortgages were given to third parties as security for money borrowed from such third parties in order that the money so obtained might be paid to the Armstrong estate as the purchase-price in full in cash. Smith was not indebted in any sum to the vendor, for the payment of which security was necessary. In *Doan* v. *Davis* (1876), 23 Gr. 207, the estate of an intestate was subject to a mortgage created by him, in which his wife had joined to bar her dower, for the purpose of securing a debt of the husband. It was held that upon a sale of the land after the husband's death the widow was entitled to dower on the whole value of the mortgaged premises and not only in the excess of the sale price over the amount due on the mortgage. Spragge C. at p. 209 used the following language of Boyd M. in *Re McMorris* (1872), 8 C.L.J. 284: "'The wife simply bars her dower with a view to secure the debt due by her husband; when that debt is paid by the husband's estate she is remitted... to her full rights as dowress in the whole estate mortgaged.'" In the case now under consideration, can it be said that the debt is for unpaid purchase-price or part of it? Nothing was owing on account of purchase-price; that debt had been discharged in full, although it is true that it was paid from the proceeds of the loans obtained from the insurance company and from Mrs. Armstrong. The debt owing by the Smith estate was to the two mortgagees. See also Falconbridge on Law of Mortgages, 3rd ed., pp. 321-2.

I have come to the conclusion that as the mortgages were not given as security for the unpaid purchase-price, that is to say, as the debt due under the mortgages was not to the vendor of the land, therefore, the mortgages were not for the unpaid purchase-money of the land and to secure the purchase-price.

The answer to the first question should be that the widow is entitled to have her dower in the surplus calculated on the full value or sale price of the property. I regret that I do not concur in the answer given by LeBel J. to this question. In view of the answer to the first question, the second question need not be answered.

I agree with the learned Judge's answer to the third question and with his answer to the fourth question, that the rate of interest and the life expectancy tables to be applied are Cameron's Tables, which have been used for many years in this Province....

Appeal allowed in part.

[LeBel J.'s answers to the third and fourth questions were as follows:

"...It is convenient to deal next with the third question, which simply asks: 'As of what date is the present value of the dower to be calculated?'

"The short answer is that the widow's inchoate right to dower ripened into an actual right on the death of her husband, *viz.*, on May 27, 1950, and the present value of the dower is to be calculated as of that date: *Johnston* v. *London & Western Trust Co.* (1929), 36 O.W.N. 176; *Whyte* v. *McNeil* (1932), 41 O.W.N. 160; *Re Auger....*

"The last question reads: '4. What rate of interest and what life expectancy tables are to be used in calculating the present value of the dower? or, alternatively, What gross sum is to be paid to the widow in satisfaction of her dower interest in the said property?'

"All that can be said in answer to the question is that nothing before me warrants a departure from the practice which has been followed in this Province for many years. It is true that Cameron's tables are of ancient vintage and that they probably bear little relation to normal life expectancy under present day conditions, but without evidence and the assistance of experts a Court is unable to say what tables should be substituted. It was suggested in argument that the tables used by the Ontario Succession Duty Department should be adopted in calculating Mrs. Smith's dower interest, but those tables, which have legislative sanction, were devised for a different purpose altogether...."]

Election: Choice of Dower or other Benefits

A wife or widow having an inchoate or actual right of dower is often required to choose between her dower and other benefits because she cannot consistently have both. Such questions of election arise between (1) dower and a widow's distributive share on an intestacy; (2) dower and provisions made for a widow under her husband's will; (3) dower and her statutory claim for an allowance by way of modification of her husband's will; and (4) dower and benefits provided for a wife under a separation agreement.

DEVOLUTION OF ESTATES ACT, R.S.O. 1960, c. 106, amended 1960-61, c. 22; 1961-62, c. 34

8. (1) Nothing in this Act takes away a widow's right to dower; but a widow may by deed or instrument in writing, attested by at least one witness, elect to take her interest under this Act in her husband's undisposed of real property in lieu of all claim to dower in respect of the real property of which her husband was at any time seised, or to which at the time of his death he was beneficially entitled, and unless she so elects she is not entitled to share in the undisposed of real property.

(2) The personal representative of the deceased may, by notice in writing, require the widow to make her election, and if she fails to execute and deliver a deed or instrument of election to him within six months after the service of the notice she shall be deemed to have elected to take her dower.

[Subsections 3 and 4 deal with election where the widow is an infant or mentally incompetent person.]

11. (1) The real and personal property of every man dying intestate and leaving a widow, whether or not he leaves issue, where the net value of such real and personal property does not exceed $20,000, belongs to his widow absolutely and exclusively.

(2) Where the net value exceeds $20,000 the widow is entitled to $20,000 part thereof, absolutely and exclusively, and has a charge thereon for such sum with interest thereon from the date of the death of the intestate at four per cent per annum until payment.

(3) The provision for the widow made by this section is in addition and without prejudice to her interest and share in the residue of the real and personal property of the intestate remaining after payment of such sum of $20,000 and interest in the same way as if such residue had been the whole of the intestate's real and personal property, and this section had not been enacted.

(4) Where the estate consists in whole or in part of real property this section applies

only if the widow elects under section 8 to take an interest in her husband's undisposed of real property in lieu of dower.

(5) In this section, "net value" means the value of the real and personal property after payment of the charges thereon and the debts, funeral expenses and expenses of administration, including succession duty.

[Section 1 of the Dower Act, R.S.N.S. 1954, c. 75 requires a widow to elect between dower and testamentary benefits where the will manifests an intention to dispose of real property in a manner inconsistent with dower.]

RE SCHOP, CLIFF v. SCHOP. Ontario High Court. [1948] O.W.N. 338

Trial of an issue to determine those entitled to share in an intestate's estate. Schop and his wife were married in 1900 and in 1917 she left him. In September of that year a separation agreement was executed by them which contained the following provisions: "5. It is further agreed that the said Laura Schop shall bar and release and discharge all her dower and thirds and her estate, right, title, and interest of, in and to the lands and property now owned by the said Conrad Schop, or which at any time hereafter may be acquired or owned by him." Para. 6 of the agreement was a covenant to execute and do "all further assurances and things for the purpose of giving full effect to the covenants, agreements and provisions herein contained". Schop's wife co-habited with two other men through the succeeding 25 years, and after her husband's death in 1945 she made a claim against his estate, followed by an election under section 8 of the Devolution of Estates Act to take her interest in his undisposed of realty in lieu of dower.

WILSON J.: I now pass to a consideration of the law applicable to the agreement. The principle of interpretation to be applied is set forth by Lord Atkin in *Hyman* v. *Hyman*, [1929] A.C. 601 at 625-6:

"Full effect has therefore to be given in all Courts to these contracts as to all other contracts. It seems not out of place to make this obvious reflection, for a perusal of some of the cases in the matrimonial Courts seems to suggest that at times they are still looked at askance, and enforced grudgingly. But there is no caste in contracts. Agreements for separation are formed, construed and dissolved and to be enforced on precisely the same principles as any respectable commercial agreement, of whose nature indeed they sometimes partake. As in other contracts stipulations will not be enforced which are illegal either as being opposed to positive law or public policy. But this is a common attribute of all contracts, though we may recognize that the subject-matter of separation agreements may bring them more than others into relation with questions of public policy."

It was submitted in argument on behalf of the plaintiff Laura Schop, however, that she had no power to contract herself out of the benefits given to a widow under s. 11 of The Devolution of Estates Act, R.S.O. 1937, c. 163, as amended by 1941, c. 19, s. 1, which, by subs. 1, gives the first $ 5,000 net value of an intestate's estate to his widow. By subss. 2 and 3, where the net value of the estate exceeds $ 5,000 she is given a charge for that sum and, in addition, her interest and share in the residue of the real and personal property remaining after payment of that sum in the same way as if the residue had been the whole of the intestate's real and personal property. By subs. 4: "Where the estate consists in whole or in part of real property this section shall apply only if the widow elects under section 8 to take an interest in her husband's undisposed of real property in lieu of dower." It will be recalled that the widow elected to take her distributive share on 9th December 1947.

In support of this argument were cited *Hyman* v. *Hyman*, *supra*, and *Jones* v. *Kline (otherwise Jones) and Hoe*, [1938] 3 W.W.R. 65, [1938] 4 D.L.R. 391, a decision of Mr. Justice Howson of the Supreme Court of Alberta in which, at page 84, he held that the principle in *Hyman* v. *Hyman* applied to an intestate succession under The Intestate Succession Act, 1928, of Alberta. From the report it is not possible to determine whether the provisions of that Act are the same as The Devolution of Estates Act of Ontario but if they are I should have to differ, with respect, from the conclusion at which he arrived, because to agree would mean that a wife could not contract herself out of the benefits given by s. 11 of The Devolution of Estates Act quoted above.

The only question before the House of Lords in *Hyman* v. *Hyman* (per Lord Hailsham L. C. at p. 608) was "whether or not the existence of the wife's covenant in the deed of separation precludes her from making any application for maintenance" under s. 190 of The Supreme Court of Judicature (Consolidation) Act, 1925, which corresponds to s. 2 of The Matrimonial Causes Act, R.S.O. 1937, c. 208 (see *Cohen* v. *Cohen and Samuels*, [1947] O.W.N. 941, [1948] 1 D.L.R. 479). In arriving at their decision their Lordships emphasized the importance of keeping in mind that the action was one for divorce: Lord Hailsham at p. 613, Lord Shaw of Dunfermline at p. 618, Lord Buckmaster at pp. 624-5, Lord Atkin at p. 630; and they all arrived at their conclusion, as stated by Lord Hailsham at p. 614: "that the power of the Court to make provision for a wife on the dissolution of her marriage is a necessary incident of the power to decree such a dissolution, conferred not merely in the interests of the wife, but of the public, and that the wife cannot by her own covenant preclude herself from invoking the jurisdiction of the Court or preclude the Court from the exercise of that jurisdiction."

The decision in that case is, therefore, in no way applicable to the argument in support of which it has been quoted, and under the ordinary principles of construction of contracts there is nothing to preclude a wife from contracting herself out of the benefits given to her by The Devolution of Estates Act....

The agreement was executed under seal.

The mutual consideration clauses are sufficient consideration to support the agreement under the authority of the numerous cases cited in Lush on Husband and Wife, 4th ed. 1933, pp. 469 *et seq.*, and it is necessary to determine the effect of the paragraphs quoted in full. Para. 5 means that Laura Schop intended to give up all claims to her husband's lands and property then owned or thereafter acquired by him. The use of the two words "lands" and "property" must be taken to express the meaning of real and personal property. Then in para. 6 provision is made for further assurances and things for the purpose of giving effect to the agreement.

If Laura Schop has any interest in the real or personal property of Conrad Schop, the administratrix, Mrs. Poore, is entitled to call upon her to release it, but the Court in cases such as this will treat as done that which ought to be done and the effect of the execution of a release by Laura Schop of her interest in the real and personal property would be to leave her without a claim against the estate and the conclusion is that she has no interest in it.

There is a further ground upon which the defendants contend, and properly so, that Laura Schop is prevented from sharing in her husband's estate, namely, that having committed adultery after leaving her husband, and never having returned to his household, she is barred forever of her action to demand her dower that she ought to have of his land, under s. 8 of The Dower Act, R.S.O. 1937, c. 112, and having no right to elect to take dower she has no right to elect to take her share under s. 11 of The Devolution of Estates Act. For Mrs. Schop it is contended that she has not lost her dower in her husband's lands, although she could not bring an action to enforce her right to it and therefore she can elect to share in her husband's estate under the provisions of s. 11 in part quoted above.

This latter argument is not now open to consideration, however, for even had Mrs. Schop been in possession or acquired possession of her husband's real estate at or after his death, she would still have had no right to claim a dower interest. By remaining away from her husband, and by living with another in adultery, she forfeited her right to dower. This is the effect of the decision of Chief Justice Falconbridge in *Bowman* v. *Thurman* (1909), 14 O.W.R. 254.

Having lost her right to dower, Mrs. Schop could not make an election, and could not therefore avail herself of the right given by s. 11 of The Devolution of Estates Act....

[If, following a release of all dower rights under a separation agreement, the spouses resume cohabitation and the husband dies intestate are the widow's rights on an intestacy, whether for her distributive share or dower, restored? See *Re Wiggins*, [1952] 1 D.L.R. 845, [1952] O.W.N. 66.

In *Moher* v. *Moher*, [1943] 2 D.L.R. 666, [1943] O.W.N. 244 (C.A.), rev'g. [1943] 1 D.L.R. 488, [1943] O.W.N. 21, the release of dower in a separation agreement was accompanied by an irrevocable power of attorney to a third person to bar the wife's dower in any present or future property. The spouses resumed cohabitation, and after the husband's death a question arose whether the power of attorney could be exercised to perfect title to land which the husband had in his lifetime contracted to sell. Was it exercisable at the request only of the husband or at the request of his executor or administrator as well, or was it also exercisable at the request of the purchaser or, indeed, at his insistence?

Cf. *Re Simpkins*, [1948] 2 D.L.R. 101 (Ont. C.A.) where the separation agreement provided that the husband would execute a mortgage of certain lands for $ 2,000 which the wife would accept "in full of all claims for support and maintenance of every nature and kind whatsoever". The wife covenanted not to take any proceedings for alimony or maintenance and also that at the request and expense of the husband she would execute such assurances as might be necessary to bar dower in the lands covered by the mortgage and in certain other lands as and when the $ 2.000 mortgage was paid by her husband. There was no other mention of dower, and in his lifetime the husband made no request for any bar of dower. Was she entitled to dower on his death (and to a right of election under s. 8 of the Devolution of Estates Act) or was it open to his personal representative to insist on a bar of dower?

Will a release or renunciation of dower in a separation agreement be construed as operable only during the husband's lifetime (to enable him to sell land free from dower) or must it also be construed to free his estate of any claims after his death? See *Re Knoll*, [1938] O.W.N. 282; *Re Jenkins*, [1951] O.W.N. 492 (Co. Ct.).]

RE HILL. Ontario High Court. [1961] O.R. 619, [1951] 4 D.L.R. 218

McRUER C. J. H. C.: This is an application for the construction of the last will and testament of Reginald Mark Hill. After making provision for payment of debts and succession duties, the testator devised and bequeathed all his estate both real and personal to his executor and trustee upon trust, to convert his estate into money and to invest the proceeds in trust securities or in securities that are a legal investment for Canadian life insurance companies, and to pay $ 1,000 to 'Sick Children's Hospital at Toronto'. Then follow six pecuniary bequests to employees and to children of gross amounts payable by instalments, each stated to be "out of the capital of my estate". The paragraphs that give rise to this application read as follows:

"(i) To pay and deliver to my wife, Isabella Christina Hill, if and while living, out of the capital of my estate, the sum of three thousand dollars ($ 3,000) six months after my death and thereafter two hundred and fifty dollars ($ 250) per month, without interest, out of capital during the natural life of my said wife.

"(j) Upon the death of my wife, Isabella Christina Hill, to pay and deliver the rest and residue of my estate, after payment of or provision for the above specific legacies, equally among my children above named, the children of any deceased child to take the parent's share per stirpes."

Nowhere in the will is the income from the estate dealt with as such.

The questions submitted to the Court are:

"1. Are the benefits given by the said Will to Isabella Christina Hill, widow of the deceased, in addition to or in lieu of her dower interest in the real proporty of the deceased?

"2. Is Isabella Christina Hill, widow of the deceased, entitled to be paid her dower interest upon the sale of the real property of the deceased, in addition to the benefits which she received under the Will?

"3. Is there an intestacy with respect to the income of the estate?

"4. To whom is the income of the estate payable and how should it be distributed?"

All parties agree that if the widow is not put to her election the estate is still sufficient to pay all the pecuniary legacies, including the payments to the widow and make provision for the widow's dower interest. The adult beneficiaries have signified their wish that a construction should be put on the will that will give their mother the maximum income possible from the estate, and through counsel representations have been made to the Court that they support their mother's contention that under the terms of the will she is not put to her election.

Mr. Beatty, on behalf of the infant, argues that on the authorities as they stand in Ontario the widow must elect as to whether she will take her dower interest or her interest under the provisions of the will.

The problem is far from a simple one and I think it can best be solved by considering the authorities here and in England having some regard for their chronological order. This is particularly necessary as I have come to the conclusion that there are some statements in the cases that are conflicting and are not fully warranted by the language used in the earlier authorities relied on.

The first and fundamental principles to be considered are laid down in *Gibson* v. *Gibson* (1852), 1 Drew. 42, 61 E.R. 367, where the Vice-Chancellor stated at pp. 51-2.:

"The question to be determined in this case is, whether the widow of the testator ought to be put to her election between her dower and the benefits given to her by the will of her husband.

"It is difficult, perhaps impossible, to reconcile all the authorities on this subject; but it is impossible to examine them without perceiving that there are certain broad and clear principles which ought to form the foundation of every decision on the subject. Putting these principles into the form of propositions, they may be stated as follows: The first is, that the doctrine of election is precisely the same, and founded on the same reasons, and governed by the same rules, when applied to dower, as when applied to any other case; there is not one doctrine of election applicable to the case of a widow claiming dower, and another doctrine of election applicable to other cases.

"The second proposition is that the doctrine of election, as applicable equally to all cases, is this: that a person who is entitled to any benefit under a will or other instrument must, if he claims that benefit, abandon every right or interest, the assertion of which would defeat, even partially, any of the provisions of that will or instrument; and, applying this to the particular case of dower, the doctrine may be thus stated: that if the testator has, by his will, made such a disposition of the real estate of which he was seised, that the assertion by the widow of her right to dower would prevent that disposition having full effect, as the testator intended, then she must elect to abandon either her dower or the benefit given to her by the will.

"The third proposition is, that in no case is a person to be put to his election unless it is clear that the provisions of the instrument, under which he is entitled to a benefit, would be in some degree defeated by the assertion of his other right. And, therefore, in the particular case of dower, unless it be clear and beyond reasonable doubt that the testator intended to make such a disposition of the real estate, that the assertion by the widow of her right to dower would prevent the giving full effect to his intention, the widow shall not be put to her election. It is not enough to say that upon the whole will it is fairly to be inferred that the testator did not intend that his widow should have her dower; in order to justify the Court in putting her to her election, it must be satisfied that there is a positive intention to exclude her from dower, either expressed or clearly implied.

"The fourth proposition is that the intention to exclude the wife from her dower must be apparent on the face of the will itself."

The precise question I have to decide may be stated thus: Where a testator has directed that his real and personal estate be disposed of so as to be blended into one trust fund out of which there are to be paid specific sums at specific times to the widow, is she put to her election where the only other interest given under the will which is affected is that of the residuary beneficiaries?

Ellis v. *Lewis* (1844), 3 Hare 310, 67 E.R. 400, is an authority of long standing. At p. 313 the Vice-Chancellor stated: "It appears from some of the earlier cases that a distinction was at one time supposed to exist between a devise of a testator's estate or interest in his lands, and a devise of the lands themselves by that description; it being considered in the former case that the devise did not, in the latter that it did, express an intention by the force of the language itself that the devisee was to take the lands discharged of the widow's right to dower. But I take the law to be clearly settled at this day that a devise of lands, *eo nomine*, upon trust for sale, or a devise of lands, *eo nomine*, to a devisee beneficially, does not *per se* express an intention to devise the land otherwise than subject to its legal incidents, that of dower included. There must be something more in the will, something inconsistent with the enjoyment by the widow of her dower by metes and bounds, or the devise standing alone will be construed as I have stated."

The Vice-Chancellor went on to say at p. 314: "The devise is of land subject to dower. The trust to sell is a trust to sell subject to dower, and the proceeds of the sale will represent the gross value of the estate *minus* the value of the dower."

Boyd C. in *Re Quimby* (1884), 5 O.R. 738, decided that the widow was put to her election where there was a blended fund created and a direction that in case of the death of a son before he reached the age of 30 years the estate, after providing for her annuity, should be distributed according to the *Statute of Distributions*, on the ground that if the widow was allowed her dower it would interfere with the equality of distribution under the *Statute of Distributions*.

In *Amsden* v. *Kyle* (1884), 9 O.R. 439, Boyd C. held that where a testator by his will left all his real and personal estate to his nephew James Kyle "subject to the following bequest, viz., to my wife Eliza Kyle, a one-third interest in all my real and personal estate, so long as she shall remain unmarried", that the widow was put to her election. The learned Chancellor stated: "The devise of one-third of the testator's land during widowhood would not *per se* interfere with the widow's right as doweress to claim another third for life. But according to judical determinations which bind me, a clue to the testator's intention is found in the direction to divide the personal as well as the real estate. He gives to his wife a one-third interest in all his real and personal estate as long as she shall remain unmarried. That imports the same manner of division in the case of the land as in the case of the personalty, i.e., a division of the entire property of each kind which would be defeated if the dower were first subtracted from the realty."

Leys v. *Toronto Gen'l Trusts Co.* (1892), 22 O.R. 603, is a case which emphasizes the distinction between a bequest to trustees to form a blended fund in which the widow is to participate with others in certain fixed proportions, and one in which she is merely to participate. The testator by his will blended his real and personal estate into a fund from which payments of income were to be made to his wife and other devisees and the division of the corpus was postponed until after the death of the wife. At p. 605 Boyd C. stated: "The testator blends the real and personal estate not for the purpose of its equal division, but in order to obtain an income out of which payments are to be made annually to his wife and other objects of his bounty, and the residue of such income to go equally during the life of his wife to his nephews and nieces. The division of the corpus is not to be made till after the wife's death."

He distinguished that case from *Re Quimby, supra*, where the blended estate was to be divided between the wife and others in equal proportions, and held that no election arose by virtue of this provision as between the wife's dower and the testamentary bestowments. The only reference that is made to *Amsden* v. *Kyle* is to correct the first sentence above quoted. The learned Chancellor stated that he could not find any manuscript of the judgment to compare with the printed text but as it stood it was misleading. He went on to say [p. 607]: "The devise of one-third for widowhood in one part, would not interfere with a claim for dower in another part, but it would be inconsistent with having the two estates in the same land concurrently."

In *Re Shunk* (1899), 31 O.R. 175, Rose J., after considering *Ellis* v. *Lewis*, *Amsden* v. *Kyle* and *Leys* v. *Toronto Gen'l Trusts Co.*, stated at p. 179: "The authorities to which I have referred shew that a devise upon trust to sell does not put the widow to any election, and here there is nothing more."

In *Re Hurst* (1905), 11 O.L.R. 6 at p. 9, Meredith C. J. outlined the principles applicable in considering whether a widow was put to her election on the facts of the case as follows: "I am unable to find in the will of this testator, or to gather from the provisions of it that his intention was to dispose of his property in a manner inconsistent with his wife's rights to dower in the thirty-three acres devised to his son Egbert Francis [subject to the right of the widow to occupy the rooms in the dwelling house and to use the drive house], which is the test, as stated in *Parker* v. *Sowerby*, 1 Dr. 488; 4 DeG. M. & G. 321; or that the provisions of the will shew clearly and beyond reasonable doubt that it was the positive intention of the testator, either clearly expressed or clearly to be implied, to exclude his wife from dower, which is the test, according to the view of the Vice-Chancellor (Kindersley) in *Gibson* v. *Gibson* (1852), 1 Dr. 42, or that the provisions of the will 'raise a necessary implication that the gift is in substitution of dower,' which must be found in order to exclude the claim to dower, according to the statement of the law by Vice-Chancellor Stuart, in *Warburton* v. *Warburton* (1854), 2 Sm. & G. 163, at p. 165."

In *Re Williamson* (1916), 11 O.W.N. 142, Middleton J. stated: "The more recent cases establish the necessity for some clear indication that the wife is to be deprived of her dower if she takes under the will; neither a direction to sell and realise nor the formation of a blended fund is a sufficient indication of the testator's intention to deprive the wife of the right to dower if she accepts the benefits given by the will."

I have examined the will Middleton J. was construing and I find that there was a bequest to trustees of real and personal property to form a blended fund and provision was made for the testator's widow as follows: "Should the principal so invested amount to no more than fifty thousand dollars, to pay to my wife during her lifetime and provided she does not marry again the sum of one hundred and fifty dollars monthly. Should the amount invested be more than fifty thousand dollars then the income to my said wife is to be increased proportionately provided there is money to pay it." The residue passed on the death or remarriage of the widow to the testator's sons.

I would have had no difficulty in this case except for some language used by Orde J. A. and Roach J. in cases with which I now deal.

In *Re De Olloqui* (1927), 32 O.W.N. 299 at pp. 300–1, Orde J.A. stated: "Here the testator has blended the whole of his personalty and realty into one mass and has given his wife an aliquot part or share of it, namely, one-third of the blended mass, and has then disposed of what is left. Where there is a gift to the widow of a proportionate share of both realty and personalty, she must elect between the gift and her dower."

I am in entire agreement that the cases relied on are authority for this statement.

In *Re Hendry*, [1931] O.R. 448 at p. 452, Orde J.A., after considering many of the authorities to which I have referred, stated:

"If the gift here were of some part of the corpus of the blended fund, the widow would clearly be put to her election under the authority of *Parker* v. *Sowerby* (1854), 4 DeG. M. & G. 321, and of the four Ontario cases above mentioned [*McGregor* v. *McGregor* (1873), 20 Gr. 450; *Re Quimby, supra; Amsden* v. *Kyle, supra; Re De Olloqui, supra*] which followed it. Does the fact that the wife is given merely one-third of the net income from the whole blended fund for her life or during widowhood, rather than a share of the fund itself, take the case out of the rule?

"Having regard to the rule itself, I am of the opinion that it does not. The testator blends the whole of his realty and personalty into one fund. Of the total net revenue derived from the whole fund one-third is to go to his widow. How can it be possible to carry out that intention if, before the creation of the blended fund, the widow is to take one-third of the realty by metes and bounds for her life, or its equivalent value in money? If she is to be permitted to do that, then the gift intended for her by the testator to be derived from the whole of his estate cannot possibly be carried out to the full. To the extent that she has asserted her right to dower, the net income available for distribution by the trustees is correspondingly reduced."

I am unable to find in any of the cases relied on any statement that goes so far as to say if the gift is of some part of the corpus of the blended fund the widow is clearly put to her election. In *Parker* v. *Sowerby* (1854), 4 De G.M. & G. 321 at pp. 325-6, 43 E.R. 531, the Lord Chancellor stated: "It is not I think quite correct to state the general rule of law as being, that, to raise a case of election against the wife, the will must shew that the testator had in his mind her right to dower, and that he meant to exclude it; the rule rather is, that it must appear from the will that the testator intended to dispose of his property in a manner inconsistent with the wife's right to dower."

In *Re Williamson*, [1943], 2 D.L.R. 726 at p. 730, O.W.N. 270 at p. 273 [affd [1943], 3 D.L.R. 809, O.W.N. 411], Roach J., after discussing several of the relevant cases, including the *Hendry* case, *supra*, stated: "The fact that the testator does not confine such payments to income is important because if the gift is out of the corpus of the blended fund, the widow is put to her election.... To that extent the will contains a gift out of the corpus of the blended fund and accordingly she is put to her election."

With the greatest respect, I cannot interpret the authorities in such a way as to warrant a statement of the applicable principle in the broad terms expressed by Orde J. A. in *Re Hendry* and Roach J. in *Re Williamson*. In the absence of written reasons in the latter case I do not think I am to assume that the Court of Appeal based its judgment on the statement I have quoted, thus overruling the decision of Middleton J. in the earlier *Williamson* case, 11 O.W.N. 142. I think the fundamental principles to which I have referred are not to be departed from. The creation of the blended fund in which the widow is to share is not in itself evidence of an intention that the benefits under the will are to be in lieu of dower. It is only to be so taken if the benefits given to the widow under the will, together with her dower interest, would in some way defeat the intention of the testator as expressed in his will, i.e., by cutting down the share of another beneficiary other than a residuary legatee, or giving the widow a greater share in the estate than on a true construction of the will the testator intended.

The law may be summed up in no better language than that used by the Master of the Rolls, Sir William Grant, in *Greatorex* v. *Cary* (1802), 6 Ves. 615 at p. 616, 31 E.R. 1223, where he said: "The question in all these cases is, whether the testator meant to give away his wife's dower; which he could not do directly. For that it must be seen clearly, that he meant to dispose so, that, if she should claim dower, it would disappoint the will. It must appear, that there is a repugnancy."

Sir William Grant stated that the case could not be distinguished from *Foster* v. *Cook* (1791), 3 Bro. C.C. 347, 29 E.R. 575. In that case the testator gave all his property to trustees and provided for an annuity for his wife. The Lord Chancellor stated at p. 351: "Then as to the other point, the wife has a charge upon the estate, paramount to the will; she has an absolute right to the third part; it is not his to deprive her of it. But, here, it is to be gathered from circumstances, that she is not to have it; and because he gives all *his* property to the trustees, I am to gather from his having given all he *has*, that he has given that which he *had not*. So far from a declaration plain, I have nothing even to lead me to think he meant to deprive her of dower. She must, therefore, have her dower."

In the will before me the direction that the real property should be sold and out of the money realized a fund blended with personalty should be set up, out of the capital of which specific payments are to be made including an annuity to the widow at the rate of $250 per month, all of which can be provided out of the testator's interest in the estate quite apart from the widow's dower interest, shows nothing inconsistent with the testator having recognized at the time the will was made that his widow should have that interest in his real estate given to her by law.

Questions 1 and 2 should be answered as follows:

1. The benefits given to Isabella Christina Hill are in addition to her dower interest.
2. Yes.

I have no doubt as to the disposition of the income of the estate. The testator is presumed to have intended to dispose of his whole estate and therefore, the income, not having been specifically disposed of, falls into the residue. The answer to Q. 3 is "No", and the answer to Q 4 is: The income falls into the residue of the estate and is to be distributed to the residuary beneficiaries according to the provisions of the will.

Order accordingly.

[In a subsequent proceeding, *Re Hill*, [1953] O.W.N. 351, the Court was asked to determine whether succession duties in respect of the widow's dower interest were payable out of the residue of the husband's estate by virtue of a testamentary provision for payment of all succession duties "that may be payable in connection with... any gift or benefit given by me either by survivorship or by this my will". The question was answered in the affirmative.

A testator gave his wife a legacy of $ 10,000 in priority over all other bequests and, subject to other legacies, also gave her one-third of his residuary realty and personalty. Is she put to her election on dower in respect of either the legacy or the residuary gift or both? See *Re Staddon*, [1955] 1 D.L.R. 756, [1954] O.W.N. 345. See also *Re Davis*, [1954] O.W.N. 187.

An execution creditor of a deceased vies with the widow (claiming dower) for priority in a situation where deceased devised to his widow a life estate in all his lands. Is she put to her election? See *Parent* v. *Drouillard*, [1937] O.W.N. 238. As to priority between dower and mechanics' liens, see Mechanics' Lien Act, R.S.O. 1960, c. 233, s. 6.]

RE GREISMAN. Surrogate Court of York County, Ontario. [1955] 1 D.L.R. 741, [1954] O.W.N. 793

Claim for the value of dower by a deceased widow's executors against her deceased husband's executors. The land out of which dower was claimed had been the subject of a contract of sale by the husband in his lifetime without bar of dower. His executors delivered a deed to the purchasers after the widow's death. The widow survived her husband by about two years but did not claim dower in the land. She had however made a claim under the Dependants' Relief Act, R.S.O. 1950, c. 101, and an order in her favour was made charging her deceased husband's estate with a monthly allowance of $ 125.00 "until the death of the applicant or until the amount to which [she] would have been entitled if [he] had died intestate is exhausted, whichever shall first occur."

MACDONELL Surr. Ct. J. (after stating the facts above set out): It is contended by counsel for the estate of Michael Greisman that the application under the *Dependants' Relief Act* amounts to an election not to claim dower. The law in this respect is dealt with in my judgment (later affirmed by the Court of Appeal) in *Re Neiman & Borovoy*, [1954] 2 D.L.R. 732, at pp. 734-5, O.W.N. 527 at p. 529, as follows:

"It is true that under the *Dependants' Relief Act* the maximum allowance which may be made is measured by what a dependant would receive under the *Devolution of Estates Act*, but I do not think that launching an application under the *Dependants' Relief Act* must be considered as an election in all cases. For instance, the will might provide that the wife should receive her dower in the real estate in addition to other benefits. It is perhaps unfortunate that the *Devolution of Estates Act* is silent on the subject. A provision to the effect that upon an application under the *Dependants' Relief Act* a widow must state whether or not she claims her dower might be appropriate.

"The law is clear that in order to exclude a widow from dower in a testator's real property there must be found from the will the intention of the testator so to dispose of his estate that the widow's claim to dower would be inconsistent with that disposition: see *Rudd* v. *Harper* (1888), 16 O.R. 422. Here the provision made for the widow by the will would not appear to be inconsisitent with her claim to dower. When we consider the provision made for the widow under the *Dependants' Relief Act*, however, I think it is plain that there is an inconsistency, as the wife has been allowed to occupy part of the real property for a period of nearly a year."

The case under consideration differs in that the testator made only nominal provision for his wife in the will. I think we must consider, however, whether the provision made on the application under the *Dependants' Relief Act* and the position taken by the applicant are inconsistent with a claim for dower. A written argument, which is in the estate file before me and which was filed by counsel for the widow on the previous application, contains the following:

"It is further respectfully submitted that, if Your Honour felt that you could not grant $150.00 a month for life, you might make an award granting her $150.00 a month up until the amount to which she would be entitled on an intestacy had been used. In other words, if the estate were a $40,000.00 estate, Mrs. Greisman would have been entitled on an intestacy to the first $5,000.00 plus one-third of the balance, which would be approximately $17,000.00. It is respectfully submitted that Your Honour could make an award then of $150.00 a month but that the payments would cease after the applicant had received $17,000.00, and the balance would then go to the estate.

"I submit that this would be a most fair provision for the estate and also would be adequate provision for Mrs. Greisman."

It will also be noted that by paragraph 2 of the above-quoted order it was intended to award the applicant no more than the maximum amount which could have been obtained on an intestacy. It follows, of course, that if the amount of the estate had been cut down by a claim of the widow for dower, such an amount could not have been awarded. I therefore think that the claim for dower on behalf of the estate of the widow cannot now be maintained.

Quite apart from the foregoing, dower is an interest of the widow in the lands. I have never heard of a claim for the value of dower against the executors of the deceased husband, although those executors might be entitled to force the widow to accept such a payment. Also dower can only be recovered by the widow; on her death the claim to dower is extinct: *White* v. *Parnther* (1829), 1 Knapp 179 at p. 226, 12 E.R. 288.

Application dismissed.

[In *Re Neiman and Borovoy* mentioned in the *Greisman* case, *supra*, the claim for dower was made after a successful application under the Dependants' Relief Act. Nothing was said as to dower on that application, by which the widow was given a lump sum and the right to occupy certain property for about one year. These benefits added to those given by the will would, if dower were also allowed, amount to more than the widow's entitlement on an intestacy, which is the maximum allowance under the Dependants' Relief Act. The claim for dower was accordingly disallowed.

Sale of land free from dower in the administration of a deceased husband's estate may be made on order of the Court with provision therein for satisfaction of the dower interest: see Devolution of Estates Act, R.S.O. 1960, c. 106, s. 10; Devolution of Estates Act, R.S.N.B. 1952, c. 62, s. 16; and see *Re Tucker*, [1947] 2 D.L.R. 382, [1947] O.W.N. 346, where the statutory provision was applied notwithstanding that the widow's whereabouts were unknown.

Wide provision for a barring order by the Court in any case where a wife having an inchoate right of dower refuses to bar it is made in the Dower Act, R.S.P.E.I. 1951, c. 46, s. 11. More limited provision (akin to that in the Ontario Dower Act) is made in Nova Scotia by the Married Women's Deeds Act, R.S.N.S. 1954, c. 167. See *Re Leahy*, [1938] 4 D.L.R. 77 (N.S.).

Extinction of dower on sale of land for taxes during husband's lifetime: see *Tomlinson* v. *Hill* (1855), 5 Gr. 231 (Ont. Ch.); Assessment Act, R.S.O. 1960, c. 23, s. 189.

Is the wife's inchoate right of dower an interest for which she may claim proportionate compensation upon an expropriation of land in her husband's lifetime? See *Flynn* v. *Flynn* (1898), 171 Mass. 312, 50 N.E. 650, answering the question in the negative; for a note opposing this result, see (1932) 80 Univ. of Pa. L. Rev. 749. It is clear that by expropriation her inchoate right disappears; the only question is whether she is entitled to share in the compensation awarded.

For the effect of the Statute of Limitations on assigment of dower and arrears of dower, see Limitations Act, R.S.O. 1960, c. 214, ss. 25, 26 and 27; Limitations of Actions Act, R.S.N.B. 1952, c. 133, ss. 29, 33 (2); Statute of Limitations, R.S.N.S. 1954, c. 153, ss. 9, 24; Statute of Limitations, R.S.P.E.I. 1951, c. 87, ss. 14, 17.]

Dower in Defeasible Estates

Whether dower (or, indeed, curtesy) should be allowed in defeasible estates in fee simple or in a fee tail is a question that does not seem to have been decisively determined in any Canadian case. The problem is of importance, of course, only when the defeasibility arises or, in the case of a fee tail, when the required line of issue has died out. If dower and curtesy are considered as derivative estates (as is argued strongly in 1 Restatement of Property, ss. 54,

75 and 84; and see Appendix to this volume, pp. 1-15) they would end when the estate on which they are dependent ends. If not, it may be urged that once they take effect, they continue to subsist despite the occurrence of the terminating event. English case law supports this latter position in the case of the estate tail, and also in the case of a fee simple subject to an executory limitation where the estate in the husband is terminated upon his death by the executory limitation over: see *Buckworth* v. *Thurkill* (1785), 4 Dougl. 323, 99 E.R. 903 (K.B.) (and more fully in 127 E.R. 347, 351n); *Moody* v. *King*, 2 Bing. 447, 130 E.R. 378 (C.P.). On the other hand, as noted earlier, dower is defeated where the husband's estate is terminated by exercise of a power of appointment operating through an executory limitation. Similarly, of course, dower would be defeated or be subordinate to interests or charges external to the limitation of the estate in question where those interests or charges arise before the inchoate right of dower attached; for example, in case of a defect of title in the husband or a vendor's prior right by reason of unpaid purchase money.

Courts in the United States have, on the whole, taken the same view as the English courts. Authority in the United States, however, recognizes the defeasibility of dower on the defeasance of determinable estates in fee simple and estates in fee simple subject to a condition subsequent. For a discussion of the problems in this area, see *Haskins*, The Defeasibility of Dower, (1950) 98 Univ. of Pa. L. Rev. 826; *Note*, (1952) 36 Minn. L. Rev. 280.

It may be noted that in so far as executory limitations are created under a trust, the dower problem will arise only if the husband dies beneficially entitled to his defeasible equitable interest.

5. HOMESTEAD (FAMILY HOME) LEGISLATION

IN ALBERTA (the Dower Act, R.S.A. 1955, c. 90), in British Columbia (the Wife's Protection Act, R.S.B.C. 1960, c. 407; and the Homestead Act, R.S.B.C. 1960, c. 175), in Manitoba (the Dower Act, R.S.M. 1954, c. 65) and in Saskatchewan (the Homesteads Act, R.S.S. 1953, c. 111, am. 1954, c. 21, 1960, c. 10) protect the wife against unilateral disposition by the husband of the family home where title is in his name. The statutes provide for the manner in which consent to a disposition or release of rights given thereby may be effected, and, in specific cases, provide for dispensing with consent. In Alberta the "dower" rights given by the statute exist in favour of husband or wife, as the case may be, and include the survivor's right to a life estate in the homestead, whether the "owner" die testate or intestate. In British Columbia, registration of the homestead is required to obtain protection of the legislation which operates only in favour of a wife. Moreover, the registered homestead is exempt from seizure or sale up to a maximum value of $2,500 for any debt or liability incurred after registration, and in case of the intestacy of the husband his widow and children acquire rights in the homestead. In Manitoba, the husband or wife as the case may be is entitled to the statutory protection given in respect of the homestead of which title is held by the other. The spouse surviving the homestead "owner" becomes entitled to a life estate in the homestead (notwithstanding any devise of the homestead), and in addition (subject to stipulated exceptions) to one-third of the deceased spouse's net estate where the testamentary provision is less; and in this latter connection, an election must be made between the statutory and testamentary benefits. In Saskatchewan, homestead protection is given to the wife only, and on the husband's death, the homestead remains exempt from seizure under execution if it is in use and enjoyment by the widow and children and is necessary for their maintenance and support (see The Exemptions Act, R.S.S. 1953, c. 88, s. 6, am. 1958, c. 51; 1960, c. 9).

The problems raised by this legislation have concerned in the main, the meaning and application of the statutory prescriptions for consent or release of the homestead rights and the extent to which the statutory homestead interests may be asserted against third persons, as for example, creditors of the homestead "owner" and purchasers from him. The following issues may be noted as arising in the cases cited:

Effect of release in a separation agreement on a widow's homestead and other statutory rights: *Pope* v. *Stevens*, [1955] 2 D.L.R. 193, 14 W.W.R. (N.S.) 71, 63 Man. R. 162 (C.A.).

Effectiveness of wife's consent to a "disposition" of the homestead by way of a renewable oil and gas lease: *McColl-Frontenac Oil Co. Ltd.* v. *Hamilton*, [1953] 1 S.C.R. 127, [1953] 1 D.L.R. 721.

Protection of purchaser or mortgagee of a homestead where genuineness of wife's consent is challenged: *Chudyj* v. *Canada Permanent Mortgage Corp.* [1937] 3 D.L.R. 261, [1937] 2 W.W.R. 225, 45 Man. R. 164 (C.A.); *Young* v. *Kinnis*, [1954] 3 D.L.R. 381, 11 W.W.R. (N.S.) 436, 61 Man. R. 374; *Friess and Friess* v. *Imperial Oil Ltd.*, [1954] 4 D.L.R. 100, 12 W.W.R. (N.S.) 151 (Sask. C.A.).

Protection of purchaser or mortgagee where husband swears falsely that property is not a homestead: *Farmers Mutual Petroleums Ltd.* v. *Jackson* (1956), 5 D.L.R. 2d 246, 19 W.W.R. (N.S.) 625 (Sask. C.A.).

Priority as between widow's homestead rights and claims of husband's creditors (where no express statutory provision exists): *Crichton* v. *Zelenitsky*, [1946] 3 D.L.R. 729, [1946] 2 W.W.R. 209, 54 Man. R. 79 (C.A.).

Is the wife's right to a life interest in the homestead after her husband's death affected where the husband's title to the homestead is extinguished by adverse possession? See *Fodchuk* v. *Fodchuk*, [1947] 3 D.L.R. 115, [1947] 1 W.W.R. 846 (Alta.).

There is no common law dower in land held on joint tenancy. Is the situation the same in respect of statutory "dower" under homestead legislation? See *Wimmer* v. *Wimmer*, [1947] 4 D.L.R. 56, [1947] 2 W.W.R. 249, 55 Man. R. 232 (C.A.).

There is no common law dower in an estate at will. Does the wife of a veteran who purchases land under the Veterans' Land Act, R.S.C. 1952, c. 280, as amended, (and is a tenant at will thereunder until he obtains a conveyance) have homestead rights in the land so purchased? See *Nelson* v. *Nelson and the Director, Veterans' Land Act*, [1954] 1 D.L.R. 465, 10 W.W.R. (N.S.) 481 (Alta. C.A.).

6. THE DESERTED WIFE'S OCCUPATION INTEREST IN THE MATRIMONIAL HOME

BENDALL v. McWHIRTER. Court of Appeal. [1952] 2 Q.B. 466, [1952] 1 All E.R. 1307

Plaintiff, as trustee in bankruptcy of defendant's husband, claimed possession, and certain money for use and occupation, of a house in which the spouses had lived and of which the husband held title subject to a mortgage. The husband had deserted defendant and she remained in the house with her children. Later she obtained a maintenance order against the husband and shortly afterwards he was adjudged a bankrupt. Defendant continued to reside in the house and plaintiff paid the taxes. She refused to vacate on his request that she do so to enable him to sell and pay off the mortgage and to distribute the surplus to other creditors. The present proceedings followed and an order was made in plaintiff's favour on the ground that defendant was a licensee whose licence was terminated when plaintiff as the husband's successor demanded possession. It was also held that plaintiff could not invoke s. 17 of the Married Women's Property Act, 1882. Defendant appealed.

DENNING L. J.: This case raises important questions about the right of a deserted wife to stay in the matrimonial home. [His Lordship stated the facts and continued:] The first question is whether the wife has any right of her own to stay in the house. Under the old common law as it existed until seventy years ago she had no rights at all apart from those of her husband. She was treated by the law more like a piece of his furniture than anything else. The husband could not sue her in ejectment or trespass, but neither could he sue a piece of furniture. He could bundle his furniture out into the street and so he could his wife. The law did not say him nay. It merely gave the wife authority to pledge his credit for necessaries. If her husband turned her out, she had to go and find lodgings elsewhere, pledging his credit for the rent, that is, if she could find anyone to trust to his credit. She could not in those days get an order for maintenance against her husband. She had to find someone who would take her in out of pity or charity or on the husband's credit. She could not pledge her own credit for she could not make a contract. Even if the husband did not turn her out, nevertheless, when he ceased for any reason to be entitled to the house she would have to leave it, for she had no right of her own to stay there. Thus, if the husband became bankrupt his assignees in bankruptcy could turn her out just as they could his furniture.

All that has changed now. A wife is no longer her husband's chattel. She is beginning to be regarded by the law as a partner in all affairs which are their common concern. Thus, the husband can no longer turn her out of the matrimonial home. She has as much right as he to stay there even though the house does stand in his name. This has only been decided in the last ten years. It started in 1942 when Goddard, L. J., said that the husband's only way of getting his wife out of the house was to make an application under s. 17 of the Married Women's Property Act, 1882: see *Bramwell* v. *Bramwell* [1942] 1 K.B. 374. That section gives the court a very wide discretion in the matter, and, accordingly, in 1947 when a husband claimed that he had an absolute right to turn his wife out it was held that he had no such right, but that it was a matter for the discretion of the court: see *Hutchinson* v. *Hutchinson*, [1947] 2 All E.R. 792. Very shortly afterwards this court took the same view (*Stewart* v. *Stewart*, [1947] 2 All E.R. 813), and it is now settled law that a deserted wife has a right, as against her husband, to stay in the matrimonial home unless and until an order is made against her under s. 17. In support of this right Judge Willes recently made an order allowing a wife to stay until the husband found alternative accommodation, and restrained the husband from selling the house over her head, and we affirmed that order: *Lee* v. *Lee*, [1952] 1 All E.R. 1299. Moreover, it has been held that the wife's right is effective, not only as against her husband, but also as against the landlord. Thus, where a husband, who was statutory tenant of the matrimonial home, deserted his wife and left the house, it was held that the landlord could not turn her out so long as she paid the rent and performed the conditions of the tenancy. This right as against the landlord is a very special right on her part. She has to assert the right in her husband's name, but the husband cannot prevent her from exercising it. Even if he gives her notice to go, or purports to surrender the tenancy or to submit to judgment, nevertheless, she is entitled to stay: see *Old Gate Estates Ltd.* v. *Alexander*, [1949] 2 All E.R. 822; *Middleton* v. *Baldock*. In the latter case, Sir Raymond Evershed, M. R., put it succinctly and simply in these words ([1950] 1 All E.R. 708, at p. 710): "It seems to me that Mrs. Baldock, as the wife of Mr. Baldock, who had deserted her, beyond doubt was entitled to be in possession and to enjoy any right the tenant had under contract, statute, or otherwise, to live on the premises." In short she has a right of her own, derived no doubt from her husband, but still a right of her own, to assert, on his behalf, the tenant-right in the premises, no matter what her husband may say or do about it.

What is the nature of this right of the deserted wife which the courts have thus evolved? It bears, I think, a very close resemblance to her right to pledge her husband's credit for necessaries. Under the old common law when a husband deserted his wife, or they separated owing to his misconduct, she had an irrevocable authority to pledge his credit for necessaries: *Bolton* v. *Prentice*, (1744), 93 E.R. 1136, quoted in the notes to *Manby* v. *Scot*, (1663), 83 E.R. 1065 (2 Smith L.C. 13th ed. 469). One of the most obvious necessaries of a wife is a roof over her head, and if we apply the old rule to modern conditions it seems only reasonable to hold that when the husband is the tenant of the matrimonial home the wife should have an irrevocable authority to continue the tenancy on his credit, and that when he is the owner of it she should have an irrevocable authority to stay there. This authority, like the old one, is based on an irrebuttable presumption of law. The husband cannot revoke it except by order of the court under s. 17 of the Act of 1882. In my opinion, therefore, the right of a deserted wife to stay in the matrimonial home proceeds out of an irrevocable authority which the husband is presumed in law to have conferred on her. This accounts for the fact that the husband cannot turn the wife out. It also accounts for the fact that, as against the landlord, the wife must assert her right in the husband's name. The authority which is thus conferred on her is an authority to stay in the house until the court orders her to go out. This authority flows from the status of marriage, coupled with the fact of separation owing to the husband's misconduct. It ceases when the marriage comes to an end by death or divorce: *Robson* v. *Headland* (1948) 64 T.L.R. 596; but it does not cease when there is a judicial separation: *Hutchinson* v. *Hutchinson*. The authority is, of course, purely personal to her. She alone can exercise it. She cannot assign it. It does not give her any legal interest in the land. She may, perhaps, sub-let some of the rooms so as to help keep herself, but even then, she does so, not out of any legal interest of her own in the land, but on the presumed authority of her husband. Her possession is not always exclusive. If the husband has only been guilty of desertion and nothing else he is entitled to come back at any time asking to be forgiven, and she is then bound to receive him. She cannot then keep him out of his house. But if he has, in addition to desertion, been guilty of cruelty or adultery, she is not bound to take him back. She can keep him out of the house. Her possession may then be quite exclusive. But, whether her possession is exclusive or not, there can be no doubt that she is not a tenant of her husband. She has only a personal privilege with no legal interest in the land, and she is, therefore, only a licensee: see *Errington* v. *Errington*, [1952] 1 All E.R. 149. Her occupation is comparable with that of a contractual licensee, the only difference being that a contractual licence is revocable in accordance with the terms of the contract, whereas her licence is not revocable except by an order of the court. Sometimes her occupation is put by the parties on a contractual footing. Thus, when they are making the necessary arrangements consequent on desertion, the husband often agrees to let the wife live in the house until he has found her other accommodation, and she in return agrees to accept a lesser amount of maintenance on that account. That is what happened in *Cristel* v. *Cristel*, [1951] 2 All E.R. 574, *Thompson* v. *Earthy*, [1951] 2 All E.R. 235, and the present case. When such arrangements are made the wife's occupation rests, not on a presumed authority of the husband, but on an express authority which is coextensive with it. In any case, however, the position of the wife is that she is a licensee with a special right under which her husband cannot turn her out except by an order of the court.

Such being the nature of the wife's right, the next question is whether it is binding on the trustee in bankruptcy....

...There is no authority on this point. I have had the advantage of reading the judgment of Romer, L. J., in which he holds that the trustee does take subject to the wife's right. I entirely agree with him, but for my own part I feel it necessary to go further and inquire what is the quality of the wife's right that it should lead to this result. I start with this. The wife's right is very analogous to a contractual licence to occupy land. It is, indeed, so analogous that I think no valid distinction can be made between them. If a contractual licence is not binding on the trustee in bankruptcy, but only gives rise to a right of proof, then I cannot think that the wife's right is binding on him, for it is of no higher quality, but if a contractual licence is binding on the trustee, like a lien, then I think the wife's right should also be binding on him.

We have recently held in this court that a contractual licence to occupy land is binding on the devisee of the licensor: see *Errington* v. *Errington*; and it seems to follow that it is also binding on his trustee in bankruptcy. Counsel for the plaintiff did not, indeed, contend the contrary. I put to him the case where a licensor grants the "front of the house" rights in a theatre to a licensee who goes into occupation of the rights and then the licensor goes bankrupt, and he conceded that the trustee in bankruptcy would be bound by the licence. Reason and justice both demand that this should be so, and I would not have felt it necessary to pursue the matter further but for the fact that the decision in *Errington* v. *Errington* was questioned before us in another case. I have, therefore, felt it necessary to re-consider the matter.

The objection that is made is that a contractual licence only gives rise to contractual obligations and not to any proprietary, rights or interests, and that the burden of it does not, therefore, run with the land. [His Lordship here reviewed the authorities on the extent to which a contractual licensee may assert his licence against successors of the licensor, and then continued as follows:] My conclusion, therefore, is that a contractual licensee, who is in actual occupation of land by virtue of the licence, has an interest which is valid, if not at law at any rate in equity, against the successors in title of the licensor, including therein his trustee in bankruptcy. It is not a legal interest in land, like a tenancy, but a clog or fetter like a lien. It is a personal right, but it is, nevertheless, binding on successors of the licensor, so long as the conditions of the licence are observed.

The third and last question is whether a deserted wife is in the same position as a contractual licensee. It has been suggested that the husband's right to apply under s. 17 of the Act of 1882 for possession is personal to the husband and does not extend to his successor. Hence it is said that the successor must be able to sue at law for possession because it is inconceivable that he should have no means of getting her out. That was the argument which prevailed with ROXBURGH, J., in *Thompson* v. *Earthy*, and with the county court judge in the present case. It seems to me, however, that one answer to it may be this: Although an application under s. 17 has to be made in the husband's name, nevertheless, a successor in title can compel the husband to allow his name to be used for the purpose. If the husband sells the house there is an implied assignment by the husband of his right to obtain possession, and equity has always compelled an assignor to allow an action to be brought in his name. So, if the husband becomes bankrupt, the trustee can compel the husband to allow his name to be used for an application under s. 17: see s. 22 (3) and s. 38 (b) of the Bankruptcy Act, 1914. Alternatively, the trustee in bankruptcy can make an application under s. 105 (1) for an order that the wife do give up possession. In either case the court which deals with the application is enabled under the relevant section to do whatever is just. I must say, however, that, even if a successor cannot compel the husband to apply under s. 17, but the successor has himself to bring an action at law, nevertheless, I should have thought the court would have a discretion whether to order possession, for that is the only way in which effect can be given to the wife's right as now established. Any other view would lead to great injustice. It would mean that a guilty husband could transfer the house into the name of his new mistress and then get her to evict his innocent lawful wife from the matrimonial home. No civilised community could tolerate such a cynical disregard of the married state. Equity demands that the successor in title should be in no better position than the husband.

The result of the whole case is that the wife's right to stay in the matrimonial home does not come to an end automatically on the husband's bankruptcy. The trustee in bankruptcy takes subject to equities. He takes, therefore, subject to her right, for it is an equity. The trustee must apply to the court for possession, and the judge who hears the case will take into account the various competing interests. He will have regard to the fact that, so far as existing assets are concerned, the general body of creditors have a substantial priority over the wife because they can prove for the debts due to them, but she cannot prove for arrears of maintenance due to her. He will also remember that, so far as the bankrupt's personal earnings are concerned, the wife has a substantial priority over the creditors because the bankrupt has to support his wife and children out of his earnings before any of it goes to the creditors. If she is allowed to stay in the matrimonial home she gets less maintenance, and the creditors get more out of his personal earnings. But if she is turned out of the matrimonial home she will be entitled to more maintenance out of his earnings and there will be less available for the creditors. In these circumstances the justice of the case may often be met by allowing the wife to stay in the house temporarily until she finds alternative accommodation, and the court can make appropriate orders to that end.

In the present action the trustee claims that in point of law as soon as the husband became bankrupt the wife became a trespasser and liable for mesne profits. I do not think the claim is well founded. The wife has an equitable right to stay which is binding on the trustee in bankruptcy. He has no absolute right to eject her. It is a matter for the discretion of the court. In my opinion, the appeal should succeed and judgment be entered for the wife.

ROMER L. J.: The position of a deserted wife who is left by her husband in occupation of the matrimonial home has been considered by the courts lately on a number of occasions. In *Errington* v. *Errington* DENNING, L. J., in referring to some of these authorities, said ([1952] 1 All E.R. 155): "... there are numerous cases where a wife who has been deserted by her husband and left by him in the matrimonial home has been held to be, not a tenant of the husband owner... nor a bare licensee... but to be in a special position—a licensee with a special right—under which the husband cannot turn her out except by an order of the court." I respectfully adopt this as a correct statement of the position of such a wife. She has no legal or equitable interest in the home which she continues to occupy and in that respect is in no better position than any other licensee. On the other hand, her husband, the licensor, cannot bring proceedings against her in ejectment, for the status of matrimony prevents it. He, accordingly, cannot effectively revoke her licence and in this respect the wife is in a more favourable position than that of an ordinary licensee.

The question is (and it is, I think, a difficult one) whether the special protection which a wife enjoys against ejectment at the instance of her husband avails her against similar action by the husband's trustee in bankruptcy. The plaintiff in the present case argues that it does not, and he says that the wife is trying to create in favour of herself a novel species of interest in property or a new kind of equity, such as the court refused to recognise in *Thompson* v. *Earthy*. It is common ground that when the debtor was adjudicated bankrupt the whole of his property (with certain irrelevant exceptions) vested in his trustee in bankruptcy and became divisible amongst his creditors: Bankruptcy Act, 1914, s. 18 (1) and s. 38. "Property" is defined by s. 167 of the Act, and, undoubtedly, included the husband's equity of redemption in the matrimonial home. It is also common ground that in general the trustee takes no better title to the property than the bankrupt had and he takes subject to the same equities as affected the property in the bankrupt's hands. DENNING, L. J., in his judgment has dealt with the latter principle and has expressed the view that the right which the deserted wife enjoyed at the date of her husband's bankruptcy constituted an enforceable equity which operated as a bar to the plaintiff's claim in these proceedings. The same result is arrived at, I think, by approaching the question from a somewhat different angle and I will confine my observations to that approach.

The debtor's right of dealing with the property was subject to the clog or fetter that the house had an occupant whom he could not, of his own volition, eject, and there was, accordingly, to this extent a restriction on his beneficial ownership of the property. If the trustee after the bankruptcy could sue the wife for possession it could only be on the footing that the property vested in him free from this restriction, and it would follow from this that he acquired a larger beneficial interest in the property than that which the debtor had previously enjoyed. It would also follow that a third person automatically lost a special feature attaching to a licence which the debtor had granted for value and was relegated to the position of an ordinary licensee, and that the deterioration of that person's position and the improvement of the trustee's would be commensurate in relation to each other.

Counsel for the plaintiff argued that these were the necessary and natural results of the bankruptcy law. What is vested in the trustee, he said, was the freehold of the property, and (apart from the mortgagee) nobody but the debtor had any legal or equitable interest in that property. The wife's licence depended on her husband's ownership of the property and could not survive the vesting thereof in the trustee. This vesting carried with it (under s. 22 (2) of the Bankruptcy Act, 1914) the right to possession and the passing of that right was destructive of licences that had been granted by the debtor previously. In this connection counsel relied on a principle which has been recognised in *Brown* v. *Draper* and other cases, namely, that a wife cannot claim the benefit of her husband's statutory tenancy after his interest as statutory tenant has been validly determined. That, of course, is true. Every subordinate interest must perish with the superior interest on which it is dependent. The argument, however, does not appear to me to be convincing. The superior interest in the present case was the ownership of the house and that has not been extinguished. It is still alive and is vested in the trustee. The real point, as I see it, is whether it became so vested subject to or free from a particular incident which was attached to it in the debtor's hands prior to the vesting. If it is now free from the bankrupt's disability to sue the wife for possession, the plaintiff's action must succeed.

This view, however, seems to me to involve a departure from the general rule, to which I have already referred, that a trustee takes no better title to property than the bankrupt had. This rule is fully, and (I think) accurately, stated in Halsbury's Laws of England, Hailsham ed., vol. 2, p. 209, as follows: "The property of the bankrupt passes to the trustee in the same plight and condition in which it was in the bankrupt's hands, and is subject to all the equities and liabilities which affected it in the bankrupt's hands, and to all dispositions which have been validly made by the bankrupt, and to all rights which have been validly acquired by third persons at the commencement of the bankruptcy, unless the property which the trustee takes is released by some express provision of the bankruptcy law." Examples of such provisions are those relating to fraudulent conveyances and preferences. A licence of the special character which the debtor in the present case created in favour of his wife appears to me to be, at all events, by analogy, prima facie within the general principle as above stated, and I can see no sufficient reason for excluding such a licence from it. In my opinion, accordingly, the trustee is no more entitled than was the debtor prior to his bankruptcy to revoke the wife's licence on his own authority and to sue her for possession of the property. It is said that if the wife's right to possession is binding on the trustee, then the title of the latter to the property is not only not better than that which the debtor had had, but is worse because he cannot, as the husband could have done, apply to the court for possession under s. 17 of the Married Women's Property Act, 1882, with the result that the wife can remain in the house without paying rent and without any fear of being dispossessed. As to this counsel for the defendant suggested that an application under s. 17 could still be made either by the husband on the compulsion of the trustee or by the trustee himself by virtue of s. 38 (b) of the Bankruptcy Act, 1914, the debtor himself being made a party to the application. I doubt this. Section 17 provides in effect that on the application of either a husband or wife the court may, in any question that arises between them, make orders as to the title to or possession of property. Theoretically the trustee might be able to compel the husband to apply: s. 22 (2) of the Bankruptcy Act, 1914, but apart from the unsatisfactory nature of such a procedure the application could scarcely be regarded as one made in a question between husband and wife, for the issue would in substance be between the husband's creditors, on the one hand, and the wife, on the other. This comment would be equally true of an application made by the trustee in bankruptcy, and, further, such an application would not be by the husband even though he were made a party to it.

I confess, accordingly, that I entertain some doubt whether the jurisdiction of the court under s. 17 could be invoked. On the other hand, if the defendant were to persist in remaining in possession without payment of rent, or if no other arrangement agreeable both to her and to the trustee can be arrived at, I see no reason why the matter should not be resolved in the bankruptcy proceedings under s. 105 (1) of the Bankruptcy Act, 1914. It is well settled that under that provision the bankruptcy court has power to determine questions affecting persons who are not parties to the bankruptcy, and, in my opinion, it would be well within the powers of the court, on a motion by the trustee, to decide whether the defendant should be permitted to remain in occupation of what was the matrimonial home, and if so on what terms, or whether she should be required to deliver up possession. On such an application the court would doubtless take into account all the matters that would be relevant to the exercise of the discretion conferred by s. 17 of the Married Women's Property Act, 1882, and, in particular, the fact that the wife cannot prove in the bankruptcy for payments due under the maintenance order and that the magistrates in making that order almost certainly regarded the wife's right to occupy the house as relevant to the amount which they directed her husband to pay. If, as I believe, the matter could be dealt with in this way, the wife's position in relation to the property would be substantially the same as it was before her husband's bankruptcy and the trustee would, in effect, succeed to the position of the debtor.

Appeal allowed.

[SOMERVELL L. J., agreed with ROMER L. J.

Section 17 of the Married Women's Property Act, 1882 (Imp.), c. 75 provides in its material part that "in any question between husband and wife as to the title to or possession of property, either party... may apply in a summary way to... a judge... [who] may make such order with respect to the property in dispute... as he thinks fit...." Similar provision is made by the Married Women's Property Act, R.S.B.C. 1960, c. 233, s. 29; Married Women's Property Act, R.S.M. 1954, c. 156, s. 8; Married Woman's Property Act, R.S.N.B. 1952, c. 140, s. 7; Married Women's Property Act, R.S.Nfld. 1952, c. 143, s. 19; Married Women's Property Act, R.S.N.S. 1954, c. 168, s. 38; Married Woman's Property Act, R.S.O. 1960, c. 229, s. 12; Married Women's Property Act, R.S.P.E.I. 1951, c. 92, s. 13; Married Women's Property Act, R.S.S. 1953, c. 304, s. 22.

The deserted wife's occupation interest has been recognized in Ontario: see *Carnochan* v. *Carnochan*, [1953] O.R. 887, [1954] 1 D.L.R. 87, aff'd [1954] 4 D.L.R. 448, [1954] O.W.N. 543; appeal quashed on one point and judgment below affirmed on another, [1955] S.C.R. 669, [1955] 4 D.L.R. 81.

Is it open to a wife, whether deserted or not, to assert an occupation interest in the matrimonial home under the homestead legislation of the Western Provinces? Distinguish the situation where a husband, in certain circumstances (as, for example, where the spouses are living apart), applies to dispense with his wife's consent to sale of the homestead: see *Re Milwarde-Yates*, [1954] 4 D.L.R. 159 (B.C.). Cf. *Re Tate and Tate* (1955), 15 W.W.R. (N.S.) 321 (B.C.).]

RE JOLLOW AND JOLLOW. Court of Appeal. [1954] O.R. 895, [1955] 1 D.L.R. 601

ROACH J. A.: The parties are husband and wife, having been married in or about the year 1920. On or about August 20, 1953, the husband left the matrimonial home and since that date they have lived separate and apart from one another.

At the date of their separation and prior thereto they occupied as their matrimonial home land and premises consisting of part of Township Lot 17 in the eleventh concession of the Township of Brock in the County of Ontario. Since their separation the wife has continued to occupy those premises. Those lands and premises are held in joint tenancy by the parties.

On an application made by the husband under the *Partition Act*, R.S.O. 1950, c. 269, for the partition or sale of those lands, His Honour Judge Pritchard, Local Judge, made an order dated March 9, 1954, that they be sold under the supervision of the Local Master at Whitby. The order is in the usual form, and in addition specifically provides that upon the sale the wife do forthwith vacate those lands.

This is an appeal by the wife against that order.

From the material filed it appears that the husband deserted his wife. From August 20th, the date on which he left the matrimonial home, until October 20th of that year, he paid his wife $10 weekly for her support and maintenance. He then stopped all payments to her. The wife then applied under the *Deserted Wives' and Children's Maintenance Act*, R.S.O. 1950, c. 102, and obtained an order against her husband for the payment to her of $10 weekly commencing on January 4, 1954. That order is still in full force and effect.

The learned local Judge in his reasons does not state in terms that the wife is a deserted wife, but I think it is inherent in his reasons that on the conflicting material before him he concluded that she was a deserted wife.

The husband in his affidavit filed stated that "in substance [he] did not desert [his] wife but was ordered by her from the property in question". I do not know what he means by "in substance".

In my opinion, a *prima facie* case of desertion has been established and not rebutted by the husband.

It was argued by counsel for the appellant, firstly, that s. 7 of the *Married Women's Property Act*, R.S.O. 1950, c. 223, is a bar to proceedings under the *Partition Act* by a husband with respect to property of which he and his wife are co-owners. Section 7 is as follows: "Every married woman shall have in her own name against all persons, including her husband, the same remedies for the protection and security of her own separate property as if such property belonged to her as a *feme sole*, but, except as aforesaid no husband or wife shall be entitled to sue the other for a tort."

[His Lordship, after considering the question raised by appellant's counsel, concluded that partition proceedings are not founded on tort, and hence s. 7 of the Married Women's Property Act was not a bar to the husband's application.]

It was next argued by counsel for the appellant that because the wife had been deserted, an order for the sale of the matrimonial home in which she was residing should not have been made under the *Partition Act* and could only be made on an application under s. 12 (1) of the *Married Women's Property Act*. That argument is sound and must prevail....

On an application made under the *Partition Act* the Judge is limited in his jurisdiction to the making of an order for partition or for sale or the dismissal of the application. On an application under s. 12 (1) of the *Married Women's Property Act* the Judge has much wider jurisdiction. He may make such order as he thinks fit.

In *Bendall* v. *McWhirter*, [1952] 1 All E.R. 1307, the Court of Appeal in England held that it is now settled law there that a deserted wife has a right as against her husband to stay in the matrimonial home unless and until an order is made against her under s. 17 of the English

Married Women's Property Act, 1882, c. 75. Section 12 (1) of the Ontario Act is substantially the same as s. 17 of the English Act....

That decision of course is not binding in this Province but in my opinion the logic of Denning L. J. is so compelling that it should be followed.

It was followed by Schroeder J. in *Carnochan* v. *Carnochan*, [1954] 1 D.L. R.87, [1953] O.R. 887, and his judgment was affirmed on appeal to this Court, [1954] 4 D.L.R. 448, O.W.N. 543.

The learned Local Judge relied upon the decision of LeBel J. in *Brown* v. *Brown*, [1953] 1 D.L.R. 158, [1952] O.W.N. 725. In that case the husband had deserted his wife, but LeBel J. nevertheless, on an application by the husband for the partition or sale of the matrimonial home of which the husband and wife were co-owners, made an order for its sale. From the reasons of that learned Judge it would appear that the question of desertion as a bar to an order under that Act was not argued before him. LeBel J.'s reasons were delivered on October 3, 1952. The judgment in *Bendall* v. *McWhirter* had been delivered on May 5, 1952, and apparently had not come to the attention of LeBel J.

If a husband who has deserted his wife is prepared to make some other provision for her in lieu of her right to continue to reside in the matrimonial home, or if he contends that there are other circumstances that render it just that she should relinquish that right, he can make his submissions to the Judge clothed with jurisdiction to make the appropriate order. A Judge hearing an application under the *Partition Act* has no such authority.

This appeal should be allowed and the order for sale should be set aside, with costs here and below.

AYLESWORTH J. A. agreed with ROACH J. A.

CHEVRIER J. A., dissenting:... The appellant's submission is that the learned County Court Judge was without jurisdiction to make this order, for the reason, he says, that this is not a case where the *Partition Act* applies, because the appellant being a deserted wife, the application should have been made under s. 12 of the *Married Women's Property Act*. That section deals with cases wherein the subject-matter as between husband and wife is the title to or possession of property.

It is submitted by the appellant that wherever the husband of a deserted wife seeks to recover possession of the matrimonial home or property he must proceed under said s. 12. With that proposition I have no quarrel. I am of the opinion that that is the proper procedure even where the wife is not a deserted wife. But the appellant argues further that even when the husband seeks partition or sale and his wife is a deserted wife, the *Partition Act* does not apply but that the application is to be made under s. 12.

This feature first came up in *Dickson* v. *Dickson*, [1948] O.W.N. 325. That was an application by a wife for an order of partition and sale of lands held by her and her husband as joint tenants. On a question of exercise of judicial discretion the learned trial Judge, LeBel J., refused the application, but he went on to say: "Furthermore, nothing in s. 12 (1) of The Married Women's Property Act, R.S.O. 1937, c. 209, affects the situation, in my view; but in any case, the section does not apply as there is here no question as to 'title or possession' between this husband and wife. The applicant makes no claim for possession of the property, and such possession as the respondent has is incidental to his title as a joint tenant." It may be noted that there the wife was the applicant and she was not shown to have been a "deserted wife".

The matter again came up in the case of *Minaker* v. *Minaker*, [1949], 1 D.L.R. 801, S.C.R. 397. That was a case where after a decree *nisi* had been granted in a divorce action at the instance of the husband, this latter demanded in an ordinary action started by writ of summons, possession and *mesne* profits. The feature of *mesne* profits being an action in tort, it could not be entertained as against the wife. But Kerwin J. (as he then was) said at p. 802 D.L.R., p. 399 S.C.R.: "The litigation has already put the parties to considerable expense and we deem it advisable to treat the matter as if proceedings under s. 12 of the *Married Women's Property Act* had been taken." And he added, on the same page: "While the husband is entitled to judgment for possession, he is not entitled to mesne profits."

That was not an action for partition and sale, nor was it the case of a deserted wife, but a straight case by the husband seeking to obtain possession of the matrimonial home after having obtained a decree nisi in an action for divorce against his wife.

[His Lordship then reviewed *Re Hutcheson and Hutcheson*, [1950] O.R. 265, [1950] 2 D.L.R. 751; *Brown* v. *Brown*, [1953] 1 D.L.R. 158, [1952] O.W.N. 725; *Carnochan* v. *Carnochan*, [1953] O.R. 887, [1954] 1 D.L.R. 87; *Davis* v. *Davis*, [1954] O.R. 23, [1954] 1 D.L.R. 827, and continued as follows:]

From the above cases in our own Courts, it would appear that an action for partition or sale at the instance of the husband or the wife, be she deserted or not, is one class of action; and that when either party seek title or possession that the issue then becomes the subject-matter of s. 12 of our *Married Women's Property Act*.

[His Lordship then referred to and considered *Bendall* v. *McWhirter* and said:]

This in my opinion is a totally different situation from that which arises in a partition or sale, where the husband does not, in either case of a partition or sale remain in or obtain possession of the matrimonial home....

But in *Lloyds Bank Ltd.* v. *Oliver's Trustee*, [1953] 2 All E.R. 1443, Upjohn J. at p. 1448 makes it clear that the wife's right to remain in the matrimonial home is not in the nature of an irrevocable licence arising on her entry therein, but arises only after she has been deserted. That again is a case where the husband sought (here he was replaced by the Trustee in Bankruptcy) to obtain full possession of the home for his own exclusive benefit.

In *Ferris* v. *Weaven*, [1952] 2 All E.R. 233, a husband after deserting his wife wrote her saying: "I will carry on paying on the house [the matrimonial home] providing you do not annoy me." The wife continued to reside in the house and the husband paid the rates. After ten years the husband sold the house to a friend at a nominal sum and the purchaser took with full knowledge of all the facts, in an attempt to enable the husband to defeat the wife's rights. Action was taken by the purchaser to obtain possession of the house. It was held that the wife was a licensee with a contractual right to remain in the house as a result of the arrangement made with her husband, and the action was dismissed.

By no stretch of the imagination can this be assimilated to an action by a husband for a partition or sale of the common property.

In *Lloyds Bank Ltd.* v. *Oliver's Trustee*, *supra*, a wife who had been deserted by her husband, the mortgagor of the matrimonial home, asserted, against the mortgagees, a right to remain in possession. The wife applied under s. 17 of the *Married Women's Property Act*, 1882, for an order against the husband to permit her and her children to reside in the matrimonial home until further order. An order was made granting her request. The right arose when the husband deserted her.

There does not appear to be in Ontario any reported case on the point at issue herein. No action for partition or sale between husband and wife has ever been decided according to the principle suggested by the appellant....

Our partition or sale practice is well known and has long been established in sound principle. In such an action neither title to nor possession of the matrimonial domicile is sought by the husband against the wife, be she deserted or not. Where, between a deserted wife and her husband, the title to or the possession of the matrimonial domicile is sought by the husband, the practice is to proceed under s. 12 of the *Married Women's Property Act*.

In conclusion, in my opinion an action for partition and sale, be it between husband and wife and be the wife a deserted one or not, is fundamentally different from an action between husband and wife, be the wife a deserted one or not, where the question between them is as to the title to or the possession of property. The conduct of each action is regulated by its own respective procedure.

I therefore find here that the action for partition and sale was well founded in law. I further see no valid reason why the learned trial Judge's findings of fact should not be accepted, as I do.

Appeal allowed.

[Is there in Ontario any incompatibility between a deserted wife's exercise of her right to occupy the matrimonial home and the continued assertion of her inchoate right of dower?

In *Vaughan* v. *Vaughan*, [1953] 1 Q.B. 762, [1953] 1 All E.R. 209 (C.A.), it was held that a deserted wife's occupation interest terminated on divorce and that she had no more than a revocable licence under her husband's statement at the time of desertion that she could "always live there".

If the matrimonial home is a leasehold held by the husband, does the deserted wife's occupation interest survive termination of the tenancy, whether by effluxion of time or expiry of a notice to quit or by surrender or otherwise? See Note, (1956) 72 Law Q. Rev. 477, commenting on *Adamson* v. *Busch*, [1955] V.L.R. 450.

Where the matrimonial home has been purchased with money contributed by both spouses and the husband, after deserting his wife, sells the property (to which he holds title) what is the wife's position? See *Rimmer* v. *Rimmer*, [1953] 1 Q.B. 63, [1952] 2 All E.R. 863 (C.A.).

The "family assets" principle of *Rimmer* v. *Rimmer* was rejected by the Supreme Court of Canada in *Thompson* v. *Thompson*, [1961] S.C.R. 3, 26 D.L.R. 2d 1, in which the Court also shied away from supporting a property interest of the deserted wife in her occupation of the matrimonial home. See *Laskin*, The Deserted Wife's Equity in the Matrimonial Home: A Dissent (1961), 14 Univ. of Tor. L.J. 67.]

WESTMINSTER BANK LD. v. LEE. Chancery Division. [1956] Ch. 7, [1955] 2 All E.R. 883

Defendant husband created an equitable mortgage on the matrimonial home in plaintiff's favour on November 10, 1948, following a deposit of the title deeds on the previous day. Some weeks earlier, on or about September 2, 1948, he had deserted his wife but plaintiff bank was unaware of this fact until after the equitable mortgage was created. In 1951 the wife obtained an order permitting her to reside in the matrimonial home unless and until the husband provided suitable alternative accommodation and restraining him by sale or assignment from evicting her: see *Lee* v. *Lee*, [1952] 1 All E.R. 1299, [1952] 2 Q.B. 489n., [1952] 1 T.L.R. 968 (C.A.).

The bank took these proceedings to enforce its equitable mortgage and it joined the wife as a defendant in order to secure an order of sale with vacant possession.

UPJOHN J. (after considering and rejecting the bank's contention that it was entitled to be subrogated to the rights of a prior legal mortgagee whose mortgage had been discharged in part by an advance from the bank): I turn, therefore, to Mr. Mills's second main point, namely, that the wife, though deserted before the date of the bank's mortgage, has no interest in the premises which can affect the bank's rights as mortgagees....

Mr. Foster, for the wife, was constrained to concede that, since *Woodcock (Jess B.) & Sons Ld.* v. *Hobbs*, [1955] 1 W.L.R. 152; [1955] 1 All E.R. 445, a decision of the Court of Appeal, she has no right to stay on in the house indefinitely, but only until such time as the court in its discretion orders the wife to go out. He submitted, however, that, in exercising its discretion, the court will recognize that the wife has been deserted, and as such has an interest in the property taking priority over the bank's mortgage, and will therefore allow a substantial period after decree of foreclosure absolute before ordering her to deliver up possession. As a practical matter, therefore, the case lies in a narrow compass and it ultimately becomes a question of how long the wife will be allowed to stay in possession; but, if the wife can establish that she has some equity having priority over the mortgage, that will enable her to plead with some force for a longer period, by some months, than if she has no rights as against the mortgagee. That may be an important matter for the wife, and I must determine it.

The first question is whether the right of the deserted wife to occupation of the matrimonial home is purely personal between husband and wife, so that an assignee of the husband (other than a trustee in bankruptcy) taking even with notice would not be affected at all by any right of the wife against the husband himself to remain in possession, or whether such right constitutes an equity binding all but purchasers for value without notice. That point was left open by the majority of the Court of Appeal in *Bendall* v. *McWhirter*, [1952] 2 Q.B. 466; [1952] 1 T.L.R. 1332; [1952] 1 All E.R. 1307.

In favour of the view that the right is purely personal is the decision of Roxburgh J. in *Thompson* v. *Earthy*, [1951] 2 K.B. 596; [1951] 2 T.L.R. 82; [1951] 2 All E.R. 235, and the remarks of Jenkins L. J. in *Bradley-Hole* v. *Cusen*, [1953] 1 Q.B. 300, 306; sub nom. *Hole* v. *Cuzen* [1953] 1 All E.R. 87. In the later case of *Woodcock (Jess B.) & Sons Ld.* v. *Hobbs*, [1955] 1 W.L.R. 152, Parker L. J. (ibid. 160) expressed great difficulty in extending the wife's right to possession against a purchaser with or without notice, and stated that he would require further argument before determining the point.

Harman J. in *Barclays Bank Ld.* v. *Bird*, [1954] Ch. 274, plainly preferred this view. In the last three cases I have mentioned the remarks were obiter.

Against that view are the observations of Denning L. J. in *Bendall* v. *McWhirter*, [1952] 2 Q.B. 466, and in *Woodcock (Jess B.) & Sons Ld.* v. *Hobbs*, [1955] 1 W.L.R. 152, and I think it is fair to say that as I read the judgment of Birkett L. J. in the last case he did not dissent from the views of Denning L. J. These observations were again obiter.

In *Ferris* v. *Weaven*, [1952] 2 All E.R. 233; [1952] W.N. 318, a decision of Jones J., the ratio decidendi was that a purchaser with notice is bound by the wife's right to possession; but it is not a satisfactory authority for the proposition under discussion because, as Parker L. J. pointed out in *Woodcock* v. *Hobbs*, [1955] 1 W.L.R. 152, and Harman J. in *Bird's* case, [1954] Ch. 274, the decision could be justified on its own special facts.

In *Street* v. *Denham*, [1954] 1 W.L.R. 624; [1954] 1 All E.R. 532, Lynskey J., against his own view, considered that he was bound to hold that a purchaser for value taking with notice was bound. It is true that in that case the plaintiff was the husband's mistress, but unlike *Ferris* v. *Weaven*, [1952] 2 All E.R. 233, the plaintiff appears to have paid the purchase-money, nor was the sale obviously collusive, as it plainly was in *Ferris* v. *Weaven*. Indeed, the husband appears to have behaved not unreasonably, being willing, at any rate at one stage, to provide alternative accommodation for the wife, which she refused.

My own view coincides closely with that of Harman J. in *Bird's* case, [1954] Ch. 274, namely, that a deserted wife has no more than a status of irremovability by the husband; but, so far as this court is concerned, I think I ought to follow the decision of Lynskey J. on this point, as he carefully considered the matter and the earlier authorities, and accordingly to hold that a wife has an equity which is enforceable against purchasers taking with notice.

Now the bank's charge is equitable, and therefore it takes subject to all equities affecting the land whether it has notice of them or not, subject only to the following qualification. The Court of Equity has been careful to distinguish between two kinds of equities, first, an equity which creates an estate or interest in the land and, secondly, an equity which falls short of that. An equitable mortgagee takes subject to all prior equitable estates or interests in the land whether he has notice of them or not, but in relation to a mere equity it is otherwise; the defence of purchaser for value without notice may be available by the owner of an equitable estate against the owner of a prior equity. The principle was laid down by Lord Westbury L. C. sitting at first instance in *Phillips* v. *Phillips* (1862) 4 De G.F. & J. 208; [and] the relevant passages in his judgment are set out and followed in a subsequent judgment of a great master of equity, Fry J., in *Cave* v. *Cave*, (1880) 15 Ch. D. 639....

The decision of the majority of the Court of Appeal in *Bendall* v. *McWhirter* is clear. Romer L. J., with whom Somervell L. J. agreed, said (at p. 485): "She has no legal or equitable interest in the home which she continues to occupy, and in that respect is in no better position than any other licensee."

In the same case Denning L. J. was careful not to describe a deserted wife as having an equitable estate or interest in the land. He described it in these terms (at p. 484): "the trustee in bankruptcy... takes therefore subject to her right, for it is an equity." It is true that the Lord Justice compared the wife's rights to that of a contractual licensee, whose rights in turn were described (at p. 483) as a "clog or fetter like a lien." A lien does not of necessity connote an interest in property, and I do not think Denning L. J. meant to suggest thereby that a deserted wife has an estate or interest in the land. If he did it was inconsistent with the view of the majority of the court. Moreover, the protection afforded to a contractual licensee, as *Winter Garden Theatre (London) Ld.* v. *Millennium Productions Ld.*, [1948] A.C. 173; 63 T.L.R. 529; [1947] 2 All E.R. 331, has made clear, does not depend upon the licensee having an estate or interest in the land, for normally at all events he will not, but upon the power of equity to restrain a breach of contract. See the judgment of Lord Greene M. R. in the Court of Appeal, [1946] 1 All E.R. 684, 685, and the speech of Lord Uthwatt in the House of Lords, [1948] A.C. 202.

In my judgment, the right of a deserted wife to remain in the matrimonial home, put at its highest, is a mere equity, and no equitable estate or interest in that home is created in her favour upon desertion. Accordingly the bank, although only a subsequent equitable mortgagee, can, like the owner of a legal estate, if the facts warrant it, plead the defence of purchaser for value without notice; and to this question I now turn.

It is not in dispute that the bank had no actual notice of the desertion before the execution of the charge, and the question is whether they had constructive notice by reason of the continued occupation of the matrimonial home by the wife as a deserted wife at the time of such execution.

Actual occupation of premises by a tenant or a stranger gives constructive notice of the rights of such tenant or stranger to a purchaser: *Hunt* v. *Luck*, a decision of Farwell J., [1901] 1 Ch. 45; 17 T.L.R. 3, affirmed in the Court of Appeal, [1902] 1 Ch. 428, 18 T.L.R. 265. Section 3 of the Conveyancing Act, 1882, only codified the law.

In *Bendall* v. *McWhirter*, [1952] 2 Q.B. 466, Denning L. J., (at p. 483) applied this doctrine without qualification to the case of a deserted wife. With all respect, I think his observations, which were obiter, went too far. In the first place, rightly or wrongly, the view is generally held in the profession that section 199 (1) (i) of the Law of Property Act, 1925, altered the law where the occupier enjoys possession of unregistered land by some instrument or matter capable of registration, for section 14 of the Law of Property Act only applied to Part I of that Act and not to section 199.

So far as this case is concerned, however, this point is academic....

Secondly, in my judgment, this doctrine that notice of the rights of those in occupation will be imputed to a purchaser must be applied to the occupation of a deserted wife with great caution. The doctrine is only an illustration of the governing principle to be found now in section 199 (1) (ii) (a) of the Law of Property Act, 1925, replacing section 3 of the Act of 1882 with amendments, that the purchaser or mortgagee will be bound by constructive notice if knowledge of the particular matter (in this case desertion) would have come to his knowledge "...if such inquiries and inspections had been made as ought reasonably to have been made by him." That is the question to be answered, and each case must depend on its own facts.

Now the facts in this case are simple. Husband and wife lived at the matrimonial home together for nine years. In 1948 the husband had been a customer of the bank at any rate for some time and was in the habit of going to the bank weekly to draw wages. The bank had his home address on their books. So far as the evidence goes, all that continued throughout the time of the negotiations and execution of the mortgage. The bank had not the slightest reason to suspect that the husband had even left home until December, 1948, a month after the mortgage was executed.

In this state of affairs it would, in my judgment, be entirely unreasonable for the bank to send an officer to inquire, not whether a stranger was in occupation but to inquire of the wife whether she has been deserted. If it be a necessary or reasonable inquiry, nothing short of that will do, for mere discovery of the absence of the husband from home is no evidence of anything. In my judgment the law does not require an intending purchaser or mortgagee, who has no reason to believe that a wife is deserted, to make any inquiry upon the footing that it is conceivably possible that she may be; that is not a reasonable inquiry. If the law were otherwise it would mean that every intending purchaser or lender must inquire into the relationship of husband and wife and inquire into matters which are no concern of his and will bring thousands of business transactions into the area of domestic life and ties. That could not be right. In my judgment the law is this, that, where a man is carrying out a perfectly normal transaction of raising money upon mortgage and the proposing lender has reasonable grounds (as in this case) for believing that the intending mortgagor, the husband, is in occupation of the security offered, he is entitled to assume that a normal relationship exists as between husband and wife and is under no obligation to make any inquiry relating to their domestic relationship. On the other hand, if the intending mortgagee has notice of any fact which may put him on further inquiry as to whether the vendor has deserted his wife, or if having some suspicion, he wilfully abstains from inquiry to avoid notice, then the doctrine of constructive notice comes into play (see *per* Farwell J. in *Hunt* v. *Leck*, [1901] 1 Ch. 52).

Each case must be dealt with according to its own circumstances. For example, if before the mortgage was completed the bank had received the unsigned letter of December from the husband asking them to send all letters to a new address as he had left the old, it may well be (though I express no concluded view upon the point) that such a circumstance might have put the bank under the duty of making some further inquiry which would have disclosed the fact of desertion.

In the circumstances, however, in my judgment the bank had no reason to make any inquiry of the wife, and therefore is not affected by any constructive notice of the wife's rights. The bank's mortgage therefore takes priority over the wife's equity.

The bank is, in my judgment, therefore, entitled to an order for the usual accounts and inquiries in a foreclosure action. Against the wife the bank only seeks an order for possession three months after the master's certificate answering the accounts and inquiries if they obtain an order for sale, and they are plainly entitled to that.

Order accordingly.

[See *Note*, (1955) Camb. L. J. 158.

Apart from any question of desertion, is a husband entitled to evict his wife from the matrimonial home to which he holds title? See *Public Trustee* v. *Kirkham*, [1956] V.L.R. 64,

See, generally, *Megarry*, The Deserted Wife's Right to Occupy the Matrimonial Home. (1952) 68 Law Q. Rev. 379.]

CHAPTER VI

NON-FREEHOLD ESTATES: INTERESTS LESS THAN ESTATES

1. NON-FREEHOLD ESTATES

1 RESTATEMENT OF PROPERTY (1936)

§ 19. Estate for Years.

An estate for years is an estate, the duration of which is fixed in units of a year or multiples or divisions thereof.

Comment: *a. Mode of expressing duration.* It is sufficient to create an estate for years, so far as the requirement of definiteness of duration is concerned, that the duration of the estate is either precisely stated or can be exactly computed at the time when the estate becomes possessory.

b. Prerequisite definiteness in duration. If the duration of the estate attempted to be created by the lease is not stated and cannot be precisely computed at the time when the estate becomes possessory, the estate is not an estate for years.

§ 20. Estate from Period to Period.

An estate from period to period is an estate which will continue for successive periods of a year, or successive periods of a fraction of a year, unless it is terminated.

Comment: *a. Varieties.* There are various kinds of periodic estates taking their names from the period which serves as the unit of duration. The most common is the estate from year to year; among others are the estate from month to month and from week to week.

§ 21. Estate at Will.

An estate at will is an estate which is terminable at the will of the transferor and also at the will of the transferee and which has no other designated period of duration.

Comment: *a. When terminable only at will of transferee.* When land is so transferred that it is held at the will only of the transferee the estate created is not an estate at will. It is either an estate for the life of the transferee or an estate in fee simple determinable dependent upon whether the required words of inheritance, if any are required for the creation of an estate of inheritance, are present.

§ 22. Estate at Sufferance.

An estate at sufferance is an interest in land which exists when a person who had a possessory interest in land by virtue of an effective conveyance, wrongfully continues in the possession of the land after the termination of such interest, but without asserting a claim to a superior title.

[A term of years, a periodic tenancy or an estate at will may be created as a determinable interest or subject to a condition subsequent or to an executory limitation.]

MITCHELL v. THE MORTGAGE CO. OF CANADA. Supreme Court of Canada. 1919. 59 S.C.R. 90, 48 D.L.R. 420

Appeal from a judgment of the Saskatchewan Court of Appeal, 11 Sask. L.R. 447, 43 D.L.R. 337, [1918] 3 W.W.R. 838, reversing the judgment of Taylor J. and dismissing plaintiff's action for specific performance. Plaintiff negotiated with defendant's agents for a lease of certain premises which were in bad condition but on which defendant was prepared to expend some money for repairs. On February 8, 1917, the agents gave plaintiff a document reading as follows: "Received from Mr. John D. Mitchell the sum of Fifty Dollars, being deposit on rental of St. Regis ground floor, building taken at $100.00 per mo., for a term of five years to start from completion of repairs or when handed over to Mitchell." Subsequently defendant leased the property to another person, and this action followed.

IDINGTON J., dissenting: The date is not given but that is supplied by the cheque of the appellant shewn to have been given at same time.

This documentary evidence read in light of the surrounding facts and circumstances leaves no doubt in my mind of a concluded contract sufficient to meet the requirements of the Statute of Frauds.

The date of the beginning of the term was made certain within the recognized maxim *id certum est quod certum reddi potest.*

Cases of this nature requiring certainty of the term of a lease are curiously enough those which the learned author of Brooms Legal Maxims puts in the foreground of his commentary on this maxim and cites in 7th ed., p. 465, as illustrative of the meaning of the maxim.

The only question raised by the Court of Appeal seems to have been the effect to be given the concluding words of the receipt "or when handed over to Mitchell" which that court seems to have read as casting a doubt upon the certainty of meaning in the receipt.

I feel no difficulty in regard thereto for obviously there is nothing more implied than if there had been added to the preceding language a stipulation that in the event of the parties agreeing on another date that might by consent be substituted for the operative words already used, which in themselves were binding.

These words on which stress is laid are clearly, as counsel for appellant suggests, mere surplusage.

The bargain thus closed could not be affected by the later correspondence between respondent and its agents, which tried to introduce a term, previously unthought of giving the right to the respondent to terminate by a three month's notice the five years' lease it was bound to give.

Nor could the doubt suggested later of the repairs and improvements contemplated throughout by the earlier correspondence being likely to exceed the estimate, affect the contract.

Any possible difficulty on that score was, as matter of fair dealing, removed by the offer of appellant to bear the extra expense.

The contract if need be might be read as one to spend at least the sum named in such repairs, alterations, or improvements and thus remove any difficulty of non-compliance with the Statute of Frauds which might in law attach to the verbal offer of the appellant to bear such extra expense.

DUFF J.: The contract, if there was one, between the appellant and the respondent company was that a certain building, of which the respondent company was the proprietor, should be altered in certain respects; and that on the date of the completion of the alterations the appellant should receive and accept a lease of part of it for five years, subject to determination on three month's notice. This contract as a whole would be a contract within the fourth section of the Statute of Frauds, the agreement to make the changes being in part consideration for the undertaking by the appellant to accept the lease.

I am inclined to think that the provision as to determination upon notice is not sufficiently evidenced in writing, but assuming it to be so, it is quite evident that it is at least doubtful whether the respondent company's agents had authority to undertake to effect alterations at a cost greater than $800.00, and there is no doubt that when it was discovered that the cost of the projected alterations would exceed this figure both the appellant and the company's agents proceeded to negotiate afresh, treating the whole matter as at large. An understanding between them was reached, but the conclusion I have arrived at, after carefully reading the statement of the 15th of February and the letters of the 20th and 24th of the same month, is that there is too much indefiniteness in the expressions used in relation to the subject of alterations to enable one to say that the beginning of the contemplated term is ascertained by reference to the date of the "completion of repairs" within the meaning of the memorandum of February 20th.

The appeal should be dismissed with costs.

ANGLIN J.: I concur with Mr. Justice Duff.

BRODEUR J., dissenting: ... There is no doubt that it is essential to the validity of a lease that it shall appear on what day the term is to commence. There must be a certain beginning: otherwise it would not be a perfect lease, and in a contract for lease, in order to satisfy the Statute of Frauds, the term of commencement must be shewn. *Marshall* v. *Berridge*, 19 Ch. D. 233.

But the commencement of the term may be collected from the memorandum or by reference to some of their writings. Then the question comes up whether we can collect from the language of the agreement at what date the lease was to commence.

In the case of *Oxford* v. *Provand*, L.R. 2 P.C. 135, it was decided that where a certain amount of rental has to be paid from the date at which a building should be completed that those terms expressed with sufficient clearness the intention of the parties to bind themselves from the time it was made to do the several acts stipulated. Mr. Justice Lamont in the Court of Appeal admitted that, if the agreement provided simply that the term should commence when the repairs should be completed, the case of *Oxford* v. *Provand* would apply; but that by inserting in the receipt given by Romeril, Fowlie & Co. an alternative time for the beginning of the term it was impossible to hold that the commencement is fixed or can with reasonable certainty be concluded from the document.

The lease stated that the term was to start from the completion of the repairs or when the building was handed over to Mitchell. I would construe this language as meaning that the lease shall commence at the termination of the repairs; but if by a new agreement between the parties the property was handed over before or after the repairs were complete, in such a case the lease would start from the latter date. But I maintain that the primary agreement of the parties was that the rent should start from the date at which the repairs would be complete and that there is no reason then to distinguish the present case from the case of *Oxford* v. *Provand.*

MIGNAULT J.: ... The rule to be applied has been authoritatively stated as follows:

"It is essential to the validity of a lease that it shall appear either in express terms or by reference to some writing which would make it certain, or by reasonable inference from the language used, on what day the term is to commence. There must be a certain beginning and a certain ending, otherwise it is not a perfect lease, and a contract for a lease must, in order to satisfy the Statute of Frauds, contain those elements. *Marshall* v. *Berridge*, 19 Ch. D 233 "

Measured by this rule, the receipt relied on by the appellant evidently fails to satisfy the requirements of the Statute of Frauds. I doubt whether the parties ever intended it to be a memorandum witnessing a contract, or anything more than a receipt for the money paid by the appellant. Even if it can be looked on as a memorandum it is impossible to determine from it the time of beginning of the lease. The term of five years is stated "to start from completion of repairs or when handed over to Mitchell".

These repairs are not described, nor is it said who is to make them. It is true that the respondent, in correspondence with the agents, expressed its willingness to spend on repairs the sum of $800.00, and that the agents, but only after the date of the receipt, sent in an estimate specifying certain repairs and improvements amounting to $1,122.00. When the respondent demurred at paying more than $800.00, the appellant says that he agreed to pay the excess in cost, over and above the $800.00, which would shew that the matter had not been finally closed by the receipt which imposed on him no such obligation.

But looking at this receipt, the time of commencement of the lease is not stated nor can it be inferred from its language. Could Mitchell be forced to take possession and pay rental before the repairs were completed? Or when these repairs, and they had not then been specified, were made, and a delay ensued before the premises were handed over to Mitchell, from which of the two events, the completion of the repairs or the handing over of the premises, would the five year lease begin? The receipt is too vague to permit any answer being given to these questions, and consequently it cannot be taken as complying with the Statute of Frauds.

The appellant relies on the decision of the Privy Council in *Oxford* v. *Provand*, but I think that this decision is clearly distinguishable from the present case. In *Oxford* v. *Provand*, the Privy Council as a court of equity considered the surrounding circumstances and the conduct of the parties in dealing with the property comprised in an agreement vague in its language, in the interval between the making of the agreement and the commencement of a suit for its enforcement. The tenant, who attacked the memorandum, had before the suit taken possession and had sub-rented a part of the buildings referred to in the agreement as having to be constructed, or the building of which had then to be completed. I would have had no hesitation in the present case had the appellant been put in possession of the premises referred to in the receipt. But such was not the case and the receipt stands alone and without the aid of any surrounding circumstances or of any conduct of the parties in dealing with the property that can shew a certain time at which the term of the lease would begin.

Appeal dismissed.

[For a discussion of the case law and considerations underlying the requirement of certainty in the commencement, duration and termination of a tenancy, see *Foa*, Landlord and Tenant (7th ed., 1947), pp. 86-96.

Is there any difference in legal effect between a stipulation for commencement *on* a named day and *from* a named day? See *West and West* v. *Barr*, [1945] 2 D.L.R. 42, 61 B.C.R. 108, [1945] 1 W.W.R. 337 (B.C.C.A.); *Lethbridge Lodge No. 2., I.O.O.F.* v. *Afaganis*, [1949] 2 D.L.R. 209, [1949] 1 W.W.R. 314 (Alta. D.C.).

A document entitled a lease purports to create a tenancy from a named date "for the duration of the war". What is its effect? See *Lace* v. *Chandler*, [1944] 1 All E.R. 305 (C.A.); *Trerise* v. *Evanocke*, [1944] 3 D.L.R. 220, 60 B.C.R. 301, [1944] 3 W.W.R. 319; and see *Note*, (1946) 62 Law Q. Rev. 12. *Cf. Eker* v. *Becker*, [1946] 1 All E.R. 721 (K.B.); *Note*, (1946) 62 Law Q. Rev. 219.]

LANDLORD AND TENANT ACT, R.S.O. 1960, c. 206

27. A week's notice to quit and a month's notice to quit, respectively, ending with the week or the month, is sufficient notice to determine respectively, a weekly or monthly tenancy.

[For similar legislation, see Landlord and Tenant Act, R.S.M. 1954, c. 136, s. 27; Tenancies and Distress for Rent Act, R.S.N.S. 1954, c. 287, s. 16 (providing, additionally, for three months' notice to quit in the case of a tenancy from year to year of a house or tenement); Landlord and Tenant Act, R.S.S. 1953, c. 312, s. 18.]

LANDLORD AND TENANT ACT, R.S.N.B. 1952, c. 126

19. (1) Subject to any express agreement to the contrary, sufficient notice to quit shall be deemed to have been given if there is given:

(a) in the case of a weekly tenancy, a week's notice ending with the week;
(b) in the case of a monthly tenancy, a month's notice ending with the month:
(c) in the case of a tenancy from year to year, three months' notice ending, in the case of a tenancy originally from year to year, with an anniversary of the last day of the first year thereof, and in the case of all other tenancies from year to year, with an anniversary of the last day of the original tenancy;

provided that, in the case of an agricultural lease, not less than six month's notice to quit shall be given.

(2) In case a tenant, upon the determination of his lease, whether created by writing or by parol, remains in possession with the consent, express or implied, of the landlord, he shall be deemed to be holding subject to the terms of the lease, so far as they are applicable.

(3) In case the tenancy created by the lease was neither a weekly nor a monthly tenancy nor a tenancy from year to year, the overholding tenant shall be deemed to be holding as a tenant from year to year.

[For similar legislation, see Landlord and Tenant Act, R.S.P.E.I. 1951, c. 82, s. 19. At common law, six months' notice is required for termination of a yearly tenancy.]

SILVER v. KELLY. Ontario Court of Appeal. [1953] 1 D.L.R. 649, [1953] O.W.N. 7

Appeal from an order granting a landlord possession of certain premises.

The judgment of the Court was delivered by HOPE J. A.: This is an appeal from the order of His Honour Judge Shea of the County Court of the County of York, dated August 6, 1952, granting to the respondent, landlord, a writ of possession of certain demised premises under the provisions of the *Landlord and Tenant Act*, R.S.O. 1950, c. 199, Part III.

The tenancy was a monthly one, starting with the first day of each month. On December 27, 1951, the landlord gave to the tenant a notice to quit requiring delivery of possession of the premises to the landlord on July 1, 1952. Counsel for the appellant contended that this notice was an invalid notice since it did not demand delivery of possession on the last day of the month, namely, June 30th, but on the first day of the next succeeding month. In support of this contention he relied on the decision of the British Columbia Court of Appeal in *Mital* v. *Andrews*, [1950] 2 D.L.R. 51, [1950] 1 W.W.R. 423.

The problem of the adequacy of a notice similar to that in the present case has come before this Court, somewhat differently constituted, in at least three appeals in recent years. The latest of such appeals was on November 18, 1949, in the unreported judgment in *Montreuil* v. *Levoy*. That appeal was heard by a Court composed of Roach, Hope and Bowlby JJ. A. I have had the advantage of consulting my notes with respect to the argument and decision therein. Since that decision there has been no material change in the pertinent statutory provisions or Rental Regulations.

In *Montreuil* v. *Levoy*, the Court accepted the statement of law with respect to the effective date of a notice to quit as found in *Sidebotham* v. *Holland*, [1895] 1 Q.B. 378. It might be useful to quote from the judgment of Lindley L. J., concurred in by Lord Halsbury and also by A. L. Smith, L. J., who, however, expressed some doubts thereon. At p. 383 Lindley L. J. states: "But, although a half-year's notice to quit on the 18th would be correct, it does not follow that a notice to quit on the 19th, which is the anniversary of the day on which the tenancy commenced, is bad, and I am clearly of opinion that it is not. I have looked at all the decisions which were referred to in the argument and at many more, and I can find none in which it has been held that a half-year's notice to quit on the anniversary of the day on which the tenancy commenced is bad. I should be very much surprised to find such a case. The validity of a notice to quit ought not to turn on the splitting of a straw. Moreover, if hypercriticisms are to be indulged in, a notice to quit at the first moment of the anniversary ought to be just as good as a notice to quit on the last moment of the day before. But such subtleties ought to be and are disregarded as out of place."

With great respect to the able judgment of the British Columbia Court of Appeal in *Mital* v. *Andrews*, *supra*, this Court prefers to follow the precedent of its earlier judgment.

Appeal dismissed.

[See *Note*, (1953) 31 Can. Bar Rev. 98; *Note*, (1950) 28 Can. Bar Rev. 212. For a vigorous criticism of the *Sidebotham* rule as adopted in Ontario, see *Note*, (1950) 28 Can. Bar Rev. 796. The author of this *Note*, Mr. Eric L. Teed, writes, *inter alia*, as follows:

"A trilogy of English cases decided by divisional courts in the 1920's provide an exhaustive discussion of the subject. *Simmons* v. *Crossley* [1922] 2 K.B. 95, was the first of these, and strangeley enough Swift J. in his judgment cited *Sidebotham* v. *Holland* as his authority for the statement:

> It is clear law that in the absence of agreement or local custom to the contrary, a yearly tenancy can only be determined by a notice to quit expiring on the last day before the anniversary of its commencement.

Thus we have the paradox of an English judge citing the *Sidebotham* case as authority supporting the Single Day Advocates and Canadian judges citing the same case in support of the Double Day Advocates. An extensive discussion of the length of notice and the date of termination of a notice to quit for monthly and weekly tenancies is to be found in *Queen's Club Gardens Estates Ltd.* v. *Bignell*, [1924] 1 K.B. 117. Lush J., in delivering the main judgment, reviewed many of the authorities and yet did not mention *Sidebotham* v. *Holland*. He summarized his findings by stating:

> I think the true view is that in any periodic tenancy, whether it be yearly, quarterly, monthly or weekly, the notice to quit must expire at the end of the current period.

The third case of the trilogy is *Precious* v. *Reedie*, [1924] 2 K.B. 149. Here Sankcy J. in presenting his view of the law said:

> In a weekly tenancy the notice to quit is a week's notice expiring at the end of the periodic week, and in a monthly tenancy a month's notice expiring at the end of the periodic month.

The failure of provincial courts in Canada to consider three cases in which such positive statements appear is presumably due to oversight.

"Two recent decisions bring the English jurisprudence on this subject up to date. Lord Greene in *Hankey* v. *Clavering* [1942] 2 K.B. 326 at p. 329, lays down a rule of construction for notice to quit which it would be well to keep in mind. He states:

> Notices of this kind are documents of a technical nature, technical because they are not consensual documents, but, if they are in proper form, they have of their own force without any assent by the recipient the effect of bringing the demise to an end. They must on their face and on a fair and reasonable construction do what the lease provides they are to do. It is perfectly true that in construing such a document, as in construing all documents, the Court in the case of an ambiguity will lean in favour of reading the document in such a way as to give validity, but I dissent entirely from the proposition that where a document is clear and specific, but inaccurate in some matter, such as that of date, it is possible to ignore the inaccuracy and substitute the correct date or other particular because it appears that the error was inserted by a slip.

In *Lemon* v. *Lardeur* [1946] 1 K.B. 613, the Court of Appeal, apparently disregarding *Sidebotham* v. *Holland*, reviewed the authorities again and approved the decisions in *Queen's Club Gardens Estate Ltd.* v. *Bignell* and *Precious* v. *Reedie*.

"Possibly the reader will say that all this leaves the problem of giving a proper notice to quit, when the exact date of the commencement of the tenancy is uncertain, in an unsatisfactory state. This problem is, however, easily met. If the date of the commencement of the tenancy is known, we have the positive rule that the notice to quit must expire on the last day of the tenancy. If the date of the commencement of the tenancy is uncertain, the courts have offered the simple remedy of adding at the end of the notice sufficient words to cure any defect in the exact date. Smith L. J. in the *Sidebotham* case, in reference to a yearly tenancy, suggested the words:

> or at the expiration of the year of your tenancy which shall expire next after the end of one half year from the service of this notice.

Lush J. in *Queen's Club Gardens Estate Ltd.* v. *Bignell* considered the problem as follows:

> If the party who desires to give notice is doubtful as to the day on which the period expires, he can make sure that the notice will be valid by adding the words that are given in the common form of notices to quit to the effect that if the date mentioned is not the real date on which the period expires then the notice to quit is to expire on the proper day of expiry next after the expiration of the current period.

"The rule of law to be taken from the various cases which have been cited in this comment is that notice to quit must expire on the last day of the tenancy. Accordingly, if a specific date unqualified by the proper additional words is named, that date must be the last day of the tenancy, or the notice is invalid. Mr. Arnup may be correct in his contention that the law in Ontario, as now settled by the Ontario Court of Appeal, allows a notice to quit to expire on either of two days. However, I suggest that this is not the accepted law in other provinces of

Canada. Statements in the judgments of the appeal courts of England, Saskatchewan, Alberta and British Columbia indicate that all these courts hold that only the last day of the tenancy is the proper day for the termination of a notice to quit. And it is submitted that the courts which still have to deal with the question of termination of a notice to quit should so hold."

Cf. Crate v. *Miller*, [1947] 2 All E.R. 45 (C.A.), noted (1947) 63 Law Q. Rev. 417. It appears from the cases that the notice to quit need not mention the specific day on which the tenant must vacate: see *Addis* v. *Burrows*, [1948] 1 K.B. 444, [1948] 1 All E.R. 177 (C.A.).

In *Eastaugh* v. *Macpherson*, [1954] 3 All E.R. 214 (C.A.), a yearly tenancy which began on April 1, 1953, was determinable by three months' notice to quit expiring at the end of any year. On December 23, 1953, the landlords wrote to the tenant asking him "to accept three months' notice to vacate... by the date March 31, 1954". Is the notice to quit valid?

As to service of a notice to quit, see Landlord and Tenant Act, R.S.O. 1950, c. 199, s. 35. If notice is given by mail, when is it effective? See *Kraszewski* v. *Old*, [1948] 4 D.L.R. 75, [1948] O.W.N. 634 (C.A.); *W. Davis Ltd.* v. *Huntley*, [1947] 1 All E.R. 246, aff'd [1947] 2 All E.R. 371 (C.A.).]

WHEELER v. MERCER. House of Lords. [1957] A.C. 416, [1956] 3 All E.R. 631

Appeal by leave by a landlord from a judgment of the Court of Appeal, [1956] 1 Q.B. 275, [1955] 3 All E.R. 455, affirming a judgment for defendant and holding that she was a tenant at will and as such entitled to the protection of the Landlord and Tenant Act, 1954 (Imp.), c. 56. Defendant had been a quarterly tenant until the expiration on September 29, 1953 of a valid notice to quit, and since that date she continued in possession while negotiations proceeded between her and plaintiff for a new lease. Being in possession with the landlord's assent, she was a tenant at will at the time the Act of 1954 came into force on October 1, 1954. The landlord changed his mind about granting a new lease and when he asked for possession in 1955, defendant claimed the protection of the Act. The question was whether a tenant at will was covered by the definition of "tenancy" in s. 69 which included a tenancy created by "a tenancy agreement". The Court of Appeal agreed that the Act covered defendant, and hence the landlord could not terminate her tenancy except by a six months' notice in accordance with s. 25. Denning L. J. after coming to this conclusion noted a further argument of the landlord as follows: "Counsel for the landlord then raised a point which he said would give rise to difficulty in the future. He took the case of a person who goes in under a treaty for purchase, and then the sale goes off. Such a person has been stated in the old books to be a tenant at will. Is he to be entitled to the benefit of the Act? I think not, for the simple reason that such a person is not a tenant at will at all; see *Errington* v. *Errington & Woods*, [1952] 1 All E.R. 149. In any case such a person does not hold under a "tenancy agreement" as that term is used in the definition of "tenancy" contained in s. 69 of the Act of 1954." The other members of the Court expressed no opinion on this point.

VISCOUNT SIMONDS (after reciting the facts and referring to the legislation): A "tenancy," then, includes a tenancy "created... out of the freehold... by a tenancy agreement." Can a tenancy at will be thus described? And, if it might in another context be so described, is the description itself at least ambiguous so that its meaning may be influenced by the context of the Act? I do not find these easy questions to answer. It may, I think, be truly said that, since a tenant at will is regarded at law as being in possession by his own will and at the will, express or implied, of his landlord, he is a tenant by their mutual agreement, and the agreement may therefore be called a tenancy agreement. He is distinguished from a tenant at sufferance in that such a tenant is said to be in possession without either the agreement or disagreement of the landlord. But, my Lords, though upon a logical analysis it is possible to regard a tenancy at will as a "tenancy created by a tenancy agreement," I am not satisfied that according to the ordinary use of language, even apart from any context, it would be so described. A tenancy at will, though called a tenancy, is unlike any other tenancy except a tenancy at sufference, to which it is next-of-kin. It has been properly described as a personal relation between the landlord and his tenant: it is determined by the death of either of them or by any one of a variety of acts, even by an involuntary alienation, which would not affect the subsistence of any other tenancy. It is true that in some cases the relation of tenant at will may be expressly created by contract (see, for example, *Morgan* v. *William Harrison Ltd.* [1907] 2 Ch. 137), but this is an exceptional case and I do not exclude the possibility of such a contract being a "tenancy agreement" even if a tenancy at will arising by implication of law is not.

If I am right in concluding, as I do, that "tenancy agreement" is itself an expression which is ambiguous in its scope, I am led by the context of the Act, which I have examined in some detail, to the further conclusion that it does not cover a tenancy at will arising by implication of law....

LORD MORTON OF HENRYTON: ... A tenancy at will can only arise with the consent, express or implied, of the landlord. I think there is much to be said for the view that the appellant never consented to the respondent's occupation after September 29, 1953, but took no active steps to recover possession, on the principle that "what cannot be cured must be endured," because he knew that any application for possession would be countered by an application for protection under section 5 (13) of the Landlord and Tenant Act, 1927. If this were the true view, the respondent would be a tenant on sufferance. I find it unnecessary to form a concluded opinion on this point, for, in my opinion, the respondent is not protected by the Act of 1954, even is she is a tenant at will....

LORD SOMERVELL OF HARROW: ... There may be some tenancies at will, and this may be one, which one would have expected to find covered by the Act, but it would be surprising if the Act were applicable to tenancies at will generally. It would be absurd if a prospective purchaser, who had entered into possession pending completion was within the Act, and yet such a purchaser, in the absence of agreement to the contrary, is a tenant at will. Permissive occupation without payment of rent would also be a relationship one would not expect to find within this Part of the Act....

Appeal allowed.

[Lord Keith of Avonholm agreed with Lord Simonds; Lord Cohen delivered a concurring opinion.

In *Humans* v. *Doyon*, [1945] 2 D.L.R. 312, [1945] O.W.N. 275 (C.A.), plaintiff and defendant executed a memorandum by which defendant was authorized to occupy certain business premises "as long as he wants to". What interest, if any, was created, and was the nature of the interest affected by evidence of payment of monthly rent? Contrast *Lapointe* v. *Cyr* (1950), 29 M.P.R. 54 (N.B.) where an agreement under seal was executed giving the use of a farm, without payment of any money by way of rent or otherwise, for "as long as he wants to live on the farm and cultivate and manage my farm as he did in the past". What interest was given by this agreement?

Where land is expropriated and the erstwhile owner is allowed to stay on, his position may be that of a tenant at will: see *Palmer* v. *The King*, [1951] Ex. C.R. 348, [1952] 1 D.L.R. 259; *Ottawa* v. *Ottawa Valley Trust Co.*, [1949] O.R. 879, [1950] 2 D.L.R. 96.

How is a tenancy at will terminated? Must the tenant be given a reasonable time to vacate?

See *Fox* v. *Hunter-Patterson*, [1948] 2 All E.R. 813, 64 T.L.R. 541 (K.B.). Is a tenancy at will terminated by the bankruptcy of the tenant? See *Re Martin*, [1953] O.W.N. 694.

Section 5 (7) of the Limitations Act, R.S.O. 1960, c. 214, provides as follows: "Where any person is in possession or in receipt of the profits of any land, or in receipt of any rent, as tenant at will, the right of the person entitled subject thereto, or of the person through whom he claims, to make an entry or distress, or to bring an action to recover the land or rent, shall be deemed to have first accrued either at the determination of the tenancy, or at the expiration of one year next after the commencement of the tenancy, at which time the tenancy shall be deemed to have determined." For an application of this provision see *Logan* v. *Campbell and Neely*, [1956] O.W.N. 177 (C.A.), in which it was held that on the assumption of proof of an oral arrangement by an "owner" of land to give possession to a person for life on the latter's agreement to pay the taxes, the interest created was a tenancy at will which, in any event, was terminated on the death of the "owner".

For legislation similar to the Ontario provision, see Limitation of Actions Act, R.S.A. 1955, c. 177, s. 30; Statute of Limitations, R.S.B.C. 1960, c. 370, s. 21; Limitation of Actions Act, R.S.M. 1954, c. 145, s. 28; Limitation of Actions Act, R.S.N.B. 1952, c. 133, s. 43; Limitation of Actions (Realty) Act, R.S.Nfld. 1952, c. 145, s. 8; Statute of Limitations, R.S.N.S. 1954, c. 153, s. 10 (f); Statute of Limitations, R.S.P.E.I. 1951, c. 87, s. 31; Limitation of Actions Act, R.S.S. 1953, c. 76, s. 30.

In *Burgess* v. *Woodstock*, [1955] O.R. 814, [1955] 4 D.L.R. 615, plaintiff was a veteran who entered into an agreement to purchase farm lands under the Veterans' Land Act, R.S.C. 1952, c. 280. In a nuisance action against defendant for pollution of a river crossing plaintiff's land, McLennan J. said, *inter alia*: "Since a weekly tenant may maintain an action for nuisance (*Jones* v. *Chappell* (1875), L.R. 20 Eq. 539), I see no reason why a tenant at will may not also do so. The duration of the tenancy may be material in considering whether an injunction ought to be refused and the plaintiff should be left to his remedy in damages, or, if an injunction is granted, it may be limited to the duration of the tenancy: *Simper* v. *Foley* (1862), 2 John & H. 555, 70 E.R. 1179, and *Jacomb* v. *Knight* (1863), 3 De G.J. & Sm. 533, 46 E.R. 743. In any event, a perusal of the Act and of the contract between the plaintiff and the Director leads me to the conclusion that even if the plaintiff, so far as the Director is concerned, is to be deemed a tenant at will, the substance of the transaction is an agreement by the veteran to purchase, and is not a tenancy at will. For these reasons I have decided the plaintiff has the status to maintain this action."]

[A tenant at will is entitled to emblements: see 1 *Coke on Littleton*, chap. 8, ss. 55a, 55b. Cf. 7 *Holdsworth*, History of English Law (1925), p. 243: "It was in the course of the sixteenth century that the estate from year to year made its appearance. The creation of these estates, rather than estates at will, was probably due to the inconvenience of estates at will. The tenant at will had no certain interest; and his right to emblements made the land of very little value to the landlord, who was practically deprived of the rent of the land while this right to emblements lasted. It was better, both from the point of view of tenant and of the landlord, that the tenant should have a better defined interest. From the point of view of the tenant, because he had a more assured position; and from the point of view of the landlord, because he was entitled to rent to the end of the term. These causes led landowners to create tenancies from year to year rather than tenancies at will. Both for these reasons, and also perhaps because it was in accordance with the agricultural policy of the state to encourage agriculture by keeping tenants on the land, the courts began to favour these tenancies; and, for these reasons, to presume that a tenancy from year to year was intended, and not a tenancy at will, whenever a tenant entering upon or remaining in possession of premises, paid rent therefor. Thus tenancies from year to year arose not only by express creation, but also by presumption of law." If a person is let into possession of another's land without any provision for payment of rent should there be the same preference for finding a periodic tenancy? See *Gibboney* v. *Gibboney* (1875), 36 U.C.Q.B. 236 (C.A.); Cf. *Swan* v. *Swan*, [1938] 1 D.L.R. 454, 12 M.P.R. 363 (N.S.C.A.). Most of the recent case law on the question has involved persons who were tenants for a term certain or for a period but who held over at the termination of their tenancies; their position is treated in chapter VII, *infra.*

In *Nelson* v. *Cook* (1854), 12 U.C.Q.B. 22 (C.A.), Robinson C. J. speaking for the Court said (at p. 29): "Still it remains to be considered that this is not an action by the proprietor who signed the instrument of the 26th of October, but by an occupant who claims on a distinct ground—not for the land taken, but for damage done to wheat which he had put in on the same farm by permission of the proprietor; and the question is, whether he may not be in a position to maintain an action, though the proprietor, John Nelson, may be unable to do so. To ascertain the precise position of the plaintiff, William Nelson, has appeared to us the most difficult part of this case. All we hear of his interest in the premises is that his father had bought the property intending to give it to him; but, though he had allowed him to cultivate it for four or five years, he had given him no title, and nothing in writing had passed between them. There is no proof either that any rent was paid or agreed upon, or any term created by verbal contract. The relation of landlord and tenant, in its proper sense, therefore did not exist. The plaintiff was at the utmost only tenant at will at any time. Great doubts have been expressed by a very learned judge in England whether since the passing of the new statute of limitations a tenancy at will can be recognized as subsisting for any purpose after the lapse of the first year; and in the case before us, if we look upon the plaintiff as being tenant at will to his father during the whole time of his occupation up to the making of the deed of the 26th October, 1852, that act of the owner must surely have terminated the tenancy at will—as to that part of the land, at least, which that deed gave the Company permission to enter and occupy forthwith. Admitting, then, that the plaintiff was tenant at will up to the execution of the deed, he could after that be but tenant at sufferance, with the right, we suppose, which a tenant at will has to the emblements, when the will is terminated not by an act of the tenant, but of the owner. That claim to the emblements would amount only to a legal right to enter for the purpose of reaping and taking away the crop. It would not put the tenant at sufferance in a position to maintain trespass against the owner of the land, or any one holding a right of possession under him, whatever might be the case as between him and a mere stranger. And this action is not for taking the plaintiff's wheat: it is strictly an action of trespass *quare clausum fregit*, charging the prostrating the fences and destroying the crops as matter of aggravation. The gist of the action we take to be the alleged illegal entry upon the land, which in our opinion was not, under the circumstances, illegal." But see 7 *Holdsworth*, History of English Law, p. 243, pointing out that since a tenant at sufferance has no estate "it follows that he has no right to emblements; and that having nothing to convey, he cannot by his alienation create another estate at sufferance. The landlord, moreover, cannot distrain; he can only bring an action for use and occupation."

In *Bloomfield* v. *Hellyer* (1895), 22 O.A.R. 232, where an issue was raised as to whether a defaulting mortgagor of land could pass a title to growing crops as against an assignee of the mortgagee who went into possession before the crops were harvested, Osler J. A. said, *inter alia*, at p. 237: "In *Scobie* v. *Collins*, [1895] 1 Q.B. 375, Williams, J., points out that a mortgagor in possession is not necessarily more than a tenant on sufferance, and occupation and payment of interest necessarily connected with the mortgage is not necessarily referable to any tenancy other than a tenancy on sufferance. In *Ex parte Temple*, 1 G. & J. 216, which is relied upon by the learned Judge in his very full and careful judgment, the mortgagor was a tenant at will by express contract, not a mere constructive or *quasi* tenant at will arising out of the relationship of mortgagor and mortgagee, and he was, therefore, entitled to emblements as upon a real tenancy at will. So in the case of *Laing* v. *Ontario Loan and Savings Co.*, 46 U.C.R. 114, which is also cited by the learned Judge, the mortgagees relied upon an unexpired contractual tenancy at will as supporting their right to distrain crops, which had as growing crops been assigned by chattel mortgage by their mortgagors to the plaintiff. The crops had been actually harvested by the mortgagors, who were still in possession of the land.... The principle on which the rights of the mortgagee and mortgagor respectively depend with regard to property of this nature, i.e., growing crops, as laid down in the authorities I have referred to, shews, in my opinion, that one who purchases them from the mortgagor does not stand in a better position than his vendor. The highest position which the mortgagor or the purchaser can take is that there is an implied assent on the part of the mortgagee to the mortgagor sowing the crops or otherwise dealing with them, arising from his remaining in possession after default, and that if he shall still be in possession when the time comes for harvesting them he may do so and if he reaps them before the mortgagee enters, so far as the crops in specie are concerned, they may belong to him or to his vendee. But, in truth, it is neither necessary nor proper to imply any assent where the mortgagor is in as tenant on sufferance and if the mortgagee obtains possession while the crops are still growing he acquires them with the land by title paramount to the mortgagor and his vendee and the latter has no better title to them when ripe than the former."

Is it accurate to speak of a mortgagor in possession as a tenant at sufferance? See *Falconbridge*, Law of Mortgages of Land (3rd ed., 1942), pp. 376, 379.]

2. INTERESTS LESS THAN ESTATES

THE LAW OF ESTATES does not exhaust the range of interests in land that may be created by one person in favour of another. Of the classes of interests that are not estates that have been recognized in judicial decision, four are of particular significance, namely, (1) licences; (2) easements; (3) profits à prendre; and (4) restrictive covenants. The existence of such interests, or any of them, qualifies the use and, indeed, the title to land against which they may be asserted. A licence, as the very term itself suggests, involves a permission to use another's land without which the use would be a trespass. There has been a recent expansion of the common law's view of licences as indicated in some of the cases set out below. Easements are interests, arising by express or implied grant or by prescription (or possibly under statute), which involve a defined use of certain land (the servient tenement) for the benefit of other land (the dominant tenement). A right of way is a common easement of an affirmative character. Easements may be negative in character, as, for example, an easement of support, obliging the holder of the servient tenement to maintain his land or buildings so as not to disturb the support they afford to buildings on the dominant tenement. Profits à prendre are interests which involve the taking of the soil or some product of the soil from the land of another, as, for example, a right to take gravel or clay or to cut timber. Similarly, a grant of mineral rights may create a profit, though as will be seen later, the interest might be something else; perhaps an estate in fee simple or a leasehold. Restrictive covenants, broadly speaking, are devices for private control of the use of land. (The easement is a more lame form of a similar device.) Thus restrictions on class and size and value of buildings in private land developments would be imposed through covenants framed to be enforceable by and against subsequent owners of land comprised in the development scheme. A fuller treatment of easements, profits and restrictive covenants will be deferred to chapter XII. It is proposed to deal here with the development of licences and, in the succeeding section of this chapter, to raise some general classification problems.

[In *Thomas* v. *Sorrell* (1673), Vaughan 330, 124 E.R. 1098, (C.P.), Vaughan C. J. said (at p. 351 Vaughan, p. 1109 E.R.):

"A dispensation or licence properly passeth no interest, nor alters or transfers property in any thing, but only makes an action lawful without which it had been unlawful. As a licence to go beyond seas, to hunt in a man's park, to come into his house, are only actions, which without licence, had been unlawful.

"But a licence to hunt in a man's park and carry away the deer killed to his own use; to cut down a tree in a man's ground and to carry it away the next day after to his own use, are licences as to the acts of hunting and cutting down the tree, but as to the carrying away of the deer killed, and tree cut down, they are grants."]

HILL v. TUPPER. Court of Exchequer Chamber. 1863. 2 H. & C. 121, 159 E.R. 51

Rule nisi to enter a nonsuit or verdict for defendant in an action arising out of a claim by plaintiff that defendant had violated an alleged exclusive right of plaintiff of letting out pleasure boats for hire upon a canal. Plaintiff claimed under a demise from the canal proprietors which, *inter alia*, conferred on plaintiff "the sole and exclusive right or liberty to put or use boats on the said canal and let the same for hire for the purpose of pleasure only". Defendant was landlord of an inn abutting on the canal bank (as did plaintiff's premises held under the demise), and it appeared that persons who came to the inn used defendant's pleasure boats for fishing and bathing. Defendant's evidence was that he kept these boats primarily for the use of his family. The trial Judge left to the jury the question whether defendant derived any pecuniary advantage from the boats. The jury brought in a verdict for plaintiff and fixed the damages at one farthing. The Act of incorporation of the canal proprietors contained the following clause:

"That it shall and may be lawful for the owners and occupiers of any lands or grounds adjoining to the said canal, to use upon the said canal any pleasure boat or boats, or any other boat or boats, for the purpose of husbandry only, or for conveying cattle from one farm, or part of a farm or lands, to any other farm or lands of the same owner or occupier, without interruption from the said Company of proprietors, their successors or assigns, agent or agents, and without paying any rate or duty for the same; and so as such boat or boats be not above seven feet in breadth, and do not pass through any lock to be made on the said navigation, without the consent of the said Company of proprietors, their successors or assigns, or be employed for carrying any goods, wares or merchandize to market or for sale, or any person or persons for hire; and so as the same shall not obstruct or prejudice the said navigation, or the towing paths, or obstruct any boats passing upon the said navigation liable to pay the rates or duties aforesaid; and the owner of all such pleasure boats, or other boats, shall, in his own lands or grounds, make convenient places for such boats to lie in, and shall not suffer them to be moored or remain upon the said canal."

One of the grounds (the second) on which the rule nisi was obtained was that even if the grant to plaintiff were within the powers of the canal proprietors, no action would lie.

POLLOCK C.B.: We are all of opinion that the rule must be absolute to enter the verdict for the defendant on the second plea. After the very full argument which has taken place, I do not think it necessary to assign any other reason for our decision, than that the case of *Ackroyd* v. *Smith* (10 C.B. 164) expressly decided that it is not competent to create rights unconnected with the use and enjoyment of land, and annex them to it so as to constitute a property in the grantee. This grant merely operates as a licence or covenant on the part of the grantors, and is binding on them as between themselves and the grantee, but gives him no right of action in his own name for any infringement of the supposed exclusive right. It is argued that, as the owner of an estate may grant a right to cut turves, or to fish or hunt, there is no reason why he may not grant such a right as that now claimed by the plaintiff. The answer is, that the law will not allow it. So the law will not permit the owner of an estate to grant it alternately to his heirs male and heirs female. A new species of incorporeal hereditament cannot be created at the will and pleasure of the owner of property; but he must be content to accept the estate and the right to dispose of it subject to the law as settled by decisions or controlled by act of parliament. A grantor may bind himself by covenant to allow any right he pleases over his property, but he cannot annex to it a new incident, so as to enable the grantee to sue in his own name for an infringement of such a limited right as that now claimed.

MARTIN B.: I am of the same opinion. This grant is perfectly valid as between the plaintiff and the canal Company; but in order to support this action, the plaintiff must establish that such an estate or interest vested in him that the act of the defendant amounted to an eviction. None of the cases cited are at all analogous to this, and some authority must be produced before we can hold that such a right can be created. To admit the right would lead to the creation of an infinite variety of interests in land, and an indefinite increase of possible estates. The only consequence is that, as between the plaintiff and the canal Company, he has a perfect right to enjoy the advantage of the covenant or contract; and, if he has been disturbed in the enjoyment of it, he must obtain the permission of the canal Company to sue in their name. The judgment of the Court of Common Pleas in *Ackroyd* v. *Smith* (10 C.B. 164), and of Lord Brougham, C., in *Keppell* v. *Bailey* (2 Myl. & K. 517, 535), are, in the absence of any case to the contrary, ample authority for our present decision.

BRAMWELL B.: I am of the same opinion. I will only add, that the defendant cannot have the verdict entered for him on the plea of not guilty, for no leave was reserved at the trial; and the defendant could only succeed on that issue by obtaining a new trial on the ground of misdirection. The rule must therefore be absolute to enter the verdict for the defendant on the second plea, unless the plaintiff elects to be nonsuited, but as he can never make a better case, the better course would be to enter the verdict for the defendant on the second plea.

Rule absolute.

[In *Keppell* v. *Bailey* (1834), 2 Myl & K. 517, 39 E.R. 1042 (Ch.), Brougham L. C. said (at p. 535 Myl. & K., p. 1049 E.R.):

"There are certain known incidents to property and its enjoyment; among others, certain burthens wherewtih it may be affected, or rights which may be created and enjoyed over it by parties other than the owner; all which incidents are recognised by the law. In respect of possession, the property may be in one, while the reversion is in another; in respect of interest, the life estate in one, the remainder in tail in a second, and the fee in reversion in a third. So in respect of enjoyment; one may have the possession and the fee-simple, and another may have a rent issuing out of it, or the tithes of its produce, or an easement, as a right of way upon it, or of common over it. And such last incorporeal heraditament may be annexed to an estate which is wholly unconnected with the estate affected by the easement, although both estates were originally united in the same owner, and one of them was afterwards granted by him with the benefit, while the other was left subject to the burthen. All these kinds of property, however, all these holdings, are well known to the law and familiarly dealt with by its principles. But it must not therefore be supposed that incidents of a novel kind can be devised and attached to property at the fancy or caprice of any owner. It is clearly inconvenient both to the science of the law and to the public weal that such a latitude should be given. There can be no harm in allowing the fullest latitude to men in binding themselves and their representatives, that is, their assets real and personal, to answer in damages for breach of their obligations. This tends to no mischief, and is a reasonable liberty to bestow; but great detriment would arise and much confusion of rights if parties were allowed to invent new modes of holding and enjoying real property, and to impress upon their lands and tenements a peculiar character, which should follow them into all hands, however remote. Every close, every messuage, might thus be held in a several fashion; and it would hardly be possible to know what rights the acquisition of any parcel conferred, or what obligations it imposed. The right of way or of common is of a public as well as of a simple nature, and no one who sees the premises can be ignorant of what all the vicinage knows. But if one man may bind his messuage and land to take lime from a particular kiln, another may bind his to take coals from a certain pit, while a third may load his property with further obligations to employ one blacksmith's forge, or the members of one corporate body, in various operations upon the premises, besides many other restraints as infinite in variety as the imagination can conceive; for there can be no reason whatever in support of the covenant in question, which would not extend to every covenant that can be devised.

"The difference is obviously very great between such a case as this and the case of covenants in a lease, whereby the demised premises are affected with certain rights in favour of the lessor. The lessor or his assignees continue in the reversion while the term lasts. The estate is not out of them, although the possession is in the lessee or his assigns. It is not at all inconsisitent with the nature of property that certain things should be reserved to the reversioners all the while the term continues; it is only something taken out of the demise, some exception to the temporary surrender of the enjoyment; it is only that they retain, more or less partially, the use of what was wholly used by them before the demise, and what will again be wholly used by them when that demise is at an end. Yet even in this case, the law does not leave the reversioner the absolute licence to invent covenants which shall affect the lands in the hands of those who take by assignment of the term. The covenant must be of such a nature as to 'inhere in the land,' to use the language of some of the cases; or 'it must concern the demised premises and the mode of occupying them,' as it is laid down in others; 'it must be *quodammodo* annexed and appurtenant to them,' as one authority has it; or, as another says, 'it must both concern the thing demised, and tend to support it and support the reversioner's estate.' Within such limits restraints upon the land demised may be imposed, which shall follow into the hands of persons who are strangers to the contract of lease, and who only become privy to the lessor through the estate which they take by assignment in the demised premises. But this is no more than saying that, within such limits, the owner of the land may retain to himself and his assignees of the reversion a certain control over or use of the property which remains in himself, or which he has conveyed to those assignees; and that he may so retain it, into whose hands soever, as lessee, the temporary possession may have come. Even he, the continuing owner, is confined within certain limits by the view which the law takes of the nature of property; and if beyond those limits he were to imagine a stipulation, the covenant in which he should embody it would not run with the land, but only bind the lessee personally and his representatives.

"It only requires a little attention to the cases to satisfy us, first, that even where the privity of lessor and lessee exists, there are bounds so narrow to the province of real covenants as would make the one in question lie on the extreme verge of it, if it did not fall without it; secondly, that there can be no doubt of such a covenant being one personal, collateral, or in gross, where there does not exist that, or some other privity of estate, which according to one or two of the authorities only, and which I venture to doubt, has been held to render real covenants which would otherwise have been personal; and, thirdly, that those covenants which have been held real, excepting, indeed, such as relate to title, would have been deemed collateral had there been no privity in respect of reversion or other unity of title."]

BENDALL v. McWHIRTER. Court of Appeal. [1952] 2 Q.B. 466, [(1952] 1 All E.R. 1307

The facts of this case are set out on p. 104 *supra*.

DENNING L. J. ...The objection that is made is that a contractual licence only gives rise to contractual obligations and not to any proprietary rights or interests, and that the burden of it does not therefore run with the land. In answer to this objection let me start with the common law. In the year 1618 and for over 200 years afterwards it was held that a contractual licence to use and occupy land, once it was acted on by entry into occupation, was binding not only on the licensor but also on his successors in title, and that it was not revocable except in accordance with the terms of the contract. If the licensor or his successor ejected the licensee or his goods in breach of the contract, he was liable in assault or trespass, as the case might be: see *Webb* v. *Paternoster*, (1618) Popham 151, where a licence to stack hay was held binding on the successors of the licensor, including his tenants: *Wood* v. *Lake*, (1751) Sayer 3, where a parol licence to stack coals for seven years was held irrevocable except in accordance with the contract: *Tayler* v. *Waters*, (1816) 7 Taunton 374, where a licence to enjoy benefical privileges in the opera house was held not to be revocable at will; and *Wallis* v. *Harrison*, (1838) 4 M. & W. 538, where a licence to make and use a railway was held not binding on successors solely because it was still executory. Those cases were much considered in *Wood* v. *Leadbitter*, (1845) 13 M. & W. 838, and the only criticism directed at them was that the licence should have been under seal. It was agreed that the licence in *Wood* v. *Leadbitter*, *Ibid.* 843, 847-8, and the other cases would have been good if they had been granted by deed. This is the very point at which the Judicature Acts come into play. Since the fusion of law and equity, there is no necessity for a seal. Every contractual licence to use and occupy land, once acted on by entry into occupation, takes effect according to its tenor. It is not revocable at will. It is only revocable in accordance with the terms of the contract. If the licensor should attempt to eject the licensee in breach of the contract he is guilty of an assault: *Hurst* v. *Picture Theatres Ld.*, [1915] 1 K.B. 1; and if he should attempt to revoke the licence in breach of the contract the court of equity will grant an injunction to restrain him: *Winter Garden Theatre (London) Ld.* v. *Millennium Productions Ld.*, *per* Lord Simon and *per* Lord Uthwatt, [1948] A.C. 173, 191, 202. This means that the law is restored to the position in which it was for 200 years before *Wood* v. *Leadbitter* came to disturb it. The Law is now just as that accomplished lawyer, Sir Vicary Gibbs C. J., stated it in 1816 in *Tayler* v. *Waters*, when delivering the reserved judgment of the full Court of Common Pleas: "A beneficial licence to be exercised upon land may be granted without deed, and cannot be countermanded, at least after it has been acted upon... and this is not such an interest in land as, by the Statute of Frauds, can only pass by writing." It is not therefore an interest in property, but nevertheless once the licensee has entered into occupation it is, as Parke B. put it in *Wallis* v. *Harrison*," a sort of interest against the licensor and "his assigns," by which he meant, as I understand it, that it was a clog or fetter, like a lien, which is not an interest in property but only a personal right to retain possession: *Legg.* v. *Evans*, (1840) 6 M. & W. 36, 42; but nevertheless it is, of course, effective against the owner and his assigns.

The truth is, I think, that the old common lawyers of the seventeenth and eighteenth centuries, without knowing it, applied to contractual licences some equitable principles which have since become well known. By dispensing with a seal when the licence had been acted on, they anticipated the doctrine of restrictive covenants. Indeed, in modern times equity lawyers have reached the same result as the old common lawyers, but they have done it in their own way.

Let me now therefore turn to equity. Every contractual licence imports a negative covenant that the licensor will not interfere with the use and occupation of the licensee in breach of the contract. This negative covenant is binding on the successors in title of the licensor in the same way as is a restrictive covenant. It does not run with the land so as to give a cause of action in damages for breach of contract against the successor; but it is binding in equity on the conscience of any successor who takes with notice of it. He cannot therefore eject the licensee in disregard of it. It is an equity within the words of Lord Cottenham L. C. in *Tulk* v. *Moxhay*, 2 Phillips 774, 778, when he said: "If an equity is attached to the property by the owner, no one purchasing with notice of that equity can stand in a different situation from the person from whom he purchased." In that case a covenant to keep the garden of a London square in its then form was held binding on successors in title who took with notice of the covenant. Suppose now that there was a covenant not only to keep the square garden in its then form but also a covenant to allow the residents of the square to use it. This second covenant is nothing more nor less than a contractual licence to use the garden; but surely both covenants would be held binding on the successors in title. There is no reason in principle to distinguish between them, and there is direct authority in favour of it. Eight years after *Tulk* v. *Moxhay* a case arose where the owners of a cemetery sold grave spaces to purchasers. There were only contractual licences to use the land for the purposes of burial; but Sir John Romilly M. R. held them to be binding on the successors in title of the licensors: see *Moreland* v. *Richardson*, (1856) 22 Beav. 596; (1857) 24 Beav. 33. So also a covenant to permit work to be done on land has been held binding on successors who take with notice, because it imports a negative covenant not to interfere with the work: see *Andrew* v. *Aitken*, (1882) 22 Ch.D. 218, 220, *per* Fry J., and *Sharpe* v. *Durrant*, (1911) 55 S.J. 423, where Warrington J. said: "This is a case where a person taking land, with notice of an obligation entered into by the previous owner, will be bound in equity to give effect to that obligation." These authorities fully support the proposition put forward by Sir John Salmond in his book on Torts that a contractual licence to enter on land "if of such a nature as to be specifically enforceable... binds and runs with the land in equity so as to be enforceable not merely against the grantor but also against all subsequent owners and occupiers of the land except purchasers for value without notice of any such equitable right" (7th ed., at p. 290).

Likewise, when the owner of goods agrees to allow another person to use them, as when he lets them out on hire, the agreement is binding not only on the original owner but also on his successors in title: *De Mattos* v. *Gibson*, (1858) 4 De G. & J. 276 and *Lord Strathcona Steamship Co.* v. *Dominion Coal Co.*, [1926] A.C. 108. I know that some people have looked askance at the principles laid down in the *Strathcona* case, but there were, on the Board of the Privy Council, three of the most distinguished equity lawyers of the day, and I fail to see why we should not follow the principles there laid down, at any rate with regard to a contractual licence tu use chattels, especially as they are so eminently just and reasonable.

It is, of course, necessary in all these cases that the party who seeks to enforce the contract against a successor in title should have a sufficient interest to warrant the intervention of equity. He must, as the Privy Council put it, "have, and continue to have, an interest in the subject-matter of the contract": see the *Strathcona* case. This does not mean that he must have a legal estate to be protected. Possession or actual occupation of the land or chattel is sufficient. Thus in the case of restrictive covenants made for the benefit of adjoining land, possession of that adjoining land is sufficient: see *London County Council* v. *Allen*, [1914] 3 K.B. 642, 672, *per* Scrutton L. J. In the case of contractual licences made for the benefit of the occupier of the land, actual occupation of that is sufficient: see *Errington* v. *Errington and Woods*, [1952] 1 K.B. 290. When a contractual licence to put up the advertisements on a wall has been acted on by putting up the advertisements, it is binding on the successors in title of the licensor, including his tenants: see *In re Webb's Lease, Sandom* v. *Webb*, [1951] Ch. 808, *per* Sir Raymond Evershed M. R. (Ibid. 821) and Jenkins L. J. (Ibid. 832). But a right to put up advertisements on a wall, not yet built, is not binding on the successors in title because that is not itself a licence but only a contract to procure that a licence will be granted in the future: *King* v. *David Allen & Sons Billposting Ld.* [1916] 2 A.C. 54. Likewise in the case of contractual licences to use chattels, entry into possession, once made, is sufficient, even though there has been a temporary lack of possession: the *Strathcona* case; but an interest in price restriction is not sufficient: *Taddy & Co.* v. *Sterious & Co.*, [1904] 1 Ch. 354.

The only case which gives rise to any difficulty is *Clore* v. *Theatrical Properties Ld. and Westby & Co. Ld.*, [1936] 3 All E.R. 483, 490, where the licensee of the "front of the house rights" in a theatre, who was in occupation of them, was held to be unable to enforce them against an assignee of the licensor. That case, however, proceeds on the assumption that the licensee had no right which equity could enforce against the licensor. That assumption is no longer true: see *Winter Garden Theatre (London) Ld.* v. *Millennium Productions Ld.*, *per* Lord Uthwatt, [1948] A.C. 173, 202; and the case may some day have to be reconsidered accordingly.

In some contractual licences over land (not amounting to occupation) there may be some nice questions whether the licence is an equitable easement which must be registered in order to be binding on successors: see an illuminating note on "Equitable Easements" by Mr. Geoffrey Cross in *The Bell Yard* (1935), No. 15, at p. 18; but no such questions arise where the licensee is in possession or actual occupation of the land, because that itself is sufficient notice of his rights: see section 14 of the Law of Property Act, 1925, and section 70 (1) (*g*) of the Land Registration Act, 1925, and *Lewisham Borough Council* v. *Maloney*, [1948] 1 K.B. 50. Statutory tenants (who have only possession) do not have to register their interests; nor does a contractual licensee so long as he is in possession or actual occupation. His interest is, therefore, binding on a trustee in bankruptcy, even though the trustee does rank as a purchaser for value: see section 43 of the Land Registration Act, 1925. I have thus shown, I hope, that equity has reached the same result as did the old common lawyers.

My conclusion, therefore, is that a contractual licensee, who is in actual occupation of land by virtue of the licence, has an interest which is valid, if not at law at any rate in equity, against the successors in title of the licensor, including therein his trustee in bankruptcy. It is not a legal interest in land, like a tenancy, but a clog or fetter like a lien. It is a personal right, but it is nevertheless binding on successors of the licensor, so long as the conditions of the licence are observed.

WINTER GARDEN THEATRE (LONDON) LD. v. MILLENIUM PRODUCTIONS LD. House of Lords. [1948] A.C. 173, [1947] 2 All E.R. 331

Appeal from a judgment of the Court of Appeal, [1946] 1 All E.R. 678, reversing an order of Roxburgh J. and holding that appellant licensors had no power to revoke a licence and that an injunction should issue to restrain them from acting on the attempted revocation.

VISCOUNT SIMON.: My Lords, the appeal relates to a licence under which the respondents were permitted to use the Winter Garden Theatre, Drury Lane, which is the property of the appellants, for the purpose of producing stage plays, concerts or ballets, in return for a weekly payment which at the time when the appellants sought to terminate the licence amounted to 300£. per week. There was no express term in the licence providing that the appellants could revoke it and the principal question of the case is whether, as the respondents contend, and as the Court of Appeal decided, the respondents are entitled to continue their use of the theatre in perpetuity if they so desire, and continue the weekly payments, or whether, as the appellants contend, the licence is revocable by reasonable notice. It is to be noted that, although the expression "rent" or "rental" was used in the relevant documents, it is agreed between the parties (as is plainly the fact) that the respondents acquired no interest in land but were pure licensees for value, the consideration taking the form of a weekly payment. Such a licence is a contract, and this contract contains the express term that if the respondents, on proper notice, opt to continue the use of the theatre beyond the first twelve months, they may do so with the right of giving one month's notice of their intention of then terminating the licence. The licensors on the other hand are given by the documents no express right to terminate the licence at all: the question is, is such a right to be implied, and if so, on what terms?

The effect of a licence by A. to permit B. to enter upon A.'s land or to use his premises for some purpose is in effect an authority which prevents B. from being regarded as a trespasser when he avails himself of the licence (*Thomas* v. *Sorrell* (1674), Vaugh. 330, 351). Such a licence may fall into one of various classes. It may be a purely gratuitous licence in return for which A. gets nothing at all, e.g., a licence to B. to walk across A.'s field. Such a gratuitous licence would plainly be revocable by notice given by A. to B. Even in that case, however, notice of revocation conveyed to B. when he was in the act of crossing A.'s field could not turn him into a trespasser until he was off the premises, but his future right of crossing would thereupon cease. There is another class of licences which may be called licences for value, in which B. gives consideration for the permission he obtains from A., and this last class may be further subdivided. In some cases the consideration may be given once for all, as for example by the payment of a capital sum or by conferring a single benefit at the beginning. The case of *Llanelly Ry, & Dock Co.* v. *London and North Western Ry. Co.*, L.R. 7 H.L. 550, to which I will refer later, is an example of this. In other cases, the consideration may take the form of a periodic payment, as is the case in the appeal we are now considering. There is yet a third variant of a licence for value which constantly occurs, as in the sale of a ticket to enter premises and witness a particular event, such as a ticket for a seat at a particular performance at a theatre or for entering private ground to witness a day's sport. In this last class of case, the implication of the arrangement, however it may be classified in law, plainly is that the ticket entitles the purchaser to enter and, if he behaves himself, to remain on the premises until the end of the event which he has paid his money to witness. Such, for example, was the situation which gave rise to the decision of the Court of Appeal in *Hurst* v. *Picture Theatres, Ld.*, [1915] 1 K.B. 1. I regard this case as rightly decided, and repudiate the view that a licensor who is paid for granting his licensee to enter premises in order to view a particular event, can nevertheless, although the licensee is behaving properly, teminate the licence before the event is over, turn the licensee out, and leave him to an action for the return of the price of his ticket. The licence in such a case is granted under contractual conditions, one of which is that a well-behaved licensee shall not be treated as a trespasser until the event which he has paid to see is over, and until he has reasonable time thereafter to depart, and in *Hurst* v. *Picture Theatres, Ld.*, where these rights were disregarded and the plaintiff was forced to leave prematurely substantial damages for assault and false imprisonment rightly resulted.

This brings up for reconsideration the oft-quoted and oft-considered decision of the Court of Exchequer in 1845 in *Wood* v. *Leadbitter*, 13 M. & W. 838. I think that this decision can only be rightly understood by bearing in mind the state of the pleadings on which the decision depended. The old system of pleading was far more strict than the system now prevailing. The action was an action for the tort assault and false imprisonment arising out of the circumstances that Wood had bought a ticket for admission to the grandstand at the Doncaster races but that while the races were going on the defendant, acting under the orders of Lord Eglintoun who was steward of the races, and must be treated as having sold Wood his ticket, turned the plaintiff out. The defendant's plea was that the plaintiff was on Lord Eglintoun's ground, to which the plaintiff filed a replication that he was there "by the leave and licence of Lord Eglintoun" (13 M. & W. 838, 839). There was a traverse to this replication and issue was joined on that traverse. Alderson B., at the beginning of his judgment, sets all this carefully out and the language of the replication is printed in italics in the report. Kennedy L. J., pointed out in *Hurst* v. *Picture Theatres, Ld.*, [1915] 1 K.B. 1, 13, that in *Wood* v. *Leadbitter* "it was not there suggested by the plaintiff 'My right to remain is not merely by leave and licence of Lord Eglintoun; I have an implied contract that I should be there and that contract is not subject to revocation'," and went on, "Therefore, as I say, one must deal with that case upon the pleading, and upon that pleading the judgment of the court cannot be put more specifically or more correctly than in the passage I have quoted from the headnote." The passage in the headnote referred to by the Lord Justice is as follows: "A right to come and remain for a certain time on the land of another can be granted only by deed; and a parol licence to do so, though money be paid for it, is revocable at any time, and without paying back the money." It seems plain, therefore, that the only issue to be decided in *Wood* v. *Leadbitter* was whether the plaintiff, when he was forcibly removed from Lord Eglintoun's land, continued to have the leave of Lord Eglintoun to be there; and he had not this leave because it had been withdrawn. On the pleadings in that case, the question was not open whether the effect of the contract was not to preserve the plaintiff from being treated as a trespasser until the races were over. Until the Common Law Procedure Act of 1852 permitted joinder of different causes of action in the same suit, a plaintiff in the position of Wood had to sue either in tort (as he did) or in assumpsit. In *Kerrison* v. *Smith*, [1897] 2 Q.B. 445, 448, Collins J. said of *Wood* v. *Leadbitter*, "It was conceded that the grantor has a right to revoke a licence but the point set up by the plaintiff, that there was a contract, for the breach of which the plaintiff was entitled to recover damages, was never properly dealt with." It does not seem necessary to discuss, now that we are more than a hundred years from the decision, whether if the Judicature Acts had then been passed, the Court of Exchequer could have protected Wood from what was an injustice; the instances given by the judges who were in a majority in *Hurst's* case show how manifest the injustice is. Wood's position really was that Lord Eglintoun had agreed with him for reward, not to treat him as a trespasser till the races were over, and till he had a reasonable time after that to withdraw, but this was not the issue directly raised by the pleadings. It is enough to say that, at any rate since the fusion of law and equity, no court in this country would refuse to a plaintiff in Wood's situation, the remedy for which he asked, and the case, in my opinion, should no longer be regarded as an authority.

I had reached this point in drafting my opinion when I had the advantage of reading in print the opinion prepared by my noble and learned friend, Lord MacDermott, in this appeal. He has so precisely and clearly expressed the view which I had formed on the case before us that it becomes unnecessary to deal independently with the application of the principles I have endeavoured to formulate to the matter in hand. I agree with him entirely that the decision of this House in *Llanelly Ry. & Dock Co.* v. *London & North Western Ry*, does not assist the present appellants, for the reasons he states. On the other hand, I accept his conclusion that when the clauses of the present licence are carefully studied, the proper inference from the language used is that the licence was not perpetual but that the intention of the parties, to be inferred from the document, though not expressly stated, was that, upon the appellant's indicating their decision that the permission given by the licence would be withdrawn, the respondents were to have a reasonable time to withdraw after which they would become trespassers. There is, in my opinion, no reason at all for saying that the only alternative to a perpetual licence is an instant termination of the respondents' right without any period of notice at all.

I entirely agree with the analysis to which my noble and learned friend, Lord MacDermott, has subjected the arrangement made between the respondents and Linnit & Dunfee, Ld. of August 22, 1945, from which it follows that this agreement was really a sub-licence entered into without the appellants' consent, thus constituting a breach of c. 6 of the letter of June 10, 1942. Consequently, the respondents are precluded from relying on it in support of their plea that, if the licence were revocable, reasonable notice had not been given. The result is, as Lord MacDermott points out, that the respondents failed to show that the time which the appellants were prepared to give them to withdraw was insufficient; the notice given by the appellants must be considered valid and effectual. I move that the appeal be allowed.

LORD PORTER: My Lords, on June 10, 1942, the appellants granted to the Countess de la Marr a licence of the Winter Garden Theatre for the purpose of producing stage plays, concerts or ballets. As I understand, the terms of this licence were meant to be a preliminary step towards establishing a contractual relationship between the appellants and the respondent company which had not then been registered. It was, however, formed shortly afterwards and on October 1, 1942, a further agreement was entered into between the appellants, the Countess, and the respondents, whereby she was authorized to assign her licence to the respondents and they in their turn were permitted to grant a sub-licence to Messrs. Arnold and Hylton for a period which by a series of options granted to those gentlemen might extend for seven years or even longer if a successful play were running at the expiry of the last optional period. The sub-licence to Messrs. Arnold and Hylton in fact expired long before any date material for your Lordships' consideration, and is, I think, only of importance as indicating that the appellants were at one time contemplating the possible continuance of the respondents' licence for seven years and upwards. Two further documents are of importance, viz.: An assignment of the licence by the Countess to the respondents on October 1, 1942, and an agreement of August 22, 1945, whereby the respondents purported to engage Linnit & Dunfee Ld., to produce a play entitled "Young Mrs. Barrington" at the theatre. A question whether this agreement constituted an unauthorized licence of the theatre to Linnit & Dunfee will have to be considered later, but cannot be solved until the terms of the original licence and the terms of the (alleged) unauthorized licence are examined.

Before these matters are considered your Lordships must, I think, decide what are the principles in the light of which a licence to enter into and carry out activities upon land has to be construed. Upon this subject there is a wide divergence of view, the appellants contending that prima facie a licence is revocable at will, though it may be that due notice of the date at which the revocation is to take place must be given and though the licensee must at least be given reasonable time to wind up his activities having regard to all the circumstances of the case. They add that this view is, of course, not inconsistent with the existence of a term in the licence whether express or implicit, making it irrevocable altogether or for a named period. The Court of Appeal, however, had held and the respondents maintain that no such principle is to be applied, even prima facie, in construing a licence. That contract, they say, must be construed in the light of its own terms and with no leaning towards revocability or irrevocability....

... It has been suggested that the decision in *Wood* v. *Leadbitter* turned merely on the pleadings and decided only that a right to enter and remain on land though for no more than a limited period required a deed to make it effective. I cannot think so. It is true that the decision ultimately turned on this point and equally true that the contention might not be good after the passing of the Judicature Act, enjoining common law courts to take into consideration the doctrines of equity. But as I read the case it is assumed that a licence is prima facie revocable. Throughout the whole of the judgment this point is stressed. Indeed Alderson B. says: "It may further be observed, that a licence under seal (provided it be a mere licence) is as revocable as a licence by parol." It was said on behalf of the respondents that this principle applied only to licences given without consideration and that the phrase "mere licence" was used in order to exclude licences given for a consideration. If the contention that licences given for a consideration are not revocable were confined to a limited licence to do a particular act or series of acts, I do not think I should disagree provided the performance of a particular act had been actually begun. So limited the proposition does not conflict with the view that normally a licence is revocable, but if applied generally it does, as I think, conflict with the principles laid down in *Wood* v. *Leadbitter*, and in particular with the statement that a licence under seal (which does not require consideration) is as revocable as a parol one. In *Wood* v. *Leadbitter* the licence was for a limited purpose and for a limited time and for valuable consideration. It may well be that now that common law and chancery remedies can be administered by any branch of the High Court, a different decision would be given, but even if that be conceded it does not seem to me to have any bearing on the case now presented to your Lordships. It is one thing to say that a limited and temporal licence remains in force until the particular object for which it is given is fulfilled or the definite period of time has elapsed, it is quite a different matter to allege that a licence once given in general terms can never be terminated. To my mind the whole historical development of the law is against such a contention. *Cornish* v. *Stubbs*, L.R. 5 C.P. 334, *Mellor* v. *Watkins*, L.R. 9 Q.B. 400, *Kerrison* v. *Smith*, [1897] 2 Q.B. 445, *Wilson* v. *Tavener*, [1901] 1 Ch. 578, *Canadian Pacific Ry. Co.* v. *The King*, [1931] A.C. 414, *Minister of Health* v. *Bellotti*, [1944] K.B. 298, are all against it and even *Hurst* v. *Picture Theatres, Ld.*, [1915] 1 K.B. 1, is not antagonistic.

The respondents, however, relied in particular on *Llanelly Ry. & Dock Co.* v. *London & North Western Ry. Co.*, (1873) L.R. 8 Ch. 942; (1875) L.R. 7 H.L. 550. Undoubtedly in that case running powers over their line given by one railway company to another were held to be irrevocable, but they formed part of a general agreement under which a large sum was lent, and formed part of the consideration for the loan. In any case running powers are in a class by themselves involving special arrangements, preparations and expenditure, which may well influence the construction of an agreement under which they are granted. The actual decision was that all the provisions of the agreement showed that it was a permanent and not a terminable one. It is true that Lord Selborne said that "an agreement de futuro, extending over a tract of time which, on the face of the instrument, is indefinite and unlimited, must (in general) throw upon anyone alleging that it is not perpetual, the burden of proving that allegation either from the nature of the subject or from some rule of law applicable thereto." Whether such a proposition is too widely stated, though in general it may be true, is not a matter which, in my opinion, it is material to decide. The other members of the House gave their decision upon the construction of the document itself and in any case qualified it by bringing to the inquiry a consideration of the nature of the subject-matter involved.

The rule of law applicable to the licence granted to the respondents in the present case, is, I think, that prima facie licences are revocable: the circumstances of the case are (1.) that this was a licence to use a theatre and (2.) are to be found in the terms of the document itself. Judging from the last consideration alone I should think it revocable. The licence is for the purpose of producing stage plays, concerts and ballets and starts with options to retain the licence for two successive periods of six months each. These provisions are succeeded by an option of further continuing the licence. Speaking for myself I should not, unless compelled, construe such a document as granting a perpetual licence. If it were a tenancy I should interpret it as requiring no more than reasonable notice, and indeed, as rent is payable weekly, it might require only a week's notice. I cannot think that the rights acquired by means of a licence exceed those which a tenancy would give. But it is said (1.) the licensees were put to considerable expense in war time in providing black-out material, and (2.) the licensees have to give a month's notice to terminate the licence whereas no provision for its termination by the licensors is to be found. As to the first objection the answer, as I think, is that the respondents were granted at least a year certain and a possibility of seven years enjoyment; and as to the second that, if my view of the law be right, the licensees are entitled to a reasonable time after notice to put an end to their commitments, whereas the licensors would have no protection against the licensees walking out at any moment and, therefore, require some notice of an intention to do so. Primarily, of course, the question whether the respondents' licence is revocable or irrevocable must depend on the language of the document of June 10, 1942, and from that contract I cannot find ground for supposing it to be irrevocable. Apart from the circumstances already mentioned, the retention of the bars and cloak rooms, the right on the part of the appellants to sell programmes, etc., their retention of the possession of the theatre and their acceptance of responsibility for payment of all rates, taxes, assessments and theatre and excise licences are not obligations which one would expect the grantor of a perpetual licence to undertake. Much less would they render themselves liable for external and structural repairs, external painting and decoration and repairs to roof and main drainage. I have not forgotten that the licence was granted and accepted in war time and at a substantial and increasing rent. Such a consideration may have some weight in a case where the construction of a document is doubtful. In the circumstances of the present case it cannot, I think, influence the decision.

There remains the subordinate question whether the appellants did not bring their action too soon. On this issue the respondents put forward two contentions (1.) that the month's notice given by the letter of September 11, 1945, is too short, (2.) that in the case of a licence they are entitled to a reasonable time to wind up their commitments after the termination of the time given by the notice for surrender of the premises. My Lords, speaking for myself on an occasion when I do not think it necessary to come to a final conclusion on the matter, I take the provisional view that a licence is prima facie terminable at once after notice to determine has been given, but that the licensee must be given a reasonable time to vacate the premises and what is a reasonable time must depend upon all the circumstances of the case. In the case of a theatre, it might even extend to the run of a play, if no suitable alternative premises could be found. But in the present instance I do not think a question of this kind which may give rise to a marked difference of view calls for decision. Whether the submission be that notice to determine a licence is required and a month was too short in the circumstances, or that a month's notice having been given the respondents were entitled to a reasonable time to dispose of their commitments and that no sufficient time had been given when the appellants delivered their counter claim for a declaration and injunction on November 27, 1945, the issue is still the same: Was a month's notice sufficient and was a reasonable time for vacating the theatre given, whether that time is to count from the date of giving the notice or from the time at which possession was demanded?

In either case the respondents sought to rely on the agreement which they had entered into with Linnit & Dunfee, Ld., and upon it alone as a circumstance to be taken into consideration in determining the time which should be given for vacating the premises. If that agreement was permissible under the terms of the licence of June 10, 1942, the time given was undoubtedly too short. For the appellants however, it is said, and Roxburgh J. who alone dealt with the matter decided that it was a sub-licence, and void under cl. 6 of that document, as it had not been authorized by the grantors. The material portion of that clause reads as follows "You are not to enter into a sub-licence of the theatre without consent of the company, but this consent would not be unreasonably withheld provided a mutual arrangement is made between us for our company to participate in any profit on any sub-licence to be entered into by you." In fact no permission to sub-licence was asked, nor was any agreement made for participation in the profit arising from the agreement between the respondents and Linnit & Dunfee, Ld. That agreement had not been authorized and if it was a sub-licence was entered into in defiance of cl. 6 and cannot be relied upon as prolonging the time to which the respondents were entitled before vacating the premises. Is it then a sub-licence? I think it is. The learned judge who tried the case has gone through the agreement clause by clause and it is not necessary for me to repeat his analysis. I think it is sufficient to say that the original licence of June 10, 1942, authorized the use of so much of the theatre as was required for the production of stage plays, concerts or ballets, reserving only an office, the right to bars and cloakrooms and some general control. Similarly, Linnit & Dunfee, Ld. obtained the right to use so much of the theatre as they required to produce a particular play with not dissimilar reservations. As the learned judge observed ((1946) 115 L.J. (Ch.) 185, 191), there is only one thing in the latter agreement which supports the contention of the respondents, viz., the phrase "The theatre company agrees to engage the production company to produce," and in his opinion those words could not prevail against the substance of the agreement as a whole. With this view I concur. I also take the same view as Roburgh J. in thinking that there is no sufficient evidence to prove that the appellants knew of and acquiesced in the impugned agreement. A knowledge that the programmes contained the words "By arrangement with Mala de la Marr, Linnit & Dunfee, present 'Young Mrs. Barrington'" seems to me quite insufficient for that purpose. On all points therefore I find myself in agreement with the learned judge who tried the case and would allow the appeal and restore his judgment.

LORD MACDERMOTT (after coming to the conclusion that the licence was revocable): But if so, how could revocation be effected? Like the first, this question involves the construction of the contract and it also requires consideration as to what term, if any, should be implied therein to give effect to the intention of the parties. My Lords, the profusion and diversity of licences and the freedom of contract regarding them are such as to discourage any unnecessary formulation of general propositions on the subject. But it is, I think, safe, as well as desirable for the decision of this case, to say that one who remains on the land of another after his licence to use it has terminated will not be considered a trespasser before he has had a reasonable time in which to vacate the premises. That is well settled, though the assessment of what is reasonable may depend on a great variety of factors and cause considerable difficulty in particular instances. This period of grace can, of course, be the subject of agreement, but it exists for gratuitous as well as for contractual licensees and, on that account, must, I think, be generally ascribed to a rule of law rather than to an implied stipulation. For that reason it need not be read into this contract. It has, however, a bearing on the question which I am now discussing. It supervenes *after* the licence has terminated. Its purpose is to enable the former licensee to adjust himself to the new situation by vacating the premises. Measured reasonably and fairly it will often provide sufficiently for the consequences of the licensor's change of will. But its object is not to prolong the user sanctioned by the licence merely for the benefit and convenience of the licensee for, ex hypothesi, the licence has ceased; and where, as for example in cases of a specialized user involving obligations to third parties or the public, the circumstances or the contract are such as to show that an immediate cessation of the authorized use or activity was not contemplated or intended, the rule of law to which I have referred may well, and notwithstanding a liberal measurement of its reasonable period, fall short of meeting the just requirements of the position.

Turning to the present case, the question then arises whether the true intendment of the contract was such as to permit an immediate withdrawal of the licence. My Lords, on that I think it is as clear that the parties did not contemplate an immediate, out-of-hand, revocation as it is that they did not intend a perpetual arrangement. What was granted was a licence to use the theatre "for the purpose of producing stage plays, concerts or ballets." That purpose, as everyone knows, connotes a wide range of activity and a highly specialized user of the premises. It involves considerable expenditure and a host of contractual relationships with those who provide and those who seek the entertainment offered. Whatever the legal attributes of a bare and unqualified licence may be, the expressed object of this licence makes it hard to believe that either of the parties ever intended that it could be withdrawn instanter, regardless of the respondents' commitments and leaving them only such time as they might require to remove themselves and their possessions from the theatre. This view must, of course, be subject to the terms to which the parties have agreed. I cannot, however, find anything in the contract to modify it. On the contrary the provisions as to (a) the payment of rent in advance, (b) the continuation of the licence after the first year, and (c) the granting of sub-licences, though insufficient to raise an implication of permanence, all go, in my opinion, to support the conclusion which the nature of the subject-matter suggests.

If this be the position, it is clear that the right to revoke must necessarily be the subject of an implied term. It is, perhaps, not so clear what, precisely, the term should be. My Lords, in approaching that question I think it well to recall the warning given by Lord Wright in *Luxor (Eastborne), Ld.* v. *Cooper*, [1941] A.C. 108, 137, when he said: "The general presumption is that the parties have expressed every material term which they intended should govern their agreement, whether oral or in writing. But it is well recognized that there may be cases where obviously some term must be implied if the intention of the parties is not to be defeated, some term of which it can be predicated that 'it goes without saying,' some term not expressed but necessary to give to the transaction such business efficacy as the parties must have intended. This does not mean that the court can embark on a reconstruction of the agreement on equitable principles, or on a view of what the parties should, in the opinion of the court, reasonably have contemplated. The implication must arise inevitably to give effect to the intention of the parties." With that caution in mind and leaving what I may call the packing-up period to the general rule of law already mentioned, the conclusion I reach is that in this contract there should be implied a stipulation to the effect that, after the expiration of the first year, the licence might be terminated by the licensors on the expiration of a reasonable notice period duly communicated to the licensees. That, to my mind, is what accords best with the express terms of the contract and the nature of the transaction. Whatever the results of disregarding such a stipulation as to notice may be (and on that I express no opinion as it does not call for decision on the view I take) it is, I think, beyond question that the parties were at liberty so to agree if they chose. I am not unmindful that an implication of this nature makes it incumbent upon the licensors to specify a reasonable period and that they may not be fully versed concerning all the relevant circumstances when they have to do so. I do not think the appellants can well complain on this score, however, when their own document is silent on the point; and, apart from that consideration, I see no practicable alternative which would not leave both parties in a state of even greater uncertainty.

It remains to be determined whether the licence has been revoked in accordance with this implied term. The precise meaning of the notice given by the appellants on September 11, 1945, is not beyond debate. But taken in conjunction with its covering letter of the same date I have little doubt that it should be read as intimating that the licence would be terminated on October 13, 1945, and it is clear that this was what it conveyed to the respondents, for their reply of September 14, inquires concerning the appellants' authority "to give a month's notice terminating the said licence." But was this a reasonable period? Apart from the term providing for payment of four weeks' rent in advance, the only evidence adduced upon this issue was the agreement dated August 22, 1945, between the respondents and Linnit & Dunfee, Ld., which the respondents pleaded and proved and under which Linnit & Dunfee, Ld. produced a play at the appellants' theatre entitled "Young Mrs. Barrington." It was admitted that the respondents were unable to terminate this agreement sooner than they did (which was on January 5, 1946), but the appellants contended that it constituted a breach of cl. 6 of the agreement of June 10, 1942, which provided that the respondents were "not to enter into a sub-licence of the theatre" without the appellants' consent and that the respondents were, accordingly, precluded from relying on it in support of their plea that, if the licence were revocable, reasonable notice had not been given. The respondents argued that this agreement was not a sub-licence and, further, that the appellants knew of the agreement and had acquiesced in the production of "Young Mrs. Barrington" so as to waive the alleged breach of cl. 6. This last point the respondents entirely failed to establish and it need not be further noticed. Nor need very much be said on the question whether the agreement of August 22, 1945, was a sub-licence of the theatre. It is true that it denied Linnit & Dunfee, Ld. the use of certain relatively small portions of the premises which were the subject of the agreement of June 10, 1942, and this, it was said, avoided a breach of cl. 6 just as a sub-lease of part only of demised premises avoids contravention of a covenant against sub-letting. My Lords, whatever the virtues of that analogy may be in the abstract, I do not consider that this contention has substance in the present case. When cl. 6 speaks of a sub-licence "of the theatre" I think that as a matter both of good sense and sound construction, it refers to the theatre premises or so much thereof as will enable the purpose of the licence, the production of "stage plays, concerts or ballets," to be achieved by the sub-licensees. Clause 6 proceeds to stipulate that the appellants' consent to a sub-licence will not be unreasonably withheld if a mutual arrangement is made between them and the respondents for sharing the profits. It is difficult to conceive that the true meaning of this clause was such as to enable this financial provision to be circumvented to the loss of the appellants and the advantage of the respondents by the reservation of a few seats in the auditorium or some unessential office accommodation. It is also difficult not to feel that this profit-sharing term of the contract may explain why the agreement of August 22, 1945, was cast in the form of an engagement. It is now admitted that Linnit & Dunfee, Ld. were not the respondents' agents or employees. They made the agreement on their own account and by its terms were given the use of the theatre for a production, the financial risks of which they were to bear. My Lords, I find it unnecessary to detail the various clauses of this somewhat peculiar document. Whatever its guise I am satisfied that, as Roxburgh J. has held, it was in its substance a sub-licence and amounted to a breach of cl. 6. It must therefore be left out of account. This means that there is virtually no evidence before your Lordships as to what would, in the circumstances, have been a reasonable period of notice. But having regard to the course of the proceedings and the issues they chose to raise, the onus in this matter rested, in my opinion, on the plaintiffs and present respondents. They have not discharged that onus and the result, in my view, is that the notice given by the appellants must be considered valid and effectual. On similar, if not identical, grounds I think the time between October 13 and November 27, 1945—the date of the counterclaim—must be taken as a sufficient period of grace to enable the respondents to vacate the theatre. . . .

Appeal allowed.

[Lord Simonds concurred with Lord MacDermott. Lord Uthwatt gave a concurring judgment to the effect that the licence was determinable by notice given at any time but that a reasonable notice was necessary. On the facts, the notice was sufficient. The learned Lord concluded as follows: "My view as to the construction of the agreement renders it unnecessary to consider whether *Hurst* v. *Picture Theatres, Ld.*, was rightly decided, or to express any concluded opinion on the question of the remedies now open in every court to a bare licensee who claims that the licensor has in breach of his bargain affected to revoke it. I merely confess my present inability to see any answer to the propositions of law stated by the Master of the Rolls in his judgment in the case under appeal. The settled practice of the courts of equity is to do what they can by an injunction to preserve the sanctity of a bargain. To my mind, as at present advised, a licensee who has refused to accept the wrongful repudiation of the bargain which is involved in an unauthorized revocation of the licence is as much entitled to the protection of an injunction as a licensee who has not received any notice of revocation;

and, if the remedy of injunction is properly available in the latter case against unauthorized interference by the licensor, it is also available in the former case. In a court of equity, wrongful acts are no passport to favour."

In *Sun Oil Co.* v. *Coveart* (1956), 4 D.L.R. 2d 303, [1956] O.W.N. 701 (C.A.), plaintiff let a service station to defendant under a monthly tenancy terminable at any time on 10 days' notice. The parties also entered into a "retailer" agreement under which defendant agreed to buy only plaintiff's products which the latter agreed to supply as required. After repeated efforts to dispossess defendant, plaintiff gave notice on November 1, 1955, to vacate on November 14 and for termination of the retailer agreement on that date. On November 10 and 11 defendant ordered gasoline and grease from plaintiff which was supplied. It was accepted that both the lease and retailer agreement had no effect after November 14. In an action for possession, defendant contended that he had a licence of occupation until disposition of the goods that he ordered and terminable on reasonable notice. The arguments were rejected. Gale J. at the trial, after considering and rejecting the contention that a licence arose, went on to consider the situation on the assumption of the existence of a licence and said, *inter alia:* "... it is the defendant's contention that he was entitled to remain after that date until reasonable notice was given revoking the licence and thereafter until he had a reasonable opportunity of quitting the premises. It would seem, however, that this contention is completely met by the judgment of the Court of Appeal in *Minister of Health* v. *Bellotti*, [1944] K.B. 298, 1 All E.R. 238. Much argument ranged around the question whether actual notice is necessary to revoke a licence and, if so, whether further time ought to be given to a licensee within which to vacate. The *Bellotti* case seems to indicate that in some circumstances a licence may be terminated without any notice at all and that proposition is confirmed to some extent in the more recent case of *Winter Garden Theatre (London) Ltd.* v. *Millennium Productions Ltd.*, *supra.* Certainly the *Bellotti* case did decide that a notice giving inadequate time within which to leave would at least effectually revoke the licence, so that if notice were necessary here ex. 3A was sufficient for the purpose. And certainly the defendant had ample time prior to the commencement of the action within which to give up the occupancy of the service station."

In *Hyslop and Hyslop* v. *M. E. Walker Ltd.* (1956), 1 D.L.R. 2d 777 (N.S.), plaintiff was awarded damages for assault where excessive force was used in ejecting him from a theatre for misbehaviour. McQuarrie J. said (at p. 778): "The defendant had the power to revoke the plaintiff's licence to remain in the theatre even if the circumstances were such that the defendant did not have the right to revoke it. In my opinion the defendant did have the right to revoke the plaintiff's licence...."

The *Hurst* case, *supra* was rejected in *Cowell* v. *Rosehill Race Course Co. Ltd.* (1937), 56 Comm. L.R. 605, but applied in *Heller* v. *Niagara Racing Assoc.*, 56 O.L.R. 355, [1925] 2 D.L.R. 286 (App. Div.) and *Barnswell* v. *National Amusement Co.* (1915), 21 B.C.R. 435, 23 D.L.R. 615 (C.A.). The general rule in the United States is contrary to the *Hurst* doctrine: see 2 American Law of Property, ss. 8.119; 8.120. See *Conard*, The Privilege of Forcibly Ejecting an Amusement Patron, (1942) 90 Univ. of Pa. L. Rev. 809; *Clark*, Licenses in Real Property Law, (1921) 21 Col. L. Rev. 757; see also, *Wade*, What is a Licence, (1948) 64 Law Q. Rev. 57; *Stoljar*, Licence, Interest and Contract, (1955) 33 Can. Bar Rev. 562.

In *Foster* v. *Robinson*, [1950] 2 All E.R. 342, [1951] 1 K.B. 149 (C.A.), a yearly tenant orally arranged with his landlord for termination of the tenancy and for his occupation of the premises rent free for life. Evershed M.R. said, *inter alia* (at p. 346 All E.R., p. 156 K.B.): "Since the recent decision in *Winter Garden Theatre (London) Ltd.* v. *Millenium Productions Ltd.* I think that although a licence of that kind may, apart from the terms of the contract, be revoked, it may now be taken that if the landlord, having made that arrangement sought to revoke it, he would be restrained by the court from so doing. Thus the result is arrived at that the tenant was entitled as licensee to occupy the premises without charge for the rest of his days, and he did so. I prefer that analysis of the case."

Assuming that a person is a licensee "with a contractual right to remain" enforceable in equity, does it follow that his licence is assignable and does it follow that the licensor's assignees are bound by the licence? See *Errington* v. *Errington*, [1952] 1 All E.R. 149, [1952] 1 K.B. 290 (C.A.).

On licences generally, see *Wade*, Licences and Third Parties, (1952) 68 Law Q. Rev. 337; *Williams*, Interests and Clogs, (1952) 30 Can. Bar Rev. 1004; *Cheshire*, A New Equitable Interest in Land, (1953) 16 Mod. L. Rev. 1; *Hanbury*, Licences, A Jonah's Gourd, (1954) Camb. L. J. 201, (1955) Camb. L. J. 47.]

WOOD v. LAKE. King's Bench. 1751. Sayer 3, 96 E.R. 783

In a case reserved, in an action upon the case, it was stated; that the defendant had agreed, by a parol agreement, that the plaintiff should have the liberty of stacking coals upon part of a close belonging to the defendant, for the term of seven years, and that, during this term, he should have the sole use of that part of the close, upon which he was to have the liberty of stacking coals; and that, after the plaintiff had, pursuant to this agreement, enjoyed the liberty of stacking coals three years, the defendant locked up the gate of the close.

The question was, whether this agreement was good for seven years?

Lee Ch. J. and Denison J. were of opinion, that it was.

And by them.—In the case of *Webb* v. *Paternoster*, Palm. 71, it is laid down, that the grant of a licence to stack hay upon land does not amount to a lease of the land; and, although it be in that case said, that such a licence, provided the grant be for a time certain, is irrevocable, it by no means follows, that an interest in the land does thereby pass. As the agreement in the present case was only for an easement, and not for an interest in the land, it did not amount to a lease, and consequently it was, notwithstanding the Statute of Frauds and Perjuries, good for seven years.

Wright J. was absent.

Foster J. concurred in opinion, that the agreement did not amount to a lease: but he inclined to be of opinion, that the words in the Statute of Frauds and Perjuries, any uncertain interest in land, do extend to this agreement, and consequently that it was not good for more than three years.

Lee Ch. J. and Denison J. inclined to be of opinion, that the words in that statute, any uncertain interest in land, do relate only to interests, which are uncertain as to the time of their duration.

After taking time to consider, it was holden that the agreement was good for seven years.

[In *Webb* v. *Paternoster* (1620), Palmer 71, 81 E.R. 983 (K.B.). A gave permission to B to stack hay on his land for a reasonable time. Thereafter A leased the land to C whose cattle ate the hay. Does B have any tenable action against A? Against C? *Cf. Winter* v. *Brockwell* (1807), 8 East 308, 103 E.R. 359 (K.B.).

In *Taylor* v. *Waters* (1817), 7 Taunt. 374, 129 E.R. 150 (C.P.) an opera house manager for consideration gave to one G., his executors, administrators and assigns, six tickets entitling the holder of each to free admission for 21 years. Plaintiff bought one of the tickets from G. and used it without objection for 15 years. Then he was refused entry at the instance of the proprietors. Is plaintiff entitled to damages from the manager by reason of his exclusion?

In *Coleman* v. *Foster* (1856), 1 H. & N. 37, 156 E.R. 1108 (Ex.), Pollock C.B. said that "a licence is a thing so evanescent that it cannot be transferred."]

KING v. DAVID ALLEN & SONS, BILLPOSTING LTD. House of Lords. [1916] 2 A.C. 54

Appeal from an order of the Court of Appeal in Ireland, [1915] 2 I.R. 448, affirming an order of the Divisional Court which affirmed a judgment of Gibson J., [1915] 2 I.R. 213, awarding damages to respondents for breach of a billposting agreement.

At the date of this agreement the appellant was the owner of certain premises situate at Madras Place and abutting on the Royal Canal Bank in the city of Dublin, and the respondents enjoyed the sole right and privilege, under an agreement dated November 1, 1889, and made between the predecessors of the respective parties, of using the whole of the surface wall of the premises for the purpose of exhibiting advertisements thereon at a yearly rent of 9£. At the date of the agreement next hereinafter mentioned the appellant was desirous of letting the lands at Madras Place to a company about to be formed for the erection thereon of a picture house, and the respondents accepted this agreement in lieu of their rights under the old agreement.

By an agreement in writing dated July 1, 1913, and made between the appellant, thereinafter called "the licensor," of the one part and the respondents, thereinafter called "the licensees," of the other part, it was agreed that the licensor thereby gave the licensees permission to affix bills, posters, and advertisements to the flank wall at side of picture house proposed to be erected at Royal Canal Bank and Madras Place, Dublin, for the term of four years from November 1, 1913, or the first day said picture house should be opened for business, whichever should first happen, thereafter terminable on six months' notice by either party as therein mentioned, the licensees to pay for such permission a rent at the rate of 12£ per annum, payable, so long as the licence remained in force, half-yearly as therein mentioned, the first payment to be made on May 1, 1914; and the licensor agreed that he would not while the licence remained in force license or permit any other person to affix any billposting or advertisement to the said flank walls or any part thereof, and would, if required by the licensees, take proceedings against any person or persons who might during the continuance of the license affix any billposting or advertisement to said flank walls, the licensees indemnifying the licensor against any costs or expenses connected therewith.

By an agreement dated August 29, 1913, and made between the appellant of the one part and Thomas C. Flinn, therein described as "trustee for the Phibsboro' Picture House, Limited," then about to be incorporated and thereinafter referred to as "the new company" of the other part, the appellant agreed to let and Flinn as trustee for the new company agreed to take a lease of the said premises in Madras Place, abutting on the Royal Canal Bank, for a term of forty years from August 1, 1913, subject to the payment of the yearly rent of 117£ and to the terms and conditions set out in the draft lease then already prepared and on which the parties thereto had signed their names; and further that the appellant should assign to Flinn as trustee for the company all his interest in the agreement of July 1, 1913; and Flinn agreed that as soon as the new company was registered he would obtain the acceptance and execution by the company of the lease and the ratification of the agreement of July 1, 1913.

The new company was duly incorporated under the Companies Act on September 2, 1913.

At a general meeting of the company held on September 13, 1913, it was resolved that the agreement of August 29, 1913, be ratified and adopted and that the seal of the company be affixed to the indenture of lease referred to in the agreement, and the lease was duly executed on that occasion. By this lease, which was expressed to be made between the appellant of the one part and the Phibsboro' Picture House, Limited, of the other part, the appellant demised the premises in question to the company for the term and subject to the rent above mentioned and the company covenanted to erect a picture house on the premises within one year from the date of the lease. The agreement of July 1, 1913, was not referred to in the lease, nor was any assignment of the interest of the appellant in that agreement ever made to the company.

The picture house was completed in May, 1914. In June, 1914, the respondents attempted to post their bills on the flank wall of the picture house, but were forcibly prevented by the servants of the company. The appellant, who was a director of the company, protested against the action of the company and his co-directors and did his best to have the agreement of July 1, 1913, honourably kept, but without success. Thereupon the respondents commenced the present action against the appellant. The appellant, while denying liability, applied to bring in the picture house company as third parties, but this application was ultimately refused.

LORD BUCKMASTER L. C.: My Lords, it is impossible to approach the consideration of this case without feeling and expressing great regret for the unfortunate position in which the appellant, Mr. King, has found himself. He seems to me to have acted throughout the whole of these transactions with perfect straightforwardness and with a sincere and anxious desire to discharge the obligation which he undertook towards David Allen & Sons, Limited; but by circumstances which have passed beyond his control there has, in my view, been a breach of his obligation to the respondents, and for that breach he must be made responsible.

... I think it is plain that Messrs. David Allen & Sons, Limited, were well acquainted with the circumstances that then existed with regard to the use of this site, and that they knew quite well that it was intended that the company should be formed for the purpose of building upon it, thus creating a new structure to which their bills might be affixed. With this knowledge they entered into an agreement with the appellant of July 1, 1913, upon which the whole of the present dispute depends. It is an agreement which was made between the appellant of the one part and the respondents of the other, and as part of the arrangement leading up to its execution the previous agreement which had been made between the predecessor in title of the appellant and the predecessor in title of the respondents was cancelled, and the new agreement took its place.

Now in the new agreement the appellant is referred to as licensor and the respondents as licensees. I only mention that fact for the purpose of making quite plain that I attach no importance whatever to these descriptions; they are nothing but a method of reference, and the names might just as well have been lessor and lessee as licensor and licensee. It is not upon the use of those phrases that my view of this contract in any way depends.

The agreement itself is quite short and begins with a clause which says that the appellant will grant to the respondents "permission to affix bills, posters, and advertisements to the flank wall" of the picture palace which is to be erected at the Royal Canal Bank "for a term of four years from the 1st November, 1913, or the first day said picture house shall be opened for business," and after that period of four years the document is to be capable of termination by either party on six months' written notice. The next clause provides that the respondents will pay a rent at the rate of 12£ per annum "so long as this license remains in force." I attach some considerable importance to this phrase; it is the description in the body of the document of what the parties intended that the document should be, and it is stated in plain language that the description of the document is that of a licence. It is not a letting or a tenancy or anything of the kind, but a licence. And the same phrase is used in a similar connection later on in the agreement, in clause 5.

My Lords, I have looked anxiously and carefully through this document to see whether it was possible to derive from its construction anything except the creation of a personal obligation between the appellant and the respondents with regard to the use of this wall, and I am unable to find it. There are two circumstances to which attention has been quite properly called by the appellant's counsel, which are no doubt important in considering what the agreement effected. The first is the fact of the rent reserved, and the next that there is a term of years granted and that arrangements are introduced into the agreement to prevent other people having competing rights with Messrs. David Allen & Sons upon this wall. Those considerations do not, in my opinion, necessarily conflict with the view that this is nothing but a licence—a licence for a fixed term of years, but a licence which creates no estate or interest in the land upon which the palace is going to be built, nor an easement to which the land would be thereafter subject.

[The Lord Chancellor recited the sequence of events and continued as follows:]

... For what has occurred is this: The company, having entered into possession of the premises under the lease and having built the picture palace, forthwith refused to permit Mssrs. David Allen & Sons to post their bills, although the company had known throughout that the lease which they had taken of the premises was a lease which had been granted by Mr. King, who had contracted with David Allen & Sons that they should possess the right of posting their bills against this wall.

My Lords, it is obviously a very undesirable thing to say any words by way of criticism of persons who are not represented before your Lordships' House, and I will therefore pass by the temptation to comment upon this action of the company, an action which appears to have been insufficiently and indeed inaccurately explained in some of their letters.

The matter then is left in this way. There is a contract between the appellant and the respondents which creates nothing but a personal obligation. It is a licence given for good and valuable consideration and to endure for a certain time. But I fail to see—although I have done my best to follow the many authorities which the learned Solicitor-General has thought it right to place before our consideration—that there is any authority for saying that any such document creates rights other than those I have described. A case of *Wilson* v. *Tavener*, [1901] 1 Ch. 578, was indeed referred to, but it really affords no assistance, for there the right conferred was to erect a hoarding upon the defendant's ground, while in the present case the sole right is to fix bills against a flank wall, and it is unreasonable to attempt to construct the relationship of landlord and tenant or grantor and grantee of an easement out of such a transaction, and I find it difficult to see how it can be reasonably urged that anything beyond personal rights was ever contemplated by the parties. Those rights have undoubtedly been taken away by the action on the part of the company, who have been enabled to prevent the respondents from exercising their rights owing to the lease granted by Mr. King, and he is accordingly liable in damages, although it was certainly not with his will, and indeed against his own express desire, that the company has declined to honour his agreement.

EARL LOREBURN: ... I have very little to add to what has been said, but I look at the case in this way. The plaintiffs say that Mr. King promised them for four years the use of a certain wall for advertising purposes by the agreement of July 1, 1913, and they say that after that Mr. King demised that land, and that Mr. King's lessees refused to make good the promise in regard to advertisement. Well, if the agreement of July 1, which purports to be on the face of it a licence, was equivalent to creating an incorporeal hereditament or a sufficient interest in land, Mr. King did not break his contract in making the lease, and would not be responsible for any trespasses that were committed by his licensees. But we must look at the document itself, and it seems to me that it does not create any interest in land at all; it merely amounts to a promise on the part of Mr. King that he would allow the other party to the contract to use the wall for advertising purposes, and there was an implied undertaking that he would not disable himself from carrying out his contract. Now Mr. King has altered his legal position in respect of his control of this land. Those to whom he granted the lease have disregarded his wishes and refused to allow his bargain to be carried out, and they have been practically enabled to do so by reason of the demise that he executed. In these circumstances it seems to me that there has been a breach in law of the contract of July 1, and Mr. King has disabled himself from giving effect to it as intended by parting with his right to present possession. That is enough to establish a case for damages against Mr. King. There may be a remedy over against the lessees. I say nothing of that, because they are not here, and I do not wish either to encourage or to discourage any further proceedings; but this I think is clear: that the existence of such a remedy, if remedy there be, does not release Mr. King from his liability to answer for breaking the contract which he made.

LORD ATKINSON: My Lords, I concur and I have nothing to add.

Appeal dismissed.

[If this case should come up again, would you advise plaintiffs to sue the company? Would it make any difference if in the lease to the company there was an express exception of plaintiffs' rights under the billposting agreement?

In *Teplitsky and Bookman* v. *O. E. Carson Ltd.* (1956), 5 D.L.R. 2d 635, [1956] O.W.N. 590, an extruding neon sign was fastened to an upper apartment leased to A. The sign was erected by B, a later lessee of the ground floor under a lease which permitted the erection of signs. A was disturbed by the flashing neon sign and moved out. The landlord sued B for a mandatory order and for damages. Should he recover? Would A have had a right of action against B or against the landlord?

In *Clapman* v. *Edwards*, [1938] 2 All E.R. 507 (Ch.), a lease of a gasoline station made between the lessor and his successors in title and the lessee and his successors in title gave the lessee the right to use the flank walls of the adjoining premises for advertising purposes. The lessor assigned his interest to plaintiff and shortly afterwards the lessee entered into a written agreement with a company giving it advertising rights in respect of the flank walls. Plaintiff sought to enjoin the lessee from permitting anyone else to advertise on the flank walls. Should he succeed?

See 2 *American Law of Property*, s. 8.122: "The question of whether a particular license is alienable is wholly a question of construction. Many licenses arise out of relations so personal in their nature that the inference that they were not intended to be assignable is one which is easy to draw.... On the other hand, many licenses have an origin much more commercial than personal in nature. This is true in the usual case of the purchase and sale of an entertainment admission ticket. Such tickets are, in the absence of special limitation, generally assignable."]

COHEN v. LIVINGSTONE. British Columbia Supreme Court. [1949] 2 W.W.R. 553

WOOD J.: The history of this matter is fully set out in the agreed statement of facts and no other evidence was given. The plaintiffs are the owners of lot 17, block 34, district lot 541, group 1, New Westminster District, plan 210, and the defendant is the owner of the adjoining lot 18. These are 25-foot lots situate in the business section of Vancouver on the west side of Richards Street between Pender and Dunsmuir Streets. On this property the plaintiffs' predecessor in title, one McPhail, and the defendant in 1928 erected a three-storey business building which has a value, aside from the land, of about $50,000; $25,000 was borrowed from the Canada Life Assurance Company on a mortgage signed by both owners.

At the time, efforts were made in a solicitor's office to have both properties put in the joint names of the two owners as tenants in common, or have a private company incorporated, but the defendant objected to this, wishing to retain the ownership of his own property, McPhail to do the same, and stipulated that either should be in a position to sell separately or put up a wall. The meeting broke up. Nevertheless, the building contemplated was erected as one unit and cannot readily be divided for on the plaintiffs' lot is the heating plant and the electrical plant, and on the defendant's lot is the elevator and the stairway.

There is no stairway on the plaintiffs' lot nor other means of access to the upper floors.

Now the defendant proposes to partition the building by erecting a wall on the boundaries of the lots so as to enjoy exclusive possession of that part of the building which is erected on his lot, asserting that the plaintiffs have no interest therein and that they have no right to the facilities or to the enjoyment of the use of any part thereof. The defendant maintains that the part of the building on each lot is part of that lot and is owned by the owner thereof—that there is no common ownership of the building and no common right of user; that there is no form of joint ownership known to the law as distinct from ownership of the land and that there can be no tenancy in common of the building unless tenants in common are tenants in common of the land itself; that one cannot be an owner of a fixture unless he is owner of the land.

On the other hand, counsel for the plaintiffs argues that the circumstances indicate an implied contract for some kind of joint ownership and right of user—a mutual easement; that each had a right to have a portion of the building on the other's land and to the user of that land for the purposes of that building. There was, of course, no express contract, but the plaintiffs contend that it must be implied notwithstanding the firm position which the defendant took that his lot was to remain his; that they erected a building of such a nature that separate ownership became impossible; that the facilities which I have mentioned were built regardless of any demarcation between the lots and that the rooms and hallways were laid out without regard to the boundary; that the building was built as a single unit and that the erection of the building was a repudiation of any suggestion that there should be two buildings, or one building to one-half of which each had ownership and right of user; that, while McPhail was the owner of the property, the building was conducted as a joint venture, although they did refer to "my half" and "your half"; that they both signed the mortgage which covered both lots and merged their interests in the construction of a single unit; that all this was consistent with and consistent only with the idea of a building owned and used in common.

At one time the defendant applied under the wartime rental regulations for a change of rental of the whole building without consulting his co-owner. There was a common business manager. They contend that all these things must have a practical application.

Counsel contends that by necessary intendment each of these lots is burdened with the building, the user thereof and the right of access thereto. In principle he contends further that there is no reason why the superstructure placed on lands should not be separated from the surface as far as the title is concerned. He refers to the law with regard to fixtures and points out that, while the degree of annexation is of evidentiary value, it is not conclusive nor material when a contrary intention has been established and that such an intention may arise out of implied agreement. He suggests that land may be divided not only perpendicularly but horizontally and that the parties are tenants in common of the building as distinct from the land.

In my view this latter contention cannot succeed. I fail to see how such a tenancy can exist apart from the land. Nor can I agree that such a building as this can be treated as a chattel—see *Cheshire on Real Property*, 5th ed., p. 102.

The only hope for the plaintiffs to succeed is indicated in the judgments of the Manitoba Court of Appeal in *Smith* v. *Curry*, 29 Man. R. 97; 42 D.L.R. 225; [1918] 2 W.W.R. 848. In that case a building was erected on two adjoining lots separately owned. There was a party wall. At p. 100 Man. R, p. 227 D.L.R., p. 850 W.W.R. Perdue, C. J. M. says:

"There is no dispute as to the main facts. The manner in which the building was constructed shows beyond a doubt that there was an agreement between the owners of the buildings that the plaintiff should have access from the street to the upper floor of his building by means of the front door, stairway and passages in the Curry building and Curry should have the use of the plaintiff's back stairs and passages to his own building. Curry was satisfied with the arrangement and agreed to it. The only matter as to which there is any question is the duration of the agreement. Nothing appears to have been said as to this before or during the construction of the building. The architect says that there was no time mentioned. He goes on to say:

"'It was agreed that the building should be built in that way. I should have said it was for all time.'

"No time having been mentioned, the agreement was either at will or for the duration of the buildings. But the whole construction of the premises, with the doors in the party wall, the passages in connection with them, the placing of the stairways, etc. points in its very nature to something more than a mere temporary arrangement. Each party received a concession from the other. Both were satisfied and we cannot now enter upon discussion as to who got the best of the bargain. The plaintiff constructed his building without a front stairway relying on the agreement that Curry would allow him the use of the front stairway in the Curry building, in return for the use by Curry of the back stairway in the Smith building. To deprive him now of this right would compel him to construct a new stairway for his building, thereby necessitating material changes in the plan and construction of it and depriving him of considerable space."

But there was an agreement for an easement as stated above and the only question was the duration of the agreement.

In the case at bar McPhail went into the deal with his eyes open. He knew the defendant's attitude but no doubt felt that no sensible man would take the attitude now taken by the defendant. He was prepared to take a chance on that.

Action dismissed.

[In *McManus* v. *Cooke* (1887), 35 Ch.D. 681, A and B were adjoining owners who entered into an oral agreement for the rebuilding of a party wall by A at their joint expense, and that each was to be at liberty to build a lean-to skylight resting on the party wall. A did the work and built his skylight. B built one too but in such a shape as to obstruct access of light to A's premises. Is A entitled to a mandatory injunction? Is the Statute of Frauds applicable, and if so, is the doctrine of part performance applicable? *Cf. Acton Tanning Co.* v. *Toronto Suburban Ry.* (1918), 56 S.C.R. 196, 40 D.L.R. 421.

In *Foster* v. *Royal Trust Co.*, [1950] O.R. 673, [1951] 1 D.L.R. 147, LeBel J. stated that the doctrine of performance or part performance to take a case out of the Statute of Frauds [or, perhaps more accurately, to take the Statute out of the case] applies to all cases in which a Court of Equity would entertain a suit for specific performance if the alleged agreement were in writing. See *Conard*, Easements, Licenses and the Statute of Frauds, (1941) 15 Temple L.Q. 222.]

RAMSDEN v. DYSON. House of Lords. 1866. L.R. 1 H.L. 129

LORD CRANWORTH L. C.: ... If a stranger begins to build on my land supposing it to be his own, and I, perceiving his mistake, abstain from setting him right, and leave him to persevere in his error, a Court of equity will not allow me afterwards to assert my title to the land on which he had expended money on the supposition that the land was his own. It considers that, when I saw the mistake into which he had fallen, it was my duty to be active and to state my adverse title; and that it would be dishonest in me to remain wilfully passive on such an occasion, in order afterwards to profit by the mistake which I might have prevented.

But it will be observed that to raise such an equity two things are required, first, that the person expending the money supposes himself to be building on his own land; and, secondly, that the real owner at the time of the expenditure knows that the land belongs to him and not to the person expending the money in the belief that he is the owner. For if a stranger builds on my land knowing it to be mine, there is no principle of equity which would prevent my claiming the land with the benefit of all the expenditure made on it. There would be nothing in my conduct, active or passive, making it inequitable in me to assert my legal rights.

It follows as a corollary from these rules, or, perhaps, it would be more accurate to say it forms part of them, that if my tenant builds on land which he holds under me, he does not thereby, in the absence of special circumstances, acquire any right to prevent me from taking possession of the land and buildings when the tenancy has determined. He knew the extent of his interest, and it was his folly to expend money upon a title which he knew would or might soon come to an end....

[A father gave to his recently married son and his wife possession of certain land to enable them to build a house on it and told them that they could have the place as long as they wished. There was no deed or writing involved. The son had the land enclosed and built a house on it. The father's devisee sued for a declaration of ownership and possession. Should he succeed? See *Campbell* v. *Campbell*, 4 M.P.R. 502, [1932] 3 D.L.R. 501 (N.S.C.A.). Would it make any difference if plaintiff was a bona fide purchaser for value of the land from the father?

Suppose that instead of giving possession to another, a landowner encourages that other to expend money and labour in improving certain land by orally promising to transfer the land to him or to leave it to him by will? Does the improver have any remedy when his expectation is disappointed? See *McBride* v. *McNeil* (1912), 27 O.L.R. 455.

In *The King* v. *Cowichan Agricultural Society*, [1950] Ex.C.R. 448, [1951] 1 D.L.R. 96, it was held that an alleged lessee of the Crown could not set up any "equitable estoppel" (in having been allowed to proceed with expensive improvements) against the express requirements of a statute governing the making of a valid lease of the lands in question, when those requirements had not been met.]

C.P.R. v. THE KING. Privy Council. [1931] A.C. 414, [1931] 2 D.L.R. 386, [1931] 1 W.W.R. 673

LORD RUSSELL OF KILLOWEN: This appeal was brought against a judgment of the Supreme Court of Canada, [1930] S.C.R. 574, [1930] 4 D.L.R. 161, which in part dismissed the appellant's appeal, and in part allowed the respondent's appeal from a judgment of the Exchequer Court of Canada, [1930] Ex.C.R. 26, [1929] 2 D.L.R. 641, in proceedings, in which the Crown, on the information of the Attorney-General of Canada, was plaintiff, and the Canadian Pacific Railway Company (the appellant here) was defendant.

The object of the proceedings was to obtain the removal from the roadway and lands of the Intercolonial Railway of the appellant's line of telegraph poles and wires. The Intercolonial Railway forms part of the Canadian Government Railways system, and its roadway lies in the Provinces of New Brunswick and Nova Scotia.

The appellant's telegraph line was, at the date of the filing of the information (September 15, 1926), substantially all erected upon and carried along the Intercolonial Railway's roadway. The telegraph line forms part of a telegraph system worked by the appellant, and is of undoubted importance both to itself and to the public, inasmuch as it connects with the cable station at Canso, as well as with Halifax and other important points in the Maritime Provinces.

For the purpose of determining the rights of the parties the Supreme Court, in considering the case, divided the appellant's telegraph line into three sections. This appears to their

Lordships to be a convenient course, and they propose to adopt it in this judgment. The three sections are as follows:—

(a) The "Main Telegraph Line"—namely, from Coldbrook near St. John through Moncton and Truro to Fairview Junction near Halifax, and from Truro to New Glasgow. This was constructed in the years 1888, 1889 and 1890.

(b) The "Branch Telegraph Line"—namely, from New Glasgow to Sydney. This was constructed in 1893, and

(c) The "Westville Telegraph Line,"—namely, from Westville to Pictou. This was constructed in 1911.

It will be necessary to consider the circumstances in which each of these sections was constructed, where the poles were placed, and how it came about that eventually substantially the whole system came to be situated on the lands of the Intercolonial Railway. But before doing so it will be advisable to state exactly what were the claims which were put forward by the Crown, and how each Court has dealt with those claims.

According to the information as it was filed and as it stood at the opening of the trial, the Crown's case was that the appellant was from the very start a trespasser in respect of its entire line. No other case was suggested....

... The relief claimed was possession and mesne profits. At the trial leave to amend was asked for and granted, with the result that damages for trespass were claimed as an alternative to the claim for mesne profits, and, as alternative relief, a declaration was sought in the following terms: "(b)—(1.) In the alternative a declaration as to the rights, if any, of the defendant in said lands in respect of the said line of poles and wires."

The appellant had pleaded licence either irrevocable or, if revocable, unrevoked, and this no doubt was the reason why it was thought prudent by the Crown's advisers to include a claim for a declaration as to the defendant's rights in the Crown lands, notwithstanding that such a claim would appear to be inconsistent with any claims founded upon trespass. It is, however, true to say that the Crown's primary contention throughout has been, that the appellant was and is a trespasser, and nothing else.

[His Lordship then considered the judgment of the trial Judge and the disposition of the appeals taken by both parties to the Supreme Court. The trial Judge held that the lines were all laid by leave and licence but that the licence was not irrevocable. The Supreme Court held that as to the first two lines, the Crown's cross-appeal should be allowed and that as to the third line the appeal of the C.P.R. should be allowed and the cross-appeal dismissed. He then proceeded to consider the facts on all three lines and concluded that with respect to all of them the C.P.R. was, before action brought, in occupation by leave and licence of the Crown. He then continued as follows:]

There remain for consideration the three further questions hereinbefore set forth, and with these their Lordships will now proceed to deal.

(i.) Was the licence, under which the appellant was in occupation of Crown land, revocable?...

It was said that the Crown encouraged the appellant to build the telegraph line upon Crown property, and that thereby the appellant acquired the right to keep the telegraph line there and use it in perpetuity. In support of this proposition reliance was placed on the case of *Plimmer* v. *Mayor of Wellington*, 9 App. Cas. 699.

As their Lordships understand that decision, it was based on contract inferred to have been made between Plimmer and the Government. As pointed out in the judgment, Plimmer in erecting his original works on Government land with Government permission, became an occupant of the land under a revocable licence. Later, by virtue of transactions for the mutual benefit of both sides, from which the Board drew the inference of a contract, Plimmer's right to occupy ceased to be revocable and became a perpetual right to occupy and use the land in question for the purposes of a jetty.

In the present case the facts appear to be very different. As regards the Main Telegraph Line there was no encouragement and no mutual arrangement of any kind. There was nothing but original trespass, which, by dint of toleration over a period of time, became an occupation by leave and licence. As regards the other two sections of the telegraph line, the original occupation was permitted by the Crown, but only upon the footing that the rights of the parties would be defined by agreement thereafter to be negotiated. Unless and until such agreements had been negotiated and had become binding, the occupation continued by leave and licence only, and the appellant must be taken to have erected the telegraph line subject to the risk of the permission being withdrawn if no agreement was effected.

In their Lordships' view *Plimmer's case* is far removed in its facts from the present case, and is of no assistance to the appellant.

It was further contended that the Crown was precluded from revoking the licence by reason of some equitable doctrine, which it was alleged was applicable to the case. The doctrine was not very clearly defined, but reference was made to *Ramsden* v. *Dyson.* In the course of the judgments in that case instances are given in which equity will intervene in favour of a litigant as against the legal owner of land. One such (see Lord Cranworth) is the case where A builds on land which he thinks is his, but is really B's, and B, knowing of A's mistake, encourages A to build either directly or by abstaining from asserting his legal right. In such a case equity will intervene for the protection of A. This, their Lordships understand to have been the equitable doctrine which was invoked by the appellant. It is a doctrine which is sometimes alluded to under the name of "equitable estoppel." Whether there can be any estoppel which is equitable as distinct from legal and whether "equitable estoppel" is an accurate phrase, their Lordships do not pause to inquire. The foundation upon which reposes the right of equity to intervene is either contract or the existence of some fact which the legal owner is estopped from denying. Thus in the case put, B's conduct is such that from it may be inferred a contract by B not to disturb A in the possession of the land, or it may amount to a statement by B that the land is A's, upon the faith of which A has acted, and built....

Upon the facts of the present case their Lordships can find no foundation for the application of any equitable doctrine in favour of the appellant. There was no mistaken belief by the appellant as to the ownership of or the rights over the Intercolonial property, still less was there any such mistaken belief, which was known to the Crown. There was no conduct on the part of the Crown which induced the appellant to build in the belief that rights in perpetuity would be acquired. There was nothing upon which to ground any estoppel. The facts are all the other way. As already stated, the Main Telegraph Line came on the roadway by way of trespass, the other two sections came there upon the footing that the rights would be subject to and would be defined by written agreements to be negotiated between the parties.

Their Lordships are of opinion that the appellant's claim that the licence is irrevocable fails, and that the Crown was at liberty to revoke the licence, and so to put an end to the continued existence of the appellant's telegraph line upon the Crown property.

(ii.) Was the licence revoked before action or by the institution of proceedings?

[His Lordship found that the licence was not revoked before action taken, and continued:]

The question next arises whether the institution of the proceedings ipso facto determined the licence. The majority of the Supreme Court apparently thought not, because as regards the Westville Telegraph Line (which is included in the information) their decision was based upon the view that the Crown had no cause of action when the information was filed. The Chief Justice of Canada thought otherwise. The point does not appear to have been taken before the trial judge; at all events it is not referred to in his judgment. Neither is the point taken in the respondent's factum before the Supreme Court.

The determination of this point involves the consideration of the third question—namely:

(iii.) If the licence is revocable but unrevoked, how and in what circumstances the licence is revocable?

Whether any and what restrictions exist on the power of a licensor to determine a revocable licence must, their Lordships think, depend upon the circumstances of each case. The general proposition would appear to be that a licensee whose licence is revocable is entitled to reasonable notice of revocation. For this proposition reference may be made to *Cornish* v. *Stubbs* (1870) L.R. 5 C.P. 334, and *Mellor* v. *Watkins* (1874) L.R. 9 Q.B. 400, in the latter of which cases Blackburn J. states that a person giving a revocable licence "is bound to give the licensee reasonable notice."

When the exercise of the rights conferred by the licence involves nothing beyond, there can be no reason to urge against the existence of a power to determine the licence *brevi manu* at the will of the licensor.

But the exercise of the rights may have involved the licensee in obligations in other directions, which the determination of the licence would disable him from fulfilling, unless the licence were determined after a notice sufficient, in point of time, for the making of substituted arrangements. In such circumstances the licensee would, their Lordships conceive, be entitled to breathing space sufficient for this purpose. The case before the Board would appear to be peculiarly a case in which grave injustice might ensue if the Crown were at liberty by the mere initiation of legal proceedings to determine summarily the rights of the appellant, and turn the appellant's occupancy into trespass. For the appellant is not the only one concerned; the telegraph line is part of a system in the existence and continuance of which the public has a very considerable interest. It appears to their Lordships that this is a case in which the licence can only be effectively ended, after notice has been served upon the appellant determining the licence on such a specified date in the future, as will give the appellant an interval of time between the service of the notice and the specified date, sufficient not only to allow the removal of the poles and wires from off the property of the Crown, but also to enable the appellant to make arrangements for the continuance of the telegraph line by the erection of poles and wires elsewhere than on Crown property. Their Lordships are accordingly of opinion that the appellant's licence was not determined by the institution of the proceedings.

In the result therefore the position is, that the appellant is in occupation as a licensee whose licence is revocable, but unrevoked. Inasmuch as the Crown, by amendment, asked for a declaration of the appellant's rights, a proper declaration of those rights should be made; but in all other respects the action fails and is at an end. There is nothing left to try.

Their Lordships feel little doubt that as between the Canadian Pacific Railway Company and the Crown suitable contractual arrangements will be made which will obviate further litigation. If, however, this anticipation proves to be ill-founded, it will be for the Crown to determine the licence by service of a notice the sufficiency of which, if called in question, will have to be decided, upon proper evidence, in subsequent proceedings. It will be for the Crown, at its risk, to fix the length of notice.... *Appeal allowed.*

[A tenant to whom certain land is demised encroaches upon and uses part of the landlord's adjoining land not included in the lease. Are the terms of the lease binding on the tenant with respect to the land on which he encroached? See *J. F. Perrott & Co. Ltd.* v. *Cohen*, [1950] 2 All E.R. 939 (C.A.). If so, for how long is he bound?]

MOHL v. SENFT. Manitoba Queen's Bench. 1956. 6 D.L.R. 2d 32, 63 Man.R. 492, 19 W.W.R. (N.S.) 481

WILLIAMS C. J. Q B.: The plaintiff and defendant are owners of adjoining lots of land in Winnipeg. The plaintiff claims to be entitled to relief under s. 28 or, alternatively, under s. 29 of the *Law of Property Act*, R.S.M. 1954, c. 138. These sections read:

"28. Where a person makes lasting improvements on land under the belief that the land is his own, he or his assigns shall be entitled to a lien upon the land to the extent of the amount by which the value of the land is enhanced by the improvements, or shall be entitled, or may be required, to retain the land if the Court of Queen's Bench is of opinion or requires that that should be done, according as may, under all the circumstances of the case, be most just, making compensation for the land if retained, as the court may direct.

"29. Where, upon the survey of a parcel of land being made, it is found that a building thereon encroaches upon adjoining land, the Court of Queen's Bench may, in its discretion,

"(a) declare that the owner of the building shall have an easement upon the land so encroached upon during the life of the building upon making such compensation therefor as the court may determine;

"(b) vest title to the land so encroached upon in the owner of the building upon payment of the value thereof as determined by the court; or

"(c) order the owner of the building to remove the encroachment."

There is little dispute about the essential facts and where there is I accept the evidence of the defendant wherever it conflicts with that of the plaintiff....

... The west boundary of the plaintiff's lot is the east boundary of the defendant's lot. There is a dwelling-house on each lot. The plaintiff purchased his property in September, 1954, without having a survey made. The defendant had owned his property for some 2 years at that time. No part of the plaintiff's house encroaches on the defendant's property and there are no overhanging eaves.

The main block of the plaintiff's house is 1.25 ft. at the south end and 1.15 ft. at the north end from the dividing line between the two lots: see ex. 6. The house was built before the coming into force of the city zoning by-laws. The land is under the *Real Property Act*, R.S.M. 1954, c. 220.

One of the plaintiff's predecessors in title, the witness Beitz, purchased the lot in September, 1924. He also did not bother to obtain a survey. At that time there was an old wooden sidewalk on the west side of what is now the plaintiff's house leading to a side door in that house. The main entrance is on the south side.

In 1928 Beitz took up the wooden sidewalk which seems to have been in poor repair and built, in the same place, a cement sidewalk about 20 ins. wide, 1-1/4 ins. thick and about 115 ft. long. There was a dispute about its condition in 1955. I find it was broken and dilapidated with many holes in it.

On July 28, 1955, the defendant instructed his then solicitor to write a letter to the plaintiff demanding that the plaintiff remove "his" sidewalk, that is the cement walk, from the defendant's land. The letter of July 28, 1955, is ex. 4.

At about this time the defendant made certain changes in the garage building at the back of his lot. On the east side of the defendant's lot there is a space between the east wall of his house and the east boundary of his lot about 10 ft. in width, unbuilt on, and the garage was in a line with that space. The defendant then found that the cement walk, or what remained of it, encroached on his property.

Surveys then showed that the walk encroached on the defendant's land and was mainly on it....

... The defendant's property is 57 ft. wide. It has three front entrances and is let out in apartments. It is a good site for an aparment block, and all the land would be required for that purpose. If the defendant wished to put in a side drive to his garage he would need all the vacant space to the east of his house.

In argument counsel for the plaintiff did not place much reliance on s. 29, *supra*. That section now only applies to "buildings" and the cement walk is not a "building". Counsel did not argue that the earlier legislation dealing with encroachments, which was formerly in force, applied because the walk was built in 1928. As will be seen, that legislation only applied to improvements made on land in consequence of unskilful survey and that is not the case here. There was no survey.

The plaintiff was driven to rely on s. 28, and to seek to establish that the cement walk was a lasting improvement made by his predecessor in title in 1928, under the belief that the land upon which it was built was his own. In this he got no help from his witness Beitz. The plaintiff relied in respect of the first branch of this argument mainly on a decision of this Court by Macdonald J. (later C.J.K.B.) in *James* v. *Brock*, [1926] 2 D.L.R. 880, [1926] 1 W.W.R. 845, and in respect of the second branch on a decision of the Saskatchewan Court of Appeal in *Schiell* v. *Morrison*, [1930] 4 D.L.R. 664, 25 S.L.R. 18.

A short answer would be that the cement walk was not a "lasting improvement" within the meaning of s. 28, and that *James* v. *Brock*, *supra*, which I shall discuss later, does not assist the plaintiff.

If I am wrong in this I am further of opinion that s. 28 applies only in cases of lasting improvements made under mistake of title; that there could be, in this case, no mistake of title, and that s. 28 does not apply.

But counsel for the plaintiff put forward his arguments with such force and personal conviction that I feel I should fully give my reasons for each of my various conclusions.

In *Tuckwell* v. *Guay* (1917), 34 D.L.R. 106, 27 Man. R. 529, [1917] 1 W.W.R. 1229, aff'd 37 D.L.R. 805, Man. R. *loc. cit.* Metcalfe J. (later J. A.) first drew attention to the difference between improvements made under mistake of title and those made because of mistake of identity. He also expressed a preference for the interpretation the Ontario Courts had placed upon the Ontario provision from which s. 28 was copied in Manitoba, namely, that it applied only to improvements made under mistake of title, but he did not need to decide the point.

In *Fletcher* v. *Claggett*, [1927] 3 D.L.R. 751, 21 S.L.R. 682, [1927] 2 W.W.R. 362, Mackenzie J., considering the Saskatchewan provision similar to s. 28, referred to *infra*, held that it applied only in cases of mistake of title. It will be seen that in 1930 the Saskatchewan Court of Appeal did not agree with this view.

In *Aumann* v. *McKenzie*, [1928] 3 W.W.R. 233, Dysart J. (later J.A.) placed the same interpretation on the Manitoba provision.

The history of what is now s. 28, *supra*, down to 1917, is, if I may say so, well set out by Metcalfe J. in *Tuckwell* v *Guay*, *supra*, and again by Dysart J. down to 1928, in *Aumann* v. *McKenzie*, *supra*.

The provision whch is now s. 28 was first enacted in Manitoba in 1910 (c. 17, s. 13) as R. 580A of the King's Bench Act, R.S.M. 1902, c. 40....

... Rule 580A was copied from an Ontario provision which had been enacted as to the first half in 1873 (c. 22), and as to the second half in 1877, by R.S.O. 1877, c. 95, s. 4, and which is now s. 37 of the Ontario Conveyancing and Law of Property Act, R.S.O. 1950, c. 68. The Ontario and Manitoba sections are identical in phraseology except that the Ontario section speaks of "the Court" while the Manitoba section adds the words "of Queen's Bench."

The Ontario Acts of 1873 and 1877 were modelled on the legislation of some of the states of the United States: See *Beaty* v. *Shaw* (1888), 14 O.A.R. 600 for the early history of the Ontario legislation.

In 1925-26, by c. 61, Saskatchewan passed legislation identical with s. 28, and this is now s. 2 of *An Act Respecting Improvements under Mistake of Title*, R.S.S. 1953, c. 116.

Section 29, *supra*, was first enacted in Manitoba in 1931, as s. 15 of the new *Law of Property Act*. For many years prior to the passing of this section there was legislation in Manitoba making provision in *ejectment actions* to assess damages which the defendant in the action might sustain by making improvements on the land in question in consequence of *unskilful survey*. This provision was first enacted when Manitoba passed an *Ejectment Act* in 1881 (3rd Sess. c. 5). It was then s. 29. Section 30 of the same Act contained provisions setting out how the defendant in the action might obtain costs.

This legislation was obviously modelled on the early Ontario legislation referred to by Hagarty C. J. O. in *Beaty* v. *Shaw*, 14 O.A.R. at p. 602. The original Ontario Act appears to have been R.S.U.C. 1818, c. 14.

The Ontario provisions passed into C.S.U.C. 1859, c. 93, dealing with *Survey of Lands*, as ss. 53 and 54. In 1877 they were taken into the *Ejectment Act* as ss. 29 and 30 (R.S.O. 1877, c. 51). In 1887 they became ss. 31 and 32 of the *Law and Transfer of Property Act*, R.S.O. 1887, c. 100. They remained in that Act (R.S.O. 1897, c. 119, ss. 31 and 32) until 1911 when a new *Law and Transfer of Property Act* (c. 25) was passed when ss. 31 and 32 were repealed by s. 53.

Sections 29 and 30 of the Manitoba *Ejectment Act* of 1881 became ss. 34 and 35 of the *Ejectment Act*, R.S.M. 1891, c. 48. When the *Queen's Bench Act* of 1895 (c. 6) was passed, ss. 34 and 35 became Rules 570 and 571. They passed into the 1913 Rules as Rules 601 and 602.

Although s. 15 of the Manitoba *Law of Property Act*, was enacted in 1931, Rules 601 and 602 were not repealed until the new King's Bench Rules were passed to come into force December 24, 1939. They were then repealed: R. 1 (2), and s. 101 of the *Queen's Bench Act*, R.S.M. 1954, c. 52.

Present s. 29 of the *Law of Property Act* is confined to encroaching "buildings" and in the instant case there is no question of an encroaching building; a cement sidewalk is not a building. The plaintiff gets no assistance from s. 29.

But the presence of that section and its forerunnners is of importance when we come to consider the decision of the Saskatchewan Court of Appeal in *Schiell* v. *Morrison, supra*, a case on which the plaintiff relied, and the plaintiff's argument based thereon.

In *Tuckwell* v. *Guay, supra*, Metcalfe J., who dismissed the plaintiff's claim as I have said, expressed a preference for the decisions in the Ontario cases that on the true construction of the legislation (now s. 28, *supra*) it was limited in its application to improvements made under mistake of title and not to cases of mistake of identity. As he had held that there was no unskilful survey he could not give relief under the then R. 601. He decided the case on this point and also on the branch of the case under then R. 603, that no "lasting improvements" had been made. His decision was affirmed by the Court of Appeal without written reasons (37 D.L.R. 805, 27 Man. R. 529). This affirmation approved the view he took on the two grounds but it cannot be said that the Court approved or disapproved his dictum about the interpretation of the section.

In *Aumann* v. *McKenzie, supra*, Dysart J., who dismissed the plaintiff's claim under R. 603, was dealing with a question of mistake of identity. He pointed out that all the Ontario decisions under the similar legislation dealt with improvements made under mistake of title and not under mistake of identity, and added, "That silence is significant."

In *Schiell* v. *Morrison*, [1930] 4 D.L.R. 664, 2 W.W.R. 737, the parties who had made the improvements obtained relief. The [W.W.R.] headnote succinctly sums up the decision. It reads:

"If there is an ambiguity or uncertainty in the language of an Act, the title may be looked to in order to ascertain the scope of the Act and to remove the ambiguity; but where the language of the Act is plain it must be given effect to notwithstanding the fact that it goes beyond the matters mentioned in the title.

"The application of ch. 61, 1925-26 (Sask.) entitled *An Act Respecting Improvements under Mistake of Title* is not confined to mistakes of title, but extends to all cases, including those of mistake of the identity of the land or of its boundaries, where a person has made 'lasting improvements under the belief that the land is his own.' It is, however, a question for the Court to determine in each case whether the person claiming for the improvements was under a *bona-fide* belief that the land was his own (Ontario and Manitoba cases discussed and dicta therein differed from)."

The judgment was written by Martin J. A., now C. J. S., whose judgments, in my respectful opinion, deserve the most careful consideration. I have endeavoured to give that judgment such consideration. I think, however, that the Saskatchewan case is distinguishable.

From 1873 to 1911, Ontario had legislation dealing with improvements made under mistake of title and improvements made because of unskilful survey. Since 1911 the latter provisions have been dropped in Ontario.

From 1881 to 1910, Manitoba had only legislation dealing with improvements made because of unskilful survey. From 1919 to 1931 (perhaps 1939 as the Rules were not repealed until then) it had legislation dealing with improvements under mistake of title and improvements because of unskilful survey (mistake of identity). Since 1931 (or 1939) s. 29 (originally s. 15) of the *Law of Property Act* has the differing provision referring only to "buildings" and not to "improvements" and making no reference to "unskilful survey".

Saskatchewan never has had, so far as I can find, any legislation such as the Manitoba and Ontario legislation relating to unskilful survey or such as our present s. 29. These are essential facts to bear in mind in considering the decision in *Schiell's* case, and the Ontario and Manitoba decisions.

In Ontario and Manitoba the Courts had, for many years, been able to give relief in cases of mistake of identity arising from unskilful survey. The later legislation dealing with mistake of title was not necessary in such cases. It was obviously designed to cover other cases, namely improvements made under mistake of title. It authorized relief only in case the improvements were "lasting improvements" while the other legislation gave relief in case there had been any "improvements".

These considerations lead me to the conclusion that the interpretation placed on the forerunners of s. 28 in the Ontario decisions and in *Tuckwell* v. *Guay* and *Aumann* v. *McKenzie*, *supra*, is the interpretation I should place upon the section. The reasoning appeals to me and I adopt it as my own.

It seems to me that this view is pointed up by the fact that in *Tuckwell* v. *Guay*, Metcalfe J. was dealing with both pieces of legislation, the then Rules 601 and 603.

The fact that in Ontario the statutes dealing with unskilful survey have been repealed and only the statute dealing with mistake of title retained does not indicate to me that the Ontario Legislature thought that the one provision covered all cases. But if it did the fact that in Manitoba we have retained a section dealing with mistake of identity (s. 29) would satisfy me that s. 28 was only intended to apply to mistake of title.

While s. 29 is limited in its operation to "buildings" it is wider in some ways than the earlier legislation. It makes no reference to "unskilful surveys," and it is not confined in its operation to actions of ejectment or for the recovery of land. Apart from the limitation to buildings it is wider in its scope than the earlier legislation and it provides for differing relief in some cases: see s-s. (a) for example.

I am not overlooking the fact that in *Aumann's* case, Dysart J. adopted the opinion expressed by Mackenzie J. in *Fletcher* v. *Claggett*, [1927] 3 D.L.R. 751, 21 Sask. L. R. 682, [1927] 2 W.W.R. 362, as to interpretation, an opinion that was not accepted by the Court of Appeal in *Schiell's* case, *supra*, a Court of which Mackenzie, then J. A., was a member. But Dysart J. adopted those opinions as his own and, with respect, he came to the right conclusion as the Manitoba law then stood and still stands.

Section 29, in my opinion, is the only provision dealing with mistake of identity; it is exclusive; and it gives a right which did not exist at common law. An encroachment is a trespass and no trespasser acquires any right by reason of his trespass as Dysart J. remarked in *Aumann's* case, [1928] 3 W.W.R. at p. 238.

I now come to the plaintiff's argument that the cement walk was a lasting improvement and for this he relies on the judgment of Macdonald J. in *James* v. *Brock*, [1926] 2 D.L.R. 880, [1926] 1 W.W.R. 845. In that case the plaintiff based his right to recover on the then R. 603. It was really a case of "unskilful" or at least erroneous survey as the report shows. A subsequent accurate survey showed that the eaves of the plaintiff's house and a side entrance to the basement encroached on the defendant's land.

Macdonald J. said *[inter alia]:*

"... The roof is a lasting improvement and I do not think the plaintiff is obliged to disfigure his dwelling to any extent by the cutting off of a portion of the roof as suggested. The plaintiff is also entitled to the ground upon which his sidewalk leading to the side entrance is built, as it existed at the time of the purchase by him of the lot in question. The side entrance to his basement is a lasting improvement, and as such the plaintiff is entitled under the rule to the ground upon which this sidewalk was originally constructed.

"I am of the opinion that R. 603 applies, and that the plaintiff is entitled to retain the land in question to the extent of the projection of the eaves and eavestrough of his dwelling over the land of the defendant, and upon making compensation for the land to the defendant is entitled to be vested with title to the same. The amount of such compensation, I find, does not exceed $10."

With respect, it seems to me that *James* v. *Brock* did not come within R. 603, and that the plaintiff's rights, if any, were governed by R. 601. The point does not seem to have been raised and the authorities were not discussed.

But assuming for a moment that R. 603 did apply, it will be observed that while the eaves and the side entrance were declared to be lasting improvements the sidewalk was not. The ground upon which it was built seems to have been given as necessary to the use of the side entrance. The plaintiff was given the land in question *to the extent of the projection of the eaves* and while accurate measurements are not given it would appear that the sidewalk was on the part of the land so given.

In the instant case there were no encroachments and no overhang so that *James* v. *Brock* is clearly distinguishable, on this ground alone.

As Macdonald J. pointed out [in] *James* v. *Brock* [it] was a case of first impression. The only other case under the provisions being considered in which overhanging eaves were under consideration is *Fletcher* v. *Claggett*, *supra*, where Mackenzie J., who refused relief, said that "perhaps" they might be lasting improvements.

With respect I am unable to see how the encroachment of a building or the overhang of its eaves could be considered to be an improvement of the adjoining owner's land. That is the test under the section....

Encroachments such as those in *James* v. *Brock* could not, in my opinion, be said to enhance the value of the defendant's property; they would rather depreciate it.

Where buildings are erected on vacant land, or buildings on the land in question are remodelled, the situation is different: See *Schiell* v. *Morrison*, *supra*, and *Welz* v. *Bady*, [1949] 1 D.L.R. 281, 56 Man. R. 374, as examples.

In many of the decisions the nature of the improvements is not disclosed as Metcalfe J. pointed out in *Tuckwell* v. *Guay*.

Scrubbing, stumping, and bringing additional land under cultivation on an improved farm constitute lasting improvements: *Mateychuk* v. *Kuchernowski*, [1930] 1 D.L.R. 367, Adamson J. (now C.J.M.), but fencing, scrubbing, clearing and breaking prairie land do not: *Tuckwell* v. *Guay*, *supra*, Metcalfe J.

The construction of a cement sidewalk such as that in the instant case cannot be said to be a lasting improvement or to enhance the value of the defendant's land.

The plaintiff in this case is deprived of the walk and may be deprived of convenient access to the side door of his house, but that fact does not enhance the value of the defendant's land. And it is only when the value of the defendant's land is enhanced that s. 28 can operate.

I have already held that s. 28 is only applicable to cases of mistake of title. The plaintiff's land is under the *Real Property Act* and there can be no mistake of title. This case differs from the cases where there was ground for an honest mistake of title. In *Chandler* v. *Gibson* (1901), 2 O.L.R. 442 the successful plaintiff had purchased the land from a person whom he believed had an estate tail in the land but who on the subsequent interpretation of the will in question was held only to have a life estate.

In *Welz* v. *Bady*, [1949] 1 D.L.R. 281, 56 Man. R. 374, [1949] 1 W.W.R. 123, the plaintiff believed he had purchased the land from a municipality when he had in fact only purchased a tax sale certificate and the land was subsequently redeemed. In *Mateychuk* v. *Kuchernowski, supra*, the plaintiff honestly believed he had purchased the land under an agreement for sale which turned out to be unenforceable, the Court holding the parties were never *ad idem*.

I have found no case that suggests there can be a mistake of title where the plaintiff's title is held by a certificate of title under the Manitoba *Real Property Act*. In my opinion the only question that can arise in such cases is that of mistake of identity and there the plaintiff's rights, if any, must be found in s. 29, a question I have already dealt with.

If I had found that there had been a mistake of title, and that s. 28 applied, and that the cement walk was a lasting improvement, I would also have found that it did not enhance the value of the defendant's land. It was completely useless to him or to his predecessors in title when new. At the time this action was brought it had no value even as a sidewalk.

The plaintiff has included a claim for damages to the cement walk. Such a claim cannot be supported. The walk being on the defendant's land was his property and he could do what he wished with it: *Nat'l Trust Co.* v. *Western Trust Co.* (1912), 4 D.L.R. 455, 5 S.L.R. 210, 2 W.W.R. 667, 21 W.L.R. 571; *Fletcher* v. *Claggett, supra.*

Action dismissed.

[S. 38 (1) of the Conveyancing and Law of Property Act, R.S.O. 1960, c. 66, reads as follows: "Where a person makes lasting improvements on land, under the belief that it is his own, he or his assigns are entitled to a lien upon it to the extent of the amount by which its value is enhanced by the improvements; or are entitled or may be required to retain the land if the court is of opinion or requires that this should be done, according as may under all circumstances of the case be most just, making compensation for the land, if retained, as the court directs."

By s. 38 (2) (3) (4) (5) of the above Act, provision is made for concurrent jurisdiction in the County or District Court subject to removal of the proceedings to the Supreme Court on application of the respondent. An appeal lies to the Court of Appeal from any order made under s. 38.

As to the application of the Ontario statute, see *Bilecki* v. *Weber*, [1942] O.R. 161, [1942] 2 D.L.R. 210 (C.A.); *Derro* v. *Dube and Boulet*, [1948] 2 D.L.R. 296 (Ont.); *Cartwright* v. *Cartwright*, [1940] S.C.R. 659, [1941] 1 D.L.R. 369. Cf. *Montreuil* v. *Ontario Asphalt Co.*, (1922), 63 S.C.R. 401, 69 D.L.R. 313, var'g 47 O.L.R. 227, 52 D.L.R. 563 which rev'd 46 O.L.R. 136.]

3. SOME PROBLEMS OF CLASSIFICATION

WEEKS AND TOPOROWSKI v. ROGALSKI. Ontario Court of Appeal. [1956] O.R. 109, 1 D.L.R. 2d 709

Appeal from a judgment of Smily J., [1954] O.R. 96, [1954] 4 D.L.R. 439, declaring plaintiff's right to a room projecting over the centre-line of semi-detached houses.

The judgment of the Court was delivered by ROACH J. A.:

... The facts out of which this litigation arose are as follows:

One Steve Zadorozny was the owner in fee simple free from encumbrances of land and premises in the City of Oshawa, composed of the whole of Lot 26 on the west side of Celina Street as shown on a registered plan known as the Arkland Plan D. On that lot are two semi-detached dwelling-houses, the most southerly being known as street No. 238 and the most northerly as street No. 236.

By a contract of purchase and sale consisting of an offer to purchase and an acceptance thereof, both dated December 2, 1950, the plaintiff Toporowski and the defendant Rogalski agreed to purchase the whole of that property. Both dwellings were tenant-occupied, and by the contract vacant possession of No. 236 was to be delivered to the purchasers by February 1, 1951, and the purchasers were to take No. 238 subject to the tenancy.

Although there was only one contract of purchase and sale and it covered the whole of the lot with the two semi-detached dwellings upon it, the purchasers, from the beginning, had intended that Toporowski would be given a deed to one of the dwellings, and Rogalski a deed to the other. It was eventually agreed between them that Rogalski would take the northerly one, that is, No. 236, and Toporowski the southerly one.

The two adjoining dwellings had, apparently from the beginning, been constructed in an unusual way. At the basement level and on the second floor a straight common wall extending from front to rear divided the two dwellings, but on the first floor, that is, the street level, this common wall did not extend in a straight line for the whole depth of the building. About 9 ft. 10-1/2 ins. from the west wall it ran at a right angle to the north for a distance of about 5 ft. and thence westerly and parallel to the outside north and south walls of the whole structure to the outside westerly wall. By adding to No. 238 the additional space thus carved out of No. 236, No. 238 had six rooms while No. 236 had only five rooms. This additional space formed part of a bedroom opening off the kitchen of No. 238.

The same solicitor acted for the vendor and the two purchasers. He recommended that the whole property be surveyed so that descriptions by metes and bounds could be provided by the surveyor for the conveyances which were to follow. The survey was made and a drawing was prepared by the surveyors. On that drawing the outside walls of the combined structure are shown by solid lines; the dividing-line between the two dwellings is shown by a broken line, but that broken line is a straight line. That broken, straight line would properly show the dividing line at the basement and second floor levels, but not on the first floor level.

The solicitor gave evidence at the trial, and the trial Judge, in his reasons, states that he accepted that evidence. According to the solicitor he discussed with the purchasers this protrusion of part of No. 238 over and into No. 236, which protrusion accounted for No. 238 having six rooms and No. 236 only five rooms, and the defendant agreed to take No. 236 subject to that protrusion.

The defendant stated in evidence that at the time of the conveyances, to which I shall refer in a moment, he had no knowledge that there was any change in the direction of any part of the common wall between the two dwellings on any floor level. There was other evidence besides that given by the solicitor that the defendant did know of the protrusion which I earlier described, and the trial Judge did not accept the defendant's evidence on that point.

The solicitor, in preparing the conveyances, used the legal descriptions provided him by the surveyor, which, of course, were not correct as applied to the first floor level of both dwellings, but were correct as applied to the basement and second floor levels.

Two deeds were prepared and executed by the vendor, both dated December 21, 1950, the one to Rogalski conveying to him the northerly 41 ft. 5-1/4 ins. from front to rear of Lot 26, the other, to Toporowski, the southerly 41 ft. 3/4 in. from front to rear of that lot. The total frontage of the lot is 82 ft. 6 ins.

The dividing-line between the two parcels, that is, the northerly boundary of the parcel conveyed to Toporowski and the southerly boundary of the parcel conveyed to Rogalski is described in each of the two deeds thus:

"COMMENCING at a point in the easterly limit of the said Lot being the westerly limit of the said Street where the same is intersected by the easterly production of the centre line of the Party Wall between the semi-detached brick dwelling houses composing the pair standing on the 19th day of December, 1950, wholly upon the said Lot and acknowledged to be a Party Wall, said point of intersection being distant forty-one feet five and one-quarter inches (41′ 5-1/4″) measured southerly in and along the said limit from the north-easterly angle of the said Lot;

THENCE westerly to and along the said centre line of the party wall and continuing westerly to a point in the westerly limit of the said lot distant forty-one feet five and one-quarter inches (41′5-1/4″) measured southerly thereon from the north-westerly angle thereof."

After the description by metes and bounds in the deed to Rogalski are added the words, "said parcel or tract comprising and being now known as premises No. 236 Celina Street, Oshawa".

After the description by metes and bounds in the deed to Toporowski are added these words, "said parcel or tract comprising and being now known as premises No. 238 Celina Street, Oshawa".

A blueprint of the surveyor's drawing which I earlier partially described was attached to each deed.

The two transactions were closed at the same time and the deeds were delivered to the respective grantees....

[The Court noted at this point that the deed to Rogalski and a mortgage which he gave were registered prior to the deed to Toporowski and a mortgage from him.]

The defendant in due course took possession of and moved into No. 236 and he is still living there. The plaintiff Toporowski some months later, when the tenant vacated, moved into No. 238 and continued in possession until in or about March, 1953.

By an agreement of sale dated March 3, 1953, Toporowski agreed to sell No. 238 to the plaintiff Weeks, who is now in possession pursuant to that agreement.

In July, 1953, the defendant Rogalski, through his then solicitor, notified Toporowski that he proposed to remove the northerly wall of the protruding room and erect a partition along the line, as shown by the survey. Toporowski told Weeks what the defendant was threatening to do. Weeks consulted the solicitor who had acted at the time of the original purchases and sales, and on behalf of Weeks that solicitor notified Rogalski's then solicitor that if Rogalski carried out his threat legal proceedings would be started against him. Rogalski carried out his threat and this action followed.

In their statement of claim the plaintiffs claim a declaration that they are entitled to the full use and enjoyment of the lands and premises known as No. 238 Celina St. and particularly the room at the north-west corner on the first floor thereof, giving the dimensions thereof; an injunction and mandatory order and damages.

The defendant pleads that he is the owner of the lands as described in the deed to him and specifically pleads sections 74, 75, 76 and 78 of the *Registry Act*, R.S.O. 1950, c. 336.

The learned trial Judge, in his reasons, held that "the plaintiff, Toporowski, received by implied grant an easement or quasi-easement of the portion of the room in question projecting over and above the property of the defendant... and there should be judgment for a declaration to such effect and a mandatory order directing the defendant to remove the partition erected by him and restoring the boundary wall to its original position."

He granted a mandatory order requiring the defendant to remove the partition-wall erected by him and to restore the former boundary-wall within 40 days, failing which the plaintiffs should recover from the defendant the sum of $200 and remove the new wall and restore the old one at their own expense. He also granted an injunction restraining the defendant, his servants and agents from removing, altering or in any way interfering with the new wall during or after its restoration by the plaintiffs. He also awarded the plaintiffs damages in the sum of $250, and costs....

It is plain from the plaintiffs' statement of claim that they are founding their claim that "they are entitled to the full use and enjoyment", etc., on an allegation that the area protruding north of the dividing-line between the two parcels according to the descriptions in the deeds, belongs to them in their respective interests, but they have not asked for rectification.

The formal judgment declares that the plaintiffs are entitled to that full use and enjoyment, etc. "without any interference by the Defendant or any persons acquiring title through or under him", etc.

But what about the title already acquired by Harry and Annie Yourkevich, the mortgagees of the northerly parcel? There is no reference in the pleadings either to them and their title-interest or to Louis and Katherine Kalynko, the mortgagees of the southerly parcel and their interest.

The relief which the plaintiffs claimed and which the judgment awards them could not be granted without the mortgagees of the northerly parcel being parties to the action.

This appeal had been argued and judgment had been reserved without any reference having been made to those mortgage interests. In this Court's later consideration of the appeal those interests came to its attention on a more careful examination of the abstract of title. Thinking that, by oversight, those interests had been overlooked, counsel for the original parties were advised and after some considerable delay the mortgagees of both parcels consented to be added as party defendants and to be bound by the judgment without further pleadings, evidence or argument, and on application by the respondent an order was so made. This accounts for the delay in the disposal of this appeal.

On the basis of the verbal agreement between Toporowski and Rogalski the former was entitled, as between himself and Rogalski, to the fee simple in that part of the building known as No. 238 which thus protruded. That part of that room contained in that protrusion, though not resting directly upon the soil but supported by surrounding parts of the building, is a corporeal hereditament, and therefore "land" within the *Conveyancing and Law of Property Act*, R.S.O. 1950, c. 68, and as such may be conveyed by grant. I refer to *Iredale* v. *Loudon* (1908), 40 S.C.R. 313, particularly the reasons of Duff J., as he then was, and the cases referred to by him; also *Kolodzi* v. *Detroit & Windsor Subway Co.*, [1931] 3 D.L.R. 337, S.C.R. 523, 38 C.R.C. 130.

On the facts as found by the trial Judge, namely, that before the conveyances from Zadorozny both Rogalski and Toporowski knew of the change in direction of the street level of the common wall between the two houses resulting in the protrusion north of the line which otherwise divided them, and that they agreed with one another that Rogalski would take the northerly house, *viz.*, No. 236, and Toporowski the southerly one, *viz.*, No 238, it was error to hold as a matter of law that Toporowski, having received the conveyance which was delivered to him, acquired an easement by way of implied grant.

Under that agreement Toporowski was to have the exclusive and unrestricted use of that part of the "land" as part of the whole "land" which comprised the premises known as No. 238.

The author of Gale on Easements, 12th ed., says at p. 25: "There is no easement known to the law which gives exclusive and unrestricted use of a piece of land. A grant of the exclusive or unrestricted use of land beyond all question passes the ownership of land."

The oral agreement between Rogalski and Toporowski was in effect an agreement for the partition of the whole lands which together they purchased or were in the process of purchasing from Zadorozny. The defendant Rogalski has not pleaded the *Statute of Frauds*, R.S.O. 1950, c. 371, and even if it had been pleaded it could be of no avail to him because there has been part performance of that agreement. Each of the parties forewent his right on the payment of his half of the purchase price to a deed to himself and the other party as tenants in common of the whole parcel which they purchased together and each went into exclusive possession of the portion which as between them each agreed to take.

The defendant Rogalski has pleaded ss. 74, 75, 76 and 78 of the *Registry Act*, R.S.O. 1950, c. 336. Sections 74, 75 and 78 are of no avail to the defendant Rogalski as against the plaintiff Toporowski because plainly the former had notice of the latter's interest in the "land" now in dispute under the oral agreement between them. Section 76 does not make Toporowski's equitable interest in the land contained in the protrusion invalid as against Rogalski.

As against the defendant Rogalski the plaintiff Toporowski was entitled to succeed. I defer for the moment discussing the exact measure of the relief to which he is entitled.

As against the defendant Rogalski is the position of the plaintiff Weeks different from that of his co-plaintiff? I think it is not. Both plaintiffs are in agreement that the land which one agreed to sell and the other agreed to purchase included the land contained in the protrusion which I earlier described. Solely by reason of the error in conveyancing there had not been a grant to Toporowski of the land in question. By that error the fee in it had been conveyed to Rogalski, but as between them Toporowski was entitled to it. He could agree to sell that to which he was thus entitled.

There remains for consideration the position of the mortgagees.

The mortgagees Harry and Annie Yourkevich are mortgagees for value without notice of the northerly 41 ft. 5-1/4 ins. from front to rear of Lot 26, that is to say, they had no notice of the equitable interest that Toporowski had in the land comprised in the protrusion under his oral agreement with Rogalski. These mortgagees are protected by s. 76 of the *Registry Act*. . . .

By the two conveyances, the one to Rogalski, the other to Toporowski, the original vendor, Zadorozny has conveyed all the lands which he had agreed to sell to them. It was by way of a convenience, not an obligation, to them that he gave the two deeds instead of one. The real dispute is between these two purchasers, and the origin of that dispute is not in the sale by Zadorozny but in the agreement between these two purchasers for the partition of those lands.

In the circumstances of this case I do not think that rectification of these deeds is the appropriate remedy. It is not asked in the pleadings, but in this Court counsel for the plaintiffs suggested that if the circumstances required it this Court should grant it. It would seem from the decision in *Ihde* v. *Starr* (1909), 19 O.L.R. 471 [aff'd 21 O.L.R. 407] that in such an action Zadorozny would have to be a party. There is no necessity for dragging him into this dispute; he is in no way concerned with it.

In this action, strangely enough, the plaintiffs ask, not for a declaration as to the title of the land contained in the protrusion, but only for a declaration that they are entitled to the full use and enjoyment of these lands as part of the lands and premises known as 238 Celina Street.

Giving effect to these reasons I would amend the formal judgment as issued so that as amended:

Paragraph 1 thereof shall declare that the plaintiffs are entitled to the full use and enjoyment of the lands and premises known as 238 Celina St., which said lands and premises may be more particularly described as follows: (1) the lands and premises contained in the legal description in the deed from Zadorozny to Toporowski, and (2) the lands and premises contained in the protrusion, without any interference by the defendant Rogalski or any persons hereafter acquiring title through or under him with notice of this judgment, subject to the rights of the defendants Harry and Annie Yourkevich, their heirs, executors, administrators and assigns under the mortgage dated December 21, 1950, and registered on December 27, 1950, as No. 63480....

Paragraph 5 should be amended by striking out the words "or in any way interfering with" contained in the third and fourth lines of the present paragraph. The reason for deleting those words is that they might be construed as at least implying that this Court was declaring some obligation on the defendant Rogalski to maintain some physical support for the wall in question. It is not my intent to do so.

The action as against the other defendants should be dismissed without costs.

Subject to those amendments the appeal should be dismissed with costs payable by the appellant.

It seems to me that all the parties should get together and tidy up the title to these lands by appropriate conveyances thus avoiding future unnecessary litigation concerning the same.

Appeal dismissed with variations.

[In *Re Interprovincial Pipe Line Co.*, [1951] 2 D.L.R. 187, 1 W.W.R. (N.S.) 479 (Sask. C.A.), the Crown in right of Saskatchewan by written agreement granted to the company "the right, licence, liberty, privilege and easement" to use certain unpatented Crown lands for its pipe lines and associated works, with right of ingress and egress, and for as long as the company desired to exercise these rights and privileges, but subject to certain conditions including an undertaking by the company to bury its pipe lines and maintain them so as not to interfere with the drainage or ordinary cultivation of the lands. There was an express reservation of mines and minerals "in or under the land comprising the said right-of-way". Each of the parties was entitled to assign on giving certain notice. What interest did the company obtain under the agreement?]

HUBBS v. BLACK. Ontario Appellate Division. 1918. 44O.L.R. 545, 46 D.L.R. 583

Appeal from dismissal of an action for damages for trespass to a cemetery plot, for an injunction and for an order that defendant remove her late husband's body from the plot.

CLUTE J.: ... From the evidence it appears that there was a grant of the portion of the plot in question, as claimed by the defendant, for the burial of herself and her husband, from William Babcock to her, for valuable consideration, and she is entitled to an order vesting the same in her in fee simple.

I am also of opinion that the defendant has been in possession of the plot for more than 10 years, and that under the Statute of Limitations her possessory title is valid. It is not denied by counsel that the possession and occupation by the defendant is complete so far as the portion of the land upon which the monument stands is concerned, but it is denied that this includes that portion of the plot required for the burial of the defendant and her husband.

In this contention I am unable to agree. The defendant was not a trespasser in what she did. The placing of the monument there had relation to the portion of the plot given to her by her brother for the purposes of burial of herself and husband, and the possession of the part occupied by the monument carried with it possession of the portion of the plot given to her by her brother.

It was urged by Mr. Porter that the defendant's claim, if any, was to an easement or licence, and he referred to *Bryan* v. *Whistler*, 8 B. & C. 288, where a rector granted to A.B., by parol, leave to make a vault in the parish church, and to bury a certain corpse there, and that he should have the exclusive use of the vault; and afterwards, without the leave of A.B., opened the vault, and buried another person there; and it was held that no action could be maintained against him for so doing; for that if the rector had power to grant the exclusive use of the vault, he could not do it by parol. Bayley, J., after saying (p. 293), "If that were an interest in land, the grant could not be binding under the Statute of Frauds, unless there were a memorandum in writing signed by the party granting," goes on to say: "If it be not an interest in land it is an easement, or the grant of an incorporeal hereditament; which could only be effectually granted by deed, and no such instrument was executed. But even had a deed been executed, I think the defendant had not the power to grant any privilege, except for the particular burial then about to take place. The rector has the freehold of the church for public purposes, not for his own emolument; to supply places for burial from time to time, as the necessities of his parish require, and not to grant away vaults, which, as it seems to me, cannot be done unless a faculty has been obtained."

It thus appears that the case has no application to the present. The plot in this case was obtained for the express purpose of burial, and there was good consideration and a part performance in refraining from purchase by the defendant of a plot and by the erection of the monument. Some agreement was intended, and parol evidence was admissible to shew what that agreement was. There was an interest in the land to which the easement could attach. It was not an easement in gross. The *Bryan* case is referred to in *Ashby* v. *Harris* (1868), L.R. 3 C.P. 523, at p. 529; see also *McGough* v. *Lancaster Burial Board* (1888), 21 Q.B.D. 323, at p. 327. But, in my view of the facts, the agreement is not for an easement, but a grant of land for valuable consideration.

RIDDELL J.: The defendant, who is now a widow, is the sister of the late William Babcock, who lived with her and her husband on their place for more than 7 years before his death in January, 1912. Babcock was the owner of a certain plot of land in a cemetery property organised under the Act respecting companies for the establishment of Cemeteries in Upper Canada, C.S.U.C. ch. 67; R.S.O. 1877, ch. 170. About 1904, the defendant intended to buy a plot for the burial of herself and her husband. Babcock said to her, "You need not buy a plot.... I will give you a plot for you and your husband," and it was agreed that the defendant should not buy another plot, but that Babcock would give her a plot and she would "put a tombstone there". She bought a tombstone, had cut thereon the names of herself and her husband, and took it to the cemetery. Babcock went with her, and then himself directed the placing of the tombstone on the plot, where it still remains.

Babcock died in 1912, leaving a will whereby he devised all his estate real and personal to the plaintiff, his nephew.

The defendant brought an action against the plaintiff as representing the estate, claiming, amongst other things, payment for the care etc. of the deceased; this action was settled, and the defendant gave to the plaintiff a release of "all claims and demands" against the estate.

The defendant's husband died in December, 1917, and his body was laid in the plot....

While one part of the defendant's evidence would indicate that she thought that she was to have the ownership of a lot, a careful perusal of the whole of what she says shews that the real agreement was that she was to give up her project of buying another lot and to place a tombstone on the plot of her brother, and in return she was to have the right of burial for herself and her husband within her brother's plot.

Whether this action comes within the Evidence Act, R.S.O. 1914, ch. 76, sec. 12, we need not consider: there is overwhelming and uncontradicted corroboration of the contract on the part of the brother.

The right to bury in another's freehold is considered an easement which can be conveyed only by deed: *Bryan* v. *Whistler*, 8 B. & C. 288; *Moreland* v. *Richardson* (1856), 22 Beav. 596; *Ashby* v. *Harris*, L.R. 3 C.P. 523, 529; *North Manchester Overseers* v. *Winstanley*, [1908] 1 K.B. 835, 843; *S.C., sub. nom. Winstanley* v. *North Manchester Overseers*, [1910] A.C. 7.

Had the Administration of Justice Act or the Judicature Act never been passed, or were the County Court not a Court with equitable jurisdiction, the defendant might be in evil plight. But now the rules of Equity prevail, and the County Court has equitable jurisdiction.

Consequently an agreement for valuable consideration, though not under seal, is sufficient here to create a right to the easement claimed, and for the purpose of lawful user is as good as a deed: *Dalton* v. *Angus* (1881), 6 App. Cas. 740, at p. 782; *White* v. *Grand Hotel Eastbourne Limited*, [1913] 1 Ch. 113; *Walsh* v. *Lonsdale* (1882), 21 Ch. D. 9; *Rogers* v. *National Drug and Chemical Co.* (1911), 23 O.L.R. 234, 24 O.L.R. 486.

The part performance by the defendant by buying the tombstone, and placing it upon the plot, etc., removes any objection under the Statute of Frauds.

Refraining from buying another plot is in itself sufficient consideration....

It is not necessary to discuss the well-known case of *Wood* v. *Leadbitter*, 13 M. & W. 838: that *crux* of the English law and stumbling block to those who wish to believe that the English law is the perfection of human reason, has been reduced to not much more than a matter of pleading by such cases as *Hurst* v. *Picture Theatres Limited*, [1915] 1 K.B. 1, 9, and *Lowe* v. *Adams*, [1910] 2 Ch. 598, 600.

What would appear at first sight a real difficulty in the way of the defendant is the principle that there can be no easement in gross, and that what purports to be such can be considered only as a personal contract sounding in damages: *Miller* v. *Tipling* (1918), 43 O.L.R. 88, 43 D.L.R. 469, and cases cited; *David Allen & Billposting Limited* v. *King*, [1915] 2 I.R. 488, and cases cited.

And were this cemetery a common law burial ground, the God's acre of an English parish, there is some authority for saying that the rule would apply to a grant of the right to bury in it to one not otherwise entitled: Comyns, Dig., "Cemetery" (B); *Bryan* v. *Whistler*, *ut supra.*

But that rule, if it ever existed, was made to depend upon the peculiar legal position of the parish graveyard, and probably in any case applied only to an exclusive right to bury.

The rule in any event never applied to burial grounds not being parish graveyards, e.g., those attached to dissenting chapels: *Moreland* v. *Richardson* (1856), 22 Beav. 596; S.C. (1857), 24 Beav. 33; or those established by burial boards under (1852) 15 & 16 Vict. ch. 85 (Imp.): *Ashby* v. *Harris*, L.R. 3 C.P. 523.

In both these cases a personal grant was made of the right to bury, not at all to the grantee as being the owner of any land or messuage, but in gross; and it was held that the grantors had no power to derogate from that grant—in the former case an injunction was granted by Sir John Romilly, M.R.; in the latter a conviction was sustained by the full Court of Common Pleas against the Board for an assault upon the grantee when planting flowers on her husband's grave. Either would be inconsistent with the proposition that the grant simply sounded in damages.

Accordingly, while the right of burial is still called an easement, it is an exception to the general rule that an easement cannot be in gross.

Neither the deceased Babcock in his lifetime nor the plaintiff, his devisee, can derogate from the right given by Babcock—the plaintiff is in no higher position than Babcock would have been....

This disposes of the first claim of the plaintiff—there was no trespass to his lot.

The second claim, the ghoulish demand that the corpse of the defendant's husband should be dug up and carried off the plot, of course falls with the first—not that the cold clay of the dead man has any rights, but that the defendant has the right to keep the body there until the end of time. It is reasonably certain that the plaintiff's ashes, if and when they are laid in the same plot, will not receive any pollution or injury from those of his dead uncle.

The claim for an injunction was not much if at all pressed upon the argument: but it was not expressly abandoned and must be dealt with. It is hardly to be expected that the plaintiff will try to prevent the defendant from having access to the grave of her dead: but the defendant is entitled to be protected against any attempt to do so....

SUTHERLAND J.: ... Here, ... William Babcock in his lifetime had entered into an agreement with the defendant in which she was to have the right of burial for herself and her husband in the lot in question. On the strength of that agreement she purchased and set up the monument in the lot. There was included in the agreement an implied term not to revoke the licence, and it would be a breach of that contract to revoke the obligation not to revoke the license.

Now under the County Courts Act, R.S.O. 1914, ch. 59, sec. 22 (1) (i), "actions for equitable relief where the subject-matter involved does not exceed in value or amount $500," are within the jurisdiction of the County Court.

The erection of the monument where it was upon the lot in question was an act of part performance so unequivocally referable to some such contract as that put forward by the defendant as, if proved, would prevent the application of the Statute of Frauds. It is such an act of part performance as would let in proper parol evidence of the contract. The contract has been fully proved, and the objection as to the Statute of Frauds therefore fails.

It may be that the plaintiff has estopped himself by standing by in so far as the burial of the defendant's husband is concerned. He is in any event a mere volunteer. He can have no higher right than the testator. It would have amounted to a fraud on the part of the testator had he been alive and sought to set up the statute against the defendant. The plaintiff can be in no better position than he....

KELLY J. agreed with SUTHERLAND J.

Appeal dismissed.

RE HEIER. Saskatchewan Court of Appeal. [1953] 1 D.L.R. 792, 7 W.W.R. (N.S.) 385

MARTIN C. J. S.: This is an application under s. 15 of the *Devolution of Real Property Act*, R.S.S. 1940, c. 108, for the approval of a petroleum and natural gas lease, granted to the British American Oil Co. by the executors of the estate of John Heier, deceased.

Section 15 of the *Devolution of Real Property Act* is in part as follows:

"15(1) The personal representative may, from time to time, subject to the provisions of any will affecting the property;

"(a) lease the real property or any part thereof for any term not exceeding one year;

"(b) lease the real property or any part thereof, with the approval of the court, for a longer term."

The application was heard by Taylor J. who dismissed it on the ground that "these so-called mining leases and oil leases" are not leases in the proper and legal sense of the term, "but are sales or agreements to sell a severable portion of the land". The learned Judge stated that he agreed with the decision of Gale J. in *Detomac Mines Ltd.* v. *Reliance Fluorspar Mining Syndicate Ltd.*, [1952] 3 D.L.R. 464, O.R. 423 [aff'd [1952] 4 D.L.R. 385, O.R. 783.]

The so-called lease was made on May 3, 1952, by Freda Stone and John George Heier, executors of the estate of John Heier, deceased, of all the petroleum and natural gas and related hydrocarbons, within, upon, or under the southwest quarter and the most easterly 60 rods in width throughout of the north-east quarter of sect. 9, tp. 8, rge. 14 W. of 2nd Meridian, containing 220 acres more or less. The lessor covenants that in consideration of the sum of $110 paid to him by the lessee and in consideration of further rentals and payments referred to in the provisions of the agreement, he "doth hereby grant and lease exclusively unto the lessee all the Petroleum and Natural Gas and related hydrocarbons except coal and valuable stone... within, upon, or under the lands hereinbefore described, and all the right, title, estate and interest of the lessor in and to the leased substances or any of them... together with the exclusive right and privilege to explore, drill for, win, take, remove, store, and dispose of the leased substances, and for the said purposes to drill wells, lay pipe lines and build and install such tanks, stations, structures and roadways as may be necessary".

It is also provided that the lessee shall have the use of such water as may be required for its purposes, provided that such use does not exclude the lessor from having sufficient water for farming purposes. The agreement is for 10 years and so long thereafter as the leased substances or any of them are produced from the lands. It is, however, provided that:

(a) If operations for the drilling of a well are not commenced within one year of the date of the agreement the lease shall be at an end, unless the lessee shall have paid or tendered the lessor the annual acreage rental "hereinafter defined", which payment shall defer the drilling operations for the period of one year.

(b) If at any time during the 10-year term the lessee shall drill a dry well or wells, the lease shall terminate at the next anniversary date, unless operations for drilling another well shall have commenced, or unless the lessee shall have paid the annual acreage rental.

(c) That if at the termination of the 10-year period the leased substances are not being produced and the lessee is engaged in drilling, the lease shall remain in force so long as operations are prosecuted, and so long as leased substances are produced.

The annual acreage rental is 50 cents per acre, and provisions are made for payment of royalties on the production of both oil and gas. The lessor covenants to pay all taxes, rates, liens and assessments that may be assessed or levied by reason of the lessor's interest or benefits in or from the lands, or by reason of his ownership of the mineral rights, and also all taxes levied against the surface of the lands. The lessee covenants to pay all taxes which may be levied in respect of the undertaking of the lessee and also all taxes levied by reason of the lessee's interest in production from the lands. There is a covenant on the part of the lessor for quiet enjoyment on the lessee's performing the covenants and conditions undertaken on his part. It is also provided that the parties, or either of them, may assign to any other person all or any of the property, powers, rights and interests obtained by, or conferred upon him or it under the agreement.

From the authorities it appears that it is often a matter of difficulty to determine the real nature of documents termed mining leases. The question is not determined by the name given to the instrument by the parties, nor by its form. The substance of the agreement must be considered and its intent is to be gathered from the entire contents. In 22 Hals., 2nd ed., p. 615, the learned author states: "It is sometimes a matter of difficulty to decide whether a particular form of words operates to grant a licence or an estate. Each case depends on its own circumstances, and it is impossible to lay down any general rule except that words denoting liberty to work minerals, if unexplained by the other parts of the deed, only amount to the grant of a licence." In support of this statement reference is made to *Sutherland (Duke of)* v. *Heathcote*, [1892] 1 Ch. 475 at p. 483, *per* Lindley L. J. Vide also 20 Hals., 2nd ed., p. 9.

In Hill & Redman's Landlord and Tenant, 11th ed., p. 603, the learned author states: "It has been said that a contract for the working and getting of minerals, though for convenience called a mining lease, is not in reality a lease at all in the sense in which one speaks of an agricultural lease, and that such a contract, properly considered, is really a sale of a portion of the land at a price payable by instalments, i.e. by way of rent or royalty, spread over a number of years."

Under the agreement it is not contemplated that the owner is to divest himself of possession; the agreement is for a limited use of the land by the company in order to permit it to get and take away the minerals purchased but the possession and control remain with the owner. To enable the company to search for the petroleum and natural gas, it is given the exclusive right "to explore, drill for, win, take, remove, store and dispose of the leased substances... and for the said purposes to drill wells, lay pipe lines, and build and install such tanks, structures and roadways as may be necessary."

The substance of the agreement is a grant to the lessee of petroleum, natural gas and all related hydrocarbons as may be found in, throughout and upon the land, and there is also a grant to the lessee of the exclusive right to enter upon the land to search for and drill for the minerals granted. Minerals while in the land are a part of the land and a grant of them is a grant of an interest in land. Petroleum and natural gas are minerals: *Landowners Mutual Minerals Ltd.* v. *Registrar of Land Titles* (1952), 6 W.W.R. (N.S.) 230.

The authorities are to the effect that what are called mineral leases are in reality sales of an estate in land. The authority which is most frequently referred to which supports this proposition is *Gowan* v. *Christie* (1873), L.R. 2 Sc. & Div. 273, where Lord Cairns is reported at p. 284 as follows: "What we call a mineral lease is really, when properly considered, a sale out and out of a portion of land. It is liberty given to a particular individual, for a specific length of time, to go into and under the land, and to get certain things there if he can find them, and to take them away, just as if he had bought so much of the soil."

This statement of Lord Cairns is cited with approval in Morine's Mining Law of Canada, 1909, p. 192. It is quoted by Lord Blackburn in *Coltness Iron Co.* v. *Black* (1881), 6 A.C. 315 at p. 335, and is referred to as "a perfectly accurate statement".

In the Province of Ontario the Courts have dealt with the subject of the so-called mining leases in several reported cases. In *McIntosh* v. *Leckie* (1906), 13 O.L.R. 54, the defendant by written lease gave the plaintiff the exclusive right to drill on certain oil lands for 5 years from December 16, 1903 "this lease to be null and void and no longer binding... if a well is not commenced... within six months... unless the lessee shall thereafter pay yearly to the lessor $50 per year for delay". It was held by Boyd C. that the legal effect of the instrument was more than a licence, that it conferred *a profit à prendre*, an incorporeal right to be exercised in the land comprised in it. In support of his conclusion Boyd C. referred to *Sutherland* v. *Heathcote*, *supra*, and cited with approval the statement of Lord Cairns in *Gowan* v. *Christie*, *supra*.

In *Can. Railway Accident Co.* v. *Williams* (1910), 21 O.L.R. 472, the oil leases were in substantially the same form as the instrument considered by Boyd C. in *McIntosh* v. *Leckie*, *supra*. Meredith C. J. was of the opinion that the document conferred the exclusive right to conduct operations on the land in order to drill for and produce oil and gas which may be there found during the specified period; that it was a *profit à prendre* an incorporeal right to be exercised on the land described. He cited *McIntosh* v. *Leckie*; *Duke of Sutherland* v. *Heathcote*, and *Wickham* v. *Hawker* (1840), 7 M. and W. 63 at p. 78, 151 E.R. 679. He quoted the statement of Lord Cairns in *Gowan* v. *Christie*, and also the reference of Lord Blackburn to the statement in *Coltness Iron Co.* v. *Black*.

In *Re Dawson & Bell*, [1946] 1 D.L.R. 327, [1945] O.R. 825, the lessee was granted, demised and leased a certain tract of land for the purpose and with the exclusive right of drilling and operating for petroleum and gas at a stipulated rent and subject to certain royalties payable in respect of the oil and gas found on the land. It was held by the Court of Appeal that the lessee had an estate in the land. McRuer J. A. at pp. 334-5 referred to the

English and Ontario decisions above cited and also to *Martyn* v. *Williams* (1857), 1 H. & N. 816 at p. 826, 156 E.R. 1430, and *Webber* v. *Lee* (1882), 9 Q.B.D. 315.

In *Detomac Mines Ltd.* v. *Reliance Fluorspar Mining Syndicate Ltd.*, [1952] 3 D.L.R. 464, O.R. 423, the so-called lease granted to the lessee "all fluorspar minerals which may or hereafter may be found in, throughout, and upon" the lands described "with full and exclusive liberty, power and authority for the lessee... to search for, dig, work, mine, procure and carry away the said fluorspar mineral wherever it may be found within the limits of the said lands". The agreement provided for the payment of a stipulated royalty by the lessee and further provided that it was to remain in "full force and effect for as long a period as the lessee makes the minimum monthly royalty payment". It was held by Gale J. that the document although called a lease was in realty not a lease but a sale of a severable portion of the land at a price payable by instalments by way of rent or royalty spread over a number of years and that it was clearly intended to convey the entire ownership of the fluorspar and was consequently a grant of an interest in land. In support of his conclusion Gale J. cited several of the authorities hereinbefore referred to. The Ontario Court of Appeal affirmed the decision of Gale J. [1952] 4 D.L.R. 385, O.R. 783, *per* Laidlaw J. A. p. 386 D.L.R., p. 788 O.R., *per* Hogg J. A. p. 389 D.L.R., pp. 791-2 O.R.

Vide also *Re Rippel*, [1948] 1 W.W.R. 695; *Kendall* v. *Smith*, [1947] 2 W.W.R. 609.

Counsel for the applicant cited the following cases: *Joggins Coal Co.* v. *M.N.R.*, [1950] 3 D.L.R. 1, S.C.R. 470; *Fraser & Co.* v. *M.N.R.*, [1947] 2 D.L.R. 321, S.C.R. 157, and in the Privy Council, [1948] 4 D.L.R. 776, [1949] A.C. 24, and *Seymour* v. *Lynch* (1885), 7 O.R. 471. In *Fraser & Co.* v. *M.N.R.* the company carried on a lumbering business in Alberta and when making its income tax return for 1941 claimed an allowance for the exhaustion of three timber limits for which it held licences from the Province. The claim was made under s. 5 (1) (a) of the *Income War Tax Act* as amended in 1940 and under which the Court held that the section gives the Minister a discretion not merely as to the amount but also as to whether any allowance for exhaustion should be made. From the judgments delivered in the Supreme Court it appears that in the opinion of the members of the Court it was not necessary to consider whether under the timber licences the company was a lessee, a licensee or owner of the timber. The Privy Council affirmed the decision of the Supreme Court and Lord Macmillan in delivering the judgment of their Lordships stated ([1948] 4 D.L.R. at p. 780): "In both of the Courts in Canada there was much argument as to the precise legal position of the appellant company as licensees of their timber limits. The Minister contended that being mere purchasers of the timber which they cut and not being lessess they were not entitled to invoke s. 5 (1) (a) of the statute and were not eligible for any depletion allowance, so that his discretion to make an allowance was not called into action. Before their Lordships counsel for the Minister abandoned this contention and no more need be said about it."

In *Joggins Coal Co.* v. *M.N.R.*, *supra*, the appellant, the Joggins Coal Co., appealed from a decision of the Exchequer Court affirming the dismissal by the Minister of an appeal in respect of its assessment for income for the years 1939, 1940 and 1941. During these years the company secured its income from mining coal from the "40 Brine Seam" the right to mine which was derived from two mining leases made by the Province of Nova Scotia. The interest of the original lessee was acquired by one Ralph Parsons by virtue of a sale under execution and he became entered as lessee in the records of the Provincial Mines Office. In 1937 Parsons sold to the Fundy Coal Co. all his right, title and interest in the mining leases and the Fundy Coal Co. almost at once assigned to the Tantramar Coal Co. all its interest in the mining leases. In 1939 the Tantramar company by agreement granted to one Winfield "the sole and exclusive right or option to mine and purchase such coal as the purchaser desires to win from the said 40 Brine Seam under the terms and conditions hereinafter recited". The agreement provided for the payment by Winfield of certain royalties to the vendors as well as the provincial royalties and obligated the purchaser to mine all the marketable coal in the seam which under sound mining practice would be practical and expedient. Later Winfield as vendor assigned to the appellant Joggins company all his rights in the lease and undertook to perform all the obligations of the vendor.

Section 5 (1) (a) with respect to the taxation year 1939 provided that in case of leases of mines "the lessor and the lessee shall each be entitled to deduct a part of the allowance for exhaustion as they agree" and if they do not agree "the Minister shall have full power to apportion the deduction". The Minister of National Revenue was of the opinion that the Province was the lessor and the Tantramar company the lessee and that the appellant company was not, therefore, within the provisions of s. 5 (1) (a) of the *Income War Tax Act* and in this opinion he was upheld by the Exchequer Court. The Supreme Court, however, held that the relationship of lessor and lessee existed between the Tantramar company and the appellant company and referred the matter back to be dealt with in accordance with this finding. The Court was of the opinion that the appellant company was a lessee within the meaning of the word in s. 5 (1) (a) of the *Income War Tax Act* and that the word "lessee" in the Nova Scotia statute, R.S.N.S. 1923, c. 22, is not used in the narrow sense attributed to it by the Minister, but that it included the interest in the leases held by the appellant under the assignment from the Tantramar company which was described by the Minister as "merely a sale and the necessary licence to mine". It is of interest to note that Kellock J. who delivered the judgment of the Court quoted with approval the statement of Lord Cairns in *Gowan* v. *Christie*, *supra.*

In *Seymour* v. *Lynch*, 7 O.R. 471, in an instrument under the *Short Forms of Leases Act* the plaintiff was described as lessor and P. and H. as lessees, the granting part being that the lessor did "give, grant, and demise and lease... the exclusive right, liberty, and privilege of entering at all times for... in and upon that certain tract of land situated... reserving that portion thereof occupied, or hereafter to be occupied as roadway by a railway company named... and with agents to search for, dig, excavate, mine, and carry away the iron ores in, upon, or under said premises". The question before the Court was whether the plaintiff at the time of the seizure of certain goods by the Sheriff, was entitled as against the defendants to a certain sum of money as one year's rent of the premises whereon the goods were seized. The case was tried by Patterson J. A. who held that the instrument was merely a licence and that at the time of seizure by the Sheriff the plaintiff was not entitled as against the defendants to any sum of money as rent of the premises.

In the Queen's Bench Division the three Judges unanimously held that the document was a lease. Armour J. stated that the document gave the exclusive right of entering at all times during the term of 10 years, that any right of entry by the lessor was excluded and that the lessor showed an intention on his part to divest himself of the possession of the land. In the Court of Appeal there was an equal division of opinion, 14 O.A.R. 738, and in the Supreme Court of Canada, 15 S.C.R. 341, three Judges held that the document was a mere licence and three that it was a lease. In the result the judgment of the Queen's Bench Division was affirmed. The arguments of counsel were devoted to the question of whether the document was a mere licence or a lease. It was not suggested by counsel nor in any of the judgments that the document constituted a sale of the minerals as an estate in the land There is no reference to *Gowan* v. *Christie*, *supra*, nor similar authorities, and while in the result it was held that the document was a lease, I must say with respect that in my opinion, had *Gowan* v. *Christie* been called to the attention of the Supreme Court, there is good reason for thinking that the result might have been different and that it might have been held that the document was a sale of an interest in the land. However the case is most unsatisfactory and I do not think it should be taken as affecting what appears to be the law with respect to the so-called mining lease established by many authorities.

Since writing the above my attention has been called to the judgment of the Privy Council in *Munro* v. *Didcott* (1910), 80 L.J.P.C. 65. The question there concerned a mining lease under a statute of Natal. Lord Atkinson in delivering the judgment of their Lordships quoted with approval the statement of Lord Cairns in *Gowan* v. *Christie, supra.* He said that the statement "may be in reality the true nature" of the document in question, but he concluded that it was unnecessary to decide it as whichever of two constructions was adopted the appellants must fail.

From the authorities it is clear that the so-called lease here under review is a sale of a portion of the land in the form of Petroleum and Natural Gas with liberty to enter upon the lands mentioned in the instrument for the purpose of searching for and severing and carrying away the Petroleum and Natural Gas within, upon or under the said lands. The application is made under s. 15 of the *Devolution of Real Property Act* for the approval of a lease and as the instrument is not a lease the application must be dismissed.

GORDON J. A., dissenting: ... With every respect I do not think it essential to define with exactitude the agreement in question. It is sufficient if it contains such covenants as to warrant a careful executor coming to the Court for its approval as a lease of part of the surface rights.

The section under which the application is made reads as follows:

"15. (1) The personal representative may, from time to time, subject to the provisions of any will affecting the property:

"(a) lease the real property or any part thereof for any term not exceeding one year;

"(b) lease the real property or any part thereof, with the approval of the court, for a longer term."

It is quite unnecessary to outline the reasons why this section of the *Devolution of Real Property Act* was passed but it seems to me that it was to prevent an executor or administrator from tying up the real property of the deceased to the detriment of the beneficiaries.

Before dealing with technical matters I should like to say that these mineral leases so called have been called "leases" for over a hundred years. Provincial statutes and Regulations refer to them as "leases". *The Mineral Resources Act*, R.S.S. 1940, c. 40, in ss. 3 and 4 makes provision for the "lease" of mines and minerals and mining rights. The Regulations passed under the provisions of this Act also provide for the terms and conditions under which such leases are issued. In the vast majority of cases the Crown in the right of the Province holds the mineral rights only, the surface rights being held by others. These Regulations call for an agreement very much in the terms of the one entered into by the parties to this so-called lease. In the case of *Lonsdale* v. *Lowther*, [1900] 2 Ch. 687, it was held that the power given to lease land included a power to lease minerals.

In considering the question it must constantly be borne in mind that under the *Land Titles Act* a certificate of title may now be issued to the owner of any minerals underlying any lands and certificates are of course issued to the owner of the surface rights. The land in this case is registered under the Act.

In by far the greatest area of the Province the owner of the surface rights is not the owner of the mineral rights. In the ordinary case the Oil Company could not acquire the rights given them under this agreement without dealing with two people, *viz.*, the owner of the mineral rights and the owner of the surface rights.

To begin with the agreement is not such a sale of the mineral rights or the leased substances as would ever lead to a certificate of title therefor being issued to the Oil Company. Further it bears no resemblance to the ordinary agreement for the sale of the surface rights of land because at no time will the so-called purchaser, the lessee, obtain a registered title to the leased substances. But even if the agreement is a sale of the leased substances that does not say that there is no lease of the surface rights.

Counsel for the applicant submitted, and with every deference, I think correctly, that the registered owner of the mineral rights under any land cannot go on that land apart from statute or regulation having the force of statute, without making an agreement with the registered owner of the surface rights.

Stating the matter in another way: The registered owner of the surface rights holds the same under s. 189 of the *Land Titles Act*, R.S.S. 1940, c. 98, absolutely free from any claim whatever unless registered on his title and subject only to those further rights or charges mentioned in s. 63 of the Act, to which it is subject by implication. If for instance the mineral rights had been reserved to the Crown, when the grant of the surface rights was made, the Crown might have rights permitting it to enter upon the land as was the fact in the case of *Fuller* v. *Garneau* (1921), 58 D.L.R. 642, 61 S.C.R. 450.

The agreement under consideration in the case referred to by the learned Judge in Chambers, namely *Detomac Mines Ltd.* v. *Reliance Fluorspar Mining Syndicate*, [1952] 3 D.L.R. 464, O.R. 423, could not possibly have been considered a lease as there was no term mentioned therein.

Counsel for the applicants referred us to the case of *Re Rippel*, [1948] 1 W.W.R. 695, which on first blush seems a strong case against the applicants but a careful reading of that case shows that the grant did not contain the following clause which appears in the agreement under consideration: "and, in so far as the lessor has the right so to grant, and for the said purposes, the right of entering upon, using and occupying the said lands or so much thereof to such an extent as may be necessary or convenient."

If for instance, the Oil Company was so fortunate as to strike a gusher, and I am sure this is the pious hope of all the beneficiaries of the estate, the Oil Company would require most of the area to properly work the wells and store the oil. No one but a lessee would have the right to enter and occupy a parcel of land even for a limited purpose, such as to remove timber, or build tanks for storing oil.

The contention was raised on the argument that the agreements dealing with the surface rights were merely ancillary to the rights given in respect to the minerals. This may be perfectly true but it does not thereby define what those rights are, lease or licence. The facts are that without the rights given in respect to the surface the Oil Company might have been put to serious expense to obtain them and if such rights had been got from an independent owner of the surface rights they would have been properly given in a lease.

In 22 Hals., 2nd ed., p. 615, the learned author states the great difficulty in deciding whether a particular document is a lease or a licence. No one can read the numerous cases on the question without being impressed by this.

Whatever doubt there may be on this question, it is beyond controversy that the agreement in question gives the Oil Company wider rights than they would have at common law or which would be implied from the fact that the owner sold it the mineral rights. It is given the right of "entering upon, using and occupying the said lands or so much thereof to such an extent as may be necessary or convenient." It seems clear that the right of possession given a tenant under a lease need not be exclusive possession for all purposes. It is sufficient if the exclusive right of possession is given for one purpose. *Glenwood Lbr. Co.* v. *Phillips*, [1904] A.C. 405.

Supposing one of the beneficiaries in this estate had not consented to an order approving of the agreement and an action was brought by him to have it declared void as being a lease for more than one year. How could the parties contend that it was a sale with a licence when throughout the agreement they have called it a lease? Why should an executor be asked to run the risk of such an action?...

In my view the agreement in question in so far as it deals with the surface rights of the land falls within the term "lease" as used in the *Devolution of Real Property Act*....

PROCTER J. A. (after reciting the terms of the transaction in question): ... The construction to be placed on these so-called "Mineral Leases" and "Petroleum and Gas Leases" has on many occasions been before the Courts for interpretation and has resulted in great difference of judicial opinion. The fact that in these documents the parties refer to themselves as lessors and lessees has little bearing on the question and does not assist in construction of the documents. Each one must be examined without regard to the form in which it has been prepared and what may be called the pith and substance of the agreement governs the effect to be given to form and words.

Here the title to the petroleum and gas and the entire fee simple belonged to the Heier estate before the document in question was executed.

It is clear from the wording of the document that much more than a mere lease or licence to work the minerals was given to the company.

The executors for a cash consideration and a royalty granted and leased exclusively all the petroleum and gas within, upon or under the lands and all the right, title and estate and interest of the lessor therein to the company and the words of grant are sufficient to constitute a sale of the minerals.

Coupled with the grant of petroleum and gas are other rights over the estate retained by the executors which affect both surface rights and other undiscovered minerals that may exist in the land. I have no difficulty in finding that as to the property rights in so far as the petroleum and gas are concerned the agreement constitutes an agreement for sale whereby the property rights are sold to the company....

The further question remains as to whether the other rights conferred make the document both an agreement of sale of minerals and a lease of surface rights in the land. Those other rights are: (1) The right to explore, drill for, win, take, remove, store and dispose of the petroleum and gas. (2) The right to drill wells, lay pipe lines and build and install tanks, storage, and make roads. (3) The right to use the surface of the land so far only as necessary for the purposes above. (4) A limited right to user of water.

These rights are granted for a period of 10 years or for so long as the petroleum and gas are produced on the land mentioned or on land with which it is unitized. They are limited by further provisions whereby drilling of a well must be commenced within one year or an annual acreage rental of 50 cents per acre must be paid until drilling is commenced. In my opinion this annual rental is paid not for the right to occupy the land but for the privilege of postponing drilling a well or wells thereon.

It is a material feature of the document that the executors, in addition to the cash monies provided to be paid in the event of petroleum or gas being produced, are to receive a further payment in money called a royalty based on the value of production but the executors do not retain ownership of any part of the petroleum or gas produced. The agreement may be surrendered at the option of the company as to part or all the land or may be terminated on notice for breach or nonperformance on the part of the company and is assignable by either party.

It is apparent that the company never becomes the owner of the soil or other minerals as distinct from the petroleum and natural gas which alone become the property of the company. The other rights granted are simply ancillary rights to enable the company to get possession of and dispose of the petroleum and gas. These rights referred to above while expressed to be exclusive are exclusive only as against others than the grantors and exclusive as against the grantors only in so far as is necessary to enable the company to enter on the land to discover, produce, and dispose of the petroleum and gas. The grantors undoubtedly continue in possession of the land for farming purposes and the company could I think be restrained from unduly interfering with the surface rights of the grantors if they sought to occupy the surface beyond what was necessary to enable them to discover, produce, and dispose of the petroleum and gas.

An essential requisite of a lease is that the lessee shall have exclusive possession of the leased property as against the lessor who retains only a right to enter upon the leased premises for purposes of inspection and repair. Another requisite is that there should be a right to the reversion at the expiration of the term. Here there is no exclusive possession of the land given by the so-called lease.

If the terms of the agreement are fully carried out the petroleum and gas are discovered, removed and disposed of. There can be no interest in them to revert to the lessors....

This Court decided in *Landowners Mutual Minerals Ltd.* v. *Registrar of Land Titles, supra*, that petroleum and gas are land.

I think, however, that the additional rights conferred are more than a bare licence since the company has more than a mere right to use the property. As was said in *Haven* v. *Hughes* (1900), 27 O.A.R. 1, the additional rights are incidental to the contract and necessary for its beneficial fulfilment. See 20 Hals, 2nd ed., pp. 8-20 and 22 Hals., pp. 614-6.

In *Warr & Co.* v. *London County Council* (1940), 73 L.J. K.B. 362, Greet and Engelbach, lessees of the Globe Theatre by an agreement in which they were described as landlords and Warr & Co. were described as tenants provided as follows:

"The landlords hereby grant and let and the tenants hereby take for the term of the landlords' lease commencing the first day of September 1900 the free and exclusive right to sell refreshment at the Globe Theatre, Newcastle Street, Strand, London, *with the necessary use of the refreshment rooms and bars and cloak rooms and wine cellars of the said theatre* together with the free right during the usual hours of the tenants their servants and agents of free access to and from all parts of the house including the front of the theatre and premises as may be necessary and is usual and proper according to the custom of the theatres for the purpose of exercising the rights granted by this agreement and *also the free and exclusive right during the aforesaid term* of supplying to the visitors and other people attending the theatre wines spirits liqueurs cigars cigarettes flowers scent and refreshments of all kinds programmes books of words books of music opera glasses and all other articles and *of providing cloak rooms and other accommodation and also the sole and exclusive privilege during the aforesaid term of advertising and letting spaces for advertisement which shall be confined to the refreshment and cloak rooms* and on all programmes used and offered for sale at the said theatre.

"The tenants shall pay to the landlords in respect of the said rights hereby granted the weekly rental of 85£."

The rights given to the company in the document before us do not seem to be wider than the rights given to Warr & Co. in their agreement. There Warr & Co. had a user of the refreshment rooms, bars, cloak-rooms and wine cellars in common with the owner of the theatre. They also had the exclusive right to provide the cloak-rooms and other accommodation and the sole and exclusive privilege of advertising and letting space in the refreshment rooms and cloak-rooms. Here the company have the exclusive right and privilege to explore, drill for, win, take, remove and store and dispose of the petroleum and gas they have purchased and *for that purpose* to drill wells, lay pipe-lines, and build and install tanks, stations structures and roadways only to the extent necessary to discover and dispose of the petroleum and gas. They also have the right to take water but must leave the executors sufficient water for their farming purposes which plainly implies that both parties contemplate the executors are to continue to farm the surface with as little interruption as possible. The executors are also to pay the taxes on the other minerals and on the soil.

The Court of Appeal in England following *Edwards* v. *Barrington* (1901), 85 L.T. 650, decided in the House of Lords, [held] that the agreement did not create in Greet and Englebach an interest in land and that it was not a lease. The same reasoning seems to have been followed in *Detomac Mines Ltd.* v. *Reliance Fluorspar Mining Syndicate Ltd.*, [1952] 4 D.L.R. 385, [1952] O.R. 783, the latest case I have been able to discover dealing with the matter.

Turning now to the royalty clause quoted above it is to be observed that not only have the executors no property in the petroleum and gas produced but the royalty payable in cash is only payable after the petroleum and gas have been marketed. It cannot therefore have been in the contemplation of the parties that the rights to use the surface of the land for the erection of storage tanks, pipe-lines, etc., were granted for general storage purposes since the company must market the petroleum and gas within a reasonable time to permit payment of the royalty and these occupational rights were merely to facilitate the marketing on which the payment is based.

If there is no right to occupy the surface for a fixed term for general storage then I think that a right to occupy the surface for so long as petroleum and gas are being produced is one for such an indefinite term that it cannot be considered to be more than a licence perhaps irrevocable so long as the agreement is complied with and giving some interest in the land short of a lease.

For the purposes of this appeal it is unnecessary to determine the precise nature of the interest created by the document in question. It is sufficient to say that it is not a lease within the meaning of s. 15 (1) (b) of the *Devolution of Real Property Act*....

MCNIVEN J. A., dissenting: ... The agreement covers:

(a) Petroleum, natural gas and related hydrocarbons within, upon or under certain defined land and for convenience referred to throughout the agreement as "leased substances".

(b) Surface rights to the said land.

By agreement rights of an infinite variety with obligations of a wide and varied nature may be established in the one document, for example the sale of land and chattels and likewise leases with an option to purchase the demised premises. A properly drawn attornment clause in an agreement for sale of land or in a land mortgage creates the relationship of landlord and tenant.

The operative words in the agreement are grant and lease. The parties to the agreement are referred to respectively as lessor and lessee, but these terms are descriptive only. The parties understood that they were dealing with rights of different kinds and must have intended that the appropriate word grant or lease would be applied to properly convey the particular right. There is frequent reference throughout the agreement to "the said lands" and "leased substances" and more particularly in the clauses providing for "quiet enjoyment" and "further assurances" where the word "demise" is also used....

Under the agreement the lessor doth hereby grant and lease exclusively unto the lessee:

(a) All the petroleum and natural gas and related hydrocarbons except coal (hereinafter referred to as the "leased substances") within, upon or under the lands hereinbefore described and all the right, title and interest of the lessor in and to the leased substances or any of them within, upon or under any lands excepted therefrom, or roadways, lanes or rights-of-way adjoining the lands aforesaid.

(b) together with the exclusive right and privilege to explore, drill for, win, take, remove, store and dispose of the leased substances and

(c) for the said purposes to drill wells, lay pipelines and build and install such tanks, stations, structures and roadways as may be convenient.

Petroleum and natural gas under our *Land Titles Act* are an interest in land for which a separate certificate of title can issue: *vide Landowners Mutual Minerals Ltd.* v. *Registrar of Land Titles*, 6 W.W.R. (N.S.) 230. The verb "lease" in its widest connotation is not applicable to the rights given—absolute ownership of all the petroleum and natural gas within, upon or under the said lands. The royalty payable to the lessor is not in kind but a percentage of the value of the marketed product. Such rights as are described in the aforementioned paragraphs are effectively transferred or conveyed by the verb grant. Upon principle and upon the authorities reviewed by the learned Chief Justice in his judgment the so-called mining leases are really a sale of the mineral as land and therefore do not require the approval of the Court as leases under the *Devolution of Real Property Act*.

Having dealt with the petroleum and natural gas as minerals the document proceeds with the surface rights of the said lands in the same paragraph:

"The Lessor doth hereby grant and lease exclusively unto the lessee and insofar as the Lessor has the right to grant and for the said purposes the right of entering upon, using and occupying the said lands or so much thereof to such an extent as may be necessary or convenient. ... To have and enjoy the same for the term of ten years from the date hereof and so long thereafter as the leased substances or any of them are produced from the said lands or on lands with which the leased premises or any part thereof is then unitized subject to the sooner determination of the said term as stipulated herein."

Here we have all the essentials of a lease—rent reserved—fixed term embodying a yardstick for the sooner determination thereof and likewise as to its extension: *vide* 20 Hals., 2nd ed., pp. 148-9, ss. 160, 161. It also provides for exclusive possession of the said lands for certain purposes as to which see *Dalton* v. *Eaton*, [1924] 1 D.L.R. 493, 18 S.L.R. 92, where Lamont J. speaking for this Court adopts the dictum of Lord Davey in *Glenwood Lbr. Co.* v. *Phillips*, [1904] A.C. 405, as expressing the law of this Province: "'If the effect of the instrument is to give the holder an exclusive right of occupation of the land, though subject to certain reservations or to a restriction of the purposes for which it may be used, it is in law a demise of the land itself.'" [p. 495]

This principle was approved by the Ontario Court of Appeal in *Brockville* v. *Dobbie & Ritchie*, [1929] 3 D.L.R. 583, 64 O.L.R. 75. This statement of the law was again under consideration in *Re Timber Dues*, [1935] 2 D.L.R. 1, A.C. 184, and adopted as an accurate expression of the law.

In *Young & Co.* v. *Liverpool Assessment Committee*, [1911] 2 K.B. 195, at p. 215, Avory J. says: "The terms of the lease, in my opinion, establish an exclusive occupation. The word 'demise' prima facie alone would be sufficient to establish that. I do not go so far as to say that where the word 'demise' is used in a lease or agreement no evidence would be admissible to displace the presumption arising from its use, but the word prima facie would establish an exclusive occupation."

This document gives the lessee the exclusive right to enter upon the said land for certain defined and restricted purposes and on the authorities cited that is equivalent to a demise of the land. The rights so given extend to the production from any land with which this land is "unitized"—such production could be piped to and stored in tanks erected upon the land described in this document. However, the intent of the parties is to be determined from the language used and all speculation as to ancillary or incidental rights is beside the point. As to the surface rights of the said lands I am of the opinion that the document before the Court is a lease thereof within the meaning of the *Devolution of Real Property Act*, s. 15 (1) (b). All the beneficiaries have consented and there is evidence before us which satisfies me that the lease of the surface rights is beneficial to the estate and I therefore approve same....

CULLITON J. A. concurs with PROCTER J. A. *Appeal dismissed.*

[In *Re Sidney Tp. School Board and McFarland*, [1955] 3 D.L.R. 142, [1955] O.W.N. 475, the parties executed a document granting quarrying rights for a six year period on certain terms "with option of leasing for another period of six years". What interest is created in the "grantee"?

S. 2 (35) of the Laws Declaratory Act, R.S.B.C. 1960, c. 213, provides that any rule of law that a lease, grant, demise or agreement is void because the term thereof is uncertain does not apply to mining or petroleum or natural gas leases.

See *Lewis*, The Canadian Petroleum and Natural Gas Lease, (1952) 30 Can. Bar Rev. 965.]

CHAPTER VII

LANDLORD AND TENANT

1. INTRODUCTORY NOTE: THE LEASE AS CONVEYANCE AND CONTRACT

Where a bargain is made for the lease of premises, whether for residential or commercial purposes, on terms embodied in a formal document of lease, the lessee (at least on entry) acquires an estate which he holds subject to those terms. The pertinent question is to what extent is the transaction regarded as the transfer of an interest in land (and hence governed by rules and doctrines developed as part of the law of estates) and to what extent is it regarded as a business dealing (and hence governed by rules and doctrines developed later as part of the law of contracts). The common law worked out certain incidents of the landlord-tenant relationship which were applicable simply because of the tenure between the parties, as, for example, distress for default in payment of rent, and a (somewhat undefined) duty of repair on the tenant (by application of the law of waste). Where the relationship was still that of lessor and lessee (before entry into possession) the common law tended to emphasize the contractual aspect of the bargain; the lessee had until entry only an *interesse termini* and thus, for example, could not sue a third person in trespass or sue his lessor for breach of a covenant for quiet enjoyment (see *Wallis* v. *Hands*, [1893] 2 Ch. 75) nor, on the other hand, was he subject to distress (*Lewis* v. *Baker*, [1905] 1 Ch. 46.) Once, however, tenure was established, whether in pursuance of a formal lease or of an agreement for a lease, property conceptions dominated. This was particularly true in respect of the covenants of the respective parties. Apart from express provision on the matter, the contract rule of dependency of promises was ignored. Thus, the tenant was not entitled to be excused from further performance or to terminate his lease unless there was a breach of condition by the landlord rather than a mere breach of covenant: cf. *Falleson* v. *Spruce Creek Mining Co.*, [1942] 4 D.L.R. 708, [1942] 3 W.W.R. 553, 58 B.C.R. 233 (C.A.). Again, contract or commercial doctrines of impossibility of performance or frustration were denied any application to leaseholds, and it is only recently that the possibility of their application to such interests has been held out.

While eviction by the landlord excused a tenant from his obligation to pay rent, anything less (for example, mere trespass or breach of the covenant for quiet enjoyment) did not unless expressly provided for: see *Kerr* v. *Maxfield* (1956), 4 D.L.R. 2d 294 (Alta.). If, as sometimes happened, a tenant vacated before expiry of his term and perhaps on a mistaken apprehension of the facts or law which would entitle him to vacate, he remained liable for rent without any duty on the landlord to mitigate damages by re-letting; see *Connolly* v. *Coon* (1896), 23 O.A.R. 37. If the landlord sues for damages for the unexpired portion of the term, he cannot (again apart from contract), if he sues before expiry of the term, recover once and for all as for an anticipatory breach of contract but must sue for his rent as it comes due under the terms of the lease. The doctrine of anticipatory breach has been applied to contracts for the sale of land (even to the point of permitting suit for specific performance: see *Kloepfer Wholesale Hardware & Automatic Co.* v. *Roy*, [1952] 2 S.C.R. 465, [1952] 3 D.L.R. 705) but there may be a justifiable distinction taken between the case of an executory contract of sale or an executory contract to lease and an executed leasing arrangement under which an estate has been acquired. Yet it may be noticed that in the United

States there is considerable, and perhaps even prevailing, authority that the anticipatory breach doctrine applies to actions for damages, brought before expiry of the lease, arising from the tenant's improper vacating of the premises: see 1 *American Law of Property*, s. 3.11; cf. *McCormick*, The Rights of the Landlord upon Abandonment of the Premises by the Tenant, (1925) 23 Mich. L. Rev. 211.

Generally, the effect of the domination of property conceptions was to subordinate the tenant to the landlord. While the balance could theoretically be redressed by covenant or simple contract obligations, their introduction depended on the parties' bargaining power. A good illustration of a standardized view of this factor and, indeed, of some of the ordinary incidents of a lease, may be seen in the Short Forms of Leases Act, R.S.O. 1960, c. 373. (See also, Short Form of Leases Act, R.S.B.C. 1960, c. 357; Short Forms Act, R.S.M. 1954, c. 243, Third Schedule; Conveyancing Act, R.S. Nfld. 1952, c. 140, s. 11; Real Property Act, R.S.P.E.I. 1951, c. 138. Part 4, Third Schedule. For a discussion of some of the unbalance in favour of the landlord, see *Plummer*, Some Aspects of the Law of Landlord and Tenant, (1946) 9 Mod. L. Rev. 42.

On the question of the leasehold as estate or contract, see *Bennett*, The Modern Lease: An Estate or a Contract, (1937) 16 Tex. L. Rev. 47; *Friedman*, The Nature of a Lease in New York, (1947) 33 Cornell L.Q. 165.

We have already seen that it is not always easy to determine whether a landlord and tenant relationship exists; the transaction may involve a licence only, especially if the test of exclusive occupation or possession is no longer conclusive of a tenancy (see *Errington* v. *Errington*, [1952] 1 K.B. 290, [1952] 1 All E.R. 149 (C.A.): *Cobb* v. *Lane*, [1952] 1 All E.R. 1199 (C.A.); *Booker* v. *Palmer*, [1942] 2 All E.R. 674 (C.A.). Cf. *Buck* v. *Howarth*, [1947] 1 All E.R. 342 (K.B.). Jenkins L. J. in *Addiscombe Garden Estates Ltd.* v. *Crabbe*, [1957] 3 All E.R. 563 (C.A.) criticised the *Errington* view of Denning L. J. that the test of exclusive possession is not decisive of a tenancy and stated (at p. 571) that "save in exceptional cases of the kind mentioned by Denning L. J. [in *Facchini* v. *Bryson*, [1952] 1 T.L.R. 1386] the law remains that the fact of exclusive possession if not decisive against the view that there is a mere licence, as distinct from a tenancy, is at all events a consideration of the first importance". Right of distress is not, of course, an incident of a licensor-licensee relationship, and a licensee (apart from contract) is not under any duty of repair. *Quaere*, whether as an occupier he is not liable to third persons in tort for the safe condition of the premises: This may well be so if the licensee is in sole occupation of a house; but what if he is merely a lodger occupying a room? Indeed, in the latter case, he himself might be entitled to protection against his "landlord" in respect of the condition of the room, and certainly of the entrance to and the hallways of the premises: see, for example, *Ottawa* v. *Munroe*, [1954] S.C.R. 756, [1955] 1 D.L.R. 465. How would you classify an apartment house dweller? Would anything turn on whether he had a "lease" of an apartment? Suppose he were merely a transient or temporary "guest"?

Similarly, a question may arise whether an occupant is a tenant or is a mere service occupant by reason of his employment, and thus not entitled to remain in possession after his employment is terminated: see *McNeely* v. *Carey* (1914), 7 W.W.R. 680 (B.C.D.C.); *Ramsbottom* v. *Snelson*, [1948] 1 All E.R. 201 (K.B.).

The matters touched on in this note suggest that drafting ability, based on an understanding of the existing law and on what your client's needs are, looms large in landlord-tenant and related transactions, even after allowance is made for any inequality of bargaining power. In assessing the cases and material in this chapter, you should consider how far proper drafting would have avoided some of the complications or (from your point of view) undesirable consequences.

[For a consideration of the Short Forms legislation, see *Delamatter* v. *Brown Bros. Co.*

(1905), 9 O.L.R. 351 (App. Div.); *Alexander* v. *Herman* (1912), 2 D.L.R. 239, 3 O.W.N. 755, 21 O.W.R. 461; *Edwards* v. *Fairview Lodge*, [1920] 3 W.W.R. 867, 28 B.C.R. 557.]

[An agreement for the sale and purchase of a house provides for a down payment by the purchaser and for monthly instalment payments. Pending payment of the price in full the purchaser is to be allowed to take possession as a tenant at will and to continue as such provided he keeps up the monthly payments. If the purchaser defaults in his payments, will it make any difference whether he is characterized as a tenant or as a purchaser? See *Dunthorne and Shore* v. *Wiggins*, [1943] 2 All E.R. 678 (C.A.).]

2. LEASES AND AGREEMENTS FOR LEASES

STATUTE OF FRAUDS, R.S.O. 1960, c. 381

1. (1) Every estate or interest of freehold and every uncertain interest of, in, to or out of any messuages, lands, tenements or hereditaments shall be made or created by writing signed by the parties making or creating the same, or their agents thereunto lawfully authorized in writing, and if not so made or created has the force and effect of an estate at will only, and shall not be deemed or taken to have any other or greater force or effect.

(2) All leases and terms of years of any messuages, lands, tenements or hereditaments are void unless made by deed.

2. Subject to section 9 of *The Conveyancing and Law of Property Act*, no lease, estate or interest, either of freehold or term of years, or any uncertain interest of, in, to or out of any messuages, lands, tenements or hereditaments shall be assigned, granted or surrendered unless it be by deed or note in writing signed by the party so assigning, granting, or surrendering the same, or his agent thereunto lawfully authorized by writing or by act or operation of law.

3. Sections 1 and 2 do not apply to a lease, or an agreement for a lease, not exceeding the term of three years from the making thereof, the rent upon which, reserved to the landlord during such term, amounts to at least two-thirds of the full improved value of the thing demised.

4. No action shall be brought whereby to charge any executor or administrator upon any special promise to answer damages out of his own estate, or whereby to charge any person upon any special promise to answer for the debt, default or miscarriage of any other person, or to charge any person upon any agreement made upon consideration of marriage, or upon any contract or sale of lands, tenements or hereditaments, or any interest in or concerning them, or upon any agreement that is not to be performed within the space of one year from the making thereof, unless the agreement upon which the action is brought, or some memorandum or note thereof is in writing and signed by the party to be charged therewith or some person thereunto by him lawfully authorized.

[For similar legislation, see Statute of Frauds, R.S.N.B. 1952, c. 218, ss. 1 (d), 7, and 8; Statute of Frauds, R.S.N.S. 1954, c. 272, ss. 2, 3 and 6 (d). Cf. Real Property Act, R.S.P.E.I. 1951, c. 138, s. 6.

In the western Provinces, provision is made for the use of specified forms of lease for the purpose of their respective land registration or land title systems: see Land Titles Act, R.S.A. 1955, c. 170, ss. 98-104; Real Property Act, R.S.M. 1954, c. 220, s. 92; Land Titles Act, 1960 (Sask.), c. 65, ss. 112-117. S. 250 of this last Act dispenses with the need of a seal, as does s. 20 of the Land Registry Act, R.S.B.C. (1960, c. 208 (except in the case of the execution of an instrument by a corporation).

What is the liability of a lessee corporation where the lease to it is not executed under its corporate seal? See *Kingston Motor Car Co.* v. *Wright*, [1941] 3 D.L.R. 778, [1941] O.W.N. 221.]

CARTER v. IRVING OIL CO. Nova Scotia Supreme Court. [1952] 4 D.L.R. 128

MacDONALD J.: The plaintiff claims damages for the defendant's breach of a lease or of an agreement to lease a service station owned by the defendant in the town of Yarmouth in failing to deliver possession thereof to him at the date therein agreed. The defendant adduced no evidence, relying upon the *Statute of Frauds* as a defence to the action.

[The learned Judge here detailed the facts which indicated that oral agreement had been reached for a one year lease. The lessor was unable to give possession on the date fixed because the existing lessee of the premises was entitled to and insisted on remaining in occupation for another month.]

Without doubt the plaintiff has suffered damage by reason of the foregoing circumstances; but any assessment thereof is futile unless it be established that he has a valid cause of action.

There being no written lease or contract upon which he may sue, he is driven to rely upon the contentions: that there was a verbal lease or present demise of the service station; or that there was a verbal agreement to lease the same; and, in either case, that there was a wrongful failure to give him possession, whereby he suffered damage.

Even assuming that there was a concluded bargain between the parties amounting to a present lease for a year beginning on May 18th or May 21st, as the case may be (as to which see *infra*), s. 3 of the *Statute of Frauds*, R.S.N.S. 1923, c. 199, stands in the plaintiff's way. By that section every lease is required to be in writing etc. and in default of this, only a tenancy at will is created. An exception is made of a lease for a term not exceeding 3 years but only if "the rent reserved amounts to two thirds at least of the annual value of the land demised". It is clear that to gain the benefit of the section enabling verbal leases for a term not exceeding 3 years (as in this case) proof must be made of the prescribed ratio between the rent reserved and the annual value of the land demised: *Power* v. *Griffin* (1887), 20 N.S.R. 52; *Smith* v. *Thomas* (1907), 41 N.S.R. 216. Since no such proof has been made, I must hold that no claim is maintainable upon the basis of there having been a lease or present demise.

The plaintiff's alternative claim upon the basis of a verbal contract of lease encounters s. 7 of the *Statute of Frauds* which applies *inter alia*, to contracts to lease land, and requires that the contract on which the action is brought, or some memorandum or note thereof, be in writing, signed by the party sought to be charged therewith or by his authorized agent. From this double-barrelled requirement relief can be had by invoking the equitable doctrine of part performance, but only in certain circumstances....

I agree that there were various acts of part performance on the part of the plaintiff (such as his public and private announcements of his change of location followed by his attempted entry into possession with the assistance of Mr. Trask). Part performance, however, is an equitable doctrine which relieves a litigant from compliance with the *Statute of Frauds* only to enable the equitable remedy of specific performance to be given.

It is clearly established (at least for this Court) that part performance can only enable an action of damages to succeed (where s. 7 of the *Statute of Frauds* is not satisfied) if the case in hand is one in which specific performance would otherwise have been granted by the Court of Chancery; and that neither *Lord Cairns' Act* of 1858 [c. 27] nor the fusion of law and equity declared by the *Judicature Act* affects this result: *Lavery* v. *Pursell* (1888), 39 Ch. D. 508 at p. 518; *Dom. Supply & Construction Co.* v. *Foley Bros.* (1919), 53 N.S.R. 333 at

p. 348; Hanbury, Modern Equity, 5th ed., pp. 107-9, 627; *cf. Bennett* v. *Stodgell* (1916), 28 D.L.R. 639 at pp. 643-5, 36 O.L.R. 45; Hill & Redman, Landlord & Tenant, 10th ed., pp. 96-7.

I am satisfied that apart from the *Statute of Frauds* the contract in this case (assuming that there was one concluded) (*cf. Harris* v. *Harris* (1920), 53 D.L.R. 389, 47 O.L.R. 321) is not susceptible of specific performance because: it is one requiring constant supervision of continuing acts of personal service (31 Hals., 2nd ed., pp. 334-5; *Bickford & Erie & Huron R. Co.* v. *Chatham* (1889), 16 S.C.R. 235; *Swan* v. *Swan*, [1938] 1 D.L.R. 454, 12 M.P.R. 363; Hanbury, Modern Equity, 5th ed., pp. 610-11; Cheshire & Fifoot on Contracts, 2nd ed., pp. 458-60); it is one in which a decree could be frustrated by termination of the lease by the defendant (31 Hals., 2nd ed., p. 343); and it is one performance of which in terms was rendered impossible by the inability of the defendant to evict LeBlanc; and had become impossible at the date of this action.

Accordingly I must dismiss the action with costs.

This is a result which can give no satisfaction to one charged with the administration of justice—according to law; for it is but one more of a long list of cases in which the successful invocation of the *Statute of Frauds* has worked patent injustice.

Action dismissed.

[See *Re Linzon and Wolfish* (1921), 20 O.W.N. 416 (C.A.); *Manchester* v. *Dixie Cup Co. (Can.) Ltd.*, [1951] O.R. 686, [1952] 1 D.L.R. 19 (C.A.). In Ontario, not only leases but agreements for leases for a term not exceeding three years from the making thereof may be enforced although made orally: see *Pain* v. *Dixon*, 52 O.L.R. 347, [1923] 3 D.L.R. 1167. (Contrast *Smith* v. *Thomas* (1907), 41 N.S.R. 216 (C.A.).) However, an oral lease for three years to begin in the future and not from the date of making is caught by the Statute of Frauds: see *Christie* v. *Clarke* (1866), 16 U.C.C.P. 544, aff'd 27 U.C.Q.B. 21 (C.A.).

What is the effect of a lease for one year with an option of renewal for three more years, where not made by deed or made orally? See the conflicting views in *Pain* v. *Dixon*, *supra*, and *R. C. Episcopal Corp. of St. Albert* v. *Sheppard & Co.* (1913), 6 Alta. L. R. 128, 9 D.L.R. 619, 3 W.W.R. 814. *Pain v. Dixon* relied on *Hand v. Hall* (1877), 2 Ex. D. 318, which had been reversed on appeal, 2 Ex. D. 355, 46 L.J.Q.B. 403.

Under the Registry Act, R.S.O. 1960, c. 348, s. 76 (2), unregistered leases for a term not exceeding seven years where actual possession goes along with the lease are protected against subsequent purchasers or mortgagees for value without actual notice. Must a lease for three years with an option to renew for five years be registered to ensure protection? Suppose that a five year lease contains an option to the lessee to purchase the land. If the document is unregistered, is the tenant in possession under the lease entitled to assert the option against a subsequent purchaser of the land from the landlord where the purchaser knows that a tenant is in possession? See *Plant* v. *Woolfe*, [1954] O.R. 726, [1954] 3 D.L.R. 700.

Where a lease for a term of more than seven years is registered, an assignee of the term is protected against subsequent *bona fide* purchasers of the land even though the assignment is not registered: see *Abraham* v. *The New York Café*, [1940] O.R. 73.

An agreement for a five year lease of certain land was not registered and thereafter a contract of sale of the land was entered into. After the contract of sale was made but before registration, the purchaser was made aware of the agreement for the lease. Who has priority? See *Paramount Theatres Ltd.* v. *Brandenberger*, 62 O.L.R. 579, [1928] 4 D.L.R. 573.]

WALSH v. LONSDALE. Court of Appeal. 1882. 21 Ch. D. 9, 52 L.J.Ch. 2

Plaintiff and defendant entered into a written agreement for the lease by defendant to plaintiff of a mill at a stipulated rent payable yearly in advance on demand. Plaintiff went into possession under the agreement and paid rent quarterly not in advance. Defendant served a written demand for rent in advance as agreed upon and when it was not paid he distrained. Plaintiff sued for damages for unlawful distress and for an injunction to restrain any sale under the distress and also for specific performance of the agreement for a lease. On a motion for an interim injunction, an order was made that on plaintiff paying into Court the amount claimed an injunction should issue and defendant should abandon the distress. Plaintiff appealed.

JESSEL M. R.: It is not necessary on the present occasion to decide finally what the rights of the parties are. If the Court sees that there is a fair question to be decided it will take security so that the party who ultimately succeeds may be in the right position. The question is one of some nicety. There is an agreement for a lease under which possession has been given. Now since the Judicature Act the possession is held under the agreement. There are not two estates as there were formerly, one estate at common law by reason of the payment of the rent from year to year, and an estate in equity under the agreement. There is only one Court, and the equity rules prevail in it. The tenant holds under an agreement for a lease. He holds, therefore, under the same terms in equity as if a lease had been granted, it being a case in which both parties admit that relief is capable of being given by specific performance. That being so, he cannot complain of the exercise by the landlord of the same rights as the landlord would have had if a lease had been granted. On the other hand, he is protected in the same way as if a lease had been granted; he cannot be turned out by six months' notice as a tenant from year to year. He has a right to say, "I have a lease in equity, and you can only re-enter if I have committed such a breach of covenant as would if a lease had been granted have entitled you to re-enter according to the terms of a proper proviso for re-entry." That being so, it appears to me that being a lessee in equity he cannot complain of the exercise of the right of distress merely because the actual parchment has not been signed and sealed.

Order varied.

[That portion of the reasons for judgment dealing with the terms of the intended lease and the amount of rent payable in advance (since rent was to be fixed according to the number of looms to be run) is omitted. Cotton and Lindley L. JJ. delivered concurring opinions. See Judicature Act, R.S.O. 1960, c. 197, s. 22.]

ROGERS v. NATIONAL DRUG AND CHEMICAL CO. Ontario Court of Appeal. 1911. 24 O.L.R. 486

Appeal from a judgment of Riddell J., 23 O.L.R. 234, dismissing plaintiff's action and allowing a counterclaim for specific performance of an agreement for a lease with an option for renewal. Plaintiff was the assignee of the original lessor who entered into an agreement with one S for a five year lease with an option to the lessee to renew for a further five years. The lessee assigned his interest to one P who in turn assigned to defendants who entered into possession and paid rent. Defendants exercised the option but plaintiff demanded possession at the end of the original five year term.

The judgment of the Court was delivered by GARROW J. A.:... I agree with the conclusion arrived at by Riddell, J.

Prior to the Statute of Frauds, a demise for a term of years by parol was perfectly lawful. That statute made a writing (subject to certain exceptions at present of no importance) necessary. And a subsequent statute, now 1 Geo. V. ch. 25, sec. 9, required the writing to be under seal. If, however, at law, possession had been taken under the parol demise, and rent paid, the tenant was regarded as a tenant, not at will merely, as described in the Statute of Frauds, but as a tenant from year to year, upon the terms contained in the writing so far as appropriate to such a tenancy; while in equity his rights were much larger, for there the Courts would in a proper case decree specific performance, treating the parol demise, if otherwise sufficient, as an agreement for a lease, with the result that the parties were regarded in equity as landlord and tenant from the time possession was taken: see *Walsh* v. *Lonsdale* (1882), 21 Ch.D. 9. And now, under the provisions of sec. 58 of the Judicature Act, the equitable rule prevails.

It is not disputed by Mr. Bicknell, counsel for the plaintiff, that in a lease under seal a covenant to renew would have run with the land. His (what I may call) major contention is, that, the present demise not being under seal, the agreement to renew did not run with the land, and hence is not binding upon the lessor's assignee. This view is, however, in my opinion, quite too narrow, in that it takes no account of the equitable rule to which effect has been, properly in my opinion, given by Riddell, J.

A minor contention was, that the option created only a personal obligation, and, therefore, did not affect the land. I am unable to see the force of this contention. It seems to me to be really included in what I have called the major contention.

The plaintiff purchased the demised premises with notice of the agreement, or so-called parol demise, which had been registered; and he, therefore, stands in the shoes of his assignor as to any rights or equities which could have been specifically enforced against the land itself while in the hands of his assignor. As I have pointed out, the Court would, or at least might, have adjudged specific performance of the agreement, and compelled the granting of a proper lease, with a proper covenant of renewal, which would have run with the land. And the land in the plaintiff's hands cannot, under these circumstances and the law, as I understand it, escape from this obligation, simply because, when he purchased, the agreement lacked a seal—which, after all, is the whole argument.

Appeal dismissed.

[In *Boyer* v. *Warbey*, [1953] 2 Q.B. 234, [1953] 1 All E.R. 269 (C.A.), Denning L. J. said (at p. 246 Q.B., 274 All E.R.): "I know that before the Supreme Court of Judicature Act, 1873, it was said that the doctrine of covenants running with the land only applied to covenants under seal and not to agreements under hand: see *Elliot* v. *Johnson* [1866), L.R. 2 Q.B. 120, but since the fusion of law and equity, the position is different. The distinction between agreements under hand and covenants under seal has been largely obliterated. There is no valid reason nowadays why the doctrine of covenants running with the land—or with the reversion—should not apply equally to agreements under hand as to covenants under seal, and I think we should so hold, not only in the case af agreements for more than three years which need the interposition of equity to perfect them, but also in the case of agreements for three years or less which do not."]

[The rule in *Walsh* v. *Lonsdale*, *supra*, does not apply to an agreement for a lease of which specific performance would not be granted either because of a want of compliance with the Statute of Frauds or for any other reason or for want of equitable jurisdiction in the Court whose aid is invoked: see *Abraham* v. *The New York Café*, [1940] O.R. 73; *Gebler* v. *Palmason*, [1930] 1 D.L.R. 475, [1929] 3 W.W.R. 534, 38 Man. R. 371 (C.A.); *Baniulis* v. *Valley*, [1950] 2 D.L.R. 619, [1950] 1 W.W.R. 758 (Sask. C.A.); *Foster* v. *Reeves*, [1892] 2 Q.B. 255 (C.A.).

In *Manchester Brewery Co.* v. *Coombs*, [1901] 2 Ch. 608, the Court enforced at the suit of a lessor's assignee a covenant by a lessee to purchase all his beer from the lessor and "its successors in business", although the covenant was contained in a sealed agreement for a lease and although the lessor did not execute the agreement. In the course of his judgment, Farwell J. said (at p. 617): "Although it has been suggested that the decision in *Walsh* v. *Lonsdale* takes away all differences between the legal and equitable estate, it, of course, does nothing of the sort, and the limits of its applicability are really somewhat narrow. It applies only to cases where there is a contract to transfer a legal title, and an act has to be justified or an action maintained by force of the legal title to which such contract relates. It involves two questions: (1.) Is there a contract of which specific performance can be obtained? (2). If Yes, will the title acquired by such specific performance justify at law the act complained of, or support at law the action in question? It is to be treated as though before the *Judicature Acts* there had been, first, a suit in equity for specific performance, and then an action at law between the same parties; and the doctrine is applicable only in those cases where specific performance can be obtained between the same parties in the same court, and at the same time as the subsequent legal question falls to be determined. Thus, in *Walsh* v. *Lonsdale* the landlord under an agreement for a lease for a term of seven years distrained. Distress is a legal remedy and depends on the existence at law of the relation of landlord and tenant; but the agreement between the same parties, if specifically enforced, created that relation. It was clear that such an agreement would be enforced in the same court and between the same parties: the act of distress was therefore held to be lawful. So in the present case I have already stated that specific performance can be granted between the parties to this action. I must treat it therefore as granted, and I then find that the result justifies this action. It is not necessary to call in aid this doctrine in matters that are purely equitable; its existence is due entirely to the divergence of legal and equitable rights between the same parties, nor does it affect the rights of third parties. Thus, a contract by a landowner to sell the fee simple of land in possession to A. would not enable A. to maintain an action of ejectment or trespass against a third person, because such actions are purely legal actions requiring the legal estate and possession respectively to support them, and the contract relied on is not made with the defendant."]

PURCHASE v. LICHFIELD BREWERY CO. King's Bench. [1915] 1 K.B. 184

Appeal by defendants from a County Court judgment holding them liable for rent.

HORRIDGE J.: By an agreement in writing purporting to be by way of lease the plaintiff or his predecessor purported to grant to Lunnis a tenancy for fifteen years at a rent of 180£ a year. That document was not under seal and therefore by s. 1 of the Statute of Frauds and s. 3 of the Real Property Act, 1845 (8 & 9 Vict. c. 106), it could not take effect as a lease for a term of years. It has been properly treated as an agreement for a lease. The day after this agreement was signed Lunnis mortgaged his interest under it to the defendants, not by way of sub-demise but by way of assignment. The defendants therefore are in the position of mortgagees who have not gone into possession. Two acts are relied on by Mr. Bosanquet as showing that the defendants had gone into possession, first that they advertised a sale of the mortgagor's interest, and secondly that they applied in their own names for a renewal of the licence so that they might get compensation as for a licensed house. Neither of these acts afford any evidence of an attornment or taking of possession; therefore unless Mr. Bosanquet can establish that the mere fact of taking an assignment by deed of an agreement for a lease makes a mortgagee liable for the rent he cannot uphold the judgment of the county court judge. He contends that Lunnis would on the authority of *Walsh* v. *Lonsdale* have been entitled to say that he was in the same position as if he had got a lease, because he was entitled to a decree for specific performance of the agreement for a lease; he says that the assignees of Lunnis were entitled in the same way to insist on specific performance; that the assignees of Lunnis must therefore be taken to be lessees under a lease and liable for the rent reserved by it. Assuming that Lunnis was in a position to have enforced specific performance against the plaintiff and had the right to treat himself as being a lessee under the lease which would have been granted under a decree for specific performance, still it does not follow that his assignee is in the same position. The only case cited to establish such a right in an assignee is *Dowell* v. *Dew* (1843), 12 L.J.Ch. 158; but in that case the assignee of the agreement had entered and paid rent and had been recognized as tenant by the owner of the property. Knight Bruce V.-C. said that the agreement was assignable "and especially with the assent of the landlord for the time being." In that case there was privity of contract. Even then the landlord was entitled if he thought fit to insist on the personal liability of his lessee on the covenants in the lease as if it had been granted to him. Such a case as the present one seems remote from the case which Jessel M. R. was considering... in *Walsh* v. *Lonsdale*.... In my opinion an assignee of a mere agreement for a lease who never took possession and never attorned tenant could not before the Judicature Acts and cannot now in his own right enforce specific performance against the landlord. He could not establish such a direct relation between himself and the landlord as would induce a Court of Equity, regarding that as done which ought to be done, to treat him as a person in whom a lease had been vested. I do not think that the case of *Williams* v. *Bosanquet* (1819) 1 Br. & B. 238, 219 E.R. 714 (C.P.) applies because in that case the lease was under seal and it was validy assigned by deed to the mortgagees.

LUSH J.: I an of the same opinion. The only point which the county court judge decided was that the present case was governed by *Williams* v. *Bosanquet*. In my view that case does not apply. The lease in question there was under seal. It was assigned by deed to mortgagees. That was a valid assignment. The only question was whether the mortgagees, not having taken possession, were bound by the covenants in the lease. It was held that they were bound. In this case there was no lease under seal. No term was created as between lessor and lessee. Therefore the question decided in *Williams* v. *Bosanquet* does not arise in this case. Consequently the judgment of the county court judge cannot stand on the grounds on which he has based it.

Then can the judgment be supported on other grounds? I do not think it is necessary to say how the case might have stood if the defendants had ever taken possession. They are liable, if at all, on the principle of *Walsh* v. *Lonsdale*. In that case the tenant was in possession under the agreement. In the present case the defendants never did take posession. The agreement contained a provision against assigning. The defendants were only mortgagees. It does not follow from *Walsh* v. *Lonsdale* that a Court of Equity would decree specific performance against mere mortgagees who only took an assignment by way of security. In my opinion it would leave the parties to their position at law. Accordingly the matter stands thus: A tenant under an agreement, whose only title to call himself a lessee depends on his right to specific performance of the agreement, assigns his right to assignees. The assignees never had a term vested in them because no term was ever created; therefore there was never privity of estate. They never went into possession or were recognized by the landlord; therefore there was never privity of contract. It is impossible that specific performance of a contract can be decreed against a person with whom there is neither privity of contract nor privity of estate. Therefore these assignees are not liable to perform the terms of the agreement and this appeal must be allowed.

Appeal allowed.

[Rules of practice now generally permit an assignee to sue in his own name on a chose in action: see, for example, Rule 88 (Ont.). Would this explain the statement of Horridge J. made in the concluding part of his judgment?

For an explanation of why the assignee of a lessee under an agreement for a lease (who has not entered) may sue the lessor or his assignee and yet the lessor or his assignee cannot sue the assignee of the lessee under the agreement, see *Ames*, Specific Performance for and Against Strangers to the Contract, (1904) 17 Harv. L. Rev. 174 (reprinted in Lectures on Legal History, 381).]

INTERESSE TERMINI AND POSSESSION

As pointed out in the Introductory Note to this chapter, at common law a lessee under a lease had no estate in the land before entry; hence he could not sue for breach of any covenants which envisaged an estate nor could he bring trespass against a third person unless there had been entry. Moreover, he himself was not liable until entry for mere use and occupation although he was liable, whether he entered or not (where entry was available), for rent reserved by his lease as by way of covenant to pay it: see *Edge* v. *Stafford* (1831), 1 C. & J. 391, 148 E.R. 1474 (Ex.); *Lowe* v. *Ross* (1850), 5 Ex. 553, 155 E.R. 242. Nonetheless, his *interesse termini* was assignable and inheritable. On the other hand, subject to any stipulation to the contrary, there was an implied obligation of the lessor that the premises, subject of the lease, would be open to actual entry by the lessee on the day specified in the lease: see *Coe* v. *Clay* (1829), 5 Bing. 440, 130 E.R. 1131 (C.P.); *Jinks* v. *Edwards* (1856), 11 Ex. 775, 156 E.R. 1045. In other terms, a person who agrees to let must be taken to promise that he has a good title to let, not necessarily a fee simple, but an interest sufficient to support the leasehold transaction: see *Stranks* v. *St. John* (1867), L.R. 2 C.P. 376, 36 L.C.J.P. 118.

If entry was denied, either because of the lessor's repudiation or because an overholding tenant was rightly or wrongly in possession, the lessee was entitled to damages and could withdraw from the lease: see *Reaume* v. *Lalonde*, [1939] O.W.N. 167 (where the measure of damages was governed by the rule in *Bain* v. *Fothergill* (1874), L.R. 7 H.L. 158); *Commercial Finance Corp.* v. *Dunlop Tire & Rubber Goods Co.*, [1942] O.R. 380, [1942] 3 D.L.R. 150 (C.A.); *Yakchuk* v. *Holgate*, [1951] O.W.N. 894. There is a line of cases in United States holding that it is sufficient if the lessor can give "legal" possession to the lessee, thus obliging the latter to sue a third person who may be wrongfully in possession, as by holding over at the expiration of his term; see 1 *American Law of Property*, s. 3.37. The preferable rule, followed by another line of United States cases, is that the lessee does not bargain for a lawsuit and hence is entitled to have the premises open to his possession at the time agreed upon.

The common law recognized the right of a lessee, who had not yet entered, to maintain ejectment against a third person wrongfully in possession, if the lessee chose thus to seek possession rather than go against his lessor for damages. In *Coe* v. *Clay* (1829), 5 Bing. 440, 130 E.R. 1131 (C.P.), it was urged on behalf of a lessor that because the lessee could bring ejectment against an occupier wrongly holding over he could not go against the lessor, but the argument was rejected The remedies are thus alternative, and the only remaining question which has been a troublesome point in connection with *interesse termini* is whether a lessee entitled to possession against his lessor may sue him for possession directly instead of relying on damages or on a claim to be relieved of his obligations. The dilemma which *interesse termini* created stemmed from the fact that a person who never had possession could not claim to recover it when he had no estate on which to found his claim. (Specific performance is inapplicable save to an agreement for a lease, but in such case the relief would be execution of a lease and hence the position is not advanced.) Yet there were dicta in a number of cases to the effect that, at least in the case of a lease to commence immediately, the lessee obtained an enforceable right to possession against the lessor: see *Doe d. Parsley* v. *Day* (1842), 2 Q.B. 147, 114 E.R. 58; *Ryan* v. *Clark* (1849), 14 Q.B. 65, 117 E.R. 26; *cf. Cole*, Ejectment (1857), pp. 72, 76.

It seems wrong today that even in the absence of legislation sweeping away *interesse termini* (as was done in England by the Law of Property Act, 1925 (Imp.), c. 20, s. 149 (1) (2)), there should be a refusal to enforce a claim to possession against a lessor where no outstanding rights of third persons would be affected: see *Note*, Is Interesse Termini Necessary?, (1918) 18 Col. L. Rev. 595. There are cases in the United States which so hold and they express a sensible position: see 51 *Corpus Juris Secundum*, p. 974. The best solution would, of course, be to abolish the doctrine.

[The need of physical entry to create a term of years was avoided where the leasehold took effect under the Statute of Uses, and this too points up the emptiness of *interesse termini* for modern purposes. A consequence of the doctrine not mentioned above was that since a lessor still retained his whole interest (before the lessee's entry), a purported release of his reversion as such accomplished nothing.

For a discussion of *interesse termini* in relation to liability for loss or destruction of the premises by fire or otherwise, see *Cole*, Interesse Termini and Risk of Loss, (1954) 19 Sask. Bar Rev. 4.]

[In *Miller* v. *Emcer Products Ltd.*, [1956] Ch. 304, [1956] 1 All E.R. 237 (C.A.), Romer L. J. said (at p. 321 Ch., 243 All E.R.): "I do not think there is any ground for implying the *Coe v. Clay* obligation in addition to the covenant for title and quiet enjoyment which is implicit in a formal instrument of demise or grant. By the very force of the liability which is imposed on a lessor under the covenant for quiet enjoyment, the tenant is entitled to be put into possession of the premises which are leased to him, at the outset of the tenancy and to remain quietly in possession thereof throughout the term". Does this mean that the covenant for quiet enjoyment is enforceable by the lessee before actual entry once the date for entry has arrived? Where does this leave *Wallis* v. *Hands*, [1893] 2 Ch. 75 (C.A.)? Note, however, the explanation of *Coe v. Clay* given in the *Emcer Products* case and the reference to the abolition of *interesse termini* in England.]

Damages on Failure or Inability of Lessor to Give Possession: Liability of Lessor and Holdover Tenant

If a person wrongfully holds over in the face of a new lease of the premises to another, or if the lessor simply refuses to give possession, the lessee is, of course, entitled to sue the lessor for damages which would ordinarily be the difference between the rental value and the actual rent reserved. Indeed, he has a cause of action against the lessor even where an existing tenant is rightfully retaining possession (but subject to the rule in *Bain* v. *Fothergill* (1874) L.R. H.L. 158 as to damages.). Special damages, if any would also be recoverable where found to be within the contemplation of the parties to the lease.

The lessor himself may sue the overholding tenant, and in such an action he may recover the general damages which he may have been obliged to pay in a suit against him by his new lessee: see *Bramley* v. *Chesterton* (1857), 2 C.B.N.S. 590, 140 E.R. 548. The intimation in *Bramley* v. *Chesterton* is that the lessor could not recover from his overholding tenant any special damages which the lessor may have had to pay to the lessee by reason of the re-letting having been for some special or extraordinary purpose. (Suppose, however, the existing tenant was made aware of the special nature of the re-letting before expiry of his term!) Ordinarily, a lessor suing his overholding tenant may recover as damages only the rental value of the premises, at least where the overholder is not made aware of any special use to which the lessor wishes to put the premises on the expiry of the existing term in the overholder: see *Cohen* v. *Godkin*, 55 O.L.R. 436, [1924] 4 D.L.R. 350 (App. Div.), noted (1925) 38 Harv. L. Rev. 1117. These damages would be recoverable either on a basis of assumpsit for use and occupation or as mesne profits for trespass on the case.

Because the ordinary common law remedy was perhaps not too much of a deterrent, a statutory remedy was given against the overholding tenant: see Landlord and Tenant Act, 1730 (Imp.), c. 28; Distress for Rent Act, 1737 (Imp.), c. 19, s. 18. He became liable (under the first mentioned Act) to double the yearly value of the land for wilfully holding over (i.e. knowing that he was not entitled to retain possession) after notice in writing by the landlord. (If there was a *bona fide* dispute as to his right to stay on, he could not be said to be wilfully holding over.) The Act in question did not apply to periodic tenancies less than yearly tenencies, and the remedy it offered was not available to a new lessee of the landlord. Moreover, the statutory damages could not be levied by distress. However, distress was available under the second of the Acts above-mentioned which applied where a tenant could terminate his tenancy by notice, and, having given such notice, he failed to vacate. Under it he became liable to double the *rent* that was payable, and distress could be invoked to collect it. For a discussion of these statutes, see *Woodfall*, Landlord and Tenant (1960, 26th ed.), pp. 1043 ff.; see also *Sayre*, Legal Remedies of Landlord against Tenant who Holds Over, (1928) 3 Ind. L. J. 555.

This English legislation has been copied in various of the Provinces: see Landlord and Tenant Act, R.S.B.C. 1960, c. 207, ss. 16, 17; Landlord and Tenant Act, R.S.M. 1954, c. 136, ss. 52, 53; Landlord and Tenant Act, R.S.N.B. 1952, c. 126, ss. 56, 57; Landlord and Tenant Act, R.S.O. 1960, c. 206, ss. 57, 58. The Ontario legislation which is typical and, in effect, a copy of the English Acts, is as follows:

"57. Where a tenant for any term for life, lives or years, or other person who comes into possession of any land, by, from, or under, or by collusion with such tenant, wilfully holds over such land or any part thereof after the determination of such term, and after notice in writing given for delivering the possession thereof by his landlord or the person to whom the remainder or reversion of such land belongs or his agent thereunto lawfully authorized, such tenant or other person so holding over shall, for and during the time he so holds over or keeps the person entitled out of possession, pay to such person or his assigns at the rate of double the yearly value of the land so detained for so long as the same is detained, to be recovered by action in any court of competent jurisdiction, against the recovering of which penalty there shall be no relief.

"58. Where a tenant gives notice of his intention to quit the premises by him held at a time mentioned in such notice, and does not accordingly deliver up the possession thereof at the time mentioned in such notice, the tenant shall from thenceforward pay to the landlord double the rent or sum which he should otherwise have paid, to be levied, sued for and recovered at the same times and in the same manner as the single rent or sum before the giving such notice could be levied, sued for or recovered, and such double rent or sum shall continue to be paid while such tenant continues in possession."

If the lessee has his action against the lessor and the lessor against an overholder, why should the lessee not be able to sue the overholder directly? Clearly he may sue him for possession, but the *interesse termini* doctrine would be a bar to an action for damages for trespass. Yet, apart from this, is there any basis on which the overholder may be liable to the lessee for damages, general and special, by reason of failing to give up possession? The lessee, to the knowledge of the overholder may have manufacturing or other obligations to fulfil. It has been suggested that the analogy of inducing breach of contract is apt where the overholder knows of the contract between the lessor and lessee, making him liable to a tort action at the suit of the lessee: see *Note*, (1925) 38 Harv. L. Rev. 991; *cf. Camden*

Nominees Ltd. v. *Slack*, [1940] 2 All E.R. 1 (Ch.), noted, (1940) 18 Can. Bar Rev. 393. Is the analogy, however, apt? Can it be said that the overholding tenant, by breaking his contract with his landlord to surrender possession at the expiry of his term, thereby subjects himself to an action at the suit of a new lessee to whom, he knows, the landlord has re-let the premises? See *Note*, (1925) 25 Col. L. Rev. 680.

The lessee cannot, of course, exercise his lessor's rights against the overholder. It is at least a tenable argument that, apart from the statutory remedy given to a landlord against an overholder, he might claim lost profits against him: see *Cohen* v. *Godkin, supra*; *cf. Note*, (1956) 41 Iowa L. Rev. 467. Equally, this could be a tenable claim against the lessor by the lessee. Why should the lessee not be able to proceed directly against the overholder for special damages, if the latter knowingly refuses to vacate?

3. ASSIGNMENT AND SUBLEASE: RENEWAL

DOE D. FREEMAN v. BATEMAN. King's Bench. 1818. 2 B. & Ald. 168, 106 E.R. 328

Abbott C. J. now delivered the opinion of the Court. This case was argued before us at Serjeants' Inn, and upon the facts found, the single question of law was this, whether a lessee for years, having made a conveyance operating as an assignment of his whole interest in the land, containing a covenant on the part of the assignee not to open a public-house on the demised premises without licence, and containing also a clause of re-entry on breach of the covenant, could upon an actual breach thereof enter upon the land and avoid his conveyance. Or, in other words, whether, if an assignment of a term of years be made upon a condition, the assignment shall be absolute and the condition void. No question arose as to the capacity of a real or personal representative to make the entry; for the entry was made by the assignor himself. The only argument adduced against the right of entry or validity of the condition was, that an entry must always be made by a person entitled to the reversion, and by no other; and consequently that as the original termor had in this case, by the deed of assignment, parted with his whole estate, and no reversion was left to him, he could not enter. And, to be sure, if the premises here assumed be true, the conclusion is properly drawn. But we think the premises from which the conclusion was drawn are untrue. And that they are untrue is manifest from the familiar case put in Lit. sect. 325, of a feoffment in fee rendering rent, with a clause of re-entry, if the rent be unpaid; in which case it is said the feoffor or his heirs may enter for the condition broken. In this case, the feoffor has no reversion; the lands are not, nor since the Statute of Quia Emptores, can be holden of him, but must be holden of the superior lord of the fee. Another instance is also mentioned in Lord Coke's commentary upon this section, Co. Lit. fo. 202. According to the text of Littleton, the party making the entry shall have and hold the land in his former estate; but according to the commentary, although this is regularly true, yet it faileth in many cases, and one of the cases of failure is that of a feoffment in fee upon condition, made by a man seised in right of his wife. The feoffor dieth, and the condition is broken. The heir of the feoffor shall enter; yet the heir at the time of his entry hath no reversion, and after the entry his estate doth vanish, and presently the estate is vested in the wife. For these reasons, we think the defendant was entitled to the verdict, and the postea must be delivered to him.

Judgment for defendant.

[In *Wulff* v. *Lundy*, [1940] 2 D.L.R. 126, [1940] 1 W.W.R. 444 (Alta. C.A.), Clarke J. A. said: "The authorities support the view that a right of re-entry for breach of a condition exists where such right is agreed upon although the grantor has no reversion." See also *Trustee of Publix Oil and Gas Co.* v. *Hinds*, [1937] 3 D.L.R. 434, [1937] 2 W.W.R. 372 (Alta. C.A.).

If on an assignment of the whole of his remaining term, a tenant reserves rent and a right of re-entry for non-payment, is the assignee liable to pay rent also to the landlord? What is the tenant's obligation as to rent to his landlord after the assignment? See *Ferrier*, Can There Be a Sublease for the Entire Unexpired Portion of a Term?, (1929) 18 Calif. L. Rev. 1; 1 *American Law of Property*, sec. 3.57.

In Ontario, s. 2 of the Landlord and Tenant Act, R.S.O. 1960, c. 206, states: "The relation of landlord and tenant does not depend on tenure and a reversion in the lessor is not necessary in order to create the relation of landlord and tenant, or to make applicable the incidents by law belonging to that relation; nor is it necessary in order to give a landlord the right of distress that there is an agreement for that purpose between the parties." What is its effect apart from an obvious application to situations where a right of re-entry is reserved upon an assignment? See *Kennedy* v. *Agricultural Development Board*, 59 O.L.R. 374, [1926] 4 D.L.R. 717; *Note*, [1942] 20 Can. Bar. Rev. 464.

A tenant under a seven year lease expiring November 28, 1944, made a "sublease" to B for one year from November 1, 1943, and thereafter quarterly until such time as either party gives three months' notice, expiring on stipulated dates in each year. In April, 1945, the tenant served notice to quit on his "sublessee". Result? See *Milmo* v. *Carreras*, [1946] 1 All E.R. 288 (C.A.).]

LA JEFFRIES v. ROBERTS. Ontario Court of Appeal. [1946] O.R. 10, [1946] 1 D.L.R. 602

The judgment of the Court was delivered by ROBERTSON C. J. O.:

This is an appeal by the tenant in a proceeding between landlord and tenant under Part III of the Landlord and Tenant Act, R.S.O. 1937, c. 219, from the order of Judge Macdonell, of the County Court of the County of York, dated October 11, 1945, by which the tenant is ordered to deliver up possession of the demised premises.

A rooming-house business had been carried on in the premises in question by the former owner of the premises, and on the sale of that business to the appellant she leased to her the premises where the business was carried on, by lease dated March 12, 1945, for the term of two years. The lease is made in pursuance of the Short Forms of Leases Act, R.S.O. 1937, c. 159, and it contains a covenant that the lessee "will not assign or sub-let without leave". This short form covenant is translated by the statute into the following:

"8. And also that the lessee shall not, nor will during the said term, assign, transfer or set over or otherwise by any act or deed procure the said premises or any of them to be assigned, transferred, set over or sub-let unto any person or persons whomsoever without the consent in writing of the lessor first had and obtained."

In July 1945 the appellant had negotiations with Mrs. Gladys Malone for the sale to the latter of the rooming-house business and the assignment to her of the lease of the premises. On July 31st there were signed and sealed a bill of sale from the appellant to Mrs. Malone of the furniture and other goods, chattels and effects of the rooming-house business, and a chattel mortgage back from Mrs. Malone to the appellant to secure the unpaid portion of the consideration of $2,500. At the same time the appellant signed under seal an assignment to Mrs. Malone of the unexpired residue of the term created by the lease held by the appellant of the premises now in question. This assignment of lease, after a recital stating the fact of the granting of the lease, contains the following further recital: "And whereas the said Assignor has agreed to sell and assign the said lease unto the said Assignee, subject to the approval of the Landlord." After the covenants in the assignment appears the following: "Provided that the assignment herein is made subject to the approval and consent of the Landlord."

These documents were all prepared by the solicitor who had acted in carrying through the transaction by which the appellant had acquired the rooming-house business and the lease. He acted for both the appellant and Mrs. Malone in the transaction of July, and prepared the several documents I have mentioned, and witnessed the signing of them by both parties. He says that he inserted the words I have quoted from the assignment of lease with respect to the assignment being subject to the approval of the landlord, to protect both of the parties because the assignment was conditional upon the landlord agreeing. He says that he told them this before they signed. The assignment of lease appears to have been left in his hands for the purpose of obtaining the consent in writing of the landlord.

Unknown to the solicitor or to the parties to the foregoing transaction, the appellant's lessor, by deed dated July 19, 1945 but unregistered until August 1st, had sold and conveyed the leased property to the respondent. No notice of this change of ownerschip was given to the appellant at the time. In the meantime the bill of sale and chattel mortgage covering the chattel property of the rooming-house business had been registered in the office of the Clerk of the County Court. Mrs. Malone, the purchaser, had taken possession and was carrying on the rooming-house business on the leased premises. The solicitor to whom had been left the obtaining of the landlord's consent to the assignment of the lease, had delayed applying for it, intending, according to the letter which he later wrote asking for it, to send along the necessary papers with the rent due on August 15th.

In the meantime the respondent had learned of the change of possession and had consulted her solicitor, who wrote Mrs. Malone with notice of the respondent's purchase of the property, and requiring that Mrs. Malone vacate the premises forthwith. In reply to that letter the solicitor who had acted for both parties in the sale of the rooming-house business to Mrs. Malone, wrote respondent's solicitor explaining the position and requesting the respondent's consent to the assignment of the lease and enclosing the rent for the ensuing month. The rent and the consent were both refused.

The respondent admits that there is no objection to Mrs. Malone that would have warranted withholding consent to an assignment to her as tenant, if the owner's consent had been requested before the covenant not to assign or sublet without leave had been broken. Her position is that there had been a breach of the covenant and her election to declare the lease forfeited had been exercised and possession had been demanded before any request was made for her consent.

There are numerous reported decisions upon the effect and operation of a covenant not to assign or sublet without the owner's consent, and as to what constitutes a breach of such a convenant. To create a forfeiture the instrument of assignment must be valid and effectual in law. An equitable assignment is not enough: *Cornish* v. *Boles* (1914), 19 D.L.R. 447 at pp. 456-7, 31 O.L.R. 505 at p. 519; *Woodfall's* Law of Landlord and Tenant (24th ed.), p. 585; *Foa's* Law of Landlord and Tenant (6th ed.), p. 318. Neither is a mere letting into possession enough where the covenant is in the terms of the covenant here. *Straus Land Corp.* v. *Internat'l Hotel Windsor* (1919), 48 D.L.R. 519, 45 O.L.R. 145, per Falconbridge C.J.K.B. at pp. 520-1 D.L.R., p. 147 O.L.R. The learned County Judge seems to have been of the opinion that letting Mrs. Malone into possession in the circumstances present here amounted to a setting over of the premises, which is contrary to the terms of the covenant. He cited the case of *Grossman* v. *Modern Theatres* (1919), 45 O.L.R. 564, where Rose J. (afterwards Chief Justice) expressed the opinion that, although an assignment that had been signed had not been delivered, as it was signed merely so that there might be something formal to submit to the landlord, yet putting the assignee into possession under the circumstances there present, even if there was no assignment, amounted to a "setting over" of the premises and to a breach of the covenant.

It has been held that when the words of the covenant were "assign, transfer or set over," and did not extend to an underlease, the words "assign, transfer and set over" were mere words of assignment: *Crusoe* v. *Bugby* (1771), 2 Bl. W. 766, 96 E.R. 448. This case is cited in the judgment of Joyce J. in *Grove* v. *Portal*, [1902] 1 Ch. 727 at p. 731, as well as in such text-books as Woodfall and Foa. I do not think, however, that the present case turns upon any nice question of the precise meaning of the words of the covenant. It seems to me that the real question here is whether that which the documents signed by the appellant and Mrs. Malone were designed to accomplish was conditional, and continued to be conditional, upon the consent and approval of the landlord being obtained. If there never was in reality such a condition, or it was waived or abandoned as a condition, either expressly or by conduct, then there was an effective and completed assignment. If, on the contrary, notwithstanding that Mrs. Malone entered into possession and carried on the rooming-house business, the condition still remained an effective condition, that condition applied no matter what term one may give to what was to be done—whether "assignment" or "transfer" or "setting over". It was only conditional, and, therefore, was ineffectual to work a forfeiture of the lease.

The learned County Judge says that there are virtually no facts in dispute. I do not find any express finding by him on the matter of whether the condition was inserted in the assignment of lease before it was signed, as the solicitor states, and whether the document was signed after he had explained the purpose of the condition, but I take it that he had accepted these important statements as true. The evidence, as well as the whole probability of the matter, fully support such a finding of fact, and counsel for the respondent made it plain that he did not question the solicitor's integrity in the matter.

The delay in asking for the consent seems to have been wholly chargeable to the solicitor. It was left for him to attend to. It is not likely that anyone contemplated that any difficulty would be made by the owner in giving consent. Mrs. Malone is admittedly unobjectionable as a tenant, and no good reason for withholding consent would seem to have been available to the owner, if she had been asked before she saw an opportunity to claim a forfeiture. Then the conduct of the appellant and Mrs. Malone when a question arose, is important. They at once, and very definitely, acted in observance of the condition and cancelled their whole transaction.

It may seem to be a case where the landlord, without much merit in her complaint of a breach of covenant, is seeking to profit by a little laxity upon the part of the solicitor in charge of the transaction. It is not necessary, however, to determine whether or not that is so, for the Courts have, for many years, required strict proof of a breach of convenant of this character before permitting a landlord the right of forfeiture, and that strict proof is, in my opinion, lacking here.

Appeal allowed.

[See *Grossman* v. *Modern Theatres Ltd.* (1919), 45 O.L.R. 564; *Rose* v. *Sharp*, [1946] O.W.N. 591 (Co. Ct. J.); *Avery* v. *Wood and Findlay*, [1947] 2 D.L.R. 790, [1947] O.W.N. 157 (C.A.).]

CARMICHAEL v. DOLMAGE AND MACINNES. British Columbia Court of Appeal. [1947] 1 D.L.R. 559, [1947] 1 W.W.R. 193

Appeal by a tenant, from a judgment declaring her lease forfeited for breach of a covenant not to assign or sublet.

O'HALLORAN J. A.: The question to be decided in the events which occurred, is whether the appellant Mary S. Dolmage broke the covenant not to assign or sublet without leave contained in her lease of an apartment suite from the respondent lessor Grace Ann Carmichael. This appeal lies from an order forfeiting the lease on that ground.

Mrs. Dolmage applied to the respondent for leave to assign the lease to her brother the appellant W. E. MacInnes. The respondent refused because she wanted the apartment for her own use. It appears there is no provision in this Province similar to the 1927 English legislation referred to in Woodfall's Landlord & Tenant, 24th ed., p. 579, which attaches to such a covenant an implied condition that leave shall not be unreasonably witheld. Mrs. Dolmage then consulted her solicitor. After perusing the lease, he advised her that if she assigned or sublet without the respondent's consent the lease would be subject to forfeiture, and that in order to avoid a forfeiture she must remain the actual tenant and maintain her rights as such.

Acting under her solicitor's advice Mrs. Dolmage so informed her brother in writing (ex. 7) adding:

"Under the circumstances, therefore I must refuse to assign or sublet to you or anyone else. Your problem is to find temporary living quarters until you can arrange for some kind of permanency. As Bill and I will, for some time at least, be busy with our West Vancouver venture, I can give you temporary shelter in the Cambie Street Suite, but such accommodation can only be given upon the following terms:

"1. I will give you leave and licence to move in and occupy the premises as my agent or representative on the distinct understanding that you do not, under this arrangement, or otherwise, acquire any rights in any way derogatory to or conflicting with, or endangering my position as tenant of said premises.

"2. This licence is terminable at my will without notice.

"3. I shall at all times during your occupancy have the right to use the premises as I may wish.

"4. You will so long as you occupy the premises pay the rent accruing thereon promptly on each gale date, and such payments shall be made as my agent and representative and shall be for my account.

"5. You will observe all the provisions of the lease under which I hold the premises, and will do nothing which could bring about a breach or forfeiture of my lease.

"6. You will safeguard at all times of your occupancy and safely keep all furniture, furnishings and equipment left by me in the said premises, and will upon termination of your occupation leave the same in the same good order and condition as when received by you.

"7. Neither this document nor anything done by either you or me in the premises shall in any way constitute you or be construed as constituting you as my tenant, or in any way create the relationship of landlord and tenant as between us."

The Dolmages then moved out, and her brother moved in. Mrs. Dolmage's solicitor wrote the respondent's solicitor to that effect stating his opinion that what was done did not amount to a breach of the covenant not to assign or sublet (ex. 4) and quoted in support *Peebles* v. *Crosthwaite* (1897), 13 T. L. R. 198; *Jackson v. Simons*, [1923] 1 Ch. 373, 92 L.J. Ch. 161, and *Chaplin* v. *Smith*, [1926] 1 K.B. 198, 95 L.J.K.B. 449. These decisions did not cause the respondent's solicitor to alter his view that a breach had occurred, for the respondent served notice demanding possession on the ground the lease had been forfeited (ex. 2). Lennox Co. Ct. J. acting under ss. 19 *et seq.* of the *Landlord and Tenant Act*, R.S.B.C. 1936, c. 143, held against the appellants. The learned Judge said: "There is little or no dispute on the facts and it all turns on the question if under all the circumstances there was in fact a subletting. I find that there was, and therefore there will be an order for possession forthwith."

It is to be observed that the learned Judge found there was a "subletting". He did not find an assignment nor its synonymous equivalent a "setting over", and see the *Short Form of Leases Act*, R.S.B.C. 1936, c. 263, and also *Crusoe* v. *Bugby* (1771), 2 Black. W. 766, 96 E.R. 448 and *Doe* v. *Hogg* (1825), 4 Dowl. & Ry. 226 at pp. 228-9. It is noted also the covenant in the lease "not to assign or sublet", remains unaccompanied by a further distinctive covenant not to part with possession which in *Chaplin* v. *Smith* (1925), 95 L.J.K.B. 449 and cases therein referred to, is found to mean something different from assigning or subletting. Nor does the amplification of the terms "assignment" and "subletting" in our *Short Form of Leases Act* include the term "part with posession". This is mentioned now to emphasize that the terms "assigning" and "subletting" by no means include every transaction by which a lessee may put a third person in legal possession or in apparent legal possession or in occupancy of the leased premises, and see *Jackson* v. *Simons* (1922), 92 L.J. Ch. 161 at p. 167.

The covenant "will not sublet without leave" is amplified by our *Short Form of Leases Act* to mean that the lessee his executors, etc. "shall not, nor will, during the said term sublet the said premises hereby granted, or any part thereof, to any person or persons without the consent in writing of the said lessor."

In comparison the covenant "will not assign without leave" is amplified by the same statute to mean"...shall not, nor will, during the said term, assign, transfer, or set over, or otherwise, by any act or deed, procure the said premises, or any of them, or the term hereby granted, *to be assigned, transferred, or set over*, unto any person or persons whomsoever, without the consent in writing of the said lessor... first had and obtained." (The italics are mine.)

The conventional distinction between assigning and subletting (*viz.*, that the former includes the full remaining term of the lease, while the latter relates to a term less than the remaining term of the lease) is preserved in the statutory amplification.

I think the learned Judge must have concluded that Mrs. Dolmage was letting the premises to her brother for some period less than her full remaining term. We have not the benefit of the reasons which led to his decision, but it seems not unlikely that the learned Judge interpreted the restricted right to occupancy given by ex. 7 as a "letting" for a period, less than the full remaining term of the lease. That may be the turning point of this case. Is that the true interpretation of ex. 7, bearing in mind that the Courts lean against forfeitures and require the person seeking to enforce a forfeiture to prove his case strictly (per Scrutton L. J. in *Chaplin* v. *Smith*, 95 L.J.K.B. at p. 455)?

One looks for some basic test by which transactions bearing the outward *indicia* of assignments, subletting, parting with possession, or letting, may be determined to fall within or without those terms as used in their legal sense. That test seems to be the right to exclusive possession. And by that is meant in my judgment legal possession which may or may not include actual occupancy. That proposition is extracted from *Taylor et al.* v. *Caldwell* (1863), 32 L.J.Q.B. 164; and from what was decided by the Court of Appeal in *Chaplin* v. *Smith*, 95 L.J.K.B. 449, and *Pincott* v. *Moorstons Ltd.* (1936), 156 L.T. 139, and see also *Woodfall's* Landlord & Tenant, 24th ed., pp. 8 and 10-11.

I think it is self-evident that actual occupancy cannot confer legal possession against the lessee where the occupant, as in this case, cannot legally refuse to vacate at any moment the lessee, who has permitted his occupancy, may choose to cancel that permission. But *Taylor* v. *Caldwell*, 32 L.J.Q.B. 164, appears to go even further. It was a case where, notwithstanding that the occupant paid a substantial sum for the use of premises for a specific period, and where it may be assumed therefore that the owner or lessor had no legal right to cancel that occupancy, yet the Court held the owner or lessor had retained possession of the premises. The defendants let a music hall and gardens to the plaintiff for four non-consecutive days at £100 per day for the purpose of giving a series of four grand concerts and day and night fetes therein. Blackburn J. said (p. 165): "The parties inaccurately call this a 'letting,' and the money to be paid a 'rent'; but the whole agreement is such as to shew that the defendants were to retain possession of the hall and gardens; so that there was to be no demise of them, and that the contract was merely to give the plaintiff the use of them on these days."

In the present case the appellant MacInnes (although he attempted to pay the rent to the lessor who refused to accept it) did not pay, and was not required to pay any consideration to his sister for his use of the suite.

In *Chaplin* v. *Smith* (where the covenant was not to assign or underlet or part with possession) Scrutton L. J. at p. 455, approved this excerpt from *Foa* on Landlord and Tenant that: "'The mere act of letting other persons into possession by the tenant, and permitting them to use the premises for their own purposes, is not, so long as he retains the legal possession himself, a breach of the covenant.'"

That language brings out in clear relief again as in *Taylor* v. *Caldwell*, the distinction which may exist between actual occupancy of premises and the right to their legal possession.

The facts in *Chaplin* v. *Smith* bear repeating. Smith, having been refused leave to assign or sublet to the "one man" company he had formed and of which he was managing director and largest shareholder, verbally entered into an arrangement with the company whereby it carried on a garage business on the premises (having its registered office there) and agreed to indemnify him against payment of the rent, rates and taxes. Smith retained a key to the premises and made use of the company office for his private correspondence. After three years this company assigned its goodwill to a second company of which Smith was also managing director, and which agreed to pay him rent for use of the same premises at which it would continue the garage business.

Before making this last agreement Smith consulted his solicitors, and under their advice wrote a letter to the second company, stating that he must remain in law the actual tenant, and subject to that, if the company wished to enter into the agreement: "The Company may have the use of these premises. I am retaining my position as lessee and remaining in possession."

It is true that Smith retained a key to the premises and used the company office for his private correspondence. But apart from the fact that such privileges were quite consistent with his duties as managing director of the company which was carrying on business there, his possession of the key could give him no greater right to immediate legal possession than the express stipulations to be found in ex. 7 in this case. Smith claimed that in the circumstances he retained the legal possession of the premises notwithstanding the company paid him rent to carry on its business there and was listed as the occupant thereof for taxation purposes. The trial Judge held Smith had commited a breach of his covenant not to part with possession and declared the lease forfeited.

The Court of Appeal reversed that judgment. Bankes L. J. at p. 451 said he attached great importance to the fact that throughout, Smith "continued to be in a position in which he could retain possession".

The learned Lord Justice did not say Smith remained in possession throughout. The carefully chosen quoted language conveys the meaning in the circumstances that although the company occupied the premises, and paid Smith a rent for that occupation, it could not acquire any legal possession, because Smith at all times retained a right to immediate legal possession, which he could enforce at any time.

That both Bankes L. J., and Warrington L. J. held that view is confirmed I think by what the former said at p. 452 and the latter developed at p. 454 regarding the trial Judge's opinion that a man could not retain possession in law and at the same time give exclusive occupation to another. Bankes L. J. said: "I think it is quite possible in law, but of course you do not ordinarily find it, and you would only find it where both persons were quite aware of the position in law, and were careful to keep themselves within the law."

Chaplin v. *Smith* was a case in which that occurred. In my judgment it has also occurred in the case at bar.

In *Pincott* v. *Moorstons Ltd.*, 156 L.T. 139, Greer L. J. (with whom Scott L. J. agreed) said (p. 140) the law must be accepted as correctly laid down by Romer J. in *Jackson* v. *Simons*, 92 L. J. Ch. 161 at p. 166 (also approved in *Chaplin* v. *Smith* at pp. 452 and 454) that "The defendant, moreover, retained the legal possession of the whole of the premises at all material times, and, as pointed out by Romer, J., in *Peebles* v. *Crosthwaite* (13 Times L.R., at p. 38, and 198) a lessee who retains such possession does not commit a breach of a covenant against parting with possession, by allowing other people to use the premises."

It is to be noted that in *Jackson* v. *Simons* the covenant was much wider than in this case and wider even than in *Chaplin* v. *Smith* for it read not to "assign or underlet or part with the said demised premises or any part thereof or part with or share the possession or occupation thereof or of any part thereof".

In *Chaplin* v. *Smith* and *Jackson* v. *Simons* rental was paid for use of the premises. No rental was paid or required in the case at bar. The test of underletting Romer J. laid down in *Jackson* v. *Simons* at p. 165, is that it must confer upon the third party some estate or interest in land. If this is the correct principle, then it is equally applicable if the third person has entire occupation instead of only part occupation as in *Jackson* v. *Simons*, for his right to legal possession must depend upon the agreement. If there is no agreement, then entire occupation may be evidence of legal possession, but if as here, there is an admitted or proven agreement or understanding denying any right to legal possession, the circumstance of entire occupation loses its significance since as Bankes L. J. put it (quoted above): "both persons were quite aware of the position in law, and were careful to keep themselves within the law."..

Persual of ex. 7 makes it clear that the relationship of landlord and tenant was never established between the two appellants. It also makes clear that Mrs. Dolmage retained at all times the legal possession and right to occupancy. At no time did she put her brother in the position where he could assert any right to occupancy against her. She did not part with the whole or any portion of her interest in the lease or in the premises. She permitted her brother to use the suite but on revocable licence only, being careful to retain legal possession at all times, and her brother availed himself of the use of the suite upon those conditions.

For these reasons, I must conclude with respect that the learned Judge erred in holding the transaction amounted to a subletting. If a lessor intends to prohibit a transaction of this kind his remedy is to provide against it in the lease. But the lessor has not done so in this case by words which admit of no other meaning. As stated before, the Courts lean against forfeitures and have always held a strict hand over covenants which are invoked to defeat leases. These covenants have always been construed with the utmost jealousy to prevent their restraint exceeding the express stipulation.

Appeal allowed.

[Robertson J. A. agreed with O'Halloran J. A. The concurring judgment of Bird J. A. is omitted.

In *Lippman* v. *Lee Yick*, [1953] O.R. 514, [1953] 3 D.L.R. 527, a lease of restaurant premises contained an absolute covenant not to assign or sublet without leave. The deceased tenant's executor entered into a "management agreement" with certain employees giving them a licence to carry on the business and providing for the sale to them of the physical assets and goodwill. The executor undertook to use his best efforts to obtain consent to an assignment of the lease, failing which he would continue the licence for the duration of the lease. *Held*, there was no breach of the covenant.

If a lessee accepts a covenant not to assign or sublet without leave, is he in breach if he enters into a mere agreement to assign? See *Cornish* v. *Boles* (1914), 31 O.L.R. 505, 19 D.L.R. 447 (C.A).

If consent is given to an assignment, is there a breach on re-assignment to the lessee? See *McEacharn* v. *Colton*, [1902] A.C. 104.

In *Dumpor* v. *Symms* (1603), 4 Co. Rep. 119b, 76 E.R. 1110 (K.B.) it was held that where a lease contains a covenant not to assign without leave, and leave is once given, it ceases to be a requirement in subsequent assignments. This common law rule was abrogated by legislation: see Landlord and Tenant Act, R.S.M. 1954, c. 136, ss. 23, 24; Landlord and Tenant Act, R.S.N.B. 1952, c. 126, s. 10; Landlord and Tenant Act, R.S.O. 1960, c. 206, ss. 23, 24; Landlord and Tenant Act, R.S.P.E.I. 1951, c. 82, s. 11; Landlord and Tenant Act, R.S.S. 1953, c. 312, ss. 14, 15.

Is a covenant not to assign or sublet without leave broken by a testamentary disposition of the leasehold? See *Crusoe d. Blencowe* v. *Bugby* (1771), 3 Wils. 234, 95 E.R. 1030 (K.B.). Cf. *Jayawardene* v. *Jayawardene*, [1939] 3 W.W.R. 88 (P.C.); *Thompson* v. *British American Oil Co. Ltd.* (1956), 7 D.L.R. 2d 116 (B.C.).

If a tenant dies and his widow continues in occupation, is she in the position of an assignee? Is it different if an executor or administrator takes over? See *Colonial Coach Lines Ltd.* v. *Nicholson*, [1949] O.R. 822, [1950] 1 D.L.R. 204 (C.A.); *Fred Long & Sons Ltd.* v. *Burgess*, [1949] 2 All E.R. 484 (C.A.). Cf. *Charles Ogilvy Ltd.* v. *Larocque*, [1952] 3 D.L.R. 241, [1952] O.W.N. 281 (C.A.).

Is a covenant not to assign or sublet broken by the lessee's bankruptcy or by a voluntary assignment for the benefit of creditors? *Cf. Magee* v. *Rankin* (1869), 29 U.C.Q.B. 257 (C.A.).

Assuming that an involuntary bankruptcy is not a breach of such a covenant, is it open to the trustee in bankruptcy to dispose of the bankrupt's leaseholds in the face of the covenant? In *Re Wright*, [1949] Ch. 729, [1949] 2 All E.R. 605, Danckwerts J. said: "It has long been accepted that.... a trustee in bankruptcy is at liberty to assign a bankrupt's leasehold property notwithstanding a covenant that the tenant or his assigns shall not assign or part with the property in question". In this case, it was held, however, that because the covenant was with "the tenant and his successors in title", the trustee in bankruptcy was bound thereby. Would this result follow if by bankruptcy legislation a trustee in bankruptcy is obliged to realize upon or liquidate the bankrupt's estate? Does it depend on whether one can "contract out" of the bankruptcy law? See Bankruptcy Act, R.S.C. 1952, c. 14, s. 10.

Section 37 (2) of the Landlord and Tenant Act, R.S.O. 1960, c. 206, provides as follows:

"Notwithstanding any provision, stipulation or agreement in any lease or agreement or the legal effect thereof, in case of an assignment for the general benefit of creditors, or an order being made for the winding up of an incorporated company, or where a receiving order in bankruptcy or authorized assignment has been made by or against a tenant, the assignee, liquidator or trustee may at any time within three months thereafter for the purposes of the trust estate and before he has given notice of intention to surrender possession or disclaim, by notice in writing elect to retain the leased premises for the whole or any portion of the unexpired term and any renewal thereof, upon the terms of the lease and subject to the payment of the rent as provided by the lease or agreement, and he may upon payment to the landlord of all arrears of rent, assign the lease with rights of renewal, if any, to any person who will covenant to observe and perform its terms and agree to conduct upon the demised premises a trade or business which is not reasonably of a more objectionable or hazardous nature than that which was thereon conducted by the debtor, and who on application of the assignee, liquidator or trustee, is approved by a judge of the Supreme Court as a person fit and proper to be put in possession of the leased premises."

For similar legislation, see Landlord and Tenant Act, R.S.B.C. 1960, c. 207, s. 33 (2);

Landlord and Tenant Act, R.S.M. 1954, c. 136, s. 46 (2); Landlord and Tenant Act, R.S.N.B. 1952, c. 126, s. 43 (2); Landlord and Tenant Act, R.S.P.E.I. 1951, c. 82, s. 74 (1); Landlord and Tenant Act, R.S.S. 1953, c. 312, s. 46. *Cf.* Landlord's Rights on Bankruptry Act, R.S.A. 1955, c. 171.

This legislation was invoked and applied in *Re Limestone Electrical & Supply Co. Ltd.*, [1955] O.R. 291, [1955] 3 D.L.R. 104 (C.A.). Presumably, it could be invoked even if the lease contained a provision for termination upon the tenant's bankruptcy.

Quaere as to the validity of provincial legislation respecting a landlord's priority for arrears of rent or for accelerated rent on his tenant's bankruptcy; *Cf.* Landlord and Tenant Act, R.S.O. 1960, c. 206, s. 37 (1), and Bankruptcy Act, R.S.C. 1952, c. 14, s. 95; see *Canadian Credit Men's Trust Association* v. *Carman Block Ltd.* (1957), 8 D.L.R. 2d 647, 22 W.W.R. (N.S.) 180 (Sask. C. A.)]

[Where consent is required to an assignment or sublease under a covenant which stipulates that consent shall not be unreasonably withheld, consent must first be asked even though refusal would be unreasonable. The tenant, intended assignor, may then proceed to assign or sublet (accepting the risk of the reasonableness of the landlord's refusal of consent) or may, under permissive legislation, apply for an order for consent, as, for example, under s. 22 (2) of the Landlord and Tenant Act, R.S.O. 1960, c. 206. *Cf. McCallum, Hill & Co.* v. *Imperial Bank of Canada* (1914), 7 Sask. L.R. 333, 22 D.L.R. 203, 7 W.W.R. 981; *Cornish* v. *Boles, supra; Childs* v. *King* (1915), 8 O.W.N. 511. The burden of showing the unreasonableness of a refusal of consent is on the tenant who seeks to assign or sublet and, as between him and his intended assignee or sublessee he is under the duty to seek the required consent: see *F. Berry Ltd.* v. *Royal Bank of Scotland*, [1949] 1 K.B. 619, [1949] 1 All E.R. 706; *Grossman* v. *Modern Theatres Ltd.* (1919), 45 O.L.R. 364; *Maas* v. *McMahon*, 19 Alta. L.R. 60, 62 D.L.R. 317, [1921] 3 W.W.R. 378 (C.A.).

What damages is a landlord entitled to for breach of a covenant not to assign or sublet? See *Straus Land Corp. Ltd.* v. *International Hotel Windsor Ltd.* (1918), 45 O.L.R. 145, 48 D.L.R. 519 (C.A.). Is a tenant or his assignee entitled to damages if consent is unreasonably withheld where the covenant against assignment is so qualified? See *Childs* v. *King, supra; Cornish* v. *Boles, supra.*

May a landlord exact a pecuniary payment for consenting to an assignment or sublease? Would it make any difference if the covenant against assigning or subletting was absolute or was qualified by an obligation not to withhold consent unreasonably? *Cf. Hilton* v. *Tipper* (1868), 18 L.T. 626 (Ch.); *Woodfall*, Landlord and Tenant (1960, 26th ed.), pp. 574-75; Law of Property Act, 1925 (Imp.), c. 20, s. 144.]

HOULDER BROS. & CO. LTD. v. GIBBS. Court of Appeal. [1925] Ch. 575

Appeal from a judgment of Tomlin J., [1925] Ch. 198 in an action for a declaration that refusal of an assent to a proposed assignment was unreasonable and that plaintiffs were accordingly entitled to assign without it.

POLLOCK M. R.: ... It is only necessary, in order to explain my judgment, to state that the plaintiffs were the lessees under a lease dated September 29, 1908, granted by the defendant of certain premises known as No. 10 Market Street, in the city of Sheffield. The plaintiffs went into possession and have held the premises under that lease, which contains the following covenant: "And the company will not, during the said term, without the consent in writing of the lessor first obtained, assign, sublet, or part with the possession of the hereby demised premises, or any part thereof, such consent not to be withheld unreasonably in the case of a respectable and responsible person or corporation." The lessees are now anxious to assign the residue of the term. The lessor has refused his consent, and he has done so candidly and avowedly on the grounds which are stated in a letter to which our attention has been called, and which is in these terms: "I withhold my consent to Houlder Brothers assigning to Roneo, Ld., on the reasonable ground that by the assignment I should lose Roneo, Ld., as good tenants of No. 12, because I should have great difficulty in finding any tenant for No. 12 in the present abnormal condition of trade in Sheffield, the loss being rent at the rate of £295 per annum, and probably for a considerable period." The premises which were granted to the plaintiffs under this lease lie contiguous to the premises No. 12, of which Roneo, Ld., are the tenants; and Roneo, Ld., are the proposed tenants to whom the plaintiffs desire to assign the residue of their term.

The short point, therefore, for us is whether or not the avowed reason of the lessor for withholding his consent—namely, that he will have great difficulty in finding a tenant for No. 12, part of his property, in the present abnormal condition of trade in Sheffield, with the consequent burden of an empty house, and possible loss of rent—is an adequate reason for withholding his consent, within the proviso in the covenant, that his consent is not to be withheld unreasonably in the case of a respectable and responsible person or corporation. It is admitted that Roneo, Ld., fulfil these last conditions, and are a respectable and responsible person or corporation, but it is claimed by the lessor that under that provision, although a respectable and responsible person or corporation is submitted to him as a proposed assignee, he nevertheless has a right to withhold his consent, subject only to the condition that that consent is not unreasonably withheld.

It is unnecessary, I think, to go through the cases, of which there are some half a dozen or more, bearing more or less upon this point, because Tomlin J. has done so, and I agree with his judgment both in its reasoning and in the conclusions at which he has arrived. Indeed I do not desire to add more than a very few words, because I think his judgment is plain and clear, and I have no wish to blur anything that he has said.

It appears to me that in construing the meaning of the words "such consent not to be withheld unreasonably" one has to bear in mind that by law in the absence of this covenant the lessees would have had a right to assign the premises as they pleased. The lessor, therefore, took this covenant from the lessees in order to cut down their rights, and to ensure that the premises would not pass into the hands of some person or corporation to whom he could reasonably take objection. Equally, the lessees by accepting the burden of this covenant, on their part, which prevented them from assigning without the leave of the lessor, obtained from him those words in the proviso which cut down the right of the lessor to withhold his consent, and prevented him from acting from caprice, or mere prejudice or the like.

It seems to me useful to call attention to the statement made by Kay L. J. in *Barrow* v. *Isaacs & Son*, [1891] 1 Q.B. 417, at p. 423. He there says: "The terms of the covenant are quite clear. If the intended lessees are respectable and responsible persons the consent is not to be 'arbitrarily withheld'." It is not contended that there is any difference between "arbitrarily" and "unreasonably". Kay L. J. continues: "Those words simply mean that the consent must be asked for before the assignment, and that it may be withheld, even though the intended lessees are proper persons, if such withholding is not arbitrary. Many cases be supposed in which it would not be." He then passes on to give instances of cases in which the withholding of consent would not be arbitrary, but those all have reference either to the user of the property, or have some connection with the actual property which is the subject of the contract between the lessor and lessee.

In *Bates* v. *Donaldson* [1896] 2 Q.B. 241, at p. 247, A. L. Smith L. J. says: "It is not, in my opinion, the true reading of this clause that the permission can be withheld in order to enable the lessor to regain possession of the premises before the termination of the term. It was in my judgment inserted *alio intuitu* altogether, and in order to protect the lessor from having his premises used or occupied in an undesirable way or by an undesirable tenant or assignee, and not in order to enable the lessor to, if possible, coerce a tenant to surrender the lease so that the lessor might obtain possession of the premises." His judgment differs, in some important respects, from the judgment which had been delivered by Kay L. J. in the same case. For my part, I agree with A. L. Smith L. J., and I think that one must look at these words in their relation to the premises, and to the contract made in reference to the premises between the lessor and lessee; in other words, one must have regard to the relation of the lessor and lessee *inter se*, or, perhaps one may add, to the due and proper management of the property, as in *Governors of Bridewell Hospital* v. *Fawkner*, 8 Times L.R. 637. The latter case is an illustration of a withholding of consent on broad grounds bearing upon the estate of the lessor, or it may be on grounds which are important between the lessor and other lessees of that property, or that estate, of which the lessee had cognizance. But I do not think the words of the covenant can be so interpreted as to entitle the lessor to exercise the right of refusal when his reason given is one which is independent of the relation between the lessor and lessee, and is on grounds which are entirely personal to the lessor, and wholly extraneous to the lessee. As an illustration of what I mean I refer to *Young* v. *Ashley Gardens Properties, Ld.*, [1903] 2 Ch. 112, where a condition was imposed, or attempted to be imposed, by the lessor, not in reference to the relation between himself and the lessee, nor in relation to the property which was the subject of the lease, but one which was wholly personal to the lessor himself, whereby he attempted to obtain immunity from possible increase in the rates.

In the present case the lessor has frankly avowed that there is no objection to Roneo, Ld., as a respectable and responsible person or corporation, and that the sole reason operating upon his mind is something extraneous to the relation of landlord and tenant, something extrinsic from the lessee, and something which is wholly personal to the lessor. To hold that such a reason absolved the lessor from the duty of giving his licence to an assignment under the terms of the covenant would, in my opinion, be to give far too wide an interpretation to the word "unreasonably", and to be going beyond the cases. While I think it is impossible to give an exact definition which will fit all cases, I prefer the reasoning which is stated by A. L. Smith L. J. in *Bates* v. *Donaldson*, which I think has been followed by Tomlin J. I agree, therefore, with the decision which Tomlin J. has reached.

WARRINGTON L. J.: ... The lessor has withheld his consent to an assignment to an admittedly respectable and responsible corporation, a company called Roneo, Ld., and the question therefore is whether he has unreasonably witheld his consent. He has withheld it on this ground: The proposed assignee happens to be tenant to himself of a shop in the same building, and adjoining that which is the subject of the lease, and the lessor is convinced on what I will assume to be sufficient ground, that if the proposed assignee is allowed to take the assignment of the plaintiffs' shop, the subject of the lease, he will give up the other shop, and the lessor will have considerable difficulty in finding a new tenant therefor. It is on that ground that the lessor has refused his consent. That is on a ground having no reference to the personality of the proposed assignee, and having no reference to the effect of the proposed assignment on the user and occupation of the demised premises.

The question whether a particular act is reasonable or unreasonable is obviously one that cannot be determined on abstract considerations. An act must be regarded as reasonable or unreasonable in reference to the circumstances under which it is committed, and when the question arises on the construction of a contract the outstanding circumstances to be considered are the nature of the contract to be construed, and the relations between the parties resulting from it. In the present case the contract is a lease, and the relation between the parties that of lessor and lessee.

The first question that arises is: What is the inference to be drawn as to the intention of the parties in inserting in the lease a provision of this kind? What was the danger which the lessor contemplated, and against which the lessee was content to allow the lessor to protect himself? It must, of course, be borne in mind that without this covenant the lessee would have had a free right to assign to whom he pleased the premises comprised in the lease, and the covenant, therefore, was inserted first as a protection of the lessor, and, secondly, the proviso was attached to it in order to prevent the lessor making an unreasonable use of that protection.

Now, what is to be inferred from what may be treated as having been in the contemplation of the parties when the contract was made? I think it must be, as I have said, that it was intended to protect the lessor as against a lessee, who, although respectable and responsible, might well be reasonably objectionable in other ways, and, secondly, from the point of view of the property, to prevent the lessor from having to accept a lessee whose user of the property might again be reasonably objectionable. The user of the property to be reasonably objectionable need not necessarily be objectionable to the lessor as lessor of that particular property. The user of the property might damage the lessor in other ways, and if it did, then an objection to that user would be reasonable; but whichever way it is looked at, I think you must find in the objection something which connects it either with the personality of the intended assignee suggested as the new tenant of the property, or with the user which he is likely to make of the property to be assigned to him.

When you look at the authorities—I do not propose to go through them—this, at any rate, is plain, that in the cases in which an objection to an assignment has been upheld as reasonable it has always had some reference either to the personality of the tenant, or to his proposed user of the property. The case which was, perhaps, most relied upon by appellant was that of *Governors of Bridewell Hospital* v. *Fawkner*, because what was there apprehended was damage to the lessor in respect of other property of his; but the damage which was apprehended would have resulted, if it resulted at all, either from the personality of the proposed assignee, who was the General of the Salvation Army, or from the user to which he was likely to put the property, so that it fell within the limitation which I have suggested. I think that even in the judgment of Kay L. J. in *Bates* v. *Donaldson* the same idea is to be found, although he puts it in more general terms. First he says: "I agree, that if the proposed assignee intended to use the house for some purpose to which the landlord might reasonably object, though such purpose was not forbidden by the lease, nor by any rule of law, the landlord might reasonably refuse to permit the assignment." Then there were the words which were much relied upon by the appellant: "So I should think there might be other reasons, personal rather to the landlord than the tenant, which might justify his refusal under the terms of this covenant." In the *Bridewell* case the refusal was personal rather to the landlord than to the tenant, but it had reference to the user by the proposed tenant of the property, and so I think it does not at all follow that Kay L. J. had in contemplation any such objection as that with which we have to deal in the present case. I think the judgment of A. L. Smith L. J. supports the view which Tomlin J. has expressed in his judgment.

SARGANT L. J.: ... In the present case the reason for refusing has nothing whatever to do with the relationship of landlord and tenant in regard to the subject matter of the demise. The sole reason is that if the property is allowed to be assigned to the new tenants, the new tenants, in respect of a tenancy of a completely different property which they hold from the lessor, will probably desire to terminate their tenancy of that other property. In my judgment that is a reason wholly dissociated from, and unconnected with, the bargain made between the lessor and the lessees under the lease that we have to consider, and is, from that point of view, a purely arbitrary and irrelevant reason. I agree with the judgment of Tomlin J., and that the appeal should be dismissed.

Appeal dismissed.

SHIELDS v. DICKLER. Ontario Court of Appeal. [1948] 1 D.L.R. 809, [1948] O.W.N. 145

Appeal by a tenant from an order dismissing his application for permission to assign a lease without the landlord's consent.

HENDERSON J. A. agreed with AYLESWORTH J. A.

HOPE J. A. (dissenting): This is an appeal from an order of Macdonell J. of the County Court of the County of York, dismissing an application made by the tenant under the provisions of s. 22 (2) of the Landlord and Tenant Act, R.S.O. 1937, c. 219 for an order permitting an assignment of a lease without the consent of the lessor.

The clause in the lease relied upon as waiving and renouncing the benefits of the Landlord and Tenant in its entirety, reads as follows: "The Lessee hereby waives and renounces the benefit of Section 29 of Chapter 190 of the Revised Statutes of Ontario, 1927, entitled 'An Act Respecting Landlord and Tenant,' or any other section of said Act or any amendment of said section or sections, or any revision of said statute which may hereafter come into force by Act of Parliament, and he also agrees that notwithstanding the said Act, the Lessor may seize upon and sell all the Lessee's goods and chattels, or such part thereof as may be necessary for payment of rent and costs as might have been done if the said Act had not been passed. And the Lessor may seize all or any of the Lessee's goods and chattels for rent in arrears in case the Lessee leaves the premises and the said Lessor may seize said goods and chattels at any place that they may have been removed to, whether on or off the premises, and the said Lessor shall also be entitled to all costs which may be incurred in the premises, including costs as between solicitor and client incurred in collecting arrears of rent, or otherwise howsoever, which terms are binding on the Lessee's heirs, executors, administrators and assigns."

In his reasons for judgment the learned trial Judge cites only the first part of this provision down to the words "come into force by Act of Parliament."

Section 29 of R.S.O. 1927, c. 190 is the same as in the present Act, and is one which deals entirely with exemption from seizure under execution by way of distress.

The whole context of the paragraph in the lease above cited deals only with this aspect of the relationship between landlord and tenant. I am of the opinion that the words "or any other section of said Act" contained in the said provision of the lease must be read in the light of the whole paragraph as though it had read "or any other section of the said Act of like effect".

To waive the provisions of the entire statute would require to be, in my opinion, in clear and unequivocal language.

I am, therefore, of opinion that the learned Judge was not deprived of the usual jurisdiction conferred upon him by s. 22 (2) of the Act.

The fact that the landlord availed himself of the provison of Wartime Prices and Trade Board Regulation Order No. 707 [[1947] S.O.R. 881] amending Order No. 294 [[1943] 3 C.W.O.R. 401], permitting him to elect to offer the tenant a two-year lease of the premises which was in turn accepted by the tenant, does not place such a lease in any different category than that of the leases contemplated under provincial law, and in dealing with the question of the reasonableness or otherwise of the action of the landlord in refusing to consent to the assignment of the lease, it is not necessary or desirable to import any other element than that which has been well recognized in cases of this kind.

It is a well-accepted rule, as set out in *Woodfall's* Law of Landlord and Tenant, 24th ed., p. 581, that: "The refusal of a licence will be unreasonable if it is on a ground having no reference either to the personality of the proposed assignee or to the effect of the proposed assignment on the user and occupation of the demised premises." This principle has been well established in a long series of cases.

In the case at bar it is agreed that the personality of the proposed assignee cannot be questioned. Furthermore the user to which the assignee proposes to put the demised premises is the same as that which is now made of the property by the appellant herein. It would appear that the reason given by the landlord for the refusal of his consent is extraneous to both principles above set out.

In *Re Gibbs & Houlder Bros. & Co.'s Lease, Houlder Bros. & Co.* v. *Gibbs*, [1925] Ch. 575, this proposition is discussed....

I would therefore allow the appeal and an order should go declaring that the consent of the landlord herein was unreasonably withheld. Costs of the appeal and of the application below to the appellant.

Since dictating the foregoing reasons for judgment I have had the advantage of reading the reasons of my brother Aylesworth, which led him to a conclusion opposite to that at which I had arrived. In the light of this and in deference to his reasons, I have given further consideration to this matter, and in particular to the judgment in *Tredegar* v. *Harwood*, [1929] A.C. 72 to which he refers.

The Court in that case consisted of Viscount Dunedin, Lord Shaw of Dunfermline, Lord Phillimore and Lord Blanesburgh. Any doubt cast upon the authority of *Re Gibbs & Houlder Bros. & Co.'s Lease, supra*, is not to be found in the judgment of the majority of the Court, as would seem to be the impression of my brother Aylesworth, but only in the form of *dicta* in the judgments of Viscount Dunedin and Lord Phillimore.

With particular reference to the doubts expressed by these two, it is of interest to note that subsequent to *Tredegar* v. *Harwood*, Bennett J. in *Premier Confectionery (London) Co.* v. *London Commercial Sale Rooms Ltd.*, [1933] W.N. 182, makes no reference to the judgment of the noble Law Lords, but bases his decision in this last-named case solely on the authority of *Re Gibbs & Houlder Bros. & Co.'s Lease, supra*, and the earlier case of *Bates* v. *Donaldson, supra*.

I also find that the question involved in the present appeal, and in circumstances practically identical thereto, was considered by Evershed J. *in Re Swanson's Agreement, Hill* v. *Swanson* (1946), 62 T.L.R. 719.

The circumstances in the *Swanson* case were that a house had been let for 2 years at a rental below standard rent, but had been increased to standard rent with the tenant remaining in possession. The tenant later agreed to assign the premises and asked for the landlord's consent. The landlord refused, not on any ground connected with the proposed assignee, but because, as in the case at present under review, as an owner of several houses in the area, she, the landlord, had a list of persons waiting to take any house which became vacant, and had promised to give the tenancy to another person on that list. It was held by Evershed J. that "according to the authorities which I have mentioned and the principles behind them, the landlord in the present case must be taken to have been unreasonable." [p. 720]

In stating the question in this respect, which was to be decided, Evershed J. said at p. 720: "The question shortly is whether it is unreasonable to refuse consent to an assignment in other respects unimpeachable in order to obtain for oneself such advantages as may be obtained in the way of getting actual vacant possession. In the absence of authority it might well be said not to be an unreasonable act for the landlord to take a step or to decline to take a step in order, as I say, to get into the best possible position for obtaining vacant possession. But the matter is not one free from authority binding on this Court. I refer first to *Houlder Brothers and Co. Limited* v. *Gibbs.*"

Then after quoting from this last-named judgment, the learned Judge continued: "The earlier case... of *Bates* v. *Donaldson* makes it, I think, clear that the reason assigned by the landlord in the present case does not fall within the grounds which have been held to be reasonable within the principle of the decisions."

The learned Judge then continues with a discussion of the opinions of two of the noble Lords in *Tredegar* v. *Harwood,* which expressed substantially doubt about the correctness of the decision in *Re Gibbs & Houlder Bros. & Co.'s Lease,* and states as follows: "But notwithstanding the dicta of Lord Dunedin and Lord Phillimore, it is plain that *Houlder Brothers and Co., Limited* v. *Gibbs* is still regarded as binding and good authority. Moreover, *Bates* v. *Donaldson* has not been adversely criticized and it is now 50 years since that decision was pronounced. It would, I think, be most dangerous and wrong for me as a Judge of first instance, on the basis of dicta in *Tredegar* v. *Harwood,* to attempt to create fine distinctions limiting the effect or questioning in any way the validity of the decision in *Houlder Brothers and Co. Limited* v. *Gibbs.*"

It is of some further interest that Evershed J. more or less invited an appeal from his decision on this point, and although the judgment was given on October 31, 1946, I have been unable to find any record of an appeal having been taken therefrom.

On a review of the evidence before the learned County Judge herein, I find it difficult to come to any other conclusion than that the appellant herein has satisfied the onus as he is called upon to do on such an application, as set out in *Grossman* v. *Modern Theatres Ltd.* (1919), 45 O.L.R. 564.

AYLESWORTH J. A.: ...The order appealed from is attacked upon two grounds: (a) that the learned County Court Judge was wrong in holding that appellant (the tenant) had waived the benefit of s. 22 (1), and, (b) that the learned County Court Judge should have found that the landlord's (respondent's) refusal to consent to the assignment was unreasonable.

As to the first ground, the lease contains the following clause: [see reasons of Hope J. A., *supra.*]

The lease also contains an agreement by the lessee not to assign without consent, and by s. 22 (1) that agreement is deemed to be subject to the proviso that such consent shall not be unreasonably withheld "unless the lease contains an expressed provision to the contrary".

Is the clause in the lease, above quoted in full, "an expressed provision to the contrary" within the meaning of s. 22 (1)? I think it may well be. I can find nothing in the clause indicating clearly that the words used therein are not to be given their plain ordinary meaning.

As to the second ground, it is said that the landlord's consent is unreasonably withheld in every case unless it be withheld upon some ground referring either to the personality of the proposed assignee, or to the effect of the proposed assignment on the user and occupation of the demised premises. Undoubtedly there are certain decisions in England to this effect, of which perhaps the most unequivocal is *Re Gibbs & Houlder Bros. & Co.'s Lease,* [1925] Ch. 575. The correctness of that decision, however, has been seriously doubted in the judgments of the majority of the law Lords who decided *Tredegar* v. *Harwood,* [1929] A.C. 72. In our own Courts, so far as I am aware, it has never been expressly decided that the reasonableness, or otherwise, of a landlord's refusal to consent to the assignment of a lease is to be determined solely and exclusively upon the two grounds above mentioned. In the absence of binding authority, I am loath to adopt such a restrictive rule, particularly where, as in this case, the ordinary rights of the parties are interfered with and to a great extent controlled by wartime regulations introduced for the benefit of the tenant and as a temporary and emergent measure. It is to be observed that the onus of demonstrating that the landlord's refusal is unreasonable rests upon the applicant for an order under s. 22 (2): *Grossman* v. *Modern Theatres Ltd.*, 45 O.L.R. 564. The effect of the finding of the learned County Court Judge is that the appellant has not satisfied that onus.

In the result I am, at the most, mildly doubtful as to the correctness of the decision appealed from. I would accordingly dismiss the appeal with costs.

Appeal dismissed.

[In *Cowitz* v. *Siegel*, [1955] 1 D.L.R. 678, [1955] O.W.N. 833 (C.A.), the Ontario Court of Appeal was content to apply (without overall approval) *Lee* v. *K. Carter Ltd.*, [1949] 1 K.B. 85, [1948] 2 All E.R. 690 (C.A.) which approved *Houlder Bros & Co. Ltd.* v. *Gibbs*, *supra.* See also *Swanson* v. *Forton*, [1949] 1 Ch. 143, [1949] 1 All E.R. 135 (C.A.); *Parker* v. *Boggan*, [1947] K.B. 346, [1947] 1 All E.R. 46.

If a tenant assigns or sublets without seeking leave where leave is required, and the landlord accepts rent from the assignee or, being aware of the sublease, accepts rent from his tenant, he loses any right of re-entry for breach of the covenant: see *Norman* v. *Simpson*, [1946] K.B. 158, [1946] 1 All E.R. 74 (C.A.). May he nonetheless claim damages?

Is it open to the parties to stipulate in a lease that the withholding of consent on certain specified grounds will not be deemed unreasonable? See *Re Smith's Lease, Smith* v. *Richards*, [1951] 1 All E.R. 346, [1951] 1 T.L.R. 254 (Ch.). Cf. *Adler* v. *Upper Grosvenor Street Investment Ltd.* [1957] 1 All E.R. 229, [1957] 1 W.L.R. 227 (Q.B.) (stipulation that lessee must offer to surrender lease before seeking consent to assign held valid).

A covenant against assigning or subletting without consent provided additionally that such consent was not to be withheld in the case of a respectable and responsible person. It was argued that this amounted to an affirmative covenant by the landlord not to require consent on an assignment to a respectable and responsible person. Do you agree? See *Mowat* v. *Martin* [1950] 1 K.B. 175, [1949] 2 All E.R. 646 (C.A.): and *cf. Wilson* v. *Flynn*, [1948] 2 All E.R. 40 (K.B.).]

[Under the Infants Act, R.S.O. 1960, c. 187, s. 9, where the landlord is an infant consent to an assignment or sublease under a covenant requiring it may be given by the Supreme Court.]

[Statutory provisions in Ontario and other provinces respecting forfeiture and relief from forfeiture for breach of covenants or conditions specifically exclude relief against forfeiture for breach of a covenant not to assign or sublet: see Landlord and Tenant Act, R.S.O. 1960, c. 206, s. 19 (7): Landlord and Tenant Act, R.S.M. 1954, c. 136, s. 19 (7); Landlord and Tenant Act, R.S.N.B. 1952, c. 126, s. 14 (9); Landlord and Tenant Act, R.S.P.E.I. 1951, c. 82, s. 15 (9); Landlord and Tenant Act, R.S.S. 1953, c. 312, s. 10 (8). These provisions were modelled on s. 14 (6) of the Conveyancing Act, 1881 (Imp.), c. 41. In England now, relief in the case of a covenant not to assign or sublet is no longer excluded: see Law of Property Act, 1925 (Imp.), c. 20, s. 146 (2). But even under the law as it stood before 1925, Courts with equitable powers asserted the right to give relief from forfeiture in the case of such a covenant through exercise of the general equity power to relieve against penalties and forfeitures. Thus in *Barrow* v. *Isaacs & Son*, [1891] 1 Q.B. 417 (C.A.) Kay L. J. said, referring to the exclusion of relief under the Conveyancing Act in respect of covenants not to assign or sublet (at p. 430): "Forfeiture for breach of this covenant is left to be dealt with according to the ordinary law and practice of Courts of Equity." See also *Eastern Telegraph Co. Ltd.* v. *Dent*, [1899] 1 Q.B. 835 (C.A.).

May we assume that in Ontario, for example, s. 19 (7) of the Landlord and Tenant Act is subject to an overriding power set out in s. 19 of the Judicature Act, R.S.O. 1960, c. 197 which reads as follows: "The Court has power to relieve against all penalties and forfeitures and in granting such relief to impose such terms as to costs, expenses, damages, compensation and all other matters as are deemed just."?

In British Columbia, where there is no express statutory provision for relief against forfeiture of leases, the Courts have indicated that they may apply their general powers to relieve against forfeitures and penalties: see *Nuytten and Bakalaryk* v. *Stein*, [1954] 2 D.L.R. 785, 12 W.W.R. (N.S.) 465 (B.C.).

For an application of the present English law, see *House Property & Investment Co. Ltd.* v. *James Walker, Goldsmith & Silversmith Ltd.*, [1947] 2 All E.R. 789 (K.B.) (relief granted); *Wilson* v. *Flynn*, [1948] 2 All E.R. 40 (K.B.) (relief refused).]

[Statutory provision for protection of a sublessee where a landlord is proceeding to exercise a right of re-entry for breach of any covenant or stipulation in a lease: Landlord and Tenant Act, R.S.M. 1954, c. 136, s. 20; Landlord and Tenant Act, R.S.N.B. 1952, c. 126, s. 15; Landlord and Tenant Act, R.S.O. 1960, c. 206, s. 20; Landlord and Tenant Act, R.S.P.E.I. 1951, c. 82, s. 16; Landlord and Tenant Act, R.S.S. 1953, c. 312, s. 11.]

[A lease containing a covenant not to assign or sublet without leave also included an option to purchase, exercisable by the lessee and assigns. The tenant assigned without leave and the assignee sought to exercise the option. Result? See *Mus* v. *Matlashewski*, [1944] 4 D.L.R. 522, [1944] 3 W.W.R. 358, 52 Man. R. 247 (C.A.).]

SPARKHALL v. WATSON. Ontario High Court. [1954] 2 D.L.R. 22, [1954] O.W.N. 101

JUDSON J.: The plaintiff leased to the defendant a golfcourse and the equipment to operate it for a term of 5 years from January 1, 1948, to December 31, 1952. The lease contained an option to renew in these terms:

"The lessor covenants with the lessee that if the lessee duly and regularly pays the rent hereby reserved and performs all and every covenant provision and agreement herein contained and on the part of the lessee to be paid and performed, the lessor will, upon the request and at the cost of the lessee, one month previous to the expiration of the said term, grant to the lessee a renewal lease of the said premises for a further term of five years."

The lessor denied the lessee's right to a renewal. The lessee refused to give up posession. The plaintiff sues for possession and the defendant counterclaims for a renewal lease.

The main issue is as to the right of renewal in view of the way the rent was paid during the first 2-1/2 years of the lease. The rent was $ 10,000 per year. The first year's rent was payable $500 on the signing of the lease, $4,500 on April 1, 1948, and $1,000 on the first days of June, July, August, September and October, 1948. The $500 was paid on the signing of the lease. The other payments were made as follows: Feb. 2—$ 200; Apr. 4—300; Apr. 7—1,000; Apr. 29—1,000; May 17—500; May 25—600; May 31—600; June 14—500; June 29—500; July 26—500; Aug. 3—500; Aug. 8—2,000; Sept. 7—1,000; Oct. 2—1,000.

The rent for 1949 was payable in the same way except that on April 1, 1949, $ 5,000 fell due. The 1949 rent was paid as follows: Feb. 9—$ 200; Mar. 7—100; Apr. 4—100; Apr. 11—1,000; Apr. 21—100; Apr. 25—200; May 3—500; May 9—500; May 17—500; May 28—800; June 7—500; June 22—420; July 3—1,000; July 28—500; Aug. 2—500; Aug. 15—200; Aug. 29—100; Sept. 7—200; Sept. 12—200; Oct. 3—1,200; Oct. 16—1,000.

The October 3rd payment of $ 1,200 was the result of a distress levied on September 17th.

The 1950 rent was payable in the same way as the 1949 rent. The $ 5,000 due on April 1, 1950, was not paid. A notice of forfeiture was served on April 17, 1950. The lessee immediately applied for relief from forfeiture, which was granted on April 25th. Since that time the rent has been paid punctually.

I have set out in detail the evidence as to the payment of the rent because of the provision in the renewal clause. It is admitted that at the end of each year of the lease, the rent had been fully paid. I mention this because the amounts I have listed may not total $ 10,000 in each year.

A lessee who seeks a renewal under a clause such as the one in question here must show that he has performed all conditions precedent. If he has not done so, he is not entitled to a renewal. The situation is not one where the lessor declares a forfeiture. None of the considerations applicable to forfeiture have any relevancy. The law I have to apply is stated by Robertson C.J.O. in *Fingold* v. *Hunter*, [1944] 3 D.L.R. 43 at p. 46, O.W.N. 287 at p. 289: "The whole clause is, however, subject to the condition precedent stated at the beginning. The clause is to operate only upon the due performance of all the lessee's covenants. There are many decisions upon the effect of similar words in the case of a true option to purchase, or to renew, and no distinction was suggested in the effect of such a condition between the clause now in question and the case of a true option, and I think no such distinction can be made. Due performance of the lessee's covenants is a condition precedent. *Finch* v. *Underwood* (1876), Ch. D. 310; *Bastin* v. *Bidwell* (1881), 18 Ch. D. 238; *Simons* v. *Associated Furnishers Ltd.*, [1931] 1 Ch. 379. The burden is upon the lessee in such a case to show that he had performed the terms upon which his right depends. *Forbes* v. *Connolly* (1875), 5 Gr. 657 at p. 661. It is, however, well settled that to show due performance the lessee need not necessarily show punctual performance. It is enough to show that the covenants have been performed at the time when the lessor is required to observe or to perform his promise. *Loveless* v. *Fitzgerald* (1909), 42 S.C.R. 254; *Starkey* v. *Barton*, [1909] 1 Ch. 284."

The first question I have to decide is whether the lessee has "duly and regularly" paid the rent reserved by the lease. The lessee says that he need not show punctual performance. He relies on *Starkey* v. *Barton*, [1909] 1 Ch. 284. There the lessee had the right to purchase at any time during the tenancy on giving 3 months' notice, provided she should "in the meantime have duly paid the said rent reserved". One instalment had not been paid at the due date but it had been paid at the time when the notice of intention to purchase was given. The *ratio* of the judgment of Parker J. is contained in the following extract [p. 290]: "I am of opinion that on the true construction of the clause creating the condition precedent in the present case 'duly' does not mean punctually, and I think that, within the meaning of the clause, the plaintiff could truly say on March 20, 1908, that she had since the commencement of her tenancy duly paid the rent reserved by the tenancy agreement. I hold, therefore, that all the conditions precedent to the exercise of the option were in fact performed."

This judgment is in line with *Finch* v. *Underwood* (1876), 2 Ch. D. 310, which held that covenants have been duly observed and performed if there is no existing right of action under them at the time when the renewal lease is applied for.

The present case appears to me to be altogether different from *Starkey* v. *Barton*. The lessee is required to show that he has "duly and regularly" paid the rent. In a phrase such as this, the word "regularly" surely must have some meaning. I think that it compels the lessee to show that he has paid at fixed intervals or periods according to the rule established by the parties themselves when they signed the lease. In other words, I am saying that it means punctually, at the due date. *Starkey* v. *Barton* does not, in my opinion, establish any general rule that delay in payment of the rent is immaterial regardless of the wording of the clause, so long as the rent is paid up to the date of the exercise of the option. This is really the submission which has to be made and which was in fact made in this case on behalf of the lessee. It ignores the fundamental problem which is to show performance of a condition precedent. This is not a case of an occasional or inadvertent or trival default. If I were to hold that in this case rent has been duly and regularly paid after the record of irregular payments extending over a period of 2-$^1/_2$ years which I have set out in detail above, then words have no meaning.

Counsel for the lessee also submitted that the order relieving against forfeiture wiped the slate clean and made it impossible to look at the prior default in the payment of rent in order to determine whether the right to renew was lost. The proposition is correct so far as the original term is concerned: *Dendy* v. *Evans*, [1910] 1 K.B. 263, but the order does not operate so as to excuse performance of conditions precedent to the right of renewal. The distinction is clearly made in *Finch* v. *Underwood*, 2 Ch. D. 310. The Court has power to relieve against forfeiture but no power to excuse performance of conditions precedent.

The plaintiff also complained of numerous breaches of covenant disentitling the defendant to a renewal. As might be expected in a lease of this kind, the covenants are numerous and onerous. I am satisfied that the defendant has performed the covenants as to maintenance of the golfcourse and equipment, and the flow of water to the plaintiff's own house on the course. Whatever interruptions there were in the supply of water to this house were due to the inadequate wells and a defective distribution system provided by the lessor. The lessee was under no obligation to increase the water supply, or to put in a new system. However, the existing installation was so inadequate that the lessee put in a supply from the township system and included the plaintiff's house in this new installation.

The buildings should all have been painted in 1948, 1950, and 1952. The evidence which I accept is that neither the club-house nor the tenant-house was painted in 1948. These are the two important buildings. They have been painted twice during the term of the lease, instead of three times. There is a breach of covenant here and it had not been remedied at the time when the notice of renewal was given.

There is another breach of covenant in the alteration of the club-house. This was done in 1952 without the written consent or any consent of the lessor. These alterations improve the property and were made to comply with the requirements of the Liquor Control Board. They will also in all probability increase the taxes which the landlord has to pay. The defendant made these alterations with his eyes open. The plaintiff told him at this time that he took the position that he had lost the right to renew.

There will be judgment for the plaintiff for possession of the demised premises and the goods and chattels mentioned in the statement of claim. There will be a reference to the Master at Toronto to determine the *mesne* profits from January 1, 1953. The plaintiff is entitled to his costs of the action and the reference. The counterclaim is dismissed with costs.

Judgment for plaintiff.

[In *McLaughlin* v. *Bodnarchuk* (1957), 8 D.L.R. 2d 596, 22 W.W.R. (N.S.) 60 (B.C.C.A.) the majority of the Court held that a covenant for renewal if the lessee "duly and regularly pays [the] rent" did not import punctuality so as to disentitle a lessee to renewal where there had been inadvertent default in three successive months.

See also *Richter* v. *Koskey and Adler*, [1953] 4 D.L.R. 509, [1953] O.W.N. 746, stating that the burden of proving compliance with conditions precedent to renewal is on the tenant. In *Young* v. *Van Beneen*, [1953] 3 D.L.R. 702, 8 W.W.R. (N.S.) 702 (B.C.C.A.), the provision for renewal was held unenforceable by reason of indefiniteness of its terms.]

[A three year lease contained a covenant by the lessor to renew it for a further three years under "the like agreements and provisions as are herein contained (including the present covenant for renewal)". Is a perpetual right of renewal created by this lease? See *Re Greenwood's Agreement*, *Parkus* v. *Greenwood*, [1950] 1 All E.R. 436 (C.A) rev'g [1950] 1 Ch. 33, [1949] 2 All E.R. 743. *Cf. Auld* v. *Scales*, [1947] S.C.R. 543, [1947] 4 D.L.R. 721, rev'g [1947] 1 D.L.R. 760, 19 M.P.R. 406 which aff'd [1946] 3 D.L.R. 613.]

[L and T entered into a five year lease, effective from April 1, 1950, which contained an option of renewal for three years on the giving of three months' notice. The lease was not registered under the Land Titles Act, R.S.O. 1950, c. 197. In 1953 L sold the premises to L^1 and the transfer was registered in June of that year. On February 9, 1955, L^1 served a notice to quit on T. In the previous November, 1954, T had served a notice exercising the option of renewal. When T did not surrender possession at the end of March, 1955, L^1 brought action. Is he entitled to succeed? Would it make any difference if L^1 knew of the lease and option before he entered into the contract of sale with L? See *Re Jung and Montgomery*, [1955] 5 D.L.R. 287, [1955] O.W.N. 931 (C.A.). See *Armour*, The Purchase of Land under Lease, (1898) 18 C.L.T. 1.]

[A covenant to renew is indivisible; and if a tenant assigns his term in part of the demised premises, neither he nor his assignee may enforce the covenant: see *Alexander Brown Milling & Elevator Co.* v. *C.P.R.* (1910), 42 S.C.R. 600.]

[On assignment of the landlord's reversion, it is no longer necessary for the tenant to attorn to the assignee: see Landlord and Tenant Act, R.S.O. 1960, c. 206, ss. 60, 61. The tenant is protected, however, against the assignee in respect of payment of rent or breach of condition for non-payment of rent before notice of the assignment. Notice is not, however, required in respect of breach of other covenants or conditions in the lease and the assignee may enforce them despite the failure to give notice of the assignment: see *Scaltock* v. *Harston* (1875), 1 C.P.D. 106, 45 L.J.Q.B. 125.

Assignees of the reversion now have the benefit of all covenants entered into between the assignor and the tenant which "touch and concern", or "run" with, the land and may assert the remedies available for their enforcement. Similarly, the tenant and his assignees may enforce such covenants which are in their favour against the landlord or his assignees: see Landlord and Tenant Act, R.S.O. 1960, c. 206, ss. 3 to 7. The common law was different: see *Cheshire*, Modern Law of Real Property (1962, 9th ed.), pp. 431-33. The problems arising in connection with enforcement of covenants by or against assignees of the original parties are considered in chapter XII, *infra*.]

4. USE AND ENJOYMENT OF LEASED PREMISES

(*a*) *Landlord's Obligations*

MARKHAM v. PAGET. Chancery Division. [1908] 1 Ch. 697

Defendant agreed "to let" certain premises to plaintiff, excepting minerals with power to work them. No power was reserved to let down the surface in working the minerals but by a previous mining lease, the lessee company had been empowered to let down the surface, and owing to its mining operations there was a subsidence which rendered plaintiff's premises uninhabitable for a certain period. The tenancy agreement between plaintiff and defendant was not made subject to the previous mining lease. Plaintiff sued for damages alleging (1) derogation from grant and (2) breach of an implied contract for quiet enjoyment.

SWINFEN EADY J. (after reciting the facts and finding that defendant was in breach of an implied obligation not to derogate from grant):... There remains the further question whether the plaintiff can recover upon an implied contract for quiet enjoyment contained in the agreement for letting the hall. It is conceded that if the word "demise" had been the operative word in the agreement there would have been an implied contract for quiet enjoyment, but it is contended that a contract will not be implied from any other words.

In *Hart* v. *Windsor*, 12 M. & W. 68, 85, Parke B., in delivering the reserved judgment of the Court of Exchequer said: "It is clear that from the word 'demise,' in a lease under seal, the law implies a covenant, in a lease not under seal, a contract, for title to the estate merely, that is, for quiet enjoyment against the lessor and all that come in under him by title, and against others claiming by title paramount during the term; and the word 'let,' or any equivalent words (Shepp. Touch. 272), which constitute a lease, have, no doubt, the same effect, but not more. Shepp. Touch. 165, 167."

In *Bandy* v. *Cartwright*, 8 Ex. 913, 919, there was a parol letting by some writing not under seal, and the tenant's quiet enjoyment was disturbed by a distress for arrears of a rent-charge lawfully claimed under a title paramount to the lessors. The language of the writing is not set out in the reports, but from the argument in the *Law Journal* it would appear that the word "demise" was not used, as counsel for the plaintiff, who was alleging an implied covenant for a good title and also for quiet enjoyment, urged that, "There is no particular virtue in the word 'demise.'" The inference rather is that the plaintiff's writing did not contain this word. In any case, however, the Court held that on an instrument of demise, not under seal, with only that contract which the law would imply, there was an implied contract for quiet enjoyment during the term, though not a covenant for title. This was followed by *Hall* v. *City of London Brewery Co.*, 2 B. & S. 737, 741. The agreement there was not under seal, and the operative words were, "The said company do hereby agree to let," and the precise point raised by the demurrer was whether upon such a contract a promise of quiet enjoyment during the term is implied in law. The Court of Queen's Bench held that it was. Cockburn C. J. said: "We cannot overrule *Bandy* v. *Cartwright*; and it is inconsistent with common sense that, when a man is let into possession for a year, a promise by the lessor for quiet enjoyment against himself and all that claim by title under him should not be implied." He also said that *Bandy* v. *Cartwright* was a direct authority that a contract for quiet enjoyment is implied in a contract of demise, and that that case was good law. Wightman and Blackburn JJ. concurred; and Compton J., without giving any opinion of his own, said that *Bandy* v. *Cartwright* was binding on that Court. Moreover, it appears from the reference during the argument to *Messent* v. *Reynolds*, (1846) 3 C.B. 194, and to the judgment of Cresswell J. in that case, that any difference between the legal effect of the word "demise" and the word "let" was a point raised and argued.

The same point was raised again in *Mostyn* v. *West Mostyn Coal and Iron Co.*, 1 C.P.D. 145. In that case there was a counter-claim for damages for breach of an implied covenant for quiet enjoyment. By the lease certain property was "let" to the defendants, but the point was taken that it did not appear that among the operative words the word "demise" was used. It was nevertheless held that the lessees could obtain damages for breach of an implied covenant for quiet enjoyment. Brett J. said: "The case of *Hart* v. *Windsor* is an authority that the word 'let' has the same effect in this respect" — i.e., as to implying a covenant — "as the word 'demise,' and that any other equivalent word would have the same effect. I think we must take it on this record that the lease did contain the word 'let' or 'demise'." Archibald J. agreed that the lease as it appeared on the record imported a covenant for quiet enjoyment, and that the lessees would be entitled to recover damages for the breach of it; and Lindley J. agreed that on the counter-claim the defendants were entitled to some damages for the breach of the implied covenant for quiet enjoyment.

In 1889 the point was again raised in the Court of Appeal in *Robinson* v. *Kilvert*, 41 Ch. D. 88, 96. The agreement there was a short agreement in writing whereby the defendants "agree to let" to the plaintiff certain premises. The plaintiff alleged a breach of the implied contract for quiet enjoyment, and this was the point pressed on the appeal. Lindley L. J. said: "*Bandy* v. *Cartwright* shews that under a demise by parol there is an implied covenant for quiet enjoyment"; and he added that if the evidence had been sufficient he would have been prepared to hold that there was a breach. Then followed *Baynes & Co.* v. *Lloyd & Sons*, [1895] 1 Q.B. 820, 826; [1895] 2 Q.B. 610, 615, 616. In that case the plaintiffs sued for breach of an implied covenant for quiet enjoyment; the document sued upon was an underlease which did not contain any express covenant for title or quiet enjoyment, nor was the word "demise" used. Lord Russell of Killowen C. J., in the Court below, held that the law imported a covenant for quiet enjoyment in all cases where the relation of landlord and tenant is established by instrument under seal, and imported a contract to the same effect where the instrument is not under seal; and added: "I think, as stated by Cockburn C. J. in the latter case" — *Hall* v. *City of London Brewery Co.* — "that the law is founded in good sense, and that a covenant for quiet enjoyment is imported *ex vi termini.*" Lord Russell C. J. however, held that the plaintiff could not recover in that case, as the implied covenant had determined with the interest of the lessor, which had expired. That case was affirmed by the Court of Appeal on the same ground as Lord Russell C. J. had decided it, namely, that any implied covenant had determined with the estate of the lessor; but Kay L. J., in delivering the judgment of the Court of Appeal, said: "The weight of authority is in favour of the view that a covenant in law is not implied from the mere relation of landlord and tenant, but only from certain words used in creating the lease." This opinion was considered by the Queen's Bench Division shortly afterwards. *Budd-Scott* v. *Daniell*, [1902] 2 K.B. 351, 356, was a case in which the defendant counter-claimed for breach of an implied contract for quiet enjoyment. There was a written agreement not under seal, whereby the plaintiff "agrees to let" a house for a year. The word "demise" was not used. Lord Alverstone C. J. considered that on principle and common sense an agreement for quiet enjoyment ought to be implied; and, after reviewing the authorities, he treated the observations of the Court of Appeal in *Baynes & Co.* v. *Lloyd & Sons* as dicta only, and said that the Court was not bound to treat that case as an authority binding on the Court on that point; and he held that, where there is a letting, a covenant for quiet enjoyment is to be implied from the mere relationship of the parties. Darling and Channell JJ. concurred, the latter pointing out that the expression of the opinion of the Court of Appeal in *Baynes & Co.* v. *Lloyd & Sons* was different from what he had always understood to be the law, and from what all the text-book writers had understood to be the law up to that time.

And in the subsequent case of *Jones* v. *Lavington*, [1903] 1 K.B. 253, the Court of Appeal did not itself treat *Baynes & Co.* v. *Lloyd & Sons* as having decided that a contract for quiet enjoyment could not be implied from the word "let".

Under these circumstances I am bound to follow what the current of authority for more than the last sixty years has determined to be the law, and what three Chief Justices of England have successively held to be the common law, both upon principle and authority, and to be the only view consistent with common sense. I therefore determine that the plaintiff is entitled to recover against the defendant on the footing that the tenancy agreement contains an implied contract for quiet enjoyment.

The further question was raised whether any implied contract extends to a disturbance by title paramount to the lessor.

[His Lordship here discussed the relevant authorities and continued as follows.]

Although *Baynes & Co.* v. *Lloyd & Sons* is not an authority that any implied covenant is limited to the acts of the lessor, or persons claiming under him, the subsequent case of *Jones* v. *Lavington* did decide that point; and although it only purported to follow *Baynes & Co.* v. *Lloyd & Sons*, and notwithstanding other decisions to the contrary, it would be my duty as a judge of first instance to follow the latest decision of the Court of Appeal, and decide — if it were necessary to decide the point — that any implied contract did not extend to persons claiming by title paramount; but as the company in the present case claim through and under the defendant, it is not in my opinion necessary that I should give any decision on this point, and accordingly, I abstain from doing so.

The result is that there must be judgment for the plaintiff against the defendant for £700 for damages for breach of the implied contract for quiet enjoyment. The measure of damages would also be the same on the footing of the defendant derogating from her grant.

Judgment for plaintiff.

[In *Miller* v. *Emcer Products Ltd.*, [1956] Ch. 304, [1956] 1 All E.R. 237 (C.A.), Romer L. J. speaking for the Court of Appeal, said:

"It has long been established that if a lessor demises property to a tenant and enters into no express covenants for title or for quiet enjoyment, certain promises are implied by him by force of the word 'demise', viz., that he is entitled to grant some term in the demised premises, and that the lessee shall have quiet enjoyment of the premises: *Burnett* v. *Lynch* (1826) 5 B. & C. at p. 609; *Hart* v. *Windsor* (1844) 12 M. & W. at p. 85. It was pointed out in *Line* v. *Stephenson* (1838) 4 Bing. N.C. 678; 5 Bing. N.C. 183, that these promises are more properly to be regarded as embodied in one single implied covenant, and that this covenant may be broken either by want of title or by the eviction of the tenant. It was also, however, decided in *Line* v. *Stephenson* that there is no room for the implication of the covenant in a demise if the lessor enters into an express covenant for quiet enjoyment. The reason for this is that an express covenant as to one branch of the covenant implied by the word 'demise' excludes the other, on the principle *expressio unius est exclusio alterius*: per LORD ABINGER, C. B. (5 Bing, N. C. at p. 184).

"Accordingly in the underlease now in question there can be no implied covenant by the landlords either as to title or for quiet enjoyment. Counsel for the tenant conceded this, but he contended that the implied promise by a lessor to put his tenant into possession at the commencement of the tenancy, which was recognised in *Coe* v. *Clay*, 5 Bing. 440, has an existence of its own which is independent of the covenant either for title or for quiet enjoyment, and which is accordingly unaffected by the principle of *Line* v. *Stephenson*. Counsel argued in the alternative that that principle only displaces implied covenants which are in *pari materia* with covenants for title and for quiet enjoyment, and that such cannot be said of the obligation in *Coe* v. *Clay*. As to the former of these submissions he relied on a passage in the judgment of Chitty. J., in *Wallis* v. *Hands*, [1893] 2 Ch 75. In that case the plaintiff in 1887 took a lease of certain minerals which, to his knowledge, had already been included in a lease to other parties which had been granted in 1884. The plaintiff never entered into possession under the lease of 1887, although it purported to be a lease in possession, and in 1888 the lessees of the lease of 1884 assigned the term thereby demised. The plaintiff then brought an action against the assigns in order to establish the priority of his own title over them and against his lessor on the implied covenant for quiet enjoyment, for the lease of 1887 contained no express covenant in that behalf. Chitty, J., held that in the circumstances the plaintiff had no more than an *interesse termini*, and accordingly could not maintain an action on the implied covenant. The decision on this point has in effect been overruled by s. 149 of the Law of Property Act, 1925, which abolished the doctrine of *interesse termini*. In so far, therefore, as the decisions in *Coe* v. *Clay* and *Jinks* v. *Edwards*, 11 Ex. 775, may have depended on the view that any covenant for quiet enjoyment, whether express or implied, could not be asserted by a tenant before actual entry, the basis of the decisions has been taken away by the Law of Property Act, 1925, since it is provided in terms by s. 149 (2) of that Act that a lease operates from the date fixed for commencement of the term without actual entry. In the course of his judgment on this matter, however, Chitty, J., expressed himself as follows, [1893] 2 Ch. at p. 85:

> 'The law provides a person having an *interesse termini* with an adequate remedy against the granter of the term, without there being any necessity to have recourse to an action on the covenant for quiet enjoyment; he can bring an action against the granter of the term for not putting him in possession: see *Coe* v. *Clay* and *Jinks* v. *Edwards*. This right of action is also founded on implied covenant. The present action is not to enforce any such right; nor are there any facts proved which would give rise to it.'

Counsel for the tenant submitted accordingly on that that the learned judge was expressing the view that the *Coe* v. *Clay* obligation (if I may so describe it) has in any event a distinct operation from that of the covenant for quiet enjoyment, and imposes on the landlords a liability separate from that which arises under the latter covenant. The isolation and independence of the obligation from the implied covenant for title and quiet enjoyment appears indeed also to be recognised in some of the text-books (see, e.g., 20 HALSBURY'S LAWS OF ENGLAND (2nd Edn.), pp. 242, 243, and HILL & REDMAN'S LAW OF LANDLORD AND TENANT (11th Edn.), para. 113). This view would also appear to receive support at first sight from the fact that in neither *Coe* v. *Clay* nor in *Jinks* v. *Edwards* did the tenants claim relief under either an implied covenant for quiet enjoyment or an implied covenant for title; in each case they rested their claim on the duty of a landlord, implicit in the relationship into which he enters with his tenant, to put the tenant into possession at the beginning of the tenancy; and it was on that ground and no other that the court awarded damages. I think, however, that even apart from the question, already mentioned, of suing on the covenant for quiet enjoyment before entry, this point is sufficiently answered by the fact that in neither of these cases was a formal lease executed by the landlord; in *Coe* v. *Clay* the letting was oral, and in *Jinks* v. *Edwards* the tenancy arose out of an agreement for a lease. It was held in *Bandy* v. *Cartwright* (1853) 8 Exch. 913, and had for long been the law that no covenant for title is implied in oral lettings. The question whether a covenant for quiet enjoyment should be implied in parol lettings and in mere agreements was an uncertain one over a period of many years, and it was not until *Markham* v. *Paget*, [1908] 1 Ch. 697, that Swinfen-Eady, J., after review of the authorities, decided definitely that it should.

"In these circumstances it may well be that the actions in *Coe* v. *Clay* and *Jinks* v. *Edwards* were not brought or decided on an implied covenant for quiet enjoyment or title because it was thought that no such implication existed or could be relied on in view of the informal character of the lettings which were there in question. For myself, I do not think that there is any ground for implying the *Coe* v. *Clay* obligation in addition to the covenant for title and quiet enjoyment which is implicit in a formal instrument of demise or grant. By the very force of the liability which is imposed on a lessor under the covenant for quiet enjoyment, the tenant is entitled to be put into possession of the premises which are leased to him at the outset of his tenancy (*Ludwell* v. *Newman* (1795), 6 Term Rep. 458) and to remain quietly in possession thereof throughout the term. Counsel for the tenant relied on the statement by Chitty, J., in *Wallis* v. *Hands*, [1893] 2 Ch. at p. 84, that

> '... the essence of a breach of a covenant for quiet enjoyment in a lease appears to me to be a disturbance of the lessee's possession.'

I do not, however, think that Chitty, J., was intending to say that the covenant does not begin to operate until the tenant has obtained possession, for it is quite clear that it operates from the moment when the demised term starts to run. There is, in my opinion, no necessity, therefore, for implying the *Coe* v. *Clay* obligation in a formal demise, and I would accordingly have felt considerable difficulty in implying it in the underlease even if no express covenant for quiet enjoyment has been incorporated. Even, however, if I am wrong in that, I am quite clear that any such implication is excluded by reason of this express covenant on the principle of *Line* v. *Stephenson.*

"Counsel for the tenant rightly said (and this was his alternative way of putting the point) that an express covenant will operate only to displace an implied covenant if they both cover the same ground—or, in other words, if they are in *pari materia* (NORTON ON DEEDS (2nd Edn.) p. 601). This is true, but it appears to me, as I have already indicated, that the purpose of the *Coe* v. *Clay* obligation is fully covered by the covenant for quiet enjoyment which is implied from the word 'demise'. Such a covenant entitles the tenant to be put into possession as well as to remain in possession thereafter, and this is exactly the purpose of the obligation which was implied in *Coe* v. *Clay*. In any case I find it impossible to regard a covenant to put the tenant in possession at the beginning of the term as being otherwise than in *pari materia* with a covenant that he should remain in possession thereafter. It was not suggested that the form of the express covenant in cl. 3 (3) of the underlease is of narrower scope than a covenant for quiet enjoyment which is implied from the word 'demise', and it accordingly follows that this covenant also answers the purpose of the obligation in *Coe* v. *Clay*.

"In these circumstances it is not possible, as I think, successfully to contend that if, contrary to my own view, the obligation on which the tenant relies can be incorporated by implication in a formal lease, it can survive the eliminating effect of an express covenant for quiet enjoyment such as that which is contained in the underlease."]

[The usual covenant for quiet enjoyment, e.g., as in the Short Forms of Leases Act, R.S.O. 1960, c. 373, does not cover acts done under title paramount. Of course, it does not make the lessor liable for acts not done under his authority, nor is he liable for tortious acts of persons claiming under him or deriving title from him: see *Matania* v. *National Provincial Bank Ltd.*, [1936] 2 All E.R. 633 (C.A.); *cf. Sandal* v. *Grand Union Holdings Ltd.*, [1955] 4 D.L.R. 266 (B.C.).

In *Owen* v. *Gadd*, [1956] 2 Q.B. 99, [1956] 2 All E.R. 28 (C.A.), Lord Evershed M. R. speaking of the scope of the covenant for quiet enjoyment said: "I am prepared to assume that the disturbance, the interruption, must at least be of what is called a direct and physical character"; and Romer L. J. in the same case stated that there must be "some physical or direct interference with the enjoyment of the demised premises", and in this latter connection the purpose for which the premises are let is a relevant consideration. The covenant is not concerned with mere interference with possession, in the sense of trespass: see *Blazewich* v. *Stefanik* (No. 2), [1947] 1 W.W.R. 627, 55 Man. R. 163.

In *Hormidge* v. *Magur*, [1947] 1 D.L.R. 415, [1946] 3 W.W.R. 668, 63 B.C.R. 188 (C.A.), the landlord slapped the tenant's children near the entrance to the tenant's apartment and threatened, on the back porch of the apartment, to cut the tenant's throat. The tenant sued for damages for breach of an implied covenant for quiet enjoyment. Any doubt about the result?

Damages for breach of the covenant may include loss of profits by reason of the landlord's interference with the tenant's use and enjoyment of the premises: see *Budnitsky* v. *Gorstein*, [1947] 3 D.L.R. 905, [1947] 1 W.W.R. 1118, 55 Man. R. 311.]

EDGE v. BOILEAU. Queen's Bench. 1885. 16 Q.B.D. 117

Motion for a new trial or to enter judgment for defendants in an action for breach of a covenant for quiet enjoyment. The covenant provided that the lessee, paying the rent when due and observing the covenants on his part to be observed (which included a covenant to repair), should peaceably and quietly hold and enjoy the premises. Plaintiff's rent was in arrear and the premises were out of repair, whereupon an agent of defendants by their authority served notices on plaintiff's sub-tenants requiring them not to pay any rent to plaintiff but to pay it to defendants, threatening legal proceedings on failure to comply with this demand. One of the sub-tenants did pay his rent to defendants before defendants, at plaintiff's insistence, withdrew the notices. Plaintiff alleged loss of rent and damage to the value of his leasehold. The jury awarded plaintiff £100 damages.

POLLOCK B.: The plaintiff claims damages for breach of a covenant for quiet enjoyment.

The defendants deny that any such breach has taken place, and say further that there was a failure to perform conditions precedent, rent being in arrear, and the covenant to repair not being performed. In my judgment there is sufficient evidence to shew that there has been a breach of the covenant for quiet enjoyment. The covenant is in the usual terms. The facts are these. During the plaintiff's term, there being some rent in arrear, the agent for the defendants, the plaintiff's lessors, by their authority sends to the tenants of the plaintiff a notice desiring them not to pay their rents to the plaintiff, but to pay them to the defendants, and threatening them with legal proceedings in default of compliance with the notice. It is obvious what the probable results of such a notice would be. It is impossible, as it seems to me, to hold that, under the circumstances of this case, and having regard to what actually followed, this notice can be treated as no more than a mere false and idle claim or threat of which no notice might be taken. To my mind there is evidence of a substantial disturbance of the plaintiff's quiet enjoyment of the property demised. The case of *Whichcot* v. *Nine*, Br. & G. 81, is the only authority to which we were referred on this subject. When the report of that is looked at, it is very short and simply comes to this, that the mere telling a tenant not to pay his rent is not necessarily a breach of the covenant for quiet enjoyment. There is nothing said as to the circumstances under which the man was told not to pay his rent, and it appears that he did pay his rent notwithstanding the notice. I can understand that there might be circumstances under which such a notice might be treated as a mere idle threat and as not amounting to a breach of the covenant for quiet enjoyment because there was no substantial interference with the enjoyment. Here I think that there is a substantial interference with the rights of the plaintiff, and one which might very well seriously affect the value of his property. Then it was contended that the covenant for quiet enjoyment and the covenants to be performed by the plaintiff were not to be read independently, but as dependent covenants, and that the payment of rent and repairing were therefore conditions precedent. I should have thought that point very clear even without authority. But there appears to be a case directly in point, viz., *Dawson* v. *Dyer*, 5 B. & Ad. 584. In that case the same argument was put before the Court as in the present case, and the Court held the argument untenable. That case seems to be conclusive in favour of the plaintiff on this point. For these reasons I think the application must be refused.

MANISTY J. concurred. *Rule refused.*

[A covenant for quiet enjoyment in a lease of unfurnished premises cannot be invoked by a tenant to support a claim for damages or to justify refusal to pay rent where the premises are infested by mice: see *Smith* v. *Galin*, (1956), 3 D.L.R. 2d 302, [1956] O.W.N. 432 (C.A.).]

HEAD v. COMMUNITY ESTATES AND BUILDING CO. LTD. Ontario High Court. [1944] O.R. 353, [1944] 3 D.L.R. 189

HOPE J.: This is an action for damages brought by eighteen tenants of an apartment house in Toronto owned by the defendant company.

The following statement of facts agreed to by counsel for both parties was filed as ex. 1:

"IT IS AGREED:—

"1. That the plaintiffs at all material times were tenants of the defendant, occupying apartments in the Avenue Homes Apartments, 869-875 Avenue Road, in the City of Toronto.

"2. That the services provided by the landlord included the supply of heat and hot and cold water.

"3. That the same written lease was in effect between the landlord and each tenant, the form used being the form provided by Grand & Toy Limited, Toronto, and described as Form 231.

"4. That the apartments were without heat from March 3 to March 11 inclusive, 1943, and were without hot water from March 3 to March 29 inclusive, 1943.

"5. That during the period March 3 to March 29 inclusive, 1943, by reason of the lack of heat and the lack of hot water, the tenants incurred respectively the disbursements set out in the Statement of Claim."

The defendant's counsel's agreement was qualified to the extent that he did not concur with the precise dates mentioned in paras. 4 and 5 above, claiming that the period in question was of slightly shorter duration. On the evidence I am however of opinion that the dates mentioned in the two paragraphs referred to must be accepted. It may be quite true that the heating equipment in the apartment building resumed operation on the evening of March 9th, at which time delivery of fuel oil was temporarily resumed to the defendant; nevertheless it is quite evident that it took approximately 36 to 48 hours for the temperature of the building to be raised to a suitable and reasonable one.

The pertinent clause in the lease referred to in para. 3 (*supra*) reads as follows: "The Lessor covenants with the Lessee that the Lessor will during the term between the 15th day of October and the 15th day of May provide suitable means for heating and furnish heat for the said premises up to a reasonable temperature for the reasonable use thereof by the Lessee, except during the making of repairs; but should the Lessor make default in so doing, he shall not be liable for indirect or consequential damages or damages for personal discomfort or illness."

The difficulties which brought about this action arose out of the Oil Controller's restrictions on the use of fuel oil in certain commercial institutions and other buildings.

The defendant received a letter from the Oil Controller dated October 8, 1941, (ex. 5) drawing attention to the uncertainty of the supplies of fuel oil and stating: "The category of heating, which includes your installation, would be one of the first to be curtailed. Therefore, since this may result in a possible shutdown of your heating plant, we urge that you seriously study the changing of your plant from oil to coal without delay."

[The learned Justice then reviewed communications and dealings between the Oil Controller and defendant, referred to the grants of temporary permits for oil coupled with insistence that the heating plant be converted, and then continued as follows:]

On March 3rd [1943] the oil supply was finally exhausted and no temporary permit issued by the Oil Controller.

It is to be noted that the defendant's covenant above quoted is firstly to "provide suitable means for heating;" secondly to "furnish heat... up to a reasonable temperature for the reasonable use... by the lessee."

In view of the repeated warnings and failure to take effective action, I am of the opinion that the defendant is guilty of a breach of the covenant to provide "suitable means for heating" in the defendant's failure to effect the conversion of his heating plant from oil to coal.

On the evidence it is abundantly clear that the defendant has also been guilty of a breach of the covenant to furnish heat up to a reasonable temperature. The evidence was that the temperature in some of the apartments during the period in question was as low as 27 and 28 degrees above zero.

The covenant contained in the lease excepts the application of the defendant's covenant during the making of repairs. It cannot, in my opinion, be reasonably argued that the conversion of the plant was in nature of the making of repairs.

The plaintiffs found their claim firstly on the covenant to supply heat as cited and secondly on an implied covenant to supply hot water.

That a breach of such covenant entitles the lessee to damages was determined in *Johnston* v. *Givens*, [1941], 4 D.L.R. 634, O.R. 281. That there was the alleged breach is amply established by the evidence.

The question of implied covenants was discussed and decided by Middleton J. in *Brymer* v. *Thompson* (1915), 23 D.L.R. 840, 34 O.L.R. 194. In my opinion there was clearly an implied covenant in the circumstances here present by the defendant to provide the lessees with water supply, both cold and hot, for the reasonable use of the lessees.

In its pleadings the defendant suggests that the doctrine of impossibility of performance, owing to circumstances beyond its control protected it from the claims of the plaintiffs—although at the trial, as I understood counsel's argument, this defence resolved itself into one of frustration.

Neither of these grounds are tenable in the light of the evidence. Measures ultimately taken by the defendant to meet the situation could have been effected much earlier by the defendant—even in summer weather—and so caused little or no trouble or inconvenience to the tenants.

I must find for the plaintiffs.

In *Inverarity* v. *Muller* (1926), 31 O.W.N. 339, it was stated that damages for the breach of a covenant to supply heat should not be pared down when the breach is due to the landlord's meanness.

The same should prevail where, as in this case, the landlord has ample warning which should have enabled him to take steps to provide "suitable means of heating" in due season —and where the landlord with rare persistence continued to rely on his oil-burning equipment, so long, in fact, that as the Deputy Oil Controller testified the defendant was the last oil consumer of its class to effect conversion for use of other fuel.

Bearing in mind the restriction on the liability of the defendant by reason of the exception in the covenant in the lease, viz., "not be liable for indirect or consequential damages or damages for personal discomfort or illness," I find on the evidence that the damages claimed by the various plaintiffs respectively, as set out in particulars filed as part of ex. 1 herein, have been substantiated save as to Jas. W. Kerr whose damages for room and board should only be computed to March 12th instead of March 17th as set out. I do not think that the defendant can complain seriously that some tenants chose accommodation in first-class hotels in comparable substitution for the apartments leased from the defendant.

The various claims for meals, for extra electricity consumed, for laundry and other out-of-pocket expenses, are fully justified. However, the exemption from liability in the covenant precludes the plaintiffs' claims for the general damages set out in the prayer.

There shall therefore be judgment for each of the plaintiffs for the respective claim of each for out-of-pocket expenses.

Judgment for plaintiffs.

[In *Regis Property Co. Ltd.* v. *Redman*, [1956] 2 Q.B. 612, [1956] 2 All E.R. 335 (C.A.), a landlord covenanted with a tenant "to use its best endeavours... to maintain at all times a reasonable and adequate supply of hot water for domestic purposes... through the central installation... and to keep the radiators in the flat sufficiently and adequately heated through the central heating installation.... Provided that the landlord shall not be liable to supply hot water for the central heating installation except during the cold season between dates to be determined at the landlord's discretion..." Jenkins L. J. referred to this covenant as follows: "...it was argued that the form of the covenant as to the supply of constant hot water and central heating was such as to impose no legal obligation on the plaintiffs, inasmuch as they only covenanted to use their best endeavours to maintain the supply of constant hot water and central heating, and were themselves to determine the dates marking the beginning and end of the cold season to which the provision of central heating was to be limited. I do not agree that the covenant imposed no legal obligation. The plaintiffs assumed a legal obligation to do their best. Nor do I think it would be open to them to nullify the covenant as regards central heating by a purely arbitrary selection of dates. It may be that a covenant in this qualified form is *qua* legal obligation to some measurable extent less valuable than an unqualified covenant (which I imagine few proprietors of flats would be prepared to enter into on a matter of this sort)."]

JOHNSTON v. GIVENS. Ontario Court of Appeal. [1941] O.R. 281, [1914] 4 D.L.R. 634

The judgment of the Court was delivered by ROBERTSON C. J. O.:

An appeal from the judgment of Judge Lovering of the County Court of the County of York, dated April 21, 1941, dismissing the plaintiff's action with costs.

The action is by a landlord for rent. By lease dated September 8, 1939, the plaintiff let to the defendant a suite in an apartment house on Chatsworth Drive, in Toronto, for the term of two years, to be computed from October 1, 1939, at a rental of $70 per month. The premises were expressly let for use and occupation as a private dwelling, for the sole occupancy of the lessee and his immediate family, and for no other purpose. The lease, which is made in pursuance of the Short Forms of Leases Act, R.S.O. 1937, c. 159, contains many special covenants. Among them is a covenant by the lessor during the continuance of the term, between October 15th and May 1st in each year of the term to provide or procure to be provided, suitable means of heating, and furnish, or procure to be furnished, heat in the demised premises up to a reasonable temperature, for the reasonable use thereof by the lessee, in such manner as is possible with the existing heating equipment. There is also a covenant by the lessor to supply hot water for domestic purposes. There is the usual covenant by the lessor for quiet enjoyment.

The lessee took possession at the beginning of the term, and continued in possession until the end of November. He paid the rent for the two months of October and November. During the time of his occupation he made many complaints that the lessor failed to live up to representations made during the negotiations for the lease, and to perform covenants contained in the lease itself. The most serious of these complaints was that the lessor failed to heat the premises, and to supply hot water for domestic purposes, according to the covenants in the lease. At the end of November the lessee vacated the leased premises and refused to pay any more rent. In April of the following year the lessor found another tenant for the apartment at a slightly reduced rent. He then brought this action for the rent accrued for the time the premises were vacant, and for the amount by which the monthly rent received from the new tenant fell short of the rent reserved by the lease in question up to the bringing of the action.

The trial Judge accepted the evidence of the lessee and his wife in respect to the failure to supply heat and hot water for domestic purposes. He found that the conditions of which they complained were drawn to the attention of the landlord many times, and were not remedied, and that the neglect of the landlord gave rise to a condition in the premises that was injurious to the health of the occupants, and caused them considerable discomfort. He held that on these grounds the defendant was justified in vacating the premises as he did, and dismissed the action.

It is not entirely clear upon what legal principle the learned County Judge proceeded in holding that the landlord's claim for rent was defeated....

The landlord's obligation to supply heat and hot water arises from contract. Beyond question, no one could live in the apartments in the winter time if they were not heated, and the only means of heating was the furnace in the landlord's control. The lessee knew that when he accepted the lease and protected himself by the covenant of the landlord already referred to. What is his remedy when the landlord has failed to fulfil the covenant?

The landlord has protected himself in respect of the tenant's breaches of covenant by a proviso for re-entry by the lessor on non-payment of rent or non-performance of covenants. There is no provision giving a corresponding remedy to the tenant against the landlord's breaches of covenant.

The rule is of general application that in default of any express provision to that effect the landlord's breaches of covenant do not entitle the tenant to declare the lease at an end. The landlord's covenant to heat the premises does not go to the whole consideration for the tenant's promise to pay rent. The tenant had still vested in him the interest in the premises created by the lease, and it cannot be said to be without any value for there are several months in each year in which the premises would be habitable notwithstanding the landlord's failure to supply heat. The term and the obligation to pay rent continue notwithstanding the landlord's breach of covenant. This is the principle established in *Surplice* v. *Farnsworth*, 7 Man. & G. 576, 135 E.R. 232: see the references to that case in *Johnstone* v. *Milling* (1886), 16 Q.B.D. 460 at p. 474, and *Hart* v. *Rogers*, [1916] 1 K.B. 646 at p. 651.

A case such as the present is to be distinguished from cases where, in the letting of furnished houses or apartments, an undertaking is implied on the part of the lessor that they are reasonably fit for the purposes of habitation. There is here no room for implying any covenant or promise in respect to supplying heat, for the written lease contains what was agreed upon. And there is the further distinction that the covenant to supply heat at certain times during the term cannot by any process be translated into a promise or undertaking as to the condition of the premises at the time of letting.

Counsel for the respondent contends, however, that there has been an eviction by the landlord. There has, of course, been no physical expulsion of the tenant from the premises —that is not what counsel contends. What he relies upon is put this way in *Upton* v. *Townend*, 17 C.B. 30 at pp. 64-5, 139 E.R. 976: "Getting rid thus of the old notion of eviction, I think it may now be taken to mean this,—not a mere trespass and nothing more, but something of a grave and permanent character done by the landlord with the intention of depriving the tenant of the enjoyment of the demised premises."

The difficulty in finding such an eviction here is in the absence of evidence of intention on the part of the landlord. The heating equipment was good. There was enough coal, and it was good coal, and there was an automatic stoker. The trouble was this—to prevent foreign substances being fed into the mechanism of the stoker with the coal and doing injury, shear-pins were so placed that any harmful foreign substance entering the automatic stoker would come in contact with the shear-pins and break them off; thereupon the automatic stoker ceased to operate until the broken shear-pin was replaced. There would have been no serious trouble if there had been some one at hand who would quickly notice when the stoker was out of operation and would be able to put things right again. There was a janitor, but he had not only this apartment-house to look after, but several others. They were all small apartment-houses, and probably for most purposes the services of one janitor were enough for all of them. There were, however, in the few weeks of respondent's occupation after the furnace went on, at least four occasions when the apartment was without heat for many hours at a time. The causes were in every case of an accidental nature....

I am unable to find in these occurrences, injurious as they were to the respondent's enjoyment of the demised premises,any evidence of an intention on the part of the landlord that they should have that effect, or indeed, that they should happen at all. They were fortuitous events, and while the landlord and not the tenant should be the one to lose by even an accidental breach of the landlord's covenant, it is impossible to find that these were acts of a permanent character done by the landlord with the intention of depriving the tenant of the enjoyment of the demised premises.

In the result, it must be held there was no eviction and that the respondent had no right to treat the lease as at an end, and to refuse to pay rent.

The learned trial Judge dismissed a counter-claim of the respondent for "damages for moving costs, pain, suffering and inconvenience to himself and his family" arising from being forced to vacate the premises. The respondent has not appealed from that dismissal. It does not seem a satisfactory way to dispose of this case to compel the tenant to pay rent for the time he was out of occupation until the landlord re-let the premises, and to give him no redress for the landlord's breach of covenant. The tenant of a leased suite of apartments is in a difficult position if the landlord fails to heat them to a livable temperature. The tenant can no doubt refuse to enter into a lease that does not adequately protect him, and the Courts cannot make a new contract for him. Whether, in circumstances such as this respondent found himself in, the Court would find a case for a mandatory injunction against the landlord within the principle first laid down in *Lane* v. *Newdigate*, 10 Ves. 192, 32 E.R. 818, may some time have to be considered. The only remedy now available to this respondent must be in damages, and in my opinion that remedy should be left fully open to him notwithstanding the dismissal of the counterclaim. It should, therefore, be a term of the allowance of this appeal and of the judgment to be entered for the appellant, that there is reserved to the respondent any right to damages he may have had arising from the breach by appellant of any of the covenants in the lease.

There remains for consideration the amount of appellant's claim. In my opinion appellant is entitled only to rent up to the time when the premises were re-let. The act of re-letting put an end to the lease. In some of the textbooks it is said that there is an exception to the rule that the landlord cannot recover rent from the time of re-letting, in case the landlord gives notice to the tenant that he is re-letting solely on the latter's account (see Foa on the Law of Landlord and Tenant, 5th ed., p. 621). *Walls* v. *Atcheson*, 3 Bing. 462, 130 E.R. 591, is commonly cited for this proposition, but the case does not really decide that. The lessor was held not entitled to recover in that case, and there is a mere dictum "that she ought to have given the Defendant notice, if her intention was to let the apartments solely on his account." [p. 463] No such notice was given in the present case, and the appellant is therefore not entitled to anything to compensate him for having re-let at a smaller rent.

Appeal allowed.

[Where do you draw the line between breach of a covenant for quiet enjoyment and eviction? There is a line of authority in the United States holding that a substantial interference by the landlord with the tenant's enjoyment amounts to "constructive" eviction, and hence suspends the obligation to pay rent or entitles the tenant to terminate the lease. See *Lloyd*, The Disturbed Tenant—A Phase of Constructive Eviction, (1931) 79 Univ. of Pa. L. Rev. 707; 1 *American Law of Property*, s. 3.51.

A landlord served upon his tenant a notice to quit which was improper but the tenant relinquished possession. Subsequently he claimed that the landlord was liable in damages for wrongful eviction. Result? See *Harrison* v. *Leopold* (No. 2), [1950] 2 D.L.R. 563, 25 M.P.R. 46 (N.S.C.A.).]

SMITH v. MARRABLE. Exchequer Court. 1843. 11 M. & W. 5, 152 E.R. 693

Action by a landlord to recover the balance of rent owing on a five weeks' lease of furnished premises. The tenant moved out at the end of the first week because the premises were infested with bugs. The jury found for the tenant and the landlord moved for a new trial.

PARKE B.: This case involves the question whether, in point of law, a person who lets a house must be taken to let it under the implied condition that it is in a state fit for decent and comfortable habitation, and whether he is at liberty to throw it up, when he makes the discovery that it is not so. The case of *Edwards* v. *Etherington* (Ry. & M. 268; S.C., 7 D. & R. 117) appears to me to be an authority very nearly in point. There the defendant, who held a house as tenant from year to year, quitted without notice, on the ground that the walls were in so dilapidated a state that it had become unsafe to reside in it; and Lord Tenterden, at Nisi Prius, held these facts to be an answer to an action by the landlord for use and occupation: telling the jury, that although slight circumstances would not suffice, such serious reasons might exist as would justify a tenant's quitting at any time, and that it was for them to say whether, in the case before them, such serious reasons existed as would exempt the defendant from the plaintiff's demand, on the ground of his having had no beneficial use and occupation of the premises. The jury found for the defendant, and the Court of King's Bench was afterwards moved for a new trial on the ground of misdirection, but they refused to disturb the verdict. There is also another case of *Collins* v. *Barrow* (1 M. & Rob. 112), in which Bayley, B., held that a tenant was justified in quitting without notice premises which were noxious and unwholesome for want of proper sewerage. These authorities appear to me fully to warrant the position, that if the demised premises are incumbered with a nuisance of so serious a nature that no person can reasonably be expected to live in them, the tenant is at liberty to throw them up. This is not the case of a contract on the part of the landlord that the premises were free from this nuisance; it rather rests in an implied condition of law, that he undertakes to let them in a habitable state....

ALDERSON B., and GURNEY B., concurred.

LORD ABINGER C. B. I am glad that authorities have been found to support the view which I took of this case at the trial, but for my own part I think no authorities were wanted, and that the case is one which common sense alone enables us to decide. A man who lets a ready-furnished house surely does so under the implied condition or obligation—call it which you will—that the house is in a fit state to be inhabited. Suppose, instead of the particular nuisance which existed in this case, the tenant discovered the fact—unknown perhaps to the landlord—that lodgers had previously quitted the house in consequence of having ascertained that a person had recently died in it of plague or scarlet fever; would not the law imply that he ought not to be compelled to stay in it? I entertain no doubt whatever on the subject, and think the defendant was fully justified in leaving these premises as he did: indeed, I only wonder that he remained so long, and gave the landlord so much opportunity of remedying the evil.

Rule refused.

[In *Sutton* v. *Temple* (1843), 12 M. & W. 52, 152 E.R. 1108 (Ex.), the Court distinguished *Smith* v. *Marrable* on the ground that it involved a lease of a house and furniture, Lord Abinger stating that "everyone knows that the furniture, upon such occasions, forms the greater part of the value which the party renting it gives for the house and its contents". Finally, in *Hart* v. *Windsor* (1843), 12 M. & W. 68, 152 E.R. 1114 (Ex.), the Court rejected the proposition that there was in general any implied condition or even covenant of fitness for habitation at the beginning of a tenancy. Baron Parke in delivering the judgment of the Court said, *inter alia*:

"... But the defendant chiefly rests his case upon the decision of *Smith* v. *Marrable*

(11 M. & W. 5). My judgment in that case certainly proceeded upon the authority of two previous decisions, which, though they contained a novel doctrine, had not been questioned in Westminster Hall, and had received, to a certain degree, the sanction of the Lord Chief Justice Tindal, in a subsequent case. Those cases were *Edwards* v. *Etherington*, before Lord Tenterden, and afterwards the Court of King's Bench (Ry. & M. 268, and 7 D. & R. 117), and *Collins* v. *Barrow* (1 M. & Rob. 112); and the last, that before Lord Chief Justice Tindal, was *Salisbury* v. *Marshall* (4 Car. & P. 65); and I thought they established the doctrine, not merely that there was an implied contract on the part of the lessor, that the house demised should be habitable, but an implied condition, that the lease should be void if it were not, and the tenant chose to quit. From the full discussion which those cases have now undergone, on the present argument, and that in the recent case of *Sutton* v. *Temple*, I feel satisfied they cannot be supported, if the reports of them are correct; and we all concur in opinion that they are not law,—an opinion strongly intimated, in the case of *Sutton* v. *Temple*, in which this Court decided, that there was no implied warranty of condition or fitness for a particular purpose on a lease of aftermath.

"We are under no necessity of deciding in the present case, whether that of *Smith* v. *Marrable* be law or not. It is distinguishable from the present case on the ground on which it was put by Lord Abinger, both on the argument of the case itself, but more fully in that of *Sutton* v. *Temple*; for it was the case of a demise of a ready-furnished house for a temporary residence at a watering-place. It was not a lease of real estate merely. But that case certainly cannot be supported on the ground on which I rested my judgment.

"We are all of opinion, for these reasons, that there is no contract, still less a condition, implied by law on the demise of real property only, that it is fit for the purpose for which it is let. The principles of the common law do not warrant such a position; and though, in the case of a dwelling-house taken for habitation, there is no apparent injustice in inferring a contract of this nature, the same rule must apply to land taken for other purposes—for building upon, or for cultivation; and there would be no limit to the inconvenience which would ensue. It is much better to leave the parties in every case to protect their interests themselves, by proper stipulations, and if they really mean a lease to be void by reason of any unfitness in the subject for the purpose intended, they should express that meaning."

The distinction between furnished and unfurnished premises so far as concerns an implied condition of fitness for habitation has been accepted in Canadian case law: see *Davey* v. *Christoff* (1916), 36 O.L.R. 123, 28 D.L.R. 447 (App. Div.); *St. George Mansions Ltd.* v. *Hetherington* (1918), 42 O.L.R. 10 (App. Div.).

Is it arguable that despite the rule in *Hart* v. *Windsor*, a condition of fitness should be implied in the case of the lease of an apartment or flat where the tenant may well be unable to effect necessary repairs because of the landlord's overall control of the building?

May the tenant raise an implied condition of fitness for habitation where the landlord defaults in an express obligation to repair? See *Cruse* v. *Mount* [1933] Ch. 278.

The rule in *Hart* v. *Windsor* compels the conclusion that a lessee in England is expected to make as careful a survey and investigation of his leasehold as a purchaser is expected to make of premises which he is buying. Do conditions in Canada justify the same conclusion as to lessees here?

The cases here and in England have recognized an implied warranty of fitness for habitation of a house still in course of erection at the time that a contract for sale thereof as a completed house is made: see *Jennings* v. *Tavener*, [1955] 2 All E.R. 769 (Q.B.); *Perry* v. *Sharon Development Co. Ltd.*, [1937] 4 All E.R. 390 (C.A.); *Croft* v. *Prendergast*, [1949] O.R. 282, [1949] 2 D.L.R. 708 (C.A.); *cf. Barak* v. *Langtry*. [1954] 4 D.L.R. 135, 12 W.W.R. (N.S.) 691 (B.C.); contrast *Hoskins* v. *Woodham*, [1938] 1 All E.R. 692 (K.B.); *Lynch* v. *Thorne*, [1956] 1 All E.R. 744 (C.A.).

In England, the Housing Act, 1936 (Imp.), c. 51, s. 2 (1), established a covenant of fitness of low rental housing for habitation both at the commencement and throughout the tenancy. It has been held that the landlord's obligation to repair a defect in discharge of the statutory covenant does not arise until he has notice or knowledge of it: see *McCarrick* v. *Liverpool Corp.*, [1947] A.C. 219. For another illustration of such a statutory covenant, see *Steers Ltd.* v. *Dakin*, [1950] 1 D.L.R. 58, 24 M.P.R. 239 (Nfld.).]

VICTOR v. LYNCH. Nova Scotia Supreme Court *en banc.* [1944] 3 D.L.R. 94, 18 M.P.R. 46

Appeal by tenants from dismissal of a counterclaim for damages by reason of the landlord's failure to repair the demised premises which had been partially destroyed by fire.

SIR JOSEPH CHISHOLM C. J.: This is an appeal from the decision of the trial Judge Mr. Justice Archibald, on the defendants' counterclaim, and is from a part only of the decision, namely, the dismissal of the defendants' claim for damages for the failure of the plaintiff to repair the demised premises; and from that part of the decision which gives the defendants only one-half of their costs on the counterclaim. It may be here noted that the learned trial Judge allowed the sum of $792.09, being part of defendants' claim.

The transactions between the parties began with a lease dated on August 1, 1938, whereby the plaintiff leased to the defendants premises on the south-west corner of Prince and Johnstone Sts. in the City of Sydney for a term of 2 years with an option of renewal for a further period of 3 years. The defendants, bakers by trade, entered into possession and began extensive operations as bakers. In August, 1941, a new lease superseding the one just mentioned was executed by the parties for a term of 10 years, with an option for a renewal for a further term of 10 years. On July 19, 1942, a fire occurred and partially destroyed the demised building. There immediately followed conferences between the parties when the question of repairing was discussed. There is some conflict in the evidence given by the parties as to these conversations, but with respect to them the learned trial Judge says that where there is a conflict he accepts the statements of the defendants respecting the conversations in preference to those of the plaintiff. The defendants owned a building adjoining and lying to the west of the demised premises, and it also had been used by the defendants for their business. It had suffered in the fire and had to be rebuilt. The learned trial Judge states that the first proposal actually agreed upon was that the work on both properties should be under the supervision of defendants, the plaintiff contributing the sum of $3,500, which he recovered as insurance on his building and the defendants were to stand the expense of rebuilding over and above that sum. The work of rebuilding proceeded for 5 days in pursuance of that understanding. On July 31, the arrangement was varied and each party agreed to carry out the repairs on his or their own building. Then, after the defendants had acted upon the agreement the plaintiff on August 1, said he would not proceed with rebuilding and on August 3rd he gave a written notice to defendants that he considered the lease as terminated—as being "null and void," and he demanded the delivery up of his premises, and he went into possession.

The defendants in their counterclaim make mention of the oral agreement with respect to the repairs under which they performed work and expended money. The defendants, as already stated, had been carrying on an extensive bakery business and had important contracts with the Army and Navy and the refusal of the plaintiff to carry out his engagement entailed great loss to them. They had to make other arrangements as quickly as possible for carrying on the business and fulfilling their contracts with the Forces and others. The learned Judge allowed the claim of the defendants for labour performed and material provided before plaintiff gave notice of a termination of the lease at $791.09 and for depriving defendants of access to the barn connected with the corner building—$1, nominal damages, in all $792.09, but he disallowed defendants' claim for damages for being obliged to acquire and equip other premises suitable for their business, and held that under the terms of the written lease under which alone defendants claimed, the plaintiff was not under any obligation to repair the building. The provisions of the lease relevant to the claim of the defendants have now to be considered.

[The provisions referred to read as follows:

"(1) Provided also that if during the term of this Lease, or any renewal thereof, the building or premises are destroyed by fire or any of the elements, or partially destroyed, so as to render the premises demised wholly unfit for occupancy or if the premises shall be so badly injured that they can not be repaired with reasonable diligence, within sixty (60) days, after the happening of such injury, then this Lease shall become null and void from the date of such injury, and the Lessee shall surrender the premises and all interest therein to the Lessor, and the Lessee shall pay rent within this term only to the time of such surrender, and in case of destruction or partial destruction, as above stated, the Lessor may re-enter and re-possess the premises and remove all parties therefrom; but if the premises shall be repairable within sixty (60) days from the happening of such damage or injury then the rent shall not run or accrue after such damage or injury while the repairs are being effected, but shall recommence after the repairs are completed; but if the premises are used by the Lessees during the time such repairs or re-building is taking place then they shall pay the rental therefor.

"(2) To pay the rent hereby reserved in the manner before stated and that at the expiration or sooner determination of this Tenancy will peaceably surrender and yield up the premises with the keys thereof, in good and tenantable repair, reasonable wear and tear and damage by fire, lightning and tempest excluded.

"(3) That they will allow the Lessor, his servants and workmen at all reasonable times, to enter the premises to examine the condition thereof, and that they will allow the Lessor and his workmen to enter and to repair any part of the said premises."]

It is agreed by counsel for both parties, and it is well-established law that there is no obligation upon the landlord to repair unless there is an express covenant to that effect; and that the landlord's covenant for quiet enjoyment does not of itself oblige him to repair or rebuild the demised premises in the event of damage or destruction by fire; it requires an express covenant on his part to cast that duty upon him. Again, the receipt of money from an insurance company by the lessor does not create an obligation to rebuild. A term in the letting exempting the tenant from an obligation on his part to repair or to pay rent if the premises should be damaged by fire does not create an obligation on the part of the landlord to repair or rebuild. Several cases were cited to support those propositions, among them the case of *Dunkelman* v. *Lister*, [1927] 2 D.L.R. 219, 60 O.L.R. 158, affirmed on appeal in [1927] 4 D.L.R. 612, 61 O.L.R. 89.

The learned trial Judge has decided that under the terms of the lease and the law governing the case the plaintiff was under no obligation to rebuild or repair in the event of fire. Looking at the proviso in the lease which becomes operative in the case of destruction or partial destruction by fire or any of the elements, we find conditions on the coming into existence of which the lease becomes null and void, and the premises have to be surrendered to the lessor. They are: (a) The destruction by fire or any of the elements, that is the total destruction; or (b) Such partial destruction as may make the premises so badly injured as being incapable of being repaired with reasonable diligence within sixty days after the date of the fire.

There was not a total destruction of the building so that the plaintiff cannot successfully invoke the first condition mentioned. As to the second condition, the learned trial Judge found that the building could easily have been repaired within the period of 60 days, and there is evidence to support the finding and that finding should not be disturbed. The result of the finding is that the plaintiff had no right in law to regard the lease as terminated when he so notified the defendants; the lease was not terminated by the events which occurred and it could not be cancelled unilaterally; it remained in force, but at that stage the plaintiff was under no obligation to repair or rebuild.

But conversations followed between the parties which resulted in an oral agreement whereby repairs were to be made at the joint expense of plaintiff and defendants, the plaintiff contributing the amount of the insurance and the balance to be borne by the defendants. This agreement was founded on a good consideration, but after 4 or 5 days the plaintiff who had control of the situation repudiated the agreement and evicted the defendants by entering into possession. The defendants to whom time was of the utmost importance, were obligated to do what best they could to obtain suitable premises in which to keep their baking operations going. They are, in my opinion, entitled to recover damages for an illegal eviction and for a breach of the oral agreement. The damages to which I refer are damages in addition to the sum of $792.09 allowed by the trial Judge. A claim for damages for the eviction is not pleaded and does not seem to have been relied on. In fact the defendants' claim is based upon the contention that the plaintiff should under the terms of the lease repair the building; and as already stated there is nothing in the lease to cast that duty upon the plaintiff. Nor again is the claim, so far as the pleadings disclose, based upon the oral agreement, the terms of which provided for repairs. I should be disposed to allow an amendment of the counterclaim to enable the defendants to clarify their claim and to take further evidence in support of it, if further evidence is available. The plaintiff wrongfully dispossessed the defendants and he is liable for the natural consequences of his act: *Grosvenor Hotel Co.* v. *Hamilton*, [1894] 2 Q.B. 836. Without suggesting what particular items of damage they can prove, I think they should not go outside of the items enumerated in para. 13 (c) nos. 2 to 8 of the particulars given in their claim. An order to amend with the amendment may be submitted to this Court, and further directions will be given.

I see no reason for disturbing the direction of the trial Judge with respect to costs of the trial. The costs of this appeal will be reserved until the referee makes a report on the matter of the damages mentioned.

GRAHAM J. concurred with DOULL J.
HALL J. concurred with SIR JOSEPH CHISHOLM C. J.

DOULL J.: I agree with the opinion of the Chief Justice although I have some doubt as to the propriety of allowing an amendment at this stage to cover a matter which the defendant seemed to deliberately reject in his pleadings and at the trial.

However, the terms of the amendment and reference are to be considered when the order is taken, and as I assume that the amendment will cover only matters now in evidence and damages, I agree that the amendment be allowed and that the costs of the appeal be reserved.

SMILEY J. concurred with SIR JOSEPH CHISHOLM C. J.

Judgment varied.

[See also *Y.M.C.A.* v. *MacDonald*, [1949] 1 D.L.R. 512, 22 M.P.R. 219 (N.B.).

In *Winbaum* v. *Zolumoff and Zolumoff*, [1956] O.W.N. 27 (C.A.), a tenant claimed that the lack of heat by reason of disrepair of a furnace would support an action for breach of covenant for quiet enjoyment when there was no express covenant by the landlord to repair. Is he right?

A landlord's repairing covenant is generally construed to require notice of want of repair from the tenant but it will suffice if the landlord knows or learns otherwise of the want of repair: see *Murphy* v. *Hurly*, [1922] 1 A.C. 369; *Morgan* v. *Liverpool Corp.* [1927] 2 K.B. 131 (C.A.); *Griffin* v. *Pillet*, [1926] 1 K.B. 17. The mere fact that the landlord may be entitled to enter and inspect the premises will not absolve the tenant of giving notice of want of repair unless notice or knowledge is acquired by the landlord independently. The foregoing principles apply even where the defect or disrepair existed at the commencement of the tenancy.

In *Uniproducts (Manchester) Ltd.* v. *Rose Furnishers Ltd.*, [1956] 1 All E.R. 146, [1956] 1 W.L.R. 45 (Q.B.), the landlord had covenanted to repair, and, owing to the rot of joists, the floor of the building fell, injuring the tenant's manager. Having been advised of its legal liability to the manager, the tenant paid him off, and then sued the landlord whose defence was that it had not been notified of the want of repair and had no knowledge of it. Result?

Where the landlord is liable on a covenant to repair, are damages measurable by the amount which the tenant may have been obliged to pay to injured third persons?

It appears to be the English and Canadian law that the injured manager in the above-mentioned case would not have a cause of action against the landlord when he was injured on premises in the tenant's occupation. This rule applies even to members of the tenant's family living with him on the demised premises: see *Cavalier* v. *Pope* [1906] A.C. 428. However the tenant himself may recover damages for personal injuries arising by reason of the landlord's breach of a covenant with the tenant to repair. In the absence of such a covenant, even the tenant must find some basis for liability of the landlord in tort: see *Devine* v. *London Housing Society Ltd.*, [1950] 2 All E.R. 1173 (K.B.); *cf. Wright*, Cases on Torts (1954), pp. 311 ff. It would be different if the injured person was a passer-by injured, say, by a falling wall, or if an adjoining owner were so injured. The landlord's duty to such third persons in tort does not depend on a covenant by him to repair but may arise if he has simply a right to enter demised premises and to do necessary repairs if he so desires; moreover, this tort liability is independent of any notice or knowledge of want of repair: see *Mint* v. *Good*, [1950] 2 All E.R. 1159, [1951] 1 K.B. 517 (C.A.), where liability to a passer-by was imposed on a landlord of premises let on a weekly tenancy in the absence both of a covenant by him to repair and of an express right to enter and do repairs. The Court said that in the circumstances there was an implied right to enter. Denning L. J. added in that case: "I venture to doubt in these days whether a landlord can exempt himself from liability to passers-by by taking a covenant from the tenant to repair the structure adjoining the highway". See also *Wright*, Cases on Torts (1963, 3rd ed.), pp. 647 ff.; *Williams*, The Duties of Non-Occupiers in respect of Dangerous Premises, (1942) 5 Mod. L. Rev. 194.

Merely because the landlord covenants to repair does not exonerate the tenant from liability to third persons whether they be injured off or on the premises: see *MacDonald* v. *Goderich*, [1949] O.R. 619, [1949] 3 D.L.R. 788 (C.A.). Can the tenant who is obliged to pay damages to a third person recover them from the landlord by reason of the latter's breach of a covenant to repair, at least where the third person was injured off the premises?

For a discussion of the law in the United States, see *Note*, Lessor's Duty to Repair: Tort Liability to Persons Injured on the Premises, (1949) 62 Harv. L. Rev. 669; *Harkrider*, Tort Liability of a Landlord, (1928) 26 Mich. L. Rev. 260; *Prosser*, Torts (2nd ed., 1955), pp. 465 ff.]

TAYLOR v. BEAL. King's Bench. 1591. Cro. Eliz. 222, 78 E.R. 478 (1 Leon. 237, 74 E.R. 216)

Debt for rent reserved upon a lease for years. The issue being joined if the rent were paid or not, the defendant gave in evidence for part of the rent, that the plaintiff by covenant was to repair the house and did not, and that thereupon he expended part of the rent in repairing the house. The question was, if this evidence will maintain the issue?—Gawdy conceived it did, for the law giveth this liberty to the lessee to expend the rent in reparations, for he shall be otherwise at great mischief, for the house may fall upon his head before it be repaired; and therefore the law alloweth him to repair it, and recoupe the rent. *Vide* 12 Hen. 8. pl. 1. 12 Rich. 2. Barr. 242. 14 Hen. 4. p. 27.—Fenner. It is no evidence; for if the lessor will not repair it, he is to have his covenants against him.—Clench seemed he might well expend the rent in reparations, but he ought to have pleaded it, and cannot give it in evidence upon the general issue; and they thereupon moved the jury to find the special matter. And as to the residue of the rent, he shewed that he paid it to others that had rent-charges out of the lands, which the lessor had covenanted to pay, and that by the commandment of the lessor he paid the rent, in discharge of the said rents: and this was clearly held good; for payment to another by the plaintiff's appointment, is payment to himself.

[In *Brown* v. *Toronto General Hospital Trustees* (1893), 23 O.R. 599, a tenant to whom the landlord had given a covenant to repair was injured because of defective front steps. The Court dismissed the action because, although the landlord had been notified of the disrepair the tenant knew of the dangerous condition. Boyd C. said: "In the case of slight repairs the tenant is justified after notice of want of repair and a reasonable time elapses, to expend what is needed in making the repairs and charging it against his landlord or taking it out of the rent."

It should be noted, however, that generally the covenant to pay rent is phrased as a covenant to pay "without any deductions whatsoever."]

PARKS v. HAMMOND. Ontario Court of Appeal. [1948] 2 D.L.R. 679, [1948] O.W.N. 383

The judgment of the Court was delivered by ROACH J. A.:

This is an appeal by the landlord against an order made by Macdonell Co. Ct. J. dismissing her application made under Part III of the Landlord and Tenant Act, R. S. O. 1937, c. 219, for an order declaring the respondents to be over-holding tenants and the landlord accordingly entitled to possession, and for a writ of possession to place her in possession.

The facts are quite out of the ordinary. The tenants are monthly tenants under a verbal letting, followed by possession, of an unfurnished dwelling and the land appurtenant thereto known as 26-1/2 Dingwall Ave. in the City of Toronto, at a monthly rental of $32.50 payable in advance on the 15th day of each month.

The sanitary sewer serving the dwelling became wholly or substantially blocked due, as was later discovered, to roots of a tree or trees getting into it. As a result the sewage from the house backed up into the basement. The Local Board of Health, having become aware of the situation and recognizing it as being most unsanitary and dangerous to health, notified the landlord to remedy it. The landlord ignored the notice.

Under date May 22, 1947, the Medical Officer of Health for the City of Toronto served a written notice on the tenants, requiring them to have the obstruction removed and the basement cleaned and disinfected. In that notice the Medical Officer of Health quoted s. 87 (4) of the Public Health Act, R.S.O. 1937, c. 299, which reads as follows: "The occupier for the time being of the premises may deduct any money recovered or collected from him which as between him and the owner, the latter ought to pay, out of the rent then due or from time to time becoming due in respect of the premises."

The tenants, with reasonable dispatch, had the condition remedied as required by the Medical Officer of Health and paid the costs thereof, amounting to $53, and thereafter deducted that amount from succeeding months' rent. The landlord treated the amount thus deducted as rent in arrear and under date July 31st notified the tenants that the rent to the extent of the deductions was in arrear for more than 15 days and required the tenants to vacate and deliver up possession on September 15th following.

Possession not having been delivered up, these proceedings were commenced. The matter came on for hearing before Macdonell Co. Ct. J. on October 30th and 31st last and at the close of the hearing His Honour held that the tenants were entitled to deduct the amounts expended by them and, therefore, that the rent was not in arrear.

In my opinion s. 87 (4) has no application to the facts of this case. The money paid by the tenants was paid by them in settlement of their contractual liability to the person whom they employed to do the work. It was not money "recovered or collected from" them by way of recoupment or recompense to the Medical Officer of Health or the Board of Health of an expense incurred, and paid by him or it in abating the nuisance. Subsection (4) is limited in its application to money "recovered or collected from the tenant" by way of such recoupment. The whole section makes that meaning plain.

Subsection (1) authorizes the Medical Officer of Health or Sanitary Inspector to take such steps as may be nesessary to abate the nuisance where the owner or occupier fails, after due notice, to abate it.

Subsection (2) provides, *inter alia*, that all reasonable costs incurred, that is by the municipal authority, "shall be recoverable from both the owner and the occupier".

Subsection (3) provides for the collection of the expenses by inserting them in the collection roll and for their collection in like manner as municipal taxes.

Subsection (5) limits the amount recoverable from the occupier from time to time to the amount of the rent due from time to time.

Where money is thus "recovered or collected from" the tenant, by virtue of the statute the tenant may deduct the same from the rent if, as between the tenant and the owner, depending on the terms of the letting, the owner ought to pay the costs of abating the nuisance.

In a lease there may be express covenants binding the owner to repair, and failure by him to repair may give the tenant the right to do so and set off the cost thereof *pro tanto* against the rent; but that is not this case.

Here, as between the owner and the tenants, there was no obligation on the owner to repair. It is trite law that in the absence of an express covenant there is no obligation on the landlord of an unfurnished house to keep it in repair and there is no implied covenant by the landlord that it is or shall continue to be reasonably fit for occupation. The tenant takes such premises as he finds them: see *Woodfall's* Law of Landlord and Tenant, 24th ed., pp. 713-4.

These premises having fallen into a state of non-repair even amounting to a nuisance, the cost of remedying the same as between the landlord and the tenants must fall on the tenants. The tenants, unfortunately for them, have misconceived their legal rights by deducting the amounts expended by them in abating the nuisance. They allowed the rent to be in arrear for more than 15 days and the landlord was within her legal rights in giving the notice to quit.

The appeal should, therefore, be allowed and the order appealed against should be varied and as varied should declare the tenants to be overholding tenants of the premises in question and require them to deliver possession thereof to the landlord and provide that, in default of their so doing, a writ of possession should issue to the Sheriff requiring him to place the landlord in possession. The landlord is entitled to her costs of the proceedings below and her costs of this appeal.

Appeal allowed.

[How far is this case an authority for the situation where as between landlord and tenant the former has covenanted to repair?

In *Gebhardt* v. *Saunders*, [1892] 2 Q.B. 452, under English legislation which was the model for the legislation discussed in *Parks* v. *Hammond*, the tenant was held entitled to recover from the landlord money expended on repairing a "nuisance" caused by a structural defect where notice to abate was served on the tenant. Is this consistent with *Parks* v. *Hammond?* Do not both cases require consideration of where the duty of repair exists apart from the statutory provisions for abatement of nuisances? *Cf. Thompson and Norris Mfg. Co.* v. *Hawes*, (1895), 73 L.T. 369 (C.A.); *Budd* v. *Marshall* (1880), 5 C.P. 481 (C.A.).]

HARMER v. JUMBIL (NIGERIA) TIN AREAS LTD. Court of Appeal. [1921] 1 Ch. 200

Plaintiff was a lessee of certain land for the purpose, known to the lessor, of maintaining explosives magazines on it. Statutory regulations required that the keeping of such magazines be licensed and it was a condition of plaintiff's licence that if other buildings were put up within specified distances of a magazine the licence would be withdrawn. The land leased to plaintiff was in a mining area but the tract of which it was part had not been worked for over 50 years. The lessor's successor in title granted mineral rights to defendants for a specified term but not so as to interfere with plaintiff's magazine or access thereto. Defendants erected certain buildings within the distances prohibited by plaintiff's licence and the latter sought an injunction and damages. The only express covenant by his lessor was a covenant for quiet enjoyment.

EVE J.: The claim to this relief is based, first, on the allegation that the acts of the defendants are in derogation of the grant in the lease under which the plaintiff holds. In this connection it is not disputed that the defendants stand in no better position than the original lessor under whom they claim, and if the acts would have amounted to a derogation from his grant, it is conceded that the defendants must abide by the consequences. The question therefore is whether John Samuel Spry after his lease to the plaintiff could have used his adjoining hereditaments as the defendants are doing, or whether he was debarred from such user on the principle that he could not derogate from his own grant. The principle is, I think, well expressed, in the judgment of Stirling J. in *Aldin* v. *Latimer Clark, Muirhead & Co.*, [1894] 2 Ch. 437, 444, 447, in the two passages I am about to read. In the earlier one the learned judge says: "Where a landlord demises part of his property for carrying on a particular business, he is bound to abstain from doing anything on the remaining portion which would render the demised premises unfit for carrying on such business in the way in which it is ordinarily carried on, but that this obligation does not extend to special branches of the business which call for extraordinary protection." And he adds: "In my opinion, Munro"—he was the grantor—"became subject to the obligation to abstain from doing anything on his adjoining property which would substantially interfere with the carrying on of that business in the ordinary course; and that obligation binds the present defendants as assigns from him." Parker J. (as he then was) puts it in this way in *Browne* v. *Flower*, [1911] 1 Ch. 219, 225: "Implications usually explained by the maxim that no one can derogate from his own grant do not stop short with easements. Under certain circumstances there will be implied on the part of the grantor of lessor obligations which restrict the user of the land retained by him further than can be explained by the implication of any easement known to the law. Thus, if the grant or demise be made for a particular purpose, the grantor or lessor comes under an obligation not to use the land retained by him in such a way as to render the land granted or demised unfit or materially less fit for the particular purpose for which the grant or demise was made." But in order to answer the inquiry whether any particular act constitutes a breach of an implied covenant founded on the principle referred to it is necessary to examine the grant and the circumstances in which it was made. There is no doubt that the premises here were demised to the plaintiff for the sole purpose of an explosives magazine. The only express covenant on the lessor's part is the covenant for quiet enjoyment, but it is not denied that some implication is raised by the fact that the demise was for a particular purpose, and that the lessor may consequently be liable for acts not covered by the covenant for quiet enjoyment. The inquiry to what acts the implication extends is one which, as I read the authorities, has to be answered upon an examination of all the circumstances surrounding the grant. I pause, before proceeding to examine those circumstances, to emphasise a point made by Mr. Courthope Wilson in his argument that the acts here sought to be covered by the implication are not acts physically affecting the demised tenement, either by direct interference with it, such as vibration, or the withdrawal of support, or indirectly by the cutting off of some easement, or the interception of some feature necessary for its proper enjoyment, such as light or means of access, or the enjoyment of a current of air required for the conduct of the business for which the premises were let, as were the acts in all the reported cases, but are acts the doing of which only affects the demised hereditaments by bringing about a condition of things in which the continued user of them for the specific purpose becomes illegal. No decision has been cited from the books which goes so far as to raise an implication covering such acts, but it does not, of course, follow from this that such an implication cannot be raised. I turn now to consider the circumstances subsisting at the date of the grant.

[His Lordship here considered the circumstances of the case, pointing out that he was bound to assume that plaintiff's lessor knew of the Explosives Act, 1875, but that he could not find that he knew the exact terms and restrictions upon which any licence would be granted, although he would know that there would be some restrictions. The learned Judge then referred to the knowledge of the parties that there had been extensive mineral workings in the area and that although they had been discontinued for many years, still they could be expected to appreciate that the time might come to resume mining operations. He then continued as follows:]

I cannot think that in these circumstances I ought to read into this transaction an agreement by the lessor not to exercise his rights as owner of the minerals to work them or to authorize others to work them. Moreover, if the plaintiff is right that under the implied agreement the lessor is not only prevented from working the minerals within the prescribed area, but is also prevented from erecting or authorizing the erection of any building within it, the result would be that he could not during the currency of the lease erect or allow any of his agricultural tenants to erect any building on his farms within the area. I think a very strong case would have to be made out before the Court would impose such restrictions as these. They seem to me to be unreasonable in a transaction of this nature, and having regard to all the circumstances, I do not think I ought to hold the acts of the defendants to be acts in breach of any covenant raised by implication against the lessor under whom they claim. I do not think in this case that the acts can properly be treated as acts done in derogation of the grant even though the result may be that the subject of the demise is by reason of such acts rendered unavailable for the use contemplated when the demise was made.

It is further and alternatively alleged that the acts complained of are in breach of the lessor's covenant for quiet enjoyment.... Now, that these acts interfere with the user of the demised premises is demonstrated by what I have already stated. They have in fact rendered it no longer a proper building for the storage of explosives; but the question whether or not they constitute a breach of the covenant for quiet enjoyment, is, I think, determined by authority, binding upon me, accepted by Lord Parker as an authority in the case which I have already mentioned. I refer to *Davis* v. *Town Properties Investment Corporation*, [1903] 1 Ch. 797, where Romer L. J. in a short judgment says this: "I only wish to add that, in the case of an alleged breach of the ordinary covenant for quiet enjoyment, where by the alleged breach neither the title to the land nor the possession of the land is affected, and what the lessee complains of is only an interruption of his enjoyment of the land by some act of the lessor, I doubt whether the act complained of is a breach of the covenant unless it amounts to a direct interference with the enjoyment."... It is true that the interference in the case before Parker J.—*Browne* v. *Flower*—was not an interference with the actual user, but with an amenity of the demised premises, but in his judgment I think the learned judge took the view that apart from the particular nature of the interference, inasmuch as the act did not affect either title or possession, it could not properly have been treated as a breach of the covenant. I adopt the same view in this case, and decline to treat the acts of the defendants as a breach of the covenant for quiet enjoyment.

Plaintiff appealed.

LORD STERNDALE M. R.:... With regard to the law on the matter, I am content to refer to the passages from *Aldin* v. *Latimer Clark, Muirhead & Co.* and *Browne* v. *Flower*, to which reference was made by Eve J. in his judgment. In fact I am content to adopt the law as stated by Eve J., and I do not think it necessary to discuss it any further. The question we have to solve, adopting the law as so laid down, is: Was there here an act by the defendants that constituted a derogation from the grant made by the original lessor in 1911? It is admitted that, for the purposes of derogation from grant, the defendants are in the same position as the original lessor, and therefore I approach the question from this point of view: Could the lessor, either immediately after the lease, or, at any rate, during the continuance of the term of twenty-one years, have done what the defendants have done without derogating from his grant of this land for the purpose of a magazine for explosives?

It has been said that the surrounding circumstances must be looked at. With that I agree. It has been laid down on more than one occasion that you must look at the surrounding circumstances in order to help you to ascertain what the grant in fact was. Two main objections were taken to the maintenance of this action. The first was that this being a mining district, it must for that reason be taken that there was a reservation, or at any rate, an implication that the grant did not extend so far as to interfere with the lessor's right to work his mines. I do not think that contention is sound....

The mines had not been worked for fifty years. I do not believe it was in the mind of either of the parties that there was any probability of their being reopened in the near future; as a matter of fact, it was the extraordinary change in value of minerals by reason of the influence of the late war that induced the reopening of these mines. That is a matter which neither party had in mind, and in that sense I think they both took the risk of it, that neither of them thought it a matter worth considering. I do not think there is anything in that point.

The next point is a more difficult one, i.e., that what the defendants have done is not a physical interference, but is only something which caused the prohibition by a third party of the carrying on of that business upon the demised premises. It was called a metaphysical interference. I am not quite clear what that means, but I am quite clear that the word "metaphysical" is not an apt word to describe what took place here. The question is whether in the circumstances of this case, doing what the defendants did, doing, that is to say, that which ipso facto as soon as it was done caused the forfeiture of the licence, and made it illegal to carry on the business in the premises, was a derogation from the grant of the lessor. I agree with the learned judge that the question has never arisen under circumstances of this kind, and I have found it a very difficult case to decide, and although I feel myself bound to differ from the conclusion at which the learned judge in the Court below arrived, I do so with great hesitation, because I think that this is a case which presents novel circumstances. The defendants, as I have said before, had to deal with the surrounding circumstances; they had to deal with the question of the mining situation. One question is what was their knowledge, or rather what was the knowledge that has to be imputed to the lessor of the circumstances connected with a magazine for explosives.... I think he must at least be taken to have known that a licence was necessary for the carrying on of this business, and that it would contain certain conditions; all the conditions I will assume he did not know, and I think he must be taken to have known that anything which violated those conditions would cause a withdrawal of the licence. As a matter of fact, according to its terms the licence was ipso facto withdrawn on the acts which happened; but I think he must be taken to have known, at any rate, that acts that violated the conditions of the licence might cause its withdrawal.

In these circumstances is there, or is there not, an implied obligation on the part of the lessor that he would not do anything which would violate the conditions of the licence which was then in existence, or which would come into existence, before the business could be carried on upon the premises? In my opinion there must be one. I do not wish to go beyond that. I do not wish to say, because it is not necessary to do so, and the point is, I think, a much more difficult one, whether that obligation extends to refraining from doing anything which may violate the conditions of any future licence that may be given upon any different terms imposed by an alteration of the Act and of the authority which granted the licence. I think it is much better to confine myself to the question which is before us—namely, whether there is implied an obligation on the part of the lessor not to do anything to violate the conditions of the existing licence. In my opinion there is such an implied obligation; therefore I think that what the defendants did, being for this purpose admittedly in the same hesition as the original lessor, were acts which if done by the lessor would have been in dorogation of his grant, and therefore that the plaintiff is entitled to the relief that he claims.

WARRINGTON L. J. (after reciting the facts and concluding that knowledge should be imputed to the lessor that the explosives magazine could not be used if the other buildings came within the distances actually specified in the licence): Now in these circumstances, is there an implied obligation, arising from the purposes for which these premises were demised, that the lessor would not do anything which would render them unfit, or materially less fit for the purpose for which they were demised? That they have become unfit, not physically, but by reason of the circumstances under which they are now situated, is quite plain. But it is contended that, when it is laid down that the lessor is under an obligation not to render the demised premises unfit for the purpose for which they were demised, all that is thereby meant is that he must not do anything which renders them physically unfit.

Undoubtedly this is the first case in which this particular question has arisen, but for myself I confess that I can see no reason why the principle should be limited in the way contended for by the defendants. The premises have become unfit for the purpose for which they were demised, and this because it is no longer legal for the plaintiff to use them for that purpose by reason of the acts of the defendants; and I cannot see why the acts of the defendants should not have the same effect in law whether the change brought about by them is a physical change in the condition of the demised premises or a change in their condition brought about by the fact that it has become illegal to use them for the purpose intended by the demise.

The only case which comes anywhere near the present is *Browne* v. *Flower*, to which I have already referred, but that case is in my judgment clearly distinguishable from the present. The learned judge there refused the injunction asked for, because in his opinion the acts of the lessor had not rendered the premises unfit or materially less fit for the purposes for which they had been demised, and for this reason. The premises had been demised as a residential flat. What the defendants had done had not in any way interfered with their use as a residential flat except in this respect, that they had made them less pleasant for the particular purpose. It had rendered it neccessary to curtain or veil a certain window looking out in a particular direction and so forth, but the premises were there and were capable of being used and fit to be used as a residential flat; all that the lessor had done was to interfere with one of the amenities which the flat had enjoyed at the time when the lease was granted. The important part of that decision is that it was based by Parker J. upon the fact that the demised premises had not been rendered unfit or materially less fit by what the defendants had done. In the present case these premises have been rendered, not only materially less fit, but absolutely unfit for the purposes for which they were demised....

YOUNGER L. J.: The question here is how far the original lessor was, or how far the defendants as now claiming under him are, bound to restrict the user of their adjoining land so as not to render illegal the only enjoyment of the demised premises which the lessee under his lease is entitled to have. Or, putting the question in another way, was the lessor, or are the defendants, as now claiming under him, entitled to use their adjoining lands in such a way as that for the convenience of such user and for the protection of their own premises the only authorized user of the demised premises by the lessee will become a statutory offence.

Now if these questions are to be answered in a sense favourable to the lessee, it must be on the principle that a grantor shall not derogate from his grant, a principle which merely embodies in a legal maxim a rule of common honesty. "A grantor having given a thing with one hand," as Bowen L. J. put it in *Birmingham, Dudley and District Banking Co.*, v. *Ross*, 38 Ch. D. 295, 313, "is not to take away the means of enjoying it with the other." "If A. lets a plot of land to B.," as Lord Loreburn phrases it in *Lyttelton Times Co.* v. *Warners*, [1907] A.C. 476, 481, "he may not act so as to frustrate the purpose for which in the contemplation of both parties the land was hired." The rule is clear but the difficulty is, as always, in its application. For the obligation laid upon the grantor is not unqualified. If it were, that which was imposed in the interest of fair dealing might, in unscrupulous hands, become a justification for oppresssion, or an instrument of extortion. The obligation therefore must in every case be construed fairly, even strictly, if not narrowly. It must be such as, in view of the surrounding circumstances, was within the reasonable contemplation of the parties at the time when the transaction was entered into, and was at that time within the grantor's power to fulfil. But so limited, the obligation imposed may, I think, be infinitely varied in kind, regard being had to the paramount purpose to serve which it is imposed. If, for instance, the purpose of a grant would in a particular case be frustrated by some act of the lessor on his own land which, while involving no physical interference with the enjoyment of the demised property, would yet be completely effective to stop or render unlawful its continued user for the purpose for which alone it was let, I can see no reason at all in principle why "*ut res magis valeat quam pereat*" that act should not be prohibited, just as clearly as an act which, though less completely effective in its result, achieved it by some physical interference. There can, in my judgment, be no valid principle in the contention which was addressed to us in this case... that, while the lease of 1911 carried with it the obligation of doing or permitting nothing on the adjoining land which would make the explosives magazine less fit for use as a magazine, that is to say, more likely to blow up, it did leave the lessor perfectly free to use his land for his own convenience in any way he chose, even although the result of his doing so would ipso facto make the continued user of a powder magazine as such a statutory offence. If that contention were to be accepted it would enable this grantor, if so minded, in pure caprice, to defeat the whole purpose of the grant and completely sterilize the property in his tenant's hands, he himself remaining entitled to the rent reserved for the whole term.

In my judgment the principle here applicable is far too great to be in effect destroyed, in the case of such a property as this, by introducing this distinction which, so far as I can see, has no sound foundation on which to rest.

Now I do not myself read, and I do not think either my Lord or the Lord Justice reads, the learned judge's judgment as dissenting from any of these views. The facts did not as he saw them call for their application. In this Court however a different complexion has been placed upon these facts, and as they are now presented, the question is whether they do not bring the case precisely within the principle which I have endeavoured to enunciate and oblige us to answer the question involved in the appeal in favour of the appellant.

This was a lease of a powder magazine which at the date of the lease was in course of erection by the lessee at his own expense. The lease was dated December 30, 1911. Before it was in fact granted, the local inquiry prescribed by the Explosives Act, 1875, had been held and an order had been obtained at Petty Sessions, approving the terms of the licence, which was subsequently made formally effective, I think, in the month of February, 1913. After that licence had been so approved at Petty Sessions, no alteration in it under the statute was possible. To its provisions the approval of the Secretary of State had to be given before it was submitted to the justices, and after it had been appoved by them, the obligation under the Act of the Secretary of State to issue the licence became imperative. In fact the licence which was formally granted in 1913 was, as we have seen from its having been shown to us, in the form originally presented by the appellant and approved, first by the Home Office, and afterwards by the magistrates. The licence, as is indicated by the statute, would be, and I do not doubt was, prepared by the lessee. The application for it, as appears by the Act, involved the statement of the precise situation and plan of the magazine, and also the boundaries of the land forming the area of the magazine, and in this case, the distances to be maintained between the magazine or any part of it and other buildings or works. These matters could not properly be described by the lessee without the knowledge and approval of the lessor or his representative, on whose land the magazine was to be erected. Further, the lessor and his representative were resident in the county of Cornwall; the proceedings at Petty Sessions were notorious. The lessor himself is now dead, but no one was called from the office of his solicitors or otherwise concerned in the transactions on his behalf to give evidence at the trial with reference to the part taken in them by himself or his representatives.

In these circumstances, no evidence to the contrary being forthcoming, I should be prepared, I think, to go further than my learned brothers on this point. The inference to my mind is really irresistible that knowledge of the terms of the proposed licence at the date of the lease was actually possessed by the lessor or his representative, and that the whole transaction, including the erection of the magazine at the lessee's expense, went through on the footing of that licence. But, if I go further in drawing that inference than the facts properly justify, then it must, I think, at least clearly be inferred that the erection of the magazine by the lessee on the lessor's land, followed by its demise for the sole purpose of its being so used, was carried out with the knowledge, common to both parties, that the lessor's adjoining land in the physical condition in which it then stood, permitted the lawful user of the magazine as a magazine in accordance with the original official requirements. Must not there then, even on that hypothesis, be taken to be imposed upon the lessor an obligation not to act in the use of his own land during the term of the lease in such a way as to make the observance by the lessee of the conditions of that original licence in that respect impossible.

When the then situation of the land is considered, I can have no doubt that this obligation must be taken to have been impliedly assumed by the lessor....

Like my Lord and the Lord Justice, I am not prepared to imply any obligation in excess of the terms of the original licence. I cannot see that anything further can reasonably be presumed to have been contemplated by the parties. The limited obligations referred to however must, I think, be taken to be binding upon the lessor and upon the defendants claiming under him, and the plaintiff is accordingly, in my judgment, entitled to relief on that footing.

Appeal allowed.

[Plaintiff was lessee of an apartment in an apartment building of which the ground floor was used for shops. His lease (as did the leases of other tenants) contained a covenant that the apartment would be used for a private dwelling only. The lessor (which was lessee of the whole building) made certain alterations, including the installation of an elevator, and turned the building into business accommodation for its business and began to use it for that purpose. This use involved alleged obstruction of access to plaintiff's apartment by the activities of the lessor's vans and also noise from the operation of the elevator and the constant banging of doors. *Held*, the lessor was liable, *inter alia*, on an implied covenant not to derogate from grant: *Newman* v. *Real Estate Debenture Corp.*, [1940] 1 All E.R. 131, 162 L.T. 183 (appeal settled: see [1940] 2 All E.R. 228n). Contrast *Kelly* v. *Battershell*, [1949] 2 All E.R. 830 (C.A.). Where do you draw the line between interference with user for the purpose for which a demise was made and interference merely with amenities of the demised premises?]

PORT v. GRIFFITH. Chancery Division. [1938] 1 All E.R. 295

Action by a tenant against a landlord for a declaration and for damages.

LUXMOORE J.: The material facts in this case are as follows. The defendants were at all material times, and still are, the owners of property in the Mile End Road, Hannibal Road, and Stepney Green, in the parish of Stepney, including premises known as 150, Mile End Road, which the defendants had, shortly before the date of the lease to the plaintiff, converted into five shops. By a lease dated July 9, 1935, the defendants demised one of these five shops, known as Shop No. 3, to the plaintiff for a term of 21 years from Mar. 25, 1930. The lease contains, among other covenants, a covenant, in cl. 2 (13), to the effect that the lessee:

> will use and occupy the said demised premises and permit the same to be used and occupied as a shop for the retail business for the sale of wool and general trimmings and for no other purpose unless the lessors their agents or surveyors shall consent in writing to the use and occupation of the same or any part thereof for any other purpose than specified.

In pursuance of this lease, the plaintiff entered into possession of Shop No. 3 and started to carry on there a retail business for the sale of wool and general trimmings, and she is still carrying on that business in the shop. On May 16, 1936, the defendants let Shops Nos. 4 and 5 to Fisher for a term of 7 years from Mar. 25, 1936. Shop No. 4 adjoins Shop No. 3, and the lease contains in cl. 2 (11) a covenant by the lessee to this effect:

> The lessee will use and occupy the demised premises and permit the same to be used and occupied as a shop for the retail business for the sale of tailor and dressmaking

> trimmings and cloths and for no other purpose unless the consent there specified should be obtained.

When the plaintiff heard that the defendants proposed to let Shops Nos. 4 and 5 to Fisher for the retail business for the sale of tailor and dressmaking trimmings and cloths, she wrote to the defendants and protested against the letting, on the ground that this business was similar to her own, and would be damaging to her. There was an attempt on the part of the defendants to prove by evidence that the two businesses were in fact different, and, while it is admitted that there is no similarity between what I might call the woollen branch of the plaintiff's business and the cloth branch of Mr. Fisher's business, I am satisfied that, so far as the sale of trimmings is concerned, the two businesses are substantially the same.

The plaintiff founds her case on derogation from grant, and relies on a number of cases which lay down the principle that every lessor is under an implied obligation not to frustrate the purpose for which, in the contemplation of both parties, the premises in question were let. My attention has been called to a number of cases, beginning with *Lyttelton Times Co., Ltd.* v. *Warners, Ltd.*, [1907] A.C. 476, in which this principle was laid down, and ending with the most recent decision, *O'Cedar Ltd.* v. *Slough Trading Co., Ltd.*, [1927] 2 K.B. 123. The earlier of these authorities relate to cases where the frustration is due to some act which has physically affected the demised premises, but in *Harmer* v. *Jumbil (Nigeria) Tin Areas, Ltd.*, this principle was applied to a case in which the act done by the lessor and resulting in the frustration had no direct physical effect on the premises. In the present case, the plaintiff is, I think, asking the court to extend the principle still further. Of the authorities to which I was referred during the argument, the two most germane to the present case appear to me to be *Browne* v. *Flower*, [1911] 1 Ch. 219, and the *O'Cedar* case to which I have just referred. In the former case, Parker J., dealt with the earlier authorities, and it is unnecessary, I think, in view of his consideration of those cases, for me to refer to them in detail.... Applying what was said by Parker J., to the facts of the present case, the question to be determined appears to be: Has the letting by the defendants to Fisher of Shops Nos. 4 and 5 rendered the plaintiff's Shop No. 3 unfit, or materially less fit, to be used for the purposes for which it was demised?

The presence of a trade rival in premises next door to those occupied by the trader may, or may not, be a detriment to any particular business. I do not think that I should be justified in saying that the presence of a trade rival next door must of necessity be a detriment, but, whatever the view may may be, the presence of a trade rival next door does not render the premises on which the trader is carrying on his business unfit for that purpose, although it may incidentally reduce the profit ratio to be earned in that business. It would be unreasonable to assume that, because the defendants let Shop No. 3 for the particular business described in the lease, the defendants were undertaking restrictive obligations which would prevent them from using or letting any of their other properties for any lawful purpose, which would include the carrying on of a rival business, and would compel them to insert a covenant restraining the carrying on of any business similar to the plaintiff's business in any subsequent lease of any of the property retained by them, for it would seem to me to be difficult to confine the case to those shops which are actually adjoining, or to draw a line defining which of the premises were to be subjected to such a restriction. As Parker, J., said in *Browne* v. *Flower*, at p. 227 ([1911] 1 Ch.):

> Much as I sympathise with the plaintiffs, it would, in my opinion, be extending the implications based on the maxim that no one can derogate from his own grant to an unreasonable extent if it were held that what has been done in this case was a breach of an implied obligation.

Those words appear to me to be applicable to express my views with regard to the present case. In my judgment, the present case is, in substance, covered by the decision in *Browne* v. *Flower*.

The matter does not stop there, however, for that case was applied and followed by Branson, J., in the *O'Cedar* case, to which I have already referred. In that case, Branson, J., after referring to *Lyttelton Times Co., Ltd.* v. *Warners, Ltd.*, and *Harmer* v. *Jumbil (Nigeria) Tin Areas, Ltd.*, said, at p. 127:

> In the case before me, however, the purpose for which the premises were demised to the plaintiffs has not been frustrated by what has been done by the defendants. The plaintiffs can still conduct their business as they were able to before the surrendered premises were let to Davies.

He goes on to state the particular facts in that case, and points out that the question which it was necessary to consider was:

> whether the principle that a lessor may not derogate from his grant extends beyond cases in which the purpose of the grant is frustrated to cases in which that purpose can still be achieved albeit at a greater expense or with less convenience.

After referring to a number of cases, to which my attention was also called, he said, at p. 129:

> The contention is that the defendants, by doing something on the adjoining land which is not in itself unreasonable or unbusinesslike, which has not affected the demised premises physically in any way, which has not rendered it less easy or less legal to carry on upon them the business for which they were demised, but which has had the effect of adding substantially to the expense of carrying on that business there, have derogated from their grant. I should be extending the application of the principle into a region quite different from that in which it has hitherto been applied if I were to hold that it applied to anything done by a lessor upon adjoining land which, while not otherwise affecting the demised premises or their user in any way, merely made it more expensive than it was before for the lessee to carry on his business on the demised premises. I do not think such a case comes within that principle at all.

He concludes by saying, at p. 130:

> I cannot think that it was within the reasonable contemplation of the parties that the defendants were putting themselves under such an obligation to the plaintiffs as that contended for in this case.

In my judgment, the decision of Branson, J., applies, and governs the present case. I am unable to hold that it was within the reasonable contemplation of the plaintiff and defendants that the defendants were putting themselves and their remaining property under such an obligation to the plaintiff as that contended for by her. For these reasons, I think that the action fails, and must be dismissed with costs.

Action dismissed.

[In view of the above case, consider how a tenant may protect himself from competition from either the landlord or others who may lease from the same landlord. The necessity for careful and precise drafting of express covenants against competition is underlined by such cases as *Labone* v. *Litherland Urban District Council*, [1956] 1 W.L.R. 522, [1956] 2 All E.R. 215 (K.B.). See *Note*, Lessor's Covenants Restricting Competition: Drafting Problems, (1950) 63 Harv. L. Rev. 1400; *1 American Law of Property*, s. 3.42.]

(*b*) *Tenant's Obligations*

WARREN v. KEEN. Court of Appeal. [1954] 1 Q.B. 15, [1953] 2 All E.R. 1118, [1953] 3 W.L.R. 702

Appeal by a weekly tenant from a judgment against him for breach of an implied covenant to make such repairs as were necessary to keep the premises in good and tenantable condition.

SOMERVELL L. J.: Counsel for the landlord did not seek to support the wide form in which the learned judge set out the obligation on the tenant which he found to be implied. That would, in fact, mean that a weekly tenant was under a general covenant to keep, and, perhaps, to put and keep, in repair. No authority was cited for such a proposition, and in principle I am clear that no such implied obligation rests on a weekly tenant. It was suggested that the words in the note were wider than those used at the hearing.

The case for the landlord before us was put in the following way. It was alleged that a tenant from year to year is under an obligation not only to use and cultivate the land or premises in a husbandlike or tenantlike manner, but also to keep the buildings wind and water tight. That will be found stated in the judgment of Swinfen Eady, L. J., in *Wedd* v. *Porter*, [1916] 2 K.B. 100, and in various other cases and in text-books. On the other hand, the researches of counsel have failed to discover any case which throws light on the scope of that obligation, in other words, any case where a tenant has been held liable for failure to keep wind and water tight where the damage would not be covered by the obligation not to commit voluntary waste or the obligation to use the premises and land in a tenantlike manner. So, whether there is an additional obligation of a limited kind as to repairs in the case of a tenant from year to year remains in a state of, at any rate, some doubt.

In *Auworth* v. *Johnson*, (1832), 5 C. & P. 239, 172 E.R. 955, Lord Tenterden, C. J., in an interlocutory observation, said (5 C. & P. 240): "A tenant from year to year is to keep the premises in a little order...", and then he said that the tenant had done nothing. When he summed up to the jury (*ibid.*, 241) he again used the words the meaning of which is obscure, "... to keep the house wind and water tight...." The argument is, first, that that obligation to keep wind and water tight applies to a weekly tenant as well as to a tenant from year to year, and then, assuming that it does, the next submission is that the matters set out in the particulars of claim come within the covenant to keep the buildings wind and water tight. I think that submission fails at both stages. If there be a, so far indefinite, obligation on a tenant from year to year to do certain minor repairs necessary to keep premises wind and water tight—and I will assume without deciding the point that there is some such limited obligation—I see no ground in principle for applying that to a tenancy from week to week. It is quite true that under the Rent Restrictions Acts many tenants from week to week are enabled to remain in premises year after year, and the landlord may find great difficulty in fulfilling the conditions which have to be fulfilled under those Acts if he is to get possession. But that consideration does not, to my mind, affect the question of what are the implications of a weekly tenancy. It seems to me that it would be absurd to suggest that a weekly tenant is under an obligation to repair. It is difficult to think of repairs which would not in themselves cost more than the weekly rent in many cases and yet it is suggested that the tenant is impliedly liable to expend that money although his right to the premises may be terminated in a week's time.

In the second place, I am myself clear that the matters particularised in the particulars of claim would not fall within the words "wind and water tight". It seems to me clear that the damage here was due to decay of the walls, and there is no suggestion that that was due to any other cause than fair wear and tear. There is no suggestion that the tenant started knocking the walls about or anything of that sort, but in the course of time they had become cracked and presumably required re-pointing, because water was seeping in through the cracks which had appeared. The same would appear to have applied to the wood of the window-sills. That may have been due, not only to age, but also to the positive failure to have the external woodwork re-painted every three years, or whatever is the normal period. Those would both be matters which, in my opinion, could not on any construction come under this formula of keeping the building wind and water tight having regard to the principles which are to be found in the cases as to the implied liability of a tenant from year to year. Therefore, for these reasons, I think this appeal succeeds and the claim made by the landlord fails.

DENNING L. J.: Apart from express contract, a tenant owes no duty to the landlord to keep the premises in repair. The only duty of the tenant is to use the premises in a husbandlike, or what is the same thing, a tenantlike, manner. That is how it was put by Sir Vicary Gibbs, C. J., in *Horsefall* v. *Mather* (Holt N.P. 9) and by Scrutton and Atkin, L. JJ., in *Marsden* v. *Edward Heyes, Ltd.* ([1927] 2 K.B. 7,8). But what does it mean—"to use the premises in a tenantlike manner"? It can, I think, best be shown by some illustrations. The tenant must take proper care of the premises. He must, if he is going away for the winter, turn off the water and empty the boiler; he must clean the chimneys, when necessary, and also the windows; he must mend the electric light when it fuses; he must unstop the sink when it is blocked by his waste. In short, he must do the little jobs about the place which a reasonable tenant would do. In addition, he must not, of course, damage the house wilfully or negligently; and he must see that his family and guests do not damage it—if they do, he must repair it. But, apart from such things, if the house falls into disrepair through fair wear and tear or lapse of time or for any reason not caused by him, the tenant is not liable to repair it.

In the present case the landlord sought to put on the tenant a higher obligation. He said that the duty of the tenant was to keep the premises wind and water tight and to effect fair and tenantable repairs thereto. That seems to be based on *Hill and Redman's* Law of Landlord and Tenant, 11th ed., p. 186. I do not think that is a correct statement of the obligation. Take the first branch, "to keep the premises wind and water tight". Lord Tenterden in one or two cases at *nisi prius* used that expression, and it was followed by the Court of Appeal in *Wedd* v. *Porter*, but it is very difficult to know what "wind and water tight" means. I asked counsel whether there was any case to be found in the books where a tenant had been found liable for breach of that obligation because I wanted to see what sort of thing it had been held to cover. But no such case was to be found. In its absence, I think that the expression "wind and water tight" is of doubtful value and should be avoided. It is better to keep to the simple obligation "to use the premises in a tenantlike manner". Take the second branch, "to make fair and tenantable repairs". Lord Kenyon used the expression in *Ferguson* v. *Anon*, (2 Esp. 590), which is reported only by Espinasse, whose reports were notoriously defective. If you read the whole sentence used by Lord Kenyon, however, it is clear that he was referring only to cases where a tenant does damage himself, such as breaking the windows or the doors. Then, of course, he must repair them. The sentence used by Lord Kenyon was explained by Bankes, L. J., in *Marsden* v. *Edward Heyes, Ltd.*, [1927] 2 K.B. 6, by saying that if a tenant commits waste—that is, if he commits voluntary waste by doing damage himself—he must do such repairs to the premises as will enable them to exclude wind and water. So explained, it does not support the proposition stated in *Hill and Redman* at p. 186.

It was suggested by counsel for the landlord that an action lies against a weekly tenant for permissive waste. I do not think that is so. It has been held not to lie against a tenant at will: see the *Countess of Shrewsbury's Case*, 5 Co. Rep. 13b, 77 E.R. 68; and, in my opinion, it does not lie against a weekly tenant. In my judgment, the only obligation on a weekly tenant is to use the premises in a tenantlike manner. That does not cover the dampness and other defects alleged in the particulars of claim. The appeal should be allowed accordingly.

ROMER L. J.: I also agree, and can express in a very few words why I think the learned judge came to a wrong conclusion in this case. He is reported (although inaccurately as we were told) to have said in his judgment as to the original contract of tenancy, which was a weekly tenancy,

> "There was an implied covenant that the tenant would keep the premises in a good and tenantable condition and do such repairs as were necessary to this end."

That language (had it been used) would be attributing to a weekly tenant a degree of liability in the matter of repairs which is higher than that imposed by the law on tenants from year to year, as has been shown by Swinfen Eady, L. J., in *Wedd* v. *Porter* and Bankes, L. J., in *Marsden* v. *Edward Heyes, Ltd.*, and in other cases to which my brethren have referred. Accordingly, counsel for the landlord is unable to support the degree of liability which the learned judge was reported to have laid down. From the cases I have mentioned I gather that, whatever may be the precise extent of the liability of a tenant from year to year, he is not liable for deterioration due to fair wear and tear, and, if so, *a fortiori*, a weekly tenant is not so liable. Counsel then submitted, (and he has authority to support him) that a yearly tenant is at all events liable to keep the demised premises wind and water tight, whatever that may mean, and that this obligation is also imposed on a weekly tenant. There is no authority supporting that proposition so far as weekly tenants are concerned, and I, for my part, find difficulty in accepting it. But, at all events, it is only necessary for me to say in the present case that, in my opinion, the deterioration of which the landlord complains and on which she is suing in these proceedings is deterioration due to fair wear and tear or failure to paint, or both, and a weekly tenant is certainly not answerable for deterioration of that character.

Appeal allowed.

[For text-book law on a tenant's obligations as to care of the premises in the absence of express covenant, see *Woodfall*, Landlord and Tenant (1960, 26th ed.), pp. 728 ff.; *Cheshire*, Modern Law of Real Property (1962, 9th ed.), p. 363. In 1 *American Law of Property*, s. 378. (at p. 347) the law is stated as follows:

"The tenant... had an implied duty at common law to make minor repairs, a duty which arose out of his duty not to commit waste. The duty was to make such repairs as would keep the buildings windtight and watertight, thus preserving the property in substantially the same condition as at the commencement of the term, ordinary wear excepted. So the tenant was required to replace broken windows and doors, repair a leaking roof, and restore boards on the side of a building. He was not required to rebuild or restore a building, or any substantial part thereof, that had been destroyed by fire or other casualty or become so dilapidated from ordinary wear that it had to be torn down. Nor was he under any obligation to correct defects existing at the commencement of his lease.

"The rule that the tenant must make repairs was probably fair when applied in an agrarian economy where the materials for repairs were simple and at hand, and the tenant capable of making them himself. At least as concerns the actual making of repairs, the rule seems archaic and completely out of harmony with the facts when applied in a complicated society to urban dwellings occupied by persons on salary or weekly wage. Common experience indicates that the tenant in such cases seldom makes or is expected to make repairs even of the minor type covered by the common law duty. Such statements of the rule as one finds in modern cases is generally in connection with the denial of a right in the tenant or his invitees to hold the lessor in tort for injuries to person or property resulting from conditions brought about by a failure to repair. It would seem that the lessor is in the better position, from the viewpoint of economic situation and interest, to make repairs, and that the tenant ought to have no duty in the absence of a specific covenant."

See *Feuerstein and Shestack*, Landlord and Tenant—The Statutory Duty to Repair, (1950) 45 I11. L. Rev. 205.

Megarry, Manual of the Law of Real Property (1955, 2nd ed.,), sums up the law of waste applicable to a tenant, as follows (at p. 390): "A tenant's liability for waste depends upon the nature of his tenancy. A tenant for a fixed term of years is liable for both voluntary and permissive waste, and must therefore keep the premises in proper repair. A yearly tenant is similarly liable save that his liability for permissive waste is limited to keeping the premises wind- and water-tight. A weekly tenant, on the other hand, is not liable for permissive waste as such, though he must take proper care of the premises, e.g., by keeping the chimneys swept and the drain-pipes unblocked; it is not clear whether the same rule applies to monthly and quarterly tenants. A tenant at will is not liable for permissive waste, although if he commits voluntary waste his tenancy is thereby terminated and he is liable to an action for damages. A tenant at sufferance is liable for voluntary waste though probably not for permissive waste." See *MacLean* v. *Valdemar*, [1953] 2 D.L.R. 702, [1953] O.W.N. 473, aff'd [1954] 1 D.L.R. 720, [1954] O.W.N. 116 (C.A.) where liability for voluntary waste in the destruction of premises by fire because of negligence was imposed on a tenant from year to year. But *cf. Martin* v. *Larsen*, [1944] 1 D.L.R. 303 (B.C. Cty. Ct.) where liability was imposed on a monthly tenant for breach of an implied covenant for tenant-like user because the premises became infested with bugs.

The problems arising from the law of waste embrace relationships in addition to that of landlord and tenant, and hence the matter is treated more fully in chapter XI, *infra*. Moreover, express covenants to repair are the rule not the exception in leases, and attention is concentrated here on the scope and meaning of such covenants. If "Short Forms" leases are used, the tenant will be bound by three covenants to repair, namely, a general covenant to repair, a covenant to repair according to notice in writing, and a covenant to yield up in repair. Generally, all three covenants are subject to exceptions, as, for example, reasonable wear and tear, and damage by fire, lightning, tempest or Act of God: see, for example, Short Forms of Leases Act, R.S.O. 1960, c. 373, Sched. B, paras. 4, 7, and 9; Short Form of Leases Act, R.S.B.C. 1960, c. 357, Second Schedule, paras. 3, 9 and 13 (first two covenants unqualified by exceptions); Short Forms Act, R.S.M. 1954, c. 243, Third Schedule, paras. 3, 6 and 8; Conveyancing Act, R.S.Nfld. 1952, c. 140, s. 11 (3) (4) (6) (first two covenants unqualified by exceptions); Real Property Act, R.S.P.E.I. 1951, c. 138, Part 4, Third Schedule, paras. 3, 6 and 8 (first two covenants unqualified by exceptions).

The differences in the operation of the three repairing covenants are explained in *Woodfall*, Landlord and Tenant (1960, 26th ed.), pp. 696-698. Some of the older English cases on absolute repairing covenants refined the duties of repair according to the formulas or terms in which the covenant was expressed: see *Hill and Redman*, Law of Landlord and Tenant (1946, 10th ed.), p. 183. It appears now that variations in the formulation of the covenant (as, for example, to repair, to keep in repair, to put and keep in repair, well and sufficiently to repair, to keep in tenantable repair, and so on) do not express different legal duties in the case of absolute repairing covenants but are all referable to one standard unless a particular variation is specified: see *Anstruther-Gough-Calthorpe* v. *McOscar*, [1924] 1 K.B. 716 (C.A.). While an absolute covenant to repair may require a tenant to put in repair premises which are let in a dilapidated condition (see *Payne* v. *Haine* (1847), 16 M. & W. 541, 153 E.R. 1304; *Proudfoot* v. *Hart* (1890), 25 Q.B.D. 42), it is construed as referable to the demised premises as at the time of commencement of the tenancy and to their maintenance as such premises: *Pembery* v. *Lamdin*, [1940] 2 All E.R. 434 (C.A.); *Gooderham & Worts Ltd.* v. *Canadian Broadcasting Corp.*, [1947] A.C. 66, [1947] 1 D.L.R. 417 (P.C.); *Sotheby* v. *Grundy*, [1947] 2 All E.R. 761 (K.B.). Trivial damage may be regarded as outside of an obligation of repair (see *Scales* v. *Lawrence* (1860), 2 F. & F. 289, 175 E.R. 1065 (N.P.)), but deterioration through age and operation of the elements will not absolve a tenant under an absolute covenant from repairing or renewing subordinate parts, as opposed to being required to reconstruct or to replace a major portion of the building, as, for example, to supply a new foundation: see *Lurcott* v. *Wakely and Wheeler*, [1911] 1 K.B. 905 (C.A.); *Lister* v. *Lane and Nesham*, [1893] 2 Q.B. 212 (C.A.). Locality and nature of the premises are important as well as their condition at the time of commencement of the tenancy in assessing the burdens of a covenant to repair. All these considerations indicate how impossible it is to lay down more than general guides to the scope of the covenant. It should be remembered too that these guides have been evolved in English cases involving long term leases with absolute repairing covenants, and hence they spring from situations which have little resemblance to conditions in Canada where home ownership (with or without mortgage) rather than a long term lease is the vogue, and where residential leases at least are for relatively short periods especially in apartment dwelling.

The absolute covenant to repair has been carried the length of requiring a tenant on pain of damages to restore or rebuild premises which were destroyed by accidental fire or by other external occurrences; and, of course, in such cases the obligation to pay rent (if unqualified) will also continue unless recognition is given to an exonerating principle of frustration: see *Redmond* v. *Dainton*, [1920] 2 K.B. 256 (which was in fact a case of repair); *Paradine* v. *Jane* (1647), Aleyn 26, 82 E.R. 897; *Woodfall*, Landlord and Tenant (1960, 26th ed.), pp. 714-15. This is a curious result in view of the distinction generally taken between rebuild or replace and repair, and is explicable perhaps by continued reliance on an old line of cases (cited in *Woodfall*, *supra*) which gave a wide construction to the meaning of repair, especially at a time when liability for loss by fire was imposed without much regard to fault. The majority view in the United States is the same as that of the old English cases but the minority opinion to the contrary makes more sense today: see 1 *American Law of Property*, p. 350. Certainly when replacement or reconstruction is not required under an absolute covenant where premises deteriorate, there is less reason to require it where an external event destroys them. This, of course, is apart from any negligence of the tenant or his servants for which he may have to respond: see *United Motors Service* v. *Hutson*, [1937] S.C.R. 294, [1937] 1 D.L.R. 737.

Where premises held under a lease containing absolute repairing covenants were damaged by enemy action, the tenant defended the landlord's action for damages on the ground that he was forbidden by war regulations to expend more than a limited sum on repairs without a licence and hence he was excused because the damages exceeded that sum. Is this a good defence? See *Maud* v. *Sandars*, [1943] 2 All E.R. 783, 60 T.L.R. 81 (K.B.).

Premises occupied by a tenant were damaged by burglars. The landlord sued for damages for breach of a repairing covenant. Result? See *Phillimore* v. *Lane* (1925) 41 T.L.R. 469, 133 L.T. 268.]

BROWN v. DAVIES. Court of Appeal. [1957] 3 All E.R. 401, [(1957] 3 W.L.R. 818

Appeal by a tenant from an order for possession. The landlord complained, *inter alia*, of breach by the tenant of covenants to repair and decorate and to cultivate the garden of the leased premises. While the tenant was a statutory one, it was conceded that under the relevant legislation there was power to make an order for possession on proof of breach of obligations of the lease.

EVERSHED M. R.:... As regards the garden it is not in issue that the tenant not only had committed breaches of his obligation, but that he was still in breach at the hearing. As the learned judge pointed out, the tenant was no gardener and apparently gardening was not a matter in which he took the smallest interest. In the result, the exterior of the place, the garden surrounding the property, had become a jungle, to use the word which was used in the evidence. That being so, it follows that the jurisdiction for the judge to make the order arose whether or not he rightly concluded that there had been, or was at the date of the hearing still subsisting, a breach of the repairing covenant.

The case, therefore, has narrowed, on any view of it, to the question whether the judge rightly exercised his discretion in making the order. The main attack on the order was to this effect: that the learned judge took into account, as relevant for the exercise of his discretion, breaches past as well as present of the covenant to repair; that he was in error as a matter of law, having regard to the construction of the covenant, in so doing; and, therefore, that the allegation that it was reasonable to make an order cannot stand. Counsel for the tenant asked in opening the case that we should say that in the circumstances the only result must be to set aside the order for possession. Again, I am far from satisfied that, given the premise, that would be the right conclusion. If the learned judge had misdirected himself, I do not think it follows that we should thereupon set aside the order for possession. It might become necessary to send the case back, but, in the circumstances stated, it might be that this court could then determine, on a true apprehension of the matters to be taken into account, what order should be made. Those considerations, however, do not arise because in my judgment, for reasons which I must now attempt to state and justify, there was no misdirection by the learned judge.

I must now read the relevant paragraphs in the covenant. I need not refer to what I will call the garden covenant [in cl. 4 (e)] because no question turns on that. Clause 4 of the tenancy agreement comprising the tenant's covenant contains many paragraphs, of which I propose to read the bulk of (c) and (i). Paragraph (c) is:

> "To use and occupy the said premises in a fair and tenantable manner and keep the interior clean and in good repair and condition and decorated except as to dilapidation or damage resulting from reasonable wear and tear, accidental fire..."

Then there are a number of calamities referred to, such as shots and shells from aircraft which need not be considered. Paragraph (i) is:

> "To permit the landlord or her agents and others with the landlord's authority and by appointment with the tenant to enter upon and view the condition of the said premises and upon notice given by the landlord or her agents to carry out any interior repairs

and decorations necessary to put the premises in as good a state of repair and condition as the same are now in."

The first thing that is obvious on a reading of those two paragraphs is that the latter, on the face of it, is or may be of much stricter incidence on the tenant than the former; for, on the face of it, if the landlord were to view the premises and then to give notice to do decorations in order to bring the premises into the condition in which they were on Oct. 1, 1938, the tenant could not evade his obligation by saying: "You cannot require me to make good that lack of repair or decoration for it can be shown to be exclusively due to reasonable wear and tear". I agree with counsel for the tenant that the duty of the court must be to construe, so far as possible, these paragraphs together so as to arrive at a coherent whole. The solution of the apparent conflict submitted by counsel for the tenant was to say that the real burden imposed on the tenant was to be found in para. (i) and that the landlord should pursue his remedy in accordance with the provisions of that paragraph; that para. (c), if not rendered wholly ineffectual, was at best a very much slighter and relatively insignificant provision. I am not satisfied that the result of putting the two together in that way is to reduce the significance of para. (c) almost to nothing. It may well be inescapable that whoever drafted the agreement succeeded in the end in producing some repugnance in the provisions of the two paragraphs. I think that one must regard para. (c) according to its own language and that the only effect of having para. (i) in the back of one's mind would rather be, contrary to the submission of counsel for the tenant, to make one disinclined to produce the somewhat absurd result that, notwithstanding para. (i), the first obligation as to repair and decoration is of practically negligible effect.

In support of the argument for reducing to minimal significance para. (c), counsel for the tenant relied strongly on a decision of this court in *Taylor* v. *Webb* ([1937] 1 All E.R. 590). The report is long and I shall not follow all through the three judgments, nor elaborate greatly the facts. I observe, however, that the facts were exceptional. It may suffice if I borrow the language of Scott, L. J., from his judgment where he says (ibid., at p. 596):

> "... our task [of construing the common exception in repairing covenants in leases, 'fair wear and tear excepted'] is not quite the ordinary one, as we have to construe the words removed from their normal context of a tenant's covenant, and transported into the text of a landlord's covenant."

Scott, L. J., referring to the circumstance that the landlord in that case was himself a lessee under a headlease, and that under the headlease there was imposed on him, as tenant or lessee, an obligation to "keep the premises... and the fixtures, painting, papering and decorations thereof in good and tenantable repair", followed by the exception familiar enough to persons who practise in this class of work, "destruction or damage by fire and fair wear and tear excepted". The lessee then being transmuted by the underlease into the situation of a landlord, assumed in the underlease a more limited obligation as to repair, for it was only to keep the outside walls and roof properly repaired, but there was added the following referential language: "as and so far only as is required to be done by them under the [headlease]". One of the first problems which the court had to decide was what was the effect of the reference to the headlease, and the court held that it imported into the obligation to keep the outside walls and roof properly repaired the exception "fair wear and tear excepted". There was, therefore, on the landlord in that case (who was also the tenant under the headlease) a repairing covenant which was limited to the outside walls and roof. At the end of his judgment Slesser, L. J., who delivered the first judgment of the court, said ([1937] 1 All E.R. at p. 594):

"It will be observed that, in this case, unlike the case of *Haskell* v. *Marlow* ([1928] 2 K. B. 45), there was no general obligation to keep the dwelling-house in good repair and condition, but only the walls and roof, and, for the reasons which I have stated, I have come to the conclusion in this case, on the facts, that the landlord had no obligations whatever with regard to reparation..."

The matter was put by Scott, L. J. in this fashion ([1937] 1 All E.R. at p. 599):

"The learned judge in effect found, and, in my view, rightly found, that the whole of the disrepair was due to the elements, coupled with the absence of any steps by anybody to prevent further progress of the decay: there was no suggestion of any 'unfair' user by anybody, either tenant or landlord."

Finally, Farwell, J., the third member of the court, said this (ibid., at p. 601):

"Under the covenant, the lessor is prima facie liable for the serious state of disrepair into which, admittedly, the walls and roof have fallen, unless he can show (and the onus is on him) that that condition is due wholly to fair wear and tear. The meaning of the exception, in such a case as this, is, in my judgment, that the lessor is under no liability for disrepair due solely to such ordinary natural causes as may fairly be said to have been in the contemplation of the parties, for example, wind and weather, assuming no abnormal use of the property by him."

The damage complained of in *Taylor* v. *Webb* was found to have been the direct and sole result of the operation of the elements on a sky-light in the roof, and so the conclusion went.

Counsel for the tenant in the present case sought to say that *Taylor* v. *Webb* lays down a broad rule that, where one finds an exception, as one finds in para. (c) of cl. 4 of the agreement in the present case, "except as to dilapidation or damage resulting from reasonable wear and tear", the effect is, for practical purposes, to negative all the preceding obligations unless it can be shown that the state of repair is due to some active or wilful damage done by the tenant as a tenant. If that were its effect, *Taylor* v. *Webb* would have operated to set at nought what was laid down as long ago as 1834 by Tindal, C. J. in *Gutteridge* v. *Munyard* ((1834), 1 Mood. & R. 334 at p. 336). I quote from WOODFALL ON LANDLORD AND TENANT (25th Edn.) (1954), p. 765, to which counsel for the landlord drew our attention.

"Tindal, C. J., stated the effect of a repairing covenant containing an exception of reasonable use and wear in these words (1 Mood. & R. at p. 336): 'What the natural operation of time flowing on effects, and all that the elements bring about in diminishing the value, constitute a loss, which, so far as it results from time and nature, falls upon the landlord. But the tenant is to take care that the premises do not suffer more than the operation of time and nature would effect; he is bound by seasonable applications of labour to keep the house as nearly as possible in the same condition as when it was demised'."

I cannot conclude that this court, in *Taylor*, v. *Webb*, intended to lay down a broad proposition inconsistent with the long-established statement of Tindal, C. J.: all the more so perhaps since *Gutteridge* v. *Munyard* was not, in fact, referred to at all. In any case, however, the question of the construction of any covenant must depend on the words of the particular covenant sought to be construed. I have already referred to the somewhat unusual terms of the covenant in *Taylor* v. *Webb*, a covenant which Scott, L. J., described ([1937] 1 All E.R. at p. 596) as being "a topsy-turvy covenant", a hybrid. In the present case the obligation of the tenant is far more extensive on the face of it than was the obligation of the landlord in *Taylor* v. *Webb*. Observe that it opens with the words:

"To use and occupy the said premises in a fair and tenantable manner and keep the interior clean and in good repair and condition and decorated..."

and the exception is limited to "dilapidation or damage resulting from reasonable wear and tear..." I do not think it necessary or right that I should attempt to give an exposition of the exact scope of this provision. I am satisfied to put it no higher than that, if proof is given that the tenant is not keeping the premises in a fair and tenantable manner and not keeping the interior clean and well repaired and decorated, then, at the very least, the tenant must establish that the matters complained of ought to be attributed to dilapidation or damage resulting from reasonable wear and tear and to nothing else. It is to my mind quite plain that the tenant in this case, having such an onus on him (and counsel for the tenant admits that he has the onus), failed so to satisfy the judge.

I must now make some reference to the evidence. [The learned Justice discussed the evidence and concluded that it was reasonable for the trial Judge to make the order].

ROMER L. J.:... It was submitted by counsel for the tenant that where one finds a covenant to repair and decorate which is qualified by excepting dilapidation or damage resulting from reasonable wear and tear, the result is that, in fact, the covenantor need do nothing active in the pursuance of his obligation; in other words, provided he just sits back and allows the elements to have such effect on the premises as naturally occurs, then it cannot be said of him that he is in breach of his covenant. Counsel for the tenant said that that was the result of the decision of this court in *Taylor* v. *Webb* ([1937] 1 All E.R. 590). In my view, that is not the result of the decision in *Taylor* v. *Webb*. As Lord Evershed, M. R., pointed out, that case was a very exceptional one, and the covenant was in a very unusual form and, although it is true that the result for which counsel for the tenant contended in this case was that at which the court in *Taylor* v. *Webb* arrived, I am quite clear that the decision had nothing like the general effect for which counsel contended. It seems to me that the law as laid down by Tindal, C. J., in *Gutteridge* v. *Munyard* ((1834), 1 Mood. & R. 334) is still the general law and was not intended to be overruled by this court in *Taylor* v. *Webb*. Nor, indeed, was the statement of the law by Tindal, C. J., brought to the attention of the court in that case. The truth is that, in order to find out the scope and effect of a qualified covenant to repair, one has to look at the document as a whole, and it appears to me to be going far beyond anything that was said by any of the judges in *Taylor* v. *Webb* to say that one merely has to find an exception for reasonable wear and tear to reduce the scope of the covenant to practically nothing at all.

In the present case, if one gave that negative effect to cl. 4 (c) of the agreement, one would come in almost direct collision with the covenant in cl. 4 (i) under which at any time the tenant is under an obligation, if so required by the landlord,

"... to carry out any interior repairs and decorations necessary to put the premises in as good a state of repair and condition as the same are now in."

One must, so far as possible, effect a reconciliation between cl. 4 (c) and cl. 4 (i) and no such reconcilation is achieved by depriving cl. 4 (c), as the contention of counsel for the tenant would have the effect of depriving it, of practically any effect at all. Therefore, I think that *Taylor* v. *Webb* must be regarded as a case (as, indeed, it was) dealing with a covenant in a very special form and with special circumstances, and that it does not form the foundation for a general statement of the law such as counsel for the tenant has laid before this court....

ORMEROD L. J.: I agree and have nothing to add. *Appeal dismissed.*

[Should it make any difference in construing an exception of fair wear and tear that it is annexed to a landlord's covenant to repair, as in *Taylor* v. *Webb*, [1937] 2 K.B. 283, [1937] 1 All E.R. 590 (C.A.) rather than to a tenant's covenant to repair?

In *Taylor* v. *Webb*, Scott L. J. speaking in relation to disrepair caused by "natural wear and tear" said: "Omission to prevent cannot give rise to a cause of action where there is no duty to prevent." He defined the expression "fair (or reasonable) wear and tear excepted" as follows: "The phrase 'wear and tear' is a very old English idiom, and the clause 'fair' (or 'reasonable') 'wear and tear excepted,' has been common in leases and tenancy agreements for two or three centuries. It is, like many idiomatic expressions, complex in meaning; it implicitly refers to both cause and effect, and, in each aspect, it covers two classes of disrepair, (a) that brought about by the normal or ordinary operation of natural causes, such as wind and weather, in contradistinction to abnormal or extraordinary events in nature, such as lightning, hurricane, flood, or earthquake; and (b) that brought about by the tenant, and other persons present in or on the premises with the consent of the tenant, either unintentionally or as a normal incident of a tenant's occupation, in the course of the 'fair' (or 'reasonable') use of the premises for any of the purposes for which they were let.... Neither, 'reasonable' nor 'fair' can apply to the elements as a cause of wear and tear; the elements cannot be either fair (except in the meteorological sense) or reasonable. Nor can either word be used as applying to the effects of the elements; the phrase cannot mean a fair amount of resultant wear and tear, as a countryman may speak of a 'fair'-sized turnip. In my view, the word 'reasonable' or 'fair' applies only to the treatment of the premises by the tenant. This reasoning leads me to the conclusion that the phrase 'fair' (or 'reasonable') 'wear and tear' is an elliptical idiom, in which only a part of the well understood meaning is expressed. The effect of either epithet is to prevent the tenant having *carte blanche* as to his user of the premises; the word is a stipulation simply and solely about his conduct, limiting his right to rely on the exception, where the state of disrepair has been caused by him or his invitees, by a proviso that such tenant's user must have been 'fair' (or 'reasonable'). If he uses the premises 'unfairly' (or 'unreasonably'), he loses *pro tanto* the benefit of his exception."

In *Arden* v. *Pullen* (1842), 10 M. & W. 321, 152 E.R. 492 (Ex.), the tenant had covenanted to repair, fair wear and tear excepted. In an action for rent his defence was that the premises had decayed and had become unsafe and that under the exception in the repairing covenant it was for the landlord to make the wear and tear good by way of implied obligation. Is this a tenable argument?

The roof of a curling rink held under a lease collapsed owing to the accumulation of an "abnormal amount" of snow. The lease contained a covenant by the tenant to repair, "reasonable wear and tear and damage by fire, lightning and tempest only excepted". The landlord's action for damages against the tenant was successful. Do you agree? See *Hall* v. *Campbellford Cloth Co. Ltd.*, [1944] 2 D.L.R. 247, [1944] O.W.N. 202.

See *Blundell*, The Fair Wear and Tear Clause, (1937) 2 Conv. & Prop. L. 1.]

MANCHESTER v. DIXIE CUP COMPANY (CANADA) LTD. Ontario Court of Appeal. [1951] O.R. 686, [1952] 1 D.L.R. 19

Appeal by landlords from dismissal of their claim for damages for breach of a covenant to repair. A separate claim for rent was held to be satisfied by a sum paid into Court by the tenant, and this conclusion was sustained on appeal. What follows below is on the issue of alleged breach of the obligation of repair.

The judgment of the Court was delivered by ROACH J. A.: ... On that branch of the plaintiffs' claim, the following covenants and agreements in the lease are relevant:

"AND the said Lessee COVENANTS with the said Lessors that it will, during the said term hereby granted, well and sufficiently repair, maintain and keep the said demised premises and every portion thereof with the appurtenances in good and substantial repair.... when and where and so often as need shall be, reasonable wear and tear and damage by fire, lightning and tempest only excepted....

"AND the Lessee further agrees to use the said premises only for the usual and ordinary business of the manufacture and distribution of sanitary drinking cups, paper containers and receptacles and other similar articles, or for such other purposes as shall not involve a greater fire hazard or be more injurious to the building or more offensive than such business, and for no other purposes, without the written consent of the Lessors first obtained.

"AND that it will leave the premises in good repair, reasonable wear and tear and damage by fire, lightning and tempest only excepted."

The plaintiffs claimed a breach of the covenants respecting repair in two particulars: first, by negligently allowing hot wax to escape during the defendant's manufacturing processes and cover the walls, floor, ceiling, pillars, pipes and fixtures and to penetrate into the inside brick; second, by damaging the floors.

Before dealing with either of those claims it is desirable that something should be said with respect to the nature of the manufacturing business conducted by the respondent in those premises, during its whole occupancy thereof.

The respondent had occupied these premises since some time in the year 1937. The appellants became owners of the building in September, 1946. As earlier stated, the respondent's lease with the former owner was not due to expire until December 31, 1946, so for the balance of the term of that earlier lease the respondent paid the rent as it became due to the appellants.

During the whole of the occupancy of the premises by the respondent there was no change in the type of business which it carried on therein, nor, subject to some deviation to which I shall later refer, was there any change in the manner in which it conducted that type of manufacturing business.

The business of the respondent is the manufacturing and sale of paper drinking-cups and other paper containers. Those products are cut and shaped and then sprayed with hot wax. The actual spraying was done by machines which were described as "treaters". The cups, or other containers, were carried into an enclosed chamber of the treater on a belt conveyor and as they passed through that chamber the hot wax was sprayed on them. As they were being carried along after emerging from the treater wax-laden vapour arose from them. Electric fans and openings had been installed at appropriate places, designed to carry the wax-laden vapour out of the building, but notwithstanding these devices some of that vapour adhered to the walls and other surfaces and in due course there was a volume of wax deposit on those surfaces, and some of it penetrated into the pores of the brick walls. The heaviest concentration of wax on the surfaces and the penetration were in the areas closest to the treaters.

The respondent at all times knew that wax was being deposited on the walls, ceilings and other surfaces which were in reasonably close proximity to the treaters, and from time to time took steps to remove those deposits. Weekly, in the room where the treaters were installed, the walls and ceiling were scraped with scrapers such as are used for scraping ice from sidewalks, and they were brushed with wire brushes and brooms. These methods sufficed to remove that part of the wax deposits which appeared as fluff on the walls and other surfaces, but there is no doubt, on the evidence, that they did not suffice to remove all the wax that was thus deposited, and the residue which was left consisted of a film of wax on the surfaces, of various thicknesses, and, of course, included in what was left was that part of the deposit which had penetrated into the pores of the brick.

Apart from the machines known as treaters, there were other pieces of machinery installed in other places throughout the plant, those other machines each performing various functions in connection with the respondent's business. To a very large extent the plaintiffs' claim with respect to floors has to do with the condition of the floors under or near to those machines, the plaintiffs' claim with respect thereto being that the floors in those areas have rotted because of the failure of the respondent to provide adequate facilities for protecting them against oil and/or grease escaping from the machines. The balance of the plaintiffs' claim with respect to the floors consists of allegations that they have been damaged, (a) by the iron wheels of carts which were pushed around the plant, and (b) by water which overflowed in the area of a drinking fountain.

The question of law arises as to the extent of the respondent's obligation to repair under the relevant covenants which I earlier quoted. In considering that obligation it becomes necessary, so far as the coating or impregnation of wax is concerned, to divide the premises into three areas—first, the annex; second, the treater-room, third, the area outside the treater-room. I divide the premises into those areas for factual reasons.

At one time the treating-machines were installed and operated in the annex, but they had been removed from the annex long before the appellants purchased the building. Unquestionably, during the time the treaters were in operation in the annex wax had escaped and been deposited on the ceiling and walls of that area. The appellants complain of that condition, but it is clear that that condition existed in that area at the time the appellants became the owners of the premises. That condition became neither better not worse in the meantime.

The condition in the treater-room, on evidence which the trial Judge accepted, was the same when the respondent vacated as at the commencement of the lease. Unquestionably, during the term of the lease wax was being deposited on the walls and ceiling of the treater-room, and weekly the methods I have earlier described for removing the same were adopted by the respondent, but any increase in the residue of wax which was deposited during the term did not make the condition of those surfaces in the treater-room appreciably worse than it was at the beginning of the lease.

In December, 1948, an additional treating machine was installed just outside the door leading into the treater-room, and it continued in operation until April, 1949. There is some evidence on behalf of the respondent that the condition with respect to wax on the walls, ceiling and other surfaces in that area was no different at the end of the term than it was at its beginning. On the other hand, there is other evidence on behalf of the appellants that the deposits in that area were greater at the end of the lease than they were at the beginning. To my mind it would be unreasonable to conclude that there had been no difference caused in the condition of the walls, ceiling and other surfaces in that area by the installation of the additional treating machine at that particular place. Wax was bound to escape in that area after the machine was installed and in operation, when formerly none escaped into that area except perhaps an inappreciable amount which might come out of the treater-room. The condition in that area, therefore, was worse at the end of the term than it was at the beginning.

If the respondent, by virtue of the covenants, was obliged to remove the wax from the walls and other surfaces in the annex, then, having failed to do so, the appellants were entitled to have it removed and to recover the cost thereof from the respondent.

So far as the condition of the treater-room is concerned different considerations apply. Because there was already a coating and impregnation of wax on and in the surfaces of that room at the beginning of the term, was the defendant obligated under its covenant, (a) to remove it, and (b) to keep it removed?

So far as the condition in the area immediately outside the door leading into the treater-room was concerned, was the respondent obligated under its covenant to keep the walls and ceiling in that area free from wax?

At least some of the questions I have posed are embodied in this more general question, namely, was the respondent, under its covenant, required to do more than maintain the premises in their condition as of the commencement of the term of the lease, subject only to reasonable wear and tear thereafter?

The covenant which I have first quoted raises a difficult question of construction. It requires that the respondent shall "well and sufficiently repair, maintain and keep the said demised premises... in good and substantial repair... reasonable wear and tear and damage by fire, lightning and tempest only excepted."

I should state at once that, in my opinion, a building of the type here in question is not in a state of good and substantial repair if its walls and ceiling are so incrusted with wax that those surfaces cannot be painted. There was evidence that at least in those sections where incrustation of wax was the thickest efforts were made by the appellants to paint those surfaces, but the paint would not adhere to the surface and would not dry. In my opinion, therefore, the annex, the treater-room and, to a lesser extent, the area outside the treater-room door, were not in a state of good and substantial repair at the commencement of the term.

In *Proudfoot* v. *Hart* (1890), 25 Q.B.D. 42, the obligation of the tenant was in terms as follows: "During the said term [to] keep the said premises in good tenantable repair, and so leave the same at the expiration thereof." It was conceded that the premises were not in tenantable repair when the tenancy commenced, and it was argued on behalf of the tenant that because they were not in tenantable repair the tenant was not obligated to put them in tenantable repair. It was held that the tenant's obligation was to put and keep the premises in such repair as, having regard to the age, character and locality of the house, would make it reasonably fit for the occupation of a tenant of the class that would be likely to take it. At p. 50 Lord Esher M. R. put it thus: "It has been decided—and, I think, rightly decided —that, where the premises are not in repair when the tenant takes them, he must put them into repair in order to discharge his obligation under a contract to keep and deliver them up in repair."

In *Proudfoot* v. *Hart* and in such other English cases as *Payne* v. *Haine* (1847), 16 M. & W. 541, 153 E.R. 1304; *Lurcott* v. *Wakely & Wheeler*, [1911] 1 K.B. 905, and *Calthorpe* v. *McOscar*, [1923] 2 K.B. 573, and in appeal [1924] 1 K.B. 716, all of which were relied upon by counsel for the appellants, the covenant to repair was absolute. Here it is subject to a limitation and because of that limitation it is impossible to give to this covenant a meaning equally extensive with the meaning of the covenants in those cases.

A building cannot at one and the same time be in a state of good and substantial repair and also in a state of non-repair. A covenant that imposed upon a tenant the duty to *put* a building in a state of good and substantial repair, except the present non-repair, would be meaningless and it would make no difference how that non-repair had been caused. Therefore, the covenant with which we are here concerned connot be construed as imposing on the tenant a duty to *put* the premises in a state of good and substantial repair. The respondent's duty under this covenant was to *keep* the premises in the state of repair in which they were at the commencement of the term, excepting only such non-repair as might be caused during the term by reasonable wear and tear, fire, lightning and/or tempest.

The respondent is, therefore, not liable for the cost of removing the wax from the annex, because no wax was deposited in that area during the term of the lease. Neither is the respondent liable for the condition in the treater-room at the termination of the lease because, though it caused wax to be deposited in that area during the term, the condition at the end of the term was not appreciably worse than at the beginning.

I think, however, that some liability attaches to the respondent for the condition existing at the termination of the lease in the area outside the treater-room where the additional treater had been installed in December, 1948.

In the treater-room itself some efforts had been made by the respondent at least to minimize the deposits of wax. The boundaries of the treater-room were as follows: On the north was an outside wall of the building; on the east and west were wooden partitions lined with gyproc; on the south was another fibre-board wall with two sliding doors. Three treaters were in operation in that room. An exhaust-fan, of a capacity recommended to the respondent as being sufficient to carry fumes from the products produced by three treaters, was installed in the north wall. In the south wall was another fan built into the fibre-board partition, so that there would be a current of air running from south to north. It was stated by Mr. Currie in his evidence that at times they found it unnecessary to keep the fan in the southern wall running.

The additional machine was installed completely outside the treater-room. A hole was cut in the southerly wall of the treater-room and the nose of the machine placed up against that hole. There is evidence that after that hole was cut one could see from outside the treater-room, through the hole and all the way across the treater-room. No further facilities were installed to take care of the extra escape of wax vapour that, to my mind, was inevitable as a result of the installation and operation of the additional treater machine. In my opinion that was not reasonable user of that particular part of the plant.

It is impossible to determine precisely from the evidence how much of the total amount spent by the appellants in removing wax should be allocated to the area outside the treater-room. Rather than direct a reference to determine that amount, I have concluded that an allowance of $300 would be reasonable.

So far as the allegation of non-repair to the floors is concerned, I would not interfere with the judgment below. It was in the contemplation of the parties that heavy machinery would be located in these premises. Indeed, the appellants saw the various machines actually installed and operating before they purchased the building. All those machines required oil and grease—some more than others. Drip-pans had been placed where there was liable to be dripping. Those pans may not have caught all the oil that dripped, but I am not prepared to hold that, having regard to the use to which the respondent was entitled to put the premises so far as this machinery was concerned, the condition of the floors of which the appellants now complain was brought about by a user that was unreasonable.

Around a drinking-fountain in a factory there is bound to be some splashing of the floor. Careless and inconsiderate employees may on occasions throw the remnants from drinking cups on the floor. An employer cannot be always on the alert to guard against that conduct. Those circumstances are almost necessarily incidental to the use of the fountain, in such premises. Moreover, there is evidence that on occasions, due to heavy rains, the drain from the fountain backed up and flooded the floor.

No doubt as a result of the use of trucks with ordinary iron wheels, some sections of the floor were gouged or the tongues in some boards were split. However, I am not prepared to hold that the use of such trucks was unreasonable. It must be remembered that this building was designed for manufacturing purposes, even heavier than the particular type of industry carried on by the respondent. In such a building, in a measure proportionate to the type of industry therein operated, wooden floors are certain to deteriorate by user. This building is about 20 years old and it is a fair inference that the condition of the floors of which the appellants complain was not all caused during the 2 years and 7 months that the respondent occupied the premises as the tenant of the appellants.

I would, therefore, allow the appeal in part by awarding to the appellants the sum of $300 and directing that judgment be entered in their favour for such amount together with their costs of the trial on the County Court scale without set-off. The appellants should also have their costs in this Court as on an appeal from the County Court.

Appeal allowed in part.

[See also *Bartram* v. *Rempel*, [1950] 4 D.L.R. 442, [1949] 2 W.W.R. 1183 (B.C.C.A.) where in view of an exception of reasonable wear and tear, the tenant was absolved of liability for failing to replace decayed fence posts.]

[It has been said that Courts will not order specific performance of repairing covenants: see *Hill* v. *Barclay* (1810), 16 Ves. 402, 33 E.R. 1037 (Ch.); subsequent proceedings (1811), 18 Ves. 56, 34 E.R. 238 (Ch.); *Holman* v. *Knox* (1911), 25 O.L.R. 588, 3 D.L.R. 207 (Div. Ct.). But *cf. Wolverhampton Corp.* v. *Emmons.* [1901] 1 K.B. 515; *Tanenbaum* v. *W. J. Bell Paper Co. Ltd.*, [1956] O.R. 278, 4 D.L.R. 2d 177.

There have been cases where Courts have issued mandatory injunctions to compel restoration in case of alterations improperly made to premises, and the principle is equally applicable to alterations made in breach of a covenant to keep in repair: see *Allport* v. *Securities Corp.* (1895), 64 L.J.Ch. 491; *Holman* v. *Knox, supra. Cf. Johnston* v. *Givens, supra*, p. 221.

Because damages are generally adequate, that is the usual remedy and, if the lease so provides, a right of re-entry or power of termination may be exercised as well, subject to relief against forfeiture which has now, generally, a statutory basis. The problems in connection with forfeiture are discussed below in section 6 of this Chapter. But it may be noted that it is open to the Court in giving relief to require restoration of premises or security for such restoration, so that in effect specific enforcement of a repairing covenant is realized: see *Hyman* v. *Rose*, [1912] A.C. 623; *Sullivan* v. *Dore* (1913), 13 D.L.R. 910, 5 O.W.N. 70.]

CONQUEST v. EBBETTS. House of Lords. [1896] A.C. 490

Appeal from a judgment of the Court of Appeal, [1895] 2 Ch. 377, affirming a report of the official referee fixing the damages for breach of a covenant to repair premises which at the time of the hearing of the case were held under a lease having an unexpired term of three and a half years. The official referee fixed the sum by ascertaining how much it would cost to put the premises in repair according to the covenant and allowing a deduction therefrom in view of the fact that the lease had some years to run.

LORD HERSCHELL: My Lords, the appellants in the present case contend that the damages for the admitted breach of contract to keep certain demised premises in repair have been assessed on a wrong principle...

Where an action for non-repair had been brought during the currency of a lease, it was said by Holt C. J. (in *Vivian* v. *Champion*, 2 Ld. Raym. 1125) in answer to the objection that it was a hard action, for maybe the lessee might leave the premises in repair at the end of the term, and that therefore it was usual to give but small damages: "We always inquire in these cases what it will cost to put the premises in repair and give so much damages, and the plaintiff ought in justice to apply the damages to the repair of the premises." In the case of *Doe d. Worcester Trustees* v. *Rowlands*, 9 C. & P. 734, Coleridge J. said: "In estimating the damages in cases where the lease has a long time to run, it is not fair to take the amount that would be necessary to put the premises into repair as the measure of the damages.... The true question therefore is, to what extent is the reversion injured by the non-repair of the premises? If the lease had ninety-nine years to run it could not make much difference in the value of the reversion whether the premises were now in repair or not. This lease, however, will expire in about six years." I may observe that what the learned judge said with regard to a lease having ninety-nine years to run would not be applicable in all cases. There are circumstances in which it might be of the utmost importance to the reversioners that the buildings should be in a proper state of repair.

Holt C. J.'s statement of the law has been subjected to criticism in other cases, and notably by Parke B. and Alderson B. in *Turner* v. *Lamb*, 14 M. & W. 412. I do not think any hard and fast rule can be laid down as to the damages which may be recovered by the covenantee during the currency of a lease in respect of the breach of a covenant to keep the demised premises in repair. All the circumstances of the case must be taken into consideration, and the damages must be assessed at such a sum as reasonably represents the damage which the covenantee has sustained by the breach of covenant. I quite agree with the criticism to which Lord Holt's view has been subjected if that learned judge intended to lay down that, whatever the circumstances and however long the term had to run, the damages must necessarily be what it would cost to put the premises into repair. On the other hand, I think it would be equally wrong to hold that this could never be the measure of damages, whatever the circumstances and however nearly the term had expired. But in the present case, if the test be applied of inquiring how much the value of the respondents' reversion has been diminished by the breach of covenant, a test for which I understand the appellants to contend, I cannot see that there has been any error in the assessment of damages. If the premises were now in good repair, the reversion of the respondents would secure them the improved rent of £100 a year to the end of the term, without any liability on their part, unless it were to the extent to which repairs subsequently became necessary. As matters stand they can only receive this rent subject to the liability of restoring the premises to good repair, so that they may in that condition re-deliver them to their lessor. The difference between these two positions represents the diminution in the value of their reversion owing to the breach of covenant, and on this basis the damages seem to me to have been properly assessed.

It was contended for the appellants that the respondents would not be bound in any case to spend upon the premises the sum necessary to put them in repair, or at the expiration of the term to pay that sum to their lessor. It was said that owing to the nature of the premises and the changed circumstances of the neighbourhood the freeholder would make an entirely different use of the site when the term he had created came to an end, that he would not desire to have the buildings then upon his land put in good repair, and that he would arrive at some arrangement with his lessee by which he would accept from him a sum less than the cost of effecting these repairs. I do not think the Court would do right, in assessing the damages in the present case, to involve itself at the instance of the appellants in considerations of that character. The duty of the appellants as between themselves and the respondents was to fulfil the obligation of the covenant into which they entered, and keep the premises in repair. If they had done so, the present question would not have arisen. They have broken their covenant, and when sued for the breach they have, in my opinion, no right to demand that a speculative inquiry shall be entered upon as to what may possibly happen and what arrangements may possibly be come to, under the special circumstances of the case, when the superior lease expires by effluxion of time.

I think the appeal should be dismissed with costs. *Appeal dismissed.*

[Lord Macnaghten and Lord Morris concurred.

In *Gooderham & Worts Ltd.* v. *Canadian Broadcasting Corp.*, [1947] A.C. 66, [1947] 1 D.L.R. 417 (F.C.), Lord Macmillan said (at p. 83 A.C., p. 428 D.L.R.): "Where a claim is made by a landlord against his tenant for breach of covenant [to repair] during the currency of the tenancy... the measure of damages is the diminution in value of the reversion resulting from the breach without prejudice to any further claim which the landlord may have at the termination of the tenancy."

Subject to any applicable statutory provision controlling any contractual right of the landlord to terminate a lease for breach of covenant to repair (see, for example, Landlord and Tenant Act, R.S.O. 1960, c. 206, s. 19), the landlord where he has reserved a right of re-entry may, of course, both terminate the lease and sue for damages. If he asserts both remedies in one action and the lease (if not terminated) would not have expired for a considerable period, are the damages assessable according to the diminution in the value of the reversion at the date of termination or according to the diminution in value at the normal expiry date of the lease? See *Hanson* v. *Newman*, [1934] Ch. 298, 50 T.L.R. 191 (C.A.). *Cf. Smiley* v. *Townshend*, [1950] 2 K.B. 311, [1950] 1 All E.R. 530 (C.A.) (premises under requisition at time of action brought after expiry of lease).

The burden of proving diminution in value of the reversion is upon the landlord but disrepair is in itself some evidence thereof: see *Smiley* v. *Townshend, supra.*]

[As to the measure of damages for breach of covenant to repair where the premises are destroyed by fire, see *Yates* v. *Dunster* (1855), 11 Ex. 15, 156 E.R. 726 (C.A.); *In re Driscoll, Driscoll* v. *Driscoll*, [1918] 1 Ir. R. 152.

Where damages are sought at the end of the term for breach of covenant to yield or deliver up in repair, the measure at common law is the cost of repairs subject to bringing into account any damages paid for breach of covenant to repair during the term and deducting a sum for depreciation as if the repairs had been then done: see *Henderson* v. *Thorn*, [1893] 2 Q.B. 164, 62 L.J.Q.B. 586.

The "cost of repairs" rule as the measure of damages under breach of a covenant to yield up in repair was accepted as the fixed rule in *Joyner* v. *Weeks*, [1891] 2 Q.B. 31, 60 L.J.Q.B. 510 (C.A.), a decision which has been followed in Canadian cases: see *Buscombe* v. *Stark*, 30 D.L.R. 736, [1917] 1 W.W.R. 204, 23 B.C.R. 155 (C.A.); *National Trust Co. Ltd.* v. *The King*, [1949] 2 D.L.R. 472 (Ex. Ct.). The application of the rule is unaffected by the fact that the landlord may have re-let the premises at as favourable a rent as was theretofore paid or even by the fact that he intends to pull down the premises.

In *James* v. *Hutton and Cook & Sons Ltd.*, [1950] 1 K.B. 9, [1949] 2 All E.R. 243 (C.A.), the rule in *Joyner* v. *Weeks* was held inapplicable to breach of a covenant to reinstate the premises (which had been altered with the landlord's consent) at the end of the term to their previous condition. Lord Goddard C. J., speaking for the Court said (at p. 15, K.B., p. 246, All E.R.):

"What then, is the measure of damages applicable to the breach of a covenant to restore on request when the only evidence is that there has been no compliance with that request? In our opinion, the general rule as to damages for breach of contract ought to be applied, namely, to ascertain what the damage actually suffered amounts to. A covenant is only a special form of contract and the same rules apply to a breach of covenant as apply to a breach of a simple contract so far as damages are concerned.

"To apply to this case the rule as to the measure of damages for a breach of contract to deliver up a house in repair is, in our opinion, wrong, for there is no true analogy between the two cases. If a tenant fails to deliver up a house in repair, the landlord must suffer some damage at least so long as the house remains in existence. Instead of getting a house in a perfect state of repair he gets one which is dilapidated. It is true that he may be able to let the dilapidated house for the same or even a higher rent than he was hitherto getting, but that may be due to market conditions and more especially to the demand for a certain class of premises. A dilapidated house must be worth less than a house in a proper state of repair. Presumably, if the house is sold in good repair, it would fetch more than a house which is out of repair. If a house can be let in good repair, it would ordinarily fetch a higher rent than one that is out of repair. Damage is, therefore, suffered. The measure of damages to be applied was laid down in *Joyner* v. *Weeks*. In that case the Divisional Court had applied the same rule as is applicable to a case where the lessee has failed to keep the house in repair during the term and ordered the damages to be assessed according to the injury done to the reversion. The Court of Appeal held that in these cases there was a well-defined rule which had become a rule of law that, on a failure to deliver up a house in good repair, the damage was the cost of the work necessary to put it into repair. Lord Esher, M. R., in giving the judgment referred ([1891] 2 Q.B. 43) to the large number of cases in which this rule had been adopted, and said that such an inveterate practice amounted to a rule of law. He said it was a highly convenient rule, avoiding all the subtle refinements with which the court had been indulged and the extensive and costly inquiries which they would involve. It was a simple and business-like rule, and he was very much inclined to think it was an absolute rule. But, as we have already said, that case must be regarded as proceeding on the footing that the landlord must have suffered damage by the tenant yielding up the house out of repair. We see no ground here for assuming that the landlord in the present case has suffered any damage at all. She has got back a shop, or would have done so if the premises had not been requisitioned, provided with a modern and convenient front, and there was no suggestion that the work had not been carried out properly. We do not for one moment suggest that it might not be possible for a landlord, in circumstances such as these to give evidence that she or her superior landlords at the end of the term desired to carry on or to let the premises for the purpose of carrying on a business for which the altered shop front would be inappropriate and the old one suitable. In that case she might well say that it is of value to her to have her shop back in its former condition and she would suffer damage if the tenant's or assignees' covenant to restore was not carried out, but if it is a mere matter of getting back a shop which has been altered and there is no suggestion that any damage whatever has been caused to the landlord thereby, it appears to us she has suffered no damage by reason of the tenant's or assignees' failure to comply with her requirements to reinstate.... In our opinion, therefore, she cannot be entitled to any more than nominal damages."

In England, the Landlord and Tenant Act, 1927 (Imp.), c. 36, provides by s. 18 (1) as follows: "Damages for a breach of a covenant or agreement to keep or put premises in repair during the currency of a lease, or to leave or put premises in repair at the termination of a lease, whether such covenant or agreement is expressed or implied, and whether general or specific, shall in no case exceed the amount (if any) by which the value of the reversion (whether immediate or not) in the premises is diminished owing to the breach of such covenant or agreement as aforesaid; and in particular no damage shall be recovered for a breach of any such covenant or agreement to leave or put premises in repair at the termination of a lease, if it is shown that the premises, in whatever state of repair they might be, would at or shortly after the termination of the tenancy have been or be pulled down, or such structural alterations made therein as would render valueless the repairs covered by the covenant or agreement." For an application of this provision, see *Salisbury* v. *Gilmore and Marcel*, [1942] 2 K.B. 38, [1942] 1 All E.R. 457 (C.A.); *Cunliffe* v. *Goodman*, [1950] 2 K.B. 237, [1950] 1 All E.R. 720 (C.A.); *Jones* v. *Herxheimer*, [1950] 2 K.B. 106, [1950] 1 All E.R. 323 (C.A.).]

[If a tenant in consideration of the diminution of rent for a specified period undertakes to repair and restore the premises, is the sum so expended deductible by him in computing his taxable income? Would it make any difference if the repairs were made in pursuance of a general covenant to repair as contrasted with the special undertaking? See *Jackson* v. *Laskers Home Furnishers Ltd.*, [1957] 1 W.L.R. 69, [1956] 3 All E.R. 891 (Ch.).]

COVENANTS TO REPAIR AND INSURANCE. If a tenant covenants to repair without excepting fire and the premises are destroyed by accidental fire or, assuming fire is excepted but the destruction by fire arises through the tenant's negligence, he may be liable for the damage, in the one case on his covenant and in the other in tort: see *United Motors Service Inc.* v. *Hutson*, [1937] S.C.R. 294, [1937] 1 D.L.R. 737. He has, of course, an insurable interest, but if he fails to insure he may be saddled with damages caused by his negligence because the exception of fire in the standard covenant to repair does not throw the liability on the landlord. If the landlord carries insurance and liability for damage by fire rests on the tenant either under an absolute covenant, or by reason of personal or vicarious liability for negligence, the tenant (in the absence of express stipulation) cannot call upon the landlord to apply the insurance money to restoration of the premises: see *Leeds* v. *Cheetham* (1827), 1 Sim. 146, 57 E.R. 533 (Ch.). Moreover, as between the landlord and his insurer, the latter on paying over the insurance money is entitled to be subrogated to the landlord's rights against the tenant; and if the tenant has repaired, in pursuance of his covenant or other obligation to do so the landlord cannot claim or keep the insurance money because he has suffered no loss and there is hence no basis for indemnity: see *Darrell* v. *Tibbitts* (1880), 5 Q.B.D. 560 (C.A.). *Cf. Baloise Fire Ins. Co.* v. *Martin*, [1937] O.R. 355, [1937] 2 D.L.R.24.

Difficulties between the parties or for either of them may be avoided by exaction of a covenant to insure covering the interests of both, with provision for expenditure of the insurance proceeds in rebuilding. A joint policy is a possibility. Of course, the landlord and tenant may each insure. If each does and a loss under the policies occurs, does the ultimate liability of the insurer depend on who repairs or on who has the obligation of repair under the lease? See *Note*, (1947) 60 Harv. L. Rev. 1348.

S. 19 (8) of the Landlord and Tenant Act, R.S.O. 1960, c. 206 provides that relief from forfeiture for breach of a covenant to insure shall not be allowed unless in addition to any other terms of relief, the insurance obligation is met. For similar legislation, see Landlord and Tenant Act, R.S.M. 1954, c. 136, s. 19 (8); Landlord and Tenant Act, R.S.N.B. 1952, c. 126, s. 14 (7); Landlord and Tenant Act, R.S.P.E.I. 1951, c. 82, s. 14 (7).

MCCUAIG v. LALONDE. Ontario Divisional Court. 1911. 23 O.L.R. 312

Appeal by a landlord from dismissal of an action for damages against a tenant.

BOYD C.: ... The reason for the defendant renting the house was that his children were taken with diphtheria, and that the medical health officer told him to remove them forthwith or he would placard the hotel. This was the reason for the urgency and the expedition manifested. Had this information as to the dangerous disease been told to Cameron, the plaintiff's agent, he would not have rented. Plainly, this is a case in which the language of Lord Eldon may be well applied: the lease was granted under surprise produced by a studious, artful, and what this Court calls fraudulent concealment for the very purpose of procuring a lease which it was known the plaintiff would not have granted except under the effect of the concealment: *Bonnett* v. *Sadler* (1808), 14 Ves. 526. Deceit is sufficiently proved to justify this action: *Keates* v. *Earl of Cadogan* (1851), 10 C.B. 591.

Apart from this, I think the law will raise an implied contract that the renting of this building was for the ordinary uses of habitation. It was a new, well-equipped house, better than most in the village of Maxville. Such a condition as to user may be implied by the Court if it appears to have been in the contemplation of both parties: see *per* Lord Esher in *Sarson* v. *Roberts*, [1895] 2 Q.B. 395, 396. The conversation of the parties at the time of renting shews that it was not contemplated that it should be used for what the plaintiff called a "pest-house". This use of the dwelling-house for diphtheretic patients was not a reasonable or ordinary use, but one which distinctly impaired the premises and deteriorated the value of the reversion. For this reason also, and on the grounds of reasoning employed in *Manchester Bonded Warehouse Co.* v. *Carr* (1880), 5 C.P.D. 507, 512, that the premises were not used in a reasonable and proper manner, having regard to their character and the purpose for which they were intended to be used, I think that the plaintiff is entitled to damages.

I agree with the appraisement of those made by my brother Riddell, for which judgment is to be given, with costs of action and of appeal, to be paid by the defendant.

MIDDLETON, J.: I agree.

RIDDELL, J.: The defendant is a hotel-keeper; his children taking diphtheria, he was informed by the medical man that, unless they were removed, the hotel must be placarded. As the defendant was making $25 to $40 a day, he did not like the idea of his hotel being in effect closed; so he went to the plaintiff, who had a small dwelling-house to let, and took the house at $8 per month rent. He lied to the plaintiff—whether before he had made his bargain or after is, in my view, immaterial—gave her to understand that the reason for his wanting the house was that his wife was near her confinement, and he wanted the house to enable her to be confined outside the hotel.

The children were taken into the house; and in fifteen minutes thereafter the house was placarded. After the children had recovered, the defendant went through a form of fumigation, which was not proved to be sufficient or efficient. The plaintiff reasonably, and, as I think, most properly, thought that, before renting her house again, she should repaper it, etc., and she did so. There was naturally delay in renting the house afterwards.

An action was brought for damages, which resulted in a dismissal by the Judge of the County Court of Stormont, Dundas, and Glengarry.

The plaintiff now appeals.

The law is correctly laid down in 24 Cyc., p. 1061: "Where the contract of lease is silent on the subject, the lessees have by implication the right to put the premises to such use and employment as they please, not materially different from that in which they are usually employed, to which they are adapted, and for which they were constructed. The law, however, implies an obligation on the part of the lessee to use the property in a proper and tenant-like manner, without exposing the buildings to ruin or waste by acts of omission or commission, and not to put them to a use or employment materially different from that in which they are usually employed...."

Lord Westbury in *Keith* v. *Reid*, L.R. 2 H.L. Sc. 39, at p. 41, says: "The law of Scotland may well be, that if there be a lease of a dwelling-house as a dwelling-house it shall not be perverted to a perfectly different purpose." And what Lord Westbury says may be the law of Scotland is, in my opinion, the law of this Province.

There is dearth of English authority, and stray expressions may be found in some of the cases like that attributed to Patterson, J., in *Leach* v. *Thomas* (1835), 7 C. & P. 327: "The defendant... tenant from year to year... was only bound to keep the premises wind and water tight." See also *Auworth* v. *Johnson* (1832), 5 C. & P. 239.

All authorities, however, agree that the tenant is bound to use the premises in a tenant-like manner, etc., and not substantially different from the purpose for which the landlord intends them.

While, as in *Nave* v. *Berry* (1853), 22 Ala. 382, the using as a young ladies' seminary of a building rented to be used either as a hotel or a private residence, is not or may not be a violation of the tenant's duty, yet that very case shews that putting the building to such a use as that inflammable substances would or might be collected therein, would be a violation of the tenant's duty.

So while, as in *Miles* v. *Lauraine* (1896), 99 Ga. 402, it is not wrong for a tenant to take into his house his own lawful wife, although she had not theretofore led a blameless private life, but been guilty of indiscretions, if she has expressed her determination thereafter to change her manner of living since she had become the lawful wife of a respectable man—still the tenant could not be allowed without the permission of the landlord to convert an ordinary respectable household into a bawdy-house.

And a case that is in point is *Hersey* v. *Chapin* (1894), 162 Mass. 176. The tenant of the plaintiff, being in possession of the house, allowed the board of health of a city to use it for a hospital for smallpox patients. In holding that the landlord had (under the facts of the case) the right of action against the individual members of the board of health, the Court said (p. 180): "The tenant... could not, as against the rights of the owner, authorise the defendants to establish a hospital for patients afflicted with an infectious disease in the plaintiff's house, and to maintain such a hospital there to the damage of the reversion."

In *United States v. Bostwick* (1876), 94 U.S. 53, the United States had rented a building which had been offered them by the owner "for the purposes of a hospital"—the letter accepting the offer expressly stated that the hiring was to be "for all purposes"—the United States used the building for a smallpox hospital. It was held that, under the terms of the hiring, no action lay; but it does not seen to have been doubted that the using by a tenant of an ordinary house as a hospital would be wrong.

Upon principle, I see no difference in the present case from a case in which the tenant had allowed a quantity of filth to be placed upon the floors, ceiling and walls of the building. The bacilli of diphtheria are infinitely more deleterious to a residence and dangerous to the health of any future occupant than mud or filth of any visible character.

The defendant does not deserve any consideration, but the only damages to be given are those proved, not vindictive damages.

The plaintiff should properly have proved damage to the reversion—the course taken at the trial was to prove what it cost her to put the house in proper condition and her loss of money. The damage to the reversion must be at least these amounts, and probably more.

I think the plaintiff should have a judgment for $240 and costs here and below.

Appeal allowed.

[Where a lease is made for a particular specified purpose, a tenant may be enjoined from using the premises for some other purpose: see *Kehoe* v. *Lansdowne*, [1893] A.C. 451; *Cockburn* v. *Quinn* (1890), 20 O.R. 519; *Tendler* v. *Sproule*, [1947] 1 All E.R. 193 (C.A.). *Cf. Hilton* v. *Donais*, [1951] 2 D.L.R. 841 (B.C.).

A leased premises to B who covenanted to use them as a private dwelling and not to alter them. B sublet to C, and C sublet to D, with the same covenants in each case. D converted the premises into apartments, and A thereupon brought forfeiture proceedings against B, and C and D were joined in the action. Should relief be granted to B, C or D? What damages are payable, the cost of reinstating the premises or what A has really suffered? See *Westminster* v. *Swinton*, [1948] 1 K.B. 524, [1948] 1 All E.R. 248.

S. 17 (2) of the Landlord and Tenant Act, R.S.O. 1960, c. 206, provides for a right of re-entry by the landlord on conviction of the tenant of keeping a disorderly house in the demised premises. For similar legislation, see Landlord and Tenant Act, R.S.M. 1954, c. 136, s. 17 (2); Landlord and Tenant Act, R.S.N.B. 1952, c. 126, s. 9; Landlord and Tenant Act, R.S.P.E.I. 1951, c. 82, s. 10; Landlord and Tenant Act, R.S.S. 1953, c. 312, s. 9 (2).]

(c) Fixtures

ELWES v. MAW, King's Bench. 1802. 3 East 38, 102 E.R. 510

The opinion of the Court was delivered by LORD ELLENBOROUGH: This was an action upon the case in the nature of waste by a landlord, the reversioner in fee, against his late tenant who had held under a term for 21 years a farm consisting of a messuage, and lands, outhouses, and barns, &c. thereto belonging, and who, as the case reserved stated, during the term and about 15 years before its expiration, erected at his own expense a beast-house, carpenter's shop, a fuel-house, a cart-house, a pump-house, and fold yard. The buildings were of brick and mortar, and tiled, and the foundations of them were about a foot and half deep in the ground. The carpenter's shop was closed in, and the other buildings were open to the front and supported by brick pillars. The fold yard wall was of brick and mortar, and its foundation was in the ground. The defendant previous to the expiration of his lease pulled down the erections, dug up the foundations, and carried away the materials; leaving the premises in the same state as when he entered upon them. The case further stated, that these erections were necessary and convenient for the occupation of the farm, which could not be well managed without them. And the question for the opinion of the Court was, whether the defendant had a right to take away these erections? Upon a full consideration of all the cases cited upon this and the former argument, which are indeed nearly all that the books afford materially relative to the subject, we are all of opinion that the defendant had not a right to take away these erections.

Questions respecting the right to what are ordinarily called fixtures, principally arise between three classes of persons. 1st, between different descriptions of representatives of the same owner of the inheritance; viz. between his heir and executor. In this first case, i.e. as between heir and executor, the rule obtains with the most rigour in favour of the inheritance, and against the right to disannex therefrom, and to consider as a personal chattel, any thing which has been affixed thereto. 2dly, between the executors of tenant for life or in tail, and the remainder-man or reversioner; in which case the right to fixtures is considered more favourably for executors than in the preceding case between heir and executor. The 3d case, and that in which the greatest latitude and indulgence has always been allowed in favour of the claim to having any particular articles considered as personal chattels as against the claim in respect of freehold or inheritance, is the case between landlord and tenant.

But the general rule on this subject is that which obtains in the first-mentioned case, i.e. between heir and executor; and that rule (as found in the Year Book 17 E. 2, p. 518, and laid down at the close of *Herlakenden's* case, 4 Co. 64, in Co. Litt. 53, in *Cooke* v. *Humphrey*, Moore, 177, and in *Lord Darby* v. *Asquith*, Hob. 234, in the part cited by my brother Vaughan, and in other cases;) is that where a lessee, having annexed any thing to the freehold during his term, afterwards takes it away, it is waste. But this rule at a very early period had several exceptions attempted to be engrafted upon it, and which were at last effectually engrafted upon it, in favour of trade and of those vessels and utensils which are immediately subservient to the purposes of trade. In the Year Book 42 E. 3, 6, the right of the tenant to remove a furnace erected by him during his term is doubted and adjourned. In the Year Book of the 20 H. 7, 13 a. & b. which was the case of trespass against executors for removing a furnace fixed with mortar by their testator and annexed to the freehold, and which was holden to be wrongfully done, it is laid down, that "if a lessee for years make a furnace for his advantage, or a dyer make his vats or vessels to occupy his occupation during his term, he may remove them: but if he suffer them to be fixed to the earth after the term, then they belong to the lessor. And so of a baker. And it is not waste to remove such things within the term by some: and this shall be against the opinions aforesaid." But the rule in this extent in favour of tenants is doubted afterwards in 21 H. 7, 27, and narrowed there, by allowing that the lessee for years could only remove, within the term, things fixed to the ground, and not to the walls of the principal building. However in process of time the rule in favour of the right in the tenant to remove utensils set up in relation to trade became fully established: and accordingly, we find Lord Holt, in *Poole's* case, Salk. 368, laying down, (in the instance of a soap-boiler, an under tenant, whose vats, coppers, &c. fixed had been taken in execution, and on which account the first lessee had brought an action against the sheriff,) that during the term the soap-boiler might well remove the vats he set up in relation to trade; and that he might do it by the common law, and not by virtue of any special custom, in favour of trade, and to encourage industry; but that after the term they became a gift in law to him in reversion, and were not removeable. He adds, that there was a difference between what the soap-boiler did to carry on his trade, and what he did to complete his house, as hearths and chimney-pieces, which he held not removeable. The indulgence in favour of the tenant for years during the term has been since carried still further, and he has been allowed to carry away matters of ornament, as ornamental marble chimney-pieces, pier glasses, hangings, wainscot fixed only by screws, and the like. *Beck* v. *Rebow*, 1 P. Wms. 94. *Ex parte Quincey*, 1 Atk. 477, and *Lawton* v. *Lawton*, 3 Atk. 13. But no adjudged case has yet gone the length of establishing that buildings subservient to purposes of agriculture, as distinguished from those of trade, have been removeable by an executor of tenant for life, nor by the tenant himself who built them during his term.

In deciding whether a particular fixed instrument, machine, or even building should be considered as removeable by the executor, as between him and the heir, the Court, in the three principal cases on this subject, (viz. *Lawton* v. *Lawton*, 3 Atk. 13, which was the case of a fire engine to work a colliery erected by tenant for life: *Lord Dudley* and *Lord Ward*, Ambler, 113, which was also the case of a fire engine to work a colliery erected by tenant for life: (these two cases before Lord Hardwicke:) and *Lawton*, *Executor*, v. *Salmon*, E. 22 G. 3, 1 H. Blac. 259, in notis, before Lord Mansfield; which was the case of salt pans, and which came on in the shape of an action of trover brought for the salt pans by the executor against the tenant of the heir at law) the Court may be considered as having decided mainly on this ground, that where the fixed instrument, engine, or utensil, (and the building covering the same falls within the same principle), was an accessory to a matter of a personal nature, that it should be itself considered as personalty. The fire engine, in the cases in 3 Atk. and Ambler, was an accessory to the carrying on the trade of getting and vending coals; a matter of a personal nature. Lord Hardwicke says in the case in Ambler, "A colliery is not only an enjoyment of the estate, but in part carrying on a trade." And in the case in 3 Atk. he says, "One reason that weighs with me is its being a mixed case, between enjoying the profits of the lands, and carrying on a species of trade; and considering it in this light, it comes very near the instances in brew-houses, &c. of furnaces and coppers." Upon the same principle, Lord Ch. B. Comyns may be considered as having decided the case of the cyder mill; i.e. as a mixed case between enjoying the profits of the land and carrying on a species of trade; and as considering the cyder mill as properly an accessory to the trade of making cyder.

In the case of the salt pans, Lord Mansfield does not seem to have considered them as accessory to the carrying on a trade; but as merely the means of enjoying the benefit of the inheritance. He says, "The salt spring is a valuable inheritance, but no profit arises from it unless there be a salt work; which consists of a building, &c. for the purpose of containing the pans, &c. which are fixed to the ground. The inheritance cannot be enjoyed without them. They are accessories necessary to the enjoyment of the principal. The owner erected them for the benefit of the inheritance." Upon this principle he considered them as belonging to the heir, as parcel of the inheritance, for the enjoyment of which they were made, and not as belonging to the executor, as the means or instrument of carrying on a trade. If, however, he had even considered them as belonging to the executor, as utensils of trade, or as being removeable by the tenant, on the ground of their being such utensils of trade; still it would not have affected the question now before the Court, which is the right of a tenant for mere agricultural purposes to remove buildings fixed to the freehold, which were constructed by him for the ordinary purposes of husbandry, and connected with no description of trade whatsoever: and to which description of buildings no case (except the Nisi Prius case of *Dean* v. *Allaly*, before Lord Kenyon, and which did not undergo the subsequent review of himself and the rest of the Court), has yet extended the indulgence allowed to tenants in respect to buildings for the purposes of trade. In the case in Buller's Nisi Prius, 34, of *Culling* v. *Tuffnell*, before Lord Ch. J. Treby, at Nisi Prius, he is stated to have holden that the tenant who had erected a barn upon the premises, and put it upon pattens and blocks of timber lying upon the ground, but not fixed in or to the ground, might by the custom of the country take them away at the end of his term. To be sure he might, and that without any custom; for the terms of the statement exclude them from being considered as fixtures; "they were not fixed in or to the ground." In the case of *Fitzherbert* v. *Shaw*, 1 H. Black. 258, we have only the opinion of, a very learned Judge indeed, Mr. Justice Gould, of what would have been the right of the tenant, as to the taking away a shed built on brick-work, and some posts and rails which he had erected, if the tenant had done so during the term: but as the term was put an end to by a new contract, the question what the tenant could have done in virtue of his right under the old term, if it had continued, could never have come judicially before him at Nisi Prius: and when that question was offered to be argued in the Court above, the counsel were stopped, as the question was excluded by the new agreement. As to the case of *Penton* v. *Robart*, 2 East. 88, it was the case of a varnish house, with a brick foundation let into the ground, of which the wood work had been removed from another place, where the defendant had carried on his trade with it. It was a building for the purpose of trade; and the tenant was entitled to the same indulgence in that case, which, in the cases already considered, had been allowed to other buildings for the purposes of trade; as furnaces, vats, coppers, engines, and the like. And though Lord Kenyon, after putting the case upon the ground of the leaning which obtains in modern times in favour of the interests of trade; upon which ground it might be properly supported; goes further, and extends the indulgence of the law to the erection of green-houses and hot-houses by nurserymen, and indeed by implication to buildings by all other tenants of land; there certainly exists no decided case, and, I believe, no recognized opinion or practice on either side of Westminster Hall, to warrant such an extension. The Nisi Prius case of *Dean* v. *Allaly* (reported in Mr. Woodfall's book, p. 207, and Mr. Espinasse's, 2 vol. 11,) is a case of the erection and removal by the tenant of two sheds, called Dutch barns, which were, I will assume, unquestionably fixtures. Lord Kenyon says, "The law will make the most favourable construction for the tenant, where he has made necessary and useful erections for the benefit of his trade or manufacture, and which enable him to carry it on with more advantage. It has been so holden in the case of cyder mills, and other cases; and I shall not narrow the law, but hold erections of this sort made for the benefit of trade, or constructed as the present, to be removable at the end of the term." Lord Kenyon here uniformly mentions the benefit of trade, as if it were a building subservient to some purposes of trade; and never mentions agriculture, for the purposes of which it was erected. He certainly seems, however, to have thought that buildings erected by tenants for the purposes of farming, were, or rather ought to be, governed by the same rules which had been so long judicially holden to apply in the case of buildings for the purposes of trade. But the case of buildings for trade has been always put and recognized as a known, allowed, exception from the general rule, which obtains as to other buildings; and the circumstance of its being so treated and considered establishes the existence of the general rule to which it is considered as an exception. To hold otherwise, and to extend the rule in favour of tenants in the latitude contended for by the defendant, would be, as appears to me, to introduce a dangerous innovation into the relative state of rights and interests holden to subsist between landlords and tenants. But its danger or probable mischief is not so properly a consideration for a Court of Law, as whether the adoption of such a doctrine would be an innovation at all: and, being of opinion that it would be so, and contrary to the uniform current of legal authorities on the subject, we feel ourselves, in conformity to, and in support of those authorities, obliged to pronounce that the defendant had no right to take away the erections stated and described in this case.

Judgment for plaintiff affirmed.

[For a critique of Lord Ellenborough's exposition, see 5 *American Law of Property*, s. 19.2, where there is also a good discussion of the subject.

The effect of *Elwes* v. *Maw* on "agricultural" fixtures has in England been removed by statute: see Agricultural Holdings Act, 1948 (Imp.), c. 63, ss. 13, 67, 68.

In *Stack* v. *T. Eaton Co.* (1902), 4 O.L.R. 335 (Div. Ct.), an issue was raised as to the ownership of certain shop and gas and electric light fittings which had been installed in business premises by the then owners, who subsequently sold the premises which, after intermediate transactions, were purchased by defendants. Plaintiff claimed the fittings as a subsequent transferee of the person who had them installed. An appeal from a judgment substantially in favour of defendants was affirmed, and Meredith C. J. speaking for the Court said, *inter alia*:

"I take it to be settled law:—

"(1) That articles not otherwise attached to the land than by their own weight are not to be considered as part of the land, unless the circumstances are such as shew that they were intended to be part of the land.

"(2) That articles affixed to the land even slightly are to be considered part of the land unless the circumstances are such as to shew that they were intended to continue chattels.

"(3) That the circumstances necessary to be shewn to alter the *primâ facie* character of the articles are circumstances which shew the degree of annexation and object of such annexation, which are patent to all to see.

"(4) That the intention of the person affixing the article to the soil is material only so far as it can be presumed from the degree and object of the annexation.

"(5) That, even in the case of tenants' fixtures put in for the purposes of trade, they form part of the freehold, with the right, however, to the tenant, as between him and his landlord, to bring them back to the state of chattels again by severing them from the soil, and that they pass by a conveyance of the land as part of it, subject to this right of the tenant.

"These propositions are the result of the decisions in *Bain* v. *Brand* (1876), 1 App. Cas. 762, 772, *Holland* v. *Hodgson* (1872), L.R. 7 C.P. 328, and *Hobson* v. *Gorringe*, [1897] 1 Ch. 182, and are in accordance with the view of the Supreme Court of Canada in *Haggert* v. *Town of Brampton* (1897), 28 S.C.R. 174, which was decided in the same month as *Hobson* v. *Gorringe*, though a few days before the judgment in that case was delivered.

"Referring to the use in one of the cases of the words 'merely for a temporary purpose,' as applied to the object of affixing an article to the soil, Lord Blackburn in *Holland* v. *Hodgson* (p. 337) points out the obvious distinction between the case of a carpet tacked to the floor (an illustration used by Mr. Smyth more than once in his argument) and the affixing by a tenant of a shop counter for the purpose, 'in one sense,' he says, 'temporary,' of more effectually enjoying the shop, whilst he continues to sell his wares there.

"If a shop counter affixed by a tenant becomes, as Lord Blackburn was of opinion that it did, a part of the freehold, subject to the right of the tenant to bring it back to its state of a chattel again by severing it, I am unable to see why the shelving affixed by Guinane, when he was the owner of the freehold, for the purpose of the business he carried on there, is not to be deemed a part of the land; and I can see nothing in the degree or object of the annexation of it to lead to the conclusion that such an intention existed as is necessary to alter the *primâ facie* character of the article arising from the fact of its being affixed, but the contrary.

"The title to the gas and electric light fittings is, as it seems to me, to be determined by the same considerations, which lead necessarily, I think, to the conclusion that, when affixed as they were, they became part of the land and passed by the conveyance of it to the respondents."

If a tenant for a term certain does not remove fixtures (where he would be entitled to remove them) before the end of his term, his interest in them is gone: see *Weeton* v. *Woodcock* (1840), 7 M. & W. 14, 151 E.R. 659 (Ex.); *Lee* v. *Gaskill* (1876), 1 Q.B.D. 700 (C.A.). What is the position of a tenant in respect of trade fixtures where he accepts a new lease on expiry of the term during which the fixtures were put in place? See *Thresher* v. *Company of Proprietors of East London Water Works* (1824), 2 B. & C. 608, 107 E.R. 510 (K.B.); *Leschallas* v. *Woolf*, [1908] 1 Ch. 641. But see *Pole-Carew* v. *Western Counties Manure Co.*, [1920] 2 Ch. 97 (C.A.).]

BADALATO v. TREBILCOCK. Ontario Appellate Division. 1923. 53 O.L.R. 359, [1924] 1 D.L.R. 465

The judgment of the Court was delivered by RIDDELL J.:

An appeal from the judgment of Macbeth, Co.Ct.J., of London, so far as it is in favour of the defendant. A very interesting and important question is raised in this case, and the law should be authoritatively declared.

The defendant, being tenant of the plaintiff, being under notice to quit, and being still in possession as such tenant, accepted a lease for one year from January 1, 1920, at an increased rental—this was on November 9, 1919—it was understood as part of the arrangement that he should continue as tenant under the old arrangement in the interim, and there was never any admission that he had ceased to be tenant.

No mention is made in the lease of the tenant's fixtures; at the termination of the lease, the defendant removed his "tenant's fixtures". On action brought in the County Court, his Honour held that he had the right to do so. The landlord appeals.

The County Court Judge has considered the law and the cases with great industry and ability; the importance and novelty in this Province of the question have made it advisable that we should examine it independently.

There is much authority or rather many authorities for the proposition that a tenant having the right to remove his fixtures loses the right if he takes a new lease without reservation of such right; and, if these authorities are binding upon us, we must follow them. *Misera est servitus ubi jus est vagum aut incertum*—although most of us at the present time would prefer the law to be uncertain rather than certain and bad.

Text-writers and their dicta may be disregarded (except perhaps in the case of Sir Edward Coke, whose dicta are often considered law); a text-writer's opinion is only his opinion, and has authority only so far as it is supported by the decisions of the Courts.

In Woodfall on Landlord and Tenant, 20th ed., p. 787, it is said, "He may lose his right at the expiration of his first term"; see, however, pp. 790-1; Foa on Landlord and Tenant, 5th ed., pp. 692-3; 2 Smith, L. C., 12th ed., p. 221.

Independently of authority the principle is clear—a tenant has the right to remove such fixtures only during his term or a reasonable time thereafter: if he does not exercise this right the fixtures become part of the freehold: *Poole's Case* (1703), 1 Salk. 368, 91 E.R. 320; and when he takes a lease of the freehold he takes a lease of it, fixtures included.

Consequently, if the tenant surrenders his lease, he loses the right: *Pronguey* v. *Gurney* (1874), 36 U.C.Q.B. 53; (1875), 37 U.C.Q.B. 347; *Ex parte Brook* (1878), 10 Ch. D. 100, at p. 110 (C.A.); even if this be done in order to obtain a new lease: *Leschallas* v. *Woolf*, [1908] 1 Ch. 641, at p. 652, "for the surrender of the demised permises *primâ facie* includes fixtures, and the subject of the new lease is *primâ facie* what is surrendered in order to be re-demised."

The same result follows as in cases where the tenant holds over after his term and the landlord puts an end to all tenancy by issuing a writ for possession followed by judgment shewing that the landlord was within his rights: *Barff* v. *Probyn* (1895), 64 L.J. (Q.B.) 557; or by re-entering: *Leader* v. *Homewood* (1858), 5 C.B. (N.S.) 546, 141 E.R. 221.

Looking now at the cases which have been thought to lay down the rule that taking a new lease in itself determines the right. In *Fitzherbert* v. *Shaw* (1789), 1 H. Bl. 258, 126 E.R. 150, a tenant held over after notice to quit and the landlord issued a writ in ejectment. (The effect of such a writ appears from *Barff* v. *Probyn*, *supra*.) A settlement was made that judgment might be signed with a stay of execution, the defendant to remain in possession, no mention being made of fixtures. Obviously the right to remove was lost, and the Court so held. In *Heap* v. *Barton et al* (1852), 12 C.B. 274, 138 E.R. 909, there was a similar state of affairs: a writ of ejectment was issued and judgment signed, but an agreement was made that the writ of possession should not issue until a later day. The right to remove was lost—the tenant for the time having remained "in possession in defiance of his landlord" (p. 280, *per* Jervis, C. J.). In *Thresher* v. *East London Water Works Co.* (1824), 2 B. & C. 608, 107 E.R. 510, a lessee took a new lease to commence on the determination of his existing term—and therein covenanted to repair all erections or buildings, etc., and "the said premises so repaired, upheld, and maintained, to leave and yield up at the end of the term". Certain brick-kilns, trade-fixtures, had been erected—and they were held not to be removable by the tenant. One rather fails to understand why they should have been by any one considered removable.

There is a dictum of Harrison, C. J., in *Pronguey* v. *Gurney et al*, 37 U.C.Q.B. 347, at p. 356, which goes the whole length, but it is *obiter*.

The Lords Justices in *Ex parte Willoughby D'Eresby* (*Baroness*) (1881), 44 L.T.R. 781, expressly declined to lay down such a rule: see p. 785.

I cannot find any case which decides that the effect of taking a new lease to begin on the termination of an existing term *simpliciter et ipso facto* deprives the tenant of an existing right.

There are many rules regarding real estate which are the legacy of the early times of the English law and which are repugnant to our modern minds—they seem sometimes to be opposed to common sense. There are the production of mediaeval lawyers with the schoolmen's logic and ingenuity—not seldom almost perverse to our mind. Parliament has had again and again to step in to get rid of these so-called principles; but all are not yet abolished.

So far as these are fixed by judicial decision, we must observe them: e.g., if a tenant take a new lease to begin during the currency of his existing lease, that may operate as a surrender in law even if not intended so to operate: *Lyon* v. *Reed et al* (1844), 13 M. & W. 285, 153 E.R. 118. But if the rule does not rest on cases binding on the Court, we should endeavour to give an effect to the transaction in accordance with the intention of the parties, expressed or implied.

In the present case it would be absurd to think that the tenant intended to give up his right to these fixtures or his right to remove them. There is nothing in the law to compel us to hold that he has lost that right—and the appeal must fail.

I cannot close without expressing our appreciation of the very excellent judgment of the County Court Judge.

Appeal dismissed.

[The *Badalato* case, in founding itself, at least in part, on the difference between surrender of a term and extension or renewal thereof was followed in *Globe Land Co.* v. *Heaslip*, 60 O.L.R. 499, [1927] 3 D.L.R. 604 (App. Div.) and *Carscallen* v. *Leeson*, [1927] 4 D.L.R. 797, [1927] 3 W.W.R. 425 (Alta. C.A.).

In *Smith* v. *City Petroleum Co. Ltd.*, [1940] 1 All E.R. 260 (C.A.), it was pointed out that a periodic tenant (in that case a weekly tenant) may have a reasonable time after termination of the tenancy to remove trade fixtures. Is the position the same in respect of a tenant for a term certain whose tenancy is terminated by the landlord's election under the lease on breach of covenant? See *Argles* v. *McMath* (1895), 26 O.R. 224, aff'd 23 O.A.R. 44.

The Short Forms of Leases Act, R.S.O. 1960, c. 373, contains a covenant (Sched. B, para. 10) for the removal of fixtures, which covers articles "in the nature of trade or tenants' fixtures or other articles belonging to or brought upon the said premises by the said lessee", subject to the lessee making good any damage to the premises.]

[A tenant of premises to which he has brought certain fixtures sells them under a bill of sale during the term while they are in place. After expiry of the term the purchaser under the bill of sale claims them against the owner of the premises. Should he succeed if the tenant himself as claimant would have failed? See *Northwest Terminals Ltd*, v. *Westminster Trust Co.*, [1939] 2 D.L.R. 343, [1939] 1 W.W.R. 642, 53 B.C.R. 463 (C.A.); *Wolf* v. *Thurm*, [1949] 4 D.L.R. 703, [1949] 2 W.W.R. 1081 (Sask. C.A.).]

DEVINE v. CALLERY. Ontario Appellate Division. 1917. 40 O.L.R. 505, 38 D.L.R. 542

Appeal by plaintiff from dismissal of an action for damages for alleged wrongful removal of a building from her land.

MEREDITH C. J. C. P.: One Deremo, or Dermo, as named in the lease in question in this action, built and owned a wooden, or "frame" as it is commonly called, house. The house was upon the plaintiff's land, of which Deremo was tenant under a lease for a term of ten years. In that tenant's time the plaintiff had, according to her testimony at the trial of this action, no interest in the house, but she "expected to have" the first chance to buy it. Deremo sold the house to the Doyles, with the knowledge and consent of the plaintiff, plainly expressed in the writing drawn up by her in her own handwriting as a lease by her of the same land to them for a term of eight years, beginning when Deremo's term ended: and, in addition to that knowledge and consent, she expressly provided in this writing that "Doyle Bros. are to have the privilege to move the house Dermo built at the end of eight years," but that "Doyle Bros. are to give Mrs. Devine the first chance to buy the house at the end of the eight years."

There was no provision against assigning the lease, or against subletting the land; and several sales of the house and assignments of the term were made, the last having been made to the defendant Callery. The sales and assignments seem to have been made to the knowledge, and with the consent, of the plaintiff, though that is immaterial.

At the end of the eight years, the defendant Callery, accompanied by one of the Doyles, went to the plaintiff and gave her "the first chance to buy the house," but she asked for the rest of the day to give her answer. No answer was given: but subsequently she claimed to be entitled to it without buying it, or paying anything for it.

The house was removed by the defendant Callery, assisted by the defendant Wright, to the land of the defendants the Deloro Smelting and Refining Company Limited, and thereupon this action was brought to recover from all of them $500 for damages for such removal of the building.

In these circumstances, the plaintiff asks us, first, to find that the wooden building was not a chattel, but was part of her land, notwithstanding the following facts: that there is no evidence, of any kind, in the case, that the building was affixed to the land; that wooden buildings are often chattels; that she, for probably eighteen years, treated it as a chattel, first the property of Deremo, then, in succession, of the several purchasers of it, as if a chattel in which she had no interest but the first chance to buy as a chattel; that fixtures can be as effectually severed from the land by a stroke of the pen as by a stroke of axe and hammer, and that she, by the strokes of her pen in her own hand, in effect, declared that the house was not hers but was her tenant's, her only right as to it being a "first chance" to purchase it;

and that standing by and consenting to a sale of the house precludes her from denying the vendor's right to sell, even if he really had none.

But such a finding, if it could be made as she asks, would be insufficient for her purposes in this action, so she is obliged to go a step further, and ask us, after finding that the house is part of her land, to rule that all the privileges to remove the house which she gave were in law invalid, because they were merely revocable licences which she revoked, or else because, though in writing, the lease in question was not granted over her seal, though it was over her signature.

Here again the plaintiff overlooks the obvious fact that her lease is not a mere licence: that the "privilege" expressed in it is not mere leave, but is an essential part of the lease, and an essential part quite common in leases. It was part of the consideration for which the rent provided for in the lease was paid throughout the term created by it.

RIDDELL J.: ...There is no evidence that the house was attached to the freehold, and that it would therefore (in the absence of other circumstances) become real property. But, even if it were proved, the plaintiff's case is not advanced. A house built by one person upon the land of another, on the agreement between them that the house shall be the property of the builder, does not, according to some authorities at least, as between them, become part of the freehold, but is the personal property of the builder. In any case the house was, as the plaintiff herself swears, the property of Deremo: by the sale to the Doyles it became theirs, and by the sales to Gilliam and Callery the property of each in succession. The agreement none the less bound the Doyles and their successors in title to give the plaintiff the option to buy on the termination of the lease: this was offered and the offer refused. Callery's house was on the plaintiff's land: under the circumstances of this case—even in the absence of the plaintiff's agreement—a right to remove within a reasonable time must be implied....

If the agreement made by the plaintiff be considered necessary to support the right of the defendant, the right of a tenant to remove buildings from land is a power, license (call it what you will), coupled with an interest—*Poole's Case* (1703), 1 Salk. 368; *Minshall* v. *Lloyd* (1837), 2 M. & W. 450—and is of course assignable.

In *Oswald* v. *Whitman* (1889), 22 N.S.R. 13, it was held that where in a lease of land there was a provision that the lessee should have the right to remove buildings thereon at the end of the term, the lessor to have the refusal of them—the buildings being affixed to the freehold—and the landlord refused to have anything to do with the buildings, the tenant had the right to remove the buildings or to sell to any other person.

The same rule was in effect laid down in *Gray* v. *McLennan* (1886), 3 Man. R. 337, where, in a very similar case, the Court said: "The plaintiff... not having made... an election" (to purchase the building)"... has forgone the right the lease gave him; and the lessee and those claiming under him have the right to it now... The lessee or his assignees had at the expiration of the term a reasonable time to remove the building..."

I agree in the law thus laid down, and would dismiss the appeal with costs.

ROSE J.: It was not clearly proved that the little house was ever affixed to the land; but the defendant tells us that when he was preparing to move it he dug and chopped around it, from which, I think, we may fairly assume in the plaintiff's favour that it was annexed.

Having been so annexed, it became, as it seems to me, part of the land: *Horwich* v. *Symond* (1914), 110 L.T.R. 1016; *S.C.*, in the Court of Appeal (1915), 84 L.J.K.B. 1083; *Hallen* v. *Runder* (1834), 1 C.M. & R. 266; *Stack* v. *T. Eaton Co.* (1902), 4 O.L.R. 335. This view is opposed to that of Buckley, J., in *In re Hulse*, [1905] 1 Ch. 406, quoted without comment in *Foa* on Landlord and Tenant, 4th ed., p. 696, and questioned in Halsbury's Laws of England, vol. 18, p. 422; but it seems to me to be the only view that is open to us, having regard to the cases referred to in *Horwich* v. *Symonds* and to the other cases to which I have referred. However, while the house became part of the land, the cases already referred to make it quite plain that, as between the plaintiff and the builder, Deremo, it remained subject to the right of Deremo to bring it back to the state of a chattel again, by severing it from the land; and such cases as *Hallen* v. *Runder*, 1 C.M. & R. 266, and *Lee* v. *Gaskell* (1876), 1 Q.B.D. 700, make it equally plain that Deremo's right was one that could be assigned, and that for its assignment no deed, or even writing, was necessary. This right of Deremo's was transferred by him to the Doyles, and by the Doyles to Gilliam, and by Gilliam to the defendant Callery; and it seems clear that the plaintiff cannot have damages against the defendant Callery for exercising it, unless that defendant lost it by not exercising it before the end of the term. Now, the plaintiff had the right to purchase the house from the defendant Callery at the end of the term, and I think that defendant, therefore, had a reasonable time, after the expiration of the term and after the plaintiff's refusal to purchase, within which to exercise his right of removal; and, there having been no unreasonable delay on his part, I think the action fails.

Appeal dismissed.

[*Cf. Haanen* v. *Decker* (1956), 1 D.L.R. 2d 425, 17 W.W.R. (N.S.) 313 (Sask. C.A.).]

[In *Haggert* v. *Brampton* (1897), 28 S.C.R. 174, the Court said (at p. 180): "A mortgagor in fee has not the same right as against the mortgagee nor a grantor as against his grantee that a person having a limited interest only, as a tenant, has to remove things annexed for the purposes of trade or domestic convenience.... Articles no further attached to the land than by their own weight may become fixtures if the circumstances are such as to show that they were intended to be part of the land, though of course the onus of shewing that they were so intended lies on those who assert that they have ceased to be chattels." *Quaere*, whether the doctrine of trade fixtures does not apply to the mortgagor-mortgagee relationship even though allegedly based on implied assent of the mortgagee to the mortgagor remaining in possession: *Cf. Gough* v. *Wood & Co.*, [1894] 1 Q.B. 713 (C.A.).]

[Should there be any difference in the rules governing the removal (or ownership) of fixtures where they are installed by the owner of premises rather than by a tenant and are claimed by a subsequent purchaser of the premises rather than by the landlord on expiry of the term? See *West Canadian Collieries Ltd.* v. *Rinaldi*, [1936] 2 D.L.R. 601, [1936] 1 W.W.R. 635 (Alta.). Would you apply the same rules to a purchaser under a contract of sale (who instals fixtures and then is unable to complete the contract), to a tenant under a lease, to an owner of land and to a mortgagor (who instals fixtures and then defaults on his mortgage)? See *Fife* v. *Hrapko*, [1936] 2 D.L.R. 383, [1936] 1 W.W.R. 627 (Alta. C.A.); *D'Augigney* v. *Brunswick-Balke-Collender Co.*, [1917] 1 W.W.R. 1331 (Alta.).]

RE MAPLE LEAF COAL CO. LTD. Alberta Appellate Division. [1951] 4 D.L.R. 210, 3 W.WR. (N.S.) 158

Appeal from a judgment of H. J. Macdonald J., [1951] 3 D.L.R. 21, upholding in part a claim that certain mining equipment must be classed as fixtures which were not removable by the trustee in bankruptcy of a sub-lessee to whom the claimant lessee had sold the equipment.

O'CONNOR C. J. A. concurs with W. A. MACDONALD J. A.

W. A. MACDONALD J. A.: At all times material to these proceedings Maple Leaf Minerals Ltd. was the lessee under coal mining lease No. 5303 from His Majesty the King in the right of the Province of Alberta, represented therein by the Minister of Lands and Mines. The term of the lease was 21 years, computed from March 22, 1938, and it covered all mines, seams and beds of coal in, on, or under the lands particularly described therein and including all of sects. 4 and 5 in tp. 28, rge. 18, W. of the 4th Meridian, and 40 acres on the east side of sect. 6, in the same township and range.

Maple Leaf Minerals Ltd. was also the registered owner in fee simple of that portion of the North-east quarter of sect. 31, tp. 27, rge. 18, W. of the 4th Meridian, which lies east of the right-of-way of the C.P.R., and containing 9.29 acres more or less.

On May 5, 1947, Maple Leaf Minerals Ltd. sublet to Maple Leaf Coal Co. Ltd. the coal and coal-mining rights under the lands particularly referred to above, that is to say, under sects. 4 and 5 in tp. 28, rge. 18, W. of the 4th Meridian, and the 40 acres on the east side of sect. 6 in the same township and range. It was a term of the sublease that the sublessee should have full, free and exclusive right to use and occupy the surface rights, owned by the lessor, in the parcel containing 9.29 acres referred to above. The evidence shows that this parcel of land was subsequently transferred to the sublessee by transfer dated December 13, 1947.

The sublease is in evidence as ex. 2 and contains a provision that the lessee will purchase from the lessor the equipment, building, tools, supplies, railway spur and all personal property belonging to the lessor and used in connection with the mine. A bill of sale (ex. 3) also dated May 5, 1947, and covering the property more particularly described therein was executed by the parties, on the same date.

The lessee went into possession of the mine and carried on mining operations for several years, but the undertaking did not prove a financial success, and on March 1, 1950, under an order of the Supreme Court, Maple Leaf Coal Co. Ltd. was declared bankrupt, and on March 14, Crown Trust Co. was appointed Trustee of the estate of the bankrupt.

On October 24, 1950, Maple Leaf Minerals Ltd. filed with the Trustee a claim, duly verified, under which it alleged that certain machinery and equipment, in possession of the bankrupt at the date of bankruptcy, were fixtures and it objected to the removal or sale of any of this property. The Trustee disallowed this claim and Maple Leaf Minerals Ltd. appealed. The learned trial Judge allowed the appeal in part and held that the trackage, the electrical system, ventilation system and pumping system in the mine, and the tipple, on sect. 32, were fixtures and not removable by the Trustee. On the other hand, he held that the main and tail hoists, machinery on the tipple, electric motors outside the mine and the motor which supplied power to the ventilation system, were not fixtures and were removable by the Trustee. The Trustee appeals and there is a cross-appeal by the claimant.

The learned trial Judge finds that the mine had been operated by Maple Leaf Minerals Ltd. prior to May 5, 1947, and that the trackage pumping system, ventilation system and electric cables were, for the most part, installed when the debtor company took possession.

I do not think there can be any doubt that the various articles which the claimant now says are fixtures were included in the bill of sale. They were part of the goods, chattels and personal property, the mining machinery, equipment, etc., used in connection with the operation of the mine, all of which were sold, transferred and delivered to the debtor company for a consideration of $40,000 and paid for in cash. The claim set up in these proceedings seems to imply that the articles involved were the property of the debtor company. If they were, it got them under the bill of sale. Nowhere in the evidence does the claimant suggest that it is entitled to retain these articles because they are its property. What it does contend is that they are fixtures, and because they are fixtures they are not removable by the Trustee.

The question whether a chattel when annexed becomes a fixture or retains its original character is mainly a question of fact, depending upon the circumstances of each case. The mode and degree of annexation, its purpose and object, and whether it can be removed without substantial injury to itself or to the freehold, are important considerations in determining the question. But to decide that a chattel is so attached to the soil as to become a fixture does not necessarily determine the further question which involves the right of the tenant to remove it.

Under the old common law rule all personal chattels when annexed to the realty became a part of the realty and could not be removed. A great deal of hardship and injustice was caused by the strict application of this rule, and from very early times it was made the subject of numerous exceptions. The reasons for this relaxation of the law are referred to in *Elliott* v. *Bishop* (1855), 24 L. J. Ex. 33. The relaxation was extended more generously to tenants than to any other class, and when the fixtures involved are trade fixtures, the greatest degree of latitude is allowed. When a tenant annexes to the realty any chattel which he brings there to be used in his trade, it may become a part of the realty, but as between him and his landlord he retains the power to bring it back to the state of a chattel by severing it from the soil. It would appear that the term "trade" is broad enough in its scope to include any calling exercised by the tenant on the leased premises for the purpose of pecuniary profit: see 26 Corp. Jur., p. 701.

The learned trial Judge says that the removal of some of the properties claimed by the debtor company might well cause serious damage, and he cites, as an example, that daily pumping is required to keep the mine free from water. It would appear that the damage which he had in contemplation was not the direct damage to the realty which would be caused by the removal of these articles, but rather damage resulting from the lack of proper maintenance of the mine after removal. On August 14, 1950, the Trustee notified the claimant of its intention to surrender the lease. By arrangement between the parties the Trustee remains in possession temporarily, and is responsible in the meantime for maintenance costs. When this temporary arrangement comes to an end and the lease is surrendered, the responsibility for maintenance will rest with the claimant, and there is no suggestion it will fail in this duty regardless of whether the present equipment is removed or not.

But in any event it seems to me the issue as between the parties to these proceedings should be decided largely, if not entirely, apart from the law of fixtures. The trial Judge has found that the trackage, pumping system, ventilation system and electric cables were, for the most part, installed when the debtor company took possession. At that date the claimant took the position that all the articles involved were chattels. There has been no substantial change in the situation since then. If the articles in dispute were fixtures then, they would have passed into the possession of the tenant under the lease. But the claimant treated them as chattels, sold them as chattels, and for a substantial consideration transferred all its interest therein to the debtor company "for its sole and only use forever". Moreover, the claimant covenanted with the bargainee (the debtor company) that it might at all times peaceably hold, possess and enjoy these chattels, for its own use and benefit without any manner of hindrance, interruption, molestation, claim or demand from or by the claimant or any other person or persons. I do not think the claimant should now be permitted to contradict or deny what it so clearly asserted in the bill of sale.

The case at bar comes within the principle of the decision of Burns J. in *Davy* v. *Lewis* (1859), 18 U.C.Q.B. 21 at p. 30, where referring to the agreement under consideration in that case, he says, "I look upon this agreement of the parties as one defining and making a law for themselves". *Davy* v. *Lewis* is quoted with approval by Ferguson J. in *Scarth* v. *Ont. Power & Flat Co.* (1894), 24 O.R. 446 at p. 451, where he says: "When a trade-fixture is attached or affixed to the freehold it becomes part of the freehold subject to the right of the tenant to remove it if he does so in proper time. In the meantime it is part of the freehold: Lord Hatherly in *Meux* v. *Jacobs*, L.R. 7 H.L. 481 at p. 490-1. But when the parties have made a special contract, as in the present case, they have, as is said by the late Mr. Justice Burns in *Davy* v. *Lewis*, 18 U.C.R. at p. 30, defined and made a law for themselves on the subject."

But it is pointed out that the sublease contains a provision under which the sublessee agreed to carry on the work of mining in accordance with the terms of the head lease and the Regulations and laws of the Province of Alberta, and clauses 9 and 14 of the head lease are invoked to show that the sublessee, or the Trustee in Bankruptcy, should not be allowed to treat the articles in dispute as chattels.

Clause 9 appears to have reference to the obligations of the lessee while the mine is in actual operation. I do not think it has been shown that the sublessee failed to comply with the requirements of this clause during the time it operated the mine. Clause 14 contemplates the situation at the termination of the lease from the Crown and within 6 months thereafter. But the lease from the Crown is now in full force and effect and its term has many years to run. One cannot forecast what the situation will be at its termination. This clause undoubtedly confers on the lessor certain rights and powers which are designed to protect the mining property and the interests of the Crown.

But in any case these proceedings raise issues as between the claimant and the Trustee. The issues raised must be determined as between these parties. The Minister of Lands and Mines is not a party thereto. His rights and powers under the head lease and under the Regulations and laws of this Province are very wide, and will be exercised, if he should decide to intervene, without regard to the question of ownership of the articles in dispute. I am unable to see how the rights of the Minister can be affected or his powers restricted in any way by the result reached in these proceedings.

The appeal is allowed and the claim is dismissed with costs. The cross-appeal is dismissed without costs.

PARLEE J. A. concurs with W. A. MACDONALD J. A.

CLINTON J. FORD J. A., dissenting: I find myself differing from the opinion of the majority of the Court, and in agreement with the conclusion of the learned trial Judge. He found that the trackage, the electrical system in the mine, the ventilation system and the pumping system, including the pipes, became part of the land; that is, of the freehold belonging to the Crown in the right of the Province of Alberta as the lessors to Maple Leaf Minerals Ltd. of the coal-mining rights. About 9 years after obtaining the lease, this company sublet these rights to the Maple Leaf Coal Co. Ltd., now in bankruptcy, for the balance of the term of 21 years of the lease.

The finding that this property is fixtures is, in my opinion, in accord with the view of Lord Shand in *Bain* v. *Brand* (1876), 1 App. Cas. 762; a colliery case. The kind of machinery there held to be fixtures was described in the following manner: "'In regard to the machinery and plant including rails which belonged to the deceased, Robert Brand, sen., and were used by him at or in connection with the colliery held on lease by him from Mr. Houldsworth: Finds that the machinery and plant and those parts thereof, are heritable and belong to the trustees of the late Alexander Brand, which were attached either directly or indirectly by being joined to what is attached to the ground for use in connection with the working and carrying away of the minerals, though they may have been fixed only in such a manner as to be capable of being removed either in their entire state or after being taken to pieces without material injury, including those loose articles which though not physically attached to the fixed machinery and plant are yet necessary for the working thereof, provided they be constructed and fitted so as to form particular machinery and not to be equally capable of being applied in their existing state to other machinery of the kind'"

This quotation appears on pp. 763-4 of the judgment of the House of Lords and is approved by them, and I think that it may be usefully added to the authorities cited by the learned trial Judge to support his finding.

The appellant, Maple Leaf Minerals Ltd., has based its objection to the removal of and sale of certain of the property in question on the ground of its being fixtures. Assuming that the several kinds of equipment of the mine are tenant or trade fixtures, and which might be removed by Maple Leaf Coal Co., or as claiming under it by the Trustee in Bankruptcy, the right of removal is subject to the condition that no damage be done to be freehold in the removal. As to this, the finding of the trial Judge is that the removal of any such property, aside from the trackage, might well cause permanent damage to the mine from the accumulation of water. He points out that for the disposal of this the pumps were required to be operated regularly, even if intermittently, and that the ventilation and electrical systems must be used for this operation. It is clear that if the water were not pumped out the floor would soften, causing the pillars or props of the roofs of the mine to sag, and bring them down with resultant irreparable damage to the mine, when there are still hundreds of thousands of tons of coal to be extracted.

It must be pointed out that Maple Leaf Coal Co., as sublessee, contracted with Maple Leaf Minerals Ltd. to abide by and perform the terms and conditions of the lease from the Crown to the same extent as it was required to do. This was for the protection of Maple Leaf Minerals Ltd., and was part of the same transaction in which it sold the property in question to Maple Leaf Coal Co. by the bill of sale; and although sold to Maple Leaf Coal Co., it, nevertheless, remained as equipment for the operation of the mine. That was the intention, and in my opinion, the real question that arises from the transfer of ownership in the equipment is whether or not Maple Leaf Minerals Ltd. is estopped by the terms of the bill of sale from objecting to the removal of the equipment as fixtures.

One must consider the purpose of the whole transaction. The property in question here, which was sold under the bill of sale, was to be continued in use, as it had been, for the operation of the mine; and used in this way in such business of Maple Leaf Coal Co. would perform its part in the skilful and proper mining operations required under clause 9 of the lease from the Crown, and was, and still is, required to keep and preserve the said mines and works from all avoidable injury and damage, also a requirement of this clause; and to make it still stronger, the clause requires that the operation of the mine shall be such that all adits, tunnels, shafts, rises, wings, levels, drifts, watercourses, roads, ways, works, erections and fixtures therein or thereon be kept in good repair and condition, except such of the matters and things last aforesaid as shall from time to time be considered by any inspector, or other person authorized by the Minister to inspect and report upon such matters and things to be unnecessary for the proper working of any such mine, but so that no supports placed in any mine, or any timbers or framework necessary for the use and maintenance of shafts or other approaches thereto or tramways thereon shall be removed or impaired, and in such state and condition shall and will at the end or sooner determination of the said term deliver peaceable possession thereof, and of the said lands to His Majesty.

Maple Leaf Coal Co., as stated, undertook in express terms to do this during the balance of the term of the lease, and since it has failed in this undertaking, Maple Leaf Minerals Ltd. must in turn take up the obligation on the surrender of the lease to it, as proposed by the Trustee, or be liable to a claim for damages. So, I think it is not estopped under such circumstances from asserting that the property constitutes fixtures that are irremovable by its lessee, which has, in fact, failed to operate for the entire term of the lease, and has left Maple Leaf Minerals Ltd. to take over the obligation that it undertook to perform.

In my opinion, it is not a question of the ownership of the property in question as between the two companies based on the contract of the bill of sale, but one that arises under the lease from the Crown, which both companies have undertaken to carry out, and that Maple Leaf Minerals Ltd. is entitled to claim that the property was and still is part of the freehold of the mine; since not being owner of the freehold it could not sever the fixtures by the bill of sale.

I think that the finding of the learned trial Judge to this effect is determinative of the real issues.

Appeal allowed.

[Plaintiff purchased a business carried on in leased premises and his bill of sale included an elevator, elevator shaft, and smokehouse which had been installed and built on the premises by the seller when he was a lessee thereof. Following the sale plaintiff obtained a lease of the premises, and upon the occurrence of a loss by fire he claimed indemnity under a fire policy which excluded the insurer's liability "for loss or damage to property owned by any person other than the insured...." The insurance company denied liability in respect of the elevator, elevator shaft and smoke-house. Would you uphold its position? See *Richardson* v. *Equitable Fire Ins. Co.*, [1953] O.R. 493, [1953] 3 D.L.R. 583 (C.A.).

A lessee of premises which included a shed containing an electric generating plant covenanted to repair. The generating plant consisted of an engine embedded in concrete in the shed and batteries set on a table and attached to the engine by wires, and by other wires attached to the light circuit of the premises. The property was requisitioned under a notice covering "brick and corrugated iron engine shed", and by statute a tenant was absolved during the period of requisition from liability on a covenant to repair for damage to "land". Is the lessee liable for disrepair of the batteries? See *Jordan* v. *May*, [1947] K.B. 427, [1947] 1 All E.R. 231 (C.A.).]

[Fixture problems arise in assorted situations. For example, where land is expropriated at a time when it is held under lease, must compensation be given for fixtures which the tenant would be entitled to remove? If so, does this mean that on expropriation the tenant loses his right of removal? Would the result be different if the Courts accepted the theory that tenant's trade fixtures belong to the tenant even while affixed? See *Selick* v. *Moncton*, [1954] 2 D.L.R. 808, 34 M.P.R. 208 (N.B.C.A.).

Again, where land is assessed for taxation, questions may arise under the provisions and definitions of the taxation statute whether certain chattels affixed to, or connected to buildings upon the land by the owner are caught by the enactment. They may be assessable under the statute even though they would not be "fixtures" in a common law sense. See *Northern Broadcasting Co. Ltd.* v. *Mountjoy Improvement District*, [1950] S.C.R. 502, [1950] 3 D.L.R. 721; *London* v. *John Labatt Ltd.*, [1953] O.R. 800, [1954] 1 D.L.R. 441. Or, even though the chattels are affixed by a tenant, taxes may be leviable against the landowner if they are brought within the statutory terms and notwithstanding that they may be removed by the tenant. (This would indicate the advisability of some provision against such a contingency in the lease.) See *Re Orr*, [1955] 4 D.L.R. 726, 16 W.W.R. (N.S.) 25 (B.C.).]

[A contractor holding a construction contract from the United States Government for certain defence works in Canada obtained a lease of land to serve as its headquarters for the job and as a place for storing equipment and supplies. It constructed certain buildings on the land for the temporary purposes of the contract, being reimbursed for them by the United States Government. The nature of the construction was as follows:

"The site on which the buildings were located was on a slope and before construction began the ground was levelled off with a grader or bulldozer. The office building was built upon stills which were supported by upright posts set at intervals which at their lower end rested on concrete footing pads set in the ground. These pads were about two feet square and four inches thick. The camp building was similarly constructed with a somewhat different type of foundation. The posts supporting the sills of the buildings were not set upon concrete footing pads but upon mud-sills so-called which were wooden timbers set upon the ground surface, which supported the posts on which the sills of the building rested. Both buildings were constructed in large measure from prefabricated materials purchased by Fraser-Brace and brought upon the site as prefabricated huts. The floors and walls were in panel form of uniform dimensions. Apparently the sills to support the floor and the beams and trusses to support the roof were cut to dimensions. The roof covering was of sheet aluminum, cut to size.

"Water and sewerage connections with the public mains were established for both buildings through pipes which were laid four feet underground below frost level.

"One portion of the office building, designed to be fireproof, was of different construction. Its walls were made of cement tile materials. It rested upon a concrete floor and was in three sections. The centre housed a common heating plant. The other two sections were designed as vaults to house plans and records.

"The buildings were clearly established for all-season occupation and appear to have been suitably constructed and serviced for such use."

On being assessed for real property tax on the buildings, the contractor contended that the buildings were not fixtures and, secondly, that they belonged to the United States Government and were exempt under principles of sovereign immunity. Both arguments were rejected: see *Fraser-Brace* v. *St. John* (1956), 39 M.P.R. 33 (rev'd on the second of the arguments, (1957), 9 D.L.R. 2d 391 (N.B.C.A.)). After discussing certain authorities on fixtures, McNair C.J.N.B., at the trial, said (at p. 65):

"According to the foregoing authorities the rule to be applied may be stated thus: If it appears from the circumstances that the buildings were erected to further some established independent use of the lands or to serve some purpose incidental to operations being carried on upon the lands, as for instance mining, manufacturing, milling or like operations, and were therefore 'accessory to a matter of a personal nature' or 'accessory to something in the nature of a personal chattel located on the land' then the buildings are in the nature of chattels; but if the purpose of their erection were to allow, or provide for, a more complete and beneficial enjoyment of the land itself and the buildings were therefore an adjunct to the land to improve its usefulness or, as it was put, were accessory to the realty as allowing a more beneficial enjoyment of it by the occupant or were calculated to enhance the value of the premises for the purpose for which those premises are applied, then the buildings are fixtures and take on the nature of realty.

"Fraser-Brace were not carrying on upon the MacDonald lot any separate or independent operations to which the buildings might be regarded as an accessory. The sole purpose that the buildings were intended to serve was to make the lands themselves useful to the occupant as its Canadian headquarters. In my view the buildings were fixtures and part of the freehold. In consequence Fraser-Brace, by reason of their proprietary interest in the lands, and later Drake-Merritt for the same reason, were liable to assessment in respect of the buildings as realty."

On further appeal to the Supreme Court of Canada, [1958] S.C.R. 263, 13 D.L.R. 2d 177, it was held, in agreement with the majority of the New Brunswick Appeal Division, that title to the property in question was in the United States and hence the property was exempt from taxation and, further (and to this extent reversing the New Brunswick Court) that although the contractor held certain leases, they were held in trust for the United States and were likewise covered by its tax immunity.]

[On deceased's death his widow claimed dower in certain realty which included premises in which deceased had carried on a bowling alley business. An issue was raised whether the valuation of the realty as a basis for determining the value of dower should cover the bowling alleys which had been installed in the premises by deceased. How should the issue be decided? See *Re Davis*, [1954] O.W.N. 187.]

[A mortgagor leased his land to a tenant for a term certain and the latter brought fixtures upon it. Subsequently the landlord-mortgagor made an assignment in bankruptcy and the mortgagee took foreclosure proceedings as a result of which it went into possession of the property. Has the tenant (now out of possession) any tenable claim to the fixtures? If not, would he have had any claim if he asserted it before the foreclosure proceedings had terminated? See *Fish Meal Co.* v. *Nickerson*, [1936] 2 D.L.R. 284 (N.S.).]

[Among the important fixture problems are those which concern the position of a conditional seller of a chattel which is affixed to or in the buyer's premises and the removal of which is subsequently sought against (1) the buyer, or (2) his prior or subsequent mortgagee of the premises. The solution to these problems will turn (apart from statute, and even under a statute where there is no clear expression of its application) on whether the underlying conception is that fixtures are part of the realty regardless of intention of the seller; or, to put the matter differently, it may turn on whether we adopt simply a title concept when there is accession of a chattel to realty. Thus, where a mortgagor brings fixtures to the property after the mortgage is put on, then, unless their removal is covered by the mortgage terms or they are removed as trade fixtures before the mortgagee takes possession, the mortgagor will be unable to remove them even though in fact the mortgagee's security is not impaired: see *Gough* v. *Wood & Co.*, [1894] 1 Q.B. 713 (C.A.); *Reynolds* v. *Ashby*, [1904] A.C. 466. If the fixtures were purchased on a conditional sale contract under which the mortgagor defaults, then under the theory above-mentioned the conditional seller would be in no better position than the mortgagor, and if the mortgage contained a provision against removal of fixtures without consent of the mortgagee, the conditional seller's right to repossess his chattels (even assuming he could remove them without injury to the freehold) would be gone: see *Ellis* v. *Glover and Hobson Ltd.*, [1908] 1 K.B. 388 (C.A.). Presumably, it would not avail as against the mortgage terms or the mortgagee if the conditional sale agreement provided for the removal of fixtures. Yet there is no good reason why the title theory should be asserted against the conditional seller's rights. *Warner* v. *Foster*, [1934] O.R. 519, [1934] 3 D.L.R. 665 (C.A.) seems to support this criticism of the English cases because there the conditional seller succeeded against a prior land mortgagee even though the latter had taken possession of the land on the mortgagor's default. The case is explicable in terms of the Conditional Sales Act, R.S.O. 1960, c. 61, s. 10 (see *Dominion Bridge Co.* v. *British-American Nickel Corp. Ltd.*, 56 O.L.R. 288, [1925] 2 D.L.R. 138); but it represents a point of view that should prevail without the statutory provision. (It may be pointed out that the Act now gives the prior land mortgagee priority over the conditional seller in respect of advances made by him under the mortgage after the goods have been affixed and up to the time of registration of the conditional sale contract: see *Poloniato* v. *Regina Macaroni Holding Ltd.*, [1955] 4 D.L.R. 845, [1955] O.W.N. 627; *cf. California Wall Bed Co. of Can.* v. *Prudential Life Assur. Co.*, [1935] O.R. 59, [1935] 1 D.L.R. 279, varied [1935] O.R. 227, [1935] 2 D.L.R. 434 (C.A.).) See also *Purmal Brick Co.* v. *General Electric Co.* (1914), 20 D.L.R. 124, 7 W.W.R. 143 (Alta.) holding that a prior land mortgagee who under Alberta legislation is not a transferee of the land but only a security holder is postponed to the rights of a subsequent conditional seller under an agreement made with the mortgagor prior to the registration of the land mortgage and without notice thereof.

Where an issue arises between a conditional seller of a chattel (which becomes a fixture) and a subsequent mortgagee, or, indeed, purchaser of the land, the matter may be considered in terms of the ordinary rule whereby subsequent takers of the legal estate for value and without notice may defeat a prior equitable interest. This has been the English and Canadian view: see *Hobson* v. *Gorringe*, [1897] 1 Ch. 182 (C.A.); *Hoppe* v. *Manners*, 66 O.L.R. 587, [1931] 2 D.L.R. 253 (App. Div.). The subsequent mortgagee may moreover be relying on the fixture as part of his security and on this basis should be protected. Moreover, if the conditional seller seeks protection in respect of his fixture against subsequent purchasers or mortgagees he can find it by recording his interest under land recording statutes: *cf. Hoppe* v. *Manners*, *supra*.

For a discussion of the mortgage situation, see *Kratovil*, Fixtures and the Real Estate Mortgagee, (1948) 97 U. of Pa. L. Rev. 180; *Osborne*, Mortgages (1951), pp. 578 ff.; *Cf. Note*, Protection of Chattel Mortgagees' and Conditional Vendors' Interests in Fixtures, (1956) 41 Ia. L. Rev. 628.

For a general discussion of fixtures, see *Niles*, The Rationale of the Law of Fixtures: English Cases, (1934) 11 N.Y.U.L.Q. 560; *Niles*, The Intention Test in the Law of Fixtures, (1934) 12 N.Y.U.L.Q. 66.

For a catalogue of things which have been held to be fixtures and things which have been held to be simply chattels, see 20 *Halsbury's Laws of England*, 2d ed., pp. 96 ff.; 8 C.E.D. (Ontario), 2d. ed., pp. 368-9; 376-8. Of course, the characterization of something as a fixture still leaves open the question of its removability (if not also of its ownership), if it falls within the class of trade or ornamental or domestic fixtures: contrast *Webb* v. *Frank Bevis Ltd.*, [1940] 1 All E.R. 247 (C.A.) and *Smith* v. *City Petroleum Co. Ltd.*, [1940] 1 All E.R. 260 (K.B.). The latter case is of interest in holding that gasoline pumps (as contrasted with the underground tanks) are removable trade fixtures.]

5. RENT

(a) The Obligation and Its Enforcement

Liability to pay reasonable compensation for the use and occupation of land does not depend on express agreement; see also Landlord and Tenant Act, R.S.B.C. 1960, c. 207, s. 10; Tenancies and Distress for Rent Act, R.S.N.S. 1954, c. 287, s. 17. Customarily, however, the covenant to pay rent is a cardinal term of a lease. One of the incidents attached at common law to rent reserved under a lease is the right of distress. There is nothing to prevent arrangements for occupation of premises "rent free", and again rent may be payable in services or goods as well as in money. There are reasons other than the advantage of distress for exacting an express covenant to pay rent. At common law rent was payable in arrear, i.e. at the end of the period or term for which it was reserved: (see *Brunner* v. *Pollock*, [1941] 4 D.L.R. 107, [1941] 3 W.W.R. 166 (Sask. C.A.)) unless the dealings between the parties established some other course of payment. Normally then, payment in advance is expressly stipulated. Since rent is regarded at common law as a profit issuing out of the land, it was necessary for the landlord, if he sought to re-enter for non-payment, to demand the rent on the land in order to put the tenant in default: see *Tom* v. *Shofer*, [1953] 1 D.L.R. 356, 30 M.P.R. 228, 240 (N.S.C.A.), dealing with the requirements of the common law rule as to formal demand of rent as a condition of re-entry; *Startup* v. *Macdonald* (1843), 12 L.J. Ex. 477, at p. 483; *Woodfall*, Landlord and Tenant (1960, 26th ed.), p. 350. The requirement of a formal demand on the land has been abolished in some jurisdictions under "Short Forms" legislation and may, of course, be qualified or excluded by express stipulation: see Short Forms of Leases Act, R.S.O. 1960, c. 373, Sched. B, para. 12; Short Form of Leases Act, R.S.B.C. 1960, c. 357, Second Schedule, para. 14; Short Forms Act, R.S.M. 1954, c. 243, Third Schedule, para. 9; Real Property Act, R.S.P.E.I. 1951, c. 138, Third Schedule, para. 9.

The common law rule as to demand on the land did not apply to enforcement of a covenant to pay rent, and here the applicable common law rule is that the debtor must seek out the creditor (if no place for payment is specified), unless the facts show payment is to be made at the demised premises or elsewhere: see *Browne* v. *White*, [1947] 2 D.L.R. 309, [1947] 1 W.W.R. 622 (B.C.C.A.); *Clarke* v. *Kirkpatrick*, [1948] O.W.N. 406 (C.A.). A good deal of the litigation in this connection has arisen where there has been a course of payment by cheque, the resulting issue being whether payment is made when the cheque is mailed or when it is actually received by the landlord (assuming that a cheque rather than legal tender is sufficient). (If remittance through the mail is proper, what is the position where the tenant puts on insufficient postage? See *Gotlieb* v. *Goldfarb*, [1951] O.R. 481, [1951] 3 D.L.R. 358 (C.A.).) Courts have not shown consistency in their decisions, but it could reasonably be expected that in some circumstances an inference of remittance by post would be made against the landlord, and in others a refusal to draw such an inference would result, leading to a decision adverse to the tenant: see *Norman* v. *Ricketts* (1886), 3 T.L.R. 182 (C.A.); *Pennington* v. *Crossley & Sons Ltd.* (1897), 13 T.L.R. 513 (C.A.); *Mitchell-Henry* v. *Norwich Union Life Ins. Soc.*, [1918] 2 K.B. 67 (C.A.); *Bolton* v. *O'Reilly*, [1952] O.W.N. 49 (Cty. Ct.). During the rent control period in the recent war years, there was a disinclination, at least by the Ontario Courts, to infer agreement or permission of the landlord for payment by use of the mails, merely because of the tenant's practice of paying by that method: see *Davidovich and Mandel* v. *Hill*, [1948] 2 D.L.R. 613, [1948] O.W.N. 201 (C.A.); *Chemarno* v. *Pollock*, [1949] 1 D.L.R. 606, [1949] O.W.N. 122 (C.A.). As already indicated whether the giving of a cheque is in itself payment, even on its receipt, may also raise a problem: see *Kamin* v. *Kirby*, [1950] 2 D.L.R. 179, [1950] O.W.N. 68.

Rent passes with the reversion on a transfer thereof, and if there is an assignment of part only of the reversion, rent is apportionable accordingly. See *Woodfall*, Landlord and Tenant (1960, 26th ed.), p. 854. By statute now, remedies on the covenant for payment or by way of re-entry for breach are as available to the assignee of part of the reversion as they were available to the assignor in respect of the whole: see *Wilkinson* v. *Benedict*, [1948] 4 D.L.R. 849, [1948] 2 W.W.R. 1128 (Man. C.A.); Landlord and Tenant Act, R.S.B.C. 1960, c. 207, s. 13; Landlord and Tenant Act, R.S.M. 1954, c. 136, ss. 4, 8; Landlord and Tenant Act, R.S.N.B. 1952, c. 126, ss. 2, 4; Landlord and Tenant Act, R.S.O. 1960, c. 206, ss. 4, 8; Landlord and Tenant Act, R.S.P.E.I. 1951, c. 82, ss. 4, 5; Landlord and Tenant Act, R.S.S. 1953, c. 312, ss. 4, 7. By statute (but not at common law) rent is, in most of the provinces, apportionable as to time, being regarded thereunder as accruing from day to day: see Landlord and Tenant Act, R.S.B.C. 1960, c. 207, s. 13; Apportionment Act, R.S.M. 1954, c. 7; Property Act, R.S.N.B. 1952, c. 177, ss. 3-7; Apportionment Act, R.S.N.S. 1954, c. 12; Apportionment Act, R.S.O. 1960, c. 16; Apportionment Act, R.S.P.E.I. 1951, c. 10. Accruing rent may itself be assigned, in which case it is rent seck in the hands of the assignee (and not a rent service), without right of distress at common law; see *Hopkins* v. *Hopkins* (1883), 3 O.R. 223, at p. 230. However, distress in the case of rents seck is now given by statute: see Landlord and Tenant Act, R.S.B.C. 1960, c. 207, s. 8; Landlord and Tenant Act, R.S.M. 1954, c. 136, s. 29 (3); Landlord and Tenant Act, R.S.N.B. 1952, c. 126, s. 20; Landlord and Tenant Act, R.S.O. 1960, c. 206, s. 39; Landlord and Tenant Act, R.S.S. 1953, c. 312, s. 19. Accrued rent which is unpaid is assignable as a chose in action.

Where the term of a lease is assigned, the assignee will become liable for rent by reason of privity of estate. However, the tenant-assignor remains liable on his covenant to pay (if there is one), and, while the landlord may sue both assignor and assignee, as between them it is the assignee who is primarily liable so long as he holds the term. Once he in turn assigns, he is no longer liable to the landlord. It is customary upon an assignment to exact from the assignee a covenant of indemnity, so that if the original tenant is sued for rent, he may put in motion a chain of indemnity based on successive covenants by successive assignees.

[A company took a lease for 99 years and assigned its unexpired term to defendants under a deed in which the latter covenanted "to pay the future rent and observe the covenants on the part of the lessee contained in the lease". The company went into liquidation and assigned to the landlord the benefit of the covenant given by defendants. The latter assigned the leasehold to another, and then the landlord sued the defendants for the amount of rent in arrears. Should he succeed if the covenant in question is merely a covenant of indemnity? See *Butler Estates Ltd.* v. *Bean*, [1942] 1 K.B. 1, [1941] 2 All E.R. 793 (C.A.); *cf. Re Perkins, Poyser* v. *Beyfus*, [1898] 2 Ch. 182 (C.A.).]

The right to rent may be enforced by (1) action; (2) distress; (3) by re-entry as permitted by the terms of the lease; and (4) by the statutory right of re-entry, provided by legislation, as hereinafter set out.

LANDLORD AND TENANT ACT, R.S.O. 1960, c. 206

17. (1) In every demise, whether by parol or in writing and whenever made, unless it is otherwise agreed, there shall be deemed to be included an agreement that if the rent reserved, or any part thereof, remains unpaid for 15 days after any of the days on which the same ought to have been paid, although no formal demand thereof has been made, it is lawful for the landlord at any time thereafter, to re-enter into and upon the demised premises, or any part thereof in the name of the whole, and to have again, re-possess and enjoy the same as of his former estate.

[For similar legislation, see Landlord and Tenant Act, R.S.M. 1954, c. 136, s. 17 (1); Landlord and Tenant Act, R.S.N.B. 1952, c. 126, s. 8; Landlord and Tenant Act, R.S.P.E.I. 1951, c. 82, s. 9; Landlord and Tenant Act, R.S.S. 1953, c. 312, s. 9 (1) (period of default after which re-entry may be made is two months).]

[Re-entry to terminate a lease may be effected by issue of a writ, or by summary proceedings for possession (under appropriate legislation), or by actual re-entry: see *Prudential Ins. Co. of America* v. *McLean*, [1943] O.R. 377, [1943] 3 D.L.R. 307 (C.A.). Service of a notice to quit does not amount to a re-entry: see *Chernec* v. *Smith*, [1946] 3 D.L.R. 765, [1946] O.W.N. 513 (C.A.); *Winbaum* v. *Ginou*, [1947] O.R. 242, [1947] 2 D.L.R. 619; *Gotlieb* v. *Goldfarb*, [1951] O.R. 481, [1951] 3 D.L.R. 358 (C.A.).

S. 17 (1) of the Ontario Landlord and Tenant Act, *supra*, provides for re-entry "if the rent . . . remains unpaid for 15 days after any of the days on which it ought to have been paid". Canadian war-time rent control regulations lifted the protection and security given to a tenant if there was "default in payment of rent for 15 days or longer". When is rent overdue under these two formulae? See *Urbach* v. *McClarty*, [1953] 1 D.L.R. 316, [1953] O.W.N. 58 (C.A.).]

[Action for arrears of rent and re-entry by proceedings for possession may be taken concurrently. If the landlord re-enters, he loses his right of distress. If he distrains and the distress proves insufficient, may he still terminate the lease through re-entry? May he terminate while he holds the tenant's chattels under distress? See *Whittaker* v. *Goggin* (1908), 38 N.B.R. 378, 4 E.L.R. 530 (C.A.); *Re Gow and Downer*, [1935] O.R. 397, [1935] 3 D.L.R. 607 (C.A.).

Is distress incompatible with an action for rent? Does it depend on which remedy is taken first? See *Naylor* v. *Woods*, [1950] 1 D.L.R. 649 (N.S.Cty.Ct.).

Distress for rent is elaborately treated in *Woodfall*, Landlord and Tenant (1960, 26th ed.), chaps 8 and 9, pp. 370-479. It is largely governed by statute in the Canadian provinces: see Distress Act, R.S.B.C. 1960, c. 115; Landlord and Tenant Act, R.S.B.C. 1960, c. 207, ss. 4-8; Landlord and Tenant Act, R.S.M. 1954, c. 136, ss. 29-45; Landlord and Tenant Act, R.S.N.B.

1952, c. 126, ss. 20-42; Tenancies and Distress for Rent Act, R.S.N.S. 1954, c. 287; Landlord and Tenant Act, R.S.O. 1960, c. 206, ss. 29-54; Landlord and Tenant Act, R.S.P.E.I. 1951, c. 82, ss. 26-72; Landlord and Tenant Act, R.S.S. 1953, c. 312, ss. 19-40.

A tenant in arrears of rent assigned its inventory to a bank as security for a debt. The goods subject to the assignment remained in the tenant's premises and the landlord distrained upon them. The bank claimed priority under the Bank Act, 1944 (Can.), c. 30, ss. 88 and 89. The landlord relied on s. 30 (2) of the Landlord and Tenant Act, R.S.O. 1950, c. 199. Result? See *Re Newmarket Lumber Co. Ltd., International Wood Products Ltd.* v. *Royal Bank of Canada*, [1951] O.R. 642, [1951] 4 D.L.R. 720.]

LANDLORD AND TENANT ACT, R.S.O. 1960, c. 206

19. (1) Where a lessor is proceeding by action or otherwise to enforce a right of re-entry or forfeiture, whether for non-payment of rent or for other cause, the lessee may, in the lessor's action, if any, or if there is no such action pending, then in an action or summary application to a judge of the Supreme Court brought by himself, apply to the court for relief, and the court may grant such relief as, having regard to the proceedings and conduct of the parties under the provisions of section 18 and to all the other circumstances, the court thinks fit, and on such terms as to payment of rent, costs, expenses, damages, compensation, penalty, or otherwise, including the granting of an injunction to restrain any like breach in the future as the court deems just.

(4) Where the action is brought to enforce a right of re-entry or forfeiture for non-payment of rent and the lessee, at any time before judgment, pays into court all the rent in arrear and the costs of the action the proceedings in the action are forever stayed.

[By s. 18 (2), notice of a particular kind must be served by the lessor on the lessee as a condition of exercising a right of re-entry for breach of covenant other than a covenant to pay rent.

For comparable and similar legislation, see Landlord and Tenant Act, R.S.B.C. 1960, c. 207, s. 29; Landlord and Tenant Act, R.S.M. 1954, c. 136, ss. 18, 19; Landlord and Tenant Act, R.S.N.B. 1952, c. 126, s. 14; Landlord and Tenant Act, R.S.P.E.I. 1951, c. 82, s. 15; Landlord and Tenant Act, R.S.S. 1953, c. 312, s. 10, amended 1959, c. 10.

The Court has no discretion to refuse a stay if the terms of s. 19 (4), *supra*, are met: see *Kamin* v. *Kirby*, [1950] 2 D.L.R. 179, [1950] O.W.N. 68. *Cf. Gill* v. *Lewis*, [1956] 1 All E.R. 844, [1956] 2 W.L.R. 962 (C.A.).

If on the tenant's default for the prescribed period in payment of rent the landlord re-enters physically, may the Court relieve against forfeiture as it might where re-entry is by judicial proceedings? See *Re Davis and Garnatz*, [1955] O.W.N. 690.]

[During the period of war-time rent control tenancies became by and large periodic. Tenant security was lost if there was default in rent for a stipulated time, but if the landlord sought to re-enter he could be met by a claim of relief from forfeiture. Landlords thereupon used the default as a basis for giving notice to quit and were able under the terms of the rent control regulations, to avoid claims for relief from forfeiture; in this way they recovered possession: see *French* v. *Harris*, [1946] O.W.N. 516 (C.A.) and *Archibald* v. *Richardson*, [1946] O.W.N. 920 (C.A.); but *cf. Gotlieb* v. *Goldfarb*, [1951] O.R. 481, [1951] 3 D.L.R. 358 (C.A.).]

PERCENTAGE LEASES. Leases of commercial premises in which the rent is fixed at a percentage of the tenant's receipts or profits, and thus varies with them, have become common in the United States and are now being used in Canada. There is, however, no developed case law on the subject here. In so far as the lease terms give rise to construction problems, they would represent nothing new for adjudication. A percentage lease may, however, also involve implied obligations as, for example, an obligation of the tenant to keep books and allow the landlord to inspect them: see 1 *American Law of Property*, s. 3.66. Consideration of some of the problems in such leases may be found in *Note*, The Percentage Lease—Its Functions and Drafting Problems, (1948) 61 Harv. L. Rev. 317; *Van Doren*, Some Suggestions for the Drafting of Long Term and Percentage Leases, (1951) 51 Col. L. Rev. 186; *Landis*, The Drafting of Percentage Leases, (1955) 11 Univ. of Tor. L. J. 43.

[Another recent development, directed to tax advantages, is the "sale and lease back" transaction, involving a sale by a corporation of its lands, as a means of raising capital, with provision for a long term lease from the purchaser: see *Cary*, Corporate Financing Through the Sale and Lease-Back of Property: Business, Tax and Policy Considerations, (1948) 62 Harv. L. Rev. 1.]

(b) Excuse for Non-Payment

GRADER v. SINGER. Ontario Court of Appeal. [1945] 1 D.L.R. 182, [1944] O.W.N. 761

The judgment of the Court was delivered by ROBERTSON C. J. O.:

This is an appeal by the landlords from the judgment of Judge Kinnear, of the County Court of the County of Welland, on the trial of an issue under Part II of the Landlord and Tenant Act, R.S.O. 1937, c. 219. The landlords having distrained goods and chattels of the tenant for arrears of rent, an issue was directed to determine whether, at the time of the seizure, any monies were owing by the tenant to the landlords, and whether or not the goods and chattels seized were distrainable. The learned County Judge determined that, at the time of the seizure on June 21, 1944, no monies were owing by the tenant to the landlords for the premises in question, and that the goods and chattels seized were not distrainable at the time of the seizure.

The tenant held the premises in question—a store on East Main St. in the City of Welland—under a lease dated August 24, 1939, made in pursuance of the Short Forms of Leases Act, R.S.O. 1937, c. 159.... The tenant covenanted by the lease to occupy, and did in fact occupy, the premises as a retail store for the sale of shoes, hosiery, leather goods and associated lines.

A fire occurred in the leased premises on April 26, 1944, and damage was done thereby, both to the tenant's goods, furnishings and fixtures, and to the demised premises. The lease contains the proviso, according to the Short Forms of Leases Act, reading as follows: "Provided, that in the event of damage by fire, lightning or tempest, rent shall cease until the premises are rebuilt."

This, as interpreted by the statute, is to be read as follows:

"Provided, and it is hereby expressly agreed, that in case the premises hereby demised or any part thereof shall, at any time during the said term, be burned down or damaged by fire, lightning or tempest so as to render the same unfit for the purposes of the said lessee, then and so often as the same shall happen, the rent hereby reserved, or a proportionate part thereof, according to the nature and extent of the injuries sustained shall abate, and all or any remedies for recovery of said rent or such proportionate part thereof shall be suspended until the said premises shall have been rebuilt or made fit for the purposes of the said lessee."

The lease also contains, in the short form provided by the same statute, an exception of "damage by fire, lightning and tempest" from the tenant's covenants to repair, and to repair according to notice in writing, and to leave the premises in good repair.

After the fire on April 26, 1944, the tenant did not pay any further rent, and the landlords made no repairs to the premises. The tenant remained in possession of the premises and retained the only key, subject to this, that for the first two weeks after the fire the Fire Marshal held possession and retained the key. No great damage was done to the demised premises. There was discoloration of the walls by smoke, and in one place some discoloration of the linoleum on the floor. One joist in the basement was charred to a depth of one-eight of an inch, and several other joists were discolored by smoke, and perhaps slightly charred. The condition was such, however, that the tenant, in the middle of July, began and carried on a fire-sale on the premises, without anything more than some cleaning up that he did. After the fire the tenant's goods were in great disorder—piled and scattered about; shelving and other fixtures of the tenant had fallen and were lying where they fell. The tenant put in a claim under the insurance that he carried on his stock and fixtures, as for a total loss amounting to some $3,600. What settlement, if any, he made with his insurers, or when he made it, if at all, does not appear, but, whether with or without an arrangement with the insurers, he advertised, in the early part of July, a fire-sale on the premises.

No doubt the premises required some minor repairs that the tenant was not required by the lease to make. Whether it was important to him to have these repairs made by the landlords before the fire-sale, or whether the appearance of a fire having been in the premises would assist him in his fire-sale, does not appear. It is noteworthy, however, that the tenant did not, at any time, ask the landlords to repair, nor did he offer them possession of the premises so that repairs might be made. He kept his stock and fixtures there, and seems never to have answered the question that had been put to him by the landlords' agent soon after the fire, as to whether or not he intended to have a fire-sale.

Another matter that is not to be overlooked is that the tenant appears to have had another occupation. When asked on cross-examination what he was doing with the store after the fire, he said that he was cleaning it up in his time off at the plant—on his off days. He proceeded to explain that he was working in some other employment for eight hours a day, the shift on which he was working not being for the same hours on each day. He was employing his time off, when he could, in cleaning up and straightening up his store premises. Then, at some time not definitely fixed by the evidence, he advertised a fire-sale for July 15th, and proceeded on that date to hold a fire-sale. In the meantime there would have accrued in the ordinary course of events, $75 rent on May 1st and $75 rent on June 1st, both prior to the seizure made by the bailiff on June 21st, for $150 rent alleged to be in arrear.

In approaching the question the learned County Judge appears to have considered that the burden of proof was on the landlords to show that the premises were fit for the purposes of the tenant, subsequent to the fire. In my opinion the burden of proof was on the tenant to show that the damage by fire rendered the premises unfit for the purposes of the tenant, and that thereby the rent reserved or a proportionate part thereof, according to the nature and extent of the injuries sustained, had abated. It would seem that the first purpose of the tenant in this case was to hold a fire-sale, after having cleared matters up with his insurers, which, no doubt, took a little time. The premises were, obviously, not unfit for the purposes of a fire-sale, for the tenant has been carrying on such a sale and gives no evidence of being in the least prevented from making the most of it, by any condition of the premises. He has brought in other goods to supplement his damaged stock, for the purposes of the fire-sale. At the time of the hearing before the County Judge on July 27th, the fire-sale, begun on July 15th, was still proceeding.

In my opinion it is to lose sight of the real facts of this case to hold that the tenant was wholly relieved of payment of rent during the period in question by reason of damage by fire rendering the premises entirely unfit for the purposes of the tenant. In the first place, he used the premises as the place where his damaged stock and fixtures were. He kept them there. He further used the premises for putting his stock and fixtures in order, and as a place to which to bring further goods to be sold at his proposed fire-sale. It is not suggested that the landlords were responsible for the fire, and so long as the tenant makes use of the premises for any purpose of his, it is not open to him to say that the premises were rendered wholly unfit for his purposes. That is the real decision in the case of *United Cigar Stores Ltd.* v. *Buller and Hughes*, [1931] 2 D.L.R. 144, 66 O.L.R. 593, cited by the learned trial Judge. In that case the provision in the event of damage by fire was substantially different from the provision here, and the tenant, in accordance with the terms of the provision in that case, gave notice to the lessor of the damage by fire, whereupon the provision required that the landlord should cause the same to be repaired, and provided that there should be a proportionate reduction of rent for the time occupied in repairing such part or parts of the premises as might be rendered untenantable and incapable of use and occupancy by the lessee. The Court held in that case, that although the premises were rendered unfit for the purpose of carrying on the ordinary business of the tenant, they were, in fact, occupied and used by him for the storage of his merchandise, and that he should be charged with a proportionate part as rent.

Beyond question, the tenant in the present case was not entitled to have the whole rent abated at any time. He had always some use of the premises. It is a fair conclusion that it was also his purpose, if he should so arrange it with his insurers, to have a fire-sale. The fact that he held a fire-sale in the premises without their being repaired, and without even asking that repairs should be made, is abundant evidence that the premises were, in his estimation, fit for that purpose. It is not clear upon the evidence whether the making of such repairs as required to be made by the landlords, such as redecorating the walls or fixing the joists in the basement, would appreciably interfere with the carrying on by the tenant of his ordinary business. Up to the time of the seizure it would seem to be obvious that the tenant was content that the landlords should not repair at that time. He probably hoped to escape payment of rent accruing in that period, and for as long thereafter as the landlords omitted to repair. In taking this position, we think the tenant has entirely misconstrued his position. He has used the premises for the purpose that suited him for the time. Some allowance may be made for the period in which the Fire Marshal retained the key, although that was, in no way, the fault of the landlords. Thereafter the tenant himself held the key, and he should pay rent.

Rather than incur the expense of a reference back to determine the allowance that might be made, we fix the sum of $50, as an ample amount to be allowed to the tenant for any use of the premises he may have been deprived of by anything that may come within the proviso upon which he relies. The order should be that the landlords were entitled, at the time of the distress, to rent in arrear to the amount of $100, and that the tenant's goods and chattels upon the premises were distrainable for that amount. The landlords are entitled to the costs of the appeal, and also to the costs of the proceedings before the County Judge.

Appeal allowed.

[A tenant took a lease of the third floor of a building for commercial purposes and elevator service was included in the transaction. The lease was under the Ontario Short Forms of Leases Act. The elevator burned and the tenant claimed that rent abated. Is he right? See *Noble Scott Ltd.* v. *Murray* (1925), 56 O.L.R. 595, aff'd 57 O.L.R. 248 (C.A.).]

GOWAN v. CHRISTIE. House of Lords. 1873. L.R. 2 Sc. & Div. 273

A lessee under a 21 year determinable mineral lease took possession of the property, and after working it for upwards of four years he brought action claiming that because the property was not workable at a profit he was entitled to be freed of his obligations under the lease. Judgment went against him in the lower Court and he appealed.

LORD SELBORNE L. C.: ... When there is that which, in the language of the law of this country, would be called a total failure of consideration—when the landlord has not the thing to let which he purports to let, and which is the consideration for the rent, it is perfectly reasonable that the whole lease should fail *ab initio*, and be subject to reduction. Nor is it a very wide extension of that principle to say that if a landlord warrants a continuation of the subject matter for a certain number of years, a total failure of the subject matter before that number of years had elapsed shall involve a reduction or termination of the contract at the time of that failure and thenceforward. Those views are perfectly intelligible. But they all resolve themselves into either the original non-existence or the subsequent exhaustion or failure of the subject matter. And when the authorities which have been referred to are considered, they will be found, with a few, if any, exceptions, to turn entirely upon that principle so understood. The Roman text, *si frui non liceat* (Dig. 19. 2. 15. 1), points at cases where possession is not given; where there is no prestation of the subject matter, or where some external *vis major*, not inherent in the subject matter, and not the fault of the tenant, takes the subject matter away, either temporarily or permanently; but the principle is always the same, resting on the destruction *pro tanto*, or entirely, of the subject matter. But Lord *Stair* (Book 1, T. 15, s. 2), the authority on the law of *Scotland* chiefly relied upon, goes further, and, as it seems to me, lays down the true principle in the most unequivocal terms. He says that there is a peril or risk undertaken by the lessee, that he is at the risk of the quantity and the value of the subject matter, but he is not at the risk of the being or existence of it.

If there had been in this case a lease of some particular description of minerals only—for instance, of a bed or seam of coal, or of a bed of freestone—and if there had been no such thing in existence, then, according to Lord *Stair's* principle, the tenant would not have been at the risk of the "being or existence" of the coal or the freestone. But that, of course, cannot apply to a case where the lease is of all minerals; for although there is necessarily some uncertainty and speculation in such a lease, because the minerals may turn out to be of greater or less value, yet some minerals there necessarily must be under every parcel of land, and therefore the peril of the "being" of the minerals is a peril which no tenant of such a mineral lease incurs; nor does the landlord incur it either. But with respect to the quantity and value, which is the whole matter in controversy here, as I understand the case, according to Lord *Stair's* doctrine, the whole peril of the quantity and value is under such circumstances upon the tenant; so that that authority is directly against the Appellant's case....

The proposition [of the Appellant] really is this, that according to the principles laid down in the Law of Scotland the landlord guarantees the tenant against loss by reason of any of those elements extrinsic to the mine and independent of the nature of the subject-matter within the mine which go to the determination of the question of profit and loss. What are those elements? The quantity, the quality, the cost of labour, the cost of materials, the demand and supply varying in the markets, the accessibility of the markets themselves, and the means of conveyance—all which are things entirely extrinsic to the mine, and certainly not within the view of the principle laid down by any of the authorities to which a reference has been made. On the contrary, they are exactly those things as to which Lord *Stair* has said that the tenant runs the "risk of quantity and value".

My Lords, it therefore appears to me that even the authorities relied upon by the Appellant are against the view of the law which he suggests. But when we come to look at the stipulations in this particular lease we find that conclusion fortified by those stipulations. It is admitted that it is a very common thing with parties entering into mining leases to contract expressly that the tenant shall not be obliged to go on with the lease when he cannot work the mine to profit, and the parties very wisely add a clause providing for an arbitration. There is nothing of that sort in the lease before us, but there is a provision that at the end of three years, or at the end of seven, or at the end of fourteen years, the tenant may "break," as it is called, or throw up the lease; a provision absolutely irreconcilable with the whole principle of the Appellant's argument; because if the lease was vitiated from the beginning, and liable to reduction, it must have been upon grounds which are wholly independent of the exercise of an option at certain periods to retain or to throw it up. I had really great difficulty in understanding whether it was seriously meant to be contended, that because the lessee had made no profit he would not only have a right to throw it up, but he would also have a right to repetition of the rent he had paid. That seemed to me to be almost a necessary consequence of the Appellant's argument, although utterly inconsistent with the whole intent and purpose of the express contract between the parties.

LORD CHELMSFORD: My Lords, I entirely agree with my noble and learned friend.

The law, as laid down by Mr. Bell (Principles, s. 1208), makes it quite clear that where there is a total destruction or exhaustion of the subject matter of a lease, there the lessee is entitled to abandon it. But I am not aware that where it is a case of sterility merely, the tenant has any such right. The old authorities upon the subject rather, to my mind, indicate directly the contrary....

Here the Appellant has fenced himself round against the possibility of loss by reason of the sterility of the subject matter. He stipulates that for the first year no rent whatever shall be payable. He then stipulates that upon giving six months' notice at the termination of the third, the seventh, and the fourteenth years respectively, he may without any cause assigned abandon the lease. Now this is entirely for the benefit of the tenant. The landlord has no corresponding right of giving notice and turning the tenant out of possession. Therefore it seems a most reasonable thing to hold that where a special contract of this description is entered into (even supposing the common law would give the right of reducing the lease, which I am quite certain from the authorities it would not) it is impossible to say that the tenant can be fairly and reasonably entitled to reduce the lease, even supposing circumstances existed which without a contract would have entitled him to do so.

LORD CAIRNS: ... The averments do not even now assert that there are no minerals, or that there is no freestone; but merely that they are not capable of being worked to profit, an averment which implies their existence.

There is a common form of covenant in mining cases, that if the minerals cannot be worked to a profit, there shall be an opportunity to the lessee of giving up the lease upon certain terms stated. That covenant is generally accompanied with a specification of means for ascertaining by the award of arbitrators, or by the opinion of experts, whether it can be predicated of the mine at a particular time, that it cannot be worked to a profit. The word "profit" is there used in a sense altogether different from that in which the Appellant would use it here; because where you have an express covenant, "profit" does not mean gain after paying for work and labour, but it means gain after paying for work and labour, and the rent of the mine—a very different position of things from that for which the Appellant contends.

There is a well-known principle of the civil law, that where the subject matter demised turns out to be non-existent, or to be exhausted, or where the working of it turns out to be utterly impracticable, the tenant is relieved from the obligations of the lease. It is attempted to bring up that principle to this case, and to say that it gives to a tenant relief in the same way that the express provision, to which I have referred as being common in mining leases, where minerals cannot be worked at a profit, would give the tenant relief.

I asked the learned counsel for the Appellant, in the first place, Is there any decided case in support of that proposition? The learned counsel who argued for the Pursuer at your Lordships' Bar were unable to produce any....

Then, my Lords, finding that there is no decided case which is an authority for the contention of the Appellant, and that there are no dicta of institutional writers which can properly be applied to a case of this kind, I have no hesitation in saying that the Appellant has utterly failed to establish that there is in the case of a lease of this kind any implied warranty in law approaching to that express warranty which, in the first instance, he asserted had been given by his landlord. It is upon this ground that I should wish to rest the decision of the case. And I do so the more particularly for this reason, that I observe that some of the learned Judges in the Court below were rather inclined to rest it upon another ground, namely, to assume that there may be the common law right for which the Appellant contends; but that, on the other hand, that common law right is ousted by the express provisions contained in this lease with regard to breaks. If I found that there was a common law right such as has been alleged, I should have great hesitation in saying that anything in this lease did oust that right. If there is such a common law right, I do not see that it is in the least degree impossible that it should co-exist with a lease containing a provision for breaks. I do not, therefore, hold, that the common law right is excluded by the provisions of this lease, but rather that these provisions are to be regarded as a proof that it never was imagined by those who entered into it that there was any such common law right; because if there was such a common law right these provisions, to a great extent at all events, would have been unnecessary.

Appeal dismissed.

[The concurring judgment of Lord Colonsay is omitted.

If an apartment, say on the top floor of a building is let and the building is destroyed by fire, does a tenant's obligation to pay rent continue if there is nothing in the lease to the contrary? See *Woodfall*, Landlord and Tenant (1960, 26th ed.), pp. 366, 1016; *cf. Packer* v. *Gibbins* (1841), 1 Q.B. 421, 113 E.R. 1194 (C.A.).

If rent is paid in advance under the terms of a lease which contains a provision for abatement in case of fire and the demised premises are destroyed by fire, may the tenant recover the "unearned" portion of the rent so paid? Suppose the rent is not actually paid at the date stipulated and the premises burn down, may the landlord recover the whole of the rent that was payable? See *Ryerse* v. *Lyons* (1862), 12 U.C.Q.B. 12 (C.A.); *cf. Patching* v. *Smith* (1896), 28 O.R. 201.]

CRICKLEWOOD PROPERTY & INVESTMENT TRUST LTD. v. LEIGHTON'S INVESTMENT TRUST LTD. House of Lords. [1945] A.C. 221, [1945] 1 All E.R. 252

Appeal by tenants under a building lease from a judgment of the Court of Appeal [1943] K.B. 493, [1943] 2 All E.R. 97, affirming a judgment of Asquith J., [1942] 2 All E.R. 580, for plaintiff landlords in an action for rent.

The facts, stated by Viscount Simon L. C. and Lord Wright, were as follows: By a lease dated May 12, 1936, the predecessors in title of the respondents demised certain land at Potters Bar to the appellant company for a term of ninety-nine years from March 25, 1936, and the other two appellants joined in the lease as guarantors for the payment of the rent and performance of the covenants. The lessors were developing a building estate for residential purposes and the lease in question was a building lease under which the appellants were to build a number of shops to form what is commonly called a shopping centre for the residents on the estate. The subject of the demise was two parcels of land adjoining the residential area, one coloured red and the other blue on the plan attached to the lease. A question had previously arisen between the lessors and the local authority under a town planning scheme for the area and there had been an appeal to the Minister. This appeal was compromised on terms which were scheduled to the lease and which in effect provided that not more than twenty-four shops in all should be built on these two parcels of land; that eight might be built at once, and, in addition, that not less than four shops to each two hundred houses occupied should be permitted to be built in the future till the total of twenty-four was reached. The rent reserved by cl. 1 was the aggregate of the following rents, (*a*) as to each of the ten shop sites on the red land a peppercorn for the first year and thereafter a yearly rent of 35£ for each site, and (*b*) as to each of the fourteen shop sites on the blue land a peppercorn till the expiration of one year from notification by the landlords that erection of a shop thereon might proceed and thereafter a yearly rent of 35£ for each site in respect of which such notification had been given. This notification that building might proceed was rendered necessary because of the compromise referred to above. Clause 2 of the lease contained covenants by the appellant company to pay the rent and outgoings and to build twenty-four shops on the demised land, ten on the red and fourteen on the blue. The first eight were to be built on the red land not later than March 25, 1937; the remainder were to be built within one year from the notification by the landlords that building might proceed, but in certain circumstances, which need not be set out in detail, an "abeyance period," as it was called, might arise which would have the effect of postponing the obligation to build beyond the year. It was, however, expressly provided that nothing in the clause which provided for this abeyance period should "in any way affect the rent or rents payable in respect of the demised property or any part thereof or the time or manner of such payment." The lease, by cl. 3, gave the appellant company the option to purchase the freehold of the demised property, both the red and blue sites. (This option was exercised as regarded the red sites and accordingly no question arose in connection with them or with the shops built on them.) By cl. 4, a right of re-entry for non-payment of rent or breach of covenant was reserved, but it was provided by cl. 5, that after any of the shops had been assigned or underlet this right should only be exercisable upon the particular shop in respect of which the breach had occurred, the intention being that each should be held separately and independently of the others. There was also a provision in cl. 6 of the lease enabling the appellant company, at the expiration of seven years from the date of the agreement, to give notice to determine the lease as to any of the sites in respect of which notice that building might proceed had not been given. As regarded the blue land, no shops had been erected when notice that building might proceed was given as to two sites on September 24, 1937. Further notices were given on May 30, 1938, and August 25, 1939, in each case as to four sites. No building was begun on any of these ten sites. On May 17, 1938, the original lessors conveyed the land subject to and with the benefit of the lease to the respondents, and as the appellant company paid no rent after the outbreak of war, the respondents issued a writ dated April 8, 1942, against the appellant company as tenants and against the other two appellants as guarantors, claiming arrears of rent since September, 1939, this being the only claim in the action. The shop sites in respect of which rent was claimed were six in the earlier period till September 30, 1940, and ten in the later period till March 25, 1942, all of them forming part of the fourteen sites included in the land marked blue on the plan.

VISCOUNT SIMON L. C.: My Lords, before this House, and apparently in both courts below, the appellants did not attempt to rely on the fact that the demand for shops had ceased, or on their inability to procure finance, as establishing a defence. They relied entirely on the impossibility of building created by the restrictions imposed on work of this character and on the acquisition of materials. Though these restrictions were not particularized it must be taken that they were imposed by valid orders or prohibitions under the Defence Regulations, and while it would have been more satisfactory if the documents relied on had been set out or referred to, the case has proceeded (as must this appeal) on the footing that the performance of the covenant to build was impossible, and continues to be so while the orders or prohibitions are in force. Asquith J., who tried the case, held on the authorities that the doctrine of frustration did not apply to a lease at all, and that for this purpose there was no distinction between a building lease and any other lease, though he said that had the doctrine applied he would have decided that the contract had been discharged. The Court of Appeal, in a judgment delivered by MacKinnon L. J., said ([1943] K.B. 493, 496) that the doctrine had never been applied to a demise of real property and that there was clear authority that it cannot be. "It is impossible for the defendants to rely on the doctrine of frustration to relieve them from their obligations as tenants under a demise of land for ninety-nine years." Against that judgment the tenants appeal to this House. Two questions are raised by the appeal: first, can the doctrine of frustration apply to determine a lease? and, secondly, even if it can, are the circumstances in the present case such as to produce the result that the lease has been determined by frustration? If, my Lords, we all agree (as I understand we do) that the answer to the second question is in the negative, it is not essential in the present case to reach a conclusion on the first question (as to which I gather that our opinions are divided). Nevertheless, I propose to express my opinion with regard to both questions, since the more general issue has been much discussed and was pronounced on in the courts below, where it was regarded as concluded by authority, including the authority of this House, in *Matthey* v. *Curling*, [1922] 2 A.C. 180.

The broad issue must first be considered as though it were *res integra*: then I propose to consider the effect of previous decisions. Frustration may be defined as the premature determination of an agreement between parties, lawfully entered into and in course of operation at the time of its premature determination, owing to the occurrence of an intervening event or change of circumstances so fundamental as to be regarded by the law both as striking at the root of the agreement, and as entirely beyond what was contemplated by the parties when they entered into the agreement. If, therefore, the intervening circumstance is one which the law would not regard as so fundamental as to destroy the basis of the agreement, there is no frustration. Equally, if the terms of the agreement show that the parties contemplated the possibility of such an intervening circumstance arising, frustration does not occur. Neither, of course, does it arise where one of the parties has deliberately brought about the supervening event by his own choice. (See the cases collected in *Joseph Constantine Steamship Line, Ld.* v. *Imperial Smelting Corporation, Ld.*, [1942] A.C. 154, 160.) But where it does arise, frustration operates to bring the agreement to an end as regards both parties forthwith and quite apart from their volition. Is there any good reason why this conception of frustration should not ever apply to a lease of land and result in its premature determination? I do not feel able to assert any *a priori* or absolute impossibility, though the instances in which the doctrine might apply to such a lease are undoubtedly very rare.

A lease of land creates in the lessee an estate, which is a chattel interest. (Law of Property Act, 1925, s. I, sub-s. I (b).) Such an estate, by the nature of the case, lasts at most for the term stipulated and may come to an end sooner. In normal circumstances, the estate continues to exist for the period of the agreed term—in the present instance, for ninety-nine years from March 25, 1936—but it is liable to be determined by the landlord's re-entry for non-payment of rent or of breach of covenant. This is expressly provided for by cl. 4 of the present lease. The question therefore is whether, in addition to pre-determination under such express provisions, it is possible that a lease for years should pre-determine from a supervening cause which amounts to frustration. If so, the term ends, no further rent is payable, and the lessor recovers the property with all permanent structures erected upon it, at once. It is said that this cannot be so, because a lease is more than a contract and amounts to an estate: but this reasoning seems to me to be dangerously near to arguing in a circle; if we assume that frustration can only arise in cases where there is a contract and nothing else, the conclusion of course follows that frustration cannot arise in the case of a lease. Where the lease is a simple lease for years at a rent, and the tenant, on condition that the rent is paid, is free during the term to use the land as he likes, it is very difficult to imagine an event which could prematurely determine the lease by frustration—though I am not prepared to deny the possibility, if, for example, some vast convulsion of nature swallowed up the property altogether, or buried it in the depths of the sea. The lease, it is true, is of the "site," but it seems to be not inconceivable that, within the meaning of the document the "site" might cease to exist. If, however, the lease is expressed to be for the purpose of building, or the like, and if the lessee is bound to the lessor to use the land for such purpose with the result that at the end of the term the lessor would acquire the benefit of this development, I find it less difficult to imagine how frustration might arise. Suppose, for example, that legislation were subsequently passed which permanently prohibited private building in the area or dedicated it as an open space for ever, why should this not bring to an end the currency of a building lease, the object of which is to provide for the erection on the area, for the combined advantage of the lessee and lessor, of buildings which it would not be unlawful to construct? It is no answer to say that it may be presumed that the legislature would make express provision, by compensation clauses or otherwise, to deal with such a case: we are entitled to test the applicability of the doctrine by assuming supervening illegality, without any qualification. Neither, I think, is the theoretic possibility of frustration got rid of by stressing the complications that might in some cases arise between the parties if the relation of lessor and lessee is prematurely terminated for all purposes by such a cause. In the case of pure contract also, the situation resulting from frustration has raised questions of difficulty which, after forty years of doubt, were only settled by the decision of this House in *Fibrosa Spolka Akcyjna* v. *Fairbairn Lawson Combe Barbour, Ld.*, [1943] A.C. 32; and even then it was considered just and necessary to modify the common law consequences by a subsequent Act of Parliament, the Law Reform (Frustrated Contracts) Act, 1943 (6 & 7 Geo. 6, c. 40.)

I now turn to the cases. A careful examination of the decided cases to which the Court of Appeal refers satisfies me that it is erroneous to suppose that there is authority binding on this House to the effect that a lease cannot in any circumstances be ended by frustration. In *Matthey* v. *Curling*, the House did not say so: the decision there was that requisitioning by the Government was no answer to a claim on the covenant for rent, any more than ouster by a trespasser would be: the remedy of the tenant was against the Government for compensation. Equally, destruction by fire, after the Government had requisitioned the place, left the tenant still liable on his covenant to deliver up in proper condition, for the tenant could have covered the risk by insurance. Thus, on the true construction of the document, the two covenants still bound the tenant. It seems clear that, if the actual decision in *Matthey* v. *Curling* is as above set out, the Court of Appeal was mistaken in treating it as "clear authority" that the doctrine of frustration "cannot" be applied to a demise of real property. It is noteworthy that when *Matthey* v. *Curling* was before the Court of Appeal, Atkin L. J., in his dissenting judgment, observed: "it does not appear to me conclusive against the application to a lease of the doctrine of frustration that the lease, in addition to containing contractual terms, grants a term of years. Seeing that the instrument as a rule expressly provides for the lease being determined, at the option of the lessor, upon the happening of certain specified events, I see no logical absurdity in implying a term that it shall be determined absolutely on the happening of other events—namely, those which in an ordinary contract work a frustration." This passage exactly expresses my view. I may further point out that in *Taylor* v. *Caldwell* (1863), 3 B. & S. 826, when the question was raised whether the hall which was burnt down was demised to the defendant or not, Blackburn J. said (at p. 832): "Nothing however, in our opinion, depends on this." The impression, which I venture to think is erroneous, that this House in *Matthey* v. *Curling* actually decided that frustration cannot arise in the case of a lease, is encouraged by the headnote to that case in the Law Reports, which states that that decision affirmed *Whitehall Court, Ld.* v. *Ettlinger*, [1920] 1 K.B. 680. It is true that Lord Atkinson in *Matthey* v. *Curling* expressed the view that the *Whitehall Court* case was rightly decided, but none of the other Lords either said or implied this. Moreover, in the *Whitehall Court* case Lord Reading C. J.'s primary decision was that the mere fact that the tenant was personally prevented from residing in the leased flat did not affect the existence of the chattel property vested in him under the lease. It is true that Lord Reading gave a further reason for his decision, which was based on the adoption of a sentence in Lush J.'s judgment in *London & Northern Estates Co.* v. *Schlesinger*, [1916] 1 K.B. 20, 24, but in this last quoted case also the actual decision of the Divisional Court was that a tenancy was not existinguished because the tenant for the time being was not allowed by law to inhabit the flat which had been leased to him. This was the ground of decision on which both members of the Divisional Court—Avory and Lush JJ:—concurred, and though Lush J. added that a tenancy agreement was more than a contract and that the chattel interest created by the lease continued to be vested in the tenant, he did not in fact, I think, advance the abstract proposition that a lease can never be determined by events equivalent to frustration. At any rate, this House is not obliged to accept such a proposition, and, as I have indicated, I think it goes too far. The occasions, however, on which frustration terminates a lease must be exceedingly rare.

So much for the abstract and theoretical question. But there remains the practical issue whether what is proved to have happened in the present case could be enough to constitute frustration of such a lease. I do not agree with Asquith J. that the orders requiring a suspension of building are sufficient to strike at the root of the arrangement. The lease at the time had more than ninety years to run, and though we do not know how long the present war, and the emergency regulations which have been made necessary by it, are going to last, the length of the interruption so caused is presumably a small fraction of the whole term. Frustration, where it exists, does not work suspension but brings the whole arrangement to an inevitable end forthwith. Here, the lease itself contemplates that rent may be payable although no building is going on, and I cannot regard the interruption which has arisen as such as to destroy the identity of the arrangement or make it unreasonable to carry out the lease according to its terms as soon as the interruption in building is over: this is the nature of the test for frustration suggested in the well-known case of *Metropolitan Water Board* v. *Dick Kerr & Co. Ld.*, [1918] A.C. 119. I therefore conclude, on the facts, that the liability for rent under the covenant continued uninterrupted, and I move your Lordships to dismiss the appeal with costs.

LORD RUSSELL OF KILLOWEN: My Lords, I share the opinion, which all your Lordships entertain, that no question as to what is called frustration can arise on the facts of the present case. Unfortunately we have no pleadings and little evidence, owing to what seems to me a regrettable attempt to take a short cut in an important case. We must therefore assume it to be true (owing to an admission made by the respondents in Judge's Chambers) that no obligation on the part of the appellant company to erect shops on any of the fourteen blue sites arose until after the outbreak of the war, and that government restrictions on buildings and building materials made if impossible to erect shops on any of those sites. It seems, however, equally true, that if it had chosen so to do, it had ample time before September 3, 1939, to erect shops on six of the sites. But apart from this last-mentioned fact, all that has happened is that for a portion of a span of ninety-nine years the erection of shops on the sites has been postponed, with the result that for a time the appellant company will be liable to pay a rent of 35£ per annum in respect of each site, although no shop has been erected thereon. But that is to carry out the provisions of the lease which is said to be frustrated. The rent thereunder is payable in respect of sites, not in respect of shops; and cl. 2, after fixing times within which the tenant has to erect shops, provides in terms that nothing in the clause should in any way affect the rent or rents payable in respect of the demised property or any part thereof or the time or manner of such payment. It seems to me clear that the intention of the parties was that rent would be payable even though the sites were vacant, and that the landlord was not to be driven to sue for damages for breach of covenant to erect shops. To such an action the war-time restrictions might well afford a defence, but that is a consequence very different and far removed from frustration. Therefore, even on the assumption that the doctrine of frustration can be applied to a lease, this appeal must fail.

On the broader question I confess that I am unable to grasp how the doctrine of frustration can ever apply so as to put an end to a lease and the respective liabilities of landlord and tenant thereunder. A lease is much more than a contract. It creates and vests in the lessee an estate or interest in the land, a chattel interest, it is true, but a vested estate or interest none the less. As was said by Lush J. in *London & Northern Estates Co.* v. *Schlesinger* "It is not correct to speak of this tenancy agreement as a contract and nothing more. A term of years was created by it and vested in the appellant, and I can see no reason for saying that because this order disqualified him from personally residing in the flat, it affected the chattel interest which was vested in him by virtue of the agreement. In my opinion it continues vested in him still." That dictum of Lush J. was approved in *Whitehall Court, Ld.* v. *Ettlinger*, a case which itself was approved by Lord Atkinson in your Lordships' House without any dissent from his colleagues in the case of *Matthey* v. *Curling*. When a contract is frustrated it is because what is called the "venture" or "undertaking" in which the parties have contracted to engage can no longer be carried out. The court in such circumstances declares the contract to be, or treats it as being, no longer binding on the parties. That is an end of the matter. But when a lease is in question, and has been granted by one to another, it is the lease which is the "venture" or "undertaking" upon which the parties have embarked. The contractual obligations thereunder of each party are merely obligations which are incidental to the relationship of landlord and tenant created by the demise, and which necessarily vary with the character and duration of the particular lease. It may well be that circumstances may arise during the currency of the term which render it difficult, or even impossible, for one party or the other to carry out some of its obligations as landlord or tenant, circumstances which might afford a defence to a claim for damages for their breach, but the lease would remain. The estate in the land would still be vested in the tenant. I know of no power in the court to declare a lease to be at an end except upon findings that some event has occurred on the happening of which the lease terminates by reason of some express provision contained in the document. In such a case the term ends not because the court exercises a power to terminate it, but because in the events which have happened the lease operated only as a demise for the shorter period. Nor do I know of any power in the court to order a tenant (who, be it observed, might have sublet part by way of mortgage or otherwise) to surrender his term to the landlord. The lease must of necessity continue. Some of the obligations thereunder may from time to time, from various circumstances, become difficult or impossible of performance by one or other of the parties; but, in my opinion, it cannot have applied to it the doctrine of frustration. The rent will continue to be payable in accordance with the terms of the document.

Since preparing my opinion in this case I have had an opportunity of perusing a print of the remarks which my noble and learned friend Lord Wright proposes to address to your Lordships and of considering the numerous references therein to a series of authorities cited by him. I wish to guard against it being said that your Lordships are in agreement with all my noble friend's statements. For myself I disagree with many of them: in particular I disagree with the view in relation to a lease of land, which is expressed in the following terms: "If the contract is avoided or dissolved, as it may be by either party, under the express terms of the lease, the estate in land falls with it." If by these words my noble friend only wishes to record the proposition that the exercise of a power to determine a lease will put an end to the lessee's estate in the land, well and good; but if he means that the estate in land necessarily comes to an end with cesser of contractual liability, I disagree. A lease may come to an end, and with it the estate in the land and all contractual liability by virtue of some provision in the lease, or by reason of some defect in the title of the person who purported to grant it. But, in my opinion, the cesser or suspension of some contractual liability under the lease will not destroy the estate in land which is vested in the lessee, unless the lease provides that in that event the term of years shall cease. Further I disagree with the view that there is anything in Lord Buckmaster's judgment in the case of *Matthey* v. *Curling* or in the cases of *Brewster* v. *Kitchell*, (1698) 1 Salk. 198, or *Baily* v. *de Crespigny*, (1869) L.R. 4 Q.B. 180, inconsistent with the view that the doctrine of frustration cannot apply to a lease of land, or favouring the view that it may so apply. I concur in the motion proposed.

LORD WRIGHT: My Lords, while I agree that the appeal must fail and the decisions of the courts below must be upheld, I prefer to base my conclusion on the ground that whether the doctrine of frustration can apply or not to a demise of land, no circumstances are shown in the present case which would excuse the appellants from their covenant to pay rent for the ten shop sites, which are the sites in respect of which rent is claimed. I think the case is concluded by the principles laid down by this House in *Matthey* v. *Curling* in the opinion delivered by Lord Buckmaster, concurred in by Lords Sumner, Wrenbury and Carson. Lord Atkinson gave a separate opinion agreeing in the result. In that case demised premises had been lawfully requisitioned by the military authorities who continued in occupation during the remainder of the term. A month before the term ended the house was destroyed by fire. The claims in the action which the lessor brought against the lessee included (1.) rent for the last quarter; (2.) damages for breach of covenants including the covenant to repair and deliver up in repair. The defence as to the former was that the lessees had been evicted by a title or authority which they could not withstand. Lord Buckmaster said that there was not an eviction by title paramount or eviction by the lessor himself, but a mere eviction. He concluded that the question was "how far the lessor has been deprived of the benefit of his covenant, and an act lawfully or unlawfully done, for which he is in no way responsible, cannot, in my opinion, have that effect, unless the covenant can be construed as excluding the event." Further, as to the repairing covenant, he held that the lessees were liable though the military had been in occupation when the house was burnt and continued in occupation until some time after the term ceased by effluxion of time. Lord Buckmaster was also of opinion that there was no impossibility of performance, though enjoyment of the premises had been interfered with by legal powers; he added "that a terminable occupation by military authorities during an uncertain time for which compensation may prove to be recoverable constitutes no answer to the obligations of this repairing covenant." It is clear that the agreed facts which the appellants rely on as relieving them from their obligation to pay rent under the covenant are not nearly so strong in their favour as those discussed by Lord Buckmaster. The appellants were not ejected in any shape or form from the demised premises. Neither the lessor nor anyone claiming under him interfered with the enjoyment of the land. All that happened was that for an uncertain term of the period, obviously likely to be short compared with the ninety-nine years of the lease, they could not proceed with their building scheme. The period of interruption is not stated, but it seems to be accepted that it is limited to the duration of the present emergency. The covenants to pay rent are absolute in terms and are expressly made independent of the progress of the building operations. It seems to me impossible to hold that these covenants are discharged by the facts alleged by the appellants in their affidavit. Even if the doctrine of frustration can be invoked in the case of a lease the interruption of the building operations cannot be regarded as likely to be so long in its duration as to destroy the basis or foundation of the lease and to lead the court to declare that it is dissolved on the principles applied by the court in order to determine if a contract is frustrated. Thus in *Metropolitan Water Board* v. *Dick Kerr & Co., Ld.*, [1918] A.C. 119, the test applied was whether the interruption was so long as to destroy the identity of the work and service when resumed with the work and service when interrupted, as Lord Dunedin put it, or in Lord Blackburn's words in *Dahl* v. *Nelson* (1881), 6 App. Cas. 38, 53, quoted by Lord Atkinson, whether the interruption was "so great and long as to make it unreasonable to require the parties to go on". But a lease is more than a contract. It creates an estate in land (Law of Property Act, 1925, s. 1, sub-s. 1 (b).) The estate so created is limited and determined by the contractual terms of the lease and is governed by the agreement between the lessor and lessee. It may be that in earlier days the element of covenant bulked sometimes more largely in the eyes of the law than the question of tenure. In *Paradine* v. *Jane* (1647), Aleyn 26, the judges do not mention the element of tenure. The claim was in debt. The court states the absolute character of the contract in language which has often been quoted: "When the party by his own contract creates a duty or charge upon himself, he is bound," they said, "to make it good, if he may, notwithstanding any accident by inevitable necessity, because he might have provided against it by his contract." Lord Atkinson in his opinion in *Matthey's* case quotes these expressions as a general statement of contract law, but so unqualified a statement would not be consistent with the modern law relative to the discharge of contractual obligations by impossibility of performance, as explained by this House in *Joseph Constantine Steamship Line, Ld.* v. *Imperial Smelting Corporation, Ld.* and other well-known authorities. Indeed, in *Constantine's* case, Lord Porter expressly enters a caveat against treating what he correctly calls the dicta which I have just quoted as universally applicable. I need not in detail refer to the mass of modern authority which would refute such a wide statement of the law. I may, however, refer to Lord Sumner's pithy description of the doctrine of frustration as "a device, by which the rules as to absolute contracts are reconciled with a special exception which justice demands": *Hirji Mulji* v. *Cheong Yue Steamship Co., Ld.*, [1926] A.C. 497, 510. But the doctrine of frustration can only be held to be applicable after a careful consideration of the particular case, and in particular after scrutinizing the nature of the contract and the particular circumstances of the case. The nature of a lease not only involves a tenure as well as a contract, but has become the subject of precise rules which must be taken to be settled law of at least general application and to be understood by those who enter into transactions of lease. Hence I think the carefully guarded way in which Lord Buckmaster deals with the question before him in *Matthey's* case. He is careful to express no opinion as to the decision in *Whitehall Court, Ld.* v. *Ettlinger*, which Lord Atkinson says expressly "was rightly decided". The majority of the House said nothing about the case, and I think the statement in the headnote that *Whitehall Court, Ld.* v. *Ettlinger* was affirmed is not accurate if intended to apply to the judgment of the House. In *Whitehall Court, Ld.* v. *Ettlinger* Lord Reading C. J. held indeed that the requisition of the flats by the military authorities did not establish a case of eviction by title paramount and held that there was "no reason why the chattel interest which was vested in the tenant by virtue of the two leases was affected merely because he was personally prevented from residing in the flats". In so deciding he seems to me to follow the same lines of reasoning as Lord Buckmaster did in *Matthey's* case. Lord Reading also did perhaps recognize the distinction between an ordinary contract and a lease. But I cannot find that his language justified the head-note to the effect that the doctrine of the termination of a contract by the frustration of the adventure did not apply to the creation of an estate by demise. He was, I think, careful to limit his observations to the facts of the case before him. And in *London & Northern Estates Co.* v. *Schlesinger*, the lessee had become by the outbreak of war an alien enemy and prohibited from residing in the area in which the flat was situated. It was not difficult to hold that the prohibition did not put an end to the tenancy or discharge the obligation to pay rent, though the tenant's personal enjoyment of the premises was prohibited. On that ground the court held that performance of the contract was not rendered impossible. The tenant could, so it was held, sublet or assign the lease. That was enough to decide the case. Lush J., however, added that nothing had happened in that case to affect the chattel interest vested by virtue of the agreement. He said, truly enough, that the tenancy agreement was not only a contract and nothing more, but a contract which created a term of years. It is clear that this is an element to be taken into account in considering whether events which have occurred, such as a requisition for a time or a destruction of the demised dwelling house by fire or the like have put an end to the tenancy or the tenant's obligations under the tenancy. It may be broadly said that as a general rule this result does not follow casualties of that character, even though the tenant is deprived of the advantages at least for a time which the parties to the lease contemplated he would normally enjoy. It has been held over and over again that a temporary interruption of the tenant's use and occupation does not affect the covenants or the chattel interest. The rule may be different, it seems, in Scotland: see *Tay Salmon Fisheries Co., Ltd.* v. *Speedie*, [1929] S.C. 593 and *Mackeson* v. *Boyd*, [1942] S.C. 56. But the Scotch authorities afford no analogy applicable to English law, because they proceed, it seems, on a different view of the contract and of the legal background. In England, since *Paradine* v. *Jane* and earlier, the law has been that in general the tenant's covenant to pay rent or repair or deliver up in repair are not affected by casualties which interfere with his enjoyment of the demised land. The lessor as a general rule gives no warranty in these respects in favour of the tenant. The tenant must perform his covenants even though the demised house is destroyed by fire (*Monk* v. *Cooper* (1727), 2 Stra. 763), quite irrespective of what covenants as to repairs there may be (*Lofft* v. *Dennis* (1859), 1 E. & E. 474), or whether the loss of enjoyment is due to the landlord's failure to fulfil his obligation to repair (*Hart* v. *Rogers*, [1916] 1 K.B. 646). In that latter case the tenant would have his cross-claim against the landlord for damages. On the same principle it has been held that a covenant in a mining lease to raise and pay for a certain amount of coal is not affected if it turns out that the mine was so exhausted that there were not coals left in it (*Bute* v. *Thompson* (1844), 13 M. & W. 487). These and many similar authorities show that by English law the lessee's covenants are generally absolute. The enjoyment and the covenant do not generally march together. I think Lord Buckmaster's judgment proceeds on this basis. He does not put it on the circumstances that the lease also creates an estate in land. But though the lessee's covenants are generally absolute, there are qualifications which the law implies in relief of the lessee, even in the absence of express terms. In other words, covenants in the lease may be suspended or terminated by operation of law and the court will decree accordingly. Thus the covenant to pay rent may be suspended: for instance, if the lessor himself evicts the tenant, as Lord Buckmaster observed in *Matthey's* case, or if there is eviction by title paramount, a term to be narrowly construed, as Lord Buckmaster points out. The law has also implied a term that a lease may be forfeited if the lessee by matter of record or the like disclaims the lessor's title. Such a case was discussed in *Doe d. Graves and Downe* v. *Wells* and *Trowbridge* (1839), 10 A. & E. 427. These results all flow from the general nature of the contract as understood in English law and its application to particular conditions of fact. I do not find that they depend on the circumstance that the lease involves a tenure and creates an estate in land. If the contract is avoided or dissolved, as it may be by either party, under the express terms of the lease, the estate in land falls with it. I do not see why this may not be also true if the lease were dissolved by operation of law. Lord Buckmaster does not mention this aspect, though *Whitehall Court, Ld.* v. *Ettlinger* was cited in argument and is referred to by

Lord Atkinson in his opinion. Lord Buckmaster deals particularly with *Baily* v. *de Crespigny*, L.R. 4 Q.B. 180. In that case a lessee claimed damages from his lessor for breach of his covenant not to permit building on a paddock facing the demised premises. The paddock was compulsorily taken by a railway company, which erected buildings on it, including a urinal, thus impairing the amenities of the dwelling. It was held by a strong Court of Queen's Bench that the lessee could not recover. Hannen J., who delivered the judgment of the court held that the lessor was "discharged on the principle expressed in the maxim '*lex non cogit ad impossibilia*'." The court said that if the position had been reversed and it was the lessee who had covenanted and was being sued for breach of covenant, he would equally have been discharged from the covenant by the change of law, on the principle laid down in *Brewster* v. *Kitchell*, 1 Salk. 198. This comes very near to the idea of frustration at least if the performance of the covenant is fundamental to the lease and so do the words of Hannen J. which Lord Buckmaster quotes with approval, though he seems to put the decision on the narrower ground that the word "assigns" as used in the covenant was to be construed in a special and limited sense which did not include compulsory acquisition by a railway company. But I cannot trace in Lord Buckmaster's judgment any suggestion that as a universal rule the doctrine of frustration or some analogous principle could not be applied to a lease, which was enunciated to be the rule by the Court of Appeal. It is true that there is no reported case in which the rule has been applied and that it could be applied only in rare and exceptional cases. But the doctrine of frustration is modern and flexible and is not subject to being constricted by an arbitrary formula. I am not therefore prepared to state as a universal principle that it can in no circumstances be applied to a lease. Let me suggest a single instance, which might some day prove to be of not merely theoretical interest. Let me put the case of a building lease for a term of ninety-nine years, and let it be supposed that a public body acting under statutory authority, soon after the lease was executed prohibited building on that site for an indefinite time, the end of which, if it ever came, could not be foreseen. In effect that would be a prohibition total for all practical purposes both in extent and time, which would override and control both lessor and lessee. Would in that event the lessee continue bound to pay under the lease the yearly rent for ninety-nine years, or would the relationship of landlord and tenant be dissolved by operation of law in respect of that site? As a matter of general principle I would say that the lease was avoided and the term came to an end. But I abstain from further discussion of the point. I agree with the opinion which my noble and learned friend the Lord Chancellor has just delivered. I would dismiss the appeal.

LORD PORTER: My Lords, the appellants relied upon the facts which have been stated by your Lordships in order to establish their contention that the agreement between the parties in relation to the fourteen sites had been frustrated and the tenancy had been determined so far as those sites were concerned. Both courts below rejected their contention broadly on the ground that the doctrine of frustration does not apply to a lease. Indeed Asquith J. indicated that if it did apply he would have found frustration in the present case. It is natural therefore that in their case as presented to your Lordships the appellants should state that the question raised by the appeal is whether the doctrine of frustration applies to a lease. That question no doubt is an interesting and difficult one, but it does not necessarily arise in the case now before the House. A narrower question may well be all that your Lordships have to determine, viz.:—whether the rent claimed to be due under the lease of May 12, 1936, is owed by the appellants to the respondents. To defeat this claim the only answer presented to your Lordships was that the lease or the agreements contained in it had been frustrated. The exact question for your Lordships therefore is not does the doctrine of frustration apply to leases generally, but in the circumstances has this lease been frustrated?

It was conceded on behalf of the appellants that the cases in which a lease can be frustrated are rare and exceptional. A lease is more than a contract. It has long been recognized as creating an estate in land and by statute is enacted to do so: see Law of Property Act, 1925, ss. 1, sub-s. 1 and 205, sub-s. 1 (xxvii.). Moreover the rent is payable for the site and issues out of the land. In these circumstances it obviously is not easy to visualize conditions in which the doctrine of frustration would apply. The land in some form is there and the payment of rent is not prohibited. Some terms of the tenancy may be impossible of performance at least for the time being but the tenancy itself is not thereby necessarily determined. Its basis still exists. Building may not be feasible, yet I do not think the tenancy has come to an end for that reason. But exceptional circumstances might conceivably arise which could be plausibly put forward as a cause of frustration and until it is necessary to pronounce definitely one way or the other I prefer to reserve the point. What I think is clear and I believe all your Lordships agree is that the lease now in question has not been frustrated by the inability of the tenants in the circumstances now existing to use the land for the purpose which both parties contemplated, viz.:—the building of shops. The lease is a long one and the interruption comparatively short. Moreover the obligation to pay rent is not dependent upon the appellant's ability to erect or upon the actual erection of shops. It is payable from a date to be ascertained from the landlords' notice that erection may proceed. If frustration can apply the fact that there are in the contract provisions dealing with the circumstances said to cause frustration is not necessarily fatal to the application of the doctrine. That circumstance is only one element to be considered. In the present case there is, it is true, a clause temporarily excusing for a time the obligation to build, but it is noteworthy that this abeyance clause, as it is called, though it excuses immediate building does not do away with the obligation to pay rent during the period of abeyance. In such circumstances I can see no reason for invoking the doctrine of frustration. The basis of the contract is not gone and if the theory of an implied term be relied on, I cannot think that a lessor, however reasonable, must be considered to have contracted on the basis that the tenancy would come to an end in case the building of shops became impossible for a number of years. I agree with the opinion of the Lord Chancellor and, agreeing with it, am of opinion that the appeal should be dismissed.

LORD GODDARD: My Lords, Asquith J., who tried this case, decided in favour of the respondents on the ground that the doctrine of law usually called frustration does not apply to a lease, and that this was as true of a building lease as of any other. But earlier in his judgment he said that had the doctrine applied he would have decided that the contract, by which he must have meant the lease, had been discharged. The Court of Appeal agreed with him that the doctrine did not apply to a lease, but, as I read their judgment, they also held that in any case it could not be said this particular lease was discharged, thereby differing from the learned judge. I agree with the Court of Appeal on both points. We are obliged, as were both courts below, to deal with the case simply on the admission, embodied in the order made by the Judge in Chambers, that the restrictions placed by the Government upon building and materials made it impossible to erect shops on any of the sites not already built on or to continue their development. No reliance was placed on the other admissions contained in the order. Obviously the restrictions referred to are those imposed by orders made under the Defence Regulations which have effect only for the period of the present emergency, though how long that will continue no one can say. On that one fact it is impossible to say, supposing the doctrine to be applicable to a lease, that one for ninety-nine years had been frustrated. Even if the restrictions remain in force for ten years that is a very small part of the life of this lease. Moreover the rent is reserved in respect of sites, not shops, and begins twelve months after notice is given that building may proceed on any site, although by reason of what the lease calls an abeyance period the tenant may not be obliged to build within that period and may not do so. This abeyance period might quite conceivably last for a considerable time, if there were no demand for shops, but the rent would none the less be payable. If however the tenants came under an obligation to build, but were prevented from so doing by the orders, they would furnish them with a good defence, were they sued for breach of their covenant to build, but not to a claim for rent under this lease. But I think it right to say that I agree also with the Court of Appeal on the wider question. There is no doubt I think that the opinion prevails generally in the profession that the doctrine in question does not apply to a lease, and if there is any doubt on the subject I venture to think that it is desirable in the interests of lessors, lessees, and their advisers that it should be resolved. I agree with the opinion of my noble and learned friend Lord Russell of Killowen, which I have had the advantage of reading, but as the matter is of obvious importance and interest I will shortly state my own reasons. The reason why the doctrine does not apply was first stated by Lush J. during the last war in *London & Northern Estates Co.* v. *Schlesinger*, and was that the lease creates a term of years which is vested in the tenant. I cannot but think that this principle was accepted by this House in *Matthey* v. *Curling*. In that case a house let on lease had been requisitioned by the War Office who remained in possession till the end of the term. Among other arguments it was contended that performance by the lessee of his covenants was thereby rendered impossible and was excused, it being an implied condition that the lessee should be allowed to continue in possession and enjoyment of the premises. Dealing with this contention Lord Buckmaster said: "There is no question here of performance having become impossible owing to its prohibition by statute, for no law has prohibited performance though enjoyment of the premises has been interfered with by legal powers." Lord Sumner and Lord Carson agreed with his opinion, and none of them expressed any dissent from Lord Atkinson who expressly approved the decision in *Whitehall Court, Ld.* v. *Ettlinger*, which in turn had approved the opinion of Lush J. It is now sought to apply this doctrine of frustration to a lease because circumstances have arisen, and restrictions have been imposed, which while not divesting the tenant of his interest do prevent him from putting the land to the use intended both by him and the landlord. Now whatever be the true ground on which the doctrine is based it is certain that it applies only where the foundation of the contract is destroyed so that performance or further performance is no longer possible. In the case of a lease the foundation of the agreement in my opinion is that the landlord parts with his interest in the demised property for a term of years, which thereupon becomes vested in the tenant, in return for a rent. So long as the interest remains in the tenant there is no frustration though particular use may be prevented. There can also be no doubt that if there be frustration the contract is destroyed so that both parties are released from its bonds. If then this doctrine applies to a lease some strange and unjust results would follow, though to use the well-known words of Lord Sumner the doctrine is "a device by which the rules as to absolute contracts are reconciled with a special exception which justice demands" *(Hirji Mulji* v. *Cheong Yue Steamship Co., Ld.)*. In the present case if some shops had been built on the blue land and the lease were held to be frustrated the landlords could presumably repossess themselves of the land with the buildings on it for which they would have to pay nothing. If the lease were now to be regarded as at an end the tenants would have no title, however willing they might be to continue to pay rent and resume building when the orders ceased to have effect. And what would then be the position of those to whom the shops had been sub-let or of mortgagees from whom finance for the building had been obtained? It is no doubt easy to envisage a hard case; building lessees may find soon after a lease has been granted that a statute is passed prohibiting building on the land in perpetuity; and if the legislature should not see fit to provide for compensation or to make provision for what is to happen to leases in such cases hardship would result, but no greater than if they had purchased the fee simple of a building estate which subsequent legislation prevented them from developing. In either case it is not the estate in the land which is affected, but the use to which it can be put. In my opinion the Court of Appeal was right on both grounds and I would dismiss the appeal.

Appeal dismissed.

[In *Vancouver Breweries Ltd.* v. *Dana* (1915), 52 S.C.R. 134, 26 D.L.R. 665, 9 W.W.R. 1018, a tenant failed to obtain renewal of his hotel licence because the landlord had failed to meet licence regulations as to enlargement of the hotel building. *Held*, the tenant remained liable for rent.

In *Denman* v. *Brise*, [1948] 2 All E.R. 141 (C.A.), the Court of Appeal held that because the House of Lords in the *Cricklewood* case left the issue of frustration open, the judgment of the Court of Appeal in that case remained binding. See also *Simper* v. *Coombs*, [1948] 1 All E.R. 306, 64 T.L.R. 131; *Foster* v. *Caldwell*, [1948] 4 D.L.R. 70, 22 M.P.R. 16 (N.B.C.A.); *Note*, (1949) 27 Can. Bar Rev. 212; *Note*, (1942) 20 Can. Bar Rev. 466. But *cf. Denny, Mott and Dickson Ltd.* v. *James B. Fraser & Co. Ltd.*, [1944] A.C. 265, [1944] 1 All E.R. 678 (option for sale or lease of purchaser's land included in contract of sale of imported timber held to fall with frustration of the contract of sale).]

MERKUR v. H. SHOOM & CO. LTD. Ontario Court of Appeal. [1954] 1 D.L.R. 85, [1954] O.W.N. 55

The judgment of the Court was delivered by PICKUP C. J. O.:

This was an appeal by the plaintiff from the judgment of His Honour Judge Factor sitting in the County Court of the County of York without a jury.

The action was to recover the sum of $900, being the balance alleged to be owing on a cheque given by the defendant to the plaintiff, payment of which was stopped. The cheque was given in payment of rental under a lease, or what is said to be a lease. The document is in writing and dated April 20, 1951, and by it the defendant purports to rent from the plaintiff from about the first week in May to about the first week in October, 1952, "summer market space; same stall occupied in previous seasons on Esplanade St. East of Scott St., at a rental consideration for the entire period paid in advance... prior to occupancy".

The defence raised by the pleadings was that the lease was made upon the express condition and warranty that the building owned by the plaintiff, of which the premises leased to the defendant formed a part, would be occupied for the season in question by dealers in fruit and produce as a summer market. There is nothing to that effect stated in the lease. The defendant also pleads that the plaintiff represented and warranted to the defendant that the remainder of the stalls in the summer market had been leased to certain specific fruit and produce merchants, from whom the plaintiff had received payment of rent, and the defendant claims to have relied, in giving the cheque in question, upon such representation and warranty.

The learned trial Judge found against the defendant on the issue of misrepresentation. He found that although the plaintiff did indicate to the defendant that seven wholesalers would move in, and they did move in, the plaintiff at no time represented that they would remain there for the duration of the summer market.

After the defendant went into possession there was a fire in adjoining premises—not the premises of the plaintiff. As a result of that fire the plaintiff's tenants moved out from the plaintiff's premises which had been used as a summer market for years.

The learned trial Judge permitted an amendment at the trial so that the defendant might raise a plea of frustration and after permitting that defence to be raised the learned trial Judge held that in the circumstances of this case the doctrine of frustration applied. He found that it was in the contemplation of both parties that the particular stall leased by the defendant was to be part of a summer market and that if anything occurred which defeated the object of the lease the doctrine of frustration came into play. In our opinion the doctrine of frustration does not apply in this case. It is not enough that the parties should have had in contemplation that the defendant and the plaintiff's other tenants would use the premises as a summer market. So far as the plaintiff was concerned there was nothing to prevent the tenants using their several stalls which they had rented from the plaintiff as a summer market. The subject-matter of the contract never ceased to exist. The learned trial Judge found against any warranty or agreement as to the existence of a summer market or the continuance of one. If the defendant company intended the contract to be dependent upon other tenants or producers being there or in the vicinity, so as to create a summer market, it should have so provided in the contract.

Many cases were cited to us, but we do not think we need discuss them. The weight of judicial authority is that the doctrine of frustration does not apply to leases, particularly where the subject-matter of the lease was in existence at the time the lease was entered into, and the tenant entered into possession thereof.

Counsel for the respondent argues, however, that this was not a lease at all but merely a licence for a particular purpose, which failed. We think it was a lease, not only in form, but in fact, and in any event the subject-matter of the contract continued, the subject-matter being the right of occupancy of certain premises during certain periods.

Appeal allowed.

[Case law in the United States has developed a doctrine of "frustration of purpose" as a ground for avoiding a lease: see 1 *American Law of Property*, s. 3.104.

Assuming that frustration or frustration of purpose became a recognized principle, how would you work out the results where frustration intervenes and rent has been paid in advance? Would apportionment legislation apply where rent is payable in arrear? Would "contract law" doctrines be apt?]

ALEXANDER v. RAYSON. Court of Appeal. [1936] 1 K.B. 169, 52 T.L.R. 131

Appeal from a judgment of du Parcq J. rejecting a plea of illegality raised by a tenant as a defence to an action for rent.

The judgment of the Court was delivered by ROMER L. J.:

Mr. Alexander, the respondent to this appeal, is the owner of a leasehold block of flats at 142, Piccadilly, in the City of Westminster. In July, 1929, the appellant, Mrs. Rayson, approached the respondent with a view to taking an underlease of the flat on the second floor of these premises at a rent of 1200£ a year, such rent to cover the provision by the respondent of the services that are usual in such cases. Mr. Alexander accordingly forwarded to Mrs. Rayson two documents, one being a draft lease of the flat at a rent of 450£ a year, the other being a draft agreement for the rendering by Mr. Alexander during the term of the lease of various services in connection with the flat in consideration of the payment by her of the additional sum of 750£ a year. It is by no means unusual in the case of a lease of a flat to have the actual lease of the premises in one document, and to provide for the rendering of the customary services in another. The strange thing in this case was that the draft lease itself provided for the rendering of such services or, at any rate, the greater part of them, without any payment by Mrs. Rayson other than the rent of 450£, and that the agreement provided for the rendering of practically the same services, with some small additions, in consideration of the extra 750£ a year. In a later part of this judgment we shall have to compare the services to be provided under the lease with those to be provided under the agreement. For the moment it is sufficient to state that, except for the provision and maintenance under the agreement of a frigidaire, they were substantially the same. In due course the two drafts were approved on behalf of Mrs. Rayson and the engrossments were prepared, executed and exchanged without any suspicion on her part, or on the part of her advisers, that there was anything sinister about the form of the two documents, or that any improper use of them could or was intended to be made of them. The instruments were both dated October 29, 1929, and Mrs. Rayson in due course entered into possession of the flat.

The annual sum of 1200£ was paid by Mrs. Rayson quarterly up to and including the instalment failling due at Midsummer, 1934; but, holding the view somewhat strongly that Mr. Alexander had failed to comply with his obligations in respect of the services to be rendered by him under the lease and agreement, she refused to pay him the quarterly instalment of the 750£ falling due on September 29 of that year. She tendered to him, however, the sum of 112£ 10s., being the quarter's rent payable on that day under the lease. This tender was refused by Mr. Alexander, and on October 12, 1934, he issued the writ in this action claiming the full sum of 300£ being the quarter's instalment payable under the two documents. By her defence, as originally delivered, Mrs. Rayson contended (1.) that there was no consideration for her agreement to pay the 750£ a year, and (2.) that the plaintiff had not performed his obligations under the lease or the agreement and had thereby repudiated them both and was not entitled to maintain the action. In addition she counterclaimed for damages in respect of the plaintiff's alleged failure to observe the covenants and agreements on his part contained in the two documents. She also pleaded the tender of the 112£ 10s. and brought that sum into Court. The action was in due course set down for trial, but shortly before it came on for hearing the defendant, by leave, amended her defence by adding the following paragraph:—"(2.) (a) The defendant will object that the said agreement is void for illegality and that its enforcement would be contrary to public policy in that its execution was obtained by the plaintiff for the purposes of defrauding the Westminster City Council by deceiving them as to the true rateable value of the said premises and by inducing them to believe that the true rent received by the plaintiff in respect of the said premises was 450£ and by concealing from them the terms of the said agreement."

If the facts alleged in this paragraph are true, it obviously raises a question of law of both difficulty and importance.... At the hearing [before du Parcq J.] it was contended on behalf of the defendant that, as the onus was upon her of establishing one or more of her defences, she had the right of opening. This contention was acceded to by the learned judge, and the defendant's counsel thereupon opened her case upon the issues (1.) of absence of consideration for the agreement of October 29, 1929, and (2.) of illegal purpose, and then called witnesses upon these two points. Her defence and counterclaim based upon the alleged repudiation by the plaintiff of both lease and agreement was not for the moment embarked upon. These witnesses deposed to the following effect: that in the valuation list for the parish of the City of Westminster made in or about January 16, 1930, the flat in question had been assessed at 720£ gross and 597£ net; that on August 9 following the plaintiff gave notice of objection to such valuation and assessment; that in support of such notice of objection the plaintiff appeared before the Assessment Committee on October 6, 1930; that he then said that the rent of the flat was 450£ a year inclusive of rent, taxes and services, and that 450£ was the only amount he received in respect of rents, services and rates; that the lease was then produced but the agreement was not; that thereupon the gross valuation of the flat was reduced in the provisional list from 720£ to 270£; that enquiry was thereafter made of the defendant on behalf of the valuation authority as to the terms of her tenancy, and that the existence of the agreement of October 29, 1929, was thereupon disclosed by her; that the plaintiff accordingly attended again before the Assessment Committee on November 12, 1930, when, in response to a request for an explanation, he gave a "rather evasive reply"; that on this occasion he contended that the agreement was confidential and that the Committee could not alter their previous decision; that the Committee did, however, alter their previous decision and restored the original figures of 720£ gross and 597£ net.

Now, if this evidence is to be accepted, it is obvious that the plaintiff attempted to perpetrate a gross fraud upon the rating authorities and through them upon the Inland Revenue. The attempt indeed failed, but only by reason of the disclosure by the defendant at the instance of the Assessment Committee of the agreement of October 29, 1929, the existence of which had been concealed by the plaintiff. The inference is that the plaintiff in causing the defendant's tenancy to be created and constituted by the unusual method that he adopted intended by means of that device to perpetrate the fraud. In these circumstances, one would have expected the plaintiff to take the earliest opportunity of going into the witness-box to repel, if he could, the serious charge that had been made against him. This course was not adopted. At the conclusion of the defendant's evidence the plaintiff's counsel submitted that there was no case to answer upon the two issues which at that stage had alone been presented to the Court, that is to say, the issues of no consideration and of illegality. [The learned Judge then pointed out that while defendant had made out a *prima facie* case for her defence yet it was irregular as well as inconvenient at the trial of an action before a Judge alone to rule on plaintiff's submission without hearing all the evidence. He then continued as follows:] The learned judge, however, acceded to the request of the plaintiff's counsel and gave a ruling of law upon the evidence as it then stood, deciding the two issues of want of consideration and want of legality in favour of the plaintiff. As the defendant's counsel desired to challenge this decision or ruling in the Court of Appeal, and considered that such an appeal would be one from an interlocutory order, he asked for and obtained from the learned judge leave to appeal. The question not unnaturally arose as to the procedure to be followed after the appeal had been disposed of, and, as we understand, both parties agreed that, if the appeal should succeed, the hearing of the action should be resumed before the learned judge himself in order that the plaintiff's evidence upon the two issues might be given. It seems also to have been agreed that the hearing of the counterclaim should be postponed until after the decision of the Court of Appeal, and that matter will presumably have to be dealt with by the learned judge whatever may be the decision of this Court.... So new indeed and so irregular did the procedure seem to us, that when the appeal came on for hearing we thought at first that we ought not to deal with it unless and until the evidence relating to the second issue had been completed. Both parties, however, urged us to hear and dispose of the appeal upon the material before us in order to save expense, and this we ultimately consented to do. The consequences may, however, be unfortunate for the plaintiff. If we allow the appeal, he will, of course, be given the opportunity of proving himself innocent; on the other hand, should we dismiss the appeal, he will be in the position of having been proved in a Court of Justice, by uncontradicted evidence, to be a fraudulent rascal.

It is in such circumstances—and we sincerely trust that the like may never occur again—that we proceed to deal with the two issues that are before us.

The first of these is the question whether there was any consideration for the agreement of October 29, 1929. The defendant contends that there was not, inasmuch as the agreement merely provided for services to be rendered by the plaintiff that he was already bound to render under the lease of the same date, such lease having in fact been executed before the execution of the agreement. [The learned Judge reviewed the lease and agreement, and then continued as follows:] The provision and maintenance of the frigidaire does, however, constitute some consideration for the agreement. It certainly would seem to be a somewhat inadequate one, but the Court is not concerned with the adequacy of consideration if consideration there be. In our opinion the learned judge was plainly right in deciding the first of the two issues in favour of the plaintiff.

The second issue raises a question of much greater difficulty.

It is settled law that an agreement to do an act that is illegal or immoral or contrary to public policy, or to do any act for a consideration that is illegal, immoral or contrary to public policy, is unlawful and therefore void. But it often happens that an agreement which in itself is not unlawful is made with the intention of one or both parties to make use of the subject matter for an unlawful purpose, that is to say a purpose that is illegal, immoral or contrary to public policy. The most common instance of this is an agreement for the sale or letting of an object, where the agreement is unobjectionable on the face of it, but where the intention of both or one of the parties is that the object shall be used by the purchaser or hirer for an unlawful purpose. In such a case any party to the agreement who had the unlawful intention is precluded from suing upon it. *Ex turpi causa non oritur actio*. The action does not lie because the Court will not lend its help to such a plaintiff. Many instances of this are to be found in the books.

In *Gas Light & Coke Co.* v. *Turner*, 5 Bing. N.C. 666, the plaintiffs had demised certain premises to the defendant to be used by him for an unlawful purpose. It was held that the plaintiffs were not entitled to sue the defendant upon the covenant for rent in the lease. We shall have to refer to this case later upon another point. In *Pearce* v. *Brooks*, L.R. 1 Ex. 213, 217, 218, a coach builder had let out a brougham on hire to a prostitute for the purpose of enabling her (to use the words of Pollock C. B.) "to make a display favourable to her immoral purposes". The coach builder subsequently sued the prostitute for moneys payable under the agreement. It was held by the Court of Exchequer that he could not recover. "I have always considered it as settled law," said the Chief Baron, "that any person who contributes to the performance of an illegal act by supplying a thing with the knowledge that it is going to be used for that purpose, cannot recover the price of the thing so supplied." He added: "Nor can any distinction be made between an illegal and an immoral purpose; the rule which is applicable to the matter is, *ex turpi causa non oritur actio*, and whether it is an immoral or an illegal purpose in which the plaintiff has participated, it comes equally within the terms of that maxim, and the effect is the same; no cause of action can arise out of either the one or the other."

In *Cowan* v. *Milbourn*, L.R. 2 Ex. 230, the defendant, who had agreed to let rooms to the plaintiff, discovered subsequently that the plaintiff intended to use them for an unlawful purpose. The defendant thereupon refused to carry out the agreement, and it was held that he was justified in so doing. It was further stated by Bramwell B. that if the defendant had carried out the agreement with knowledge of the plaintiff's unlawful intention and let the plaintiff into possession of the rooms he could not have recovered the price for their letting. This dictum of the learned Baron was, of course, abundantly justified by the decision of the Court of Common Pleas in *Gas Light & Coke Co.'s* case and by the decision of the Court of Exchequer in *Pearce* v. *Brooks*, where the brougham had been delivered to the defendant. To the same effect was a decision of the King's Bench Division in *Upfill* v. *Wright*, [1911] 1 K.B. 506. The plaintiff in that case had let a flat to the defendant whose intention was to use it for an immoral purpose, and this intention was known to the plaintiff. The plaintiff sued for the rent, and it was held that he could not maintain the action.

It will be observed that in all these cases the plaintiff was endeavouring to enforce by action an agreement, or a clause in an agreement, which was tainted by the unlawful intention of the plaintiff, or the unlawful intention of the defendant known to the plaintiff, as to the purpose for which the subject matter of the agreement was to be used. To such an action the maxim, *ex turpi causa non oritur actio* applies. But the maxim does not require, nor does the language of it suggest, that a completely executed transfer of property, or of an interest in property, made in pursuance of such an agreement must be regarded as being invalid. This is laid down in clear terms in the well-known case of *Feret* v. *Hill*, 15 C.B. 207. In that case A. procured B.

to grant him a lease of premises by means of a false representation that he intended to carry on a certain lawful trade therein. Having obtained possession, A. converted the premises into a brothel, whereupon B. forcibly expelled him. It was held that A. might maintain ejectment—the fraudulent misrepresentation and the subsequent illegal use of the premises not being sufficient at law to avoid the lease. As the lease had been obtained by fraudulent misrepresentation it could have been set aside in equity, and since the Judicature Act, in any division of the High Court. With that aspect of the matter we are not now concerned. The importance of the case lies in the fact that the lease was held to be a valid one notwithstanding the intention of A. to use the demised premises for an unlawful purpose. On this question Maule J. expressed himself as follows (Ibid. 224): "The plaintiff is not calling upon the Court to enforce any agreement at all. The agreement was an agreement on the part of the defendant to demise certain premises to the plaintiff for a given term. When the instrument was executed, and possession was given under it, it received its full effect: no aid of a court of justice was required to enforce it. This action of ejectment is brought, not for the purpose of enforcing the agreement, but the plaintiff asks the Court to afford him a remedy against one who has extruded him from a lawful possession. There is, therefore, a manifest distinction between this case and those where the Court was called upon to assist the plaintiff in enforcing an agreement the object of which was to do an illegal act, as in *Ritchie* v. *Smith* (1848) 6 C.B. 462. In that case both plaintiff and defendant were parties to an agreement, the very object and intention of which was, to enable one of them to commit an infraction of the law. If the Court there had refused to listen to the defence, they would have been helping the plaintiff to enforce something which lay in contract, namely, the payment of rent, when both parties to the agreement were intending to apply the premises to an illegal purpose and the plaintiff was seeking to enforce the performance of an illegal agreement. Such was also the case of *Gas Light & Coke Co.* v. *Turner*." Crowder J. said much the same thing (15 C.B. 227): "He," that is the plaintiff, "is not calling upon the Court to aid him in enforcing or carrying into effect an illegal agreement: all he seeks, is, to recover the possession of premises to which he is lawfully entitled."

This distinction between an action brought to enforce an unlawful agreement and one brought to assert a right of property already acquired under such an agreement is further illustrated by *Taylor* v. *Chester* (1869), L.R. 4 Q.B. 309. The defendant in that case was the keeper of a brothel and as such had supplied wine and supper to the plaintiff "for the purpose of being consumed there by the plaintiff and divers prostitutes in a debauch there, to incite them to riotous, disorderly, and immoral conduct." When the debauch was over there followed in due course the reckoning. Being unable or unwilling to pay it at once, the plaintiff deposited with the defendant the half of a 50£ note as security. He subsequently repented of this action, and instituted proceedings against the defendant for the purpose of obtaining the return of the half bank note. It was held that he was not entitled to recover. The property in the half note had passed to the defendant, and in spite of the illegality of the agreement under which it had passed, the defendant was entitled to keep it. As was said by Parke B. in *Scarfe* v. *Morgan* (1838), 4 M. & W. 270, 281, in a passage quoted by Hannen J. in the course of the argument: "if the [illegal] contract is executed, and a property either special or general has passed thereby, the property must remain." The plaintiff, on the other hand, could not maintain his action without asserting and relying upon the unlawful agreement. He could not, to use the language of Mellor J. in delivering the judgment of the Court, recover without showing the true character of the deposit; and that being upon an illegal consideration, to which he himself was a party, he was precluded from obtaining "the assistance of the law" to recover it back.

Much to the same effect is *Gordon* v. *Chief Commissioner of Metropolitan Police*, [1910] 2 K.B. 1080. The money that the plaintiff was claiming in that action had been earned by him in carrying on an illegal business. But the money had become his property and he was held entitled to recover it. He was not asking the Court to enforce any illegal contract or to grant relief dependent in any way on any illegal transaction on his part, but solely on the unjustifiable detention of his money by the defendant.

In view of these various authorities it seems plain that, if the plaintiff had let the flat to the defendant to be used by her for an illegal purpose, he could not have successfully sued her for the rent, but the leasehold interest in the flat purporting to be granted by the lease would nevertheless have been legally vested in her. The result would have been that the defendant would be entitled to remain in possession of the flat without payment of rent until and unless the plaintiff could eject her without having to rely upon the lease or agreement. This curious aspect of the matter was alluded to by Tindal C. J. in *Gas Light & Coke Co.* v. *Turner*. "It was observed," he said, "in the course of argument for the plaintiffs, that, as they had granted a lease for twenty-one years, such term was vested in the defendant, and that he would be able to hold himself in for the remainder of it without payment of any rent. That point is not now before us; but, without giving any opinion how far the position is maintainable, it is obvious that, if an ejectment should be brought upon the breach of any condition in the lease, the action of ejectment would, at all events, be free from the objection that the Court was lending its aid to enforce a contract in violation of law." In the present case the defendant does not, as a matter of fact, desire to remain in possession of the flat. She is, and has for some time been, anxious to leave it. But, if the plaintiff has by his conduct placed himself in the same position in law as though he had let the flat with the intention of its being used for an illegal purpose, he has no one but himself to thank for any loss that he may suffer in consequence.

That brings us to the real crux of this case. Has the plaintiff placed himself in that position? Now, in the cases to which we have referred, there was an intention to use the subject-matter of the agreement for an unlawful purpose. In the present case, on the other hand, the plaintiff's intention was merely to make use of the lease and agreement, that is the documents themselves, for an unlawful purpose. Does that make any difference? In our opinion it does not. It seems to us, and it is here that we respectfully disagree with du Parcq J., that the principles applicable to the two cases are identical. That this is so, seems to be established by the decision of this Court in *Scott* v. *Brown, Doering, McNab & Co.*, [1892] 2 Q.B. 724. In that case the plaintiff brought an action against some stockbrokers through whom he had purchased shares in a certain company to obtain rescission of the purchase contract and repayment of the purchase money on the ground that the defendants, while acting as the plaintiff's brokers, had delivered their own shares to him instead of purchasing them upon the Stock Exchange. At the trial it appeared from the plaintiff's own evidence that the money sought to be recovered had been paid by the plaintiff in pursuance of an agreement between him and one of the defendants by which such defendant was with the money to purchase upon the Stock Exchange a number of shares in the company at a premium with the sole object of inducing the public to believe that there was a real market for the shares and that they were at a real premium. The object, in other words, was "to rig the market." It was held by this Court, applying the principle *ex turpi causa non oritur actio*, that the action was based upon an illegal contract and that the money could not be recovered. It will be observed that there was no intention on the part of the plaintiff in that case to use the shares in an unlawful way. The intention was merely to make use of the existence of the share contract in order to defraud the public by inducing them to believe that it recorded a genuine transaction.... It was the transaction of purchase on the market at a particular price and not the thing purchased, of which an illegal use was to be made. So in the present case, it was the formulation of the transaction in a particular way by means of the lease and agreement, and not the subject-matter of the transaction, of which an illegal use was to be made. In one sense, no doubt, it may be said that the plaintiff intended to use only the lease for an unlawful purpose, and not to use, but to conceal, the agreement. In reality there was only one transaction between the parties. The splitting of it up into two documents was a device essential for the success of the plaintiff's fraud and both documents must be regarded as equally fraudulent in purpose.

For these reasons we are of opinion that the plaintiff is not entitled to seek the assistance of a court of justice in enforcing either the lease or the agreement. du Parcq J. (who came to a different conclusion) considered that the present case was much the same as one in which a party to an agreement enters into it with the intention of altering it at a later date and using the document so altered for his own fraudulent purposes. "I cannot think," said the learned judge, "that if a man says, When I have got this agreement I am going by forgery to alter it,' he is thereby precluded from getting his rights against the other party to the agreement under the agreement in fact made." He thought that in such a case it was something altogether too remote from the contract itself to say that the contract was illegal. In that we respectfully agree with him. But, with all deference, it seems to us that the case he supposed is fundamentally different from the case now before us. In the former case the document is a harmless one, and can only be rendered dangerous by a subsequent act. We see no reason why, before the commission of that act, the document should not be used for an innocent purpose. The intention was mental only and no overt step in carrying out the fraudulent intention was taken in the transaction itself. In the present case, however, the documents themselves were dangerous in the sense that they could be and were intended to be used for a fraudulent purpose, without alteration, and the splitting of the transaction into the two documents was an overt step in carrying out the fraud. We cannot think that the plaintiff is entitled to bring these documents into a court of justice and ask the Court to assist him in carrying them into effect. The plaintiff's counsel contended that this view is inconsistent with the decision in *In re Thomas*, [1894] 1 Q.B. 747. But there is no such inconsistency. In that case one Jaquess had handed over money to Thomas, who was a soliciter, to be used by Thomas in conducting certain litigation. Jaquess subsequently sought to obtain from Thomas an account of the money so handed over to him and a taxation of his bill of costs. Thomas sought to resist the claim on the ground that the money in question had been subscribed by various persons under a champertous and therefore illegal agreement. It is not surprising that he failed in his defence, for, apart altogether from the fact that Thomas was an officer of the Court, a fact upon which the Court commented with some vigour, Thomas could not justify misappropriating the money of Jaquess merely because it had come to Jaquess from a tainted source. Nor, of course, was Jaquess in any way asking the Court to enforce the champertous agreement. In these respects the case is not unlike that of *Gordon* v. *Chief Commissioner of Metropolitan Police*, [1910] 2 K.B. 1080.

Plantiff's counsel further contended that inasmuch as the plaintiff had failed in his attempted fraud, and could therefore no longer use the documents for an illegal purpose, he was now entitled to sue upon them. The law, it was said, would allow to the plaintiff a *locus poenitentiae*. So, perhaps, it would have done, had the plaintiff repented before attempting to carry his fraud into effect: see *Taylor* v. *Bowers*, 1 Q.B.D. 291. But, as it is, the plaintiff's repentance came too late—namely, after he had been found out. Where the illegal purpose has been wholly or partially effected the law allows no *locus poenitentiae:* see *Salmond and Winfield's* Law of Contract, p. 152. It will not be any the readier to do so when the repentance, as in the present case, is merely due to the frustration by others of the plaintiff's fraudulent purpose.

In our opinion the appeal as to the second issue must be allowed and the order directing payment by the defendant of the costs of that issue should be discharged. It is true that this issue (being the issue raised in paragraph 2A of the defence) goes only to the validity of the agreement. But this, in our opinion, is immaterial. The moment that the attention of the Court is drawn to the illegality attending the execution of the lease, it is bound to take notice of it, whether such illegality be pleaded or not. It had not been pleaded in the case of *Scott* v. *Brown, Doering, McNab & Co.* See, too, the observations of Vaugham Williams L. J. in *Gordon* v. *Chief Commissioner of Metropolitan Police.*

If, therefore, when the trial is resumed before du Parcq J. the plaintiff should fail to disprove the charge of fraud made against him, his action so far as it is based on the lease and the agreement, should be dismissed. It will, however, apparently still be open to the plaintiff to ask for leave to amend his statement of claim by alleging an oral agreement and claiming relief based upon it. His application for this purpose was ordered by du Parcq J. to stand over until after the hearing of this appeal. But we do not intend to suggest that if and when the application is made it should be granted. It should be added that the defendant seems not unwilling to pay the rent accrued due under the lease. Should she do so the plaintiff is, of course, entitled to retain it. But if he seeks the assistance of the Court to recover it, such assistance must be refused.

On the other hand, if the plaintiff succeeds in clearing himself, the issue of repudiation raised in the defence will have to be decided. In either case the counterclaim will have to be proceeded with. *Appeal allowed.*

[Is there no escape from the result of this case that the tenant may retain possession for the duration of the tenancy without paying rent? See *Hamson*, Illegal Contracts and Limited Interests, (1949) 10 Camb. L.J. 249; *Higgins*, The Transfer of Property under Illegal Transactions, (1962) 25 Mod. L. Rev. 149; and see *Mistry Amar Singh* v. *Kulubya*, [1963] 3 All E.R. 499 (P.C.).]

EDLER v. AUERBACH. King's Bench. [1950] 1 K.B. 359, [1949] 2 All E.R. 692

Action to recover money paid to defendant, for a declaration that a leasing agreement was void and, alternatively, for rescission and, alternatively, for damages for breach of contract. Defendant counterclaimed for rent and for damages for breach of contract to deliver up in repair.

Defendant, an accountant, looking for premises which he could use partly as an office, took a lease in December, 1945, of certain premises which had been used for residential purposes after December 31, 1938. They were thus "controlled" premises under the Defence (General) Regulations, 1939, reg. 68 CA (1), which was effective on October 20, 1945, and provided as follows:

"No person shall except with the consent of the local housing authority use for purposes other than residential purposes any housing accommodation which has been used for residential purposes at any time since December 31, 1938."

The lease provided that the tenant might use the premises as a private dwelling house or for office purposes and the tenant covenanted to obtain any necessary consent for use of any part of the premises for non-residential purposes. By way of exception to the regulations defendant could himself have used part of the premises as an office if he himself resided in them. He found, however, that it would cost too much to repair them to make them fit for residential purposes so he used them simply as an office in breach, therefore, of reg. 68 CA. He took no steps to obtain the required consent for such use despite the covenant in his lease.

In March, 1947, defendant agreed to sub-let to plaintiff, a solicitor, the second and third floors of the premises, telling plaintiff that it was all right to let the space for office purposes and that the premises had not been used for residential purposes after the date fixed in the regulations. Plaintiff made no further inquiries and the leasing agreement to him, for a term of six months from March 31, 1947, and thereafter until termination by either party on six month's notice, was for use of the two floors for professional purposes only. The rent was payable quarterly in advance. Plaintiff decided to sublet one of his rooms, and his required application for a licence for electrical work put in motion an inquiry as to the use of the whole of the premises. The local housing authority informed defendant that his business user contravened reg. 68 CA and defendant, after expressing surprise at this, applied for consent to such user. A hearing held by the local housing authority was attended by both plaintiff and defendant. Consent was given to business user of the ground and first floors only but because of plaintiff's bona fide error the regulation would not be enforced in respect of present occupants of the second and third floors on defendant undertaking to re-allocate accommodation on the ground and first floors so as to release the other floors for residential use. This undertaking was given. Prior to the hearing plaintiff had written to defendant demanding return of the first quarter's rent which he had prepaid. Certain negotiations between the parties came to nought and plaintiff sued. Thereafter as a matter of precaution he gave appropriate notice to terminate the tenancy on March 31, 1948.

DEVLIN J.: ... I am now in a position to consider the questions of law which arise, and I shall take, first, the issue of illegality. It is well settled that an agreement may be unenforceable either because on the face of it it cannot be performed without breaking the law, or because, although capable of being performed legally, it was made with the object of breaking the law. The statement of claim pleads *ex facie* illegality only; it contains no allegation about the object of the agreement, or about the state of mind of either party. I am bound to consider any sort of illegality, but I must first consider the case as pleaded.

In my judgment it fails. The regulation does not touch the letting of premises: it concerns only their use. The lease contains a covenant by the tenant to use the premises for professional purposes and not otherwise. Though positive in form, this is really a negative covenant; it should more correctly be phrased as a covenant not to use the premises otherwise than for professional purposes. Counsel for the plaintiff rightly concedes that it cannot be construed as imposing any obligation on the tenant to use the premises at all. The plaintiff can legally perform all his obligations under the agreement. He can get no benefit from it, because he could not, assuming the prohibition in the regulation to be absolute, enter into occupation; but that is immaterial. This is enough to dispose of the point. But, since the prohibition is not absolute, it is unnecessary to take quite such a legalistic view of the position. The regulation forbids non-residential user without the consent of the authority. There would be nothing remarkable in a man's taking a lease in this form if he had previously satisfied himself that consent would be granted, or if he were willing to take the risk of its refusal. The agreement would be *ex facie* illegal only if, expressly or impliedly, it required the tenant to enter into occupation without first obtaining consent to professional user.

Mr. Lloyd-Jones argues, alternatively, that, if the agreement could be performed lawfully, the covenant as to use is at least clear evidence that the parties contemplated an unlawful performance. That is to say, they contemplated that the premises should be used for professional purposes, and that would be unlawful use. The object of the agreement was therefore unlawful, and it is immaterial, counsel argues, whether the parties appreciated that their object was unlawful. Thus, he says, there is no need to investigate the state of mind of either the plaintiff or the defendant: he can establish that the agreement had an illegal object from the document itself and without going outside his pleading.

The fallacy in this argument is in the assertion that the covenant by itself shows that the parties contemplated an unlawful performance. It might, if the prohibition in the regulation were absolute; but, as I have pointed out, it is consistent with the hypothesis that the parties intended first to obtain the consent of the local authority. Whether or not they had such an intention can be shown only by extraneous evidence; the covenant by itself proves nothing. I am not accepting the view that, when the agreement is one which can be performed lawfully, it does not matter that the parties may not have intended to break the law if their object or intended mode of performance is in fact illegal. Such authority as there is suggests the contrary: see *Waugh* v. *Morris* (1873), L.R. 8 Q.B. 202, 208. But I need not determine that point.

Before I consider the other issues raised on the pleadings it is covenient that I should complete what I have to say on illegality. I am satisfied that the defendant knew that his use of No. 9, Mansfield Street, was a breach of the law. Since he was using it illegally throughout 1946 without attempting to regularize his position by applying for the council's consent, I infer that he had no intention of making the application: doubtless he thought that the risk of refusal was greater than the risk of discovery. I am satisfied that when, at the end of 1946, he decided to sublet part of the premises for office accommodation, he did not intend that either he or the plaintiff should apply for the council's consent; if he had, he would not have deceived the plaintiff about the position. Accordingly, when he granted the tenancy, he expected and intended that the premises demised would be used by the tenant for an illegal purpose. It is, I suppose, notorious that a higher rent is obtainable for premises of this class if let for offices than if the user is restricted to dwelling.

The relevant principle of law is expressed by the Court of Appeal in *Alexander* v. *Rayson*, [1936] 1 K.B. 169, 182, as follows: "But it often happens that an agreement which in itself is not unlawful is made with the intention of one or both parties to make use of the subject matter for an unlawful purpose.... In such a case any party to the agreement who had the unlawful intention is precluded from suing upon it." Counsel for the defendant submits that I ought not in the circumstances of this case to apply that principle at all. Subject to this objection, which I shall consider later, he distinguishes it in three ways: first, he says that there is here no question of the defendant's himself using the demised premises illegally: the only person who could use them is the plaintiff. This is a distinction of form but not, I think, of substance. If both parties intend to use the subject-matter illegally, it is clear that the agreement is enforceable by neither. If one party intends to use the subject-matter illegally, it is clear that the agreement is not enforceable by him. If one party intends that the other should use the subject-matter illegally, I think that it is a logical and necessary extension of the principle that the agreement should be unenforceable by the first party. The plaintiff in this case is the innocent instrument through which the defendant sought to effect his intention that the law should be broken, and the defendant's position is, therefore, no better than if he were using the subject-matter himself.

Secondly, it is said that all that is shown against the defendant is an intention to break the law, and that that is not enough to attract the principle: see *Alexander* v. *Rayson*. I do not think that this is a case of mere intention. The granting of the lease which permitted only professional use was itself an overt step in carrying out the illegal intention which the defendant had already formed. Indeed, when the defendant, having deceived the plaintiff, had granted him the lease, there was nothing left for him to do: the breach of the law would follow naturally the steps which he had taken. There was more than an intent to break the law: there was an attempt to break it; and the fact that the attempt was frustrated because, before the premises were actually used, the borough council discovered the position is immaterial.

Thirdly, the defendant says that on May 22 the borough council consented, in effect if not in form, to the plaintiff's professional use of the premises, and that accordingly the lease can be enforced by the defendant after that date. I think that this plea fails. I doubt whether the borough council's resolution legalizes the professional use of the premises: but, assuming that is does, what has to be considered in the application of this principle is not whether the premises can legally be used for the purpose contemplated, but whether the defendant's conduct has been such as to disentitle him from obtaining the aid of the court to enforce the agreement to his own advantage. The agreement was part of the illegal scheme conceived by the defendant; it succeeded to this extent, as is clear from the minute of the meeting, that if the committee had not considered the plaintiff as being in actual occupation by reason of a bona fide error they would not have given him any relief. To allow the defendant to take advantage of a consent obtained in those circumstances would give him a profit from his own wrong. But in truth neither success nor failure of the scheme matters; neither would atone for the fact that it was conceived in wrongdoing. That is what matters, and what debars the defendant from invoking the aid of the court.

I turn now to the objection that I ought not to be considering any illegality except that which is pleaded. I accept the submission of counsel for the defendant that the illegality which I have found depends on the knowledge or intention of the defendant, that this is not pleaded, and that it ought to have been pleaded if it was to be relied on. Counsel then cited *North-Western Salt Company Ld.* v. *Electrolytic Alkali Company Ld.*, [1914] A.C. 461. That case, I think, authorizes four propositions: first, that, where a contract is *ex facie* illegal, the court will not enforce it, whether the illegality is pleaded or not; secondly, that, where, as here, the contract is not *ex facie* illegal, evidence of extraneous circumstances tending to show that it has an illegal object should not be admitted unless the circumstances relied on are pleaded; thirdly, that, where unpleaded facts, which taken by themselves show an illegal object, have been revealed in evidence (because, perhaps, no objection was raised or because they were adduced for some other purpose), the court should not act on them unless it is satisfied that the whole of the relevant circumstances are before it; but, fourthly, that, where the court is satisfied that all the relevant facts are before it and it can see clearly from them that the contract had an illegal object, it may not enforce the contract, whether the facts were pleaded or not.

The last proposition is the most important for the purpose of this case, and I think that it fairly synthesizes the relevant dicta. The court must pronounce on the transaction if, in the words of Viscount Haldane L.C. (at p. 469), the "case has been completely presented," or, in Lord Moulton's words (at p. 476) "the contract and its setting be fully before the court". What I have expressed as the third proposition is not so much an exception to the principle as an exemplification of it: the court must be satisfied of the illegality of the transaction; that means that it must be satisfied that it knows all the relevant facts. On any issue which is raised on the pleadings the court may safely assume that the relevant facts will be brought before it by one side or the other; where notice of the issue is not given on the pleadings, there is a danger that that assumption may break down, and the decision in *North-Western Salt Company Ld.* v. *Electrolytic Alkali Company Ld.* is a warning against overlooking that danger. In *Rawlings* v. *General Trading Company*, [1921] 1 K.B. 635, 645, Scrutton L. J. treated the decision as making it clear "that where all the facts are before the court, and it can see clearly that it is contrary to public policy to enforce the agreement, the court should act, though the pleadings do not raise the point". This dictum is in a dissenting judgment; but the point of dissent was whether the agreement in that case was in restraint of trade or not.

I must now apply these propositions to the circumstances of this case. The plaintiff called the defendant's agent, and the only point of his evidence was to establish that the defendant at all material times knew quite well that the premises were subject to the regulation. Fraudulent misrepresentation is not pleaded: the only issue in the statement of claim to which the defendant's state of mind might relate is mutual mistake, and the agent's evidence was inconsistent with the plea on that point. Nevertheless, his evidence was taken without objection; I think that, if objection had been made, I should have upheld it. It was not until after his evidence, including cross-examination, had been completed that it was submitted for the defendant that it ought not to have been received and that I ought to disregard it. That is in effect inviting me to ignore an illegality that has been brought to my attention. I cannot do that. When the court comes to know of an illegality, public policy requires that it should refuse any help to the wrongdoer; and public policy cannot be circumvented by the court's fictitiously deeming itself not to have heard that which in truth it has heard. Things might be different if the illegality depended on evidence received after an objection made in time had been wrongly overruled; but I have not to consider that.

If the matter had been left there, I might, applying the third of the propositions expressed above, have concluded that I had heard only one side of the case and have refused to act upon the agent's evidence, even though unchallenged. But the defendant went into the box and dealt fully with the point. I am satisfied that I have all the relevant material before me; indeed, it was not suggested that I had not or that there was any aspect of the point insufficiently exposed. I am satisfied that the evidence leads clearly and inevitably to the inferences which I have set out above, and that I must refuse to allow the defendant to enforce the tenancy agreement.

Accordingly, the counterclaim, in so far as it consists of a claim for rent, fails, as it would have failed in *Alexander* v. *Rayson*, had it been pursued. Similarly, the other claim in the counterclaim for alleged failure to repair, which depends on the terms of the lease, must fail. It is agreed, and I hold, that the claim for compensation for damage done to the structure of the building during the removal of the bath, arises independently of the lease. The issues raised by that claim and the corresponding paragraph in the plaintiff's reply will be referred to an official referee for determination.

The illegality does not affect the validity of the lease: see *Alexander* v. *Rayson*, and so the prayer in the statement of claim for a declaration that the lease is void fails. *Prima facie* the rent, which the plaintiff is seeking to recover, was properly paid under a valid agreement, and the defendant is entitled to retain it: see *Alexander* v. *Rayson*. The defendant's illegality prevents him from enforcing his rights under the lease, but does not by itself give any right of action to the plaintiff. If the plaintiff is to sustain his claim he must show a good cause of action entitling him to repayment of the money either as a liquidated sum or by way of damages or equitable relief based on rescission or otherwise; and I must therefore resume consideration of the causes of action pleaded in the statement of claim.

I take, first, misrepresentation about the use of the premises in 1939. I find the misrepresentation proved, but it is pleaded only as innocent misrepresentation and can therefore lead only to the remedy of rescission. *Angel* v. *Jay*, [1911] 1 K.B. 666, clearly decides that innocent misrepresentation is not a ground for the rescission of an executed lease. I treat that decision as binding upon me, and so need not consider the effect of the plaintiff's acts after the lease was executed, or indeed after May 15 when he discovered the truth. This claim fails. Mutual mistake of fact about the user of the premises fails also, because on the facts which I have found the mistake was not mutual.

The statement of claim next pleads an implied warranty that the plaintiff could use the premises for professional purposes. The relevant principle of law was enunciated by Parke B. in *Hart* v. *Windsor* (1843), 12 M. & W. 68, 87, and quoted with approval by Scrutton L. J. in *Bottomley* v. *Bannister*, [1932] 1 K.B. 458, 468, and is as follows: "There is no contract, still less a condition, implied by law on the demise of real property only, that it is fit for the purpose for which it is let." This principle has often been applied in cases where the premises are physically unfit for the purpose. I think it equally applicable where premises are, so to speak, legally unfit. It is the business of the tenant, if he does not protect himself by an express warranty, to satisfy himself that the premises are fit for the purpose for which he wants to use them, whether that fitness depends upon the state of their structure, the state of the law, or any other relevant circumstances.

Even if in the ordinary case of this type the law implied a warranty, it must still remain true that it is based on the presumed intention of the parties. Where, as in this case, the point is expressly canvassed and a specific representation is made during the negotiations leading to the agreement, it seems to me that the plaintiff's case must be an express collateral warranty or nothing. If the representation is made with the intention that it should be a warranty, it will be one; if it was made without such an intention, how is the intention, which is necessary for implied warranty, to be presumed? The refusal of an express warranty would clearly negative any implication; I think that what I might call the withholding of it must have the same effect. No express warranty is pleaded here, doubtless because the plaintiff did not regard the statement as a warranty; if he had, it would be difficult to explain how as a solicitor with a knowledge of these distinctions, he did not ask for it to be incorporated in the draft agreement which he was then considering. In my opinion the plea of implied warranty fails.

I take next the plea that the money was paid for a consideration that has failed. The money was paid because it was due under a valid lease, by which an estate passed to the plaintiff. The defendant has not broken or repudiated any covenant in the lease. The plaintiff, once implied warranty is negatived, has obtained all that he bargained for. He may have derived no benefit from the consideration which he obtained, but that is not the same thing as failing to get it.

Next, there is a plea that the money was paid under a mistake of fact. This is pleaded sufficiently widely in the writ, but in the prayer of the statement of claim it is restricted to mutual mistake. During the trial I permitted an amendment to the statement of claim to enable the plaintiff to rely on unilateral mistake. The mistake relied upon is the plaintiff's mistake in supposing that the premises had not been used for residential purposes since December 31, 1938. I think that the plaintiff made this mistake, but I do not think that he paid the money because of it. The effect of the mistake was exhausted when the lease was made, and the plaintiff made the payment because the lease compelled him to do so. The lease could be rescinded only if the mistake was mutual. Presumably the plaintiff would not contend, leaving illegality, which is irrelevant on this point, on one side, that he could escape payment of rent and at the same time hold the defendant to his obligations under the lease. But if the tenant is released from paying rent and the landlord released from his obligations, it would amount to a rescission of the lease on the ground of unilateral mistake.

If the plaintiff had known from the start the facts showing illegality, he could have resisted the first payment of rent on the same ground as that on which the counterclaim has been dismissed. It may at first sight seem odd that he should not now be allowed to recover it. It may be that if the plaintiff had pleaded that he made the payment under the mistaken belief that the lease was enforceable by the defendant he could have recovered it. I do not have to consider this point. It is not the mistake pleaded; and if the necessary amendment had been asked for I should not have allowed it. The facts necessary to support it would have involved the allegation that the defendant at the material time knew of the 1939 residence and was engaged in a deliberate attempt to defeat the law. The allegation of knowledge would almost inevitably have turned the plea of innocent misrepresentation into one of fraudulent misrepresentation. It is one of the unfortunate aspects of this case that I have been compelled, as I think, on grounds of public policy to give effect to what is tantamount to a finding of fraud against the defendant although fraud is not pleaded. In so doing I must be careful to limit myself to that which public policy requires, namely, the denial of relief to the defendant. In the matter of the relief to be granted to the plaintiff, he must be held most strictly to his pleading.

This last point is relevant also to the final plea raised by the plaintiff. This is the action of money had and received, which his counsel invoked in wide terms, pleading that the defendant had been unjustly enriched and that it would be unconscientious of him to retain the money. Counsel relied on a passage in Lord Wright's speech in *Fibrosa Spolka Akcyjna* v. *Fairbairn Lawson Combe Barbour Limited*, [1943] A.C. 32, 64. I am not going to explore the boundaries of the action for money had and received. I do not think that any question of injustice or unconscientiousness arises in this case, or that the law need fear any reproach if it refuses relief. The plaintiff can legitimately complain that he was misled by the defendant: that is his real grievance. It was open to him to allege and, if he could, to prove that the defendant had acted fraudulently; and, if he had proved it, the law would have granted him a remedy. Since he does not allege it, it would be unjust to the defendant to assume that he acted otherwise than innocently. It is never easy to decide which of two innocent men should bear a loss that has fallen upon them both; for it must be remembered that, while the plaintiff has paid his rent without benefit to himself, the defendant, if the rent were repaid, would have given up, without any return, the use of his premises from the beginning of the lease until the plaintiff elected to claim relief. It would be inequitable, therefore, to grant the plaintiff unconditional relief. Equity will grant relief, but only upon terms as to restitution with which in this case the plaintiff cannot comply. The last plea of the plaintiff's is in reality therefore only a plea that the well-settled principles upon which relief is granted for innocent misrepresentation should be overturned; and as such it must fail.

Judgment for defendant on the claim and for plaintiff on the counterclaim.

[If there had been a supervening illegality in this case touching the only use to which the premises could be put under the terms of the leasing agreement, would the result have been different? See *Note*, (1951) 51 Col. L. Rev. 1058.

Suppose that the lessee had an illegal purpose in view when entering into the leasing agreement and uses the property accordingly. May he set this up as a defence to a claim for rent? Does it matter when the lessor knew of the illegal purpose?

For a discussion of these matters see 1 *American Law of Property*, ss. 3.43, 3.44.]

[A tenant leased the ground floor of a building as store premises. The only washroom was on the second floor and it could be reached through a door in the rear of the store and up a stairway. The lease made no mention of the washroom but the lessor had orally agreed that the lessee and his customers could use it. A municipal licence was required for operation of the tenant's business and he obtained it; but the following year, on being informed that a new licence was needed, the tenant applied and was informed that written authority of the landlord as to use of the washroom would have to be filed with the Department of Health. The landlord refused to give any written authorization and the tenant had to close down his business. Is he entitled to relief? Is he excused from rent? See *Silverstein and Jonas* v. *Applebaum*, [1953] 4 D.L.R. 637, [1953] O.W.N. 754 (C.A.).]

RE SILLS, TIDY v. MERKUR AND MERKUR. Ontario Court of Appeal. [1956] O.R. 494, 4 D.L.R. 2d 432

Appeal from dismissal of an application by a lessee's trustee in bankruptcy to recover a prepayment of rent under a lease.

HOGG J. A.: I agree with SCHROEDER J. A.

F. G. MACKAY J. A.: I have had the privilege of reading the reasons for judgment of my brother Schroeder and I agree that the appeal should be dismissed. In reaching this conclusion I think that on the facts of this case reliance need not be placed on the case of *Re Abraham*,

[1926] 3 D.L.R. 971, 59 O.L.R. 164, and I prefer not to do so because the terms of the lease in that case were entirely different from the present case. I shall briefly state my reasons....

By [the] provisions of the lease the parties agree that the sum of $1,200, due and payable by the lessee on September 15, 1952, is to be applied in payment of the rent for the first month of the term and the last 5 months of the term. The sum of $1,200 payable on September 15, 1952, is expressed to be paid to the lessors for one purpose only, and that is to prepay the rent on the demised premises for the two periods to which I have referred. It is not being held by the landlord as a deposit, nor is it available to compensate the landlord for any damages he may suffer by reason of breach by the lessee of any of the covenants or conditions of the lease. In the result, the position of the parties on September 15, 1952, was that the tenant was in possession of the leased premises on which the rent had been paid for the first and the last 5 months of the term. In the event of bankruptcy, which did occur, it was not the sum of $1,000 that was to be forfeited; it was the remainder of the term of the lease, including the last 5 months of the term, for which the rent had been paid. In these circumstances the Trustee in Bankruptcy cannot make any claim to the money on the ground of relief against forfeiture. His only right was to relief against forfeiture of the remainder of the term of the lease. The Landlord and Tenant Act, R.S.O. 1950, c. 199, s. 37 (2) provides that notwithstanding any provision in the lease a Trustee in Bankruptcy may elect to retain the leased premises for the remainder of the term of the lease, and subject to the approval of a Judge of the Supreme Court may assign the lease. In this case the Trustee in Bankruptcy has not so elected, but has served notice disclaiming the lease.

In *Re Abraham*, [1926] 3 D.L.R. 971, the money, prepaid by the tenant on entering into the lease, was to be held by the landlord as a deposit to be available as liquidated damages to compensate the landlord in the event of the tenant failing to pay the instalments of rent or taxes, with a provision that if the tenant complied with all the terms and covenants of the lease the deposit, with interest, would be repaid to him by applying it on the rent in the last months of the term when the rent for those last months became due. There was also a provision in the lease in that case for forfeiture of the money in the event of the tenant becoming bankrupt.

In that case the Court was concerned with the right to relief from forfeiture of money belonging to the tenant which was being held by the landlord for certain agreed purposes, and I think it may be that the statement of Middleton J.A. that it was prepaid rent, may be *obiter*.

SCHROEDER J. A.: The appellant seeks the reversal of a judgment of Smily J. delivered on June 21, 1955, whereby he dismissed the appellant's application for an order requiring the respondents to pay to him the sum of $1,000, the amount prepaid by the debtor under the terms of a lease of commercial property to which further reference will be made.

There is no controversy as to the facts, which may be summarized as follows: The debtor was a merchant carrying on business in the Township of East York. He became bankrupt on June 18, 1954, and the appellant was appointed trustee of the estate in bankruptcy. The business had been conducted on premises owned by the respondents and known and described for municipal purposes as 889 O'Connor Drive. The debtor as lessee and the respondents as lessors entered into a written lease on August 28, 1952, for a term of 5 years commencing on September 15, 1952, and expiring on September 14, 1957. The clause relating to the rent payable reads as follows:

"Yielding and paying therefor yearly and every year during the said term unto the said Lessors their heirs, executors, administrators or assigns, the sum of TWENTY FOUR HUNDRED ($2400.00) Dollars, of lawful money of Canada, without any deduction, defalcation or abatement whatsoever to be payable in advance on the following days and times, that is to say:

the sum of ($1200.00) TWELVE HUNDRED DOLLARS shall become due and payable on the 15th day of September 1952, and the sum of ($200.00) TWO HUNDRED DOLLARS shall become due on the 15th day of each and every month and payable thereafter up to and including the 15th day of March 1957. The sum of ($1000.00) ONE THOUSAND DOLLARS shall therefor be applied on the last five months of this lease ending the 14th day of September 1957. The first of such payments to become due and be made on the 15th day of September next, and the last payment to become due and be paid in advance on the 15th day of March one thousand nine hundred and fifty-seven."

The following clause is also relevant:

"AND ALSO that if the term hereby granted shall be at any time seized or taken in execution or in attachment by any creditor of the said Lessee or if the said Lessee shall make any assignment for the benefit of creditors, or becoming bankrupt or insolvent shall take the benefit of any Act that may be in force for bankrupt or insolvent debtors, the then current month's rent and the 3 month [*sic*] following shall immediately become due and payable, and the said term shall immediately become forfeited and void, and in such case it shall be lawful for the Lessor at any time thereafter into and upon the said demised premises, or any part thereof, in the name of the whole to re-enter, and the same to have again, repossess and enjoy as of former estate; anything herein contained to the contrary notwithstanding."

Following the bankruptcy of the lessee the respondent lessors filed proof of claim in bankruptcy claiming $400 as a secured debt and $200 as an unsecured debt. The trustee disallowed this claim and advised the respondents that the claim should have been for the sum of $300 as a preferred claim for rent from June 15th to July 31st and $400 as an ordinary or unsecured claim for the period extending from April 15th to June 14th. It is not clear just how this result was reached but apparently the amount is limited to some extent by the fact that assets on the property which were subject to distress did not have sufficient value to cover the amount that was due, and it was also affected by the fact that the trustee disclaimed the lease and the premises were rented by the respondents to a new tenant for a term commencing on August 1, 1954.

The landlord having refused to comply with the trustee's demand for payment, the application to Smily J. followed and, as stated, was dismissed with costs. The learned Judge of first instance held that it was the intention of the parties that the sum of $1,000 paid in advance by the debtor should compensate the lessors in the event of the debtor failing to perform his covenants as required by the terms of the lease. He further held that the refusal of the lessors was not based on a claim for damages and that there was nothing in s. 37 or s. 38 of the Landlord and Tenant Act which prohibited the retention of this sum. He was also of the opinion that the money had been paid to induce the landlords to grant the 5-year lease to the debtor and concluded that the case was governed by the decision of this Court in *Re Abraham*, [1926] 3 D.L.R. 971, 59 O.L.R. 164. Counsel for the appellant sought to distinguish the case cited on the ground that it was provided in the lease that the sum of $1,000 prepaid by the lessee under the terms of the lease there in question should be forfeited in the event of default in payment of rent and taxes by the lessee.

In the *Abraham* case the matter first came before the late Mr. Holmested, K. C., Registrar in Bankruptcy. He dealt with the case as a problem involving the determination of the question whether the $1,000 was to be regarded as a penalty or liquidated damages and in the end determined that the deposit was to be regarded as a penalty, against which he relieved, allowing the lessors the sum of $100 to cover damages sustained by them. This order was reversed by Fisher J. [[1926] 1 D.L.R. 939] who appeared to hold that the case was not to be considered as one of penalty or liquidated damages. His reasoning, which appears on pp. 942-4 D.L.R., pp. 172-3 O.L.R., makes the *ratio decidendi* of his judgment clear and in the concluding paragraph he said:

"If, however, I am wrong, and the case must be considered strictly as one of penalty or liquidated damages, and also as to whether or not the lessor (Francke) by his conduct surrendered the lease to the trustee and any right he had to retain the $1,000, then I am in accord with the findings and conclusions of the Registrar, and the measure of damage he has allowed."

An appeal from the judgment of Fisher J. was dismissed by the Court of Appeal. After referring to the contentions that the sum in question was a penalty and should be treated as a penalty even though the parties had chosen to describe it as liquidated damages, or that, on the other hand, it was a genuine pre-estimate and assessment of damages and should be treated as liquidated damages, Middleton J. A. continued at p. 973 D.L.R., p. 177 O.L.R.:

"If this test be applied here, it will be at once obvious that the rule can have no application, because the sum which is to be paid by the tenant to the landlord is never to be repaid to the tenant. If the tenant makes no default this sum is to be applied as part payment of the last gales of rent falling due under the lease, and interest earned upon it is to be applied in like manner. If the tenant makes default, the money which has been paid to the landlord is to remain his and is to be accepted by him as the damages flowing from the tenant's breach of his contract. If effect is to be given to the contract between the parties, in no possible event is this money to be actually repaid to the tenant, and the assignee of the tenant has no greater right than the tenant himself. No matter what the parties have called it, it was a partial prepayment of rent and nothing more.

"Upon this short ground, I think the appeal fails and must be dismissed with costs."

I have come to the conclusion that the presence of the forfeiture clause in the lease involved in *Re Abraham* made no difference and that the same result would have been reached by Fisher J. and by the Court of Appeal if that clause had not been included as one of the terms.

This decision is also in harmony with other cases dealing with this subject or with a subject bearing a close analogy thereto. In *Re Bradley* (1921), 21 O.W.N. 216, the order of Holmested, K. C., Registrar in Bankruptcy, declared that the Bankruptcy Act did not give the trustee the right to demand from the landlord repayment of rent paid by the debtor in advance for a period following the authorized assignment. Mr. Holmested, as has been pointed out, took a different view in *Re Abraham* where the amount paid in advance was expressly stated to be paid as a deposit subject to forfeiture in the event of default occurring. The judgments reversing his order would appear to support his decision in *Re Bradley* as the use of the term "deposit" with reference to the money paid on the execution of the lease was held not to deprive it of its character of a partial prepayment of rent and nothing more, regardless of what the parties chose to call it.

A distinction is to be made, of course, between cases in which a lessee has not entered into possession and enjoyed a part of the term and cases in which he has done so. This point was emphasized in *Colton* v. *Dorrell* (1869), 17 W.R. 672, where Keating J. stated: "There has been a part performance of the contract; the defendant has taken possession of the premises, and paid the plaintiff £42 on account. This sum cannot be used as a set-off, as the consideration has not wholly failed, and the parties cannot be put in *statu quo*, for the defendant has been let into possession."

Counsel for the lessors cited two Quebec decisions, *Re Yaffy Systems Inc.* (1952), 32 C.B.R. 202, and *Re Flomen & Lussier Inc. et al*, (1952), 33 C.B.R. 1. Both cases were decided under the provisions of the Civil Code of Lower Canada, but the same result was reached as in *Re Abraham*. *Re Beider & Lapids* (1921), 1 C.B.R. 547, is not in accord with these two later decisions. It should be stated that since s. 105 of the Bankruptcy Act, R.S.C. 1952, c. 14, provides that except as therein stated the rights of landlords shall be determined according to the laws of the Province in which the leased premises are situate, Quebec cases dealing with the rights of lessors and lessees *inter se* may not always be relied upon in Ontario as it is possible that there may be substantial differences between the laws of the two Provinces bearing on such rights and obligations. In any event, *Re Beider & Lapids* is a judgment of a single Judge and is in conflict with the judgment of this Court in *Re Abraham.*

In *Fong* v. *Kerwin*, [1929] 3 D.L.R. 612, 36 O.W.N. 129, the Court of Appeal was concerned with a case in which the lessee had paid $120 in advance for rent, the essential basis of the agreement between the parties being that the premises were to be available for use by the tenant as a laundry. Through some action on the part of the municipality the performance of the agreement became impossible from a cause for which neither party was responsible, viz., the refusal of the municipal authorities to grant the licence which was sought. In these circumstances Masten J. A., writing the majority judgment of the Court, held that both parties were relieved from performance of the contract and that the well-established rule applied that each party must rest in the position in which he is found when the event occurs which makes the fulfilment of the agreement impossible. There was a frustration of the contract for a lease, and neither party could recover from the other.

In support of this proposition Masten J. A. cited *Goulding* v. *Rabinovitch*, [1927] 3 D.L.R. 820, 60 O.L.R. 607, and the cases referred to therein. That was a case which involved the element of impossibility of performance. The plaintiff had been granted an option by the defendant to purchase lands which were subsequently expropriated by a railway company. He had paid $1,000 for the option and in the action sought to recover that sum when completion of the contract had become impossible. The Court of Appeal held that the plaintiff had had the benefit of the option for the period between the making of the option contract and the registration of the railway company's plans and that during that period the defendant was unable to sell the land. The defendant eventually had to accept from the railway company a sum which was less than the price named in the option agreement, and applying the same principle which was referred to by Masten J. A. in *Fong* v. *Kerwin, supra*, the Court held that each party had to bear his own loss. Middleton J. A. reviewed several English authorities in which this principle was recognized.

In both of the two cases above mentioned impossibility of performance or completion of the contract was due to causes beyond the control of both contracting parties and if that principle is applicable in cases of that nature, it should apply *a fortiori* in a case such as this where the impossibility of performance arises from the insolvency of the debtor and he is the party in default.

It is *nihil ad rem* that the parties have provided in this lease that in the event of bankruptcy or certain other causes the lease shall become forfeited and void. Under s. 37 (2) of the Landlord and Tenant Act, notwithstanding any provision in any lease similar to the one which appears in this lease, the trustee may elect to retain the leased premises for the whole or any portion of the unexpired term and, on payment of all arrears of rent, may assign the lease to any person who will covenant to observe and perform its terms, provided that he does not conduct an objectionable business on the premises and that the assignment is approved by a Judge of the Supreme Court. The Act also provides for the right of the trustee to disclaim the lease, in which event liability for payment of future rent ceases (subject to the lessor's right to three months' accelerated rent) and no claim for damages can be asserted by the lessor. This was determined by Rose C. J. H. C. in *Re Mussens Ltd.*, [1933] O.W.N. 459.

I cannot agree with the submission that s. 37 of the Landlord and Tenant Act and s. 95 (1) (f) of the Bankruptcy Act, have the effect of prohibiting a landlord from accepting in advance and retaining more than 3 months' rent. The provision for a statutory preference in favour of landlords cannot supersede an express contract made between the parties at a time when the lessee (debtor) was solvent. This was the view expressed by Fisher J. in *Re Abraham* and the Court of Appeal did not dissent from that view. In discussing this point Fisher J. said at pp. 943-4 D.L.R., p. 172, O.L.R.:

"There was nothing to prevent the landlord in this case from making a contract with the tenant providing that all the rent must be paid in advance before he would agree to lease the store, and if the tenant was solvent and agreed to the landlord's terms, and the transaction was a bona fide one, and not entered into with a view of giving the landlord a fraudulent preference, and bankruptcy intervened before the expiration of the term, the trustee would not, in my opinion, be entitled to a return of so much of the money as represented the unexpired term. Could a tenant in such circumstances, after retaining the demised premises for any part of the term, say to the landlord:—'I am not going to continue,' then vacate the premises and demand his money back? I do not think he could, and a trustee occupies no higher position than the tenant, but in this particular case there was no thought or attempt on the part of either the landlord or tenant to evade the statute or to obtain an undue advantage. The tenant had every reason to believe that it was 'a good stroke of business' to obtain a lease of this particular store, and that he would prosper, and his creditors not suffer. I cannot see that there was any attempt on the part of either the landlord or tenant to 'contract out of the statute' and there are no express words in the statute prohibiting such a contract as was made here."

In my view *Re Mussens Ltd.* has no application to the facts of the present case because the respondents are not asserting a claim for damages. There is no doubt that the parties anticipated the bankruptcy of the lessee as a possible event and the lessee could have stipulated for repayment of the prepaid rent if that event occurred, but he failed to do so. The lease does provide for repayment in a specific manner, namely, by crediting the sum prepaid against the last five gales of rent, and in no other manner.

It is contended on behalf of the trustee that this sum of $1,000 has become impressed with a constructive trust on equitable principles. This argument is based on the supposition that the money was paid for a consideration that has failed. This reasoning is fallacious, in my view.... Had the trustee not disclaimed the lease but chosen to assign or sublet the premises, it may be that he could in that manner have obtained the benefit of the prepayment.

It was argued on the authority of *Ex p. Glegg* (1881), 19 Ch. D. 7, and *Ex p. Stephens* (1877), 7 Ch. D. 127, that the trustee, in disclaiming the lease, became a mere stranger and thereafter he had no status to claim repayment of moneys prepaid under the lease. In both these cases the right in question was the right to remove the tenant debtor's fixtures and it was held that after the disclaimer was executed the term was at once gone as from the date of his appointment and that the removal of the fixtures months afterwards could not be said to be a removal during the term or within a reasonable time after its expiration. Those decisions are not applicable to the point involved here. Even if the term was at an end as soon as the disclaimer was made effective, the trustee could still make any claim which was open to the lessee in respect of the sum of $1,000, but his rights could not be placed on any higher basis.

The trustee's claim is not founded upon the doctrine of frustration and for good reason, because it is well established that that doctrine does not apply to leases once the tenant has gone into possession....

Notwithstanding the very able argument of counsel for the appellant, I have concluded that he has not effectively distinguished the judgment in the case of *Re Abraham, supra*, and despite the absence in the present case of a forfeiture clause the principle laid down in that case must govern the rights of the parties in the case at bar.

Appeal dismissed.

6. TERMINATION: CREATION OF NEW TENANCY ON LANDLORD'S FAILURE TO REPOSSESS

IT HAS ALREADY BEEN SEEN that tenancies for a term certain end by effluxion of time and without the need of notice, although it is open to the parties to prescribe for termination on notice (see *P. M. Fleming Ltd.* v. *Hadley*, [1954] O.W.N. 87 (C.A.)). Periodic tenancies are brought to an end by appropriate notice to quit. In either case, statutory protection may qualify ordinary provisions for termination (see, for example, Leasehold Regulation Act, R.S.S. 1953, c. 313.). There are, however, other ways in which a tenancy may be brought to an end. Thus, for example, the property may be expropriated (as distinguished from being merely requisitioned for public use) and while the tenant may be entitled to compensation as well as the landlord, his tenancy is effectively terminated. Again, a tenancy may end by merger or release, as where the tenant acquires the reversion; or by surrender, as where the landlord accepts a surrender of the lease. Some of the problems in connection with surrender are noted below.

[Surrender may take place by deed, or by an enforceable written agreement or even by an oral arrangement for surrender where the doctrine of part performance may be applied: see *Foster* v. *Robinson*, [1951] 1 K.B. 149, [1950] 2 All E.R. 342 (C.A.); *Canadian Oil Companies* v. *McManus Petroleums*, [1947] O.W.N. 813. More difficult problems arise in surrender by operation of law, involving acts not in pursuance of any surrender agreement but which are inconsistent with continuance of the tenancy. Examples are where a tenant accepts a new lease from his landlord or where the landlord takes possession when the tenant vacates.

"The principle is that if a new lease is not effective but would, if it were effective produce a surrender, then by reason of the fact that the new lease is not effective, there is not an effective surrender.": Danckwerts J. in *Barclays Bank Ltd.* v. *Stasek*, [1957] Ch. 28, [1956] 3 All E.R. 439.

A tenant desired to sell his business and sought the landlord's permission to assign his lease to a prospective purchaser. The landlord agreed to accept the purchaser as tenant but wished to hold the tenant as well and thereupon entered into a lease with the purchaser which provided that upon default the lease should terminate and become vested in the (prior) tenant for the remainder of the term. Did a surrender of the original tenancy take place? See *Ferguson* v. *Craig*, [1954] 4 D.L.R. 815, [1954] O.W.N. 631.

A monthly tenant gave notice to quit and then vacated the premises but left behind a neon sign which had been erected on the outside of the premises by arrangement between him and a sign company. The landlord claimed rent for two months during which the sign remained on the premises after the tenant vacated. Should he succeed? See *Oakville Investments Ltd.* v. *Dauphinee*, [1955] 3 D.L.R. 415, [1955] O.W.N. 645 (C.A.).

In *Woodall* v. *Gusa* (1951), 1 W.W.R. (N.S.) 403 (Sask. C.A.), a claim was made for two months' rent from a tenant who had vacated a monthly tenancy without proper notice. Rent was payable on the first of the month and the tenant vacated on the tenth. The landlord re-let at the end of the next succeeding month. There was evidence that when the tenant vacated the landlord entered to clean and decorate. Dismissal of the action was affirmed on equal division. McNiven J. A. who would have allowed the appeal said, *inter alia*, at p. 407:

"If a tenant on, or between, two rent days leaves without notice and the landlord relets before the following rent day, this amounts to an eviction and the landlord cannot recover for a portion of the rent: *Hall* v. *Burgess* (1826) 5 B & C 332, 108 E.R. 124; *Hartcup* v. *Bell* (1883) 1 Cab. & El. 19; *Baynton* v. *Morgan* (1888) 21 Q.B.D. 101, 57 L.J.Q.B. 465 (affirmed 22 Q.B.D. 74, 58 L.J.Q.B. 139).

"Though not pleaded, there was some evidence given that might amount to a surrender of the term and acceptance thereof by the landlord. When the defendant vacated the suite the plaintiff entered, cleaned up the premises and did some painting and decorating. To be effective a surrender must be based upon some act inconsistent whith the term granted and it was held in *Oastler* v. *Henderson* (1877) 2 Q.B.D. 575, 46 L.J.Q.B. 607, that entry for the purpose of making repairs was not inconsistent with the term granted—was not such an unequivocal act as showed an intention on the part of the landlord to no longer hold the tenant to his lease. This case was followed in *Ont. Industrial Loan Etc. Co.* v. *O'Dea* (1895) 22 O.A.R. 349. These cases along with others are noted and reviewed at 25 *Can. Abridgment,* 618 and 619."

Suppose a tenant vacates and improperly refuses to pay further rent. Is there any obligation on the landlord to re-let the premises? If the landlord re-lets, is there a surrender by operation of law? Suppose the landlord notifies the tenant that he is re-letting on the tenant's account, or suppose that the lease with the tenant provides for such re-letting. If the landlord re-lets for a term which is to endure beyond the period of the tenant's lease is there a surrender as of the time of re-letting? See *Hill and Redman,* Law of Landlord and Tenant (1955, 12th ed.), p. 299; *Woodfall,* Landlord and Tenant (1960, 26th ed.), p. 362.

In *Crozier* v. *Trevarton* (1914), 32 O.L.R. 79, 22 D.L.R. 199 where the tenant vacated and the landlord, without notifying the tenant that he was doing so on the latter's account, re-let the premises, Boyd C. held that the re-letting extinguished the term. Contrast *Noble Scott Ltd.* v. *Murray* (1925), 56 O.L.R. 595, aff'd 57 O.L.R. 248 (C.A.) where the landlord notified the tenant that he was re-letting on the tenant's account.

Is it arguable that if a tenant vacates during the currency of his lease and the landlord re-lets without notifying the tenant then there is an eviction, which, while suspending the tenant's obligation to pay rent, does not terminate his tenancy? *Cf. Hall* v. *Burgess* (1826), 5 B. & C. 332, 108 E.R. 124 (K.B.). Of course, the tenant could not get back in, if there was eviction by title paramount. But may he assert a possessory claim against his own landlord, unless the case is one of surrender, or may he recover possession from the new tenant? Or, is the situation explicable as one where the old tenant remains liable on his covenants but subject to a power in the landlord to re-let? See 1 *American Law of Property*, s. 3.99. The problem in question may be distinguished from the situation where the landlord can re-enter and terminate for breach of covenant and does so by re-letting to another tenant: see *Edward H. Lewis & Son Ltd.* v. *Morelli*, [1948] 1 All E.R. 433 (K.B.). However there may still be a question whether by re-letting the landlord has abandoned any claim to damages.].

[If a tenant moves out while his term is still on foot and the landlord puts a "to let" sign on the premises, is there a surrender? *Cf. Redpath* v. *Roberts* (1800), 3 Esp. 225, 170 E.R. 596 (N.P.) and *Rumball* v. *Hoskings* (1909), 11 W.L.R. 250 (B.C. Cty. Ct.); *Yukon Trust Co.* v. *Popich* (1908), 8 W.L.R. 852 (Y.T.).

If a surrender occurs does it relate merely to the term of the lease in question or does it destroy also other rights or privileges stipulated therein, as, for example, an option to purchase? It may be conceded that, unless there be any agreement to the contrary, surrender does not affect accrued claims, as for example unpaid overdue rent. But what of other matters provided for in the lease? See *Mathewson* v. *Burns* (1914), 50 S.C.R. 115, 18 D.L.R. 399; *A.-G. Sask.* v. *Whiteshore Salt & Chemical Co. Ltd. and Midwest Chemicals Ltd.* [1955] S.C.R. 43, [1955] 1 D.L.R. 241.

As to the effect of surrender on right to remove fixtures, see *Badalato* v. *Trebilcock*, *supra*, p. 266; *Ex parte Glegg, Re Latham* (1881), 19 Ch. D. 7.

If a tenant who has sublet surrenders his lease, what is the effect upon the sublease? See *Shapiro* v. *Handelman*, [1947] O.R. 223, [1947] 2 D.L.R. 492 (C.A.); *Kowalski and Shoota* v. *Gale*, [1947] 1 D.L.R. 354, [1946] O.W.N. 893 (C.A.).

For a collection of English and Canadian cases on surrender, see *Williams*, Canadian Law of Landlord and Tenant (1957, 3rd ed.), pp. 456 ff.]

[Disclaimer involving a denial of the landlord's title will entitle the landlord to terminate a tenancy but it is a question of fact whether there is such a denial: see *Wisbech St. Mary Parish Council* v. *Lilley*, [1956] 1 All E.R. 301, [1956] 1 W.L.R. 121 (C.A.), where Romer L. J. said: "As Evershed M. R. has pointed out, the law on this subject is archaic in some degree and is founded upon feudal principles which certainly do not loom very large in modern life. But I accept Mr. Bridge's submission that, even now, if a tenant does in fact deliberately assert a title in himself adverse to his landlord, or if he lets a stranger into possession with the intention of enabling him to set up a title adverse to the landlord, then that amounts to a repudiation of the landlord's title; and it would seem that where the tenancy in question is a yearly tenancy it is sufficient to constitute a repudiation if the assertion of title against the landlord is made orally. But, as Evershed M. R. has pointed out, it is a question of fact as to what intention underlies the words or the actions of a tenant, as to whether in fact he is definitely asserting a title adverse to the landlord, or, as the case may be, intending to enable somebody else to set up such a title."]

While mere breach of covenant will not give a power of termination, breach of condition will or, as is usual, a power of termination may be reserved by the terms of the lease. Short Forms legislation contains a standard proviso for re-entry by the landlord on non-payment of rent or non-performance of covenants by the tenant. Landlord and tenant legislation in the Canadian provinces provides that save as to "forfeiture" for default in rent, "a right of entry or forfeiture under any proviso or stipulation in a lease... shall not be enforceable by action, entry or otherwise unless the lessor serves on the lessee a notice specifying the particular breach complained of, and if the breach is capable of remedy requiring the lessee to remedy the breach, and, in any case, requiring the lessee to make compensation in money for the breach, and the lessee fails within a reasonable time thereafter to remedy the breach, if it is capable of remedy, and to make reasonable compensation in money to the satisfaction of the lessor for the breach." (Landlord and Tenant Act, R.S.O. 1960, c. 206, s. 18 (2)). See also, Landlord and Tenant Act, R.S.M. 1954, c. 136, s. 18 (2); Landlord and Tenant Act, R.S.N.B. 1952, c. 126, s. 14 (1); Landlord and Tenant Act, R.S.P.E.I. 1951, c. 82, s. 15 (1); Landlord and Tenant Act, R.S.S. 1953, c. 312, s. 10 (2), amended 1959, c. 10.

What particulars should a notice contain? See *Fox* v. *Jolly*, [1916] 1 A.C. 1. The elements of a valid notice under s. 18 (2) of the Ontario Landlord and Tenant Act for the purpose of forfeiture proceedings for breach of a covenant to pay taxes are discussed in *Perrett* v. *Perrett*, [1944] 1 D.L.R. 673, [1944] O.W.N. 21.

In the absence of a valid notice, re-entry by the landlord is a trespass: *Canadian Silk Mfg. Co. Ltd.* v. *Badalato*, [1950] 2 D.L.R. 77, [1950] O.W.N. 186.

Where a tenant is convicted of keeping a disorderly house in breach of covenant, is the required notice (preliminary to forfeiture proceedings) defective if it fails to require the tenant to remedy the breach? See *Egerton* v. *Esplanade Hotels (London) Ltd.*, [1947] 2 All E.R. 88 (K.B.); *Hoffman* v. *Fineberg*, [1948] 1 All E.R. 592 (Ch.). Relief from forfeiture has been refused in the disorderly house cases: see *Borthwick-Norton* v. *Romney Warwick Estates Ltd.*, [1950] 1 All E.R. 798 (C.A.).

[Statutory provision exists for preservation by the Court of the position of a sublessee where the head landlord is proceeding to "forfeit" the head lease: see Landlord and Tenant Act, R.S.M. 1954, c. 136, s. 20; Landlord and Tenant Act, R.S.N.B. 1952, c. 126, s. 15; Landlord and Tenant Act, R.S.O. 1960, c. 206, s. 20; Landlord and Tenant Act, R.S.P.E.I. 1951, c. 82, s. 16; Landlord and Tenant Act, R.S.S. 1953, c. 312, s. 11.]

[Occurrence of an event entitling a landlord to re-enter gives him an election but he may by acts or conduct disentitle himself to terminate for the particular breach. For example, if, being aware of the breach, he accepts rent accruing due after the breach, he has recognized the tenancy as subsisting: see *Re Bagshaw and O'Connor* (1918), 42 O.L.R. 466, 42 D.L.R. 596 (C.A.). Suppose, however, the breach is a continuing one (as, for example, breach of a covenant to repair) and rent is accepted: See *Thompson* v. *Baskerville* (1877), 40 U.C.Q.B. 614 (C.A.).

It is possible for the parties to agree in a lease that upon the happening or non-happening of a certain event, the lease will terminate automatically without manifestation of an election one way or the other: see *Setter & Hurlbut* v. *Mander & Red-Man Oils Ltd.* (1952), 6 W.W.R. (N.S.) 577 (Man.).]

[A lease of an ice cream parlour contained a covenant by the tenant to buy all ice cream from the landlord who covenanted to supply the tenant. On breach of this covenant by the tenant, the landlord gave the required notice of the breach preliminary to taking forfeiture proceedings and the tenant did nothing to remedy his default. The landlord continued to supply ice cream, and on his taking proceedings for possession he was met by the argument of "waiver" of forfeiture. Result? See *Re Jackson Ltd. and Gettas* (1926), 58 O.L.R. 564 (C.A.).

In *Oak Property Co. Ltd.* v. *Chapman*, [1947] K.B. 886, [1947] 2 All E.R. 1 (C.A.), Somervell L. J., speaking for the Court of Appeal, said (at p. 898, K.B., p. 5, All E.R.):

"By the common law, which tended to construe forfeiture provisions as effective to render leases voidable and not void, a landlord was bound, as soon as he was fully aware of a non-continuing breach of covenant by the tenant entitling the landlord to avoid the lease, to elect at once for or against avoidance and to notify the tenant if he elected for the former. On this principle, acceptance of any rent accrued due after the landlord's knowledge of the tenant's breach was regarded necessarily as inconsistent with an election to avoid the lease and consistent only with its affirmance. The acceptance of the rent being, in the circumstances, an unequivocal act, waiver of the breach followed as a matter of law, according to Parker, J. ([1910] 1 Ch. 786, 787) in *Matthews* v. *Smallwood.* And so unequivocal was the act of acceptance of rent that the landlord was held disentitled to get the best of both worlds by attempts to qualify the acceptance by stating that he accepted the rent without prejudice to his rights of forfeiture: see the notes to *Dumpor's Case* in Smith's Leading Cases, 13th ed., vol. 1, p. 38, *et seq.* Nor do we think that these principles have been in any way qualified by the decision of this court in *Elliott* v. *Boynton*, [1924] 1 Ch. 236, relied on by the sub-tenant. That case only decided that the obligation to pay rent under a contractual tenancy continues until the tenancy is determined in fact by re-entry, namely, the issue of the writ for possession.

"It must, in our judgment, be conceded that the principles of the common law above stated cannot apply, or cannot wholly apply, to a statutory tenancy. In the first place, the landlord of a statutory tenant has no right to avoid the tenancy. His only right is to invoke the jurisdiction of the court to make an order for possession and the tenancy continues until at least the date of the order. Secondly—and consequentially—the obligation of the tenant to pay rent and the right of the landlord to accept it continues notwithstanding the breach of covenant and notwithstanding the landlord's election to invoke the court's jurisdiction and the issue by him of his summons pursuant to his election. In our judgment, therefore, it may fairly be said that the acceptance of rent by a landlord after knowledge of a non-continuing breach of covenant by a tenant entitling the landlord to go to the court is not so unequivocal an act of affirmance of the tenancy as is acceptance of rent in like circumstances from a contractual tenant. On the other hand, it is, we think, important to bear in mind that under the scheme of the Rent Acts the incidents of tenancy as understood by our law continue to apply to a statutory tenancy so far as they are consistent with the provisions of the Acts. From long usage the acceptance of rent by a landlord after knowledge of circumstances giving rise to a claim for possession has come to be regarded by landlords and tenants alike as evidence of an intention to affirm the tenancy. Moreover, the landlord has, in the case of a statutory tenancy, a choice—he may either rely on the breach and go to the courts, or he may waive it—though his choice is not the same as that presented to the common law landlord. Finally, (and to this extent *Elliott* v. *Boynton*, in our view, assists the sub-tenant) the continuance of the obligation to pay rent under a contractual tenancy accruing after the breach for some period is not itself inconsistent with the landlord's election to forfeit.

"If, therefore, it is not justifiable to treat the common law rule as entirely applicable to a statutory tenancy (as the county court judge implied), we think that the question whether in any case the acceptance of rent by the landlord is an unequivocal act of affirmance of the tenancy is a question of fact for the judge to determine in the circumstances of the case, and, if he decides that question of fact affirmatively, then the ordinary legal consequences would *prima facie* follow. Thus, we are strongly inclined to think that the strict common law rule in regard to a qualified acceptance of rent is not applicable to a statutory tenancy and that a qualified acceptance of rent from a statutory tenant is not necessarily fatal to the landlord's rights to seek an order for possession. As at present advised, we think that the fair rule is that a landlord who has acquired full knowledge of a non-continuing breach of covenant by a statutory tenant entitling him to invoke the court's jurisdiction should be entitled thereafter to receive rent and should not by reason of such receipt be held to have waived the breach, provided he makes it clear to the tenant at the time of or prior to the receipt that his receipt is without prejudice to his right to go to the court and provided he issues his summons for possession within such time as, having regard to all the circumstances of the case, the court hearing the summons regards as reasonable."

See also *Carter* v. *Green*, [1950] 2 K.B. 76, [1950] 1 All E.R. 627 (C.A.).

In *Burns* v. *Hodgson*, [1945] O.R. 876, [1946] 1 D.L.R. 510 (C.A.), the Ontario Court of Appeal considered a similar question in respect of the purported termination of a periodic tenancy by notice to quit where statutory provisions supervened to protect the tenant and the landlord accepted rent during the statutory "freeze" but later, on its removal, sought possession. McRuer J. A. said (at p. 886 O.R., p. 517 D.L.R.):

"The acceptance of rent after a notice to quit by the landlord, and permitting the tenant to remain in the premises, may be evidence of an agreement for a new tenancy on the old terms. But how is the mere acceptance of rent evidence of such an agreement in the circumstances of this case, where the landlord was powerless to get possession of the premises? The view adopted in all the English cases subsequent to *Hartell* v. *Blackler*, [1920] 2 K.B. 161, is that where the tenant remains in possession after the notice to quit expires and the landlord is prevented by statute from taking proceedings that he would have been entitled to take otherwise, a new statutory tenancy is created for the term that the tenant occupies under the protection of the statute, and that the mere acceptance of rent during the term of the statutory tenancy does not affect the termination of the previous tenancy by the notice to quit when the statutory protection is lifted.

"In *Hartell* v. *Blackler* a Divisional Court applied to a case where the landlord accepted rent after a notice to quit, the same common law principles that are applied in cases of the acceptance of rent after circumstances have arisen to the knowledge of the landlord giving a right to forfeiture. In *Davies* v. *Bristow*, [1920] 3 K.B. 428, a Divisional Court expressly dissented from this application of the law and refused to follow *Hartell* v. *Blackler*. Shearman J. at p. 440 said:

"'As long as s. 1, sub-s. 2, of the Rent Restriction Act, 1915, and s. 1 of the Act of 1919 are in force and a landlord is prevented from getting recovery of possession of premises after the expiration of a notice to quit, I think it is correct to say the former tenant by holding over no longer becomes a trespasser but is in lawful statutory occupation of the premises unless there is proved in fact any other lawful agreement subject to the provisions of the Act, which the landlord and tenant choose to make. I am the more ready to agree with *Hunt* v. *Bliss*,

[1919] W.N. 331, in preference to *Hartell* v. *Blackler*, [1920] 2 K.B. 161, because I notice that in the latter case the expression 'waiver of notice to quit' is used throughout the report. It may be that it is not open to objection if it is clearly understood as referring to an agreement for a new tenancy, but at the same time it cannot be disputed that it is a loose and unscientific expression in that connection. A notice to quit can be withdrawn at any time before the date fixed for the termination of the tenancy. But after the time has expired the lease is at an end and a landlord can no more waive his notice to quit than he can waive the effluxion of time. I infer that the expression 'waiver of notice to quit' wherever it is used in the report merely means that the parties have arrived at a new agreement, but that agreement to be any other agreement must be proved in the ordinary way. I think that what was decided in *Hunt* v. *Bliss* was this, that after the expiry of the notice to quit the tenant is entitled to continue in occupation under the provisions of the statute until those conditions arise which enable the judge in his discretion to order recovery of possession, or until the parties have arrived at a fresh agreement.'"

See also *Serbu* v. *Feinstein*, [1952] 1 D.L.R. 98, 3 W.W.R. (N.S.) 545 (Sask. C.A.).

Hartell v. *Blackler*, referred to *supra*, was expressly overruled in *Clarke* v. *Grant*, [1950] K.B. 104, [1949] 1 All E.R. 768 (C.A.).]

[Where a right of re-entry arises on breach of covenant or a periodic tenancy is terminated by notice to quit or a tenancy for a term certain expires, the landlord may take summary proceedings for possession as provided by overholding tenants' legislation which has been extended in some jurisdictions to "forfeiture" proceedings and thus enables the Court in the summary proceedings to grant relief from forfeiture: see Landlord and Tenant Act, R.S.O. 1960, c. 206, ss. 18, 75 ff.; Landlord and Tenant Act, R.S.M. 1954, c. 136, ss. 18, 70 ff.; Landlord and Tenant Act, R.S.N.B. 1952, c. 126, ss. 58 ff.; Landlord and Tenant Act, R.S.P.E.I. 1951, c. 82, ss. 78 ff. Landlord and Tenant Act, R.S.S. 1953, c. 312, ss. 10 (amended 1959, c. 10), 49 ff..

In British Columbia there are no express statutory provisions respecting relief from "forfeiture" of leases, but the general statutory power to relieve against penalties and forfeitures has been construed to permit the Court to relieve not only in cases of default in rent but in case of other breaches: see *Nuytten and Bakalaryk* v. *Stein*, [1954] 2 D.L.R. 785, 12 W.W.R. (N.S.) 465 (B.C.).]

[The summary procedure does not preclude resort to formal Court action or to physical re-entry, but it is available only against a tenant and not against a trespasser and only at the instance of a landlord: see *Courville* v. *Pretty*, [1948] 2 D.L.R. 430, [1948] O.W.N. 359 (C.A.) and *Altbaum* v. *Northover*, [1949] 3 D.L.R. 337, [1949] O.W.N. 415 (C.A.). *Cf. Kruciak* v. *Antoniuk*, [1947] 1 D.L.R. 445, [1946] 3 W.W.R. 252, 54 Man. R. 281 (C.A.).

It has been held that the Judge hearing a summary application for possession has no jurisdiction to provide for payment of "occupation" rent.: *Ashwin* v. *Lash*, [1948] O.W.N. 277 (C.A.).

On physical re-entry by a landlord, see *Hemmings* v. *Stoke Poges Golf Club Ltd.*, [1920] 1 K.B. 720, 36 T.L.R. 77 (C.A.); *Richter* v. *Koskey and Adler*, [1953] 4 D.L.R. 509, [1953] O.W.N. 746. *Cf.* Cr. Code, 1953-54 (Can.), c. 51, ss. 73, 74.

If money is sent as rent, and accepted by the landlord after proceedings for possession have been initiated, is this necessarily recognition of the continuation of the existing tenancy or creation of a new one, as the case may be? See *Sammon* v. *Cawley* (1919), 53 Ir. L. T. 224; *Ucci* v. *Livingstone*, [1946] O.W.N. 861 (C.A.); *McIntyre* v. *Bird*, [1946] O.W.N. 905 (C.A.); *Suwala* v. *Prociw*, [1949] 1 D.L.R. 340, [1949] O.W.N. 33.]

[Mere overholding by a tenant on the expiry of a term certain or on the expiry of a notice to quit in case of a periodic tenancy does not *ipso facto* result in a new tenancy: see *Jones* v. *Shears* (1836), 4 A. & E. 832, 111 E.R. 997; *Gasner* v. *Bellak Bros. Ltd.*, [1945] O.R. 499, [1945] 3 D.L.R. 365 (C.A.). A new tenancy may arise where the holding over is with consent of the landlord (see *Right* v. *Darby* (1786), 1 T.R. 159, 99 E.R. 1059 (K.B.) and *Waring* v. *King* (1841), 8 M. & W. 571, 151 E.R. 1166 (Ex.)), but is it open to the landlord to elect to treat the overholder as a tenant so as to oblige him to pay rent under a new "imposed" tenancy? *Cf. Dougal* v. *McCarthy*, [1893] 1 Q.B. 736; and see *Blyth* v. *Dennett* (1853), 13 C.B. 178, 138 E.R. 1165 (C.P.) (demand for rent which overholder did not satisfy; landlord entitled to insist on repossession). The majority position in the United States gives the landlord such an election: see 1 *American Law of Property*, ss. 3.33, 3.34.

A holding over and payment of money as rent provide evidence of a new tenancy. There are really two questions involved in overholding situations: (1) whether a new tenancy is created; and (2) if so, what kind of tenancy? A central problem in the first question is what should the legal conclusion be where an overholder sends money *as rent* and the landlord takes it, say, for use and occupation, thus negating any implication of a new tenancy. It may be easier to fix the landlord with consent to a new tenancy if he receives the money and says nothing for a time. But if having received it, he purports to keep it and yet to insist on recovering possession, should he be permitted thus to devote it to a purpose other than that for which it was sent? And should it make any difference if he acknowledges receipt of the rent and takes it "without prejudice"? In *Sikorski* v. *Hunter*, [1949] 4 D.L.R. 607, [1949] O.W.N. 361 (C.A.), Roach J. A. speaking for the Court said: "If it was not being accepted in payment of rent, it should have been returned to the tenant"; see also *Clarke* v. *Fitzpatrick*, [1950] 1 D.L.R. 137, [1949] O.W.N. 526 (C.A.); *Park* v. *Shell Oil Co. of Can. Ltd.*, [1950] 4 D.L.R. 283, [1950] O.W.N. 543. Of course, the landlord may safely accept rent for the period running to the expiry of the tenancy (see *Banrevi* v. *Larman*, [1953] 2 D.L.R. 619, [1953] O.W.N. 210), but is there not a practical difficulty for a landlord who insists on possession and yet, having money on hand sent in by the tenant as rent, wishes to apply it for use and occupation for the period that the tenant overholds, thus avoiding the need of another lawsuit? But if he is insisting on possession, and hence on treating the overholder as a trespasser, is he entitled thus to fix his damages and collect them as well?

Should there be a difference in the legal conclusion, where money is sent as rent for a succeeding period and retained by the landlord for "use and occupation", when his claim for possession is asserted (1) for breach of the lease entitling him to re-enter and (2) after ordinary termination of the tenancy? Should the Courts not lean more strongly against a forfeiture than in favour of finding a new tenancy? See *Croft* v. *Lumley* (1858), 6 H.L.C. 672, at p. 706, 10 E.R. 1459, at p. 1472; 6 *Williston on Contracts*, (rev. ed.) s. 1856. But *cf. Nuytten and Bakalaryk* v. *Stein*, [1954] 2 D.L.R. 785, 12 W.W.R. (N.S.) 465 (B.C.).

Should the legal effect, where money sent as rent is accepted for another purpose, turn on the intention of the payee as a question of fact or should intention be ignored? See *Day* v. *McLea* (1889), 22 Q.B.D. 610; *Hirachand Panamchand* v. *Temple*, [1911] 2 K.B. 330; *Coastal Estates Ltd.* v. *Dales*, [1952] 3 D.L.R. 422 (B.C.). *Cf. Neuchatel Asphalte Co. Ltd.* v. *Barnett*, [1957] 1 All E.R. 362 (C.A.).]

[Where rent is paid and accepted on a holding over so that a new periodic tenancy results, should the governing consideration in determining the kind of periodic tenancy be the term or period length of the original lease, or should it be the way in which or the time unit for which rent was reserved? The following situations may be envisaged:

(1) Tenancy for year or more; rent reserved and payable on a yearly basis.
(2) Tenancy for year or more; rent reserved on a yearly basis but payable monthly or weekly.
(3) Tenancy for year or more; rent reserved and payable on a monthly or weekly basis.
(4) Tenancy for less than one year; rent reserved and payable on a yearly basis.
(5) Tenancy for less than one year; rent reserved on a yearly basis but payable monthly or weekly.

6) Tenancy for less than one year; rent reserved and payable on a monthly or weekly basis. The following cases are illustrative:

(1) *Young* v. *Bank of Nova Scotia* (1915), 34 O.L.R. 176, 23 D.L.R. 854 (App. Div.): lease for 18 months; rent reserved on yearly basis but payable monthly. *Held*, tenancy from year to year.

(2) *Re Lyons and McVeity* (1919), 46 O.L.R. 148, 49 D.L.R. 635 (App. Div.): lease for 14 months; rent reserved and payable monthly. *Held*, tenancy from year to year.

(3) *Covered Markets Ltd.* v. *Green*, [1947] 2 All E.R. 40 (K.B.): lease for 7 years at rent payable weekly in advance. *Held*, tenancy from year to year.

(4) *Adler* v. *Blackman*, [1953] 1 Q.B. 146, [1952] 2 All E.R. 41: weekly tenancy at weekly rent followed by agreement for 12 month tenancy at a weekly rent. *Held*, weekly tenancy. (*Cf. Ladies Hosiery & Underwear Ltd.* v. *Parker*, [1930] 1 Ch. 304.)

(5) *Grant* v. *Rutledge*, [1950] 3 D.L.R. 447, [1950] O.W.N. 560 (C.A.): monthly tenancy at monthly rent followed by statutory two-year lease at monthly rent. *Held*, tenancy from year to year.

(6) *Eastman* v. *Richards* (1898), 3 Terr. L. R. 73, aff'd (1899), 29 S.C.R. 438: lease for 11 months "at the rate of $400 per year", payable monthly. *Held*, monthly tenancy.

(7) *Grumbacher* v. *Booster Nut Ltd.*, [1948] O.R. 945, [1949] 1 D.L.R. 157 (C.A.): lease for 5 months at monthly rent. *Held*, monthly tenancy. Contrast, *Charles Ogilvy Ltd.* v. *Larocque*, [1952] 3 D.L.R. 241, [1952] O.W.N. 281 (C.A.): lease for 9 months at rent of $288 payable $32 per month. *Held*, yearly tenancy.]

[Premises are let to a tenant "as a monthly tenant from August 20, 1942, to August 20, 1943", with rent payable semi-monthly. Prior to August 20, 1943, the landlord wrote to the tenant saying "I'll keep you on as a monthly tenant and not by the year" and requesting that rent be paid monthly. *Held*, no implication of a yearly tenancy on a holding over and continued payment of rent: *Burns* v. *Hodgson*, [1945] O.R. 876, [1946] 1 D.L.R. 510 (C.A.). Would the result be the same if the landlord had not written but the tenant stayed on, paying rent as before?

A tenant under a lease providing for successive tenancy periods of 364 days at a stipulated rent payable monthly stays on after expiry of a notice to quit and pays rent as before. What is the nature of his holding? See *Swift* v. *Ambrose* (1931), 47 T.L.R. 594 (K.B.); *Land Settlement Association Ltd.* v. *Carr*, [1944] K.B. 657, [1944] 2 All E.R. 126 (C.A.).]

[A tenant under a two year lease with rent payable monthly remained in possession after expiry of the term and shortly afterwards agreed to pay an increased monthly rent. Is the new implied tenancy a monthly one or a yearly one? See *Paterson* v. *Zhilat*, [1953] O.W.N. 415 (C.A.).

A provision in a lease reads as follows: "In the event that the lessee holds over after expiration of the term hereby granted, the lessee shall be a monthly tenant or tenant from year to year as the lessor may elect." Does this provision entitle a tenant to stay on without the landlord's consent?]

[A tenant under a lease for a term certain which contained an option to purchase stayed on after expiration of the term and as a periodic tenant claimed to exercise the option. Result? See *Re Leeds and Batley Breweries Ltd.*, [1920] 2 Ch. 548, 124 L.T. 189; *Re Devine and Ferguson*, [1946] O.R. 736, [1947] 1 D.L.R. 76. Contrast *Hill* v. *Hill*, [1947] Ch. 231, [1947] 1 All E.R. 54 (C.A.).]

[A yearly tenant is entitled to emblements at common law unless the tenancy is terminated owing to his default, but not a tenant for a term certain unless the term ends prematurely without his fault, e.g., owing to termination of the landlord's interest. See *Atkinson* v. *Farrell* (1912), 27 O.L.R. 204, 8 D.L.R. 582 (C.A.); 5 *American Law of Property*, s. 19.16.]

CHAPTER VIII

COMMON LAW FUTURE INTERESTS

A DOCTRINE OF ESTATES which measured interests in land in terms of duration and recognized that interests could arise successively as segments of an ultimate estate in fee simple invited the working out of a law of future interests. "A future interest may be described as an interest in land or other things in which the privilege of possession or of enjoyment is future and not present. It should be emphasized that the interest is an existing interest from the time of its creation, and is looked upon as a part of the total ownership of land or other thing which is its subject matter." (1 *Simes and Smith*, Law of Future Interests (1956, 2d ed.) p. 2.) Thus, a future interest is an interest capable of becoming possessory and, being regarded as a segment of ownership, is distinguishable on these two counts from interests like easements which may never be possessory and are qualifications of another's ownership outside of a doctrine of estates.

The common law recognized the following types of future interests: (1) reversionary interests, which include the reversion after a fee tail, after a life estate, and after a leasehold or term of years; (2) possibility of reverter; (3) right of entry for condition broken; (4) remainders, vested and contingent. These interests emerged under the rules of common law conveyancing referred to in part on pp. 37-39, *supra*. In addition to the methods noted there for transferring possessory and non-possessory freehold interests, it should be recalled that nonfreehold interests, specifically a term of years, may arise through a mere agreement followed by entry into possession; and that surrenders and releases were and are significant in connection with leaseholds, although having a wider application. A surrender occurs when a present interest is transferred to the holder of a future interest, being the next vested estate in the same land. By statute now (e.g., Conveyancing and Law of Property Act, R.S.O. 1960, c. 66, s. 9 and Statute of Frauds, R.S.O. 1960, c. 381, s. 2) surrenders other than those arising by operation of law must be by deed or in writing to be enforceable (subject, presumably, to the part performance doctrine). A release occurs where a future interest is transferred to the holder of a present interest in the same land and the common law required a deed.

Why the aforementioned interests were the only ones recognized at common law is more readily appreciated in the light of the role of seisin in conveyancing, and the fact that a grant of a fee simple exhausted all that a grantor could give. The feudal conveyancing rule which prohibited an abeyance of seisin was given practical expression by the fact that the writs in real actions lay only against a tenant of the immediate freehold and similarly feudal services could be demanded only from such tenant.

The result may be expressed in two fundamental propositions:

1. No freehold estate may be created or transferred to begin in the future; that is, the common law did not recognize springing interests in freehold.

2. No freehold estate may be created to arise in a third person in defeasance of another estate by cutting the latter off on the occurrence of some event other than its ordinary or natural termination; that is, the common law did not recognize shifting interests in freehold. This was so whether the estate sought thus to be defeated was an estate in fee simple or a fee tail or a life estate.

It will be seen that reversionary interests (in which category one may include the possibility of reverter and the reversion upon a leasehold) are future interests left in the grantor; that the right of entry for condition broken (or power of termination) is a future interest created in a grantor of an estate given subject to a condition subsequent; and that remainder interests arise in grantees and become (and, indeed, must become) possessory on the ordinary or natural termination of prior supporting interests.

[1 *Simes and Smith*, Law of Future Interests (1956, 2nd ed.), p. 42:

"One of the most potent concepts of the feudal land law, so far as the law of future interests is concerned, was the notion of livery of seisin, the typical form of conveyance, as a present transaction, a present symbolical delivery of the land. While even before the Statute of Uses, this was not the only mode of alienation of present possessory freehold interests, it was the type form about which the feudal picture of conveyancing was sketched in. One might infer, if the notion of conveyancing as a present delivery of seisin were to be laid down as a major premise, that no future interests at all were possible. But, as we have seen, even the rigidity of feudal logic drew no such conclusion. The reversion and the remainder were fully recognized, but the theory of their creation was this. The holder of the preceding particular estate, be it life estate or fee tail, was regarded as taking the seisin both for himself and for the remainderman. And, when the particular estate terminated, the seisin was regarded as passing instantly to the holder of the next vested estate. In theory it was all a part of the same seisin; there was no break; the remainderman did not take by way of cutting off the preceding estate, but only on the instant of its termination. In so far as a reversion was concerned, the theory of a present passing of seisin required even less stretching to compass it. Since the reversioner or his ancestor had once had seisin, it was in accord with feudal notions for it to revest in him on the termination of any outstanding estates. The reversion was not looked upon as something newly created, but as a present estate previously existing from which the particular estate had been carved. Thus, so far as the common law was concerned, seisin could only pass from one person to another in the future if it passed at the instant of the termination of the preceding estate of freehold. The future interest could not take effect by way of cutting off the preceding estate; nor could it take effect after an interval of time following the termination of the preceding estate.

"At first blush the right of entry for condition broken might be regarded as an exception to that proposition; but a little thought will make it clear that such is not the case. If A, owning in fee simple, conveyed to B in fee simple with a common-law condition subsequent, it was true that the happening of the condition might result in the cutting off prematurely of B's estate. But it was not cut off by virtue of the original act of livery of seisin. It was cut off only when, after the breach of the condition, A entered. In other words seisin revested in A only as a result of a present act, the act of re-entry."

Consider the interests that arise under the following limitations:

(1) A grants to B.
(2) A grants to B and his heirs so long as C lives.
(3) A grants to B and his heirs until C returns from Paris.
(4) A grants to B for life remainder to the heirs of C.
(5) A grants to B for life remainder to C and his heirs when C reaches age 21.
(6) A grants to B and his heirs but if B dies without children him surviving, then to C and his heirs.
(7) A grants to B and his heirs provided B does not sell liquor on the premises.
(8) A grants to B for life provided B pays $100 per year.
(9) A grants to B for life provided he pays $100 per year, remainder to C.
(10) A grants to B for life and if he does not pay $100 per year, then to C and his heirs.
(11) A grants to B for life remainder to C and his heirs provided the land is farmed.
(12) A grants to B for life remainder to C and his heirs so long as C remains a widower.
(13) A grants to B for life or during widowhood remainder to C and his heirs.

(14) A grants to B for 10 years and then to C and his heirs.
(15) A grants to B for 99 years if he should so long live remainder to C and his heirs.
(16) A grants to B for 21 years if he should so long live and after B's death to C and his heirs.
(17) A grants to B for 21 years remainder to the heirs of C.
(18) A grants to B for life remainder to C for 21 years remainder to D and his heirs.
(19) A grants to B for life and after C's death to D and his heirs.
(20) A grants to B for life and one day after his death to C and his heirs.

Would it make any difference in the effect of any of the foregoing limitations if each was a devise?

After the Statute of Uses, 1536 and the Statute of Wills, 1540, shifting interests (limitation no. 6 and no. 10) and springing interests (limitation no. 16, no. 17 and no. 20) could be created as legal interests. This is treated in the next chapter. Determinable interests (see limitation no. 3, no. 12, no. 13, no. 15 and no. 16) could be created at common law in accordance with the strict rules governing seisin and conveyancing.

It is unnecessary to comment extensively on reversionary interests. Such interests (excluding the possibility of reverter) are *vested* interests, although there may be situations where they may be divested. (See limitation no. 5, reversion subject to a contingent remainder in fee simple.) Another way of putting the matter is to say that reversions may be indefeasible or defeasible. Reversions in the sense here considered are alienable *inter vivos*, devisable and devolve on an intestacy.

Where reversions arise *inter vivos* they are in the grantor; where they arise under a will, they are in the testator's statutory heirs as being entitled to interests undisposed of by the will.]

The possibility of reverter as the interest remaining in the grantor of a determinable fee simple or in the statutory heirs of a testator who devises a determinable fee simple is a contingent interest because subject to a condition precedent. [The position that a possibility of reverter is a contingent interest is taken by the *Restatement of Property*, s. 154; by 1 *American Law of Property*, s. 4.12; and by *Simes and Smith*, Law of Future Interests (1956, 2nd ed.), s. 281. *Megarry*, Manual of Law of Real Property, (1955, 2nd ed.), p. 157 refers to it as a vested interest (but see *Megarry and Wade*, Law of Real Property (1959, 2nd ed.), at p. 243, contra); so does *Gray*, Rule against Perpetuities (1942, 4th ed.), s. 113.3.] It may be released to the holder of the determinable fee, or the nature of the contingency may be such as to result in destruction of the possibility of reverter and consequent enlargement of the determinable fee simple into an absolute fee simple. For example, if A grants to B and his heirs so long as C remains unmarried and C dies without marrying, the event upon which the determinable fee will be automatically terminated will never happen, and hence B's interest becomes a fee simple absolute. We know that a fee simple determinable is alienable *inter vivos* and devisable and that it will devolve upon an intestacy, subject in all cases to its attendant defeasibility in the hands of any subsequent holder. Does this hold true for a possibility of reverter?

While there were doubts whether a possibility of reverter was alienable *inter vivos* at common law (see *Gray*, Rule against Perpetuities (1942, 4th ed.), p. 8, and 1 *American Law of Property*, s. 4.70), statute has resolved the doubts in England (see Real Property Act, 1845 (Imp.), c. 106, s. 6, now Law of Property Act, 1925 (Imp.), c. 20, s. 4 (2)) and in some of the provinces of Canada. In the United States, the majority case view is that such interests (being existing interests even if contingent rather than vested) are alienable: see 1 *American Law of Property*, s. 4.70.

The English legislation just referred to was copied in some of the Provinces of Canada as indicated below.

CONVEYANCING AND LAW OF PROPERTY ACT, R.S.O. 1960, c. 66

10. A contingent, an executory, and a future interest, and a possibility coupled with an interest in land, whether the object of the gift or limitation of such interest or possibility is or is not ascertained, also a right of entry, whether immediate or future, and whether vested or contingent, into or upon land, may be disposed of by deed; but no such disposition, by force only of this Act, defeats or enlarges an estate tail.

[See also Property Act, R.S.N.B. 1952, c. 177, s. 14; Real Property Act, R.S.N.S. 1954, c. 244, s. 26; Real Property Act, R.S.P.E.I. 1951, c. 138, s. 9.]

Possibilities of reverter are devisable within the general run of Wills Acts: see Wills Act, 1960 (Alta.), c. 118, s. 3; Wills Act, R.S.B.C. 1960, c. 408, s. 3; Wills Act, R.S.M. 1954, c. 293, s. 3; Wills Act, R.S.N.B. 1952, c. 251, s. 2; Wills Act, R.S.N.S. 1954, c. 315, s. 2; Wills Act, R.S.O. 1960, c. 433, s. 8; Wills Act, R.S.P.E.I. 1951, c. 124, s. 70; Wills Act, R.S.S. 1953, c. 120, s. 3.

Does a possibility of reverter devolve upon an intestacy? Some provincial statutes of distributions cover them fairly clearly: see Probate Act, R.S.P.E.I. 1951, c. 124, s. 119; Intestate Succession Act, R.S.S. 1953, c. 119, s. 4; and *cf.* Intestate Succession Act, R.S.A. 1955, c. 161; Intestate Succession Act, R.S.Nfld. 1952, c. 153. The Descent of Property Act, R.S.N.S. 1954, c. 69 deals in s. 2 (1) only with the descent of real property held in fee simple or for the life of another. In British Columbia (Administration Act, R.S.B.C. 1960, c. 3, s. 95), in Manitoba (Devolution of Estates Act, R.S.M. 1954, c. 63, s. 17 (1)), in New Brunswick (Devolution of Estates Act, R.S.N.B. 1952, c. 62, as amended, s. 3), and in Ontario (Devolution of Estates Act, R.S.O. 1960, c. 106, s. 2) the legislation speaks of devolution of interests in land "vested in any person". Does this exclude possibilities of reverter (and also rights of entry on condition broken) so as to remit the descent of these interests to another scheme of devolution, e.g., that under which descent of future interests was traced from the last purchaser: see 1 *American Law of Property*, ss. 4.73, 4.74? It may be, of course, that the term "vested" is used in the statutes in a sense that would cover such interests (e.g., see *Megarry*, Manual of Law of Real Property (1955, 2nd ed.), p. 157). The matter has not been the subject of any specific decision.

[Consider the following limitations:

(1) A devises to B and his heirs so long as B pays $100 per year to C, and if B dies in C's lifetime then to D and his heirs.

(2) A devises to B and his heirs until B ceases to support C and if B dies without children him surviving then to D and his heirs.

(3) A devises to B and his heirs so long as the land is farmed and if not then to D and his heirs.

What interests do B and D have in each case?]

The right of entry for condition broken, arising in a grantor of an estate subject to a condition subsequent (or power of termination) or arising in the statutory heirs of a testator who devises such an estate is, to be accurate, a mere possibility of a right of entry until the condition is broken or the power of termination is exercisable. When exercised the right of entry or power of termination cuts short the estate to which it is subjoined. At common law it could exist only in favour of a grantor or his heirs and the "revesting" of the seisin in him was not regarded as violating the common law rules of conveyancing, as would be the case if the right of entry or power of termination were by the same limitation given to a third person. *Littleton's Tenures* (1481), where the fee simple on condition subsequent and consequent right of entry, were considered, laid down, in s. 347, a rule to this effect as follows: "No entry or re-entry... may be reserved or given to any person but only to the feoffor, or to the donor or to the lessor, or to their heirs; and such re-entry cannot be given to any other person".

By subsequent statutory modification rights of entry for condition broken, where incident to a reversion (as upon a life estate or a leasehold) passed *inter vivos* along with alienation of the reversion: see Grantees of Reversions Act, 1540, c. 34, s. 1. (This provision is reproduced in part in the Landlord and Tenant Act, R.S.O. 1960, c. 206, s. 3 which, however, does not make it clear that the Act of 1540 applied to life interests as well as to leaseholds; see also, for similar legislation, Landlord and Tenant Act, R.S.M. 1954, c. 136, s. 3; Landlord and Tenant Act, R.S.N.B. 1952, c. 126, ss. 2 and 3; Landlord and Tenant Act, R.S.P.E.I. 1951, c. 82, ss. 2, 3 and 4; Landlord and Tenant Act, R.S.S. 1953, c. 312, s. 3.)

There was, of course, no reversion upon a fee simple subject to a condition subsequent; and the right of entry in that connection, while it could be released to the holder of the defeasible fee simple, was not alienable *inter vivos* in England until 1845: see Real Property Act, 1845 (Imp.), c. 106, s. 6, now Law of Property Act, 1925 (Imp.), c. 20, s. 4 (2). Even so, there were some decisions that the term "right of entry" in s. 6 of the 1845 statute referred to the right of entry upon a disseisin. Thus it was said in *Hunt* v. *Bishop* (1853), 8 Ex. 675, 155 E.R. 1523, at p. 680 Ex., p. 1525 E.R., "we think that the 8 & 9 Vict. c. 106 does not relate to a right to repossess or re-enter for a condition broken but only to an original right where there had been a disseisin, or where the party has a right to recover land, and his right of entry and nothing but that remains"; see also *Hunt* v. *Remnant* (1854), 9 Ex. 635, 156 E.R. 271. This view was adopted in *Baldwin* v. *Wanzer* (1892), 22 O.R. 612, at p. 641 in interpreting similar Ontario legislation, now s. 10 of the Conveyancing and Law of Property Act, R.S.O. 1960, c. 66, reproduced, *supra*, p. 330. It is submitted that this interpretation is indefensible, and that it may properly be taken that rights of entry for condition broken are now freely alienable *inter vivos*: see *Gray*, Rule against Perpetuities (1942, 4th ed.), p. 7n; *Cheshire*, Modern Law of Real Property (1954, 7th ed.), p. 313.

[There was authority in the United States that having regard to the common law rule against alienability of rights of entry for condition broken, an attempted alienation at least before the right became exercisable destroyed the right in the assignor and his heirs while failing to give anything to the assignee: see *Rice* v. *Boston & Worcester Railroad Corp*, (1866), 12 Allen 141 (Mass.). The *Restatement of Property* adopted this position originally (see volume 2, s. 160, comment C) but in the 1948 Supplement (at p. 415) its position was changed as a result of, *inter alia*, *Jones* v. *Oklahoma City* (1943), 193 Okl. 637, 145 P. 2d 971 which expressed a view in opposition to the *Rice* case.]

Rights of entry for condition broken are, like possibilities of reverter, devisable under the Wills Acts referred to *supra*, p. 330. Again, where incident to a reversion, they would clearly devolve with it upon an intestacy; and it is submitted that a right of entry for condition broken that is not so incident is nonetheless likewise a descendible interest, even under the provincial legislation which deals only with devolution of interests "vested in any person"; and this is so regardless of whether the condition has or has not been broken.

[See, generally, *Dunham*, Possibility of Reverter and Powers of Termination—Fraternal or Identical Twins, (1953) 20 U. of Chi. L. Rev. 215; *Goldstein*, Rights of Entry and Possibilities of Reverter as Devices to Restrict the Use of Land, (1940) 54 Harv. L. Rev. 248.]

["It is true that words of an express condition may in certain cases be intended as a limitation, but the rule is that it will not ordinarily be so construed, and there does not appear to be any reason in the present case why it should be construed as a limitation rather than as a condition": Byrne J. in *In re Trustees of Hollis' Hospital and Hague's Contract*, [1899] 2 Ch. 540, where land was conveyed to trustees of a hospital for certain purposes provided that if the land should at any time be used or converted to any other purposes, then it should revert. What interests arose under this conveyance and was there any tenable objection to their validity?

Construction of an apparent condition as a "limitation" is justifiable in a case such as this: A grants to B for life provided that B does not sell liquor on the premises remainder to C in fee simple. Why? See 1 *Simes and Smith*, Law of Future Interests (1956, 2nd ed.) p. 289.]

IN RE MELVILLE. Ontario Chancery Division. 1886. 11 O.R. 626

Petition for a declaration that devisees under a will and their successors were entitled to certain land or to the proceeds from the sale thereof.

PROUDFOOT J.: On the 26th September, 1844, John LeBreton, by deed bargained and sold, &c., to the Municipal Council of the Dalhousie District, in consideration of five shillings, a parcel of land, now within the City of Ottawa, for the purpose of erecting thereon a school-house for the use of the District of Dalhousie, to have and to hold the same for the purpose aforesaid unto the Municipal Council for ever. The deed was subject to a proviso that unless the said Municipal Council should within the space of one year from the date of the deed, build or erect on the said land a school-house, to belong exclusively to the said Municipal Council for the use of the said district; or if the said Municipal Council should at any time thereafter erect or build upon the said land any other house or building save the said school-house and the necessary outhouses and offices appurtenant thereto, or if the Municipal Council should at any time thereafter sell, lease, alien, transfer or convey the said land, or any part thereof, then the indenture was to be null and void, and it should be lawful for the said John LeBreton and his heirs to re-enter the said land and premises and avoid the estate of the said Municipal Council.

On the 23rd July, 1847, John LeBreton made his will. He devised to certain nieces, naming them, all his real estate, to have and to hold the same to them and their heirs for ever share and share alike.

The Municipal Council of Dalhousie District complied with the condition by building a school-house on the land and at the time of the making of the will the condition had not been violated.

The successors of the District of Dalhousie have dealt with the land otherwise than was authorized by the deed, and have broken the condition.

The land has been sold and the purchase money is in Court, and the question is whether the devisees of John LeBreton or his heirs-at-law are entitled to the money.

It was contended for the heirs-at-law, that under the law existing when the will was made, that future estates would not pass,—that when the will was made John LeBreton had no estate, legal or equitable, in the land—and that a mere possibility of reverter was not devisable,—and that the condition was itself void—that the only way the object of the parties could have been effected, was by a conditional limitation.

It was decided in *Whateley* v. *Whateley*, 13 Gr. 436, 14 Gr. 430, that a general devise, not containing any words referring to such estate as the testator should die seized of, did not pass after acquired estates.

The question then is: Whether a possibility of reverter was devisable?

The R.S.O. ch. 106, sec. 2, repeating C.S.U.C. ch. 82, sec. 14, defines the meaning to be given to the word *land* in wills before the 1st January, 1874, and says it shall extend among other things, not applicable to the present case, "to any possibility, right or title of entry or action and any other interest capable of being inherited," whether the same "are in reversion, remainder or contingency".

In the same Revised Act, ch. 106, sec. 10, in declaring what property may be devised by wills after the 1st January, 1874, copies the clause on that subject in the Imperial Act, which mentions among other things, "all rights of entry for condition broken," which are not included in sec. 2, and omits "possibilities," which are included in sec. 2.

If sec. 10 had mentioned "possibilities" there would have been some reason for arguing that they differed from rights of entry for condition broken. But not having done so, it is thus left open to infer that "possibilities" may include rights of entry for condition broken.

Some help towards ascertaining the meaning of "possibility" may perhaps be found in R.S.O., ch. 98, sec. 5, which specifies interests in land that may be conveyed by deed, and among others "a possibility coupled with an interest in any land, whether the object of the gift or limitation of such interest or possibility be or be not ascertained, also a right of entry, whether immediate or future, and whether vested or contingent, into or upon any land".

That section seems to be copied from the Imperial Statute, 8 & 9 Vic., ch. 106, sec. 6, and under that statute it has been held that this section 6, does not relate to a right of entry for condition broken: *Smith's* Real and Personal Property, 6th ed., sec. 2424; *Shelford* Real Property Stat., 8th ed., 639; *Hunt* v. *Remnant*, 9 Exch. 640, per Maule, J.; *Hunt* v. *Bishop*, 8 Exch. 680. It would seem to follow that such a right of entry does not come under the words "possibility coupled with an interest," or these cases would have been argued on that ground, and decided the other way.

That does not determine, however, the meaning of possibility, when not limited by being coupled with an interest.

In *Smith's* Real and Personal Property, 6th ed., sec. 890, it is said that "the word possibility has a general sense, in which it includes even executory interests which are the objects of a limitation. But in its more specific sense it is that kind of contingent benefit which is neither the object of a limitation, like an executory interest, nor is founded in any lost but recoverable seisin. Of this nature is a possibility of reverter on the grant of a qualified or determinable fee.... And of the same nature is a contingent right of entry in case there should be a breach of a condition subsequent."

Hence it would seem that "possibility" in R.S.O. ch. 106, sec. 2, includes a right of entry for condition broken, mentioned in the 10th section, and is more extensive than that phrase, and might therefore be the subject of a devise, and is covered by the general name of "land".

Upon the happening of the breach of condition, in this case, which took place after the death of the testator, and it would have been the same if it had happened after the making of the will, and before the death of the testator, no new estate was acquired so as to require words applicable to after acquired estates to be found in the will. The possibility of reverter was a contingent interest that existed in the testator when the will was made. The subsequent breach of the condition gave a right of entry, by which the contingent interest might be converted into an estate in possession.

It remains therefore to consider whether the condition in this deed was void. The subject is discussed in *Leake's* Digest of the Law of Property in Land, p. 214, *et seq.*, and in *Smith's* Real and Personal Property, 6th ed., p. 76, *et seq.* Conditions subsequent appear in the two forms of *conditional limitations*, and *conditions of re-entry*, or *conditions* strictly so called at common law. A conditional limitation operates to determine the estate by the intrinsic force of the limitation; in the event prescribed by the terms of the condition the estate ceases. A condition operates by reserving a right of re-entry to the grantor and his heirs; in the event prescribed the estate becomes defeasible by entry, but until entry the estate continues. Apt words of limitation are *durante viduitate*, or *durante vita*, &c., words of conditions are *sub conditione proviso*, &c. In the present case the condition is under the shape of a proviso, and is a condition subsequent, giving a right of entry upon breach. A condition can be reserved in a conveyance at common law only to the grantor or lessor of the estate, and to his heirs, and to no other person. A condition may be reserved upon a conveyance in fee simple, leaving no reversion, or upon an assignment of a term of years leaving no reversion. The sentence in *Smith's* Real and Personal Property, 6th ed., appears in sec. 170 of the 8th ed., and is to the effect that "these limitations can only be by way of use or devise. They would be void if inserted in a deed at common law, being foreign to the simplicity of the conveyances before uses and devises were introduced." But the learned author is there speaking of conditional limitations, not of conditions. But when speaking of conditions, in sec. 154, he refers to subsequent conditions as a means by which an estate or interest is to be prematurely defeated or determined, and no other estate is to be created in its room.

I think, therefore, that the condition was perfectly valid.

My conclusion is that the devisees, and not the heirs of John LeBreton are entitled to the land or to the money representing it.

Judgment accordingly.

[In *McKinnon* v. *Lundy* (1893), 24 O.R. 132, rev'd on other grounds (1894), 21 O.A.R. 560 and restored (1895), 24 S.C.R. 650, a testatrix devised certain land to her husband "he to pay off the mortgage to McCulla. Should he not pay the said mortgage off at maturity, the said land to become the property of my children...." After making her will (which she left unchanged) the testatrix paid off the mortgage. She was killed by her husband who was convicted of manslaughter and who sold the land to provide money for his defence. While it was ultimately decided that he could not take any benefits under his wife's will, the trial Judge's ruling on the nature of the testamentary interest was affirmed. Ferguson J., the trial Judge, said, *inter alia* (at p. 137 ff.):

"As will be observed, this devise is a gift of the land to James B. Lundy, 'he to pay off the mortgage to McCulla,' and upon his failure to pay it off at maturity, then a gift over to and in favour of others.

"The arguments upon the subject seemed to me to embrace the whole field of inquiry as to whether this devise really contained or was upon a condition, and, if so, whether such condition was and must be considered to be a condition precedent, or a condition subsequent, or, whether a charge only was created.

"To constitute a condition it must be clear that the testatrix intended the gift to take effect or continue only in a certain event, and it has been frequently said that there is no distinction in the way of technical words between conditions precedent and conditions subsequent, that the distinction is matter of construction dependent upon the intention of the testator as manifested by the will. This is stated in many of the books, and must, I think, be received as a general proposition of law....

"I may here say that I am entirely unable to take the view or arrive at the conclusion that the devise in question is a gift of the land subject merely to a charge upon it for the amount of the mortgage to McCulla. The sense of the language employed in the gift appears to me to be against this view, and I think the gift over incompatible with it.

"I am of the opinion that the devise is a conditional one, and the question as to whether the condition is a condition precedent or a condition subsequent arises and seems of great materiality so far as the construction of the devise alone has concern in determining the rights of the parties.

"In the contention that the gift was upon a condition precedent reference was made to the agreement of the 25th of April, 1887, about one year and a half before the making of the will, counsel suggesting and contending that in viewing the whole case and all the circumstances, a fair conclusion would be that this devise was made for the purpose and with the intention of 'carrying into effect' the provisions and terms of the agreement. That agreement, as before stated, provided for a conveyance by the wife to the husband of the then interest in the land 'upon payment' by him of the mortgage to McCulla. These words 'upon payment' were relied upon as constituting or shewing a condition precedent in the agreement, and the contention was that the words of the devise should be construed in the same way, the words in the devise 'he to pay off the mortgage to McCulla', being capable of receiving this construction. The words 'he to pay off the mortgage' might, I think, if looked at alone, be so construed. The authority referred to by counsel, or rather one of the authorities referred to, was the case *Large* v. *Cheshire*, Vent. 147, a case that I find referred to in *Acherley* v. *Vernon*, Willes 153, where the Lord Chief Justice, in discussing the effect of the words 'upon condition that she release,' says they are the same in effect as 'she releasing'. The expression under discussion in that case was in this way reduced to this: 'I give her the annuity, she releasing,' and the learned Chief Justice said, at p. 159-60: 'This expression has always been holden to make a condition precedent,' referring to *Large* v. *Cheshire*, which was a case of a man agreeing to pay £50 to J.S., *he making him a good estate in the lands.*

"So far as the construction and meaning of the expressions themselves have concern, I do not perceive any very material difference between the expressions: He making him a good estate, and, he to make him a good estate, or between she releasing, and, she to release, or between *he paying off the mortgage*, and, *he to pay off the mortgage.* Yet, and notwithstanding the use of the word 'always' by Chief Justice Willes as above, it seems clear that in construing such an expression it must be taken and considered in the setting in which it is found. In the case before the Chief Justice the annuity was the consideration for the release, and so in *Large* v. *Cheshire*, the one thing was the consideration for the other; and it is said in *Theobald on Wills*, 3rd ed., p. 374, and seems to be a general rule, that a condition which involves anything in the nature of a consideration is in general a condition precedent.

"It is also said in *Theobald*, at the same page, that when the condition requires something to be done that requires time, the argument is in favour of construing it as a condition subsequent.

"The mortgage to McCulla did not fall due for some three years after the date of the will. 'He to pay this off' must be taken to mean he to pay it off at maturity, and in the gift over that follows, this expression is used, and the testatrix might have died at any time after the making of the will during these three years.

"As I have already said, one must in endeavouring to ascertain the effect of the words 'he to pay off,' etc., take them in the connection in which they are in the devise, and in so doing one is bound to read the whole devise including the gift over in favour of the children, and in regard to the effect of this gift over, I do not at present see that I can do better than refer to the cases found in *Hawkins* on the Construction of Wills, at p. 240 *seq.*, under the case *Edwards* v. *Hammond*, 1 B. & P.N.R. 324, n.

"... Then, shortly, I think this devise in the will is a gift of the land to James B. Lundy, with a condition subsequent that he should pay off the mortgage to McCulla at maturity, and in default of his so doing, a gift over in favour of the children. The estate, marked out in this devise, to be taken by James B. Lundy was, as I think, an estate known as a conditional limitation, one that would cease upon breach of condition and this without entry by the heir: 4 Kent's Com. on Amer. Law, 12th ed., at p. 126.

"In *Jarman* on Wills, 6 Am. ed., vol. 2, p. 12 (the author referring to Coke Litt. 206 b, and several American cases), it is said to be clear that where a condition precedent annexed to a devise of real estate, or a charge on realty, becomes impossible of performance, and though there be no default or laches on the part of the devisee himself, the devise fails. And, on the other hand, it is clear that if performance of a condition subsequent be rendered impossible the estate to which it is annexed, whether in land or money legacies, by that event becomes absolute. I need not, I think, delay by referring to cases on these subjects. This general statement seems to me, after having looked at several cases, to be the law. So where the condition is impossible in its creation, if the condition is precedent, the devise being of real estate is itself void; if, however, the condition is subsequent, the devise, whether of real or personal estate, is absolute: *Jarman, ib.*, at pp. 14 and 15.

"From what has been said in respect of the transaction between the husband and wife of the 6th of April, 1892, and the payment and satisfaction by her thereafter of the mortgage to McCulla, it appears, as I think, plainly enough that this condition subsequent though perfectly possible of performance at the time of the making of the will, became impossible of performance before the death of the testatrix; then, whether the will is considered as speaking from the time of the death of the testatrix, or from the time of its execution, the devise to James B. Lundy is as if no condition had been annexed to it; that is to say, whether the condition being a condition subsequent is looked upon as a condition possible of performance, that became impossible of performance, or a condition that was in its creation impossible of performance, the estate would pass to the devisee without the condition. The condition, being a condition subsequent, either was or became void, and the estate given absolute."]

[Differences between a "determinable" limitation and an interest on condition subsequent exist in the consequence that flows from invalidity of the limitation on the one hand and of the condition subsequent on the other; they exist also in the fact that the same circumstance expressed in a determinable limitation may not affect its validity but if expressed as a condition subsequent may result in an invalid condition.

Land was devised to A "until he shall assign, charge, or otherwise dispose of the same, or some part thereof or become bankrupt" and if he should die without leaving a male heir of the body then to B. What is the nature of A's interest? Would its validity be affected if it were formulated as an interest subject to a condition subsequent? See *In re Leach, Leach* v. *Leach*, [1912] 2 Ch. 422.

It is beyond the scope of this casebook to deal with restraints on alienation, but some awareness of the problems involved may properly be aroused. Thus, to take the limitation above set out, would its validity be affected if disposition to a particular person or to a class of persons was alone prohibited, or if the prohibition on alienation generally was limited in time? See *In re Macleay* (1875), L.R. 20 Eq. 186; *Re Rosher* (1884), 26 Ch. D. 801. See, generally, on the subject, 6 *American Law of Property*, Part 26; 4 *Restatement of Property*, Part II; *Schnebly*, Restraints upon the Alienation of Legal Interests, (1935) 44 Yale L.J. 964.

It may be difficult in particular situations to determine whether a condition has been created or a determinable limitation, or a trust or a charge or merely a covenant: see *Walsh*, Conditional Estates and Covenants Running with the Land, (1937) 14 N.Y.U. Law Q. Rev. 162. Again, it may be that a statement in a conveyance as to use of land should not be given any effect at all: see 1 *Restatement of Property*, p. 143. Where a condition is created, it may fail because it is void for uncertainty, or it may be unlawful or it may offend recognized public policy, or it may be an improper restraint on alienation. The following are some illustrative cases:

Land is conveyed to A and his heirs so long as he continues to reside in Canada. What is the nature of A's interest and is its validity affected by the condition? See *Sifton* v. *Sifton*, [1938] A.C. 656, [1938] 3 D.L.R. 577, [1938] 3 All E.R. 435; *cf. Re Gape's Will Trusts*, [1952] Ch. 743, [1952] 1 All E.R. 827; *Re Switzer*, [1951] O.W.N. 786.

Land is conveyed to A "so long as he shall occupy the same". In considering the effect and validity of the limitation, contrast *Re Field's Will Trusts, Parry-Jones* v. *Hillman*, [1950] Ch.

520, [1950] 2 All E.R. 188 and *Moore* v. *Royal Trust Co.*, [1956] S.C.R. 880, 5 D.L.R. 2d 152.

If a condition is precedent rather than subsequent, and is invalid for some reason, does the interest which is contingent thereon necessarily fail? See *Re Going*, [1951] O.R. 147, [1951] 2 D.L.R. 136 (C.A.). For refinements applicable in the case of invalid conditions precedent in gifts of personalty, see *Re Elliott*, [1952] Ch. 217, [1952] 1 All E.R. 145.

A condition under which a named beneficiary will lose a benefit unless at a prescribed time she has "shed" or "divested" herself of her husband (who was objectionable to the testator) is void as contrary to public policy: see *Re Hurshman, Mindlin* v. *Hurshman* (1956), 6 D.L.R. 2d 615 (B.C.). *Cf. Re Piper, Dodd* v. *Piper*, [1946] 2 All E.R. 503, 62 T.L.R. 618 (Ch.).]

MATHESON v. TOWN OF MITCHELL. Ontario Appellate Division. 1919. 46 O.L.R. 546, 51 D.L.R. 477

Appeal from a judgment of Rose J., 44 O.L.R. 619, dismissing an action brought by executors of the will of one Matheson for mandamus to compel defendant to keep in proper repair as a public park certain land devised to it or, alternatively, for a declaration that the land formed part of the estate. The trial Judge found that from a year or two after the testator's death in 1883 there had been continuous neglect by the town council to keep the property in repair as a public park. However, he refused a mandamus because the Court would not undertake supervision of the performance of a continuous obligation. He held also that the action was barred by the Statute of Limitations.

MACLAREN J. A.: ... In my opinion, the appeal must also fail on another and perhaps a stronger ground. The clause of the will making the bequest reads as follows:—

"I give and devise to the Corporation of the Town of Mitchell in the County of Perth lots numbers 7 and 8 ... in the first concession of the Township of Fullarton ... to have and to hold to the said Corporation of Mitchell and its successors in office for ever and to be used and kept as a place of recreation and amusement for the inhabitants of the said Town of Mitchell for ever and to be called and known as the Matheson Park: Provided that if the said corporation neglects or refuses to keep the same and the fences surrounding it in proper order and repair and as a public park should be kept I hereby in that event cancel the said gift and direct that the said lands shall revert to and form part of my estate."

It is to be observed that the devise is to "the Corporation of the Town of Mitchell," and the habendum "to the said Corporation of Mitchell and its successors in office for ever". According to the authorities, the proviso is an express common law condition subsequent, and is obnoxious to the rule against perpetuities, and consequently void. If the land had been granted to the town corporation so long as it should be used and maintained and kept in proper order and repair and as a public park should be kept, the result might have been different, but it has been granted for ever, and the proviso is wholly inoperative for the reason above stated.

The case is practically on all fours with *Re St. Patrick's Market* (1909), 1 O.W.N. 92; and the conclusion above stated is supported by *In re Trustees of Hollis' Hospital and Hague's Contract*, [1899] 2 Ch. 540; *In re Ashforth*, [1905] 1 Ch. 535; *In re Da Costa*, [1912] 1 Ch. 337; Halsbury's Laws of England, vol. 22, p. 315.

I am consequently of opinion that the appeal should be dismissed, but under the circumstances without costs.

MAGEE, J. A., and LATCHFORD, J., agreed with MACLAREN, J. A.

MASTEN, J.: I agree in the result at which the other members of the Court have arrived, but desire to add a word explaining the views which I entertain.

I have had an opportunity of perusing the judgment prepared by my brother Maclaren and agree entirely with his view that this is not a proper case for a mandatory order and with the grounds stated by him for so holding.

In regard to the alternative claim of the plaintiff seeking a declaration that the property in question has reverted to the testator's estate, and the holding of the trial Judge that the right of the plaintiff to declare a forfeiture is barred by the Statute of Limitations, the impression created on my mind at the argument and by a perusal of the evidence was that grounds of forfeiture for breaches of the condition arose from an early period, but that these were from time to time waived by the action of the plaintiff in demanding that the condition be fulfilled and by his acquiescence in the partial fulfilment of the same at his request, so that the statute did not begin to run until very recently. However, after further consideration of the matter, the course of events appears so confused and obfuscated, and the conclusion to be drawn from all the evidence so doubtful and dependent to so great an extent on the manner in which the evidence was given in the witness-box, that I find myself unable to reverse the finding of the trial Judge in this respect, and consequently agree with his holding that the right of forfeiture is barred, and that the plaintiff's claim on this branch of the case fails. This suffices to dispose of this appeal.

In regard to the last point discussed in the judgment of my brother Maclaren, viz., that the proviso in the will is an express common law condition subsequent to and limiting an estate in fee simple, and that it is obnoxious to the rule against perpetuities, and void, I prefer to express no opinion. I find the point exceedingly difficult: see *In re Randell* (1888), 38 Ch. D. 213, at p. 218; and, as it is not necessary to the disposition of this appeal, I prefer to reserve any expression of opinion until the point necessarily arises.

Appeal dismissed.

[In *Fitzmaurice* v. *Board of School Trustees of Township of Monk*, [1950] 1 D.L.R. 239, [1949] O.W.N. 786, land was granted in 1910 to defendant "to have and to hold... for their sole and only use forever subject... to the said land reverting to [the grantor] should the said land not be required or used for public school purposes". A school was built on the land and used until 1945 when it was temporarily closed. Plaintiff, son of the grantor and beneficiary under his will, sued for a reconveyance of the land. Should he succeed?]

[On the validity of conditions, generally, see *Cheshire*, Modern Law of Real Property (1962, 9th ed.), pp. 285-292.]

[Restrictive covenants no less than conditions may be void for uncertainty: see *Noble and Wolf* v. *Alley*, [1951] S.C.R. 64, [1951] 1 D.L.R. 321; *cf. Clayton* v. *Ramsden*, [1943] A.C. 320.]

"*Reverter*" *on Dissolution of a Corporation*

RE STOWELL-MACGREGOR CORP. AND JOHN MACGREGOR CORP. New Brunswick Chancery Division. [1942] 4 D.L.R. 120, 16 M.P.R. 343

Application to determine rights to realty vested in a corporation which had been dissolved and petition for appointment of a trustee.

BAXTER C. J.: Prior to June 28, 1932, there existed two companies incorporated under the laws of the State of Maine. One was called the "John MacGregor Corporation" which was seized in fee simple of numerous parcels of wild land situate in the Counties of Madawaska, York, Sunbury, Queen's, King's and Charlotte in this Province. All of these lands had been purchased for valuable consideration from the grantors. The other company, similarly incorporated was the "N.S. Stowell & Company, Incorporated". On the date mentioned these companies entered into what is termed under the laws of the State of Maine, an agreement of consolidation. Section 63 of the Revised Statutes of Maine, 1930, c. 56, enacts that any two or more corporations organized under the provisions of that chapter or existing under the laws of the State, may consolidate into a single corporation which may be any one of the said corporations or a new corporation organized under the laws of the State to be formed by means of such consolidation, by entering into an agreement duly authorized by a majority of the directors of the respective corporations and signed by the duly authorized officers and under the respective seals of said corporations prescribing the terms and conditions of the consolidation, the mode of carrying the same into effect, whether or not the consolidated corporation shall be one of the constituent corporations or a new corporation created by such consolidation, etc., etc. Provision is made for the execution of such agreement. Subsection (7) provides that when said agreement is so signed, acknowledged, adopted, recorded and filed *the separate existence of all of the constituent corporations*, or all of such constituent corporations except the one into which such constituent corporations shall have been consolidated *shall cease*, and *the constituent corporation*, whether consolidated into a new corporation or merged into one of such constituent corporations, as the case may be, *shall become the consolidated corporation by the name provided in said agreement*, possessing all the rights, privileges, powers, franchises and immunities as well of a public nature, and being subject to all the liabilities, restrictions and duties of each of such corporations so consolidated and all and singular the rights, privileges, powers, franchises, and immunities of each of said corporations, and all property, real, personal and mixed, wheresoever located, and all debts due to any of the said constituent corporations on whatever account, and all other things in action of or belonging to each of said corporations, shall be vested in the consolidated corporation; and all property, rights, privileges, powers, franchises and immunities, and all and every other interest shall be thereafter as effectually the property of the consolidated corporation as they were of the several and respective constituent corporations, and the title to any real estate whether by deed or otherwise, under the laws of this state, vested in any of such constituent corporations, shall not revert or be in any way impaired by reason thereof, provided, that all rights of creditors and all liens upon the property of any of said constituent corporations shall be preserved unimpaired, limited to the property affected by such liens at the time of the consolidation, and all debts, liabilities and duties of the respective constituent corporations shall thenceforth attach to said consolidated corporation and may be enforced against it to the same extent as if said debts, liabilities and duties had been incurred or contracted by it.

By an agreement of consolidation dated June 28, 1932, these companies were consolidated into a single corporation under the name of "Stowell-MacGregor Corporation" which was declared to be a new corporation.

The agreement continues:

"All and singular the rights, privileges, powers, franchises and immunities of each of the said Constituent Companies, and all property, real, personal and mixed, and all debts due to either of the said Constituent Companies on whatever account, and all other things in action of or belonging to each of said companies, shall be vested in the Consolidated Corporation; and all property, rights, privileges, powers, franchises and immunities, and all and every other interest shall be as effectually the property of the Consolidated Corporation as they were of the respective Constituent Companies, and the title to any real estate, whether by deed or otherwise, under the laws of the State of Maine, vested in either of said Constituent

Companies, shall not revert or be in any way impaired by reason of this consolidation; provided, that all rights of creditors and all liens upon the property of the respective Constituent Companies shall be preserved unimpaired, limited to the property affected by such liens at the time of such consolidation, and all debts, liabilities and duties of the respective Constituent Companies shall attach to the Consolidated Corporation and may be enforced against it to the same extent as if said debts, liabilities and duties had been incurred or contracted by it."

The objects and purposes of the consolidated corporations were declared by the agreement to be the same as those set forth in the respective certificates of organization of the constituent companies.

It was further agreed that:

"Each of the Constituent Companies shall take all such further steps, do and perform all such further acts, and make, execute, acknowledge and deliver all such deeds, bills of sale, assignments and other documents of title and transfer as may be necessary or proper to effectually vest title to all of the property, real, personal and mixed, of said Companies in the Consolidated Corporation, and otherwise carry out the purposes of this agreement."

In order to have its rights determined in respect of the real estate in this Province acquired by the John MacGregor Corporation, the new corporation applied for an originating summons and also petitioned under the Trustee Act, R.S.N.B. 1927, c. 175.

There seemed to be some difficulty in ascertaining the parties who should be served. But for some cases to which I shall refer there appeared to be no reason for bringing the former owners or their heirs before the Court. Yet as late as 1845 in *Mayor etc., of Colchester* v. *Brooke*, 7 Q.B. 339 at p. 384, 115 E.R. 518, Lord Denman C. J. delivering the judgment of the Court said: "in the case of mere dissolution, as by the death of all the members, the real property of a corporation does not escheat to the Crown, but reverts to the donor or his heir." In that case it was held that there had been no actual dissolution so it was unnecessary to apply this dictum. There appears also in 8 Hals. (1st ed.), p. 373, para. 825, "And in every case where lands are granted, whether in fee or any less estate, to a corporation, there is an implied condition that if the corporation is dissolved the lands will thereupon revert to the grantor." Citing 1 Bl. Com. 484 and Co. Litt. 13b.

In *Hastings Corp.* v. *Letton* (1907), 77 L.J.K.B. 149, it was held that a term of years vested in a limited company came to an end upon the dissolution of the company. By the *Companies Act* of 1862 [(Imp.), c. 89] the company, in liquidation, was deemed to be dissolved. Darling J. held that the term reverted to the grantors and was merged in the reversion. Phillimore J. did not think that there could be a lease without a leaseholder. He pointed out that if the lease remained in existence after the dissolution of the corporation there ought not to have been a dissolution at all. He said (pp. 151-2):

"There is no authority that leasehold estates as such vest in the Crown. But what does happen in such a case to estates and interests in land? Corporations may often receive grants not merely of estates in fee simple, but of long leases. What is to happen in such cases? The law considers them as being grants by which the freeholder carves some interest out of his estate. Then *Blackstone* says in these cases the property in the land is held to have been given by the grantor on the implied condition that the corporation is to hold it as long as it remains a corporation. Corporations are supposed to be created for beneficial purposes, and the land is given to them for such purposes. When they cease to exist, the public spirit of the landowner is rewarded by the property coming back to him. I do not see why there should be any difference between a life estate, a freehold, or a term of years. In any case, I think that land given to a corporation for a particular purpose would revert to the landlord. It may be put in another way. The property is given to the corporation for a term of years if they are there to enjoy it. If the corporation ceases, the reversion is accelerated and the grantor comes into possession so much the sooner. On these grounds I am of opinion that this lease ceased to exist when the lessee ceased to exist."

The lease, in this case, was made to a limited company which was wound up and under the provisions of the *Companies Act* ceased to exist. It is difficult to conceive that this lease was other than a commercial transaction. How, then, could there be any public spirit to be rewarded? It may be that as the freehold has never passed out of the lessor there is no one in existence to dispute his entry upon the land.

The John MacGregor Corporation in the present case did not take an estate for the life of the corporation. If it had alienated its lands, its after dissolution would not destroy the estate. That a corporation takes in fee simple was decided in *March* v. *Newman*, Popham, 163, 79 E.R. 1261. Upon its dissolution therefore it would seem from *Letton's* case (*supra*) that the grantor or his heirs would take the real estate which he had sold to the corporation—a clear case of eating his cake and having it as well. Can this be so? The scant authorities on the subject all go back to Co. Litt. 13b which I reproduce *in extenso* from the edition of 1670:

"And it is to be well observed that our author saith *sil ad nascun heire etc. la terre eschoetra.* In which words is implied a diversity (as to the escheate) between fee simple absolute, which a natural body hath, and fee simple absolute which a body politique or incorporate hath. For if Land holden of I.S. *be given* to an Abbott and his successors: In this case if the Abbott and all the convent die so that the body politick is dissolved, the *Donor* shall have again this land and not the Lord by escheat. And so if land be *given* in fee simple to a Dean and Chapter, or to a Maior and Commonalty, and to their successors and after such body politick or incorporate is dissolved, the *donor* shall have again the land, and not the Lord by escheat. And the reason and the cause of this diversity is, for that in the case of a body politick or incorporate the fee simple is vested in their politick or incorporate capacity created by the policy of man and therefore the law doth annex a condition in law to every such *gift and grant*, that if such body politick or incorporate be dissolved, that the *Donor or grantor* shall re-enter, for that the *cause of the gift or grant faileth*, but no such condition is annexed to the estate in fee simple vested in any man in his natural capacity, but in case where the *Donor or Feoffor* reserveth to him a tenure and then the law doth imply a condition in law by way of escheat." (The italics are mine.)

Surely the author is referring to voluntary donations made by deed of gift or in case of incorporeal hereditaments by grant. Such would naturally be made for religious purposes or possibly to a "Maior and Commonalty". To such bodies would be applicable the failure of "the cause of the gift or grant" but not to a commercial body, utterly unknown to the law of that time and which would obtain its holdings by bargain and sale rather than by gift or feoffment. It may be noted that Coke speaks only of the "donor" or "grantor" as having the right of re-entry and does not mention "his heirs". These words were introduced by Blackstone and repeated by Lord Denman. Assuming that Coke intended to include the heirs of the donor, there might have been little difficulty while the law of primogeniture obtained in ascertaining in whom the right of re-entry was vested but under our modern conditions by which an intestate succession goes to all the children of the intestate and the ability to dispose of the right of re-entry by will exists, in many cases it would be well nigh impossible to ascertain the persons to whom the summons in this case should go. Phillimore J. seems to have appreciated the reasons underlying the rule given by Coke but I am not clear that he has adequately applied them. It seemed to me that I should order public advertisement in the Royal Gazette so that if any one desired to raise the question of the original grantor's right or that of his representatives they might have an opportunity of doing so. No one has come forward and I shall take the risk of deciding that if there is an escheat in the present case it is to the Crown and not to the grantor who bargained and sold the lands to the Company. In *Re Woking Urban Council (Basingstoke Canal) Act*, (1913), 83 L.J. Ch. 201, the Court of

Appeal assumes that the contrary opinion is the law but the point does not seem to have been argued by counsel and the lapse of time rendered it unnecessary to decide it. I cannot, with all respect, agree with the judgment of Proudfoot, V.C. in *Lindsay Petroleum Co.* v. *Pardee* (1875), 22 Gr. 18. In the present case it would be a mere matter of form to obtain a release from the Crown to the new company.

But it does not follow that there has been an escheat. The alienation of all its lands and possessions does not extinguish a corporation: *Anon.*, Bro. N.C. 82, 73 E.R. 883. A corporation, under a new charter, could exercise powers which the same body at common law could exercise even though such powers were not mentioned in the new charter: *Haddock's Case*, Raym. T. 435 at p. 439, 83 E.R. 227. Acceptance of a new charter does not destroy the old corporation: *Mayor and Commonalty of Colchester* v. *Seaber*, 3 Burr. 1866, 97 E.R. 1140. See also *Luttrel's Case*, 4 Co. 86a at p. 87b, 76 E.R. 1065.

Then we have *per Lord Kenyon* C. J., in *The King* v. *Pasmore*, 3 T.R. 199 at p. 241, 100 E.R. 531:

"The several inconveniences, which have been pointed out, namely, that the corporation lands would revert to the donor, by which the means of carrying into execution public and charitable trusts would be defeated, and that various privileges would be destroyed, would, if true, have considerable weight.... But if the King choose that all their rights shall be revived, it is competent to him to do so, either with the old or new corporators; and thereby no person is injured, nor is any rule of law infringed. And by the new charter the King did not consider the old corporation as dissolved to all purposes; but he granted those rights to a new set of men, and superadded such other powers as he deemed necessary."

And by the same Judge in *The King* v. *Knight*, 4 T.R. 419, at p. 430, 100 E.R. 1096:

"The new modification of the common council cannot make any difference; because, as the whole corporation accepted this charter, they assented to it; and by that acceptance the same powers which were exercised by the old body... are now vested in the new body."

In *Re Higginson & Dean, Ex p. Attorney-General* (1898), 68 L.J.Q.B. 198 at p. 202, Wright J. for the Court, referring to the old authorities as to the effect of dissolution of municipal or other companies, says: "I cannot find that in any case the rights or obligations of a corporation were held to be affected by a technical dissolution. Nor, on the other hand, can I find a case in which such a question has been decided where the corporation had not been revived or some provision made by statute or charter with reference to its obligations."

He also cites *Mumma* v. *Potomac Co.* (1834), 8 Peters (U.S.) 281, a case of dissolution of an insolvent incorporated company under a statute of a State Legislature in which Story J. said (p. 285): "The obligations of those contracts survive; and the creditors may enforce their claims against any property belonging to the corporation, which has not passed into the hands of bona fide purchasers; but is still held in trust for the company or for the stockholders thereof, at the time of its dissolution, in any mode permitted by the local laws."

There can be no difference between the charters which proceed from the King and those which emanate from a State so far as the questions which arise here are concerned. It seems to me that the MacGregor Corporation still lives though under another name and that if there is any apparent dissolution it is only as Wright J. suggests, a technical one, and I so decide.

Let us assume, however, that the John MacGregor Corporation has been dissolved. At the time of its dissolution it held certain lands which had been purchased by it and which it had agreed to convey to the new corporation. Are these to revert to any grantor? In *Lindsay Petroleum* v. *Pardee (supra)*, Proudfoot V.C. could find no English case to support the doctrine of Chancellor Kent that "'The received doctrine now is, ... that the capital and debts of banking and other moneyed corporations constitute a trust fund for the payment of creditors and stockholders.'" (22 Gr. at p. 21.) Since that time the English Courts have applied the notion of a trust to precisely this class of matters and Mr. Dougherty has referred me to the following cases which are emphatically in point: *Re General Accident Ass'ce Corp. Ltd.*, 73 L.J. Ch. 84, [1904] 1 Ch. 147; *Re No. 9 Bomore Road*, 75 L.J. Ch. 157, [1906] 1 Ch. 359; *Re Albert Road, Norwood*, 85 L.J. Ch. 187, [1916] 1 Ch. 289, in which *Hastings Corp.* v. *Letton*, 77 L.J.K.B. 149, [1908] 1 K.B. 378, and the *Woking Case*, 83 L.J. Ch. 201, [1914] 1 Ch. 300, were considered; and *Re Crichton Ltd.*, [1932] W.N. 208. From the *Bomore Road* case (*supra*) it is apparent that it is not necessary to serve any person who might be a claimant under the reverter theory. The U.S. view as expounded in *Mumma* v. *Potomac Co.*, 8 Peters (U.S.) 281, by Mr. Justice Story is now in practice acted upon by the English Courts.

The *Trustee Act*, R.S.N.B. 1927, c. 175, s. 35, applies when it is found inexpedient, difficult or impracticable to appoint a new trustee without the assistance of the Court. In the present case it is impossible to do so. The MacGregor Corporation by the agreement of consolidation declared a trust, including all real estate, in favour of the new corporation. There is no one now empowered to affix the seal of the John MacGregor Corporation to a deed. The trust has been declared and is evident. In such case the Court is empowered to make an order for the appointment of a new trustee. I think without the amendment made at the recent session of the Legislature that the language of the section is wide enough to cover the present case.

I hold, therefore, that there has been no reverter to the grantors of the company's lands; that there has only been a change of name and not an actual dissolution of the John MacGregor Corporation; that all its rights and titles have passed to the new corporation and that in so far as they have not been formally conveyed to the new corporation that its real estate is subject to a trust in favour of the Stowell-MacGregor Corporation; that the John MacGregor Corporation is not at present capable of acting as a trustee, there being no one in a position to execute the necessary documents and that the assistance of the Court is necessary for the appointment of a new trustee. I, therefore, appoint William J. West of the City of Fredericton, barrister-at-law to be and act as a trustee in the place and stead of the John MacGregor Corporation and order that the lands in the Counties of Madawaska, York, Sunbury, Queen's, King's and Charlotte now held in the name of that corporation be vested in the said trustee upon trust to convey the same to the Stowell-MacGregor Corporation.

Application granted.

[An Editorial Note to this case in [1942] 4 D.L.R. 120, reads as follows: "A similar point arose in *Re Canadian Fertilizer Co. & Canadian Industries Ltd.* [1938], 3 D.L.R. 765, O.W.N. 335, which was not cited by the Court. Roach J. held, following *Robinson v. Moffatt* (C.A.), 31 D.L.R. 490, 37 O.L.R. 52, that when a provincial company, which had agreed to sell its assets to a Dominion company, surrendered its charter without executing a conveyance of lands to the Dominion company, the provincial company held title as a bare trustee for the Dominion company. It would seem that in light of the sections of the Ontario Trustee Act cited, all that was required was the appointment of a trustee to make the conveyance in place of one who had ceased to exist. While this in effect was done, even as in the present case, Roach J. stated that the legal title passed by reverter to the grantor of the land who had sold to the dissolved company, following *Lindsay Petroleum Co.* v. *Pardee*, *supra.* As he later stated it was unnecessary to serve such grantor with notice of the motion, it is difficult to understand why he was mentioned at all. The reasoning of Baxter C. J. against any reverter to the grantor, (even where no trust is involved) has the support of the American authorities, and the error of Coke's statement is exhaustively dealt with in *Gray*, Rule Against Perpetuities, 4th ed., pp. 49-55, where it is pointed out that while the doctrine of reverter or escheat to the donor or grantor to a corporation on its dissolution has been frequently referred to as law (see *Hastings Corp.* v. *Letton*, *supra; Re Woking Urban Council (Basingstoke Canal) Act*, [1914] 1 Ch. 300; *Cheshire*, Modern Real Property, 3rd ed., p. 467) it is not supported by the

English decisions. See Lawrence L. J. in *Re Wells*, [1933] Ch. 29 at p. 54 who supports Gray's view. The judgment of Baxter C. J. is valuable in its refusal to be misled by *Lindsay Petroleum Co.* v. *Pardee* and the passage from Coke. Some of the English cases cited by Roach J. in the Ontario decision, as indicating that the grantor of land to a company which is dissolved has an interest in the property, involved leasehold interests, in which the issue was different, since if a lease is determined by dissolution the title to the reversion is still in the grantor: not so in case of a fee. Unfortunately some English cases dealing with leases, e.g., *Hastings Corp.* v. *Letton, supra*, quote Coke's passage with approval—which has not made for clarity. Even as to leases, however, see Lawrence L. J. in *Re Wells, supra.*" See also *Re Strathblaine Estates Ltd.*, [1948] Ch. 228, [1948] 1 All E.R. 162. *Cf. Hughes*, Reverter to Donor of Legal Fee Vested in Dissolved Corporation, (1935) 51 Law Q. Rev. 347; Reply, *Farrer*, (1935) 51 Law Q. Rev. 361; 1 *Simes and Smith*, Law of Future Interests (1956, 2nd ed.), s. 291.]

[In Ontario, the Corporations Act, R.S.O. 1960, c. 71, provides by s. 330 that "any real or personal property of a corporation that has not been disposed of at the date of dissolution is forfeit to the Crown". See also, Companies Act, R.S.M. 1954, c. 43, s. 330; Dissolved Corporations' Property Act, R.S.N.S. 1954, c. 72; Property of Dissolved Corporations Vesting Act, R.S.Nfld. 1952, c. 169.

For similar provisions, see Companies Act, 1948 (Imp.), c. 38, ss. 354, 355. *Cf.* Law of Property Act, 1925 (Imp.), c. 20, ss. 7 (2), 181.]

Remainders

"ALL FUTURE INTERESTS which are created in someone other than the grantor or his successors are either remainders or executory interests" (1 *Simes and Smith*, Law of Future Interests (1956, 2nd ed.), p. 79). The common law recognition of the remainder as a future interest which could be created in a third person was bound up in a number of requirements for its validity which may be summarized as follows:

1. Remainders are interests in freehold estates and must be supported (i.e. preceded) by either a life estate or a fee tail, for two reasons: first, because there must be a present livery of seisin to someone before a remainder may be limited in the same instrument; and secondly, there can be no remainder after a present estate in fee simple.

2. Unless it is capable of taking effect as a possessory interest on the termination of its supporting or preceding estate (and without at the same time cutting short that estate), the future interest is not a remainder but rather an executory interest. If it is capable of so taking effect, it will fail at common law if it does not "vest" at or before the termination of the supporting estate. This aspect of "destructibility" related, and still relates, to contingent remainders. It is a different thing from the mere acceleration of interests, e.g., by the disappearance of intermediate life estates or even a fee tail (through death) under an instrument which ends with an ultimate remainder in fee simple: for example, A grants to B for life, to C for life, to D for life, to E in fee tail and then to F in fee simple. D dies during the lives of B and C, and E dies without any issue during the life of C but after the death of B.

3. The common law did not recognize remainders in a grantor or his heirs (using this word in its technical meaning), and they took by descent and not as purchasers because in this way tenurial incidents consequent upon descent remained enforceable. This position also obtained in respect of equitable interests.

[See *Warren*, A Remainder to the Grantor's Heirs, (1943) 22 Tex. L. Rev. 22.

The result of the rule was to leave the grantor with a reversion. The rule is allied to another doctrine often referred to as the "worthier" title doctrine which applies to wills giving a devisee a freehold estate of the same quality and quantity which would have devolved upon him upon the testator's intestacy. Again because of the store placed on feudal incidents on descent, the title by descent was preferred to the title under the devise, and the devisee took under the former.

Both rules were abolished in England by the Inheritance Act, 1833 (Imp.), c. 106, s. 3, thus allowing the "heirs" in the one case and the person who turned out to be the "heir" (if the technical designation "heirs" was not used) in the second case, to take as purchaser and devisee respectively; and see now Law of Property Act, 1925 (Imp.), c. 20, s. 132.

The English provision of 1833 was adopted in Upper Canada by s. 2 of the Real Property Act, 1834, c. 1, and was carried down to s. 26 of the Devolution of Estates Act, R.S.O. 1897, c. 127. A new Devolution of Estates Act, 1910 (Ont.), c. 56 replaced the former one, and by s. 35 repealed it save for ss. 22—58. Of the preserved sections, only ss. 25 to 27 are of any particular value today. They are still in force although not introduced into succeeding statute revisions.]

Remainder interests were given protection through the writ of formedon in the remainder but for a long time only *vested* remainders were recognized, i.e. interests which were present estates although enjoyment was postponed. Vested remainders could be made determinable or given on condition subsequent. Contingent remainders developed in the fifteenth century, first under defined contingencies, and ultimately (subject to the rule against remainders to the grantor's heirs), free range was given to the contingencies with which they could be associated. This development was undoubtedly helped by the development of uses in Chancery and by the Statute of Uses, 1536. Vested and contingent remainders are distinguishable according to whether the remainder (1) is or is not in favour of a living, ascertained person and (2) is or is not subject to any condition precedent. (The ordinary termination of a supporting estate according to the nature of the limitation does not, of course, raise any issue of condition precedent.) Considerations of seisin, i.e., that there must be someone available at any time to hold the seisin of a freehold, meant that there was always a vested reversion in fee simple where a contingent remainder in fee simple was limited (and was subject to be defeated on the vesting of the remainder); and, more importantly, a contingent remainder was irretrievably destroyed if the contingency or contingencies involved did not occur at or before the termination of the supporting estate so as to enable seisin to pass to the remainderman. This involved a "wait and see" attitude to the vesting of contingent remainders. Recall too that it was necessary not only that the remainder actually vest as indicated but that the interest to be a remainder be limited so as to be capable of so vesting.

In *Reeve* v. *Long* (1694), 3 Lev. 408, 1 Salk. 227, 83 E.R. 754, 91 E.R. 202 (H.L.), land was devised to A for life remainder to A's eldest son in fee tail. A died childless but a son was born posthumously. Does he take? The answer in the House of Lords was "yes" because it was a devise which should not be construed in strict common law terms. Legislation was subsequently enacted (10 Will. III, c. 22 (1698)) enabling posthumous children to take even under an *inter vivos* settlement. The legislation was adopted in Ontario and is now s. 46 of the Conveyancing and Law of Property Act, R.S.O. 1960, c. 66.

[Consider the following limitations:

(1) A devises to B for life remainder to A's eldest son.
(2) A grants to B for life, remainder to C for life, remainder to the heirs of A.
(3) A grants to B for life or until remarriage and on such remarriage to C.
(4) A grants to B for life until C marries, and on such marriage to D.
(5) A grants to B for life remainder to C for life and if C outlives B then to D.

(6) A grants to B for 80 years if C should so long live and on C's death to D.
(7) A grants to B for life remainder to C if B dies without children him surviving, and if not then to D.
(8) A grants to B for life and if C survives D remainder to C and his heirs and if not remainder to D and his heirs.
(9) A grants to B for life remainder to the children of C.
(10) A grants to B for life remainder to C for life on reaching age 21 remainder to D's eldest son.
(11) A devises to B for life remainder to C and his heirs, but if C dies without children him surviving then to D and his heirs.

How do limitations nos. 7 and 11 differ?

What is the effect on limitation no. 9 where some of C's children are born in B's lifetime and some after B's death? If the limitation were to B for life remainder to the children of C who reach age 21, would it make any difference whether children born before B's death reached age 21 after his death? See *Festing* v. *Allen* (1843), 12 M. & W. 279, 152 E.R. 1204 (Ex.).

In connection with limitation no. 3, see *Re McLean* (1956), 6 D.L.R. 2d 519 (Ont. C.A.) which arose out of a devise of realty "to my wife so long as she remains my widow or at her death but should she again marry then the property shall be divided equally among my sisters' children". The widow died without remarrying. Did the devise give her (1) a life estate or a fee simple? (2) If a life estate determinable on death or remarriage, was the interest over to the sisters' children a vested or a contingent remainder? See *Luxford* v. *Cheeke* (1683), 3 Lev. 125, 83 E.R. 611 (K.B.).

In limitation no. 6 is D's interest vested or not? See *Fearne*, Essay on Contingent Remainders (1824, 8th ed.), p. 21.]

[In *Egerton* v. *Massey* (1857), 3 C.B.N.S. 338, 140 E.R. 771 (C.P.), land was devised to B for life, remainder to the children of B or their issue, living at B's death, and, in default of such children or issue, to C in fee simple. The residue of the estate was left to B who never married and who conveyed all her interest in the land to D. After B's death the question was raised whether C's interest took effect. It was held that it was destroyed by B's conveyance. This could only be so if D obtained a fee simple under the conveyance. How did this occur? What was B's residuary interest, a reversion or a remainder in fee simple? While there may be a reversion subject to a contingent remainder in fee simple, is it possible to have a vested remainder after a contingent remainder in fee simple? Did the devise create alternative contingent remainders one of which was in C or did C get an executory interest? For explanations of the case see *Gray*, Rule against Perpetuities (1942, 4th ed.), s. 113.1; *1 Simes and Smith*, Law of Future Interests (1956, 2nd ed.), s. 145; *Casner and Leach*, Cases and Text on Property, p. 355n.]

At common law, destructibility of contingent remainders (illustrated in *Egerton* v. *Massey*, *supra*) could be accomplished artificially as well as by the failure of the remainder to vest in the ordinary course of events. (Once vested, a remainder in fee simple passed, of course, to the remainderman's heirs or devisees even though he himself died before expiration of the supporting estate.) Artificial destruction of the supporting estate (usually a life estate) could be accomplished by (1) forfeiture; or (2) merger by surrender or release, and remainders which were then still contingent fell with it. The following is a short explanation of how this came about:

(1) Forfeiture

The denial of the life tenant's feudal tie to his overlord, as by making a tortious feoffment in fee simple, gave rise to a forfeiture entitling the next vested estate holder to possession; this was usually the holder of the reversion where there was a contingent remainder in fee simple. See *Archer's Case* (1597), 1 Co. Rep. 66b, 76 E.R. 146 (Q.B.).

(This case suggested another point, not now of any importance. Suppose the supporting life tenant was disseised before the contingent remainder vested. He had a right of entry which would still support the contingent remainder but if the disseisor died and his heirs held the land for five years the right of entry (tolled by descent cast) became a right of action which would not support a contingent remainder. The Real Property Limitation Act, 1833 (Imp.), c. 27, abolished the distinction between rights of action and of entry and preserved rights of entry despite a disseisor's death. See Limitations Act, R.S.O. 1960, c. 214, s. 10.)

(2) Merger by Surrender or Release

If the supporting estate and the next vested estate came into the hands of the same person, any contingent remainders were destroyed by the disappearance of the supporting estate. Thus, if A grants to B for life, remainder to C on reaching age 21 and B surrenders to A (the reversioner) before C attains the required age, C's interest is defeated. Similarly, if A grants to B for life, remainder to C in fee tail on attaining age 21, remainder to D in fee simple, and D releases to B before C reaches age 21, C's interest is defeated. See *Purefoy* v. *Rogers* (1671), 2 Wms. Saund. 380, 85 E.R. 1181 (K.B.); *Thompson* v. *Leach* (1698), 2 Ventr. 198, 86 E.R. 391 (K.B.).

There were two exceptions to the merger doctrine: (1) there is no merger of a fee tail in a fee simple. Of course, the tenant in tail might suffer a common recovery or disentail by any other available method but if not, a person to whom a fee tail and a remainder in fee simple in the same land were conveyed held these interests separately to preserve the rights of issue in a fee tail; (2) the second exception arose in a case such as this: A devises to his eldest son for life remainder to C in fee simple on attaining age 21. If A's eldest son is also A's heir he would have simultaneously the life estate and reversion in the land as the next vested estate, and merger would destroy C's interest. This was not permitted. Similarly, if today A granted to himself for life remainder to B in fee simple on reaching age 21. However, if the holder of the two interests conveyed them to a third person, the contingent remainder if it had not previously vested was destroyed. (Note: the merger doctrine should not be confused with the Rule in Shelley's Case considered *infra*.)

To avoid artificial destruction of contingent remainders, conveyancers developed the device known as "trustees to preserve contingent remainders" which in simple form involved this type of limitation: A grants to B for life and on the determination of B's estate by forfeiture or merger or otherwise in B's lifetime then to trustees during the life of B, in trust for C and to preserve contingent remainders, remainder in trust for C on reaching age 21. The vital issue in this device was whether the remainder to the trustees was vested; if not, B could destroy it. It was held in *Smith* v. *Packhurst* (1741-2), 3 Atk. 135, 26 E.R. 881 (H.L.), (see also *Willes* 327, 125 E.R. 1197) that it was vested. Of course, if the trustees tried to destroy contingent remainders by artificially terminating their estate they would be liable for breach of trust, and purchasers with notice would in any event be bound.

This device became unnecessary when statutory relief was provided against artificial destruction of contingent remainders by the Real Property Act, 1845 (Imp.), c. 106, s. 8. This provision is in force in Ontario as s. 36 of the Conveyancing and Law of Property Act, R.S.O. 1960, c. 66, reading as follows: "Every contingent remainder is capable of taking effect notwithstanding the determination by forfeiture, surrender or merger of any preceding estate of freehold." (For similar legislation see Property Act, R.S.N.B. 1952, c. 177, s. 8.)

England went further with a Contingent Remainders Act, 1877 (Imp.), c. 33 which apparently purported to deal with (1) the situation left after the 1845 Act which was that thenceforward a contingent remainder would fail only if it failed to vest at or before the termination of the supporting estate; and (2) the situation created by what is known as the *Rule in Purefoy* v. *Rogers* (1671) 2 Wms. Saund. 380, 85 E.R. 1181 (K.B.). The English Act is substantially reproduced in s. 11 of the Real Property Act, R.S.P.E.I. 1951, c. 138, which reads as follows: "Every Contingent Remainder created by an Instrument executed after the second day of October, 1939, or by any will or codicil revived or republished by any will or codicil executed after that date in tenements or hereditaments of any tenure, which would have been valid as a springing or shifting use or executory devise or other limitation had it not had a sufficient estate to support it as a Contingent Remainder, in the event of the particular estate determining before the Contingent Remainder vests, shall be, and if created before the second day of October, 1939, shall be deemed to have been, capable of taking effect in all respects as if the Contingent Remainder had originally been created as a springing or shifting use or executory devise or other executory limitation." It is curious that while Ontario has the 1845 English provision on contingent remainders but not the 1877 one, Prince Edward Island has the latter but not the former.

It could be regarded as doubtful whether the 1877 Act really covered situation (1) abovementioned (see *Megarry*, Manual of Law of Real Property (1955, 2nd ed.), pp. 137-139; but see *Cheshire*, Modern Law of Real Property (1962, 9th ed.), p. 228; 1 *Simes and Smith*, Law of Future Interests (1956, 2nd ed.), p. 207). The fact that it followed closely upon *Cunliffe* v. *Brancker* (1876), 3 Ch. D. 393 (C.A.) where a contingent remainder under a devise failed because it did not vest at or before the termination of the preceding life estate may support Cheshire's confident view that the 1877 Act was designed to cure this remaining aspect of destructibility, especially so in view of the severe criticism heaped by the Court upon the state of the law.

Situation (2) is more clearly covered by the 1877 Act. The *Rule* in *Purefoy* v. *Rogers* was a rule of law applicable to ordinary grants *inter vivos*, to legal interests under the Statute of Uses and to devises (but not to equitable interests) which was expressed as follows by Lord Hale: "Where a contingency is limited to depend on an estate of freehold which is capable of supporting a remainder, it shall never be construed to be an executory devise [interest] but a contingent remainder only and not otherwise". Since executory interests were (before the development of the rule against perpetuities) indestructible, the possibility that every contingent remainder (at least those under an executed use or a will) would be construed as an executory interest was not favourably regarded by the common law lawyers. In the result, *Purefoy* v. *Rogers* required that a future interest which at the time of its creation could take effect as a contingent remainder should be so considered and not be construed in the light of subsequent events as an executory interest. The following limitations illustrate the problem:

(1) A devises to B for life remainder to the children of C who reach age 21.
(2) A devises to B for life but if B leaves Canada then to C.
(3) A devises to B for life then to C for 21 years then to C's eldest son in fee simple.
(4) A grants to B for life and two years after B's death to C in fee simple.
(5) A grants to and to the use of B for life remainder to and to the use of C's eldest son.
(6) A grants to X to the use of B for life remainder to the use of C on reaching age 21.

For a discussion of the rule in *Purefoy* v. *Rogers* see *Gray*, Rule against Perpetuities (1942, 4th ed.), appendix J.; 1 *Simes and Smith*, Law of Future Interests (1956, 2nd ed.), ss. 204-206.

[It would appear that the Contingent Remainders Act, 1877, also did away with destructibility arising from disclaimer by a life tenant of his interest whereby contingent remainders depending thereon would be defeated.]

[Suppose the limitation of an interest which is capable of taking effect as a remainder would be void if it were construed as an executory interest, e.g. because of the rule against perpetuities. Does the Act of 1877 apply or does the *Purefoy* v. *Rogers* rule still obtain? See *Megarry, op. cit.*, at p. 137.

It has been held that the rule against perpetuities applies to contingent remainders: see *In re Frost* (1889), 43 Ch. D. 246; *Re Ashforth,* [1905] 1 Ch. 535; 2 *Simes and Smith,* Law of Future Interests (1956, 2nd ed.), s. 1237.

In *Re Ashforth, supra,* a testatrix devised realty to trustees on trust to pay the rents and profits in equal shares to A, B and C and to the survivors of them for their lives and then to the ultimate survivor for life and after the death of the survivor to pay the rents and profits equally to all children of A, B and C born in the testatrix's lifetime or within 21 years after her death, and after the death of all such children except one, then to such surviving child in fee tail remainder to the right heirs of the testatrix's uncle. C survived A and B but left no children. B likewise left no children. However A did leave children who were born within the period limited by the will. In holding that the remainder in fee tail infringed the rule against perpetuities Farwell J. said, *inter alia*:

"Then it is said that this is a legal contingent remainder supported by a particular estate vested in trustees during the lives of the grandchildren and of the survivor of them, and this was not disputed. But the plaintiffs argue further that such a remainder is not affected by any doctrine of remoteness, except the rule that estates cannot be limited to unborn persons for life with remainders to the issue of such unborn persons. I might have contented myself with following Kay J.'s decision in *In re Frost*, 43 Ch. D. 246, 253; but it is said that this was only the second or alternative reason for his judgment, and I have accordingly considered the point for myself.

"It is very difficult to say when the conception of perpetuity in its modern meaning first appeared in our Courts. There is no doubt that the common law regarded all attempts to restrict the free alienation of property with extreme disfavour. As is stated in Mr. Butler's note to Coke on Littleton, 342 b, i., although the suspense or abeyance of the inheritance (as distinguished from the freehold) was allowed by the common law, it was discountenanced and discouraged as much as possible, and modern law has added her discouragement of every contrivance which tends to render property inalienable beyond the limits settled for its suspense, because it is clear that no restraint on alienation would be more effectual than a suspense of the inheritance. He adds: 'The same principles have, in some degree, given rise to the well-known rule of law, that a preceding estate of freehold is indispensably necessary for the support of a contingent remainder; and they influence, in some degree, the doctrines respecting the destruction of contingent remainders.' There was also the rule that an estate by purchase cannot be limited to the unborn child of an unborn child: *Whitby* v. *Mitchell* (1890), 44 Ch. D. 85. With all respect to Kay J., I do not think that much reliance can be placed on the existence of an independent rule of law forbidding a possibility on a possibility: see *Gray* on Perpetuities, p. 86, and *Williams* on Real Property, 6th ed. p. 245. The phrase seems due to Lord Coke's unfortunate predilection for scholastic logic, and may possibly be a pedantic and inaccurate reason for avoiding remoteness: see *Blamford* v. *Blamford* (1615), 3 Bulst. 98, 108; S.C. 1 Roll. Rep. 318, 321, cited in *Gray* at p. 86. 'Coke moves another matter in this case on Popham's opinion, Coke I., Rector de Chedington, that a possibility on a possibility is not good, for here in our case is a possibility on a possibility... yet it seems that it is good, for if Popham's opinion should be law, it would shake the common assurances of the land.... But I agree that in divers cases there shall not be a possibility upon a possibility, and he puts the diversities in *Lampet's Case* (1612), 10 Rep. 46 b, 50 b.' It seems probable that contingent remainders could not anciently have been created at all: see *Williams* on Seisin, p. 190; and that down to the time of the Commonwealth the usual mode of settlement on marriage was by giving vested estates tail to living persons, and not estates tail to unborn children: ibid. 189. Although, therefore, there was a general principle that alienation should not be restricted by the creation of estates beyond a particular estate for life with a remainder in fee, or in tail, I can find no trace of any statement of the present rule in terms in any of the old books. But the general principle was well established, and as the ingenuity of real property lawyers invented new devices for rendering land inalienable for as long a time as possible, it became necessary to mould the expression of the old law so as to meet new emergencies. Thus in *Cadell* v. *Palmer* (1833), 1 Cl. & F. 372, 36 R.R. 128, the House of Lords settled the question of the extent to which executory limitations and shifting uses, which had become possible under the Statute of Uses, could be lawfully carried, and they did this, not by creating any new law, for that would have been legislation, not decision, but by applying the old law to the new circumstances. The judges who advised the House supported their opinion by numerous authorities, and I would refer in particular to the quotation from Lord Kenyon's judgment in *Long* v. *Blackall* (1796-97), 7 T.R. 100, 102; 4 R.R. 73: 'The rules respecting executory devises have conformed to the rules laid down in the construction of legal limitations, and the Courts have said that the estate shall not be unalienable by executory devises for a longer time than is allowed by the limitations of a common law conveyance.' Here, then, is an authoritative statement in terms of precision of the rule of law which had existed for centuries, but had not been theretofore defined, and had been applied from time to time, as occasion arose, by judges who, without formulating the precise limits of the rule, held, as Lord Nottingham said in the *Duke of Norfolk's Case* (1681), 3 Ch. Cas. 14, 31: 'If it tends to a perpetuity, there needs no more to be said, for the law has so long laboured against perpetuities, that it is an undeniable reason against any settlement, if it can be proved to tend to a perpetuity.' The rule, however, was only to be applied to cases where it was really necessary in order to defeat remoteness, and, accordingly, Lord St. Leonards in *Cole* v. *Sewell*, 4 D. & War. 1; S.C. 2 H.L.C. 186, points out that it has no application to remainders limited to arise after an estate tail, because they are destructible by barring such estate tail, and are no more open to objection than the estate tail itself; and this is the meaning of the reference to destructibility in the passage that I read above from *Lewis* on Perpetuity, p. 164. But this reason has no application to contingent remainders not so limited and destructible; nor do I think that Lord St. Leonards so intended: see *Sugden's* Law of Property, pp. 116-121, and Lord Brougham's speech in the same case in the House of Lords, 2 H.L.C. at p. 234, where he puts this ground plainly as the reason for his observations. It would be very strange indeed that Lord St. Leonards should have referred to the 'sacred rule' enunciated in *Purefoy* v. *Rogers* (1669) 2 Wm. Saund. 768, 781, n. 9, that no limitation shall be construed as an executory or shifting use which can by possibility take effect by way of remainder—a rule which probably owes its origin to the chance of destruction by the failure of the particular estate incident to the one and not to the other—and should at the same time have affirmed that the rule against perpetuities had no application to such contingent remainders, although they might exceed the limits allowed for executory limitations, because they could not exceed the limits of perpetuity, for the proposition is self-contradictory.

"Assuming that the doctrine of the destructibility of contingent remainders by failure of the particular estate is due to the desire of the Courts to avoid remoteness, as Mr. Butler suggests, it does not follow that such remainders should be free from all other bonds. Liability to destruction for a particular cause at or before a given period is not incompatible with, or any ground for immunity from, destruction at the same period for a cause common to all other interests, executory, equitable, or otherwise, which may lead to remoteness. It is plain, moreover, that the Courts have acted upon the principle that the rule against perpetuities is to be applied where no other sufficient protection against remoteness is attainable. Thus, inasmuch as equitable contingent remainders never failed for want of a particular estate, it was held that the rule must apply to them. In *Abbiss* v. *Burney* (1881), 17 Ch. D. 211, the gift was to trustees on trust for A. for life, and, after his death, on trust to convey to such son of his as should first attain twenty-five. Sir George Jessel M.R. said (ibid. 230): 'Where the legal fee is outstanding in the trustees, that doctrine of contingent remainders which, until the recent statute, prevented contingent remainders from taking effect at all unless they vested at the moment of the termination of the prior estate in freehold, has no operation, and on that ground I think that this appeal should be allowed.' In *In re Trustees of Hollis' Hospital*, [1899] 2 Ch. 540, the late Mr. Justice Byrne held that the rule against perpetuity applied to a common law condition. He says (ibid. 552): 'The Courts have first to find what is the common law—that is, the principle embodied in what is called the common law—and then to apply it to new and ever varying states of fact and circumstances.... New statutes and the course of social development give rise to new aspects and conditions which have to be regarded in applying the old principles. The policy of the law against the creation of perpetuities was certainly asserted at a very early date, as was also the policy of discountenancing unrestricted restraints upon alienation.' In *Chudleigh's Case* (1589-95) 1 Rep. 120 a, (the Case of perpetuities) the Court defeated an attempt to make the Statute of Uses serve as the means of protecting contingent remainders from destruction, lest lands should remain too long in settlement. In *Abbiss* v. *Burney*, 17 Ch. D. 211, the Court of Appeal defeated an attempt made by vesting all the legal estate in the property in trustees. The present attempt is made by vesting a legal estate *pur autre vie* in trustees and limiting the contingent remainders as a legal use. In my opinion, the Court is equally bound to defeat this; nor can I find any rule of law or decision or principle to the contrary. The opinion of the late Mr. Challis (Real Property, 2nd ed. pp. 174-177) is, I think, sufficiently displaced by Byrne J.'s judgment in the *Hollis' Hospital Case*, and that of the late Mr. Joshua Williams by *Gray* on Perpetuities, pp. 283-298; and the conclusion at which I have arrived is supported by (in addition to the text-writers cited in that case and in *In re Frost*) an argument in the first edition of *Jarman* on Wills, vol. ii., p. 727, and repeated in some of the later editions, by Mr. Serjeant Stephen's note in his Commentaries, 8th ed. vol. i., p. 554, and by Mr. Gray's excellent Treatise on Perpetuities. The rule against perpetuities applies to all contingent equitable limitations of real estate and all contingent limitations of personalty, including leaseholds. It would certainly be undesirable to add another to the anomalies that adorn our law, as I should succeed in doing if I held that the rule did not apply to legal contingent remainders."]

[A first legal contingent remainder would not be destroyed by the rule against perpetuities, but why should the rule not apply to succeeding legal contingent remainders limited in the same instrument? *Cf. Farrer*, Remainder to "Survivor" of Persons for Life Only: Vested or Contingent? (1938), 2 Conv. & Prop. L. (N.S.) 307.]

WHITBY v. MITCHELL. Court of Appeal. 1890. 44 Ch. D. 85

Appeal from a judgment of Kay J., 42 Ch. D. 494.

COTTON L. J.: This is an appeal from a decision of Mr. Justice Kay declaring that certain limitations treated as introduced into an antenuptial settlement by virtue of a post-nuptial appointment under a power contained in the settlement, being limitations of legal estates, were void, not on the ground that they were void for remoteness, but that they were limitations which the law does not allow of legal estates. Now, what are these limitations? First, there is a limitation of a legal estate to an unborn child of the marriage for life, and then, after that, there is a limitation to the children of that unborn child. It is said that this latter limitation does not come within the rule against perpetuities, and that there is no other rule preventing this limitation from being good. Mr. Justice Kay has decided, and in my opinion rightly, that there is a rule in existence which does prevent the limitation from being good, namely, that you cannot have a possibility upon a possibility; or, to state the rule in a more convenient form, that you cannot have a limitation for the life of an unborn person, with a limitation after his death to his unborn children to take as purchasers. That is the same thing as what has been called "a possibility upon a possibility".

But it is said that, although there is such a rule in existence, that is superseded by the more modern rule against perpetuities. In my opinion the old rule with regard to a possibility on a possibility has not been done away with by this modern rule. It is conceded that the rule against a possibility upon a possibility existed long before the rule prohibiting the limitations of estates tending to a perpetuity existed. Can we say that the old rule has been put an end to or superseded? Mr. Joshua Williams lays it down that the rule still exists; while other text-writers say it does not exist. In this difference of opinion we must see what aid we can obtain from Judges and others in high position. First of all, we have *Butler's* note to *Fearne*—and the same thing is expressed in the works of other writers—to the effect that the rule of law against double possibilities is a rule still existing, prohibiting limitations of estates in such a way as that, although they may not offend against the rule of perpetuities, they are bad as being objectionable to the law. Then Lord Kenyon, referring to that point in *Hay* v. *Earl of Coventry*, says (3 T.R. 86): "It is not necessary for me to say what effect that would have had in the present case, if that point"—that is, whether an estate for life could be given to unborn issue—"had remained undecided; because the law is now clearly settled that an estate for life may be limited to unborn issue, provided the devisor does not go farther and give an estate in succession to the children of such unborn issue." It is said that only meant that a limitation to the children of unborn issue generally, without any limit as to the time within which such children should be born, would offend against the rule of perpetuities; but in my opinion Lord Kenyon was referring to the old rule against double possibilities. It is clear, in my opinion, that the rule under which Mr. Justice Kay has decided this case is a rule which Judges treated as still subsisting long after the rule against perpetuities had been crystallised and laid down in definite and distinct terms.

Then, again, in *Monypenny* v. *Dering*, 2 D. M. & G. 145, Lord St. Leonards says (*ibid.* p. 170): "Then the rule of law forbids the raising of successive estates by purchase to unborn children, that is, to an unborn child of an unborn child. With this rule I have never meant to interfere, for it is too well settled to be broken in upon." According to the argument addressed to us on behalf of the Appellants that old rule has been superseded by the modern rule against perpetuities; but here we have Lord St. Leonards treating it as still subsisting in 1852.

Then we have besides, *Butler's* note to *Fearne*, 10th ed. vol. i. p. 565, n., in which he lays down what he takes to be the law—that there was no decision superseding the old rule. He says this: "The cases of a possibility upon a possibility may be considered as exceptions from the rule. They proceeded on a different ground, and gave rise to this important rule, that, if land is limited to an unborn person during his life, a remainder cannot be limited so as to confer an estate by purchase on that person's issue." He there quite treats it as the true rule still subsisting. And then we have a statement by *Burton*, in his Compendium, 7th ed. p. 255, shewing that he did recognise clearly that the old rule was still subsisting. He says: "Life estates may by law be given in succession to any number of persons in existence, and ulterior estates in succession to their children yet unborn.... But no remainder can be given to the child of a person who is not in existence."

Therefore, although very ingenious and learned arguments have been addressed to us to shew that the old rule has been superseded and put an end to, it is, in my opinion, well established that the rule is still in existence.

There is a passage in Lord St. Leonards' judgment in *Cole* v. *Sewell*, 4 D. & War. 1, 32, in which he speaks of the rule as being obsolete, but he nowhere lays down that the rule is no longer existing. He only means that the rule is no longer necessary to be referred to because, through the introduction of shifting uses and executory devises, the law is now governed rather by the rule against perpetuities. When Mr. Marten referred us to *Sugden* on Powers, I referred him to the opinion expressed by the learned author, when sitting as Lord Chancellor, in *Monypenny* v. *Dering*, 2 D. M. & G. 145, 170, in the passage which I have read, and which shews he did not consider the old rule to have been abrogated. In my opinion the decision of Mr. Justice Kay is right.

LINDLEY L. J.: I entertain no doubt myself that Mr. Joshua Williams' observations on this subject are correct from beginning to end, and I do not know that I could express my views better than he did. I do not know, any more than he seems to have done, the exact meaning of the old rule as to a possibility upon a possibility; and if anyone turns to the passage in *Coke* upon *Littleton* where it is discussed, I hope he will understand it better than I do. I confess I do not understand it now, and never did. But, at all events, it gave rise to the rule which everyone can understand, and which is expressed by *Butler* in the note to *Fearne*, 10th ed. vol. i. p. 565, n., where he says that "the cases of a possibility upon a possibility... gave rise to this important rule, that, if land is limited to an unborn person during his life, a remainder cannot be limited, so as to confer an estate by purchase on that person's issue." That is intelligible; and there are other passages on pages 502 and 503 shewing this was the author's settled opinion.

I have always understood that to be the settled rule of law, and I am not aware of any decision or dictum which in any way impugns it. But it is said that the old rule became obsolete, or merged or confused in the more modern law of perpetuities. Butler, however, shews that this is a mistake. The rule against perpetuities was invented much later, on account of the law of shifting uses and executory devises. When shifting uses and executory devises were invented it became necessary to impose some limit upon them, and the doctrine of perpetuities has arisen from that necessity. The old rule against double possibilities is a rule that has not been abrogated, and it is founded on very good sense; because it is not desirable that land should be tied up to a greater extent than that allowed by the rule. So far from supporting ingenious devices for tying up land longer, the time has long gone by for that; and, as the law is against the Appellant's contention, in my opinion the appeal should be dismissed.

Appeal dismissed.

[Lopes L. J. delivered a concurring judgment.]

The rule in *Whitby* v. *Mitchell* is criticized by *Gray*, Rule against Perpetuities (1942, 4th ed.), appendix K. It was abolished in England by s. 161 of the Law of Property Act, 1925 (Imp.), c. 20, and also in British Columbia by what is now s. 2 (36) of the Laws Declaratory Act, R.S.B.C. 1960, c. 213. It was regarded as applicable to both legal and equitable interests in realty. In wills, the effect of the rule was qualified by the so-called cy-près doctrine where realty was devised to an unborn person for life remainder to that person's children successively in fee tail. In such case, rather than allow the remainder in fee tail to fall, the Courts would give the unborn life tenant a fee tail. See *Megarry*, *op. cit.*, p. 144.

In some cases the rule was interpreted as in effect one which prohibited successive contingent remainders to unborn persons. For example, land is granted to A (a bachelor) for life, remainder to such woman as he may marry for life, remainder to their children in fee simple: see *Re Park's Settlement*, [1914] 1 Ch. 595. Later cases have rejected this view: see *In re Bullock's Will Trusts*, [1915] 1 Ch. 493; *cf. In re Garnham*, [1916] 2 Ch. 413. Unfortunately, *Re Park's Settlement* was acted on in Ontario in *Stuart* v. *Taylor* (1914), 33 O.L.R. 20, 22 D.L.R. 282 (App. Div.) where Middleton J. at the trial referred to it for the proposition that "there cannot be a contingent remainder upon a contingent remainder". On appeal, only

Clute J. dealt with the point; the other members of the Court construed the devise in the case as conferring only a life estate. As construed by Middleton J. and Clute J., it was as follows: to A, B and C for life and if they should marry then to their respective surviving wives for life and on the death of each wife to their respective children in fee simple. In his judgment Clute J. said (at p. 46): "While I agree with my brother Middleton that the gift to the children was void, it would also appear to follow from *Whitby* v. *Mitchell* that the gift to the wives of the three sons was also void as offending the rule against perpetuities, inasmuch as they were unmarried at the time of the death of the testator, and might not be married until more than twenty-one years thereafter, and so there would be a gift for life with a further gift which might extend more than twenty-one years thereafter". Do you agree with this application of the rule against perpetuities?

[Suppose the limitation in *Stuart* v. *Taylor* was by devise to A for life, remainder to such woman as he may marry for life remainder to their children living at her death. Any question as to its validity?

In *Chandler* v. *Gibson* (1901), 2 O.L.R. 442 (C.A.), a testator devised "to my son M for life and then to his children if any, but should he have no issue then equally among all my grandsons". Is the devise valid?

T devised "to A for life, then to his sons successively in tail male and in default of such issue to the eldest or other son of B who should first attain age 21 in tail male and in default of such issue to C". Is the devise valid? See *White* v. *Summers*, [1908] 2 Ch. 256.]

Note on Equitable Contingent Interests

STRICTLY SPEAKING, reversions and remainders assume doctrines of seisin and tenure, and hence equitable interests akin to legal reversions and legal remainders ought not to be subject to common law rules, such as the destructibility rule governing contingent remainders, because the seisin remains in the legal titleholder, e.g., a trustee. The development of uses and, later, the Statute of Uses and the Statute of Wills, permitted not only the creation of equitable interests similar to those at common law, but also the creation of equitable springing and shifting interests and legal executory interests which were not cognizable at common law. Such interests (not recognized at common law) were indestructible subject, however, to the rule against perpetuities. They are considered in the next chapter. Mention is made of them here only to point up that the destructibility rule governing legal contingent remainders did not apply to equitable contingent "remainders", and since modern devolution statutes establish a statutory trust of a deceased's estate it is arguable that all limitations in a devise are equitable. One consequence would then be that the rule in *Purefoy* v. *Rogers* would have no application to devises.

[Consider the following limitations:
A grants to B in trust to pay the income to C for life remainder to D on reaching age 21.
A (a mortgagor) grants his interest to B for life remainder to C on reaching age 21.
A grants to B to the use of C for life remainder to the use of D on reaching age 21.]

DEVOLUTION OF ESTATES ACT, R.S.O. 1960. c. 106

2. (1) All real and personal property that is vested in a person without a right in any other person to take by survivorship, on his death, whether testate or intestate, and not-

withstanding any testamentary disposition, devolves to and becomes vested in his personal representative from time to time as trustee for the persons by law beneficially entitled thereto and, subject to the payment of his debts, and so far as such property is not disposed of by deed, will, contract or other effectual disposition, it shall be administered, dealt with and distributed as if it were personal property not so disposed of.

(2) This section applies to property over which a person executes by will a general power of appointment as if it were property vested in him.

(3) This section does not apply to estates tail or to the personal property, except chattels real, of any person who, at the time of his death, is domiciled out of Ontario.

[See, for similar legislation, Devolution of Real Property Act, R.S.A. 1955, c. 83, s. 4; Devolution of Estates Act, R.S.M. 1954, c. 63, s. 17; Devolution of Estates Act, R.S.N.B. 1952, c. 62, s. 3; Probate Act, R.S.P.E.I. 1951, c. 124, s. 119; Devolution of Real Property Act, R.S.S. 1953, c. 118, s. 5.]

IN RE ROBSON, DOUGLASS v. DOUGLASS. Chancery Division. [1916] 1 Ch. 116

Originating summons to determine who was entitled to certain land in view of the terms of a will and of the events that happened. A testator devised this land "unto and to the use of my said daughter Helen... during her life and from and after her decease to the use of such of her children in fee simple as shall attain the age of twenty-one years and if more than one in equal shares as tenants in common". The testator died on January 21, 1905. Helen, the life tenant, died on April 27, 1915, survived by four children, two of whom had attained age 21 before her death and two of whom were under that age at her death.

ASTBURY J. (after stating the facts): The question is whether the life tenant's children who attained twenty-one during her life are now entitled to "The Oaks" to the exclusion of the infants.

The solution depends on the answer to one or other of the following questions: First, whether, in the events that have happened, the interests which the testator undoubtedly intended the infants to take are preserved by the Contingent Remainders Act, 1877—a moot point that has never been decided; secondly, whether those interests are preserved by the Land Transfer Act, 1897.

I will deal with the point on the Land Transfer Act, 1897, in a moment, but before doing so I will just state the nature of the question under the Contingent Remainders Act, 1877. That Act was passed on August 2, 1877. It provided that "Every contingent remainder created by any instrument executed after the passing of this Act," which would have been valid as a springing or shifting use or executory devise or other limitation had it not had a sufficient estate to support it as a contingent remainder, "shall, in the event of the particular estate determining before the contingent remainder vests," be capable of taking effect in all respects as if the contingent remainder had originally been created as a springing or shifting use or executory devise or other executory limitation.

In a case like the present, if the life tenant had died when all the children were infants, there would have been no difficulty. The devise would have operated under the statute as an executory devise. But where, as in the present case, some children have attained twenty-one during the life tenancy and others are still infants there are two possible views: Either the remainder in its entirety is vested in the children who attained twenty-one during the life tenancy, or the possible contingent interests of the infants are saved by the statute. The former view is preferred by most text-books, but, having regard to the view I take as to the effect of the Land Transfer Act, 1897, I do not propose to decide this point.

I will now deal with the question under the Land Transfer Act, 1897.

It is clear on the authorities that the difficulty arising from the old doctrine of seisin applies only to legal and not to equitable remainders: *In re Eddels' Trusts*, L.R. 11 Eq. 559; *Berry* v. *Berry*, 7 Ch. D. 657; *Astley* v. *Micklethwait*, 15 Ch. D. 59, 63.

In *Astley* v. *Micklethwait* a testator devised a freehold estate to the use of his son for life, and after his decease to the use of the son's children who should attain twenty-one in equal shares. The testator had mortgaged part of the estate, and at his death the legal estate was outstanding in the mortgagees. The son died leaving four infant children. Malins V.-C. held that as to the mortgaged portion the contingent remainders were preserved from failure by the legal estate outstanding in the mortgagees, but as to the unmortgaged portion the remainders failed on the son's death. During the argument he said: "The testator had not the legal estate at the date of his will or death. His will never operated upon the legal estate. Why am I to go out of my way to destroy the will instead of preserving it? Anything that would enable the Court to get out of the monstrous doctrine of *Festing* v. *Allen*, 12 M. & W. 279, ought to be adopted. You cannot have a more forcible illustration than this very case." This "monstrous doctrine" was that the property vested in the children who attained twenty-one during the life tenancy to the exclusion of children who might subsequently attain that age.

In *In re Freme*, [1891] 3 Ch. 167, 170, an equitable contingent remainder created before the Contingent Remainders Act, 1877, became clothed with the legal estate after that Act. North J. held not only under but also independently of the Act that the contingent remainder was not defeated by the failure of the life interest. In that case a testator died in 1873 having devised freeholds to his son for life and after his decease (subject to a power of appointment in the son) to the son's children who being a son should attain twenty-one or being a daughter should attain that age or marry equally between them. A portion of the freeholds was in mortgage at the date of the testator's will and death. During the life tenancy the mortgage was discharged and the property reconveyed to the uses of the will. The son then died intestate and without appointing, leaving three infant children. North J. said: "I think that all that was created by the will was an equitable contingent remainder that was not subject to the defect of failure by reason of the absence of a sufficient freehold to support it;"—the will in fact only operated on the equity of redemption—"and I do not think that the subsequent acquisition of the legal estate by the deed of 1887, can do any harm, whatever effect it might have produced if that deed had been dated before the time when the Act in question came into operation." This was the actual decision, namely, that the equitable contingent remainder having been turned into a legal contingent remainder by an instrument subsequent to the Act was preserved by the Act, the whole remainder being still contingent at the life tenant's death, as all the children were infants. North J. then proceeded to give an alternative ground for his decision: "In addition to that my impression is that there is another answer to this case, namely, the point that the contingent limitations being equitable only are not subject to being defeated by the absence of any freehold to support them, even though they had while contingent been clothed with the legal estate, and I think that that in effect is to be gathered from what fell from Vice-Chancellor Malins in *Astley* v. *Micklethwait*. I think, therefore, that there are two reasons that prevent the failure of this contingent remainder." That view comes to this. Where there is a devise of an equity of redemption to a life tenant with a contingent remainder to a class of children who attain twenty-one the subsequent clothing of the equitable life estate and contingent remainder with the legal estate during the life tenancy is not enough to defeat the testator's intention that all children who attain twenty-one shall take, although their interests are still contingent at the life tenant's death.

The infants contend that the Land Transfer Act, 1897, which came into operation on January 1, 1898, brings the present case within *In re Freme.*

Sect. 1, sub-s. 1, provides that "Where real estate is vested in any person without a right in any other person to take by survivorship it shall, on his death, notwithstanding any testamentary disposition, devolve to and become vested in his personal representatives or representative from time to time as if it were a chattel real vesting in them or him." This freehold therefore vested, not in the life tenant under the legal limitation, but in the executors.

Sect. 2, sub-s. 1, provides that "Subject to the powers... hereinafter mentioned, the personal representatives... shall hold the real estate as trustees for the persons by law beneficially entitled thereto,..." The executors therefore held the real estate as trustees for the persons by law beneficially entitled thereto, i.e., for persons who, having regard to the law, including the Land Transfer Act, 1897, were at the testator's death and prior to any assent under s. 3 entitled to equitable and not legal estates.

Sect. 3, sub-s. 1, provides that "At any time after the death of the owner of any land, his personal representatives may assent to any devise contained in his will, or may convey the land to any person entitled thereto as heir, devisee, or otherwise...." In the present case there was clearly an assent to the devise at some time during the life tenancy. From the date of this assent the property vested in the life tenant and remaindermen according to the limitations of the will; but it follows, in my judgment, from the view expressed by North J. in *In re Freme*, with which I respectfully agree, that the equitable contingent remainders which, having regard to the provisions of the Land Transfer Act, were originally created by the will retained their initial immunity from destruction though clothed from the date of such assent with the legal estate.

Before parting with the case I may mention that in two colonies where the old English common law prevails and there are statutes similar to the Land Transfer Act, 1897, a similar view as to the initial preservation of contingent remainders by the estate vested in the executors was taken, though the question as to the effect of a subsequent assent or registered transfer was not raised: see *In re Beavis*, 7 N.S.W. State Rep. 66; *In re Campion* (1908), South Australian L.R. 1.

I therefore hold that the plaintiffs are not entitled to "The Oaks" to the exclusion of the infants.

[*In re Robson* is doubted by *Cheshire*, Modern Law of Real Property (1954, 7th ed.), p. 259n, but, *semble*, approved by *Megarry and Wade*, Law of Real Property (1959, 2nd ed.), p. 213. In England now all future interests in freeholds are equitable; Law of Property Act, 1925 (Imp.), c. 20, s. 1. The Statute of Uses, the Real Property Act, 1845 and the Contingent Remainders Act, 1877 are among the statutes that were repealed by the Law of Property Amendment Act, 1924 (Imp.), c. 5, 10th Schedule.

The Conveyancing Act, 1956 (N.S.), c. 3 provides by s. 3 (3) that "feoffment and livery of seisin are abolished". This, quite clearly, refers to a method of conveyancing and does not make it possible to create springing and shifting interests *inter vivos* as legal interests apart from the Statute of Uses.]

Contingent remainders are now by statute alienable *inter vivos* (see legislation on p. 330, *supra*), and are also transmissible on death where they are limited to an ascertained person in fee simple on a contingency not personal to himself. Thus in *Re Stewart*, [1939] O.R. 153, [1939] 2 D.L.R. 185, a testator left property to A for life and if she die leaving a child or children surviving remainder to such children when they severally attain age 21, but if A die without leaving any child or children her surviving, then to S and C equally. A died without issue but S had predeceased A. It was held that S's executors shared the property with C.

(Note the devise is an illustration of alternative contingent remainders.) Contingent remainders are devisable (see legislation referred to on p. 330, *supra*).

The Rule in Shelley's Case

SHORTLY STATED, the rule in *Shelley's Case* (see (1579-1581), 1 Co. Rep. 93b, 76 E.R. 206 (Q.B.)) is a rule of law, applicable to deeds and wills of realty , which comes into operation when an estate of freehold is created in a person and by the same instrument a remainder is limited to the heirs or heirs of the body of such person. In such case, if the limitation to heirs or heirs of the body (or by way of equivalent expression) is to an indefinite line of succession of heirs or heirs of the body (and not to designated persons), and the estate to the ancestor and that given in remainder, mediately or immediately, to heirs or heirs of the body are both legal or both equitable, the remainder is construed as a fee simple or fee tail, as the case may be, to the ancestor.

The classical statement of the rule and a survey of its history may be found in *Van Grutten* v. *Foxwell*, [1897] A.C. 658. Reasons for the rule are examined by *Megarry and Wade*, Law of Real Property (1957), pp. 57-63, and discussed in detail in 3 *Simes and Smith*, *op. cit.*, chap. 45, where it is pointed out (at p. 430) that although the modern justification for it is that it increases alienability, this is not enough to outweigh its arbitrary effect. "The operation of the rule is two-fold; first, it denies to the remainder the effect of a gift to the heirs; secondly, it attributes to the remainder the effect of a gift to the ancestor himself" (1 *Hayes*, Conveyancing (5th ed.), at p. 542-3).

The rule has not generally been applied to personalty and, indeed, it cannot be if a requirement is an estate of freehold in the ancestor (see 1 *Simes and Smith*, *op. cit.*, s. 367). It was, however, held to be applicable to personalty in *Re Woods*, [1946] O.R. 290, [1946] 3 D.L.R. 394, a holding which it is impossible to support unless it be by way of a mere analogical rule of construction: see *Re Woodward*, [1945] 2 D.L.R. 497, [1945] 1 W.W.R. 722, 61 B.C.R. 298; and *Editorial Note*, [1946] 3 D.L.R. 394, referring to English cases.

In *Re Simpson*, [1927] 4 D.L.R. 817, [1927] 3 W.W.R. 534, 23 Alta. L. R. 374 (C.A.), the Alberta. [On further appeal to the Supreme Court of Canada ([1928] S.C.R. 329, [1928] 3 W.W.R. 107) that the rule, founded as it was on feudal conditions which never prevailed in the North-West Territories, was not introduced there and hence was not part of the law of Alberta. On further appeal to the Supreme Court of Canada ([1928] S.C.R. 329, [1928] 3 D.L.R. 773) it was held to be unnecessary to consider whether the rule is in force in Alberta because, even assuming it was, it did not apply.] *Re Simpson* was followed in *Re Budd* (1958), 12 D.L.R. 2d 783, 24 W.W.R. 383 (Alta.).

The rule has been abolished in England: see Law of Property Act, 1925 (Imp.), c. 20, c. 131.

[Lord Mansfield's disregard of the rule in *Perrin* v. *Blake* (1769), 1 Wm. Bl. 672, 96 E.R. 392 (K.B.) in favour of giving effect to a testator's intention provoked a fierce controversy which was not altogether stilled by the reversal of his judgment in the Court of Exchequer Chamber in 1772 (see 4 Burr. 2577, 98 E.R. 355). A further appeal to the House of Lords was taken but the matter was dropped when the parties reached a settlement in 1777. The controversy is recounted by *Leach*, Cases on Future Interests (1940, 2nd ed.), pp. 132-136.]

[Should the fact that "heirs" is now statutorily defined (e.g., Wills Act, R.S.O. 1960, c. 433, s. 31) to mean those persons who would take on an intestacy make any difference in the application of the Rule in Shelley's case? See 3 *Restatement of Property*, s. 312, Comments and g.]

Consider the following limitations relative to the application of the rule:

(1) A grants to B for life remainder to C for life on reaching age 21, remainder to the heirs of B.

(2) A grants to B for life remainder to C in trust for the heirs of B.

(3) A grants to B for life remainder to C for life on reaching age 21 remainder to the heirs of C.

(4) A devises to B for life and if B survives C remainder to the heirs of B.

(5) A devises to B for life remainder to the issue of B who reach age 21.

(6) A devises to B for life remainder to C for 21 years and on the termination of C's lease remainder to the issue of B.

(7) A grants to B for life or during widowhood remainder to the heirs of B.

(8) A grants to B in trust for C for life, remainder to D for life, remainder to the issue of C.

(9) A grants to B and C for their joint lives remainder to the heirs of C.

(10) A grants to B and C as tenants in common for their respective lives remainder to the heirs of C.

(11) A devises to B for life remainder to C for life remainder to the heirs of B and C. (See 3 *Simes and Smith*, *op. cit.*, s. 1560.)

[If A devises to B for life, remainder to the heirs of B, and B dies before the testator, is the Rule in Shelley's case applicable? See 3 *Simes and Smith*, *op. cit.*, s. 1561.]

The following cases offer further illustrations of the rule:

(1) T left his whole estate, whether realty or personalty, to his wife for life remainder to his brother J. if he should survive the wife and if he should predecease her, then equally "between the heirs of my wife and the heirs of my said brother J." J. died in the wife's lifetime leaving a widow but no children. Does the rule apply? See *Stewart* v. *Murray*, [1951] 1 D.L.R. 299, 26 M.P.R. 147 (P.E.I.).

(2) T devised to A for life and after his death to the lawful issue of A to hold in fee simple, with a gift over in default of surviving issue. Does the rule apply? See *King* v. *Evans* (1895), 24 S.C.R. 356.

(3) T devised to A and B as tenants in common for life, and "on their death the undivided share of each to their respective issue in fee so that the child or children of each will take his or her or their mother's share". Does the rule apply? See *Re Taylor* (1916), 36 O.L.R. 116, 28 D.L.R. 488 (C.A.).

(4) T devised to G "for his own use and benefit during his natural life and from and after that to such uses as he shall by will appoint and in default of appointment to his heirs living at his death". Does the rule apply? See *Re Gracey* (1932), 41 O.W.N. 1. *Cf. Richardson* v. *Harrison* (1885), 16 Q.B.D. 85 (C.A.); *Archer's Case* (1599), 1 Co. Rep. 66b, 76 E.R. 146 (Q.B.).

On the effect of such superadded words as "living at his decease", contrast *Re Armstrong*, [1943] O.W.N. 43 and *Re Routledge*, *Marshall* v. *Elliott*, [1942] Ch. 457, [1942] 2 All E.R. 418.

(5) T devised land to A and after his death "to any lawful issue that may survive him, their heirs and assigns absolutely... as tenants in common". Does the rule apply? See *Re Badgerow*, [1940] 1 D.L.R. 140 (Ont.).

(6) T devised to trustees in trust to pay the income to two daughters and a granddaughter during the lifetime of the survivor of certain named persons (including these beneficiaries), and on the termination of this period to sell the land and divide the proceeds into as many shares as there were daughters of his then deceased and having descendants them surviving, and to divide each stirpital share among the descendants of each of such daughters. Does

the rule apply? See *Re Woodward*, [1945] 2 D.L.R. 497, [1945] 1 W.W.R. 722, 61 B.C.R. 298.

(7) T devised to trustees to hold for the benefit of A for life "and upon his death they are to convey [the property] or the proceeds thereof to his lawful issue" but if he die without issue, then over. Does the rule apply? See *Re Fanning*, [1934] O.W.N. 397 (C.A.).

(8) T devised land "to the use of my son during his life... with remainder to the use of his first and other sons successively according to seniority in tail male...." Does the rule apply? See *In re Williams, Tucker* v. *Williams*, [1952] Ch. 828, [1952] 2 All E.R. 502.

CHAPTER IX

EQUITABLE ESTATES AND THE STATUTE OF USES

1. USES BEFORE THE STATUTE OF USES

IT IS A TRITE OBSERVATION that the use is the forerunner of the modern trust. The present chapter is intended to show how the exercise of jurisdiction by the Court of Chancery led to the recognition of equitable interests in land which could be asserted against holders with notice or not for value of the outstanding legal title; how the attempt to effect a statutory conversion of these interests into legal estates was but partially and temporarily successful; how the device of uses provided a vehicle for limiting shifting and springing interests which under the Statute of Uses survived as legal executory interests, and by virtue of the Statute of Wills operated as executory devises; and how these developments were a prelude to a distinct law of trusts, a subject which is itself beyond the scope of this casebook.

[The developments referred to are traced by *Maitland*, Equity (1936 ed.); 1 *Scott on Trusts* (1956, 2nd ed.), Introduction; 1 *American Law of Property*, ss. 1.17-1.33; 4 *Holdsworth*, History of English Law (1937), pp. 407 ff.]

The following stages in the development of uses may be noted:

(*a*) Available evidence shows that general resort to uses began in the 13th century with conveyances being made whereby land was to be held for the use of ("ad opus" i.e. for the need or benefit of) religious orders. It should be noted that by s. 43 of Magna Carta it was declared that "it shall not be lawful from henceforth to any to give his lands to any religious house and to take the same land again to hold of the same house; nor shall it be lawful to any house of religion to take the lands of and to lease the same to him of whom they were received to be holden". The device of uses offered an escape from this and other mortmain legislation.

(*b*) This escape was blocked by legislation in 1391 prohibiting conveyances of land to persons to hold to the use of religious orders. In the meantime conveyances to uses for other purposes had spread, as, for example, to escape feudal burdens, usually accomplished by feoffments to joint tenants; to escape common law methods of conveyancing, as by oral or written transfers of the beneficial interest since no tenure was involved in equity; to enable a feoffor to uses to defeat his creditors, a practice that was blocked by statute in 1376; and to enable wills of land to be made, this being accomplished by arrangement between the feoffor and the feoffees to uses to whom the legal title was given for designated purposes, e.g. to hold to the use of a named beneficiary (cestui que use) or to hold to the use of such persons as may be named in a testament by the feoffor, and so on.

(*c*) Since the feoffee to uses held title recognized by the common law courts, the beneficiary's interest (which might rest on merely an oral declaration) was a fragile one depending originally on a sense of moral obligation and later on the interposition of Chancery to protect it against a faithless feoffee to uses.

(*d*) When Chancery for the first time enforced a decree in favour of a cestui que use against a feoffee to uses (the first recorded one was in 1446), we had the beginnings of a new scheme of interests in land, especially with the recognition of such features as inheritability and assignability of the beneficiary's interest and the recognition of quantums of interest comparable to the estate system at common law. In time the use or beneficial interest became enforceable in the Court of Chancery not only against feoffees to uses but against their heirs, their donees and even against their assignees for value with notice. Only a subsequent *bona fide* purchaser for value and without notice of the equitable interest could take the land unburdened by such interest. However, when a person took an interest in land held to uses, otherwise than through the feoffee, he was not subject to any use affecting it; for example, the lord who took by escheat, the wife of the feoffee to uses (who was originally entitled to dower), and a disseisor.

2. RAISING A USE

FOUR METHODS of raising a use (i.e. an equitable interest in land) were developed: (1) by express declaration, even if gratuitous, under a feoffment; (2) by implication by way of resulting use where a feoffment was made without consideration and without declaration of a use (it should be noted that if the feoffment created a tenurial relationship between grantor and grantee the feudal obligations arising therefrom were considered as sufficient to keep the beneficial interest in the grantee unless a use was expressly declared); (3) by a bargain and sale (which required no formality or even writing) for consideration; and (4) by a covenant to stand seised to the use of a blood relation or a person connected by marriage to the covenantor.

It will be noticed that methods (1) and (2) involved transfer of the land, while methods (3) and (4) enabled the holder of an estate to raise a use thereon without transferring it. Where the land was transferred to a grantee for consideration or by way of creation of a relationship of tenure, no use arose in the absence of proof of a declaration of a use. However, a use gratuitously declared upon a common law feoffment was enforceable in equity even if the feoffment itself was purely voluntary. A bargain and sale for consideration (in effect, a contract selling the beneficial interest, whether for life or for years or in fee) raised a use enforceable by Chancery but not a bargain or sale where there was no consideration; nor would a gratuitous promise under seal (as opposed to a conveyance) be enforceable in equity unless it was a covenant to stand seised to a relative. In one situation, both before and after the Statute of Uses, equity would not enforce a declared use and that was where it was declared upon a fee tail; the *Statute De Donis* was regarded as having fixed the beneficial interest: see *Cooper* v. *Franklin* (1616), Cro. Jac. 400, 79 E.R. 342 (K.B.).

Consider the following limitations:

1. A enfeoffs B and his heirs to the use of C for life then to the use of D and his heirs.
2. A enfeoffs B and his heirs to the use of A for life remainder to the use of C and the heirs of his body.
3. A bargains and sells to B for life then to C for 21 years.
4. A bargains and sells to B and the heirs of his body and then to C and his heirs.
5. A covenants to stand seised to the use of B and his heirs.
6. A enfeoffs B and his heirs to the use of A for life.
7. A enfeoffs B and his heirs to the use of C for life.

3. SPRINGING AND SHIFTING USES

CHANCERY'S ENFORCEMENT of uses or directions for the holding and disposition of beneficial interests in land (all done behind, or superimposed upon, the legal title) was without regard to the common law doctrines of seisin and tenure as it was without regard to common law forms of disposition. The opportunity was thus afforded to create equitable interests of a kind that were impossible at common law; as for example, interests that would arise in the future unsupported by any preceding estate of freehold and without affecting any prior interest, or, interests that would take effect by defeating an existing estate on the occurrence of some contingency. In the latter case the interest shifted automatically on the occurrence of the specified event. Springing and shifting uses were the means of establishing interests that were enforceable in equity even though, if created at common law, they would fail because of either (1) abeyance of seisin; or (2) violation of the principle that there can be no remainder after a fee simple; or (3) violation of the principle that no interest can be limited in favour of a third person to take effect by cutting short a prior estate.

Consider the following limitations:

1. A enfeoffs B and his heirs to the use of C and his heirs on reaching age 21.
2. A enfeoffs B and his heirs to the use of C and his heirs but if C dies without issue him surviving then to the use of D and his heirs.
3. A enfeoffs B and his heirs to the use of C for life then to the use of D and his heirs on D reaching age 21.
4. A enfeoffs B and his heirs to the use of C for life and if D dies without issue him surviving then to the use of E and his heirs.
5. A grants to B for 99 years to the use of C and his heirs.
6. A grants to B for 99 years to the use of C for life and then to the use of D and his heirs when D reaches age 21.

[Suppose A enfeoffs B and his heirs to the use of C and his heirs from and after next Christmas. Before the stipulated time arrives A dies without heirs. What is the effect on the interests that were created? Suppose B dies without heirs. What effect then?]

4. THE STATUTE OF USES

A SHORT RECITAL of the considerations which variously underlay the Statute of Uses is given in 1 *Scott on Trusts* (1956, 2nd ed.), at p. 19, as follows: "Every advantage which a tenant gained by enfeoffing others to his use involved a corresponding disadvantage to someone else: to his heirs, who were disinherited in favor of younger sons or daughters or strangers; to the overlords, who were deprived of their feudal rights; above all to the Crown, which was always lord and never tenant. It was indeed the king, Henry VIII, who insisted that something should be done about it. Professor Holdsworth [4 History of English Law (1937), pp. 407 ff.] has told at length of the measures proposed by the king to Parliament, of the opposition which he met on various hands, of the compromises which were effected, and of the final result, namely, the enactment of the Statute of Uses. Of this statute Professor Holdsworth says that it is 'perhaps the most important addition that the legislature has ever made to our private law.' In the preamble of the statute are enumerated at length certain disadvantages and abuses flowing from the employment of uses. By the employment of uses lands were devised and heirs disinherited; conveyances were secretly made to the detriment of creditors and subsequent purchasers; lords lost their rights of ward, marriage, relief, heriot, escheat and aids; married men were deprived of their tenancy by the curtesy and married women of their dower; the king was deprived of his rights in the property of persons attainted of treason and his right to waste for a year and a day the lands of persons attainted of felony; aliens were enabled to enjoy English lands; and in general 'many other inconveniences have happened, and daily do increase among the king's subjects, to their great trouble and inquietness, and to the utter subversion of the ancient common law of this realm.' Although these reasons for the enactment of the statute are all good lawyerlike reasons, they do not of course tell the whole story of the struggle between the king, the nobility and other landholders, and the lawyers, as Professor Holdsworth points out. And what was the remedy which Parliament provided? It was a very simple one. Uses were not made illegal, the cestui que use was not deprived of his beneficial interest; but on the contrary the cestui que use was given the legal title." The legal title did not, however, go to the cestui que use in all cases; there were important qualifications in the application of the Statute of Uses as indicated below.

The terms of the Statute (1536, 27 H. 8, c. 10), so far as relevant, read as follows:

"... where any person or persons stand, or be seised, or at any time hereafter shall happen to be seised of and in any honours, castles, manors, lands, tenements, rents, services, reversions, remainders, or other hereditaments, to the use, confidence, or trust of any other person or persons, or of any body politick, by reason of any bargain, sale, feoffment, fine recovery, covenant, contract, agreement, will, or otherwise, by any manner means whatsoever it be; that in every such case, all and every such person and persons, and bodies politick, that have or hereafter shall have any such use, confidence, or trust, in fee simple, fee tail, for term of life, or for years, or otherwise; or any use, confidence, or trust, in remainder or reverter, shall from henceforth stand and be seised, deemed, and adjudged in lawful seisin, estate, and possession of and in the same honours, castles, manors, lands, tenements, rents, services, reversions, remainders, and hereditaments, with their appurtenances, to all intents, constructions, and purposes in the law, of and in such like estates, as they had or shall have in use, trust, or confidence of or in the same; and that the estate, title, right, and possession that was in such person or persons that were or hereafter shall be seised of any lands, tenements, or hereditaments, to the use, confidence, or trust of any such person or persons, or of any body politick, be from henceforth clearly deemed and adjudged to be in him or them that have, or hereafter shall have such use, confidence, or trust, after such quality, manner, form, and condition as they had before, in or to the use, confidence, or trust that was in them.

"2. And be it further enacted by the authority aforesaid. That where divers and many persons be or hereafter shall happen to be jointly seised of and in any lands, tenements, rents, reversions, remainders, or other hereditaments, to the use, confidence, or trust of any of them that be so jointly seised, that in every such case that or those person or persons which have or hereafter shall have any such use, confidence, or trust, in any such lands, tenements, rents, reversions, remainders, or hereditaments, shall from henceforth have and be deemed and adjudged to have, only to him or them that have, or hereafter shall have, such use, confidence, or trust, such estate, possession, and seisin of and in the same lands, tenements, rents, reversions, remainders, and other hereditaments, in like nature, manner, form, condition, and course, as he or they had before in the use, confidence, or trust of the same lands, tenements, or hereditaments....

"3. And where also divers persons stand and be seised of and in any lands, tenements, or hereditaments in fee-simple or otherwise, to the use or intent that some other person or persons shall have and perceive yearly to them and to his or their heirs one annual rent of x. li. or more or less out of the same lands and tenements, and some other person one other annual rent to him and his assigns for term of life, or years, or for some other special time, according to such intent and use as hath been heretofore declared, limited, and made thereof: Be it therefore enacted by the authority aforesaid, that in every such case the same persons, their heirs, and assigns, that have such use and interest to have and perceive any such annual rents out of any lands, tenements, or hereditaments, that they and every of them, their heirs and assigns be adjudged and deemed to be in possession and seisin of the same rent of and in such like estate as they had in the title, interest, or use of the said rent or profit, and as if a sufficient grant or other lawful conveyance had been made and executed to them by such as were or shall be seised to the use or intent of any such rent to be had, made, or paid according to the very trust and intent thereof, and that all and every such person and persons as have or hereafter shall have any title, use, and interest, in or to any such rent or profit shall lawfully distrain for non-payment of the said rent, and in their own names make avowries, or by their bailiffs or servants make cognisances and justifications, and have all other suits, entries, and remedies, for such rents as if the same rents had been actually and really granted to them with sufficient clauses of distress, re-entry, or otherwise, according to such conditions, pains, or other things limited and appointed upon the trust and intent for payment or surety of such rent...."

[In the same session in which the Statute of Uses was passed, Parliament enacted the Statute of Enrolments, 1536, 27 H. 8, c. 16 to require recording of legal titles created by the effect of the Statute of Uses on bargains and sales of freeholds; otherwise such titles could have rested on merely oral transactions with resulting opportunities for secret and fraudulent transfers. The Statute of Enrolments, in its relevant provisions reads, as follows: "no manors, lands, tenements, or other hereditaments, shall pass, alter, or change from one to another, whereby any estate of inheritance or freehold shall be made or take effect in any person or persons, or any use thereof to be made, by reason only of any bargain and sale thereof, except the same bargain and sale be made by writing indented, sealed, and enrolled in one of the King's Courts of Record at Westminster, or else within the same county or counties where the same manors, lands, or tenements so bargained and sold lie or be, before the *Custos Rotulorum* and two Justices of the Peace, and the Clerk of the Peace of the same county or counties, or two of them at the least, whereof the Clerk of the Peace to be one; and the same enrolment to be had and made within six months next after the date of the same writings indented."]

The effect of the Statute of Uses was to "execute" uses and turn them into legal interests corresponding to the interests that existed previously as equitable ones. What then happened to the legal estate of the feoffee to uses? It was destroyed by the operation of the Statute of Uses and (to use a sophisticated explanation) the seisin in the feoffee to uses was drawn to feed the use interests. In view of *Pimbe's Case* (1585), Moore 196, 72 E.R. 528 (K.B.), it must be taken that the feoffee to uses had seisin for at least an instant, because there T, who had committed treason, was convicted thereof after land was conveyed to him to the use of S (who in turn conveyed his interest to P). It was held that the land was forfeited to the Crown, a holding that depended on T being seised of land at the time of or after committing treason. This doctrine of "scintilla juris" was also invoked in the case of a shifting interest to support the execution of the use in the taker of that interest. For example, if A enfeoffed B and his heirs to the use of C and his heirs and if C died without issue him surviving then to D and his heirs, the seisin on which the execution of the use in D was based was found in a scintilla juris in B notwithstanding that the seisin in B had already "fed" the use in C. The doctrine was formally abolished in England by 1860 (Imp.), c. 38, s. 7, legislation which was copied in Ontario: see Conveyancing and Law of Property Act, R.S.O. 1960, c. 66, s. 35. See also, Property Act, R.S.N.B. 1952, c. 177, s. 17.

[For an account of the exposition of the Statute of Uses, see *Digby*, History of the Law of Real Property (1897, 5th ed.), pp. 344 ff.]

[The Statute of Uses is in force in the common law provinces, either as English law introduced as of a particular date, or by specific enactment; for an instance of the latter situation, see Statute of Uses, R.S.O. 1897, c. 331 (unrepealed). The Real Property Act, R.S.N.S. 1954, c. 244, s. 7 provides that "contingent uses and powers may be created by a deed of bargain and sale or by a covenant to stand seized to uses". For case law in Nova Scotia and New Brunswick treating the Statute of Uses as in force (there was a difference of opinion on the Statute of Enrolments because it assumed that machinery for recording was available), see *Shey* v. *Chisholm* (1853), 2 N.S.R. 52 (C.A.); *Doe d. Hanington* v. *McFadden* (1836), 2 N.B.R. 260 (C.A.). In *Sinclair* v. *Mulligan* (1888), 5 Man. R. 17, aff'g 3 Man. R. 481, the Statute of Uses (but not the Statute of Enrolments) was held to be in force in Manitoba.

In England the Statute of Uses was repealed by the Law of Property Act, 1925 (Imp.), c. 20, 7th Sched.; all future interests in land in England are now equitable only.]

5. EFFECT OF THE STATUTE OF USES

THREE MAIN EFFECTS of the Statute of Uses may be noted; first, its effect on conveyancing; secondly, its effect on future interests; and thirdly, its effect on equitable interests and the law of trusts.

(a) Effect on Conveyancing

The effect of the Statute of Uses on a feoffment on which a use was (even orally) declared was to give the cestui que use the legal title. Thus, a feoffment would not have the effect at law which it formerly had where a use was declared; and to avoid the possible entanglements that would beset an allegation of a legal title based on an oral declaration of use, section 7 of the Statute of Frauds, 1677, required all declarations or creations of trusts or confidences of land (except resulting trusts or confidences) to be in writing: see now, for example, Statute of Frauds, R.S.O. 1960, c. 381, ss. 9 and 10; Statute of Frauds, R.S.N.B. 1952, c. 218, s. 9; Statute of Frauds, R.S.N.S. 1954, c. 272, s. 4.

Where a use arose to the payer of consideration or because no consideration was given upon a feoffment, the result of the Statute of Uses was to vest or keep the legal title in the cestui que use despite the feoffment. Chancery required a purchaser to prove the consideration. A change was effected in some jurisdictions by legislation operating in favour of a subsequent *bona fide* purchaser and enabling him to rely on a recital of consideration in the conveyance to the grantee under whom the purchaser was claiming.

CONVEYANCING AND LAW OF PROPERTY ACT, R.S.O. 1960, c. 66

7. A receipt for consideration money or other consideration in the body of a conveyance or endorsed thereon is, in favour of a subsequent purchaser, not having notice that the money or other consideration thereby acknowledged to be received was not in fact paid or given, wholly or in part, sufficient evidence of the payment or giving of the whole amount thereof.

[See also Conveyancing Act, 1956 (N.S.), c. 3, s. 6 (b).

There may, of course, be a "presumption of advancement" where the payer of consideration takes title in the name of his wife or a child.]

The bargain and sale for consideration was put to good use by conveyancers after the Statute of Uses in the fashioning of a method of conveyance which avoided the unsatisfactory feoffment and livery of seisin. The Statute of Enrolments applied only to a bargain and sale of a freehold. Hence the effect of the Statute of Uses upon the bargain and sale of a leasehold was to create a tenancy not only without any need of entry (as was required at common law) but without the need of recording the transaction. The bargainor was left with a reversion which he could release by deed to the tenant. The "lease and release" became the common method of conveying a fee simple until legislation in the 19th century substituted a simple deed of grant and abolished the necessity of either a feoffment or a resort to executed uses: see *Lutwich* v. *Mitton* (1620), Cro. Jac. 604, 79 E.R. 516 (Ct. of Wards).

(b) Effect on Future Interests

Springing and shifting legal interests became possible under the Statute of Uses, giving grantors methods of disposition and control which they never had at common law. The likely adverse effects on the marketability of land were later mitigated to some extent by the rule against perpetuities. When the Statute of Wills was enacted in 1540, the same flexibility in the creation of future interests by will was permitted as had been developed and recognized by way of use. Subject to the rule against perpetuities, springing and shifting interests or executory devises (as they were called when created under a will) were indestructible in contrast to the legal contingent remainder.

[See *Pells* v. *Brown* (1620), Cro. Jac. 590, 79 E.R. 504 (K.B.).

In *Re Tanqueray-Willaume and Landau* (1882) 20 Ch. D. 465 (C.A.), Jessel M.R. said at p. 478: "... As has been often observed, the Statute of Uses does not apply to wills. It is used sometimes as a mode of construing wills where it is obvious that the testator, so to say, had the Statute in his mind...."

Powers of appointment had become familiar devices under uses, and after the Statute of Uses and the Statute of Wills they came into more extensive use. The subject is beyond the scope of this casebook but for an illustration of the reliance on powers of appointment in deeds to uses to bar dower, see pp. 79 ff., *supra*.]

(c) Effect on Equitable Interests and the Law of Trusts

The Statute of Uses, even by its own terms, did not exclude the continued operation of uses as equitable interests. It applied only where *one* person was *seised* to the use of *another* and thus was inapplicable where (1) a use was raised upon a leasehold; and (2) a person was seised to his own use. A third class of unexecuted use was recognized where the feoffee to uses had active duties to perform (over and above the pre-Statute of Uses duties of protecting the title and conveying at the direction of the cestui que use). In an active as opposed to a passive trust the legal title remained in the feoffee to uses; and the modern rationalization of this result is that it is necessary to enable the trustee to administer the trust. In the evolution of trusts, the legal and equitable interests in land were separated whenever active duties of administration were specified or could be imported from the terms of the document in question; they did not arise from the mere use of the phrase "on trust".

A fourth class of unexecuted use developed about 100 years after the Statute of Uses through the "use upon a use". In *Tyrrel's Case* (1557), 2 Dyer 155a, 1 And. 37, 73 E.R. 336 (K.B.), it was held, in obedience to pre-Statute of Uses decisions of Chancery, that "an use cannot be engendered of an use", a holding based on alleged repugnancy. Thus, only the first use was executed and the second was completely ignored. After *Sambach* v. *Dalston* (1634), Toth. 188, 21 E.R. 164 (Ch.) equity enforced the second use (following the execution of the first by the Statute of Uses) on the same basis as it had originally enforced a first use before the Statute. Evasion of the Statute could hence be accomplished by passive trusts arising either by a use upon a use or by enfeoffing a person to his own use. Hence the reproach that the Statute of Uses did nothing more than add three, or five, words to a conveyance.

But the survival and development of unexecuted uses into a rounded law of trusts make the reproach of little consequence.

[See *Ames*, Lectures on Legal History, Lectures 20 and 21.

The "use upon a use" which remains unexecuted, should be distinguished from what has been called the "use after a use" which is executed, and which is merely the projection of one use through a life estate and remainder in different persons or through a shifting interest to another person or through these or other forms of such limitations in combination.]

Consider the following limitations:

1. A bargains and sells to B for 99 years.
2. A grants to B and his heirs on trust to permit C to collect the rents and profits.
3. A grants to B and his heirs on trust to collect the rents and profits and pay them to C.
4. A grants to B and his heirs on trust to pay the income to C for life remainder on trust for D and his heirs.
5. A grants to and to the use of B and his heirs in trust for C and his heirs.
6. A grants to B and his heirs to the use of C and his heirs to the use of D and his heirs.
7. A bargains and sells to B and his heirs to the use of C and his heirs.
8. A grants to B and his heirs to the use of C for life remainder to the use of D and his heirs but if D dies without issue him surviving then to the use of E and his heirs.
9. A grants to B and his heirs to such uses as C shall by deed or will appoint, and in default of and until appointment to the use of C and his heirs.
10. A grants to and to the use of B for life remainder to and to the use of C and his heirs when C reaches age 21.
11. A grants to B and his heirs to the use of C and his heirs to the use of D for life remainder to the use of E on reaching age 21.

[In connection with limitation no. 5, see *Doe d. Lloyd* v. *Passingham* (1827), 6 B. & C. 305, 108 E.R. 465 (K.B.) where Bayley J. said, *inter alia*: "Ever since I have belonged to the profession of the law, I have invariably understood that an use cannot be limited upon an use. That is admitted to be so in general, but a distinction has been taken where the limitation is to A., to the use of A. in trust for B., and it is said that then A. is in by the common law. That is true; but he is in of the estate clothed with the use, which is not extinguished, but remains in him. In the case of *Meredith* v. *Jones*, Cro. Car. 244, cited in argument to shew that where an estate is limited to A., to the use of A., he is in by the common law, it is said, ‚For it is not an use divided from the estate, as where it is limited to a stranger, but the use and the estate go together.' That case therefore shews, that although the trustees in this case might be in by the common law, yet they were in both of the estate and the use. There are two cases expressly in point. *Lady Whetstone* v. *Bury*, 2 P.W. 146, is a very clear case, and the words used were precisely the same as those found in the deed in question, and it was there decided, and also in *The Attorney-General* v. *Scott*, Cas. temp. Talb. 138, which came before Lord Talbot, one of the greatest real property lawyers that ever filled the office of Lord Chancellor, that the legal estate vests in him to whom by the words of the instrument the use is limited. Upon the authority of these two cases, I am of opinion that the use of the estate in question was executed in the trustees."

And Holroyd J. said, in part: "Upon the first perusal of the deed in question I had no doubt that the legal estate was vested in the trustees, having always understood that an use cannot be limited upon an use; and although I was struck by the ingenuity of the distinction pointed out by Mr. Taunton, yet upon further consideration it appears to me that his argument does not warrant it. The argument is, that as the trustees did not in the first instance take to the use of another, but of themselves, they were in by the common law, and not the statute;

that the first use was, therefore, of no effect, and the case was to be considered as if the deed had merely contained the second limitation to uses. But that is not so, for although it be true that the trustees take the seisin by the common law, and not by the statute, yet they take that seisin to the use of themselves, and not to the use of another, in which case alone the use is executed by the statute. They are, therefore, seised in trust for another, and the legal estate remains in them."

Is the rule in *Purefoy* v. *Rogers* applicable to limitations nos. 10 and 11?

Questions touching the vested or contingent character of interests, whether remainders or not, as affected by executory gifts over, and constructional problems in connection with contingent remainders and executory limitations are beyond the scope of this casebook. *Cf. Doe d. Evers* v. *Challis* (1859), 7 H.L.C. 531, 11 E.R. 212, and *Hancock* v. *Watson*, [1902] A.C. 14. See *Simes and Smith*, Law of Future Interests (1956, 2nd ed.), vols. 1 and 2, ss. 491 ff.]

[For additional reading on uses, see *Bigelow*, Introduction to the Law of Real Property (1945, 3rd ed.), pp. 90 ff.; *Bordwell*, The Repeal of the Statute of Uses (1926), 39 Harv. L. Rev. 466.]

Note on Future Interests in Chattels

Common law future interests in land were, as has been seen, intimately connected with and, indeed, governed by doctrines of tenure and seisin. Although, historically, "seisin" of chattels was not unknown (see *Maitland*, The Seisin of Chattels, (1885) 1 Law Q. Rev. 324, and *Ames*, The Disseisin of Chattels, in Lectures on Legal History, p. 172) it did not have the lasting feudal significance that it had for land. Absent then such doctrines as tenure and seisin, could future interests in chattels be created at law, especially when in the case of chattels personal (as opposed to chattels real like leaseholds) there was no system of estates?

We may put to one side equitable future interests in chattels operating under a trust and, equally, there has been no difficulty in recognizing future interests in chattels arising under testamentary dispositions. While originally a distinction was taken between a testamentary gift of the use of a chattel for life with remainder over and a gift of the chattel itself for life (the gift being regarded as absolute in the latter case) it was subsequently held that a gift of a limited interest by will would be construed as a *use* interest only: see *Hide* v. *Parrat* (1696), 2 Vern. 331, 23 E.R. 813 (Ch.); *Leath, Note*, Future Interests in Chattels Personal, (1936) 14 N. C. L. Rev. 196. For Canadian authorities, see *Osterhout* v. *Osterhout* (1904), 7 O.L.R. 402, affd. (1904), 8 O.L.R. 685 (C.A.); *Re Turnbull Estate* (1906), 11 O.L.R. 334; *Re McLaughlin* (1915), 8 O.W.N. 277. *Cf. In re Ridd Estate*, [1947] 2 W.W.R. 369, 55 Man. R. 300. However, where the chattel is of the class of things "quae ipso usu consumuntur" a gift for life only carries the title because "the use and the property can have no separate existence": see *Randall* v. *Russell* (1817), 3 Mer. 190, at p. 195, 36 E.R. 73, at p. 75 (Ch.); *cf. Re Elliott* (1916), 10 O.W.N. 378.

Future interests in personal chattels may be created by deed *inter vivos* in the United States but this is not so in England or in Canada: see 1 *American Law of Property*, s. 4.4; *Leach*, Cases and Materials on Future Interests (1940, 2d ed.), pp. 207 ff. The Privy Council stated in *Bennett and White (Calgary) Ltd.* v. *Sugar City*, [1951] A.C. 786, at p. 812, [1951] 4 D.L.R. 129, at p. 143 that "the law knows nothing of successive estates in [personal] property". *Gray*, Rule against Perpetuities (1942, 4th ed.), Appendix F, comments (at p. 749) that "the American doctrine [which prevails everywhere except in North Carolina] is the better for there is no rational distinction in this respect between deeds and wills".

The development of future interests in the case of chattels real was first inhibited by the conceptualistic notion (founded on the doctrine of estates) that a life estate was larger than a term of years. This was overcome in the English cases in the case of wills by construing a gift for life of a leasehold with a remainder over as an executory devise after the death of the life tenant who would have the residue of the term: see *Leach*, *op. cit.*, pp. 198-207 for the case law; 1 *American Law of Property*, s. 4.4. In the United States, it is regarded as possible to create future interests in leaseholds by deeds *inter vivos* as well as by wills, without regard to artificial feudal doctrines: see *Gray*, *op. cit.* English or Canadian authority, however, is lacking to support enforceability under a deed *inter vivos* of a future interest in a leasehold after grant of a life estate therein unless (as *Gray* points out) it can be good as an executory limitation, and this could not be so under a common law conveyance. Again, *Gray* says (at p. 749) that "the American doctrine is the better, as there is no rational distinction in this respect between deeds and wills, and no judicial authority in favour of such a distinction."

Further elaboration of the subject of this *Note* is beyond the scope of this casebook.

CHAPTER X

CONCURRENT ESTATES

1. CONCURRENT ESTATES AT COMMON LAW AND IN EQUITY

IN MODERN DEALINGS, concurrent interests may exist in land or in goods, in a fund, in the beneficial enjoyment of a trust, in a partnership, and in ownership (of the stock) of a corporation. The particular concern of this chapter is with the kinds of concurrent estates in land (whether in fee simple or for life or for years) that developed at common law and were recognized in equity, and with their position today both as respects the holders of the concurrent interests *inter se* and as against third parties. Four kinds developed: Joint tenancy, tenancy in common, co-parcenary and tenancy by the entireties.

At common law, a conveyance to two or more persons without more (where such persons did not include a husband and wife) created a joint tenancy. This type of estate which could arise only by act of the parties (i.e. deed, will or length of possession) and not by operation of law (e.g. descent), was characterized by the right of survivorship. Each joint tenant was seised *per my et per tout*, and the death of any one (without severing the joint tenancy in his lifetime) resulted in the joint estate remaining with the survivors; he had nothing to pass by will or descent. The ultimate survivor, on becoming solely seised, was of course in a different position. (Recall that there is no dower or curtesy in a joint tenancy in fee simple or fee tail.)

At common law the joint tenancy was distinguished by four unities: unity of estate or interest, unity of title, unity of time and unity of possession. Briefly, these requirements were, respectively, that the several persons concerned must obtain the same quantum of estate; that it must arise by the same act, whether grant or devise or dispossession which ripens into title; that it must commence or have vested at the same time; and, finally, that it must be held by one and the same undivided possession. (Each joint tenant has possession of the whole as well as of every parcel; each has an undivided moiety of the whole, and not the whole of an undivided moiety.) In equity or by devise it was possible to have a joint tenancy although there was no unity of time; as where by use or devise land is given to A for life remainder to the children of A so that the interests of the children as born vest at different times.

Destruction of any of the constituent unities results in destruction of the joint tenancy and hence of the right of survivorship, at least as between those joint tenants in respect of whom the unities are destroyed. Partition, or sale under a partition order may, of course, result in complete termination of all co-ownership. Alienation by a joint tenant (and for this purpose he can control an undivided interest) will result in destroying unity of title and time between his grantee and the remaining joint tenants, and thus will create a tenancy in common to that extent. Similarly, if one joint tenant acquires a greater interest than his co-tenants, as where A, a joint tenant for life, acquires the reversion or remainder in fee simple, the joint tenancy would be gone and in its place (assuming there were originally two joint tenants, A and B), A would hold an undivided half in fee simple, and B would hold an undivided half for life, with A holding the reversion or remainder of that half in fee simple. Other severance problems will be considered in the succeeding section of this chapter.

A tenancy in common is characterized only by unity of possession. There is no right of survivorship, and as between themselves tenants in common may have unequal shares; each has a share in the undivided whole and this share may be alienated or devised or left to devolve on an intestacy. Dower and curtesy in jurisdictions where they survive are of course applicable to the interests of tenants in common.

Co-parcenary, now practically extinct, arose on a descent of land to two or more. In view of the English rule of primogeniture it arose there on an inheritance by two or more females. While, in origin, it exhibited unity of interest or estate, title and possession (unity of time was not required because the heirs of female co-parceners even if they were males, were themselves co-parceners), it was akin to tenancy in common. Once any co-parcener alienated or devised his interest the tenancy became one in common. It was thus a tenancy which arose and continued by operation of law. Perhaps on this account, a co-parcener could compel partition at common law at a time when this remedy was not available (unless by consent of the concurrent owners) in other kinds of co-tenancy.

A tenancy by the entireties arose at common law by a conveyance to persons who were husband and wife where the estate would have been a joint tenancy if they were not. The spouses were seised *per tout* only; in other words, a fifth unity (of the person) was added to the four unities of a joint tenancy. The right of survivorship was a feature of this co-tenancy as well but, subject only to the husband's rights of enjoyment and limited disposition during the joint lives of the spouses, a tenancy by the entireties was unseverable. While neither spouse could destroy the right of survivorship they could together alienate the estate. If a conveyance, otherwise apt to create a joint tenancy, was made to three or more persons of whom two were husband and wife, the spouses were as between themselves tenants by the entireties, but in respect of the other grantees, the spouses (considered as one person) were in a joint tenancy.

The common law predisposition in favour of joint tenancies was modified in equity in a number of cases. Thus, mortgagees who held as joint tenants were regarded in equity as tenants in common (regardless of whether their advances on the mortgage were in equal or unequal sums) and the survivors or survivor at law were bound in equity in favour of the personal representatives of any deceased mortgagee. (This was as between the mortgagees, but in respect of the mortgagor's right to secure a discharge on repayment of the debt other considerations were involved which turned more on mortgage law: see, for example, Mortgages Act, R.S.O. 1950, c. 239, ss. 7 and 10, am. 1952, c. 61.) Again, joint purchasers of land were regarded in equity as tenants in common if they had advanced unequal sums for the purchase, although this might be subject to a "presumption of advancement" as in the case of husband and wife. Further, where land was bought by persons for the purpose of a partnership equity treated them as tenants in common in respect thereto; and see for example, Partnership Act, R.S.O. 1950, c. 270, ss. 21, 22 and 23.

[See, generally, on the various forms of co-tenancy, 2 *American Law of Property*, ss. 6.1 ff.; *Blackstone*, Commentaries, Book II, ss. 180-195; *Cheshire*, Modern Law of Real Property (1962, 9th ed.), pp. 293-315.]

[Reference may usefully be made to two other forms of concurrent ownership, namely (1) the community property system which is in force in Quebec as well as in a number of states of the United States; and (2) so-called co-operative ownership in apartment and office buildings. On the former, see *Beaulieu*, Community of Property in the Law of Quebec, (1939) 17 Can. Bar Rev. 486; 2 *American Law of Property*, ss. 7.1-7.36. *Cf.* Communal Property Act, R.S.A. 1955, c. 52. On the latter, see 1 *American Law of Property*, s. 3.10; *Note*, Co-Operative Apartment Housing, (1948) 61 Harv. L. Rev. 1407; 4 *Powell on Real Property*, s. 633.

Partnership is outside the scope of this casebook as is concurrent ownership of personalty.]

2. STATUTORY REFORM

CONVEYANCING AND LAW OF PROPERTY ACT, R.S.O. 1960, c. 66

13. (1) Where by any letters patent, assurance or will, made and executed after the 1st day of July, 1834, land has been or is granted, conveyed or devised to two or more persons other than executors or trustees in fee simple, or for any less estate, it shall be considered that such persons took or take as tenants in common, and not as joint tenants, unless an intention sufficiently appears on the face of such letters patent, assurance or will, that they are to take as joint tenants.

(2) This section shall apply notwithstanding that one of such persons is the wife of another of them.

14. Where two or more persons acquire land by length of possession they shall be considered to hold as tenants in common and not as joint tenants.

41. Any property may be conveyed by a person to himself jointly with another person by the like means by which it might be conveyed by him to another person, and may in like manner be conveyed or assigned by a husband to his wife, or by a wife to her husband alone or jointly with another person.

42. A person may convey property to or vest property in himself in like manner as he could have conveyed the property to or vested the property in another person.

43. Two or more persons, whether or not they are trustees or personal representatives, may convey and shall be deemed always to have been capable of conveying property vested in them to any one or more of themselves in like manner as they could have conveyed the property to a third party; but, if the persons in whose favour the conveyance is made are, by reason of any fiduciary relationship or otherwise, precluded from validly carrying out the transaction, the conveyance is liable to be set aside.

44. (1) A corporation is and has been capable of acquiring and holding real or personal property in joint tenancy in the same manner as if it were an individual, and where a corportation and an individual, or two or more corporations, became or become entitled to any such property under circumstances or by virtue of any instrument that would, if the corporation had been an individual, have created a joint tenancy, they are and have been entitled to the property as joint tenants; but the acquisition and holding of property by a corporation in joint tenancy has been and is subject to the like conditions and restrictions as attach to the acquisition and holding of property by a corporation in severalty.

(2) Where a corporation is joint tenant of property and the corporation dissolves, the property devolves on the other joint tenant.

DEVOLUTION OF ESTATES ACT, R.S.O. 1960, c. 106

18. Where real property becomes vested under this Act in two or more persons beneficially entitled under this Act, they take as tenants in common in proportion to their respective rights, unless in the case of a devise they take otherwise under the will of the deceased.

[For similar legislation, see Transfer and Descent of Land Act, R.S.A. 1955, c. 342, s. 9; Land Registry Act, R.S.B.C. 1960, c. 208, ss. 21; 22 (1); Law of Property Act, R.S.M. 1954, c. 138, ss. 16, 17, 18; Property Act, R.S.N.B. 1952, c. 177, ss. 19, 20, 22, 23; Real Property Act, R.S.N.S. 1954, c. 244, s. 4; Real Property Act, R.S.P.E.I. 1951, c. 138, s. 14; Land Titles Act, 1960 (Sask.), c. 65, ss. 234, 235, 238, 239.

In England the Law of Property Act, 1925 (Imp.), c. 20 abolished legal tenancies in common (see s. 1 (6)), and a trust for sale arises upon any attempted creation of legal concurrent interests. The legal holders are joint tenants upon trust for sale and severance is in consequence forbidden (see s. 36 (2)). As to the rights of equitable tenants in common *inter se* (e.g. co-possession) until sale, see *Bull* v. *Bull*, [1955] 1 Q.B. 234, [1955] 1 All E.R. 253 (C.A.).]

SPRING v. KINNEE. Ontario Appellate Division. 62 O.L.R. 562, [1928] 4 D.L.R. 723

The judgment of the Court was delivered by MIDDLETON, J. A.:

The sole question involved in the appeal is the effect of a conveyance to a husband and wife in terms which, prior to the Conveyancing and Law of Property Act, would have created a joint tenancy and which under that statute would create a tenancy in common were it not for the matrimonial relationship existing.

At common law because of this matrimonial relationship the husband and wife would have taken an estate by entireties, but the effect of the Married Women's Property Act is to enable the wife to take as though she were a *feme sole*, and so the effect of the marital relationship is ended so far as real property is concerned. This view was adopted by Falconbridge, J., in 1891, in *Re Wilson and Toronto Incandescent Electric Light Co.*, 20 O.R. 397, after some conflict had arisen in England, and this has never been questioned since. The English cases are discussed in *Challis*, 3rd ed., p. 378; and, though there remains some doubt as to the effect of a conveyance to a husband and his wife and a third party, I do not gather that there is now any real difference of opinion in England as to the effect of a conveyance to the husband and the wife. In England they would still take as joint tenants, but the effect under our Conveyancing and Law of Property Act is different. They take as tenants in common.

Appeal dismissed.

[Before the enactment of reforming legislation, if land was conveyed to three persons two of whom were husband and wife, the two took as one person vis à vis the third grantee. It was held in *Thornley* v. *Thornley*, [1893] 2 Ch. 229 that on a conveyance to husband and wife after the Married Women's Property Act they took as joint tenants only and no longer by the entireties. (Before this legislation, a divorce would simply turn the estate by the entireties into a joint tenancy.) If the conveyance after the Married Women's Property Act were to husband and wife and a third person, there was no logical reason why, even if a joint tenancy arose, husband and wife should be treated as one as against the third person. Kay J. in *Re Jupp* (1888), 39 Ch. D. 148 took the position that the Act altered a married woman's status only as between herself and her husband, a conception which is difficult to appreciate. The case was distinguished if not rejected in *Re Jeffery*, [1914] 1 Ch. 375, 83 L.J.Ch. 251 following *Re Dixon* (1889), 42 Ch.D. 306, so that on a devise to "H, W and their daughter", husband and wife were treated as separate persons. This result is certainly reinforced by legislation such as that expressed in s. 12 of the Ontario Conveyancing and Law of Property Act. In England, s. 37 of the Law of Property Act, 1925 (Imp.), c. 20 has destroyed whatever force *Re Jupp* has.

What has been said does not, however, touch mere questions of construction; and, indeed, *Re Jeffery* treated the problem under discussion as in truth a matter of construction. It is thus quite possible that by the terms of a deed or will a husband and wife may be given but one share together of an estate or fund which is being distributed among a number of named persons: see *Re Todd*, [1946] O.W.N. 727.

See *Note*, Effect of Married Women's Property Acts upon Estates by the Entirety, (1924) 37 Harv. L. Rev. 616. Tenancy by the entireties is abolished by the Transfer and Descent of Land Act, R.S.A. 1955, c. 342, s. 6; cf. Land Titles Act, 1960 (Sask.), c. 65, s. 238.

[At common law, if a husband was solely seised, what was the effect of a conveyance to himself and his wife? After the Married Women's Property Act, would a conveyance by a husband to himself and his wife create a joint tenancy? See *Note*, (1946) 32 Cornell L. Q. 291. Under legislation such as s. 42 of the Ontario Conveyancing and Law of Property Act, there is no doubt but that a husband may create a joint tenancy by a conveyance to himself and his wife as joint tenants: see *Re Sherrett and Gray*, [1933] O.R. 690, [1933] 3 D.L.R. 723, where the argument as to absence of unity of time was rejected. Armour J. said in that case:

"Before [the present s. 41] came into operation by The Conveyancing and Law of Property Act, 1886 (49 Vic. ch. 20, sec. 6), a person could not make a direct conveyance of freehold land to himself jointly with another, on account of the rule of law, that a man cannot make any conveyance to himself. For the same reason, and because of the rule, that a husband and wife are one in law, a husband could not previously make a direct conveyance of freehold land to his wife, nor a wife to her husband, partly for the same reason, but also because, being under coverture, the wife could not convey at all. But freehold land might be conveyed from a person to himself, or from a husband to a wife, and vice versa, by means of the Statute of Uses. For a person could convey the land to another, to the use of himself or herself or the wife or her husband; and of course this method can still be adopted. See *Williams* on Real Property, 23rd ed., ch. 13.

"Until the Statute of 1933 above referred to, it was still necessary to convey by means of the Statute of Uses whenever a person desired to convey freehold land to himself alone, as sometimes happens upon a settlement or re-settlement of land, for sec. 39 [now s. 41] of the Conveyancing and Law of Property Act only enabled the man to convey to himself jointly with another person. But the new sec. 39a [now s. 42] now permits the conveyance of property by any person to himself."]

[Where legislation such as that in s. 18 of the Ontario Devolution of Estates Act is in force, co-parcenary remains for all practical purposes only upon the descent of an estate tail to two or more daughters. Since its only real difference from tenancy in common was that at common law a co-parcener could compel partition, it has no longer any special significance because partition is available now to all classes of co-tenants.]

[T devised land to A and B "as their property jointly and should they decide to sell the said property each of them is to have an equal share of the proceeds of the said sale". What is the nature of the co-tenancy thus created? See *McEwen* v. *Ewers and Ferguson*, [1946] 3 D.L.R. 494, [1946] O.W.N. 573.

A and B took premises under a lease in which they "jointly and severally" covenanted to pay the rent. After A's death B made a payment of rent and sought contribution from A's estate. Result? Would the result be different if contribution had been sought in the lifetimes of both A and B when B paid the rent? See *Cunningham-Reid* v. *Public Trustee and Underwood*, [1944] K.B. 602, [1944] 2 All E.R. 6 (C.A.).

A and B were joint tenants of land which they mortgaged jointly to C under a mortgage deed in which they covenanted jointly and severally to pay the mortgage debt. Thereafter A died. You are asked to advise (1) whether B is now the sole beneficial owner of the land subject to the mortgage; (2) whether A's estate is liable on the covenant for payment, and what the effect would be as against B if A's estate discharged the mortgage debt to C. (See Mercantile Law Amendment Act, R.S.O. 1960, c. 238, s. 4.) What is your advice?

A testator devised certain land to his sons A and B "on condition that they agree to pay in equal shares to my wife for the remainder of her life after my death" a specified weekly sum. After the testator's death the sons paid the specified sum for a number of years and then A died. What was the effect on the title to the land and on the obligation to the testator's widow? See *Re North, North* v. *Cusden*, [1952] Ch. 397, [1952] 1 All E.R. 609.]

3. SEVERANCE OF JOINT TENANCIES: SOME PROBLEMS

FLANNIGAN v. WOTHERSPOON. British Columbia Supreme Court. [1953] 1 D.L.R. 768, 7 W.W.R. (N.S.) 660

COADY J.: The above-named deceased William Wotherspoon and the defendant James Wotherspoon are registered in the Land Registry Office, Vancouver, B.C. in joint tenancy of Lot 2 of Lots 1 to 5 and 11 to 15, Block 44, D.L. 301, Group 1, New Westminster District, Plan 3197. On or about September 6, 1950, they sold as joint tenants the said lands and premises by way of agreement of sale and purchase to the defendants Cecil William Robinson and Georgina Elsie Robinson as joint tenants for the sum of $5,250 on terms of $800 in cash and the balance payable at the rate of $40 per month. The deceased William Wotherspoon died on November 8, 1950, leaving a will dated November 1, 1950, in which he left all his "real and personal estate of ever kind and nature wheresoever situate absolutely and forever unto my daughter Margaret Malcolm Flannigan", the plaintiff herein.

This action is brought by the plaintiff against the defendant James Wotherspoon for a declaration that the plaintiff is entitled to an undivided one-half interest in and to the lands and premises above referred to, and in the moneys payable by the other defendants, on the agreement of sale and purchase, or alternatively for a declaration that the defendant James Wotherspoon stands possessed of an undivided one-half interest in the said lands and premises in trust for the plaintiff and for rectification of the Register. The defendants Cecil William Robinson, and Georgina Elsie Robinson are joined as defendants as the registered holders of a right to purchase. The plaintiff alleges in effect that, while the deceased and the defendant James Wotherspoon were and are registered as joint owners of the said lands and premises, there was a severance of title by mutual agreement between them. In *Williams* v. *Hensman* (1861), 1 John & H. 546 at pp. 557-8, 70 E.R. 862, Sir W. Page Wood V.-C. says: "A joint-tenancy may be severed in three ways: in the first place, an act of any one of the persons interested operating upon his own share may create a severance as to that share. The right of each joint-tenant is a right by survivorship only in the event of no severance having taken place of the share which is claimed under the jus accrescendi. Each one is at liberty to dispose of his own interest in such manner as to sever it from the joint fund—losing, of course, at the same time, his own right of survivorship. Secondly, a joint-tenancy may be severed by mutual agreement. And, in the third place, there may be a severance by any course of dealing sufficient to intimate that the interests of all were mutually treated as constituting a tenancy in common. When the severance depends on an inference of this kind without any express act of severance, it will not suffice to rely on an intention, with respect to the particular share, declared only behind the backs of the other persons interested. You must find in this class of cases a course of dealing by which the shares of all the parties to the contest have been affected, as happened in the cases of *Wilson* v. *Bell* and *Jackson* v. *Jackson.*"

The plaintiff herein relies upon the third mode of severance referred to above. We have then to consider whether or not the acts of the parties, and course of conduct, indicate a mutuality of agreement from which the Court will infer a mutual agreement to sever.

The plaintiff herein contends that while no direct evidence of an express mutual agreement can be submitted there is nevertheless strong evidence based on the acts and conduct of the parties from which the existence of such mutual agreement ought to be inferred. The acts, statements and conduct relied upon, and clearly established by the evidence are as follows:

1. When the sale was made by the deceased and the defendant Wotherspoon on or about September 6, 1950 to the other defendants, the cash payment made by these defendants amounting to $800 after the payment to William Wotherspoon, now deceased, of certain

moneys previously advanced by him for payment of taxes, was divided equally between the two Wotherspoons.

2. On or about September 13, 1950 the defendant James Wotherspoon took the agreement of sale and purchase to the bank and gave instructions to the bank to collect the payments from the Robinsons from month to month and to deposit the moneys so collected, less collection charges, to the credit of himself and his brother William Wotherspoon in equal shares, and pursuant to this arrangement two accounts were opened at the said bank by the defendant James Wotherspoon, one for himself and one for William Wotherspoon, now deceased.

3. The payments made by the Robinsons prior to the death of the deceased were in fact divided by the bank and deposited in the said two accounts as instructed.

4. The defendant James Wotherspoon having made this arrangement at the bank wrote to his brother William Wotherspoon as follows: "I made arrangements at the Bank of Toronto, at Fraser and Kingsway, for the Robinsons to make their payments there. That is what we agreed upon. The Bank look after it for fifty cents a month. I figure that is reasonable don't you? So neither of us has to worry about anything."

5. The foregoing arrangement with the bank was made by the defendant Wotherspoon when his brother William Wotherspoon was ill and unable personally to attend to such matters of business for himself.

6. That on the evening of November 2, 1950, the deceased William Wotherspoon, being then confined to his bed through illness, advised the defendant James Wotherspoon in the presence of the plaintiff that the doctor had told him he had not long to live and that he had made a will the day before and had left all his property including his interest in the property in question to his daughter the plaintiff in this action, and that the defendant James Wotherspoon, when advised of this, did not indicate any opposition to it or indicate that he was entitled to or would claim by survivorship.

7. That immediately following the said conversation referred to above, and after the plaintiff and the defendant James Wotherspoon had left the sickroom, the matter of the will which the deceased had referred to and the property in question herein was further discussed by the plaintiff, and her husband, with the defendant James Wotherspoon as they sat in the kitchen of the deceased's house at which time the defendant James Wotherspoon in effect said that the plaintiff should not rely too much on receiving these payments due under the agreement of sale from the Robinsons because the house might not stand up long enough to permit them to make payment—in other words, the purchasers would not likely complete the payments, and live up to the contract, the house being in such poor condition.

The point now is whether this course of conduct, and these acts are sufficient to establish that mutuality of agreement necessary to effect a severance.

It will be noted that the defendant James Wotherspoon in his letter referred to in cl. 4 above says: "for that is what we agreed upon", namely, this arrangement at the bank for the collection and division of the payments to be received on the agreement. Had William not died obviously this question of severance would never have arisen. The payments under the agreement, if made, would have been equally divided as received. Then there is this significant statement: "So neither of us has to worry about anything." It must be noted that at this time the defendant James Wotherspoon knew that his brother William Wotherspoon was ill, and whether James Wotherspoon then knew the serious nature of this illness or otherwise, he apparently wanted to assure his brother that there was nothing to worry about now with regard to these payments, the bank had instruction to divide the money as received. This is strong evidence of a mutual agreement in relation to the division of the proceeds and not confined to payments made during the lifetime of either.

Then again while the silence of the defendant Wotherspoon when advised of the will as set out in cl. 6 above, may not afford any very strong evidence of a mutual agreement to sever, and while the will itself could of course not effect a severance, yet when the surrounding circumstances are considered, along with his statement in the conversation immediately thereafter with the plaintiff and her husband, it affords strong evidence of a mutual agreement by the Wotherspoons to treat the tenancy as a tenancy in common. The clear inference to be drawn, it seems to me, from the statement made by James Wotherspoon as set out in cl. 7 above is that the plaintiff, on the death of her father, would, along with him, be the owner of an undivided one-half interest in the said property and in the payments to be made under the agreement of sale and purchase, and if the payments were not made and the property reverted to them they would be entitled as tenants in common. It was in effect an admission of the mutual agreement already arrived at between the two brothers. It seems to me in view of all the foregoing that one is driven to the almost irresistible conclusion that the parties by their conduct and acts had effected a severance by mutual agreement.

But it is suggested by the counsel for the defendant that these acts, statements and conduct do not constitute sufficient evidence of a mutuality of agreement for severance with respect to the balance of the moneys payable on the agreement but, at most, severance only to the moneys already collected and to be collected under the agreement of sale up to the time of the death of William Wotherspoon.

Furthermore it is contended that while William Wotherspoon knew of the joint tenancy and the incidents thereof the defendant James Wotherspoon did not, and the acts done by him and his conduct throughout must be viewed in the light of his lack of knowledge of the existence of a joint tenancy and the incidents thereof. With respect to that lack of knowledge this further observation should be made that while James Wotherspoon claims in effect that he did not know the property in question was held by himself and his brother in joint tenancy, I have some difficulty in accepting that statement. He had been informed by his mother in a letter received from her when he was overseas that if he died the property would go to William. Conversely one would think he would assume if William died the property would go to him as the survivor—if in fact he gave any thought to the matter. Then again if the defendant had no knowledge of the joint tenancy, it is difficult to understand that something he saw in the legal column of a daily newspaper in December 1950 relating to joint tenants and their respective rights, should be of any significance to him, unless he already knew of the joint tenancy existing between himself and his brother. I am rather inclined to think that he knew this property was held in joint tenancy by himself and his brother.

But whether he had such knowledge or not would seem to be immaterial when we come to consider the matter of severance arising from the acts of the parties. In *Williams* v. *Hensman*, 1 John. & H. at p. 560, the Vice-Chancellor says: "*In Jackson* v. *Jackson* [(1804), 9 Ves. 591, 32 E.R. 732], it is laid down, that, where you find in point of fact a dealing as tenants in common, it is not material whether that was or was not done in ignorance of the existence of a joint-tenancy. And there is good reason for this, for it must be borne in mind that a joint-tenancy is a right which any one of the joint-tenants may determine when he pleases; and, if all continue to deal on the footing of their interests not being joint, it would be most inequitable to treat it as a joint-tenancy when all the parties, whether in ignorance or not, have dealt with their interests in several."

Now the authorities are clear that an agreement of sale and purchase such as entered into here will not of itself operate as a severance: *Re Hayes' Estate*, [1920] 1 Ir. R. 207; the headnote which would appear to be a correct summation of the decision reads as follows: "An agreement for sale entered into by the persons who were together joint tenants of real property does not in itself, and in the absence of evidence of intention, operate as a severance of a joint tenancy in the purchase-money."

O'Connor L. J. at p. 221 says: "A mere agreement by persons entitled as joint tenants to convert their property from one species to another does not operate to work a severance."

And he continues: "It is true that when the transaction comes to be completed they may effect a severance: in the case of money converted into land, by the limitations in the conveyance; in the case of land converted into money, by taking and dividing the money."

This case was followed in the case of *Re Allingham, Allingham* v. *Allingham,* [1932] V.L.R. 469, in which Lowe J. at p. 472 says: "Apart from authority, I see no reason why a change in the form of the property should in itself effect an alteration in the nature of the ownership. The law permits a joint tenancy in personal property no less than in realty. Neither can I see that a contract to sell the property will be any more effective to work that change, that is, to work a severance, if nothing more appears. In my opinion the joint tenants of the land became the joint tenants of the proceeds of the sale of the land. But, of course, the joint tenants may effect a severance of their interest in the proceeds of sale, as, for instance, by dividing the proceeds of sale equally between themselves."

However it is largely then a matter of what inference can reasonably be drawn from the evidence and while the agreement itself does not operate as a severance there may be conduct and acts of the parties from which severance can be inferred. In *Crooke* v. *De Vandes* (1805), 11 Ves. 330, 32 E.R. 1115, the headnote reads as follows: "An agreement for severance as to the whole may be inferred from their conduct; dividing, as the property was received."

At p. 333 the Lord Chancellor says: "The other question, as to the severance of the joint-tenancy, is mere matter of evidence. It is not necessary to shew a specific art [act] of division of each part of the property, if there has been a general dealing, sufficient to manifest the intention to divide the whole. The acts, done as to parts, may be evidence as to the rest; as to which no act has been done. Their division of all the other parts of the estate is evidence of their intention to divide this, whenever they could lay hold of it."

The defendant submits however that a division of purchase-money on a sale is not sufficient evidence of a severance and relies on *Leak* v. *Macdowall* (1862), 32 Beav. 28 at p. 30, 55 E.R. 11, wherein it is stated by Sir John Romilly M. R.:

"A separate dealing by joint-tenants of the property may sever the joint-tenancy and create a tenancy in common. But I do not think this inference is to be drawn merely from the circumstance that a trustee, having realised part of the estate, has paid the money received, in certain proportions, to the parties in severalty. As to the money not received, they still remain joint-tenants.

"If a testator were to devise twenty houses to a trustee, in trust to sell and pay the proceeds to ten persons as joint-tenants, though one house were sold and the purchase-money divided, that would not shew that the other nineteen houses were to be held by the owners as tenants in common, and that when sold, the produce was to be divided equally between the surviving owners and the representatives of those who had died. Until some act is done to sever, the interest remains as it previously was, an interest in joint-tenancy. The burthen of proof lies on those who contend that a joint-tenancy has been severed."

Now this case is considered by Jenkins J. in *Re Denny, Stokes* v. *Denny* (1947), 177 L.T. 291. Here Jenkins J. points out that while at first sight it would appear that the decision of the Master of Rolls in the *Leak* case is in conflict with the decision of the Lord Chancellor in *Crooke* v. *De Vandes* he says at p. 294: "I do not think on examination of it that there is really any conflict, but if there was I should have no hesitation in preferring the authority of *Crooke* v. *De Vandes,* a decision of Lord Eldon, L. C. to the authority of *Leak* v. *Macdowall,* a decision of Sir John Romilly, M. R., in the later period of his career."

The learned Judge then quoted that part of the judgment of Lord Romilly above set out and continues: "Now if that decision really was a decision that division in portions of a fund can never support an inference of severance as a whole, then it would be in conflict with *Crooke* v. *De Vandes* and I would reject it accordingly, but in my judgment it really decides no such thing. It is merely a decision on the particular facts of the case to the effect that such distributions of portions on account as had there taken place were not sufficient to support the inference of severance any more than the sale of one out of the twenty houses held in joint tenancy and division in severalty of that one house would ordinarily be sufficient to support an inference to sever as to the remaining nineteen. The matter can, I think, be regarded as one of degree, so that while it is perfectly clear from the judgment of Lord Eldon that distribution in severalty of portions of the fund or estate may well be evidence of an intention to sever as to the whole, it is not every distribution, no matter how small and unimportant, that will support such an inference."

In this case Jenkins J. came to the conclusion that on the principles laid down in *Crooke* v. *De Vandes* there was a severance not only of the moneys received but of the reversionary interest.

Stirling J. in *Re Wilks, Child* v. *Bulmer*, [1891] 3 Ch. 59 at p. 62 says: "Without going so far [i.e. to say that jointure can only be severed by assignment by one, or by mutual agreement by all], I think that if the act of a joint tenant amounts to a severance it must be such as to preclude him from claiming by survivorship any interest in the subject-matter of the joint tenancy."

In *Wilson* v. *Bell* (1843), 5 Ir. Eq. Rep. 501, it is said by Lefroy B. at p. 507: "It was not argued that this was not in its origin a joint-tenancy; but it was contended, and upon undoubted authority, that joint-tenants may so act in respect to the property, as in equity, to sever the joint-tenancy; that if the acts and dealings of the parties in respect to the joint property *indicate an intention* to treat it as property held in common and not jointly, the Court will, from those acts and dealings, infer an agreement to sever the joint-tenancy; and that it is settled, that an agreement to sever will in equity amount to a severance."

The defendant relies on *Randall* v. *McLaughlin*, [1950] 1 D.L.R. 736, S.C.R. 291, where it was held that following the death of one of two joint tenants the division of rentals collected thereafter, between the survivor and the estate of the deceased joint owner was insufficient under the circumstances to effect a severance. But in that case it is clear there was not that mutuality of acts from which a severance could be inferred, because the division of the rents following Hill's death gives no help in inferring mutuality, and because that same division of rents prior to Hill's death is consistent both with a tenancy in common and a joint tenancy. Rents must not be confused with assets realized from a disposition of the land.

While by inference from the *Hayes' Estate* case and the *Allingham* case it would seem that had there been in either case a division of the principal sums received the Court would have held in favour of severance, I do not have to go so far as to decide in this case that that would be sufficient, since here we have not only such a division but such other mutual acts and conduct as to establish clearly it seems to me the agreement to sever.

Each case it seems to me must depend on its own facts and the reasonable inference which ought to be inferred therefrom.

In the present case therefore it seems to me the only reasonable inference that can be drawn is the existence of a mutual agreement to sever.

Judgment for plaintiff.

[A husband, holder in fee simple, conveyed to himself and his wife as joint tenants. Thereafter he entered into a contract to sell the land to plaintiff. The wife refused to join in a conveyance and plaintiff sought specific performance. Should he succeed and, if so, to what extent? See *Hurley* v. *Roy* (1921), 50 O.L.R. 281, 64 D.L.R. 375 (App. Div.); cf. *Freedman* v. *Mason*, [1957] O.R. 441, 9 D.L.R. 2d. 262, rev'g [1956] O.R. 849, 4 D.L.R. 2d 576.

In *Hurley* v. *Roy*, Riddell J. said that "the agreement to sell itself puts an end to the joint tenancy in equity". In this statement consistent with the view expressed in *Re Hayes' Estate*, as set out on p. 378, *supra*? See *In re Hewett*, [1894] 1 Ch. 362.

Suppose in *Hurley* v. *Roy* that the husband died after making an agreement to sell his interest. What is the purchaser's position, and is it affected by the co-tenant's knowledge or lack of knowledge of the agreement to sell?]

[Where spouses holding in joint tenancy execute a joint will with an agreement not to revoke it, the joint tenancy is severed: see *Re Kerr*, [1948] O.R. 543, [1948] 3 D.L.R. 668, aff'd [1949] 1 D.L.R. 736, [1949] O.W.N. 71 (C.A.).]

[A and B are joint tenants of land. A brings an action for partition. What is the state of the title if A dies (1) before judgment in the action or (2) after judgment ordering partition or sale? See *In re Wilks, Child* v. *Bulmer* [1891] 3 Ch. 59, 60 L.J. Ch. 696; *Grant* v. *Grant*, [1952] O.W.N. 641.

An assignment by a joint tenant for the benefit of creditors effects a severance: see *Re White*, [1928] 1 D.L.R. 846, 33 O.W.N. 255.

For a general treatment, see *Swenson and Degnan*, Severance of Joint Tenancies, (1954) 38 Minn. L. Rev. 466.]

POWER v. GRACE. Ontario Court of Appeal. [1932] O.R. 357, [1932] 2 D.L.R. 793

Appeal from a judgment of Widdifield Co. Ct. J., [1932] 1 D.L.R. 801, dismissing an action by an execution creditor. Plaintiff had filed a writ of execution against a joint tenant of land but before anything was done by the sheriff under the execution the debtor joint tenant died. Defendant, the surviving joint tenant claimed the whole estate free of the execution.

RIDDELL, J. A.: ... In my view, there is little advantage to be gained by an elaborate discussion of the principles of joint estates and their destruction, as the question here may be made to rest upon a few simple considerations.

In the first place, it has been undoubted law for centuries that where a writ under which an interest in land may be taken by the sheriff has been placed in his hands against a joint-tenant, and the joint-tenant dies before execution, the other joint-tenant surviving holds it discharged of the execution. *Lord Abergavenny's Case* (1607), 6 Co. 78a, 79a. This law has never been doubted; and the sole question for decision is whether the delivery of the writ to the sheriff is "execution". The proposition that such is the case, is conclusively met by the language of the statute and rules.

That "delivery" of the writ to the sheriff is not the equivalent of "seizure" by him is plain from the Execution Act, R.S.O. 1927, c. 112, s. 9(3) in the case of goods and s. 8 in the case of lands—it would savour of absurdity to say that a sheriff "to whom a writ of execution against lands is delivered for execution may seize and sell thereunder" if the delivery itself was equivalent to seizure. But still stronger, if possible, is the effect of our R. 564, corresponding to former statutory provisions; the rule says that the advertisement in the Ontario Gazette of any lands for sale under a writ of *fi. fa.*, during the currency of the writ shall be deemed a sufficient commencement of the execution. This would be nonsense if the delivery of the writ to the sheriff, itself, was *ipso facto*, the commencement of the execution. It is argued, however, that the statute, s. 9 providing that the "writ shall bind the... lands... from the time of the delivery thereof...," gives the delivery of the writ the effect of severing the joint-tenancy; but it must always be borne in mind that "statutes are not presumed to make any alteration in the Common Law, further or otherwise than the Act does expressly declare": *Arthur* v. *Bokenham* (1708), 11 Mod. 150; see Craies on Statute Law, 3rd ed., pp. 112, 278 *et seq.*

Sufficient effect is given to the statute by interpreting it according to its language, and I see no necessity for extending its meaning.

Restating in tabular form, the principles upon which I proceed:

(1) At the Common Law, a joint-tenancy is not affected by the delivery of a writ which may be effective against land, to the sheriff;

(2) Even after such delivery, the death of the joint-tenant before the "execution" of the writ at once terminates the joint-tenancy in favour of the other joint-tenant; delivery is not any part of "execution".

(3) Our statute does not expressly or by necessary implication change the Common Law in that regard—the implication, if any, being the other way. The result is that the Common Law is still in force, and the joint-tenancy was dissolved on the death of the mother.

The case was argued with great learning and ingenuity; but I think these elementary considerations are sufficient to dispose of it.

I think the appeal must be dismissed with costs.

HODGINS, J. A.: I agree.

GRANT, J. A.: ... It is elementary law that the destruction of any one of the four unities of joint-tenancy, namely, possession, interest, title or time, will terminate the tenancy and therewith the right of survivorship. To the continued existence of this right, the maintenance of these unities is essential. Not every dealing with the interest of one of the joint-tenants will operate to sever or terminate the tenancy. For example, a lease for years, by one of two joint-tenants in fee, of his share, does not sever the tenancy; but where they hold for a term of years only, it will do so. Where one of two joint-tenants in fee, grants his interest to a stranger for life, the joint-tenancy is merely suspended; if during such life estate, either of the joint-tenants dies, there is no right of survivorship and the joint estate is permanently severed; but if the life tenant dies before either of the joint-tenants, the joint estate is revived. (Vide 24 Hals., pp. 204-5, and cases cited.)

"In order that a grant by one joint-tenant may bind his fellows, it must be the grant of an estate, and not the grant of a mere incumbrance or burden on the estate, such as a rent-charge or a right of common." Co. Litt., p. 185a, cited in footnote to Challis on Real Property, 3rd ed., p. 367.

Turning to the statutory provisions regarding execution, we find that the Execution Act, s. 9 (1), reads in part, as follows: "Subject to the provisions of The Land Titles Act, a writ of execution shall bind the goods and lands against which it is issued from the time of the delivery thereof to the sheriff for execution."

It is to be noted in passing that the delivery of the writ to the sheriff, is "for execution"; the mere delivery is not execution, but empowers the sheriff to take the steps necessary to obtain or effect execution: i.e., "seizure, selling or disposing" as mentioned in s. 10, relating to lands. The meaning to be given to the word "bind" as used in s. 9 has been stated in numerous authorities.

"The writ is said to 'bind' the property in the goods of the judgment debtor in the bailiwick. Where it is said that the goods, or the property therein, are 'bound', what is meant is that the sheriff acquires a legal right to seize such goods. The ownership or general property, notwithstanding the binding effect of the writ, continues in the judgment debtor until the sale, and he can legally, until seizure, deal with the goods himself or, until sale, pass the property to others. Any transfer or assignment of the goods after the date at which the binding power of the writ operates will (except in the cases of a purchaser in market overt or of a bona fide purchaser for value without notice) be subject to the sheriff's right to follow up and seize the goods under the writ:" 14 Hals., p. 42, para. 87.

"The meaning of the expression, that the property of the goods is 'bound' is not that the property in them is altered but the defendant... cannot dispose of them, unless in market overt, so as to prevent their being taken in execution:" Edward's Law of Execution, p. 114.

Also, to the same effect is Anderson's Law of Execution, pp. 219-21.

The point is discussed at some length by Mellish, L.J. (with whom James, L.J., concurred) in *Ex p. Williams, Re Davis* (1872), L.R. 7 Ch. 314, at pp. 317-8, a decision that has been cited with approval, and followed in many later cases.

... As will have been noted, s. 9 of the statute uses the words "shall bind" with respect to goods and lands indiscriminately. The seizure to be made of goods or lands, thereby putting them "in execution" is covered by other sections of the Act and by the Consolidated Rules, to which reference has been made by my brother Riddell in his opinion which I have been privileged to read. The effect of the authorities to which I have referred is, as I understand them, that, until execution against the lands is actually commenced by advertisement (R. 564) or probably by an actual seizure upon the lands themselves, as illustrated in *Doe d. Miller* v. *Tiffany* (1848-50), 5 U.C.Q.B. 79, 6 U.C.Q.B. 426, cited in *Bradbourn* v. *Hall* (1869), 16 Gr. 518, there is no such effect wrought upon the title or interest of the joint-tenant (the judgment debtor) as will operate to sever the joint-tenancy. The filing of the writ of fi. fa. with the sheriff merely gives the right to seize the lands, and until the withdrawal, discharge or expiry of the writ, the lands continue "bound" in that sense. The change which may subsequently be made in "title and interest" is potential only, contingent upon the lands being placed in execution by seizure with a view to sale as by law provided.

Appeal dismissed.

[In *In re Penn* (1951), 4 W.W.R. (N.S.) 453 (B.C.), the Court purported to distinguish *Power* v. *Grace* by holding that registration of a judgment against a joint tenant (which, by statute, had the effect of a lien and charge upon which the judgment creditor might forthwith proceed) effected at least a suspension of the joint tenancy, and on the debtor's death before discharge of the judgment her heirs took rather than the surviving joint tenant. The principle expressed in *In re Penn* was rejected in *Re Brooklands Lumber & Hardware Limited* v. *Simcoe* (1956), 3 D.L.R. 2d 762, 18 W.W.R. (N.S.) 328 (Man.) where the Court applied *Power* v. *Grace* by analogy and held that registration of a judgment under legislation similar to that in *In re Penn* did not effect a severance of the joint tenancy. However, the judgment creditor was entitled to have the debtor's interest sold to realize on his judgment.

United States cases on the effect of a judgment lien favour the view in the *Brooklands Lumber* case; they are divided on the effect of a mere levy of execution: see 2 *American Law of Property*, s. 6. 2.]

[Where, as in Ontario, an execution debtor's interest in land may not be sold until 12 months after delivery of the writ of execution to the sheriff (see Ont. Rule 566), and even then must be preceded by advertising of the sale (see Ont. Rules 570 and 571), does this mean that in the interval or at least until seizure by commencement of the execution through advertising (see *Hall* v. *Goslee* (1864), 15 U.C.C.P. 101; *Bradburn* v. *Hall* (1869), 16 Gr. 518, and *Merchants Bank* v. *Campbell* (1881), 32 U.C.C.P. 170 (C.A.)) an execution debtor who is a joint tenant may pass a title to a purchaser free of the execution? The better answer would appear to be "no". Cf. *Re O'Brien*, [1943] O.W.N. 436, 24 C.B.R. 266; *Greiger* v. *Pye* (1941), 210 Minn. 71, 297 N.W. 173.

Should the answer be any different if all joint tenants join in selling to a purchaser while an execution subsists against one of them? And should it make any difference whether they are selling legal or equitable interests? It has been held that the interest of a joint tenant of an equitable fee simple is exigible and may be sold under an execution: see *Re Craig* (1928), 63 O.L.R. 192, [1929] 1 D.L.R. 142 (App. Div.), a judgment without written reasons. However, in *Re Tully and Klotz*, [1953] 4 D.L.R. 798, [1953] O.W.N. 661, it was held (also without written reasons) that equitable joint tenants of land (subject to a mortgage) could together pass a good title to a purchaser, although an execution was filed against one of the joint tenants before the agreement of sale was made. The Court apparently accepted the argument that the interest of one equitable joint tenant was not exigible because the equity of redemption is one and indivisible in that anyone with an interest therein is entitled to redeem the whole. Statutory provisions relative to execution against a mortgagor's interest were (so it was argued) applicable only to the case of a single mortgagor. In the result, while the execution creditor could follow the purchase-money into the hands of the debtor, he lost his claim against the latter's interest in the mortgaged land. *Re Tully and Kloz* was disapproved in *Re Klagsbrun and Stankiewicz*, [1954] 1 D.L.R. 593, [1953] O.W.N. 910 but a decision on the point at issue did not have to be made in the latter case. See also *Kates* v. *Morrison*, [1951] 4 D.L.R. 260, [1951] O.W.N. 701. *Quaere*, whether the "one and indivisible" argument is not more appropriate to the mortgagor-mortgagee relationship only, in that the mortgagee may insist on redemption of the whole mortgage and refuse to allow partial redemption by one of several joint tenants. If, as seems clear, an equitable (mortgagor) joint tenant may sell his interest, why is it not exigible?]

RE PUPKOWSKI. British Columbia Supreme Court. 1956. 6 D.L.R. 2d 427

Application to register a transmission of interest to a surviving joint tenant.

MACFARLANE J.: This matter came before me by way of petition under the *Land Registry Act*, R.S.B.C. 1948, c. 171, for an order that the Registrar of Titles for the Victoria Land Registration District do register two applications in respect of property registered under Indefeasible Title No. 1474821. The property is described as Lot 20 of Sect. 9 Beckley Farm Victoria City Plan 359. There is registered against this property a right to purchase in favour of Chester (who it appears is properly described as Czeslaw) Pupkowski and Cecilia Pupkowski as joint tenants. Cecilia Pupkowski met her death on March 24, 1956. Czeslaw Pupkowski was charged with the murder of the said Cecilia Pupkowski, his wife. After a preliminary hearing, Czeslaw Pupkowski was committed for trial on April 19, 1956, on the charge of murder. The first application No. 195383-G is an application made for the transmission as surviving joint tenant under the right to purchase to which I have referred. The second application is for registration of an assignment of the right to purchase executed under power of attorney which is filed with the application. The power of attorney was executed under date of March 26, 1956, and the assignment of the right to purchase on April 6, 1956. The applications to register were filed on April 10, 1956. On April 16, 1956, the Registrar of Titles by notice under the *Land Registry Act* refused to effect registration, in accordance with the tenor of the said application on the ground that he has been advised by the Deputy Attorney-General that a charge has been laid against Czeslaw Pupkowski charging him with the murder of his wife and that if the said Czeslaw Pupkowski is convicted, he could not obtain or enforce any right resulting to him from his own crime nor could his personal representative claiming under him enforce any such rights and that therefore the said Registrar says he is not satisfied that Czeslaw Pupkowski is now entitled to a good safe holding and marketable title to be registered in accordance with the tenor of this application, meaning application number 195383-G, and that application number 195384-G in respect to the assignment of the right to purchase must also be rejected because the said Registrar says the title claimed in part is founded upon the right of Czeslaw Pupkowski to survivorship under the joint tenancy referred to....

It is necessary to deal with the right of the Registrar to refuse transmission to the surviving joint tenant, when there is some evidence before the Registrar that the right of the survivor, though not adjudicated upon, may be affected or taken away by reason of the application of an aspect of the principle that a person is not entitled to benefit from his own wrong. The position the Registrar takes is that his acceptance of the application is only possible if he can find on the registration that the surviving joint tenant would be entitled to a good safe holding and marketable title by transmission under the *jus accrescendi.*

Section 164 of the *Land Registry Act* provides that: "Upon application being made for registration of a charge, and upon the Registrar being satisfied that a good safeholding and marketable title to the charge has been established by the applicant, and after giving notice if he sees fit, as provided in section 141, the Registrar shall register the title claimed by the applicant by endorsing a memorandum thereof on the register. The memorandum shall also be endorsed on the duplicate certificate of title if it has been produced."

Section 233 of the Act provides for notice by the Registrar in case of refusal to effect registration in accordance with the tenor of any application, first made or of any subsequent application affected by his refusal.

Section 234 also provides for an appeal to the Supreme Court, and for service with the petition and copies of all material and exhibits proposed to be used at the hearing.

Section 235 provides that upon the petition being made the application shall remain in good standing until the final disposition of the petition and if the petition is dismissed, the application shall forthwith become null and void and be cancelled unless an appeal is lodged and a stay of proceedings is obtained.

This petition is filed under the provisions of s. 234. The situation here is one that so far as I can find has not been dealt with by our Courts or in fact elsewhere. Somewhat similar problems have arisen in connection with the right of a person who brings about the death of another to take a benefit under the will of the person killed, or upon an intestacy and there are some cases which deal with the right of an insane person in such circumstances. I do not think these cases are in point here because the succession claimed here does not fall within either of the categories mentioned nor has the sanity or insanity of the husband at the time of the killing been adjudicated upon.

In a joint tenancy, although the parties are together interested in the whole of the property, and while one may sever a joint tenancy by certain methods, all that one party alone can deal with is his own right. It was pointed out long ago in Blackstone's Commentaries (1773 ed.), vol, 2 at p. 183 that "one joint-tenant is not capable by himself to do any act which tends to defeat or injure the estate of the other; as to let leases, or to grant copyholds", and that any such attempt was void. The authority given was *Lancaster and Lucas Case* (1591) 1 Leon. 233, 74 E.R. 214, where Lord Anderson put this case, "two joynt tenants of a manor, the one of them doth grant a copy, the same is void, for he is not dominus pro tempore". It would seem to me clear on principle that one joint tenant if he had no control over the interest of the other joint tenant could not take away entirely the right or interest of the other joint tenant by his own act. By his own act, he can sever the joint tenancy and upon severance, the joint tenants become tenants in common.

Now it is quite true that one of the incidents of a joint tenancy is the *jus accrescendi* which the survivor enjoys upon the death of the other but I think it is entirely contrary to the inherent conception of a joint tenancy that one joint tenant can defeat the right of the other or bring into being the *jus accrescendi* by his own act.

I am not called on in this case I think to decide whether such an act effects a severance for the application is not to register an assignment of his interest alone.

The condition upon which the Registrar exercises the power given him by s. 164 is that he be "satisfied that a good safeholding and marketable title to the charge has been established by the applicant" and the nature of his power has been settled in this Province by the Court of Appeal in *Re Land Registry Act and Shaw* (1915), 24 D.L.R. 429, 22 B.C.R. 116. I will content myself with a reference to the passages quoted by the late Chief Justice Farris in *Re Application of Penn* (1951), 4 W.W.R. (N.S.) 452 at p. 454. I think the language of the late Chief Justice Martin at p. 132 (B.C.R.) quoted there to be most apt to the situation here.

While I do not intend to discuss the cases dealing with the right to share in the estate of the deceased woman based upon a will or intestacy most of which are collected on pp. 10 and 11 of 1 Hals., 3rd ed., I might refer to the case of *Re Pollock*, [1941], Ch. 219, 1 All E.R. 360, where it was held that the onus was on the claimant to show that the act was done while the killer was of unsound mind. There is no evidence and certainly no adjudication as yet to that effect here.

I base my decision on the right of the Registrar to hold "that the documents and evidence produced to the Registrar have failed to establish a good safeholding and marketable title because of the palpable blot upon the face of the title which no examiner of titles could safely pass in the discharge of this duty".

Application dismissed.

[*Re Pupkowski* is discussed in a note by *Macdonald*, (1957) 35 Can. Bar Rev. 966. See also *Wade*, Acquisition of Property by Wilfully Killing Another—A Statutory Solution, (1936) 49 Harv. L. Rev. 715.

Apart from the effect of a land titles system (which, in any event, does not prevent voluntary severance: see *Re Cameron* (1957), 11 D.L.R. 2d 201 (Ont.)), legal title would pass to the surviving joint tenant who kills his co-tenant, but the Court should impose a constructive trust upon this title. The question that arises is whether the constructive trust should extend to the whole of the estate or to part only. See *Note*, (1952) 37 Minn. L. Rev. 71; *Note*, (1952) 27 Tulane L. Rev. 131. *The Restatement of Restitution* (1937), Comment *a* to s. 188, states that if one joint tenant murders his co-tenant "the murderer takes by survivorship the whole legal interest... but he can be compelled to hold the entire interest upon a constructive trust for the estate of his co-tenant, except that he is entitled to one-half of the income for life".]

[Suppose two joint tenants, say a husband and a wife, die in a common disaster and there is no evidence that either survived the other. Result, in the absence of legislation? Cf. Commorientes Act, R.S.A. 1955, c. 51, amended 1957, c. 8; 1958, c. 82; Survivorship and Presumption of Death Act, R.S.B.C. 1960, c. 375; Survivorship Act, 1962 (Man.), c. 73; Survivorship Act, R.S.N.B. 1952, c. 224, amended 1954, c. 81; 1958, c. 54; Survivorship Act, 1963 (Nfld.), c. 3; Survivorship Act, R.S.O. 1960, c. 391; Commorientes Act, R.S.P.E.I. 1951, c. 25, amended 1957, c. 5; Survivorship Act, 1962 (Sask.), c. 7.]

[Husband and wife were joint tenants of land under a conveyance thereof by the husband to his wife and himself. Subsequently the spouses separated (with the wife leaving the property) and later the marriage was annulled. On the (former) husband's death, she claimed the land by survivorship. Would you uphold her claim? See *Dunbar* v. *Dunbar*, [1909] 2 Ch. 639; *Crawford* v. *Crawford*, [1953] O.W.N. 781.]

4. INCIDENTS OF CO-TENANCY

(a) Possession and Accounting between Co-Tenants

HENDERSON v. EASON. Exchequer Chamber. 1951. 17 Q.B. 701, 21 L.J. Q.B. 82, 117 E.R. 1451

Writ of error in respect of a judgment for plaintiff in an action of account, founded on the statute 4 Anne, c. 16, brought by Robert Eason against the executor of his co-tenant Edward

Eason. Robert and Edward were tenants in common in fee simple of a farm from November 1833 to November 1838 during which time Edward occupied the whole on his own account, cultivating it and receiving and selling all produce to his own use.

The judgment of the Court was delivered by PARKE B.: ... There is no doubt as to the law before the statute of 4 Ann. c. 16. If one tenant in common occupied, and took the whole profits, the other had no remedy against him whilst the tenancy in common continued, unless he was put out of possession, when he might have his ejectment, or unless he appointed the other to be his bailiff as to his undivided moiety, and the other accepted that appointment, when an action of account would lie, as against a bailiff of the owner of the entirety of an estate.

Until the Statute of Anne this state of the law continued. That statute provides by section 27, that an action of account may be brought and maintained by one joint tenant and tenant in common, his executors and administrators, against the other, for receiving more than comes to his just share or proportion, and against the executor and administrator of such joint tenant or tenant in common; and the auditors are authorized to administer an oath.

Declarations framed on this statute vary from those at common law, as it is an essential averment in them that the defendant has received more than his share. This was held in the case of *Wheeler* v. *Horne* (Willes, 208), and in *Sturton* v. *Richardson* (13 M. & W. 17).

Under the Statute of Anne he is bailiff only by virtue of his receiving more than his just share, and as soon as he does so, and is answerable only for so much as he actually receives, as is fully explained by Lord Chief Justice Willes in the case above cited. He is not responsible, as a bailiff at common law, for what he might have made without his wilful default.

Is is to be observed that the statute does not mention lands or tenements, or any particular subject. Every case in which a tenant in common receives more than his share is within the statute; and account will lie when he does receive, but not otherwise. It is to observed, also, that the receipt of issues and profits is not mentioned, but simply the receipt of more than comes to his just share; and further, he is to account when he receives, not takes, more than comes to his just share. What, then, is a "receiving" of more than comes to his just share, within the meaning of that provision in the Statute of Anne?

It appears to us that, construing the Act according to the ordinary meaning of the words, this provision of the statute was meant to apply only to cases where the tenant in common receives money or something else, where another person gives or pays it, which the co-tenants are entitled to simply by reason of their being tenants in common, and in proportion to their interests as such, and of which one receives and keeps more than his just share according to that proportion.

The statute, therefore, includes all cases in which one of two tenants in common of lands leased at a rent payable to both, or of a rent charge, or any money payment or payment in kind, due to them from another person, receives the whole or more than his proportionate share according to his interest in the subject of the tenancy. There is no difficulty in ascertaining the share of each, and determining when one has received more than his just share: and he becomes, as to that excess, the bailiff of the other, and must account.

But when we seek to extend the operation of the statute beyond the ordinary meaning of its words, and to apply it to cases in which one has enjoyed more of the benefit of the subject, or made more by its occupation, than the other, we have insuperable difficulties to encounter.

There are obviously many cases in which a tenant in common may occupy and enjoy the land or other subject of tenancy in common solely, and have all the advantage to be derived from it, and yet it would be most unjust to make him pay anything. For instance, if a dwelling house, or barn, or room, is solely occupied by one tenant in common, without ousting the other, or a chattel is used by one cotenant in common, nothing is received; and it would be most inequitable to hold that he thereby, by the simple act of occupation or use, without any agreement, should be liable to pay a rent or anything in the nature of compensation to his cotenants for that occupation or use to which to the full extent to which he enjoyed it he had a perfect right. It appears impossible to hold that such a case could be within the statute; and an opinion to that effect was expressed by Lord Cottenham in *M'Mahon* v. *Burchell* (2 Phillips's Rep. 134). Such cases are clearly out of the operation of the statute.

Again, there are many cases where profits are made, and are actually taken, by one cotenant, and yet it is impossible to say that he has received more than comes to his just share. For instance, one tenant employs his capital and industry in cultivating the whole of a piece of land, the subject of the tenancy, in a mode in which the money and labour expended greatly exceed the value of the rent or compensation for the mere occupation of the land; in raising hops, for example, which is a very hazardous adventure. He takes the whole of the crops: and is he to be accountable for any of the profits in such a case, when it is clear that, if the speculation had been a losing one altogether, he could not have called for a moiety of the losses, as he would have been enabled to do had it been so cultivated by the mutual agreement of the cotenants? The risk of the cultivation, and the profits and loss, are his own; and what is just with respect to the very uncertain and expensive crop of hops is just also with respect to all the produce of the land, the fructus industriales, which are raised by the capital and industry of the occupier, and would not exist without it. In taking all that produce he cannot be said to receive more than his just share and proportion to which he is entitled as a tenant in common. He receives in truth the return for his own labour and capital, to which his cotenant has no right....

We therefore think that, upon the evidence set out in this case, there was nothing to warrant the jury in coming to the conclusion that the defendant received more than his just share within the meaning of the Act; and that the direction of the learned Judge as to the second issue was therefore wrong. And we also think that there was no conclusive or sufficient, or indeed any, evidence that he had the care and management of the farm for their common profit, as averred in the declaration.

Judgment reversed.

[The statute (1704), 4 Anne, c. 16, s. 27 is in force in the common law provinces; in most of them by virtue of the introduction of English law as of specified dates (see *Spelman* v. *Spelman*, [1944] 2 D.L.R. 74, [1944] 1 W.W.R. 691, 59 B.C.R. 551 (C.A.); *King* v. *King*, [1944] 4 D.L.R. 796, [1944] 3 W.W.R. 242 (Sask.); *Crane* v. *Blackadar* (1894), 40 N.S.R. 100 (C.A.); *Field* v. *Field* (1910), 8 E.L.R. 374 (P.E.I.); and in some by specific enactment; s. 133 of the Judicature Act, R.S.O. 1960, c. 197 reads as follows:

> Actions of account may be brought and maintained against the executors or administrators of a guardian, bailiff or receiver, and also by one joint tenant or tenant in common, his executors or administrators, against the other as bailiff for receiving more than comes to his just share or proportion, and against the executor or administrator of such joint tenant or tenant in common.

(See *Munsie* v. *Lindsay* (1883), 10 P.R. 173.) See also Administration Act, R.S.B.C. 1960, c. 3, s. 87.]

[Notwithstanding the extinction of title of a co-tenant, e.g. by the running of the Statute of Limitations against him in favour of his co-tenant, he may (if otherwise entitled) obtain an accounting of rents and profits from the land for the limitation period prior to the date of extinction of title: see *Isaryk* v. *Isaryk*, [1955] O.W.N. 487, where a wife, joint tenant with her husband, left him in possession and he remained in occupation, taking in roomers. Nine years and eleven months after the wife left, the husband sold the property. Some six months later she sued for an accounting of rents and profits for the six years prior to her action and an accounting of the proceeds of sale and obtained judgment. See Limitations Act, R.S.O. 1960, c. 214, ss. 4, 5 (1), 11. *Quaree*, whether *Isaryk* v. *Isaryk* is consistent with *Spelman* v. *Spelman* and *King* v. *King*, *supra*.

The position in an action of account is to be distinguished from that in an action for partition, a matter considered below.

In the United States, where most states have legislation similar to that of 4 Anne, c. 16, s. 27, a somewhat broader view has been taken than that in England, and a co-tenant is liable to account, not only for rents received from a third person (as in England) but also for profits earned from a depletion of the land, as by mining, oil production or timber cutting; see 2 *American Law of Property*, s. 6.14 and compare *Job* v. *Potton* (1875), L.R. 20 Eq. 84. See *Weible*, Accountability of Cotenants (1944), 29 Iowa L. Rev. 558.

There is some Canadian authority which appears to be in line with this United States view, but the basis of relief is more a matter of damages and injunction in respect of waste than an obligation to account: see *Proudfoot* v. *Bush* (1859), 7 Gr. 518 (cutting of timber by one co-tenant restrained at suit of other where land suitable as timber land only and cutting operated to destruction of the subject matter of the co-tenancy); cf. *Hersey* v. *Murphy* (1920), 48 N.B.R. 65, where the Court stated that "as between tenants in common acts of destructive waste only will be restrained," and dismissed an action by a co-tenant, holding a five-eighths interest in a 65 acre lot, to enjoin licensees of his co-tenants who had cut 8 cords of wood thereon. In the course of his judgment Grimmer J. said (at p. 73):

"When property is held by several persons as joint tenants or tenants in common, each has an equal right with his co-tenants to the entry and possession of the entire estate, and each co-tenant may use and enjoy the common property in a reasonable manner to the extent of his own interest, but cannot in any way impair or interfere with the equal right of his co-tenants to a similar use and enjoyment. What is a reasonable use depends upon the nature of the property and the fact that some of it is consumed or its value impaired by the use does not necessarily render the use unlawful where such is a natural result of the usual and legitimate exercise of the right of enjoyment, as in the case of timber or mineral lands held in common. If one tenant in common has used the property unlawfully or to the exclusion of his co-tenant he may become liable to the latter either in an action of tort for an accounting, or for possession, as the case may be. Also one co-tenant may license a stranger to use the property in such manner as would be permissible in himself, but such licence will not affect the interest or rights of the other co-tenants. Ordinarily one tenant in common of real property cannot maintain trespass *quare clausum fregit* against his co-tenant unless the act complained of amounts to an injury to or destruction of the common property or to the expulsion of the plaintiff from the property or an interference with his enjoyment thereof: *Murray* v. *Hall* (1849) 7 C.B. 439; *Stedman* v. *Smith* (1857) 8 E. & B. 1; *Wilkinson* v. *Haygarth* (1847) 12 Ad. El. N.S. 835.

"The general rule of liability between co-tenants for rents and profits received from the common property is that a tenant in common who has received the whole or more than his proper share of the rents and profits of the common estate is liable to his co-tenants for the amount of the excess received by him above his just proportion, each being entitled to a share of the rents and profits in proportion to his interest in the common property.

"Then did the cutting of the defendants amount to an injury to or destruction of the common property, to the expulsion of the plaintiff therefrom, or an interference with his enjoyment thereof?...

"Having reached [the] conclusion [that it did not], it is quite unnecessary to labor the matter further, but as an injunction was applied for and obtained, and I am asked to continue it, I desire to say that the trend and bulk of authority is that in some cases Courts of Equity will grant an injunction in favor of one co-tenant against another, to prevent waste (which is not the case here) but the jurisdiction is sparingly exercised, and the Court will grant an injunction only where the waste complained of is malicious or destructive, or attended with peculiar circumstances warranting such relief. As between tenants in common, acts of destructive waste only will be restrained: *Hole* v. *Thomas*, 7 Ves. Jr. 589. The note to this case is of such importance I deem it advisable to state it here:

"In case of coparceners and tenants in common, no legal remedy is provided as to acts of waste or trespass between themselves: *Matts* v. *Hawkins*, 5 Taunt. 24, but Courts of Equity will interfere not only when (as in the principal case) one tenant in common is committing acts which, if suffered to go on, would amount to a destruction of the property, (*Norway* v. *Rowe*, 19 Ves. 159), but also, whenever it appears that any sort of waste has been committed, or threatened, by one tenant in common, who has, by contract, become the occupying tenant of the other, and who is consequently bound to treat the property as any other occupying tenant should treat it, (*Twort* v. *Twort*, 16 Ves. 132), though prospective relief cannot be given, as against tenants in common against acts of mere equitable waste: *Smallman* v. *Onions*, 3 Brown 622. The remedy, in such cases, is to apply for a partition: *Goodwin* v. *Spray*, 2 Dick. 667."

See also *Jacobs* v. *Seward* (1872), L.R. 5 H.L. 464.]

[In *Lehman* v. *Hunter* (1939), 13 M.P.R. 553 (N.B.), an issue was raised in a partition action between co-tenants that one group had acquired title to a portion of the land by length of possession against a second group. In rejecting this contention, Baxter C. J. said, *inter alia*:

"One joint tenant or tenant in common of land cannot maintain an action of trespass against another in respect of the exercise of any acts of ownership on the land by the latter consistent with the right of the former: *Martyn* v. *Knowlys*, 8 T.R. 145; *Jacobs* v. *Seward*, L.R. 4 C.P. 328, L.R. 5 H.L. 464, 41 L.J.C.P. 221, but only for an actual expulsion or destruction of some part of the common property.

"Now what is the nature of the property? Essentially it is fishing property: The 400 acres of land is of no practical value except as it subserves the enjoyment of fishing for salmon. No one pretends for a moment that it was either purchased or held for the sake of its timber or for any other reason than that it was adjacent to the fishing waters. How could it be used for fishing purposes? Just as it was used: by constructing some sort of reservoir for a water supply, an ice house and a house for a caretaker. But what about the joint owners? Where were they to lodge? If one set up a tent or a shelter of any kind must the others regard it as an ouster or an adverse possession and begin to count time under the statute? Surely each owner had a right to use the property consistently with the opportunities for enjoyment of his co-owners. I have to say whether the building of the Mitchell-Hunter-Olds camp was an act of dispossession of the Ehrich-Lehman interest. I think I am entitled to have regard to the nature of the property which these parties used together for upwards of twenty years as a fishing resort, in considering the question whether the building of the Mitchell-Hunter-Olds lodge was or was not an act of dispossession and I am of opinion that it was not. Neither was it one of discontinuance. To come to a contrary conclusion I would have to satisfy myself that the moment Mitchell-Hunter-Olds broke ground for their camp and thus commenced its erection, an action of trespass could have been brought against them by the other owners. As said by Lord Hatherley, L.C. in *Jacobs* v. *Seward*, L. R. 5 H.L. 464: 'so long as a tenant in common is only exercising lawfully the right he has as tenant in common, no action can lie against him by his co-tenant', and by Lord Westbury in the same case: 'It is undoubtedly settled law that (one tenant in common) cannot maintain trespass unless there is a case of ouster'. There was, in the present case, no intention of ouster. All that took place is perfectly compatible with the intention of the parties to enjoy the whole property in common. Of course one of the parties would not be sleeping in the camp of the other, but it does not follow that there was any intention of putting any part of the property in severalty. Surely the use of the property by any tenant in common in a manner which is necessary for its enjoyment cannot be taken, in the absence of any other evidence to be an ouster of the other tenants in common."]

[Legislation based on the Statute of Westminster 11 (1285) enables one co-tenant to sue another for waste; see for example, Conveyancing and Law of Property Act, R.S.O. 1960, c. 66, s. 32: "Tenants in common and joint tenants shall be liable to their co-tenants for waste, or in the event of a partition, the part wasted may be assigned to the tenant committing such waste at the value thereof to be estimated as if no such waste had been committed"; and see chap. XI, *infra.*]

Co-tenants in fee simple are, of course, in a more favourable position respecting waste than holders of more limited interests. As put in 2 *American Law of Property*, s. 6.15, "a cotenant in fee is properly liable for waste when his use of the property is not in the exercise of his right of reasonable enjoyment, and when such use results in permanent injury to the property". See *Martyn* v. *Knowllys* (1799), 8 T.R. 145, 101 E.R. 1313 (K.B.) (action for waste does not lie where no injury done to inheritance but there was mere felling of trees that were fit to be cut); *Wilkinson* v. *Haygarth* (1847), 12 Q.B. 837, 116 E.R. 1085 (carrying away of turf by a licensee of one co-tenant held actionable waste at suit of another co-tenant because an act of destruction and not mere realization of the yield or profits of the property.) In *Martyn* v. *Knowllys*, would the co-tenant who cut the grown timber be liable to account for the proceeds of its sale? See *Rice* v. *George* (1873), 20 Gr. 221.

Leases by a co-tenant. Among the problems that arise under this heading are (1) the effect upon a joint tenancy in fee of a lease by a joint tenant of his interest and (2) the effect upon other co-tenants of a lease by one of them of the whole of the land held in co-tenancy.

It is clear that a co-tenant may lease his interest putting his lessee in his position *qua* the other co-tenants. Where the lease is by a joint tenant, there are alternative views open on whether a severance results, each supported by some authority. Thus (1) the lease effects a complete severance: see *Clerk* v. *Clerk* (1694), 2 Vern. 323, 23 E.R. 809 (Ch.); 2 *American Law of Property*, s. 6.3; (2) the right of survivorship subsists as to the reversion with the lease being binding on the surviving joint tenant: see 27 *Halsbury's* Laws of England (1937, 2nd ed.), p. 662n; and (3) the joint tenancy is severed (suspended) during the term of the lease but is re-established upon termination of the lease during the lessor's lifetime: *cf. Napier* v. *Williams*, [1911] 1 Ch. 361, at p. 368. See, generally, *Note* (1937), 25 Calif. L. Rev. 203, at p. 206.

[What is the effect upon a joint tenancy in fee of a grant by one joint tenant of his interest to a third person for life? If one of two joint tenants of a leasehold sub-lets his interest, is there a severance? See 32 *Halsbury* (1960, 3rd ed.), p. 335 n; *Cheshire*, Modern Law of Real Property (1962, 9th ed.), p. 299.]

If one co-tenant purports to lease the whole of the land held in co-tenancy, the other co-tenants may resist its effect as to their interests, and so too where the lease is of a defined part of the whole: see *Goodenow* v. *Farquhar* (1873), 19 Gr. 614 (one co-tenant entitled to injunction against lessee of other co-tenant and to accounting of moiety of proceeds of quarrying in the portion of the land specified in the lease.). The lease is good only as a transfer of the lessor's interest (see *Vasiloff* v. *Johnson* (1932), 41 O.W.N. 139) but it may be ratified by his co-tenants, e.g., if they share in the rent.

(b) Repairs and Improvements

LEIGH v. DICKESON. Court of Queen's Bench. 1883. 12 Q.B.D. 194

A tenant in common of land to the extent of three fourths thereof leased her interest to one who subsequently assigned to defendant. During the currency of the lease defendant purchased the one-fourth interest of the other tenant in common. When the lease expired defendant continued in possession. Negotiations for renewal of the lease foundered and the lessor's trustees sued for use and occupation from the expiration of the lease. Defendant counter-claimed for contribution in respect of money expended by him as a co-tenant for repairs.

POLLOCK B.: ... On behalf of the defendant it was contended that the action would not lie, because one tenant in common cannot sue another tenant in common for the rent of premises owned by them. It is, however, unnecessary to deal with this general proposition, because in the present case a claim is made by the plaintiffs against the defendant not simply to recover the value of premises occupied by him as tenant in common, but it is brought for the use and occupation of the three-fourths of the premises which were let by the plaintiffs' cestui que trust to Prebble in 1860, by a lease which was afterwards assigned by Prebble to the defendant, who entered and paid rent. Having carefully considered the correspondence that passed between Mrs. Eyles and her solicitors and the defendant and his solicitors, I have come to the conclusion that the occupation by the defendant, which occurred after the expiration of the lease in question on the 6th of January, 1881, must be referred, not to his right as tenant in common, but to his continuing in occupation as tenant as sufferance. Now it is quite clear from the authority of Lord Coke in Co. Litt. 186a, which was adopted by the Court in *Cowper* v. *Fletcher*, 6 B. & S. 464, that one joint tenant may let his part for years or at will to his companion, and I think it is equally clear that if after the expiration of such a lease the tenant holds over, the same consequences must be taken to follow as would arise in the case of a lease between strangers, and that the lessor would have a right to treat the defendant as a tenant at sufferance for the period during which he held after the expiration of the lease, and to sue him for use and occupation in respect thereof. If any authority were required for this, the case of *Bayley* v. *Bradley*, 5 C.B. 396, seems to suffice. Looking, therefore, at the case in this light, my judgment will be for the amount claimed, 241£, 9s. 6d. being the amount recoverable for 264 days' occupation at the same rate as was reserved by the lease.

This disposes of the plaintiffs' claim. The defendant, however, by way of counter-claim, charges the plaintiffs with a sum of 801., which, he alleges, he laid out and expended in substantial and other proper repairs and improvements upon the premises since the expiration of the lease. With regard to this claim, it is first to be observed that it is made not in respect of any breach by Mrs. Eyles or her trustees of the covenant contained in the lease, but for what are called substantial and proper repairs and improvements. To this set-off and counter-claim the plaintiffs demur, and it was admitted by counsel that if the demurrer should be overruled, the defendant was entitled to judgment upon the counter-claim, so that any question of amount, and any distinction which might be taken between repairs and improvements, is apparently waived, and the question is broadly raised whether, having reference to the legal relation which existed between the parties, the plaintiffs are liable to recoup the defendant for money so laid out by him in repairing the premises in the absence of any express contract. There is, however, nothing to shew that but for them the subject-matter of the tenancy in common would have perished, so as to bring the case within the principle of those decisions in which it has been held that, where an outlay is in the nature of salvage, all interested in the thing saved are bound to contribute.

No case or authority was cited by counsel to shew that going back for a long period of years effect has ever been given by the Courts to a claim by action by one tenant in common against another for money which had been expended upon the repair of their common property, nor have I been able to find any such case or authority, although the claim deals with a matter of common occurrence, and the question must often have arisen if the defendant's contention be correct. It becomes necessary, therefore, to refer to the older law, and to see upon what principle any claim of a like nature has been rested, and how far, if at all, it would govern a case like the present. The writ by one of two tenants in common against the other de reparatione faciendâ is mentioned by the earlier law writers. Coke, in his Commentary upon Littleton, Co. Litt, 200 b, speaks of it thus: "If two tenants in common, or joint tenants, be of an house or mill, and it fall in decay, and the one is willing to repaire the same and the other will not, he that is willing shall have a writ de reparatione faciendâ, and the writ saith, ad reparationem et sustentationem ejusdem domûs teneantur; whereby it appeareth that owners are in the case bound pro bono publico to maintain houses and mills which are for habitation and use of men."

The right to this writ is also mentioned in almost similar terms in *Lewis Bowles' Case* (11 Co. Rep. 82b), where it is said: "If there be two joint tenants of a wood, or arable land, the one has no remedy against the other to make inclosure or reparations for safeguard of the wood, or corn, but if there be two joint tenants of an house the one shall have a writ de reparatione faciendâ against the other, and the words of the writ are ad reparationem et sustentationem ejusdem domûs tenetur." Similar statements of the law will be found in 2 Co. Inst. 402, and Moor's Rep. 374. The writ is also mentioned in 2 Cruise's Dig. 377, as a common law writ.

The later authorities in substance adopt these two, and refer to them in much the same language. It is curious to observe that the remedy between the joint tenants is spoken of as if it was one which existed rather for the benefit of the community than of the joint tenant, but what is more to the purpose is to notice that in these passages and in the books in which the form of the writ itself is given, as in Fitzherbert's N.B. p. 127, and the Registrum Brevium, p. 153 b, the writ is to be found amongst those which require acts to be done by way of reparation, such as the repairing of mills either by the county or by an individual who is liable, the repairing of a bridge, wall, road, sewer, or pavement, the repairing by a neighbour of his house which is so in decay as to be dangerous; and in all these cases the ground of the claims seems to be such as to presuppose that the condition of the things to be repaired would be dangerous or useless unless the repairs in question were effected. This procedure differs widely from the right alleged in the present case of one tenant in common to expend money in the ordinary repairs of a house, and then recover from his co-tenant his share. In *Dering* v. *Earl of Winchelsea* (1 Cox, 318) Eyre, C. B. speaking of the right to contribution among sureties, mentions the case of tenants in common, and refers to the writ in Fitzherbert. He speaks of contribution generally as being founded upon an equitable right based upon general principles, and in the recent case of *Leslie* v. *French* (23 Ch. D. 552) this dictum was cited by counsel, but I do not find that it received any assent in the judgment of Fry, L. J., and in neither of these cases—one being a claim between co-sureties, and the other a claim between co-owners of a policy of insurance—was it necessary to consider what was the law as applicable to tenants in common.

In Story's Eq. Jurisp. s. 1235, the subject is treated of, and the writer refers to some cases which have arisen in the Courts of America, but the only one which bears upon the question now before the Court is that of *Converse* v. *Ferre* (11 Mass. 326), in which Parker, C. J., says that, "At common law no action lies by one tenant in common who has expended more than his share in repairing the common property against the deficient tenants," and he goes on to say that for this reason the legislature of the state provided a remedy which was applicable however to mills only.

An interesting judgment by Chancellor Kent, upon the subject of contribution will be found in the case of *Campbell* v. *Mesier*. (4 John. 344.) A bill was filed by one of two owners of adjoining houses separated by a party-wall. It was an old party-wall between the two houses, and the owner of one of them being desirous to build a new house on his lot, pulled down the old house, and with it, the party-wall, which was ruinous, and rebuilt it with his new house. The owner of the adjoining house and lot was held to be bound to contribute rateably to the expense of the new wall of partition. The particular case was decided expressly upon the ground that it was absolutely necessary to have the wall rebuilt, and therefore it furnishes no authority for the right to contribution where ordinary repairs are done. In the course of the judgment Chancellor Kent refers to dicta expressed by different writers upon the civil law. One of these, Papinian (Dig. 17, 2, 52, 10), states it as a rule of the civil law, that if one part owner of a house in decay, repairs it at his own expense, upon the refusal of the others to unite in the expense, he can compel them to contribute their proportion, with interest, or, upon their default, at the end of four months, the house, at his election, becomes his sole property. This would seem only to apply to the case of such decay as would if not arrested by repair produce ruin. Pothier, speaking of party-walls, Contrat de Société, Première Appendice, No. 199, 203, accords the right to contribution for the rebuilding of a party-wall only where it is ruinous and needs to be rebuilt, independently of the raising of it by the part owner on one side.

I was referred during the course of the argument to a form of order which is to be found in Seton on Decrees, vol, 11., 1024, wherein an inquiry is directed as to what, if any, substantial repairs have been done by one or more of several tenants in common. This occurs in an order made in a suit for partition and sale, in which it is obvious the direction would be necessary, quite apart from such a right as is insisted upon by the defendant in the present action.

At common law no action of account lay by one joint tenant or tenant in common against his co-tenant. By the statue of 4 Anne, c. 16, s. 27, a tenant in common could be charged by his co-tenant in an action at law as bailiff for money received, a share of which the plaintiff was entitled to. The same end could also be better attained by a bill in equity. The history of the action of account will be found in Viner's Abridgment "Account," and under the same title in Selwyn's Nisi Prius. Except, however, in the case of a bill for partition I can find no trace of any action or claim in equity for contribution in respect of money expended for repairs.

This being the state of the authorities, the conclusion I arrive at is that the defendant has failed to establish his counter-claim against the plaintiffs. It may be said that this leaves the defendant to bear the costs of repairs which in equity and fair dealing ought to be borne in part by the plaintiffs. There is something no doubt in this argument, but it must be remembered that the relation which exists between tenants in common is peculiar. In cases where the money expended is for ordinary repairs, and not such as are absolutely necessary for the prevention of ruin, the inconvenience of taking an account between the co-tenants whenever one has paid more than his share would be great, and in almost every case in which they are unable themselves to agree as to what repairs are needed and how the costs of them should be divided, the only efficient remedy would be attained by a partition.

Judgment for plaintiffs.

[The judgment of Pollock B. was affirmed on appeal, (1884), 15 Q.B.D. 60, where Cotton L. J. said, *inter alia* (at p. 66): "I think that it must be assumed that the house was in a bad state of repair, and that the repairs executed by the defendant were necessary. As to the claim for improvements, it has been urged that no tenant in common is entitled to execute improvements upon the property held in common, and then to charge his co-tenant in common with the cost. This seems to me the true view, and I need not further discuss the question as to improvements. As to the question of repairs, it is to be observed that when two persons are under a common obligation, one of them can recover from the other the amount expended in discharge or fulfilment of the common obligation; but that is not the position of affairs here: one tenant in common cannot charge another with the cost of repairs without a request, and in the present case it is impossible even to imply a request. No action for money paid will lie at common law; and in equity there is no remedy against a co-tenant in common, except in the case which I will presently mention. It was suggested, however, that at common law a right of contribution existed between tenants in common; and reference was made to Fitz. Nat. Brev. 127: a form of the writ, de reparatione faciendâ, is there set out: but the language of the writ assumes that the tenants in common or joint tenants are bound to repair the mill or house; it assumes an obligation or duty towards third persons. The existence of this obligation or duty explains the writ. A similar explanation may be given of the writ of contribution mentioned in Fitz. Nat. Brev. 162. Reference was also made to Co. Litt. 200, where it is said that one tenant in common or joint tenant may have a writ de reparatione faciendâ against another; but Lord Coke is there referring to the form of writ given in Fitz. Nat. Brev. 127. I cannot assent to the suggestion that the passage in Co. Litt. 200, shews that one tenant in common may compel at his pleasure another tenant in common to contribute to the repairs of a house. I think that the passages in Fitz. Nat. Brev. 127, 162, do not present any difficulty, and are not inconsistent with the conclusion at which I have arrived. Therefore, no remedy exists for money expended in repairs by one tenant in common, so long as the property is enjoyed in common; but in a suit for a partition it is usual to have an inquiry as to those expenses of which nothing could be recovered so long as the parties enjoyed their property in common; when it is desired to put an end to that state of things, it is then necessary to consider what has been expended in improvements or repairs: the property held in common has been increased in value by the improvements and repairs; and whether the property is divided or sold by the decree of the Court, one party cannot take the increase in value, without making an allowance for what has been expended in order to obtain that increased value; in fact, the execution of the repairs and improvements is adopted and sanctioned by accepting the increased value. There is, therefore, a mode by which money expended by one tenant in common for repairs can be recovered, but the procedure is confined to suits for partition. Tenancy in common is an inconvenient kind of tenure; but if tenants in common disagree, there is always a remedy by a suit for a partition, and in this case it is the only remedy."

The English cases proceed on the principle that in the absence of agreement there is no common liability to repair: see *Bonner* v. *Tottenham*, [1899] 1 Q.B. 161, at p. 175. It is stated in 2 *American Law of Property*, s. 6. 18 that, notwithstanding the views of some authors to the contrary, the position in the United States is the same, even though repairs are made for preservation and use of the property. Expenditures for repairs are, of course, considered in an accounting for rents and profits and in partition actions. Where a co-tenant on his own effects capital improvements, should he be entitled to exact contribution in an action for an account of rents and profits, as opposed to an action of partition?]

RUPTASH AND LUMSDEN v. ZAWICK. Supreme Court of Canada. [1956] S.C.R. 347, 2 D.L.R. 2d 145

Appeal from a judgment of the Alberta Appellate Division, [1955] 4 D.L.R. 195, 15 W.W.R. (N.S.) 518, affirming with a variation a judgment of Primrose J., 14 W.W.R. (N.S. 683, continuing certain caveats. Two tenants in common entered into a written agreement respecting the management of the common property by one of them with authority to repair and improve it, to collect rents and pay the cost of repairs, improvements and the charges out of the rents. Provision was made for an accounting and division of profits and for payment to the managing co-tenant by the other of the latter's share of the cost of repairs, and the latter also agreed to give possession to the former. Mutual rights of pre-emption were stipulated, and by an amended agreement neither co-tenant could sell his interest without the other's consent. The issues in this case arose when the managing co-tenant took proceedings on caveats filed by him when the other co-tenant sold his interest to the appellants. He claimed, inter alia, a charge on the land under the agreement for the other co-tenant's share of the cost of repairs. The appellants sought a declaration that their title was free of any charge or equitable interest in the managing co-tenant.

The judgment of the Court was delivered by CARTWRIGHT J. (who after reciting the facts and reviewing the agreement continued as follows):

For the above reasons I conclude that on its proper construction the agreement did not by its terms grant any estate or interest to the respondent in the undivided share in the land owned by William Zawick or give him any charge thereon or any assignment of the future rents. It gave him rather a terminable right to manage the property and collect the rents on behalf of William Zawick as well as on his own behalf and the personal covenant of William Zawick to pay his proportionate share of the cost of the repairs.

This leaves for consideration the respondent's contention secondly mentioned above. This may be briefly stated as follows. Firstly, even if it should be held that the agreement of June 23, 1951, in so far as it relates to the repairing of the building, did not in terms give the respondent any charge on the undivided share owned by William Zawick but only his personal covenant to pay his proportion of the cost, it is clear that the repairs were made and paid for by the respondent with the consent and approval of William Zawick who accepted the benefit of the resulting increase in value of the property, and in such circumstances, by operation of law an equitable lien on the undivided share owned by William Zawick was conferred upon the respondent until his claim for payment of the proportion of the cost of repairs chargeable to William Zawick was satisfied; and, secondly, even if it should be held that the caveat of November 19, 1951, was ineffective to protect or give notice of such lien, the title of the appellants is nonetheless subject to it as s. 189 of the *Land Titles Act* has no application to the equities of tenants in common or to their consequent rights to liens.

The first branch of this argument appears to have been accepted by Clinton J. Ford, J. A. but not the second. The learned Justice of Appeal says in part:

"I do not think that the lack of a restrictive covenant running with the land could be said to override what I have just concluded to be the rights of co-tenants to contract with respect to improvements and repairs to the premises held in common so as to bind themselves and their assignees who had actual knowledge of the agreement under a caveat filed pursuant to s. 131 of the Act.

"In this connection I quote from 86 C.J.S. p. 460: 'Recording laws have no application to the equities of tenants in common, or to their consequent rights to liens. Where one co-tenant agreed to pay his proportionate share of necessary expenditures, but sold his interest without making payment thereof, his co-tenant has a lien on the interest conveyed for the amount due him.'

"I think that the last part of this statement is true in this jurisdiction only where the purchaser had, as here, notice in accordance with the provisions of the *Land Titles Act*."

Immediately after the passage from Corpus Juris Secundum quoted by Clinton J. Ford J. A. this sentence follows: "While a proportionate share of necessary expenditures could have been impressed as a lien on the noncontributing cotenant's interest in the realty prior to conveyance of such interest to a bona fide purchaser for value without notice, on failure to do so, the cotenant making the expenditure is merely a creditor of the noncontributing cotenant as against a purchaser of the latter's interest."

And earlier on the same page there is the following statement: "A claim for contribution does not of itself constitute a lien on the premises but only a right to have a lien decreed on a cotenant's interest for the protection of the claim against such cotenant."

In 20 Hals., 2nd ed., p. 573, under the title "Lien" the learned author says: "Thus a tenant in common has been held to have no lien against the share of his co-tenant for payments made for the benefit of the estate."

I have examined all the cases cited as authority for this statement and they appear to me to support it. The contrary view which was expressed by Lord Hardwicke L. C. in *Doddington* v. *Hallet* (1750), 1 Ves. Sen. 497, 27 E.R. 1165, has been overruled by the cases collected in Halsbury at the page mentioned above.

In view of the wording of the passage from Corpus Juris Secundum quoted by Clinton J. Ford J. A. it may be observed that the following passage from the judgment of Sir James Wigram V.-C. in *Green* v. *Briggs* (1848), 6 Hare 395 at p. 401, 67 E.R. 1219, indicates that a different view of the law was adopted in America: "The case of *Doddington* v. *Hallet* (1 Ves. 497) was referred to in argument by the Plaintiff's counsel, but only (as I understand) for the purpose of excluding the suggestion that the Plaintiff relied upon it, or upon the doctrine it contains, for supporting his claim in this suit. I collect from Stroy on Partnership (sect. 444) that upon principles of public policy and convenience, America has adopted *Doddington* v. *Hallett*. But, however that may be, it is certain that Lord Eldon, in *Ex parte Harrison* (2 Rose, 76), and in *Ex parte Young* (2 Rose, 78, n), deliberately overruled it."

In the case at bar the respondent had a contractual right to recover from William Zawick the latter's proportionate share of the moneys expended by the former on repairs. I have already stated my reasons for concluding that on its proper construction the contract did not create a lien or charge. The nature of the rights of the respondent apart from contract is, I think, accurately stated in the judgment of Cotton L. J. in Leigh v. Dickeson (1884), 15 Q.B.D. 60 at p. 67....

In my opinion, apart from contract the right of a tenant in common who has made repairs to the property of which his co-tenant has taken the benefit is limited to an equitable right to an accounting which can be asserted only in a suit for partition; he does not acquire a lien or charge on the property itself. This view is I think supported not only by the English cases referred to in Halsbury but also by at least some of the American decisions referred to in Corpus Juris. For example, in *Dietsch* v. *Long* (1942), 43 N.E. 2d 906, one of the questions which arose was whether the purchaser in good faith of the share of one of several tenants in common took such share subject to a claim for contribution to the cost of repairs made prior to the transfer and which could have been enforced against the transferor by his co-tenants. In holding that the purchaser did not take subject to such claim it was said, *per curiam*, at p. 917: "The persons seeking to impress their claims on the real estate conveyed were not at any time owners of any interest in the real estate conveyed but had only equitable rights for an accounting against the grantor, which, if they had pursued their remedies prior to the transfer, by proper proceedings in equity, they could have had impressed as liens on the real estate conveyed. Hence they were creditors."

The second branch of this argument was not accepted by Clinton J. Ford J.A., as appears from the last sentence in the passage from his reasons last quoted above; he was however of opinion that the interest claimed by the respondent was sufficiently protected by the caveat filed.

I have already indicated my reasons for holding that the caveat noted on the register when the appellants obtained title did not give notice of the claim for the proportionate share of the cost of repairs. [The caveat in question referred only to the right of pre-emption.] It follows that the appellants are in the position of purchasers in good faith and for value who have obtained the legal title to the land formerly owned by William Zawick without notice of an equitable right claimed against him. While in my opinion that right was a personal one only and did not amount to a charge on the land, the appellants having acquired the legal estate would (fraud having been negatived) hold it free of an equitable charge of which they had no notice; this would be so apart from the provisions of the *Land Titles Act*; and s. 189 of that Act appears to me to provide in plain terms that as purchasers from a registered owner who have received a certificate of title they take free from such a charge, even if they had notice of its existence, unless it is registered. To hold that a purchaser from the registered owner of an undivided fractional share in a parcel of land is put upon inquiry as to the state of the accounts between his vendor and the latter's co-tenants and takes the land subject to a charge for the balance if any in favour of such co-tenants as of the date of purchase would, I think, be to disregard the plain wording of s. 189.

The fact that the contract of June 23, 1951, was expressed to enure to the benefit of and be binding upon each of the parties and their respective assigns does not assist the respondent, in the circumstances of this case, as the covenant to pay for repairs being positive would not run with the land and there is no question of novation. In the result the respondent is left to his rights against William Zawick personally under the contracts referred to above.

Appeal allowed.

MCINTOSH v. THE ONTARIO BANK. Ontario Court of Chancery. 1873. 20 Gr. 24

Limited rehearing in respect of the decree of Spragge C., 19 Gr. 155, in an action arising out of a will by which certain mill property was left to sons of the testator as tenants in common. One of them William McIntosh, believed he was sole owner, and he insured the property, paying all premiums. On the destruction of the mill by fire he received all the insurance moneys. Later he entered into an agreement to sell the property to one Wagstaff who went into possession and erected a new mill but, being unable later to complete the purchase, he gave up his right to William McIntosh. The latter executed a mortgage to the defendant bank and later gave a second mortgage to the defendant Dixon. The bank shortly after went into possession and collected rents. Co-tenants under the will filed a bill claiming an accounting for their share of the rents and an accounting of the insurance money, and, further, a declaration that the mortgages did not affect their interests. They succeeded at the trial but the Court directed that the value of the new mill should be set off against the insurance money.

STRONG V. C.: The case as to the insurance moneys is, as I understand the evidence, shortly this. William McIntosh, being one of several tenants in common, under his father's will, though believing himself to be the sole owner as heir-at-law, insured the mill, paying the premiums himself. At the same time he had in his hands moneys received for rents, for which he was accountable, under the Statute of Anne, to his co-tenants. The mill having burnt, William McIntosh received the insurance money, for which the plaintiffs now insist he is accountable to them. I take it to be clear, that neither in an action of account by the plaintiffs to recover the rents, nor under a decree of this Court for a like account, could William McIntosh have insisted on charging his co-tenants with the premiums of insurance. A mortgagee insuring without the concurrence of his mortgagor, is not accountable for insurance moneys, on the ground that he could not charge the mortgagor, in account, with the premiums, the contract being considered one for the mortgagee's own personal benefit, which there is nothing in the relationship of mortgagor and mortgagee to incapacitate him from entering into.

The same principle, in my opinion, applies with even greater force to the present case. There is nothing of a fiduciary character in the relationship of tenants in common; such a tenant is not even accountable for an occupation rent, and he can in no sense be considered as a trustee for his co-tenant, though the Statute of Anne does make him legally liable to account as bailiff for rents and profits received.

I think therefore, that William McIntosh ought not to have been charged with the insurance moneys.

On the other hand, it appears to me that Mr. Hoskin's objection, that William McIntosh ought not to have any allowance in respect of the improvements made by Wagstaff, must prevail. Not being charged with the insurance moneys, it cannot be considered that those funds were laid out in building the new mill, and the case is therefore the naked one of a tenant in common assuming to sell the whole estate to a purchaser who makes improvements and then abandons his purchase. This is totally unlike cases where the expenditure having been by a tenant in common of his own moneys in improvements, he has had the benefit of the outlay given to him on a partition. I can see no equity which this defendant can claim in respect of Wagstaff's improvements. As well might the defendant set up a claim to be allowed for permanent improvements made by his tenant and afterwards abandoned; or to the increased value of the property occasioned by any other accident. I think the decree should be varied in both the respects indicated.

BLAKE V. C.: The judgment of the Chancellor finds that the defendant William McIntosh, is, as co-tenant, entitled to seven-fifteenths, and that the co-defendants, the Ontario Bank and Dixon, as mortgagees, can claim a charge only upon this portion of the premises in question.

The parties assent to this portion of the decree, but the Ontario Bank and Dixon contend that certain moneys received by William McIntosh, before he gave the security to the Bank and Dixon, upon an insurance of the whole of the premises, should not be charged against his share and the interest mortgaged to them be thus incumbered.

The true position of the parties must be taken to have been, as is declared by this decree, that from the death of the testator, William McIntosh was, as co-tenant, entitled to the interest above mentioned; and in his dealings with the premises, the plaintiffs cannot ask that William should be viewed otherwise than as is insisted upon by them namely, a co-tenant with them....

I cannot see what there is in the position of a tenant in common that enables him to call on his co-tenant for a portion of insurance money received under a policy effected by the co-tenant in his own name and at his own risk and expense, upon the premises liable to be partitioned. Here William McIntosh could not charge against the co-tenants any portion of the premiums paid by him. He could not, it is true, by rights effect the insurance he actually did, nor could he, in my opinion, have claimed the insurance money from the Company, as he represented to them that he had an interest which he did not possess; but he chose to speculate in the matter, he insured the whole premises instead of his interest in them, the Company paid him the money, and I fail to see what right they have to any portion of the insurance money, who have in no way contracted for any insurance in the matter, and who were not responsible for or chargeable with the premiums paid. It is true that an action would lie against William McIntosh for the share of the rents to which his co-tenants were entitled, but as the premiums paid would not form the subject of a set-off in such an action, so I think where the account is taken here, in place of at law, the premiums would not and could not form an item in the account; and, if these be thrown out of the account on the one side, that which the premiums earned, namely, the insurance money, should be thrown out on the other. The case cannot be placed more strongly for the plaintiffs than that, as the mill in question formed a part of the freehold, and, when it was destroyed by fire and the defendant received this insurance money, he thus received that which represented the freehold, and in this way obtained his share or a portion of his share of the premises about to be partitioned, he should give credit for this on a division. But in the case of mortgagor and mortgagee, where the land mortgaged is only a security and is held until repayment of the debt, if the mortgagee insures, and the house be destroyed by fire, the insurance money is received by the mortgagee, without any credit to the mortgagor in respect thereof. Now, there it might as well be said the mortgage debt is paid out of that which represents the property mortgaged, the mortgagee has received a part of the premises of the mortgagor, and to the extent of the amount thus received the mortgage must be discharged. Yet in such a case the authorities shew clearly that the mortgagee can claim the insurance money and also the whole amount due on the mortgage. If the mortgagee can thus claim the insurance money, and also the mortgage money, I cannot see why a co-tenant has not the right to claim the insurance money earned by the premiums he paid, and also his share of the premises to be divided.He chose, as I said, to speculate on the chances of his receiving a return for the money he expended in insuring. He could not make any claim against his co-tenants in respect of these premiums —there was no duty cast upon him to keep insured the premises—and I cannot find any principle or authority that would warrant the placing a tenant in common in the position in which the plaintiffs contend William McIntosh should stand. If the rent received by the tenant in possession be large compared with the value of the property, he may desire to effect an insurance for a greater sum than he could insure his interest for, and for such a sum as, if the property be burned, would, when invested, produce an amount equal to the share of the rent coming to him. Should he arrange with the Insurance Company to accept a risk as if he were the owner of the whole premises, I cannot see what equity there arises out of such an insurance in another who, with the right to insure, is satisfied to run his risk, or to be his own insurer....

I do not think that William is entitled to any allowance for the increase of the value of the estate by the mill placed thereon by Wagstaff. This is not an improvement made by William, nor were his money or means expended in it. He simply makes an agreement for the sale of the premises to Wagstaff, which proves abortive. Wagstaff improves the premises, which revert to the estate. If this sale were adopted by all parties interested, each would share in all the benefits to be derived from it. William could not demand a special benefit from the sale, and what was done to the premises by Wagstaff must enure to the benefit of all the co-tenants. There was no expenditure on the part of William; there was not anything to raise an equity in his favour....

In my judgment the insurance money should not have been charged against William, and the so-called improvements should not have been allowed him.

SPRAGGE C.: I agree with the judgment of my learned brothers that the moneys expended by Wagstaff in putting up the grist mill, taking that transaction by itself, cannot be considered as money expended by William McIntosh: or to the benefit of which he is entitled beyond his share as a tenant in common.

I am not so clear as to the other point. William McIntosh might have insured his interest as a tenant in common. He had in his hands rents and profits of the premises, and he did, in fact, insure the whole premises. He had not an insurable interest in his own right beyond a certain proportion, but he insured the whole—for whom? Granted, that he was not bound to insure, yet, as a fact, he did insure, and I cannot free myself from the doubt that it does not lie in his mouth to say that the insurance was wholly on his own account....

I incline to think that in accounting for rents and profits he could have charged the premiums paid for insurance, but if he could not I still incline to think that having insured, and insured the whole interest as he did, he is accountable to his co-tenants for a proportion of the insurance moneys received commensurate with their interests.

I am not at all events prepared to agree with the opinion of my learned brothers that they are not.

Decree varied.

[Note the statement of Strong V.C. that "there is nothing of a fiduciary character in the relationship of tenants in common". This is certainly true in the sense that the mere existence of a co-tenancy does not give rise to any reciprocal fiduciary obligations. See *Kennedy* v. *De Trafford*, [1897] A.C. 180. Nor does any such obligation arise on the purchase by a co-tenant of the mortgaged common property on a *bona fide* sale under a power of sale in the mortgage: see *Fleet* v. *Fleet* (1925), 28 O.W.N. 193 (C.A.); nor upon a purchase at a tax sale after the period for redemption has expired: see *Janisse* v. *Stewart* (1925), 28 O.W.N. 446. Should the same conclusion apply, however, in respect of redemption by one co-tenant in foreclosure proceedings or redemption in tax sale proceedings? In *Sproule* v. *McConnell*, [1925] 1 D.L.R. 982, [1925] 1 W.W.R. 609, 19 Sask. L.R. 319 (C.A.), the Court refused to hold as a fiduciary a co-tenant who purchased the common property immediately after final order of foreclosure in proceedings in which the other co-tenants refused to take part, although duly served. However, there was a finding that these co-tenants had left the defendant to carry the burden of the property and had abandoned the undertaking. Should this have made any difference in view of evidence that before foreclosure proceedings were begun the mortgagee indicated that he would look to defendant only for payment and it was arranged that on final foreclosure the mortgagee would convey to defendant who in turn would give a mortgage back for the full amount of the pre-existing mortgage?

See the discussion in 2 *American Law of Property*, s. 6.16 where it is said, *inter alia*: "Historically, cotenants have been regarded in equity as fiduciaries of one another where they have acquired their interests at the same time, either by inheritance from a common ancestor or by the same deed or will. In such case, the principle that a cotenant who has acquired an outstanding title holds it for the benefit of his cotenants is applicable." See *Kennedy* v. *De Trafford*, *supra*, at p. 189 where Lord Herschell, in rejecting the contention that co-tenants in fee simple were in a fiduciary relationship said: "Cases have been referred to of a very different description, where the owner of an estate under a settlement, a tenant for life for example, has been held incapable of obtaining an enlargement of that estate for himself alone. It has been said that whatever benefit he gets must enure to the benefit of all taking under the settlement. That is a totally different case from this case."]

5. PARTITION

PARTITION BY AGREEMENT has always been open to co-tenants (except tenants by the entireties) but originally compulsory partition was available only to co-parceners. Voluntary partition to-day is properly accomplished by deed (cf. Conveyancing and Law of Property Act, R.S.O. 1960, c. 66, s. 9 "a partition . . . shall be void at law unless made by deed"), or by writing to satisfy the Statute of Frauds, but, no doubt, it is equally enforceable in equity if done parolly where acted upon so as to set up an estoppel. Compulsory partition for joint tenants and tenants in common originated in legislation of 1539 and 1540 and Chancery almost concurrently developed its jurisdiction in this area. This Chancery jurisdiction superseded in practice the writ of partition given by the old statutes, and in 1833 the Real Property Limitation Act, 1833 (Imp.), c. 27, s. 36 abolished the writ. The Partition Act, 1868 (Imp.), c. 40

empowered the Court of Chancery to order a sale (which theretofore it could only do on consent) instead of actual partition. (For the parallel legislative history of partition jurisdiction in Ontario, see *Ontario Power Co.* v. *Whattler* (1904), 7 O.L.R. 198 (Div. Ct.)) With the virtual abolition of legal co-tenancy in England by the statutory creation of a trust for sale, partition legislation there became unnecessary and was abolished: see Law of Property Act, 1925 (Imp.), c. 20, 7th Sched.

Partition legislation founded on the English legislation of 1539-1868, is in force in the common law provinces, as follows: Partition Act, R.S.B.C. 1960, c. 276; Law of Property Act, R.S.M. 1954, c. 138, ss. 19-27; Partition Act, R.S.N.S. 1954, c. 211; Partition Act, R.S.O. 1960, c. 287; Real Property Act, R.S.P.E.I. 1951, c. 138, ss. 19-52. The English Partition Act, 1868 (Imp.), c. 40 is in force in Alberta and Saskatchewan: see *Robertson* v. *Robertson* (1951), 1 W.W.R. (N.S.) 183 (Alta.). Jurisdiction in partition or sale is exercised in New Brunswick by the Chancery Division of the Supreme Court under Rules of Court: see Judicature Act, R.S.N.B. 1952, c. 120, ss. 9(b), 23, and *Lehman* v. *Hunter* (1939), 13 M.P.R. 553 (N.B.).

No attempt is made here to detail any variations in substantive law and procedure governing compulsory partition in the various provinces. In general, an order for partition or sale is discretionary, which, in practice, means that while an applicant's right thereto is not absolute the burden is on an opposing co-tenant to persuade the Court to deny partition (or sale in lieu thereof): see *Re Hutcheson and Hutcheson* [1950] O.R. 265, [1950] 2 D.L.R. 751; *Davis* v. *Davis* [1954] O.R. 23, [1954] 1 D.L.R. 827 (C.A.); *Watts* v. *Watts*, [1952] 1 D.L.R. 652, 4 W.W.R. (N.S.) 566 (B.C.); *Fritz* v. *Fritz*, [1950] 2 D.L.R. 104, 1 W.W.R. (N.S.) 446, 57 Man. R. 510 (C.A.). Cf., however, *Robertson* v. *Robertson* (1951), 1 W.W.R. (N.S.) 183 (Alta.) (right to partition absolute but does not prevail against "homestead" legislation); but see *Mitchelson* v. *Mitchelson* (1953), 9 W.W.R. (N.S.) 316 (Man.) (statutory provision for partition or sale without obtaining consent of spouse under homestead legislation).

[It has been held that an applicant for partition under the general run of legislation in the common law provinces must have an estate in possession or have the immediate right to its possession; hence a registered judgment creditor of a joint tenant has no standing to seek partition (see *Morrow* v. *Eakin*, [1953] 2 D.L.R. 593, 8 W.W.R. (N.S.) 548 (B.C.)), nor has a claimant of a legacy charged on land (see *Re Fidler and Seaman*, [1948] 2 D.L.R. 771, [1948] O.W.N. 454), nor has a widow who is entitled to dower out of the land held in co-tenancy (see *Morrison* v. *Morrison* (1917), 39 O.L.R. 163, 34 D.L.R. 677 (App. Div.)), nor has a mortgagee of a co-tenant who is still in possession (see *Mulligan* v. *Hendershott* (1896), 17 P.R. 227 (Ont.)).

In so far as partition legislation in Canada may be invoked only by persons in possession or entitled to immediate possession, neither reversioners nor remaindermen who are co-owners of such interests may seek partition either against an existing tenant for life, in any event because there is no co-tenancy with a life tenant (see *Murcar* v. *Bolton* (1884), 5 O.R. 164) or as against each other (see *Morrison* v. *Morrison*, *supra*), even though there is no intention to disturb an existing life tenant (see *Bunting* v. *Servos* [1931] O.R. 409, [1931] 4 D.L.R. 167 (C.A.)). *Quaere*, however, whether reversioners upon a leasehold may not have partition since they have present seisin: see 2 *American Law of Property*, s. 6.23.

Of course, the fact that land held in co-tenancy is subject to dower or to other incumbrances is not a bar to partition by a person entitled to apply therefor but it depends on the particular statute whether such outstanding interests may be liquidated by compensation or otherwise in a partition proceeding or whether the partition (or sale), if ordered, will be subject thereto. In *Re McCully, McCully* v. *McCully* (1910), 23 O.L.R. 156 (Div. Ct.) it was held that a co-tenant who had mortgaged his undivided interest should not be granted partition if the unpaid mortgagee or the other co-tenants object, but it is not clear why objection of the latter should be automatically a bar.

As to the relation between partition where sought by a husband and his deserted wife's claim to occupation of the matrimonial home, see *Re Jollow and Jollow*, [1954] O.R. 895, [1955] 1 D.L.R. 601 (C.A.), reproduced *supra*, at p. 111.

The conferring of jurisdiction to order a sale instead of partition means that proceedings must be taken to partition unless it appears that it cannot be made without prejudice to the holders of or parties interested in the estate; and if that is shown then proceedings for sale are to be taken: see *Ontario Power Co.* v. *Whattler* (1904), 7 O.L.R. 198 (Div. Ct.).]

MASTRON v. COTTON. Ontario Appellate Division. 58 O.L.R. 251, [1926] 1 D.L.R. 767.

FERGUSON J. A. (for the Court): ... While the general rule is that one joint tenant, unless ousted by his co-tenant, may not sue another for use and occupation, it seems clear that when the joint tenancy is terminated by a court order for partition or sale, the Court may in such proceedings make all just allowances and should give such directions as will do complete equity between the parties: *Gage* v. *Mulholland* (1869), 16 Gr. 145; *Rogers* v. *Mackenzie* (1799), 4 Ves. 751; 33 Corpus Juris, p. 909; Taylor's Equity, para. 376.

What is just and equitable depends on the circumstances of each case. For instance, if the tenant in occupation claims for upkeep and repairs, the Court, as a term of such allowance, usually requires that the claimant shall submit to an allowance for use and occupation: *Rice* v. *George* (1873), 20 Gr. 221; *Pascoe* v. *Swan* (1859), 27 Beav. 508. Again, if one tenant has made improvements which have increased the selling value of the property, the other tenant cannot take the advantage of increased price without submitting to an allowance for the improvements: *Leigh* v. *Dickeson*, 15 Q.B.D. 60, *per* Cotton, L. J., at p. 67; Halsbury's Law of England, vol. 21, p. 851. And, once again, when, as here, one tenant has paid more than his share of encumbrances, he is entitled to an allowance for such surplus: *In re Curry, Curry* v.*Curry* (1898), 25 A.R. 267; 33 Corpus Juris, p. 909.

These allowances being made as equitable allowances, there may as a matter of course be circumstances under which they should not be made. For instance, the circumstances may indicate that the improvements were made or the surplus payments were made or intended to be made as gifts by one tenant to the other—as by the husband for the benefit of the wife; and it may be that had the surplus payments in this case been made by the husband rather than by the wife the Court would, in the absence of something to shew a contrary intention, presume that they were gifts to the wife: *Dunbar* v. *Dunbar*, [1909] 2 Ch. 639. But the circumstances under which these payments were made by the wife clearly indicate that the defendant was not, in reducing the encumbrance, imbued with the idea of making gifts to her husband; and I am therefore of opinion that as between herself and the plaintiff she is, on the distribution of the money arising from the sale of the property, entitled to have taken into account all payments made on the purchase-moneys or on principal moneys secured by the mortgages, irrespective of whether such payments were made before or after divorce, and all payments made on interest, taxes, and repairs after she ceased to occupy; but that she should only be allowed payments on account of interest, taxes, and repairs during the period of occupation if she elects to submit to an allowance for use and occupation; and I would, for these reasons, allow the appeal in part and amend the judgment accordingly.

[Where in a partition action against a co-tenant who had mortgaged his interest it was found that he was liable for occupation rent and the property was sold pursuant to Court order, *held*, the occupation rent could not be charged against this co-tenant's share of the proceeds to the prejudice of his mortgagee but only against him personally: see *Hill* v. *Hicklin*, [1897] 2 Ch. 579.

For illustrations of an accounting between co-tenants upon a sale of the property in partition proceedings, see *Szuba* v. *Szuba*, [1951] O.W.N. 61; *Macdonald* v. *Macdonald*, [1953] O.W.N. 232.]

6. CO-OWNERSHIP OF PERSONALTY

CONSIDERATION of co-ownership of personalty is beyond the scope of this casebook, but it may be noted that much of the litigation in this connection has arisen from joint bank accounts. For theories underlying such transactions, see *Willis*, The Nature of a Joint Account, (1936), 14 Can. Bar Rev. 457; and see also *Wright*, Note, (1937), 15 Can. Bar Rev. 371; *Bruce*, Note, (1955) 33 Can. Bar Rev. 345; *Niles* v. *Lake*, [1947] S.C.R. 291, [1947] 2 D.L.R. 248; *Edwards* v. *Bradley*, [1957] S.C.R. 599, 9 D.L.R. 2d 673.

The common law rules applicable to determine whether a co-tenancy of realty was joint or in common are applicable to personalty, so that, in the absence of words of severance (e.g. to A and B equally) or of modifying statute, a transfer of personalty to two or more persons makes them joint owners. A co-owner of personalty like a co-tenant of realty is under no liability to his co-owners by virtue of his sole possession or use of the property. Destruction of the property or an unauthorized sale thereof makes him liable in conversion, but it should be pointed out that there are English cases, which have been adopted in some instances in Canada, holding that a sale by a co-owner is not a conversion. These decisions have no modern justification: see *Derham*, Conversion by Wrongful Disposal as between Co-Owners (1952), 68 Law Q. Rev. 507.

CHAPTER XI

BENEFITS AND BURDENS AS BETWEEN OWNERS OF LIMITED INTERESTS: WASTE

1. INTRODUCTORY NOTE

If land is held by A for life, remainder to B in fee simple, the limited nature of their respective interests qualifies the extent to which each can deal with the land or use and enjoy it in relation to the other. Similarly, their respective limited interests may involve an apportionment between them of the burden of obligations, such as taxes or mortgage payments, which attach to the fee simple interest as a whole. The problem of distributing benefits and burdens in accordance with the valuation of present and future interests in the same land becomes more complicated if the interests are determinable or in any way contingent. If a trustee holds the legal title and manages the property accordingly, the accounting as between successive beneficiaries, for which he is responsible, will eliminate many problems that arise where life tenant and remainderman (to take the simplest example) must thresh these problems out between themselves directly because they "share" the legal title. The trust situation, save for incidental reference, is outside the scope of this casebook.

Among the common situations requiring valuation of interests and apportionment of benefits or burdens are expropriation of the land or sale (e.g. under statutory power), exploitation of mineral resources, realization of insurance policies, assessment for improvements, and discharge of mortgages or other encumbrances. The paucity of Canadian case law on these matters in their common law aspect may be some measure of the extent to which the trust has been utilized for easier control for the mutual advantage of all concerned; and, of course, this is usually so under wills, especially in view of legislation vesting title in executors as trustees for the persons beneficially entitled.

2. BENEFITS AND BURDENS

HOMFRAY v. HOMFRAY. British Columbia Supreme Court. 1936. 51 B.C.R. 287

Hotel property which was left by will to a life tenant and remaindermen was destroyed by fire during the life tenancy. It was agreed by all concerned that it should be rebuilt and this was done with money provided in large part by the life tenant and through a mortgage accepted by the contractors who did the work. The hotel was leased to a third person and defendant, one of the remaindermen, looked after the accounts. She paid the life tenant only small amounts of the rents and profits, devoting most of them to liquidation of the expenses of rebuilding. The life tenant thereupon sued for a declaration of her rights, including possession, and for a charge on the property for her advance. Plaintiff life tenant and defendant were the present trustees of the estate.

FISHER J.: In this matter counsel for the parties agree that the hotel property in question herein is a settled estate within the meaning of the Settled Estates Act, R.S.B.C. 1924, Cap.

228 but they disagree as to the claim of the plaintiffs for a declaration that one of them, *viz.*, Alice Kathleen Homfray, as tenant for life, is entitled to possession of the said property. It is, or must be admitted, that, though the said Alice Kathleen Homfray is entitled to receive the net rents and profits of the said property she is not entitled as of right to the declaration asked for but it is a discretionary matter with the Court. In the case of *In re Bagot's Settlement* (1893), 63 L.J. Ch. 515, Chitty, J. says in part as follows at pp. 517 and 518:

"Now the application is addressed to the judicial discretion of the Court; and this discretion has to be exercised on reasonable grounds, the Court looking to the convenience of the parties, to the question of expense—which falls, of course, on the tenant for life—and to other circumstances of a like kind. It is clear that Mrs. Bagot has no right to claim to be let into possession, and she can only claim to be let into possession through the exercise of the Court's judicial discretion.

"It seems to me that it is convenient and proper under the circumstances of the case to allow her, as I do, to exercise all the powers of the tenant for life, with the exception of the power of sale and exchange."

In the *Bagot* case reference was made by Chitty, J. to the Settled Lands Acts as affording an additional ground for exercising the discretion favourable to a tenant for life under these Acts but it must be noted that such Acts are not in force in this Province...

I think it is apparent that though the life tenant may be entitled under ordinary circumstances to the declaration now asked for there may be cases where the circumstances are such that the discretion should not be so exercised in favour of the life tenant. In the present case I have come to the conclusion that the powers of management or leasing should be left with the trustees and that the life tenant should not be let into possession of the property...

The parties also disagree as to the adjustment of burdens as between capital and income. I will deal first with the issue on the cost of the reconstruction or repairs commenced in or about the month of February, 1933, and made necessary by the fire of September, 1931. Counsel seem to disagree as to whether the proper term to be used is "reconstruction" or "repair" but I might say that upon my view of the issue I do not think the terminology is material. However, as the parties apparently agreed at the time of the consent order made the 7th of April, 1933 (Exhibit 35), that the proposed work could be properly described as "repairs, alterations and improvements". I do not think that either party should now be heard to object to the work being treated as such and I deal with the matter on that basis. In any event the issue must be determined only after taking into consideration the circumstances and bearing in mind the equitable rules laid down by the authorities....

It is quite apparent from the evidence, including the correspondence filed (see Exhibits 3 and 4) that the defendant now agrees that the life tenant is entitled to a first charge for all moneys advanced by her to the trustees. The real dispute is as to whether or not the life tenant is entitled to a first charge for all moneys paid out of the rents on account of the repairs, alterations and improvements. On this issue I think it is worthy of note that the parties did not know exactly how much such repairs, alterations and improvements would cost and that the defendant tried, unsuccessfully, to get a loan from other parties for $15,000. The result was that approximately $8,000 was advanced by the life tenant and the defendant (who were then the trustees), approximately $3,000 by the contractors, Miller & Lewis, on a mortgage and the balance required was paid out of the rents from time to time. I think it is quite apparent however and I find that it was the intention of the parties to renew the efforts to obtain from other parties all the money required so soon as the building was completed. If the moneys were so obtained undoubtedly a mortgage would have to be given....

I am satisfied and find, therefore, that it was intended to give a mortgage later on to other parties if the money should be obtained from them. Under such circumstances the question arises as to what are the rights of the parties now. Is the life tenant entitled to a first charge upon the property for moneys paid out of the rents? Obviously the property has been greatly increased in value by the work which was done and which no doubt had to be paid for before the money could be raised by a mortgage. The income however has also been greatly increased. Thus the work has been for the benefit of both the remaindermen and the life tenant. My first impression was that the Court might have some discretion to adjust the burden between capital and income in proportion to the benefits received from the work and expenditure. I have come to the conclusion however that upon the facts of this case, as I find them, and the law applicable I have no such discretion. As already intimated I find the parties never intended that the rents should be used for the repairs as aforesaid at the expense of the life tenant and with no attempt made to reimburse her. I find the interim arrangements were intended to be temporary only but unfortunately the parties did not foresee a time when, as the defendant suggests in one of her later letters (Exhibit 16) the whole matter would have to be dealt with "on a strictly business basis" without any sentiment.

In the case of *In re Hotchkys* (1886), 32 Ch. D. 408 Lindley, L. J. says at p. 420:

"As regards the substantial question, that of the repairs, it appears to me there is no avoiding the application to this case of the rule laid down by Lord Hatherley in *Powys* v. *Blagrave* [(1854)], Kay 495. The tenant for life is equitable tenant for life and the remainderman is not entitled to throw upon her the burthen of keeping the property in repair."

In the case of *In re Freman*, [1898] 1 Ch. 28, North, J. said at pp. 32-3, in part, as follows:

"*Powys* v. *Blagrave* [(1854)], 4 De G.M. & G. 448, and the subsequent case *In re Cartwright* [(1889)], 41 Ch. D. 532, before Kay, J., make it perfectly clear that the tenant for life is under no obligation to keep the property in repair. That is so as to lands settled by the will....

"I can see no distinction in principle in this respect between a tenant for life of land purchased under a direction in the will and the tenant for life of land devised by the will itself. I do not think I am in any way extending the principle of *Powys* v. *Blagrave* and *In re Cartwright* by saying that it applies to this case.

"Then there is the question, What is to be done about the repairs? What was pointed out in *In re Hotchkys* [(1886)], 32 Ch. D. 408 as the right thing to be done is the right thing to be done here. The property ought to be kept in repair. As was pointed out there, it must be done by an equitable arrangement between the tenant for life and remainderman. I think the right thing to do in this case is this—that the money required for the repairs should be borne by capital; but of course the tenant for life will have to keep down the interest upon that capital."

In neither the *Hotchkys* nor the *Freman* case did the Court have to deal with a case where the repairs had actually been made without the Court having ordered how they were to be paid for as between capital and income. In the present matter I have to deal with such a case but the circumstances being as I have found them I think the ordinary rule of law laid down in the above mentioned cases must be applied and that the application of such rule of law to the condition of circumstances existing obliges me to hold, as I do, that the plaintiff Alice Kathleen Homfray is entitled to the declaration asked for with respect to both the moneys actually advanced by her and the moneys paid out of the rents on account of the repairs, alterations or improvements or on account of the principal of the Miller & Lewis mortgage, and such moneys will, therefore, be a charge on the property. Such charge will also include the expenses of and incidental to the repairs, alterations and improvements as claimed by the plaintiff in paragraph 12 of the statement of claim with the exception at present of the items of November 26th, 1932, May 9th, 1933, August 11th, 1933, September 7th, 1933, and October 25th, 1934, which may be further spoken to. If any further inquiry is necessary to determine the exact amount of the charge there will be a reference. The said plaintiff, as life tenant, will be entitled to receive from the trustees the net income of the property but she must pay or keep down the interest. See *Freman* case, *supra.*

Dealing further with the adjustments of burdens as between capital and income, I will next deal with the question of insurance. Section 9 (1) of the Trustee Act, Cap. 262, R.S.B.C. 1924, reads as follows:

A trustee may insure against loss or damage by fire any building or other insurable property to any amount (including the amount of any insurance already on foot) not exceeding three equal fourth parts of the full value of such building or property, and pay the premiums for such insurance out of the income thereof or out of the income of any other property subject to the same trusts, without obtaining the consent of any person who may be entitled wholly or partly to such income.

Counsel for the plaintiffs relies especially upon *Re McEacharn*; *Gambles* v. *McEacharn* (1911), 103 L.T. 900 where the Court dealt with section 18 (1) of the Trustee Act 1893 which is similar to our said section 9 (1). In order to show just exactly what the circumstances and decision in that case were I think I should here set out a considerable portion from the judgment of Eve, J. at pp. 901-2:

"During the testator's lifetime and at the date of his death the mansionhouse and other insurable parts of the premises comprised in this devise were insured against fire in amounts falling far short of their respective values, and the question now raised is whether the devisees in trust ought to increase the subsisting insurances to adequate amounts—that is, to amounts not exceeding three fourth parts of the value of the premises insured—and to pay the annual premiums in respect of such insurances out of the rents and profits of the estate. The tenant for life, who is one of the devisees in trust, objects to any increase being made in the insurances at her expense; those entitled in remainder urge that the insurances ought to be substantially increased and that the annual premiums ought to be borne by the income.... At p. 702 of Lewin on Trusts (11th edition) the position prior to the Trustee Act 1893 is thus stated: 'The duty of a trustee in reference to insuring the property was until recently not very clearly defined; it was conceived that under special circumstances and in due course of management he would be justified in insuring, but that where there was a tenant for life, he could not be advised to do so out of the income without the tenant for life's consent.' The learned editor then proceeds to draw attention to sect. 18 of the Trustee Act 1893, but he does not suggest, nor can I hold, that this section imposes on the trustee a statutory obligation to insure and on the tenant for life a statutory liability to pay the cost of such insurance. The section appears to me to confer powers not to impose obligations on trustees, and, inasmuch as the trustees are not unanimous in this case as to the exercise of the powers so conferred upon them, I think I ought to answer the question put to me by saying that 'the devisees in trust of Galloway House and buildings ought not to keep such house and buildings insured against fire out of the rents and profits arising therefrom and from the other property devised therewith up to three equal fourth parts of the value of such house and buildings.' In so answering the question, I answer it as it is put, and I say nothing as to whether the trustees ought to insure the premises at the expense of the estate generally, because the only point which has been argued on this part of the summons is that such insurance ought to be maintained at the expense of the tenant for life, and, as I have already said I do not think that this has been established either under the trusts of the testator's will or under the statute."

From the passages as above set out it would appear that the Court in the *McEacharn* case decided that the trustees were not obliged to insure and charge the premiums to the life tenant but it did not decide that they could not do so. In the case now before me the trustees have actually done so and said section 9 (1) authorizes, though it does not oblige, them to do so.

As to insurance, therefore, on the said property already effected by the trustees or either of them I refuse to make any declaration that the trustees had or have no power or authority to pay the premiums for such insurance out of income arising from the property but with regard to any further insurance, in case the trustees are not unanimous as to the exercise of the powers so conferred upon them, I will make a declaration similar to that made in the

McEacharn case, *viz.*, that the trustees ought not to keep the property insured out of the rents and profits arising therefrom and I will also state, as was stated by the Court in the said case, that I say nothing as to whether the trustees ought to insure the premises at the expense of the estate generally. I express the hope that the trustees will be able to agree upon some equitable division of the cost of adequate insurance.

Order accordingly.

[While an obligation of repair rests upon a trustee in whom title is vested for life tenant and remainderman, yet in the absence of trusteeship, a life tenant is under no obligation to repair unless so directed by the settlement under which he holds and, moreover, in such case the obligation may not be enforceable in respect of repairs existing at the date the settlement took effect: cf. *Re Hotchkys* (1886), 32 Ch. D. 408 (C.A.); *Re Elliot* (1917), 41 O.L.R. 276, 40 D.L.R. 649 (App. Div.).

In the case of a trustee's duty of repair, the substantial question is the apportionment of the cost between life tenant and remainderman, and if money is not available and must to be raised (by way of mortgage), an application to the Court will be necessary under "Settled Estates" legislation: see *Re Elliot*, *supra*. There is no invariable rule that the capital burden will be imposed on the remainderman and the burden of interest on the life tenant; it depends on the nature of the repairs: cf. *Re Vair* (1923), 54 O.L.R. 497 (repairs to building charged against remainderman); *Re Dwyer*, [1930] 2 D.L.R. 897 (N.S.) (permanent non-recurring repairs charged on capital; taxes and water rates as annual outgoings charged on income); *Re Stevens* (1929), 35 O.W.N. 359 (cost of renewal of heating equipment and of painting assessed against reversion); *Wilson* v. *Whelpley* (1929), 1 M.P.R. 196 (N.B.C.A.) (repairs made by life tenant, who was also trustee, chargeable against remainderman to the extent to which they were "salvage" repairs and not ordinary, common repairs); *Re Rose*, [1940] 1 D.L.R. 139, 14 M.P.R. 223 (N.B.) (where life tenant entitled to net income from estate including a business, depreciation on business building charged against business as current expenditure payable out of income; consumption of capital should not enter into profits); and see *Re Robertson*, [1951] O.R. 309, [1951] 3 D.L.R. 241, *infra*, under "Waste".]

[Under United States law, a tenant for life is under a duty to the reversioner or remainderman to make ordinary repairs (i.e. he is liable for permissive waste), to the extent of the total income received from the property or to the extent of its fair rental value where he is himself in occupation: see 1 *Restatement of Property*, s. 139; 1 *American Law of Property*, s. 2.18. This American rule, which follows Coke and Blackstone, is at variance with the rule in England and (so it would seem) that in Canada in relation to life tenants where there is no trust; see *infra* under "Waste".

Generally, even in United States a life tenant who voluntarily makes improvements (as contrasted with repairs) has no claim for contribution from the remainderman. For illustrations of exceptions and a reference to evolving case law in United States, see 1 *Restatement of Property*, s. 127; *Restatement of the Law, 1948 Supplement*, pp. 404-5; 1 *American Law of Property*, s. 2.21.]

[Land was devised to A for life remainder to B in fee simple and by the will the life tenant was required to pay, out of the income of the property, insurance premiums, taxes and other rates, and to repair and keep in repair except in case of loss by fire. A went into possession, and on her death the remainderman found the property out of repair and, having expended money to repair it, he claimed the sum from the life tenant's estate. The Court, in allowing the claim, applied the principle that "where a person accepts a benefit under a will on condition that he shall discharge a certain liability he takes the benefit *cum onere*"; see *Re Andrews, Andrews* v. *Board*, [1952] O.W.N. 163. Could the claim for repairs exceed the income of the life tenant?]

[The holder of an estate for life, as between him and holders of future interests limited thereafter, is under a duty (subject to the settlement under which he holds and to the extent of the rents and profits of the property) "(a) to keep paid all current taxes, periodic charges and interest on incumbrances on the land, when such tax, charge or interest, if left unpaid, may result in a lien effective against the interests subsequent to the estate for life; and (b) to pay any expense incidental to the management of the land, when such sum, if left unpaid, may result in a lien effective against the interests subsequent to the estate for life": 1 *Restatement of Property*, s. 129; and see *Restatement of the Law, 1948 Supplement*, pp. 405 ff; and see *White* v. *White* (1804), 9 Ves. Jr. 554, 32 E.R. 718 (Ch.).

A life tenant who pays off a mortage on the land which becomes due during his lifetime may, of course, take an assignment thereof but even if he does not, he is deemed to have a charge on the land by subrogation to the rights of the discharged mortgagee; the burden of proof is on those who allege that in paying off the mortgage he intended to exonerate the reversioner or remainderman: *Macklem* v. *Cummings* (1859), 7 Gr. 318. It was held in *Re Harvey, Harvey* v. *Hobday*, [1896] 1 Ch. 137 (C.A.) that the fact that the life tenant and remainderman were parent and child did not establish an intention to relinquish the charge; and see also *Currie* v. *Currie* (1910), 20 O.L.R. 375.

English and Canadian case law give the paying life tenant a charge to the extent of the whole of the principal of the mortgage. United States case law follows a more equitable rule of requiring the life tenant to assume the burden of interest for his life, and hence to reduce his charge by the present value of such interest. The situation would be the same if the remainderman paid off the mortgage; he would be entitled to a charge on the life estate to the extent of the present value of the interest on the mortgage for the life tenant's life expectancy. See 1 *American Law of Property*, s. 2.22; 1 *Restatement of Property*, s. 132. The English and Canadian rule would not require the life tenant to contribute where the remainderman pays off a mortgage which falls due during the life tenancy. Of course, even under the English and Canadian rule a life tenant who pays off a mortgage and asserts a right of subrogation may not charge interest against the remainderman.]

[Where mortgaged property is left to a life tenant and remainderman, a payment by the former on account of the mortgage debt will stop the running of the Statute of Limitations against the mortgage obligation. Why? See *Official Guardian* v. *Sadecki*, [1946] 2 D.L.R. 733, [1946] 1 W.W.R. 593 (Alta.).]

IN RE WARWICK'S SETTLEMENT TRUSTS. Chancery. [1937] Ch. 561

An equitable tenant for life of certain property which was subject to various charges sold his interest to a company which thereupon became entitled to rents and profits. In three successive years, the amounts of such rents and profits were insufficient to pay in full the charges on the property. The company paid the deficiency out of its own funds without any arrangement for recoupment from those entitled to the corpus. It then moved for a declaration of its right to be recouped out of the corpus for the deficiency so paid.

FARWELL J.: The question how far the company is entitled, if at all, to any such declarations as is claimed is one which, so far as I know, is not covered exactly by authority. The plaintiff company relies, and I think the whole of its case is based, upon *Kensington* v. *Bouverie*, a decision of the House of Lords (1859), 7 H.L.C. 557, 11 E.R. 222. It will be necessary to consider how far that authority supports this application, and whether the company is entitled, having regard to it, to any such charge as is claimed; but that case differs materially from the case with which I am dealing, and it is impossible to say that it is an authority which is exactly in point. There are three obvious differences. Firstly, in that case the payments which were made, in respect of which recoupment was claimed, were made by a person who was the tenant for life and not, as in this case, the assignee of the rents and profits of the estate; secondly, the claim for recoupment was made after the cessor of the life interest, the claim being a claim by the legal personal representative of the deceased tenant for life; thirdly in that case the remainderman was a person in existence who was known, whereas in this case who may ultimately become entitled to the estate as tenant in tail is not known and cannot be known for many years. That authority, however, does assist the plaintiff to this extent, that all the learned Lords who were parties to that decision appeared to recognize that there might be a right to recoupment in certain circumstances in the tenant for life or his legal personal representative in respect of interest on mortgages which the tenant for life had paid out of his own resources. To that extent that decision assists the plaintiffs; but the question which I have to determine requires consideration from a rather wider aspect and I propose in the first instance to consider it apart from any difficulty which may arise owing to the fact that the plaintiff company is not the tenant for life. I will, so far as it is necessary, deal with that matter a little later, but for the moment I am going to consider this matter disregarding that factor, and as though the plaintiff company was strictly speaking tenant for life.

It is well settled that, where a tenant for life pays off a capital charge on the estates out of his own moneys, he is entitled prima facie to keep that charge alive for his own protection, but I have found no case which in terms explains the principle upon which that rule rests. Generally speaking where a person out of his own moneys voluntarily chooses to pay off a charge on the property of another without taking an assignment of the charge, the charge goes, and the person making the payment has no claim against the estate or against the owner of the estate. What is sometimes called the right of subrogation is a right which is extremely limited in its application. There are rights of subrogation at common law in respect of insurance. There are rights in equity of subrogation in cases of sureties and in some cases of trustees, and there may be other cases; but the right is a limited one, and it may be useful to consider how the right of recoupment in a tenant for life, who pays off a capital charge, arose. In my judgment it is clearly an equitable and not a legal right, and I think that it originated in the Court of Equity, when administering an estate, coming to the conclusion that as both the tenant for life and the person entitled in remainder had some interest in the estate as a whole, if the tenant for life paid off a charge on the whole estate out of his own moneys, it was inequitable to permit the remainderman to have the benefit of such a payment, and in order to do equity between the parties the Court held that the tenant for life in those circumstances was prima facie entitled to stand in the shoes of the mortgagees or chargees. However that may be, it is now well settled there is an equity in favour of the tenant for life to be recouped moneys which he has paid to discharge a capital charge on the estates, and one which, prima facie, he is entitled to enforce. In such a case the onus rests on those who say that by such payment the tenant for life did not intend to keep the charge alive, and in the absence of any satisfactory evidence to the contrary, the tenant for life is entitled to be recouped. Whether such an equitable right exists in a tenant for life to recover interest paid out of his own moneys on such charges is a question which, so far as I know, has never been exactly decided, but having regard to the case to which I have already referred, *Kensington* v. *Bouverie*, it is difficult to say that there can never be any such equity in his favour because, although the learned Law Lords differed as to whether or not in the particular circumstances of that case the equity could be successfully asserted by the legal personal representative of the tenant for life, they all appear to have recognized that there might be such an equity, and that in certain circumstances a claim for recoupment could be successfully asserted.

But that case deals only with the claim of a tenant for life or his legal personal representative to recoupment of interest so paid after the determination of the life interest. Other considerations must necessarily apply when the Court is dealing with the equity of a tenant for life to a charge or a declaration of charge in respect of interest during the continuation of the life interest. It is clear from the decision in the House of Lords that in order successfully to assert an equity in the tenant for life to be recouped for payment out of his own moneys of interest charges, it is necessary firstly, for the claimant to show that there has actually been payment out of his own moneys; secondly, he must show not merely what the actual amounts were that he paid and received, but he may have to satisfy the Court that the sums which he has paid out are more than the sums which he ought to have received had the estate been properly managed. If it could be shown that there had been mismanagement or misuser of the property so that the income received was less than the income which could have been received, given good management, that authority appears to show that if the income which could have been received would have been sufficient to satisfy the interest, no such equity would exist. Further, it is for the tenant for life or his legal personal representatives to show that there is nothing inequitable in the particular facts of the case in his setting up such a claim. In the case in the House of Lords, the majority of the House held that the equity could not be successfully asserted because the payments had been made by the tenant for life without communication or notice to the remainderman, and the majority of the Court seems to have thought that it was not equitable that the tenant for life should assert such a claim if he had not given the remainderman an opportunity to object, if he so desired, to such payments being made.

It is, I think, obvious from that authority that, when a tenant for life or his legal personal representative is asserting an equity in his favour with respect to payment of interest, his position is one of much greater difficulty than where a tenant for life is asserting his equity to the benefit of a charge on the estates which he has himself discharged out of his own money, and when one considers the circumstances, the difficulty of the claim in this case must be apparent. The interest on the portions and the jointure are continuing charges upon income as well as upon capital and it therefore appears to me to be quite impossible for a tenant for life, while alive, or at any rate so long as the properties remain unsold, to show that there is, or rather will be, a deficiency in the total of the rents and profits. It is not, in my judgment right to say that because there has been a deficiency in one or two or more years, there will necessarily be a deficiency when the whole account comes to be taken. It may well be that when the whole amount received, or which ought to have been received during the tenancy for life, is calculated against the sums paid for interest over the same period, it will then appear that there had been sufficient, notwithstanding that in some years the income had been insufficient, and a claim by the tenant for life for a charge or declaration of charge, because in one year or in more than one year, there was a deficiency which he chose to pay out of his own pocket, seems to me to be a claim which this Court cannot sustain. As I have said there may or may not be a right to recoupment at the end of the period, but there can be no present right to a charge. Presumably if the tenant for life was entitled to a charge he would be entitled to interest on the charge, and possibly compound interest, so that having the benefit of that charge he would still remain in possession of the income in the future years, which income might in the years to come be more than sufficient to pay the whole of the interest and leave a surplus in hand for the tenant for life.

In those circumstances it seems to me that even in the case of a tenant for life it is impossible for him to claim, during his lifetime, that he has a right to be recouped then or at some other time, money which he has chosen to pay out of his own pocket for interest on the charges. It may be that it suits his own purpose to make these payments, but there is no obligation upon him to make them, and if he elects to do so, he does it, in my judgment, at his own risk. When the tenancy for life comes to an end, or possibly if and when the estates are sold, and the proceeds of sale invested in securities, the position is different. But until then there can be no means by which the question, whether or not there is a right to recoupment, can properly arise, or properly be determined. While I am not denying that there may ultimately be some right to recoupment, and that when the due time comes, a tenant for life or his legal personal representatives may be entitled, having regard to the decision in the House of Lords, to assert an equity in his favour for recoupment of moneys paid for interest, until that event happens, in my judgment he is not entitled to any such relief. This Court will not make a declaration that there may be a charge in the future, but it will leave the tenant for life to see, or rather it may be for his legal personal representatives to see whether such an equitable right can be successfully asserted after the determination of the tenancy for life....

If, when the final account of the life tenancy can be taken, it can then be shown that, given proper management of the estate and allowing for that, there was not sufficient income to pay the whole of the interest on the charges, then and only then in my judgment can the plaintiff company make the claim to be recouped which it is seeking to make today. Whether that claim will succeed or not will depend upon the circumstances at the time and the equities existing as between the tenant for life and the persons entitled in remainder in the particular circumstances of the case as it then appears. So far as this summons is concerned, in my judgment it is misconceived and must be dismissed with costs.

Application dismissed.

RE DENISON, WALDIE v. DENISON. Ontario Chancery Division. 1893. 24 O.R. 197

Lands which were held by a tenant for life with remainder to his children were in part under lease and in part vacant; other parts had been sold under Court order. A considerable sum of money had accumulated from rent of the parts leased and from the proceeds of sale. Arrears of taxes had accumulated on the vacant parts. The life tenant claimed that he was entitled to the rents on the leased parts without being obliged to pay the taxes on the other parts. The receiver of the rents applied to the Court for directions.

BOYD C.: The person entitled to possession is the person to pay the taxes yearly chargeable on the property, and the fund out of which taxes are ordinarily payable is the rents of the land: *Fountaine* v. *Pellet*, 1 Ves. Jr. 337, and R.S.O. ch. 193, s. 24.

This charge for taxes is one of the things which should be paid by the tenant for life, so as to protect the property for the remaindermen. As between him and the remaindermen the Court would not allow him to receive rents from part of the property, while he allows taxes to accumulate on another part.

The fund is now in the hands of the Court through the receiver, and the equity of the infants to have the taxes paid out of the fund is superior to the claim of execution and other creditors of the tenant for life. There is nothing in the will to interfere with these relations between the tenant for life and remaindermen, and my order will be so to apply the fund in hand derived from the rents.

[Suppose there are arrears of taxes at the time land is settled upon a tenant for life with remainder over. How would you apportion the burden?

Assuming that the vacant land was unproductive, why should the tenant for life be obliged to pay taxes thereon out of income from productive land? See 2 *American Law of Property*, at p. 152.]

[If a life tenant fails to pay taxes and subsequently acquires title at a tax sale, he will not be permitted to hold it free of the remainderman's rights: see *Mayo* v. *Leitovski*, [1928]

1 W.W.R. 700 (Man.), where the Court, in the absence of English or Canadian authority, examined and applied American principles.

In *Biscoe v. Van Bearle* (1858), 6 Gr. 438, on a life tenant's failure to pay taxes a portion of the land was sold but was redeemed by the remainderman. *Held*, the latter was entitled to recoupment from the life tenant.]

[Ordinarily, a lease by a life tenant terminates on expiration of the life estate, but legislation such as the Settled Estates Act, R.S.O. 1960, c. 369 gives a life tenant (who is not otherwise prevented by the settlement) a power to lease for a period up to 21 years and makes the lease binding on holders of future interests, provided it conforms to the requirements of the Act. Leases for longer periods may be made on approval of the Court. In *Hunter* v. *Doan*, [1942] O.W.N. 291, a 90 year old life tenant gave a 2 year lease containing an option of renewal for 3 more years. He died less than 2 years later. The tenant was unable to show that the terms of the lease conformed to the Settled Estates Act, and hence could not rest on the lease as against the remainderman.

Settled estates legislation also provides for applications to the Court for authority to mortgage settled land to raise money for repairs or improvements and even for authority to sell outright: see, in addition to the Ontario Act quoted above, Settled Estates Act, R.S.B.C. 1960, c. 351; Judicature Act, 1950 (N.S.), c. 60, ss. 15 and 16 (applying Settled Estates Act, 1877, (Imp.), c. 18, s. 16); and see *Re Baugild and Baugild*, [1954] 3 D.L.R. 586, 34 M.P.R. 346 (N.S.C.A.).

Where the property is sold, ordinarily a tenant for life is not entitled to a lump sum payment but only to the income on the proceeds of sale. Legislative patterns are not, however, uniform; for example, some partition legislation contemplates that on a sale the inchoate dower rights of the wife of a co-tenant may be valued and paid for either by a lump sum or by an annual sum: see Partition Act, R.S.O. 1960, c. 287.]

[Where settled land is leased and the lessee on the expiration of the lease pays for breach of covenant to yield up in repair, does the money belong to the life tenant or to the remainderman? Must it be applied to repairs? See *In re Lacon's Settlement*, [1911] 2 Ch. 17 (C.A.).]

Insurance

A life tenant and a reversioner or remainderman have separate insurable interests, but apart from any express obligation imposed by the settlement or other instrument under which they take, neither is bound to insure either for his own benefit or for the benefit of the other. Both may, of course, join in effecting insurance on the entire interest in the land, but if the life tenant purports to insure the entire interest in his own name and a loss occurs, the central questions are whether the insurer is obliged to pay for any loss beyond the life tenant's interest and, if it does pay, whether the reversioner or remainderman has any claim to the excess or any right to have it applied for his benefit.

[In *In re Bennett*, [1896] 1 Ch. 778, (C.A.) at p. 787, A. L. Smith L. J. said: "... in the case of insurance the payment [of premiums] is a voluntary one made by the tenant for life out of his own income without any obligation on his part to do so".

If land held by a life tenant and remainderman is subject to an overriding mortgage which requires that the property be kept insured, is the burden of insurance premiums to be borne by the life tenant or by the remainderman?]

CASTELLAIN v. PRESTON. Court of Appeal. 1883. 11 Q.B.D. 380

BOWEN L. J.: ... It seems to me that it is an ocular illusion to suppose that under any circumstances more may be obtained by the assured than the amount of the loss. I think this illusion can be detected if it is recollected what are the ordinary business rules according to which insurances are made. It is well known in marine and fire insurances that a person who has a limited interest may insure nevertheless on the total value of the subject-matter of the insurance, and he may recover the whole value, subject to these two provisions; first of all, the form of his policy must be such as to enable him to recover the total value, because the assured may so limit himself by the way in which he insures as not really to insure the whole value of the subject-matter; and secondly, he must intend to insure the whole value at the time. When the insurance is effected he cannot recover the entire value unless he has intended to insure the entire value. A person with a limited interest may insure either for himself and to cover his own interest only, or he may insure so as to cover not merely his own limited interest, but the interest of all others who are interested in the property. It is a question of fact what is his intention when he obtains the policy. But he can only hold for so much as he has intended to insure. Let us take a few of the cases which are most commonly known in commerce of persons who insure. There are persons who have a limited interest and yet who insure for more than a limited interest, who insure for the total value of the subject-matter. There is the case, which is I suppose the most common, of carriers and wharfingers and commercial agents, who have an interest in the adventure. It is well known what their rights are. Them, to take a case which perhaps illustrates more exactly the argument, let us turn to the case of a mortgagee. If he has the legal ownership, he is entitled to insure for the whole value, but even supposing he is not entitled to the legal ownership he is entitled to insure primâ facie for all. If he intends to cover only his mortgage and is only insuring his own interest, he can only in the event of a loss hold the amount to which he has been damnified. If he has intended to cover other persons beside himself, he can hold the surplus for those whom he has intended to cover. But one thing he cannot do, that is, having intended only to cover himself and being a person whose interest is only limited, he cannot hold anything beyond the amount of the loss caused to his own particular interest. Suppose for a moment the case of a ship and a mortgagee who has lent £500 on the ship. The ship is worth £10,000. If he insures for £10,000, meaning only to cover his own interest, and not the interest of anybody besides, can it for a moment be supposed that the mortgagee who insures under those circumstances can hold the £10,000? That would be an over insurance, and to treat it in any other way would be to make a marine policy not a contract of idemnity, but a wager, a speculation for gain. Suppose, again, there are several mortgagees for small sums, can they all recover and hold (having ex hypothesi insured their separate interests only) the entire value of the ship? It seems to me they cannot. They can recover only what they have lost. That being, as I apprehend, the law about mortgages of ships, is there any real distinction between that and the mortgagee of a house? I can see none. It seems to me that the same principle applies, and here as in many other problems of insurance law, the problem will be solved by going back and resting upon the doctrine of indemnity.

Let us take another instance which had been much pressed upon us in the course of the argument, the case of a tenant for years or a tenant from year to year. We have been asked to hold that a tenant from year to year can always recover the full value of the house from the insurance company, although he has intended to insure only his limited interest in it. There is some justification for that in the language of James, L. J., in *Rayner* v. *Preston*, 18 Ch. D. 1, at p. 15. He says this: "In my view of the case it is perhaps unneccesary to refer to the Act of Parliament as to fire insurance. But that Act seems to me to shew that a policy of insurance on a house was considered by the legislature, as I believe it to be considered by the universal consensus of mankind, to be a policy for the benefit of all persons interested in the property, and it appears to me that a purchaser having an equitable interest under a contract of sale is a person having an interest in the house within the meaning of the Act. I believe that there is no case to be found in which the liability of the insurance office has been limited to the value of the interest of the insured in the house destroyed. If a tenant for life having insured his house has the house destroyed or damaged by fire, I have never heard it suggested that the insurance office could cut down his claim by shewing that he was of extreme old age or suffering from a mortal disease." Now, with the greatest possible respect and reverence for all that is left to us of the judgments of a great judge like James, L. J., I confess I do not follow that. I have no doubt the insurance offices seldom take the trouble to look to the exact interest of the tenant who insures, or perhaps of the landlord who insures, and for the best of all reasons because it is generally intended that the insurance shall be made, not merely to cover the limited interest of the tenant, but also to cover the interest of all concerned. In most cases the covenants as to repair throw liability on one side or the other, and in a large class of leases the liability to repair is by the provisions of the lease thrown upon the tenant. Therefore, in these cases no question ever can arise between the insurance office and the tenant from year to year, or the tenant for years, as to the amount which the insurance office ought to pay. But if a tenant for a year, or a tenant for six months, or a tenant from week to week, insures, meaning only to cover his interest, does anybody really suppose that he could get the whole value of the house? It is true that in most cases the claim of the tenant from year to year, or for years, cannot be answered by handing over to him what may be the marketable value of his property; and the reason is that he insures more than the marketable value of this property, and he loses more than the marketable value of his property; he loses the house in which he is living and the beneficial enjoyment of the house as well as its pecuniary value. That I think is all that was meant by the Vice-Chancellor in *Simpson* v. *Scottish Union Insurance Co.* 1 H. & M. 618, at p. 628. I will pass on to the case of a life tenant. I will take the case of a life tenant who is a very old man, and whose house is burnt down, but who has intended only to insure his own interest. I am far from saying that he could not under any conceivable circumstances be entitled to have the house reinstated. A man cannot be compensated simply by paying him for the marketable value of his interest. But it does not follow from that that he gets or can keep more than he has lost. I very much doubt whether, if a life tenant, having intended to insure only his life interest, dies within a week after the loss by fire, the Court would award his executors the whole value of the house. In all these difficult problems I go back with confidence to the broad principle of indemnity. Apply that and an answer to the difficulty will always be found.

[The judgments of Brett and Cotton L. JJ. are omitted. *Castellain* v. *Preston* involved a claim by an insurer against the vendor of land to recover insurance money paid to the vendor who had insured the property which was damaged by fire after a contract of sale had been made which contained no reference to the insurance. The sale was subsequently carried through, the vendor receiving the full price agreed upon. *Held*, on appeal, the insurer was entitled to recover.]

[In *Gaussen* v. *Whatman* (1905), 93 L.T. 101 (Ch.), a tenant for life, although not so obliged, maintained insurance on settled property. A loss having occurred, the insurer paid the insurance money to the trustees of the settlement. Is the life tenant entitled to recover this money from the trustees?

If a life tenant insures the whole of the property and a loss occurs, may the remainderman take advantage of the insurance by ratifying the life tenant's act? Must there be express mention in the policy of an intention to insure the remainder interest as well, or may this intention be shown in some other way? See 1 *American Law of Property*, s. 2.23; *Note*, (1929) 42 Harv. L. Rev. 581. On ratification after loss, see *Goulding* v. *Norwich Union Fire Ins. Society*, [1947] 4 D.L.R. 236, [1947] 2 W.W.R. 4 (Sask.); cf. *Rayner* v. *Preston* (1881), 18 Ch. D. 1 (C.A.).

See, generally, *Preston*, Life Tenants and Remaindermen: Insurance (1944), 8 Convey. & Prop. L. (N.S.) 201.]

[Where settled property is held by a trustee having active duties of management, is he (apart from the terms of the trust) under an obligation to insure at least against loss by fire? The authorities in the United States say "yes": see 2 *Scott on Trusts* (1956, 2nd ed.), p. 1306. English cases have emphasized the trustee's power to insure but without obligation to do so: see *Re McEacharn* (1911), 103 L.T. 900 (Ch.); but cf. *Kingham* v. *Kingham*, [1897] 1 Ir. R. 170. In *Re Gamble* (1925), 57 O.L.R. 504, Mowat J. refused to follow the English cases (the more so because they were lower Court decisions) and held that apart from statute or specific terms of the trust, a trustee is bound to insure; "It is the custom in this country to insure and failure to do so is negligent conduct on the part of executors".

Where a trustee effects insurance, there is a question of how the burden of premiums must be borne, in the absence of direction in the trust instrument. In the United States, they are regarded as a recurring charge payable out of income, although in some cases they have been apportioned between income and capital: see 3 *Scott on Trusts* (1956, 2nd ed.) p. 1752. In Ontario, after some disparate decisions in the lower Courts (see *Re Cunningham* (1917), 12 O.W.N. 268 and *Re Stevens* (1929), 35 O.W.N. 359), it has come to be accepted that insurance premiums are properly chargeable to capital: see *Re Rutherford*, [1933] O.R. 707, [1933] 4 D.L.R. 222 (C.A.) (holding also that the permissive terms of the Trustee Act, now R.S.O. 1960, c. 408, s. 21 enabling the trustee to pay premiums out of income did not settle the ultimate incidence): *Re Davis Estate*, [1942] O.W.N. 26; *Leonard and Hall* v. *Crown Trust & Guarantee Co.*, [1949] O.R. 678, [1949] 3 D.L.R. 815 (C.A.) (majority holding that Surrogate Court's finding that insurance premiums are income disbursements is *res judicata* so far as concerns a later action by executors to recover the amounts paid); *Re Tuckett*, [1954] O.R. 973 (at p. 979), [1955] 1 D.L.R. 643 (at p. 648), and see *Note*, (1934) 12 Can. Bar Rev. 459.

In *Re Barr*, [1935] O.W.N. 134, the Court purported to follow *Re Rutherford* (wrongly it would now appear) by holding that premiums were apportionable between life tenant and reversioner.

English cases appear to be in accord with the prevailing American line that insurance premiums are chargeable to income: see *In re Egmont's Trusts*, [1908] 1 Ch. 821. In *In re Mitchell Estate*, [1936] 3 W.W.R. 249 (Sask.), it was held that "premiums of insurance on buildings against loss by fire are chargeable against capital [because] they are a speculative investment to safeguard capital. On the other hand, premiums of insurance against loss of crops by hail are a speculative investment against loss of income and should be chargeable to income" (p. 252).]

[Provision for insurance and for the burden of premiums may properly be made by a Court which is asked to approve, under Settled Estates legislation, a mortgage on the property to raise money for repairs or improvements: see *Re Darch* (1914), 6 O.W.N. 107.]

EMBLEMENTS

The personal representatives of a life tenant (or the tenant himself in the case of an estate *pur autre vie*) are entitled to emblements, that is, to reap annual crops sown by the life tenant even though the estate has terminated (provided that it was without his act or default) before they matured. This extension of his interest in the land was recognized because of the uncertain duration of a life tenancy (and hence, by contrast, a tenant for a term certain was not entitled to emblements), and, moreover, emblements would encourage cultivation.

ATKINSON v. FARRELL. Ontario Divisional Court. 1912. 27 O.L.R. 204, 8 D.L.R. 582

Appeal by defendant, who was the remainderman in respect of certain land, from a judgment in favour of the executors of the deceased life tenant for damages by reason of the conversion of certain wheat, straw and manure allegedly belonging to plaintiffs. The life tenant had leased the land for five years to one Hanley but about two years later the life tenant died and it was agreed that this brought the lease to an end. In the previous fall, Hanley had planted some wheat which was still growing at the life tenant's death and there was also some straw and manure on the land at the time.

The judgment of the Court was delivered by BOYD C. (who referred first to the fact that the lease terminated on the life tenant's death along with the life tenancy): . . . This being so, the wheat then sown and in the ground became emblements belonging to the tenant Hanley. These emblements were purchased by the executors of the lessor, Patrick Farrell, and an assignment thereof obtained under seal on the 9th March, 1911. The reversioner, the defendant, assumed to deal with as his property and make sale and conveyance of the land and these crops in July, 1911, to one Maher, whereby he became liable for their conversion under the circumstances and evidence set forth below.

The action is well-founded in this regard, and the judgment as to them in favour of the executors is right.

The other branch of the appeal is as to straw and manure on the farm at the determination of the lease. By the terms of the lessee's covenant, these were to be kept and utilized on and for the land; and, according to the authorities, they were not the property of or removable by the tenant. So that the neat point is, whether this straw and manure passed to the reversioner with the land freed from the demise, or did they pass to the executors of the lessor? The judgment in appeal decides in favour of the plaintiffs, the executors, grounded on the decision of Osler, J. A., to that effect in a like case, *Gardner* v. *Perry*, 2 O.W.R. 681. The correctness of that decision is impeached by this appeal.

The straw-stacks and the manure-piles are the chattels of the tenant to be used in a particular way; the straw as bedding and fodder for the cattle is to be turned into manure, and the manure is to be turned into the land so as to enrich the soil and become part of it. While the tenant may be called the owner in one sense, the effect of his covenant not to remove from the premises, but to use and spend thereon, the straw and manure, is, that he has no right to take these things away from the place, nor when left on the place has he any right to be paid for them: *Beaty* v. *Gibbons* (1812), 16 East 116, 118; and *Roberts* v. *Barker* (1833), 1 Cr. & M. 808.

The law is obscure on the precise point. The dung made on the farm is spoken of as "belonging to the farm" in *Hindle* v. *Pollitt* (1840), 6 M. & W. 529, 533. To remove this stuff, even apart from the covenant, would be a failure to work in a husbandlike manner, and would be an injury done to the inheritance: *Cheetham* v. *Hampson* (1791), 4 T.R. 318, 319; *Walton* v. *Johnson* (1848), 15 Sim. 352; *Powley* v. *Walker* (1793), 5 T.R. 373. The tenant, being unable to remove because of his covenant, is to leave the straw and manure on the farm for the landlord; so it is put in *Massey* v. *Goodall* (1851), 17 Q.B. 310, 316. The provision is with a view to benefit of the land: *Richards* v. *Bluck* (1848), 6 C.B. 437, 441. In the last case I have found, Vaughan Williams, L. J., deals with the situation in this way: the provisions in the lease are intended for the purpose of ensuring proper cultivation of the land according to the rules of good husbandry. One thing which is clearly for the advantage of the land is that the crops should be dealt with in such a manner that the land may not become impoverished. The straw and manure clauses relate to things which have existence on the farm and which can be dealt with actively or left passively for the benefit of the farm: *In re Hull and Lady Meux*, [1905] 1 K.B. 588, 590.

Now these chattels are the tenant's but he cannot avail himself of them in any way, because, by the death of the life-tenant, the tenancy is at an end—the estate and interest of the lessor as landlord is at an end. No title was in him during his life which could at his death pass to his executors, as was held by the learned County Court Judge in this case, following the decision under consideration of *Gardner* v. *Perry*. In the case of a living landlord, the straw and hay at the end of the tenancy would be left on the land, and would fall under the control of the landlord by virtue of his ownership of the land. The straw and manure may be regarded as constructive fixtures, the destiny of which is to be incorporated in the soil. That points the way to the proper conclusion in this appeal, viz., the death of the life-tenant ended his interest in the land and everything lying upon it that could not be legally removed; but his death brought, forthwith and *eo instanti*, into virtual possession the estate in fee of the remainderman, who, as lord of the land, takes the farm with the straw and manure thereon as "accessories of the soil". (See Amos and Ferard on Fixtures, 3rd ed., p. 215, n.)

I think the decision in 2 O.W.R. is not to be followed on this point, and that the judgment in appeal should be varied by restricting it to the value of the wheat in the ground, $90, and dismissing it as to the straw and manure on the ground ($35), which passed to the defendant as remainderman, to the exclusion of any claim on the part of the executors of the life-tenant.

This conclusion is fortified in another way. The provisions of the lease to till and manure in good husbandlike and proper manner, and to spend, use, and employ in a proper husbandlike manner, all the straw and manure which shall grow, arise, or be made thereon, and not to remove or permit to be removed from the premises any straw of any kind, manure, etc., are usual and customary provisions for the right farming of the land, which apply generally not only when expressly set out, but as of course, in farming leases, unless the contrary is expressed. Such is the law of England, and is alike applicable to the farm lands of this Province: *Brown* v. *Crump* (1815), 1 Marsh. 567, 569, quoting the language of Buller, J.

This rule of proper use of the land applies as between landlord and tenant and also between tenant for life and remainderman. To neglect these precautions against the deterioration and impoverishment of the land savours of waste. While the life-tenant is entitled to the use of the property and to the receipt of all the income and profits, he is in such fiduciary relationship to the remainderman that he is not allowed to injure or to deal with the estate to the detriment of the inheritance. To allow the executors of the life-tenant to take away from the land, after death has freed the estate for the remainderman, the straw and manure left on the land for its nourishment, would be to reduce unduly the rights of the land-owner.

Appeal allowed in part.

[On emblements see 1 *American Law of Property*, s. 2.16 (g) (where it is said: "An estate for a fixed term held from a life tenant as landlord, or otherwise subject to termination on the ending of a life or lives is subject to this right."); 5 *American Law of Property*, s. 19.16; *Armour*, Real Property (1901, 1st ed.), p. 111; *Cheshire*, Modern Law of Real Property (1962, 9th ed.), pp. 185, 364; *Graves* v. *Weld* (1833), 5 B. & Ad. 105, 110 E.R. 731 (K.B.).

For an application of *Atkinson* v. *Farrell* to a crop-share lease see *Peck and Peck* v. *Veiner*, [1950] 1 W.W.R. 293 (Alta.).]

[A life tenant's position as to "fixtures" which he has brought on the land is, in general, subject to the same considerations as those arising in the landlord-tenant situation: see *Leigh* v. *Taylor*, [1902] A.C. 157; *In re Hulse*, [1905] 1 Ch. 406; *McLaren* v. *Coombs* (1869), 16 Gr. 587; and see, *supra*, pp. 261-277.]

3. WASTE

COMMON LAW, equity and statute have all contributed to the development of this branch of the law. It is concerned with restrictions upon user of land by the holder of a limited interest therein by reason of interests (usually future) in the same land held by others. (Waste between co-tenants has been referred to in chapter x, *supra*, at p. 389.) The law of waste, hence, is based on different considerations from nuisance, and differs again from restrictions on user, such as easements or profits, arising from grants or contracts.

There is some dispute among writers on the subject on the extent to which liability for waste rested upon various kinds of holders of limited interests before the enactment of the Statute of Marlbridge, 1267 and the Statute of Gloucester, 1278. The dispute need not concern us here. Those statutes, whether considered as mainly remedial or partly substantive as well, provided a basis for subsequent evolution of the law both in England and in common law jurisdictions elsewhere, e.g. Canada and United States, with considerable contribution on the remedial side from equity.

[On the history of waste, see *Holdsworth*, History of English Law, vol. 3, pp. 121-3; vol. 7, pp. 275-281; 2 *Pollock and Maitland*, History of English Law (1898, 2nd ed.), p. 9; *Kirchwey*, Liability for Waste, (1908) 8 Col. L. Rev. 425, 624.

The Statute of Marlbridge (or Marlborough), 1267 (52 Hen. 3, c. 23), was as follows:

> Also fermors during their terms shall not make waste, sale nor exile of houses, wood and men, nor of anything belonging to the tenements they have to ferm, without special licence had by writing of covenant, making mention that they may do it; which thing, if they do and therof be convict, they shall yield full damage and shall be punished by amerciament grievously.

The Statute of Gloucester, 1278 (6 Edw. 1, c. 5), was as follows:

> It is provided also that a man from henceforth shall have a writ of waste in the chancery against him that holdeth by law of England, or otherwise for term of life, or for term of years, or a woman in dower; and he who shall be attainted of waste shall lose the thing which he hath wasted, and moreover shall recompense thrice so much as the waste shall be taxed at.

The Statute of Gloucester was repealed in England by 1879 (Imp.), c. 59. The defect of the writ of waste provided by that statute was that it could be invoked only by the person having the immediate estate of inheritance. However, Chancery in developing its jurisdiction over waste did not follow this common law view: see *Anon.* (1599), Moore 554, placitum 748. The writ of waste was abolished in England by 1833 (Imp.), c. 27, s. 36; and see also 1834 (U.C.), c. 1, s. 39.]

CONVEYANCING AND LAW OF PROPERTY ACT, R.S.O. 1960, c. 66

30. A tenant by the curtesy, a dowress, a tenant for life or for years, and the guardian of the estate of an infant, are impeachable for waste, and liable in damages to the person injured.

31. An estate for life without impeachment of waste does not confer upon the tenant for life any legal right to commit waste of the description known as equitable waste, unless an intention to confer the right expressly appears by the instrument creating the estate.

33. Lessees making or suffering waste on the demised premises without licence of the lessors are liable for the full damage so occasioned.

[For provincial legislation on waste similar to s. 30 of the Ontario Act, *supra*, see Law of Property Act, R.S.M. 1954, c. 138, s. 14; Landlord and Tenant Act, R.S.N.B. 1952, c. 126, s. 6; Landlord and Tenant Act. R.S.P.E.I. 1951, c. 82, s. 7.

For provincial legislation similar to s. 31 of the Ontario Act, *supra*, See Judicature Act, R.S.A. 1955, c. 164, s. 34 (3); Laws Declaratory Act, R.S.B.C. 1960, c. 213, s. 2 (9); Law of Property Act, R.S.M. 1954, c. 138, s. 13; Judicature Act, R.S.N.B. 1952, c. 120, s. 30; Judicature Act, R.S.Nfld. 1952, c. 114, s. 25 (8); Queen's Bench Act, 1960 (Sask.), c. 35, s. 44 (2).

The Judicature Act, R.S.O. 1960, c. 197, s. 16 (1) empowers the Court to grant an injunction against any threatened or apprehended waste. For similar legislation, see Judicature Act, R.S.P.E.I. 1951, c. 79, s. 15 (5).]

DRAKE v. WIGLE. Ontario Court of Common Pleas. 1874. 24 U.C.C.P. 405

Demurrer to a plea arising out of an action by a reversioner against a lessee of the life tenant for damages for cutting down trees to clear wooded land for cultivation.

HAGARTY C. J.: As I understand it, "Waste" is a spoil or destruction in houses, gardens, trees or other corporeal hereditaments to the disherison of him in remainder or reversion, &c., or to the prejudice of the heir or reversioner: 1 Co. Litt. 53.

There is a summary of the cases in the notes to *Greene* v. *Cole*, Wm. Saund. ed. 1871, vol. ii., p. 651: "There is no authority for saying that any act can be waste which is not injurious to the inheritance, either, first, by diminishing the value of the estate, or, secondly, by increasing the burden upon it, or by impairing the evidence of title."

This is the language used by Lord Denman in *Doe dem. Grubb* v. *Earl of Burlington*, 5 B. & Ad. 507, at p. 517.

He also says, speaking of some authorites, "they are illustrations of the principle, that where there are no damages there can be no waste; and to this effect is *Barrett* v. *Barrett*, Hetley 35."

He concluded by adding, "As the jury have found that the defendant did no damage to the estate, it follows there was no waste and no forfeiture."...

Waste seems to me to be an expression necessarily bearing upon an actual injury to the estate of the reversioner, as has been said by diminishing the value, increasing the burden, or impairing the evidence of title.

Under this last head may be classed the alteration of the estate, e.g., by turning pasture into arable, &c.

"I agree," says Knight Bruce, Lord Justice, in *Morris* v. *Morris*, 3 DeG. & J. 323, at p. 327, "That an act may be reasonable, may be judicious, may be beneficial to all the parties interested in a settled property, and yet it may be an act prohibited to a tenant for life, if a person interested in remainder chooses to interfere. I do not put the case, therefore, merely on the reasonableness, on the judiciousness, and on the beneficial nature of what was done, but they are ingredients in it."

Turner L. J.: "I apprehend that the principle upon which the Court proceeds in these cases is, that the tenant for life of an estate is liable to account in equity for profit derived by him from an improper user of his legal powers, in committing equitable waste."

In *Coppinger* v. *Gubbins*, 9 Ir. Eq. 304, Sir E. Sugden, Chancellor, at p. 309, discusses the rights of tenants for life to cut turf for sale on bog land: "There may be such a demise, as referred to by the learned Judges, with whom I entirely agree in the cases cited; e.g., where bog and nothing else is demised, and turf could be cut for no valuable purpose except for sale; or if it was a bog always cut for sale, and demised as such in the same manner as an open mine. Such cases depend on contract, and must be considered as standing on their own ground, and no doubt the lessees would have a right to cut turf and sell it."...

If there be any analogy between the manner in which an open mine or bog held as such, apart from other land on a life estate, and a parcel of wild land in a state of nature covered with trees, it would seem that it ought not to be waste to cut such a reasonable portion of the trees as would render the land fit for cultivation according to the custom of the country.

I have been disappointed, so far, in not finding in our old books and Digests some reference to the clearing up of lands at a period when a large portion of England was covered with forest. Long after the beginning of legal memory or of reported law, there were extensive forest tracts, and we can hardly suppose that land was not brought into cultivation by the clearance of the woods and the agency of fire for the consumption of the encumbering timber.

For some time, even in this forest land, timber has become a most valuable article of sale, at least as much so as in England six centuries back, when statutes were passed on the subject of Waste in the reigns of Henry III. and his son, Edward I.

Yet the destruction of the forest by fire, for the purpose of clearing and cultivating, has still to be resorted to in Canada as the only means available to the settler in large sections of the country.

From all we know or read of the England of the first Edward, it is difficult to believe but that the same process was as necessary and as common as it is still here.

I am not aware of any express decision of our own Courts....

In Kent's Commentaries, 11th ed., vol. iv., p. 82, the subject is well discussed from a point of view worthy of a Canadian Court. It is said the tenant may clear part of wild land for the purpose of cultivation. "But he must leave wood and timber sufficient for the permanent use of the farm. And it is a question of fact for a jury, what extent of wood may be cut down in such cases, without exposing the party to the charge of waste. The American doctrine on the subject of waste is somewhat varied from the English law, and is more enlarged, and better accommodated to the circumstances of a new and growing country." But he adds that in Massachusetts the Supreme Court seemed to be "in favour of the strict English rule; and that was one of the reasons assigned for holding the widow not dowable of such lands."

A very recent judgment of Sir George Jessel, M.R., *Honywood* v. *Honywood*, L.R. 18 Eq. 306, is instructive on some points as to waste.

After mentioning that by the general law of England oak, ash, and elm, twenty years old and upwards, are timber, and that the kind of tree which may be called timber may be varied by local custom, he proceeds, at p. 309: "Once arrived at the fact of what is timber, the tenant for life, impeachable for waste, cannot cut it down. That I take it to be the clear law, with one single exception, which has been established principally by modern authorities in favour of the owners of timber estates, that is, estates which are cultivated merely for the produce of saleable timber, and where the timber is cut periodically. The reason of the distinction is this, that as cutting the timber is the mode of cultivation, the timber is not to be kept as part of the inheritance, but part, so to say, of the annual fruits of the land, and in these cases the same kind of cultivation may be carried on by the tenant for life that has been carried on by the settlor on the estate, and the timber so cut down periodically in due course is looked upon as the annual profits of the estate, and, therefore, goes to the tenant for life."

It seems to me on all the authorities that "Waste," is a flexible term varying with local and other circumstances; that its essence is injury to the reversion; and that, if there be no damage thereto, especially in the action on the case for waste, there can be no recovery.

In the case before us there is no such injury, I think, as impairing the evidence of title, or imposing a greater burden on the inheritance.

The exception as to a "timber estate," mentioned by Sir George Jessel, shews how a law like that of waste is made to adapt itself to the varying circumstances of life, and the dictates of common sense.

When the state of England in the olden time more resembled that of our comparatively new country, I do not see anything in the authorities to have prevented the allowance to a life tenant of the right to resort to the only method by which any benefit whatever could be derived from a piece of aboriginal forest, namely, the clearance of a moderate part for cultivation, by removal of the trees.

Judgment for defendant.

[Gwynne J. concurred. The separate concurring judgment of Galt J. is omitted.

A similar approach to voluntary or commissive waste is adopted by 1 *Restatement of Property*, s. 138. The approach is criticized in 5 *American Law of Property*, s. 20.1 which emphasizes that "it seems safer... to recognize in each case that a particular act results in legal liability not because it injures other interests in the land but because it contravenes or frustrates the intention of the grantor.... Where no intention is expressed, a reasonable use, in light of all the facts must be presumed. The inheritance is what is left."]

HIXON v. REAVELEY. Ontario Chancery Division. 1904. 9 O.L.R. 6

Action by remaindermen for waste arising out of the following circumstances. Buildings were in need of repair and the timber on the property was unsuitable. The life tenant thereupon arranged to procure suitable lumber and to sell a sufficient amount of the timber on the land to pay for it.

BOYD C.: All the niceties of the ancient learning as to waste which obtain in England are not to be transferred without discrimination to a new and comparatively unsettled country like this Province. It is no doubt laid down in the books that the tenant for life cannot cut down trees for repairs and sell the same, and that he must use the timber itself in making the repairs, and that the sale is waste: *Gower* v. *Eyre*, G. Coop., at p. 161. And this doctrine was reluctantly applied by Lord Thurlow in a case where the tenant felled timber and applied the produce instead; but he called it a hard demand and refused to give costs: *Lee* v. *Alston* (1789), 1 Ves. Jr. 78, S.C. 3 Bro. C.C. 37. This case, however, turned very much on the pleadings, wherein the defendant admitted wrongful cutting. So in *Simmons* v. *Norton* (1831), 7 Bing. 640, and 5 M. & P. 645, at p. 660, the Court held that in the absence of a proper plea evidence could not be given that the tenant had bought and applied for repairs other timber bought with proceeds of the timber cut, which was unsuitable for the purpose. This line of defence may, however, even in England be set up by way of set-off in mitigation of damages, so that in a case of reasonable dealing of the tenant he may escape with nominal damages: See *Rennell* v. *Wither* (1818), Manning's Index of Cases, cited in Bewes' Waste, p. 54.

In England consideration is extended to ecclesiastical bodies—tenants for life—who are allowed not only to fell timber and dig stone to repair, but may sell such produce in order to expend the money in repairs: *Knight* v. *Mosely* (1753), Amb. 176, and *Wither* v. *Winchester* (1817), 3 Mer. 421. This may be explained on the grounds that proper reparation is essential for the proper use of the whole property, and that such cutting and selling and using the money on the dilapidated buildings is not "waste," but really going to the betterment of the whole property.

A like relaxation of the strict rule obtains in the United States, and the authorities of that country, so much alike in its territorial conditions to our own, may well be regarded by Canadian courts, as was done in *Drake* v. *Wigle*, 24 C.P. 405.

I am content to adopt the language of Mr. Justice Story as found in *Loomis* v. *Wilbur* (1827), 5 Mason 11, at p. 15. If the cutting down of the timber was without any intention of repairs but for sale generally, the act itself would doubtless be waste, and if so it would not be purged or its character changed by a subsequent application to repairs. But if the cutting down and sale were originally for the purpose of repairs, and the sale was an economical mode of making the repairs, and the most for the benefit of all concerned, and the proceeds were bonâ fide applied for that purpose in pursuance of the original intention, it does not appear to me possible that such a cutting down and sale can be waste. It would be repugnant to the principles of common sense that the tenant should be obliged to make the repairs in the way most expensive and injurious to the estate. See *Miller* v. *Shields* (1887), 55 Ind. 71....

On the present evidence there does not appear to me to be any case of waste made out to justify granting an injunction, nor nothing on which to award damages if the timber is cut with due regard to the situation of the bush and cleared land, and no unreasonable amount is taken off to recoup the cost of timber and shingles used and to be used in the repairs.

Action dismissed.

[Land which was subject to a mortgage to secure an annuity was devised for life, remainder in fee simple. The life tenant sold standing timber to her co-defendant; and in an action for an injunction and damages brought by the remainderman the life tenant claimed that, having paid a number of instalments of the annuity, she was entitled to be subrogated to the mortgagee's claim against the land, and because the land was an insufficient security she had the right to cut down timber. What are the relevant considerations for a proper disposition of the case? See *Whitesell* v. *Reece and Payne* (1903), 5 O.L.R. 352 (Div. Ct.); *Brethour* v. *Brooke* (1893), 23 O.R. 658, aff'd (1894), 21 O.A.R. 144.

As to waste as between mortgagor and mortgagee, see *Falconbridge*, Law of Mortgages of Land (1942, 3rd ed.), pp. 611, 626.]

[Where land which is settled on a life tenant and remainderman (or which is leased for a term of years to a tenant) is a timber estate, there may be a right in the life tenant (or tenant for years, as the case may be), subject to the terms of the settlement or instrument under which he takes, to cut the timber periodically as a matter of ordinary, reasonable enjoyment of the estate. No actionable waste is committed; and the "inheritance" is simply limited by this right of enjoyment of the preceding estate: see *Honywood* v. *Honywood* (1874), L.R. 18 Eq. 306; *Dashwood* v. *Magniac*, [1891] 3 Ch. 306 (C.A.); *A.-G. of Nova Scotia* v. *McDougall*, [1930] 2 D.L.R. 479, 2 M.P.R. 332 (N.S.C.A.). In the latter case, Mellish J. said, *inter alia*: "The very nature of a timber lease I think implies that the lessee is to have the benefit of the trees not as standing timber but as trees to be cut for use as timber, whatever the size of the trees may be. As restricting this benefit there may be, of course, express or implied provisions to prevent premature cutting, but a breach of such provisions would not I think alter the lease or make the product of the soil when severed the property of the lessor. Such a conclusion is not met by the suggestion that a tenant cannot have the advantage of his own wrongdoing as a principle of equity. He cannot do so, he is liable in damages for the injury to the reversion whatever that damage may be, having regard to the length of the lease, the size of the timber cut, the period during the lease when the timber was cut, and other relevant considerations. But his conduct does not in opinion give the lessor the right to treat him as though the lease never existed in respect of the trees cut or inequitably, by taking from him as in the present case many times more than such damage could possibly amount to. By paying 10 cents more per acre or in all $29.40 the lessor might have got from the Crown a lease permitting him to cut timber down to five inches in diameter. The 65 cords of wood taken are worth, I have no doubt, more than ten times that amount. If such a right of forfeiture exists equitable considerations should I think give relief against it and remit the lessor to his right of relief in damages, on the principle that he who invokes equity should do equity. In a lease of timber lands I think the trees which may not be cut until they reach a certain size are in the same position as bushes 'the general property' in which in an ordinary lease by the demise passes to the lessee. When severed the property remains in the lessee, even though they may have been severed in such a way as to render the tenant liable in an action of waste. *Berriman* v. *Peacock* (1832), 9 Bing. 384, 131 E.R. 660. And even in a lease which is not a timber lease a wrongful cutting by the tenant of trees not yet timber trees, does not at law give the property to the lessor. *Honywood* v. *Honywood* (1874), L.R. 18 Eq. 306, at pp. 311-2."]

PATTERSON v. CENTRAL CANADA LOAN AND SAVINGS CO. Ontario Divisional Court. 1898. 29 O.R. 134

In an action for damage to a reversionary interest by reason of commissive and permissive waste by mortgagees of life tenants the trial Judge gave damages for commissive waste only. Plaintiffs appealed.

The judgment of the Court was delivered by BOYD C.: It appears unnecessary to delve into the ancient law with a view of impeaching the decision of Mr. Justice Kay in *In re Cartwright* (1889), 41 Ch. D. 532. That case is apparently supported by the authority of a Divisional Court consisting of Lopes and Stephen, JJ., not there cited, although decided in 1881. It is *Barnes* v. *Dowling* (1881), 44 L.T.N.S. 809, where it is laid down that the weight of authority in equity is clearly opposed to an action for permissive waste against a tenant for life, and assuming that there was doubt or conflict as to the legal liability, and that there was variance between the rules of equity and those of common law with reference to permissive waste, they were bound to give effect to the former, and therefore held that an action for permissive waste will not lie against a tenant for life. We have the same provision in the Judicature Act as to the prevalence of the rules of equity in case of conflict as is alluded to in *Barnes* v. *Dowling*, and that is authority which concludes us in this appeal so far as the relief sought is in respect of permissive waste. *In re Cartwright*, is also affirmed in *In re Freman, Dimond* v. *Newburn*, [1898] 1 Ch. 28, 32.

It may be noted that the subject of waste was a familiar one to Mr. Justice Kay, and the whole subject was dealt with by him in *Re Williames, Andrew* v. *Williames* (1884), 52 L.T.N.S. 40, which was affirmed in appeal (1885), 54 *ib.* 105. The opinions of the text writers cannot be weighed against their judgments, and as a matter of fact they neutralize each other by a process of set-off. For against Roscoe, Addison, and Woodfall (or the modern editor thereof), can be set Pollock, Bewes, and White & Tudor, who support *In re Cartwright*.

The finding of the trial Judge as to active or commissive waste is limited to two heads, first, in regard to the stone taken away from the base of the fence, and second, in regard to trees cut. As to these, I think he has perhaps allowed too little for the stone placed as it was in the fence, but he could well have disallowed anything for the trees. I should on the evidence say that there was no waste in cutting or disposing of these—some were blown down—others interfered with the utilization of arable land, and they were not in all more than enough for fire-wood. Still there is no cross-appeal and these findings in money value may, therefore, be allowed to stand.

A strong argument was made about the deterioration of the farm on account of the spread of mustard seed and quack grass. Had these been sowed by the tenant it would have been an act of actionable waste: *Pratt* v. *Brett* (1817), 2 Madd. 62. But the spread of these weeds from natural causes, or by the action of cattle depasturing or eating hay or straw that came from the fields where the mustard was, and the failure to overcome the growth and spread of these and thistles by a process of summer fallowing, or by a process of handpicking, is no evidence of waste, but only of ill-husbandry: 2 Rolle Abr. 814, 22 Viner's Abr., p. 437, Tit. Waste D. 2. The same result would have followed had the land been left uncultivated, for it is in evidence that the farm was injured by the presence of these noxious weeds in many places before the defendants took possession. And to leave the land uncultivated is not waste either wilful or permissive: Parke, B., in *Hutton* v. *Warren* (1836), 1 M. & W. 466, 476.

That there is an Ontario statute for the prevention of the spread of noxious weeds, R.S.O. ch. 202, does not change the character of the inaction attributed to the defendant. He is not thereby made liable *qua* tenant for life to the remainderman, though there may be a direct remedy against the occupant or owner of the farm under provisions of the statute: *Osborne* v. *Corporation of the City of Kingston* (1893), 23 O.R. 382.

I agree with what the learned Judge says about the fences. They were old ones to begin with; many of the rails were useless with age, and the fences had to be reconstructed in a more economical manner (I mean in the way of saving material, for the Russel fence is better than the old fences), and new rails were brought in to assist in the change which had to be made. It is said for the defence that allowing for necessary decay of material the fencing on the whole is as extensive now as in 1889. And a tenant for life is not called on to bring in new rails for fences if there is no suitable material on the place, which was the case here: see *Whitfield* v. *Weedon*, (1772), 2 Chit. 685.

The buildings were very old, and have suffered from decay and exposure; but the tenant is not legally bound to repair, in the absence of a direction to that effect in the instrument creating the present and the reversionary estates. If premises are suffered to become dilapidated by omission to repair, and so run down through mere neglect, that is no more than permissive waste for which an action does not lie: *Gibson* v. *Wells* (1805), 1 B. & P.N.R. 290. Though it may be the duty of the tenant for life, and in his own interest to keep up the buildings in habitable shape, he cannot charge the expense on the inheritance, nor can he be dispunishable for waste if he abstains: *In re Leigh's Estate*, L.R. 6 Ch. 887, 892; *In re Freman, Dimond* v. *Newburn*, [1898] 1 Ch. 28.

Appeal dismissed.

[An injunction was refused in respect of the commissive waste because "the acts of spoliation as proved were of minor importance—none of recent date—no likelihood of their repetition, and any intention to commit torts repudiated by the defence".

The *Patterson* case was followed in *Monro* v. *Toronto Railway Co.* (1904), 9 O.L.R. 299, and in *Currie* v. *Currie* (1910), 20 O.L.R. 375, where a life tenant under a will was held not liable for permissive waste, "no express duty to repair being imposed by the will".

Kirchwey, Liability for Waste, (1908) 8 Col. L. Rev. 624 regards *In re Cartwright* as clearly wrong in so far as it assumed that at common law a life tenant is not liable for permitting buildings on the land to fall into a state of dilapidation.

In the United States, life tenants and lessees, being under some duty to repair, are to that extent liable for permissive waste: see 5 *American Law of Property*, s. 20.12, stating that the matter is a factual one under the broad principle that the property must be preserved in a reasonable state of repair. See also pp. 243-244, *supra*.]

[Damage to premises resulting from negligence is voluntary or commissive waste: see *Kokatt* v. *Melidonis*, [1920] 3 W.W.R. 800, 55 D.L.R. 155, 13 Sask. L.R. 470 (C.A.) (premises damaged by fire resulting from negligence of tenant at will in filling a gasoline tank); *MacLean* v. *Valdemar*, [1953] 2 D.L.R. 702, [1953] O.W.N. 473, aff'd [1954] 1 D.L.R. 720, [1954] O.W.N. 116 (C.A.) (tenant from year to year liable for voluntary waste where premises destroyed by fire because of negligence).

On the other hand, accidental damage involves no liability (in the absence of express covenant) if a tenant is not liable for permissive waste: see *Wolfe* v. *McGuire* (1896), 28 O.R. 45 (Div. Ct.).

Accidental fires legislation has moreover, removed liability for waste where premises are destroyed by accidental fire: see *United Motors Service* v. *Hutson*, [1937] S.C.R. 294, [1937] 1 D.L.R. 737.

At common law, liability for waste rested on a tenant in possession, whether for life or otherwise, for damage caused by strangers (other than by Act of God or of the King's enemies). The explanation for this result lay in the fact that originally no action could be brought by a reversioner or remainderman directly against the trespasser because the former did not have possession. The tenant, however, could maintain trespass and, having relief over, he was made answerable in the first place. With the development of the action on the case, the basis for the tenant's liability disappeared: see 1 *American Law of Property*, s. 2.16c; 1 *Restatement of Property*, s. 146; 2 *Restatement of Property*, s. 191.]

MORRIS v. CAIRNCROSS. Ontario Divisional Court. 1907. 14 O.L.R. 544

Appeal from a judgment of Boyd C. dismissing an action to nullify a 21 year lease executed in 1895 in favour of defendant by a tenant for life who died in 1905. The lease was defended under the Settled Estates Act, 1895 (Ont.), c. 95, but plaintiffs (who were entitled to the fee simple in possession on the termination of the life estate) contended, *inter alia*, that the lease was in violation of that statute which stipulated that it must not be without impeachment of waste.

The judgment of the Court was delivered by MEREDITH C.J.C.P.: . . . The other ground of objection on this branch of the case—that the demise is without impeachment of waste—is based upon the proposition that the covenants to repair and to repair according to notice are qualified by the exceptions in the covenant to leave the premises in good repair, namely, "reasonable wear and tear and damage by fire or tempest," and that, being so qualified, the effect of them is that the lessee is freed from liability for waste, for which, as was contended, both voluntary and permissive, a tenant for years is answerable.

The lease is made in pursuance of the Act respecting Short Forms of Leases, which was then ch. 106 of the Revised Statutes of Ontario, 1887. It contains on the part of the lessee covenants to repair and to repair according to notice, according to statutory short forms 3 and 6, and a covenant on his part to leave the premises in good repair, according to the statutory short form 8, with the words added to the last of these covenants, "reasonable wear and tear and damage by fire and tempest only excepted," and the effect of this departure from the statutory form is to bring within the exception "damage by tempest," in addition to the two subjects of exception which are named in the long form 8.

The Chancellor was of opinion that the covenants to repair and to repair after notice were not qualified by the exceptions included in and engrafted on the statutory covenant to leave the premises in good repair. He distinguished *Davies* v. *Davies*, 38 Ch. D. 499, in which Kekewich, J., held that the exception in a covenant in these words: "at all times during the said term keep the said premises in good and substantial repair and the same in good and substantial repair deliver up to the lessor at the expiration or sooner determination of the said term, fair wear and tear and damage by tempest excepted," referred not only to the latter branch of the covenant, but to it as a whole.

Emmett v. *Quinn*, 7 O.A.R. 306, not cited to the Chancellor, is, however, an express decision that statutory covenants 3 and 6 are qualified by the exception contained in statutory covenant 8. . . .

I refer also to the observations of my brother Magee as to the effect of *Emmett* v. *Quinn*, in *Delamatter* v. *Brown Brothers Co.* (1905), 9 O.L.R. 351, at pp. 361-2.

There remain to be considered two questions:

(1) Whether a tenant for years is answerable for permissive waste;

(2) If answerable, whether the terms of the lease are such as to relieve the respondent from any liability which otherwise he would be under for permissive waste.

Had it been possible to do so, I would willingly have followed the course taken by the Chancellor in *Patterson* v. *Central Canada Loan and Savings Co.*, 29 O.R. 134, and have refrained from "delving into the ancient law," as to the liability of a tenant for years for permissive waste. I am not, however, at liberty to do so, because in the case at bar it is necessary for the Court, for the solution of the questions raised, to determine whether such a liability exists, and if it does the nature and extent of it.

I would have been justified in resting my decision as to the existence of the liability upon *Yellowly* v. *Gower*, 11 Exch. 274, had it not been that it was argued that the authority of that case has been shaken, if not destroyed, by subsequent decisions and by the effect of the Judicature Act, and that if I had come to that conclusion it would still be necessary to ascertain what are the nature and extent of the liability of a tenant for years for the state and condition of the demised premises.

Yellowly v. *Gower* was decided in 1855 by the Court of Exchequer, the judgment of the Court being delivered by Baron Parke, and was supposed, as the text writers say, to have "stifled the doubt" that had before existed as to the liability of a tenant for years for permissive waste.

This doubt, as Baron Parke points out, was raised by three cases in the Common Pleas: *Gibson* v. *Wells* (1805), 1 Bos. & P.N.R. 290; *Herne* v. *Bembow* (1813), 4 Taunt. 764; and *Jones* v. *Hill* (1817), 7 Taunt. 392; and as to them he said, at p. 292; "Upon examining these cases, none of which appears to be well reported, the Court seems to have contemplated the case only of a tenant at will in the two first cases, and in the last no such proposition is stated that a tenant for years is not liable for permissive waste."

The opinion of the Court was stated in no uncertain terms (at p. 292): "We conceive that there is no doubt of the liability of tenants for terms of years, for they are clearly put on the same footing as tenants for life, both as to voluntary and permissive waste...."

The remarks of Baron Parke as to the three cases in the Common Pleas were, I think, well founded....

That the case of a tenant at will is not within the statutes is clear. The Statute of Marlbridge, 1267, 52 Hy. III. ch. 23, sec. 3, forbade *fermors (firmarii)* during their terms to make waste without license to do so, and extended only to those who held for life or for a term of years, 2 Inst. 145; and the Statute of Gloucester, 1278, 6 Edw. I. ch. 5, extended the right to the writ of waste so that it would lie "against him that holdeth by law of England or otherwise for term of life or for term of years or a woman in dower."

Other reasons why the writ did not lie against a tenant at will are given in Smith's Landlord and Tenant, 2nd ed., pp. 20, 217, *et seq.*

I have been unable to find any reported case since *Yellowly* v. *Gower* in which the question of the liability of a tenant for years was dealt with, until 1880, when it was thus referred to by Lopes, J., in *Woodhouse* v. *Walker* (1880), 5 Q.B.D. 404, at p. 407: "It is not necessary in this case to enter into the question whether an action on the case for permissive waste can be maintained against a tenant for life or years, upon whom no express duty to repair is imposed by the instrument which creates the estate. The modern authorities, or rather the dicta upon this point, appear to be strangely in conflict with the ancient reading of the statutes. See notes to *Greene* v. *Cole* (1670), 2 Wm. Saunders 644."

Next came the case of *Davies* v. *Davies*, 38 Ch.D. 499, already referred to. There the question arose, as it does in the case at bar, in an action to declare a lease not to be a valid exercise of the leasing power conferred by the Settled Estate Act, and Kekewich, J., held that a tenant for years was impeachable for permissive waste, founding his judgment not only upon his own opinion but also upon the authority of *Yellowly* v. *Gower*....

The learned Chancellor declined to follow *Yellowly* v. *Gower* and *Davies* v. *Davies*. He had already, in *Patterson* v. *The Central Canada Loan and Savings Co.*, *supra*, adopting the view of Kay, J. in *In re Cartwright*, *Avis* v. *Newman*, 41 Ch. D. 532, determined that a tenant for life was not impeachable for permissive waste, and that determination logically required the same holding as to a tenant for years, for tenants for years are by the statutes put on the same footing as tenants for life.

I am, with great respect, of opinion that even if *In re Cartwright* was well decided, we ought to follow *Yellowly* v. *Gower*, followed as it was by Kekewich, J., in *Davies* v. *Davies*, unless the Judicature Act makes it necessary to follow the rule in equity which undoubtedly was not to interpose its aid in the case of permissive waste.

This rule of equity was not based upon any different view as to the legal liability from that entertained by Courts of common law, and I do not find anywhere any clear statement of the reason for its adoption....

The rule probably had its origin in the difficulty which Courts of equity found in enforcing by their process the performance of the tenant's duty, and in the absence of jurisdiction to give relief by mandatory injunction, that jurisdiction being strictly confined to cases where the remedy by damages was inadequate for the purposes of justice, and the restoring of things to their former condition was the only remedy which would meet the requirements of the case: Kerr on Injunctions, 4th ed., p. 31.

Nor did Courts of equity entertain a bill for an account, except where the account was asked as an incident to an injunction. As James, L. J., said, in *Higginbotham* v. *Higgins* (1872), L.R., 7 Ch. 676, at p. 679: "It is clearly established that a bill will not lie for an account of timber felled any more than for any other money demand, except when account is asked as incident to an injunction, and that where the plaintiff has no right to an injunction he has no right to an account, and his remedy is at law alone."

In *Barnes* v. *Dowling*, 44 L.T.N.S. 809, it was, however, held that since the Judicature Act, an action for permissive waste is not maintainable. That case was decided by Lopes, J., who delivered the judgment of the Court, and Stephen, J. The estate of the plaintiff was equitable, and his claim was for permissive waste against the tenant for life. The Court said, at p. 810: "The legal liability of a tenant for life for waste may be doubtful, but authority is strong to shew there is no liability for permissive waste in equity:" and after referring to certain equity cases, the learned Judge proceeded to say: "The weight of authority in equity is therefore clearly against an action for permissive waste, and if there is any variance between the rules of equity and the rules of common law with reference to permissive waste, we are bound to give effect to the former. We think this action is not maintainable for permissive waste."

The ratio decidendi in *Barnes* v. *Dowling* is criticised by the writer of an able article on Permissive Waste, in the Solicitors' Journal of October 5th, 1889, vol. 33, at p. 744. The writer points out that the liability of a tenant for life, who has the legal estate vested in him, "depends upon statute, and is not imposed by a mere rule of the common law," and expresses the opinion that the provision of the Judicature Act upon which the Court proceeded cannot for that reason alter the liability of such a tenant for life, and a similar view is taken by Mr. C. B. Labatt in an article in the Canada Law Journal, vol. 37, at pp. 533-4.

I entirely agree with this view, even if it be that the rule in equity to which I have referred depended upon a different view being taken in Courts of equity of the effect of the statutes from that which was entertained by the common law Courts.

As put by Lord Esher, in *Harrison* v. *The Duke of Rutland*, [1893] 1 Q.B. 142, at p. 149, "The intention of the Judicature Acts, no doubt, was that, where the principles of law and of equity differed, the principles of equity should prevail."

The most that can be said as to the course of Courts of equity in regard to claims for permissive waste is that they did not actively interfere where the estates were legal, but left the claimant to his remedy at law, and that they did not interfere where the estates were equitable, and I see in this course nothing that involves any conflict or variance between the rules of equity and the rules of common law as to the remedy by a legal remainderman for permissive waste by a legal tenant for life or for years.

The Chancellor refers to the incisive criticism of *Davies* v. *Davies* by Mr. Bewes (pp. 216-219), in his Law of Waste, ed. 1894. That criticism is not, however, directed against the holding by Kekewich, J., that a tenant for life is impeachable for permissive waste, but against his decision that the exception to the lessee's covenant to repair, of "fair wear and tear and damage by tempest," rendered the lessee free in respect of these matters from a liability which but for the exception would have rested upon him.

Mr. Bewes says (p. 216): "It is submitted in advance that *Yellowly* v. *Gower* is correct, and that *Davies* v. *Davies* is incorrect," and referring to the former he says (p. 217); "This case seems quite consistent with the cases already mentioned, from which it appears that a tenant is obliged to do such repairs as will prevent the premises from decaying."

If the question were as to the liability of a tenant for life, we would be bound by *Patterson* v. *The Central Canada L. & S. Co.*, to hold that such a tenant is not liable. The effect of that decision and of my conclusion in this case leads to the illogical result, so far as a decision of a Divisional Court can be said to settle the law, that though by the statutes both classes of tenants are put on the same footing as to waste, tenants for years are liable for permissive waste, but tenants for life are not; and were it not for that consideration, I should have refrained from adding anything further on this branch of the case.

Apart from *Barnes* v. *Dowling*, the only English case supporting the view of the Divisional Court in *Patterson* v. *The Central Canada L. & S. Co.*, is *In re Cartwright*, *Avis* v. *Newman*, 41 Ch. D. 532, referred to with approval by North, J., in *In re Freman*, *Dimond* v. *Newburn*, [1898] 1 Ch. 28, 32, and followed by the same Judge in *In re Parry & Hopkin*, [1900] 1 Ch. 160. Mr. Justice Kay, though *Yellowly* v. *Gower* was cited by counsel, does not refer to it in his judgment, unless it be when he speaks of "certain dicta of Baron Parke and the late Lord Justice Lush": *In re Cartwright*, *Avis* v. *Newman*, 41 Ch. D., at p. 536.

I do not understand how the decision of the Court in *Yellowly* v. *Gower* can properly be referred to as a dictum of Baron Parke. Probably the reference is to what is to be implied from Baron Parke's observation that he would have held that a tenant for life was impeachable for permissive waste, just as the Court held a tenant for years to be....

The main ground of Mr. Justice Kay's decision, however, is stated on p. 536: "Since the Statutes of Marlbridge and of Gloucester there must have been hundreds of thousands of tenants for life who have died leaving their estates in a condition of great dilapidation. Not once, so far as legal records go, have damages been recovered against the estate of a tenant for life on that ground. To ask me in that state of the authorities to hold that a tenant for life is liable for permissive waste to a remainderman is to my mind a proposition altogether startling. I should not think of coming to such a decision without direct authority upon the point."

For an able criticism of this judgment, I refer again to the article on Permissive Waste in the Solicitors' Journal, and to Mr. Labatt's article in the Canada Law Journal, vol. 37, p. 535 *et seq.*

Text writers and others have suggested reasons for the absence of adjudged cases since the time of Charles I. In the notes on *In re Cartwright*, in the Law Quarterly Review, vol. 5, at p. 449, it is suggested that this may be explained by the rule "*actio personalis,*" and Mr. Smith, in his Lectures on the Law of Landlord and Tenant, 2nd ed., p. 266, speaking of tenants for years, says that the reason of the "paucity of information is, that in practice a case rarely, if ever, occurs in which it is necessary to inquire what the general law is on the subject; for every lease of any importance contains stipulations upon the subject of repairs, and where those are inserted they supersede the law, as it would stand without them; and of course, therefore, the question of what that law is, in the absence of express stipulations, rarely if ever occurs."

These reasons appear to me to afford a satisfactory explanation of the absence of decided cases as to both tenants for life and tenants for years.

That down to the time of Charles I. cases did occur in which the question arose is beyond question, and there is abundant authority in the earlier cases to support the statement of Lord Coke that the statutes applied to permissive as well as to voluntary waste.

The early cases are referred to and commented upon by Mr. Bewes at pp. 211-216 of his book, and the principle he deduces from them is that "a tenant is not in general responsible for permissive waste where not followed by actual, substantial damage to the premises": p. 213.

It appears to me, however, that the cases establish that as far as liability of tenants for life and for years for waste is concerned, there is no difference between permissive and voluntary waste, and that the questions which have arisen were not as to the existence of the liability but as to what acts or omissions of the tenant constitute waste, and that the result of the cases is that the tenant is not liable for mere wear and tear, but that he is liable for his failure to make such repairs as are necessary to prevent the decay or destruction of the premises as where a small breach is made in the roof of a building by tempest and the tenant permits it to remain unrepaired, and the roof is afterwards blown off or the house blown down for want of repairing the breach: 6 Eliz., Moore, p. 62, case 173; or where the tenant neglects to paint or plaster a chamber of the house, which results in the timbers of the house becoming putrid: *Corbet* v. *Stonehouse*, 9 Car., 2 Rolle Abr. 816-7; or neglects to scour a ditch, which results in the groundsells of the house becoming putrified: *Sticklehorne* v. *Hatchman*, 28 Eliz., Owen, p. 43.

[The learned Justice then reviewed certain English, Irish and American authorities, referred to the civil law of usufruct, and then concluded as follows:]

An independent inquiry into the question, fortified by the result of this examination of the principal cases, in England, Ireland and the United States, and of the opinions of text writers and commentators, leads me to the conclusion that *Yellowly* v. *Gower* was rightly decided, and that its authority has not been impugned or affected by any subsequent case, or displaced by the provisions of the Judicature Act, and I may point out that the Commissioners by whom the Laws of England introduced into this Province by the Constitutional Act of 1792, 32 Geo. III, ch. 1, were revised and consolidated, must have reached the same conclusion as that to which I have come, for as revised the Statute of Marlbridge reads: "Lessees making or suffering waste on the demised premises without license of the lessors shall be liable for the full damage so sustained": R.S.O. 1897, ch. 330, sec. 23; *ibid.* ch. 342, sec. 22.

There remains to be considered the question whether the modifications of the covenants in the lease to which I have referred have the effect of relieving the respondent from any liability which but for them he would have been subject to for permissive waste; and I am of opinion that they do not. That a tenant for years is not liable to make good the results of reasonable wear and tear of the demised premises is clear upon the authorities to which reference already has been made, and the exception in respect of it does not, in my opinion, relieve from liability for decay or destruction of the premises occurring from his failure to make such small repairs as according to the cases it is his duty to make. Nor does the exception of damage by fire or tempest modify the obligation which but for the exception would rest upon him. The exception extends, I think, only to such damage as is the result of accident, and is not due to his negligence. Though, since the Imperial statute, 14 Geo. III, ch. 78, sec. 86, a tenant, in the absence of contractual obligation to the contrary, is not liable for damage done by an accidental fire occurring on his premises, the statute has no application to protect him from legal liability as a consequence of his negligence: *Canada Southern Ry. Co.* v. *Phelps* (1884), 14 S.C.R. 132; and so I think the exception to the covenant must be construed as not exempting the respondent from liability for damage by fire occasioned by his negligence. In the same way, the exception as to damage by tempest, does not, I think, relieve the respondent from liability should a building on the demised premises be destroyed or damaged by tempest, if its destruction or the injury to it be due primarily to his failure to make such reasonable repairs as were necessary to prevent the destruction of it, or the injury to it, happening in the event of a tempest, and for damage resulting from tempest alone a tenant was never apart from contract liable: *Nugent* v. *Cuthbert* (1822), Sugden's Law of Property, p. 475.

The exceptions no doubt modify the contractual obligation which the respondent would have been subject to if his covenants in respect of repairing were unqualified, but that is, of course, a different matter.

If I had reached a different conclusion on this branch of the case the provisions of R.S.O. (1897), ch. 330, sec. 24, would have applied to prevent the lease from being avoided because of the departure by the tenant for life from the provisions of sec. 42 of the Settled Estates Act.

This enactment provides that in the cases to which it applies the lease if made *bonâ fide* and the lessee have entered under it "shall be considered in equity as a contract for a grant at the request of the lessee his heirs, executors, administrators or assigns (as the case may require) of a valid lease under such power to the like purport and effect as such invalid lease as aforesaid, save so far as any variation may be necessary in order to comply with the terms of such power, and all persons who would have been bound by a lease lawfully granted under such power shall be bound in equity by such contract."

The result is that in my opinion the appeal fails and should be dismissed with costs.

Appeal dismissed.

[Omission of a tenant for a term certain to clean out flues, resulting in damage to a furnace was held to be actionable permissive waste in *Roberts* v. *McMannis*, [1933] 1 W.W.R. 193, aff'd [1933] 3 W.W.R. 248 (Sask. C.A.).

Kirchwey, Liability for Waste, (1908) 8 Col. L. Rev. 624, states the position on permissive waste in accord with *Morris* v. *Cairncross*. The author's comment on *Davies* v. *Davies* is that while it went beyond the old law in holding a tenant for years liable for ordinary wear and tear, this did not impair its value as an assertion of the general liability of such a tenant for permissive waste even where no active negligence is imputed to him.]

[Is there compatibility on the effect of the exception of reasonable wear and tear as expounded in *Morris* v. *Cairncross*, *supra*, in *Brown* v. *Davies*, *supra*, at p. 246, and in *Manchester* v. *Dixie Cup Company (Canada) Ltd.*, *supra*, at p. 250? Should it be said that liability for permissive waste is, to all intents and purposes, gone and that it is now a matter of negligence and, on this basis, it is better to talk of voluntary waste? See *Warren* v. *Keen*, *supra*, at p. 241.]

[In *Monro* v. *Toronto Railway Co.* (1904), 9 O.L.R. 299, Teetzel J. followed *Davies* v. *Davies* in holding that a lease by a tenant for life exempting the lessee from liability for "fair wear and tear and damage by tempest" was void under the Settled Estates Act which forbade such leases if made without impeachment of waste. On appeal, see 9 O.L.R. at p. 308, the validity of the lease was not pressed by defendants but the trial judgment was varied on other grounds. *Quaere*, whether this judgment is or ever was a supportable one. How can it be said that an exception of reasonable wear and tear makes a tenant dispunishable for waste if the exception does not cover voluntary waste, whether the result of deliberate acts or of negligence?]

RE ROBERTSON. Ontario High Court. [1951] O.R. 309, [1951] 3 D.L.R. 241

Appeal from an order of the Surrogate Court on a passing of accounts. A testator who owned a newspaper directed his executors and trustees to carry on the business. In their administration, they set aside annually certain sums out of the gross proceeds to cover depreciation on buildings, plant and equipment, and this reduced the aggregate annual income payable to certain life tenants. The business was subsequently sold, and an issue arose whether the total sum set aside for depreciation should be paid to the income beneficiaries or to those entitled to the capital. The Surrogate Judge held that the income beneficiaries were entitled to the money but that, as to the larger part of it, they were not entitled (for reasons not material here) to question the sums charged for depreciation. The trustees of the estate and the remaindermen appealed. The judgment on the appeal is reproduced in part only.

GALE J.: ... If one accepts, as I do, the theory that depreciation is the loss sustained by a capital asset during its serviceable existence due to wear and tear, decay, inadequacy and obsolescence and that provision is ordinarily made for such loss in business practice by the adoption of one of several methods of allocation, then the questions to be decided here are whether the executors and trustees of this estate were right in taking depreciation into consideration when computing the amount of income earned by the estate each year, and if so, whether the amounts set aside by them were fair and reasonable. I am satisfied that both of those questions are to be answered in the affirmative.

In the first place let me say that there does not appear to be any good reason for suggesting that executors who are directed to carry on the business of a deceased may not allocate proper amounts for depreciation in computing the annual income from the business. In his lifetime the wise testator does so and I believe his policy should be followed by his executors. Ample authority for that view is to be found in the judgments in *Re Crabtree*, *Thomas* v. *Crabtree* (1912), 106 L.T. 49, and *Re Rose*, [1940] 1 D.L.R. 139, 14 M.P.R. 223. In the former there was a direction to the trustees to continue the testator's business and to pay "the profits arising from my business" to his widow during her life. In pursuance of their duties the trustees deducted from profits not only the cost of repairs to the machinery but also an annual sum for depreciation at the rate of 7 1/2% on its original value. It was held by Swinfen Eady J. and by the Court of Appeal that they had taken the proper course. Two of the Judges in Appeal expressly approved of certain language used by the Judge of first instance, and I believe it is well worth quoting here, though all the judgments are most pertinent. The passage to which I refer is as follows (p. 50):

"But in the ordinary course of ascertaining the profits of a business where there is power machinery and trade machinery which is necessary in order to perform the work of the business, it is, in my opinion, essential that, in addition to all sums actually expended in repairing the machinery, or in renewing parts, that there should be also written off a proper sum for depreciation, and that sum ought to be written off before you can arrive at the net profits of the business, or at the profits of the business; and it is not profit until a proper sum, varying with the class of machinery, with the nature of the business and with the life of the machinery, has been written off for depreciation."

Re Rose is a decision of Harrison J. of the Supreme Court of New Brunswick. After the business formerly conducted by the deceased was sold on account of a loss it was held that the depreciation of the building and of the equipment used in the business was chargeable against the income from the business and not against capital. At p. 144 the learned Judge says:

"In my opinion the business should be charged with depreciation on this building as a current expenditure payable out of income, because there is a consumption of capital to that extent which ought not to enter into profits.

"For the same reasons I consider that depreciation on 'the furniture and fixtures and delivery equipment' used in the business is a proper charge against the income of such business."

Those judgments express with clarity the opinion which I formed at an early stage in this matter, not only that the executors and trustees of this estate were permitted to charge depreciation to income but that it was incumbent upon them to do so in order to determine the net profits distributable under the will....

It was said that although *Re Crabtree*, *supra*, did fortify the conclusion that depreciation in respect of machinery could be debited against gross revenue, with the exception of the judgment in *Re Rose*, *supra*, the Courts have steadfastly turned against the idea of charging the income with depreciation upon buildings unless there is express permission to that effect in the will and since there is none here, the life tenants ought not to be burdened with that portion of the charge. Mr. Mason mentioned certain American authorities including 31 C.J.S. p. 65; Scott on Trusts, 1939, vol. II, p. 1342; *Laflin* v. *Com'r of Internal Revenue* (1934), 69 Fed. (2d) 460; *Dixon* v. *Com'r of Internal Revenue* (1934), 69 Fed. (2d) 461; and *Re Matthews' Estate* (1932), 245 N.W. 122, all of which refer to "the Pennsylvania rule" that extraordinary dividends or proceeds upon a sale are apportionable, and to the extent to which they represent earnings accruing during the period of the trust they are allocatable to income, and so far as they do not they are assigned to principal. It should be mentioned at once, however, that what is known as "the Massachusetts rule" prescribes that extraordinary dividends are wholly principal; *cf. Scott, op. cit.*, pp. 1259, 1316, 1342-4. Thus it will be seen that there is no unanimity of opinion on the point south of our border.

In an argument somewhat paralleling that which I have just discussed, Mr. Denison contended that the life tenants, not being liable for permissive waste, were not chargeable for any depreciation in respect of the buildings. The cases of *Re Hotchkys* (1886), 32 Ch. D. 408; *Re Cartwright* (1889), 41 Ch. D. 532; *Patterson* v. *Central Can, Loan & Savings Co.* (1898), 29 O.R. 134; *Monro* v. *Tor. R. Co.* (1904), 9 O.L.R. 299, and *Currie* v. *Currie* (1910), 20 O.L.R. 375, all substantiate the proposition that unless there is an express duty to repair, a legal tenant for life of land is not liable for permissive waste. Mr. Denison submits that while the executors and trustees of this estate were required to repair generally, they had no right to throw the load of those repairs upon the life tenants.

This will prevents the application of either of those two rules. Clause 15 contains unequivocal instructions to the executors and trustees to carry on the newspaper business, and I cannot avoid the conclusion that implicit in that direction was authority to charge repairs and depreciation in the same way and to the same extent as in any other commercial enterprise. While depreciation upon buildings may not be allocated against income in certain American States, and while the burden of permissive waste is not ordinarily cast upon a tenant for life, it is my view that such is not the case in any instance where the testator has directed his executors to carry on his business and depreciation and repairs are rightly incurred in the conduct of that business. The decision in the *Rose* case, *supra*, is authority for that statement....

Appeal allowed.

[The learned Judge's discussion of whether the sums allocated to depreciation were proper is omitted. His judgment was affirmed on appeal (by a majority), [1952] O.R. 283, [1952] 2 D.L.R. 594, and this judgment was in turn affirmed by the Supreme Court of Canada, *sub nom. Chartered Trust Co.* v. *Trustees of the Estate of John Ross Robertson*, [1953] 2 S.C.R. 1, [1953] 4 D.L.R. 225.]

TURNER v. WRIGHT. Chancery. 1860. 2 De G. F. & J. 234, 45 E.R. 612

LORD CAMPBELL L. C.: In this case the plaintiff, by his bill, prayed an injunction "to restrain the cutting of any timber, or at any rate of any ornamental timber," growing upon the lands devised in fee to the defendant, subject to an executory devise over to the plaintiff.

The decree of the Vive-Chancellor declared, "that the defendant is entitled to fell all such timber on the devised estates as is mature and fit to be cut, except as has been planted or left standing by way of ornament or shelter with reference to the occupation of the mansion-house on the said devised estates; but that he is not entitled to fell any unripe timber or any timber planted or left standing for ornament or shelter aforesaid."

The result of the decision is, that the defendant is dispunishable of legal, but not of equitable, waste. After great consideration, I agree with the Vice-Chancellor on both questions....

Decree affirmed.

[The principle of *Turner* v. *Wright* was followed in *In re Hanbury's Settled Estates*, [1913] 2 Ch. 357.]

NEW WESTMINSTER v. KENNEDY. British Columbia, New Westminster County Court. [1918] 1 W.W.R. 489

Plaintiff municipality became the purchaser at a tax sale of certain land which had belonged to defendants. Just before the redemption year expired, defendants stripped the house on the land of its doors, windows, bathtub, toilet, boilers and other fixtures. Plaintiff sued to restrain defendants and also asked for a mandatory order for return of what was taken.

HOWAY CO. CT. J. (after holding that the tax sale purchaser obtained a real interest in the land, "an inchoate right in, or title to, the property which may ripen into a complete title"): ... Two persons being thus interested in the title will not equity interfere to prevent him who happens to be in possession from so acting as to injure the other, that is, apply to them the principles of equitable waste, as it is called?

The law of waste originating in the common law extended by the *Statutes of Marlbridge and Gloucester* was very inelastic and strictly limited to certain classes of estates and interests in land. Only where the land was held by a tenant (in dower, by the curtesy, for years, for life, etc) could the remainderman by this proceeding recover for permanent depreciation to the estate committed by the tenant in possession; in all other cases of conflicting interests the wrong was without remedy.

Here was a principle which particularly appealed to equity, which it soon adopted, and which under its fostering care continued to grow. Under the name of "equitable waste" it reached many cases within the mischief though not within the legal remedy. It was sometimes said to be merely such conduct as a prudent man would not follow in the management of his own property. Sometimes it was said to be the unconscientious exercise of a legal right to the prejudice of others, and there the expression "unconscientious" meant contrary to the dictates of prudence and reason even though it might be clear that the person from his peculiar frame of mind or from some other cause was not acting with any malicious motive.

The term "equitable waste" is not felicitous when applied to a person who is at law the absolute owner but is only subject to the equitable rules of the Court. See *Millett* v. *Davey*, 31 Beav. 470, at p. 475; 32 L.J. Ch. 122. This principle that one in possession will be restrained from using his legal power unfairly—unconscientiously—so as to destroy or depreciate the subject-matter (Jessel, M.R., *Baker* v. *Sebright*, 13 Ch. D. 179, at p. 185; 49 L.J. Ch. 65) has been applied to tenants in tail after possibility of issue extinct; *Williams* v. *Williams*, 15 Ves. 427, at p. 428; tenants in common and joint tenants, *Hole* v. *Thomas*, 7 Ves. 589; 6 R.R. 195; *Clegg* v. *Clegg*, 8 Giff. 322, at p. 336; 31 L.J. Ch. 153; mortgagor and mortgagee, *King* v. *Smith*, 2 Hare 239; *Millett* v. *Davey*, *supra*; tenant in fee subject to an executory devise over, *Turner* v. *Wright*, 2 DeG. F. & J. 234; 29 L.J. Ch. 598; rector or vicar as regards the rectory or glebe lands, *Marlborough (Duke)* v. *St. John*, 5 Deg. & Sm. 174; 21 L.J. Ch. 381; partners, *Marshall* v. *Watson*, 25 Beav. 501; against a purchaser who "is in equity by the effect of the contract the owner of this estate," having taken possession under the contract, at the suit of the vendor who is in the "situation of an equitable mortgagee," *Crockford* v. *Alexander*, 15 Ves. 138; 10 R.R. 44.

In the *Raby Castle case*, (*Vane* v. *Barnard [Lord]*) 2 Vern. 738; Pre. Ch. 454; Gilb. Eq. Rep. 127; 1 Salk. 161, Lord Barnard had on his son's marriage settled the castle on himself for life without impeachment of waste, remainder to his son for life and then to his first and other sons. Having taken some displeasure against his son Lord Barnard got 200 workmen together, and of a sudden, in a few days stripped the castle of the lead, iron, glass-doors, boards, etc. Upon the son's application an injunction was issued to restrain further waste and to compel the defendant to repair the castle.

The words of Lord Campbell in *Turner* v. *Wright*, *supra*, at p. 243 (2 DeG. F. & J.)—a case similar in principle to the present—are apt....

I pause to add that a tenant in fee with executory devise over is the nearest possible approach to a tenant in fee, because executory devises are so repugnant to the essentials of such a tenancy that they are only creatable by will.

Should this principle be applied here? In my judgment it should. It is true that the interest of the plaintiff here arises not by act of parties, or by settlement, but has been created by statute, I cannot, however, bring myself to believe that such adventitious circumstance affords any real ground for differentiation.

The plaintiff has asked for an order restraining the defendants from removing or disposing of the fixtures taken from the building and also for an order for their return. I hold, following the *Raby Castle case*, *supra*, that the plaintiff is entitled to [a mandatory] order....

Judgment for plaintiff.

DOHERTY v. ALLMAN. House of Lords. 1878. 3 App. Cas. 709

Respondent was tenant under two leases, one granted in 1798 for 999 years and the other in 1824 for 988 years, and the reversion in each case was in appellant. Each lease contained a covenant by the lessee to uphold, support, maintain and keep the premises, and all improvements thereon in good and sufficient order, repair and condition. There was no power of re-entry reserved in either lease for breach of covenant save in the case of default of rent and insufficient distress to satisfy the arrears. Nor did either lease contain any express negative covenant against change in the use of the premises. The buildings on the premises at the time the leases were made consisted of stores for corn. Later, they were used for other purposes but they became dilapidated over the years. At the same time the demand for such buildings dried up, and respondent proposed to remodel them and convert them into dwelling houses. Appellant objected on the ground that this was enjoinable waste. The case came before the Vice-Chancellor of Ireland who held that he was bound to treat the proposed alterations as waste, impairing evidence of title, and he granted an injunction. On appeal, 10 Ir. Eq. 362, the injunction was dissolved, without prejudice to appellant's right to proceed at law.

On appeal to the House of Lords appellant claimed relief on the grounds of waste and of contract. On the latter point, the Law Lords concluded that the case did not call for the exercise of equity jurisdiction to enjoin breach of a negative covenant or one negative in substance.

LORD O'HAGAN: ... Now we have, I think, established for the purposes of this decision the principles in this case by which we ought to abide. In the case of *Mollineux* v. *Powell*, 3 P. Wms. 268, n., which contains perhaps the clearest dictum we have upon the matter, two conditions as to the exercise of jurisdiction in cases of waste have been very clearly pointed out, and one at least of those conditions is expressly recognised afterwards in the Irish case of *Coppinger* v. *Gubbins* 3 J. & Lat. 411. Those conditions are that the waste with which a Court of Equity, or your Lordships acting as a Court of Equity, ought to interfere, should be not ameliorating waste, nor trivial waste. It must be waste of an injurious character—it must be waste of not only an injurious character, but of a substantially injurious character, and if either the waste be really ameliorating waste—that is a proceeding which results in benefit and not in injury—the Court of Equity, and your Lordships acting as a Court of Equity, ought not to interfere to prevent it. I think that is perfectly well established. On the other hand, if the waste be so small as to be indifferent to the one party or the other—if it be, as has been said by a great authority in our law, such a thing as twelvepence worth of waste, a Court of Equity, and your Lordships acting as a Court of Equity, ought not to interfere on account of the triviality of the matter. Now, in my view of the case, those principles decide the question so far as this portion of it is concerned; for it appears to me that we have here established to the full satisfaction of your Lordships, by a series of authorities to which I shall not refer, that the waste, to be of any sort of effect with a view to an injunction, must be a waste resulting in substantial damage. Your Lordships are the Judges not only of the propriety of exercising your discretion, but of the facts by which the exercise of that discretion ought to be regulated. Now, with reference in the first place to the materiality of the waste, we have in the analogy of proceedings in the Courts of Law a very important guide for the exercise of our equitable jurisdiction. It is established not only in the case of *The Governors of the Harrow School* v. *Alderton* 2 B. & P. 86, before Lord Eldon, but in every case, that if there be a trial at law, and if the result of such trial is that the jury is compelled to give nominal damages, such as three farthings in that case, the verdict will be entered, not for the man who obtained the nominal damages, but for the Defendant in the case. It is rather an extraordinary jurisdiction, no doubt—it is an equitable jurisdiction exercised by a Court of Law—but it seems to be quite established and quite recognised, and being so I think it is impossible to say that when we come to exercise our jurisdiction, which is a discretionary jurisdiction, we should act upon any other principle, or to say that if we see that the damage has not really been substantial and important, we should do that in a Court of Equity according to our discretion, which even in the strictness of a Court of Common Law is not done because of the reason given.

I think that the judgment in the Court below in the first instance went very much upon the view that the waste here had the effect of destroying the evidence of title. A great deal was said also at the Bar upon that subject, and a great deal certainly was said by the learned Judge who pronounced the original judgment in this case. Now I cannot myself see that there is anything at all in that. I do not think that in the particular circumstances of this case there is any interference with the evidence of title. You may do what you please with this particular building (according to the plans and views of the parties connected with it), and yet not destroy any evidence of title at all. The building is to be modified—is to be improved—but it is to remain where it was, it is to be of the same proportions, it is to have the same position, it is to have the same surroundings; and I cannot see how what is proposed to be done would injure or affect the Appellant's evidence of title. Independently of that, I think we must take this into account, that owing to the circumstances in which property is now situated in this country, in Scotland, and in Ireland, evidence of title of this kind is not at all of the same importance as it was in other times and other circumstances. When you have an Ordinance Survey, when you have a Registry of Deeds, when you have a system of conveyancing, the value as evidence of title, of a place of this sort retaining its particular position, is very sensibly diminished. At all events, I see no reason upon that ground to hold that there has been any diminution of the evidence of title of which the lessor of these premises can properly complain.

We have heard much comment, on the one side and the other, with reference to the length of the term in this case. I do not rely upon that as the only circumstance in the case on which the judgment of the Court of Appeal should be sustained; but when, in a case of this sort, we are asked to exercise our discretionary jurisdiction, it surely is material to see that the interest of the individual who is only to come into possession of the premises at the end of 900 years is infinitesimally small compared with the interest of the man who is the tenant, and who, with his successors, is to hold the premises all that time, upon whom the effect of our exercise of this jurisdiction would be to tie up his hands, to destroy their property, and to inflict great damage upon them during the course of these many centuries that are yet to come. I think, that being so, we have only to say this in addition, that it is scarcely a matter of possible controversy here whether or not this change is a beneficial change. We have most conclusive evidence that the change will be beneficial. We have the most clear evidence that, as the matter stands, this old dilapidated store has become useless, I presume, to any human being. Circumstances have changed; the necessity for a store of that kind has ceased, and the result has been that the store, if it be allowed to continue in its present condition—because the parties are compelled to leave it in its prevent condition—till the end of this term of 999 years, the whole premises will be utterly valueless; whereas, upon the other side, if you substitute for this store the houses which are contemplated you double, you treble the security of the landlord, and give him, or whoever may live at the end of the term of 999 years, certainly not an injured property but an improved one. Therefore, inasmuch as the waste, if waste there be, is ameliorating waste, and the injury to the property produced by the waste is not merely trivial but absolutely non-existent, it appears to me that upon that ground the judgment of the Court below may very fairly be maintained.

Appeal dismissed.

[The concurring judgments of Lord Cairns L.C. and Lord Blackburn are omitted.]

SMYTH v. CARTER. Rolls Court. 1853. 18 Beav. 78, 52 E.R. 31

Motion by defendant to dissolve an interlocutory injunction restraining him from pulling down a house (which was allegedly in poor condition) and erecting a brewery in its place.

SIR JOHN ROMILLY M. R.: Assuming the plaintiffs to be landlords, and the defendant tenant, I entertain no doubt that this court will restrain a tenant from pulling down a house and building any other which the landlord dislikes. It is not sufficient to show that the house proposed to be built is a better one; and the fact of the defendant's showing that the landlord does not know his own interest will not affect the judgment of the court in any respect whatever. The landlord has a right to exercise his own judgment and caprice, whether there shall be any change; and if he objects, the court will not allow a tenant to pull down one house and build another in its place.

Motion dismissed.

[Lord O'Hagan in *Doherty* v. *Allman*, *supra*, commented on this case as follows: "... Now there was one case, I think it is the only case, referred to by the very able and learned Judge who had this matter first before him, the case before Lord Romilly to which reference has been made from time to time, *Smyth* v. *Carter*, which would be very strong authority if we are to take it as expressing, in the words that are used, the full opinion of that learned Lord, and an opinion reached with reference to facts which have analogy to the facts before your Lordships. But in the first place, that was a mere *obiter dictum* of Lord Romilly. It was in an interlocutory proceeding. It was without any sort of argument; and the case has, I think, no application to the case before your Lordships, and for this important reason, that in that case the observations may have been applied to the limited interest of a tenant from year to year, whereas we have to deal here with the interest of a tenant for 900 years. The circumstances are wholly different, the conditions are wholly unlike, and, therefore, the authority does not, in my opinion apply at all to the case before us."]

[In 5 *American Law of Property*, s. 20.11, footnote 4, it is said that "the more desirable way to describe the doctrine of meliorative waste... seems to be something like this: any alteration of the premises which is injurious to the inheritance is waste, even though it increases the value of the land. There is nothing contradictory in such a statement since 'inheritance' and 'land' do not mean the same thing. The difficulty in many cases is that the words 'which is injurious to the inheritance' have been omitted from the court's working definition."]

RENÉ v. CARLING EXPORT BREWING AND MALTING COMPANY LIMITED.
Ontario Appellate Division. 63 O.L.R. 582, [1929] 2 D.L.R. 881

Appeal by defendant from a judgment for plaintiffs in an action to annul a lease and for a mandatory order to yield up the demised premises in good order. The trial Judge refused to declare the lease forfeited because of waste but he gave damages and an injunction.

The judgment of the Court was delivered by HODGINS J. A.: ... It was argued, however, that waste was shewn and was a ground for forfeiture. Waste, however, is a tort (*Defries* v. *Milne*, [1913] 1 Ch. 98), and not a ground for forfeiture unless there is an express covenant against it. Damages or an injunction may be given in proper cases restraining the further commission of the tort. In a case for injunction it must be of "a substantially injurious character." per Lord O'Hagan in *Doherty* v. *Allman* (1878), 3 App. Cas. 709, at p. 724. But what was done here could not be waste if judged by the rules mentioned and discussed by Buckley, J. (afterwards Lord Wrenbury), in *West Ham Central Charity Board* v. *East London Waterworks Co.*, [1900] 1 Ch. 624. In that case Buckley J., says (p. 636):—

"If the permanent character of the property demised is not substantially altered, as for instance, by the conversion of pasture land into plough land, by breaking up ancient meadows, or the like, I conceive that the law is that it is not now waste for the tenant to do things which within the covenants and conditions of his lease he is not precluded from doing. Within those covenants and conditions he may use his holding as he pleases."

In the lease in this case there are no restrictive covenants dealing with waste, repair, etc., and there is in law no implied covenant against waste: Foa on Landlord and Tenant, 5th ed., p. 280.

There are expressions in many cases shewing how closely waste is distinguished from the intended or proper use of the demised premises. In *Saner* v. *Bilton* (1878), 7 Ch. D. 815, Fry, J., said (p. 821): "I should be prepared to hold that no user of a tenement which is reasonable and proper, having regard to the class to which it belongs, is waste." In *Manchester Bonded Warehouse Co.* v. *Carr* (1880), 5 C.P.D. 507, the Court said: "In the absence of an express agreement to that effect, a tenant is not liable for the destruction of the property let to him if such destruction is in fact due to nothing more than a reasonable use of the property, and any use of it is in our opinion reasonable provided it is for a purpose for which the property was intended to be used, and provided the mode and extent of the user was apparently proper, having regard to the nature of the property and to what the tenant knew of it and to what as an ordinary business man he ought to have known of it."

And there is here no negative covenant, the importance of which is pointed out in *Doherty* v. *Allman (ante)*.

In a later case on the subject, *Rose* v. *Spicer*, [1911] 2 K.B. 234, 254, Buckley, L. J., whose dissenting judgment was adopted by the House of Lords, *Hyman* v. *Rose*, [1912] A.C. 623, said: "The thing demised is premises which the lessee may consistently with the lease use for many purposes for which they are without alteration and adaptation not suitable. A right reasonably to alter and adapt is to be implied."

What was done here was merely the shifting of land not covered by water to adjoining land, leaving the water to flow over the space thus cleared, and occupying, with the earth so taken out, a space adjoining the new bank.

The making of slips is evidently contemplated by the lease, and the mode in which the slip has been enlarged seems unobjectionable, as the earth is there to be filled back again, which can readily be done if desired, and it cannot be said that there is any substantial alteration in the permanent character of the property demised.

For these reasons, I think a case of waste has not been made out in any way, either in the enlargement of the slip or in anything else that is complained of. There is no loss to the inheritance as such, and nothing in the evidence brings it within measurable distance of any of the considerations which were given effect to in the *West Ham* case....

The position of the plaintiffs remains to be considered. The Ohio Realty Ltd., which is shewn to be the beneficial owner of the property under an agreement with the assignees of the Renés, dated the 14th July, 1927, would not be entitled to any of the damages which might arise had waste been proved prior to the 14th July, 1927. The right to recover for a tort such as waste is not assignable: *Defries* v. *Milne (ante)*. The Renés themselves, for the reasons I have given, are not entitled under the facts of the case to any such damages.

Appeal allowed.

[In *Toronto Harbour Commissioners* v. *Royal Canadian Yacht Club* (1913), 29 O.L.R. 391, 15 D.L.R. 106, the Yacht Club was lessee at a nominal rent of certain land under a lease by which it covenanted to use the land only for mooring purposes, and for reasonable access to its club house by the construction of wharves (with consent of the proper governmental authority), and save as might be necessary for such construction no filling would be done so as to interfere with navigation. The club proposed to dredge sand from that portion of the demised premises which was covered by water, relying on *Lewis* v. *Godson* (1888), 15 O.R. 252 where it was held that a tenant, in order to clear land for cultivation, could lawfully collect and remove stones from the land in the same way as he could cut down timber to prepare the land for cultivation. Moreover, *Lewis* v. *Godson* held (and in this respect in effect overruled *Saunders* v. *Breakie* (1884), 5 O.R. 603) that the tenant was entitled to the proceeds of sale of the stones (or timber, as the case might be). In enjoining the yacht club, Middleton J. distinguished *Lewis* v. *Godson*, stating that "the case does not determine that a tenant has the right to take and remove the body of the soil itself, which is what is being done here". Removal of stones and timber by a tenant holding a lease for agricultural purposes could not be regarded as waste because such removal was contemplated by the lease, and the reversion was not injured but rather improved. He then continued as follows:

"That which is suggested as the test, namely, is there injury to the reversion or not? has long been recognised as the touchstone. The old cases are collected in *Doe dem. Grubb* v. *Burlington* (1833), 5 B. & Ad. 507, which adopts the statement of Richardson C. J.: 'The law will not allow that to be waste which is not any ways prejudicial to the inheritance.'

"In furtherance of this idea, it has always been held that a tenant has no right 'to take the substance of the estate by opening mines or clay pits;' an exception being recognised where the property leased is being already operated as a mine or clay pit; for there the presumption is, that the tenant is intended to continue to work the mine or pit, leased to him, as the landlord had done before. See cases collected in *Dashwood* v. *Magniac*, [1891] 3 Ch. 306.

"Perhaps the most complete statement of the law is found in the judgment of Buckley, J., in *West Ham Central Charity Board* v. *East London Waterworks Co.*, [1900] 1 Ch. 624; where he states the test of injury to the reversion in practically the same words as in the later judgment which has the approval of the Lords [i.e., *Hyman* v. *Rose*, [1912] A.C. 623].

"In the case at bar it is established, I think beyond peradventure, that what is proposed by the tenant will, in the circumstances which exist, be a most substantial injury to the reversion. Further, if it be material to the case, I do not think that the lease in any way contemplated any excavation. It contemplated a user of the water lots as they were at the time of the demise. If these were unsuitable for the purposes of the Club, that was the Club's misfortune. No right was given to take away the sand—something far more analogous to the opening of a new mine than to the prudent conduct of husbandry, and in no sense permissible under such a lease as that in question."]

[In *In re Hall, Hall* v. *Hall*, [1916] 2 Ch. 488, Peterson J. said (at p. 492):

"Apart from any statutory provisions a tenant for life who is expressed to be unimpeachable for waste can open and work mines and receive all the profits arising therefrom. If he is impeachable for waste he cannot open mines; but if the mines in question have been opened before the settlement (*Dashwood* v. *Magniac; In re Ridge*, 31 Ch. D. 504, 508), or have been opened by a person interested under the settlement and entitled to open mines, e.g., a tenant in tail (*Clavering* v. *Clavering*, 2 P. Wms. 388), a tenant for life can continue to work the mines and receive all the profits derived therefrom.

"So, too, where the owner of an estate has contracted to lease mines and dies before the grant of the lease or the opening of the mines, the tenant for life under his will is entitled to receive the rents and royalties payable under the lease: *In re Kemeys-Tynte*, [1892] 2 Ch. 211."]

[*The West Ham case*, [1900] 1 Ch. 624, referred to with approval in the Ontario cases, *supra*, is criticized, in its application of principle, in *Note*, (1900) 14 Harv. L. Rev. 226.

Ameliorating waste is discussed by *Bathurst*, The Strict Common Law Rules of Waste and their Apparent Modification, (1949) 13 Conv. & P.L. (N.S.) 278; and *Yardley*, Ameliorating Waste in England and the United States, (1956) 19 Mod. L. Rev. 150.]

BAKER v. SEBRIGHT. Chancery. 1879. 13 Ch. D. 179

JESSEL M. R.: ... An equitable tenant for life unimpeachable for waste cut ornamental timber, and he alleged that he cut it, not only properly, but beneficially for the ornamental timber which remained; and accordingly an inquiry was directed in this form:—[His Lordship read it, and continued:] I need not trouble myself about the last part of the inquiry, because the first part of it has been answered in favour of the tenant for life; that is, in effect, that the trees which he did cut injured or impeded the growth of other trees which were of essential importance for ornament or shelter: in other words, he did that which the Court directed to be done in the cases of *Lushington* v. *Boldero* 6 Madd. 149 and *Ford* v. *Tynte* 2 D.J. & S. 127, 129. It seems that the trees cut were of considerable value, and of a value very much in excess of the cost of cutting; that is admitted; and consequently there was a considerable sum arising from the proceeds of the sale of the timber cut which went into the pocket of the tenant for life.

The question I have now to decide on further consideration is, whether the equitable tenant for life unimpeachable for waste is entitled to retain the proceeds of the timber so cut for his own use. If he is not, a second question arises which otherwise it is not necessary to discuss.

The point... does not appear to have been directly decided; but, from the cases,... it seems to have been indirectly decided or assumed in favour of the tenant for life; and in deciding it, apparently for the first time, I have no hesitation in saying that, looking at the principles which have been laid down by the Court of Chancery as, so to say, the ground of its interference with the tenant for life in respect of what is commonly called "ornamental timber," that is, timber planted for ornament or shelter, it is impossible to hold that this tenant for life ought to be interfered with at all; that is to say, his rights, such as they would have been had the timber not been ornamental, remain unaffected by what has occurred.

The way to look at the matter is this: Courts of Equity restrained a legal tenant for life unimpeachable for waste from committing some kinds of waste which are called equitable waste. Why? Because it was considered that, though he had legal powers, he was not using them fairly—he was abusing them so as to destroy the subject of the settlement. That was the only ground, as it was said. Sometimes he was making an unconscientious use of his powers; and in fact the first case on the subject, the case of Lord Barnard 2 Vern. 738, 23 E.R. 1082, who, to spite the remainderman, took off the roof of *Raby Castle*, was a very striking case of the unconscientious use of those powers....

Judgment for defendant.

CHAPTER XII

ENHANCING AND LIMITING THE USE OF LAND: BENEFITS AND BURDENS THROUGH COVENANTS, EASEMENTS AND PROFITS

1. INTRODUCTORY NOTE

THIS CHAPTER is concerned with what is commonly known as land use control through private agreement or arrangement. It does not purport to deal with public planning statutes and zoning regulations, of which account must be taken by anyone who would presume to advise on title to land or on its use by a purchaser or lessee. So restricted, the material in this chapter is further limited to specified means of private control. In chapter III of this casebook some attention was paid to determinable limitations and to conditions subsequent which, as devices for land use control, suffer because they involve forfeiture of the controlled estate; thus, they are met more frequently in wills and in voluntary conveyances than in transfers for value. In chapter VI, passing reference was made to interests less than estates, and these, as there enumerated (with the exception of licences which were treated at some length in chapter VI), form the subject matter of the present chapter.

Enforcement of the interests arising under covenants or easements and profits is usually by injunction, with additional or alternative resort to damages. It will have been noticed, however, that forfeiture is commonly introduced in respect of covenants as between landlord and tenant (by reason of express provision for re-entry), but there is some opportunity in such cases to seek relief therefrom through the Courts.

2. COVENANTS

(a) *Validity: Problems of Construction*

NOBLE AND WOLF v. ALLEY. Supreme Court of Canada. [1951] S.C.R. 64, [1951] 1 D.L.R. 321

Appeal from a judgment of the Ontario Court of Appeal, [1949] O.R. 503, [1949] 4 D.L.R. 375, affirming a judgment of Schroeder J., [1948] O.R. 579, [1948] 4 D.L.R. 123, declaring that a certain "racial" restrictive covenant was valid and enforceable.

The judgment of KERWIN and TASCHEREAU JJ. was delivered by KERWIN J.:... In the Courts below emphasis was laid upon the decision of MacKay J. in *Re Drummond Wren*, [1945] 4 D.L.R. 674, O.R. 778, and it was considered that the motion was confined to the consideration of whether that case, if rightly decided, covered the situation. The motion was for an order declaring that the objection to the covenant made on behalf of the purchaser had been fully answered by the vendor and that the same did not constitute a valid objection to the title or for such further and other order as might seem just. The objection was: "REQUIRED in view of the fact that the purchaser herein might be considered as being of the Jewish race or blood, we require a release from the restrictions imposed in the said clause (f) and an order declaring that the restrictive covenant set out in the said clause (f) is void and of no effect."

The answer by the vendor was that the decision in *Re Drummond Wren* applied to the facts of the present sale with the result that cl. (f) was invalid and the vendor and purchaser were not bound to observe it. In view of the wide terms of the notice of motion, the application is not restricted and it may be determined by a point taken before the Court of Appeal and this Court, if not before Schroeder J.

That point depends upon the meaning of the rule laid down in *Tulk* v. *Moxhay* (1848), 2 Ph. 774, 41 E.R. 1143....

Whatever the precise delimitation in the rule in *Tulk* v. *Moxhay* may be, counsel were unable to refer us to any case where it was applied to a covenant restricting the alienation of land to persons other than those of a certain race. Mr. Denison did refer to three decisions in Ontario: *Essex Real Estate Co.* v. *Holmes* (1930), 37 O.W.N. 392 [affd 38 O.W.N. 69]; *Re Bryers & Morris* (1931), 40 O.W.N. 572; *Re McDougall & Waddell*, [1945] 2 D.L.R. 244, O.W.N. 272; but he was quite correct in stating that they were of no assistance. The holding in the first was merely that the purchaser of the land there in question did not fall within a certain prohibition. In the second an inquiry was directed, without more. In the third, all that was decided was that the provisions of s. 1 of the *Racial Discrimination Act*, 1944 (Ont.), c. 51, would not be violated by a deed containing a covenant on the part of the purchaser that certain lands or any buildings erected thereon should not at any time be sold to, let to or occupied by any person or persons other than Gentiles (non-semitic [*sic*]) of European or British or Irish or Scottish racial origin.

It was a forward step that the rigour of the common law should be softened by the doctrine expounded in *Tulk* v. *Moxhay* but it would be an unwarrantable extension of that doctrine to hold, from anything that was said in that case or in subsequent cases, that the covenant here in question has any reference to the use, or abstention from use, of land. Even if decisions upon the common law could be prayed in aid, there are none that go to the extent claimed in the present case.

The appeal should be allowed....

The judgment of RAND, KELLOCK and FAUTEUX JJ. was delivered by RAND J.: Covenants enforceable under the rule of *Tulk* v. *Moxhay*, 11 Beav. 571, 50 E.R. 937, are properly conceived as running with the land in equity and, by reason of their enforceability, as constituting an equitable servitude or burden on the servient land. The essence of such an incident is that it should touch or concern the land as contradistinguished from a collateral effect. In that sense, it is a relation between parcels, annexed to them and, subject to the equitable rule of notice, passing with them both as to benefit and burden in transmissions by operation of law as well as by act of the parties.

But by its language, the covenant here is directed not to the land or to some mode of its use, but to transfer by act of the purchaser; its scope does not purport to extend to a transmission by law to a person within the banned class. If, for instance, the grantee married a member of that class, it is not suggested that the ordinary inheritance by a child of the union would be affected. Not only, then, is it not a covenant touching or concerning the land, but by its own terms it fails in annexation to the land. The respondent owners are, therefore, without any right against the proposed vendor.

On its true interpretation, the covenant is a restraint on alienation. The grantor company which has disposed of all its holdings in the subdivision has admittedly ceased to carry on business and by force of the provisions of the *Companies Act*, R.S.O. 1937, c. 251, s. 28, its powers have become forfeited; but by s-s. (4) they may, on such conditions as may be exacted, be revived by the Lieutenant-Governor in Council. Assuming the grantor would otherwise be entitled to enforce the covenant in equity against the original covenantor—and if he would not the point falls—it becomes necessary to deal with the question whether for the purposes of specific performance the covenant is unenforceable for uncertainty.

It is in these words: "The lands and premises herein described shall never be sold, assigned, transferred, leased, rented or in any manner whatsoever alienated to and shall never be occupied or used in any manner whatsoever by any person of the Jewish, Hebrew, Semitic, Negro or coloured race or blood, it being the intention and purpose of the Grantor, to restrict the ownership, use, occupation and enjoyment of the said recreational development including the lands and premises herein described, to persons of white or Caucasian race not excluded by this clause."

If this language were in the form of a condition, the holding in *Clayton* v. *Ramsden*, [1943] A.C. 320, would be conclusive against its sufficiency. In that case the House of Lords dealt with a condition in a devise by which the donee became divested if she should marry a person "not of Jewish parentage and of the Jewish faith" and held it void for uncertainty. I am unable to distinguish the defect in that language from what we have here: it is impossible to set such limits to the lines of race or blood as would enable a Court to say in all cases whether a proposed purchaser is or is not within the ban. As put by Lord Cranworth in *Clavering* v. *Ellison* (1859), 7 H.L.C. 707 at p. 725, 11 E.R. 282, the condition "must be such that the Court can see from the beginning, precisely and distinctly, upon the happening of what event it was that the preceding vested estate was to determine".

The effect of the covenant, if enforceable, would be to annex a partial inalienability as an equitable incident of the ownership, to nullify an area of proprietary powers. In both cases there is the removal of part of the power to alienate; and I can see no ground of distinction between the certainty required in the one case and that of the other. The uncertainty is, then, fatal to the validity of the covenant before us as a defect of or objection to the title.

ESTEY J.: The appellants Noble as vendor and Wolf as purchaser were negotiating relative to a summer residence in an area known as the Beach O'Pines on Lake Huron. In the course thereof questions were raised as to the validity of cl. (f) (hereinafter quoted) in the agreement under which the appellant Noble acquired the premises on January 16, 1933, from the Frank S. Salter Co. The appellant Noble, therefore, brought a motion under the *Vendors and Purchasers Act*, for an order, *inter alia*, that the restrictive covenant (cl. (f)) did not constitute a valid objection to the title. Schroeder J. held the covenant to be valid and his judgment was affirmed by the Court of Appeal for Ontario.

The appellants contend this cl. (f) is contrary to public policy, constitutes a restraint upon alienation and is void for uncertainty.

Clause (f) reads:

"And the Grantee for himself, his heirs, executors, administrators and assigns, covenants and agrees with the Grantor that he will carry out, comply with and observe, with the intent that they shall run with the land and shall be binding upon himself, his heirs, executors, administrators and assigns, and shall be for the benefit of and enforcible by the Grantor and/ or any other person or persons seized or possessed of any part or parts of the lands included in Beach O'Pines Development, the restrictions herein following, which said restrictions shall remain in full force and effect until the first day of August, 1962, and the Grantee for himself, his heirs, executors, administrators and assigns further covenants and agrees with the Grantor that he will exact the same covenants with respect to the said restrictions from any and all persons to whom he may in any manner whatsoever dispose of the said lands....

"(f) The lands and premises herein described shall never be sold, assigned, transferred, leased, rented or in any manner whatsoever alienated to, and shall never be occupied or used in any manner whatsoever by any person of the Jewish, Hebrew, Semitic, Negro or coloured race or blood, it being the intention and purpose of the Grantor, to restrict the ownership, use, occupation and enjoyment of the said recreational development, including the lands and premises herein described, to persons of the white or Caucasian race not excluded by this clause."

This restrictive covenant literally construed would prohibit any person possessing the slightest degree of race or blood specified purchasing any land in this area. So construed it would be necessary to determine whether it constituted such a substantial restraint upon alienation as to make the clause void "as being repugnant to the very conception of ownership": Cheshire's Modern Real Property, 6th ed., p. 523.

It is, however, submitted that the parties never intended that the language should be so strictly construed. Once, however, another or more liberal construction be given the issue becomes one of what degree of race or blood would be permitted. As to what degree, the contract is silent. A Judge, therefore, called upon to determine this issue, finds in the contract no standard or other assistance that would constitute a basis upon which the issue might be determined.

[The learned Judge then discussed *Sifton* v. *Sifton*, [1938] A.C. 656, [1938] 3 D.L.R. 577, *Clayton* v. *Ramsden*, [1943] A.C. 320 and *Clavering* v. *Ellison* (1859), 7 H.L.C. 707, 11 E.R. 282 and continued as follows:]

The foregoing are cases of conditions subsequent providing for the divesting of vested estates. It is contended that such precise and distinct language is not required in restrictive covenants. On the contrary, both upon principle and authority, the same clarity would appear to be essential.

Restrictive covenants constitute "an equity attached to land by the owner": Lord Cottenham L. C. in *Tulk* v. *Moxhay*, 2 Ph. at p. 779; and in *Hall* v. *Ewin* (1887), 37 Ch. D. 74 at p. 81, Lindley L. J. states: "The principle of *Tulk* v. *Moxhay*... imposes a burden on the land." This burden passes with the land against all but purchasers without notice thereof and parties interested are entitled to ascertain from the covenant the exact nature, character and extent of the restriction.

Moreover, these covenants constituting a burden upon the land must, in general, interfere with the right of disposition thereof. Lord Dunedin, in speaking of a condition restricting land, and the same rule of construction would apply to a covenant, stated, in *Anderson* v. *Dickie* (1915), 84 L.J.P.C. 219 at p. 227: "Far earlier than this it had been held that all conditions restricting the use of land must be very clearly expressed, the presumption being always for freedom."

In *Murray* v. *Dunn*, [1907] A.C. 283, a covenant, by way of a servitude, provided that "any building of an unseemly description" should not be erected upon the premises. Lord Kinnear in the First Division of the Court of Session for Scotland delivered a judgment which was approved of in the House of Lords. In the course of his judgment he stated that the bond of servitude "provides no standard for the specific application of the terms" and at p. 287:

"So far as my own opinion goes, I cannot say that it is unseemly; the utmost that can be said for the pursuers' case is that that is matter of opinion, and if there may be a reasonable difference of opinion as to the specific application of the terms in which a servitude is expressed to the facts of a particular case, it is not a well-defined servitude."

In Brown, Covenants Running with Land, 1907, p. 126, the author states: "A restrictive covenant as to letting or user of property will be construed strictly; the Court will not extend it on the ground of presumed intention."

See also Jolly, Restrictive Covenants Affecting Land, 1909, pp. 77 and 79.

These authorities support the view that the language of a restrictive covenant must set forth clearly and distinctly the intent of the parties. The general language in cl. (f), with great respect to those learned Judges who hold a contrary view, fails to indicate the intention of the parties as to the amount or degree of the prohibited race or blood that might be permitted. It must, therefore, upon the authorities, be held void for uncertainty.

Appeal allowed.

[The dissenting opinion of Locke J. is omitted. That learned Judge took the position that the question whether the covenant was one that would run with the land should not be considered by the Supreme Court because the provincial Court of Appeal had refused to consider it when it had been newly raised before that Court. Locke J. then concluded as follows: "As to the remaining matters argued so fully before us, I agree with the learned Chief Justice of Ontario".

The Conveyancing and Law of Property Act, R.S.O. 1960, c. 66, s. 22 provides as follows: "Every covenant made after the 24th day of March, 1950, that but for this section would be annexed to and run with land and that restricts the sale, ownership, occupation or use of land because of the race, colour, nationality, ancestry or place of origin of any person is void and of no effect." For similar legislation, see Law of Property Act, R.S.M. 1954, c. 138, s. 7; cf. Saskatchewan Bill of Rights Act, R.S.S. 1953, c. 345, ss. 10, 16.

In view of the Supreme Court's judgment in *Noble and Wolf* v. *Alley*, does the Ontario (and Manitoba) legislation, *supra*, have any real effect?

On "racial" restrictive covenants, see *Smout*, An Inquiry into the Law on Racial and Religious Restraints on Alienation, (1952) 30 Can. Bar Rev. 863; *Robinson*, Limited Restraints on Alienation, (1950) 8 Advocate (B.C.) p. 250.

In the United States, "racial" restrictive covenants are no longer enforceable by State Courts, either by way of injunction or by actions for damages, because such enforcement would constitute state action in violation of the Fourteenth Amendment: see *Shelley* v. *Kraemer*, *McGhee* v. *Sipes* (1948), 334 U.S.1, 68 S. Ct. 836; *Barrows* v. *Jackson* (1953), 346 U.S. 249, 73 S. Ct. 1031. Cf., however, *Charlotte Park and Recreation Commission* v. *Barringer* (1955), 242 N.C. 311, 88 S.E. 2d 114, cert. denied (1956), 350 U.S. 983, holding that the Fourteenth Amendment is not involved where the "racial" restriction operates by way of a determinable fee so that there is automatic reverter on breach of the limitation. For a discussion of the United States cases, see *Note*, Equal Protection and the Racial Restrictive Covenant, (1955) 30 Ind. L. J. 366; *Note*, (1956) 29 So. Calif. L. Rev. 498; cf. *Comment*, (1956) 44 Calif. L. Rev. 718.]

HALIFAX v. VAUGHAN CONSTRUCTION COMPANY. Nova Scotia Supreme Court. 1957. 9 D.L.R. 2d 431

Action by the city of Halifax for a declaration of its right to share in the compensation awarded to defendant in certain expropriation proceedings. The city was a grantee from the Crown (Canada) of land which it sold to a telegraph and telephone company under a conveyance containing covenants by the company (1) to construct certain buildings on the land "as soon as practically may be after delivery of these presents"; and (2) to reconvey the land to the city if the company does not proceed with construction of the buildings. By novation, the land was sold to defendant which gave a deed to the city embodying covenants aforementioned. The deed concluded as follows:

"It is intended by the parties hereto that the burden of the foregoing covenants shall run with the lands hereinbefore described until such building or buildings shall have been constructed and no longer; and that upon the construction of such building or buildings in compliance with the foregoing covenants the burden of the foregoing covenants shall no longer run with the lands; and this Deed of Covenants is accepted by the City of Halifax and the said consideration paid upon such intent and understanding."

Defendant did nothing about its covenant to build. About nine months after it acquired the land, notice of expropriation thereof was given by the Province of Nova Scotia. The land thus vested in the Crown (Nova Scotia) and compensation was fixed in a judicial proceeding. Plaintiff claimed the compensation money over and above the price that defendant had paid for the land. The effect of applicable expropriation legislation was that any claim or encumbrance that plaintiff could assert against the land became, after expropriation, a claim against the compensation money.

DOULL J. (after reciting the facts and rejecting the argument that the covenants were void on the grounds of vagueness and uncertainty): The defendant also says that if the covenants are not void on the ground of vagueness or uncertainty, the 6th covenant, which is a covenant to reconvey, is void as offending against the rule against perpetuities. The argument is that there is no limit of time within which the right may arise.

I think that if this covenant creates an equitable interest in the land in question, the rule applies, and if the time within which the city may make its demand is unlimited, the covenant is void.

This covenant does refer to and bind the particular land in question and I am of opinion that it does create an equitable interest in the land in favor of the city: *London & S.W.R. Co.* v. *Gomm.* (1881), 20 Ch. D. 562; Challis Real Property 3rd Ed. 183-189. That the covenant continues indefinitely is, however, another question. In the *Gomm* case it will be noted Jessel M. R. said: (p. 580)

"The very essence of the contract is that it shall be indefinite in point of time. You cannot, as in *Kemp* v. *South Eastern Railway Company*, Law Rep. 7 Ch. 364, insert by intendment the limitation that the land is to be taken before the time for executing the works had expired, for in this case the time for the execution of the works had already expired."

In Kemp v. *S.E.R. Co.* (1872), L.R. 7 Ch. 364, the work was to be completed within 5 years from the passing of the Act and on the expiration of that period the compulsory powers were to cease. The company entered into an agreement which provided:

"If the company shall require more than one acre of ground for the site of the said station, or any additional ground for any purpose beyond that specified in the said schedule hereto, they shall pay for the same at the rate of £100 per acre."

Lord Hatherley L. C. said that this agreement was not unlimited as to time.

In the present case I think that the whole agreement is governed by the provision that the buildings are to be commenced, "as soon as practicably may be after the delivery of these presents". The covenants are to run only until the construction of these buildings and within a reasonable time. Certainly the time when the right of the city would arise would be after a reasonable time for the commencement of the work, and I hold that it could not continue in perpetuity.

It may be noted that the dispute in *Tulk* v. *Moxhay* (1848), 2 Ph. 774, 41 E.R. 1143, 18 L.J. Ch. 83, was between a vendor and a successor in title of the purchaser and not between the original parties to the agreement as here. The following, however, from Lord Cottenham L. C. is interesting (18 L.J. Ch. at p. 88):

"Of course, the party purchasing the property under such restriction, gives less for it than he would have given if he had bought it unincumbered. Therefore, can there be anything more inequitable or contrary to good conscience, than that a party who takes property at a less price because it is subject to a restriction, should receive the whole value from a third party, and that such third party should then hold it unfettered by the restriction under which it was granted?"

In my opinion the covenants were binding upon the defendant and were in equity an interest in the land. There is nothing in *Irving Oil Co.* v. *The King*, [1946], 4 D.L.R. 625, S.C.R. 551, 60 C.R.T.C. 309 or in *Diggon-Hibben Ltd.* v. *The King*, [1949], 4 D.L.R. 785, S.C.R. 712, 64 C.R.T.C. 295, to suggest that this is not so.

The defendant also says that upon the expropriation taking place, the covenants in the Deed of Covenants were frustrated and the defendant was relieved of any liability thereunder and discharged therefrom.

It is quite certain that the result of the expropriation was to work frustration. The defendant cannot construct any building upon the lands in question and it is clear that the defendant cannot reconvey the land to the plaintiff.

The question is whether or not the defendant is wholly relieved of the burden of his covenants.

The rule established at common law is that the occurrence of the frustrating event "brings the contract to an end forthwith, without more and automatically".

The rule adopted by the Judges until 1943 is thus stated:

"Each party must fulfil contractual obligations so far as they have fallen due before the frustrating event, but he is excused from performing those that fall due later,"...

In *Chandler* v. *Webster*, [1904] 1 K.B. 493, the plaintiff, whose rent was payable in advance and who had paid £140, could not only not recover his money that he had paid, but was liable to pay the balance which was due at the time of the frustration.

The decision in *Chandler* v. *Webster* was the subject of criticism and indeed caused general dissatisfaction. See Williston on Contracts. It was not adopted in the American Restatement of the Law of Contract and was said by Lord Birkenhead in *Cantiare San Rocco* v. *Clyde Shipbuilding & Engineering Co.*, [1924] A.C. 226, to be not in accordance with the law of Scotland.

It was not until 1942 that the decision in *Chandler* v. *Webster* came for review in the House of Lords. In the case of *Fibrosa Spolka Akcyjna* v. *Fairbairn Lawson Combe Barbour Ltd.*, [1943] A.C. 32, [1942] 2 All E.R. 122, the respondents contracted to deliver certain machinery to the appellants, the delivery to be c.i.f. at Gdynia. The contract provided that one-third of the purchase-price should be paid at the time when the order was given. The appellants in fact paid £1000 although the one-third amounted to £1600 and never paid the balance of £600. War broke out in September, 1939, and Gdynia was within enemy territory. It was held that the outbreak of war worked a frustration and it was further held that the appellants were entitled to a return of the money paid upon a consideration which had wholly failed. The decision in *Chandler* v. *Webster*, *supra*, was overruled.

Following these cases, the Legislatures in many jurisdictions took a hand and passed Acts entitled "*Frustrated Contracts Act*". It is not necessary to refer to these Acts which extend somewhat the decision in the *Fibrosa case*, *supra*, for the reason that while such an Act has been passed in seven of the nine common law Provinces, it has not been passed in Nova Scotia.

In my view the discussions in these cases do not affect the present case. It is quite true that the owner of a ship, if it be requisitioned by the Admiralty, is relieved of his covenant to freight coal to London, but in the case of an interest in land, there is something more than a contract.

In *London & Northern Estates Co.* v. *Schlesinger*, [1916] 1 K.B. 20, the defendant had a lease. On war breaking out he, being an alien enemy, was required by an Order in Council to move from that district, it was held that he had an estate in the realty and notwithstanding this order, he must pay rent. The matter is perhaps clearer in *Whitehall Court Ltd.* v. *Ettlinger*, [1920] 1 K.B. 680. In this case certain flats belonging to the plaintiff were requisitioned by military authorities. The defendant was a tenant for a term of 3 years. The defendant paid the rent to the date of requisition. It was held that he must pay the rent and recover his damages from H.M. Office of Works. The Earl of Reading C. J. said (p. 687): "The agreements contained in the leases are not only contracts, they also create an estate by demise for a term of years."

True these are cases of tenancy, but they depend in some part at least on the fact that a tenancy is an interest in land and it follows that if the interest is destroyed, temporarily or permanently, the authority which destroys it must pay the owner of the interest for its value. Let us suppose that the interest in question is a mortgage, or the lien of an unpaid vendor, it is quite clear that the result would be that the owner of the interest must share the compensation. It is so here.

It may be added that it seems to be the effect of the evidence that the defendant had been negotiating with the Crown authorities before the date of the expropriation and desired that there be expropriation proceedings for the express purpose of wiping out his obligations....

While in the view which I take, this does not affect the question, it may well be argued that the frustration in the present case does not relieve the defendant of any obligation, being a self-induced frustration as in *Maritime National Fish Ltd.* v. *Ocean Trawlers Ltd.*, [1935], 3 D.L.R. 12, A.C. 524.

In the result I am of opinion that the plaintiff is entitled to receive payment out of the compensation money, to the extent of the value of its interest in the property expropriated, *viz.*, the Bellevue property in the City of Halifax, such interest being $280,000. less $87,520., plus 5% of the balance so found and interest on the sum from July 18, 1956.

Judgment for plaintiff.

[On appeal this judgment was reversed on other grounds: (1958), 12 D.L.R. 2d. 159. Suppose that defendant had sold the land to another prior to the expropriation. Could plaintiff have sued the subsequent purchaser by relying on the stipulation in the deed of covenants that it was intended that the burden of the covenants should run with the land?]

[In *Kerrigan* v. *Harrison* (1921), 62 S.C.R. 374, 65 D.L.R. 95, aff'g 47 O.L.R. 548, 54 D.L.R. 258, A granted land to B and gave B a right of way to that land over a certain road which A covenanted to maintain. Owing to erosion resulting from encroachment of the waters of a lake, the road disappeared. C, a purchaser from B, sued A on the covenant. *Held*, the covenant assumed the continued existence of the road, and upon its disappearance A was excused from further performance.]

LONDON AND SOUTH WESTERN RAILWAY CO. v. GOMM. Court of Appeal. 1882. 20 Ch. D. 562, 51 L.J.Ch. 530

Appeal from a judgment of Kay J., decreeing specific performance. Plaintiffs were holders in fee simple of land which in 1865 they conveyed to one Powell, an adjoining owner, under a deed in which Powell convenanted for himself, his heirs, executors, administrators and assigns that whenever the land would be required by plaintiffs for their works and upon request by this company, its successors or assigns, on six calendar months' notice, the land would be reconveyed upon payment of £100. The land passed to Powell's son and heir from whom defendant purchased it in 1879 with full notice of the covenant in the original deed from the company. On defendant's refusal to reconvey after proper notice from the company, action for specific performance was brought. Kay J., after holding that the original transaction was within the company's powers, considered whether the covenant to reconvey violated the rule against perpetuities. He was of opinion that "a present right to an interest in property which may arise at a period beyond the legal limit is void notwithstanding that the person entitled to it may release it"; however, "a contract not creating any estate or interest properly so-called, at law or equity, is not... obnoxious to the rule. For instance, a covenant to pay £1000 when demanded, with interest meanwhile, if not barred by the Statute of Limitations, might be enforced by an action of covenant at any time. A contract to buy or sell land and covenants restricting the use of land, though unlimited, are not void for perpetuity. In these latter cases the contracts do not run with the land, and are not binding upon an assign, unless he takes with notice. They are not, properly speaking, estates or interests in land, and are therefore not within the rule. I think that this is the true test to apply to this case, and am of opinion that this covenant does not create any interest in land. A purchaser without notice from Powell would not be bound by it. It is not, I think, within the rule against perpetuities at all. Consequently I hold that objection to fail; and as the defendant took the land with notice, I hold that he is bound in Equity by the covenant, on the principle of *Tulk* v. *Moxhay*, 2 Ph. 774."

JESSEL M. R. (after stating the facts and referring to the covenant to reconvey): Now that is unlimited in point of time, and it does not appear to me to be possible to insert a limit of time, because to put in the words "within a reasonable time," or any other words limiting the time, would be exactly contrary to the intention of the parties. It is not only unlimited in point of time but it is obviously intended so to be. The railway company do not want the land now, and they do not know that they ever will want it, but their bargain is that whenever it may be required for the works of the company the owners or owner for the time being of the land are or is to convey to the company. The very essence of the contract is that it shall be indefinite in point of time. You cannot, as in *Kemp* v. *South Eastern Railway Company*, L.R. 7 Ch. 364, insert by intendment the limitation that the land is to be taken before the time for executing the works had expired, for in this case the time for the execution of the works had already expired. It appears to me therefore plain (and indeed it was admitted in argument by the Respondents) that the option is unlimited in point of time.

If then the rule as to remoteness applies to a covenant of this nature, this covenant clearly is bad as extending beyond the period allowed by the rule. Whether the rule applies or not depends upon this as it appears to me, does or does not the covenant give an interest in the land? If it is a bare or mere personal contract it is of course not obnoxious to the rule, but in that case it is impossible to see how the present Appellant can be bound. He did not enter into the contract, but is only a purchaser from Powell who did. If it is a mere personal contract it cannot be enforced against the assignee. Therefore the company must admit that it somehow binds the land. But if it binds the land it creates an equitable interest in the land. The right to call for a conveyance of the land is an equitable interest or equitable estate. In the ordinary case of a contract for purchase there is no doubt about this, and an option for repurchase is not different in its nature. A person exercising the option has to do two things, he has to give notice of his intention to purchase, and to pay the purchase-money; but as far as the man who is liable to convey is concerned, his estate or interest is taken away from him without his consent, and the right to take it away being vested in another, the covenant giving the option must give that other an interest in the land.

It appears to me therefore that this covenant plainly gives the company an interest in the land, and as regards remoteness there is no distinction that I know of (unless the case falls within one of the recognised exceptions, such as charities) between one kind of equitable interest and another kind of equitable interest. In all cases they must take effect as against the owners of the land within a prescribed period.

It was suggested that the rule has no application to any case of contract, but in my opinion the mode in which the interest is created is immaterial. Whether it is by devise or voluntary gift or contract can make no difference. The question is, what is the nature of the interest intended to be created?...

Now is there any substantial distinction between a contract for purchase, or an option for purchase, and a conditional limitation? Is there any difference in substance between the case of a limitation to A. in fee, with a proviso that whenever a notice in writing is sent and £100 paid by B. or his heirs to A. or his heirs the estate shall vest in B. and his heirs, and a contract that whenever such notice is given and such payment made by B. or his heirs to A. or his heirs, A. shall convey to B. and his heirs? It seems to me that in a Court of Equity it is impossible to suggest that there is any real distinction between these two cases. There is in each case the same fetter on the estate and on the owners of the estate for all time, and it seems to me to be plain that the rules as to remoteness apply to one case as much as to the other.

That appears to me to dispose of the case, unless we agree with the conclusion of Mr. Justice Kay on the last point considered by him. Down to that point I agree with him. I consider that he is quite right in the view he takes of the doctrine of remoteness and of the authorities cited before him, not forgetting the case of the *Birmingham Canal Company* v. *Cartwright*, 11 Ch. D. 421, which must be treated as overruled. But Mr. Justice *Kay*, having, as I think he has, most correctly and accurately defined the law, thinks that this case is not within it, because he comes to the conclusion that "this covenant does not create any interest in the land". But he had forgotten that if that were so he could not make a decree against Mr. *Gomm.* If it were a mere contract it was not *Gomm's* contract, and if it did not in equity run with the land so as to give an interest in the land, it could not have been enforced against him. It is clear from his Lordship's judgment that if he had been of opinion that this covenant gave the company an interest in the land (which, I think, is the correct view) he would have decided the case the other way.

With regard to the argument founded on *Tulk* v. *Moxhay*, that case was very much considered by the Court of Appeal at Westminster in *Haywood* v. *The Brunswick Permanent Benefit Building Society* 8 Q.B.D. 403, and the Court there decided that they would not extend the doctrine of *Tulk* v. *Moxhay* to affirmative covenants, compelling a man to lay out money or do any other act of what I may call an active character, but that it was to be confined to restrictive covenants. Of course that authority would be binding upon us if we did not agree to it, but I most cordially accede to it. I think that we ought not to extend the doctrine of *Tulk* v. *Moxhay* in the way suggested here. The doctrine of that case, rightly considered, appears to me to be either an extension in equity of the doctrine of *Spencer's Case* to another line of cases, or else an extension in equity of the doctrine of negative easements; such, for instance, as a right to the access of light, which prevents the owner of the servient tenement from building so as to obstruct the light. The covenant in *Tulk* v. *Moxhay* was affirmative in its terms but was held by the Court to imply a negative. Where there is a negative covenant expressed or implied, as, for instance, not to build so as to obstruct a view, or not to use a piece of land otherwise than as a garden, the Court interferes on one or other of the above grounds. This is an equitable doctrine, establishing an exception to the rules of Common Law which did not treat such a covenant as running with the land, and it does not matter whether it proceeds on analogy to a covenant running with the land or on analogy to an easement. The purchaser took the estate subject to the equitable burden, with the qualification that if he acquired the legal estate for value without notice he was freed from the burden. That qualification, however, did not affect the nature of the burden; the notice was required merely to avoid the effect of the legal estate, and did not create the right, and if the purchaser took only an equitable estate he took subject to the burden, whether he had notice or not. It appears to me that, rightly considered, that doctrine is not an authority for the proposition that an equitable estate or interest may be raised at any time, notwithstanding the rule against remoteness. It is, if I may say so, another exception to the rules against remoteness, exceptions which had previously been thoroughly established in many cases at law as regards easements, and in equity as regards charities. That being so, it does not appear to me that *Tulk* v. *Moxhay* has any direct bearing on the case which we have to decide.

Appeal allowed.

[The concurring judgments of Sir James Hannen and Lindley L. J. are omitted. The Court also held that the sale by the company, conditioned by the covenant to reconvey, was beyond its statutory powers and that the land vested in Powell after 10 years (under a statutory provision) free of any restriction.]

[A lease creating a tenancy from year to year, terminable on 12 months' notice in writing, gave to the lessee at all times "the right, privilege and option of purchasing the said premises from the lessor" on payment of a stated sum. *Held*, the option did not violate the rule against perpetuities because the person for the time being entitled to the property subject to the option could destroy the option by terminating the lease by proper notice and without the concurrence of the person holding the option: *Auld* v. *Scales*, [1947] S.C.R. 543, [1947] 4 D.L.R. 721. The holding assumes that an option in the terms set forth creates an interest in land. That this is so is doubted in *Re Devine and Ferguson*, [1946] O.R. 736, [1947] 1 D.L.R. 76.

[In *Forseth* v. *Prudential Trust Co. Ltd. and Canadian Williston Minerals Ltd.* (1956), 7 D.L.R. 2d 44, 20 W.W.R. (N.S.) 282 (Sask.) a landowner who had given an indeterminate oil "lease" to A subsequently gave B an option to lease the mineral rights should the existing lease terminate. The landowner brought a declaratory action to set aside the option as violating the rule against perpetuities but the trial Judge considered that the plea was premature until B sought to enforce the option. He then went on, as follows:

"This plaintiff asked for a declaration that the option is void. It is true that many learned Justices have used the term 'void' somewhat loosely in reference to perpetuities but it is clear that a transaction offending against perpetuities is neither void nor illegal but merely unenforceable in some circumstances. The failure to perform a contract which does offend against the rule frequently gives rise to a right in damages. Furthermore, the authorities lean to the view that as between the parties (as distinct from a successor to the grantor) the rule has no application, and particularly where the enforcement is sought within the limits of the rule. *Stocker* v. *Dean* (1852), 16 Beav. 161, 51 E.R. 739; *Kenrick* v. *Dempsey* (1856), 5 Gr. 584 at p. 586; *Worthing Corp* v. *Heather*, [1906] 2 Ch. 532; *South Eastern R. Co.* v. *Associated Portland Cement Mfrs. (1900) Ltd.*, [1910] 1 Ch. 12; *Hutton* v. *Watling*, [1947] 2 All E.R. 641; confirmed on appeal, [1948] 1 All E.R. 803; *McClement* v. *Lovatt* (1954), 13 W.W.R. (N.S.) 695; revd (1955), 15 W.W.R. (N.S.) 426."]

RE ALBAY REALTY LTD. v. DUFFERIN-LAWRENCE DEVELOPMENT LIMITED.

Ontario High Court. 2 D.L.R. 2d 604, [1956] O.W.N. 302

GALE J.: Here the Court is asked for an order declaring that the respondent Dufferin-Lawrence Development Ltd., and its predecessors in title have no title or interest whatsoever in the lands purchased by the applicant because of certain covenants contained in a deed to which I shall make more specific reference in a moment.

On February 14, 1947, Mary E. Sanders conveyed certain lands in the Township of North York, which I shall hereafter designate as parcel "A", to Leavens' Bros. Air Services Limited. Apparently at that time Mrs. Sanders owned other neighbouring lands and there was contained in the deed just mentioned the following covenant: "The Grantor further covenants and agrees on behalf of herself, her executors, administrators, successors and assigns, that no part of the three parcels of land next hereinafter described shall be sold to any person other than the Purchaser without the same first being offered to the Purchaser, who shall have three days exclusive of Sundays and holidays to accept such offer and that none of the said lands shall be sold to any other person on more favourable terms than previously shall have been offered to the Purchaser."

The property with which I am concerned was secondly described in the covenant and for the sake of clarity I shall call it parcel "B". Generally speaking, it adjoins parcel "A" to the west.

By deed dated July 30, 1953, Leavens' Bros. Air Services Ltd. conveyed a major portion of parcel "A" to Dufferin-Lawrence Development Ltd. and included in that conveyance was an assignment from the grantor to the grantee of "all the right, title and interest of the said Grantor to and in any right of first refusal which the Grantor may have acquired" under the earlier conveyance.

In April, 1955, Mrs. Sanders received an offer from the applicant, Albay Realty Ltd., to purchase that part of parcel "B" which had not in the meantime been expropriated by the municipality of Metropolitan Toronto and other lands, the offer with respect to the part of parcel "B" which remained being at a price of $13,000 per acre. Earlier in the month, and prior to that offer, the solicitors for Mrs. Sanders had offered to sell the portion of parcel "B" which was left to her to Dufferin-Lawrence Development Ltd. for the price of $13,000 per acre. While there is further evidence as to what developed between the solicitors for Mrs. Sanders and the Dufferin-Lawrence Development Ltd., I do not need to explore that phase of the matter for reasons which will appear later on. Eventually parcel "B" was sold to the applicant, Albay Realty Ltd., a company which is now interested in developing the lands, and it has met with difficulties in arranging financing because of the alleged impediment created by the covenant which I have described. Hence this motion....

In the first place, Mr. Morden (for the applicant) argued that quite apart from the question of whether or not compliance was made with the covenant, his client and the lands are not now bound by it for the reason that while the benefit of the covenant could be assigned by Leavens' Bros. Air Services Ltd. to Dufferin-Lawrence Development Ltd., as was done, its burden could not be transferred by Mrs. Sanders to the Albay company; 8 Hals., 3rd ed., p. 258 was cited for that proposition. I should say at once that I agree with that contention, and accordingly, to have the covenant effective as against the applicant, the Dufferin-Lawrence company would have to show that it is one which runs with the land and is not personal to the grantor and grantee who brought it into existence. At most the covenant created an option; indeed, it might be said to be something less than that for it is described in the assignment as "a right of first refusal". In any event, plainly it is personal to the grantor or grantee and does not run with the land. In this regard several authorities might be cited. I have in mind particularly *Rogers* v. *Hosegood*, [1900] 2 Ch. 388; *Woodall* v. *Clifton*, [1905] 2 Ch. 257, and the earlier case of *London & South Western R. Co.* v. *Gomm* (1882), 20 Ch. D. 562. In the last of these cases the Court was considering a covenant to reconvey land and it was held that the benefit of a stipulation of that character did not pass to successive owners.

Perhaps the clearest statement on the subject is to be found in 29 Hals., 2nd ed., s. 649, p. 442, where this appears: "In order that a covenant may run with the land it must be of such a nature as to 'touch or concern' the land; that is, it must either affect the land as regards mode of occupation, or it must be such as per se and not merely from collateral circumstances, affects the value of the land."

It is my view that this option or right was a personal one only and did not touch or concern the land itself. Accordingly, it is not binding upon the applicant and for that reason alone the declaration ought to be made.

In addition, it seems to me that as to the applicant the right or option is void as offending the rule against perpetuities. It is unlimited in time and no interest would have accrued to the grantee of the right unless and until an agreement to purchase the land was entered into. The Dufferin-Lawrence company has not entered into such an agreement and theoretically might never do so. Accordingly the right or condition violates the rule against remoteness. In this connection reference might be made to Gray on the Rule Against Perpetuities, 4th ed., pp. 362, et seq. ss. 330, 330-1. *United Fuel Supply Co.* v. *Volcanic Oil & Gas Co.* (1911), 3 O.W.N. 93, and *Rutherford* v. *Rispin*, [1926] 4 D.L.R. 822, 59 O.L.R. 506, demonstrate that the law of England as exemplified by the judgments in the *Gomm* case, *supra*, is also the law of this Province.

For the foregoing reasons I hold that the applicant is entitled to the declaration it seeks. However, I wish it clearly understood that my judgment is based on considerations of law and not upon a finding of fact that Mrs. Sanders fulfilled her obligations under the covenant. She may have done so but I would not care to decide that issue on the evidence before me.

Order accordingly.

[In the *Manchester Ship Canal Co.* v. *Manchester Racecourse Co.*, [1901] 2 Ch. 27, 70 L.J. Ch. 468 (C.A.), a racecourse company whose land adjoined a canal entered into an agreement under seal with the canal company under which it agreed that if the racecourse should cease to be used as such or should it be proposed to be used for dock purposes, "then and in either of such cases the racecourse company shall give to the canal company the first refusal of [the racecourse lands]". The agreement was given statutory force so that no issue could arise as to invalidity because of remoteness or uncertainty. The racecourse company offered the land to a third company at a price lower than that originally sought from the canal company and, ultimately, agreed to sell it to the third company, subject to the canal company's right of first refusal. The price was less than the offering price to the purchaser but more than the canal company's offer and more than the price finally asked of the canal company. Declaratory and injunctive relief was obtained by the canal company against the other two: see [1900] 2 Ch. 352. In dismissing an appeal, Vaughan Williams L. J. for the Court said, in part:

"The main question in this action is whether or not, according to the true construction of the scheduled agreement, the defendants did give a 'first refusal' of the racecourse land to the canal company. There appear to be two possible meanings of the words 'first refusal': One is that they mean the opportunity of refusing a 'fair and reasonable offer' by the racecourse company to sell the lands en bloc to the canal company; the other is that they mean the opportunity of refusing the land at a price acceptable to the racecourse company offered by some person other than the canal company, which is what we understand by the term 'right of pre-emption'....

"We think that the very words 'first refusal' in clause 3 import that the price at which the racecourse company give the canal company the 'first refusal' is a price at which the racecourse company will offer the land to other would-be buyers in the event of the refusal of the canal company to buy at that price. If there is no person negotiating a purchase it may not be easy to prove that the price offered to the canal company is above the price which the racecourse company are willing to take from persons other than the canal company; but whenever this can be proved, it seems to me that there is a clear infraction of the right of pre-emption given to the canal company by clause 3. In the present case, however, there is no difficulty of proof....

"Then it was objected that clause 3 could not be enforced against the Trafford Park Company, who are only alienees of the land. Farwell J., thought that clause 3 created an interest in land, and that this objection could be thus answered. We do not think that clause 3 does create an interest in land, nor do we think that there is anything in the decisions in

Tulk v. *Moxhay* or in *London and County Banking Co.* v. *Lewis* 21 Ch. D. 490 which gets over the objection.

"It seems, however, from the decision in *Willmott* v. *Barber* 15 Ch. D. 96, that the Trafford Park Company could not obtain a decree for specific performance of a contract for sale and purchase of land, if that sale would be a breach of a prior contract with a third person; and it seems to us to follow that one ought to treat this case on the basis of an action to restrain a breach of a contract threatened to be carried out in pursuance of a subsequent contract by the defendant with a third person having full knowledge of the first contract. This seems to bring the case within the principle of *Lumley* v. *Wagner*, 1 D.M. & G. 604. The contract here to give the canal company the 'first refusal' involves a negative contract not to part with the land to any other company or person without giving that first refusal. If the action had been brought against the racecourse company, the party to the contract, alone, the injunction asked for could not have been granted without affecting the rights and interests of the Trafford Park Company. They are necessary parties to the action, just as Mr. Gye was a necessary party to the action of *Lumley* v. *Wagner*, for to grant the injunction in that case was to prevent Miss Wagner from carrying out her contract to sing at Mr. Gye's opera-house; and, if the defendant, thus brought in, comes and insists on his right to have the second contract carried out, we do not see why the injunction should not be granted against him....

"It is said that, if the agreement for the sale of the racecourse to the Trafford Park Company is carried out, the plaintiffs will not be hurt, because the contract of sale is expressly subject to their rights. But the answer to this is, on the question of the amount of compensation to be paid on compulsory purchase, it may make a great difference to the canal company, who are the claimants."]

AAROE AND AAROE v. SEYMOUR. Ontario High Court. [1956] O.R. 736, 6 D.L.R. 2d 100

Purchaser's action for damages against his vendor and against his solicitors.

LEBEL J.: The plaintiffs are husband and wife who purchased lands from the defendant Brisson for the purpose of building their residence thereon. The lands consist of Lot 24, Plan 182, "Glen Acres Extension", in the City of St. Catharines. The defendant Brisson is a real estate broker in St. Catharines, and the defendants Seymour, Lampard, Goldring and Young are the firm of solicitors practising there who searched the title to the property and acted for the plaintiffs in connection with their purchase. I shall refer to them hereafter as "the solicitors".

On September 24, 1951, the approximate date the purchase was closed, the title to Lot 24 was subject to the terms of an agreement registered on March 29, 1950. This document created an easement over the easterly 6 ft. of the westerly 7 ft. of the lot for the construction and maintenance of a sewer by the Corporation of the City of St. Catharines. The solicitors did not disclose the existence of this agreement to the plaintiffs, and the house was completed early in 1952. About a year later serious cracks and other defects began to show up in the masonry, walls and floor.

The City's sewer was laid before the end of 1950 and the soil on both sides of the main was disturbed in consequence. It is common ground, I think, that the westerly foundation wall of the plaintiffs' house was built upon the easterly edge of the easement for some distance and that the disturbed soil there should not have been built upon, at least, not until special construction safeguards had been taken. These safeguards were not taken, and I find upon the evidence that about 80% of the damage to the plaintiffs' house was caused for that reason.

The plaintiffs claim that the solicitors were negligent in failing to report the existence of the easement and also that Mr. Brisson breached certain covenants in his deed, and they ask for substantial damages against both defendants.

[The learned Judge first considered the case against the solicitors and concluded that they were liable for negligence in passing title as they did without requiring a survey. He then continued as follows:]

The action as pleaded against the defendant Brisson is for breach of the covenant or covenants for "quiet possession... free from all encumbrances". Better to consider the meaning of the words "free of all encumbrances" it is necessary to look at the extended meanings given these words in cl. 4 of Sch. B. of the *Short Forms of Conveyances Act*, R.S.O. 1950, c. 360. The relevant part of the clause reads:

"4. And that free and clear and freely and absolutely acquitted, exonerated and for ever discharged or otherwise by the said grantor or his heirs well and sufficiently saved, kept harmless and indemnified of, from and against *any and every former and other gift, grant*,... and every other estate, title, charge, trouble and encumbrance whatsoever, made, executed, occasioned or suffered *by the said grantor or his heirs*." (The italics are mine.)

Strictly speaking an easement is not an encumbrance. It is an interest in land—a hereditament; but since by the statutory covenant the grantor promises that he will keep harmless and indemnify his grantee against any gift, grant, etc., made by him or his heirs, his promise is the equivalent of the old implied covenant for quiet title dealt with in *Turner* v. *Moon*, [1901] 2 Ch. 825 (a case of an undisclosed right-of-way). In its extended meaning the statutory covenant for quiet possession, free of encumbrances, is thus wider in its scope than the simple covenant for quiet possession or for quiet enjoyment (dealt with in Mayne on Damages, 11th ed., p. 238, and in Dart on Vendors & Purchasers, 8th ed., vol. II, p. 666), the purpose of which is simply to secure the grantee against dispossession or other physical disturbances, there being no breach until such event takes place.

In my opinion the defendant Brisson is therefore liable for breach of his express covenant....

Both the defendants are liable to [plaintiffs] in contract, and the measure of damages is the difference between the value of the land conveyed and the value of the land that Brisson had the power to convey: Mayne *op.cit.*, 11th ed., p. 236, and *Turner* v. *Moon*, [1901] 2 Ch. at pp. 829-30. The only evidence on the point is that Lot 24, encumbered as it is by the easement agreement, is worth some $300 less than it would otherwise be. The plaintiffs are therefore entitled to damages against both defendants in the sum of $300....

Judgment for plaintiffs.

[An appeal taken by defendant Brisson only was dismissed: (1957), 7 D.L.R. 2d 676 (Ont. C.A.). In giving the judgment of the Court, Laidlaw J. A. said, *inter alia*:

"The learned trial Judge was of the opinion that there is liability on the part of the appellant because of breach of the covenant for quiet possession, free from encumbrances. Counsel for the appellant in this Court argued that there is no liability by reason of alleged breach of that covenant, because the covenant that a grantee shall have quiet possession free from all encumbrances is a single covenant indivisible in its terms and provisions, and that no action will lie for breach of the covenant until the occupier of the land proves that there has been a disturbance, in fact, of his possession. He contends that the mere existence of an encumbrance does not give a right to sue under this covenant. He refers to the pleadings in the action and maintains that the claim is founded solely on the alleged breach of covenant for quiet enjoyment. He argues that the case ought to be disposed of by a determination of that issue, and that issue alone, and that when the law is properly applied to that issue the action fails. He concedes at once that if the action had been founded on an alleged breach of the covenant that there was no act done by the grantor to encumber the land, he would have no defence to it, but he resists any amendment to the pleadings except upon terms that will adequately and fairly compensate him in the matter of costs.

"I examine the statement of claim and find that in para. 8 thereof it is alleged that: 'The deed to the plaintiffs by the defendant vendor was in pursuance of The Forms of Conveyances Act and contained covenants that the land was "free from all encumbrances" and that the plaintiffs "shall have quiet possession".' I refer also to para. 10 which I quote as follows: 'The plaintiffs have sustained loss and damage by reason of the negligence and breach of duty of the defendant solicitors and by reason of breach of covenants of the defendant vendor.'

"In the statement of defence to the allegations made by the plaintiff, it is set forth in para. 6, as follows: 'The Defendant Gordon Brisson specifically denies that he has broken any covenants contained in the grant from him to the Plaintiffs.'

"When one examines the record of proceedings at trial it is apparent that the case was not limited specifically to the allegation in respect of the covenant for quiet possession, nor do we think that the pleadings should be construed in such a limited manner. It became apparent, particularly from the statement of defence filed by the appellant Brisson, that he was putting in issue the matter of all covenants in the deed delivered by him. He expressly denied that there was a breach of any of those covenants.

"It appears to this Court that it is unnecessary, in the circumstances, to express an opinion as to whether or not the covenant for quiet enjoyment free from all encumbrances can in all cases be regarded as a covenant in respect of title. It may well be, as argued by counsel for the appellant, that that covenant is applicable only to future acts and damage subsequent to the time of the conveyance; but in the facts of this case, even if the covenant for quiet possession be so regarded, it is proper to hold that the existence of the sewer on the lands of the appellants was a continuing encumbrance and that when disturbance to the landowner occurred by reason of the existence of that structure, that then the possession of the landowner was disturbed in fact. It was because of the existence of this sewer structure that the building of the respondent did, in fact, collapse. That collapse was obviously a disturbance to his possession. It was a disturbance to his possession by reason of the encumbrance on the land and the exercise of the right on the part of the city to put that structure there. If the covenant for quiet possession is not so regarded, and, in particular, is not regarded as a covenant in respect to title, nevertheless there is liability on the part of the appellant by reason of the breach of covenant on the part of the appellant that he had done no act to encumber the land. There is no denial of liability for that breach, and the liability may properly be placed on that basis without the necessity of amendment of the pleadings. In either case, it is the opinion of the Court that the amount of damages as assessed by the learned Judge cannot be disturbed.

"It is no doubt the law that the measure of damages for breach of the covenant for quiet possession must be determined on a different basis than for breach of the covenant that there had been no act done to encumber the lands. If the liability be placed on the ground that there was breach of the covenant for quiet possession, then there is evidence that clearly established a quantum of damages suffered by the landowner much in excess of that awarded by the trial Judge. The only reason greater damages were not allowed to the plaintiffs on that basis is by reason of the fact that some knowledge should be attributed to them of the existence of this easement. If the damages are to be assessed on the basis of breach of the covenant that no act was done to encumber the land, then the sum of $300 properly represents the depreciated market value of this land by reason of the existence of this easement."]

[A purchaser under an agreement for the sale of land may insist on a good title before completing the transaction. Once he takes a deed, however, he must, generally speaking, rely on the covenants therein, if any, to protect him against any title defects which may be subsequently discovered: see *Hansen* v. *Franz* (1918), 57 S.C.R. 57, 41 D.L.R. 457; *Angel* v.

Jay, [1911] 1 K.B. 666; *Thurston* v. *Streilen*, [1951] 4 D.L.R. 724, 59 Man. R. 55. Readers should contrast the position in respect of executed contracts for the sale of personalty.

In those jurisdictions which have merely a system of registration of documents of title and where, accordingly, the purchaser must satisfy himself by a search of documents that he is getting the title he contracted for, there is little likelihood of litigation after the deed is taken if the search is a careful one. These jurisdictions deal in different ways with covenants for title. For example, in Ontario, s. 23 of the Conveyancing and Law of Property Act, R.S.O. 1960, c. 66 stipulates that there are implied in every conveyance covenants for (1) the right to convey; (2) quiet enjoyment; (3) freedom from encumbrances; and (4) further assurances. In Prince Edward Island, these covenants are included in the standard form of conveyance which may be used as provided by s. 53 of the Real Property Act, R.S.P.E.I. 1951, c. 138. On the other hand, in Nova Scotia, s. 7(2) of the Conveyancing Act, 1956 (N.S.), c. 3 states that unless a conveyance is required to be by warranty deed or unless an express enactment so requires, no covenants or conditions are implied in any conveyance, either by the mode of conveying or by the use therein of any such words as "grant", "give", or "demise", or other terms of art. This statute is reminiscent of the period of the common law warranty (referred to in chapter IV, p. 61, *supra*) which antedated coveyances under the Statute of Uses through which covenants for title in the modern sense came into vogue: cf. *Holmes*, Common Law, pp. 371 ff.

Under a land titles system, where the state of the title appears on and is represented by a public register, covenants for title have little significance. However, in some provinces which have such a system, short forms legislation providing for standardized deeds include the covenants for title hereinbefore referred to: see Short Form of Deeds Act, R.S.B.C. 1960, c. 356; Short Forms Act, R.S.M. 1954, c. 243.]

[For the historical background of covenants for title, see *Rawle*, Covenants for Title (1887, 5th ed.), chap. 1; and see also 3 *American Law of Property*, chap. 6; *Burby*, Real Property (1954, 2nd ed.), chap. 24; 34 Halsbury (1960, 3rd ed.), pp. 369-378.

It may be noted here that the "running" of covenants for title arises only in respect of benefit and not of burden (save as to personal representatives of the covenantor.): see *Megarry and Wade*, Law of Real Property (1959, 2nd ed.), p. 596.]

[Where land is conveyed by a deed with covenants for title which run therewith (in this case a covenant for seisin in fee free from incumbrance), an assignee of part only of the land may sue on the covenants and recover in proportion to his interest: see *Keyes* v. *O'Brien* (1860), 20 U.C.Q.B. 12 (C.A.), where Robinson C. J. said (at p. 14): "The little that can be found bearing upon the question in the general form is chiefly, if not altogether, in cases upon leases, in which cases the statute 32 H. 8, c. 34 has been relied on for giving assignees a right to sue; but it seems to us that such cases on the statute apply in principle to the present, as does also in a measure the language of the judges who have decided them.... In American courts the ability of such assignees of part to sue had been recognized in many cases, though they seem to have been unable to cite English decisions supporting that view."]

[The English and Canadian cases regard the "usual covenants for title" as capable of running in favour of a remote grantee: see 34 Halsbury (1960, 3rd ed.), p. 373; *Gamble* v. *Rees* (1850), 6 U.C.Q.B. 396 (C.A.); *Platt* v. *G.T.R.* (1892), 19 O.A.R. 403, at pp. 414-416; *Trust & Loan Co.* v. *Ruttan* (1877), 1 S.C.R. 564; cf. *Harry* v. *Anderson* (1863), 13 U.C.C.P. 476; *Leeming* v. *Smith* (1877) 25 Gr. 256. The prevailing American rule is that only the covenants for quiet enjoyment and for further assurances run; that the covenants for seisin and for the right to convey do not run because they are broken if at all when the conveyance is made and this indicates that they are not of a continuing nature; and, similarly, the covenant against encumbrances is not regarded as a covenant which can run: see 3 *American Law of Property*, ss. 12. 127 to 12. 130.]

[An interim receipt given upon payment of a deposit on the purchase price of land stipulated that "an agreement of sale containing the usual covenants contained in agreements for sale of land within British Columbia to be entered into on the terms hereof". What is the effect of the stipulation? Is there an enforceable contract? See *Buyers* v. *Begg*, [1952] 1 D.L.R. 313, 3 W.W.R. (N.S.) 673 (B.C.C.A.); *Parento and Parento* v. *Jacobsen*, [1955] 2 D.L.R. 510 (B.C.). Would your answer be any different if the matter arose in Ontario?]

BANK OF MONTREAL v. UNIVERSITY OF SASKATCHEWAN. Saskatchewan Queen's Bench. 1953. 9 W.W.R. (N.S.) 193

THOMSON J.: The facts in this matter are not in dispute. Possibly for that reason the material filed in the first instance was not as complete as it otherwise might have been. It, however, has been supplemented from time to time by the filing of various documents and by admissions made by counsel during the course of argument. Under these circumstances, it would be well to summarize the facts as finally presented to me.

The Bank of Montreal is now and, for many years, has been the owner of lots 38, 39 and 40, all in block 307, in the city of Regina, Saskatchewan, Plan Old No. 33. In fact, it has been the registered owner of lot 38, with which we are particularly concerned in these proceedings, ever since September 27, 1896. On these lots the bank erected a building in which its main branch in Regina was located. The building, however, did not cover the entire area of the said lots. According to the sketch filed by consent of counsel, there is a strip of land slightly more than 15 feet in width lying between the said building and the southerly limit of lot 38, on which no building has ever been erected. Incidentally, it should be noted that the bank's building did not, at any time material to these proceedings, extend all the way back to the lane as shown on the said sketch. The wider portion of the building shown on the sketch, extending from the jog in the northern wall thereof to the said lane, was added some years later and was not in the contemplation of the parties at the time the agreement hereinafter mentioned was made or entered into.

The bank was also the owner of lots 36 and 37, in said block 307. Those lots lie to the south of and adjoin the other lots above described. By an agreement in writing and under seal bearing date August 1, 1906, the bank agreed to sell said lots 36 and 37 to Norman Mackenzie and George William Brown for $15,000, payable $3,000 in cash on the execution of the agreement and the balance in deferred instalments with interest at the rate of 6 per cent per annum. The agreement, in the main, follows the form ordinarily used by conveyancers when land is sold on the deferred instalment plan but omits a number of the provisions usually found in agreements of that kind.

The main difficulty arises from the inclusion in the agreement of certain special provisions contained in a paragraph of which the following is a copy, viz:

"And the Purchasers agree to erect (commencing not later than the first day of June, 1907) a building, to be constructed out of brick, concrete or stone or partly of one and partly of another of said materials, to be not less than three stories in height and to be in keeping with the Bank Building of the Vendors now constructed on the adjoining Lots northerly thereto and taking into consideration in the Plans of such intended erection the South Fifteen (15) Feet, between the said land agreed to be sold herein and the said Bank Building agreed by the Vendors to remain vacant and being reserved for the purpose of fire protection and light for the benefit of the Vendors and Purchasers; and the Plans and Specifications showing the windows on the Northerly wall of the building so to be erected shall be first submitted to the Vendors for approval."

It is admitted by counsel that following the execution of the said agreement, Mackenzie and Brown erected a building on the lots they had agreed to purchase and, in due course, paid the purchase-price of the said lots in full. It is also agreed that the bank thereupon transferred and conveyed to Mackenzie and Brown the title to the said lots in fee simple and clear of encumbrances in accordance with the provisions in that behalf contained in the said agreement. Apparently, the parties then assumed that the matter was closed. In any event, there is no evidence that Mackenzie and Brown (or either of them) at that time or at any other time ever demanded from the bank any transfer or other instrument capable of registration under *The Land Titles Act* granting to or conferring upon them any easement or any other interest in or right over any portion of the property retained by the bank. I think that it may now be assumed that no such transfer or instrument was ever demanded by or given to the said purchasers.

There the matter rested until after the death of George William Brown. On August 8, 1921, National Trust Company Ltd., Brown's executor, and Mackenzie, the surviving purchaser, caused a caveat to be registered against the title to lot 38, claiming an interest therein under the special provision of the agreement of August 1, 1906, above set forth. Subsequently, Mackenzie, the surviving purchaser, died.

On January 24, 1930, the defendant Beatrice Annie Brown became the registered owner of an undivided half interest in lots 36 and 37 and on March 10, 1938, the defendant, the University of Saskatchewan, became the registered owner of the remaining undivided half interest therein. There is nothing in the record to indicate how the defendants acquired their respective interests but, on the argument before me, counsel assumed that Miss Brown acquired her interest as devisee under the will of her father George William Brown and that the university acquired its interest as devisee under the will of Norman Mackenzie. It was admitted, however, that the present owners have never received any assignment or other conveyance of the interest in lot 38 which, it is now alleged, was taken or acquired by Mackenzie and Brown under the original agreement of August 1, 1906.

Shortly after the argument before me, it was found that the university and Miss Brown had entered into an agreement to sell said lots 36 and 37 to Steen & Wright Furriers, Limited. An application was made by the plaintiff bank to add the said purchaser as a party defendant and with the consent of counsel for all parties (including Steen & Wright Furriers, Limited) the said company was added as a party defendant so that they might be bound by any order made in these proceedings. Here again there is no suggestion that the benefit of the restrictive covenant in the original contract of August 1, 1906, has been assigned to Steen & Wright Furriers, Limited. That, however, is not surprising because the personal representatives of Mackenzie and Brown, having parted with the title to the property, would not now be able to effectively assign the benefit of the covenant in question to any of the defendants: *Cheshire's Modern Real Property*, 5th ed., pp. 305 and 312, and *In re Union of London and Smith's Bank Conveyance; Miles* v. *Easter* [1933] 1 Ch 611, 102 L.J. Ch. 241.

While it is true that no building has ever been erected on the most southerly 15 feet in width of said lot 38, it, nevertheless, should here be noted that the said strip of land has never, at any time since August 1, 1906, been entirely unused. The bank building which is now situate on lots 38, 39 and 40 is not the building which was in existence when the agreement of August 1, 1906, was entered into. The building then in existence had a side entrance from the south with steps leading up to it. This entrance and the said steps projected out over the 15 foot strip for some feet and there was a sidewalk some three feet in width leading from Scarth Street to the said entrance. For something more than 30 years, the bank also maintained a lattice work fence about 5½ feet in height across the said strip of land which extended from the south wall of its bank building to the north wall of the building erected by Mackenzie and Brown. It is not clear, however, whether that fence was first erected before or after the caveat, above mentioned, was filed by National Trust Company Ltd. and Mackenzie on

August 8, 1921. Furthermore, a considerable portion of the said strip of land has been for many years, used by the bank as a parking space for automobiles.

For some time past, the bank has been negotiating for the removal of the said caveat but the parties have been unable to come to any agreement. The bank now applies, by originating notice, for the following relief:

"That it may be determined whether upon the true construction of an agreement dated August 1st, A.D. 1906, whereby the plaintiff agreed to sell and one, Norman Mackenzie, and one, George William Brown, agreed to purchase Lots Thirty-six (36) and Thirty-seven (37), in Block Three Hundred and Seven (307), in Regina, aforesaid, as shown in Plan Old No. 33, and more particularly the clause of said agreement set forth below, the defendants have any right or interest in Lot Thirty-eight (38), in said Block and Plan; and

"(a) If it be determined that the said clause is vague, uncertain, indefinite, incomplete or for any other reason entirely void and ineffective as against the Plaintiff, an order removing from the title to said Lot Thirty-Eight (38), the Caveat registered as instrument No. CF2167; and

"(b) If it be not so determined, then a declaration as to what the rights of the interested parties are."

For the bank, it is contended that the special provision of the agreement of August 1, 1906, now under consideration, is altogether too vague and uncertain to be enforceable. It is quite obvious that the draftsmanship leaves much to be desired. Counsel for the bank points out that there is nothing in the agreement indicating how long or wide the proposed building was to be or the time within which the erection thereof was to be completed. The agreement stipulated that the said building was to be "in keeping with" the bank building of the vendors situate on the adjoining property. Whether a building is in keeping with some other building is always a matter of opinion on which there might well be an honest difference of opinion. In this connection, counsel has called my attention to *Murray* v. *Dunn* [1907] A.C. 283, 97 L.T. 112, in which the House of Lords decided that a condition against the erection of buildings of "an unseemly description" was too vague and indefinite to be enforceable as a permanent restraint on the use of the property....

As above stated, the purchasers did erect a building. It is admitted that it is three storeys in height and there is no suggestion that the bank has ever objected to its size, type or location or complained that it was not in keeping with its own building. Furthermore, the bank accepted the purchase moneys and, apparently, without protest transferred and conveyed the title to the purchasers.

In my opinion, it is now too late to complain of any ambiguity or uncertainty in the agreement in so far as it relates to the erection of the said building or to the size, type or location thereof. After all, when there is ambiguity in an agreement, there is no better way of determining what the parties intended than to look to what they did under it: *Hoefle* v. *Bongard & Co.* [1945] S.C.R. 360, Kellock, J. at 377; *Watcham* v. *Atty.-Gen for East Africa Protectorate* [1919] A.C. 533, 87 L.J.P.C. 150, Lord Atkinson at 152; *Firestone Tire & Rubber Co.* v. *Commr. of Income Tax* [1942] S.C.R. 476 (reversing [1941] 3 W.W.R. 635, 56 B.C.R. 328) Rinfret, J. at 482; and *Van Dieman's Land Co.* v. *Marine Board of Table Cape* [1906] A.C. 92, 75 L.J.P.C. 28. Under the circumstances, it must now be assumed that the bank approved and accepted the building erected by Mackenzie and Brown as a building of the kind and description which the said purchasers, by their agreement, were required to erect on the land they were purchasing from the bank.

That, however, does not end the matter. It is still necessary to determine whether the defendants have any interest in or rights over lot 38 which adjoins their property and, if so, to determine just what interest or rights they have. That involves an interpretation of that portion of the paragraph above quoted which reads as follows: "... agreed by the Vendors to remain vacant and being reserved for the purpose of fire protection and light for the benefit of the Vendors and the Purchasers."...

The defendants contend that the benefit of the covenant did pass to them. In support of that contention they invoke the rule set forth in *Tulk* v. *Moxhay* (1848) 2 Ph. 744, 18 L.J. Ch. 83, 41 E.R. 1143.

... Wide though the rule or doctrine of *Tulk* v. *Moxhay*, *supra*, may be, the mere fact that the owner of a parcel of land, for good and valuable consideration, gives to the owner of adjoining land a covenant restricting the use to which he may put his land does not necessarily mean that the benefit of such restrictive covenant will automatically pass to successive owners of the land of the covenantee merely because it is shown to be advantageous to that land.

Unless the agreement, expressly or by necessary implication, annexes the benefit of the covenant to the land of the covenantee so as to show that the primary object of the covenant is to protect or benefit his land and not the covenantee personally, the benefit of the covenant will not pass automatically to those who may, from time to time, become the owners or possessors of the said land. A covenant drafted in personal terms, without express or implicit reference to the land of the covenantee, does not automatically run with a conveyance of that land: *Cheshire's Modern Real Property*, 5th ed., p. 308; *Brown on Covenants Running with Land*, p. 106; and *Renals* v. *Cowlishaw* (1878) 9 Ch. D. 125, 48 L.J. Ch. 33, affirmed 11 Ch. D. 866, 48 L.J. Ch. 830. This principle is concisely stated by Cozens-Hardy, M.R. in *Reid* v. *Bickerstaff* [1909] 2 Ch. 305, at 320, 78 L.J. Ch. 753....

Whether the benefit of the covenant passes to subsequent owners of the land of the covenantee is in each case primarily a question of intention to be determined by the court on the construction of the particular document, and with due regard to the nature of the covenant and the surrounding circumstances: *Cheshire's Modern Real Property*, p. 308. It is necessary, therefore to examine the agreement in this case with some care.

I can find no provision in the agreement which definitely annexes the covenant to the land the bank was selling to Mackenzie and Brown or which states, in express terms, that the benefit of the covenant was to protect or benefit that land. Even the usual provision that the covenant was to run with the land is conspicuous by its absence and no attempt has been made to follow the pattern set by the draftsman who drew the deed considered by the courts in *Rogers* v. *Hosegood*, *supra*, now frequently followed by conveyancers. In that case the deed specifically stated that it was made with the intention that the covenants of the grantee were, so far as possible, to bind the premises thereby conveyed and every part thereof "into whosesoever hands the same might come" and that they were to enure to the benefit of the grantors, their heirs and assigns and "others claiming under them to all or any of their lands adjoining or near the said premises." In my opinion, it is significant that the agreement in this case contains none of these provisions or any term or condition to the like effect.

It is even more significant that there is nothing in the agreement to indicate that the benefit of this particular covenant [as contrasted with other covenants, such as those for title.—ED.] was to extend to the heirs or assigns of Mackenzie and Brown, the said purchasers....

There may be cases in which the courts should read in the word "assigns" when not expressed in a document to be interpreted, but that should never be done where there is nothing in the context requiring it to be done: *Anglo-Newfoundland Dev. Co.* v. *Newfoundland Pine and Pulp Co.* (1913) 83 L.J.P.C. 50, at 52, 110 L.T. 82:

"It is of course possible in certain cases to read in the word 'assigns' when not expressed in the document, though their Lordships know of no case in which the words 'assigns or nominees' have been thus supplied. But whether or not it is proper so to do must depend on the context in each case."

It should also be borne in mind that the purchasers were lawyers. The agreement (as appears from the endorsement on the back thereof) was drawn by the firm of Mackenzie,

Brown & Thom, of which they were the senior partners. In view of those facts, I think that it would be fair to assume that they must have known the significance and importance of including a reference to heirs and assigns if, in fact, they actually intended that the benefit of this restrictive covenant should pass to successive owners of the property they were purchasing. In any event, they were careful to include a reference to executors, administrators and assigns where that was deemed necessary.

In these days everyone has become so used to dealing with land under the Torrens system of land registration as established in this province by *The Land Titles Act* that they are apt to forget that at common law a conveyance of land to a person without mention of his heirs or assigns or the specific estate he was to take conferred an estate for life only: *Williams on Real Property*, 24th ed., p. 213. As to the reasons for this see pp. 155 and 156. Indeed, that continued to be the law in England until 1926 when the *Law of Property Act*, 1925, ch. 20, came into force: *In re Whiston's Estate; Lovatt* v. *Williamson* [1894] 1 Ch. 661, 63 L.J. Ch. 273; *In re Irwin; Irwin* v. *Parkes* [1904] 2 Ch. 752, 73 L.J. Ch. 832, and *In re Bostock's Settlement; Norrish* v. *Bostock* [1921] 2 Ch. 469, 91 L.J. Ch. 17. The covenant in this case is contained in a document which is not capable of registration under *The Land Titles Act* and that Act would not apply thereto. If the covenant is to be considered as a grant or conveyance of an estate or interest in lot 38 to Mackenzie and Brown, the original purchasers, then the common-law rule may be applicable thereto and, in the absence of any mention of heirs or assigns or the estate which they were to take thereunder, it may well be that the said estate or interest came to an end on the death of the said purchasers. However, it is not necessary for me, in this case, to decide that particular question and I make no finding in that regard.

After carefully considering the provisions of the agreement and all of the surrounding circumstances, I have finally come to the conclusion, though with some hesitation, that the restrictive covenant now under consideration is a purely personal covenant which was binding only as between the bank and Mackenzie and Brown, the original purchasers, and that the benefit of the said covenant has not passed to the defendants or any of them.

The foregoing, however, are not the only reasons why I think that the defendants are not entitled to the interest in or rights over lot 38 they now claim. It is a well-established principle of law that where, as in this case, there is a preliminary agreement in writing which is afterwards carried out or completed by the execution and delivery of a deed, the rights of the parties are governed entirely by the deed. If there should be any difference between the written agreement and the deed the provisions of the deed alone will prevail: *Millbourn* v. *Lyons* [1914] 2 Ch. 231, 83 L.J. Ch. 737, Cozens-Hardy, M. R., at 741; *Leggott* v. *Barrett* (1881) 15 Ch. D. 305, 51 L.J. Ch. 90, James, L. J. at 309, and *Knight Sugar Co. Ltd.* v. *Alta. Ry. & Irrigation Co.* [1938] 1 W.W.R. 234, at 237 and 238 (P.C.). It has now been established that this principle applies to agreements for the sale of land and that transfers under *The Land Titles Act* differ in no relevant respect from an ordinary conveyance or deed of unregistered land: *Knight Sugar Co. Ltd.* v. *Alta. Ry. & Irrigation Co.*, *supra*, at 238; *Franz* v. *Hansen* [1918] 2 W.W.R. 40, 57 S.C.R. 57, and *Stuart* v. *C. & E. Ry.* [1927] 1 W.W.R. 639, at 651 (varied [1927] 3 W.W.R. 678, 23 Alta. L.R. 205)....

Finally, I am of the opinion that the defendants cannot succeed in this case because I am unable to distinguish it from *In re Jamieson Caveat* (1913) 4 W.W.R. 475, 6 Sask. L.R. 296, 23 W.L.R. 921. In that case the Grand Trunk Pacific Development Co. Ltd. sold certain lots in Nokomis, Saskatchewan, to the trustees of a church under an agreement in which the purchasers covenanted that they would use the property for the erection of a church and buildings in connection therewith and for no other purpose. Upon payment of the purchase-price, the vendors executed and delivered to the purchasers a transfer of the property and filed a caveat against the land to protect their rights under the said covenant.

Proceedings were commenced to remove the caveat and the company's application to continue it was heard by Lamont, J. who, in a judgment which is reported under the name of *In re G.T. Pac. Dev. Co.'s Caveat* (1912) 2 W.W.R. 1068, 5 Sask. L.R. 313, 22 W.L.R. 193, decided that the covenant did not confer on the company an interest in the lots which would support a caveat and ordered that it be discharged. An appeal was taken to the court en banc. The position taken by counsel for the company was almost the same as that taken by counsel for the defendants in this case. A summary of his arguments will be found in 6 Sask. L.R. at 297. In particular, he too contended that the doctrine of *Tulk* v. *Moxhay*, *supra*, applied and also that the covenant was not merged in the transfer. The court en banc, however, was unanimous in rejecting those contentions and the appeal was dismissed. Newlands, J. in his judgment, 4 W.W.R. at 476-7, 6 Sask. L.R. at 299, said:

"Mr. T. D. Brown argued that the covenant in question created a right in the company, they being the owners of adjoining lands, in the nature of an easement, for although it was affirmative in form, it had the effect of a negative covenant on the part of the trustees that they would not use the land for any other than church purposes. If this argument is correct, and such a covenant should be construed as creating an easement, then, in order to be effective under *The Land Titles Act*, it should have been created and registered as provided by ss. 71 and 73 of that Act."

It is true, as pointed out by counsel for the defendants, that the judgment of Newlands, J. was not the only judgment in *In re Jamieson Caveat*, *supra*. Brown, J. also delivered a judgment which was concurred in by Haultain, C. J. and his judgment must, therefore, be regarded as the majority judgment. There is nothing in the judgment of Brown, J., however, to indicate that he disagreed with the reasoning of Newlands, J. It is also quite clear that Haultain, C. J. did not disagree with the judgment delivered by Newlands, J. because he later expressly approved of and followed it in *Sumner* v. *McIntosh* [1917] 1 W.W.R. 1404, at 1407, 10 Sask. L.R. 63. The appeal from his judgment in that case was dismissed: See [1918] 2 W.W.R. 293, 11 Sask. L.R. 152. The judgment delivered by Newlands, J. in the *Jamieson* case was also followed and applied by Mackenzie, J. in *Franco Canadian Corpn.* v. *Johnson* [1923] 1 W.W.R. 790, at 795, 16 Sask. L.R. 345. Under these circumstances, I am of the opinion that I am bound by the said judgment of Newlands, J. For the reasons stated in that judgment, I hold that the defendants cannot now assert any interest in or rights over said lot 38 or any part thereof. It follows that the caveat filed against the title to that lot by National Trust Company, Ltd. and Norman Mackenzie must now be discharged and removed from the plaintiff's title.

Judgment for plaintiff.

MAHONE OAR & BLOCK WORKS LIMITED v. RECTOR. Nova Scotia Supreme Court. [1953] 3 D.L.R. 609

Land was mortgaged to a named mortgagee, his heirs and assigns and the covenant for payment was made in favour of the mortgagee, his heirs and assigns by the mortgagors, their heirs, executors, administrators and assigns. The mortgagee died intestate and no administrator of his estate was appointed. The heirs-at-law of the deceased mortgagee, being those persons entitled under the Descent of Real and Personal Property Act, R.S.N.S. 1923, c. 147, purported to assign their interests in deceased's personalty, and questions arose whether the assignment was effective to pass the chose in action created by the mortgage and also whether the legal estate in the land passed to the heirs-at-law.

ILSLEY C. J.: ... First, has the chose in action created by the mortgage instrument, since A. Claremont Zwicker's death ever become vested in his heirs-at-law—or next-of-kin (who are the same persons)? There are three possible grounds on which it may be argued that this vesting has taken place.

The first ground is the wording of the covenant in the mortgage. The defendants covenanted with A. Claremont Zwicker, his heirs and assigns that they would pay unto A. Claremont Zwicker, his heirs and assigns the principal and interest of the mortgage. Moreover, they covenanted on behalf of themselves, their and each of their heirs, executors, administrators and assigns thereby giving some ground for the conclusion that while they intended their executors and administrators to be bound by the covenant, they did not intend the executors or administrators of A. Claremont Zwicker to have the benefit of the covenant. At the same time I do not think that I would be justified in concluding that that was their intention. It seems to me that the covenant was a covenant with A. Claremont Zwicker and with him alone. Such a covenant could, of course, after his death be enforced by his executors or administrators. A covenant with his heirs purported to be a covenant with non-existent persons. Such a covenant would be meaningless. There could be no privity between the mortgagors and the heirs-at-law of the mortgagee. *Nemo est haeres viventis.* In my opinion the words "covenant with the said mortgagee, his heirs and assigns" mean either "covenant with the said mortgagee and his assigns" or "covenant with the said mortgagee, his executors, administrators and assigns". The word "heirs" in wills is variously interpreted depending upon the intention to be gathered from the will. In other documents, too, "heirs" has been variously construed (at least in the American Courts) as meaning something else, sometimes as "representatives" or "personal representatives": 29 Corp. Jur., p. 295. I do not think there was any enforceable covenant by the mortgagors with the heirs-at-law of the mortgagee. The only enforceable covenant was with the mortgagee himself. Unless the heirs can enforce the covenant as representing the covenantee, they cannot enforce it at all. The fact that the covenant is expressed to be with them does not make them covenantees.

This covenant was however not only expressed to be with the heirs but was to pay the heirs. But this additional fact could not give the heirs a right to recover the mortgage debt because not being parties to the contract they would simply be future donee third-party beneficiaries. Moreover, it would in my opinion, on a literal construction of the word "heirs", not give the executors or administrators a right to collect, because on such a construction the heirs and not the executors or administrators would be entitled to the money. See Vandepitte's case [*Vandepitte* v. *Preferred Acc. Ins. Co.*], [1933] 1 D.L.R. 289, A.C. 70. A literal construction of the word "heirs" in the clause "shall and will well and truly pay unto the said Mortgagee, his heirs and assigns" would therefore lead to the absurd conclusion that the mortgagors if they did not pay off the mortgage in the mortgagee's lifetime, would not have to pay anybody. I think, therefore, that "heirs" in the last-quoted clause cannot be construed as meaning the persons entitled under the *Descent of Real and Personal Property Act*, but must be construed as meaning personal representatives—either that or disregarded altogether. The covenant is in my opinion nothing more or less than a covenant with the mortgagor to pay the mortgagee, or—which is the same thing—to pay the mortgagee, his executors, administrators and assigns. If the heirs had an action against the mortgagor upon the death of the mortgagee by virtue of the peculiar wording of the covenant, neither the appointment of an administrator of the mortgagee or the existence of creditors would make any difference. Still the heirs could collect the interest and principal of the mortgage and snap their fingers both at the administrator and the creditors. This, in my judgment, was certainly never the intention of the parties to the mortgage.

Falconbridge on the Law of Mortgages, 3rd ed., p. 395, says: "Even if the heirs of the mortgagee are named in the covenant for payment, the personal representatives will not thereby be deprived of their ordinary right to the money as being personalty, or of the right to sue for the money in their own names."...

The second ground on which it may be argued—and was argued—that the chose in action created by the mortgage was vested in the heirs-at-law is that upon the death of an intestate, his choses in action must vest in somebody and that as no administrator has been appointed, they vested in his next-of-kin.

The theory underlying this ground may be tested by applying it to the following not unusual situation: A., the owner of a chose in action, dies intestate owing debts. One month after his death B. is appointed his administrator. C. is his widow and D. and E. his only next-of-kin. The theory of succession of the chose in action under consideration is that during that month the chose in action is vested in C., D. and E., subject of course to being divested when the administrator is appointed. The reasons given in support of the theory are: (1) that the chose in action must be vested in someone during that month, and (2) that B., C. and D. are the persons to whom the personal property of an intestate must be distributed under s. 6 of the *Descent of Real and Personal Property Act*. Both reasons in my judgment are invalid.

As to the first reason, I cannot find that there is any rule that property must at all times be vested in someone. True, the common law is stated by Leake on Property in Land, 2nd ed., p. 33 to have been as follows: "The exigencies of tenure required that the seisin or immediate freehold should never be in abeyance, but that there should at all times be a tenant invested with the seisin ready, on the one hand, to meet the claims of the lord for the duties and services of the tenure, and, on the other hand, to meet adverse claims to the seisin, and to preserve it for the successors in the title."

And Williams on Personal Property, 18th ed., p. 50 says: "Ownerless things, however, are rare in civilised countries. Indeed they appear to be limited to wild animals, which are not the object of property until they are killed or caught."

But *quaere* whether abandoned chattels are not after abandonment ordinarily ownerless, at least until someone takes possession of them. Williams at p. 26 says: "It appears that the ownership of goods may be ended by their abandonment". And see Goodeve on Personal Property, 8th ed., p. 93.

The immediate question is dealt with in Salmond on Jurisprudence, 10th ed., pp. 234-5. While Salmond says that an ownerless right does not appear to be recognized by English law, he goes on to say that the ownership of a right may be merely contingent or uncertain, that the owner of it may be a person indeterminate, and that although every right has an owner, it need not have a vested and certain owner. He gives what he regards as an example, asks who is the owner of a debt in the interval between the death of the creditor intestate and the vesting of his estate in an administrator, refers to the Roman law personifying the inheritance (*haereditas jacens*) and refers to the English statutes which have vested and now vest the personal property of an intestate in such interval in certain Judges and then goes on to say: "But neither the Roman nor the English fiction is essential. There is no difficulty in saying that the estate of an intestate is presently owned by an *incerta persona*, namely by him who is subsequently appointed the administrator of it. The law, however, abhors a temporary vacuum of vested ownership. It prefers to regard all rights as presently vested in some determinate person, subject, if need be, to be divested on the happening of the event on which the title of the contingent owner depends. As to ownerless rights, see Windscheid, I. sect. 49, n. 3. Dernburg, *Pandekten*, I. sect. 49."

But there are or have been at least two situations in which rights have been regarded by the English common law as ownerless for the time being or vested in an *incerta persona*. One is the situation which arises when the individual constituting a corporation sole dies and a period elapses before his successor is appointed. There is an "abeyance of seisin" during this period. See Salmond, page 234, note (1), and Gray on the Nature and Sources of the Law, 1938 ed., p. 316, note 4. The other situation was one which obtained before 1677, the situation which arose when an estate *per autre vie* was granted to A without any mention of his heirs....

The good, chattels and credits of an intestate from very early times down to 1857 vested in the Ordinary from the intestate's death until the appointment of an administrator: *Dyke* v. *Walford* (1846), 5 Moo. P.C. 434, 13 E.R. 557. By the *Probate Act*, 1858 (Imp.), c. 95, s. 19, the personal estate and effects of an intestate were vested in the Judge of the Court of Probate for the time being until an administrator was appointed. I suggest that if that section had not been enacted, the termination of the jurisdiction and authority of the Ecclesiastical Courts by statute in 1857 would have left the personal property of an intestate ownerless or vested in an *incerta persona* between the date of the death of an intestate and the appointment of an administrator.

In this Province we have no legislation vesting the personal property of an intestate in anyone during this interval unless the *Descent of Real and Personal Property Act* by implication vests it in the widow or next-of-kin, or both. Now does it? I think not. Descent is different from distribution. The real property under s. 2 descends. The personal property under s. 6 is distributed, and this I should think means distributed by the personal representative. In my opinion there is no vesting of the personal property of an intestate in the widow or next-of-kin or both when an intestate dies and they do not have the right to bring action for recovery of a debt due the deceased. The right to bring that action in the absence of an administrator is in my opinion vested in no one or, which for practical purposes is the same thing, in an *incerta persona*, which we may give any name we like, such as "the estate" or "the administrator".

It may be added that even if there were such a vesting in the widow and next-of-kin, it would clearly be subject to a divesting upon the appointment of an administrator. Whether a vesting subject to a divesting would give the vestees right to bring an action for the recovery of a debt, is a question which I shall not try to answer as it is unnecessary to do so in this case.

Thirdly, it is argued by counsel for the plaintiff that *where there are no creditors* the widow or next-of-kin or both, as the case may be, may bring an action for the recovery of a debt due the deceased. He bases this contention on decisions in several American jurisdictions. Curiously enough the question as to whether the personal property of an intestate is vested in anybody, and if so, in whom, between the death of the intestate and the appointment of an administrator, has been discussed little, if at all, in the United States: Gray, p. 317. But without discussion of the question of vesting, it is said (in effect) in Corpus Juris that in some jurisdictions in the United States there are exceptions to the rule that the title to choses in action and the right to sue thereon are in the administrator so that actions thereon cannot be maintained by the heirs or distributees either at law or in equity, and that one of these exceptions is that the heirs or distributees may sue on a chose in action where there is no administration and where there are no debts of the estate, or they have all been paid and nothing remains but to reduce the assets to possession and distribute them to the heirs or next-of-kin: 18 Corp. Jur., p. 903. However, it is said in 18 Corp. Jur., p. 904 that "also in certain states the courts do not recognize some of the exceptions already mentioned, such as the exceptions which allow the distributees to sue where there are no debts and no administration". I can find no English or Canadian authority for the principle applied in the American jurisdictions first mentioned. The inconvenience of applying such a principle is obvious. How is a debtor when asked by the next-of-kin to pay a debt which he owed the deceased to satisfy himself that there are no creditors? If it be said that this can be determined in the action, must he in all cases, in order to be safe, defend the action at the risk of losing it if it is proved that there are no creditors? I cannot hold that widows and next-of-kin of intestates, even when there are no creditors, have actions for the recovery of debts owing the intestate. I think they have no such actions.

It follows that the chose in action created by the mortgage instrument has never vested in the first assignors of that mortgage, that their assignment of it is invalid for the purposes of this action, and that the second point of law mentioned above must be decided in favour of the defendants.

It was argued on behalf of the defendants not only that the chose in action never vested in the heirs or next-of-kin, but that the legal estate in the mortgaged land never vested in them. A decision of this point is unnecessary and I should like my opinion on it to be so regarded. Still, it was thoroughly argued and counsel may expect some opinion. The argument of counsel for the defendant is that by s. 6 (1) of the *Law and Transfer of Real Property Act*, R.S.N.S. 1923, c. 140, the heirs are deprived of the legal estate in the land. Section 6 (1) is as follows: "Where an estate or interest of inheritance or limited to the heir as special occupant in any lands, is vested on any trust or by way of mortgage in any person solely, the same shall on his death, notwithstanding any testamentary disposition by such person, devolve to and become vested in his personal representatives in like manner as if the same was a chattel real vesting in them; and accordingly all the like power to dispose of and otherwise deal with the same shall belong to the personal representatives of the deceased, with all the like incidents, but subject to the like rights, equities, and obligations as if the same was a chattel real vesting in them; and for the purposes of this section the personal representatives for the time being of the deceased shall be deemed in law his heirs and assigns within the meaning of all trusts and powers."

An almost identical section (s. 30) of the *Conveyancing and Law of Property Act*, 1881 (Imp.), c. 41, has been considered by the English Courts in its application to land vested on trusts. Three cases were cited: *Re Pilling's Trusts* (1884), 26 Ch. D. 432; *Re Rackstraw's* Trusts (1885), 52 L.T. 612; and *Re Williams' Trusts* (1887), 36 Ch. D. 231.

In *Pilling's* case Fry J. had made an order in January, 1883, upon the death intestate of a sole surviving trustee for the appointment of new trustees, and vesting the trust estates in such new trustees. No administration had then been taken out to the intestate's estate, and the order, as drawn up, passed and entered, directed certain lands which formed part of the trust estate to vest in the new trustees "for the estate therein now vested in the heir-at-law of the deceased intestate trustees". After the date of the order administration of the intestate's estate was taken out, and a question had been raised whether the legal estate in the real estate did not thereupon vest in his administratix notwithstanding the vesting order. Upon a motion to correct the order, Pearson J. said the following: "This motion raises a question of great importance on the construction of sect. 30 of the *Conveyancing Act*, 1881, which provides that the legal estate vested in a trustee or mortgagee shall 'on his death' 'devolve to and become vested in his personal representatives or representative from time to time'. The question is, what happens when there is no personal representative? If the legal estate does not vest in the heir, where is it? On the other hand, the wording of the section seems to evince an intention to exclude the heir. As there is now a legal personal representative I will make a new order, on the motion, that, notwithstanding the previous order the land shall vest in the new trustees for all the estate therein now vested in the legal personal representative. I cannot alter the order made by my predecessor so long ago."

Curiously enough this case has been interpreted in two opposite ways. The editors of 14 Hals., 2nd ed., p. 310. note (n) cite it as supporting the proposition that upon the death intestate of a sole surviving trustee the legal estate is vested in the heir in the absence of a personal representative. But Coote on Mortgages, 9th ed., vol. 2, p. 869 cites the same case as supporting the proposition that the effect of the statute seems to have been to exclude the heir from trust and mortgage estates.

Rackstraw's case is of little assistance. Kay J. escaped the necessity of deciding the point under consideration by vesting the property in the new trustees for all the estate and interest which the deceased trustee had in him immediately before his death.

In *Williams'* case, North J. did the same thing as Kay J. did in *Rackstraw's* case. In

Williams' case a trustee had been appointed by a testator but predeceased him. The testator's heiress-at-law, Mary Jenkins, therefore took the land impressed with the trust and was therefore the trustee. She died intestate. North J. expressed no opinion as to whether the legal estate became vested in Mary Jenkins' heir-at-law, and upon the appointment of new trustees, made an order vesting the property in them for all such estate as was vested in Mary Jenkins at the time of her death.

None of these cases is very helpful. There are however expressions of opinion in two other cases as to the effect of s. 1 (1) of the *Land Transfer Act*, 1897 (Imp.), c. 65, which is as follows: "Where real estate is vested in any person without a right in any other person to take by survivorship it shall, on his death, notwithstanding any testamentary disposition, devolve to and become vested in his personal representatives or representative from time to time as if it were a chattel real vesting in them or him."

The two cases are *John* v. *John*, [1898] 2 Ch. 573, and *Re Griggs*, [1914] 2 Ch. 547. These cases are cited in 10 Hals., 2nd ed., p. 575, note (a) as supporting the proposition that "in the case of an intestacy before 1926 the legal estate in real property vested in the heir-at-law". The note goes on to say, "in respect of the real estate of persons dying intestate between January 1, 1898, and December 31, 1925, upon a grant of administration being made, the heir was divested of such legal estate, which thereupon vested in the personal representative as such".

If this statement of the law is correct and can be applied to transmitted estates held on trust or by way of mortgage on the ground that the wording of s. 1 (1) of the *Land Transfer Act*, 1897, is very similar to that of the relevant parts of s. 30 of the *Conveyancing Act*, 1881, and if such an application ought to be made by the Courts of this Province, then the heirs-at-law of A. Claremont Zwicker at the time they made the assignment to W.H.S. Zwicker had the legal estate in the mortgaged lands subject to a divesting of such legal estate if and when an administrator of A. Claremont Zwicker is appointed. This is the very most that can be said in favour of the proposition that the legal estate in the mortgaged lands is vested in the plaintiffs in this action. However, there are differences between s. 30 of the *Conveyancing Act*, 1881, and s. 1(1) of the *Land Transfer Act*, 1897, particularly the concluding provision of the former that for the purposes of the section the personal representatives for the time being of the deceased shall be deemed in law his heirs and assigns within the meaning of all trusts and powers and there is some ground for the view that s. 30 of the *Conveyancing Act*, 1881, and s. 6 (1) of R.S.N.S. 1923, c. 140, evince an intention that the heirs are not to take the legal estate at all. In my opinion, however, and in the absence of any judgment of our Supreme Court in banco on the point, an estate of inheritance vested by way of mortgage in a person who dies intestate does devolve to and become vested in his heirs-at-law in the absence of an administrator, subject to a divesting in favour of the administrator if and when an administrator is appointed. I base this opinion upon the statement above quoted from Salmond that the common law prefers to regard all rights as presently vested in some determinate person, subject, if need be, to be divested on the happening of the event on which the title of the contingent owner depends, upon the *Descent of Real and Personal Property Act*, providing as it does for the descent of real property held in fee simple to the persons therein mentioned, and upon the expressions of judicial opinion in the English cases above cited in which the *Land Transfer Act* (1897) was interpreted. The situations in which the point has any importance must be rare indeed although it conceivably might have some practical importance if the heirs-at-law of an intestate mortgagee undertook to take possession under the mortgage, instead of suing for payment and, in default thereof, foreclosure and sale.

As indicated above, I have left undecided the question as to whether the assignment from the heirs-at-law to W.H.S. Zwicker was sufficient to convey the legal estate in the mortgaged lands, but as in my view the plaintiff cannot effect a foreclosure of this mortgage without procuring the appointment of an administrator, the decision of this question is really unnecessary. Once an administrator is appointed, that administrator will be vested not only with the chose in action for the mortgage debt but with the legal estate in the mortgaged lands. The assignment from the heirs-at-law to W.H.S. Zwicker is sufficient to transfer the beneficial interests of the assignors in the amount of the mortgage debt subject, of course, to any claims of creditors. If there are no creditors, foreclosure by an administrator would therefore result in the plaintiffs ultimately obtaining the full amount of the mortgage debt. It would appear that the Court of Probate would have jurisdiction under s. 21 of the *Probate Act*, R.S.N.S. 1923, c. 217, to appoint a nominee of the plaintiffs as administrator.

(b) Running of Covenants: In General

3 HOLDSWORTH, HISTORY OF ENGLISH LAW (1923, 3rd ed.), 158

As a general rule a covenant binds only the parties to it or their representatives. But the mediaeval land law recognized certain covenants which had a wider operation. They were regarded as being in a sense annexed to an estate in the land, so that they could be enforced by any one who took that estate in the land. In this respect they have some analogy to easements. They differ from easements in that they can be enforced only by the person who has the same estate as the original covenantee. "If," says Coke, (Co. Ltt. 385b) "a man hath a warranty to him, his heirs and assigns and he make a lease for life or a gift in tail, the lessee or donee shall not vouch as assignee, because he hath not the estate in fee simple whereunto the warranty was annexed." In the case put above it would only be the person who took A's actual estate who could enforce such a covenant made with him. Neither his tenants nor his lord who took by escheat could enforce it. At law, therefore, covenants do not run with the land: they run with the estate in the land to which they are annexed. The conception of covenants running with the land is a later conception due to equity; and, because these covenants running with the land in equity really run with the land, and not merely with an estate in it, they have many more of the characteristics of true easements than the covenants which run at law with an estate in the land.

For the origin of these covenants thus annexed to an estate in land we must look at the old obligation of warranty. A warranty might be implied; but, as we have seen, from a very early date express warranties were entered into with a view of securing greater freedom of alienation. These warranties, if contained in a deed, could operate as covenants; and, though they operated as covenants, they, together with other covenants relating to the land, were still regarded as annexed to the estate in the land. During the course of the sixteenth and seventeenth centuries these old warranties impled or express gave way to the modern covenants for title. The old warranties having disappeared, the law was concerned only with covenants annexed to the estate in the land; and so the modern law as to these covenants is gradually built up....

The combined effect of the Statute de Bigamis and the Statute Quia Emptores made these express warranties essential on a conveyance in fee simple. The former statute enacted that if a gift were made to be held of the lord of the fee, or of persons other than the feoffor, and no express clause of warranty was inserted, only the feoffor and not his heirs were impliedly bound to warrant. But the result of the Statute Quia Emptores was that all land given in fee simple was held, not of the feoffor, but of his lord. Therefore express covenants of warranty became necessary to secure the estate of the feoffee. Hence these express covenants of warranty became almost universal. Therefore the question, how far their benefit or burden could be made to run with the estate in the land, was a question of the greatest practical importance.

(i) *Benefit*

These covenants could be used either as a warranty, i.e. the person entitled to the benefit of the warranty could by the process of voucher or by writ of *Warrantia Cartae* get lands of equal value; or they could be used as a covenant on which an action for damages could be brought. In either case they were annexed to the estate in the land, and could be enforced by persons other than the original feoffee with whom they were made. Thus if A enfeoffed B and his heirs of land, and covenanted to warrant their title, either B or his heirs could call upon either A or his heirs to fulfil this obligation. Moreover, if A's covenant were to B and his heirs and assigns, not only B but any person who became entitled to the estate in the land as B's assign was able to sue if B's heirs failed. Later the assign could sue the original grantor whether or no the heirs of the grantor had failed. Possibly this was the result of the Statute Quia Emptores. As we have seen, that statute made the mention of assigns as well as heirs unnecessary when a grant in fee simple was made, because the statute allowed assignment, and put the alienee into the place of the alienor. It was only natural therefore to give the assign a right of recourse directly against the original grantor. The explanation which Bracton gives of this fact is that the assign comes in because he is named as a quasi-heir. He explains it by the analogy of succession; and it was probably because this analogy was used that assigns must be named if they were to be able to make use of the covenant as a warranty which would enable them to recover lands of equal value, and not merely as a covenant which would only enable them to recover damages. But a right of this kind which was in a manner attached to an estate in land looked rather like an easement; and it could equally well be explained on this analogy. Hence it came to be said that such a covenant ran with the estate in the land, on the analogy of an easement; and, if we adopt this analogy, there will be no need to mention assigns, because the land will pass to the assignee with its appurtenances whether or no they are named in the grant. Hence, whether or no assigns are named, they can sue on such a covenant annexed to the land and recover damages. This mode of regarding the matter comes out clearly in the much discussed case of *Pakenham*, Y.B. 42 Ed. III, Hil. pl. 14. Pakenham sued a prior for breach of the prior's covenant made with Pakenham's great-grandfather that the prior and convent should celebrate divine service weekly in his chapel. The plaintiff claimed not as heir but as assignee; and it was held that he was entitled to recover—"he is tenant of the land, and it is a thing which is annexed to the chapel, which is in the manor, and so annexed to the manor". Similarly it was held in 1582 that where A had enfeoffed B in return for certain services, and granted that if the feoffee his heirs or assigns were distrained for greater services, he (the feoffee) his heirs or assigns could levy a distress in A's manor, the assign of B could take advantage of the covenant.

It is clear from *Pakenham's Case* that the covenantor need not necessarily be connected with the land. In that case the prior was a stranger; and this was one of the cases cited by Coke to illustrate his remark that "a covenant is in many cases extended further than a warranty". But as early as 1401 it was recognized that the assign must, to enable him to sue, have the land to which the covenant was annexed. An assign cannot, like an heir, rely on the privity of contract; he can only rely on privity of estate. Hence we get the modern rule that the benefit of covenants made with the purchaser of land will, if they relate to the land, run with that purchaser's estate in the land, that is they can be enforced by successive tenants of that estate. It was partly this settlement of modern rule as to the conditions under which the benefit of covenants will run with the estate in the land, and partly the inconvenience of the procedure available to enforce a warranty, which has led to the substitution of the modern covenants for title for the old warranties express or implied. In the course of the sixteenth and seventeenth centuries covenants for seisin, for the right to convey, for quiet enjoyment, for freedom from incumbrances, and for further assurance, became usual covenants on a conveyance of land. They are at the present day by far the commonest class of covenants, the benefit of which runs with the estate in the land.

(ii) *Burden*

Whether or not the burden of a covenant made by a purchaser of land could be annexed to it so as to run with the land was long an unsettled question. Bracton seems to think that land might be so bound to warranty that the burden of warranty would pass to the assignee of the land. This would imply that a man might by a covenant bind his land and subject it to something very like an easement. Probably such covenants were rare. The more usual case would be where land was charged with rent, which, as we have seen, was regarded as an independent incorporeal hereditament, or with other services, which were similarly regarded. Any covenants which fettered the freedom of alienation would probably have been held to be void as inconsistent with the nature of the estate granted. In fact the power to burden the land by such covenants seems to be negatived by the dictum laid down in a Year Book of Edward I.'s reign to the effect that "No one can bind his assigns to warranty, because the burden of warranty always extends only to heirs who claim by succession, and not to those who claim by assignment." And it should be noted that, if a feoffee vouched his feoffor to warranty, or sued him by a writ of Warrantia Cartae he could only get such lands as the feoffor had at the date of the purchase of the writ. There is nothing in Coke's commentary which gives colour to the view that the burden of such covenants could be annexed to the land, though he has much to say of the manner in which these benefits might be so annexed. Holt, C. J., was clearly of the opinion that the burden could not be annexed to the land, for he decided that, though land might be charged with a rent, it could not be bound by a covenant.

This conclusion is clearly in accordance with the principles of our modern land law. To allow the burden of a covenant to be attached to the land would be tantamount to allowing landowners to subject it to something very like an easement; and it is well settled that it is not possible for landowners to create new easements at their will and pleasure. Moreover, such a covenant would obviously tend to restrict free alienation, and so would infringe the policy of the modern rule against perpetuities.

7 HOLDSWORTH, HISTORY OF ENGLISH LAW (1926, 1st ed.), 287

With respect to the benefit of covenants relating to the land, the law in the case of landlord and tenant started from somewhat the same general principles as in the case of similar covenants between the vendor and purchaser of an estate in fee simple. We have seen that on a lease for life, when rent was reserved, the warranty implied from the use of the word "dedi," enabled the assignee of the lessee to sue; and there can be little doubt that express or implied covenants relating to the land, entered into between landlord and tenant, could be enforced by the assignee of the tenant. There seems no reason why such an assignee should not sue in covenant, just as the assignee in *Pakenham's Case* sued, and it is clear that Coke considered that the principles there laid down were applicable as between landlord and tenant. But with respect to the burden of covenants relating to the land, the law as to covenants as between landlord and tenant departed from the law as to covenants between vendor and purchaser of an estate in fee simple. In the case of rent the law seems to have allowed that a lessor could bring debt against an assignee of the lessee. Whether or not the burden of other covenants would run with the land, and whether or not the assignee of the land could be sued by writ of covenant, seem to have been matters upon which there is little or no mediaeval authority.

The question whether or not the benefit or burden of a covenant could run with the reversion, was one upon which the rules relating to covenants on the sale and purchase of an estate in fee simple could shed no light; for on such a sale there was no reversion. It would seem, however, that the benefit of the obligation to pay rent, and the benefit of implied conditions, the breach of which gave the lessor the right to enter, were regarded as attached to the land itself, and not merely to the estate in land; so that, not only the assignee of the lessor, but also the lord who took by escheat, could enforce them—these obligations were in fact very completely assimilated to easements. On the other hand, the burden of a warranty implied by law, and, according to a case of 1346, the burden of an express warranty, would, if rent were reserved, bind the assignee of the lessor. Whether a covenant for title in a lease for years, implied by the word demise or equivalent words, would have the same effect must be regarded as a doubtful question; and whether the benefit or burden of any other covenants would run with the reversion is equally doubtful. The preamble to the statute of 1540 (32 H.8, c.34) would seem to negative the idea that the benefit or burden of any covenant would run with the reversion, so as to entitle the assignee to sue by writ of covenant. But it is clear that some of the statements in the preamble are too wide, as they would negative the possibility of any covenant running, not only with the reversion, but also with the land; and, as we have seen from the preamble to the statute of Uses, we cannot place very much reliance on the preambles to the Tudor statutes. Authority is scanty and conflicting; and there are two good reasons why this is so. In the first place, it would seem from Coke's report of *Spencer's Case* that there was very little mediaeval authority on this matter—if he had known of more it is quite clear that he would have cited more. In the second place, the new rules introduced by the statute of 1540, and the decision in *Spencer's Case*, really made a new starting point in this branch of the law, behind which it was rarely necessary to go.

The occasion for the passing of the statute of 1540 was the large transfer of reversionary interests, which followed on the dissolution of the monasteries, and on the gift of these reversions by the King to various favoured persons. It enacted that the grantees of the reversions of lands formerly belonging to the religious houses, and all other grantees of other reversions, should have the same rights against the lessees and their assigns by entry or action for non-payment of rent, or waste, or non-performance of other conditions or covenants, as the original lessors had; and, conversely, that lessees and their assigns should have "like action advantage and remedy" against the assignees of the reversion and their assigns, as they had against their original lessors—except only that they could not take advantage of "any warranty in deed or in law by voucher or otherwise".

This statute applied only to reversions on leases for life or years, and not to gifts in fee or in tail. It is clear that it made a wholly new departure in this part of the law of landlord and tenant. In the first place, it gave to assignees of the reversion a right to enforce, and put these assignees under a duty to fulfil, covenants in leases. In the second place, it gave to assignees of the land the right to enforce, and put them under a duty to fulfil these covenants. The existing duties as to warranties, express or implied, were excepted from the Act; and this is perhaps an additional proof that these duties were becoming obsolete, and were giving place to the duties based on express covenants contained in leases. But the provisions of the Act were very wide. It contained no sort of definition as to the kind of covenants which were to run with the land or the reversion. This and other matters were left for the courts to elucidate, in the light of the scanty authority which they possessed. As we shall now see, in the light of the guidance given by the Act and of the existing principles of the law, and in the light of the new situation created by the Act, they performed their task of interpretation with considerable skill.

[The statute (1540) 32 H.8, c.34 (Grantees of Reversions Act) is in force in Ontario as ss. 3 and 6 of the Landlord and Tenant Act, R.S.O. 1960, c. 206; and see also ss. 4, 5, 7 and

8. For similar legislation, see Landlord and Tenant Act, R.S.M. 1954, c. 136, ss. 3 and 6; Landlord and Tenant Act, R.S.N.B. 1952, c. 126, s. 2; Landlord and Tenant Act, R.S.P.E.I. 1951, c. 82, s. 2; Landlord and Tenant Act, R.S.S. 1953, c. 312, ss. 3 and 5.

In *Rogers* v. *National Drug and Chemical Co.* (1911), 23 O.L.R. 234, Riddell J. said (at p. 236):

"At the 'common law, covenants ran with the land, but not with the reversion. Therefore the assignee of the lessee was held to be liable in covenant and to be entitled to bring covenant, but the assignee of the lessor was not:' 1 Wms. Saund. 240 (a), note; and see also per Lefroy, C. J., in *Butler* v. *Archer* (1860), 12 Ir. C.L.R. 104, at p. 127.

"The statute 32 Hen. VIII, ch. 34 does not apply to leases not under seal: *Bickford* v. *Parson* (1848), 5 C.B. 920, and the many other cases cited in 1 Sm. L.C. 59, 60. Nor does the principle of *Cornish* v. *Stubbs* (1870), L.R. 5 C.P. 334, based upon *Buckworth* v. *Simpson* (1835), 1 C.M. & R. 834, apply. While the plaintiff accepted the rent, he never had an opportunity or the right to give notice to quit; and, therefore, it could not be said, in the words of Willes, J. (L.R. 5 C.P. at p. 339), 'a conventional law is thus made equivalent to that of Henry VIII, in the case of leases under seal'—there is nothing from which it can be inferred that the plaintiff considered himself bound by the option for a term beyond that provided for in the document itself.

"Neither are there any letters or negotiations indicating anything in the way of waiver, such as are relied upon by Farwell, J., in *Manchester Brewery Co.* v. *Coombs*, [1901] 2 Ch. 608, at p. 615. . . .

"[However, the doctrine of *Walsh* v. *Lonsdale* (1882), 21 Ch. D. 9, 52 L.J. Ch. 2 is applicable, and the] defendants, then, being before a Court with equitable jurisdiction, must, I think, be considered as though the lease had actually been made—in which case the statute of Henry VIII, would apply: *Manchester Brewery Co.* v. *Coombs*, [1901] 2 Ch. 608."

The judgment of Riddell J. was affirmed on appeal: (1911), 24 O.L.R. 486, reproduced *supra*, at p. 185; and see also *Boyer* v. *Warbey*, referred to *supra*, at p. 186.]

SPENCER'S CASE. King's Bench. 1583. 5 Co. 16a, 77 E.R. 72

Spencer and his wife brought an action of covenant against Clark, assignee to J. assignee to S. and the case was such: Spencer and his wife by deed indented demised a house and certain land (in the right of the wife) to S. for term of 21 years, by which indenture S. covenanted for him, his executors, and administrators, with the plaintiffs, that he, his executors, administrators, or assigns, would build a brick wall upon part of the land demised, &c. S. assigned over his term to J. and J. to the defendant; and for not making of the brick wall the plaintiffs brought the action of covenant against the defendant as assignee: and after many arguments at the Bar, the case was excellently argued and debated by the Justices at the Bench: and in this case these points were unanimously resolved by Sir Christopher Wray, Chief Justice, Sir Thomas Gawdy, and the whole Court. And many differences taken and agreed concerning express covenants, and covenants in law, and which of them run with the land, and which of them are collateral, and do not go with the land, and where the assignee shall be bound without naming him, and where not; and where he shall not be bound although he be expressly named, and where not.

1. When the covenant extends to a thing *in esse*, parcel of the demise, the thing to be done by force of the covenant is *quodammodo* annexed and appurtenant to the thing demised, and shall go with the land, and shall bind the assignee although he be not bound by express words: but when the covenant extends to a thing which is not in being at the time of the demise made, it cannot be appurtenant or annexed to the thing which hath no being: as if the lessee cove-

nants to repair the houses demised to him during the term, that is parcel of the contract, and extends to the support of the thing demised, and therefore is *quodammodo* annexed appurtenant to houses, and shall bind the assignee although he be not bound expressly by the covenant: but in the case at Bar, the covenant concerns a thing which was not *in esse* at the time of the demise made, but to be newly built after, and therefore shall bind the covenantor, his executors, or administrators, and not the assignee, for the law will not annex the covenant to a thing which hath no being.

2. It was resolved that in this case, if the lessee had covenanted for him and his assigns, that they would make a new wall upon some part of the thing demised, that for as much as it is to be done upon the land demised, that it should bind the assignee; for although the covenant doth extend to a thing to be newly made, yet it is to be made upon the thing demised, and the assignee is to take the benefit of it, and therefore shall bind the assignee by express words. So on the other side, if a warranty be made to one, his heirs and assigns, by express words, the assignee shall take benefit of it, and shall have a *warrantia chartae*, F.N.B. 135. & 9 E. 2. Garr' de Charters 30. 36 E. 3. Garr. 1. 4 H. 8. Dyer 1. But although the covenant be for him and his assigns, yet if the thing to be done be merely collateral to the land, and doth not touch or concern the thing demised in any sort, there the assignee shall not be charged. As if the lessee covenants for him and his assigns to build a house upon the land of the lessor which is no parcel of the demise, or to pay any collateral sum to the lessor, or to a stranger, it shall not bind the assignee, because it is merely collateral, and in no manner touches or concerns the thing that was demised, or that is assigned over; and therefore in such case the assignee of the thing demised cannot be charged with it, no more than any other stranger.

3. It was resolved, if a man leases sheep or other stock of cattle, or any other personal goods for any time, and the lessee covenants for him and his assigns at the end of the time to deliver the like cattle or goods as good as the things letten were, or such price for them; and the lessee assigns the sheep over, this covenant shall not bind the assignee, for it is but a personal contract, and wants such privity as is between the lessor and lessee and his assigns of the land in respect of the reversion. But in the case of a lease of personal goods there is not any privity, nor any reversion, but merely a thing in action in the personalty, which cannot bind any but the covenantor, his executors, or administrators, who represent him. The same law, if a man demises a house and land for years, with a stock or sum of money rendering rent, and the lessee covenants for him, his executors, administrators, and assigns, to deliver the stock or sum of money at the end of the term, yet the assignee shall not be charged with this covenant: for although the rent reserved was increased in respect of the stock or sum, yet the rent did not issue out of the stock or sum, but out of the land only; and therefore as to the stock or sum the covenant is personal, and shall bind the covenantor, his executors and administrators, and not his assignee: and it is not certain that the stock or sum will come to the assignee's hands, for it may be wasted, or otherwise consumed or destroyed by the lessee, and therefore the law cannot determine at the time of the lease made, that such covenant shall bind the assignee....

6. If lessee for years covenants to repair the houses during the term, it shall bind all others as a thing which is appurtenant, and goeth with the land in whose hands soever the term shall come, as well those who come to it by act in law, as by the act of the party, for all is one having regard to the lessor. And if the law should not be such, great prejudice might accrue to him; and reason requires, that they, who shall take benefit of such covenant when the lessor makes it with the lessee, should on the other side be bound by the like covenants when the lessee makes it with the lessor....

See the statute of 32 H. 8. c. 24. 34. which Act was resolved to extend to covenants which touch or concern the thing demised and not to collateral covenants.

NOTE ON PRIVITY OF ESTATE. In *Webb* v. *Russell* (1789), 3 T.R. 393, at p. 402, 100 E.R. 639, at p. 644 (K.B.), Lord Kenyon stated that "it is not sufficient that a covenant is concerning the land, but in order to make it run with the land, there must be a privity of estate between the covenanting parties". This dictum, referable to the running of covenants at law, became established in the English and Canadian cases so as to require a relationship of tenure between covenantor and covenantee before the burden of a covenant (which was one "touching and concerning" the land) would run against the covenantor's assignee. This view of privity of estate restricted the running of the burden at law substantially to landlord and tenant cases: tenure would be present as between assignees of the landlord and of the tenant. The resulting inhibition of the running of the burden at law as between holders in fee simple was partly alleviated by equity in respect of restrictive covenants only.

The tenurial view of privity of estate has been criticized by writers in the United States, and, indeed, the august authority of the late Mr. Justice Holmes is opposed to it. In *The Common Law* (1881), he referred to this matter as follows (at p. 404):

"According to the general opinion there must be a privity of estate between the covenantor and covenantee in the latter class of cases [i.e. of covenants running with the land] in order to bind the assigns of the covenantor. Some have supposed this privity to be tenure; some, an interest of the covenantee in the land of the covenantor; and so on. The first notion is false, the second misleading, and the proposition to which they are applied is unfounded. Privity of estate, as used in connection with covenants at common law, does not mean tenure or easement; it means succession to a title. It is never necessary between covenantor and covenantee, or any other persons, except between the present owner and the original covenantee. And on principle it is only necessary between them in those cases—such as warranties, and probably covenants for title—where, the covenants being regarded wholly from the side of contract, the benefit goes by way of succession, and not with the land."

The reference, in the passage just quoted, to "easement" is to the so-called Massachusetts rule under which an easement relationship between holders in fee is regarded as satisfying the requirement of privity to enable "real" covenants to run.

The severest criticism of the received notion of privity of estate will be found in *Clark*, Covenants and Interests Running with Land (1947 2d ed.), pp. 116 ff. and Appendices I and III. It is his view that the burden ran at law in early English cases and that "privity in the sense of succession to the estate of a party to the covenants is the only privity which should be required in the case of real covenants [and] that this requirement should not be applied technically so as to require succession to the identical estate of the assignor, but merely to his general legal position as regards the specified land; that where such privity exists and either benefit or burden is intended to run and 'touches or concerns the land' it should be held to pass freely with the land, either alone or together with its accompanying burden or benefit where that too satisfies the necessary legal requisites; and that failure of one end of a covenant to run should not prevent the other end from running to assignees where otherwise it may properly be so transferred" (at pp. 136-7). For a further critical appraisal based on historical inquiry, see *Sims*, The Law of Real Covenants: Exceptions to the Restatement of the Subject by the American Law Institute, (1944) 30 Cornell L.Q. 1, especially at p. 16 where he sums up the English law.

The Restatement of Property has accepted privity of estate (in its succession or easement senses) as necessary to enable the burden of real covenants to run at law as between holders in fee but not necessary to enable the running of the benefit: see vol. 5, ss. 534, 548. For a survey of the existing American law as between holders in fee, see 2 *American Law of Property*, ss. 9.8 ff.

AUSTERBERRY v. OLDHAM. Court of Appeal. 1885. 27 Ch. D. 750

Appeal from dismissal of a declaratory action involving the question whether defendant corporation was subject to the burden of a covenant, entered into by its predecessor in title with plaintiff's predecessor in title, to keep in repair a road which defendant's predecessor had constructed after a conveyance to him of land as a site for the road. The conveyance contained a covenant by the grantee, his heirs and assigns to construct the road and keep it in repair. The land so granted was bounded on both sides by other lands belonging to the grantor, and the road gave access to such lands.

COTTON L. J.: ... In my opinion, if this is not a covenant running at law, there can be no relief in respect of it in equity; it is not a restrictive covenant; it is not a covenant restraining the corporation or the trustees from using the land in any particular way, at least so far as this case is concerned. If either the trustees or the corporation were intending to divert this land from the purpose for which it was conveyed, that is, from its being used as a road or street, that would be a very different question; then one would have to consider this—how far, having regard to the Act of 1880, the equitable right would travel; because, undoubtedly, where there is a restrictive covenant, the burden and benefit of which do not run at law, Courts of Equity restrain anyone who takes the property with notice of that covenant from using it in a way inconsistent with the covenant. But here the covenant which is attempted to be insisted upon on this appeal is a covenant to lay out money in doing certain work upon this land; and, that being so, in my opinion—and the Court of Appeal has already expressed a similar opinion in a case which was before it—that is not a covenant which a Court of Equity will enforce: it will not enforce a covenant not running at law when it is sought to enforce that covenant in such a way as to require the successors in title of the covenantor, to spend money, and in that way to undertake a burden upon themselves. The covenantor must not use the property for a purpose inconsistent with the use for which it was originally granted: but in my opinion a Court of Equity does not and ought not to enforce a covenant binding only in equity in such a way as to require the successors of the covenantor himself, they having entered into no covenant, to expend sums of money in accordance with what the original covenantor bound himself to do. The case principally relied upon by the Appellant was one before Vice-Chancellor *Malins*. That was the case of *Cooke* v. *Chilcott* 3 Ch. D. 694. Now undoubtedly the Vice-Chancellor did decide that case on the equitable doctrine, and said that he would enforce the covenant; but that is an authority which in my opinion was not right on that point. In the subsequent case of *Haywood* v. *Brunswick Permanent Benefit Building Society*, 8 Q.B.D. 403,—both Lord Justice Lindley and myself were members of the Court which decided that case—we expressed our opinion against *Cooke* v. *Chilcott* being a correct development of the doctrine established by *Tulk* v. *Moxhay*, 2 Ph. 774, or for which *Tulk* v. *Moxhay* was an authority.

Then there was another case, before the late Lord Romilly, of *Morland* v. *Cook* L.R. 6 Eq. 252, which was relied upon; but that was really a case not turning upon that doctrine, because it was this: There was a deed of partition of land all of which was below the sea level and was protected by a river or sea wall, and a covenant was entered into by the different parties to pay their proportion of the expense of repairing the sea wall, whoever should do it; and that covenant was enforced for and against the successors of those who were parties to the deed. But in that case it appeared that there was, according to the view of the Master of the Rolls, a common law liability, independently of that covenant, to repair the sea wall, so that it would be very different from the case of creating a new liability: the covenant there was framed in such a way as to create a grant by the different persons who took, on partition, portions of the property, of a rent-charge out of their lands in order to provide for the expense. The covenant was in this form. The parties covenanted for themselves, &c., "severally and respectively, in manner following, that is to say, that the charges, damages, and expenses of or attending the keeping and maintaining the walls and gutts of or belonging to the said lands, fresh marsh lands, hereditaments and premises hereby granted and released, or intended so to be, in good order and repair, shall be borne and paid by them (naming them), their respective heirs and assigns, out of the said lands and hereditaments hereby divided in proportion, and by an acre-scot to be from time to time for that purpose made thereon and payable thereout in the same proportions in ready money." So, although in terms it was a covenant, it was a covenant by these parties that the expense should be paid out of their proportions of the land by an acre-scot payable thereout in the same proportions in ready money. That is, therefore, really a grant by each of the parties of a rent-charge of so much money as would be equivalent to his proportion of the total expense of repairing the sea wall....

Then, is there here a covenant enforceable at law? For this there are two things to be considered—the burden of the covenant, and the benefit of the covenant; and unless the Plaintiff can shew, he being as assign of the original covenantee, that he is entitled to the benefit of the covenant, and unless he can also shew that the corporation, being assigns of the original covenantor, are subject to the burden of the covenant, he cannot establish in this Court any covenant which can be enforced at law. If the Plaintiff fails in either of these two points, he fails on this part of the case. As I think my learned brethren will consider more particularly the question whether this burden runs with the land, I do not propose to enter into this part of the case. If I had to do so, I ought to give my opinion upon the debated point whether the burden of a covenant can properly run with the land; and for that purpose I should like, before giving any opinion on the subject, to consider the authorities which are supposed to lay down the proposition that it can; but I in no way say that the burden of a covenant can be so annexed to the land as to run properly with the land. But does the benefit of the covenant in the present case run with the land? In order that the benefit may run with the land, the covenant must be one which relates to or touches and concerns the land of the covenantee. Here, undoubtedly, what was to be done was not to be done on the land of the covenantee at all, but simply on the land of the purchasers from him—these trustees; and when we look at the particular form of covenant entered into with him it is clear that it was not pointedly with reference to his land that this covenant was entered into—it was a covenant that this strip of land should be kept as a road for the use of the public....

Then as to the other case of *Morland* v. *Cook*, I have explained what the case really is, and although Lord Romilly did decide that the covenant would run with the land, I do not think, having regard to the explanation which I have given, one need consider that an authority which ought to trouble one either as regards the benefit to or burden of the covenant; but, as regards benefit, a covenant for the keeping up of a sea wall which would prevent the land in question owned by the plaintiff from being flooded was undoubtedly a covenant with reference to the benefit to be enjoyed by the land by the keeping of the sea out.

Then *Western* v. *Macdermott* L.R. 1 Eq. 499; 2 Ch. 72 was another decision of Lord Romilly, and he did express his opinion that there the covenant ran with the land; but there the covenant was one which was much more pointedly and directly for the benefit of the land of the plaintiff, or the predecessor in title of the plaintiff, because it was a covenant not to build on adjoining land, the evidence being that it was not for the benefit of mere members of the public other than the owner of the adjoining land, but to prevent the adjoining land being made less commodious by the erection of buildings on the land of the covenantor.

Then there is the case of *Cooke* v. *Chilcott* 3 Ch. D. 694, which was before Malins, V.C. where he likewise expressed an opinion that the covenant ran with the land. He did not base his opinion on the cases I have mentioned, but the case was one in which there was very little, if any, difficulty as regards the benefit of the covenant touching and relating to land of the plaintiff, because it was to erect a pump and pump water from the land of the defendant's predecessor in title to the land of the plaintiff's predecessor in title, and there was reference to the benefit of the land, which shewed that that was the object of the covenant. As to whether it was right to express any opinion as to the burden running with the land I say nothing; but there is no authority which can in any way interfere, when fairly regarded, with the opinion which I express, that the covenant in the present case was neither in terms nor in its obvious sense such as to be a covenant relating to, or touching and concerning, the land of the Plaintiff's predecessor in title. So, in my opinion, this point that there is a covenant on which the Plaintiff can sue the corporation at law is one which cannot be maintained, and, so far as this case depends on that, in my opinion the appeal fails.

LINDLEY L. J.: ... The first question which I will consider is whether that covenant runs with the land, as it is called—whether the benefit of it runs with the land held by the Plaintiff, and whether the burden of it runs with the land held by the Defendants; because, if the covenant does run at law, then the Plaintiff, so far as I can see, would be right as to this portion of his claim. Now, as regards the benefit running with the Plaintiff's land, the covenant is, so far as the road goes, a covenant to repair the road; what I mean by that is, there is nothing in the deed which points particularly to that portion of the road which abuts upon or fronts the Plaintiff's land—it is a covenant to repair the whole of the road, no distinction being made between the portion of that road which joins or abuts upon his land and the rest of the road; in other words, it is a covenant simply to make and maintain this road as a public highway; there is no covenant to do anything whatever on the Plaintiff's land, and there is nothing pointing to the Plaintiff's land in particular. Now it appears to me to be going a long way to say that the benefit of that covenant runs with the Plaintiff's land. I do not overlook the fact that the Plaintiff as a frontager has certain rights of getting on to the road; and if this covenant had been so worded as to shew that there had been an intention to grant him some particular benefit in respect of that particular part of his land, possibly we might have said that the benefit of the covenant did run with this land; but when you look at the covenant it is a mere covenant with him, as with all adjoining owners, to make this road, a small portion of which only abuts on his land, and there is nothing specially relating to his land at all. I cannot see myself how any benefit of this covenant runs with his land.

But it strikes me, I confess, that there is a still more formidable objection as regards the burden. Does the burden of this covenant run with the land so as to bind the Defendants? The Defendants have acquired the road under the trustees, and they are bound by such covenant as runs with the land. Now we come to face the difficulty; does a covenant to repair all this road run with the land—that is, does the burden of it descend upon those to whom the road may be assigned in future? We are not dealing here with a case of landlord and tenant. The authorities which refer to that class of cases have little, if any, bearing upon the case which we have to consider, and I am not prepared to say that any covenant which imposes a burden upon the land does run with the land, unless the covenant does, upon the true construction of the deed containing the covenant, amount to either a grant of an easement, or a rent-charge, or some estate or interest in the land. A mere covenant to repair, or to do something of that kind, does not seem to me, I confess, to run with the land in such a way as to bind those who may acquire it.

It is remarkable that the authorities upon this point, when they are examined, are very few, and it is also remarkable that in no case that I know of, except one which I shall refer to presently, is there anything like authority to say that a burden of this kind will run with the land. That point has often been discussed, and I rather think the conclusion at which the editors of the last edition of *Smith's* Leading Cases have come to is right, that no case has been decided which does establish that such a burden can run with the land in the sense in which I am now using that expression. The case of *Holmes* v. *Buckley* 1 Eq. C. Ab. 27, looks a little like it at first; but the observation to be made on that case I think is this: In the first place it is quite plain that there the plaintiff had a cause of action; he was entitled to an injunction of some sort to restrain the defendants from interrupting his watercourse. The right of the plaintiff to enforce specifically the covenant to repair, or rather to cleanse the watercourse, is obscure, and we have not got the decree which was pronounced; and I confess that having only that short note of it which is to be found in 'Equity Cases Abridged', I fail to understand the exact grounds of that decision, specifically enforcing that covenant to cleanse. I doubt whether it was a decision to that effect; but the case is too loosely reported to be a guide on the point.

Morland v. *Cook*, another case in which it was said that the covenant ran with the land, is intelligible on this ground—that there was there that which amounted to the creation of a rent-charge for the repair of the sea wall which was in question. That is intelligible enough, and if the covenant in the present case amounted to anything of the kind, of course the observations I am now making would not be applicable.

The case before Vice-Chancellor *Malins* of *Cooke* v. *Chilcott* has been so shaken that I cannot rely upon it as an authority at all. I think the Vice-Chancellor did intimate an opinion that the covenant there would run with the land. I confess I doubt the correctness of that opinion. He decided the case upon another point, and upon that other point only has it been followed. There is no other authority that I am aware of that such a covenant as this runs with the land, unless it is *Western* v. *Macdermott*, where the Court of Appeal did not sanction the notion that the covenant in that case ran with the land, although the covenant was a purely restrictive covenant. I am not aware of any other case which either shews, or appears to shew, that a burden such as this can be annexed to land by a mere covenant, such as we have got here; and in the absence of authority it appears to me that we shall be perfectly warranted in saying that the burden of this covenant does not run with the land. After all it is a mere personal covenant. If the parties had intended to charge this land for ever, into whosesoever hands it came, with the burden of repairing the road, there are ways and means known to conveyancers by which it could be done with comparative ease; all that would have been necessary would have been to create a rent-charge and charge it on the tolls, and the thing would have been done. They have not done anything of the sort, and, therefore, it seems to me to shew that they did not intend to have a covenant which should run with the land. That disposes of the part of the case which is perhaps the most difficult.

The last point was this—that even if it did not run with the land at law, still, upon the authority of *Tulk* v. *Moxhay*, the Defendants, having bought the land with notice of this covenant, take the land subject to it. Mr. Collins very properly did not press that upon us, because after the two recent decisions in the Court of Appeal in *Haywood* v. *Brunswick Permanent Benefit Building Society* and *London and South Western Railway Company* v. *Gomm* 20 Ch. D. 562, that argument is untenable. *Tulk* v. *Moxhay* cannot be extended to covenants of this description.

FRY L. J.: ... In the first place, did the benefit of this covenant run with the land—the land of Mr. Elliott? Upon that point my opinion is perhaps not quite as confident as that of my learned brothers. I am rather more inclined to think that the road connecting the land with the public highway was so far an incident to the use and occupation of the remainder of Mr. Elliott's land that it might be conceivable that it came within the principles of covenants relating to things incident to the land; but, at the same time, I do not desire to express any difference of opinion upon that. But upon the point whether the burden of the covenant ran with the land of the covenantors, I am clearly of opinion that it did not so run; and I share the doubt which has been expressed by my learned brothers whether in any case, except that of landlord and tenant, the burden of covenants of this description does ever run with the land.

There is one authority which appears to me very closely parallel to the present case. I think the most favourable way of stating the case for the Appellant is to hold that there was the grant by the covenantors to Mr. Elliott of a right of way over the land of the covenantors, with a covenant by the covenantors that they would maintain the land subject to the right of way in repair as a road. Now, putting the case in that manner, it is extremely like the circumstances which occurred in the case of *Brewster* v. *Kidgill*, which is best reported in 12 Modern Reports, 166. That was a case which came before Lord *Holt* and the King's Bench, and was evidently very elaborately argued. There was one *Brewster*, who was seised in fee of a manor, in consideration of £800 granted a rent-charge in fee of £40 per annum, and on the back of the deed was indorsed a memorandum declaring it to be the true intent and meaning of that deed, "that the grantee and her heirs shall for ever hereafter be paid the said rent-charge without any deduction or abatement of taxes, charge or payment out of, for or concerning the said rent, or the said manor or lands charged herewith". The question then arose whether the memorandum was really part of the grant of the rent-charge, or a covenant collateral to the grant. Lord *Holt* conceived it to be a collateral covenant; the other Judges of the King's Bench thought that it was part of the grant. They all agreed in the view that if it was a part of the grant it ran with the land; but that if it was a covenant to pay it did not run with the land. Now what Lord *Holt* said upon that point is this (12 Mod. 170): "I make no doubt, but that the assignee of the rent shall have covenant against the grantor, because it is a covenant annexed to the thing granted; but that covenant should run with the rent against the assignee of the land, I see no reason. If this rent was granted so to be paid, it would be another matter; but here is only a covenant, and no words amounting to a grant; and therefore there can be no relief in this case against the terre-tenant, but," his Lordship added, "in equity";—I will consider that point presently—"and, therefore for this point I do not see how the plaintiff can have his judgment." The learned Judges differed on the question of construction, but they do not appear to have differed on the point of law which Lord *Holt* discussed.

There remains, therefore, only the question whether there is any relief in equity in a case of this description where there is none at law. The point is not pressed upon us by the Appellant. I do not think it is arguable after the recent decisions. A covenant of this description requiring the outlay of money upon the land is not a covenant which, if it does not run at law, runs at equity by reason of any doctrine such as that in *Tulk* v. *Moxhay*. I agree, therefore, that this appeal must be dismissed with costs.

Appeal dismissed.

[A mortgaged his land to B who gave a covenant to renew the mortgage. Subsequently A assigned his equitable interest to C who, on the maturity of the existing mortgage, sought renewal. Is B's covenant enforceable by C? Would the case be any different if C sought to enforce it against an assignee of B?

A, owner of a gasoline service station, mortgaged the property to X. At the same time A and X entered into a 5 year agreement (which the parties designated as a "lease") under which A granted to X the exclusive privilege of installing oil and gasoline dispensing equipment on the service station property, and A agreed to purchase all oil and gasoline supplies from X. It was also agreed that if A should sell the business during the 5 year period, a covenant to observe the terms of the agreement would be exacted from the purchaser. Some months later, A sold the property (subject to the mortgage) and the business to B but did not obtain any covenant from B to observe the agreement. X continued to supply B with gasoline and oil, but after a few months B entered into a contract with a third person to install other oil and gasoline dispensing equipment on the premises and excavations were made on the land for the installation of such equipment which had been delivered to the premises. X consults you on whether any relief is open against B. Result? See *Cities Service Oil Co. Ltd.* v. *Pauley*, [1931] O.R. 685.]

[A conveyed certain land in fee simple to a company which covenanted for itself, its successors and assigns to give annually to A, his heirs and assigns 60 loads of coal. The company also agreed to build a fence along the boundary of the land so conveyed and to pay A, his heirs and assigns the sum of $6.00 annually to keep the fence in repair. After several years the company transferred the land to B by a conveyance which referred to the covenants mentioned above. On B's failure to observe the covenants A sued claiming that (1) a rent charge had been created in his favour and, alternatively, (2) B was bound by the covenants. Result? See *Carroll* v. *Dominion Coal Co. Ltd.* (1910), 44 N.S.R. 209 (C.A.).]

[On a conveyance of certain land to him in fee simple, the grantee entered into a bond conditioned on his keeping in repair a certain dam on the land. Does the obligation constitute a valid objection to title by a subsequent purchaser of the land? See *Ferris* v. *Ellis* (1920), 48 O.L.R. 374.]

[A granted certain land to a municipality for a highway and reserved the right to a cattle-pass (under the highway) which the municipality agreed to maintain and keep in repair. By his will A devised his farm half to B and half to C. The latter complained that the municipality was defaulting in its obligation to maintain and repair the cattle-pass. Is he entitled to relief, and on what basis? Suppose the municipality had conveyed the highway land to another municipality. What then? See *Freeman* v. *Camden* (1917), 41 O.L.R. 179.]

[There is some English authority for enforceability of the burden of covenants to repair private ways and line fences: see 12 *Halsbury* (1955 3rd ed.), p. 521n; *Rider* v. *Smith* (1790), 3 T.R. 766, 100 E.R. 848 (K.B.); *Gale on Easements* (1950, 12th ed.), p. 422; but see (1959, 13th ed.), p. 42. In so far as an easement exists which the grantor thereof covenants to maintain the result has been explained in some American cases on the "easement" theory of privity of estate. Otherwise, these cases may be regarded as exceptions to the English and Canadian view respecting the burden of affirmative covenants: see *Clark*, Covenants and Interests Running with Land (1947, 2nd ed.), p. 133; *Note*, (1927) 12 Cornell L.Q. 404; cf. *Haywood* v. *Brunswick Permanent Benefit Building Society* (1881), 8 Q.B.D. 403 (C.A.).]

HALSALL v. BRIZELL. Chancery. [1957] Ch. 169, [1957] 1 All E.R. 371

Motion to determine whether defendants as owners of a dwelling house and land were obliged to make certain annual payments under a deed of covenant executed in 1851. In that year two persons, O and J, purchased a large tract of land which they sold off in lots to various purchasers under a building scheme. There remained vested in O and J the roads laid out in connection with the scheme and a promenade along a sea wall. Purchasers of the lots entered into a deed of covenant with O and J which declared that the roads and promenade were vested in O and J on trust to permit them to be forever used by the parties, their heirs and assigns and by the occupiers for the time of the lots and of the dwelling houses erected or to be erected thereon. The purchasers covenanted for themselves, their heirs and assigns, with O and J, their heirs and assigns that they would pay in respect of their lots and dwelling houses a reasonable porportion of all costs charges and expenses incurred in maintaining, *inter alia*, the roads and sea wall promenade. The deed provided for annual meetings of owners for the time being of any lots at which levies for maintenance expenses would be made. Defendants were executors of one F, who had purchased one of the lots in 1931 under a conveyance made subject to the covenants in the deed of 1851.

UPJOHN J.: ... In so far as the deed of 1851 purports to make the successors of the original contracting parties liable to pay calls, is it valid and enforceable at all? I think that this much is plain: that the defendants could not be sued on the covenants contained in the deed for at least three reasons. First, a positive covenant in the terms of the seventh covenant does not run with the land. Secondly, these particular provisions with regard to the payment of calls plainly infringed the rule against perpetuities. Of course, these parties are not parties to the contract. Finally, it is conceded that the provision for distraining on failure to pay is not valid. A right to distrain can only be annexed to a rent charge which this certainly is not. It is, however, conceded to be ancient law that a man cannot take benefit under a deed without subscribing to the obligations thereunder. If authority is required for that proposition, I refer to one sentence during the argument in *Elliston* v. *Reacher* ([1908] 2 Ch. 665), where Sir Herbert Cozens-Hardy, M. R., said (ibid., at p. 669):

"It is laid down in *Coke* on *Littleton*, 230b, that a man who takes the benefit of a deed is bound by a condition contained in it though he does not execute it."

If the defendants did not desire to take the benefit of this deed, for the reasons that I have given they could not be under any liability to pay the obligations thereunder. They do desire, however, to take the benefit of this deed. They have no right to use the sewers which are vested in the plaintiffs, and I cannot see that they have any right, apart from the deed, to use the roads of the park which lead to their particular house, No. 22, Salisbury Road. The defendants cannot rely on any way of necessity nor on any right by prescription, for the simple reason that, when the house was originally sold in 1851 to their predecessor in title, he took the house on the terms of the deed of 1851 which contractually bound him to contribute a proper proportion of the expenses of maintaining the roads and sewers, and so forth, as a condition of being entitled to make use of those roads and sewers. Therefore, it seems to me that the defendants here cannot, if they desire to use their house, as they do, take advantage of the trusts concerning the user of the roads contained in the deed and the other benefits created by it without undertaking the obligations thereunder. On that principle it seems to me that they are bound by this deed, if they desire to take its benefits.

[The judgment is reproduced on one only of the two points raised in the case. The case is noted in (1957) 73 Law Q. Rev. 154.]

SMITH AND SNIPES HALL FARM LD. v. RIVER DOUGLAS CATCHMENT BOARD.
Court of Appeal. [1949] 2 K.B. 500, [1949] 2 All E.R. 179, 65 T.L.R. 628

Appeal from a judgment of Morris J. [1948] W.N. 414, dismissing an action for damages in tort and for breach of contract. The first plaintiff was transferree of the land of one of the original covenantees to the agreement hereinafter referred to, such transfer being with the benefit of the agreement. The second plaintiff was a company which was a yearly tenant of the land. The trial Judge found that the covenants in the agreement were not "running" covenants.

TUCKER L. J. (after reciting the facts, which are set out in the judgment of Denning L. J. below):... It remains to consider whether, in these circumstances, the plaintiffs, or either of them, can sue in respect of this breach. It is said for the defendants that the benefit of the covenant does not run with the land so as to bind a stranger who has not and never had an interest in the land to be benefited and there being no servient tenement to bear the burden. Further, it is contended that such a covenant must by the terms of the deed in which it is contained relate to some specific parcel of land, the precise extent and situation of which can be identified by reference to the deed alone. It is first necessary to ascertain from the deed that the covenant is one which "touches or concerns" the land, that is, it must either affect the land as regards mode of occupation, or it must be such as per se, and not merely from collateral circumstances, affects the value of the land, and it must then be shown that it was the intention of the parties that the benefit thereof should run with the land. In this case the deed shows that its object was to improve the drainage of land liable to flooding and prevent future flooding. The location of the land is described as situate between the Leeds and Liverpool Canal and the River Douglas and adjoining the Eller Brook. In return for lump sum payments the board covenants to do certain work to the banks of the Eller Brook, one of such banks being in fact situate upon and forming part of the plaintiffs' lands, and to maintain for all time the work when completed. In my view the language of the deed satisfies both tests. It affects the value of the land per se and converts it from flooded meadows to land suitable for agriculture, and shows an intention that the benefit of the obligation to maintain shall attach thereto into whosesoever hands the lands shall come.

With regard to the covenantor being a stranger the case of *The Prior* is referred to in *Spencer's* case, in these words: "In the case of a grandfather, father and two sons, the grandfather being seised of the manor of D, whereof a chapel was parcel: a prior, with the assent of his convent, by deed covenanted for him and his successors, with the grandfather and his heirs, that he and his convent would sing all the week in his chapel, parcel of the said manor, for the lords of the said manor and his servants, etc.; the grandfather did enfeoff one of the manor in fee, who gave it to the younger son and his wife in tail; and it was adjudged that the tenants in tail, as terre-tenants (for the elder brother was heir), should have an action of covenant against the prior, for the covenant is to do a thing which is annexed to the chapel, which is within the manor, and so annexed to the manor, as it is there said." The notes to *Spencer's* case state: "When such a covenant (namely, covenants running with the land made with the owner of the land to which they relate) is made it seems to be of no consequence whether the covenantor be the person who conveyed the land to the covenantee or be a mere stranger." In volume 4 of Bythewood & Jarman's Conveyancing, 4th ed., at p. 268, the following passage from the third report of the Real Property Commissioners is quoted with approval: "Expressions found in some books would lead to the opinion that, in considering this class of covenant with reference to the benefit of them, there is a distinction between those cases where the covenantor is a party by whom the estate is, or has been, conveyed, and those in which he is a stranger to the estate. We think the authority of Lord Coke on this point (which is express (Co. Litt 384b)) sufficient to warrant us in disregarding this distinction."

In *Rogers* v. *Hosegood* [1900] 2 Ch. 388, 395, Farwell J. in a passage where he refers, amongst others, to the *The Prior's* case—and I quote from Farwell J.'s judgment because, although this case went to the Court of Appeal, his judgment was approved, and the Court of Appeal had to deal with a rather different point—after stating what are the requirements in order that the covenant may run with the land, proceeds: "It is not contended that the covenants in question in this case have not the first characteristic, but it is said that they fail in the second. I am of opinion that they possess both. Adopting the definition of Bayley J. in *Congleton Corporation* v. *Pattison* 10 East 130, 135 the covenant must either affect the land as regards mode of occupation, or it must be such as per se, and not merely from collateral circumstances, affects the value of the land. It is to my mind obvious that the value of Sir J. Millais's land is directly increased by the covenants in question.... I see no difficulty in holding that the benefit of a covenant runs with the land of the covenantee, while the burden of the same covenant does not run with the land of the covenantor."

In this state of the authorities it seems clear, despite some dicta tending to the contrary view, that such a covenant if it runs with the land is binding on the covenantor though a mere stranger, and that this point will not avail the defendant board. As to the requirement that the deed containing the covenant must expressly identify the particular land to be benefited, no authority was cited to us and in the absence of such authority I can see no valid reason why the maxim "Id certum est quod certum reddi potest" should not apply, so as to make admissible extrinsic evidence to prove the extent and situation of the lands of the respective land owners adjoining the Eller Brook situate between the Leeds and Liverpool Canal and the River Douglas....

I do not find anything in the judgments in *Austerberry* v. *Corporation of Oldham* which conflicts with the law as I have endeavoured to set it out above, and I have accordingly arrived at the conclusion that the covenant by the board in the agreement of April 25, 1938, is one which runs with the land referred to therein, which land is capable of identification, and that it is binding on the defendant board; and, further, that by virtue of s. 78 of the Law of Property Act, 1925, it can be enforced at the suit of the covenantee and her successors in title and the persons deriving title under her or them so that both the plaintiff Smith and the plaintiff company can sue in respect of the damage resulting to their respective interests therein by reason of the defendants' breach of covenant.

DENNING L. J.: There is in Lancashire a river called Eller Brook, which is liable to overflow its banks and flood the adjoining land. In 1938, in order to prevent the flooding, eleven owners of land through which the river ran made an agreement with the local catchment board, whereby the board undertook to widen, deepen and make good the banks of the river, and thereafter to maintain them, and the landowners paid a contributon towards the cost. The board did the work and practically completed it by 1940, but they did it so unskilfully that, in the opinion of experts, it was from the first doomed to failure. The landowners, of course, did not know this and set about cultivating the land. The low meadows, which had been rough marshland, were broken up and brought under the plough. Crops were sown and harvested. But the banks of the river were not strong enough to stand serious floods. In 1944 they burst. The breach on that occasion was soon closed, but the board's engineer was aware of the danger. He reported to the board that "the bank is a bad one under any conditions." In 1945 there was another burst near by, and he reported that "this bank is largely composed of sand. I propose to put a machine on to strengthen it as soon as one is available." But apparently he did nothing, or at any rate nothing effective. The landowners and their tenants went on cultivating the land. They did not know that the banks were doomed to failure. Then in 1946 the worst happened. Serious floods arose, the banks burst, the fields were flooded, and the crops ruined. This action is brought by a tenant of the fields against the board to recover the value of the crops he has lost. The present owner joins in the action, claiming his loss of rent, but the substantial claim is by the tenant company.

On those facts it is my opinion that the board broke their contract. It was an implied term that they should do the work with reasonable care and skill, so as to make the banks reasonably fit for the purpose of preventing flooding. The proper way of doing this, according to the experts, was to put a clay core in the banks, or to make them very much wider, but they did not do either. It may be that the board had not sufficient funds available to carry out such works; but that seems to me to be an irrelevant consideration, or, at any rate, just as irrelevant in the case of a public board as in the case of a private contractor. No private contractor who was engaged to make works for a specific purpose could excuse himself for bad results by saying that he had not sufficient money to erect proper works. It follows, therefore, that if the original landowner with whom the agreement was made had himself cultivated the fields, and suffered damage by the breach, he could recover from the board. But he sold the land and he has suffered no damage. The damage has been suffered partly by the man who purchased the land, but principally by the tenants, and the question is whether they can sue on the contract.

Mr. Nield says that the plaintiffs cannot sue. He says that there is no privity of contract between them and the board, and that it is a fundamental principle that no one can sue upon a contract to which he is not a party. That argument can be met either by admitting the principle and saying that it does not apply to this case, or by disputing the principle itself. I make so bold as to dispute it. The principle is not nearly so fundamental as it is sometimes supposed to be. It did not become rooted in our law until the year 1861 (*Tweddle* v. *Aktkinson* 1 B. & S. 393), and reached its full growth in 1915 (*Dunlop* v. *Selfridge* [1915] A.C. 847)... It has never been able entirely to supplant another principle whose roots go much deeper. I mean the principle that a man who makes a deliberate promise which is intended to be binding, that is to say, under seal or for good consideration, must keep his promise; and the court will hold him to it, not only at the suit of the party who gave the consideration, but also at the suit of one who was not a party to the contract, provided that it was made for his benefit and that he has a sufficient interest to entitle him to enforce it, subject always, of course, to any defences that may be open on the merits. It is upon this principle, implicit if not expressed (i.) that the courts, ever since 1368 have held that a covenant made with the owner of land for its benefit can be enforced against the covenantor, not only by the original party, but also by his successors in title. (See *The Prior's* case, which is set out by Lord Coke in his work on Littleton, at p. 384a, and in his report of *Spencer's* case; (ii.) that the Courts of Common Law in the seventeenth and eighteenth centuries repeatedly enforced promises expressly made in favour of an interested person; (See *Dutton* v. *Poole*, 2 Lev. 210, approved by Lord Mansfield in *Martyn* v. *Hind*, 2 Cowp. 443); (iii.) that Lord Mansfield held that an undisclosed principal is entitled to sue on a contract made by his agent for his benefit, even though nothing was said about agency in the contract; (See *Rabone* v. *Williams* cited in *George* v. *Clagett*, 7 Term R. 359); and (iv.) that Lord Hardwicke decided that a third person is entitled to sue if there can be spelt out of the contract an intention by one of the parties to contract as trustee for him, even though nothing was said about any trust in the contract, and there was no trust fund to be administered. (See *Tomlinson* v. *Gill*, Ambler 330.)

Throughout the history of the principle the difficulty has been, of course, to say what is a sufficient interest to entitle the third person to recover. It has sometimes been supposed that there must always be something in the nature of a "trust" for his benefit. (See *Vandepitte's* case [1933] A.C. 70, 79.) But this is an elusive test which does not explain all the cases, and it involves the trustee being made a nominal party to the action either as plaintiff or defendant, unless that formality is dispensed with, as it was in *Les Affréteurs Réunis Société Anonyme* v. *Leopold Walford Ld.* [1919] A.C. 801. The truth is that the principle is not so limited. It may be difficult to define what is a sufficient interest. Whilst it does not include the maintenance of prices to the public disadvantage, it does cover the protection of the legitimate property, rights and interests of the third person, although no agency or trust for him can be inferred. It covers, therefore, rights such as these which cannot justly be denied; the right of a seller to enforce a commercial credit issued in his favour by a bank, under contract with the buyer; the right of a widow to sue for a pension which her husband's employers promised to pay her under contract with him; (See *Dutton* v. *Poole* and cf. *In re Schebsman* [1944] Ch. 83, 103, 104); or the right of a man's servants and guests to claim on an insurance policy, taken out by him against loss by burglary which is expressed to cover them; cf. *Prudential Staff Union* v. *Hall* [1947] K.B. 685. In some cases the legislature itself has intervened, as, for instance, to give the driver of a motor car the right to sue on an insurance policy taken out by the owner which is expressed to cover the driver. But this does not mean that the common law would not have reached the same result by itself.

The particular application of the principle with which we are concerned here is the case oi covenants made with the owner of the land to which they relate. The law on this subject was fully expounded by Mr. Smith in his note to *Spencer's* case which has always been regarded as authoritative. Such covenants are clearly intended, and usually expressed, to be for the benefit of whomsoever should be the owner of the land for the time being; and at common law each successive owner has a sufficient interest to sue because he holds the same estate as the original owner. The reason which Lord Coke gave for this rule is the reason which underlies the whole of the principle now under consideration. He said in his work upon Littleton that it was "to give damages to the party grieved." If a successor in title were not allowed to sue it would mean that the covenantor could break his contract with impunity, for it is clear that the original owner, after he has parted with the land, could recover no more than nominal damages for any breach that occurred thereafter. It was always held, however, at common law that, in order that a successor in title should be entitled to sue, he must be of the same estate as the original owner. That alone was a sufficient interest to entitle him to enforce the contract. The covenant was supposed to be made for the benefit of the owner and his successors in title, and not for the benefit of anyone else. This limitation, however, was, as is pointed out in Smith's Leading Cases, capable of being "productive of very serious and disagreeable consequences," and it has been removed by s. 78 of the Law of Property Act, 1925, which provides that a covenant relating to any land of the covenantee shall be deemed to be made with the covenantee and his successors in title, "and the persons deriving title "under him or them" and shall have effect as if such successors "and other persons" were expressed.

The covenant of the catchment board in this case clearly relates to the land of the covenantees. It was a covenant to do work on the land for the benefit of the land. By the statute, therefore, it is to be deemed to be made, not only with the original owner, but also with the purchasers of the land and their tenants as if they were expressed. Now if they were expressed, it would be clear that the covenant was made for their benefit; and they clearly have sufficient interest to entitle them to enforce it because they have suffered the damage. The result is that the plaintiffs come within the principle whereby a person interested can sue on a contract expressly made for his benefit.

I would not wish to leave this subject without referring also to s. 56 of the Law of Property Act, 1925, which says that a person may take the benefit of any covenant or agreement respecting land or other property, although he may not be named as a party to the instrument. That section is no doubt, as Lord Greene has said, confined to cases when the person seeking to take advantage of it is a person "within the benefit" of the covenant or agreement; (See *White* v. *Bijou Mansions* [1938] Ch. 351); but, subject to that limitation, there is no reason why the section should not be given its full scope, just as Lord Dunedin was prepared to give full scope to its narrower predecessor, s. 5 of the Real Property Act, 1845. (See *Dyson* v. *Forster* [1909] A.C. 98.) Section 56 means, therefore, that a person may enforce an agreement respecting property made for his benefit, although he was not a party to it. So construed it is a clear statutory recognition of the principle to which I have referred and it is applicable to this case. If the principle had been canvassed in *In re Miller's Agreement* [1947] Ch. 615, it should, I think have been held there that the daughters had a right at common law to sue for their pension, a right which was reinforced by s. 56. I cannot believe that the covenantors there could break their contract with impunity. So much for the question of principle.

Mr. Nield did urge that the benefit of the covenant should not run with the land here because there was no clearly defined piece of land to which it was attached. It is true that the agreement did not describe the lands by metes and bounds, but it did give a description of them which was capable of being rendered certain by extrinsic evidence; and that is sufficient. Id certum est quod certum reddi potest. Mr. Nield also argued that there was no servient tenement. But that is only material when there is a question whether the burden of a covenant runs with the land. This is a question of the benefit running, and ever since *The Prior's* case it has been held that the covenantor is liable because of his covenant given to the owner of the dominant tenement and not because of his relationship to any servient tenement. In my opinion, therefore, the board are liable to the plaintiffs in damages for breach of covenant.

Appeal allowed.

[The concurring judgment of Somervell L. J. is omitted. The Court made no finding on whether there was any liability in tort. See *Scammell*, Positive Covenants in Conveyances of the Fee Simple, (1954) 18 Conv. & Prop. L. (N. S.) 546.]

[Is a covenant to pump water on to adjoining land and a covenant to keep the pump in repair enforceable without express assignment by an assignee of the covenantee. See *Shayler* v. *Woolf*, [1946] 1 All E.R. 464, aff'd [1946] Ch. 320, [1946] 2 All. E.R. 54 (C.A.).]

[Section 24 of the Conveyancing and Law of Property Act, R.S.O. 1960, c. 66 is in somewhat similar terms to s. 78 of the English Law of Property Act, 1925, referred to in the case above and reads as follows:

"(1) A covenant relating to land of inheritance or to land held for the life of another shall be deemed to be made with the covenantee, his heirs and assigns, and has effect as if heirs and assigns were expressed.

"(2) A covenant relating to land not of inheritance or to land not held for the life of another shall be deemed to be made with the covenantee, his executors, administrators and assigns, and has effect as if executors, administrators and assigns were expressed."

The Ontario provision is in the terms of the predecessor of the present English provision which was s. 58 of the Conveyancing Act, 1881 (Imp.), c. 41.

What is the difference in the effect or application of the present Ontario and English provisions? Cf. *Radcliffe*, Some Problems of the Law Relating to Restrictive Covenants, (1941) 57 Law Q. Rev. 203, at pp. 204 ff.

The Conveyancing Act, 1956 (N.S.), c. 3 provides by s. 6 (c) that except where a contrary intention appears by the conveyance the parties are deemed to agree that it shall enure to the benefit of and bind them and their respective representatives and assigns.]

[Section 79 of the Law of Property Act, 1925 (Imp.), c. 20 makes it unnecessary to add the terms "heirs, executors, administrators and assigns" so far as concerns a covenantor just as s. 78 made it unnecessary in relation to a covenantee. However, it must not be thought from this that there has been any change in England in the law governing the running of the burden of real covenants: see *Megurry and Wade*, Law of Real Property (1959, 2nd ed.), pp. 699-700. Its main effect would seem to be on the *in posse* and *in esse* distinction made in *Spencer's Case*, as is indicated by the last sentence in s. 79 (1) reading as follows: "This subsection extends to a covenant to do some act relating to the land, notwithstanding that the subject matter may not be in existence when the covenant is made." (There is no comparable legislation in Canada.) Thus, in relation to burden under s. 79 of the English Act (as in relation to benefit under s. 78 or the similar s. 24 of the Ontario Conveyancing and Law of Property Act) the statutory inclusion of successors in title, such as assigns, satisfies the required manifestation of intention that a covenant relating to a thing *in posse* should run. Since the distinction between things *in esse* and *in posse* is at best an artificial one, the absence, in s. 78 of the English Act or s. 24 of the Ontario Act, of such a clause as is quoted above from s. 79 (1) of the English Act should not militate again holding that a covenant runs as to benefit although relating to a thing *in posse.*

The distinction in question has not passed without criticism even in the English cases: see *Minshull* v. *Oakes* (1858), 2 H. & N. 793, 157 E.R. 327 (Ex.) (covenant by a lessee, his heirs, executors and administrators, that he would repair the premises and all other buildings which should or might be erected during the term, *held*, binding on an assignee although not named because there was one covenant to repair, and as to part it was only conditionally in posse.). Equally, it has been criticised in United States where, in some states, it has been rejected: see 2 *American Law of Property*. s. 9. 3.

The distinction has been accepted and acted upon in Canadian case law, but there are no recent cases by which to test its survival at the present time: see *Emmett* v. *Quinn* (1882), 7 O.A.R. 306 (covenant by lessee to build and to rebuild in case of destruction by fire, *held*, not binding upon remote assignee where building erected before remote assignment but destroyed by fire afterwards, and where "assigns" of lessee not mentioned in the lease nor effectively incorporated under purported "short form" lease). *Emmett* v. *Quinn* points up that in the case, at least, of the prescribed covenants under Short Forms legislation the problem under discussion is covered by the extension of "lessee" to include "executors, administrators and assigns": see, for example, Short Forms of Leases Act, R.S.O. 1960, c. 373, s. 2 (5).

In *McLary* v. *Jackson* (1887), 13 O.R. 310, where a lessor, without mentioning assigns, covenanted to buy a building if erected by the lessee and the latter did erect a building, it was held that the covenant was not binding on the lessor's devisee but only on his executors. The Court refused to follow *Minshull* v. *Oakes* although the situations in the two cases were comparable.]

[What has been said above on the effect of ss. 78 and 79 of the English Law of Property Act is subject to qualification based on the use (following the references, respectively, to "the covenantee and his successors in title" and to "the covenantor on behalf of himself, his successors in title") of the phrase "and the persons deriving title under him or them". In the *River Douglas Catchment Board case*, this phrase was interpreted to cover a mere tenant of the covenantee and thus to enable the benefit to run in favour of a person who did not succeed to the whole interest of the covenantee (which was the common law requirement). If the same broad view is taken of this phrase so far as the running of burden is concerned under s. 79, would it not follow that a sublessee may become bound by positive covenants in the head lease, and even a mortgagee of a freehold or an assignee of a freehold, without regard to privity of estate? The question was raised but not decided in *Williams* v. *Unit Construction Co. Ltd.*, a 1951 judgment of the English Court of Appeal which remained unreported until reproduced in (1955) 19 Convey. & Prop. L. (N.S.) 262. The Court was concerned with the running of benefit under s. 78 and refused to express any view on s. 79; see Positive Covenants and Third Parties, (1955) 19 Convey. & Prop. L. (N.S.) 261.]

[A covenant by a lessee to pay for improvements, given under a lease in which assigns were not mentioned is not enforceable against his assignee: see *Hilliard* v. *Beck* (1889), 9 C.L.T. 90 (Ont. C.A.).]

[A vendor on the sale of certain land covenanted with the purchaser that the building thereon, used for apartment housing, complied with municipal building, zoning and licensing regulations. Is this a covenant which runs so as to be enforceable against the vendor by the purchaser's assignee? See *Welch and Welch* v. *White and Brezden* (1957), 10 D.L.R. 2d 83 (B.C.).]

[At common law, where any immediate estate or interest in land was conveyed to a person who was not a party he could not take if the conveyance was by way of indenture but he could take under a deed poll. The same disability existed with respect to the benefit of covenants; hence, ordinarily, a covenantee had to be party to the deed. The Real Property Act, 1845 (Imp.), c. 106, s. 5 cured this defect by providing that "an immediate interest in any tenements or hereditaments, the benefit of a condition or covenant respecting any tenements or hereditaments, may be taken although the taker thereof be not named a party to the same indenture". The Law of Property Act, 1925 (Imp.), c. 20 s. 56 extended this provision to apply to "land or other property". The original English provision, confined to land is in force in New Brunswick (see Property Act, R.S.N.B. 1952, c. 177, s. 13) and in Prince Edward Island (see Real Property Act, R.S.P.E.I. 1951, c. 138, s. 8).

The common law rule did not apply to future interests. However, the effect of the legislation referred to was not simply to enable an unnamed person to sue on the benefit of a covenant; he could do so only if, although not being a party to the deed, he was named as covenantee or, if not named, was an ascertainable person at the time of the execution of the deed in whose favour the covenant was expressed: see *White* v. *Bijou Mansions Ltd.*, [1938] Ch. 351, [1938] 1 All E.R. 546 (C.A.), aff'g [1937] Ch. 610, [1937] 3 All E.R. 269; *Re Foster, Hudson* v. *Foster*, [1938] 3 All E.R. 357, 54 T.L.R. 993 (Ch.).

In *Keoughan* v. *Holland*, [1948] 1 D.L.R. 605, 21 M.P.R. 168 (P.E.I.), grantors under an indenture conveyed to F.K. as grantee their interests in certain land and personalty, and F.K. covenanted (for himself, his heirs, personal representatives and assigns) with the grantors that he would support M.K., his mother, for her lifetime, "the support and maintenance... to be a lien and charge on the said lands". M.K. claimed the benefit of the covenant and F.K. brought a declaratory action to establish that she had no enforceable claim. *Held*, M.K. had no enforceable claim either at common law or under what is now s. 8 of the Real Property Act, R.S.P.E.I. 1951, c. 138. However, the covenantees were entitled to enforce F.K.'s covenant.

Would M.K. be entitled to insist that the covenantees enforce the covenant and would she be entitled to claim from them what they recover from F.K.?]

[A deed of licence to assign a leasehold term given by the landlord to the tenant included an option to the proposed assignee to purchase the reversion. Is the option enforceable by the assignee of the term? See *Stromdale and Ball Ltd.* v. *Burden*, [1952] Ch. 223, [1952] 1 All E.R. 59.]

(c) Touching and Concerning: Landlord and Tenant Cases

CLEGG v. HANDS. Court of Appeal. 1890. 44 Ch. D. 503, 59 L.J. Ch. 477

Clegg and Wright, who were brewers, gave a lease of a certain public house to Hands for a specified term and the lessee covenanted, *inter alia*, that he would not buy or sell any ale or stout other than such as shall have been purchased from the lessors. The lease purported to be between the lessors, their heirs, executors, administrators, and assigns and the lessee, his executors, administrators and permitted assigns. A few years later the lessors agreed to sell their brewery plant, the business and goodwill to one Cain who was a brewer carrying on business at a different address. In carrying out the sale they assigned to Cain the leasehold premises occupied by Hands with the full benefit of the covenants contained in the lease to Hands and in particular the "tied house" covenant. Shortly afterwards, Clegg and Wright retired from business and the brewery premises they occupied were closed down. Hands refused to purchase any ale or stout from Cain whereupon Clegg and Wright joined with Cain in an action for an injunction against Hands. The trial Judge held that Clegg and Wright were not entitled to any relief because they were no longer in business but he granted relief to Cain. Defendant Hands appealed.

COTTON L. J.:... But then it is said, as I understand the argument, that it can only have been intended to include such assigns as carry on the business of brewers at the particular brewery which was assigned to Cain, and where the business of brewing is no longer carried on. The case of *Doe* v. *Reid*, 10 B. & C. 849, was much relied upon for the purpose of that construction, but it was a case where the language was different, and in my opinion there is nothing here to shew such an intention. Then there is this clause: "Providing they or he shall at such time deal in or vend such liquors as aforesaid, and shall be willing to supply the same to the lessee of good quality and at the fair current market price." Well, it was pointed out by one of us in the course of the argument, that there is some protection granted here to the publican by the provision that the beer shall be of good quality, and that it shall be supplied at the fair current market price.

That, in my opinion, shews clearly that it was not intended in this case to restrict the benefit of the covenant to the persons who carried on this brewery at this particular place, for it does not in any way refer to the beer which is to be provided, as being beer made by the landlords or their assigns. The words are "provided they or he shall at such time deal in or vend such liquors." It shews that there was no intention whatever to stipulate that the persons entitled to the benefit of the covenant were to be persons who made beer. It was not provided that they should continue to make the beer they were selling; but it was provided that it should be of good quality and be supplied at the fair current market price, and that they should deal in and vend beer. Considerable light was to my mind thrown upon the true intention of the parties by what was put before us by Mr. Collins in his reply, that at the time the covenant was entered into these landlords not only made beer, but bought beer, and supplied those who were not bound by any restrictive covenants to take beer from them alone. That, I think, shews what they were intending to provide for, viz., not that they should only supply beer which they themselves made, but that they should go on doing what they were then doing, supply beer either by making it, or by buying it, so long as they were able to supply it of good quality and at the fair market price. Then there is the case of *Doe* v. *Reid*, to which I have already referred. Now cases, as far as they give us a rule of construction, are very useful; but it is very seldom, to my mind, that a case upon the construction of one particular document tells us much about the construction of another ducument unless it lays down some principle to guide us. In *Doe* v. *Reid*, the Defendant Reid, in taking a lease of a public-house from John Phillips & Samuel Miall, covenanted to purchase and take of and from Phillips & Miall, their executors, administrators, or assigns, or their successors in their late or present trade as brewers, all the porter, ale, and twopenny or amber, or such of the said liquors as by them should be brewed for sale, as should be sold or disposed of on the premises. Phillips & Miall sold their business and trade premises to Stanley & Cass, who again assigned to Calvert & Co., and these assignees shut up the old brewery and removed the plant, so that though they carried on the original lessors' brewing business, they did not carry it on at the place where the original lessors carried it on. The case turned almost entirely upon the construction of the covenant, and the words, "or their successors in their late or present trade as brewers," though not in terms limiting the assigns to assigns in that position, afforded in that case a rule of construction. The Court accordingly held, that what was meant was successors carrying on the same trade—not merely carrying on the trade of brewers, but carrying on the trade which was carried on by Phillips & Miall at that particular brewery. Now this particular clause which governs the construction of the covenant in *Doe* v. *Reid* does not occur in the present case, and its absence leads me to put a different construction and effect upon this covenant from that which was put by the Court in *Doe* v. *Reid* upon the different words occurring in that case. It cannot, in my opinion, be said here that this was a personal covenant with the particular landlords who granted the lease, or that it was impossible for the benefit of that covenant to be conveyed to anybody else who did not carry on their trade. It is not like entering into a contract with a particular painter to paint your picture. That is a contract made with him personally, and he must not hand it over to anybody else. In my opinion, this is not a contract which is incapable of being assigned.

Then it is said that this covenant does not run with the land. I think it does run with the land. That is my opinion; but there are other points on which this case may be decided independently of that question. It is a contract relating to the way in which the business at a particular house is to be carried on—therefore it is a contract relating to the public-house, just as much, in my opinion, as a contract as to the mode in which the cultivation of a particular bit of land is to be carried on relates to the land. It affects the value of the reversion, it affects the house, and in my opinion it is a contract running with the land. If that is so, that will enable the judgment to be supported, and will enable the present owner of the reversion in this case to sue.

But there is another ground on which I think the judgment may be supported. Here there has been a sale to the Plaintiff by the lessors of the goodwill of the business. The Plaintiff is therefore, independently of the question whether the covenant runs with the land, entitled to sue so far as by assignment the landlord who entered into this covenant could give him the right. That being so, the difficulty as to the title to sue which there was in the case *Renals* v. *Cowlishaw*, 9 Ch. D. 125, before Vice-Chancellor Hall, is got rid of. There is no doubt that there is here an actual assignment of the benefit of the covenant to Cain, even if that benefit did not pass by the mere assignment to him of the reversion of this public-house. Then, in my opinion, as he is thus entitled to sue, the doctrine of *Tulk* v. *Moxhay*, 2 Ph. 774, properly applied, will enable him to enforce that right as against the Defendant—that is to say, considering that the Defendant obtained this public-house at a less rent, as we may assume he did, by reason of the covenant, we ought not, as against the person entitled to the benefit of that covenant, to allow him to deal with the public-house in a way inconsistent with the covenant by reason of which he got it at a lower rent. Therefore, in my opinion, on that ground, even if this covenant did not run with the land, the judgment of the Vice-Chancellor is right.

LINDLEY L. J.:... The whole question here to my mind turns upon the true construction of this agreement, and the only difficulty that I think serious is to find out whether this agreement is or is not assignable—that is to say, whether the tenant here entered into a contract with certain persons relying upon their personal skill and reputation, and agreed to buy beer of them and them alone, or whether he did not enter into a very much wider contract, and agree to buy beer from them or anybody to whom they might assign their business or the public-house. The answer to the question whether this is a personal unassignable contract or not must be gathered from the instrument itself, having regard of course to the position of both parties.

The lease has been gone through, and I will refer to it very shortly. The lessors are described as brewers; there is no reference to any particular place of business or anything of that kind; and the lessee is described as a licensed victualler. Then there is an ordinary lease of a public-house, and then, reading it shortly, there come covenants by the tenant that he will use and occupy the premises demised as and for and in a tavern or public house only, and will conduct the same so as not to forfeit his license, and will keep open the premises for the sale of the articles before mentioned, which I will call ale and beer. Then there is a covenant about not getting ale or beer from other people. Now, just let us see whether this lease does or does not contain any indication either one way or the other as to whether the benefit of this was capable of being assigned. The very first thing that one comes across is the interpretation clause saying that the term "lessors," which applied to the brewers, shall include "each of them and their and each and every of their heirs, executors, administrators, and assigns." Those words are never found in what are called personal contracts. If I were to enter into an engagement with an artist to paint my picture, I should not put those words in. If he died, I should not leave it with his executors to finish what he had done. Such words are out of place altogether in a contract which is personal in that sense....

That being the case, I think there can be no reasonable doubt that this contract is not a personal unassignable contract. The question then arises whether it has been assigned to Mr. *Cain*. It unquestionably has. If it is capable of being assigned it has been assigned. It has been assigned without any controversy in equity by the brewers to *Cain*, and, inasmuch as he and his assignors are both suing, I see no answer whatever to this action upon that ground.

It has also been said that it is assigned to Mr. *Cain* by virtue of his being an assignee of the reversion in the lease. That raises a technical question which, stated in legal language, amounts to this: whether the benefit of this covenant runs with the land. We have heard the authorities discussed by Mr. *Collins*, who has studied this branch of the law probably more carefully than anybody living, and he has not persuaded me, I confess, that this is a covenant which does not run with the land. I rather think it does. If you look at the authorities which he has cited, and look at them carefully, this does, in lawyers' language, so "touch and concern" the land demised as to run with it at Common Law. But whether that is so or not, the benefit of the contract has been assigned to Mr. *Cain*, and Mr. *Cain* is entitled to it.

LOPES L. J.: ... A question is raised as to whether the benefit of this covenant runs with the reversion. It was contended by Mr. *Collins* that it did not run with the reversion, and that it was purely collateral. The benefit to run with the reversion must touch or concern the demised premises. Now, does this covenant touch or concern the demised premises? It relates to the mode of enjoyment of a public-house. The thing demised is a public-house, and the covenant compels the covenantor to buy the beer of the covenantee and his assigns.

In my opinion, it touches and concerns the demised premises; it affects the mode of enjoyment of the premises, and therefore it runs with the reversion.

Appeal dismissed.

[Suppose Hands had assigned his leasehold. Would Cain have succeeded against the assignee?]

[A lessee of a hotel covenanted in his lease that at the expiration thereof he would assign his hotel licence to the lessor. Is the covenant enforceable against an assignee of the lessee? See *Walsh* v. *Walper* (1901), 3 O.L.R. 158 (C.A.).]

[That the benefit of a covenant is assignable as a chose in action (apart from the question whether it "runs") is made clear in *Manchester Brewery Co.* v. *Coombs*, [1901] 2 Ch. 608, at p. 619, 70 L.J. Ch. 814, at p. 820.]

RE LEADER DRESS CO. LTD. Ontario Supreme Court in Bankruptcy. 1932. 41 O.W.N. 338, 14 C.B.R. 92

SEDGEWICK J.: The landlord demised the premises to lessees by a lease which contained the usual provision for accelerated rent in case of the bankruptcy of the lessees. The lessees assigned the lease to the debtors against whom a receiving order has been made.

The claim for accelerated rent was disallowed on the ground that the landlord is not able to enforce the provision referred to against the assignees of the lease. The Registrar has upheld the disallowance.

I am afraid that I must dismiss the appeal because I think I am bound by the judgment in *Mitchell* v. *McCauley* (1893), 20 O.A.R. 272, where three of the four Judges held that a similar condition did not run with the land but was personal to the original lessor and his lessee and "altogether collateral" having "no relation to the land." It is true that the judgment was that the assignee of part of the reversion could not enforce the condition against the original lessee, but I think the language of the majority is too clear to permit me to distinguish the case now under consideration.

Appeal dismissed.

[In *Horsey Estate Ltd.* v. *Steiger*, [1899] 2 Q.B. 79 (C.A.), a lease of premises provided for re-entry if the lessees became bankrupt or went into liquidation. *Held*, the provision, whether it be a condition or a covenant, was binding on an assignee of the lease and enforceable by an assignee of the reversion. Is this consistent with *Re Leader Dress Co. Ltd.?*

[The point made in *Mitchell* v. *McCauley*, referred to in *Re Leader Dress Co. Ltd.*, *supra*, that an assignee of the reversion in part of the demised land could not enforce a condition of re-entry is now changed by legislation: see Landlord and Tenant Act, R.S.O. 1960, c. 206, s. 8; Landlord and Tenant Act, R.S.M. 1954, c. 136, s. 8; Landlord and Tenant Act, R.S.N.B. 1952, c. 126, s. 4; Landlord and Tenant Act, R.S.P.E.I. 1951, c. 82, s. 5; Landlord and Tenant Act, R.S.S. 1953, c. 312, s. 7. The benefit and burden of covenants also now go with any part of the reversionary estate; and moreover, the benefit of a covenant goes with the reversion (or part thereof), even though the assignment of the reversion took place after a breach of the covenant in question: see Landlord and Tenant Act, R.S.O. 1960, c. 206, ss. 5 and 7; Landlord and Tenant Act, R.S.M. 1954, c. 136, ss. 5 and 7; Landlord and Tenant Act, R.S.N.B. 1952, c. 126, ss. 2 and 3; Landlord and Tenant Act, R.S.P.E.I. 1951, c. 82, ss. 2 and 4; Landlord and Tenant Act, R.S.S. 1953, c. 312, ss. 4 and 6. For background material on this legislation, see *Woodfall*, Landlord and Tenant (1960, 26th ed.), pp. 540-542; *Williams*, Canadian Law of Landlord and Tenant (1957, 3rd ed.), pp. 694-700.

In *Wilkinson* v. *Benedict*, [1948] 4 D.L.R. 849, [1948] 2 W.W.R. 1128, 56 Man. R. 340 (C.A.), where after a yearly lease of two lots to one tenant the lessor sold one of the lots to X to whom the tenant paid apportioned rent, *held*, X was entitled, under s. 8 of the Landlord and Tenant Act, R.S.M. 1940, c. 112 to terminate the lease, by a proper notice to quit, as to the one lot in which he held the reversion. However, the result would have been different if rent had not been apportioned and X had not been recognized by the tenant as his landlord at the time notice to quit was given. This latter situation is now taken care of in England by s. 140 (1) (2) of the Law of Property Act, 1925 (Imp.), c. 20; see *Smith* v. *Kinsey*, [1938] 3 All E.R. 73 (C.A.). The legislation in Canada is not as comprehensive; in Saskatchewan, for example, it is required that the rent upon severance of a reversion be first legally apportioned; and in no case does provincial legislation define right of entry to include termination by notice to quit.

Surrender or merger of a reversion no longer operates to destroy covenants that "go" with the reversion but they survive as incident to the estate which confers the next vested right to the land as against the tenant: see Landlord and Tenant Act, R.S.O. 1960, c. 206, s. 16; Landlord and Tenant Act, R.S.M. 1954, c. 136, s. 16; Landlord and Tenant Act, R.S.N.B. 1952, c. 126, s. 5; Landlord and Tenant Act, R.S.P.E.I. 1951, c. 82, s. 6; Landlord and Tenant Act, R.S.S. 1953, c. 312, s. 8.]

[A provision in a lease providing for its termination upon sale of the property and the giving of notice to the tenant is binding on the tenant's assignee: see *Re Snazel and Ding Pong* (1925), 29 O.W.N. 104 (C.A.)

Does a covenant in a lease for renewal run in favour of the tenant's assignee and against the assignee of the reversion? See *Rogers* v. *National Drug and Chemical Co.* (1911), 23 O.L.R. 234, aff'd 24 O.L.R. 486 (C.A.), where Riddell J. said (at p. 236): "This is not, it is argued, a mere personal option but in law an interest in the land—an advantage... which the assignee took with his assignment—and which he may enforce against the assignee of the original lessor, who took with notice." Suppose the lessor's assignee had no notice of the provision for renewal. Would he be bound? See *Anon* (1584), Moore 159, 72 E.R. 504 (K.B.).

A, a lessee for a long term, sub-let to B and covenanted to renew B's sub-lease. Subsequently A assigned his head-lease to C who acquired the fee simple in the land. Is B's covenant for renewal enforceable against C.? See *Brereton* v. *Tuohey* (1858), 8 Ir. C.L. Rep. 190; cf. *Muller* v. *Trafford*, [1901] 1 Ch. 54.

In *Alexander* v. *Herman* (1912), 3 O.W.N. 755, 2 D.L.R. 239, a provision in a lease for a one year term gave the lessee "the privilege of renewing the said lease from year to year at the expiration of any year, so long as he may care to do so". *Held*, this provision was not a covenant and did not "bind" the land or the heirs, assigns or personal representatives of the lessor; and, moreover, it conferred no rights on the heirs, assigns or personal representatives of the lessee. Do you agree?]

GRIFFITH v. PELTON. Court of Appeal. [1957] 3 All E.R. 75, [1957] 3 W.L.R. 522

Appeal by a landlord's executrix from a judgment of Vaisey J. declaring that the benefit of an option to purchase had been validly vested in an assignee of the term by an assignment of the lease.

The judgment of the Court was delivered by JENKINS L. J.: In this case the plaintiff, Herbert Charles Griffith (who is the respondent to this appeal and is called herein "the assignee"), claimed against the defendant, Ethel Elizabeth Pelton (who is the appellant on this appeal and is herein called "the freeholder"), as executrix of Aubrey John Pelton, deceased, a declaration to the effect that the assignee had by a notice in writing dated Mar. 22, 1956, effectually exercised an option contained in a lease dated May 17, 1935, and made between the deceased of the one part and Winifred Martha Blaker of the other part, to purchase the property comprised therein, and consisting of No. 1, The Broadway, Mount Pleasant, Tunbridge Wells, together with a leasehold interest in a certain right of way, with consequential claims for specific performance of the agreement constituted by his exercise of the option, and further or other relief.

On an application by the assignee for summary judgment under R.S.C., Ord. 14a, an order was made by consent for the setting down of certain questions of law for argument under R.S.C., Ord. 34, r. 2.

The questions of law thus raised, so far as immediately material, were (shortly) whether the benefit of the option was effectually vested in the assignee, either (1) by an assignment dated Aug. 3, 1948 (being an assignment of the lease by Miss Blaker to the assignee), or alternatively (2) by a deed dated Mar. 22, 1956 (being an assignment, or purported assignment, of the benefit of the option by Miss Blaker to the assignee).

Vaisey, J., by his order dated Mar. 18, 1957, made a declaration answering the first of these questions in the assignee's favour, and from that order the freeholder now appeals to this court.

The lease of May 17, 1935, was, as we have said, made between the deceased of the one part and Miss Blaker of the other part. The parties were thereinafter respectively described as "'the lessor', which expression shall include the estate owner or estate owners for the time being of the reversion of the premises hereby demised expectant on the term hereby granted, where the context so admits", and "'the lessee' which expression shall include her executors, administrators and assigns where the context so admits."

The lease was for twenty-one years from Mar. 25, 1935 (determinable as thereinafter mentioned) at the yearly rent of £450. There was a proviso that "if the lessor survives the term hereby granted [which event did not happen] he will grant to the lessee a further term of fourteen years subject to the rent terms and conditions of this lease."

There was also a proviso enabling the lessee to determine the lease at the expiration of the first fourteen years of the term.

Finally, there was this proviso conferring the option which has given rise to the present litigation:

"Provided always and it is hereby agreed that if the lessee shall within the period hereinafter prescribed give to the lessor or leave at his last known place of abode in England six months' notice in writing of the desire of the lessee to purchase the fee simple of the demised premises and his leasehold interest in the right of way over the passageway coloured yellow on the said plan then the lessor shall on the expiration of such notice and upon payment of the sum of £7,000 together with interest thereon at the rate of £5 per centum per annum from the expiration of such notice till the completion of the purchase and of all rent hereby reserved up to such expiration assure the said premises unto the lessee for an estate in fee simple in possession free from incumbrances except as already disclosed to the lessee and assign his interest in the said right of way to the lessee Provided nevertheless that this option to purchase the fee simple of the demised premises shall not be exercised during the lifetime of the present lessor the said Aubrey John Pelton but shall be exercised within one year next after his death if he shall die during the term hereby granted and nothing herein contained shall be construed as giving to the lessee any option to purchase the fee simple of the demised premises at any time after the expiration or sooner determination of the term hereby granted unless the aforesaid notice shall have been given by her before such expiration or determination."

By the assignment of Aug. 3, 1948, to which we have already referred, Miss Blaker (having first duly obtained a licence so to do from the deceased as required by the lease) assigned to the assignee at the price of £3,200 "all that the property comprised in and demised by the lease" for the residue of the term thereby granted, subject to the rent thereby reserved and the lessee's covenants and conditions therein contained. This document contained no reference to the option. It included, in addition to the lease, an assignment of the goodwill of a business carried on at the premises to which the purchase consideration was no doubt to some extent attributable.

The deceased died on Mar. 2, 1956, and probate of his will was granted to the freeholder on Apr. 13, 1956. By the deed dated Mar. 22, 1956, to which we have already referred, Miss Blaker gratuitously assigned (or purported gratuitously to assign) the benefit of the option to the assignee if and so far as not already vested in him. On the same day the assignee by his solicitors gave notice in writing of this assignment to "the personal representative or personal representatives" of the deceased. Also on the same day the assignee by his solicitors gave to "the personal representative or personal representatives" of the deceased notice in writing exercising the option. The term granted by the lease expired on Mar. 25, 1956. On these facts counsel for the freeholder contends that both the questions shortly stated above should be answered in the negative.

As to the first question, counsel for the freeholder submits that the benefit of the option cannot have been effectually vested in the assignee by the assignment of Aug. 3, 1948, because the benefit of the provision in the lease whereby the option was conferred did not run with the land. He invokes the second and sixth resolutions in *Spencer's Case* ((1583), 5 Co. Rep. 16a), the effect of which is conveniently stated by Jelf, J., in *Dewar* v. *Goodman* ([1907] 1 K.B. 612 at p. 620) as establishing the proposition that neither the benefit nor the burden (as the case may be) of a lessor's covenant runs with the land unless it touches or concerns the thing demised, or, as s. 142 (1) of the Law of Property Act, 1925, now has it, is entered into "with reference to the subject-matter of the lease." As illustrations of the application of the general principle he referred to *Thomas* v. *Hayward* ((1869), L.R. 4 Exch. 311), where a lessor's covenant in a lease of a public house not to keep any house for the sale of spirits or beer was held not to be enforceable by an assignee of the lease against the lessor because it did not touch or concern the thing demised and therefore the benefit of it did not run with the land; and to *Dewar* v. *Goodman*, where an under-lessor's covenant to perform the covenants in the superior lease as regards land not included in the sub-demise was on like grounds held not to be enforceable by an assignee of the underlease against an assignee of the under-lessor. The general principle on which counsel for the freeholder relies is, of course, well settled, and he submits that its application to the case in point of an option contained in a lease to purchase the freehold is established by authority binding on us in the shape of the case in this court of *Woodall* v. *Clifton* ([1905] 2 Ch. 257), where it was held that such an option did not touch or concern the thing demised, and therefore did not run with the land so as to be enforceable against the assigns of the lessor. Counsel for the freeholder's submissions, if well founded, would produce the surprising result that although the intention of the parties to the present lease as expressed in the document plainly was that either Miss Blaker herself as the original lessee, or her executors, administrators and assigns, who were included in the term "lessee" by virtue of the definition to which I have referred, should be entitled to exercise the option by giving the prescribed notice and otherwise complying with the conditions laid down for its exercise, the option was nevertheless not assignable by Miss Blaker even by an assignment of the term which expressly included the benefit of the option. This, says counsel for the freeholder, necessarily follows from the principle established by *Spencer's Case*, that where a provision does not run with the land (as in his submission the present option does not), the parties cannot make it run, even where they show by express words their intention that the burden and benefit of it, as the case may be, should pass to the respective assignees.

Counsel for the assignee traverses the argument of counsel for the freeholder and submits that the benefit of an option such as this, expressly made exercisable not only by the original lessee but also by her executors, administrators and assigns, is an assignable interest which will pass to any assignee of the lease under a mere assignment of the term even though such assignment (like the assignment of Aug. 3, 1948, in the present case) contains no express reference to the option. Support for this view is to be found in the following authorities.

[The learned Justice here referred to and discussed the following cases: *Re Adams & Kensington Vestry* (1883), 24 Ch. D. 199, aff'd (1884), 27 Ch. D. 394 (C.A.); *Friary Holroyd & Healey's Breweries Ltd.* v. *Singleton*, [1899] 1 Ch. 86, rev'd [1899] 2 Ch. 261 (C.A.); *Batchelor* v. *Murphy*, [1925] Ch. 220 (C.A.), aff'd [1926] A.C. 63; and *Re Johnston's Application*, [1950] 1 All E.R. 613 (Ch.). He then continued as follows:]

In this state of the authorities, counsel for the freeholder urges us to follow *Woodall* v. *Clifton*, which he says concludes the present case in his favour, and to reject all observations to the contrary in the other authorities to which we have referred as made obiter or alio intuitu or on the strength of admissions. In particular, he adopts this comment by Romer, L. J., towards the end of the judgment of the court in *Woodall* v. *Clifton* ([1905] 2 Ch. at p. 279), as disposing of what is perhaps the most difficult case from his point of view:

"There are cases where the option has been exercised by the tenant and accepted by the landlord, and subsidiary questions have had to be decided which naturally would be dealt with on the footing that what had already been done could not or need not be questioned by the court; as, for example, *Re Adams & Kensington Vestry*. But such cases are really of no assistance for the decision of the present case."

On the other hand, counsel for the assignee submits that the cases above referred to relating to options to purchase, other than *Woodall* v. *Clifton*, taken together afford a strong body of judicial opinion in favour of the assignee's contention by which, in preference to *Woodall* v. *Clifton*, the court should be guided in deciding the present case.

In order to resolve this conflict it will be necessary to examine with some care *Woodall* v. *Clifton*, to see what was actually decided by that authority. However, before doing so, we may perhaps be permitted some general observations of an elementary kind as to the nature of options to purchase land. It is by no means uncommon for leases to contain (as did the present lease) provisions conferring on the lessee an option to purchase the freehold. Options to purchase land are also, however, not uncommonly granted in cases where the grantor and the grantee of the option do not stand in the relationship of landlord and tenant. Options of the latter class may conveniently be referred to as "options in gross". An option in gross for the purchase of land is a conditional contract for such purchase by the grantee of the option from the grantor, which the grantee is entitled to convert into a concluded contract of purchase, and to have carried to completion by the grantor, on giving the prescribed notice and otherwise complying with the conditions on which the option is made exercisable in any particular case. The conditional contract constituted by the grant of the option is a chose in action the benefit of which can (if the terms of the contract are such as to show that it is not merely personal to the grantor) be assigned by the grantee to anyone he chooses, subject to any restriction imposed by the contract as to the persons in whose favour assignment is permissible. The burden of the contract qua contract does not, in the absence of novation, pass to a third party acquiring the land; but inasmuch as the option creates in favour of the grantee of the option a contingent interest in the land, it may, provided that its exercise is limited to a period permissible under the rule against perpetuities, and provided that the appropriate precautions as to registration are taken, be exercised and enforced against the land in the hands of such third party—see as to the rule against perpetuities in relation to options the judgment of Warrington, J., in *Woodall* v. *Clifton* ([1905] 2 Ch. 257), and of Jenkins, J., in *Hutton* v. *Watling* ([1947] 2 All E.R. 641 at pp. 643 et seq., affd., [1948] 1 All E.R. 803) in which two cases the authorities on this matter are discussed. An option contained in a lease for the lessee to purchase the freehold differs from an option in gross only in the respects that the grantor and the grantee stand in the relationship of landlord and tenant, and that the contract creating it is made part of the terms on which the lease is granted. However, albeit collateral to the lease, it is in itself a distinct contract possessing all the essential characteristics of an option in gross. These general observations lead us to the conclusion that under the option provisions in the present case Miss Blaker was entitled as a matter of contract to assign the benefit of the option contained in the lease to the assignee as her assignee of the term, so as to entitle the assignee to enforce it against the freeholder, who, be it observed, was not an assignee of the reversion but the executrix of the original lessor, and as such bound by her testator's contract.

Returning to *Woodall* v. *Clifton*, we would observe that the plaintiff there seeking to enforce the option was an assignee of the original lessee to whom and whose heirs and assigns the option to purchase had been granted, while the defendants were assignees of the original lessor: and that the term during which the option was expressed to be exercisable was ninety-nine years from June 24, 1866. The assignment of the reversion prevented the plaintiff from enforcing the option against the defendants as a matter of contract, and the plaintiff could only rely on the contingent or conditional interest in the land created by the option, because the period during which it was exercisable exceeded the limit of time imposed by the rule against perpetuities. Warrington, J., held in those circumstances that the option to purchase was void on the ground of remoteness. The Court of Appeal apparently accepted this view so far as the plaintiff's claim involved the assertion that the option created an interest in the land which had devolved on him by assignment, but went on to consider an alternative contention to the effect that the burden of the proviso creating the option ran with the land so as to bind the assignees for the time being of the reversion at any distance of time. That was the contention which Romer, L. J., in delivering the judgment of the court, was concerned to repel, and he did so by holding that the burden of the proviso did not run with the land so as to make the option enforceable against the assignees of the reversion. He did not hold that if there had been no assignment of the reversion the plaintiff as assignee of the term could not as a matter of contract have enforced the option against the original lessor or his personal representative. We think that it is reasonably plain that he was deciding nothing of the sort. This sufficiently appears from the opening passage of his judgment, where he said ([1905] 2 Ch. at p. 278):

"A contract in a lease giving an option of purchase might be good, without regard to the provisions of the statute of Henry VIII, as binding the land in the hands of the heirs or assigns, provided it did not infringe the law as to perpetuities. It would not be the less a binding contract because it was contained in a lease. But in the present case it is clear that the plaintiff cannot succeed on such a ground. Unless the covenant or proviso giving the option of purchase can be said to run with the land by virtue of the provisions of the statute, then the plaintiff must fail."

If it has been his view (as counsel for the freeholder now would have us hold) that the plaintiff could not enforce the option because he was an assignee of the term, but not the original lessee, that would have been a short answer to the whole case, and his discussion of the question whether the assignees of the reversion were bound would have been wholly otiose. The same may be said of Warrington, J.'s full and careful discussion of the rule against perpetuities in its application to options to purchase land. We would add that *Friary Holroyd & Healey's Breweries, Ltd.* v. *Singleton* was referred to in argument in *Woodall* v. *Clifton* ([1905] 2 Ch. at p. 269), when Romer, L. J. said of it: "In that case the question was, assuming the validity of the covenant, who was the person entitled to give notice to exercise the option." That comment does not appear to us to cast any doubt on the correctness of view that he had expressed in the former case on the point now in hand

In our view, therefore, there is nothing in *Woodall* v. *Clifton* to prevent us from holding that it was competent to Miss Blaker to assign the benefit of the option to the assignee so as to make it exercisable and enforceable by him against the freeholder as executrix of the deceased original lessor. We agree with Vaisey, J. (as indeed was held in *Re Adams & Kensington Vestry* (27 Ch. D. 394, per Cotton, L. J. at p. 420, and per Lindley, L. J., at p. 404, and in *Re Friary Holroyd & Healey's Breweries. Ltd.* v. *Singleton*) that the reference to the assignees of the lessee, imported by definition into the option provision, must be construed as referring to assigns of the term, and consequently as limiting the assignability of the benefit of the option to assigns of that description. So far as assigns of that description are concerned, however, the language of the proviso conferring the option expressly entitles them to exercise it.

The first of the two questions stated above therefore seems to us to come down to the narrow issue whether the assignment of Aug. 3, 1948, being on the face of it a mere assignment of the term, without any reference to the benefit of the option, operated, in view of the terms of the proviso, or, in other words, the contract creating the option, as an assignment of the benefit of the option; or whether an express reference to the benefit of the option in the assignment of the term was necessary to produce that result. We think that, on the true construction of the proviso, including the definition to be read into it of the term lessee as including the lessee's assigns, the original parties to the lease must be taken to have agreed that the option should be exercisable by Miss Blaker herself or by any assignee of the term to whom she might assign the benefit of the option, and that a mere assignment of the term should operate as an assignment of the benefit of the option to the assignee of the term. On this point we find ourselves in complete agreement with the following passage from the judgment of Vaisey, J.:

"I now come to what seems to me to be the main point of the case, which is whether the benefit of the option passed by the assignment of 1948, or, if not, then by the assignment of 1956. Taking the assignment of 1948 first, it seems to me that the benefit of the option did pass by it to the [assignee] notwithstanding the omission of any reference to it. Admittedly it was a collateral contract, independent in some respects of the main contract between the parties as lessor and lessee. I think that the point is covered by *Re Adams & Kensington Vestry* ((1883), 24 Ch. D. 199); see per Pearson, J., at p. 206"—.

Then Vaisey, J., reads part of what I have already quoted from the judgment of Pearson, J., including "If the lease had been simply assigned, without any more words, the option would have passed with it...." Then the learned judge continues: "In the same case in the Court of Appeal ((1884), 27 Ch. D. 394), the decision of Pearson, J., was affirmed." Then Vaisey, J., quotes Cotton, L. J.'s observations (27 Ch. D. at p. 402), and goes on: "To the same effect is *Batchelor* v. *Murphy* ([1925] Ch. 220)." Vaisey, J., then, after briefly stating the nature of that case and quoting a passage from the judgment of Warrington, L. J. (ibid., at p. 228), to which we have already referred, continues:

"And the authority of that decision is enhanced and certainly in no way diminished by the report of the same case in the House of Lords ([1926] A. C. 63) and support is given to the same view by *Re Johnston's Application* ([1950] 1 All E.R. 613)."

For these reasons we are of opinion that the first of the two questions raised should be answered in the affirmative, that is to say, in the sense that the assignment of Aug. 3, 1948, did, as Vaisey, J., held, effectually vest the benefit of the option in the assignee.

That conclusion makes it strictly unnecessary to answer the second question, concerning the efficacy of the deed of Mar. 22, 1956, which purported to assign the benefit of the option to the assignee, if and so far as not already vested in him by the assignment of Aug. 3, 1948, and Vaisey, J., did not deal with it. However, in case we are wrong in holding the assignment of Aug. 3, 1948, to have included the benefit of the option, we should perhaps briefly indicate our view on this second question also.

If the assignment of Aug. 3, 1948, did not pass the benefit of the option to the assignee, then in our view the benefit of the option remained vested in Miss Blaker. True it is that by the terms of the option provision Miss Blaker could only assign it to an assignee of the term, but we fail to see why it should not have been competent to her to assign it to the assignee who was in fact the assignee of the term.

Counsel for the freeholder contended that the benefit of the option if, contrary to his submission on the first question, it was assignable at all, was only assignable along with and by the same instrument as the term; and accordingly that by assigning the term without including the option, Miss Blaker destroyed the option, which thus became incapable of assignment to the assignee or anyone else. We find it impossible to accede to this argument and are clearly of opinion that the deed of Mar. 22, 1956 must have constituted an effective assignment of the benefit of the option to the assignee if the assignment of Aug. 3, 1948, did not.

Appeal dismissed.

[Petition for leave to appeal to House of Lords dismissed: [1958] 1 W.L.R. 65. See also *Re Maynard and Regent Refining (Canada) Ltd.*, [1956] O.W.N. 251, where King J. held in a short judgment that an assignment of a lease "together with all benefit and advantage to be derived therefrom" enabled the assignee to enforce an option to purchase against the original lessor.]

[*In Quee* v. *Jany* (1957), 7 D.L.R. 2d 596 (Ont. C.A.), the Court, citing *Woodall* v. *Clifton* held that an option to purchase, given to a lessee, was not enforceable against an assignee of the reversion because it was "a collateral right and not a right running with the reversion".

Does it not follow from *Griffith* v. *Pelton* and *Quee* v. *Jany* that one end of a covenant may run but the other end may not? For a development of this thesis, see *Bigelow*, The Content of Covenants in Leases (1914), 12 Mich. L. Rev. 639, 30 Law Q. Rev. 319; cf. 2 *American Law of Property*, s. 9.13.

While it may be quite proper, in landlord and tenant cases, to hold that if only one end of a covenant "touches and concerns", it may "run" although the other end will not, is it good policy to apply this view to the running of restrictive covenants in equity? For example, should the benefit be enforceable at the suit of a person who has no land to be benefited although the burden will run in equity? See *London County Council* v. *Allen*, [1914] 3 K.B. 642 (C.A.); and see section 3 of this chapter, *infra*.]

[A leased land to B for a term certain and gave B an option to purchase. B did not register the option, and because of this he was advised that he would be unable to exercise it against X, A's assignee. B thereupon gave notice to A of his exercise of the option and sued A for damages. Should he succeed? See *Wright* v. *Dean*, [1948] Ch. 686, [1948] 2 All E.R. 415. Would it have made any difference if the option had been registered?]

[A lease which provided for assignment only by leave of the lessor contained an option to purchase in favour of "the lessee, his heirs and assigns". The lease was assigned, without the lessor's consent, with all rights of action, benefits and interest of the lessee, and, in particular, all rights under the option. The assignee gave the lessor notice of the assignment and at the same time purported to exercise the option. Has he an enforceable claim against the lessor? See *Mus* v. *Matlashewski*, [1944] 4 D.L.R. 522, [1944] 3 W.W.R. 358, 52 Man. R. 247 (C.A.).]

[The usual covenants found in leases such as the covenant to repair, the covenant against assignment, the covenant to pay rent and the covenant for quiet enjoyment are all binding on or enforceable by assignees. Some covenants are just as obviously covenants which do not bind assignees; for example, a covenant to pay taxes on other than the leased premises (*Gower* v. *Postmaster-General* (1887), 57 L.T.N.S. 527 (Ch.)), a covenant to pay a sum of money in consideration of obtaining a lease (see *Regor Estates Ltd.* v. *Wright*, [1951] 1 K.B. 689, [1951] 1 All E.R. 219 (C.A.)), or a covenant to sell other land (see *Collison* v. *Lettsom* (1815), 6 Taunt. 224, 128 E.R. 1020 (C.P.)).

See *Note*, Landlord and Tenant: Covenants Running with the Land (1946), 201 L.T. 52.]

[A lessee covenanted to insure the leased property against fire in the lessor's name and the latter agreed to expend the insurance money in rebuilding. The leasehold term was assigned to defendant. No insurance was effected, and when the buildings were destroyed by fire the lessor sued for damages. Result? See *Douglass* v. *Murphy* (1858), 16 U.C.Q.B. 113 (C.A.). See also *Vernon* v. *Smith* (1821), 5 B. & Ald. 1, 106 E.R. 1094 (K.B.), where the assignee of the reversion sued the lessee for breach of a covenant to insure.

Should there be any difference in result in the two situations?]

[The burden of a covenant to insure does not run as between vendor and purchaser: see *Lampert* v. *Weber and Doyle*, [1923] 2 W.W.R. 1148 (Sask. C.A.).]

[Does a covenant by a lessor not to compete in business with his lessee bind an assignee of the reversion? Does it bind the lessor in favour of an assignee of the lease? See *Thomas* v. *Hayward* (1869), L.R. 4 Ex. 311.

Certainly, a covenant by the lessee not to carry on particular kinds of businesses on the premises will bind his assignees. Should this be so if the covenant by the lessee is one not to compete with a business carried on by the lessor? Even if it should run as to burden, what about benefit? Is such a covenant any different from a covenant like that in *Clegg* v. *Hands*, *supra*, requiring the lessee to do business only with the lessor? Cf. *Cities Service Oil Co. Ltd.* v. *Pauley*, [1931] O.R. 685.]

[A lessor covenanted that he would not erect or permit to be erected on adjoining land (which he held) any building in front of a defined building line on the adjoining land. Is this covenant enforceable by the assignee of the lease? Is it enforceable against the assignee of the lessor? See *Ricketts* v. *Enfield Churchwardens*, [1909] 1 Ch. 544. Cf. *Sampson* v. *Easterby* (1829), 9 B. & C. 505, 109 E.R. 182 (K.B.), aff'd (1830), 6 Bing. 644, 130 E.R. 1429 (Ex. Ch.).]

[An 89-year lease made in 1820 contained a covenant by the lessee to repair, with a proviso for re-entry on breach of covenant. In 1886 the then lessee gave a sublease of part of the demised property to one H and covenanted with him for quiet enjoyment and also to observe the covenants in the head lease so far as they affected land covered by the head lease and not included in the sublease; and also to indemnify the sublessee against breaches of these covenants. H assigned the sublease to D. The head lease became vested in G, and on his failure to keep the premises in repair, including those covered by the sublease, the then head lessor recovered possession of the property. D was consequently ejected and he sued G for breaches of the covenants given by the sublessor. Should he succeed? See *Dewar* v. *Goodman*, [1909] A.C. 72.]

[In *Breams Property Investment Co. Ltd.* v. *Stroulger*, [1948] 2 K.B. 1, [1948] 1 All E.R. 758 (C.A.), the lessor of premises let on a quarterly tenancy covenanted not to terminate the tenancy (by notice to quit) for three years from a specified date unless he required the premises for himself. The lessor assigned the reversion to X who was unaware of the covenant. X purported to terminate the tenancy by notice to quit within the three year period. Result?

A lessor of apartments in an apartment building included in the leases a covenant on his part to supply maid service to the various tenants. Is the lessor's assignee bound by the covenant? See *Barnes* v. *London Real Property Co.*, [1918] 2 Ch. 18, 119 L.T. 293. *Cf. Lewin* v. *American and Colonial Distributors Ltd.*, [1945] 1 All E.R. 592, 173 L.T. 416, aff'd [1945] Ch. 225, [1945] 2 All E.R. 271 (C.A.).]

A lease made in 1802 for 89 years included a covenant by the tenant to repair. One G took possession in 1836, as against the tenant (who disappeared), and remained in possession until 1876, paying rent to the landlord during that period. In 1876 G assigned his interest to defendant. Plaintiff, assignee of the reversion, subsequently sued defendant for breach of the covenant to repair. Result? See *Tichborne* v. *Weir* (1892), 67 L.T. 735 (C.A.); *cf. O'Connor* v. *Foley*, [1906] 1 Ir. R. 20 (C.A.)]

[As is evident from *Wright* v. *Dean*, referred to *supra*, at p. 502 a covenantor remains contractually liable on his covenant although he has assigned the land or estate burdened by the covenant. Two questions are material: (1) Does the covenantor, if held liable on his covenant, have any right of redress against any subsequent assignee of the burdened estate? (2) Does the covenantee or any assignee of his have standing to enforce the covenant against the covenantor (or any assignee) after such covenantee or assignee has parted with the benefited interest? On the first question, see *Moule* v. *Garrett* (1872), L.R. 7 Ex. 101, 41 L.J. Ex. 62; *Boulton* v. *Blake* (1886), 12 O.R. 532; and *cf. Magill* v. *Young* (1853), 10 U.C.Q.B. 301 (C.A.). On the second question, see *Brett* v. *Cumberland* (1619), 2 Rolle 63, 81 E.R. 661 (K.B.); *Re Rabinovitch and Booth* (1914), 31 O.L.R. 88, 19 D.L.R. 296 (C.A.); and *cf. Stuart* v. *Joy*, [1904] 1 K.B. 362, 73 L.J.K.B. 97 (C.A.). See, generally, 23 Halsbury (1958, 3rd ed.), pp. 644 ff.; 2 *American Law of Property*, s. 9.5.]

3. RESTRICTIVE COVENANTS BETWEEN HOLDERS IN FEE SIMPLE

(a) *Conditions of Enforceability*

TULK v. MOXHAY. Chancery. 1848. 2 Ph. 774, 41 E.R. 1143

Motion to vacate an injunction originally granted *ex parte* by the Master of the Rolls, Lord Langdale, and continued by him in refusing a motion to dissolve it, 18 L.J. Ch. 83.

The facts giving rise to the injunction were as follows: In the year 1808 the Plaintiff, being then the owner in fee of the vacant piece of ground in Leicester Square, as well as of several of the houses forming the Square, sold the piece of ground by the description of "Leicester Square garden or pleasure ground, with the equestrian statue then standing in the centre thereof, and the iron railing and stone work round the same," to one Elms in fee; and the deed of conveyance contained a covenant by Elms, for himself, his heirs, and assigns, with the Plaintiff, his heirs, executors, and administrators, "that Elms, his heirs, and assigns should, and would from time to time, and at all times thereafter at his and their own costs and charges, keep and maintain the said piece of ground and square garden, and the iron railing round the same in its then form, and in sufficient and proper repair as a square garden and pleasure ground, in an open state, uncovered with any buildings, in neat and ornamental order; and that it should be lawful for the inhabitants of Leicester Square, tenants of the Plaintiff, on payment of a reasonable rent for the same, to have keys at their own expense and the privilege of admission therewith at any time or times into the said square garden and pleasure ground."

The piece of land so conveyed passed by divers mesne conveyances into the hands of the Defendant, whose purchase deed contained no similar covenant with his vendor: but he admitted that he had purchased with notice of the covenant in the deed of 1808.

The Defendant having manifested an intention to alter the character of the square garden, and asserted a right, if he thought fit, to build upon it, the Plaintiff, who still remained owner of several houses in the square, filed a bill for an injunction.

COTTENHAM L. C.: That this Court has jurisdiction to enforce a contract between the owner of land and his neighbour purchasing a part of it, that the latter shall either use or abstain from using the land purchased in a particular way, is what I never knew disputed. Here there is no question about the contract: the owner of certain houses in the square sells the land adjoining, with a covenant from the purchaser not to use it for any other purpose than as a square garden. And it is now contended, not that the vendee could violate that contract, but that he might sell the piece of land, and that the purchaser from him may violate it without this Court having any power to interfere. If that were so, it would be impossible for an owner of land to sell part of it without incurring the risk of rendering what he retains worthless. Is is said that, the covenant being one which does not run with the land, this Court cannot enforce it; but the question is, not whether the covenant runs with the land, but whether a party shall be permitted to use the land in a manner inconsistent with the contract entered into by his vendor, and with notice of which he purchased. Of course, the price would be affected by the covenant, and nothing could be more inequitable than that the original purchaser should be able to sell the property the next day for a greater price, in consideration of the assignee being allowed to escape from the liability which he had himself undertaken.

That the question does not depend upon whether the covenant runs with the land is evident from this, that if there was a mere agreement and no covenant, this Court would enforce it against a party purchasing with notice of it; for if an equity is attached to the property by the owner, no one purchasing with notice of that equity can stand in a different situation from the party from whom he purchased. There are not only cases before the Vice-Chancellor of England, in which he considered that doctrine as not in dispute; but looking at the ground on which Lord Eldon disposed of the case of *The Duke of Bedford* v. *The Trustees of the British Museum* (2 My. & K. 552), it is impossible to suppose that he entertained any doubt of it. In the case of *Mann* v. *Stephens* (15 Sim. 379), before me, I never intended to make the injunction depend upon the result of the action: nor does the order imply it. The motion was, to discharge an order for the commitment of the Defendant for an alleged breach of the injunction, and also to dissolve the injunction. I upheld the injunction, but discharged the order of commitment, on the ground that it was not clearly proved that any breach had been committed; but there being a doubt whether part of the premises on which the Defendant was proceeding to build was locally situated within what was called the Dell, on which alone he had under the covenant a right to build at all, and the Plaintiff insisting that it was not, I thought the pendency of the suit ought not to prejudice the Plaintiff in his right to bring an action if he thought he had such right, and, therefore, I gave him liberty to do so.

With respect to the observations of Lord Brougham in *Keppell* v. *Bailey*, (2 My. & K. 547) he never could have meant to lay down that this Court would not enforce an equity attached to land by the owner, unless under such circumstances as would maintain an action at law. If that be the result of his observations, I can only say that I cannot coincide with it.

I think the cases cited before the Vice-Chancellor and this decision of the Master of the Rolls perfectly right, and, therefore, that this motion must be refused, with costs.

Motion dismissed.

[For subsequent, though unrelated, proceedings involving Leicester Square and an account of the devolution of title thereto, see *Tulk* v. *Metropolitan Board of Works* (1867), L.R. 3 Q.B. 49 (C.A.).]

[It is now clear that notice is significant not to the running of covenants in equity but to the question (on the assumption that they otherwise run) whether a purchaser holds the legal title in the burdened land free of restrictive covenants. On this score, registration legislation, whether in respect of documents or of title, is important.

The existence of an enforceable restrictive covenant on land contracted to be sold constitutes a valid objection to title: see *Re Hunt and Bell.* (1915), 34 O.L.R. 256, 24 D.L.R. 590 (App. Div.); *Re Bowes Co. Ltd. and Rankin* (1924), 55 O.L.R. 601, [1924] 4 D.L.R. 406 (App. Div.).

A purchaser agreed to buy certain land and a building thereon "subject to the restrictions and covenants that run with the land". The building was in fact put up by the vendor in breach of a restrictive covenant but this was not known to the purchaser when he entered into the agreement for sale. Is the purchaser entitled to withdraw from the contract? Would it make any difference if he knew, when making the contract, of the vendor's breach of covenant? See *McAleer* v. *Desjardine*, [1948] O.R. 557, [1948] 4 D.L.R. 40 (C.A.).]

[Land burdened by a restrictive covenant is occupied by a stranger for a period and in circumstances sufficient to extinguish title of the former holder. Is the burden enforceable against the stranger? Suppose that he subsequently sells the land to a purchaser for value who has no actual notice of the restrictive covenant but it is included in the registered deed to the dispossessed holder. (It is material here to consider (1) the effect of the applicable Statute of Limitations, and (2) the effect of legislation or other rule of law governing the length of required search through the chain of title). See *Re Nisbet and Potts' Contract*, [1906] 1 Ch. 386 (C.A.), aff'g [1905] 1 Ch. 391.

In *Re Hunt and Bell, supra*, land burdened by a restrictive covenant was sold for taxes pursuant to legislative authority, and a tax sale deed was given to the purchaser without mention of the covenant. *Held*, on appeal, reversing the trial Judge, the tax sale and the deed given in consequence thereof extinguished the covenant. It was pointed out by a member of the Court that the applicable legislation provided for sale of the land itself and not merely of the defaulting taxpayer's interest therein. On this interpretation, the result is clear and it would be immaterial whether or not the purchaser knew of the restrictive covenant.]

[A defendant, against whom it is sought to enforce a restrictive covenant which is included in a registered deed of the burdened land, urges that he is not bound unless the deed contains or discloses facts from which it may be ascertained that the covenant is one which validly runs. Is the argument tenable? See *Besinnett* v. *White*, 58 O.L.R. 125, [1926] 1 D.L.R. 95 (App. Div.), aff'g 57 O.L.R. 171, [1925] 3 D.L.R. 560.]

LONDON COUNTY COUNCIL v. ALLEN. Court of Appeal. [1914] 3 K.B. 642, 83 L.J.K.B. 1695

Appeal from a judgment of Avory J. in an action for breach of covenant. The material facts as set out in the judgment of Buckley L. J. were as follows.

This action was brought by the London County Council upon an indenture dated January 24, 1907, made between the defendant Morris Joseph Allen of the one part and the London County Council of the other part, claiming certain mandatory injunctions and damages for breach of a covenant contained in that indenture. Before the date of the execution of the deed the defendant M. J. Allen had applied to the London County Council for their permission under s. 7 of the London Building Act, 1894, to his laying out a certain new road, called Galloway Road, running from south to north, and a further small portion of road at the northern end of Galloway Road running from east to west in continuation of a road called Dunraven Street. The London County Council gave their permission upon the terms, amongst other things, that this defendant should enter into a certain deed of covenant, and that was the deed of January 24, 1907. The covenant in question was as follows: "The applicant" (that is to say, the defendant M. J. Allen) "doth hereby for himself, his heirs and assigns, and the other persons claiming under him, and so far as practicable to bind the land and hereditaments herein mentioned into whosesoever hands the same may come, covenant and agree with the council that he and they will not erect or place, or cause or permit to be erected or placed, any building, structure, or other erection upon the land shewn by green colour on the said plan without the previous consent in writing of the council so to do, and that on every conveyance, sale, charge, mortgage, lease, assignment, or other dealing with the land herein mentioned or any part thereof he will give notice of the aforesaid covenant in every conveyance, transfer, mortgage, charge, lease, assignment, or other document by which such dealing is effected." The deed recited (but contrary to the fact) that the applicant was the owner in fee simple of the land in question. He was not. He had at the date of this deed of covenant merely an option of purchase, which might or might not result in his becoming owner of the land. The portions coloured green were two, namely, plot No. 1, being the continuation of Dunraven Street to the west of Galloway Road, and plot No. 2, being the continuation of Galloway Road to the north of Dunraven Street. It is necessary to deal with these two plots separately.

First as regards plot No. 1. On July 3, 1908, this was conveyed to the defendant M. J. Allen in fee. On the same day he mortgaged it with other land to one Willcocks to secure a sum of £3600. On August 1, 1911, the mortgage was redeemed, and Willcocks with the concurrence of Allen conveyed the land discharged from the incumbrance to the defendant Emily Allen in fee. On October 9, 1911, Mrs. Allen charged the land together with the three messuages then recently erected thereon to the defendant Norris in fee by way of mortgage. In the interval, namely, in July, 1911, Mrs. Allen built on plot No. 1 and completed by the end of that month three houses. The writ in this action was issued on August 5, 1911.

By virtue of ss. 7 and 9 of the London Building Act, 1894, the London County Council have certain powers of control over land which the owner proposes to form or lay out in streets. But they have no estate or interest in such land. The plaintiffs at the date of the deed of covenant had no estate or interest in any land adjoining or in any manner affected by the observance or non-observance of the covenant contained in the deed.

The trial Judge in the exercise of discretion declined to grant a mandatory injunction to pull down the houses erected by Mrs. Allen on one plot or the wall erected by M. J. Allen on the other. However, he apparently treated the duty and interest of the county council in the matter of new streets as sufficient to make the covenant bind the land in the hands of assigns from Allen. Accordingly, he gave judgment for 40 s. nominal damages against the defendants M. J. Allen and Mrs. Allen and he gave judgment for the defendant Norris but ordered him to pay his own costs. On appeal by all defendants, argument proceeded first on the point of law whether, assuming that defendants Mrs. Allen and Norris had notice of the restrictive covenant, it was enforceable against them.

SCRUTTON J. (ad hoc):... Counsel on each side agreed that the burden of this covenant would not run with the land at law, so as to bind assigns, for the reason stated in the notes to *Spencer's Case* that "there appears to be no authority which has decided, apart from the equitable doctrine of notice" (by which is meant, as hereinafter explained, the doctrine identified with the case of *Tulk* v. *Moxhay* "that the burden of a covenant will run with land in any case except that of landlord and tenant." This opinion appears to be justified by the judgments of the Court of Appeal in *Austerberry* v. *Oldham Corporation*, 29 Ch. D. 750, especially that of Lindley L. J. at p. 781 and of Fry L. J. at p. 784.

The question then is whether it is essential to the doctrine of *Tulk* v. *Moxhay* that the covenantee should have at the time of the creation of the covenant, and afterwards, land for the benefit of which the covenant is created, in order that the burden of the covenant may bind assigns of the land to which it relates. It is clear that the covenantee may sue the covenantor himself, though the former has parted with the land to which the covenant relates: *Stokes* v. *Russell*, 3 T.R. 678. To answer the question as to the assigns of the covenantor, and the land in their hands, requires the investigation of the historical growth of the doctrine of *Tulk* v. *Moxhay*. Though the covenantee in that case did hold adjacent land, there is no trace in the judgment of Lord Cottenham of the requirement that the covenantee should have and continue to hold land to be benefited by the covenant. I read Lord Cottenham's judgment as proceeding entirely on the question of notice of the covenant, and on the equitable ground that a man purchasing land with notice that there was a covenant not to use it in a particular way would not be allowed to violate the covenant he knew of when he bought the land. Lord Cottenham states the question, "Whether a party shall be permitted to use the land in a manner inconsistent with the contract entered into by his vendor and with notice of which he purchased," and answers it: "If there was a mere agreement and no covenant, this Court would enforce it against a party purchasing with notice of it; for if an equity is attached to the property by the owner, no one purchasing with notice of that equity can stand in a different situation from the party from whom he purchased."

Up to 1881, when counsel in *Haywood* v. *Brunswick Permanent Benefit Building Society*, 8 Q.B.D. 403, stated (at p. 405) that *Tulk* v. *Moxhay* had been applied in fifteen cases, I cannot trace, nor could counsel before us discover, that *Tulk* v. *Moxhay* had been based on anything but notice of the covenant by the assignee. In the case cited, in which the Court of Appeal refused to extend the doctrine to an affirmative covenant to repair, Lindley L. J. said (at p. 410): "The result of these cases is that only such a covenant as can be complied with without expenditure of money will be enforced against the assignee on the ground of notice." Brett L. J. said (at p. 408): "That case" (*Tulk* v. *Moxhay*) "decided that an assignee taking land subject to a certain class of covenants is bound by such covenants if he has notice of them, and that the class of covenants comprehended within the rule is that covenants restricting the mode of using the land only will be enforced." Cotton L. J., after citing Lord Cottenham that "No one purchasing with notice of that equity can stand in a different situation from the party from whom he purchased," said (at p. 409): "This lays down the real principle that an equity attaches to the owner of the land." Meanwhile in *De Mattos* v.

Gibson, 4 De G. & J. 276, at p. 282, in 1858, Knight Bruce L. J. had put the principle as applying to all property thus: "Reason and justice seem to prescribe that, at least as a general rule, where a man, by gift or purchase, acquires property from another, with knowledge of a previous contract, lawfully and for valuable consideration made by him with a third person, to use and employ the property for a particular purpose in a specified manner, the acquirer shall not, to the material damage of the third person, in opposition to the contract and inconsistently with it, use and employ the property in a manner not allowable to the giver or seller," resting the matter on knowledge of the previous contract, that is notice. In *Catt* v. *Tourle*, L. R. 4 Ch. 654, in 1869, A., a brewer, had sold land to B. with a covenant that he should have the exclusive right to supply all ale consumed in any public-house erected on the land. C., with knowledge of the covenant, bought part of the land from B., erected a public-house on it, but did not take his beer from A. The Court of Appeal, citing *De Mattos* v. *Gibson*, restrained C., treating the covenant as negatave, and resting the judgment on the ground that C. "clearly purchased with notice of the present covenant, and... cannot be heard to say that he is now entitled to disregard its provisions." It is to be noted that A. is not stated to have owned any land, and as he might brew beer anywhere, the covenant could not relate to any particular land of his.

In *Luker* v. *Dennis*, 7 Ch. D. 227, in 1877, A., a brewer, granted a lease to B. of public-house X., with a covenant that B. should take from him all beer consumed not only in X., but also in public-house Y., which B. held of a different landlord. C. took public-house Y. from B. with notice of the covenant, and did not take his beer from A. It was argued before Fry J. that notice was not enough unless the covenantee had some interest in the land bound by the covenant, either as vendor or lessor. That learned judge refused to accede to this argument, and, citing *De Mattos* v. *Gibson* and *Catt* v. *Tourle*, granted the injunction, giving, as he said (at p. 236), "effect to the equitable doctrine of notice." I think up to this point the doctrine had been rested on notice, and did not depend on the covenantee having land in favour of which the covenant was created.

The first departure from this position occurs in the judgment of Jessel M. R. in *London and South Western Ry. Co.* v. *Gomm*, 20 Ch. D. 562, in March, 1882. The contract to be enforced was one to reconvey land on notice, and clearly therefore an affirmative covenant, and, as such, within the doctrine laid down in *Haywood's Case* in December, 1881, excluding such contracts from the doctrine of *Tulk* v. *Moxhay*. The Court also held that the sale was ultra vires the railway company, and void for remoteness. But Sir George Jessel, holding that the covenant did, but for its being ultra vires and void, create an interest in the land, discussed the nature of the right. He said: "The doctrine of that case,"—*Tulk* v. *Moxhay*—"rightly considered, appears to me to be either an extension in equity of the doctrine of *Spencer's Case* to another line of cases, or else an extension in equity of the doctrine of negative easements; such, for instance, as a right to the access of light, which prevents the owner of the servient tenement from building so as to obstruct the light. The covenant in *Tulk* v. *Moxhay* was affirmative in its terms, but was held by the Court to imply a negative. Where there is a negative covenant expressed or implied, as, for instance, not to build so as to obstruct a view, or not to use a piece of land otherwise than as a garden, the Court interferes on one or other of the above grounds. This is an equitable doctrine, establishing an exception to the rules of common law which did not treat such a covenant as running with the land, and it does not matter whether it proceeds on analogy to a covenant running with the land or on analogy to an easement. The purchaser took the estate subject to the equitable burden, with the qualification that if he acquired the legal estate for value without notice he was freed from the burden. That qualification however, did not affect the nature of the burden; the notice was required merely to avoid the effect of the legal estate, and did not create the right, and if the purchaser took only an equitable estate he took subject to the burden, whether he had notice or not." It will be noticed that the equitable estate or burden was held to arise independent of notice; which I respectfully think was contrary to the previous authorities; and that in Sir George Jessel's view it did not matter whether it was by analogy to covenants running with the land, or on analogy to an easement. Both, however, had this in common, that some land belonging to the covenantee was required, either for him to let, that the covenant might run with the land, or as a dominant tenement for the easement, an easement in gross being merely a personal right. Whether the "analogy" or "extension" spoken of by Sir George Jessel involved this condition as to land is not discussed. The other members of the Court did not discuss the foundation of *Tulk* v. *Moxhay*, though Lindley L. J. seems again to put it on notice. *Catt* v. *Tourle* a decision of the Court of Appeal—and *Luker* v. *Dennis* were not cited to the Court.

In 1890, in *Clegg* v. *Hands*, 44 Ch. D. 503, the doctrine of *Tulk* v. *Moxhay*, was applied by the Court of Appeal to a case somewhat similar to *Catt* v. *Tourle*, without any discussion of Sir George Jessel's explanation of the doctrine, the case, however, being one of landlord and tenant. In *Rogers* v. *Hosegood* [1900] 2 Ch. 388, in 1900, A., the mortgagor, and B., the mortgagee, of some land, conveyed plot X. to C., who entered into a restrictive covenant with the mortgagor only, who had not the legal estate in the land. This plot X. was purchased by D. with notice of the restrictive covenant. A. also conveyed some of his adjoining land, plot Y., to E., who had no notice of the restrictive covenant on plot X. D. then proceeded to erect buildings on plot X. said to contravene the restrictive covenant. E. then sued D. to enforce the covenant. Farwell J. (at p. 394) treated D. as obviously bound by the covenant. "He is obviously bound, by reason of notice, whether the covenant as regards him runs with the land or not." (This expression of the reason why he is bound does not harmonize with the later decisions, but does, I think, with all the earlier ones.) And he held that the benefit of the covenant passed to E. at law running with his land. There was an appeal. In the course of the argument of Mr. Haldane, Q.C., that the covenant ran with the land in equity, Rigby L. J. said: "I do not think any covenant runs with the land in equity. The equitable doctrine is that a person who takes with notice of a covenant is bound by it"; a remark again which seems to me to harmonize with the earlier authorities. The Court held that the benefit of the covenant did not run with the land at law, as the covenantee, the mortgagor, had no legal interest in the land, but did run with the land in equity, as there was a clear intention to benefit that land, and equity would regard the mortgagor as the owner, and, citing Jessel M. R. in *London and South Western Ry.* v. *Gomm*, continued at p. 405: "These observations, which are just as applicable to the benefit reserved as to the burden imposed, shew that in equity, just as at law, the first point to be determined is whether the covenant or contract in its inception binds the land. If it does, it is then capable of passing with the land to subsequent assignees; if it does not, it is incapable of passing by mere assignment of the land. The benefit may be annexed to one plot and the burden to another, and when this has been once clearly done the benefit and the burden pass to the respective assignees, subject, in the case of the burden, to proof that the legal estate, if acquired, has been acquired with notice of the covenant." This makes land bound or benefited by the covenant essential to bind or benefit assigns. The judgment proceeds: "These authorities"—*Renals* v. *Cowlishaw*, 9 Ch. D. 125, and *Child* v. *Douglas*, Kay, 560—"establish the proposition that, when the benefit has been once clearly annexed to one piece of land, it passes by assignment of that land, and may be said to run with it, in contemplation as well of equity as of law, without proof of special bargain or representation on the assignment. In such a case it runs, not because the conscience of either party is affected, but because the purchaser has bought something which inhered in or was annexed to the land bought. This is the reason why, in dealing with the burden, the purchaser's conscience is not affected by notice of covenants which were part of the original bargain on the first sale, but were merely personal and collateral, while it is affected by notice of those which touch and concern the land. The covenant must be one that is capable of running with the land before the question of the purchaser's conscience and the equity affecting it can come into discussion." This again appears to me to treat land as essential, on both sides of the covenant, to affect assigns whether of the benefit or burden.

This view seems to me to be adopted also by the Court of Appeal in *Formby* v. *Barker* [1903] 2 Ch. 539. A., the owner of land, conveyed all his land with a restrictive covenant against its being used in particular ways to B., who assigned it to C., who had notice of the covenant. A. died; C. began to use the land in a way forbidden by the covenant; the administratrix of A., who had no land, sued C. It was argued that the right to enforce such a covenant depended entirely on notice; members of the Court suggested in argument that the benefit of the covenant, if not pursued by the covenantee, must follow some land; and this was the argument put forward for the defendant, that without land the covenant was only one in gross. Romer L. J. asked (at p. 546), "Is there any case in which it has been held that such a covenant purporting to bind land for ever is valid except for the protection of an estate?" and counsel for the plaintiff did not refer him, as they might have done, to *Catt* v. *Tourle* and *Luker* v. *Dennis*, in neither of which cases had the plaintiff an estate, but only a trade. In the judgments, Vaughan Williams L. J. points out that A. conveyed his whole estate and had no contiguous estate which would be benefited by the covenant in question. I refer to, but do not read, the Lord Justice's judgment on pp. 550-552, but it seems to me, adopting the language of Collins L. J. in *Rogers* v. *Hosegood*, to negative the view that the doctrine of *Tulk* v. *Moxhay* depends on notice, and to make it depend, where there is no contractual privity, on a "relation of dominancy and serviency of lands" (p. 552), and to fail if the covenantee or his assign has no land to which the covenant relates. Romer L. J. thought that the assign of a covenantee could not sue unless the covenant related to or concerned some ascertainable property belonging to him or in which he was interested. Stirling L. J., while saying that different considerations would apply if the covenantee sued, a remark which leaves it doubtful whether he thought the covenantee could, though owning no land, have sued assigns of the land restricted, rested his judgment on the ground that damages, not injunction would be the appropriate remedy.

The doctrine was again considered, and I think further developed, in *In re Nisbet and Potts' Contract* [1905] 1 Ch. 391 in 1905. The owner of certain land had entered into restrictive covenants with the vendor, who owned an adjoining estate. A squatter, without notice of these covenants, acquired a title by adverse possession, and sold to A., who did not require a forty years' title, which would have disclosed the restrictive covenants. A. sold to B., who, having reason to believe there were restrictive covenants, declined to complete. B. took out a summons for a declaration that the title was not one which he ought to be compelled to accept. Farwell J. treated the nature of the right of action created under the doctrine of *Tulk* v. *Moxhay* as analogous to an equitable charge on real estate, not depending in any way on notice for its validity, but only defeated by a legal estate acquired for value and without notice. He held therefore that the squatter, though he had no notice and had the legal estate, was bound by the restrictive covenants, as apparently he only took the land subject to the equitable interest in it, and that as the purchaser from the squatter of the legal estate for value would, of he had required a forty years' title, have had notice of the covenants, he had constructive notice and was bound by the covenants. In the Court of Appeal [1906] 1 Ch. 386, the appellant argued that notice was part of the cause of action, the respondent that the doctrine rested on an interest in land, binding on the land itself, with a dominant and servient tenement. The Court of Appeal adopted the latter argument, and held that the restrictive covenant was an equitable interest in the land, whether the occupier of the land had notice of it or not, unless he had purchased the legal estate for value without notice. They do not expressly refer to the necessity of there being a dominant tenement to enforce the interest, but there was in fact such a dominant tenement in the case.

Lastly, in *Millbourn* v. *Lyons* [1914] 1 Ch. 34, where a person who had agreed to sell with a restrictive covenant died, and his personal representatives, having sold all their land, conveyed with a similar restrictive covenant, Neville J. enforced the title against a purchaser who knew of the restrictive covenant, and therefore objected to complete, on the ground that there was no restriction against him, as the vendors, at the date of the covenant, had no land to which the benefit of the covenant could be attached, and the Court of Appeal affirmed his judgment on similar grounds.

I think the result of this long chain of authorities is that, whereas in my view, at the time of *Tulk* v. *Moxhay* and for at least twenty years afterwards, the plaintiffs in this case would have succeeded against an assign on the ground that the assign had notice of the covenant, since *Formby* v. *Barker*, *In re Nisbet and Potts' Contract*, and *Millbourn* v. *Lyons*, three decisions of the Court of Appeal, the plaintiffs must fail on the ground that they have never had any land for the benefit of which this "equitable interest analogous to a negative easement" could be created, and therefore cannot sue a person who bought the land with knowledge that there was a restrictive covenant as to its use, which he proceeds to disregard, because he is not privy to the contract. I think the learned editors of Dart on Vendors and Purchasers, 7th ed., vol. ii, p. 769, are justified by the present state of the authorities in saying that "the question of notice to the purchaser has nothing whatever to do with the question whether the covenant binds him, except in so far as the absence of notice may enable him to raise the plea of purchaser for valuable consideration without notice." If the covenant does not run with the land in law, its benefit can only be asserted against an assign of the land burdened, if the covenant was made for the benefit of certain land, all or some of which remains in the possession of the covenantee or his assign, suing to enforce the covenant. It may be, if the matter is considered by a higher tribunal, that tribunal may see its way to revert to what I think was the earlier doctrine of notice, or at any rate to treat it as co-existing with the later refinement of "an equitable interest analogous to a negative easement" binding on persons who are ignorant of it. The remarks of Lord Selborne in *Earl of Zetland* v. *Hislop*, 7 App. Cas. 427, at pp. 446, 447, are not favourable to the too rigid development or enforcement of the latter alternative; and the observations of Lord Macnaghten (p. 32), Lord Davey (p. 35), and Lord Lindley (p. 36) in *Noakes & Co.* v. *Rice* [1902] A.C. 24 seem to suggest that the doctrine of *Tulk* v. *Moxhay* may well be reconsidered and put on a proper footing. For I regard it as very regrettable that a public body should be prevented from enforcing a restriction on the use of property imposed for the public benefit against persons who bought the property knowing of the restriction, by the apparently immaterial circumstance that the public body does not own any land in the immediate neighbourhood. But, after a careful consideration of the authorities, I am forced to the view that the later decisions of this Court compel me so to hold.

In my opinion, therefore, the demurrer of Mr. Norris and of Mrs. Allen succeeds. The action against Mr. Norris must be dismissed with costs. I regret that I do not see my way to depriving Mrs. Allen of her costs, as whatever may be her equitable rights, I am not at all favourably impressed with her conduct as a good citizen. I see no reason for interfering with the judgment against Mr. Allen in respect of plots No. 1 and No. 2, and his appeal must be dismissed with costs.

Appeal allowed in part.

[The concurring judgments of Buckley L. J. and of Kennedy L. J. are omitted. *London County Council* v. *Allen* was followed in *Page* v. *Campbell*, 61 S.C.R. 633, 59 D.L.R. 215, [1921] 2 W.W.R. 552; see also *Playter* v. *Lucas* (1921), 51 O.L.R. 492, 69 D.L.R. 514.]

[While mere regulatory control by a municipality over land laid out or proposed to be laid out for streets may not establish a sufficient basis for enforcement by it of a restrictive covenant, is there any reason why a street may not be "benefited" land for that purpose if the municipality has in truth a proprietory interest therein? See *Re Daly and Vancouver* (1956), 5 D.L.R. 2d 474 (B.C.); *Re McKillop and Vancouver*, [1954] 3 D.L.R. 63, 11 W.W.R. (N.S.) 593 (B.C.), rev'd on other grounds, sub nom. *Vancouver* v. *Registrar Vancouver Land Registration District*, [1955] 2 D.L.R. 709, 15 W.W.R. (N.S.) 351 (B.C.C.A.); and cf. *Registrar of Titles* v. *Vancouver*, [1945] 3 D.L.R. 304, [1945] 2 W.W.R. 348, 51 B.C.R. 211 (C.A.).

It may be noted that there is legislation, e.g., Town Planning Act, R.S.N.S. 1954, c. 292, s. 11 (4), empowering a municipality to impose, by agreement with owners, building restrictions or easements without acquiring title to land to which to attach the benefit.]

[What sort of interest in a covenantee or his assigns will support a right to enforce a restrictive covenant (or, to put the matter another way, what is meant by "benefited land")? Similarly, what sort of interest in land is sufficient in the covenantor to make the burden of a restrictive covenant enforceable against his assigns? The following cases are illustrative.

In *A.-G.* v. *Comox Logging Co.*, [1955] 2 D.L.R. 211 (B.C.), the Crown created a subdivision of 18 lots subject to a uniform set of building restrictions. Assignees of the purchaser of two of the lots proposed to use them in breach of the restrictions and the Crown sued for an injunction. On a motion for an interim injunction (which was granted), defendants argued that the Crown had no land left in the subdivision for the benefit of which it could enforce the restrictions. On this point Macfarlane J., distinguishing *London County Council* v. *Allen*, said: "For the purposes of this motion, I do not think I could hold that the Crown has no estate or interest in the lands sold and not paid for or unsold. I do not think that the intention of the Crown to use Lot 6 and Lot 18 for road purposes, if such is its intention, or that the statutes require access to be given, deprives the Crown of its estate or interest in the lands until the intention is carried into action or access provided. Nor do I think that the Crown is without interest in the land sold and not paid for. I think too I can go so far as to say that whether or not there is what is known as a building scheme that where uniform restrictive conditions are imposed on all the lots in the subdivision, the same considerations apply as in a building scheme, *vide* Smith's Leading cases, 13th ed., vol. 1, p. 91, also *Hudson* v. *Cripps*, [1896] 1 Ch. 265. But I do not think that is the only footing on which the plaintiff stands here. The Crown has granted to Anderton the title to Lots 11 and 12 upon certain conditions, of which conditions, it is admitted, a breach has been made or is threatened. Those conditions by the terms in which they are expressed extend to the heirs and assigns of Anderton. *Prima facie* that would seem to me to give a right to an injunction. At least it raises a substantial question to be tried. I do not think that I should here attempt to consider at length the legal effect of a condition as that may be a matter to be determined on the trial of the action."

In *Besinnett* v. *White*, 58 O.L.R. 125, [1926] 1 D.L.R. 95 (App. Div.), aff'g 57 O.L.R. 171, [1925] 3 D.L.R. 560, the restrictive covenant in question was taken by the covenantee for the benefit of land which she did not then own (although she acquired title about 17 months later) but in respect of which she had the verbal (and, hence, unenforceable) agreement of the then owner to convey it to her. Middleton J. A., for the Court concluded that "the question is in each case one of intention—was the covenant taken to protect or benefit land in which the covenantee had an interest, using this term in its widest sense, or was it merely personal and collateral to the conveyance. If the former, then so long as the interest intended to be protected remains, or is augmented as in the case in hand, there is no reason why the Court should not compel... regard [for] the terms of the covenant". *Held*, the interest under the verbal agreement was a sufficient interest to support the benefit of the covenant even though that interest might have been defeated by repudiation of the verbal agreement.

The position is apparently not the same so far as the burden of a covenant on a fee simple interest is concerned. In *Besinnett* v. *White*, the Court said that "no one doubts that in order that the lands may be bound by the covenantor he must own the lands". If the state of affairs at the date of a conveyance governs, it would follow that an assignee of the interest of a purchaser under an agreement for sale would not be bound by a restrictive covenant included in the agreement: see *Millbourn* v. *Lyons*, [1914] 1 Ch. 34, aff'd [1914] 2 Ch. 231 (C.A.).

It should be noted that in *London County Council* v. *Allen*, *supra*, the covenantor had merely an option to purchase the land but for the purposes of the case he was treated as the owner at the date of the covenant: see [1914] 3 K.B. 643n. Suppose he had assigned the option instead of himself exercising it. Would his assignee have been bound?

Where the matter of binding the fee simple interest is not in issue, there is no doubt that restrictive covenants may run against assigns of a mortgagor or of a lessee so long as the estates to which they are attached subsist. See *Preston and Newsom*, Restrictive Covenants Affecting Freehold Land (1955, 2nd ed.), pp. 61 ff.]

The fact that a grantee of land does not execute the conveyance in which there are restrictive covenants does not in itself affect either his liability or that of his assigns where the conveyance is acted upon, e.g. by registering it or by assigning the land subject to the covenants: see *Re Rowan and Eaton*, 60 O.L.R. 245, [1927] 2 D.L.R. 722, aff'g 59 O.L.R. 379, [1926] 4 D.L.R. 582 (App. Div.); see also *Re Wheeler*, 59 O.L.R. 223, [1926] 4 D.L.R. 392 (App. Div.).]

RE UNION OF LONDON AND SMITH'S BANK LIMITED'S CONVEYANCE, MILES v. EASTER. Court of Appeal. [1933] Ch. 611, 102 L.J. Ch. 241

Appeal from a judgment of Bennett J. in favour of plaintiff, declaring that certain restrictive covenants were not enforceable against him by defendant. In 1908, a vendor company sold part of its land to purchasers under a deed in which they entered into restrictive covenants for themselves, their heirs and assigns, one of which was a covenant not to put up certain kinds of buildings on the land conveyed. A plan annexed to the conveyance showed the purchased land in the colours pink, violet, brown and red; and it showed other land retained by the vendor in the colour green. Plaintiff became owner of part of the land coloured pink (with knowledge of the restrictive covenants), and defendant became owner of the larger part of the land coloured green. He had, however, sold some parts of it, and at the time of the action there were about 14 or 15 other persons who held in fee simple some of the land coloured green on the plan.

After the vendor had sold its retained land (the greater portion to defendant), it executed an express assignment to defendant of the benefit of the restrictive covenants. Plaintiff's title to part of the "pink" land was derived from P who in turn had purchased from one P.B., an assignee of the original purchasers. P had entered into a restrictive covenant with P.B. and plaintiff had notice thereof at the time of his purchase. Some years later, P.B., who had in the meantime sold all the land which he had obtained from the original purchasers, assigned the benefit of this covenant to defendant who was holder in fee of a considerable part of the land purchased by P.B.

The conveyance by the vendor company to the original purchasers contained a restrictive covenant in favour of the latter, and it was given by the vendor "for themselves, their successors and assigns as owners of the land coloured green", in favour of "the purchasers, their heirs and assigns, the owners or owner for the time being of the land coloured pink or any part thereof". However, there was no similar reference to the parties as owners of land coloured green or pink in respect of the covenants on which this action was based.

The judgment of the Court was delivered by ROMER L. J.:... The relevant facts, as to which there is no dispute, are fully stated in the judgment of the learned judge and need not be repeated here. The questions arising on the appeal depend upon the application to those facts of the law relating to restrictive covenants affecting land. That the plaintiff is bound by the covenants in question is not disputed, in view of the fact that he purchased his lands with notice of them. What is in dispute is the question whether the defendants are entitled to the benefit of such covenants. Now the defendants are not the original covenantees, and it therefore becomes necessary to ascertain what person other than the original covenantee is entitled to the benefit of a restrictive covenant affecting land. This question was put to himself by Hall V.-C. in *Renals* v. *Cowlishaw*, 9 Ch. D. 125, and the answer was given in a judgment so well known that it is unnecessary to refer to it at length. It is a judgment that has received the approval both of this Court and of the House of Lords, and has always been regarded as a correct statement of the law upon the subject. Stated shortly it laid down this: that, apart from what are usually referred to as building scheme cases (and this is not a case of that sort), a purchaser from the original covenantee of land retained by him when he executed the conveyance containing the covenant will be entitled to the benefit of the covenant if the conveyance shows that the covenant was intended to enure for the benefit of that particular land. It follows that, if what is being acquired by the purchaser was only part of the land shown by the conveyance as being intended to be benefited, it must also be shown that the benefit was intended to enure to each portion of that land. In such cases the benefit of the restrictive covenant will pass to the purchaser without being mentioned. It runs with the land. In all other cases the purchaser will not acquire the benefit of the covenant unless that benefit be expressly assigned to him—or, to use the words of the Vice-Chancellor (9 Ch. D. at p. 130). "it must appear that the benefit of the covenant was part of the subject-matter of the purchase."

In *Renals* v. *Cowlishaw*, the covenant was entered into with the covenantee, his heirs and assigns, and it appears to have been argued that the use of the word assigns showed an intention that the benefit of the covenant should run with the land. But, to use the language of Farwell J. in *Rogers* v. *Hosegood* [1900] 2 Ch. 388, 396, "there was nothing to shew what assigns were intended by the words of the covenant; there was no necessary implication that each assign of each parcel of the vendor's land, whether acquired before or after the date of the deed, was to have the benefit of the covenant; the inference, indeed, was to the contrary, and the Courts accordingly held that the covenant did not run, but must be expressly assigned in order to pass. Contrast this with the case of the ordinary covenants for title: these undoubtedly run with the land, and each purchaser of each portion of the land gets the benefit of the covenants so far as they relate to the land purchased by him. In both these cases the covenants are entered into with the heirs and assigns, but in the first case the word 'assign,' on the true construction of the deed, means 'assign of the covenant,' in the latter 'assign of the land, to which is annexed the benefit of the covenant by virtue of the evidence of intention so to contract which is found in the deed and the surrounding circumstances.'" In *Rogers* v. *Hosegood* itself the benefit of the covenant was held to run with the land of the covenantees, for the covenant had been entered into with them, their heirs and assigns, with the express intent that the covenant would enure to the benefit of the covenantees, their heirs and assigns and others claiming under them to all or any of their lands adjoining or near to the premises then being conveyed to the covenantor. In *Renals* v. *Cowlishaw* the benefit of the covenant had never been expressly assigned by the covenantee. In neither of these cases, therefore, did it become necessary for the Court to inquire into the circumstances in which an express assignee of the benefit of a covenant that does not run with the land is entitled to enforce it. In the present case, however, it is necessary to do so, inasmuch as the defendants claim to be the express assignees of the benefit of the restrictive covenants contained in the deeds of October 23, 1908, and May 11, 1909.

Now it may be conceded that the benefit of a covenant entered into with the covenantee or his assigns is assignable. The use of the word "assigns" indicates this: see Williams on Personal Property, 18th ed., p. 33. But it by no means follows that the assignee of a restrictive covenant affecting land of the covenantor is entitled to enforce it against an assign of that land. For the burden of the covenant did not run with the land at law, and is only enforceable against a purchaser with notice by reason of the equitable doctrine that is usually referred to as the rule in *Tulk* v. *Moxhay*. It was open, therefore, to the Courts of Equity to prescribe the particular class of assignees of the covenant to whom they should concede the benefit of the rule. This they have done, and in doing so have included within the class persons to whom the benefit of the covenant could not have been assigned at law. For at law the benefit could not be assigned in pieces. It would have to be assigned as a whole or not at all. And yet in equity the right to enforce the covenant can in certain circumstances be assigned by the covenantee from time to time to one person after another. Who then are the assignees of the covenant that are entitled to enforce it? The answer to this question is to be found in several authorities which it now becomes necessary to consider.

In *Formby* v. *Barker* [1903] 2 Ch. 539, a vendor, on the occasion of the sale of the whole of his land, exacted from the purchaser a restrictive covenant as to its user. The vendor having died, his executor sought to enforce the covenant against an assignee of the purchaser. Inasmuch as there was no land retained by the vendor on the occasion of the sale the covenant was merely personal to the vendor, and was accordingly held to be unenforceable by the vendor's executor as his assignee against the assignee of the purchaser. "If restrictive covenants," said Romer L. J., "are entered into with a covenantee, not in respect of or concerning any ascertainable property belonging to him, or in which he is interested, then the covenant must be regarded, so far as he is concerned, as a personal covenant—that is, as one obtained by him for some personal purpose or object. It appears to me that it is not legally permissible for him to assign the benefit of such a covenant to any person or persons he may choose, so as to place the assign or assigns in his position." To a like effect was the decision in *London County Council* v. *Allen* [1914] 3 K.B. 642. In that case the covenantees had never had any interest at all in the land in respect of which the owner had entered into a restrictive covenant. It was held that the covenantees were not entitled to enforce the covenant against an assignee of the covenantor. Buckley L. J. said that the "doctrine in *Tulk* v. *Moxhay* does not extend to the case in which the covenantee has no land capable of enjoying, as against the land of the covenantor, the benefit of the restrictive covenant." Scrutton J. said: "If the covenant does not run with the land in law, its benefit can only be asserted against an assign of the land burdened, if the covenant was made for the benefit of certain land, all or some of which remains in the possession of the covenantee or his assign, suing to enforce the covenant."

It is plain, however, from these and other cases, and notably that of *Renals* v. *Cowlishaw*, that if the restrictive covenant be taken not merely for some personal purpose or object of the vendor, but for the benefit of some other land of his in the sense that it would enable him to dispose of that land to greater advantage, the covenant, though not annexed to such land so as to run with any part of it, may be enforced against an assignee of the covenantor taking with notice, both by the covenantee and by persons to whom the benefit of such covenant has been assigned, subject however to certain conditions. In the first place, the "other land" must be land that is capable of being benefited by the covenant—otherwise it would be impossible to infer that the object of the covenant was to enable the vendor to dispose of his land to greater advantage. In the next place, this land must be "ascertainable" or "certain," to use the words of Romer and Scrutton L. JJ. respectively. For, although the

Court will readily infer the intention to benefit the other land of the vendor where the existence and situation of such land are indicated in the conveyance or have been otherwise shown with reasonable certainty, it is impossible to do so from vague references in the conveyance or in other documents laid before the Court as to the existence of other lands of the vendor, the extent and situation of which are undefined. In the third place, the covenant cannot be enforced by the covenantee against an assign of the purchaser after the covenantee has parted with the whole of his land.

This last point was decided, and in our opinion rightly decided, by Sargant J. in *Chambers* v. *Randall*, [1923] 1 Ch. 149. As pointed out by that learned judge, the covenant having been entered into to enable the covenantee to dispose of his property to advantage, that result will in fact have been obtained when all that property has been disposed of. There is therefore no longer any reason why the Court should extend to him the benefit of the equitable doctrine of *Tulk* v. *Moxhay*. That is only done when it is sought to enforce the covenant in connection with the enjoyment of land that the covenant was intended to protect. But it was also held by Sargant J. in the same case ([1923] 1 Ch. 149), and in our opinion rightly held, that although on a sale of the whole or part of the property intended to be protected by the covenant the right to enforce the covenant may be expressly assigned to the purchaser, such an assignment will be ineffective if made at a later date when the covenantee has parted with the whole of his land. The covenantee must, indeed, be at liberty to include in any sale of the retained property the right to enforce the covenants. He might not otherwise be able to dispose of such property to the best advantage, and the intention with which he obtained the covenant would be defeated. But if he has been able to sell any particular part of his property without assigning to the purchaser the benefit of the covenant, there seems no reason why he should at a later date and as an independent transaction be at liberty to confer upon the purchaser such benefit. To hold that he could do so would be to treat the covenant as having been obtained, not only for the purpose of enabling the covenantee to dispose of his land to the best advantage, but also for the purpose of enabling him to dispose of the benefit of the covenant to the best advantage. Where, at the date of the assignment of the benefit of the covenant, the covenantee has disposed of the whole of his land, there is an additional reason why the assignee should be unable to enforce it. For at the date of the assignment the covenant had ceased to be enforceable at the instance of the covenantee himself, and he cannot confer any greater rights upon the assignee than he possessed himself. In opposition to this view we were very properly pressed by counsel with two earlier decisions of Sargant J.

The earlier of these is *Ives* v. *Brown* [1919] 2 Ch. 314. In that case the survivor of two joint covenantees was the owner of other land held by herself as trustee for herself for life with remainder to her testamentary appointees. By her will she appointed the lands to the plaintiff Ives for life, but not in such a way as to pass to him the benefit of the restrictive covenant which accordingly devolved upon her death upon her two executors, of whom the plaintiff Ives was one. In an action brought by Ives alone to enforce the covenant against an assignee of the covenantor, it was objected that he was not entitled to maintain the action. The learned judge thereupon gave leave to the plaintiff to amend by adding as a co-plaintiff the other executor, and eventually granted an injunction to restrain a breach of the covenant. After holding that the testamentary appointment did not amount to an assignment of the benefit of the restrictive covenant, he added: "and it was, therefore, necessary in my judgment that her legal personal representatives should be joined in the action." The learned judge does not, however, appear to have addressed his mind to the question whether the legal personal representatives of a covenantee can enforce a restrictive covenant unless they are possessed of land that the covenant was intended to protect, and that question does not appear to have been argued. But it may well have been that the executors still had the legal estate of the land vested in them, and if that were so, then they could not be said to have had no interest in the land.

The second case was that of *Lord Northbourne* v. *Johnston & Son* [1922] 2 Ch. 309. But the assignment of the benefit of the covenant in that case was made by a representative of the covenantees who, at the time of the assignment, held such benefit as a bare trustee for the plaintiff, to whom had been conveyed at an earlier date the land for the protection of which the covenant had originally been obtained. It is true that after the conveyance the covenantees were not possessed of any of that land, but they continued to hold the benefit of the covenant as trustees for the plaintiff, and the right to enforce it was treated accordingly as being kept alive for his benefit. In neither of these two cases did the learned judge intend to decide, nor did he in fact decide, that a covenantee who has parted with all the land for the protection of which the covenant was imposed can thereafter confer upon an assignee of the covenant the right to enforce it. Indeed, in *Chambers* v. *Randall*, as already stated, it was definitely decided by the learned judge that he could not.

Such being the law, it only remains to apply it to the facts of the present case; and the first question that has to be considered is whether or no an intention is shown in the deed of October 23, 1908, that the restrictive covenants should enure for the benefit of any particular land of the covenantees. As to this, it is contended on behalf of the appellants that an intention is shown in the deed to attach the benefit to the land coloured green upon the plan annexed to it. It is conceded by them that if they are wrong in this contention there is no other land of the vendors for the benefit of which the covenants can be said to enure. Now for the purpose of considering this question there is one outstanding fact to be borne in mind, a fact that naturally had considerable effect upon the mind of Bennett J. It is this. In the indenture are contained certain restrictive covenants on the part of the vendors as to the user of the land coloured green, and those covenants are expressed to be made with the "purchasers their heirs and assigns or other the owner or owners for the time being of the land coloured pink or any part or parts thereof." These are apt words to ensure that the benefit of the covenant should run with the pink land and every part of it, and one cannot doubt that in framing them the author had *Renals* v. *Cowlishaw* and *Rogers* v. *Hosegood* in mind. To use the words of Bennett J., "the draftsman has shown that when he desires to annex the benefit and burden respectively of restrictive covenants to different parcels of land he knows the appropriate language to use in order to do so." No such language is, however, used in relation to the restrictive covenants entered into by the purchasers. If the omission were due to design it would be conclusive of the matter. It would, however, be possible to attribute the omission to carelessness, if one could find elsewhere in the deed a strong indication of intention to make the benefit of the purchasers' covenant enure to the green land. The appellants contend that this strong indication is afforded by the fact that the restrictive covenants entered into by the vendors in relation to the green land and those entered into by the purchasers in relation to the pink land are more or less reciprocal covenants, and that just as the vendors' covenants were entered into for the benefit of the pink lands, so too were the purchasers' covenants entered into for the benefit of the green lands. But an examination of the two sets of covenants renders this argument untenable. For though the vendors covenant not to do anything upon the green land that may be a nuisance or damage to the owner of the land coloured pink or any part thereof, the corresponding covenant on the part of the purchasers is not to do anything on the land coloured pink that might be a nuisance or damage to the vendor or to the Bank (who were the mortgagees), no mention being made of the green land or any other land of the vendors or the Bank. It is hardly permissible to regard this further omission as being unintentional. There must be some limit to the carelessness to be attributed to the draftsman. But the appellants also rely upon the fact that the purchasers covenant not to erect any factory upon the lands coloured pink within 460 yards of the land coloured green, and not to authorize more than one grocer's licence for the sale of wine, beer or spirits to be applied for or used within the same distance. This circumstance does, no doubt, give some ground for the suggestion that these two restrictions were intended for the benefit of the green land as distinct from any other lands of the vendors and that, therefore, the restrictions as a whole should be so regarded. But these two references to the green land do no more than define the part of the pink land that was to be subject to the two restrictions in question, and such restrictions may quite conceivably have been intended also to protect the land coloured yellow on the plan, land that, as is shown by the conveyance itself, was also land of the vendors, and land of which part at any rate was, as appears from the plan, capable of being benefited by such restrictions. In these circumstances it is impossible, having regard to the remarkable difference between the wording of the covenants by the vendors and purchasers respectively, to avoid drawing the inference that it was not intended to annex the benefit of the purchasers' covenant to the land coloured green. That is the inference that Bennett J. drew, and in our opinion he was right in so doing. The benefit of such covenant did not, therefore, run with the green land, and the next question is whether the defendant Easter is entitled to enforce the covenant as express assignee of the benefit of it. In our opinion he is not. To start with, it is impossible to ascertain with any certainty what lands retained by the covenantees when the conveyance of October 23, 1908, was executed were intended to be protected by the covenant so that the covenantees might thereafter dispose of them to greater advantage. That conveyance shows that the vendors were possessed of other land in the vicinity, reference being made in the deed to "foreshore belonging to the vendors west of the harbour entrance," without further defining it, and to land coloured yellow on the plan attached to the deed in terms that clearly indicate their ownership of such land. But our attention is also called to certain transactions between the covenantees and a company called The Service Land Company, Ltd., in the month of January, 1912, that show that in October, 1908, the covenantees were possessed of still other lands at Lancing and Shoreham of considerable, though, so far as the Court is concerned, of undefined extent. Referring to these other lands, Bennett J. said: "There was no evidence before me as to where such other lands were situate or as to the area thereof. There was no evidence before me as to the purposes for which the Shoreham Company acquired these lands, whether for the purpose of resale or for development as a building estate... I am really left to guess at the reasons, if any, which led to the introduction in the conveyance of October 23, 1908, of the purchaser's covenant." In these circumstances, the learned judge declined to draw the conclusion that the covenant was inserted in the conveyance for the protection of all the other lands of the Shoreham Company so as to enable them to dispose of such lands to the best advantage. And he was justified in so doing. It is impossible to ascertain whether all or some, and if so, which part of such lands were capable of being protected by the reservation of the covenant. When, therefore, by indentures of October 19, 1920, and October 15, 1921, the Shoreham Company and the Seaside Company (to whom the Shoreham Company had previously sold the whole of their still unsold lands) purported to assign to the defendant Easter the benefit of the restrictive covenant, there can be no sure ground for thinking that any of such still unsold lands were lands for the protection of which the covenant had been obtained. It is plain that at that time all the lands coloured green had been disposed of. The defendants have accordingly failed to show that there is now vested in them, or either of them, the right to enforce the restrictive covenant contained in the deed of October 23, 1908. It is not necessary, in these circumstances, to consider the question whether, in any case, the right to enforce the restrictive covenant against the assigns of the covenantors had not come to an end when the Shoreham Company conveyed to the Seaside Company the whole of their lands still remaining unsold without assigning at the same time the benefit of the covenant. It is only necessary to say that it appears to us more than doubtful whether in the contract for sale that preceded that conveyance the benefit of the covenant was included•

It only remains to consider the question whether the restrictive covenant contained in the deed of May 11, 1909, is enforceable against the plaintiff by the defendants. This question can be dealt with quite shortly. There is no indication whatsoever to be found in the conveyance that the benefit of the restrictive covenant by Phillips was annexed to any other defined land belonging to Bury so as to pass with it to subsequent purchasers from him of such land. The right to enforce the covenant would not therefore pass to any such purchaser, unless the covenant was obtained by Bury for the purpose of enabling him to dispose of the remainder of his land to the greatest advantage, and unless the benefit of the covenant were expressly assigned by Bury to such purchaser before Bury had disposed of the whole of his land. Inasmuch as at the date of the assignment by Bury to the defendants of the benefit of the covenant, Bury had disposed of the whole of his land, the defendants could not in any case acquire from him any right to enforce the covenant, and it is unnecessary to consider whether such covenant was or was not imposed for the benefit of any and what other land retained by Bury on the occasion of the sale to Phillips.

Appeal dismissed.

[For an evaluation of the above case, see *Preston and Newsom*, Restrictive Covenants Affecting Freehold Land (1955 2nd ed.,), pp. 26 ff.

On the question of identification or ascertainment of the benefited land, see *Newton Abbott Co-Operative Society Ltd.* v. *Williamson and Treadgold Ltd.*, [1952] Ch. 286, [1952] 1 All. E.R. 279, reproduced in part, *infra*, at p. 529. For a critical comment, see *Elphinstone*, Assignment of the Benefit of Covenants Affecting Land, (1952) 68 Law Q. Rev. 353.]

[In *Re Campbell and Cowdy*, 61 O.L.R. 545, [1928] 1 D.L.R. 1034, Orde J. A. stated that "when restrictive conditions are registered under [The Land Titles] Act [R.S.O. 1914, c. 126], if those who impose the conditions intend the benefit of them to attach and run with other lands, those other lands ought to be clearly defined and set forth in the register and in the certificate of ownership".]

[If the benefit of a restrictive covenant (which is capable of running with the land) has not been originally annexed but is expressly assigned at the time of a conveyance of the land intended to be protected, does it thereafter run to succeeding assignees without further express assignment or must there be an express assignment on each change of ownership? See the conflicting opinions expressed by *Megarry and Wade*, Law of Real Property (1959, 2nd ed.), p. 740 and *Preston and Newsom*, Restrictive Covenants Affecting Freehold Land (1955, 2nd ed.), p. 26.]

[In *Re Pidgeon*, [1938] 3 D.L.R. 494, [1938] O.W.N. 292 (C.A.), A sold part of a parcel of land to B by an absolute deed which contained a building restriction on the "grantee and her successors in title". While it was not in the form of a covenant, the restrictive provision was declared to "run with the lands and shall be exacted from purchasers from the grantee". The deed to B's immediate grantee contained the restrictions but subsequent conveyances did not. A remote grantee of A's remaining land sought to enforce the restrictions against a remote grantee of B's land. In denying enforceability, the Court said (in part): "It will be observed that the deed contains nothing which on its face stipulates that this restriction is for the benefit of the adjacent land or the future owners thereof. It is not in form... a covenant, and the deed is not executed by the grantee".]

[What is the effect, on the running of the burden of a restrictive covenant, of the draftsman's failure to mention that the covenant is entered into not only by the covenantor but also by his assigns? See *Re Rowan and Eaton*, 60 O.L.R. 245, [1927] 2 D.L.R. 722, aff'g 59 O.L.R. 379, [1926] 4 D.L.R. 582 (App. Div.).]

[Does the retention of a power to vary restrictions affect their enforceability? See *Ex parte Little*, [1954] O.W.N. 610; and cf. *Re Campbell and Cowdy*, 61 O.L.R. 545, [1928] 1 D.L.R. 1034.]

(b) Some Problems of "Touching and Concerning"

ZETLAND v. DRIVER. Court of Appeal. [1939] Ch. 1, [1938] 2 All E.R. 158

Appeal from a judgment of Bennett J., [1937] Ch. 651, [1937] 3 All E.R. 795, dismissing an action to enjoin breach of a restrictive covenant. The facts out of which the action arose were as follows.

By a settlement dated August 2, 1871, land at Redcar in Yorkshire (including a piece of land subsequently known as No. 200 Lord Street) was settled to uses under which, on September 10, 1928, the first Marquess of Zetland was tenant for life in possession and the first plaintiff was entitled to an entailed interest in remainder. On June 15, 1926, a vesting deed was executed in favour of the first Marquess.

By a conveyance dated September 10, 1928, the first Marquess conveyed to David Goodswen in fee simple the piece of land subsequently known as No. 200 Lord Street. Clause 2 of the conveyance provided: "The purchaser to the intent and so as to bind as far as practicable the said property hereby conveyed into whosesoever hands the same may come and to benefit and protect such part or parts of the lands in the Borough Township or Parish of Redcar, in the North Riding of the County of York, now subject to the settlement (a) as shall for the time being remain unsold or (b) as shall be sold by the vendor or his successors in title with the express benefit of this covenant, covenants with the vendor that the purchaser will at all times observe, perform and keep the said stipulations contained in the Second Schedule hereto." The Second Schedule provided: "(a) that the property hereby conveyed shall not (except with the previous consent in writing of the vendor, which expression in this Schedule includes where the context admits his successors in title) be used for any other purpose than the erection of a shop and dwelling-house... (d) that no intoxicating or spirituous liquors shall be sold from the premises and in particular that no part of the land hereby conveyed shall be used for the purposes of a club and that no act or thing shall be done or permitted thereon which in the opinion of the vendor may be a public or private nuisance or prejudicial or detrimental to the vendor and the owners or occupiers of any adjoining property or to the neighbourhood." The covenant was duly registered as a land charge.

On March 11, 1929, the first Marquess died and the first plaintiff, who succeeded to the title, became entitled in possession as tenant in tail male to the land comprised in the settlement dated August 2, 1871. On July 10, 1929, a vesting assent was made in favour of the first plaintiff. On March 11, 1929, and at all material times thereafter portions of the land at Redcar were unsold and remained subject to the settlement.

On April 2, 1935, David Goodswen conveyed No. 200 Lord Street, on which a shop had been erected, to the first defendant, William Driver, in fee simple, with notice of the restrictive covenants. Thereafter the first defendant and the second defendant, Eric Wilson, carried on at No. 200 Lord Street the business of keeping an eating-house for the consumption of fried fish and other food. In April, 1936, the defendants obtained a licence from the local authority authorizing the sale of fried fish at the premises for consumption off the premises, and thereafter the defendants carried on that business on the premises in addition to the business theretofore carried on by them.

As a result of complaints as to the carrying on by the defendants of the business of selling fried fish for consumption off the premises, the first plaintiff formed the opinion that such sales were detrimental to the amenities of the neighbourhood and to his own property.

The defendants were duly informed of this and requested to give up the business, but they refused so to do. On July 7, 1936, the first plaintiff, together with the second plaintiffs, the Zetland Estates Company (in whom by a conveyance dated March 5, 1927, the first plaintiff had vested his equitable reversionary interest), commenced this action, claiming an injunction to restrain the defendants, their servants, workmen or agents, from using any part of No. 200 Lord Street for the frying of fish or other substances for consumption off the premises or from doing or permitting any other act or thing which in the opinion of the first plaintiff or other the successor in title of the late Marquess might be a public or private nuisance or prejudicial or detrimental to the first plaintiff or his successor in title as aforesaid and to the owners or occupiers of any adjoining premises or the neighbourhood. No evidence was called to show that the defendants were committing a nuisance. The parties agreed that the lands, for the benefit of which the covenant was taken, included (i) a small portion of land contiguous to No. 200 Lord Street; (ii) a number of scattered parcels of land to the north and west with houses built on them; and (iii) to the south, beyond a large area covered with buildings, certain land part of which was more than a mile away.

The judgment of the Court was delivered by FARWELL J.:... The first appellant (hereinafter referred to as "the appellant") is the estate owner in fee simple of certain lands and hereditaments in Redcar in the county of York and the beneficial interest in the property is vested in the second appellant during the appellant's life... The respondents by their defence put in issue the right of the appellant to enforce the covenant. They deny that the business complained of is a breach of the covenant. They further say that the opinion of the appellant was wholly unreasonable and capricious and that in forming an opinion he was acting in a quasi-judicial capacity and was, therefore, bound to give the respondents an opportunity of being heard before coming to any conclusion and that this he had failed to do. In addition, they plead laches and acquiescence as a bar to the relief sought.

It will be convenient to dispose at once of those last mentioned pleas. In our judgment, there is no foundation for the plea of laches or acquiescence, nor is there anything in the evidence to support the contention that the opinion which the appellant formed as to the respondents' business was capricious or other than a bona fide opinion formed after a proper consideration of the facts. In forming his opinion the appellant was in no sense performing a judicial or quasi-judicial function, and he was, therefore, under no obligation to give the respondents an opportunity of being heard....

There remains to be considered the real issue in this appeal—namely, whether the covenant is enforceable by the appellant. Covenants restricting the user of land imposed by a vendor upon a sale fall into three classes: (i) covenants imposed by the vendor for his own benefit; (ii) covenants imposed by the vendor as owner of other land, of which that sold formed a part, and intended to protect or benefit the unsold land; and (iii) covenants imposed by a vendor upon a sale of land to various purchasers who are intended mutually to enjoy the benefit of and be bound by the covenants: *Osborne* v. *Bradley*, 2 Ch. 446, 450.

Covenants of the first class are personal to the vendor and enforceable by him alone unless expressly assigned by him. Covenants of the second class are said to run with the land and are enforceable without express assignment by the owner for the time being of the land for the benefit of which they were imposed. Covenants of the third class are most usually found in sales under building schemes, although not strictly confined to such sales. It is not suggested that the present covenant falls within this class. Nor will it assist the appellant if it falls within the first class, since he was not the original covenantee or an express assignee from him. If, therefore, the appellant is entitled to sue on this covenant it must fall within the second class above mentioned.

Such covenants can only be validly imposed if they comply with certain conditions.

Firstly, they must be negative covenants. No affirmative covenant requiring the expenditure of money or the doing of some act can ever be made to run with the land. Secondly, the covenant must be one that touches or concerns the land, by which is meant that it must be imposed for the benefit or to enhance the value of the land retained by the vendor or some part of it, and no such covenant can ever be imposed if the sale comprises the whole of the vendor's land. Further, the land retained by the vendor must be such as to be capable of being benefited by the covenant at the time when it is imposed. Thirdly, the land which is intended to be benefited must be so defined as to be easily ascertainable, and the fact that the covenant is imposed for the benefit of that particular land should be stated in the conveyance and the persons or the class of persons entitled to enforce it. The fact that the benefit of the covenant is not intended to pass to all persons into whose hands the unsold land may come is not objectionable so long as the class of persons intended to have the benefit of the covenant is clearly defined. Finally, it must be remembered that these covenants can only be enforced so long as the covenantee or his successor in title retains some part of the land for the benefit of which the covenant was imposed. Applying those conditions to the present case, the covenant sued upon appears to comply with them. The covenant is restrictive; it is expressly stated in the conveyance to be for the benefit of the unsold part of the land comprised in the settlement and such land is easily ascertainable, nor is it suggested that at the date of the conveyance the land retained was not capable of being benefited by the restrictions, and lastly the appellant is the successor in title of the original covenantee and as such is the estate owner of part of the land unsold which is subject to the settlement. That being so, the appellant is the person now entitled to the benefit of the covenant and, prima facie, is entitled to enforce it against the respondents who, although not the original covenantors, took their land with notice of the restrictions and are, therefore, bound by them.

It is said, however, on behalf of the respondents, that this covenant is not one which can run with the land because it is imposed for the benefit, not only of the unsold land of the vendor, but also for the benefit of the adjoining owners and the neighbourhood. If that were the true construction of the covenant, that might be so; but in our judgment, reading the covenant as a whole, it cannot be so construed. The paramount purpose of the covenant, as appears from the conveyance itself, is to benefit and protect the unsold land of the vendor, and only such acts or things as are, in the opinion of the appellant or his successors in title, injurious to that land are within the restrictions, and consequently nothing which would be a nuisance or annoyance to an adjoining owner of the neighbourhood is within the covenant, unless it is also detrimental or injurious to the unsold land of the vendor. The covenant is, therefore, not impeachable on this ground. Then it was said that it was open to objection as offending the rule against perpetuities, but in our judgment there is no ground for such contention. The formation of an opinion by a successor in title of the original vendor at whatever time cannot operate to create any new estate or revest the land and, consequently, the rule against perpetuities has no application.

Under those circumstances, there does not appear to be any ground on which the appellant can properly be refused the relief which he seeks; but Bennett J. took the opposite view and held that the benefit of the covenant had not passed to the appellant. In coming to that conclusion he founded himself upon a decision of Clauson J. in *In re Ballard's Conveyance* [1937] Ch. 473, [1937] 2 All E.R. 691, which he considered to be exactly in point and binding upon him. In our judgment the learned judge was wrong in thinking that *In re Ballard's Conveyance* was an authority in this case. It is not necessary for us, and we do not propose, to express any opinion as to that decision beyond saying that it is clearly distinguishable from the present case, if only on the ground that in that case the covenant was expressed to run with the whole estate, whereas in the present case no such difficulty arises because the covenant is expressed to be for the benefit of the whole or any part or parts of the unsold settled property.

It is to be noticed in the present case that the benefit of the covenant is not intended to pass to a purchaser without express assignment. It is not necessary for us to express any opinion as to what would be the effect of a sale of part of the settled property with an express assignment of the covenant; but, if such a purchaser could enforce the covenant, it could only be for so long as some successor in title of the original covenantee retained some part of the settled property, since such a person alone can form the requisite opinion.

For these reasons the appeal must be allowed. The appellant is entitled to the injunction which he seeks subject to two limitations. In the first place the injunction must be limited to fried fish and the words "other substances" deleted, because the opinion of the appellant as to the nuisance was confined to fried fish, and secondly, the period of the injunction must be confined to so long as the appellant or some other successor in title of the original vendor retains unsold any part of the settled property for the benefit of which the covenant was imposed. *Appeal allowed.*

[*In Re Ballard's Conveyance*, [1937] Ch. 473, [1937] 2 All E.R. 691, two lots, comprising about 18 acres, were sold by auction subject to certain building restrictions. The conveyance to the purchaser stated that he "doth hereby covenant with the said [vendor] her heirs and assigns and successors in title owners from time to time of the Childwickbury Estate... that he the said [purchaser] his heirs and assigns will perform and observe the conditions and stipulations set forth in the schedule hereto so far as the same relate to, affect or concern the said premises hereinbefore expressed to be hereby conveyed". One of the stipulations in the schedule defined "vendor" to include her and her successors in title owners of any part of the above-mentioned estate for the time being remaining unsold. The vendor sold the Childwickbury Estate to J. by a conveyance which made no reference to the restrictions, and J. in turn sold the Estate to a company which was the respondent in this action. The purchaser sued for a declaration that the restrictions were not enforceable against him by the company. In giving judgment for the purchaser, Clauson J. said in part:

"I accordingly hold that the land for the benefit of which the covenant was taken was the land (about 1,700 acres) now vested in Childwickbury Stud, Ltd., by conveyance from Mr. Joel, and that the fact that it claims by virtue of a purchase from Mrs. Ballard would not affect its title to sue.

"That brings me to the remaining question, namely: Is the covenant one which, in the circumstances of the case, comes within the category of a covenant the benefit of which is capable of running with the land for the benefit of which it was taken? A necessary qualification, in order that the covenant may come within that category, is that it concerns or touches the land with which it is to run: see per Farwell, J., in *Rogers* v. *Hosegood* [1900] 2 Ch. 388, at p. 395. That land is an area of some 1,700 acres. It appears to me quite obvious that, while a breach of the stipulations might possibly affect a portion of that area in the vicinity of Mr. Wright's land, far the largest part of this area of 1,700 acres could not possibly be affected by any breach of any of the stipulations....

"The result seems to me to be that I am bound to hold that, while the covenant may concern or touch some comparatively small portion of the land to which it has been sought to annex it, it fails to concern or touch far the largest part of the land. I asked in vain for any authority which would justify me in severing the covenant, and treating it as annexed to or running with such part of the land as is touched by or concerned with it, though, as regards the remainder of the land, namely, such part as is not touched by or concerned with the covenant, the covenant is not, and cannot be, annexed to it, and accordingly does not, and cannot, run with it. Nor have I been able, through my own researches, to find anything in the books which seems to justify any such course. In *Rogers* v. *Hosegood*, the benefit of the covenant was annexed to all or any of certain lands adjoining or near to the covenantor's land, and no such difficulty arose as faces me here; and there are many other reported cases in which, for similar reasons, no such difficulty arose. But the requirement that the covenant, in order that the benefit of it may run with certain lands, must concern or touch those lands, is categorically stated by Farwell, J., in the passage I have cited, in terms which are unquestionably in accord with a long line of earlier authority.

"I would observe that the construction of the document and the intention of the parties to be gathered therefrom are material on the question what is the area of land to which the covenantor and covenantee intended to annex the benefit of the covenant, or, in technical language, what is the land with which the parties intended the covenant to run; but that, on the question whether, in the circumstances of the case, this covenant is capable of being annexed to, or of running with, the land to which it is sought to annex it, it is necessary, first, to ascertain whether, in fact, the covenant touches or concerns that particular land. If, on the facts, it appears that the covenant does not touch or concern that particular land, the only question which remains is whether, by the law in regard to annexation of a covenant to land, as recognised as long ago as 1368 in the *Prior's Case*, such annexation can take place unless it can be predicated of the covenant that it touches or concerns the land to which it is sought to annex it. That is a question of dry technical law, on which it would not be right, at all events for a judge of first instance, to go beyond settled authority, or, at all events, beyond that which can logically be deduced from settled authority, though, in the result, the intention of the parties to the original covenant may be frustrated. As I have not been referred to, and I cannot find, any authority for the proposition that a covenant which it has been sought to annex to a particular area of land can be enforced by the person seised of that land, not being the original covenantee, in a case where it cannot truly be said that the covenant touches or concerns the land to which it was sought to annex it, I must hold that the attempted annexation has failed, and that the covenant has not been effectually annexed to the land, and does not run with it. The consequence is that I am bound to hold that the respondent company, the Childwickbury Stud, Ltd., cannot sue Mr. Wright on the covenant."

On the constructional question whether a restrictive covenant is for the protection of the whole of the land retained by the vendor or for the protection of the whole or any part thereof, see *Drake* v. *Gray*, [1936] Ch. 451, [1936] 1 All E.R. 363 (C.A.). Is there anything more involved than proper draftsmanship?]

CANADIAN CONSTRUCTION CO. LTD. v. BEAVER (ALBERTA) LUMBER LTD.

Supreme Court of Canada. [1955] S.C.R. 682, [1955] 3 D.L.R. 502

Appeal from the Alberta Appellate Division, [1954] 2 D.L.R. 702, 11 W.W.R. (N.S.) 494, reversing a judgment of Egbert J., [1953] 4 D.L.R. 834, 9 W.W.R. (N.S.) 489, which ordered removal of a caveat to support a restrictive covenant.

LOCKE J.:... I am unable, with great respect, to agree with the view that, in construing this agreement, oral evidence was admissible. I do not consider that the cases referred to in the judgment at the trial [[1953] 4 D.L.R. 834] support that view. In *Re Bowes Co. & Rankin*, [1924] 4 D.L.R. 406, 55 O.L.R. 601, the report does not indicate whether the agreement sought to be enforced identified the dominant estate, and the question as to the admissibility of the evidence does not appear to have been argued. In *Zetland* v. *Driver*, as pointed out by Farwell J. at p. 162, the conveyance of the lands referred to the settlement in which the lands, of which those conveyed formed part, were referred to and expressly stated that the covenant was for the benefit of the unsold part of the land comprised in the settlement.

In *Smith* v. *River Douglas Catchment Bd.*, [1949] 2 All E.R. 179, the conveyance to the plaintiff Smith, in terms, provided that it was conveyed with the benefit of the agreement of April 25, 1938, which referred to, though it did not describe by metes and bounds, the lands entitled to the benefit of the covenant and the learned Judges of the Court of Appeal considered that evidence to identify these lands might be given. In *Laurie* v. *Winch*, [1952] 4 D.L.R. 449, [1953] 1 S.C.R. 49, there was ambiguity in the terms of the grant which, Kellock J. held, might be explained by oral evidence, relying upon *Waterpark* v. *Fennell* (1859), 7 H.L.C. 650, 11 E.R. 259, and other authorities to the like effect. In that case, the headnote is to the effect that, where parcels are described in old documents by words of a general nature or of doubtful import, evidence of usage is proper to be received to show what they comprehend. There is no ambiguity in the language of the agreement of March 7, 1944, and, in my opinion, its provisions cannot be supplemented by oral evidence, not explanatory of its terms or identifying its subject-matter but adding a term calculated to bring the covenant within the second class referred to by Farwell J. in *Zetland's* case.

I respectfully agree with the conclusion of the learned trial Judge that the covenant in question was merely personal to the respondent and did not create an interest in the lands in question and was not binding upon the appellant.

I have had the advantage of reading the reasons for judgment to be delivered in this matter by my brother Cartwright and concur in his opinion that, even if the evidence which I think to have been inadmissible is considered in construing the agreement, the covenant was a covenant in gross and did not run with the land.

CARTWRIGHT J.:... The question raised is whether the respondent can enforce as against the appellant the observance of certain restrictions upon the use of lands of which the appellant is the owner.

The case was dealt with on an agreed statement of facts, no witnesses being called. We were informed by counsel that the making of this agreement as to the facts was not to prejudice the appellant's argument that extrinsic evidence was inadmissible to vary or add to the terms of the agreement of March 7, 1944, hereinafter set out.

The statement of facts agreed to may be summarized as follows. In 1927, or earlier, the respondent became the owner of Lots 3 to 8 inclusive in Block 11 Plan T 3 in the Townsite of Leduc (hereinafter referred to for convenience as "Parcel A"). It used this land as a branch yard where it carried on the business of selling lumber and other building materials until November, 1942, when it purchased Lots 4, 5, and 6 in Block 18, Plan T 5 in the same townsite (hereinafter referred to for convenience as "Parcel B"). In November, 1942, the respondent moved its business from Parcel A to Parcel B and up to the date of the trial it continued to carry on at Parcel B the same sort of business which it had proviously carried on at Parcel A. These parcels are distant approximately 1,000 ft. from each other and are on different streets, Parcel B being four blocks to the north and one block to the east of Parcel A.

In March, 1944, the respondent agreed to sell Parcel A to one Henderson and entered into an agreement with him dated March 7, 1944, which is set out in full hereafter. A transfer of Parcel A to Henderson was registered and the respondent filed a caveat in the Land Titles Office with a copy of the agreement of March 7, 1944, attached thereto. Thereafter Henderson sold Parcel A to the Municipal District of Leduc No. 75 and that corporation became the registered owner thereof. In August, 1950, the appellant purchased Parcel A from the Municipal District of Leduc No. 75 with actual knowledge of the agreement of March 7, 1944, but reserving its rights to maintain that the covenants therein contained were not enforceable against it. The appellant served a notice on the respondent, pursuant to s. 137 of the *Land Titles Act*, requiring it to take proceedings on its caveat and this action followed.

The agreement of March 7, 1944, reads as follows:... "Whereas the Purchaser is at present the owner of certain buildings situated upon the under-described lands, which said lands are the property of the Vendor, and

"Whereas the Vendor has agreed to sell the said under-described lands without any improvements to the Purchaser, subject to the terms and conditions hereinafter set out,

"Now therefore this agreement witnesseth and it is mutually covenanted and agreed between the parties hereto as follows:—

"1. The Vendor does hereby agree to sell and transfer unto the Purchaser Lots Three (3) and Four (4) in Block Eleven (11) in the Townsite of Leduc in the Province of Alberta, of record in the Land Titles Office for the North Alberta Land Registration District as Plan T-3, excepting thereout all mines and minerals and the right to work the same, and Lots Five (5) to Eight (8) in Block Eleven (11) in the Townsite of Leduc in the Province of Alberta, of record in the Land Titles Office for the North Alberta Land Registration District as Plan T-3, excepting out of the said Lot Five (5) all mines and minerals and the right to work the same in consideration of the Purchaser paying to the Vendor the sum of One Hundred and Three and Sixty-Two Hundredths ($103.62) Dollars and covenanting and agreeing that the said Lots or any part thereof shall not for the period of twenty-five (25) years from the date hereof be used for the purpose of manufacturing, storing, buying, selling or otherwise acquiring or disposing of any lumber or building materials of any kind whatsoever.

"2. The Purchaser does hereby covenant and agree with the Vendor that each and every part of the said Lots shall be subject to the above restriction and condition for the said period of twenty-five (25) years and that the said restriction and condition shall be binding upon each of the said Lots hereby conveyed for the benefit of the Vendor and the said restriction and condition shall be a restrictive covenant attached to and running with the said lots for the said period of twenty-five (25) years.

"3. It is further covenanted and agreed that the Vendor shall transfer Title to the said lands to the Purchaser by a separate Transfer and that the above set out restriction and condition shall be deemed to be a term and condition of the said Transfer and that the Vendor shall have the right and privilege of filing a Caveat against the Titles to the said lands to protect its interests under this Agreement.

"4. The Purchaser covenants and agrees that he will not transfer, sell, lease, mortgage, encumber or otherwise dispose of all or any part of the said lands and premises, except such transfer, sale, lease, mortgage, encumbrance or disposition be made subject to the above set out restriction and condition.

"These presents shall enure to the benefit of and be binding upon the successors and assigns of the Vendor and the heirs, executors, administrators and assigns of the Purchaser...."

This agreement is sealed by the respondent but not by Henderson the purchaser. It will however be convenient to refer to the agreements made by Henderson as "covenants" as was done in the Courts below and in argument.

In its amended statement of claim the respondent sets out the making of the agreement of March 7, 1944, the registration of the caveat, the purchase by the appellant of the lands described in the agreement with notice of the restrictions and continues:

"9A. The Plaintiff, prior to the 7th day of March, 1944, was the registered owner and has continued to be the registered owner and still is the registered owner of the lands described as (Parcel B) and it was for the protection of such land and in order to preserve, maintain and enhance its value that the Plaintiff obtained the covenants hereinbefore set forth at the time of selling the lands described in paragraph 1 hereof, and the said (Parcel B) constitutes the dominant tenement owned by the Plaintiff for the benefit of which the lands referred to in paragraph 1 hereof (Parcel A) were made subject to the said restrictive covenants."

On this record the learned trial Judge was of opinion (i) that the covenant sought to be enforced was clearly negative; (ii) that to be enforceable against the appellant it must have been given for the benefit of and must touch and concern some neighbouring land of the respondent, that "there must co-exist the dominant estate of the covenantee and the servient estate of the covenantor, and the covenant itself must 'touch and concern' the dominant estate of the covenantee in such manner as to affect its mode of occupation or be such a covenant as per se, and not merely from collateral circumstances, affects its value"; (iii) that the respondent's land, Parcel B, was so situate in relation to the appellant's land, Parcel A, that the former was capable of being regarded as a "dominant tenement" and the latter as a "servient tenement" within the rule stated in (ii) above; (iv) that the covenant was one which could affect per se the value of such "dominant tenement;" (v) that the "dominant tenement" was still owned by the respondent; but (vi) that on the true construction of the agreement of March 7, 1944, with due regard to the surrounding circumstances, the covenant was intended by the parties to be personal to the respondent and not for the benefit of its land, Parcel B.

Frank Ford J.A., who delivered the unanimous judgment of the Appellate Division, differed from the learned trial Judge only as to item (vi) above, as to which he reached a directly opposite conclusion. The accuracy of the views of the learned trial Judge set out in items (i), (ii) and (v) above was not questioned before us. I have reached the conclusion that the learned trial Judge was right in his view which is summarized in item (vi) above. This makes it unnecessary for me to express any opinion in regard to the questions, fully argued before us, on which the views of the learned trial Judge are summarized in items (iii) and (iv) above.

In approaching the question of the construction of the agreement of March 7, 1944, it may first be observed that it is a formal and carefully prepared instrument obviously intended to be a complete statement of the whole bargain between the parties so that, according to the general rule, extrinsic evidence is inadmissible to contradict, vary or add to its contents. It was argued for the appellant that as there is nothing in the agreement to indicate the existence or situation of other land of the covenantee intended to be benefited the Court cannot allow the identity of such land to be deduced from the surrounding circumstances This argument raises a difficult question as to which the authorities, a number of which are collected and discussed in a most helpful article by Sir Lancelot Elphinstone in 68 L.Q.Rev. 353, are not easy to reconcile. However I do not find it necessary to decide this question because, assuming that all the evidence in the record was admissible to aid in the construction of the agreement, I would, for the reasons given by the learned trial Judge, interpret it as he has done.

Having already expressed my concurrence with the reasons of the learned trial Judge as to the interpretation of the agreement, I wish to stress one feature of the matter. The question is whether, on the true construction of the agreement, the respondent and Henderson intended the restrictive covenant therein contained to be (a) for the vendor's own benefit and personal to it, or (b) for the protection or benefit of the vendor's land, Parcel B. As was said by Lord Shaw in *Lord Strathcona SS. Co.* v. *Dom. Coal Co.*, [1926], 1 D.L.R. 873 at p. 879, A.C. 108 at p. 119, the cases on the branch of the law dealt with in *Tulk* v. *Moxhay* (1848), 2 Ph. 774, 41 E.R. 1143, are legion. In the cases and in the text-books dealing with them the importance of the difference between covenants intended to be for purpose (a) and those intended to be for purpose (b) is repeatedly stressed, and can hardly be supposed to have been absent from the mind of the draftsman of the agreement under consideration when he made no mention of any lands retained by the vendor and inserted in para. 2 the words "the said restriction and condition shall be binding upon each of the lots hereby conveyed for the benefit of the vendor". I cannot accept the view that the mere fact that at the date of the agreement the respondent owned another parcel of land so situate that it might be capable of being regarded as "a dominant tenement" within the rule stated above furnishes a sufficient reason for construing the agreement otherwise than the learned trial Judge has done.

It remains to consider Mr. Morrow's submission that, whatever might have been the result of the appeal apart from the provisions of the *Land Titles Act*, ss. 51 and 131 of that statute require a decision in favour of the respondent. We were informed by counsel that this point was argued in both Courts below although there is no mention of it in the reasons for judgment. In my view there is nothing in these sections that alters the general law as to restrictive covenants running with land. Their purpose appears to be merely to provide methods of registering covenants so as to bring them to the notice of persons intending to deal with lands registered under the Act and to confer power upon the Court to modify or discharge such covenants in certain circumstances. The intention of the Legislature not to alter the general law appears to me to be indicated by the words in s. 51 (3), "if it is of such nature as to run with the land", and by the words of s. 51(4) reading as follows:

"51(4) The entry on the register of a condition or covenant as running with or annexed to land shall not make it run with the land, if the covenant or condition on account of its nature, or of the manner in which it is expressed, would not otherwise be annexed to or run with the land."

I have already expressed my view that the covenant in question was a covenant personal to the respondent not touching or concerning any land retained by it. That is to say, it was a covenant in gross and so on account of its nature would not run with the land.

Appeal allowed.

[Taschereau, Rand and Estey JJ. concurred with Cartwright J.

A canning company operated three canning factories in a village and it sold to B the land on which one of the factories stood, exacting a covenant from B that neither B, its successors and assigns would thereafter use the land as a canning factory without the consent of the vendor, its successors or assigns. B agreed to sell the land to R, and an issue was raised as to the enforceability of the covenant against R by the successors in title to the vendor of its remaining two canning factories. It was argued that (1) the covenant was unenforceable because in restraint of trade; (2) in any event, it was merely personal to the vendor, being for the protection of its business. In upholding a judgment that the covenant was enforceable, Middleton J. A., speaking for the Ontario Appellate Division in *Re Bowes Co. Ltd and Rankin* (1924), 55 O.L.R. 601, [1924] 4 D.L.R. 406, said in part:

"The covenant was imposed upon the sale of one parcel for the benefit of the parcel retained; and, although it relates to the business to be carried on by the purchaser, and is intended to protect the business carried on by the vendor, it must be kept in mind that on each parcel of the vendor's property there was a canning factory, and that the benefit of the covenant, if it passed upon any sale, would tend to enhance the price to be obtained.

"I quite agree with Mr. McMaster that the mere fact that the covenant falls within this rule does not render valid any covenant which would in itself offend against any principle of public policy, and would for that reason be void. I have found no case shewing that a covenant such as this offends any rule of public policy. The purchasing company does not covenant not to carry on its business, but not to carry on another business entirely different, and the effect of the covenant is to prevent the sale of the factory to one contemplating a canning business. Any canner is at perfect liberty to buy any other site, and erect a factory, and to compete with the covenantee. The canning company was under no obligation to sell the factory, and might have kept it idle as long as it chose. By selling it to a non-competing industry rather than adopting this course, the public interest is served rather than prejudiced. The covenant is quite outside the principle involved."]

NEWTON ABBOTT CO-OPERATIVE SOCIETY LTD. v. WILLIAMSON AND TREADGOLD LTD. Chancery. [1952] Ch. 286, [1952] 1 All E.R. 279

Action to enjoin breach of a covenant against the carrying on of the business of an ironmonger on certain land. M. owned premises, known as Devonia, in which she carried on business as an ironmonger. She also owned premises on the opposite side of the street which she sold in 1923 to a grocery partnership under a deed by which the purchasers covenanted not to carry on any business on the purchased land which would compete with the business of an ironmonger. This land subsequently came into the lands of defendants who had notice of the covenant. M. remained in occupation of her business premises until her death in 1944. She devised these premises to her son, and her executors assented to the vesting of title in him. There was no assent in writing as to the benefit of the restrictive covenant exacted in the 1923 conveyance. The son carried on the business until 1948 when he agreed to sell it to a society and to give it a lease of the premises in which the business was conducted. In the assignment of the goodwill of the business he purported to assign the benefit of the covenant aforesaid. The purchasing society which became a lessee of the premises amalgamated with plaintiffs in 1949. When defendants began to expose for sale articles of ironmongery plaintiffs complained and then brought this suit.

UPJOHN J.:... The sole issue before me is whether the plaintiffs are entitled to the benefit of the restrictive covenant, and, if so, whether they are entitled to enforce it against the defendants. I will deal with the first point first. Counsel for the plaintiffs submitted, first, that the benefit of the restrictive covenant was annexed to Devonia so as to pass with the assignment of Devonia in equity without any express mention in such subsequent assignment—in other words, that the covenant runs with the land. Alternatively, he said that the plaintiffs are the express assigns of the benefit of the covenant, and as such are entitled to enforce it. In this difficult branch of the law one thing, in my judgment, is clear, *viz.*, that in order to annex the benefit of a restrictive covenant to land so that it runs with the land without express assignment on a subsequent assignment of the land, the land for the benefit of which it is taken must be clearly identified in the conveyance containing the covenant. That has been established in a number of cases of high authority, and I need only refer shortly to two.

[The learned Judge then referred to *Renals* v. *Cowlishaw*, 11 Ch. D. 861, at p. 868 and to *Re Union of London and Smith's Bank Ltd.'s Conveyance.* [1933] Ch. 611, at p. 627, and continued as follows:]

Looking at the 1923 conveyance, I can find nothing whatever which identifies the land for the benefit of which the covenant is alleged to be taken. Counsel for the plaintiffs relies on the fact that Mrs. Mardon is described as of Devonia, Fore Street, but that, in my judgment, is quite insufficient to annex the benefit of the covenant to those premises. There is no other mention whatever of Devonia in the conveyance. In my judgment, therefore, the plaintiffs fail on this point.

I turn, then, to his second submission, *viz.*, that the plaintiffs are express assigns of the benefit of the restrictive covenant. Counsel for the defendants contends that, even if his submissions (with which I shall deal later) are wrong and the covenant was taken by Mrs. Mardon for the benefit of Devonia to enable her to dispose of it to better advantage, yet there is here no complete chain of assignments vesting the benefit in the plaintiffs. He says that there was never any assignment of the benefit of the covenant by the executors of Mrs. Mardon to Leonard Soper Mardon, and, therefore, he was not in a position to assign the benefit of the covenant to the plaintiffs' predecessors in title. He relied on *Ives* v. *Brown*, [1919] 2 Ch. 314 and *Lord Northbourne* v. *Johnston & Son*, [1922] 2 Ch. 309. In my judgment, those authorities do not support his contention. The position as I see it was this. On the footing that the restrictive covenant was not annexed to the land so as to run with it, the benefit of the covenant is capable of passing by operation of law as well as by express assignment and formed part of Mrs. Mardon's personal estate on her death: see *Ives* v. *Brown.* It follows, therefore, that when her estate was duly wound up and administered—and this case has been argued before me on the footing that that happened many years ago—the benefit of the covenant was held by the executors as bare trustees for the residuary legatee, Leonard Soper Mardon, who was himself one of the executors. He, therefore, became entitled to the benefit of this restrictive covenant in equity, and, in my judgment, he was entitled to assign the benefit in equity on an assignment of Devonia. No doubt, had the covenant been assigned to him by the executors, he could also have assigned it at law. That this is the position is, in my judgment, made clear by [a] passage in the judgment of SARGANT, J., in *Lord Northbourne* v. *Johnston & Son*, [1919] 2 Ch. 309 at p. 317.

... The second main point was the question whether the defendants are liable to have the covenant enforced against them. This was the defendants' main defence in this action and counsel says that the restrictive covenant was not taken for the benefit of Devonia. He puts his case in this way. First, he says that in any event this was not taken for the benefit of any land, but was a covenant with Mrs. Mardon personally, solely for the benefit of her business. Secondly, he says that in order that an express assign of the benefit may sue an assignee of the burden of a covenant there must be some reference in the conveyance creating such covenant to the land for the benefit of which it was taken. It will be convenient to deal with the first point first.

Counsel for the defendants strongly urged that the covenant was taken solely to protect the goodwill of the business carried on at Devonia, that it had no reference to the land itself, and that it was not taken for the benefit of such land—in brief, that it was a covenant in gross incapable of assignment. He urged that taking such a covenant would benefit the business in that an enhanced price could be obtained for the business, but no such enhanced price would be obtained for the land. He relied on the fact that the covenant did not mention the vendors' assigns and that it was a covenant against competition. Further, he pointed out that when Leonard Soper Mardon assigned to the Bovey Tracey Co-operative Society the benefit of the covenant was assigned in the deed which assigned the business and not in the lease of Devonia. If that be the right view, then he said there could be no right to enforce the covenant against the defendants because the mere fact that the defendants took with notice is not sufficient to bind their consciences in equity, and he relied on *Formby* v. *Barker*, [1903] 2 Ch. 539, and *London County Council* v. *Allen*. Those cases show, he submitted, and I agree with him, that in order to enforce a covenant such as this against an assign of the covenantor, you must show that the covenant created something in the nature of an equitable easement. You must find something in the nature of a dominant tenement for the benefit of which the covenant was taken and a servient tenement which was to be subject to that covenant. Here he says there was no dominant tenement. The covenant was taken, not for the benefit of any land, but for the benefit of the business. I do not accept this view of the transaction in 1923. In that year Mrs. Mardon was carrying on the business of an ironmonger at Devonia. No doubt, the covenant was taken for the benefit of that business and to prevent competition therewith, but I see no reason to think, and there is nothing in the 1923 conveyance which leads me to believe, that that was the sole object of taking the covenant. Why should not Mrs. Mardon have sold her land and the business and the benefit of the covenant in such manner as to annex the benefit of the covenant to Devonia, for, by so doing, she would get an enhanced price for the totality of the assets she was selling? A purchaser would surely pay more for a property which would enable him to pass on the benefit of the covenant and to sue in equity assigns of the defendants' premises taking with notice, than for a property which would only enable him to sue the original covenantor, for that is the result of the view urged on me by counsel for the defendants. Further, Mrs. Mardon may well have had it in mind that her own business might be closed down or the goodwill thereof sold to someone who was going to carry it on some other premises. She would then be left with Devonia, and Devonia could be sold at an enhanced price to someone intending to carry on the business of an ironmonger because, if as part of the sale transaction he obtained the benefit of the covenant, he could prevent competition from the defendants' premises opposite in that trade. In my judgment, it was always open to Mrs. Mardon, when she desired to dispose either of the land or the business, to assign the benefit of the covenant with the one or the other or both as she chose. By taking this covenant, she was thereby enabled to sell her premises, or her business, to better advantage as she thought fit.

... Accordingly, in my judgment, the defendants fail on this point.

Counsel's second point was that in order that the benefit of the covenant may be assignable the land for which the benefit of the covenant is taken must in some way be referred to in the conveyance creating the covenant, and I was naturally pressed with the headnote in the *Union of London & Smith's Bank* case, which reads as follows:

"Where on a sale otherwise than under a building scheme a restrictive covenant is taken, the benefit of which is not on the sale annexed to the land retained by the covenantee so as to run with it, an assign of the covenantee's retained land cannot enforce the covenant against an assign (taking with notice) of the covenantor unless he can show (i) that the covenant was taken for the benefit of ascertainable land of the covenantee capable of being benefited by the covenant, and (ii) that he (the covenantee's assign) is an express assign of the benefit of the covenant."

In his judgment, Bennett, J., says ([1933] Ch. 625):

"In my judgment, in order that an express assignee of a covenant restricting the user of land may be able to enforce that covenant against the owner of the land burdened with the covenant, he must be able to satisfy the court of two things. The first is that it was a covenant entered into for the benefit or protection of land owned by the covenantee at the date of the covenant. Otherwise it is a covenant in gross, and unenforceable except as between the parties to the covenant: see *Formby* v. *Barker*. Secondly, the assignee must be able to satisfy the court that the deed containing the covenant defines or contains something to define the property for the benefit of which the covenant was entered into: see James, L. J., in *Renals* v. *Cowlishaw*."

With all respect to the statement of the learned judge, I am unable to agree that where a person is suing as an assign of the benefit of the covenant there must necessarily be something in the deed containing the covenant to define the land for the benefit of which the covenant was entered into. In the first place, the passage in the judgment of James, L. J., in *Renals* v. *Cowlishaw*,... on which the learned judge relies, does not, in my judgment, support the statement of the law for which it was cited. In *Renals* v. *Cowlishaw* there was no question of there being any express assignment of the benefit of the restrictive covenant: see the statement of fact (9 Ch. D. 127); and when James, L. J., says that to enable an assign to take the benefit of restrictive covenants there must be something in the deed to define the property for the benefit of which they were entered into, he is, I think, dealing with the case where it is contended that the benefit of the covenant has been annexed to the land so as to run with the land. When he uses the word "assign" he is using the word as meaning an assign of the land and not an assign of the benefit of the covenant. Secondly, the views expressed by Bennett, J., appear to me to be inconsistent with the views expressed in some of the earlier decisions.... Finally, in the *Union of London & Smith's Bank* case itself, Romer, L. J., reading the judgment of the Court of Appeal, having considered the cases where the benefit of the covenant is annexed to land so as to run without express mention, says ([1933] Ch. 628):

"In all other cases the purchaser will not acquire the benefit of the covenant unless that benefit be expressly assigned to him—or, to use the words of [HALL, V.-C., in *Renals* v. *Cowlishaw* (9 Ch. D. 130)], 'it must appear that the benefit of the covenant was part of the subject-matter of the purchase'."

Later, he says (*ibid.*, 631):

"It is plain, however, from these and other cases, and notably that of *Renals* v. *Cowlishaw*, that if the restrictive covenant be taken not merely for some personal purpose or object of the vendor, but for the benefit of some other land of his in the sense that it would enable him to dispose of that land to greater advantage, the covenant, though not annexed to such land so as to run with any part of it, may be enforced against an assignee of the covenantor taking with notice, both by the covenantee and by persons to whom the benefit of such covenant has been assigned, subject however to certain conditions. In the first place, the 'other land' must be land that is capable of being benefited by the covenant—otherwise it would be impossible to infer that the object of the covenant was to enable the vendor to dispose of his land to greater advantage. In the next place, this land must be 'ascertainable' or 'certain,' to use the words of Romer, L. J., and Scrutton, L. J., respectively. For, although the court will readily infer the intention to benefit the other land of the vendor where the existence and situation of such land are indicated in the conveyance or have been otherwise shown with reasonable certainty, it is impossible to do so from vague references in the conveyance or in other documents laid before the court as to the existence of other lands of the vendor, the extent and situation of which are undefined."

In my judgment, therefore, the problem which I have to consider is, first, when Mrs. Mardon took the covenant in 1923, did she retain other land capable of being benefited by the covenant? If not, *cadit quaestio*. Secondly, was such land "ascertainable" or "certain" in this sense, that the existence and situation of the land must be indicated in the conveyance or otherwise shown with reasonable certainty. Apart from the fact that Mrs. Mardon is described as of Devonia, there is nothing in the 1923 conveyance to define the land for the benefit of which the restrictive covenant was taken, and I do not think that carries one very far, but, for the reasons I have given, I am, in my judgment, entitled to look at the surrounding circumstances to see if the land to be benefited is shown "otherwise" with reasonable certainty. That is a question of fact, and, on the admitted facts, bearing in mind the close juxtaposition of Devonia and the defendants' premises, in my judgment, the only reasonable inference to draw from the circumstances at the time of the 1923 conveyance was that Mrs. Mardon took the covenant restrictive of the user of the defendants' premises for the benefit of her own business of ironmonger and of her property Devonia where at all material times she was carrying on that business, which last-mentioned fact must have been apparent to the purchasers in 1923. I should, perhaps, mention that at the date of her death, Mrs. Mardon owned other property in Fore Street, but counsel on neither side founded any argument on that circumstance. It follows, therefore, in my judgment, that Mrs. Mardon could on any subsequent sale of her land Devonia, if she so chose, as part of the transaction of sale, assign the benefit of the covenant so as to enable the purchaser from her and his assignees of the land and covenant to enforce it against an owner of the defendants' premises taking with notice and her legatee, Leonard Soper Mardon, was in no worse position. I do not regard the fact that he assigned the covenant in the deed containing the assignment of the business as affecting the matter. I say nothing as to the position when the plaintiffs' lease expires so that their estate in Devonia comes to an end, nor whether Leonard Soper Mardon, having apparently assigned away the entire benefit of the covenant, will then be in any position further to enforce it.

Counsel for the defendants took one further point. He submitted that a covenant restrictive of business could not be annexed to land unless it was a covenant not to carry on a business so as to be a nuisance or annoyance to an adjoining occupier, but he cited no authority for that proposition, and, in my judgment, it cannot be maintained: see *Nicoll* v. *Fenning*, 19 Ch. D. 258. Accordingly, in my judgment, the plaintiffs are entitled to succeed in this action and to an injunction as claimed and to costs.

Judgment for plaintiffs.

[For a discussion of some of the problems raised by this case see *Preston and Newsom*, Restrictive Covenants Affecting Freehold Land (1955, 2nd ed.), pp. 70 ff., Excursus B.]

[Owners of a certain hill, being a place of interest and natural beauty, became party to a deed with an owner of other land in the area, under which the latter covenanted "with intent and so as to bind as far as practicable [his land] into whatsoever hands the same may come and to benefit and protect Midsummer Hill" that "no act or thing shall be done or placed or permitted to remain upon the land which shall injure prejudice affect or destroy the natural aspect and condition of the land except as hereinafter provided". *Held*, the covenant was void for uncertainty, and in any event the restriction (having regard to the events which occured, viz., the erection of electricity poles, which were at least 1100 yards distant form Midsummer Hill) could not protect or benefit Midsummer Hill. See *National Trust for Places of Historic Interest or Natural Beauty* v. *Midlands Electricity Board*, [1952] Ch. 380, [1952] 1 All E.R. 298.]

(c) Building and Other Schemes of Development

ELLISTON v. REACHER. Chancery. [1908] 2 Ch. 374, 77 L.J.Ch. 617

PARKER J.:... In my judgment, in order to bring the principles of *Renals* v. *Cowlishaw*, 9 Ch. D. 125; 11 Ch. D. 866 and *Spicer* v. *Martin*, 14 App. Cas. 12 into operation it must be proved (i) that both the plaintiffs and defendants derive title under a common vendor; (ii) that previously to selling the lands to which the plaintiffs and defendants are respectively entitled the vendor laid out his estate, or a defined portion thereof (including the lands purchased by the plaintiffs and defendants respectively), for sale in lots subject to restrictions intended to be imposed on all the lots, and which, though varying in details as to particular lots, are consistent and consistent only with some general scheme of development; (iii) that these restrictions were intended by the common vendor to be and were for the benefit of all the lots intended to be sold, whether or not they were also intended to be and were for the benefit of other land retained by the vendor; and (iv) that both the plaintiffs and the defendants, or their predecessors in title, purchased their lots from the common vendor upon the footing that the restrictions subject to which the purchases were made were to enure for the benefit of the other lots included in the general scheme whether or not they were also to enure for the benefit of other lands retained by the vendors. If these four points be established, I think that the plaintiffs would in equity be entitled to enforce the restrictive covenants entered into by the defendants or their predecessors with the common vendor irrespective of the dates of the respective purchases. I may observe, with reference to the third point, that the vendor's object in imposing the restrictions must in general be gathered from all the circumstances of the case, including in particular the nature of the restrictions. If a general observance of the restrictions is in fact calculated to enhance the values of the several lots offered for sale, it is an easy inference that the vendor intended the restrictions to be for the benefit of all the lots, even though he might retain other land the value of which might be similarly enhanced, for a vendor may naturally be expected to aim at obtaining the highest possible price for his land. Further, if the first three points be established, the fourth point may readily be inferred, provided the purchasers have notice of the facts involved in the three first points; but if the purchaser purchases in ignorance of any material part of those facts, it would be difficult, if not impossible, to establish the fourth point. It is also observable that the equity arising out of the establishment of the four points I have mentioned has been sometimes explained by the implication of mutual contracts between the various purchasers, and sometimes by the implication of a contract between each purchaser and the common vendor, that each purchaser is to have the benefit of all the covenants by the other purchasers, so that each purchaser is in equity an assign of the benefit of these covenants. In my opinion the implication of mutual contract is not always a perfectly satisfactory explanation. It may be satisfactory where all the lots are sold by auction at the same time, but when, as in cases such as *Spicer* v. *Martin*, there is no sale by auction, but all the various sales are by private treaty and at various intervals of time, the circumstances may, at the date of one or more of the sales, be such as to preclude the possibility of any actual contract. For example, a prior purchaser may be dead or incapable of contracting at the time of a subsequent purchase, and in any event it is unlikely that the prior and subsequent purchasers are ever brought into personal relationship, and yet the equity may exist between them. It is, I think, enough to say, using Lord Macnaghten's words in *Spicer* v. *Martin*, that where the four points I have mentioned are established, the community of interest imports in equity the reciprocity of obligation which is in fact contemplated by each at the time of his own purchase.

[The judgment of Parker J. was affirmed on appeal, [1908] 2 Ch. 665 (C.A.).

In *Reid* v. *Bickerstaff*, [1909] 2 Ch. 305 78 L.J. Ch. 753 (C.A.), the Court pointed out that it was a requirement of a building scheme that the area in which it is to operate be clearly defined.

The English rules on building schemes have been adopted in Canada: see *Re Wheeler*, 59 O.L.R. 223, [1926] 4 D.L.R. 392 (App. Div.); *Re Section 51, Land Titles Act (Grieve's Application)* [1954] 1 D.L.R. 301, 10 W.W.R. (N.S.) 49 (Alta.); *West* v. *Hughes*, 58 O.L.R. 183, [1926] 1 D.L.R. 359; *Re Campbell and Cowdy*, 61 O.L.R. 545, [1928] 1 D.L.R. 1034.]

[Omission to impose restrictions in respect of a number of lots comprised in a plan or in a defined area may invalidate an intended building scheme: see *Re Wallace and Bremner*, [1954] O.W.N. 826. Again, if contemplated restrictions are carried out in some sales but not in others, supporting an inference that the common vendor has a discretion whether to impose restrictions or not, there is no enforceable building scheme: see *Re Zierler* (1957), 8 D.L.R. 2d 189 (Ont.).]

[Is the reciprocal enforcement of restrictions affected where the common vendor has reserved a power to vary or "waive" the restrictions in respect of any lot in the area? Is this situation different from the case where varying restrictions are imposed on the lots comprised in the scheme? See the opposing views in *Whitehouse* v. *Hugh* [1906] 1 Ch. 253, aff'd [1906] 2 Ch. 283, 75 L.J. Ch. 677 (C.A.) and *Re Lankin*, [1951] O.W.N. 821; and cf. *White* v. *Bijou Mansions Ltd.*, [1938] Ch. 351, [1938] 1 All E.R. 546 (C.A.) and *Re Wheeler*, 59 O.L.R. 223, [1926] 4 D.L.R. 392 (App. Div.).]

[A common vendor subdivided his land into 23 lots, all of which he sold to four purchasers subject to certain restrictions constituting a building scheme. The purchasers subsequently entered into a deed by which they "released and discharged" each other from the restrictions and covenanted to accept different restrictions with intent to bind their respective lots. The common vendor was not a party to this deed which, moreover, did not indicate that the covenants thereof were in modification or supplement of the original building scheme. A successor in title to some of the lots sought to enforce the second set of restrictions against a successor in title to other lots. Result? See *Re Pinewood Estate, Farnborough*, [1957] 2 All E.R. 517 (Ch.).]

[May a building scheme exist where a vendor has only two parcels of land which on the sale of one parcel, he purports to subject to reciprocal restrictions? See the conflicting views in *Re Rowan and Eaton*, 59 O.L.R. 379, [1926] 4 D.L.R. 582, aff'd 60 O.L.R. 245, [1927] 2 D.L.R. 722 (App. Div.) and *Re Pidgeon*, [1938] 3 D.L.R. 494, [1938] O.W.N. 292 (C.A.).]

[A building scheme may encompass provision for common use of recreation grounds or park land by purchasers of lots in the defined area, and such "commons" must then be maintained by the common vendor or his successors in title: see *Re Lorne Park* (1914), 33 O.L.R. 51, 22 D.L.R. 350 (App. Div.), aff'g 30 O.L.R. 289, 18 D.L.R. 595.]

(d) Modification and Discharge of Restrictive Covenants

RE SECTION 51 LAND TITLES ACT (GRIEVE'S APPLICATION). Alberta Supreme Court. [1954] 1 D.L.R. 301, 10 W.W.R. (N.S.) 49

Petition for modification or discharge of building restrictions. Petitioner was registered owner of two lots which were part of a block of land which had been owned by the C.P.R. By an agreement of sale made in 1911, the C.P.R. sold some of its land to A under certain conditions and covenants which the C.P.R. covenanted to observe, "the intention being to create these conditions and limitations for the benefit of all the owners of the [C.P.R.'s] lots from time to time". A registered a caveat against all the land described in the agreement. Petitioner was a remote assignee of the C.P.R. and proposed to build an apartment house upon his lands. The petition was opposed by one adjacent owner B whose title was also derived from the C.P.R. A finding was made that B, as assignee of the covenantor, could enforce the restrictions in question because there was a building scheme.

EGBERT J.:... The question which remains, then is whether, despite Blundun's opposition, I should modify or discharge the covenants, by virtue of the statutory authority conferred upon the Court by the provisions of s-s. (3) of s. 51 of the *Land Titles Act*, R.S.A. 1942, c. 205, which, as amended by 1950, c. 35, s. 2, reads in part as follows:

"51 (3)... but any such condition or covenant may be modified or discharged by order of the Court, on proof to the satisfaction of the Court that the modification will be beneficial to the persons principally interested in the enforcement of the condition or covenant, or that the condition or covenant conflicts with the provisions of a zoning by-law, official plan or scheme of development under *The Town and Rural Planning Act* and the modification or discharge is in the public interest."

The condition or covenant referred to in this subsection is that described in s-s. (1) of the same section: "A condition or covenant that the land, or any specified portion thereof, is not to be built on, or is to be or not to be used in a particular manner, or any other condition or covenant running with or capable of being legally annexed to land."

The situation here is that it is proposed to build on the land now owned by the petitioner a modern apartment building containing fifteen suites or apartments at a cost of approximately $150,000. As part of a general scheme, and under the provisions of Interior Development By-law No. 4271, the use classification of all lands in the City of Calgary was revised, and the present classification of the petitioner's land is "R. 3", i.e., classified for multiple-family dwellings. Mr. Martin, employed by the City of Calgary as City Planner, states that he verily believes there is a housing shortage in Calgary, and, in his belief, it would be in the public interest to permit the erection of an apartment building on these lands. He further says that an application has been received, and approved by the City Planning Department for the erection of the said apartment block, and permit therefor will issue subject to the Anderson caveat being removed. The apartment, if built, would accordingly comply with the zoning by-laws or regulations of the City of Calgary.

The first situation in which the Court may discharge or modify covenants such as these, is where the modifications will be beneficial "to the persons principally interested in the enforcement" thereof. It seems to me that the application cannot be based on that ground. That provision seems to contemplate the case where all those persons principally interested in the enforcement of the covenant are agreed that a modification of it will be to their mutual interest, and not to the case where some of those persons are persuaded it is in their interest while some of them are equally persuaded it is not in their interest, and refuse to consent to such modification. It seems to me that it was never intended that the Court should act the part of a benevolent despot and say to this latter class, "A modification of this covenant is in your interest whether you think so or not; and you are going to have it whether you want it or not". It would undoubtedly be in the interest of the petitioner, as she would receive a better price for her now vacant lots than she would otherwise receive, but there is no evidence before me that it would be in the interest of Blundun or of any other of "the persons principally interested in the enforcement" of the covenants, which incidentally appears to me to be a question quite different from the question of whether or not a modification might be in the public interest.

Since the petitioner is not entitled to succeed under the first set of conditions laid down is s-s. (3) of s. 51, my one remaining consideration is whether she is entitled to succeed under the second part of that subsection—"that the condition or covenant conflicts with the provisions of a zoning by-law, official plan or scheme of development under *The Town and Rural Planning Act* and the modification or discharge is in the public interest". I can find nothing in the material before me to indicate that the conditions or covenants sought to be modified conflict with the provisions of any zoning by-law, official plan or scheme of development. It is true that Mr. Martin, City Planner, says in his affidavit that "as part of a general scheme and under the provisions of the Interior Development By-law, Number 4271, the use classification of all lands in the City of Calgary was revised and that the present classification of Lots 11 and 12, Block 233, Plan 5700 A.G., is R.3, that is classified for multiple family dwellings". But surely all that means, all it can possibly mean is that insofar as the City of Calgary is concerned, its zoning by-laws or regulations have been altered so as to permit of multiple-family dwellings being erected in an area where only single-family dwellings might have been erected before. There is nothing whatsoever to suggest that the present classification is obligatory, that only multiple-family dwellings may be erected in the area, and that the erection of further single-family dwellings is prohibited. How then can it be said that a covenant enforceable by and against each individual owner in the area conflicts with a provision which is merely permissive and not obligatory? The city has said "In this area you may, at your discretion, build either multiple or single family dwellings", to which the owners promptly reply "We have already agreed among ourselves that we will build only single-family dwellings". How can it be said that there is anything conflicting between the two statements?

If I am right in my opinion that no conflict exists such as is contemplated by the statute, the matter is disposed of as the second part of the subsection is not then applicable, but if I am wrong in this opinion, I must still consider whether the proposed modification or development is in the public interest.

A similar provision of the Ontario *Conveyancing and Law of Property Act*, R.S.O. 1937, c. 152, was considered by the Ontario Court of Appeal in *Re Moody*, [1941], 3 D.L.R. 768, O.W.N. 167. Middleton J. A. pointed out that no provision is made in the section for compensation to anyone and so the statute was not in the nature of an expropriation statute, and so was not entitled to any wide effect and is only to be used where the character of the neighbourhood is so changed that an order can be made without doing violence to the rights of other land owners. He referred to various earlier Ontario cases, including *Re Ontario Lime Co.* [1927] 1 D.L.R. 765 at p. 768, 59 O.L.R. 646 at p. 651, in which he had said "the jurisdiction is one to be exercised with the greatest caution, and an order should seldom, if ever be made which will in truth operate to the prejudice of the adjacent landowner who has any real rights". And he concluded by saying that the function of the statute is to enable the Court to get rid of a condition or restriction which is spent, or so unworkable as to be of no value, and under circumstances where its assertion would be clearly vexatious.

In the later case of *Re Toronto and Lot 23, Plan M206*, [1945], 4 D.L.R. 590, O.W.N. 723, Urquhart J. proceeded on the same principle and held that an order should not be made unless the benefit to the applicant greatly exceeds any possible detriment to the respondents.

It is urged here on behalf of the petitioner that a housing shortage exists in the City of Calgary, and that it would be in the public interest to alleviate that shortage by permitting the erection of an apartment building on those lands. Unless I take judicial notice of the nationwide housing shortage, there is practically no evidence before me of the alleged housing shortage in Calgary, and even if I take judicial notice of such shortage, there is no evidence whatever before me that that shortage cannot be better and more fully alleviated by the erection of apartment houses on locations other than the petitioner's property.

The onus is surely on the petitioner to prove that the public interest will be peculiarly or particularly furthered by the modification which she proposes. This onus has not been in any way discharged. There is no evidence whatsoever that the character of the neighbourhood has been materially changed, so that an order can be made without doing violence to the rights of other landowners. There is no proof whatever that the covenant is spent, that it is so unworkable as to be of no value, or that the circumstances are such as to make its assertion clearly vexatious. To modify the covenant would clearly operate to the prejudice of Blundun, who I have already found has "real rights". I am of the opinion that even if the covenant is in conflict with the provisions of a zoning by-law, etc., its modification or discharge has not been proved by the petitioner to be in the public interest.

Petition dismissed.

[The Conveyancing and Law of Property Act, R.S.O. 1960, c. 66, s. 62, provides in part, as follows:

"(1) Where there is annexed to land a condition or covenant that the land or a specified part of it is not to be built on or is to be or not to be used in a particular manner, or any other condition or covenant running with or capable of being legally annexed to land, any such condition or covenant may be modified or discharged by order of a judge. . . . .

(7) Nothing in this section applies to building restrictions imposed by a by-law passed under the Municipal Act or the Planning Act."

The sparing exercise of the power so conferred is indicated by *Re Beardmore*, [1935] O.R. 526, [1935] 4 D.L.R. 562 (refusal to follow a mere "balance of convenience" rule under the present wording of the statute and application of rule that injury to covenantees must be negligible before restrictions are modified or removed or restrictions have become vexatious).

If restrictions are spent there is no need to obtain an order under s. 62 of the Ontario Act: see *Re Bartley*, [1950] 3 D.L.R. 705, [1950] O.W.N. 648 (C.A.), also holding that a person entitled to land under an agreement for sale only has no status to apply for discharge of restrictive covenants.

See also, for statutory authority to modify or discharge restrictive covenants, Land Titles Act, R.S.A. 1955, c. 170, s. 52 (3).]

[In England, statutory provision for the discharge or modification of restrictive covenants is made by s. 84(1) of the Law of Property Act, 1925 (Imp.), c. 20 which delineates the jurisdiction of the Lands Tribunal (the authority which now administers the provision, subject to an appeal to the Court of Appeal) in much more elaborate terms than are found in Canadian legislation. For a discussion of s. 84(1) and a collection of decisions of the Lands Tribunal and of the Courts, see *Newsom*, The Discharge and Modification of Restrictive Covenants (1957).]

SHAUGHNESSY HEIGHTS PROPERTY OWNERS' ASSOCIATION v. CAMPBELL AND CAMPBELL. British Columbia Supreme Court. [1951] 2 D.L.R. 62, 3 W.W.R. (N.S.) 407

Action to enjoin breach of restrictions established under a private Act. The Act, in brief, restricted a defined area to private dwelling houses. Defendants owned a large house in the area and operated it as caterers to persons holding private or public entertainments.

WILSON J. (after considering the Act in question and upholding plaintiff's status to sue although it was not a property owner):... There is evidence before me that out of some 450 houses in that part of the restricted area known as 1st Shaughnessy about 150 are now being put to uses in violation of the Act. It must here be stressed that the area comprised in 1st Shaughnessy, the northern part of the restricted district, is the only area as to which I have any evidence. I have no proof of violations in the remainder of the district to which the restrictions apply and, since the presumption is against breaches of the law, I assume that there are none.

It is necessary to consider the nature of these violations. It can generally be said that practically all of them are by owners or occupiers who are operating their houses as boarding or rooming-houses. There are some possible exceptions, as for instance a doctor and an optician who practice their professions in their homes, a nursing home and a home for the aged, operated by the provincial Government. The exception would not exceed 4% of the total violations, and the characteristic violator is a rooming or boarding-house operator. These apparent violations are not, in fact, violations because of the provisions of Order in Council No. 200 [[1942] C.W.O.R. 310] of the Wartime Prices and Trade Board, made under the authority of the *War Measures Act*, R.S.C. 1927, c. 206, of the Parliament of Canada. It is not disputed that the effect of this Order was to override the *Shaughnessy Heights Building Restriction Act*, insofar as the two were in conflict, and to permit, during the wartime emergency, the operation of premises within the restricted area as rooming-houses, boarding-houses and apartments. Therefore, the operation of these rooming and boarding-houses is presently legal, but, since O. 200 does not cover the type of business carried on by the defendants, they are still contravening the Act.

The evidence above referred to was introduced by the defendants in an effort to bring this case within the purview of the principles stated in *Knight* v. *Simmonds*, [1896] 2 Ch. 294, and *Sobey* v. *Sainsbury*, [1913] 2 Ch. 513.

The applicability of these cases was questioned by plaintiff's counsel on the ground that they deal with the enforcement of restrictive covenants in private contracts, and not with the interpretation and enforcement of statutes. The answer to that argument is simple. I have already decided that the statute in question is a private Act. I have cited and adopted Maxwell's statement, based on the rulings in *Milnes* v. *Mayor etc. of Huddersfield* (1886), 11 App. Cas. 511 at p. 523, and *Ayr Harbour Trustees* v. *Oswald* (1883), 8 App. Cas. 623, that "The Courts take notice that the statutory powers are obtained on the petitions framed by their promoters and, in construing them, regard them, as they are in effect, as contracts between those persons, or those whom they represent, and the Legislature on behalf of the public and for the public good". I shall, therefore, interpret this statute as I would a contract. It follows that the cases cited by the defendants are applicable.

Knight v. *Simmonds*, [1896] 2 Ch. 294, involved an attempt to enforce a covenant by a purchaser of lands that no trade or business should be carried on upon the lots bought by him. The defence set up was that laundries had been carried on for years upon nearby lots subject to similar restrictions without objection by the plaintiff, and that some other trades had been carried on for a length of time. The principle under which such a defence might be valid was stated by Lindley L. J. at pp. 297-8:

"When a Court of Equity is asked to enforce a covenant by decreeing specific performance or granting an injunction, in other words, when equitable as distinguished from legal relief is sought, equitable as distinguished from legal defences have to be considered. The conduct of the plaintiff may disentitle him from relief; his acquiescence in what he complains of or his delay in seeking relief may of itself be sufficient to preclude him from obtaining it. *Sayers* v. *Collyer*, 28 Ch. D. 103, and *Roper* v. *Williams*, T. & R. 18, illustrate this. In both of those cases the Court refused to enforce restrictive covenants at the instance of the particular plaintiffs. But, further, before granting equitable relief, Courts of Equity look not only to the words of a covenant, but to the object to attain which it was entered into, and if, owing to circumstances which have occurred since it was entered into, that object cannot be attained, equitable relief will be refused. This doctrine was laid down and acted upon by Lord Eldon and Sir Thomas Plumer in *Duke of Bedford* v. *Trustees of the British Museum*, 2 My. & K. 552, and by Wood V.-C. in *Peek* v. *Matthews*, L.R. 3 Eq. 515, and was recognised in *German* v. *Chapman*, 7 Ch.D. 271. It is upon this ground that restrictive covenants intended to preserve the character of land to be laid out and used in a particular way will not be enforced if the land has already been so laid out or used that its preservation as intended is no longer possible. Such a state of things can seldom if ever have arisen except from a departure by the vendor and the purchasers from him from the scheme, or from the acquiescence or laches of those entitled to enforce the observance of the covenants in question; but, whatever the explanation of the altered state of things may be, if the object to be attained by the covenant cannot be attained, equitable relief to enforce it will be refused."

Again, Kay L. J. at p. 301 says, in defining the nature of the defence: "What is the answer? The answer is twofold. The answer is, 'First of all, you, the plaintiff, have by your conduct disentitled yourself to obtain such an injunction because you have acquiesced in many people carrying on laundry businesses, not upon this particular plot bought by the defendant, but upon other parts of the estate, and, secondly, even if your conduct does not disentitle you, still the character of the whole property has been so changed that it is no longer a residential property upon which no one may carry on a trade or business.'"

In *Knight* v. *Simmonds* the Court held that, as to part of the plaintiff's claim, the defence was not established. I quote further from Lindley L. J. at p. 299: "The evidence in the present case shews that, except in a few instances of no real importance, the restrictive covenants entered into with the vendor when the property was sold in lots for building purposes have always been observed. There has been no departure worth mentioning from the scheme originally adopted."

It remains for me to decide whether there has been proved, in this case, any "departure worth mentioning from the scheme originally established".

The boarding-houses, rooming-houses and apartments which constitute 97% of the premises used otherwise than as private dwelling-houses carry on solely by virtue of the existence of Order in Council No. 200. This Order was made under the authority of the *War Measures Act*, which is emergency legislation of a temporary nature. Order 200, a product of the emergency statute, must also be considered, not as permanently changing the law, but as dealing with a situation created by the emergency, by a measure only intended to remain in effect during the emergency. The *War Measures Act*, the *National Emergency Transitional Powers Act*, 1945 (Can.), c. 25, and the *Continuation of Transitional Measures*

Act, 1947 (Can.), c. 16 have all lately been before the Supreme Court of Canada in *Reference re Leasehold Regulations*, [1950] 2 D.L.R. 1, S.C.R. 124. The judgments make it clear that all this Federal legislation, infringing as it does on provincial powers in respect to property and civil rights, is only supportable as emergency legislation. Therefore, the condition created by O. 200, the operation of these boarding-houses, rooming-houses and apartments within the restricted area, is only a temporary condition. Further, it is not a condition acquiesced in or consented to by the plaintiff, but one which they are powerless to remedy. I have no doubt, from the evidence, that the plaintiff has taken all steps in its power to enforce the Act and to preserve the character of the area.

I must, therefore, hold that there has been neither "a change in the character of the neighbourhood nor an acquiescence in breaches" (cf. Lindley L. J. in *Knight* v. *Simmonds*, [1896] 2 Ch. at p. 297).

It follows that the plaintiff's action must succeed.

In fairness to the defendants I should add that there is not the slightest evidence that the commercial business carried on in their premises has any of the aspects of a nuisance, as that word is understood in law. They conduct an orderly, decent establishment, and maintain their premises well.

I think the enforcement of the injunction sought should be postponed for a reasonable time to enable the defendants to close out their business and fulfil outstanding engagements.

Judgment for plaintiff.

[For a decision to the same effect on somewhat similar facts, see *Alexander* v. *Malcheski* (1953), 8 W.W.R. (N.S.) 73, 61 Man. R. 139, aff'd with a variation, 9 W.W.R. (N.S.) 334, 61 Man. R. at p. 145 (C.A.), where Tritschler J., at the trial, said, *inter alia*: "Defendants are not entitled to take advantage of non-observance or non-enforcement of building restrictions during this temporary period of housing shortage and to seek to perpetuate the situation which grew up against the wishes of many owners. In any event, whatever the number of two-family occupancies there may be in the area, I am satisfied that there has not been so complete a change in the character of the neighbourhood that there is no longer any value left in the agreement at all, and this is what defendants must show to succeed on that ground: *Chatsworth Estates Co.* v. *Fewell*, [1931] 1 Ch. 224, at 230, 100 L.J. Ch. 52".

In *Cowan* v. *Ferguson* (1919), 45 O.L.R. 161, 48 D.L.R. 616 (App. Div.), the Court refused to enforce a restrictive covenant taken in 1842 against the use of certain land for a foundry where there was no competition between the parties. It held that the applicable principle was "that where... there has been a general change in the character of the neighbourhood, the Court will not enforce the covenant," and it went on to say that this principle was not confined to cases where the person seeking to enforce the covenant, or his predecessor in title, had been a party to the changes. (For a contrary view based on the older English authorities, see *Van Koughnet* v. *Denison* (1885), 11 O.A.R. 699). Moreover, enforcement may be refused if plaintiff has stood by and, knowing that defendant was erecting a building in breach of the covenant, acquiesced in what was being done, as by making suggestions on the mode of construction.

A covenantee, estopped by conduct from enforcing one of a number of covenants, is not thereby disabled from enforcing the others: see *Re Second Church of Christ Scientist and Dods* (1920), 18 O.W.N. 409.

On acquiescence by failure to enforce against others restrictions which a plaintiff now seeks to enforce against defendant, see *Roper* v. *Williams* (1822), Turn. & R. 18, 37 E.R. 999 (Ch.) (injunctive relief refused.)

See, generally, on defences to enforcement of restrictive covenants, 2 *American Law of Property*, ss. 9.38, 9.39.]

4. EASEMENTS

(a) Characteristics and Types

NAEGELE v. OKE. Ontario Appellate Division. 1916. 37 O.L.R. 61, 31 D.L.R. 501

Appeal by defendant from a judgment for plaintiffs enjoining defendant from interfering with plaintiffs' right to maintain a hydraulic ram upon and take water from defendant's land. The alleged right was based on an oral agreement with defendant's predecessor in title and about eight years later it was reduced to writing and described therein as a lease for 49 years of a "hydraulic water privilege". A few years later defendant bought the land from his predecessor and almost immediately denied to plaintiffs the use of the ram and the water.

MASTEN J:... Is is important, in dealing with this appeal, first to ascertain within what legal category the rights of the parties fall....

Is the right claimed an easement, a lease, or a license?

It is of the essence of an easement that a dominant tenement be specified, and that the grantee of the easement shall have an estate or interest in the dominant tenement at the time of the grant: *Rymer* v. *McIlroy*, [1897] 1 Ch. 528.

No authority need be quoted for the proposition that there cannot be an easement in gross.

It is manifest, therefore, upon the facts as above stated, that the interest in question is not an easement.

Neither can the arrangement be construed to be a lease, though the parties so characterise it, for it is of the essence of a lease that the lessee acquire the exclusive possession of the leased premises: *Watkins* v. *Milton-next-Gravesend Overseers* (1868), L.R. 3 Q.B. 350; *Glenwood Lumber Co.* v. *Phillips*, [1904] A.C. 405.

No exclusive possession of any part of Halliday's lands was acquired by Naegele.

In *Ward* v. *Day* (1863), 4 B. & S. 337, it was held that a license to get all the copperas stone which might be found in part of a manor for twenty-one years at the yearly rental of £25 was not a demise and would not support a distress for rent.

In *Stockport Water Works Co.* v. *Potter* (1864), 3 H. & C. 300, it was held that the grant by a riparian proprietor of a right to take water from a natural stream on which his land abutted operated as a license in gross, and not as a mere demise, and would not enable the grantee to maintain an action in his own name against a wrong-doer.

The written agreement of September, 1911, is, I think, to be construed as relating to the existing ram and pipes and to their then use for supplying water to lot 13. The evidence shews clearly that it was drawn to confirm and continue that which had been in existence and in actual use under an oral agreement for seven or eight years, and was not a general right to take water. That which the plaintiff Naegele acquired under his agreement with the Hallidays was, therefore, I think, a license personal to himself, good for 49 years, subject to earlier determination by his death, or because he was no longer in occupation of the Naegele farm, so as to enable him to enjoy the benefits of the license.

No estate in the lands of Halliday (or Oke) was acquired by Naegele. The license does not include "assigns" and so was not transferable.

At the time this action was instituted, Francis Naegele had sold the lands to which the hydraulic ram conveyed the water, and Pitblado, the purchaser, was in possession, so that, on the date when the writ was issued, he (Francis) had no rights capable of enforcement by the Court.

As Naegele's interest amounts only to a personal license by his grantors and not to any estate or interest in the lands of his grantors, I do not think that Oke was in any way bound (even with notice) by the license granted by his predecessor in title. The right was a personal right given by the Hallidays to Naegele. Not being an interest in the lands, Oke on his purchase took the land clear of any right or license.

The result is, that Naegele's enjoyment of the personal right given him by the Hallidays has been interrupted. But that gives him no claim against Oke, who bought the lands clear and free of any claim against them.

If Naegele has any claim, it is not against Oke, but against Mrs. Halliday [defendant's predecessor]. This action, being against Oke, must be dismissed.

If Naegele were to sue Mrs. Halliday for breach of agreement, he must also fail, on the ground first mentioned.

It is therefore unnecessary to consider other interesting and important questions raised on this appeal—which should be allowed and the action dismissed.

MEREDITH C. J. C. P.:... It must not be forgotten that the title to the land in question is a registered title, and that the defendant, being the duly registered owner of the land, is entitled to the protection which the Registry Act affords, except in so far as he had actual notice of any adverse right; and the actual notice which the defendant had was of the Halliday-Naegele agreement in question, and so he is in the same position as, but not worse in any way than, if that agreement had been registered: he is not chargeable with any notice beyond that which the writing conveys: and that is really nothing affecting the title to the land in question, or the adjoining Naegele farm to which the water in question is conveyed: because neither party to the writing had any estate or interest in either farm; it is an agreement between persons strangers to such titles.

... I agree that the writing would not, if made by the owner, effect a demise of any part of the farm in question: there is no rent reserved; the possibility, depending on Naegele's willingness, and other chances, of Halliday getting some "waste water" is very far removed from the annual certainty of even a peppercorn. Nor could it create an easement, in the strict sense of the term "easement;" and, if a right in gross only, would not be assignable: see *Ackroyd* v. *Smith* (1850), 10 C.B. 164, and *Thorpe* v. *Brumfitt* (1873), L.R. 8 Ch. 650; and, as the right is to be used only in connection with land in which the owner of the right has now no substantial interest, I am unable to imagine any kind of legal or equitable right the plaintiffs can have against the defendant, under the writing in question, enforceable in this action. *Appeal allowed.*

[Riddell and Lennox JJ. concurred on the ground that only a personal licence had been granted.

Two points made in the above case require elaboration, viz; the specification of a dominant tenement and that the grantee of an easement have an estate or interest in such tenement at the time of creation of the easement.

On the first point, express specification is not a prerequisite; parol evidence is admissible to show what was the tenement to which it was intended that the easement be appurtenant: see *Laurie* v. *Winch*, [1953] 1 S.C.R. 49, [1952] 4 D.L.R. 449, rev'g in part [1951] O.R. 505, [1951] 3 D.L.R. 81 which rev'd [1950] O.R. 626, [1950] 4 D.L.R. 577; and cf. *Conn* v. *Zostantos*, [1950] O.W.N. 277 (C.A.); *Hayes* v. *Hayes* (1901), 40 N.S.R. 320 (C.A.).

On the second point, note that in *Rymer* v. *McIlroy*, cited in the principal case, the claimant of the easement was a lessee at the time of its creation but subsequently acquired the fee simple interest. Is there anything more involved here than the issue of duration of the easement?

In 5 *Restatement of Property*, s. 453, Comment a, the following appears: "Usually the owner of an easement appurtenant is, at the time of its creation, in possession of the land to which it becomes appurtenant. Ordinarily, also, the tract to which it becomes appurtenant is defined at the time of the creation of the easement. However, it is conceivable that an easement appurtenant may be created to benefit a person as the possessor of certain land contingently upon his obtaining possession thereof, or upon his future selection of land to which the easement will then become appurtenant." Cf. *Lindenmuth* v. *Safe Harbor Water Power Corp.* (1932), 309 Pa. 58, 163 Atl. 159.]

[Is physical contiguity as between dominant and servient tenement necessary to support an easement? Where the easement is a right of way, must the dominant tenement be one of the termini of the way in question? In *Todrick* v. *Western National Omnibus Co.*, [1934] Ch. 561, 103 L.J. Ch. 224 (C.A.), aff'g on other grounds [1934] Ch. 190, 103 L.J. Ch. 57, Lord Hanworth M. R. said, *inter alia*, that "the real test... does not require physical contiguity... The only consideration is whether or not there can be a better enjoyment of the land by virtue of this right of way, whether the right of way is beneficial in respect of the ownership of the land". The test is no different in respect of other easements, but as in the case of restrictive covenants there may be a question whether the alleged dominant tenement is capable of being benefited by the easement claimed. See also *Guthrie* v. *C.P.R.* (1900), 27 O.A.R. 64, rev'd on other grounds (1901), 31 S.C.R. 155 (prescriptive right to easement of way denied where access thereto involved crossing land of a third person against whom no prescriptive right asserted).

See *Laurie* v. *Winch*, *supra*, for a review of authorities that evidence of existing circumstances may suffice to define the precise limits of an easement of way subject to consideration of the terms of the grant; and, similarly, that such circumstances may be relevant to the nature of the intended user.]

[May an easement be appurtenant to an easement? Cf. *Re Salvin's Indenture*, *Pitt* v. *Durham County Water Board*, [1938] 2 All E.R. 498 (Ch.) (undertaking of waterworks company, composed of land compulsorily taken for erection of reservoirs and statutory right to lay pipes along defined route, held capable of supporting an easement of right to lay pipes through non-contiguous land where such right acquired from plaintiffs' predecessor in title).].

RE ELLENBOROUGH PARK, RE DAVIES, POWELL v. MADDISON. Court of Appeal. [1956] Ch. 131, [1955] 3 All E.R. 667

Appeal from a judgment of Danckwerts J., [1955] 2 All E.R. 38, holding that certain house owners were entitled to an easement of enjoyment of certain land as a pleasure ground or park.

The judgment of the Court was delivered by EVERSHED M. R.: The substantial question raised in this appeal is whether the respondent, or those whom he has been appointed to represent, being the owners of certain houses fronting upon, or, in some few cases, adjacent to, the garden or park known as Ellenborough Park in Weston-super-Mare, have any right known to the law, and now enforceable by them against the owners of the park, to the use and enjoyment of the park to the extent and in the manner later more precisely defined. Both the premises now belonging to the respondent, or to the owners for whom he acts as champion, and also the park itself, were originally part of an estate known as the White Cross Estate. The houses in question were built and the park laid out in the middle of the last century. None of the owners of the houses is an original grantee from the proprietors of the White Cross Estate. Similarly, the present owners of the park are the successors in title of the original grantors of the premises of the house owners....

The substantial question in the case, which we have briefly indicated, is one of considerable interest and importance. It is clear from our brief recital of the facts that, if the house owners are now entitled to an enforceable right in respect of the use and enjoyment of Ellenborough Park, that right must have the character and quality of an easement as understood by, and known to, our law. It has, therefore, been necessary for us to consider carefully the qualities and characteristics of easements, and, for such purpose, to look back into the history of that category of incorporeal rights in the development of English real property law. It may be fairly assumed that, in the case of *Duncan* v. *Louch*, 16 Q.B. 904, the Court of Queen's Bench in the year 1845, and particularly Lord Denman C. J., who delivered the first judgment in the court, was of opinion that such a right as the respondent claims was capable of fulfilling the qualifying conditions of an easement. And Buckley J., in the case in 1904 of *Keith* v. *Twentieth Century Club Ltd.*, (1904) 73 L.J. Ch. 545; 20 T.L.R. 462 answered certain questions which Byrne J. had ordered to be set down to be argued before the court, themselves depending upon the assumption that such a right could exist in law. On the other hand, Farwell J., a judge peculiarly experienced and learned in real property law, on two occasions, namely in 1903 in the case of *International Tea Stores Co.* v. *Hobbs*, [1903] 2 Ch. 165 and, in 1905 in *Attorney-General* v. *Antrobus*, [1905] 2 Ch. 198, used language appearing to treat as axiomatic the proposition, that a right, which should properly be described as a jus spatiandi, was a right excluded by English law, as by Roman law, from the company of servitudes.

The four cases which we have mentioned must be considered hereafter at greater length. But it can be said at once that, with the possible exception of the first, none of them constitutes or involves a direct decision upon the question now before us: and although the existence of gardens surrounded by houses, the owners or occupiers of which enjoy in practice the amenities of the gardens, is a well-known feature of town development throughout the country, no other case appears to have come before the courts in which the validity of the rights in fact enjoyed in the gardens has ever been tested.

A full statement of the facts of the present case was contained in the judgment of Danckwerts J.... Save in two respects, therefore, we do not think it useful or necessary to set the facts out again in this judgment. But, having regard particularly to certain of the arguments by way of analogy put before us by Mr. Cross, it is necessary to decide what precisely was the nature of the rights which, under the original conveyances, the owners of the estate purported to grant to the purchasers of the relevant plots of land; and what corresponding obligations the vendors undertook. We shall therefore have to examine closely the exact form of the conveyances, one of which has been before the court, and has been accepted by counsel as typical of all the relevant conveyances.

And, secondly, by reason of Mr. Cross's more general argument, based on the alleged absence of the required connexion between the rights to enjoy the garden and the premises themselves (as distinct from the persons of their owners), which are said to constitute the dominant tenements, we must also state precisely, by reference to further evidence filed before us and by our leave, where these premises are situated.

But, before we proceed to those matters of fact, it will be proper, as a foundation for all that follows in this judgment, to attempt a brief account of the emergence in the course of the history of our law, of the rights known to us as "easements," and thereafter, so far as relevant for present purposes, to formulate what can now be taken to be the essential qualities of those rights. For the former purpose we cannot do better than cite a considerable passage from the late Sir William Holdworth's Historical Introduction to the Land Law (Clarendon Press, 1927, p. 265). The author states: "Both the term 'easement' and the thing itself were known to the mediaeval common law. At the latter part of the sixteenth century it was described in Kitchin's book on courts, and defined in the later editions of the 'Termes de la Ley.'" After stating the definition and observing its obvious defects from the point of view of modern law, Sir William proceeds: "But these defects in the definition are instructive, because they indicate that the law as to easements was as yet rudimentary.

"It was still rudimentary when Blackstone wrote. In fact, right down to the beginning of the nineteenth century, there was but little authority on many parts of this subject. Gale, writing in 1839, said: 'The difficulties which arise from the abstruseness and refinements incident to the subject have been increased by the comparatively small number of decided cases affording matter for defining and systematising this branch of the law. Upon some points indeed there is no authority at all in English law.'

"The industrial revolution, which caused the growth of large towns and manufacturing industries, naturally brought into prominence such easements as ways, watercourses, light, and support; and so Gale's book became the starting-point of the modern law, which rests largely upon comparatively recent decisions.

"But, though the law of easements is comparatively modern, some of its rules have ancient roots. There is a basis of Roman rules introduced into English law by Bracton, and acclimatized by Coke.... The law, as thus developed, sufficed for the needs of the country in the eighteenth century. But, as it was no longer sufficient for the new economic needs of the nineteenth century, an expansion and an elaboration of this branch of the law became necessary. It was expanded and elaborated partly on the basis of the old rules, which had been evolved by the working of the assize of nuisance, and its successor the action on the case; partly by the help of Bracton's Roman rules; and partly, as Gale's book shows, by the help of the Roman rules taken from the Digest, which he frequently and continuously uses to illustrate and to supplement the existing rules of law."

The reference to Sir E. Coke we take to be a reference to Coke upon Littleton, citations from which and criticisms of which will be found, for example, in Gale on Easements, 12th ed., p. 305.

The passage which we have read from Sir William Holdsworth sufficiently serves to explain the appearance and the prominence of Roman dicta in the English law of easements, commonly called, indeed, by the Latin name of "servitudes": and it may well be possible that Farwell J.'s rejection of the jus spatiandi as a legal right by English law was derived in part from its similar rejection by the law of Rome.... Apart from the opinion of Farwell J., there has been, as we have already observed, no judicial authority for adopting the Roman view in this respect into the English law. Moreover, the exact characteristics of the jus spatiandi mentioned by the Roman lawyers has to be considered. It by no means follows that the kind of right which is here in question, arising out of a method of urban development that would not have been known to Roman lawyers, can in any case be said to fall within its scope. And, in any event, its validity must depend, in our judgment, upon a consideration of the qualities which must now be attributed to all easements by the law relating to easements as it has now developed in England.

For the purposes of the argument before us Mr. Cross and Mr. Goff were content to adopt, as correct, the four characteristics formulated in Dr. Cheshire's Modern Real Property, 7th ed., pp. 456 et seq. They are (1) there must be a dominant and a servient tenement: (2) an easement must "accommodate" the dominant tenement: (3) dominant and servient owners must be different persons, and (4) a right over land cannot amount to an easement, unless it is capable of forming the subject-matter of a grant.

The four characteristics stated by Dr. Cheshire correspond with the qualities discussed by Gale in his second chapter, sections 2, 5, 3, and 6 and 8 respectively. Two of the four may be disregarded for present purposes, namely, the first and the third. If the garden or park is, as it is alleged to be, the servient tenement in the present case, then it is undoubtedly distinct from the alleged dominant tenements, namely, the freeholds of the several houses whose owners claim to exercise the rights. It is equally clear that if these lands respectively constitute the servient and dominant tenements then they are owned by different persons. The argument in the case is found, accordingly, to turn upon the meaning and application to the circumstances of the present case of the second and fourth conditions; that is, first, whether the alleged easement can be said in truth to "accommodate" the dominant tenement—in other words, whether there exists the required "connexion" between the one and the other: and, secondly, whether the right alleged is "capable of forming the subject-matter of a grant." The exact significance of this fourth and last condition is, at first sight perhaps, not entirely clear. As between the original parties to the "grant," it is not in doubt that rights of this kind would be capable of taking effect by way of contract or licence. But for the purposes of the present case, as the arguments made clear, the cognate questions involved under this condition are: whether the rights purported to be given are expressed in terms of too wide and vague a character; whether, if and so far as effective, such rights would amount to rights of joint occupation or would substantially deprive the park owners of proprietorship or legal possession; whether, if and so far as effective, such rights constitute mere rights of recreation, possessing no quality of utility or benefit; and on such grounds cannot qualify as easements.

It will now be convenient for us to state the terms of the conveyance dated December 23, 1864, and made between Henry Davies and Joseph Whereat of the one part and John Porter of the other part which, as we have said, has been taken for the purposes of the case as typical of all the conveyances.

[The learned Justice then reviewed the terms of the conveyance which included "the full enjoyment... at all times hereafter in common with the other persons to whom such easements may be granted of the pleasure ground set out and made in front of the said plot of land... in the centre of the square called Ellenborough Park... but subject to the payment of a fair and just proportion of the costs charges and expenses of keeping in good order and condition the said pleasure ground". The vendor covenanted in the deed that the plot of land aforesaid "shall at all times remain as an ornamental garden or pleasure ground". The learned Justice concluded that the right of enjoyment of the garden or park was intended to be annexed to the premises sold rather than given as a personal privilege to their purchasers, and he dealt with the question of what were the premises to which this right was annexed. He then continued as follows:]

It remains to interpret the actual terms of the grant itself—"the full enjoyment of the pleasure ground set out and made", etc. Mr. Cross fastened upon the presence of the word "full", and the absence of any indication of the way in which the pleasure ground was to be used—or of any limitations upon its use—and contended that the right or privilege given was a jus spatiandi in its strict sense, that is, a right to go or wander upon the park and every part of it and enjoy its amenities (and even its produce) without stint. We do not so construe the words in their context. Although we are now anticipating to some extent the question which arises under the fourth of Dr. Cheshire's conditions, it seems to us, as a matter of construction, that the use contemplated and granted was the use of the park as a garden, the proprietorship of which (and of the produce of which) remained vested in the vendors and their successors. The enjoyment contemplated was the enjoyment of the vendors' ornamental garden in its physical state as such—the right, that is to say, of walking on or over those parts provided for such purpose, that is, pathways and (subject to restrictions in the ordinary course in the interest of the grass) the lawns; to rest in or upon the seats or other places provided; and, if certain parts were set apart for particular recreations such as tennis or bowls, to use those parts for those purposes, subject again, in the ordinary course, to the provisions made for their regulation; but no to trample at will all over the park, to cut or pluck the flowers or shrubs, or to interfere in the laying out or upkeep of the park. Such use or enjoyment is, we think, a common and clearly understood conception, analogous to the use and enjoyment conferred upon members of the public, when they are open to the public, of parks or gardens such as St. James's Park, Kew Gardens or the Gardens of Lincoln's Inn Fields. In our judgment, the use of the word "full" does not import some wider, less well understood or less definable privilege. The adjective does not in fact again appear when the enjoyment of the garden is later referred to. It means no more than that to each plot was annexed the right of enjoyment of the park as a whole—notwithstanding that it was divided by Walliscote Road. Nor does any difficulty arise out of the condition as to contribution, and Mr. Cross did not, indeed, so suggest. The obligation being a condition of the enjoyment, each house would be bound to contribute its due (that is, proportionate) share of the reasonable cost of upkeep....

We pass, accordingly, to a consideration of the first of Dr. Cheshire's conditions—that of the accommodation of the alleged dominant tenements by the rights as we have interpreted them. For it was one of the main submissions by Mr. Cross on behalf of the appellant that the right of full enjoyment of the park, granted to the purchaser by the conveyance of December 23, 1864, was insufficiently connected with the enjoyment of the property conveyed, in that it did not subserve some use which was to be made of that property; and that such a right accordingly could not exist in law as an easement. In this part of his argument Mr. Cross was invoking a principle which is, in our judgment, of unchallengeable authority, expounded, in somewhat varying language, in many judicial utterances, of which the judgments in *Ackroyd* v. *Smith*, 10 C.B. 164, are, perhaps, most commonly cited. We think it unnecessary to review the authorities in which the principle has been applied; for the effect of the decisions is stated with accuracy in Dr. Cheshire's Modern Real Property, 7th ed., at p. 457. After pointing out that "one of the fundamental principles concerning easements is that they must be not only appurtenant to a dominant tenement, but also connected with the normal enjoyment of the dominant tenement" and referring to certain citations in support of that proposition the author proceeded: "We may expand the statement of the principle thus: a right enjoyed by one over the land of another does not possess the status of an easement unless it accommodates and serves the dominant tenement, and is reasonably necessary for the better enjoyment of that tenement, for if it has no necessary connexion therewith, although it confers an advantage upon the owner and renders his ownership of the land more valuable, it is not an easement at all, but a mere contractual right personal to and only enforceable between the two contracting parties." In the course of the argument before us it was suggested that the principle thus formulated lacked completeness having regard to the judgment of Willes J. in *Bailey* v. *Stephens*, 12 C.B.N.S. 91. The effect of the decision of the Court of Common Pleas in that case is sufficiently stated in the sidenote, which is as follows: "A claim of a prescriptive right in the owners or occupiers of close A to enter close B (belonging to a third person), and to cut down and carry away and convert to their own use all the trees and wood growing and being thereon, 'as to the said close A appertaining' is void, as being too large."... It will be observed that in this judgment Willes J. twice incorporated, in his definition of incidents which run with the land, that they were not (or could not be) of benefit to persons other than the grantees thereof; and Mr. Cross submitted that the judge was intending to indicate that this isolation of benefit constitutes an essential ingredient of every right granted to a purchaser over the vendor's land, if it is to qualify as an easement which the law will recognize. If Willes J. did in fact intend to introduce this qualification, and if he were right in doing so, the appellant would be much assisted in the present case; for it is clear that a right to use and enjoy the amenities of Ellenborough Park could be appreciated by and could benefit many inhabitants of Weston-super-Mare besides the persons to whom in fact the right was granted. We do not think, however, that Willes J. was intending to say that the right of a man to use another person's property for the purposes of his own estate cannot amount to an easement, unless it is incapable of being in fact enjoyed by anyone other than the grantee of the right.... In our judgment Willes J., in expressing himself as he did,... was merely emphasizing that an easement must be appurtenant to an estate for the benefit of that estate and its owner and that it cannot at the same time lawfully be enjoyed by any other person. If, however, the judge was intimating that, if a right be of such a character that it can factually (as distinct from lawfully) be of benefit to persons other than the owner of the estate to whom the right is granted, it is incapable of legal recognition as an easement, the judge was enunciating a principle which, so far as we are aware, has no other authority to support it. It is true that the observations of Willes J. were quoted without disapproval by Hamilton L. J. in *Attorney-General* v. *Horner* (No. 2), [1913] 2 Ch. 140, 196, but there is no reason to suppose that the particular point which we are now considering received his attention, for the point was as unnecessary for the determination of the case which was before him as it was, in fact, for the determination of *Bailey* v. *Stephens* itself. Willes J.'s judgment was also briefly referred to by Lord Hanworth M. R. in *Todrick* v. *Western National Omnibus Co. Ltd.*, [1934] Ch. 561; but as to this it is to be observed that, if he or Romer and Maugham L.JJ., who sat with him, had regarded the language of Willes J. as establishing the principle now in question, it is difficult to imagine why they expressed no view upon it; for it would have been directly relevant to the decision of the court. The effect of that decision, so far as material to present purposes, was that a right to use a way as appurtenant to land can exist as an easement, even though the dominant tenement is not one of the termini of the way. It is clear that such a way is capable of benefiting any passer-by, wholly unconnected with the dominant tenement, who chooses to use it as a short cut; nevertheless, this court held that a way of this kind could constitute an easement. In our judgment, accordingly, the statement of the law in Dr. Cheshire's book, to which we have referred, is unaffected by the judgment of Willes J. in *Bailey* v. *Stephens.*

Can it be said, then, of the right of full enjoyment of the park in question, which was granted by the conveyance of December 23, 1864, and which, for reasons already given, was, in our view, intended to be annexed to the property conveyed to Mr. Porter, that it accommodated and served that property? It is clear that the right did, in some degree, enhance the value of the property, and this consideration cannot be dismissed as wholly irrelevant. It is, of course, a point to be noted; but we agree with Mr. Cross's submission that it is in no way decisive of the problem; it is not sufficient to show that the right increased the value of the property conveyed, unless it is also shown that it was connected with the normal enjoyment of that property. It appears to us that the question whether or not this connexion exists is primarily one of fact, and depends largely on the nature of the alleged dominant tenement and the nature of the right granted. As to the former, it was in the contemplation of the parties to the conveyance of 1864 that the property conveyed should be used for residential and not commercial purposes.... We have already stated that the purchasers of all the plots, which actually abutted on the park, were granted the right to enjoy the use of it, as were also the purchasers of some of the plots which, although not fronting upon the park, were only a short distance away from it. As to the nature of the right granted, the conveyance of 1864 shows that the park was to be kept and maintained as a pleasure ground or ornamental garden, and that it was contemplated that it should at all times be kept in good order and condition and well stocked with plants and shrubs; and the vendors covenanted that they would not at any time thereafter erect or permit to be erected any dwelling-house or other building (except a grotto, bower, summer-house, flower-stand, fountain, music-stand or other ornamental erection) within or on any part of the pleasure ground. On these facts Mr. Cross submitted that the requisite connexion between the right to use the park and the normal enjoyment of the houses which were built around it or near it had not been established. He likened the position to a right granted to the purchaser of a house to use the Zoological Gardens free of charge or to attend Lord's Cricket Ground without payment. Such a right would undoubtedly, he said, increase the value of the property conveyed but could not run with it at law as an easement, because there was no sufficient nexus between the enjoyment of the right and the use of the house. It is probably true, we think, that in neither of Mr. Cross's illustrations would the supposed right constitute an easement, for it would be wholly extraneous to, and independent of, the use of a house as a house, namely, as a place in which the householder and his family live and make their home; and it is for this reason that the analogy which Mr. Cross sought to establish between his illustrations and the present case cannot, in our opinion, be supported. A much closer analogy, as it seems to us, is the case of a man selling the freehold of part of his house and granting to the purchaser, his heirs and assigns, the right, appurtenant to such part, to use the garden in common with the vendor and his assigns. In such a case, the test of connexion, or accommodation, would be amply satisfied; for just as the use of a garden undoubtedly enhances, and is connected with, the normal enjoyment of the house to which it belongs, so also would the right granted, in the case supposed, be closely connected with the use and enjoyment of the part of the premises sold. Such, we think, is in substance the position in the present case. The park became a communal garden for the benefit and enjoyment of those whose houses adjoined it or were in its close proximity. Its flower beds, lawns and walks were calculated to afford all the amenities which it is the purpose of the garden of a house to provide; and, apart from the fact that these amenities extended to a number of householders, instead of being confined to one (which on this aspect of the case is immaterial), we can see no difference in principle between Ellenborough Park and a garden in the ordinary signification of that word. It is the collective garden of the neighbouring houses, to whose use it was dedicated by the owners of the estate and as such amply satisfied, in our judgment, the requirement of connexion with the dominant tenements to which it is appurtenant. The result is not affected by the circumstance that the right to the park is in this case enjoyed by some few houses which are not immediately fronting on the park. The test for present purposes, no doubt, is that the park should constitute in a real and intelligible sense the garden (albeit the communal garden) of the houses to which its enjoyment is annexed. But we think that the test is satisfied as regards these few neighbouring, though not adjacent, houses. We think that the extension of the right of enjoyment to these few houses does not negative the presence oft he necessary "nexus" between the subject-matter enjoyed and the premises to which the enjoyment is expressed to belong....

For the reasons which we have stated, we are unable to accept the contention that the right to the full enjoyment of Ellenborough Park fails in limine to qualify as a legal easement for want of the necessary connexion between its enjoyment and the use of the properties comprised in the conveyance of 1864, and in the other relevant conveyances.

We turn next to Dr. Cheshire's fourth condition for an easement—that the right must be capable of forming the subject-matter of a grant. As we have earlier stated, satisfaction of the condition in the present case depends on a consideration of the questions whether the right conferred is too wide and vague, whether it is inconsistent with the proprietorship or possession of the alleged servient owners, and whether it is a mere right of recreation without utility or benefit.

To the first of these questions the interpretation which we have given to the typical deed provides, in our judgment, the answer; for we have construed the right conferred as being both well defined and commonly understood. In these essential respects the right may be said to be distinct from the indefinite and unregulated privilege which, we think, would ordinarily be understood by the Latin term "jus spatiandi", a privilege of wandering at will over all and every part of another's field or park, and which, though easily intelligible as the subject-matter of a personal licence, is something substantially different from the subject-matter of the grant in question, namely, the provision for a limited number of houses in a uniform crescent of one single large but private garden.

Our interpretation of the deed also provides, we think, the answer to the second question; for the right conferred no more amounts to a joint occupation of the park with its owners, no more excludes the proprietorship or possession of the latter, than a right of way granted through a passage, or than the use by the public of the gardens of Lincoln's Inn Fields (to take one of our former examples) amount to joint occupation of that garden with the London County Council, or involve an inconsistency with the possession or proprietorship of the council as lessees. It is conceded that, in any event, the plaintiff owners of the park are entitled to cut the timber growing on the park and to retain its proceeds. We have said that in our judgment, under the deed, the flowers and shrubs grown in the garden are equally the park owners' property. We see nothing repugnant to a man's proprietorship or possession of a piece of land that he should decide to make it and maintain it as an ornamental garden, and should grant rights to a limited number of other persons to come into it for the enjoyment of its amenities.

Mr. Cross relied, upon this part of his case, on the recent decision of *Copeland* v. *Greenhalf*, [1952] Ch. 488, [1952] 1 All E.R. 809 and the ratio of Upjohn J.'s judgment. The relevant facts were that a claim was made to a prescriptive right to deposit and leave, for an indefinite time, vehicles upon an undefined part of a strip of land which was subject to a right of way. It appeared that the claimant was by trade a wagon repairer and that the vehicles were deposited by him on the land in the course of his business and while awating repairs. It further appeared that wagons were commonly repaired while remaining so deposited. On these facts the judge—very justifiably (if we may say so)—found that the claimant was occupying and seeking the right to occupy an unspecified part of the land for the purpose of his business, and carrying on such business upon the land so occupied. "I think," said the judge, "that the right claimed goes wholly outside any normal idea of an easement, that is, the right of the owner or the occupier of a dominant tenement over a servient tenement. This claim (to which no closely related authority has been referred to me) really amounts to a claim to a joint user of the land by the defendant. Practically, the defendant is claiming the whole beneficial user of the strip of land on the south-east side of the track there; he can leave as many or as few lorries there as he likes for as long as he likes; he may enter on it by himself, his servants and agents to do repair work thereon. In my judgment, that is not a claim which can be established as an easement. It is virtually a claim to possession of the servient tenement, if necessary to the exclusion of the owner; or, at any rate, to a joint user, and no authority has been cited to me which would justify the conclusion that a right of this wide and undefined nature can be the proper subject-matter of an easement. It seems to me that to succeed, this claim must amount to a successful claim of possession by reason of long adverse possession. I say nothing, of course, as to the creation of such rights by deeds or by covenant; I am dealing solely with the question of a right arising by prescription."

We do not think that the facts of *Copeland* v. *Greenhalf* bear any real relation to the present case, and Upjohn J.'s judgment constitutes no authority relevant to our decision.

The third of the questions embraced in Dr. Cheshire's fourth condition rests primarily on a proposition stated in Theobald's The Law of Land, 2nd ed. (1929), at p. 263, where it is said that an easement "must be a right of utility and benefit and not one of mere recreation and amusement." It does not appear that a proposition in similar terms is stated by Gale. The passage in Theobald in justified by reference to two cases: *Mounsey* v. *Ismay*, (1865) 3 H. & C. 486, 498 and *Solomon* v. *Vintners Co.*, (1859) 4 H. & N. 585, 593. The second of these cases was concerned with a right of support, and appears only to be relevant for present purposes on account of an intervention in the course of the argument on the part of Pollock C. B. and Baron Bramwell, in which it was suggested that one who had for a long period played rackets against the wall of a neighbour would have a right not to have the wall pulled down. We were also referred in argument to the Scottish case in the House of Lords of

Dyce v. *Lady James Hay*, 1 Macq. 305, and to the earlier case before Lord Eldon therein referred to of *Dempster* v. *Cleghorn*, 2 Dow. 40. The former of these two cases was concerned with a claim on the part of the inhabitants of Aberdeen to roam at will over a piece of land bordering upon the River Don, and for such purpose to use every part of the land to the practical exclusion of any right of user on the part of the owner. The case was therefore one involving what could strictly be called a claim by a large and ill-defined number of people to a jus spatiandi. In Lord Eldon's case (in which the only decision was to refer the matter back to the Court of Session), the dispute was between certain persons, inhabitants of the City of St. Andrews and others, claiming the right of playing golf on the St. Andrews' Golf Links, and a tenant whose rabbits were said to be interfering with the proper maintenance of the golf course. Lord Eldon observed that the case had excited great warmth of feeling—which indeed may sufficiently appear from the allegation that some of the rabbits on the course were English rabbits. Neither that case nor the case of *Dyce* v. *Lady James Hay* appear to us to lend real support to the proposition stated by Theobald, at least in its application to such a case as the present.

But the observations of Martin B., who delivered the judgment of the court in *Mounsey* v. *Ismay* (the first case mentioned in Theobald), are much more to the point. The case concerned a claim under the Prescription Act for the freemen and citizens of a town on a certain day to enter upon a close for the purpose of holding horse races thereon. The opinion of the court was that the right claimed failed, in any event, to qualify as an easement by reason of the absence of a dominant tenement. Baron Martin considered, without deciding, the question whether an easement of the kind claimed could in any case exist as an easement in gross: and proceeded as follows: "But, however this may be, we are of opinion that to bring the right within the term 'easement' in the second section (of the Prescription Act) it must be one analogous to that of a right of way which precedes it and a right of watercourse which follows it, and must be a right of utility and benefit and not one of mere recreation and amusement."

The words which we have quoted were used in reference to a claim for a right to conduct horse races and, in our judgment, the formula adopted by Theobald should be read in the light of that circumstance. In any case, if the proposition be well-founded, we do not think that the right to use a garden of the character with which we are concerned in this case can be called one of mere recreation and amusement, as those words were used by Martin B. No doubt a garden is a pleasure—on high authority, it is the purest of pleasures—but, in our judgment, it is not a right having no quality either of utility or benefit as those words should be understood. The right here in suit is, for reasons already given, one appurtenant to the surrounding houses as such, and constitutes a beneficial attribute of residence in a house as ordinarily understood. Its use for the purposes, not only of exercise and rest but also for such domestic purposes as were suggested in argument—for example, for taking out small children in perambulators or otherwise—is not fairly to be described as one of mere recreation or amusement, and is clearly beneficial to the premises to which it is attached. If Baron Martin's test is applied, the right in suit is, in point of utility, fairly analogous to a right of way passing over fields to, say, the railway station, which would be none the less a good right, even though it provided a longer route to the objective. We think, therefore, that the statement of Baron Martin must at least be confined to exclusion of rights to indulge in such recreations as were in question in the case before him, horse racing or perhaps playing games, and has no application to the facts of the present case.

As appears from what has been stated earlier, the right to the full enjoyment of Ellenborough Park, which was granted by the 1864 and other relevant conveyances, was, in substance, no more that a right to use the park as a garden in the way in which gardens are commonly used. In a sense, no doubt, such a right includes something of a jus spatiandi, inasmuch as it involves the principle of wandering at will round each part of the garden, except of course, such parts as comprise flower beds, or are laid out for some other purpose, which renders walking impossible or unsuitable. We doubt, nevertheless, whether the right to use and enjoy a garden in this manner can with accuracy be said to constitute a mere jus spatiandi. Wandering at large is of the essence of such a right and constitutes the main purpose for which it exists. A private garden, on the other hand, is an attribute of the ordinary enjoyment of the residence to which it is attached, and the right of wandering in it is but one method of enjoying it. On the assumption, however, that the right now in question does constitute a jus spatiandi, or that it is analogous thereto, it becomes necessary to consider whether the right, which is in question in these proceedings, is, for that reason, incapable of ranking in law as an easement.

Farwell J. twice indicated that in his opinion the jus spatiandi is an interest which is not known to our law; and we think it is true to say that this principle has been widely accepted in the profession without sufficient regard being had, perhaps, to the exact language in which Farwell J. expressed himself or the circumstances in which his view of the matter was propounded. The first of the two cases, in which he intimated that a jus spatiandi is not known to the law, was *International Tea Stores Co.* v. *Hobbs*, [1903] 2 Ch. 165. The actual decision in that case had nothing to do with a jus spatiandi, nor did the facts before the judge require of themselves any pronouncement by him upon that subject. The question which was in issue was whether the right or privilege of using a way by a lessee over the land of his lessor passed under section 6 of the Conveyancing Act, 1881, upon a subsequent conveyance to the lessee of the demised property, notwithstanding that the enjoyment of the way had been wholly permissive and precarious. That being the issue, it is not surprising that the arguments of counsel on both sides, as reported in the Law Reports, did not travel outside it. It appears, however, from Farwell J.'s judgment that, in the course of Lord Coleridge's submission on behalf of the defendant that the user by the lessee of the way had been merely permissive and precarious and was therefore outside the scope of section 6, he had introduced a right of user of a park and gardens as an illustration of the argument which he was presenting. Farwell J. in his judgment described and dealt with the illustration [in part] as follows:... The instance suggested by Lord Coleridge in his argument illustrates my meaning; he put the case of a man living in a house at his landlord's park gates, and having leave to use and using the drive as a means of access to church or town, and to use and using the gardens and park for his enjoyment, and asked, "Would such a man on buying the house with the rights given by section 6 of the Conveyancing Act acquire a right of way over the drive, and a right to use the gardens and park? My answer is 'Yes' to the first, and 'No' to the second question, because the first is a right the existence of which is known to the law, and the latter, being a mere jus spatiandi, is not so known."

Farwell J. was a judge of great learning and all his judicial utterances merit and are accorded more than ordinary respect; but in his, as in all, judgments more weight should be attached to that which was necessary for the decision of the case than to that which was merely obiter. It is plain that Farwell J.'s reference, in the passage quoted, to the jus spatiandi formed no necessary part of his judgment, and it is to be noted that he did not refer to any authority in support of it. It must nevertheless be conceded that in the view of a very learned judge the right of a man to use, as appurtenant to his own property, the gardens and park of another is a right the existence of which is not known to the law, even though that right be expressly granted.

The second of the two cases in which the jus spatiandi was considered by Farwell J. was *Attorney-General* v. *Antrobus*, [1905] 2 Ch. 188. That was an action which was brought by the Attorney-General at the relation of the chairman of the local parish council and certain gentlemen interested in the preservation of public rights in open spaces and footpaths against the then owner of the land upon which Stonehenge stands, for an order for the removal of certain fences which the defendant had erected round Stonehenge. It will be seen accordingly that the object of the action was to establish public, as distinct from private, rights; and the public rights, as so asserted, were to have free access to Stonehenge by means of roads running up to and through the same, such rights being founded upon an alleged trust, created by a lost grant or declaration or by lost statute, for the free user by the public of Stonehenge as a place of resort and for the free access of the public thereto by means of the said roads. At the trial, as appears from the judgment of Farwell J., the plaintiffs produced no evidence that Stonehenge was subject to a trust for its free user by the public but asked the court to presume a lost grant or statute because for many years past the public had been in the habit of visiting the place.... Now it is quite true that in this judgment Farwell J. said that the jus spatiandi is not "known to our law as a possible subject-matter of grant or prescription" and that this formula is on its face wide enough to exclude the purported grant in express terms of such a right to a purchaser as appurtenant to his property. But no such grant was in question in the case, which was solely concerned with the alleged rights of the public as a whole; and, in our judgment, the judge was addressing his mind to those rights and to those alone, and he held that, as they could not be the subject-matter of a grant, he was unable to presume a lost grant which purported to create them. He held also that a jus spatiandi cannot be acquired by public user as an easement, and this is clearly so, if only for the reason that there can be no dominant tenement to which the easement could be said to be appurtenant. It does not necessarily follow from this, however, that no such jus could be acquired by individuals by prescription, and still less does it follow (which is the material point for present purposes) that no such jus could be created in favour of an individual for the better enjoyment of his property by a grant which was express in its terms. As in the *International Tea Stores* case so in *Attorney-General* v. *Antrobus*, Farwell J. refrained from citing authority in support of his observations with regard to the jus spatiandi.

It will be noted that in both of these cases the judge said that a jus spatiandi is "not known to our law" and the question arises as to what precisely he meant by using that phrase. He may have meant: (a) that it was unknown to our law, because it found no place in the Roman law of servitudes; (b) that it was repugnant to the ownership of land that other persons should have rights of user over the whole of it; (c) that the law will not recognize rights to use a servient tenement for the purposes of mere recreation and pleasure; or (d) that such rights are too vague and uncertain to be capable of definition. Which of these meanings the judge had in mind it is difficult to know; and indeed, he may have had some other meaning. If, however, one attributes to the phrase "not known to the law" its ordinary signification, namely, that it was a right which our law had refused to recognize, it is clear, we think, that he would at least have expressed himself in less general terms had his attention been drawn to *Duncan* v. *Louch*, 6 Q.B. 904. That case was not, however, cited to him in either the *International Tea Stores* case or in *Attorney-General* v. *Antrobus* for the sufficient reason that it was not relevant to any issue that was before the judge upon the questions which arose for decision. There is no doubt, in our judgment, but that *Attorney-General* v. *Antrobus* was rightly decided; for no right can be granted (otherwise than by Statute) to the public at large to wander at will over an undefined open space, nor can the public acquire such a right by prescription. We doubt very much whether Farwell J. had in mind, notwithstanding the apparent generality of his language, a so-called jus spatiandi granted as properly appurtenant to an estate; for the whole of his judgment was devoted to a consideration of public rights; and, although this cannot be said of his observations as to the gardens and park in the *International Tea Stores* case the view which he there expressed was entirely obiter upon a point which was irrelevant to the case and had not been argued. Inasmuch, therefore, as this observation is unsupported by any principle or any authority that are binding upon us, and is in conflict with the decision in *Duncan* v. *Louch*, we are unable to accept its accuracy as an exhaustive statement of the law and, in reference, at least, to a case such as that now before the court, it cannot, in our judgment, be regarded hereafter as authoritative.

Duncan v. *Louch*, on the other hand, decided more than 100 years ago but not, as we have observed, quoted to Farwell J. in either of the two cases which we have cited, is authoritative in favour of the recognition by our law as an easement of a right closely comparable to that now in question which, if it involves in some sense a jus spatiandi, is nevertheless properly annexed and appurtenant to a defined hereditament.

Duncan v. *Louch* was an action brought by the plaintiff as owner of premises No. 15, Buckingham Gate, Adelphi, London, on account of obstruction by the defendant of what the plaintiff alleged to be a right of way from Buckingham Gate over or across Terrace Walk to a watergate on the Thames River. On the trial before Wightman J. it was objected on the defendant's part that, though the plaintiff had alleged a right of way from terminus to terminus, the right which he had in fact proved under his documents of title was a right to use Terrace Walk for the purpose of pleasure, that is, to pass and repass over every part of the close. The objection was overruled by the trial judge. The plaintiff showed cause before the Queen's Bench why the rule nisi obtained by the defendant for a verdict in his favour should be discharged; and the matter, as so often was the case in like circumstances, strictly turned upon the narrow question whether the alleged variance between the allegation and the proof was fatal to the plaintiff's case. The decision in the plaintiff's favour was to the effect that, although the right proved exceeded the allegation, nevertheless the former necessarily embraced the latter....

The reasoning of the decision and the circumstances of the case, no less than the language used, particularly by Lord Denman C. J., involve acceptance as an easement of a right such as that with which, according to our interpretation of the effect of the relevant deeds, we are here concerned.

The remaining one of the four cases mentioned at the beginning of this judgment, *Keith* v. *Twentieth Century Club*, 73 L.J.Ch. 545, is however, in our view, of much less assistance. There, the plaintiffs were owners and occupiers of two rows of houses in London and claimed the right to use the garden between these rows. The plaintiffs sought in the action an injunction to restrain the defendants (who were owners of certain other houses in one of the rows and carried on the business there of a Proprietary Ladies' Club) from authorizing members of the club to use the garden: and the questions formulated by Byrne J. in an order made by consent were (briefly) whether certain classes of the club members were, during membership, and having regard to the terms of the defendants' title deeds, entitled as of right to use the garden or could be authorized by the defendants so to do.

The original grant to the defendants' predecessor in title purported to grant to the purchaser "his heirs, executors, administrators and assigns, and his or their lessees and sublessees or tenants (being occupiers for the time being) of the" premises in question the use of the garden or pleasure ground.

The argument before Buckley J. turned, according to the report, upon the question whether the members or particular categories of the members were "tenants" or mere licensees for the purposes of the deed, and the judge decided in favour of the latter view.

As Buckley J. observed at the beginning of the judgment, the freehold owner of the garden, that is of the alleged servient tenement, was never before the court at all.... The whole of the rest of the judgment was devoted to consideration of the question whether the members were tenants or licensees.

It is no doubt true, as Mr. Goff contended, that if any right of the nature of a jus spatiandi is incapable of being an easement under our law, the questions submitted to and determined by Buckley J. were open to a simple and conclusive answer—or were, at best, questions of merely academic interest. On the other hand, as Mr. Cross observed, the questions had been formulated by another judge of the Chancery Division, Byrne J., under the Rules of the Supreme Court for the court to answer; and they had, moreover, been submitted in an action to which the owner of the "servient tenement" was not a party. The *International Tea Stores* case had been before the Chancery Court in the immediately preceding year, and it seems at the least unlikely that Buckley J. (and all the experienced counsel before him) were wholly unaware of Farwell J.'s views. It appears more reasonable to us to assume that Buckley J. felt it his duty to determine the questions which had been properly submitted to him under the Rules without questioning the basis on which they had been or might have been formulated. In the circumstances, therefore, we cannot regard *Keith's* case as having authoritative force. On the other hand, we agree with Danckwerts J. in regarding *Duncan* v. *Louch* as being a direct authority in the defendants' favour. It has never, so far as we are aware, been since questioned, and we think it should, in the present case, be followed.

Appeal dismissed.

[The *Ellenborough Park* case is noted in (1955) 18 Mod. L. Rev. 599; (1955) 71 Law Q. Rev. 324; (1956) 72 Law Q. Rev. 16; (1956) 100 Sol. J. 6.

Having regard to this case, is there any reason why a mere "right to a view" may not be acquired by grant or prescription? See *Brummell* v. *Wharin* (1866), 12 Gr. 283. And if this is so would it not provide a basis for justifying so-called "spite" fences to prevent the running of the prescriptive period? See *Knowles* v. *Richardson*, (1669), 1 Mod. 55, 86 E.R. 727 (K.B.); *McBean* v. *Wyllie* (1902), 14 Man. R. 135; *Wright*, Cases on the Law of Torts (1963, 3rd ed.), p. 921; cf. *Cable* v. *Bryant*, [1908] 1 Ch. 259; *Bryant* v. *Lefever* (1879), 4 C.P.D. 172 (C.A.).

5 *Restatement of Property*, Comment to s. 450 (e), reads as follows:

"For a privilege of use of land to constitute an easement the privilege must be capable of creation by conveyance. Not all privileges of use have this capacity. A conveyance presupposes the existence as an entity of the subject matter of the conveyance. Since the subject matter of all conveyances consists only of aggregations of legal relations, the existence as an entity of such a subject matter consists merely in a way of looking at it. Nevertheless, a conveyance is regarded as an executed transaction by virtue of which something is transferred from one person to another. In order that an aggregation of legal relations may have the capacity to be the subject matter of a conveyance, the aggregation must have such a unity that it can be and is conceived of as an entity. Whether an aggregation of legal relations which includes the privilege to use land in the possession of another can be and is so conceived of is determined largely by considerations of the traditional way of looking at the aggregation and the precision of the pattern created by the use. Many privileges of use have long been regarded as the proper subject matter of conveyance.

"... Whether a particular privilege of use of land in the possession of another may be deemed an entity so as to enable it to be conveyed depends in part upon the recognition the use has previously received. Though the mere fact that a use is novel is not sufficient to prevent the privilege of making it from being an easement, its novelty does tend in that direction. Out of the infinite variety of possible privileges of use of land relatively few have received recognition in the law as property interests. That recognition has taken the form of a gradual evolution. It cannot be said that the list of easements is closed, but it is nevertheless true that the law hesitates to recognize new easements, the hesitancy being due, in part, to the fear of increasing the range of possible burdens upon land and, in part, to the extent to which the concept of covenant, especially as developed in equity, has proved to be adapted to promoting purposes which could otherwise be accomplished only through easements.

"... Some degree of definiteness in the scope or extent of an interest is essential to its recognition as a property interest. Some privileges of use of land are quite definite in outline;

others are altogether lacking in definiteness. An example of a privilege of the first sort is the right of way with prescribed boundaries, of the second, the privilege of strolling at pleasure through a field. When an interest is definite and precise in its extent it is more readily recognized as an entity which can be the subject matter of a conveyance than when it is indefinite. In order that privileges of use may be recognized as easements there must be some degree of definiteness in the privileged use. When a use has not the degree of definiteness necessary to the creation of an easement, the privilege to make it can be nothing more than a licence. The required degree of definiteness varies to some extent with the novelty of the particular use. A new privilege of use is not so readily regarded as an entity as is a long-known one. On the other hand, even a novel privilege of use may be so definite in content and so obviously subject to the considerations which have led to the recognition of new easements in the past as to warrant its being presently considered an easement. Whether a particular privilege may be an easement or can be only a licence depends, therefore, upon a consideration both of the definiteness of the use privileged and of the extent to which like privileges have received recognition as easements in the past."

See also *Megarry*, Manual of Law of Real Property (1955, 2nd ed.), at pp. 437-9; *Conard*, Easement Novelties (1942), 30 Calif. L. Rev. 125, at p. 143: "The rules about novelty and grantability have been distilled to a residue which consists chiefly of certain legal incidents—definiteness of dominant and servient owners, of scope and duration, completeness of judicial protection, appurtenancy".]

[A grant of a right of way "for all purposes" may be invalid as an easement appurtenant because it may fail to meet the test of benefiting or "accommodating" the dominant tenement in view of its wide terms: see *Ackroyd* v. *Smith* (1850), 10 C.B. 164, 138 E.R. 68 (C.A.); and see the explanation given in *Todrick* v. *Western National Omnibus Co.*, [1934] Ch. 561, 103 L.J.Ch. 224 (C.A.).]

[The general rule in English and Canadian law (see, for example, *Adamson* v. *Bell Telephone Co. of Canada* (1920), 48 O.L.R. 24, 55 D.L.R. 157 (App. Div.)) is that no easement (as distinguished from a profit à prendre) can exist in gross. This rule does not obtain in the United States: see 2 *American Law of Property*, s. 8. 9n; 5 *Restatement of Property*, ss. 454, 489 ff. *Quaere*, however, whether "executed" and irrevocable licences are not easements in gross under another title. The substantial issues are how far the benefit is assignable and how far the burden passes to a succeeding holder of the servient land: see *Clark*, Covenants and Interests Running with Land (1947, 2nd ed.), chap. 3; *Welsh*, The Assignability of Easements in Gross, (1945) 12 U. of Chi. L. Rev. 276.

The principal kinds of easements in gross recognized in cases in the United States have been so-called public service easements as, for example, for railroad lines, pipe lines and telephone lines. In Canada, legislative intervention has been necessary to provide for enforcement of such interests by the holders (beneficiaries) thereof: see Real Property Act, R.S.M. 1954, c. 220, s. 111; Land Registry Act, R.S.B.C. 1960, c. 208, s. 24. Cf. *Consumers' Gas Co.* v. *Toronto* (1897), 27 S.C.R. 453, aff'g 23 O.A.R. 551 which aff'd 26 O.R. 722.

For recognition of a right of burial in another's land as an easement in gross, see *Hubbs* v. *Black*, *supra*, at p. 166.

The holder of a burial right in a certain cemetery plot covenanted with the cemetery operator to maintain a certain tree. Is the covenant enforceable against an assignee of the burial right? What does this depend on? Cf. *London Cemetery Co.* v. *Cundey*, [1953] 2 All E.R. 257, [1953] 1 W.L.R. 786 (Q.B.).]

[No valid easement exists if there is no capable grantor or grantee: see *Industrial Molasses Corp.* v. *H. Corby Distillery Ltd. and Empire-Hanna Coal Co.*, [1952] O.R. 50; *Paine & Co. Ltd.* v. *St. Neots Gas & Coke Co.*, [1939] 3 All E.R. 812, 55 T.L.R. 1062 (C.A.).]

[Easements are legal interests in land and caught by the Statute of Frauds but equitable doctrines are also applicable to permit enforcement of easements in equity: see *Craig* v. *Craig* (1878), 2 O.A.R. 583; *Toronto* v. *Jarvis* (1895), 25 S.C.R. 237; *Hubbs* v. *Black* (1918), 44 O.L.R. 545, 46 D.L.R. 583 (C.A.); *Anderson* v. *Ontario Rock Co.* (1924), 26 O.W.N. 458, aff'd 27 O.W.N. 241 (C.A.); but cf. *Smith* v. *Curry*, [1918] 2 W.W.R. 848, 42 D.L.R. 225, 29 Man. R. 97 (C.A.).]

[A and B, adjoining landowners, agreed orally to search for water and to build a well for mutual benefit if water was found. Water was found near the boundary of the two properties and a well was built on B's land. A used the well and in connection therewith traversed B's land. Subsequently, A sold his land to C who was refused use of the well. What is C's position? See *Bruce and Bruce* v. *Dixon*, [1957] O.W.N. 489 (C.A.).]

[For a catalogue of easements recognized in the English cases, see *Megarry and Wade*, Law of Real Property (1959, 2nd ed.), pp. 828-836; *Cheshire*, Modern Law of Real Property (1962, 9th ed.), pp. 454-455. The following are illustrative:

1. Right to use a lavatory: see *Miller* v. *Emcer Products Ltd.*, [1956] Ch. 304, [1956] 1 All E.R. 237 (C.A.); see *Note*, (1956) 72 Law Q. Rev. 172.
2. Right to project roof over adjoining land: see *De Vault* v. *Robinson* (1920), 48 O.L.R. 34, 54 D.L.R. 591 (C.A.); cf. *Hall* v. *Alexander* (1902), 3 O.L.R. 482 (C.A.).
3. Right to emit sounds or noise: see *Duchman* v. *Oakland Dairy Co.*, 63 O.L.R. 111, [1929] 1 D.L.R. 9 (App. Div.).
4. Right to discharge substances through air and deposit them on neighbouring land: see *Russell Transport Ltd.* v. *Ontario Malleable Iron Co.*, [1952] O.R. 621, [1952] 4 D.L.R. 719; *British Columbia Forest Products Ltd.* v. *Nordal* (1954), 11 W.W.R. (N.S.) 403 (B.C.).
5. Right to use of another's steam power to drive machinery: see *Brewing* v. *Berryman* (1873), 15 N.B.R. 115 (C.A.).
6. Right to drain surplus water on to adjoining land: see *McGillivray* v. *Millin* (1867), 27 U.C.Q.B. 62 (C.A.); cf. *Brown* v. *Street* (1844), 1 U.C.Q.B. 124 (C.A.); *Morrison* v. *Weller*, [1951] 3 D.L.R. 156, 4 W.W.R. (N.S.) 160 (B.C.).
7. Right to take water from a spring: see *McKay* v. *Bruce* (1891), 20 O.R. 709 (C.A.); *Corbitt* v. *Wilson* (1891), 24 N.S.R. 25 (C.A.); and see also *Race* v. *Ward* (1855), 4 El. & Bl. 702, 119 E.R. 259 (K.B.).
8. Right to supply of water from town reservoir: see *Fergusson* v. *Public Utilities Commission of Dundas*, [1953] O.R. 980 (C.A.)
9. Right to have a dock kept open: see *Morton* v. *Snow* (1873), C.R. 14 A.C. 140, 29 L.T. 591, rev'g 8 N.S.R. 237.
10. Right to pollute the air: see *Radenhurst* v. *Coate* (1857), 6 Gr. 139 (C.A.)
11. Right to use chimney flue on another's land: see *Lane* v. *George* (1904), 4 O.W.R. 539; *Culverwell* v. *Lockington* (1875), 24 U.C.C.P. 611 (C.A.)
12. Right to lay and maintain a pipe-line: see *Smith* v. *Inland Gas & Oil Co. Ltd.* (1955), 14 W.W.R. (N.S.) 558 (Alta.).
13. Right on notice to open up a natural runway on another's land: see *Rystephaniuk* v. *Prosken* (1951), 3 W.W.R. (N.S.) 76, 59 Man. R. 142.]

[A grant of land contained a "reservation" to the grantor of "the sole and exclusive permission, right and privilege at any time of constructing and maintaining on the surface any... structures not requiring excavations or cellars, with rights of ingress and egress to and from the said land". What is the nature of the interest under the reservation? See *Re Ottawa* (1931), 40 O.W.N. 521.]

(b) Creation

Easements may arise by conveyance or enforceable agreement or by testament or by implication or by prescription. At common law, an easement could arise only under a deed of grant; and a grantor of an estate in land who wished at the same time to retain a right against it by way of an easement (which was an "incorporeal hereditament") could not do so either by way of an "exception" or a "reservation" in the deed of grant. An "exception" was referable to a "corporeal" interest and a "reservation" was referable to rights incident to a tenurial relationship, such as rent. Hence, the development of the theory of regrant, so that at common law the grantee of land over which an easement was created in the conveyance thereof, was required to execute the deed: see *Bigelow and Madden*, Exception and Reservation of Easements, (1924) 38 Harv. L. Rev. 180; *Attrill* v. *Platt* (1884), 10 S.C.R. 425; *Miller* v. *Tipling* (1918), 43 O.L.R. 88, 43 D.L.R. 469 (C.A.). In equity this was not required, and to all intents and purposes the common law technicalities are now obsolete: see *Adamson* v. *Bell Telephone Co.* (1920), 48 O.L.R. 24, 55 D.L.R. 157 (App. Div.); *Patterson* v. *Bignall*, [1948] 1 D.L.R. 702 (P.E.I.).

[A, the owner of a block of land conveyed a lot out of the block to B by a deed which described the lot as abutting on a "proposed 66 foot roadway". The proposed roadway was shown on an unregistered plan but nothing was specifically said at the time of the conveyance about the road, although B understood that he was getting a lot abutting on a road. B sold his lot to C by a deed containing a similar description. C did not see the plan until after he obtained his deed from B. Should C succeed in a claim of an easement against A and his successor in title? See *Raab* v. *Smith*, [1950] O.R. 589, [1950] 4 D.L.R. 123 (C.A.); cf. *Carpenter* v. *Smith*, [1951] O.R. 241, [1951] 2 D.L.R. 609.]

Although not expressed in the terms of a grant, easements may arise through the circumstances in which a grant is made. Thus, where the Crown made a grant of land on which the grantee, with the Crown's approval, erected a mill and cut an artificial channel from a lake bay to the mill and the grantee used the water power to work the mill, held, an easement existed in the grantee's favour which it could assert against a subsequent grantee from the Crown of the banks and bed of an outflow of the lake and of the water power: see *Keewatin Power Co.* v. *Lake of the Woods Milling Co.*, [1930] A.C. 640, [1930] 4 D.L.R. 961, [1930] 3 W.W.R. 260 (P.C.).

RE WEBB, SANDOM v. WEBB. Court of Appeal. [1951] Ch. 808, [1951] 2 All E.R. 131

Appeal from a judgment of Danckwerts J., [1950] 2 All E.R. 828, holding that an easement to display two advertisements on the outer walls of certain premises was to be implied in favour of a landlord against a tenant to whom the premises had been let by the landlord. The landlord was in fact a head lessee of certain premises on the ground floor of which he carried on a meat and grocery shop. He sub-let the two upper floors to the tenant under a 21 year lease which made no reference to the upkeep of the exterior walls although the tenant covenanted to keep the interior in repair. It was conceded that the outer walls passed to the tenant under the lease. The tenant had been in possession of the upper floors for 10 years prior to the lease above mentioned, and during this time the landlord had maintained the two advertisements in question on the outer walls of the tenant's premises. The landlord in these proceedings asserted an easement by implied reservation, relying on his user and the tenant's acquiescence.

JENKINS L. J.: . . . There are, and have at all times since a date prior to the commencement of the tenant's original tenancy been the following advertisements painted on or affixed to the exterior surfaces of the outside walls of the two upper floors demised to the tenant, *viz:* (i) Painted directly on the brickwork of the wall over the door into the landlord's shop in black letters on a white ground an advertisement of the landlord's own business in these terms: "Webb's for meat grocery & provisions. Phone ELT. 2047." (ii) Displayed on a billboard affixed to the upper part of one of the flank walls of the premises a poster advertising Brymay safety matches. This poster surmounts another similarly affixed to the lower part of the same wall advertising Oxydol, the upper poster apparently extending downwards to approximately the level of the first floor, although it is impossible to say exactly where its lower edge is placed in relation to the interior division between the ground and first floors. The tenant never raised any objection to the presence on the exterior of the outer walls comprised in his tenancy or lease of the advertisement and poster I have mentioned until January, 1950, when through his solicitors he opened a correspondence on the subject of the Brymay poster. Bryant & May, Ltd., who were first approached, referred the tenant's solicitors to the Borough Billposting Co., to whom they paid rent for the display of the poster, and reference to that company (with a demand for payment to the tenant of all further rent in respect of the Brymay poster) elicited information to the effect that they held a licence from the landlord under which they used the part of the wall occupied by the poster as an advertising site. The tenant's solicitors next wrote to the landlord's solicitors claiming that the landlord should account to the tenant for all sums received by him since Mar. 6, 1939, from the Borough Billposting Co. in respect of the Brymay poster, and also asking what payment the landlord was prepared to offer for his own advertisement. After further correspondence (including a letter dated Mar. 15, 1950, whereby the tenant's solicitors gave notice terminating "all licences if any" from the tenant to the landlord in respect of the display of advertisements on the outer walls of the two floors demised to the tenant) the present proceedings ensued. . . .

The landlord did not include in the provisions of the lease, as executed, any reservation of advertising rights over any part of the outer walls. At the date of the lease the advertisements now in dispute were in their present positions on the walls and plainly to be seen. Moreover, they had existed in their present positions continuously since before the commencement of the tenant's original tenancy in 1939, and the tenant never objected to their presence at any time during his original tenancy or at the time of the granting of the lease of Aug. 11, 1949, or thereafter until January, 1950. There is no evidence that either party ever even mentioned the subject of the advertisements to the other during the whole of this period of more than ten years. This being in substance the whole of the available facts, the question is whether on those bare facts, without more, the court can and ought as a matter of law to imply in favour of the landlord a reservation during the term of twenty-one years granted by the lease of Aug. 11, 1949, of advertising rights over the outer walls demised, at all events, to the extent required to enable him to maintain the existing advertisements and to retain for his own benefit any periodical payments receivable from the Borough Billposting Co. in respect of the site of the Brymay poster.

As to the law applicable to the case, it is not disputed that as a general rule a grantor, whether by way of conveyance of lease, or part of a hereditament in his ownership, cannot claim any easement over the part granted for the benefit of the part retained unless it is expressly reserved out of the grant: see, e.g., *Suffield* v. *Brown* (1864), 4 DeG. J. & Sm. 185, *Crossley & Sons, Ltd.* v. *Lightowler* (1867), 2 Ch. App. 478 and *Wheeldon* v. *Burrows* (1879), 12 Ch. D. 31. There are, however, certain exceptions to the general rule. Two well-established exceptions relate to easements of necessity and mutual easements such as rights of support between adjacent buildings. It is, however, recognised in the authorities that these two specific exceptions do not exhaust the list, which is, indeed, incapable of exhaustive statement as the circumstances of any particular case may be such as to raise a necessary inference that the common intention of the parties must have been to reserve some easement to the grantor or such as to preclude the grantee from denying the right consistently with good faith, and there appears to be no doubt that where circumstances such as these are clearly established the court will imply the appropriate reservation. For statements of the general rule and observations on the types of case which should be treated as exceptions to it, reference may usefully be made to the following authorities.

In *Wheeldon* v. *Burrows*, Thesiger, L. J. (12 Ch. D. 49), states two propositions as "the general rules governing cases of this kind." The first concerns easements passing to the grantee and is not relevant here. The second he states (*ibid.*) as being

"... that, if the grantor intends to reserve any right over the tenement granted, it is his duty to reserve it expressly in the grant. Those are the general rules governing cases of this kind, but the second of those rules is subject to certain exceptions. One of those exceptions is the well-known exception which attaches to cases of what are called ways of necessity; and I do not dispute for a moment that there may be, and probably are, certain other exceptions, to which I shall refer before I close my observations upon this case. Both of the general rules which I have mentioned are founded upon a maxim which is as well established by authority as it is consonant to reason and common sense, *viz.*, that a grantor shall not derogate from his grant."

The learned lord justice deals further with the question of exceptions (*ibid.*, 59), but, apart from the case of easements of necessity, he does not appear to have been disposed to admit any further exceptions other than cases of mutual easements and cases in which the same vendor sells by auction different lots to different persons at the same time, where the purchaser of one lot may be entitled to an easement over another lot even though the latter was in fact actually conveyed before the former: see *Swansborough* v. *Coventry* (1832), 9 Bing. 305. In *Russell* v. *Watts*, 10 App. Cas. 590 the Earl of Selborne, L. C. after referring to the general rule that a man cannot be prevented from darkening his neighbour's windows by a lawful act done on his own land unless light has been enjoyed through those windows for twenty years and also to the second of the two propositions in *Wheeldon* v. *Burrows*, said (10 App. Cas. 596):

"It is manifest, however, that neither of those rules can be invoked in defence of any act contrary to the good faith of a particular contract."

In *Aldridge* v. *Wright* Scrutton, L. J. said ([1929] 2 K.B. 124):

"There are exceptions to the doctrine of *Wheeldon* v. *Burrows*. I do not see my way to attempt an exhaustive statement of those exceptions, as facts would immediately present themselves to prove my absence of foresight, and I find some of the suggested exceptions difficult to understand—but I do not find any suggested exception which covers the facts of this case," and, after citing (ibid., 125) the well-known statement of Lord Parker of Waddington in *Pwllbach Colliery Co., Ltd.* v. *Woodman* ([1915] A.C. 646) (to which I will return), he stated his conclusions thus ([1929] 2 K.B. 127):

"I think the grantee of No. 30, when his grantor claims to have impliedly reserved such a right from his grant, though it is not mentioned in his grant, is entitled to require the clearest evidence of an 'intention of the parties' that there should be reserved for the benefit of No. 28 an easement or quasi-easement to be used and enjoyed as of right. In my opinion the defendant has failed to show such a common intention or implied reservation in this case; the doctrine of *Wheeldon* v. *Burrows* applies; the decision of the Divisional Court must be affirmed, and the appeal dismissed."

Greer, L. J. (*ibid.*, 129) quoted the general rule as enunciated by Thesiger, L. J., in *Wheeldon* v. *Burrows* and stated five classes of exceptions which he thought to be the only ones warranted by the authorities and of which it is only necessary to mention the third, which is thus stated (*ibid.*, 130):

"3. If the owner of two adjoining properties, A and B, grants to the tenant of A a tenancy from year to year with a right of way during his tenancy over B, and subsequently leases B, the lease of B is subject to a reservation of the right of way which has ex hypothesi been granted to the tenant of A if it is shown that the lessee of B was aware of a long-continued exercise of the right by the tenant of A: *Thomas* v. *Owen*, 20 Q.B.D. 225."

Sankey, L. J., said (*ibid.*, 134):

"I do not think it is possible, at any rate I propose to resist the dangerous ambition of trying, to lay down a rule which will cover all exceptions. It is impossible to foresee facts; all that can be said is that the onus is upon the grantor to establish the facts to prove that his case is an exception to the rule. In *Wheeldon* v. *Burrows* he failed to do so."

In *Liddiard* v. *Waldron*, *Thomas* v. *Owen* was distinguished and Greer, L. J., after referring to *Aldridge* v. *Wright* and the rule in *Wheeldon* v. *Burrows* said ([1934] 1 K.B. 447):

"The courts have been faced with the questions whether or not in some cases there are exceptional circumstances which justify departure from that rule. One of those exceptional cases was established in *Thomas* v. *Owen*, the effect of which I ventured to summarise in these words...."

Greer, L. J., then set out and re-affirmed his statement of the effect of that case in *Aldridge* v. *Wright* and added (*ibid.*):

"*Thomas* v. *Owen* is only an illustration of the proposition that a man cannot grant to A what he has already given to B, and, therefore, in order to give effect to what he has already given to B, if the grantee knows the facts, there nust be an implied reservation of that which would enable him to perform his obligation to his tenant under his existing lease."

The most comprehensive statement of the area of potential exceptions is probably that contained in the speech of Lord Parker of Waddington in *Pwllbach Colliery Co., Ltd.* v. *Woodman*, where his Lordship, after referring to the exception with respect to easements of necessity, said this ([1915] A.C. 646):

"The second class of cases in which easements may impliedly be created depends not upon the terms of the grant itself, but upon the circumstances under which the grant was made. The law will readily imply the grant or reservation of such easements as may be necessary to give effect to the common intention of the parties to a grant of real property, with reference to the manner or purposes in and for which the land granted or some land retained by the grantor is to be used: see *Jones* v. *Pritchard* [1908] 1 Ch. 630 and *Lyttelton Times Co., Ltd.* v. *Warners, Ltd.* [1907] A.C. 476. But it is essential for this purpose that the parties should intend that the subject of the grant or the land retained by the grantor should be used in some definite and particular manner. It is not enough that the subject of the grant or the land retained should be intended to be used in a manner which may or may not involve this definite and particular use."

The illustrations given by Lord Parker in support of this general proposition seem, however, to show that it is of less comprehensive import than would at first sight appear. He refers to *Jones* v. *Pritchard*, which was, in effect, a case of mutual easements; to *Lyttelton Times Co., Ltd.* v. *Warners, Ltd.*, where both parties contemplated at the time of the grant that the grantor should carry on his printing works on the part of the premises retained and it was held that the grantee could not in those circumstances complain of a nuisance to the premises granted due to noise and vibration unavoidably occasioned by the carrying on as contemplated of printing operations on the grantor's part of the premises; and to two other cases which appear to have proceeded on similar principles.

The case which in point of actual decision goes furthest in the direction of implying reservations of easements in favour of a grantor is, undoubtedly, *Simpson* v. *Weber*, (1925), 133 L.T. 46. The question there was whether the grantor of one of two adjoining houses owned by him had by implication reserved the right to have a creeper growing in the garden of the house retained supported by a wall of the house granted over which its foliage had spread, and the right to continue the attachment of a gate forming part of the premises retained to a wall forming part of the premises granted, and the Divisional Court, reversing a county court judge, decided in favour of the grantor's successor in title on both points. Of this case I need only say that while the physical circumstances at the date of the severance may, perhaps, have sufficed to support an implication of an intention common to grantor and grantee that the easements in question should be reserved, I cannot agree that the decision is good law so far as it proceeds on the ground, given in both the two not very satisfactory reports, that (133 L.T. 47; 41 T.L.R. 304), "there was no evidence that it was not the intention of the parties that the creeper and gate-post should stay."

In his judgment in the present case Danckwerts, J., after citing at length from *Simpson* v. *Weber*, and also referring to *Liddiard* v. *Waldron*, *Wheeldon* v. *Burrows* and *Thomas* v. *Owen*, expressed his conclusion thus ([1950] 2 All E.R. 831):

"It does seem to me that there may be exceptional circumstances in which it is only common sense to imply some reservation, and that such an implication should be made in the circumstances of the present case. When I see from the photograph which is before me that when the parties entered into their transaction there was an enormous advertisement painted on the wall advertising Webb's for meat, grocery and provisions, and a very large advertisement advertising Brymay safety matches, which had been there at least since 1939, and when no evidence is given that anything was said by either of the parties about the removal of those advertisements, it appears to me to be common sense to imply an intention on the part of the parties that they should remain. Therefore, I am prepared to hold that there was in favour of the landlord implied in this lease an easement until the termination of the lease to keep those two advertisements in the position in which they were, and, by necessary implication, a right to repair them, paint them, and do whatever may be necessary from time to time to preserve them as effective advertisements."

I find myself unable to agree with the learned judge's conclusion. The question is whether the circumstances of the present case as proved in evidence are such as to raise a necessary inference that the common intention of the parties was to reserve to the landlord during the twenty-one years' term some, and, if so, what, rights in regard to the display of advertisements over the outer walls of the demised premises, or such as to preclude the tenant from denying the implied reservation to the landlord of some such rights consistently with good faith.

That question must be approached with the following principles in mind: (i) If the landlord intended to reserve any such rights over the demised premises it was his duty to reserve them expressly in the lease of Aug. 11, 1949: *Wheeldon* v. *Burrows*. (ii) The landlord having failed in this duty, the onus was on him to establish the facts to prove, and prove clearly, that his case was an exception to the rule: *Aldridge* v. *Wright*. (iii) The mere fact that the tenant knew at the date of the lease of Aug. 11, 1949, that the landlord was using the outer walls of the demised premises for the display of the advertisements in question did not suffice to absolve the landlord from his duty of expressly reserving any rights in respect of them he intended to claim, or to take the case out of the general rule: see *Suffield* v. *Brown* (4 De G.J. & Sm. 199), *Crossley & Sons, Ltd.* v. *Lightowler* (2 Ch. App. 486).

Applying these principles to the present case, I ask myself whether on the meagre facts proved the landlord has discharged the onus which lies on him of proving it an exception to the general rule. He can, so far as I can see, derive no assistance from the passage quoted from the speech of Lord Parker of Waddington in the *Pwllbach Colliery* case. It might, I suppose, be said to have been in the contemplation of the parties that the landlord would continue to use the ground floor of the premises for the purposes of his business as a butcher and provision merchant, but it cannot, in my view, be contended that the maintenance during the term of the lease of his advertisement over the door was a necessary incident of the user so contemplated. This applies a fortiori to the Brymay advertisement, the display of which on the outer wall of the demised premises by the Borough Billposting Co. as licensees of the landlord was, so far as I can see, not related in any way to the use or occupation of the ground floor for the existing or any other purpose. The transaction with that company was simply a hiring out for reward of part of an outer wall of the demised premises for use as an advertising or billposting site or station. The mere fact that the tenant knew of the presence of the advertisements at the date when the lease of Aug. 11, 1949, was granted being beside the point, nothing is left beyond the bare circumstance that the advertisements were not only present at the date of the grant, but had been continuously present without objection by the tenant since the commencement of his original tenancy in 1939. Does this circumstance suffice to raise a necessary inference of an intention common to both parties at the date of the lease that the landlord should have reserved to him the right to maintain these advertisements throughout the twenty-one years' term thereby granted? I cannot see that it does. The most that can be said is that the facts are consistent with such a common intention. That will not do. The landlord must surely show at least that the facts are not reasonably consistent with any other explanation. Here he manifestly fails. It may be that neither party ever applied his mind at all to the question whether the outer walls were included in, or excluded from, the original tenancy or the lease ultimately granted, or what their respective rights as to the use of such walls for any purpose might be. It may be that the tenant, so far as he applied his mind to the matter at all, merely refrained from objecting to the presence of the advertisements because, whether the landlord was within his rights in maintaining them or not, he, the tenant, did not for the time being think it worth his while to object. As to the landlord, he may have been under the erroneous impression that, notwithstanding the tenancy and, subsequently, notwithstanding the lease, he was entitled to use the outer walls for advertising purposes. If so, his own mistake will not avail him, at all events in the absence of evidence that the tenant was aware of it. On the other hand, the landlord may have thought, when he came to grant the lease, that, as the tenant had never objected to the advertisements during all the ten years of his previous tenancy, it could be assumed that the tenant would not object in the future, and have preferred, accordingly, to let the matter rest at that rather than raise the question by claiming a reservation. In short, I can hold nothing more established by the facts proved than permissive user of the outer walls by the landlord for the display of the advertisements during the original tenancy and thereafter from the granting of the lease until the tenant's objection in January, 1950, with nothing approaching grounds for inferring, as a matter of necessary inference, an intention common to both parties that such permissive user should be converted by the lease into a reservation to the landlord of equivalent rights throughout the twenty-one years' term thereby granted. If the hypothetical officious stranger, sometimes used as a test of implied terms, had intervened in the course of the negotiation of the lease and had said: "What about Mr. Webb's advertisements?" would both parties have exclaimed with one voice: "Of course they are to stay"? I see no justification for this assumption. The landlord might well have said: "Of course I want them to stay", but, as likely as not, the tenant would have said: "At present I have no objection to the advertisements, but I cannot bind myself to allow them for twenty-one years. For all I know, I may at any time during that period for one reason or another want them removed. If the landlord insists on reserving rights in the matter, he must reduce the rent or find some other tenant." So far as the Brymay advertisement is concerned, the present case resembles *Thomas* v. *Owen* in that the right in question was granted by the landlord to the Borough Billposting Co. before the date of the lease. This means only that *prima facie* the demise to the tenant took effect subject to the company's right, and cannot, so far as I can see, afford any ground for implying a reservation by the landlord to himself of the proceeds accruing subsequently to the date of the lease from thus hiring out a part of the demised premises or any right to grant any further licence for a similar purpose.

Appeal allowed.

[The concurring judgments of Evershed M. R. and Morris L. J. are omitted.

For an illustration of an easement by implied reservation in favour of a grantor, see *Duchman* v. *Oakland Dairy Co.*, 63 O.L.R. 111, [1929] 1 D.L.R. 9 (C.A.).]

RE TORONTO AND STUTCHBURY. Ontario Court of Appeal. [1942] O.R. 665, [1942] 4 D.L.R. 749

Appeal from an order on a vendors and purchasers application, declaring that applicant, a tax sale purchaser, was entitled to a way of ingress and egress over certain land of a municipality. The land purchased at the tax sale was part of a block of land which had belonged to one W, who had sold off the other lots in the block, leaving the parcel which was sold for taxes. This parcel was alleged to be land-locked. The municipality owned a lot (which it had acquired by tax deed) which lay between applicant's parcel and a public street.

The judgment of the Court was delivered by ROBERTSON C. J. O.:... The rule of law upon which respondent's case is rested is a rule that works both ways. A way of necessity arises by implication not only in favour of a purchaser of a land-locked parcel; it also arises by implication in favour of a vendor over the land he has sold where the land that is sold affords the only access to land that the vendor retains. As it is put in the headnote to *Howton* v. *Frearson*, 8 T.R. 50, 101 E.R. 1261, "If the owner of two closes, having no way to one of them but over the other, part with the latter without reserving the way, it will be reserved to him by operation of law." If, therefore, when Annie E. Welch sold the frontage on Lorindale Ave. she was left without any other means of access to the parts of lots that she retained, and of which the respondent has now become the purchaser, she would become entitled by implication of law to a way of necessity over the land she had sold. Respondent's counsel does not dispute that proposition. His answer to it is that, granting that Annie E. Welch did become so entitled to a way of necessity to Lorindale Ave., she lost it by the operation of the *Registry Act*, R.S.O. 1937, c. 170, when her grantees registered their conveyances. He refers particularly to s. 75 of the *Registry Act*, which is as follows:—

"75. No equitable lien, charge or interest affecting land shall be valid, as against a registered instrument executed by the same person, his heirs or assigns, and tacking shall not be allowed in any case to prevail against the provisions of this Act."

I do not think that section has any application to such an "interest affecting land" as is assumed to have been vested in Annie E. Welch as a way of necessity. It was not an equitable right or interest, and while s. 75 no doubt applies to equitable liens, charges or interests affecting land that are not created or evidenced by writing, and are, therefore, incapable of registration, in which respect an implied right-of-way resembles them, the section applies only where the lien, charge or interest is equitable in its nature. *Israel* v. *Leith* (1890), 20 O.R. 361.

None of the owners of the Lorindale Ave. frontages are before us in this matter, nor is there evidence on the record of the facts and circumstances attending the disposal by Annie E. Welch of that property, nor of the time or times when it was disposed of, nor of its use and occupation since. It is, therefore, impossible to make any finding upon this application that at the time of the tax-sale there was appurtenant to the land respondent then purchased a right-of-way to Lorindale Ave. over the front part of any of the lots that had been sold by Annie E. Welch. I think, however, that it was incumbent upon the respondent to establish that Annie E. Welch did not have any such means of access to the lands that she retained, that passed on the tax-sale to respondent under s. 15 of the *Assessment Act*, R.S.O. 1937, c. 272. The facts in evidence are consistent with the contrary. The basis of respondent's application is that she has no means of ingress to or egress from the lands she bought at the tax-sale unless she is allowed a way of necessity over appellant's adjoining land, and, in my opinion, appellant's point is well taken and respondent's application fails upon that ground at the outset,

I am further of the opinion that on a sale of land for taxes a purchaser acquires only what the *Assessment Act* provides. The sale is made under the authority of that statute and that authority alone. Section 181 provides a form of tax-deed, which is required to describe the lands sold at the tax-sale according to the provisions of s. 175, and is declared to have the effect of vesting the land so described in the purchaser, his heirs or assigns or legal representatives, in fee simple, or otherwise according to the nature of the estate or interest sold. Section 15 makes express provision as to easements. Subsection (1) provides what easements shall pass to the purchaser, and is as follows:—

"Where land sold for arrears of taxes was a dominant tenement at the time of sale and was so sold after the 3rd day of April, 1930, the easements appurtenant thereto shall be deemed to have passed to the purchaser."

The land purchased by respondent was not "at the time of sale" a dominant tenement in relation to appellant's land adjoining, and the easement now claimed does not come within the subsection.

I am further of the opinion that appellant was not the grantor of the lands that respondent acquired at the tax-sale. No title to these lands was vested in the municipality. The *Assessment Act* creates a lien for unpaid taxes in favour of the municipality, and provides for the enforcement of that lien by sale in the manner prescribed by the Act. While the municipal officers who, by the Act are authorized to execute the tax-deed, may be considered, in making the sale and in executing the tax-deed, as officers, and in a sense the agents, of the corporation (*Langdon* v. *Holtyrex Gold Mines*, [1937] 2 D.L.R. 364, S.C.R. 344) their power to convey the lands that have been sold is derived from the *Assessment Act*. The corporation can give them no other authority to sell and convey as might be the case if some title to the lands was vested in it, and it in no way purports to do so. The tax-deed is expressly made in pursuance of the *Assessment Act*. A way of necessity arises from implied grant, and can arise only where such a grant can be implied (*Pomfret* v. *Ricroft*, 1 Wms. Saund. 321, 85 E.R. at p. 462). There is no warrant for the assumption that the municipal officers carrying out their duties under the *Assessment Act* could grant to the purchaser of lands sold for taxes a right-of-way over other lands vested in the corporation....

Appeal allowed.

[By statute in some jurisdictions, neither easements nor restrictive covenants are affected by a tax sale of the servient tenement: see *Assessment Act*, R.S.O. 1960, c. 23, s. 15; *Land Registry Act*, R.S.B.C. 1960, c. 208, s. 25 (a).]

[Even where a way of necessity by implied reservation in favour of a grantor is admitted, the easement terminates when the necessity ceases: see *McCulloch* v. *McCulloch* (1910), 2 O.W.N. 331; *Carpenter* v. *Smith*, [1951] O.R. 241, [1951] 2 D.L.R. 609.]

[Does a way of necessity by implied grant arise whether the granted land is completely enclosed or surrounded by land retained by the grantor or partly by that of the grantor and partly by land of third persons? See *Barry* v. *Haseldine*, [1952] Ch. 835, [1952] 2 All E.R. 317.]

DUVERNET v. EISENER. Nova Scotia Supreme Court en banc. [1951] 4 D.L.R. 406

Appeal from an award of damages for trespass and from a declaration of the boundary line between the parties' lands. A driveway had been used in common and the effect of the judgment, now appealed, was that the entire driveway was on plaintiff's land and defendant had no interest therein. At the time the driveway was established, one L owned the land now held by defendant and he also held the equity of redemption in the land now owned by plaintiff. L used the driveway for the benefit of both parcels. Subsequently he conveyed to T the land that was later acquired by defendant.

The judgment of the Court was delivered by PARKER J.:... The law relating to an implied grant of a right-of-way in a case of a grant by an owner of a tenement of part of that tenement is, I think, clearly stated by Thesiger L. J. in the case of *Wheeldon* v. *Burrows* (1879), 48 L.J. Ch. 853 at p. 856: "A number of cases have been cited to us, and on them, I think two propositions arise which may be stated as the general rules governing cases of this kind. The first proposition is, that on the grant by the owner of a tenement of part of that tenement, as it is then used and enjoyed, there will pass to the grantee all those continuous and apparent easements (by which of course I mean *quasi* easements), or, in other words, all those easements which are necessary to the reasonable enjoyment of the property granted, and which have been and are at the time of the grant, used by the owners of the entirety for the benefit of the part granted." See also *Brown* v. *Alabaster* (1887), 37 Ch. D. 490; *Hart* v. *McMullen* (1899), 32 N.S.R. 340, confirmed on appeal to Supreme Court of Canada 30 S.C.R. 245; *Fullerton* v. *Randall* (1918), 44 D.L.R. 356, 52 N.S.R. 354.

In 11 Hals., 2nd ed., p. 287, the law is stated as follows: "Upon the grant by the owner of a tenement of part of that tenement as it is then used and enjoyed, there will pass to the grantee all those continuous and apparent accommodations afforded by the part retained to the part granted which (1) are of such a nature that they might form the subject-matter of an easement, (2) are necessary to the reasonable enjoyment of the property granted, and (3) have been and are at the time of the grant used by the owner of the entirety for the benefit of the part granted. This rule is founded upon the principle that a man shall not derogate from his grant. There is no corresponding implied reservation in favour of the grantor."

Gale on Easements, 12th ed., pp. 102-3 states the law as follows: "On the grant by the owner of a tenement of part of that tenement, a grant will be implied of (1) all those continuous and apparent easements which are necessary to the reasonable enjoyment of the part granted, and which have been, and are at the time of the grant, used by the owner of the entirety for the benefit of that part; and (2) of all those easements without which the enjoyment of the part granted could not be had at all."

The law as stated by the foregoing authorities and in many other cases is applicable only to cases where the grantor at the time of the grant is also the owner of the land over which the alleged right-of-way extends: *Rangeley* v. *Midland R. Co.* (1868), L.R. 3 Ch. 306; *Hunter* v. *Richards* (1912), 5 D.L.R. 116, 26 O.L.R. 458 [affd 12 D.L.R. 503].

As already indicated, however, the respondent's land over which the right-of-way is claimed, was at the time of the grant of appellant's land to Teasdale mortgaged, and all the grantor had was an equity of redemption.

I shall assume, as Lindley, Fry and Lopes L. JJ., all assumed in the case of *Taws* v. *Knowles*, [1891] 2 Q.B. 564, but without expressing any opinion on the point, that had there been no mortgage and the matter turned upon the conveyance alone, that Teasdale would have acquired by way of implied grant a right to use the driveway.

To decide whether the user of the driveway by the grantor was "continuous" or "apparent" or "necessary for the reasonable enjoyment" of the land granted to Teasdale, it would be necessary "to look at a great many cases, and the cases upon the point run very fine" to use the words of Lindley L. J. in *Taws* v. *Knowles, supra.* In my opinion, the law applicable as a result of the mortgage is correctly stated in that case and the existence of the mortgage on the respondent's land at the time of the grant to Teasdale, precludes me from holding that a right-of-way passed to him by way of an implied grant.

Appeal dismissed.

[A, the common owner of lots 1 and 2 conveyed lot 1 to a predecessor in title of B who claimed and exercised a right of way over lot 2. There was a mortgage on lot 2 at the time of the conveyance to B's predecessor in title, and the mortgaged land was subsequently sold under a power of sale in the mortgage and came into the hands of C who disputed B's claim of a right of way. Result? See *Ker* v. *Little* (1898), 25 O.A.R. 387.]

[The Conveyancing and Law of Property Act, R.S.O. 1960, c. 66, s. 15, provides as follows: (1) Every conveyance of land, unless an exception is specially made therein, includes all houses, out-houses, edifices, barns, stables, yards, gardens, orchards, commons, trees, woods, underwoods, mounds, fences, hedges, ditches, ways, waters, water-courses, lights, liberties, privileges, easements, profits, commodities, emoluments, hereditaments and appurtenances whatsoever, to such land belonging or in anywise appertaining, or with such land demised, held, used, occupied and enjoyed or taken or known as part or parcel thereof, and if the conveyance purports to convey an estate in fee simple, also the reversion or reversions, remainder and remainders, yearly and other rents, issues and profits of the same land and of every part and parcel thereof, and all the estate, right, title, interest, inheritance, use, trust, property, profit, possession, claim and demand whatsoever, of the grantor, into, out of, or upon the same land, and every part and parcel thereof, with their and every of their appurtenances.
(2) Except as to conveyances under former Acts relating to short forms of conveyances, this section shall apply only to conveyances made after the 1st day of July, 1886.

For similar legislation, see Land Titles Act, R.S.A. 1955, c. 170, ss. 2(l), 57; Law of Property Act, R.S.M. 1954, c. 138, s. 6; Property Act, R.S.N.B. 1952, c. 177, s. 21; Conveyancing Act, 1956 (N.S.) c. 3, s. 6 (d); Real Property Act, R.S.P.E.I. 1951, c. 138, s. 55; Land Titles Act, 1960 (Sask.), c. 65, ss. 2(10), 66.

An easement by implied grant may be enforced under a specifically enforceable contract of sale even though such a contract is outside of the terms of the above-noted legislation: see *Borman* v. *Griffith*, [1930] 1 Ch. 493, 99 L.J. Ch. 205.]

SORRENTE v. RICE AND MCCOLL-FRONTENAC OIL CO. LTD. Ontario High Court. [1950] O.R. 479, [1950] 3 D.L.R. 246

Action for damages for trespass to an oak tree and for an injunction to restrain interference with an alleged right of way and interference with light enjoyed by windows of plaintiff's residence. Two adjoining lots, on one of which there was a house, which had separate owners, were acquired by one T who gave an option to McColl-Frontenac to purchase the southerly portions of both lots for purposes of a service station. Shortly afterwards, T agreed to sell the northerly portion of the two lots (and this included the house) to plaintiff who, on the evidence, was aware of the outstanding option to McColl-Frontenac. The latter exercised the option but the sale to plaintiff and registration of the deed to him was effected before a deed was acquired by McColl-Frontenac.

A cement walk had existed from the house to the street, traversing part of the property sold to McColl-Frontenac. After the sale, plaintiff re-laid the walk so as to confine it wholly to his land. McColl-Frontenac sold its land to Rice who began to build a service station thereon. The line between the lands of the parties passed through about six inches of the southerly side of an oak tree at ground level, the bulk of the tree being on plaintiff's property. In laying the foundation wall, Rice severed one surface root extending southerly from the tree.

GALE J.: . . . In these circumstances the plaintiff asks for damages for trespass to the oak tree. This part of his claim must fail. Quite apart from all other considerations, there have been no damages shown me with respect to this item, and I am not going to assume because one root is cut the oak tree has suffered. Mr. Clarke argued that Sorrente was to have the entire tree, but this contention cannot stand in view of the evidence that the oil company were required to have 65 ft. of depth, and in addition Sorrente admitted that before he purchased he sighted along the Archibald stakes, which marked the true boundary line between the two properties, and if he misjudged the location of the tree he cannot now complain.

The next claim is for an injunction to protect the right-of-way which Sorrente claims along the ground formerly occupied by the cement walk leading from the rear verandah to Goderich St. It is perfectly obvious that the purpose of the action is not so much to maintain the way as to prevent construction of any sort on the southerly portion of the lands, but if the plaintiff has the legal right to maintain that way, then, of course, that legal right must be upheld.

In the first place, let me say that it cannot be supported by way of an implied grant upon the severance by Teall of the whole of the two lots united in him. I say that because the walk has not been shown on the evidence to be either a way of necessity or necessary to the reasonable enjoyment of the Sorrente property. Much time and evidence was devoted to the desirability of the walk and its convenience to those occupying the house, but in my view that evidence fell hopelessly short of demonstrating that its continuance is necessary for the reasonable enjoyment of the plaintiff's lands.

However, Mr. Clarke, in his careful argument, contended that the right-of-way over the walk must be maintained by reason of the fact that the deed from Teall to Sorrente was made pursuant to the *Short Forms of Conveyances Act*, which had the effect of incorporating in it the provisions of s. 14(1) of the *Conveyancing and Law of Property Act*, R.S.O. 1937, c. 152, and my attention was called to a great many cases in which that situation has been discussed. It is unnecessary for me to examine those cases further because I am convinced that there are two short but complete answers to the application of the statute.

The first answer, in my opinion, is to be found in the doctrine expressed in *Beddington* v. *Atlee* (1887), 35 Ch. D. 317. In that case the owner of a parcel of land on part of which a house was erected entered into an agreement for purchase by A of the unencumbered lands. Then the lands upon which the house was situate were conveyed to B. Subsequently the transaction with A was carried out and the vacant lands were conveyed to him. B contended that he was entitled to a right of light by reason of his prior deed and the provisions of the English Act corresponding to s. 14 (1) of our Act, which I have just mentioned. There is also a discussion, of course, about an implied grant of an easement. At pp. 330-1 Chitty J. disposes of the effect of the *Conveyancing and Law of Property Act*, 1881, which really constitutes the basis of the argument put forward by Mr. Clarke. After discussing what would otherwise be the result in view of the form of the deed given to B and the language of the Act (with particular reference to whether there was expressed in the deed a contrary intention denying the right to light), His Lordship concludes:

"What there is in the deed is an expression that something shall pass, and something less than would pass under the Act"—(I pause to point out that that is the exact situation in this case)—"and the question is, whether the maxim *expressio unius est exclusio alterius* is strong enough to apply to such a case as is before me. But I refrain from deciding the point, because I think it does not really arise. It appears to me that whether the plaintiff claims by express grant or implied grant he is equally thrown upon the investigation of the title to the adjoining land; and that the observations I have made with regard to the implied grant apply."

At pp. 326-7, His Lordship deals with the question of implied grant in this way: "Now I go to the question which has been so much argued, as to the grant to be implied on the conveyance. The first observation I make is this: on reading the conveyance no implication whatever arises. It is not like the case of an implied grant when, upon reading the instrument, you say the terms employed mean so and so; and it is necessary, in order to give effect to the intention, as manifested by the deed, to imply something which is not expressed in so many words. In this case, in order to raise any implied grant, it is necessary to look outside the deed of conveyance, and to consider the surrounding circumstances. That observation appears to me to be important. It is necessary to make an inquiry in regard to the adjoining land, that is to say, the alleged servient tenement. To make what I have said plain, I will put it in this way: if the adjoining land is owned by a stranger, of course there is no implied grant. The allegation that there is an implied grant over the adjoining land necessarily involves an investigation of the circumstances, and especially of the title, to the adjoining land. As I say, where a stranger is the owner there is no implication whatever; but if the grantor,—I am now taking the simple case as the best illustration—who is seised of the fee simple in law of the house, is shewn by proper evidence to be also seised in fee simple of the field, then the implication arises, but not till then perfectly. If it appears that the grantor of the house has a term, and only a term, in the adjoining land, then the implied grant would be to the extent of the term, and not more. If he has got a short and temporary interest, the implied grant would be only to the extent of the short and temporary interest. That appears to me to be a plain way of reasoning out the case according to principle."

I apply that reasoning here. At the time that Sorrente signed his offer to purchase, the title of the offeree (Teall) in the southerly portion of the lot was subject to the outstanding interest acquired by McColl-Frontenac by reason of the option to purchase, and any grant to be implied at that time would be subject to the limits of the interest then vested in Teall. At most, all that Teall could pass to Sorrente in respect of the southerly lands was a right-of-way over the walk in the event that the option was not exercised by the McColl-Frontenac Co., and since that option was subsequently taken up by the Company Sorrente acquired no such right-of-way either by implied grant or by the operation of the statute.

The *Beddington* case is on all fours with the present case with the exception that there the person who turned out to be the servient owner had a prior agreement to purchase. Here the servient owner, McColl-Frontenac, held an option to purchase. In principle, there is no substantial distinction that I can see between the positions of the two so-called servient owners. It should also be observed that the grant of any right-of-way by reason of s. 14(1) would become operative only when the conveyance was given from Teall to Sorrente. By that time the option had been exercised by the oil company, so that the similarity between this and the *Beddington* case may be greater than suggested above. Reference might also be made to *Lysaght* v. *Edwards* (1876), 2 Ch. D. 499, and to the fact that in *Webb* v. *Dipenta*, [1925] 1 D.L.R. 216, S.C.R. 565, our Supreme Court of Canada speaks almost as if options to purchase and agreements to purchase carried substantially the same incidents.

There is another reason why I cannot give effect to the claim for the right-of-way. It was well known by and between Sorrente and Teall prior to the execution of the offer by Sorrente to purchase the northerly 57 ft. that McColl-Frontenac Oil Co. had acquired the southerly 65 ft. and were intending to erect a service station on that property. As I have already said, it does not require much stretch of the imagination to conclude also that Sorrente would at the same time be fully cognizant of the fact that any service station to be erected on those lands would interfere with the walk and with his right to light. In those circumstances it has been decided that s. 14(1) does not operate. I have in mind the case of *Birmingham*, *Dudley &*

Dist. Banking Co. v. *Ross* (1888), 38 Ch. D. 295, a decision of the Court of Appeal in England. The facts, of course, are quite different except that there, too, both parties were deemed to be aware of the fact that the right to light which might otherwise be vested in the plaintiff was not intended to be transferred to him. Cotton L. J., in upholding the judgment of Kekewich J., states at p. 307:

"But in my opinion, even with the assistance afforded us by the language of this deed, this could not be said to be a light, within the meaning of this section [The comparable section of the English Act], enjoyed with the house. The house had only recently been erected; and at the time when this lease was granted it was obvious to both parties that this was a large tract of land bought by the corporation of Birmingham for the purpose of effecting an improvement, and for the purpose of the land being laid out so as to have buildings upon it, and at the time when the lease was granted Corporation Street had only just been formed... Therefore, I think it could not be said that the light coming over that low building to these windows could be considered as enjoyed with it within the meaning of this section. The light did in fact at the time come over that building; but it came over it under such circumstances as to shew that there could be no expectation of its continuance."

It is true that on the following page the Lord Justice indicates that the case against the enjoyment of the right is stronger because of the terms of that deed, but I do not read his statement to that effect as being intended to cut down the passages which I have quoted from p. 307. In this case there can be no question on the findings which I have made that there was no expectation by Sorrente that he would have continued use of the walk or that his light would not be diminished. It is absurd to come to any other conclusion once one appreciates the fact that he did know when he purchased his house that the southerly portion of the lands was going to be used for the purposes which I have described.

The same principle was enunciated in *Godwin* v. *Schweppes Ltd.*, [1902] 1 Ch. 926. At p. 933 Joyce J., who delivered the judgment in that case, stated as follows: "But in the very important case of *Birmingham, Dudley and District Banking Co.* v. *Ross*, 38 Ch. D. 295, it was determined that, although a grantor shall not derogate from his own grant, this rule does not entitle the grantee of a house with the lights, under the words imported into the grant by the *Conveyancing Act*, 1881, to any easement of light to an extent inconsistent with the intention to be implied from the circumstances existing at the time of the grant and known to the grantee. The expression 'lights enjoyed' in the statute is confined to the light enjoyed under such circumstances as would reasonably and properly lead to an expectation that the enjoyment of that light would be continued."

As I have already said, the plaintiff had no expectation whatever that full enjoyment of light and the right-of-way would continue once the lands to the south were put to the purpose for which they had been purchased. The plaintiff's own evidence demonstrates the absence of any such expectation.

Mr. Clarke relied upon s. 73 (1) of the *Registry Act*, R.S.O. 1937, c. 170, to defeat the effect of the option to purchase and subsequent acceptance of it by McColl-Frontenac Oil Co. That section can have no application to the circumstances of this case because here Sorrente had actual notice when he signed his offer to purchase that McColl-Frontenac had already acquired the lands to the south.

The two matters above mentioned may be invoked as answers also to the claim for the easement with respect to light. Mr. Clarke conceded that to be so if I favoured those defences, and so I did not hear argument from him on the existence of the easement relating to light....

Action dismissed.

[See 2 *American Law of Property*, ss. 8. 31 to 8. 43.

Suppose a common owner of a block of land makes simultaneous sales of different parcels to different purchasers. Will an easement by implication arise as between the purchasers in the same circumstances in which one would have arisen as between a common owner and one purchaser? See *Hart* v. *McMullen* (1900), 30 S.C.R. 245 (implication of easement denied where no existing user at time of severance); *Schwann* v. *Cotton*, [1916] 2 Ch. 120, 459 (C.A.) (easement by implication recognized where water pipe from one parcel to other existed and was used at time of severance—in this case by will).]

[For an illustration of an easement by implied grant as between landlord and tenant, see *Wright* v. *Macadam*, [1949] 2 K.B. 744, [1949] 2 All E.R. 565 (C.A.).]

ISRAEL v. LEITH. Ontario Queen's Bench. 1890. 20 O.R. 361

Appeal from dismissal of an action in which the issue was whether plaintiff as owner of a house was entitled to an easement of drainage and aqueduct against adjoining land. Both parcels were at one time owned by B who sold one to plaintiff's predecessor in title under a deed which was registered some months later. There was no express mention therein of any easement. At that time the water and sewer pipes ran first to the land retained by the grantor and from there to the property now owned by plaintiff and were the only means by which the house thereon obtained water and drainage. B subsequently sold the adjoining land to defendant who registered his deed. Defendant cut off the pipes and plaintiff sued for damages.

The judgment of the Court was delivered by STREET J.: It is clearly established law that where the owner of two adjoining lots conveys one of them he impliedly grants to the grantee all those continuous and apparent easements which are necessary to the reasonable use of the property granted, and which are at the time of the grant used by the owner of the entirety for the benefit of the part granted: *Suffield* v. *Brown*, 4 D. J. & S. 185; *Watts* v. *Kelson*, L. R. 6 Ch. 166; *Wheeldon* v. *Burrows*, 12 Ch. D. 31; *Bayley* v. *Great Western R. W. Co.*, 26 Ch. D. 434; *Birmingham, &c.*, v. *Ross*, 38 Ch. D. at p. 308; and the rights of drainage and of aqueduct are within this category of easements. See *Pyer* v. *Carter*, 1 H. & N. 916, which does not seem to have been doubted in this respect. Therefore, the conveyance made in 1882 by Thomas Bryce to Emily Maddox passed to the grantee, her heirs and assigns, a right to have uninterrupted use of the drain leading from house No. 118, which was the house conveyed to her, through house No. 116, which the grantor retained, and a right to have the water conveyed to house No. 118 through the pipes leading to it from house No. 116.

The grant of these rights would have been implied under the circumstances as an incident to the express grant of house No. 118. There are also in the conveyance general words sufficient to pass the rights claimed, and so to give them to the grantee by way of express grant. It is, however, here immaterial whether these rights are to be treated as arising under an implied or an express grant, in my opinion, because in either case the plaintiff is entitled to them as against the defendant....

If the Registry Act is to be left out of consideration, there can equally, I think, be no doubt that the plaintiff, claiming under a prior legal grant, although an implied one, would not be affected by the fact that the defendant, claiming under a subsequent grant, although an express one, was a purchaser without notice.

The only question therefore remaining is whether the rights of the plaintiff have been taken from him by the Registry Act.

The Registry Act requires instruments affecting lands to be registered; originally it did not interfere with rights, legal or equitable, arising otherwise than by instruments capable of being registered: *Harrison* v. *Armour*, 11 Gr. 303. Then it was amended so as to postpone in certain cases unregistered equitable rights whether based upon written instruments or not, but this left untouched the case of legal rights arising otherwise than under written instruments. If, therefore, the rights in question here are to be treated as arising under an implied grant, they are outside the effect of the Registry Act; and, being prior in point of time, and arising under a grant, they must prevail over the defendant, a subsequent purchaser of the estate out of which they were granted.

If they are to be treated as arising under express grant, undoubtedly the Registry Act applies, but I am unable to see that the defendant's position is strengthened. There is nothing in the Act requiring the creation of legal rights or their transfer to be evidenced by any new forms of words; it only requires that the instruments creating or transferring rights to land shall be registered; and when registered in the due order of their dates, no provision in the Act disturbs the effect which would have been given to them had no registry law prevailed. Here the plaintiff's conveyance is prior in point of time to the defendant's; it passed certain legal rights to the plaintiff in the land which the defendant subsequently purchased. The instrument under which these rights passed is first in point of time and first in point of registration, and therefore there is nothing in the Registry Act to take away the rights acquired by the plaintiff under it.

I find myself obliged, with great respect, to differ from the dicta of Mr. Justice Patterson found in *Carter* v. *Grasett*, 14 A.R. at pp. 709, 710, in so far as they affect this question....

Appeal allowed.

[The doctrine of *Israel* v. *Leith* has been followed consistently: see *Duchman* v. *Oakland Dairy Co. Ltd.* (1928), 63 O.L.R. 111, [1929] 1 D.L.R. 9 (App. Div.); *Torosian* v. *Robertson*, [1945] 3 D.L.R. 142, [1945] O.W.N. 427.

Should the doctrine be applied in favour of a person who holds land under an unregistered agreement for sale? See *Donaldson* v. *Lapp*, [1953] O.R. 178, [1953] 2 D.L.R. 166.

Israel v. *Leith* has also been applied to easements acquired by prescription: see *Myers* v. *Johnston* (1922), 52 O.L.R. 658, [1923] 4 D.L.R. 1152 (App. Div.); *Garfinkel* v. *Kleinberg and Kleinberg*, [1955] O.R. 388, [1955] 2 D.L.R. 844 (C.A.).

In *Morrison* v. *Weller*, [1951] 3 D.L.R. 156, 4 W.W.R. (N.S.). 160 (B.C.), it was held that an easement acquired by prescription is not an interest in possession under s. 38 (2) of the Land Registry Act, now R.S.B.C. 1960, c. 208 and hence is not protected by that provision against the holder of a certificate of indefeasible title to the servient land. Only if the prescriptive easement is acquired before the first issue of such a certificate and is marked thereon as a restriction will it be enforceable.]

RUETSCH v. SPRY. Ontario High Court. 1907. 14 O.L.R. 233

Action for a mandatory injunction to remove a boundary fence which cut off light and air and collected snow and ice so as to interfere with plaintiff's enjoyment of his house and land. Plaintiff had bought the house from defendant who for some 50 years had owned the lot on which it stood. The house was, as to its main part, more than 60 years old, and an addition thereto was more than 40 years old. Light to the windows was from the west; and no other buildings stood on the westerly part of the lot. In selling off the house defendant retained part of the lot, and the boundary line was at some points only 8 inches and at others about 2 feet from plaintiff's house. Defendant built a 7 foot board fence on his side of the boundary line, thus cutting off the light (the windows in the additon were some 18 inches from the ground) and air and impairing ventilation. Moreover, snow and ice collected in the narrow area between the house and the fence, and it was difficult to get at it to remove it; in the result, water soaked into the house. The fence was, in short, a spite fence built after plaintiff had brought a successful action to have his conveyance rectified.

RIDDELL J.:... The claim of the plaintiff is, briefly, this: I bought the land, including the house, with all its appurtenances. At the time I bought, the house had the full benefit of light and air from the west and also the benefit of an outlet for snow and ice and water, so that these would not pile up against the house, and do damage by the water making its way in through the windows and otherwise. I claim (1) that an easement passed by the deed; (2) and, if not, the defendant cannot derogate from his own deed.

The defendant claims: (1) The deed of 1903 is plain, and there was no grant of anything but the very land mentioned therein, as admittedly there was no parol agreement or any agreement outside of the conveyance, if, indeed, that would make a difference.

(2) If there was any doubt before, there is none since the judgment of the Court in the former action, in which the rights of the parties were declared.

(3) That being so, the defendant is at liberty to do as he pleases upon his own property; and (4) the fact that the fence may have been or was placed from a motive to do injury to the plaintiff is immaterial.

As to the last point urged by the defendant, I agree with him: "No use of property which would be legal if due to a proper motive can become illegal because it is prompted by a motive that is improper or even malicious": *The Mayor, Aldermen and Burgesses of the Burrow of Bradford* v. *Pickles*, [1895] A.C. 587.

There may be some doubt how it is in the law of Scotland as to the action "*in aemulationem vicini*" (see per Lord Watson, at p. 598), but by the law of England no action will lie at the instance of a neighbour for an act done by one on his own land unless such act be attended with offence or injury to the legal rights of such neighbour; and improper or malicious intent or motive is immaterial.

The second ground taken is untenable. The whole question in dispute in the former action between the parties is the location on the ground of the land conveyed or intended to be conveyed by the deed.

As to the first and third, the statute R.S.O. 1897, ch. 124, shews that the effect of the deed is, to entitle the grantee to the quiet possession of the lands, "with their and every of their appurtenances" (Sch. B, column 2 (3)), and the word "appurtenances" will not cover these quasi easements, which have never existed or which have ceased to exist, as easements properly so-called, by reason of unity of ownership: see per Harrison, C. J., at p. 39 of *Harris* v. *Smith* (1876), 40 U.C.R. 33; Goddard on Easements, 3rd ed., at pp. 131, 132; cf. Gale's Law of Easements, 7th ed., p. 78; Tudor's L.C., R.P., 3rd ed., at p. 170; although the question does not seem to be free from doubt and difficulty.

So that, if the plaintiff was relying simply upon the wording of his deed, as interpreted by the statute, he might fail.

But the other ground upon which he relies is, I think, inexpugnable. Since ever the question was raised in England, it has been held, that "where the owner of two tenements sells one, a grant will be implied of those continuous and apparent easements which during the unity of possession were enjoyed under the title of ownership. For instance, where the same person possesses a house, having the actual use and enjoyment of certain rights and also possessing the adjoining land, sells the house to another person... he cannot... build upon the adjoining land so as to obstruct or interrupt the enjoyment of those rights. The reason is founded on the rule that 'a man cannot derogate from his own grant,' for it would be manifestly unjust, when a person had purchased the house, having the apparent and continuous enjoyment of the lights, that he should be deprived of this by the act of the person from whom he purchased": Tudor's L.C., R.P., 3rd ed., p. 173. And the same rule will apply to air as to light: *Kelk* v. *Pearson* (1871), L.R., 6 Ch. 809, *per* Mellish, L. J., at p. 813; such right not being different from that which might be gained under the statute: cf. Gale's Law of Easements 7th ed., p. 100.

But there is a distinction between easements which are continuous and easements which are used from time to time only. "There is a distinction between easements such as a right of way or easements used from time to time, and easements of necessity or continuous easements. The cases recognize this distinction; and it is clear law that, upon a severance of tenements, easements used as of necessity, or in their nature continuous, will pass by implication of law, without any words of grant; but, with regard to easements which are used from time to time only, they do not pass, unless the owner by appropriate language shews an intention that they should pass: pp. 109, 110: *Poldon* v. *Bostard* (1865), L.R. 1 Q.B. 156, at p. 161, *per* Erle, C. J. cited with approval by Sir Geo. Mellish, L. J. giving the judgment of the Court in *Watts* v. *Kelson* (1871), L.R., 6 Ch. 166, at p. 173.

As regards the light and air, I had no difficulty, and at the trial so expressed myself. Mr. O'Connell, however, urges that it would not be sufficient to cut down the fence to within eighteen inches of the ground, but that the plaintiff is entitled to have a surface exit for the snow and water from the heavens direct and from the roof.

That raises a question which, so far as I can find, has not been decided. If the water falling, either in liquid or crystalline form, from the roof had been accustomed to be carried away by a drain over some defined channel, no doubt that would establish an easement which would pass by implication: *Pyer* v. *Carter* (1856), 1 H. & N. 916.

And, again, if it were a case of determining the naked right of one neighbour to discharge surface water upon the lands of another jure naturae, the plaintiff must fail: *Darby* v. *The Corporation of the Township of Crowland* (1876), 38 U.C.R. 338, *per* Hagarty, C. J., at p. 343; *Williams* v. *Richards* (1893), 23 O.R. 657. And the Massachusetts cases cited by Hagarty, C. J., at p. 343, shew that the same rule applies whether the water be from rain or melted snow.

This rule is apparently drawn by our Courts ultimately from the case of *Rawstron* v. *Taylor* (1855), 11 Ex. 369. There the plaintiff had received from the defendant a conveyance of certain land, "together with all... waters, watercourses,... privileges, rights,... and appurtenances to the same... piece of land belonging or appertaining," p. 376. The land conveyed adjoined land retained by the defendant, and from two parts of this land so retained, surface water sometimes came upon the land sold to the plaintiff. At another point there was a defined flow. It was held, that, notwithstanding the deed and the maxim that a grantor cannot derogate from his own grant, no cause of action lay for the acts of the defendant, in stopping the flow of mere surface water which was wont to come from the two places first mentioned...

This case seems to be authority for the converse of what is under discussion; and it seems to me, that if the right to the flow of surface water to the granted property does not pass by implication, neither does the right to the flow of surface water from the granted premises, speaking in the abstract.

But if the damming back of the surface water would have the effect of interfering with the reasonable enjoyment of the property granted, this is a violation of the rights of the grantee. The grantor cannot be permitted to do any act which, e.g., would cause the land granted to be or become a mere water-table (to use the expression of Platt, B., in *Rawstron* v. *Taylor*, at p. 383) or a morass: Angell on Watercourses, 6th ed., par. 166a. It is to my mind clear that the reasonable enjoyment of the premises sold includes the comfortable enjoyment of them; and that, under the circumstances of this case and the condition of the house, involves the non-prevention of the natural flow of the water, etc., from the side of the house. Whether this fence interferes with the reasonable enjoyment of the remainder of the lot sold does not appear. If the whole fence be removed, there will be no necessity of determining that matter; if not, the matter may require to be determined on a motion to commit for breach of the injunction to be ordered.

There will be an injunction restraining the plaintiff from continuing the fence erected by him in such a way as to interfere with the comfortable and reasonable enjoyment of the premises conveyed, and an order that he forthwith remove the same or so much thereof as interferes with such enjoyment.

Judgment for plaintiff.

[See also *Carter* v. *Grasett* (1888), 14 O.A.R. 685, rev'g 11 O.R. 331.

In *Simpson* v. *Eaton* (1907), 15 O.L.R. 161 (Div. Ct.), the owner of certain land sold part of it to S and it ultimately came into the hands of plaintiff. A few months after the sale to S, the remaining part of the land was sold to another and it ultimately came into the hands of defendant. Plaintiff claimed access of light to the windows of his house as it was enjoyed on the day of the original sale to S, and he alleged that defendant's building obstructed the light. The trial Judge proceeded on the basis of an admission by defendant that plaintiff had by implied grant acquired the right to access of light to his property but he found that there was no actionable privation of light by reason of any obstruction caused by defendant's building so as to make the occupation of plaintiff's house uncomfortable. On appeal, the judgment was reversed and Boyd C. (with whom Magee J. concurred, the third Judge, Mabee J., delivering a separate judgment) said, in part:

"The plaintiff has a substantial grievance, and his action should not have been dismissed. The judgment appears to err in applying the rules settled by the Courts in the case of interference with ancient lights by extension to the present case where the plaintiff's rights depend upon conveyances to him from the common owner of his lot and the adjoining lot now owned by the defendant.

"This case is one of modern windows which are to receive such access of light as they had at the time the plaintiff's lot was severed from that now owned by the adjoining proprietor. Lake, the common owner of both, severed the lots by first granting under a short form conveyance to the plaintiff's predecessor, his lot. That grant by express terms carried the lights as appurtenant, or quasi-appurtenant, and over and above that it was subject to the well established rule that one cannot derogate from his own grant being applied to the case in hand; that means that Lake having conveyed this lot with house and windows in question, the owner could not by himself or by anyone claiming under him thereafter do anything on the next adjoining lot he retained which would materially diminish the light coming to the windows.

"But a change has been made by the defendants, who have erected a wall on this lot about twice as high as that which existed at the time of severance. This structure has the effect of obstructing the passage of light whereby the plaintiff's rooms have been darkened and artificial light has to be used early in the evenings. The structure complained of occasions perceptible and material detriment to the plaintiff's premises, and lessens the beneficial enjoyment of them to an easily measurable extent. By this act the defendants have derogated from the grant made by Lake, and the plaintiff has the right to complain of it.

"The plaintiff's inertness has been such that the defendants have changed their position, so that the proper method of relief is not by way of mandatory injunction, but by way of award of damages."

The "ancient light" cases, on which the trial Judge relied, were cases in which the right to access of light was gained by prescription. In such cases, as was pointed out in *Colls* v. *Home and Colonial Stores Ltd.*, [1904] A.C. 179, the test applied by the trial Judge in *Simpson* v. *Eaton*, *supra*, would have been appropriate. The cases dealing with "ancient lights" show that not every diminution or privation of light (occurring after the prescriptive right has been gained) will support an action. The reason is disclosed in Lord Hardwicke's oft quoted statement in *Fishmongers' Company* v. *East India Co.* (1752), 1 Dick. 163, 21 E.R. 232 (Ch.), where he said, of an alleged obstruction to light: "It is not sufficient to say that it will alter the plaintiffs' lights, for then no vacant piece of land could be built on in the city". Indeed, the test applied is essentially one of "nuisance": see 12 *Halsbury's Laws of England* (1955 3rd ed.), pp. 582 ff. *Quaere*, whether the same test should not be applied to easements of light or air arising by implication.

See *Radcliffe*, The Easement of Light and Air and Its Limitations under English Law, (1908) 24 Law Q. Rev. 120, 247.]

[Legislation has prohibited the acquisition of easements of light and air by prescription, and in some cases the prohibition extends to any easement or profit a prendre: see Limitation of Actions Act, R.S.A. 1955, c. 177, s. 49 (no easement or right in gross or profit a prendre may be acquired by prescription); Prescription Act, R.S.B.C. 1960, c. 296, ss. 4 and 5 (no prescriptive rights to light or air); Law of Property Act, R.S.M. 1954, c. 138, s. 30 (no prescriptive right to light); Easements Act, R.S.N.B. 1952, c. 67, ss. 8 and 9 (no prescriptive rights to light or air or in respect of wires or cables); Limitation of Actions Act, R.S.N.S. 1954, c. 153, s. 32 (2) (no prescriptive rights to light or air in any city or incorporated town); Limitations Act, R.S.O. 1960, c. 214, ss. 33 and 35 (no prescriptive rights to light or air or in respect of wires or cables); Land Titles Act, 1960 (Sask.), c. 65, s. 71 (no easement or right in gross or profit a prendre may be acquired by prescription).

The prevailing rule in United States is that no easement of light or air or lateral support can be acquired by prescription: see *Burby*, Real Property (1954 2d ed.), p. 95.]

[In addition to statutory limitations on the acquisition of easements by prescription, the Courts have held that acts which amount to a public nuisance (as contrasted with a private wrong) or which involve a statutory offence will not ripen into prescriptive easements: see *Hunter* v. *Richards* (1912), 26 O.L.R. 458, 5 D.L.R. 116, aff'd 28 O.L.R. 267, 12 D.L.R. 503 (C.A.); *A.-G.* v. *Harrison* (1866), 12 Gr. 466.]

A NOTE ON PRESCRIPTION. The basic assumption of prescription (and this is hardly less true of limitations legislation governing "corporeal" as contrasted with "incorporeal" hereditaments) is that the use claimed as an easement had a valid (or legal) origin, which may be presumed in case of long-continued enjoyment. The presumption, which would be of a grant, operated originally under the rules of common law prescription, by which a continuous use (of the kind hereinafter considered) back to 1189 (specifically to the date of accession of Richard I, the date of "legal memory") was conclusively presumed to be founded upon a grant of the alleged easement prior to that time. This meant, of course, that any claim of an easement by common law prescription would be defeated on a showing that the alleged easement could not or did not exist at some particular time after 1189. Moreover, the farther 1189 receded the more difficult it became to prove continuous use back to that time, and, in consequence the Courts modified the required proof by accepting proof of use for as long as living witnesses could remember: see 7 *Holdsworth, History of English Law* (1926, 3rd ed.), pp. 343-350. As before, however, this did not help where the evidence showed that the easement did not or could not have existed at some time after 1189; for example, the "dominant" and "servient" tenements might have come into common ownership since that time, or, in the case of an easement of support of buildings, the buildings were not put up until after 1189.

We need not be concerned in this country with common law prescription. It is inapplicable because, as Masten J. said in *Abell* v. *Woodbridge and York* (1917), 39 O.L.R. 382, 37 D.L.R. 352, rev'd on other grounds 45 O.L.R. 79, 46 D.L.R. 513, but restored 61 S.C.R. 345, 57 D.L.R. 81, "the Court may take judicial notice of the fact that America was discovered in

1492"; see also *Ring* v. *Pugsley* (1878), 18 N.B.R. 303, rev'd on other grounds Cassels S.C. 243.

The absurdity of the rule of "legal memory" led to the development of the doctrine of lost (modern) grant, based on a presumption of grant since 1189 but before the commencement of the long-continued use on which a claimant relied. Thus, a period of no less than 20 years' unexplained continuous use (adopted by analogy to Statutes of Limitation) would suffice to justify a finding that a grant, now lost, had been made; and, further, the period of use did not have to be immediately before action.

The defects of lost modern grant were not quite as formidable as those of common law prescription. However, the presumed grant would have to be by a capable grantor to a capable grantee. The use in question had to be in respect of a fee simple interest as against a similar interest (although if it had its beginning in this way the fact that leases were subsequently made would not affect the matter); and it could not involve an illegality, as, for example, breach of a statute. But apart from these qualifications (and the required proof of the user and its accompanying elements), the Courts apparently would not listen to an argument that no grant was in fact made. The "lost grant" doctrine was accepted in the common law provinces as part of the applicable common law: see *Watson* v. *Jackson* (1914), 31 O.L.R. 481, 19 D.L.R. 733 (App. Div.); *Jones* v. *Jones* (1843), 4 N.B.R. 265 (C.A.).

[On whether unity of interest or of possession defeats a claim under lost grant, see *Robson* v. *Wilson* (1919), 45 O.L.R. 296, 48 D.L.R. 437 (App. Div.).

A claim of easement by prescription was made against B by A who, during most of the alleged period of user, was a mortgagor in possession of B's predecessor in title. Result? See *Walker* v. *Hennigar*, [1935] 1 D.L.R. 285 (N.S.).]

It may be astonishing that legislative relief should not have come in England until the 19th century when such relief in respect of estates in land had come much earlier. The Prescription Act, 1832 (Imp.), c. 71 supplements the common law and the scheme and substance of the Act have been adopted in some of the common law provinces: see Prescription Act, R.S.B.C. 1960, c. 296; Easements Act, R.S.N.B. 1952, c. 67; Limitation of Actions Act, R.S.N.S. 1954, c. 153, ss. 31, 33-36; Limitations Act, R.S.O. 1960, c. 214, ss. 30-32, 34, 39-41. It will be convenient, for general purposes, to set out the key provisions of the British Columbia Prescription Act, as follows:

2. No claim which may be lawfully made at the common law, by custom, prescription or grant, to any right of common or other profit or benefit to be taken and enjoyed from or upon any land of the Crown, or any land of any ecclesiastical or lay person, or body corporate, except such matters and things as are herein specially provided for, and except rent and services, shall, where such right, profit, or benefit has been actually taken and enjoyed by any person claiming right thereto without interruption for the full period of thirty years, be defeated or destroyed by showing only that such right, profit, or benefit was first taken or enjoyed at any time prior to such period of thirty years, but nevertheless the claim may be defeated in any other way by which the same is now liable to be defeated; and when the right, profit, or benefit has been so taken and enjoyed as aforesaid for the full period of sixty years, the right thereto shall be deemed absolute and indefeasible, unless it appears that the same was taken and enjoyed by some consent or agreement expressly made or given for that purpose by deed or writing. [2 & 3 Will. 4, c. 71, s. 1]

3. No claim which may be lawfully made at the common law, by custom, prescription,

or grant, to any way or other easement, or to any watercourse, or the use of any water, to be enjoyed or derived upon, over, or from any land or water of the Crown, or being the property of any ecclesiastical or lay person, or body corporate, when such way or other matter as herein last before mentioned has been actually enjoyed by any person claiming right thereto without interruption for the full period of twenty years, shall be defeated or destroyed by showing only that such way or other matter was first enjoyed at any time prior to such period of twenty years, but nevertheless the claim may be defeated in any other way by which the same is now liable to be defeated; and where such way or other matter as herein last before mentioned shall have been so enjoyed as aforesaid for the full period of forty years, the right thereto shall be deemed absolute and indefeasible, unless it shall appear that the same was enjoyed by some consent or agreement expressly given or made for that purpose by deed or writing. [2 & 3 Will. 4, c. 71, s. 2].

6. Each of the respective periods of years hereinbefore mentioned shall be deemed and taken to be the period next before some suit or action wherein the claim or matter to which such period may relate has been or is brought into question, and no act or other matter shall be deemed to be an interruption, within the meaning of this Statute, unless the same has been or is submitted to or acquiesced in for one year after the party interrupted had or has notice thereof, and of the person making or authorizing the same to be made. [2 & 3 Will. 4, c. 71, s. 4].

8. In the several cases mentioned in and provided for by this Act, no presumption shall be allowed or made in favour or support of any claim, upon proof of the exercise or enjoyment of the right or matter claimed for any less period of time or number of years than for such period or number mentioned in this Act as may be applicable to the case and to the nature of the claim. [2 & 3 Will. 4, c. 71, s. 6].

9. The time during which any person otherwise capable of resisting any claim to any of the matters before mentioned has been or is an infant, idiot, non compos mentis, or tenant for life, or during which any action or suit has been pending, and which has been diligently prosecuted, until abated by the death of any party or parties thereto, shall be excluded in the computation of the periods hereinbefore mentioned, except only in cases where the right or claim is hereby declared to be absolute and indefeasible. [2 & 3 Will. 4, c. 71, s. 7].

10. When any land or water upon, over, or from which any such way or other convenient watercourse or use of water has been or is enjoyed or derived has been or is held under or by virtue of any term of life, or any term of years exceeding three years from the granting thereof, the time of the enjoyment of any such way or other matter as herein last before mentioned, during the continuance of such term, shall be excluded in the computation of the said period of forty years, in case the claim is within three years next after the end or sooner determination of such term resisted by any person entitled to any reversion expectant on the determination thereof. [2 & 3 Will. 4, c. 71, s. 8].

[For a discussion of the legislation and its effect, see *Cheshire*, Modern Law of Real Property (1962, 9th ed.), pp. 477-486; *Megarry and Wade*, Law of Real Property (1959, 2nd ed.), pp. 810-822; *Gale*, Law of Easements (1959, 13th ed.), pp. 126 ff.; *Note*, (1956) 72 Law Q. Rev. 32.]

What is the nature of or what are the elements of the user necessary to found a prescriptive claim of easement? The applied formula that the user must be a continuous one "*nec vi, nec clam, nec precario*" is elaborated in the cases and notes set out below.

GARFINKEL v. KLEINBERG AND KLEINBERG. Ontario Court of Appeal. [1955] O.R. 388, [1955] 2 D.L.R. 844

Appeal from a judgment for plaintiff upholding his claim of a prescriptive right to use a chimney on defendants' premises.

The judgment of the Court was delivered by F. G. MACKAY J. A.:... The plaintiff is the owner of the premises known as 120 Markham St. in the City of Toronto and the defendants are the owners of the premises immediately adjoining on the south, known as 118 Markham St. There is a party-wall between the two houses. The plaintiff's claim is that he has acquired a prescriptive right to use a chimney in the wall of the defendants' house. This chimney is entirely on the property of the defendants and is located at a point close to where the walls of the two houses join to become a party-wall. The defendants plead that if the plaintiff used the chimney he did so secretly and without their knowledge, and they plead the provisions of the *Registry Act*, R.S.O. 1950, c. 336....

The evidence relating to the ownership and occupancy of the two properties is as follows: The plaintiff purchased the property known as 120 Markham St. from Gustave and Oscar S. Kling by deed dated July 31, 1911, and registered on January 10, 1912. The vendors also owned the property immediately adjoining on the south and in their deed to the plaintiff they reserved the right to use the south wall of the plaintiff's house as a party-wall for a house to be built on their remaining land. The plaintiff's evidence is that this house, now known as 118 Markham St., was built in 1912. Prior to the building of that house there was a chimney built against the south wall of the plaintiff's house and used by him in connection with his furnace. In building No. 118 Markham St., the Kling brothers tore down this chimney and erected the chimney that the plaintiff now claims a prescriptive right to use. He says that at that time the workmen made an opening to the chimney through his south wall and the adjoining wall of house No. 118 for this purpose, with the knowledge and consent of the Kling brothers, and that he has used it continuously from that time until the difficulties arose between himself and the defendants in 1952, when this action was commenced. There was no agreement in writing nor was there any further oral discussion as to the plaintiff's use of this chimney during the occupancy of 118 Markham St. by the Kling brothers or by any subsequent owners of that property, although there was a written agreement in the year 1913 relating to overhanging eaves and drains. By deed dated September 15, 1921, the Kling brothers sold house Number 118 to one Harry Hurovitz. Hurovitz sold the property in 1922 and repurchased it by deed dated May 25, 1925. He remained the owner and occupant until 1942, when it was rented to the present defendants. It was sold by deed dated August 1, 1946, to one Nestor Lotosky, and he in turn sold it by deed dated October 31, 1947, to the defendants. The defendants have been in possession as either tenants or owners since 1942. The defendant's evidence is that they had no knowledge of the use of the chimney by the plaintiff until 1949. They say they became aware of the use because of fumes coming into their house from the chimney.

The learned trial Judge found as a fact that the plaintiff had used the chimney continuously since 1912. From the plaintiff's own evidence it is clear that he commenced to use the chimney with the knowledge and permission of the then owners of house Number 118 Markham St. The plaintiff's claim to an easement is based on user for more than 20 years and comes within the provisions of the first part of s. 34 of the *Limitations Act*, R.S.O. 1950, c. 207, the relevant part of which is as follows: "No claim which may lawfully be made at the common law by custom, prescription or grant, to any way or other easement, or to any water-course, or the use of any water to be enjoyed, or derived upon, over, or from any land or water of the Crown or being the property of any person, when the way or other matter as herein last before mentioned has been actually enjoyed by any person claiming right thereto without interruption for the full period of 20 years shall be defeated or destroyed by showing only that the way or other matter was first enjoyed at any time prior to the period of 20 years, but, nevertheless the claim may be defeated in any other way by which the same is now liable to be defeated."

The wording of this section is the same as that of s. 2 of the English Act (the *Prescription Act*, 1832 (Imp.), c. 71) and the cases decided under that Act are relevant in considering the Ontario Act.

A distinction between the cases where an easement is claimed at common law and where it is claimed under the *Prescription Act* is stated in Gale on Easements, 12th ed. p. 218, as follows:

"Before the Prescription Act, any admission, whether verbal or otherwise, that the enjoyment had been had by permission of the owner of the servient tenement was sufficient to prevent the acquisition of the right, however long such enjoyment might have continued.

"Since the Prescription Act, where an easement is claimed under the Act, the effect of permission for the enjoyment having been given by the owner of the servient tenement has been considered in many cases.

"An easement other than light may be claimed under section 2 of the Act on the ground of an enjoyment for twenty years; and in that case it has been laid down that a parol permission, if it extends over the whole period of twenty years, is consistent with, and will not *per se* prevent the enjoyment from being, an enjoyment as of right. On the other hand, if the parol permission be given from time to time within the twenty years, this would prevent the enjoyment from being an enjoyment as of right."

The words "claiming right thereto" used in the *Prescription Act* have been held to have the same meaning as "user as of right". *Tickle* v. *Brown* (1836), 4 Ad. & El. 369, 111 E.R. 826, and *Gardner* v. *Hodgson's Kingston Breweries Co.*, [1900] 1 Ch. 592 and [1903] A.C. 229. "User as of right" is defined in 11 Halsbury, 2nd ed., pp. 296-7, s. 537, as follows:

"The user or enjoyment of an alleged right in order to support a prescriptive claim, under the doctrine of prescription at common law, must be shown to have been user 'as of right', having been enjoyed *nec vi, nec clam, nec precario*, neither as the result of force, secrecy, or evasion, nor as dependent upon the consent of the owner of the servient tenement. Consent or acquiescence on the part of the servient owner lies at the root of prescription. He cannot be said to acquiesce in an act enforced by mere violence, or in an act which fear on his part hinders him from preventing, or in an act of which he has no knowledge actual or constructive, or which he contests and endeavours to interrupt, or which he sanctions only for temporary purposes, or in return for recurrent consideration.

"Actual ignorance of the exercise or enjoyment of the alleged right will not in every case prevent the enjoyment from being as of right. There are some things which every man ought to be presumed to know. Very slight circumstances may put the servient owner upon inquiry, and if he neglects to make inquiry it may be that knowledge must be imputed to him. Where an ordinary owner of land, diligent in the protection of his interests, would have a reasonable opportunity of becoming aware of the enjoyment by another person of a right over his land, he cannot allege that it was secret. If, however, the enjoyment be fraudulent or surreptitious, it cannot support a prescriptive claim."

A reading of the cases referred to in the footnotes to this section makes it clear that the statemants that "consent or acquiescence on the part of the servient owner lies at the root of prescription" and that "the user must not be dependent on the consent of the owner of the servient tenement" are not inconsistent. Where the right is claimed under the *Limitations Act*, consent to the user, unqualified as to time, will not be a bar to the owner of the dominant tenement obtaining a prescriptive right; if the user following the consent or permission is as of right by reason of the consent, and if the user continues for the full period of 20 years after the consent a prescriptive right is acquired under the statute; but permission asked and granted, periodic payments, acknowledgment by the dominant owner that his user is not as of right, at any time during the 20-year period will prevent his acquiring a prescriptive right; *Kinloch* v. *Nevile* (1840), 6 M. & W. 796, 151 E.R. 633; *Tickle* v. *Brown*, 4 Ad. & El. 369; *Gardner* v. *Hodgon's Kingston Breweries Co.*, [1900] 1 Ch. 592 and [1903] A.C. 229; *Myers* v. *Johnston*, [1923] 4 D.L.R. 1152, 52 O.L.R. 658, and *Bowes* v. *Reid*, [1924] 2 D.L.R. 399, 54 O.L.R. 253.

The questions that arise for determination are:

(1) Did the plaintiff use the chimney continuously from 1912?

(2) Does the fact that the original use of the chimney was by permission prevent the plaintiff from acquiring a prescriptive right to its use?

(3) Was the use secret?

(4) What is the effect of the *Registry Act*?

In the case at bar the only evidence is that the user began by arrangement between the adjoining owners in 1912 without any time limit expressed. From that date on the user by the plaintiff was "as of right" within the definitions laid down in the cases I have referred to.

A more difficult question is whether the user was "clam" or secret. On the evidence it is clear that the original owner of the servient tenement unquestionably had knowledge of the use by the plaintiff of the chimney. Hurovitz, who owned the property from May, 1925, to August, 1946, was said to be dead prior to the time of the trial of this action. His son, Harry Hurovitz, gave evidence. He said that he had lived in the house with his father for some years. He was asked as to his knowledge of the use of the chimney. His evidence on this point was very brief and is as follows:

"Q. Do you recall a chimney in the premises of 118 Markham? A. Well, offhand I cannot say. The only thing I do recall is the warmth of the north wall at 118. Q. Yes? A. And I imagine their chimney was on the same side of the house as ours.... Q. And do you know what chimney they [the Garfinkels] used for their furnace? A. Well, offhand I cannot say but I had an idea that it was a mutual chimney."

I think the only inference that can be drawn from his statement as to the north wall being warm and that he thought it was a mutual chimney is that it was warm when their own furnace was not on and that therefore the warmth was caused by the use of the chimney by the plaintiff. It would be a most unusual coincidence if the owners of both houses ceased having fire in their furnaces on the same day and started them at the same time in each year. It is also, I think, of some significance that the learned trial Judge found on the evidence that the only other chimney in the plaintiff's house was a kitchen-chimney that did not go down to the basement. Whether the user is "secret" is a question of fact to be decided on the evidence in each case: *Dalton* v. *Angus* (1881), 6 App. Cas. 740; *Union Lighterage Co.* v. *London Graving Dock.*, [1902] 2 Ch. 557.

I think, on the evidence in this case, that the defendants and their predecessors in title must be held to have had knowledge, or the means of knowledge, that the chimney was being used by the plaintiff.

As to the effect of the *Registry Act*, it was held in *Israel* v. *Leith* (1890), 20 O.R. 361, and *Myers* v. *Johnston*, [1923] 4 D.L.R. 1152, 52 O.L.R. 658, that an easement or other legal right or interest, arising by implication but not expressed in an instrument which can be registered, may be good as against a subsequent purchaser or mortgagee, without notice, claiming under a registered instrument. The effect of *Israel* v. *Leith* is discussed in Falconbridge, Law of Mortgages, 3rd ed., pp. 129-30.

The appellant also contends that a right such as that asserted by the plaintiff is not an easement and cannot be acquired by prescription. I do not agree with this contention. The right to pass smoke through flues was held to be an easement in *Jones* v. *Pritchard*, [1908] 1 Ch. 630.... *Appeal dismissed.*

[In 5 *Restatement of Property*, the elements of prescription are set out as follows:

S. 457. Creation of Easements by Prescription.
An easement is created by such use of land, for the period of prescription, as would be privileged if an easement existed, provided the use is
(a) adverse, and
(b) for the period of prescription, continuous and uninterrupted.

S. 458. Adverse Use.
A use of land is adverse to the owner of an interest in land which is or may become possessory when it is
(a) not made in subordination to him, and
(b) wrongful, or may be made by him wrongful, as to him, and
(c) open and notorious.

S. 459. Continuous and Uninterrupted Adverse Use.
(1) An adverse use is continuous when it is made without a break in the essential attitude of mind required for use.
(2) An adverse use is uninterrupted when those against whom the use is adverse do not
(a) bring and pursue to judgment legal proceedings in which the use is determined to be without legal justification, or
(b) cause a cessation of the use without the aid of legal proceedings.

FRANKLIN & HERSCHORN THEATRE CO. LTD. v. ODEON THEATRES OF CANADA LIMITED. Nova Scotia Supreme Court. [1949] 1 D.L.R. 651

Action under ss. 31 and 33 of the Nova Scotia Statute of Limitations (now R.S.N.S. 1954, c. 153) to establish a prescriptive right of way over land owned by defendant. The land lay between two theatres, called the Vogue and the Casino, owned by plaintiff and defendant respectively. The Vogue was in a new building opened in April, 1948, and it replaced an old building which had been a church but which, in 1923, was converted into a theatre called the Community. This theatre was closed in February, 1947 and the building itself was torn down between that time and April, 1947 to make way for the new building. The Casino had been in its present position for more than 20 years. Defendant began to erect a fence on the line between the two properties and plaintiff issued a writ on September 30, 1948, claiming a right of way by prescription over the whole of the vacant land owned by defendant and extending from the street to the rear of plaintiff's land. The acts of user on which plaintiff relied were acts of its predecessor Community Realty Ltd. during the period 1923 to 1947 at a time when defendant's predecessor Casino Co. Ltd. owned the land now held by defendant.

DOULL J. (after reviewing the evidence of user and quoting ss. 31 and 33 of the applicable statute): The result of these two sections is that an easement is not actually acquired until some "action or proceeding" is begun in which the easement is "brought into question". The writ in this action was issued on September 30, 1948. The period of 20 years must therefore be counted from September 30, 1948, and the plaintiff must show that it has been actually enjoyed by the plaintiff or some one under whom the plaintiff may claim, such person "claiming right" to the said easement and enjoying the same without interruption. An interruption to be effective against such a claim must have been submitted to or acquiesced in for more than a year.

The rights which might accrue to the plaintiff under the facts of this case are of two kinds: First, the right to use the eastern part of the land as an exit for patrons of the Community Theatre, and second, the right to use the western part of the land as an entrance to the back part of the Community premises and for purposes of repair to the Community building.

If we deal first with the claim of a right-of-way extending to the back of the lot, the claim is that this was used for the repairing and painting of the building and for a passageway to the back of plaintiff's building for foot passengers. We have to consider whether there was an enjoyment as of right uninterrupted during the period September 30, 1928 to September 30, 1948. The interruptions proven consist of requests for permission to take a truck of coal in on two occasions during the period in question. The plaintiff counters this by stating that it does not now claim a right for vehicles. Second, the placing of a gate which closed the passage except when under Mr. McAdam's orders the gate was opened, usually it was open in the daytime but sometimes it was closed even then; this continued for some years. Finally the period from February 18, 1947 to the date of the writ. On February 18, 1947, the Community Theatre was closed and certainly no more painting or repairing was done to it after that date; the Community was torn down and a fence was erected between the plaintiff's property and the alleyway in question. As far as I can see no claim to an easement as of right was made from that time up to the date of the writ. There were negotiations between the parties for the purchase of a right-of-way. These finally fell through in April, 1948....

The right to use the eastern portion of the right-of-way as an exit for patrons of the theatre, gives rise to other considerations.

On first impression, it might seem clear that there had been no user of this right-of-way from February, 1947 to the date of the issue of the writ and that consequently the plaintiff has not shown enjoyment for 20 years before the issue of the writ.

The cases on this section, however, are to the effect that a discontinuance even at the end of the period, if for the convenience of the dominant tenement is not an interruption by the servient owner. See Gale on Easements, 11th ed., pp. 205, 206, notes.

The section is rather difficult and, no doubt, if the Community Theatre had been closed for repairs, or because of the prevalence of smallpox, there might not be an interruption of enjoyment, if, when the cessation had ended, actual enjoyment began again. In the present case I think that the cessation was of a nature that would exclude an inference of enjoyment, *viz.*, the tearing down of the old building, the closing of the exit and opening it in a different place, the building of the wall in a different place and the much greater size and seating capacity of the building.

Whether or not it is correct that there was not actual enjoyment for the statutory period immediately before the issue of the writ, I am clearly of opinion that the plaintiff never enjoyed as of right, the easement which is claimed in this action.

In regard to the general right-of-way over the area to the rear of plaintiff's land, plaintiff has made the most of the acts of putting up ladders and repairing the wall of the old Community Theatre, but these acts were either casual acts of trespass or more likely acts with the permission of Mr. McAdam, Manager of the Casino. It would seem inconsistent with a claim to use the alleyway "as of right" that the plaintiff's predecessor asked on more than one occasion for permission to take in a load of coal, or that a gate was erected which was directed to be opened or closed at the pleasure of Mr. McAdam. The use made of the alleyway to put up ladders, was simply the tacit permission of a neighbour, which occurred only at irregular intervals and which were not exercised as of right and which gave rise to no easement. What I am about to say in regard to the eastern part, applies also to this part.

As to the right to use the eastern section of the alley as a way to Gottingen St., it must not be forgotten that this was kept open for the use of defendant's theatre. The exit to this space from the Casino Theatre is back beyond the old exit from the Community Theatre and was constantly used by patrons of the Casino. There is ample American authority that under such circumstances, no inference arises that a neighbouring owner makes use of the passage "as of right". The following is from 19 Corp. Jur., p. 898: "Where a space is left open by the owner for his own convenience the presumption ordinarily is that the use of such space by another, even for his own purpose, is permissive." For this proposition a number of American cases are cited. A somewhat similar case is *Adams* v. *Fairweather* (1906), 13 O.L.R. 490. See also *Rogers* v. *Duncan* (1890), 18 S.C.R. 710, and particularly the judgment of Strong J. in Can. S.C. Cas. 352 at p. 362.

Whatever use was made of this space by patrons of the Community was in common with patrons of the Casino. Indeed there was more space belonging to the Community Theatre towards the street, than there was of the Casino. No right arises from a policy of give and take even if it ran on over many years or indefinitely.

But in any case if there was a right-of-way, it has been abandoned. When the building was torn down, it became a question of intention whether or not there was an abandonment of any right which plaintiff might have in this disputed area. Plaintiff did not immediately claim any rights, but probably if they had built a new building at the same distance from the boundary line as the old, of the same seating capacity and with exits in the same place as in the old, they might have been held to be continuing any rights which were theirs previously. The case is otherwise. The new building is larger and has a larger seating capacity. The new exit is further from the street, necessitating the use of a greater area of the alley and finally in the area over which patrons formerly walked, the new building narrows up the area formerly left open by the Community Theatre, to 3 ft. 2 ins. The plaintiff now claims to throw the traffic which formerly used 7 to 10 ft. of the Community Theatre land, practically all upon the defendant. The former space was from the exits to the street about half on each property and if patrons of the Community Theatre sometimes spread over the Casino part, it was equally true that Casino patrons sometimes spread over the Community part. The present contention means that the plaintiff may build upon its land, but the defendant cannot build upon its part. All these actions are so inconsistent with the continuance of any prior rights that they amount to an abandonment.

In the result, I am of opinion that the plaintiff or its predecessors never enjoyed an easement over the lands in question as of right and even if they had such an enjoyment they must now be held to have abandoned it....

Action dismissed.

[While uninterrupted user for the requisite period is not inconsistent with intervals in enjoyment (see *Younghusband* v. *McRae*, [1937] O.W.N. 218), yet where during the alleged period of user there is non-user for a considerable time (and this is established by positive evidence so as to foreclose an inference of user based on active user before and after this "gap" period), the prescriptive claim will fail: see *McIlmurray* v. *Brown*, [1954] 1 D.L.R. 458, [1954] O.W.N. 121.

In *Hunter* v. *Richards* (1913), 28 O.L.R. 267, 12 D.L.R. 503 (C.A.), the Court said: "In dealing with questions of this nature, the character of this country in the earlier days of its settlement, and the needs of the earlier civilised inhabitants, must never be overlooked if justice is to be done. Things which were then the order of the day would mightily surprise land-owners of older settled countries, and even many of us of this country of later birth or adoption. The needs of the earlier settlers in their gigantic and heroic task of entering into the primeval forests and converting them into fertile lands brought about a fellowship and liberality which gave, by leave to one another, rights of entry, rights of passage, and other rights such as if all were members of one great family. Indeed, until later years any one, even the greatest stranger, was permitted to shoot, trap, hunt, and fish, and gather natural fruits, where he would; but gradually these privileges are being withdrawn: "accommodation roads" are closed, and "trespassing is forbidden" is coming to be the rule rather than the exception; but all these things when done, including the fouling of streams, was seldom as of right, but only as of neighbourliness—tacit license."]

RUSSELL TRANSPORT LTD. v. ONTARIO MALLEABLE IRON CO. LTD. Ontario High Court. [1952] O.R. 621, [1952] 4 D.L.R. 719

Action in nuisance for damages and an injunction to restrain defendant from discharging corrosive substances from its foundry upon plaintiffs' land. Plaintiffs carried on a motor transport business and used the land for office and garage servicing purposes. The trial Judge concluded, on the evidence, that "defendant emits from its plant particles of iron and iron oxide together with other matters which settle on the plaintiffs' lands, rendering the plaintiffs' property unfit for the purpose for which it was purchased and developed". Defendant's foundry had been in operation at least since 1907 when it bought the land on which the foundry stood, and it was alleged to have been in operation since 1876 although the character of operation had changed in that time. Among the defences to the action was that of prescriptive right, and it was contended, in reliance on ss. 34 and 35 of the Limitation of Actions Act, R.S.O. 1950, c. 207, that defendant and its predecessors in title had for a period of 40 years or more before this action was begun, enjoyed as of right and without interruption the right to do what is now complained of as a ground of action.

McRUER C. J. H. C.:... In asserting the defence of prescription the onus rests on the defendant: *Crossley and Sons Ltd.* v. *Lightowler* (1867), L.R. 2 Ch. 478 at p. 482. The defendant must not only show that it has exercised the right to deposit the substances herein complained of on the plaintiffs' lands, for the prescribed period, but that the exercise of the right amounted to a nuisance actionable at the instance of the plaintiffs and their predecessors in title for the full period of 20 years: *Sturges* v. *Bridgman*, 11 Ch. D. 852; *Danforth Glebe Estates Ltd.* v. *W. Harris & Co.* (1919), 16 O.W.N. 41.

The latter case was a case arising out of the emission of offensive odours from the defendant's plant. After referring to *Sturges* v. *Bridgman*, Riddell J. said: "So long as the adjoining land remained wholly vacant, and no attempt was made to sell it, and no other damage could be shewn, the time did not begin to run. Nothing of the kind was shewn to have taken place 20 years before this action."

In *Hollins* v. *Verney* (1884), 13 Q.B.D. 304 at p. 315, Lindley L. J. said: "It is sufficient for the present case to observe that the statute expressly requires actual enjoyment as of right for the full period of twenty years before action. No user can be sufficient which does not raise a reasonable inference of such a continuous enjoyment. Morever, as the enjoyment which is pointed out by the statute is an enjoyment which is open as well as of right, it seems to follow that no actual user can be sufficient to satisfy the statute, unless during the whole of the statutory term (whether acts of user be proved in each year or not) the user is enough at any rate to carry to the mind of a reasonable person who is in possession of the servient tenement, the fact that a continuous right to enjoyment is being asserted, and ought to be resisted if such right is not recognized, and if resistance to it is intended."

In judgments of Middleton J. at the trial, and Clute J. in the Court of Appeal in *Watson* v. *Jackson* (1914), 30 O.L.R. 517, and on appeal, 19 D.L.R. 733, 31 O.L.R. 481, the defence of prescription is comprehensively discussed, and for a veritable textbook on the whole subject see *Dalton* v. *Henry Angus & Co.* (1881), 6 App. Cas. 740.

The evidence in support of prescriptive right consists of proof that for over 40 years the defendant's predecessors in title and the defendant carried on foundry operations on the property in question. Two cupolas were in use for some time for the purpose of casting grey iron, the last of which was demolished in the year 1932, and the casting of grey iron was then discontinued. From 1932 to 1946 no cupolas were in use. For the casting of malleable iron a batch-type melting process was used. I think it unnecessary to go into the details of the different processes of casting grey iron and malleable iron, but the process of melting and the material used in the melt between 1932 and 1952 are of considerable importance in relation to the defence of prescription. Between 1932 and 1946 the total melt increased from 2,257 tons to 21,050 tons. [The learned Judge then pointed out that up to 1946 pig-iron and sprue (cuttings from new castings and defective new castings) were the substantial raw materials with only 10 to 15 per cent. of scrap iron, but from 1946 on when the present cupola was built and the melting process was changed from an air furnace to the cupola, a substantial change occurred by increased use of scrap iron proportionately to pig iron. On the evidence, increased use of scrap iron would increase the amount of iron oxide and the amount of iron particles that would be emitted into the air. This was because in proportion to weight the exposed surface of scrap iron was much greater than that of pig iron, and a greater amount of oxide forms on scrap iron in proportion to weight than on pig iron. All iron oxide is driven off through the stack. He then went on to describe the methods of operation of the air furnace and of the cupula, pointing out that the former was connected with a stack 125 feet high while the latter had a stack that was 54 feet 8 inches high. Prior to 1946, the charge was composed mostly of pig iron with some cast iron. In the cupola operation the charge consisted of 10 per cent. pig iron, 40 per cent. steel scrap iron and 50 per cent. sprue, with coke and lime. The learned Judge then continued as follows:]

Section 37 of the *Limitations Act* provides: "In the cases mentioned in and provided for by this Act, of claims to ways, water-courses or other easements, no presumption shall be allowed or made in favour or support of any claim upon proof of the exercise or enjoyment of the right or matter claimed for any less period of time or number of years than for such period or number mentioned in this Act as is applicable to the case and to the nature of the claim."

Having regard to the fact that the number of tons melted has increased almost ten times since the year 1933, and that the amount of case-metal, malleable and steel scrap consumed has increased 566 times, that any particles of iron oxide or steel that might have been driven from the charge passed through flues of a different character and the emissions from the stack were dispersed into the air at a height of 125 ft., and the method of charging the cupola is entirely different from the method of charging the air furnaces in use prior to 1946, I think the evidence, rather than affording satisfactory proof that the nuisance giving rise to this action has existed for the past 20 years, establishes that it is highly unlikely that emissions of the character and to the extent shown to be now deposited on the plaintiffs' lands were throughout that time being so deposited.

It may be that injurious matter of another character was escaping from other parts of the foundry to some greater degree in previous years than it now is. The methods of dust control which have been installed did not previously exist; but because the defendant may in previous years have exercised a right not now the subject of complaint does not give it the easement now claimed over the plaintiffs' lands.

Even if on any view of the evidence it could be considered that iron oxide and iron particles were being emitted from the defendant's plant for a period of 20 years next preceding the issue of the writ in this action, to the same extent and in the same manner as they are now being emitted, I think the defence of prescriptive right would still fail. In order to obtain a prescriptive right, the enjoyment of the right must not be secret and the servient owner must have either actual or constructive knowledge of it.

The evidence clearly shows that neither the plaintiffs nor the defendant's officers had any knowledge that any injurious particles were being deposited on the plaintiffs' lands as emissions from the defendant's plant until late in the autumn of 1951. *Sturges* v. *Bridgman*, 11 Ch. D. 852, has always been recognized as the leading authority for the proposition stated therein at p. 863: "The law governing the acquisition of easements by user stands thus: Consent or acquiescence of the owner of the servient tenement lies at the root of prescription, and of the fiction of a lost grant, and hence the acts or user, which go to the proof of either the one or the other, must be, in the language of the civil law, *nec vi nec clam nec precario*; for a man cannot, as a general rule, be said to consent to or acquiesce in the acquisition by his neighbour of an easement through an enjoyment of which he has no knowledge, actual or constructive or which he contests and endeavours to interrupt, or which he temporarily licenses. It is a mere extension of the same notion, or rather it is a principle into which by strict analysis it may be resolved, to hold, that an enjoyment which a man cannot prevent raises no presumption of consent or acquiescence."

In that case a confectioner had for more than 20 years used a pestle and mortar in his back premises, which abutted on the garden of a physician, and the noise and vibration were not felt as a nuisance and were not complained of, but in 1873 the physician erected a consulting-room at the end of his garden, and then the noise and vibration became a nuisance to him. It was held that there being no right of action against the defendant until the plaintiff had built the consulting-room the time for prescription did not commence to run until the offensive trade became actionable.

The history of the plaintiffs' property, which I have outlined in detail, shows that for more than 20 years prior to the commencement of the action it was low-lying vacant land, formerly the site of a disused foundry. At that period there were only sixteen dwelling-houses on the assessment roll in the area of one hundred acres covered by registered Plan 148 of which the plaintiffs' land forms a part. Applying the principle followed in *Sturges* v. *Bridgman, supra*, and *Danforth Glebe Estates Ltd.* v. *Harris & Co.*, 16 O.W.N. 41, I do not think it can be said that the evidence would warrant me in finding that for the whole period of 20 years prior to 1952 the plantiffs or their predecessors in title could have maintained an action against the defendant for nuisance....

Judgment for plaintiff.

[A owned lana in 1861 on part of which there was a wharf and shipbuilding yard. The other part consisted of a dock of which the underground supports extended to the first part. On A's death, his devisees conveyed the first part in 1877 to plaintiffs with no express reservation of support. Defendants subsequently became owners of the dock, which had been conveyed by the devisees in 1886. In making excavations to improve their property plaintiffs came across the supports and an issue arose between the parties as to whether defendants were entitled to have the dock so supported. Result? See *Union Lighterage Co.* v. *London Graving Dock Co.*, [1902] 2 Ch. 557 (C.A.).]

In order to prevent acquisition of an easement of support of buildings, must the "servient" owner excavate on his own land regardless of any utility in such excavation? And what of the resulting damage to the building on the "dominant" land? See *Foster* v. *Woolworth Co. Ltd. and Galloway* (1930), 38 O.W.N. 448.

The problem arises because the Courts recognize prescriptive easements both where the user relied on is actionable and physically interruptible and where such user is either actionable or physically interruptible. Where the user is actionable only (as in the nuisance cases) there is no serious problem involved in holding the "servient" owner bound by an easement unless he asserts a right of action within the prescriptive period. Where the user is physically interruptible only, as in the right of support cases, it is harsh to require physical interruption with the consequent damage to adjoining property, where no purpose is served other than to prevent acquisition of a prescriptive easement. In *Webb* v. *Bird* (1863), 13 C.B.N.S. 841, 143 E.R. 332 (Ex. Ch.), aff'g 10 C.B.N.S. 268, 142 E.R. 455, where the question at issue concerned a prescriptive claim to have the free flow of air for the working of a windmill, Wightman J. for the Court said: "We think, in accordance with the judgment of the court of Common Pleas, and the judgment of the House of Lords in *Chasemore* v. *Richards*, 7 House of Lords Cases, 349, that the presumption of a grant from long-continued enjoyment only arises where the person against whom the right is claimed might have interrupted or prevented the exercise of the subject of the supposed grant. As was observed by Lord Wensleydale, it was going very far to say that a man must go to the expense of putting up a screen to window-lights, to prevent a right being gained by twenty years' enjoyment. But, in that case, the right claimed, which was the percolating of water underground, went far beyond the case of a window. In the present case, it would be practically so difficult, even if not absolutely impossible, to interfere with or prevent the exercise of the right claimed, subject, as it must be, to so much variation and uncertainty, as pointed out in the judgment below, that we think it clear that no presumption of a grant, or easement in the nature of a grant, can be raised from the non-interruption of the exercise of what is called a right by the person against whom it is claimed, as a non-interruption by one who might prevent or interrupt it." This suggests a rule that does not oblige a "servient" owner to interrupt at any cost or merely because it is possible. Yet in *Dalton* v. *Henry Angus & Co.* (1881), 6 App. Cas. 740, the House of Lords indicated that a "servient" owner takes the risk of a prescriptive easement of support of buildings if he does not physically interrupt. Lord Selborne L. C. dealt with this matter as follows: "The policy and purpose of the law on which both prescription and the presumptions which have supplied its place, when length of possession has been less than immemorial, rest, would be defeated, or rendered very insecure, if exceptions to it were admitted on such grounds as that a particular servitude (capable of a lawful origin) is negative rather than positive; or that the inchoate enjoyment of it before it has matured into a right is not an actionable wrong; or that resistance to or interruption of it may not be conveniently practicable. I assume, for the present purpose, that a man who places on his own land, where it adjoins that of his neighbour, a weight which increases its pressure upon his neighbour's land, is not thereby guilty of an actionable wrong. If this be so, the reason probably is, that the act is lawfully done upon his own land, and that the owner of the adjoining land suffers no actual or appreciable damage from the increased amount of pressure which it has to bear, except so far as the continuance of that pressure, if uninterrupted, may tend to ripen into a right, and so to enlarge the servitude to which this land was previously subject. But against this he has his own remedy, if he chooses to prevent and interrupt it. That power of resistance by interruption does and must in all such cases exist, otherwise no question like the present could arise. It is true that in some cases (of which the present is an example) a man acting with a reasonable regard to his own interest would never exercise it for the mere purpose of preventing his neighbour from enlarging or extending such a servitude. But, on the other hand, it would not be reasonably consistent with the policy of the law in favour of possessory titles, that they should depend, in each particular case, upon the greater or less facility or difficulty, convenience or inconvenience, of practically interrupting them. They can always be interrupted (and that without difficulty or inconvenience), when a man wishes, and finds it for his interest, to make such a use of his own land as will have that effect. So long as it does not suit his purpose or his interest to do this, the law which allows a servitude to be established or enlarged by long and open enjoyment, against one whose preponderating interest it has been to be passive during the whole time necessary for its acquisition, seems more reasonable, and more consistent with public convenience and natural equity, than one which would enable him, at any distance of time (whenever his views of his own interest may have undergone a change), to destroy the fruits of his neighbour's diligence, industry, and expenditure."

The right of support of buildings (by other buildings or by adjoining land) was held by Lord Selborne to be an easement within the English Prescription Act, 1832. Support of land only by adjoining land and subjacent support of land are not matters of easement but stand on a different footing: see *Bonomi* v. *Backhouse* (1859), El. Bl. & El. 646, 120 E.R. 652 (Ex. Ch.), aff'd (1861), 9 H.L.C. 503, 11 E.R. 825. There is a legally protected interest in support of land in its natural state, and interference (as by excavation on adjoining land) which results in injury (e.g. by subsidence) is actionable: see *Cleland* v. *Berberick* (1916), 36 O.L.R. 357, 29 D.L.R. 72 (App. Div.). While damage must be shown (see *Bremner* v. *Bleakley* (1923), 54 O.L.R. 233, [1924] 2 D.L.R. 202 (App. Div.)), *quaere* whether nominal damages at least should not be awarded where subsidence occurs as a result of another's excavations on his own land, even though no appreciable injury results: see *Boyd* v. *Toronto* (1911), 23 O.L.R. 421 (Div. Ct.); but cf. *Smith* v. *Thackerah* (1866), L.R. 1 C.P. 564. However, where damage is established to the land in its natural state (and not simply to buildings thereon and by reason only of the presence of buildings) recovery may be had for the damage resulting at the same time to buildings: see *Boyd* v. *Toronto, supra; Gordon Mackay & Co.* v. *North American Life Assur. Co.*, [1934] O.W.N. 101; but see, *contra, Joss* v. *Uhryniuk and Stelmach* (1957), 10 D.L.R. 2d 630, 22 W.W.R. (N.S.) 12 (Man.).

However, the interest in support of land in its natural state will not be protected if the excavation on the adjoining land results in subsidence not because of such excavation (vis-à-vis the subsiding land) but because of the weight of buildings on the subsiding land: see *Gillies* v. *Bortoluzzi and Benjamin Bros. Ltd.*, [1953] 1 D.L.R. 335, 6 W.W.R. (N.S.) 633, 60 Man. R. 397. Of course, if the excavation disturbs the vertical support of such buildings (i.e. it amounts to a trespass) the resulting damage is actionable: see *Achdus Free Loan Society* v. *Shatsky and Gus Arnaud Ltd.*, [1955] 3 D.L.R. 249, 14 W.W.R. (N.S.) 481 (Man.); *Joss* v. *Uhryniuk and Stelmach, supra*; see *Note*, (1953) 31 Can. Bar Rev. 85, 220-225.

The recognition of the reciprocal obligation of adjoining landowners to maintain support for their respective lands in their natural state (and, indeed, the recognition of the right of the surface owner to support from the owner of the underlying stratum) makes it all the more strange that protection should be given by prescription to support of a building which one owner erects near the boundary line of his land. Should the fact that he has built first entitle him to limit the adjoining owner's use of his land? See *Metropolitan Life Ins. Co.* v. *McQueen* [1924] 2 D.L.R. 942, [1924] 2 W.W.R. 981 (Alta.). And if not, should he not bear the risk of damage resulting from a reasonable use of the adjoining land? See 6-A *American Law of Property*, pp. 101 ff. If this be so, why should the adjoining owner be required to make this use of his land within a specified (prescriptive) period? Cf. *Backus* v. *Smith* (1880), 5 O.A.R. 341.

See, generally, *Salmond on Torts* (1961, 13th. ed.), pp. 220-224, and for a "tort" rather than a "property" approach see 4 *Restatement of Torts*, chap. 39.

[If one adjoining owner puts up a building and the other owner subsequently builds so as to engage the support of the former's building, is the former thereby prevented from altering his structure if the support has continued for the prescriptive period? Further, is the owner of the supported buildings entitled to insist on a right of support although he has made changes in his structure? See *Lloyds Bank Ltd.* v. *Dalton*, [1942] Ch. 466, [1942] 2 All E.R. 352.]

[A and B were adjoining owners and B excavated on his own land and built a retaining wall to prevent subsidence of A's land. Subsequently B sold his land to C and owing to decay of the retaining wall a subsidence of A's land occurred. Is there any liability on the part of B or C or both? Would your answer be any different if A's land enjoyed an easement of support? See *Foster* v. *Brown* (1920), 48 O.L.R. 1, 55 D.L.R. 143 (App. Div.).]

NOTE ON PARTY WALLS. While an easement of support may exist in respect of a wall built wholly on the land of one of two adjoining owners a different problem is presented where the wall straddles the boundary between such owners. The wall may have been so built under agreement between the adjoining owners or it may have been built by a common owner who has subsequently sold to two different persons. To the extent to which the wall rests on the respective parcels, ownership of the wall may be in severalty, with cross-easements of support, which is the prevailing rule in United States, or there may be ownership in common of the wall, subject to explicit agreement otherwise as to title. The English cases show a disposition to the "tenancy in common" construction, but no invariable rule can be postulated: see 2 *American Law of Property*, s. 9.21; 3 *Halsbury*, Laws of England (3rd ed. 1953), pp. 376 ff. The few reported cases from the common law provinces do not disclose any decided preference between the "severalty" view and the "tenancy in common" view: see *Alberta Loan & Investment Co.* v. *Johnson* (1913), 4 W.W.R. 995, 12 D.L.R. 292, 6 Alta. L.R. 212 (C.A.); *Lewis* v. *Allison*, (1899), 30 S.C.R. 173; *Woodrow* v. *Connor* (1922), 52 O.L.R. 631 (App. Div.).

Apart from questions of title, party wall agreements may involve covenants as to repair or as to payment for cost of construction and the like, raising issues of enforceability between remote parties on either a covenant or an easement basis: see *Clark*, Covenants and Interests Running with Land (1947, 2nd ed.), chap. 5.

KENNY v. MACKENZIE. Ontario Court of Appeal. 1885. 12 O.A.R. 346

Plaintiffs were purchasers from one Chapman who had entered into an agreement with defendant, the adjoining owner, to build a party wall on the dividing line between the two lots and equally on both. Chapman was to erect the wall and defendant agreed to pay half the cost of the front 40 feet of the wall at the time of its erection and to pay half of the cost of the remaining portion when he would require use of the wall. After the conveyance to plaintiffs, defendant erected a building on his land and made use of the party wall. Plaintiffs demanded payment pursuant to the agreement, and, on defendant's refusal, brought an action which was dismissed. Plaintiffs appealed.

HAGARTY C. J. O. (for the Court): I am of opinion that the learned Judge in the Court below was right in holding that the plaintiffs could not recover.

When they purchased from Chapman they might have bargained for the advantage of this contingent claim against defendant, and had it assigned to them as a chose in action; that is, if they had been aware of its existence.

Chapman and his personal representatives would have had the right to enforce the claim whenever the contingency happened.

The plaintiffs bought Chapman's lot. They find a party wall running from front to the rear, built equally on the two lots.

They and the defendant thus own this wall in severalty. It became a party wall built by agreement under seal between the then owners on good consideration, and neither they, nor any person in privity of estate with them, could I think, interfere with its existence as such party wall.

The defendant then uses that part of the wall resting on his own land, not intruding on the plaintiffs' land in any way.

I cannot see how it could be successfully contended that his covenant to pay Chapman and his assigns whenever he used it, was covenant so running with the land as to pass to the plaintiffs under their deed.

The user of the wall on defendant's own land was not anything done to, or on, or affecting the plaintiffs' lot; and I see nothing in the extended words of our statutory conveyance form to enlarge or change the nature of the right, estate, or interest conveyed, so as to pass such a claim as this to the purchaser.

The ordinary rule as stated in *Platt* on Covenants, 461, is that, "in order to make a covenant run with the land, whether the estate be granted for an estate of inheritance, or for a term of years, the performance or non-performance of it must affect the nature, quality, or value of the property conveyed independently of collateral circumstances, or must affect the mode of enjoying it".

... No case like this in its facts appears among the English cases.

The learned Judge cites the case from Indiana, of *Bloch* v. *Isham*, 6 Am. Law Reg. 8, and which refers to *Weld* v. *Nichols*, 17 Pick. 538, where Shaw C. J., takes the same view.

Mr. Aylesworth refers to *Burlock* v. *Peck*, 2 Duer 90, in which the New York Court differs from the Indiana decision.

Mr. Lash then refers to *Cole* v. *Hughes*, 54 N.Y. 444, (1873), a much later case, which supports the learned Judge's decision, and questions *Burlock* v. *Peck*.

In *Cole* v. *Hughes* there is an extract from *Washburn* on Real Property strongly supporting the decision. *Cole* v. *Hughes* is noticed in notes to *Spencer's Case*, 1 Sm. L.C. 179 (Ed. of 1885); *Joy* v. *Boston Savings Bank*, 115 Mass. 60, is to the same effect; also *Scott* v. *McMillan* (1879), 76 N.Y. 141.

There is a summary of cases in which the covenant is held not to run with the land in *Woodfall*, L. & T. 149 (Ed. 1877). No case is as to party walls, but the general subject is well illustrated by the authorities. At p. 575 it is stated according to *Matts* v. *Hawkins*, 5 Taunt. 20, that the proprietors are not tenants in common of a wall built half on the land of each. "In contemplation of law such wall constitutes two distinct walls, and had to be so described under the old system of pleading," citing *Murley* v. *McDermott*, 8 A. & E. 138.

I think the later American decisions are in favor of defendant's view, and in accordance (as I think) with the principles of law which we find in the English books.

There is neither privity of estate nor privity of contract between the plaintiffs and defendant, and I think the judgment below is right, and that the appeal must be dismissed, with costs.

Appeal dismissed.

[See *Aigler*, The Running with the Land of Agreements to Pay for a Portion of the Cost of Party-Walls, (1912) 10 Mich. L. Rev. 187.

C and M were adjoining lot owners, and M built a wall which extended 80 feet along the assumed boundary line but which in fact encroached to a depth of 4 feet on C's land. C and M used the wall as a party wall. Subsequently C continued the wall another 20 feet along the assumed boundary line but M did not use this part. Thereafter the mistake made by M was discovered and the parties (acting without solicitor's advice) purported to rectify the mistake by a conveyance of the 4 foot strip from C to M, so that the north side of this strip ran along the north side of the wall built by M. The conveyance also contained a reservation by C of the right to build into the wall to the depth of 80 feet, and stipulated that should M desire to build into the wall to the extent of the 20 foot continuation (built by C) he would have the privilege of doing so by paying one-half the value of the 20 foot section, and should either of the parties wish to carry the wall any higher, he could do so at his own expense (provided it was of the same thickness) and, further, if either wished to extend the wall the extra 12 feet to take it to the street line, they might do so either separately or jointly as might be agreed upon at the time. The conveyance containing these stipulations was registered. On C's death his executors conveyed his land to plaintiff "together with rights and privileges as to party wall contained in [the registered conveyance]". Some years later M conveyed to defendant who used the 20 foot section as a party wall but refused to pay for the "privilege". He also built a frame building along the remaining 12 foot open section. Plaintiff sued for trespass in respect of the use of the 20 foot section and sought a mandatory injunction for removal of the frame building. Does plaintiff have any enforceable easement against defendant? Is the latter under any obligation to pay half the cost of the 20 foot section? See *Roche* v. *Allan* (1911), 23 O.L.R. 300 (Div. Ct.), where the first question was answered in the affirmative and the second in the negative; but note the dissenting judgment of Boyd C. who distinguished *Kenny* v. *Mackenzie* on the ground that there "the defendant had paid half the value of the wall which he used to Chapman, who had built the wall, and the action was to recover it again, by the plaintiff, who had bought Chapman's lot, but had taken no assignment of his interest in the money claim which was properly regarded as not attaching to the land."]

[A and B, adjoining landowners, entered into a party wall agreement under which B was authorized to build a party wall of not less than 24 inches in thickness of which the centre line would be on the boundary line between the two lots. B built the wall on these terms to a height of 12 feet but in the subsequent 36 feet of its height he reduced the thickness progressively on his own side of the boundary so that near or at the top the wall was almost completely on A's land. The wall formed part of a building put up by B. When A discovered (some years later) what B had done, he sued for relief. What remedies were open to him? See *Gross* v. *Wright*, [1923] S.C.R. 214, [1923] 2 D.L.R. 171, [1923] 1 W.W.R. 882. Suppose that B had conveyed to C who was unaware of what B had done. Would A be entitled to any relief against C?]

(c) Scope

MALDEN FARMS LTD. v. NICHOLSON. Ontario Court of Appeal. [1956] O.R. 415, 3 D.L.R. 2d 236

Appeal from a judgment of Spence J., [1954] O.R. 740, [1955] 1 D.L.R. 339, enjoining excessive user of a right of way.

The judgment of the Court was delivered by AYLESWORTH J. A.: ... At the trial appellant raised the defence of laches and although that defence had not been pleaded, the learned trial Judge considered it but held against appellant. In this Court counsel conceded that there was insufficient evidence upon which, successfully, to raise this defence. Appellant's main argument attributes error to the learned trial Judge in unduly restricting appellant's rights under the express grant to his predecessors in title of a right-of-way over the lands in question. Respondent, on the contrary, moves to vary the judgment, complaining that it does not properly reflect the conclusions reached by Spence J. and expressed in his reasons in that the injunction as granted does not afford respondent all of the protection to which he has been found to be entitled.

The facts as to the prior respective titles of the parties are stated exhaustively by the learned trial Judge and are not in dispute. The lands in question lie along the edge of Lake Erie south of Provincial Highway 18, also known as the Lake Shore Road, in the Township of Malden in the County of Essex, and are a part of Lot 56 in the 5th Concession and Lot 57 in the 6th Concession and of a tract of land known as the Caldwell Grant.

In 1916 one Barron owned the easterly portion of these lands extending westerly from the lands of Lake Erie Country Club and the Lake Shore Road. The westerly portion of the lands in question was owned by Ledyard and Bulkley (respondent's predecessors in title) and was chiefly marsh lands, used and of much value for duck-hunting. The marsh cut across Barron's lands also, which to the north thereof were farm lands and which to the south thereof were in a state of nature with a wide sand beach extending to the lake. By conveyance dated January 26, 1916, and duly registered, Barron granted to Ledyard *et al.* "their heirs and assigns and their agents, servants and workmen, a free uninterrupted right-of-way, ingress and egress for persons, animals and vehicles through along and over" a 20 ft. strip of land on the easterly boundary of his lands from the Lake Shore Road towards the lake and then across the southern portion of his lands to the boundary of the grantees' lands. The grantor, for himself, his heirs and assigns, covenanted with the grantees, their heirs and assigns, to keep the way in proper repair and condition and to maintain fences on both sides of the way at his own expense and it was further agreed that the grantees "shall have the right to maintain a gate at each end of the said way with the privilege of having the said gates opened or locked, whichever they desire".

By conveyance dated March 10, 1917, and duly registered, Barron conveyed to Wallace and Marentette (appellant's predecessors in title) two parcels of land at the southerly portion thereof and abutting on either side of the east-west portion of the right-of-way previously granted to Ledyard *et al.*, "together with a right of way for the Grantees their heirs and assigns over and upon the lands shown on each of the plans hereto attached marked Ledyard, Bulkley and Chappus right of way". Forming part of this conveyance is a plan attached thereto which sets out the right-of-way granted to Ledyard *et al.* and the lands being conveyed to Wallace and Marentette; in the conveyance itself, each of the two parcels conveyed is described by metes and bounds commencing at points in the Ledyard *et al.* right-of-way limits and the prior grant of that right-of-way is referred to by registered instrument number.

By later conveyances the remaining lands of Barron, including the fee in his lands made subject to the rights-of-way mentioned and the Ledyard and Bulkley lands, became vested in respondent and the Wallace and Marentette lands similarly became vested in appellant and his father as joint tenants. In July 1953 the father conveyed his interest to appellant. The predecessor in title to appellant and his father, one Frank Dayus, had acquired Wallace and Marentette's lands in 1941, and shortly thereafter, by agreement with respondent, the east-west portion of the right-of-way was shifted northward approximately 300 ft., respondent, however, never relinquishing the fee in any portion of the way as originally delimited. On July 16, 1952, Dayus threw open his premises as a beach-resort and, by extensive advertising, attracted large numbers of patrons who flocked to the premises by automobile over the right-of-way. In that year the travelled portion of the right-of-way was widened to 18 ft., gravelled, calcimined and rolled to a full two-car width. Appellant and his father in their turn, and later appellant, continued to advertise the premises as "Holiday Beach" and, in addition, held them out as a trailer-park and camp-site. It is unnecessary to detail the extent of the user of the right-of-way resulting from the establishment and maintenance of "Holiday Beach". Suffice it to say that, in the picnic and camping season each year, cars and patrons by the hundreds travelled up and down the way, cars were parked on appellant's lands, and the picnickers and campers spread out not only over those lands, but over the respondent's lands comprising the original east-west portion of the way. In other words, the burden of the easement has been markedly increased.

The fee in the way is now burdened, not with a private right-of-way in favour of appellant, his heirs and assigns, as originally contemplated, but with a use of the way for appellant's commercial purposes by great numbers of the public who travel over respondent's lands much as though the same constituted a public highway or a busy toll-road. At the time appellant's easement was created it was subject to the prior "free uninterrupted right-of-way" in respondent's predecessors in title. The chronology and contrasting language of the two grants, together with the surrounding circumstances as referred to by the learned trial Judge, established very clearly, in my opinion, that appellant's present user is much beyond the extent of his legal right and ought to be restrained. Appellant's use of the way constitutes an unauthorized enlargement and alteration in the character, nature and extent of the easement.

In ascertaining the rights of the parties I have applied the principles enunciated in Gale on Easements, 12th ed., p. 324, and in the judgment pronounced by the Supreme Court of Canada in *Laurie* v. *Winch*, [1952] 4 D.L.R. 449, [1953] 1 S.C.R. 49. I quote from Gale on pp. 324-5: "According to the present state of the authorities, it appears that the grantee of a right of way is not entitled to increase the legitimate burden. But, on the other hand, the legal extent of his right may entitle him to increase the amount of inconvenience imposed upon the servient tenement—e.g., by placing on the dominant tenement new buildings or increasing the size of old buildings. And the legal extent of the right (in other words, the mode as distinct from the extent of user) must, it seems, be ascertained from the intention of the parties at the time when the right was created."

It is useful, also, to quote two passages from *Laurie* v. *Winch*. At p. 455 D.L.R., p. 56 S.C.R., Kellock J., delivering the judgment of the Court, said: "With respect to the nature and extent of the easement granted, it is to be observed that the grant is one of a right-of-way *simpliciter* with no express restriction as to use. Just as the circumstances existing at the time of the grant may be looked at for the purpose of ascertaining the intention of the parties as to the dominant tenement and as to the location and termini of the way, the circumstances may also be looked at for the purpose of construing the conveyance as to the nature and extent of the rights conveyed."

Later in his judgment Kellock J. adopts the statement of the same principle as expressed in the Court of Appeal in England:

"In *Todrick* v. *Western Nat'l Omnibus Co.*, [1934] Ch. 190 at p. 206, Farwell J. at the trial said: 'In considering whether a particular use of a right of this kind is a proper use or not, I am entitled to take into consideration the circumstances of the case, the situation of the parties and the situation of the land at the time when the grant was made: see *United Land Co.* v. *Great Eastern Ry. Co.*, L.R. 10 Ch. 586 at p. 590, per James L. J.; and in my judgment a grant for all purposes means for all purposes having regard to the considerations which I have already mentioned.'

"It was held by the Court of Appeal in *Todrick's* case, [1934] Ch. 561, that having regard to the width of the land over which the right-of-way there in question was granted, it was not within the intention of the parties to the grant that it should be used for heavy omnibus traffic.

"In *Robinson* v. *Bailey*, [1948] 2 All E.R. 791 at p. 795, Lord Greene M. R. referred to the language of Farwell J. in *Todrick's* case, *supra*, and said: 'While not in any way dissenting from that statement as a general proposition, I would like to give this word of caution, that it is a principle which must not be allowed to carry the court blindly. Obviously the question of the scope of the right of way expressed in a grant or reservation is *prima facie* a question of construction of the words used. If those words are susceptible of being cut down by some implication from surrounding circumstances, it being, to construe them properly, necessary to look at the surrounding circumstances, of course they would be cut down. *Todrick's* case is a very good example of the sort of application of the rule which Farwell J. was enunciating.'"

For these reasons I agree with the conclusion of the learned trial Judge that the appellant ought to be restrained from continuing to use the right-of-way as he has been using it. I think, however, that respondent is entitled to his injunction in somewhat broader terms than those contained in para. 2 of the judgment. In the first place, since the original east-west portion of the way is no longer used as such, the parties by consent having substituted therefore a way of equal width lying to the north thereof, respondent is entitled to an order restraining appellant from any use of the lands comprising that original east-west portion. Then as to the whole of the way as presently constituted, appellant, his servants and agents, ought to be restrained from using it as a means for members of the public to have access to or egress from appellant's lands while used as a public commercial bathing-beach, public picnic ground or trailer-camp, and from inviting members of the public so to use the way or any part thereof, and from otherwise using the way so as substantially to interfere with respondent's user thereof: see *Taff Vale R. Co.* v. *Canning*, [1909] 2 Ch. 48 at p. 58.

Appeal dismissed; judgment varied.

[Use of an easement of way to benefit other than the dominant land will be enjoined. The question whether the way is used for the convenience of the dominant tenement or for other land reached through the dominant tenement poses the issue in this line of cases: see *Friedman* v. *Murray*, [1953] 3 D.L.R. 313, [1953] O.W.N. 486, aff'g [1952] 3 D.L.R. 159, [1952] O.W.N. 295 (C.A.); *Howell* v. *King* (1674), 1 Mod. 190, 86 E.R. 821 (K.B.); *Williams* v. *James* (1867), L.R. 2 C.P. 577.]

[Comment c to s. 483, 5 *Restatement of Property* reads as follows: "The process of ascertainment of the extent of an easement created by conveyance differs markedly from the process of ascertainment of the extent of an easement created by prescription. In both cases the facts which evidence the creation of the easement must also evidence its extent. In the case of prescription, however, the creation is evidenced by a long course of use adverse to the owner of the servient tenement. From such use must be ascertained not only the creation of the easement but also its extent. In the case of easements created by conveyance, the creation is evidenced by the language and the circumstances of the conveyance. In them is to be found the meaning of the conveyance. From them is to be ascertained the extent of an easement created by it. Any use of the servient tenement which may have been made before or which may be made after the conveyance was made is relevant to the object of ascertaining the extent of the easement only in so far as it aids in ascertaining the meaning of the conveyance. To the extent to which such a use does aid in ascertaining the meaning of the conveyance it is one of the circumstances in the light of which the conveyance is to be construed."

A common vendor registered a plan of subdivision showing seven lots (numbered 1 to 7 from west to east) extending northerly from a river (which marked their south boundary) with a right of way extending across the northerly limits of the lots from the westerly boundary of lot 1 to the boundary between lots 6 and 7 where it joined a private road leading north to a public highway. The lots were sold to various purchasers under deeds which referred to the right of way on the plan (and, in some cases, to the private road) to and from the public highway. Subsequently the vendor conveyed to the owners of lots 1 and 2 land in that part of the right of way contiguous to those lots, and these owners put a building on that land with a fence along the easterly boundary of lot 2. The owner of lot 6 complained of obstruction of an alleged right to use the right of way as a westerly as well as an easterly way. Reliance was also placed on s. 84 (14) of the Registry Act, R.S.O. 1950, c. 336 which provides that "any public or private street, way, lane or alley... being the only access to a lot or lots laid down on a plan of survey and subdivision shall, for the purposes of this section, be deemed to be a street or highway". Result? See *Van Alstyne* v. *Ruck*, [1957] S.C.R. 142, 7 D.L.R. 2d 1, rev'g [1955] O.R. 738, [1955] 4 D.L.R. 41.

A change in the character of the dominant tenement, e.g. by the erection of a building thereon or extension of a building, may result in loss of right to assert an easement: see *Allen* v. *Gomme* (1840), 11 Ad. & E. 759, 113 E.R. 602 (K.B.); (right of way to open space lost where building erected in that space); *Pearsall and Pearsall* v. *Power Supermarkets Ltd.* (1957), 8 D.L.R. 2d 270 (Ont.) (right of way appurtenant to lot A lost where dominant owner purchased adjoining lot B and built store on both lots); *Bell* v. *Marsh*, [1951] 3 D.L.R. 486, [1951] O.W.N. 433 (C.A.) (prescriptive easement of way acquired in respect of farm not exercisable in respect of apartment building); *Wimbledon & Putney Commons Conservators* v. *Dixon* (1875), 1 Ch. D. 362 (C.A.) (similar decision on facts similar to those in *Bell* v. *Marsh*); but cf. *Lloyds Bank Ltd.* v. *Dalton*, [1942] Ch. 466, [1942] 2 All E.R. 352 (easement of support of building not affected by change in internal arrangement of dominant tenement, as by substitution of water closets for earth closets, where no substantially greater weight imposed on servient building); *White* v. *Grand Hotel Eastbourne Ltd.*, [1913] 1 Ch. 113, 84 L.J.Ch. 938 (C.A.) (right of way granted for general purposes when dominant tenement had dwelling house on it held exercisable although house replaced by hotel).

Similarly, enjoyment of an easement may be affected by a change in the mode of user, subject, however, to construction of the terms of the grant in the case of an easement so created: see *Golisky* v. *Romanuik*, [1951] 2 D.L.R. 475, [1951] O.W.N. 401 (C.A.), (right of way granted "for the purpose of a driveway" not exercisable to enable picnic parties to be held on dominant tenement); *Pickard* v. *Kernick*, 63 O.L.R. 225, [1929] 1 D.L.R. 493 (App. Div.) (prescriptive easement of way acquired when horse-drawn vehicles in vogue held exercisable for motor cars); but cf. *Todrick* v. *Western National Omnibus Co. Ltd.*, [1934] Ch. 190, 103 L.J. Ch. 57, aff'd [1934] Ch. 561, 103 L.J.Ch. 224 (reservation of right of way, while construed as grant for all purposes within reasonable contemplation of parties, held in particular circumstances not exercisable through use of motorbuses); and see *Robinson* v. *Bailey*, [1948] 2 All E.R. 791 (C.A.) (grant of right of way held exercisable for business purposes although dominant land had been part of residential estate).

What is the effect of a severance of the dominant tenement upon an easement? See *Golisky* v. *Romanuik* [1951] 2 D.L.R. 475, [1951] O.W.N. 401 (C.A.); *Laurie* v. *Winch*, [1953] 1 S.C.R. 49, [1952] 4 D.L.R. 449; 5 *Restatement of Property*, s. 488.]

[Ordinarily, existence of an easement does not, save to the extent necessary to give effect to it, limit a servient owner's use of his land: see *Devaney* v. *McNab* (1921), 51 O.L.R. 106, 69 D.L.R. 231 (App. Div.). Subject to the terms of the grant or to the limits of the prescriptive right, as the case may be, the class of users may include licensees of the dominant owner no less than licensees of the servient owner; and it is not a tenable objection to an easement that its exercise by the dominant owner benefits other persons or other landowners: see *Simpson* v. *Godmanchester Corp.*, [1897] A.C. 696.

Subject again to the terms of the grant or other agreement on the matter, the duty to repair the servient tenement in reference to the easement rests on the dominant owner who may enter the servient land for that purpose: see *Macpherson* v. *London Passenger Transport Board* (1946), 175 L.T. 279 (K.B.); cf. *Campbell, Wilson & Horne Co.* v. *Great West Saddlery Co.* [1921] 2 W.W.R. 63, 59 D.L.R. 322, 16 Alta. L.R. 465 (C.A.). It is, of of course, open to the servient owner to make the repairs, if he so wishes, or to take any other steps, as owner, towards the upkeep of his land, so long as he does not interfere with or disturb (apart from temporary inconvenience) the easement right: see *Kain* v. *Norfolk and Baker (Hauliers) Ltd.*, [1949] Ch. 163, [1949] 1 All E.R. 176 (servient owner entitled to clean pond from which dominant owner entitled to draw water but breach of retaining wall of pond held actionable).

A dominant owner is entitled to protect his easement against disturbance by third persons as well as by the servient owner: see *Canada Trust Co.* v. *Strathroy*, [1955] O.W.N. 840, aff'd [1956] O.W.N. 474 (C.A.); *Northern Agency Ltd.* v. *Army & Navy Department Store Ltd.*, [1939] 1 D.L.R. 44, [1939] 1 W.W.R. 21 (Alta. C.A.); *Industrial Molasses Corp.* v. *H. Corby Distillery Ltd. and Empire-Hanna Coal Co.*, [1952] O.R. 50. However, the grantee of an easement may himself be enjoined at the suit of the servient owner where he obstructs the latter in his equal right to use the servient tenement: see *Bridgman* v. *Loblaw Groceterias Co.* (1929), 35 O.W.N. 353, aff'd 36 O.W.N. 214 (C.A.) (right of way not a right to tarry, as by prolonged parking of trucks by dominant owner in a "blind" lane).

Interference with an easement may be remedied by abatement or by suing in nuisance but trespass does not lie.]

(d) Termination

Easements may be created for periods of duration similar to those obtaining in the case of estates. Whatever may have been the true view at common law of the requirement of words of limitation to create an easement in fee (see *Sweet*, The True Nature of an Easement, (1908) 24 Law. Q. Rev. 259; 2 *American Law of Property*, ss. 8.22, 8. 23), modern legislation dispensing with obligatory use of the technical term "heirs" in the creation of estates in fee has destroyed any rational basis for subjecting easements to rules no longer applicable to estates. So far as there is any guide in the Canadian case law to determination of the duration of an easement, where there is no express specification, it is that set out in *Craig* v. *Craig* (1878), 2 O.A.R. 583, rev'g 24 Gr. 573, where the Court, in refusing to find that an agreement for an easement of way was for such way in perpetuity, declared (at p. 592) that "the nature and character of the easement, the purposes which it is intended to serve, the relations of the parties to each other, and other circumstances, may require to be taken into account"; see also *Smith* v. *Curry*, [1918] 2 W.W.R. 848, 42 D.L.R. 225, 29 Man. R. 97 (C.A.).

Apart from termination by expiry of the period of its duration (which in some cases may be reflected in cessation of the purpose for which it was established), an easement will be extinguished where the dominant and servient tenements "both belong absolutely to the same owner who has in the exercise of his own unrestricted right of enjoyment, the power of using both as he thinks fit" (per Strong J. in *Attrill* v. *Platt* (1884), 10 S.C.R. 425, at p. 463); *Brightman* v. *Hazel* (1920), 54 N.S.R. 81 (C.A.). However, unity of ownership alone may not result in an extinction: see *Richardson* v. *Graham*, [1908] 1 K.B. 39 (C.A.) (dominant tenement leased to plaintiff and subsequently conveyed to owner of servient tenement; tenant entitled to assert easement for duration of lease). Similarly, unity of possession alone may not extinguish an easement but will suspend it: see *Re Cockburn* (1896), 27 O.R. 450 (Div. Ct.) (owner of servient tenement becoming tenant of dominant tenement); see also *McLean* v. *Davis* (1865), 11 N.B.R. 255 (C.A.).

Extinction may also occur under statute (see *Abell* v. *York* (1920), 61 S.C.R. 345, 57 D.L.R. 81) or by release or by abandonment (referred to in some cases as implied release): see *Liscombe* v. *Maughan*, 62 O.L.R. 328, [1928] 3 D.L.R. 397 (App. Div.). Mere non-user, it is clear, is not abandonment: see *Baker* v. *Harris*, 64 O.L.R. 513, [1930] 1 D.L.R. 354 (App. Div.). In *Cook* v. *Bath* (1868), L.R. 6 Eq. 177, a right of way over the servient tenement extended from the back door of a house on the dominant tenement and this door had been bricked in for 30 years. Four years before the action in this case it was re-opened and user was resumed, and thereafter the servient owner proceeded to erect buildings which would obstruct the right of way. In awarding an injunction to the dominant owner, the Court said (at p. 179) that "it is always a question of fact... from the surrounding circumstances whether the act amounts to an abandonment or was intended as such. If in this case the defendants had commenced building before this back door had been re-opened I should have been of opinion that the plaintiff had by allowing it so to remain closed led them into incurring expense, and therefore could not prevent their acting on the impression that he intended to abandon this right". *Moore* v. *Rawson* (1824), 3 B. & C. 332, 107 E.R. 756 (K.B.) was a case where the servient owner acted on the evidence of non-user before the dominant owner resumed use of the easement, and in consequence the easement was lost; see also *Bell* v. *Golding* (1896), 23 O.A.R. 485 (abandonment may be found in acquiescence by the dominant owner in obstruction of the easement by the servient owner). A different result was reached in *Pharand* v. *Jean Louis*, [1952] O.R. 665 (C.A.) where non-user for 21 years accompanied by actual obstruction of an easement of way by the servient owner was held to be without effect upon the easement when the parties were mistaken as to the location of the right of way from the time the servient owner erected his obstructing fence.

It is simpler to explain cases like *Cook* v. *Bath* and *Bell* v. *Golding*, *supra*, on principles of estoppel (see 5 *Restatement of Property* s. 505) rather than on any doctrine of abandonment or implied release: see *Note*, (1948) 36 Calif. L. Rev. 490. They are cases where acts were done by the servient owner on his land, as contrasted with abandonment through act and intention of the dominant owner with respect to his land. A remaining question of importance is whether a servient owner may invoke prescription (or adverse possession) in addition to estoppel, to extinguish an easement: see 5 *Restatement of Property*, s. 506. The difficulty faced here by the Courts in the common law provinces was that prescription legislation, copied from England, did not deal with extinction of easements by prescription but only with their acquisition in that manner: see *Currah* v. *Ray* (1909), 13 O.W.R. 652, aff'd 13 O.W.R. 1071 (Div. Ct.). There were suggestions in the case law, both English and Canadian, that just as 20 years' user was necessary to acquire an easement by prescription, so 20 years' non-user may be evidence of its extinction. This, however, was addressed to the doctrine of abandonment or implied release, and it was pointed out, quite properly, in *Baker* v. *Harris*, *supra*, that "there is no hard and fast rule that 20 years' non-user raises even a prima facie presumption of a release", and in *Bell* v. *Golding* it was said that a presumption of abandonment may be made after a shorter period of non-user than 20 years. Resort was, therefore, had to the general Statutes of Limitation which in their definition of "land" covered both "corporeal" and "incorporeal" hereditaments. In *Mykel* v. *Doyle* (1880), 45 U.C.Q.B. 65 (C.A.), however, a majority of the Court held that the Ontario Statute of Limitations, in its substantive provisions, did not encompass extinction of an easement by adverse possession but was referable to "corporeal" interests only. This view has been followed in later cases, particularly in deference to its long standing authority (see *Midanic* v. *Gross*, [1957] O.W.N. 35 (C.A.); *Ihde* v. *Starr* (1910), 21 O.L.R. 407, aff'g 19 O.L.R. 471 (C.A.)), but not without a doubt as to its correctness having been expressed not too many years after it was decided (see *Bell* v. *Golding* (1896), 23 O.A.R. 485, per Burton J. A. at p. 489; *Ihde* v. *Starr* (1909), 19 O.L.R. 471, per Meredith C. J., at p. 478).

5. PROFITS

BERKHEISER v. BERKHEISER AND GLAISTER. Supreme Court of Canada. [1957] S.C.R. 387, 7 D.L.R. 2d 721

Appeal from a judgment of the Saskatchewan Court of Appeal, [1955] 5 D.L.R. 183, 16 W.W.R. (N.S.) 459, aff'g a judgment of Graham J., 16 W.W.R. (N.S.) 172.

RAND J. (Cartwright J. concurring): The facts in this appeal are these. By will dated May 2, 1947, a testatrix devised to the appellant a quarter-section of land in Saskatchewan; under date of December 18, 1951, with an incorporated company, she entered into what is called a "lease" of all petroleum and natural gas "within, upon or under" the quarter-section for a term of 10 years "and so long thereafter as the leased substances or any of them are produced" from the land; on July 9, 1953, she died. The lease called for a down payment of $320; it provided, in the event of deferred operations, for an annual acreage rental of $160, for certain royalties related to the oil and gas as they were produced, and for other matters mentioned later. Following the death of the lessor a payment of rental was made to the executors which deferred drilling to December 18, 1954. Under a clause headed "Surrender", the lease was terminated by notice given after the death but before April 15, 1955, when these proceedings were launched. The respondents are the residuary beneficiaries under the will, and the substantial question raised is whether the interest of oil and gas is now vested in them or in the appellant.

In the Courts below the transaction was treated as an out-and-out sale or agreement of sale of minerals *in situ*, the sale of a corporeal hereditament; the title to the minerals in fee simple was thereby severed from the rest of the fee; this worked an ademption of the devise to the extent of the oil, gas and royalties, and on termination the title fell into the residue. Apart from any question of the effect of a "termination" by notice of an estate, legal or equitable, in fee simple, or any question of a determinable fee or a fee on condition, the controversy hinges on the validity of that interpretation of the lease and it becomes necessary to examine its terms.

The operative words in the premises are:

"The Lessor... doth hereby grant and lease... all the petroleum and natural gas... within, upon or under the lands... together with the exclusive right and privilege to explore, drill for, win, take, remove, store and dispose of, the leased substances and... to drill wells, lay pipe lines, and build and install such tanks, stations, structures and roadways as may be necessary...."

Provisos were stipulated, (a) in effect, that if the drilling of a well was not commenced within the second year (the first year having been carried over by the down payment) the lease should terminate unless the lessee should pay the rental which would defer the work for a further year, with like payments for like deferred periods thereafter; (b) that if, at any time within the 10-year period and prior to discovery, a dry well or wells should have been drilled, or if after the discovery, during that term, production should cease, the lease should terminate at the next anniversary date unless operations for further drilling had been commenced or the rental paid, in which event thereafter the rental proviso would continue in force; and (c) that if at any time after the 10-year period production had ceased but the lessee had begun further work, the lease should remain in force so long as the operations were prosecuted and, if successful, so long thereafter as production continued. In any case, the time of any cesser of drilling, working or production from any cause beyond the lessee's control should not be counted against it. Royalties were provided, (1) on crude oil, of $12^1/_2$ per cent. of the current market value at the point of measurement; (2) on natural gas, of $12^1/_2$ per cent. of the current value at the point of measurement, and on gas treated in a plant, that percentage of the residual gas therefrom marketed; (3) on plant products, related to the current market-price at the plant where produced on a basis, the details of which are not material. The lessor might, in lieu of the cash royalty, on notice, take one-eighth of the oil, for collecting which the lessee would provide free of cost tanks for not more than 10 days' accumulation. The lessee agreed to drill offset wells whenever and wherever they might be required by reason of production on lands laterally adjoining the quarter-section and not owned by the lessor.

The language of the provision for surrender reads:

"Notwithstanding anything herein contained, the Lessee may at any time or from time to time determine or surrender this Lease and the term hereby granted as to the whole or any part or parts of the leased substances and/or the said lands, upon giving the Lessor written notice to that effect, whereupon this Lease and the said term shall terminate as to the whole or any part or parts thereof so surrendered and the annual acreage rental shall be extinguished or proportionally reduced as the case may be, but the Lessee shall not be entitled to a refund of any such rent theretofore paid."

If within 90 days of notice of default given by the lessor for breach, non-observance or non-performance by the lessee of any covenant, proviso, condition, restriction or stipulation, the default was not remedied, the lease would thereupon terminate.

Whether petroleum and natural gas *in situ* are to be classed as corporeal hereditaments and sold as land has been the subject of a great deal of consideration by Courts, particularly in the United States, and the application of common law conceptions to substances of such character, whose utility was little appreciated before this century, has produced a wide variance of opinion; but for the reasons following, the determination of that question here becomes unnecessary.

A corporeal hereditament was looked upon at common law as property of a permanent and indestructible character. When land was spoken of there was in mind not only the substances of the soil but also the space in which the substances were contained. To the ownership of land applied the maxim *cujus est solum, ejus est usque ad coelum.* In this conception of space filled with substance there is, for the purposes of law, an indestructible base to which incorporeal rights can be related.

But as stated in Challis's Real Property, 3rd ed. 1911, at p. 54, the classification of minerals—and the illustration there given of coal indicates the kind of mineral in mind—as corporeal hereditaments, is, in the foregoing respect, an anomaly; the use of minerals has, as its primary object, their removal from the soil and to that extent, their destruction as part of it. A *fortiori* would that consideration operate in respect of the fugacious minerals we are dealing with.

What as a practical matter is sought by such a lessor is the undertaking of the lessee to explore for discovery and in the event of success to proceed with production to its exhaustion. Neither presence nor absence of the minerals was here known, and the initial task was to verify the existence or non-existence of the one or the other. The fugitive nature of each is now well known; a large pool of either, underlying many surface titles, may in large measure be drained off through wells sunk in one of them; tapping the reservoir against such abstraction may, then, become an urgent necessity of the owner.

In that situation the notion of ownership *in situ* is not the likely thing to be suggested to the mind of any person interested because primarily of the difficulty of the factual conception itself. The proprietary interest becomes real only when the substance is under control, when it has been piped, brought to the surface and stored. Any step or operation short of that mastery is still in the stage of capture. To the ordinary producer that course of action is compatible with the risk of discovering nothing, but an initial grant of a title to something that may prove to be non-existent can scarcely be said to be so.

The language of the lease confirms this. The word "grant" is no more significant to a fee title than to an easement or a *profit à prendre* or, apparently, under the land law of Saskatchewan, an irrevocable licence to take. Indeed it is more appropriate to incorporeal than it is to corporeal rights. At common law a grant of a freehold title was ineffectual unless accompanied by livery of seisin, and, in the case of a tenement, attornment. Livery in relation to mines involves difficulties and, in later conveyancing, a transfer of minerals of an open mine appears to have been limited in practice to a bargain and sale under the statute of uses, or a lease of the surface and a release of the minerals, or by a statutory deed: *Challis*, *op. cit.*, p. 58. An unopened mine has been referred to as an incorporeal hereditament, but that is considered by Challis to be an unsound view. The word "lease" in its ordinary meaning implies in relation to land the possession of an indestructible substance (although at common law the lessee for years held the seisin or possession for the freeholder). For oil or gas, livery would seem to be out of the question and for the reasons mentioned other modes of conveyance appropriate to a corporeal hereditament would not accord with the notion of ownership of those substances.

The idea suitable to the partial use of the surface of lands as a necessary means of seeking for and drawing off these fluid substances, apart from the influence by analogy of existing concepts related to different substances, is that of operations to reduce to possession something by its nature generally ready for flight, which, as embodying a property interest, is adequately symbolised by the general term incorporeal right. The word "grant", then, not being significant of title and the word "lease" not carrying with it the possession with which it is ordinarily associated, we look to the detailed description of the acts authorized for the true intendment of the instrument and doing that here I interpret it as either a *profit à prendre* or an irrevocable licence to search for and win the substances named.

This view is strengthened by the provision for payment of taxes. The lessor is to pay "all taxes, rates and assessments" levied directly or indirectly against her by reason of her interest in production or her ownership of mineral rights, as well as those assessed against the surface of the land. On the other hand, the lessee is to pay all taxes levied in respect of the undertaking and operations and of the lessee's interest in production. The effect of this is not modified by the stipulation that the lessee shall reimburse the lessor for seven-eighths of any taxes imposed on the latter by reason of being the registered owner of the leased substances. This treats the legal title to the substances as remaining in the lessor and the interest of the lessee as analogous to that of an ordinary lessee of land, that is, as having only an interest in relation to them.

Rights of this nature have long been recognized in coal and other minerals and profits. In *Muskett* v. *Hill et al.* (1839), 5 Bing. N.C. 694, 132 E.R. 1267, the instrument was construed to be a licence coupled with a grant and the interest of the assignee held to be assignable. Tindal C. J. quoted the following language from *Thomas* v. *Sorrell*, (1673), Vaugh. 330 at 351, 124 E.R. 1098 at 1109: "But a licence to hunt in a man's park, and carry away the deer kill'd to his own use; to cut down a tree in a man's ground, and to carry it away the next day after to his own use, are licences as to the acts of hunting and cutting down the tree; but as to the carrying away of the deer kill'd and tree cut down, they are grants."

In *Wilkinson* v. *Proud et al.* (1843) 11 M. & W. 33, 152 E.R. 704, the decision went on the distinction between such a right and title; in the language of Parke B.: "This is not a claim of a prescriptive right to take coal in the plaintiff's close, but a prescription for all the strata and seams of coal lying under it, that is, for a part of the soil itself, and not for the right to get the coal, which would be the subject of a grant."

In *Martyn* v. *Williams* (1857), 1 H. & N. 817, 156 E.R. 1430, a licence was granted to the defendant "to dig, work, and search for china clay, and to raise, get, and dispose of the same... for the term of 21 years". The grantee covenanted, among other things, that at the expiration of the term he or his assigns would deliver up the works to the grantor in good repair. The grantor assigned and an action was brought by the assignee against the grantee on the covenant. It was held that the grant created an incorporeal hereditament, the covenants relating to which under 32 Hen. VIII, c. 34, ran with the land. Martin B., in delivering the judgment, made observations which are of special interest here:

"These cases [*Doe* d. *Hanley* v. *Wood* (1819), 2 B. & Ald. 724, 106 E.R. 529, and *Muskett* v. *Hill et al., supra*] establish that it is an incorporeal hereditament, a property, and an estate capable of being inherited by the heir, and assigned to a purchaser, or otherwise conveyed away. It is in truth 'a tenement' within the definition of Lord Coke in the First Institute, 20 a., who says that the word 'tenement includeth not only corporate inheritances, but also all inheritances issuing out of them or concerning or annexed to, or exercisable within them, as rent, estovers, common, or other profits whatever, granted out of land.'... The statute in express terms therefore extends to incorporeal hereditaments and tenements, and is not confined merely to lands. If, therefore, there had been an estate in fee of the right or interest created by the indenture mentioned in the declaration, and the owner in fee of the right had demised it for twenty-one years, and there had been a covenant such as that secondly declared on, we should have been of opinion, that the assignee of the reversion could have sued upon it for a breach committed in his own time. But in the present case no estate in fee in the right to take the china clay has been created. The owners of the fee simple merely granted the right for a term of years, and after the expiration of this term, the plaintiff, who was then the owner of the land, was entitled to do all which the defendant was authorised and licensed by the indenture to do, not by virtue of the same estate which the defendant had, having reverted and continuing an existing estate, but by virtue of his ownership of and dominion over his own land; (for the owner of land exercises his right over it, not by virtue of any licences or liberties or easements, but by virtue of his ownership in which all interests of this kind merge: *Greathead* v. *Morley*, 3 M. & G. 139); and the question is, whether the conveyance or assignment of the land to the plaintiff, during the existence of the term in the incorporeal tenement, was an assignment of the reversion within the statute of 32 H. 8. We think that it was. There is in reality the relation of reversioner and ownership of particular estates between them; there is exactly the same privity of estate as exists between reversioner and tenant properly so called, and upon the determination of the term the entire interest in the land reverted to the plaintiff, as upon the expiration of an ordinary lease."

In *Hooper et al.* v. *Clark* (1867), L.R. 2 Q.B. 200, an exclusive right and licence to take and kill game on certain land with the use of a cottage was similarly treated; Blackburn J. at pp. 202-3 said: "The first question is, this being the demise of an incorporeal hereditament, do convenants which would run with a demise of land, run with it? *Martyn* v. *Williams* [*supra*] decides that they do."

To the like effect was the decision in *Lord Hastings* v. *North Eastern Railway Company* [1898] 2 Ch. 674, where a covenant to pay for the privilege of a way-leave on which to make and use a railway, based on a rate on the coal carried to a certain port, was held to run with the reversion.

In such cases the title to the substances as part of the land remains in the owner and upon it is imposed the incorporeal right which the termination of the lease, as in this case, extinguishes. As stated in Jarman on Wills, 8th ed. 1951, p. 939 (vol. 2), an immediate devise of land in fee to a person in esse, carries the rents and profits of the land from the death of the testator. The rents and royalties here are obviously profits and like rent from a leasehold, in the absence of a specific bequest of them, which, if an assignment of the lessor's interest in the lease, would require a grant of the minerals themselves, are embraced in the devise. It follows that both the right to the payment of $160 and the reversionary interest in the petroleum and gas enured to the appellant.

The interpretation given the instrument is not all affected by the judgment of this Court in *McColl-Frontenac Oil Company Limited* v. *Hamilton et al.* [1953] 1 S.C.R. 127, [1953] 1 D.L.R. 721. In the majority reasons written by Kellock J. at pp. 136-7, dealing with that question, he says: "Whether the proper construction of the instrument is that, with respect to minerals, it is a grant of the minerals as land, as in *Gowan's* case (1873) L.R. 2 Sc. & Div. 273, or a demise of the surface to which is super-added a profit à prendre, the result is, in my opinion, the same."

The finding that the agreement was a sale of property within the Act there being examined was satisfied by the transfer of title as the oil or gas was obtained in production; but that piecemeal sale and acquisition is the completion of the exercise of the right to win them, in contrast to the out-and-out conveyance of them in situ.

I would, therefore, allow the appeal, set aside the judgment below by declaring the petroleum and natural gas rights to be vested in the appellant and that the appellant is entitled to the sum of $160 received by the executors....

KELLOCK J. (Locke and Nolan JJ. concurring): It is quite competent for an owner of land so to convey mineral lying in or under the land that thereafter two separate estates in fee exist, the one in the mineral conveyed and the other in that which is retained. The respondents contend that this is the result of the instrument here in question....

In Armour on Real Property, 2nd ed. 1916, the following is stated on p. 47:

"... a grant of all the coal or other mineral in or upon certain land, is a grant of the land itself, and passes complete ownership in the mineral to the grantee."

But the learned author continues:

"But a grant of the right to enter, search for and dig coal, and carry away as much as may be dug, is a grant of an incorporeal right to enter and dig, and passes the property in such coal only as shall be dug."

As stated in 11 Halsbury, 2nd ed. 1933, p. 386, s. 678:

"A *profit à prendre* may be created for an estate in perpetuity analoguous to an estate in fee simple, or for any less period or interest such as a term of years...."

In the case at bar the Courts below have construed the instrument as a conveyance in fee....

While what is referred to as a "mining lease" commonly amounts to a "sale of land", so to characterize any given instrument does not necessarily equate it with either a grant in fee simple of the mineral in place or of a *profit à prendre*. For example, the grant in question in *Gowan* v. *Christie et al.*, was only for a term of 21 years. Nevertheless, the oft-quoted citation from the judgment of Lord Cairns, on pp. 283-4, was quite properly applicable to it. Lord Cairns was there differentiating a mineral from an agricultural lease in that the agricultural lessee, while entitled to "fruits", is not entitled to either a corporeal or an incorporeal interest in the lands.

The words of Lord Cairns were also cited in *Joggins Coal Company Limited* v. *The Minister of National Revenue* [1950] S.C.R. 470, [1950] 3 D.L.R. 1, [1950] C.T.C. 149, but the decision of the issue there arising did not require the Court to determine anything more with respect to the instrument before the Court than that the appellant had such an interest in the mineral that it was entitled to claim a share in depletion allowance as a "lessee" within the meaning of the *Income War Tax Act*.

The question which arose in *McColl-Frontenac Oil Company Limited* v. *Hamilton, et al.* [1953] 1 S.C.R. 127, [1953] 1 D.L.R. 721, was whether the instrument before the Court was "a contract for the sale of property" within the meaning of the Alberta *Dower Act*. Whether the agreement was one for the sale of the mineral in place or of a *profit à prendre* was immaterial. In either case the Court considered the language of the statute to apply.

In the case at bar it is necessary to decide whether the interest in the mineral created in favour of the grantee was of such a nature that the devise to the appellant was, *pro tanto*, adeemed. In my opinion, this is not so. The provisions of the instrument as analyzed above are, in my opinion, quite inconsistent with any conception of a grant in fee whether of the minerals in place or of a *profit à prendre*. In my opinion, the instrument is to be construed as a grant of a *profit à prendre* for an uncertain term which might be brought to an end upon the happening of any of the various contingencies for which it provides. It did not bring about that separation of the estate in the minerals from the estate in the land apart from the minerals which is the necessary basis for the operation of the doctrine of ademption....

Accordingly, upon the termination of the interest of the grantee under the lease here in question, the estate of the appellant in the lands was no longer subject to it. The doctrine of ademption does not apply. Equally the appellant is entitled to the amount paid for acreage rental by the lessee following the death of the testatrix....

Appeal allowed.

[In *Cherry* v. *Petch*, [1948] O.W.N. 378 Wells J. said:

"It has been said that a *profit à prendre* is a right to take something off the land of another person. It may be more fully defined as a right to enter on the land of another person and take some profit of the soil such as minerals, oil, stones, trees, turf, fish or game, for the use of the owner of the right. It is an incorporeal hereditament, and unlike an easement it is not necessarily appurtenant to a dominant tenement but may be held as a right in gross, and as such may be assigned and dealt with as a valuable interest according to the ordinary rules of property. It is in effect a grant of the ownership of such portions of the land as are conveyed.

"If this is so, there is no necessity for such a grant being for a definite term, as is necessary in the case of a lease....

"It therefore becomes necessary to see on what principles the deed of 1926 should be construed. Documents such as this are very similar to grants of coal and other minerals in Great Britain, and these rights have been discussed in many cases. In the decision of the Court of Appeal in *Duke of Sutherland* v. *Heathcote*, [1892] 1 Ch. 475, Lindley L. J., delivering the judgment of the Court, said at pp. 484-5: 'A *profit à prendre* is a right to take something off another person's land; such a right does not prevent the owner from taking the same sort of thing from off his own land; the first right may limit, but does not exclude, the second. An exclusive right to all the profit of a particular kind can, no doubt, be granted; but such a right cannot be inferred from language which is not clear and explicit.'

"There follows a discussion of a number of old cases which, in my opinion, bear out this statement.

"In this case, the grant is one of 'all the gas, petroleum and other petroliferous products in and under the following described premises'. In my view the word 'all' makes it clear that what was given to the grantees in the deed of August 1926 was precisely what it says, that is, 'all the gas, petroleum and other petroliferous products in and under' the lands. Such a grant, however, while it was a grant of these products as they existed in and under the soil of the land in question would not, unless it strictly said so, interfere with the normal use of the land by the owners of the fee on which the *profit à prendre* was granted and was a burden. I am therefore constrained to look at the other provisions of the deed, and I think I must construe them strictly. [After a discussion of other terms in the grant, his Lordship concluded as follows:]

"While the grant is an exclusive one of all the gas, petroleum and other petroliferous products in and under the land, it is not a grant of anything else, and therefore, in my view, the owners of the fee in the land are entitled to build on it, to dig wells for water in it, and to use the land in any way which to them may seem fit. They cannot, however, preclude the plaintiff from exercising his rights, but if he exercises them in such a way as to damage crops, orchards, buildings and fences on the property then, on the request of the party of the first part and his successors in title, who are the defendants in this action, he (Cherry) is obliged to pay any damages caused by reason of his operations and through his fault."

See, for a general treatment, *Hahner*, An Analysis of Profits A Prendre, (1946) 25 Ore. L. Rev. 217.]

[Heirs of an intestate who left them a farm conveyed their respective interests in a certain portion of the farm to a power company, the deed in each case containing the following clause: "Excepting and reserving... unto the said grantors, their heirs and assigns, the right to cultivate any part of the above described lands not damaged by the flowage due to the development at Grand Falls". The municipality purported to sell the farm (including the portion sold to the power company) for taxes assessed against the estate. One M purchased the property at the tax sale and later sold it to defendant. Plaintiff, one of the heirs, had accepted a small sum representing his share of the surplus over and above the taxes and expenses of the sale. On being excluded from use of the land sold to the power company, he sued defendant for damages. What was the nature of his interest, and was it enforceable against defendant? See *Akerley* v. *Bellefleur* (1937), 12 M.P.R. 299 (N.B.C.A.).

A 21 year lease of a house and land and of fishing rights, made between V as "owner" and T as "tenant", provided that "the owner shall retain for her own use a rod in the said fishing...." The fishing rights were the most valuable of the interests covered by the lease and this was reflected in the rent. Elaborate terms were laid down for T's exercise of the right of fishing. On V's death during the term of the lease, a question arose whether V obtained a regrant of a profit, exercisable by her or her successors during the term of the lease or alienable by her in her lifetime, or whether she had merely a personal contractual right. *Held*, the right conferred was personal and not alienable and ended with V's death. See *Re Vicker's Lease, Pocock* v. *Vickers*, [1947] Ch. 420, [1947] 1 All E.R. 707 (C.A.).

Defendants who admittedly had a right to fish, as members of the public, in certain waters, claimed a prescriptive right of putting boats and nets on the shore of plaintiff's island and using the property as a fishing station. What is the nature of the right claimed? See *Pitman* v. *Nickerson* (1891), 40 N.S.R. 20.]

[Land granted by the Crown in 1831 to plaintiff's predecessor in title had certain mineral springs on it, and in 1837 the property was laid out in streets and lots. The plan of subdivision showed a square on which the mineral springs were located, and this square and some of the land leading thereto were ultimately developed as a hotel property. From the time of the Crown grant to 1877, members of the public were permitted to drink the waters of the spring without charge or hindrance but a charge of 5 cents a gallon was made for water taken away. In 1877 plaintiff began to charge for drinking at the springs, and defendant invited an action of trespass by breaking down a gate and drinking from the springs without paying. He pleaded that he had a right by custom to use the springs, a right which had been exercised for more than 40 years. *Held*, defendant's claim could not be upheld. Apart from the fact that there was no time immemorial on which to found it, a custom claimed on behalf of the whole world was bad. Moreover, a right to take water from a well or spring is not claimable as a profit but only as an easement. While rights in the nature of easements may be acquired by custom by fluctuating bodies of persons (but profits may not be so acquired), the only basis for acquiring the right claimed here was statutory prescription and it had been held in *Shuttleworth* v. *Le Fleming* (1865), 19 C.B.N.S. 687, 144 E.R. 956, that the Prescription Act, 1832 did not apply to interests in gross, even if they be profits: see *Grand Hotel Co.* v. *Cross* (1879), 44 U.C.Q.B. 153 (C.A.); and see also *Rice Lake Fur Co. Ltd.* v. *McAllister*, 56 O.L.R. 440, [1925] 2 D.L.R. 506 (App. Div.) (right to trap muskrats on another's land, as a right in gross, cannot be acquired by prescription). It appears, however, that a profit in gross could be acquired by common law prescription: see *Goodman* v. *Saltash* (1882), 7 App. Cas. 633.

If the right to take water from a spring or pond is assertable only as an easement, is the same true when the water solidifies into ice, and the right asserted is to cut and take ice? See *Note*, (1954) 53 Mich. L. Rev. 306.]

BRATT v. TOWNSHIP OF MALDEN. Ontario High Court. 1927. 60 O.L.R. 102, [1927] 1 D.L.R. 1116

Action to determine validity and duration of an agreement between plaintiffs' predecessor in title and defendant township.

WRIGHT J.:... The material parts of the agreement are as follows:

"The said party of the first part doth grant and sell unto the said parties of the second part all the sand and gravel and right of way thereto as hereinafter described upon his lot known as the middle part of lot No. 59 in the 7th concession in the said township of Malden described as follows... and a right of ingress, egress and regress *to all this gravel and sand until it is all gone* as now staked out commencing at the Lake road... The dirt or earth may be taken from either side of the said lot to grade up the roadway and for all bridging purposes in grading up the said road to said sand and gravel pit but not to interfere with any tile drainage existing at the time of grading... This agreement is to be in full force and virtue until ."

This artless document has had the usual result of bringing about this litigation.

At the time the agreement was entered into, there was some sand and gravel on the beach and from time to time accretions to this deposit were made by the action of the waters of Lake Erie, so that since the date of the agreement a very large quantity of sand and gravel has been so deposited, and the defendant corporation has used the same for the purpose of road repair and construction. It apparently was in the contemplation of the parties at the time that there would be very considerable accretions to the deposit of sand and gravel from the causes already mentioned, and it was never the intention of the parties that the amount of sand and gravel covered by the agreement should be restricted to the quantities that were deposited on this land at the date of the agreement.

As already stated, the defendant corporation has removed large quantities of this sand and gravel and now claims a perpetual right to remove the same.

For the plaintiffs it is contended: (1) that the grant is void for uncertainty and as being for an indefinite period; (2) that it was clearly in contemplation of all parties to the agreement that there should be a limited time for the removal of the sand; (3) that, in the absence of a provision as to time, the rights of the defendant corporation should be exercised in a reasonable time, and that such reasonable time has elapsed.

It appears clear that this grant is of a *profit à prendre*, as distinguished from an easement, and as such would amount to an interest in land.

Dealing first with the contention of the defendant that the grant is perpetual, I accept the view of the law stated by the late Chief Justice Thomas Moss in *Craig* v. *Craig* (1878), 2 A.R. 583, at p. 592, that in an instrument relating to or purporting to grant an easement the absence of a provision as to time does not necessarily mean that the grant is in perpetuity, and that in determining the duration of the grant the surrounding circumstances and the relations of the parties may be taken into account.

In the present case the wording of the document would appear to shew that it was not intended to be perpetual. The phrase "until it is all gone" would lead to that conclusion. Also the uncompleted clause, "this agreement to be in full force and virtue until ." favours a like inference. It would, in my view, be unreasonable to assume that the grantor ever intended to impose a burden on the owner of the lands for all time. Had this been the intention of the parties the agreement would most likely have taken the form of a deed of the parcel in question in fee simple.

Viewing all the circumstances, I am of the opinion that the grant was not intended to be in perpetuity, but only for a limited period, which by accident or mistake was omitted to be stated in the deed.

In arriving at this conclusion I am not overlooking the contention of counsel for the defendant to the effect that it was in contemplation of the parties that there would be from time to time accretions of sand and gravel, and that the agreement was made in contemplation of such a condition, and therefore ought to continue so long as sand and gravel were washed or deposited upon the lands by the action of the waters of Lake Erie.

The question as to the duration of the grant or agreement, if it is not a perpetual grant, now remains to be determined. The principle to be applied in deciding this is, I think, that enunciated by Mr. Justice Bruce in *Nosotti* v. *Auerbach* (1898), 79 L.T.R. 413, at p. 414:

"When all the terms of an agreement are stated except the term as to the time when it is to be carried out and there is no expressed stipulation as to time, then in the case of agreements relating to the sale of real property as well as in the case of agreements relating to the sale of personal property, it is an implied term that the agreement is to be performed within a reasonable time."

The principle of this decision was applied and approved in our own Courts in *Dolan* v. *Baker* (1905), 10 O.L.R. 259, and commends itself to me as the proper rule to be applied in the present case. The subject-matter in *Dolan* v. *Baker* was trees and timber which were then on the lands, and which might be increased by natural growth, so that it would not be exactly parallel to the facts in the present case, where it was contemplated that in the future there would be accretions as distinguished from natural growth. Notwithstanding this difference, I think the same principle should be applied.

This naturally leads to the question as to what in the present case was a reasonable time for the operation of the agreement. Almost 17 years had elapsed from the date of the agreement, the 3rd July, 1909, to the issue of the writ, the 15th April, 1926, and in my view this period was more than a reasonable time for the defendant corporation to exercise its rights.

In view of these findings, it follows that the rights of the defendant corporation have been determined, and that the corporation is no longer entitled to remove sand or gravel or make any entry upon the lands....

Judgment for plaintiffs.

[An appeal by defendant township was dismissed for the reasons assigned by the trial Judge: see 60 O.L.R. at p. 106, [1927] 1 D.L.R. at p. 1119.

In *Post* v. *Bean*, [1947] 3 D.L.R. 513 (Can.), aff'g 20 M.P.R. 168 (N.B.C.A.), P entered into an agreement with M in 1928 for the purchase of fishing rights in a river for 5 years, and paid a deposit on the purchase price. P went into "possession" at once, but in the meantime a paper company began to buy up rights along the river for a proposed development and sought to acquire M's lands. On being advised by M of the arrangement with P, the company entered into an agreement with P to give him the fishing rights until the proposed development took place. In fact, P enjoyed fishing rights from 1928 to 1944 without further payments. The development contemplated never took place and in 1944 the company leased the fishing rights to another. *Held*, on appeal, P had no enforceable claim. Kellock J. said (at p. 516): "The right claimed by the appellants is a *profit à prendre*: *Wickham* v. *Hawker* (1840), 7 M. & W. 63 at p. 79, 151 E.R. 679; *Fitzgerald* v. *Firbank*, [1897] 2 Ch. 96. While at law such a right may be granted by deed only, the position in equity is that where the grantees have entered into possession, specific performance of the agreement will be granted: *Frogley* v. *Lovelace* (1859), Johns. 333, 70 E.R. 450. However, while a *profit à prendre* is a good subject of demise, it may be demised only subject to the rules of law applicable to demises of real property. Accordingly, the duration being uncertain, the case is, in my opinion, completely governed by the decision in *Lace* v. *Chandler*, [1944] 1 All E.R. 305."

Land was let to defendant by an owner who reserved to himself all game, rabbits, fowl and fish with liberty to preserve, hunt, kill and carry the same away, and defendant agreed not to shoot or sport on the land. The owner's (landlord's) rights in the land passed to a company which (holding a *profit à prendre* in the land by regrant—this being the effect of the reservation) sold the rabbiting rights to plaintiff under an oral agreement. The sum agreed upon was acknowledged by a receipt, and although it was contended that the receipt was false and was designed to defraud the revenue it was ultimately held that plaintiff was not implicated in any fraud. He began to exercise his rights under the oral agreement but defendant interfered by kicking over snares laid by plaintiff and by ordering him off the land. Later the company and plaintiff reduced their oral agreement to writing. *Held*, on appeal, plaintiff was entitled to damages. On the evidence, the setting of rabbit snares was a reasonable exercise of the rabbiting rights even though sheep were pastured in the field. While plaintiff had no legal right to a profit at the time of the oral agreement, he had a clear equitable title because he had entered into possession of the profit by exercising his rights under the agreement. His acts of setting snares, taking rabbits and paying helpers were exclusively referable to the oral agreement so as to entitle him to specific performance of a contract for a profit. Accordingly he could properly sue in trespass: see *Mason* v. *Clarke*, [1955] A.C. 778, [1955] 1 All E.R. 914, rev'g [1954] 1 Q.B. 460, [1954] 1 All E.R. 189 (C.A.). See also *James Jones & Sons Ltd.* v. *Tankerville*, [1909] 2 Ch. 440 (injunction granted against interference with contract for purchase of timber to be cut on defendant's land).]

[Profits which are appurtenant to a dominant tenement are exercisable only for the benefit thereof, as in the case of easements. In *Clayton* v. *Corby* (1843), 5 Q.B. 415, 114 E.R. 1306, defendant owner of a brick kiln asserted a prescriptive right (based on exercise by him and his predecessors for more than 30 years before action) to dig and take away as much clay from plaintiff's land as was at any time required by him for the purpose of making bricks in his kiln, in every year and at all times of the year. *Held*, defendant's contention was bad because of the vagueness and uncertainty of the right claimed. Do you agree? See also *Drury* v. *Kent* (1603), Cro. Jac. 14, 79 E.R. 13 (K.B.); *Harris* v. *Chesterfield*, [1911] A.C. 623.]

RE DAWSON AND BELL. Ontario Court of Appeal. [1945] O.R. 825, [1946] 1 D.L.R. 327

Appeal from a judgment of Mackay J. ordering that payments due under an oil and gas "lease" be divided between the owners of the "reversionary" estate in proportion to their respective interests. In 1913 one J. F. Dawson, now deceased, entered into an agreement and lease for 10 years "and as much longer as oil and gas shall be found in paying quantities on the premises", granting to an oil and gas company the exclusive right of drilling and operating for petroleum oil and gas in and on a 125 acre tract of land. Certain compensation was provided under the agreement. Two producing gas wells were brought in on part of the tract within the 10 year period; and this part, consisting of 75 acres, subsequently came into the hands of D. L. Dawson after the death of the original grantor. No producing wells were drilled on the remaining 50 acres which came into the hands of Helen Lucille Bell, and the question that arose was whether she was entitled to share in the compensation.

McRUER J. A.:... In determining the rights of the parties it is a first essential to consider the legal rights conferred on the lessee under the lease, and what rights attached to the land owned by the deceased at his death, for which compensation was to be paid to him, his heirs, executors and assigns.

The estate granted under the lease was an exclusive and continuing right extending to the whole of the demised farm, to enter upon the land and occupy it for the purpose of "drilling and operation for Petroleum Oil and Gas", for a period of ten years and for such further term as oil and gas might be produced thereon. There is in addition a right to use water for necessary purposes which may be taken from any portion of the lands, except the wells on the lands, and an exclusive right-of-way to lay pipes and move machinery on any portion of the land. In case the lessee recovers oil or gas it becomes the property of the lessee with full liberty to remove it from the demised lands. There is no doubt that the lands of the respondent, as well as the appellant, are burdened with the rights conferred on the lessee under the lease. In return for the rights conferred the lessee agrees to pay compensation fixed at one dollar per acre until the completion of a well on the premises. If an oil well is completed, the compensation is based on the number of gas wells yielding gas in paying quantities, and in addition thereto "enough gas to heat dwelling on premises".

It is well established in English law that a mining lease "is liberty given to a particular individual, for a specific length of time, to go into and under the land, and to get certain things there if he can find them, and to take them away, as if he had bought so much of the soil": *Gowan* v. *Christie* (1873). L.R. 2 H.L. Sc. 273, per Lord Cairns at p. 284; *Coltness Iron Co.* v. *Black* (1881), 6 App. Cas. 315, per Lord Blackburn at p. 335. In *McIntosh* v. *Leckie* (1906), 13 O.L.R. 54, Boyd C. held that a gas lease not dissimilar to the lease here in question, was more than a mere licence, and that it conferred an exclusive right to conduct operations on the land in order to drill for and produce the subterranean oil and gas which might be found during the specified period. "It is a *profit à prendre* an incorporeal right to be exercised in the land described." The same views were expressed by Meredith C.J.C.P. in *Can. Ry. Acc. Co.* v. *Williams* (1910), 21 O.L.R. 472. These cases follow and apply to oil and gas leases the principles set out in *Sutherland* v. *Heathcote*, [1892] 1 Ch. 475, particularly at p. 483, where Lord Justice Lindley states: "A right to work mines is something more than a mere license: it is a *profit à prendre*, an incorporeal hereditament lying in grant. The distinction between a license and a profit à prendre was pointed out in *Wickham* v. *Hawker* (1840), 7 M. & W. 63 at p. 78, 151 E.R. 679, a leading case on rights of sporting."

It is therefore clear that, according to our law, the right granted under the lease here in question is more than a licence of limited occupancy, and is a right to enter upon and occupy the whole farm for the purposes named therein and to recover and take away oil and gas, which, until they are liberated from confinement by the soil, form part of the soil. It is a *profit à prendre* in gross, an incorporeal hereditament, which is an estate in the whole land and which will continue to exist, unless otherwise terminated, as long as oil or gas is produced under the provisions of the lease. As to the nature of the estate, see *Martyn* v. *Williams* (1857), 1 H. & N. 816 at p. 826, 156 E.R. 1430; *Webber* v. *Lee* (1882), 9 Q.B.D. 315; *Shuttleworth* v. *Le Fleming* (1865), 19 C.B.N.S. 687 at p. 709, 144 E.R. 956.

There can be no doubt that had the lessor, within the ten-year period and prior to the completion of a well, divided the farm, as it subsequently was divided, the appellant and the respondent would have been entitled to an apportionment of the money received as consideration for the lease. I fail to see why in such case the law laid down in Redman's Law of Landlord and Tenant, 7th ed., p. 451, and Woodfall's Law of Landlord and Tenant, 22nd ed., p. 513, would not apply and why the right to receive the proportionate part of the rent would not pass to the respondent under the grant of the land to her according to the provisions of the *Conveyancing and Law of Property Act*, R.S.O. 1937, c. 152, s. 14(1).

That being so, are the rights of the parties altered by the fact that two producing gas wells were completed prior to the division of the freehold? As I interpret the lease, no new rights accured to the lessee following the completion of a well, except the extension of the term of the lease, but a different measure of payment for those rights was provided. The lessee's right to remove oil or gas, if found, remains the same. Prior to the completion of a gas well the measure of compensation was fixed by the number of acres leased. Following the completion of a well the measure of compensation was fixed at $100 per annum for each well yielding gas in paying quantities and free gas for the dwelling-house on the premises, or in the case of a producing oil well being completed the measure of payment was one barrel in ten, or its equivalent for every barrel of oil obtained on the premises. I think the compensation might just as well have been fixed by the number of wells drilled on any other property if the parties had so agreed.

I do not think the amount paid for these privileges can under the English law be considered the purchase-price of a chattel, *viz.*, gas or oil when the same has been severed from the realty at the head of the well, as is suggested in some of the American cases. It is the compensation that is paid for the right to exercise the privileges conferred under the lease. The land conveyed to the respondent was subject to the exercise of those rights and will continue to be subject to the exercise of those rights as long as gas is produced in paying quantities anywhere on the 125-acre tract demised.

The compensation payable under the lease is referred to in popular language as a royalty; the nature of a royalty payable under leases that, in my opinion, do not differ in principle from the lease being considered, has been well decided by English law.

In *Reg.* v. *Westbrook* (1847), 10 Q.B. 178, 116 E.R. 69, Lord Denman, C. J. was called upon to decide what was the legal nature of a royalty derived from a lease of land held for the purpose of getting clay to make bricks. The royalty was fixed at £2 per acre and 2s. 6d. for every 1,000 bricks moulded in a year. It was argued that it was altogether wrong in principle to consider the royalty as rent. This argument was founded on the contention that it is a sum paid not in respect of renewing produce of the land but a *portion of the land itself* (the italics are mine) and that not consumed by slow degrees and to be exhausted at the end of a long period, as in the case of a coal mine, under which circumstances it was admitted that it might be treated as produce, but in such large proportions that the whole would in a few years be exhausted. Lord Denman says at p. 203: "It does not appear to us that the circumstance of a more or less rapid consumption can make any difference in the principle."

And at pp. 204-5: "We come, then, to the bare objection that the royalty is paid, not for the renewing produce of the land, but for several portions of the land itself, mixed up with foreign matter: the expense of this, however, must of course have been cast off before the royalty itself was fixed. That was a sum which, after all such expenses paid, the occupier could afford to render to the landlord. When the case is thus laid bare, there is no distinction between it and that of the lessee of coal mines, of clay pits, of slate quarries: in all these the occupation is only valuable by the removal of portions of the soil: and whether the occupation is paid for in money or kind, is fixed beforehand by the contract, or measured afterwards by the actual produce, it is equally in substance a rent: *it is the compensation which the occupier pays the landlord for that species of occupation which the contract between them allows.*" (The italics are mine.)

In *Daniel* v. *Gracie* (1844), 6 Q.B. 145, 115 E.R. 56, Lord Denman held that where an agreement provided that the plaintiff should take a certain marl and slack pit and pay yearly 8d. per yard for all the marl and slack, and the right to work a brick mine and pay 1s. 8d. per 1,000 for all bricks made, the owner of the land had the rights of a landlord and was entitled to distrain for rent.

In *Coal Com'n* v. *Earl Fitzwilliam's Royalties Co.*, [1942] 1 Ch. 365, Bennett J. at p. 374 said: "In *The Queen* v. *Everist* (Reg. v. Westbrook) (1847), 10 Q.B. 178 at p. 193, 116 E.R. 69, it was decided by the Court of Queen's Bench that a royalty is a true rent."

Counsel for the appellant argues that notwithstanding that the respondent's land is burdened with the lease and the rights granted thereunder, the respondent is to be entitled to no compensation for the burden imposed on her land, unless and until the lessee might choose to complete a gas or oil well thereon. To admit this argument is to deny that the royalty is rent and to hold that upon the division of the freehold the profit à prendre in a sense became severed, and the lessee held the same on terms to pay to the owner of the 75 acres the whole compensation therefor, while precisely the same rights were held from the owner of the 50 acre block, for which the lessee is liable to pay no compensation, unless and until a producing well is brought in on her property. So to hold, in my opinion, would be inconsistent with the terms of the lease or with long established principles of English law. The money paid is the consideration for the right to enter upon the land and drill for oil or gas and to take away the same when it is recovered, as distinct from the purchase-price of oil or gas reduced to possession.

The appellant, in an able argument, relied strongly on certain decisions in the Courts of States of the United States of America. These decisions are only useful in so far as they may expound the law consistently with the principles of English law, and in this light I have given them careful consideration. There are two conflicting lines of authorities, one holding that when there has been a transfer of a part of the leased premises the transferee, in the absence of a contract to the contrary, is entitled to all royalties accruing from producing wells on the portion transferred, and not merely to a *pro rata* interest in the royalty from production on the part not transferred. The other line of authorities held that royalties should be apportioned according to the proportion that the area of the part of the land transferred bears to the whole of the leased premises. Thornton on Oil and Gas, 5th ed., vol. 2, p. 669, adopts the former proposition, but points out that contrary views have been expressed in a number of cases. I have read with care all the decisions cited by the author for both propositions, in an effort to reconcile one or the other with the underlying principles of English law, and to ascertain the fundamental principles on which they differ. I have come to the conclusion that the difference of opinion in the American Courts flows from the views held by the respective Courts on the nature of the rights granted under the lease.

In the States of Pennsylvania and Texas, the Courts have consistently held that the purchaser or the devisee of a part of land subject to a gas and oil lease is entitled to a proportionate share of the royalty payable under the lease: *Wettengel* v. *Gormley* (1894), 160 Pa. 559; 184 Pa. 354; *Gillette* v. *Mitchell* (1918), 214 S.W. 619; *McRae* v. *Japhet* (1925), 269 S.W. 829; *Hoffman* v. *Magnolia Petroleum Co.* (1925), 273 S.W. 828.

In Ohio, West Virginia, Oklahoma, Arkansas and Kentucky, the Courts have held that upon partition of a tract of land subject to an oil and gas lease, the royalties are not apportioned, but the right thereto passes with the conveyance of the land on which the wells are situate: *Northwestern Ohio Natural Gas. Co.* v. *Ullery* (1903), 67 N.E. 494; *Pittsburgh & West Virginia Gas Co.* v. *Ankrom* (1918) 97 S.E. 593; *Musgrave* v. *Musgrave* (1920), 103 S.E. 302; *Pierce Oil Corp.* v. *Schacht* (1919), 181 Pac. 731; *Osborn* v. *Arkansas Territorial Oil & Gas Co.* (1912), 146 S.W. 122; *Hurst* v. *Paken Oil Co.* (1941), 152 S.W. (2d) 181.

I have come to the conclusion that the cases in support of the latter proposition are dependent on the adoption of a principle that cannot be reconciled with English law. As I read these cases, the Courts proceed on the principle that the absolute ownership of the oil or gas under a tract of land subject to an oil and gas lease is in the owner of the land and that what the lessee holds is a licence to go on the land and reduce the oil or gas to possession, whereupon it becomes a chattel and his property. On this theory, the royalty is the purchase-price of a chattel reduced to possession on the land of another under licence....

I do not think that the royalty provided under the lease we have to consider can in any sense be interpreted to be rental for the gas wells sunk on the 75-acre portion of the farm....

I can find nothing in the reasoning of the American Courts that take a contrary view from the conclusion to which I have come to warrant me in departing from the principles of English law which so clearly establish that a royalty is compensation for the right to occupy land, and that in its essence it is rent, and, being rent, must necessarily be apportioned among the owners of the separate parts of the freehold. I have, therefore, come to the conclusion that the learned trial Judge was right in holding that the royalty of $200 a year payable under the lease should be apportioned in proportions 75/125 and 50/125....

Appeal on this point dismissed.

[Henderson J. A. agreed with McRuer J. A. Laidlaw J. A. dissented on another point in the case involving a clause of the oil and gas agreement giving the grantor the privilege of using enough gas to heat the dwelling on the premises. There was a dwelling on the 75 acre part of the tract, and McRuer J. A. held that this right was appurtenant to that part of the land and hence that there should be no apportionment of the value of the gas supplied to the dwelling.

Where oil or mineral land is left to a life tenant and remainderman, may either separately give an oil or general mineral "lease"? If the executors give such a lease, what allotment should be made of the rents and royalties? See *Re Moffatt Estate* (1955), 16 W.W.R. (N.S.) 314 (Sask.).

Oil and gas rights as such are beyond the scope of this casebook. See generally, Oil and Gas Rights, 2 *American Law of Property*, pp. 507 ff.; *Laycraft and Head*, Theories of Ownership of Oil and Gas, (1953) 31 Can. Bar Rev. 382.

The grant of oil and gas rights in mortgaged lands where the mortgagee is not a party thereto is subject to the mortgagee's prior right to protect his security: see *Stevenson* v. *Westgate*, [1942] 1 D.L.R. 369 (Ont. C.A.).]

[A profit, whether in gross or appurtenant, is normally assignable; but see 5 *Restatement of Property*, ss. 487, 489-492. Where appurtenant, it passes with an assignment of the dominant tenement, and severance of this tenement will result in apportionment of the total benefit among the severed parts (see 5 *Restatement of Property*, s. 488) unless the profit is indivisible. Where the profit is in gross the question is whether (especially in the case of a non-exclusive or common profit) the owner may assign the full benefit to each of several persons (otherwise than as co-tenants or as a group) either in respect of the servient land as a whole or in respect of particular parts thereof. Apportionment of this kind has been rejected by the Courts, although the decisions are few. In *Earl of Huntington and Lord Mountjoyes Case* (1583), 4 Leon. 147, 74 E.R. 786 (K.B.) (also reported 1 And. 307, 123 E.R. 488) an issue was raised whether an assignment of a profit (which was held to be non-exclusive) to two persons was good because "if to two, so he might do to twenty, and so a surcharge might be to the tenant of the soil". It was held that the assignment was good "but the two assignees ought not to work severally but together, with one stock and with such workmen as belonged to them both". See also *Stanton* v. *T. L. Herbert & Sons* (1919), 141 Tenn. 440, 211 S.W. 353. Cf. 2 *American Law of Property*, ss. 8.84-8.86; 5 *Restatement of Property*, s. 493.]

[The grantor of a profit in his land reserved a royalty the right to which by assignment came into the hands of plaintiff. The grantor conveyed the land to defendant subject to the royalty. Subsequently defendant acquired the profit from the grantee thereof, and thereafter made a new grant of a profit to others. Plaintiff sued defendant and his grantees for the royalty reserved in the original grant of a profit. Result? See *Fuller* v. *Howell*, [1942] 1 D.L.R. 462 (Ont.).

On extinction of profits by release or where the owner becomes also owner of the servient land, see *Rotherham* v. *Green* (1597), Cro. Eliz. 593, 78 E.R. 836 (K.B.) and *Tyrringham's Case* (1584), 4 Co. 36b, 76 E.R. 973 (K.B.).]

CHAPTER XIII

ADVERSE POSSESSION

1. INTRODUCTORY NOTE

IN THE PRECEDING CHAPTER, consideration was given to prescription as it affects such "incorporeal" interests as easements and profits. Although subsequently enshrined in and developed by statute, prescription originated as a common law doctrine through which easements and profits could arise. By contrast, limitations operating upon title to land are purely statutory and are not as much a means of creating interests as they are of extinguishing existing claims. The effect of limitations legislation is to protect a possessor against a paper titleholder if the circumstances set out in the statute are present.

Protection of possession has been a cardinal policy of the law both in respect of chattels and in respect of land. Indeed, seisin and disseisin, referring to the quality of possession of a freehold, were key concepts in the possessory assizes which lay for recovery of land; and while, theoretically, the results of such actions did not foreclose resort to such proprietary remedies as the writ of right, yet, practically speaking, seisin was the root of title. This is shown by one of the earliest limitation statutes, that of (1275) 3 Edw. I, c. 39 which provided, *inter alia*, that "forasmuch as it is long time passed since the writs undernamed were limited, it is provided that in conveying [i.e. in tracing] a descent in a writ of right, none shall presume to declare of the seisin of his ancestor further or beyond the time of King Richard ... and that a writ of novel disseisin, of partition ... have their limitation since the first voyage of King Henry, father to the King that now is, into Gascoin...". Most of the learning on seisin and disseisin as related to possession and dispossession (which were, of course, not necessarily equivalent to seisin and disseisin) has now become unimportant, but it should be noticed that limitations legislation played upon seisin through to the sixteenth century. "The Statute of 32 Henry VIII, c. 2, s. 3 limited real actions by providing that if the claimant rested his title on the ground of former seisin by himself, he was limited to a seisin within thirty years before the teste or date of the original writ, as regards both droitural and possessory actions; if on the ground of a seisin by his ancestor, to a seisin within fifty years as regards possessory actions and within sixty years as regards droitural actions. The demandant in a writ of right must allege and prove seisin in his ancestor within sixty years. Hence seisin that could be traced back sixty years became a good root of title. This was for the reason that no older seisin which had been lost could be resorted to." (*Ballantine*, Title by Adverse Possession, (1918) 32 Harv. L. Rev. 135, at p. 138; see also *Bordwell*, Disseisin and Adverse Possession, (1923) 33 Yale L. J. 141, 285.) Not until the statute of (1623), 21 Jac. 1, c. 16, the forerunner of modern limitations legislation, did the emphasis shift from a time limitation on tracing back seisin to a time limitation on asserting a right of entry. Since the older real actions had become obsolete in the face of the remedial advantages of ejectment, the effect of the statute was to protect possession against a titleholder's failure to assert his right of possession within the prescribed 20 year period after his right accrued. However, an action by writ of right was still possible for 40 years more, and the Real Property Limitation Act, 1833 (Imp.), c. 27 expressly abolished real actions and also provided by s. 34 that "at the determination of the period limited... to any person for making an entry... or bringing any... action or suit, the right and title of such person to the land... shall be extinguished". (The general limitation period in respect of land was reduced to 12 years in

England in 1874 and this is still operative under the Limitation Act, 1939 (Imp.), c. 21.)

Despite the abolition of the old action of ejectment (e.g. in England by the Common Law Procedure Act, 1852 (Imp.), c. 76, and in what is now Ontario by the Upper Canada Act, 1851 (U.C.) c. 114 and the Common Law Procedure Act of Upper Canada, 1856, c. 43) and despite the final abolition of forms of action by the Judicature Acts, "our substantive law is still that developed from the action of ejectment so that to-day it is still true that possession is a root of title. Any distinction between seisin and possession as the basis of title is obscured by the well-established rule that possession of land, unless otherwise explained, is evidence of seisin in fee simple.... Where the possession is truly adverse, there is little merit to-day in preserving...any distinction between seisin and possession; it is possession that forms the recognized root of title. Titles are not absolute but relative; ownership, as between two rival claimants, is the better right to possession": *Megarry and Wade*, Law of Real Property (1959, 2nd ed.), pp. 956-957.

[That seisin rather than possession is still the basis of title is the thesis of *Hargreaves*, Terminology and Title in Ejectment, (1940) 56 Law Q. Rev. 376; and see reply by *Holdsworth*, *ibid.*, at p. 479.]

[The Judicature Acts have eliminated the old defence to an action at law for possession that only an equitable title was proved by plaintiff. Such proof now entitles plaintiff to recover without first getting in the legal title: see *Thorne* v. *Williams* (1887), 13 O.R. 577 (C.P.); *Forrest* v. *Howe*, [1952] 1 D.L.R. 717, 4 W.W.R. (N.S.) 300 (B.C.C.A.).]

A distinction must be made between an action merely for trespass and an action to recover possession (formerly sounding in ejectment). In trespass, it is sufficient for plaintiff to show that at the material time he was in possession, but in the case of unoccupied land proof of title in the plaintiff or in the person under whom he claims would have to be established to show possession (properly characterized here as "constructive") for the purposes of trespass: see *Patterson* v. *De Smit*, [1949] 3 D.L.R. 178, [1949] O.W.N. 338 (C.A.); *MacKay* v. *Meikle*, [1953] 1 D.L.R. 695 (N.S.); cf. *Gahagan* v. *Sisson*, [1943] O.W.N. 619 (C.A.). While defendant may defend through an assertion of possession or even title in himself, it will not avail him to show that plaintiff's interest is subject to a superior claim of a third person unless defendant is himself claiming through that third person (i.e. setting up the *jus tertii*): see, for example, *Smith* v. *Ontario and Minnesota Power Co.* (1918), 44 O.L.R. 43, 45 D.L.R. 266 (App. Div.) (squatters disentitled to damages for flooding of lands where defendants authorized by owners). In proceedings for the recovery of possession, on the other hand, the frailty of defendant's holding will not help a plaintiff who is himself unable to prove a better right to possession, either by right thereto or title in himself or through a third person.

There is an exception, in the case of possession of Crown land, to the rule that a possessor without title may assert trespass against an intruder. A line of authority has established that plaintiff must be in possession with consent or privity of the Crown if he is to succeed: see *Bruyea* v. *Rose* (1890), 19 O.R. 433; *Marchischuk* v. *Lee*, [1954] 2 D.L.R. 484 (Man. Co. Ct.).

ASHER v. WHITLOCK. Queen's Bench. 1865. L.R. 1 Q.B. 1

Action of ejectment. In 1842, one Williamson enclosed a piece of waste land and extended the enclosure in 1850 when he built a cottage on the land. He remained in occupation until his death in 1860. By will he devised the property to his wife for life or during widowhood, remainder to his daughter Mary. The widow and daughter remained in possession and in

1861 the widow remarried. Mary died in 1863 at which time the widow and her second husband remained in possession until the widow's death shortly afterwards. Plaintiff, as heir-at-law of Mary, then sued the second husband. A verdict was given for plaintiff but a rule nisi was obtained on the ground that the testator had no devisable interest and hence plaintiff had no title.

COCKBURN C. J.: I am of opinion that this rule should be discharged. The defendant, on the facts, is in this dilemma; either his possession was adverse, or it was not. If it was not adverse to the devisee of the person who inclosed the land, and it may be treated as a continuance of the possession which the widow had and ought to have given up, on her marriage with the defendant, then, as she and the defendant came in under the will, both would be estopped from denying the title of the devisee and her heir-at-law. But assuming the defendant's possession to have been adverse, we have then to consider how far it operated to destroy the right of the devisee and her heir-at-law. Mr. Merewether was obliged to contend that possession acquired, as this was, against a rightful owner, would not be sufficient to keep out every other person but the rightful owner. But I take it as clearly established, that possession is good against all the world except the person who can shew a good title; and it would be mischievous to change this established doctrine. In *Doe* v. *Dyeball*, (Mood. & M. 346) one year's possession by the plaintiff was held good against a person who came and turned him out; and there are other authorities to the same effect. Suppose the person who originally inclosed the land had been expelled by the defendant, or the defendant had obtained possession without force, by simply walking in at the open door in the absence of the then possessor, and were to say to him, "You have no more title than I have, my possession is as good as yours," surely ejectment could have been maintained by the original possessor against the defendant. All the old law on the doctrine of disseisin was founded on the principle that the disseisor's title was good against all but the disseisee. It is too clear to admit of doubt, that if the devisor had been turned out of possession he could have maintained ejectment. What is the position of the devisee? There can be no doubt that a man has a right to devise that estate, which the law gives him against all the world but the true owner. Here the widow was a prior devisee, but *durante viduitate* only, and as soon as the testator died, the estate became vested in the widow; and immediately on the widow's marriage the daughter had a right to possession; the defendant however anticipates her, and with the widow takes possession. But just as he had no right to interfere with the testator, so he had no right against the daughter, and had she lived she could have brought ejectment; although she died without asserting her right, the same right belongs to her heir. Therefore I think the action can be maintained, inasmuch as the defendant had not acquired any title by length of possession. The devisor might have brought ejectment, his right of possession being passed by will to his daughter, she could have maintained ejectment, and so therefore can her heir, the female plaintiff. We know to what extent encroachments on waste lands have taken place; and if the lord has acquiesced and does not interfere, can it be at the mere will of any stranger to disturb the person in possession? I do not know what equity may say to the rights of different claimants who have come in at different times without title; but at law, I think the right of the original possessor is clear. On the simple ground that possession is good title against all but the true owner, I think the plaintiffs entitled to succeed, and that the rule should be discharged.

MELLOR J. I am of the same opinion. It is necessary to distinguish between the case of the true owner and that of a person having no title. The fact of possession is *primâ facie* evidence of seisin in fee. The law gives credit to possession unless explained; and Mr. Merewether, in order to succeed, ought to have gone on and shewn the testator's title to be bad, as that he was only tenant at will, but this he did not do. In *Doe* v. *Dyeball* possession for a year only was held sufficient against a person having no title. In *Doe* v. *Barnard*, 13 Q. B. 945, the plaintiff did not rely on her own possession merely, but shewed a prior possession in her husband, with whom she was unconnected in point of title. Here the first possessor is connected in title with the plaintiffs; for there can be no doubt that the testator's interest was devisable. In the common case of proving a claim to landed estate under a will, proof of the will and of possession or receipt of rents by the testator is always *primâ facie* sufficient, without going on to shew possession for more than twenty years. I agree with the Lord Chief Justice in the importance of maintaining, that possession is good against all but the rightful owner.

LUSH J., concurred. *Rule discharged.*

[In 1836, W, holder in fee simple of certain land, conveyed to G but remained in possession. In 1850, F falsely represented to W that he had obtained a conveyance of the land from G's son and heir-at-law, and took possession. G in fact died in 1850 and his only son (who had not conveyed to F) died in 1854. Plaintiff, a daughter of G and heiress-at-law of him and of her deceased brother, sought recovery of the land in 1868 from F's grantee. *Held*, the title of G, if he were alive, would be statute-barred and hence plaintiff could not recover. Do you agree? See *Butterfield* v. *Mabee* (1872), 22 U.C.C.P. 230 (C.A.).

H remained in possession of her husband's land after his death intestate, and leased it to defendant, telling him that she claimed no more than a life interest and after her death he could take the matter up with her late husband's heirs-at-law. On H's death, her heir-at-law purported to convey the land to a predecessor of plaintiff, and the latter subsequently sued defendant for arrears of rent. *Held*, the defendant was entitled to show that after H's death he was no longer in possession under the lease, and consequently he was not liable for any rent: see *Patterson* v. *Smith* (1877), 42 U.C.Q.B. 1 (C.A.).]

PERRY v. CLISSOLD. Privy Council. [1907] A.C. 73

Certain land "resumed" in 1891 by the Crown (in right of New South Wales) for public purposes under statutory authority had been in possession of C to whom notice was given but who died shortly afterwards. C had entered the land in 1881 when it was open and vacant, and he fenced it and remained in possession without interruption or notice of any competing claim until its resumption. In 1902, 10 years after C's will was proved, his trustees claimed compensation for the land. The Minister denied the claim and his decision was upheld by the state Supreme Court but the High Court of Australia issued mandamus to have the land valued. On appeal the case was twice argued before the Judicial Committee.

The judgment of the Privy Council was delivered by LORD MACNAGHTEN:... On the part of the Minister it was contended that, upon the plaintiffs' own showing, Clissold was a mere trespasser, without any estate or interest in the land.

Their Lordships are unable to agree with this contention.

It cannot be disputed that a person in possession of land in the assumed character of owner and exercising peaceably the ordinary rights of ownership has a perfectly good title against all the world but the rightful owner. And if the rightful owner does not come forward and assert his title by process of law within the period prescribed by the provisions of the Statute of Limitations applicable to the case, his right is for ever extinguished, and the possessory owner acquires an absolute title.

On behalf of the Minister reliance was placed on the case of *Doe* v. *Barnard*, 13 Q.B. 945, which seems to lay down this proposition, that if a person having only a possessory title to land be supplanted in the possession by another who has himself no better title, and afterwards brings an action to recover the land, he must fail in case he shews in the course of the proceedings that the title on which he seeks to recover was merely possessory. It is, however, difficult, if not impossible, to reconcile this case with the later case of *Asher* v. *Whitlock*, L.R. 1 Q.B. 1, in which *Doe* v. *Barnard* was cited. The judgment of Cockburn C. J. is clear on the point. The rest of the Court concurred, and it may be observed that one of the members of the Court in *Asher* v. *Whitlock* (Lush J.) had been of counsel for the successful party in *Doe* v. *Barnard*. The conclusion at which the Court arrived in *Doe* v. *Barnard* is hardly consistent with the views of such eminent authorities on real property law as Mr. Preston and Mr. Joshua Williams. It is opposed to the opinions of modern text-writers of such weight and authority as Professor Maitland and Holmes J., of the Supreme Court of the United States.

Their Lordships are of opinion that it is impossible to say that no prima facie case for compensation has been disclosed.

They do not think that a case for compensation is necessarily excluded by the circumstance that under the provisions of the Act of 1900 the Minister acquired not merely the title of the person in possession as owner, but also the title, whatever it may have been, of the rightful owner out of possession, who never came forward to claim the land or the compensation payable in respect of it, and who is, as the Chief Justice says, "unknown to this day".

The Act throughout from the very preamble has it apparently in contemplation that compensation would be payable to every person deprived of the land resumed for public purposes. It could hardly have been intended or contemplated that the Act should have the effect of shaking titles which but for the Act would have been secure, and would in process of time have become absolute and indisputable, or that the Governor, or responsible Ministers acting under his instructions, should take advantage of the infirmity of anybody's title in order to acquire his land for nothing. Even where the true owner, after diligent inquiry, cannot be found the Act contemplates payment of the compensation into Court to be dealt with by a Court of Equity....

Appeal dismissed.

[Does the conclusion of the Court mean that the occupier will necessarily receive the expropriation compensation after it has been fixed? See *C.P.R.* v. *Brown Milling* Co. (1909), 18 O.L.R. 85 (C.A.), aff'd (1910), 42 S.C.R. 600.]

THE LIMITATIONS ACT, R.S.O. 1960, c. 214

3. (1) No entry, distress, or action shall be made or brought on behalf of Her Majesty against any person for the recovery of or respecting any land or rent, or for or concerning any revenues, rents, issues or profits, but within 60 years next after the right to make such entry or distress or to bring such action has first accrued to Her Majesty.

(2) Subsections 1 to 3, 5 to 7, and 9 to 12 of section 5 and sections 6, 8 to 11 and 13 to 15 shall apply to rights of entry, distress or action asserted by or on behalf of Her Majesty.

4. No person shall make an entry or distress, or bring an action to recover any land or rent, but within 10 years next after the time at which the right to make such entry or distress, or to bring such action, first accrued to some person through whom he claims, or if the right did not accrue to any person through whom he claims, then within 10 years next after the time at which the right to make such entry or distress, or to bring such action, first accrued to the person making or bringing it.

5. (1) Where the person claiming such land or rent, or some person through whom he

claims, has, in respect of the estate or interest claimed, been in possession or in receipt of the profits of the land, or in receipt of the rent, and has, while entitled thereto, been dispossessed, or has discontinued such possession or receipt, the right to make an entry or distress or bring an action to recover the land or rent shall be deemed to have first accrued at the time of the dispossession or discontinuance of possession, or at the last time at which any such profits or rent were so received.

(6) Where a person is in possession or in receipt of the profits of any land, or in receipt of any rent as tenant from year to year or other period, without any lease in writing, the right of the person entitled subject thereto, or of the person through whom he claims, to make an entry or distress, or to bring an action to recover the land or rent, shall be deemed to have first accrued at the determination of the first of such years or other periods, or at the last time when any rent payable in respect of such tenancy was received, whichever last happened.

(7) Where any person is in possession or in receipt of the profits of any land, or in receipt of any rent, as tenant at will, the right of the person entitled subject thereto, or of the person through whom he claims, to make an entry or distress, or to bring an action to recover the land or rent, shall be deemed to have first accrued either at the determination of the tenancy, or at the expiration of one year next after the commencement of the tenancy, at which time the tenancy shall be deemed to have determined.

(9) Where the person claiming such land or rent, or the person through whom he claims, has become entitled by reason of any forfeiture or breach of condition, such right shall be deemed to have first accrued when the forfeiture was incurred or the condition broken.

(10) Where any right to make an entry or distress, or to bring an action to recover any land or rent, by reason of any forfeiture or breach of condition, has first accrued in respect of any estate or interest in reversion or remainder and the land or rent has not been recovered by virtue of such right, the right to make an entry or distress, or to bring an action to recover the land or rent, shall be deemed to have first accrued in respect of such estate or interest at the time when it became an estate or interest in possession as if no such forfeiture or breach of condition had happened.

(11) Where the estate or interest claimed is an estate or interest in reversion or remainder, or other future estate or interest, and no person has obtained the possession or receipt of the profits of the land, or the receipt of the rent, in respect of such estate or interest, such right shall be deemed to have first accrued at the time at which such estate or interest became an estate or interest in possession.

(12) A right to make an entry or distress, or to bring an action to recover any land or rent, shall be deemed to have first accrued, in respect of an estate or interest in reversion or remainder or other future estate or interest at the time at which it became an estate or interest in possession, by the determination of any estate or estates in respect of which the land has been held or the profits thereof or the rent have been received, notwithstanding that the person claiming the land or rent, or some person through whom he claims, has, at any time before the creation of the estate or estates that have determined, been in possession or receipt of the profits of the land, or in receipt of the rent.

6. (1) If the person last entitled to any particular estate on which any future estate or interest was expectant has not been in the possession or receipt of the profits of the land, or in receipt of the rent, at the time when his interest determined, no such entry or distress shall be made and no such action shall be brought by any person becoming entitled in possession to a future estate or interest, but within ten years next after the time when the right to make an entry or distress, or to bring an action for the recovery of the land or rent, first accrued to the person whose interest has so determined, or within five years next after the time when the estate of the person becoming entitled in

possession has become vested in possession, whichever of those two periods is the longer.

8. No person shall be deemed to have been in possession of any land within the meaning of this Act merely by reason of having made an entry thereon.

9. No continual or other claim upon or near any land preserves any right of making an entry or distress or of bringing an action.

10. No descent cast, discontinuance or warranty, which has happened or been made since the 1st day of July, 1834, or which may hereafter happen or be made, shall toll or defeat any right of entry or action for the recovery of land.

11. Where any one or more of several persons entitled to any land or rent as coparceners, joint tenants or tenants in common has or have been in possession or receipt of the entirety, or more than his or their undivided share or shares of the land, or of the profits thereof, or of the rent for his or their own benefit, or for the benefit of any person or persons other than the person or persons entitled to the other share or shares of the same land or rent, such possession or receipt shall not be deemed to have been the possession or receipt of, or by the last-mentioned person or persons or any of them.

13. Where any acknowledgment in writing of the title of the person entitled to any land or rent has been given to him or to his agent, signed by the person in possession or in receipt of the profits of the land, or in the receipt of the rent, such possession or receipt of or by the person by whom the acknowledgment was given shall be deemed, according to the meaning of this Act, to have been the possession or receipt of or by the person to whom or to whose agent the acknowledgment was given at the time of giving it, and the right of the last-mentioned person, or of any person claiming through him, to make an entry or distress or bring an action to recover the land or rent, shall be deemed to have first accrued at and not before the time at which the acknowledgment, or the last of the acknowledgments, if more than one, was given.

15. At the determination of the period limited by this Act to any person for making an entry or distress or bringing any action, the right and title of such person to the land or rent, for the recovery whereof such entry, distress or action respectively might have been made or brought within such period, is extinguished.

16. Nothing in sections 1 to 15 shall apply to any waste or vacant land of the Crown, whether surveyed or not, nor to lands included in any road allowance heretofore or hereafter surveyed and laid out or to any lands reserved or set apart or laid out as a public highway where the freehold in any such road allowance or highway is vested in the Crown or in a municipal corporation, commission or other public body, but nothing in this section shall be deemed to affect or prejudice any right, title or interest acquired by any person before the 13th day of June, 1922.

[Under ss. 28 and 29, the right of action to recover land of which a person has been deprived by concealed fraud is deemed to have first accrued at the time at which the fraud was or, with reasonable diligence might have been, first discovered, subject, however, to protection of a subsequent innocent *bona fide* purchaser for value.]

36. If at the time at which the right of a person to make an entry or distress, or to bring an action to recover any land or rent, first accrues, as herein mentioned, such person is under the disability of infancy, mental deficiency, mental incompetency or unsoundness of mind, such person, or the person claiming through him, notwithstanding that the period of ten years or five years, as the case may be, hereinbefore limited has expired, may make an entry or distress, or bring an action, to recover the land or rent at any time within five years next after the time at which the person to whom the right first accrued ceased to be under any such disability, or died, whichever of those two events first happened.

[By s. 37, the right of entry or action by a person who at the time of first accrual was under any of the specified disabilities, or by any person claiming under him, must in any event be made or brought within 20 years after first accrual even though the disability subsists during the whole of the 20 years, or though 5 years have not elapsed after cessation of disability or death. By s. 38, if a person under disability at time of accrual of his right of entry or action dies in that condition, no time beyond the 10 year period after his right first accrued or the period of 5 years after his death shall be allowed by reason of any disability of any other person.]

[For similar legislation, see Limitation of Actions Act, R.S.A. 1955, c. 177, ss. 18-32, 43-47; Statute of Limitations, R.S.B.C. 1960, c. 370, ss. 15-48; Limitation of Actions Act, R.S.M. 1954, c. 145, ss. 16-30, 43-48; Limitation of Actions Act, R.S.N.B. 1952, c. 133, ss. 29-45, 59, 60, 62, 63; Limitation of Actions (Realty) Act, R.S.-Nfld, 1952, c. 145; Limitation of Actions Act, R.S.N.S. 1954, c. 153, ss. 9-21, 28, 29; Statute of Limitations, R.S.P.E.I. 1951, c. 87, ss. 17-34, 46-50; Limitation of Actions Act, R.S.S. 1953, c. 76, ss. 17-32, 45-49.

Land titles legislation has, in the main, excluded the acquisition of "possessory" titles once land has been properly brought under the land titles system: see Land Registry Act, R.S.B.C. 1960, c. 208, s. 38(3); Real Property Act, R.S.M. 1954, c. 220, s. 66(2); Land Titles Act, R.S.O. 1960, c. 204, s. 57; Land Titles Act, 1960 (Sask.), c. 65, s. 70(2). An exception is Alberta where a "possessory" title may still be acquired against a registered titleholder, although if not properly protected it may be defeated upon a subsequent registered transfer from the previous registered titleholder: see *Harris* v. *Keith* (1911), 3 Alta. L.R. 222, 16 W.L.R. 433; *Boyczuk* v. *Perry*, [1948] 2 D.L.R. 406, [1948] 1 W.W.R. 495 (Alta. C.A.). *Quaere* whether a person who had possession for the full limitation period against a registered titleholder in Alberta and who subsequently vacates may regain possession against the registered holder. While he may be a successful defendant would he be a successful plaintiff? See *Sinclair* v. *McLellan*, [1919] 2 W.W.R. 782, 15 Alta. L.R. 86.

In *Gatz* v. *Kiziw*, [1959] S.C.R. 10, 16 D.L.R. 2d 215, rev'g [1957] O.W.N. 313, 8 D.L.R. 2d 292, it was held that the exception in favour of possessory interests as between adjoining owners under s. 23 (1) (c) [now s. 51 (1), para. 3] of the Ontario Land Titles Act operated only to protect possessory interests at the time of first registration and did not otherwise qualify the exclusion of possessory interests under s. 28 [now s. 57].

2. RUNNING OF THE LIMITATION PERIOD

AGENCY COMPANY LIMITED AND TEMPLETON v. SHORT. Privy Council. 1888. 13 App. Cas. 793

Appeal from a judgment of the Supreme Court of New South Wales, (1886), 7 N.S.W. 365, refusing a rule nisi for a new trial in an action of ejectment to recover 50 acres of land.

The judgment of their Lordships was delivered by LORD MACNAGHTEN: On the 3rd of December, 1885, the appellants, as plaintiffs, brought an action against the respondent, as defendant, to recover fifty acres of land situated in the district of Botany Bay, in the county of Cumberland, in the colony of New South Wales.

The defence was the Statute of Limitations (3 & 4 Will. 4, c. 27), which was adopted in the Colony by the Act No. 3 of 1837.

The action came on for trial in September, 1886, before the late Chief Justice Martin and a jury.

For the present purpose the facts of the case may be stated very shortly. The land in dispute was, until recently, waste open bush. The plaintiffs at the trial proved a complete documentary title deduced from a Crown grant in 1810. But they failed to prove to the satisfaction of the learned judge at the trial that they or any person through whom they claimed had been in actual occupation of the land at any time during the period of twenty years immediately preceding the commencement of the action. On the other hand the defendant, who claimed to have purchased the land within the last few years, did not prove to the satisfaction of the learned judge that he and the person or persons through whom he claimed had been in continuous possession during the statutory period.

The Chief Justice told the jury that when any person went into possession of another person's land, and exercised dominion over it, with the intention of claiming it, and the Statute of Limitations thereupon began to run as against the owner of the land, such running was never stopped, notwithstanding that the intruder abandoned the land long before the expiration of twenty years from his first entry, and no other person took possession of such land, and the right of the true owner to the land would not again arise without an entry by such true owner with the intention of repossessing himself of such land. The Chief Justice also told the jury that at the expiration of the twenty years after such taking possession of the land, as against the true owner, his right of action was defeated, notwithstanding there may not have been twenty years' possession as against him.

A verdict was found for the defendant.

On the 27th of October, 1886, the plaintiffs applied for a rule nisi for a new trial on the ground of misdirection. The application was heard before the late Chief Justice, Faucett, J., and Windeyer, J., who refused the rule. The Chief Justice is reported to have said: "There is no doubt that there was evidence sufficient to justify the verdict of the jury as to the occupation of the land more than forty years ago, which caused the statute to run against the legal owner. That being so, there was no evidence whatever that the legal owner during that time ever retook possession, or even walked over the land. The statute having been set running there was nothing to stop it."

To this report Faucett, J., has been good enough to append the following memorandum for the information of their Lordships:—

"This is substantially a correct note of the reasons given by the late Chief Justice for refusing the rule in this case. His judgment was given in very few words.

"I may add that it has been before held by this Court that when the rightful owner of land has been dispossessed, and the statute has once begun to run against him, the statute does not cease to run; in other words, the operation of the statute is not suspended until the rightful owner has exercised some act of ownership on the land; and that if the rightful owner allows twenty years to elapse, from the time when the statute so first began to run, without exercising any such act of ownership, he cannot recover in ejectment against any person who may happen to be in possession at the end of the twenty years, although there may have been an interval in the twenty years during which no one was in possession.

"To stop or suspend the operation of the statute there must be some new act of ownership on the part of the rightful owner. There must be, as it were, a new departure."

The doctrine appears to have had its origin in the case of *Laing* v. *Bain*, which was before the Supreme Court on a motion for a new trial in March, 1876. Their Lordships were referred to a note of the case in Oliver's Real Property Statutes, p. 79. Martin, C. J., is there reported to have said that "it was clear law that if the statute once commenced to run it would not stop except by the owner going into possession and so getting, as it were, a new departure."

Their Lordships are unable to concur in this view. They are of opinion that if a person enters upon the land of another and holds possession for a time, and then, without having acquired title under the statute, abandons possession, the rightful owner, on the abandonment, is in the same position in all respects as he was before the intrusion took place. There is no one against whom he can bring an action. He cannot make an entry upon himself. There is no positive enactment, nor is there any principle of law, which requires him to do any act, to issue any notice, or to perform any ceremony in order to rehabilitate himself. No new departure is necessary. The possession of the intruder, ineffectual for the purpose of transferring title, ceases upon its abandonment to be effectual for any purpose. It does not leave behind it any cloud on the title of the rightful owner, or any secret process at work for the possible benefit in time to come of some casual interloper or lucky vagrant.

There is not, in their Lordships' opinion, any analogy between the case supposed and the case of successive disabilities mentioned in the statute. There the statute "continues to run" because there is a person in possession in whose favour it is running.

There is no direct authority on the point in this country. But such authority as there is seems to be opposed to the doctrine laid down by the Supreme Court. It is sufficient to refer to *McDonnell* v. *McKinty*, 10 Ir. L.R. 514, Lord St. Leonards' Real Property Statutes, p. 31, and *Smith* v. *Lloyd*, 9 Exch. 562. In the latter case, which was decided in 1854, Parke, B., giving the judgment of the Court, says:—"We are clearly of opinion that the statute applies, not to want of actual possession by the plaintiff, but to cases where he has been out of, and another in, possession for the prescribed time. There must be both absence of possession by the person who has the right, and actual possession by another, whether adverse or not, to be protected, to bring the case within the statute. We entirely concur in the judgment of Blackburne, C.J., in *McDonnell* v. *McKinty*, and the principle on which it is founded."

Their Lordships have only to add that, in their opinion, there is no difference in principle as regards the application of the statute between the case of mines and the case of other land where the fact of possession is more open and notorious. It is obvious that, in the case of mines, the doctrine contended for might lead to startling results and produce great injustice.

In the result, therefore, their Lordships have come to the conclusion that the direction given to the jury by the learned Chief Justice was not law, and they think that there was substantial miscarriage in the trial....

New trial ordered.

[Acts amounting to a "series of petty trespasses to which no owner would be likely to object" do not constitute such evidence of actual and constant possession as is necessary to extinguish the paper title: see *Carson* v. *Musialo*, [1940] 4 D.L.R. 651, [1940] O.W.N. 398 (C.A.); *Stackhouse* v. *Morin*, [1948] O.R. 864.

Conversely, a paper titleholder will not be regarded as having been dispossessed of vacant land on which he intended to build where there is evidence of isolated acts of user on his part even though another has made use of the land for the limitation period: see *Williams Bros. Direct Supply Stores Ltd.* v. *Raftery*, [1957] 3 All E.R. 593, [1957] 3 W.L.R. 931 (C.A.). Cf. *Leigh* v. Jack (1879), 5 Ex. D. 264 where Bramwell L. J. said, *inter alia*, at p. 273: "...acts of user are not enough to take the soil out of the plaintiff and her predecessors in title and to vest it in the defendant; in order to defeat a title by dispossessing the former owner, acts must be done which are inconsistent with his enjoyment of the soil for the purposes for which he intended to use it."]

PIPER v. STEVENSON. Ontario Appellate Division. 1913. 28 O.L.R. 379, 12 D.L.R. 820

Appeal by defendant from a judgment for plaintiff in an action for trespass to land. In September, 1901, plaintiff enclosed by a fence eight lots, six of which he had contracted to buy from one Whaley from whom he received the deeds thereof in 1902. The eight lots were cultivated by plaintiff as one, and in 1905 and 1906 buildings were put up and plaintiff who had theretofore lived on a rented farm, went to live on the land. In October, 1911 defendant obtained from the registered owner a conveyance of the two lots enclosed by plaintiff with the six he had bought, and he made an entry thereon in November, 1911. In June, 1912, he fenced and cultivated the two lots and shortly afterwards plaintiff brought his action.

The judgment of the Court was delivered by CLUTE J.:... As to the entry, such as it was, under the law as it now stands, it could have no effect. Since the Act [The Real Property Limitation Act, R.S.O. 1897, ch. 133.], sec. 8, no person shall be deemed to have been in possession of any land within the meaning of the Act merely by reason of having made an entry thereon. "Under the old law a merely formal entry by the person entitled was sufficient to vest the possession in him: Co. Litt. 253b; though under 4 & 5 Anne ch. 16, sec. 16, such an entry or claim was not effectual to avoid the statute 21 Jac. I. ch. 16, unless an action was commenced within a year and prosecuted with effect.... The result is that an entry, to vest the possession in the person entering and prevent the bar of the statute, must be effective as opposed to merely formal. 'The making an entry amounts to nothing unless something is done to divest the possession out of the tenant, and revest it in fact in the lord': *Doe* v. *Coombes* (1850), 9 C.B. 714, at p. 718. And it must be made *animo possidendi*: *Solling* v. *Broughton*, [1893] A.C. 556." In the *Coombes* case, after the encroachment, the lord of the manor, accompanied by the steward, entered. The lord stated that he took possession, and directed that a stone should be taken out of the wall of the hut, and that a portion of the fence should be removed. This was held no more than a mere entry, and not sufficient to vest the possession in the lord. See Lightwood's Time Limit on Actions, pp. 11, 12.

It is said in *Worssam* v. *Vandenbrande* (1868), 17 W.R. 53, that slighter acts will be sufficient if no person is actually on the land at the time of re-entry, although the possession may not be vacant. In that case the predecessors in title went to the land, broke down the fence, and erected a post with the announcement that applications for a lease of the land were to be made to them. They remained on the land three-quarters of an hour. Three days later, the post was gone, but there was no evidence to shew who had removed it. For the next five years no one, so far as appeared, did anything on the land, and then the defendant re-entered and built upon it. It was held that the plaintiffs' predecessors had effectually resumed possession.

The present case differs from that quoted in several particulars. The land has been continuously used and occupied down to the present time by the plaintiff. The plaintiff was in fact residing upon the land at the time the alleged entry was made, that is, upon the block of which the lands in question form a part, being one enclosure for the whole. Also here the ten years had elapsed after the enclosure and before the entry; and the entry was such as, I think, expressly falls within sec. 8 of the Act.

There remains, therefore, for consideration, only the question as to whether or not a piece of land entirely enclosed with other lands by the plaintiff, used and occupied by her continuously for over ten years, her possession all along being "open, obvious, exclusive, and continuous," does not come within the statute, simply because in the earlier four or five years she did not live upon the land; that is, was personally absent during the winter, although the land remained still enclosed by the fence and was used and occupied as an owner would use and occupy in such a case.

The authority chiefly relied on by Mr. Armour was *Coffin* v. *North American Land Co.*, 21 O.R. 80. In several respects the facts in that case are similar to the facts in the present case, but in others they widely differ. In that case, during the statutory period, the true owners entered upon the land, pulled down the old and built a new fence. Here, as already pointed out, entry was not made until after ten years had elapsed from the time the lots were enclosed, in September, 1901. Further, the plaintiff in the *Coffin* case entered into an agreement, after a threat that he would be evicted unless he acknowledged himself to be a tenant, and promised to give up possession when required, and he did give up possession, and, although living on the adjoining land, he made no claim of any kind until five years after he had given up possession.

The points of difference are sufficient, I think, to distinguish the *Coffin* case from the present. But I desire to refer to some observations made in the judgment of the *Coffin* case to which I cannot accede. It is said there (p. 87): "The plaintiff here cropped the land in question during the summer; during the winter he did nothing to it but draw some loads of manure upon it.... During the summer months and during the months when he was sowing the land and reaping his crop, his possession was clearly sufficient beyond question, but during the rest of the year his possession was not actual, nor constant, nor visible. During each winter he says that he drew some manure upon the place and in the spring he spread. Excepting for this he withdrew absolutely to his own lot, which adjoined but was separated by a fence from that of which he claims the possession"— Differing in this respect also from the present. "The winter months must be separated from the summer and we must look at the acts of possession done during those winter months by themselves. Doing this, I think the acts done in the winter did not constitute an occupation of the property to the exclusion of the right of the true owner, but were mere acts of trespass, covering necessarily but a very short portion of the winter, and that the possession must be taken to have been vacant for the remainder of it. The right of the true owner would attach upon each occasion when the possession became thus vacant, and the operation of the Statute of Limitations would cease until actual possession was taken in the spring again by the plaintiff:" citing *Trustees Executors and Agency Co.* v. *Short*, 13 App. Cas. 793.

To this proposition of the law I cannot assent.

[The learned Judge then pointed out that the law stated in the *Short* case was applied to the *Coffin* case on the finding that there was an abandonment of the premises for some four or five years. However in the instant case there was no abandonment unless it be based on the fact that the land lay idle in the winter. He then continued as follows:]

I cannot assent to the general statement of Street, J., in the *Coffin* case that the winter months must be separated from the summer months, and that we must look at the acts of possession during those months by themselves, nor to the view there expressed that the acts done in the winter months did not constitute an occupation of the property to the exclusion of the right of the true owner, nor that the property thus became vacant during the winter, and that the right of the true owner would attach, and that the operation of the Statute of Limitations would cease until actual possession was taken in the following spring. No doubt, the statute ceases to run if the adverse possessor quits the land and leaves the possession vacant, as there is no person in whose favour it can run: Lightwood's Time Limit on Actions, p. 12.

But, where the property is entirely enclosed by the person claiming by possession, his mere absence does not, in my opinion, amount to abandonment or make the premises vacant. It may still be considered under his control, inasmuch as it excludes all others therefrom by his enclosure. If the owner himself claimed before the statute had barred him, he could not reach his land without doing some act. He could not make an entry without at least breaking down, if not destroying, the fence. It is a notice to all the world that the property is claimed by some one and that all others are excluded, and unless there is some act on the part of the true owner to create a new starting-point, and the intruder retains possession by the enclosure, and uses and cultivates the land as his own, either by himself or his servants, although not actually present, in person or by his servants, during portions of the year, the owner is excluded and his title barred after the statutory period....

Appeal dismissed.

[See also *Warren* v. *Yeoll*, [1943] O.R. 762, [1944] 1 D.L.R. 118 (C.A.) (enclosure of portion of a neighbour's back yard by a line fence though originating in error as to true boundary line held to result in extinction of title after expiry of limitation period).]

IRELAND v. CUTTEN. Ontario High Court. [1940] O.R. 12, [1939] 4 D.L.R. 681

Action by plaintiff for a declaration of her right to occupy certain land for life pursuant to an alleged oral agreement under which she went into possession. The trial Judge upheld the claim but also went on to deal with an alternative claim by plaintiff that she had acquired a "possessory" title. The judgment is reproduced on the limitations point only.

J. G. KELLY J.: ... By virtue of secs. 4 and 15 of The Limitations Act, the title of the owner of any land which is in the possession of another is extinguished at the expiration of ten years from the date when his right to make an entry first accrued. By virtue of sec. 5(7), where the person in possession is a tenant at will, the right of entry is deemed to have accrued at the end of one year from the date when such tenancy began, or from the date when such tenancy actually determined, whichever is the earlier date. It is clear, therefore, that, without anything more, if the plaintiff went into possession of No. 63 Regal Road on 4th March, 1920, as tenant at will of Lionel Cutten, the ten-year period began to run on 4th March, 1921. The running of the statute may be interrupted in various ways, but if it is not interrupted for a period of eleven years from the commencement of a tenancy at will, the title of the owner is extinguished in favour of the tenant, who then becomes owner in fee simple. The leading case is *Day* v. *Day* (1871), L.R. 3 P.C. 751, and I quote two passages from the Privy Council judgment in that case, at page 761: "When the Statute has once begun to run it would seem on principle that it would not cease to run unless the real owner, whom the Statute assumed to be dispossessed of the property, shall have been restored to the possession. He may be so restored either by entering on the actual possession of the property, or by receiving rent from the person in the occupation, or by making a new lease to such person, which is accepted by him; and it is not material whether it is a lease for a term of years, from year to year, or at will."

And, at page 763, "The language and policy of the Statute require that to constitute this new *terminus a quo* the agreement for a new tenancy should be made by the parties with a knowledge of the determination of the former tenancy, and with an intention to create a fresh tenancy at will."

The *Day* case is authority for the proposition that mere determination of a tenancy at will is not sufficient to interrupt or stop the running of the statute. There must be evidence of a new tenancy. Two other sections of the Act should be noticed—sec. 8, which provides that no person shall be deemed to have been in possession of any land merely by reason of having made an entry thereon, and sec. 9, which provides that a right of entry cannot be kept alive merely by making a continual claim on the land. The authorities also make it clear that a tenancy at will is determined by any act of the owner done with the knowledge of the tenant inconsistent with the continuance of such tenancy: *Turner* v. *Doe d. Bennett* (1842), 9 M. & W. 643; *Doe d. Baker* v. *Coombes* (1850), 9 C.B. 714.

Turning to the facts of this case, I think I should have to hold that the payment of one dollar to Lionel Cutten in 1922 gave a new starting-point to the statute: *Day* v. *Day* (1871), L.R. 3 P.C. 751; sec. 13 of the Act. Whether or not it was a joke, it was called rent and Lionel kept it.

The next incident that could affect the running of the statute was the cheque and letter of 4th March, 1927. The cheque was never indorsed, nor paid, and nothing passed to Lionel Cutten thereby. It was not, I think, a payment of rent within the meaning of sec. 13. In my opinion the letter was not an acknowledgment within that section either. The essentials of an acknowledgment are discussed in Armour on Real Property, 2nd ed., at page 502 *et seq.* The acknowledgment must be made to the owner or his agent. Mr. Hughes argues that Mrs. Cutten was Lionel Cutten's agent for this purpose. With respect, I can find no evidence whatever that Lionel Cutten ever constituted his wife his agent for any purpose connected with No. 63 Regal Road and, more particularly, there is no evidence that he ever heard of the letter or cheque. It is true that it was perhaps chiefly because of his wife that Lionel purchased the land and built the house and, knowing this, she may have spoken of it as a house that she built for her sister; but I think the affectionate relations of husband and wife are not to be confused with agency. I am unable to find that the running of the statute, if it were running, could have been interrupted by this cheque or this letter.

If we suppose the payment of one dollar to have been made on the last day of 1922, the eleven-year period would have expired on 31st December, 1933, and I can find nothing in that period to interrupt the running of the statute. On the assumption, with which of course I disagree, that the plaintiff commenced her occupation as a tenant at will, she would have a good title in fee simple at least by 1st January, 1934, and nothing short of a reconveyance after that date could affect her title: *Doe d. Perry et al.* v. *Henderson* (1847), 3 U.C.Q.B. 486; sec. 15 of the Act. Even if 4th March, 1927, was constituted a new starting point, I think that nothing in the next eleven years occurred to interrupt the running of the statute. There was no payment, taxes not being rent: *Finch* v. *Gilray* (1889), 16 O.A.R. 484. The placing of "For Sale" signs on the lawn may have been sufficient to terminate the tenancy at will, but, if so, there is clearly no evidence that there was ever a new agreement for a fresh tenancy at will. Arthur Cutten certainly does not pretend ever to have agreed to any tenancy, and the placing of the signs was his doing. At most they constituted a mere entry within the provisions of sec. 8 of the Act. It would follow that, before the death of Lionel Cutten in August, 1938, eleven years had run from 4th March, 1927, and the plaintiff, if originally a mere tenant at will, had acquired a good title in fee simple.

Generally, with regard to the nature of the plaintiff's occupation as a tenant at will, the payment of taxes and insurance by Lionel Cutten was in no way inconsistent with such a tenancy: *Noble* v. *Noble* (1912), 27 O.L.R. 342; the assessment of Lionel Cutten as owner, and Lionel's friendly visits to the property, equally gave no new starting-point to the statute as being inconsistent with the original tenancy at will: *McCowan et al.* v. *Armstrong* (1902), 3 O.L.R. 100.

It is my opinion, therefore, if the defendant is correct in saying that the plaintiff occupied No. 63 Regal Road as tenant at will, that Lional Cutten's title has been extinguished by virtue of The Limitations Act, and that the plaintiff is the owner in fee simple.

The defendant's counsel, however, argues that in no event can the plaintiff be entitled in fee. The principle he relies on appears most plainly in *Board* v. *Board* (1873), L.R. 9 Q.B. 48. In that case, a tenant by the curtesy, having nothing to devise, nevertheless by his will purported to devise a life estate to his daughter, Rebecca, with remainder to his grandson William. Upon his death, Rebecca went into possession and the true owner stood by and allowed his title to be barred by her possession. By her conduct in paying certain annuities charged against the land by the invalid will, Rebecca clearly showed that she took possession thereunder. After Rebecca's death, it was contended that the will being void, William, the grandson, took nothing thereunder, and that Rebecca had acquired, by possession, a title in fee simple for her own benefit. It was held that as against the grandson, William, entitled in remainder under the will, Rebecca had taken only a life estate. Blackburn J., at page 53, says: "My brother Martin, in *Anstee* v. *Nelms* (1856), 1 H. & N. 232, says that the Statute of Limitations can never be so construed that a person claiming a life estate under a will shall enter and then say that such possession was unlawful, so as to give to his heir a right against a remainderman. That seems directly in point. It is good sense and good law.

All that we have to decide here is that Rebecca, having entered under the will, William, the remainderman under the same will, has a right to say that she and all those claiming through her are estopped from denying that the will was valid."

The cases, *Re Defoe* (1882), 2 O.R. 623, and *Bartels* v. *Bartels* (1877), 42 U.C.Q.B. 22, so far as they are relevant, add nothing new to the statement of Blackburn J., in the *Board* case. I think that the position of the defendant here in no way resembles the position of the grandson in that case. If it is borne in mind that the plaintiff claims a title in fee simple only if the defendant succeeds in destroying the validity of the contract under which she claims to have entered, the distinction between the case at bar and the *Board* case becomes apparent. It is one thing to say that Mrs. Ireland cannot deny the validity of the agreement under which she took possession so as to bar the claim of a person who would be entitled in remainder if the agreement were in truth valid; that is the *Board* case. It is a quite different thing to say that the defendant may by his conduct before trial deny the existence and validity of any such agreement and, when he has succeeded in having the Court declare the agreement invalid, or void, or non-existent, that he may then claim as against the plaintiff that he must be given all the rights to which he would have been entitled if he himself had not successfully shown that the alleged agreement in fact conferred no right: that is the defendant's contention. In effect, the defendant would be saying to the plaintiff, "You are estopped as against me from denying the validity of an agreement which in this very action I have succeeded in showing to be invalid." I should require the strongest authority to compel me to accede to such a proposition, which is not supported by any case cited by counsel before me....

Judgment for plaintiff.

[See also *Berube* v. *Cameron*, [1946] S.C.R.74, [1946] 1 D.L.R. 561 (payment by a tenant at will or from year to year of annual taxes (assessed against the registered owner) as a fluctuating rent, pursuant to an agreement with such owner, held to prevent the running of the Statute of Limitations).]

[Successive periods of "adverse" possession by different persons which together make up the required limitation period may be relied upon by the person in possession at the expiry of such period to extinguish the paper title: see *Robertson* v. *Tucker*, [1954] 2 D.L.R. 736, 34 M.P.R. 164 (N.B.C.A.).]

A.-G. OF CANADA v. KRAUSE. Ontario Court of Appeal. [1956] O.R. 675, 3 D.L.R. 2d 400

Appeal from a judgment of Kelly J. [1955] 5 D.L.R. 19, [1955] O.W.N. 827, dismissing an action for a declaration of title to and for possession of certain land.

The judgment of the Court was delivered by ROACH J. A.:... The plaintiff's claim was to recover possession of certain lands on Point Pelee in the Township of Mersea, in the County of Essex, which lands are described by metes and bounds in the statement of claim and are said to contain 1.6 acres more or less, and for a declaration that the plaintiff is the rightful owner thereof and that the defendant has no right, title or interest therein. The defendant pleaded that he and his predecessors have been in continuous and uninterrupted possession of part of the lands described in the statement of claim for a period in excess of 100 years and he makes no claim to the balance of those lands and he pleaded the *Nullum Tempus Act*, 1769 (Imp.), c. 16.

The defendant is a commercial fisherman residing on Point Pelee and fishing in Lake Erie. The lands to which he claims he has acquired title by possession are not described in his statement of defence by metes and bounds or otherwise than as "the property presently used by him in his fishing operations" (para. 2) and "that property occupied by him in his business comprising the parcel of land between his residence and the shore of Lake Erie having a frontage of approximately five hundred (500′) feet" (para. 6).

Point Pelee is a peninsula shaped like a long and narrow triangle running into Lake Erie from the north shore....

When a litigant asserts that as against the otherwise lawful owner he has title to land by possession the onus rests upon him to prove it. This requires that the land be described with reasonable certainty. From the pleadings, the admission filed and the evidence, all that can be said with respect to the location and area of the lands in dispute is that they consist of, first, the land upon which stand two buildings consisting of a storehouse 20 ft. by 60 ft. and an ice-house 18 ft. by 30 ft. in dimension and some undefined area of land surrounding those buildings, the whole having a frontage of 500 ft. approximately measured along some line which may be, for all that appears, the road shown on the plan, the shore-line, or, indeed, a line described in the evidence as a trail running from the road toward the beach and which is used by the public for access to the beach and by the defendant for access to those buildings. I rather suspect that the defendant, when he refers in his pleading to a frontage of 500 ft. approximately, means a frontage measured along the westerly side of the road shown in the plan. On that assumption where are the northerly and southerly boundaries of the parcel? I do not know.

Apart from the road there are not now and never have been any visible boundary-lines, either natural or man-made, of lands of which the defendant claims he has title and possession. To the north and to the south of the lands occupied by the buildings and the lands in front thereof there is a beach running for a great distance in both directions. It would, of course, be possible to determine by a survey the exact location of the buildings presently occupied by the defendant, but by reason of the paucity and vagueness of evidence no surveyor could run boundary-lines around any larger area and then say that they enclose the area to which the defendant has said in evidence that he has possession and title.

Counsel agreed that the *Nullum Tempus Act* applies to this case. Under that Act the right of the Crown is barred with respect to and the defendant is entitled to "have, hold and enjoy", as against the Crown, those lands, if any, that the defendant or those under whom he claims "have held or enjoyed" for the space of 60 years prior to the issue of the writ unless within that space of 60 years the Crown, by virtue of its right or title has been, in the words of the Act, "answered the rents", therof or "that the same have or shall have been duly in Charge, or stood insuper of Record."

The writ was issued on August 26, 1953. In order to succeed, the defendant would have to prove that he and those through whom he claims were in continuous, open or visible and notorious possession of whatever land he now claims for a period commencing not later than August, 26, 1893....

[The learned Judge then reviewed defendant's evidence which showed that the total area of land on which his present buildings stood had not continuously since 1893 been covered by a building. He then continued as follows:]

It is my opinion that the defendant has failed to prove that for a continuous period of 60 years prior to the issue of the writ, lands upon which the defendant's buildings now stand, and any definite area around them, had been in the continuous and exclusive possession of the defendant and those through whom he claims, so as to bar the Crown and to give to the defendant the right "to have, hold and enjoy" them against the Crown.

So far as the land upon which the present buildings stand is concerned, there has been adverse and continuous and exclusive possession since they were erected, but at the risk of repetition I point out that there is no evidence that prior to their erection there were any buildings continuously since August, 1893, on any part of the sites of the present buildings.

So far as the surrounding land to which the defendant now claims title is concerned, and excluding therefrom the part or parts, if any, on which a building or buildings from time to time stood, the evidence establishes no more than this, namely, that over the years dating back to 1893 and earlier, there have been in each year seasonal trespasses on the whole or parts thereof.

The occupation, the holding or enjoying contemplated by the *Nullum Tempus Act* and which would bar the Crown, is such as would constitute a civil possession against a subject owner: see the reasons of Duff J., as he then was, in *Hamilton* v. *The King* (1917), 35 D.L.R. 226, at p. 253, 54 S.C.R. 331 at p. 371. This means that throughout the statutory period as against the Crown, there must have been if the defendant is to succeed, (1) exclusive occupation in the physical sense, i.e., detention, and (2) the *animus possidendi.*

What constitutes exclusive possession? It must be actual possession, an occupation exclusive, continuous, open or visible and notorious. It must not be equivocal, occasional or for a special or temporary purpose. What the law requires is the ouster of the Crown: *Sherren* v. *Pearson* (1887), 14 S.C.R. 581....

At p. 595 Taschereau J. said this: "The effect to be given to repeated entries upon the land, or acts of user or possession, depend largely upon the nature of the property. What might be sufficient evidence in the case of cultivated lands to go to a jury would not constitute any evidence in those of wilderness lands. If the property is of a nature that cannot easily be protected against intrusions, mere acts of user by trespassers will not establish a right."

Applying what Taschereau J. there said to the instant case: Here was an open strip of beach several miles in length extending back from the water's edge to some higher land that was wooded and from that point the terrain extended out to the road to which I earlier made reference. That extensive strip of beach and higher land could not be easily protected against trespassers intruding thereon. There would be no practical way of doing so. What was more natural than that fishermen fishing the waters of Lake Erie on the west side of Point Pelee would during the fishing season as a matter of convenience, and unless there was objection from the Crown or its lessee—in this case, as will later appear, there was a lessee—use the beach for the purpose of landing thereon and departing therefrom, leaving excess equipment here and there along the beach, perhaps not more than once in the same spot, drying their nets and in the winter piling such of their equipment as they were willing to have exposed to the weather, some safe distance back from the water's edge and at a place which would be convenient when they would resume operations in the following spring? In doing those things fishermen would be using parts of this strip of beach for a temporary and special purpose, not with the intention of excluding others from the beach and not always using the same precise areas. Such acts, in my opinion, were mere seasonal acts of trespass and no more.

The instant case bears some resemblance in its facts to *McLean* v. *Wilson* (1916), 31 D.L.R. 260, 36 O.L.R. 610. In that case the defendant, a fisherman, built a shack near the shore of Lake Huron on land belonging to the plaintiff. In an action by the plaintiff to recover possession, the defendant alleged that for over 20 years he had continuous, peaceable and undisputed possession of the land on which the shack was erected, a right-of-way thereto from the water's edge and a right-of-way from a side-road to the shack. Writing the judgment of this Court Meredith C.J.O. at p. 263 said this: "I am also of opinion the appellant [defendant] failed to shew a possession of any part of the land of which possession is claimed, except that part of it which was occupied by the original shack or hut which he built, sufficient to extinguish the title of the respondent. Such use as he made of the strip of land between the road allowance and the water's edge of the lake was as a mere trespasser; and, being but a trespasser, it was necessary for him to shew pedal possession. Apart from the occupation of the site of the shack or hut, he went upon the land only for a few days in the spring or autumn, when he was engaged in fishing, and at all other times the true owner was, in the eye of the law, in possession. It is well settled that possession, in order to extinguish the title of the owner, must be actual, continuous, and visible. The appellant's possession was not of that character and indeed was not a possession at all, but his acts were but a series of successive trespasses with long periods of time between them".

I earlier made reference to a lessee of these lands from the Crown. These are the particulars. On April 6, 1885, the Crown granted to the South Essex Gun Club a lease for 21 years of the property known as the Naval Reserve containing 3, 190 acres. It is admitted that the lands thereby demised included the lands in question in this action. That lease was in effect until it was cancelled on December 5, 1902. The yearly rent thereby reserved was the sum of $400 and it was paid by the lessee to the Crown. If the Crown from time to time was not in actual possession of part of the lands in question in this action, the Crown was during the term of that lease being "answered the rents" therefor.

What is meant by being "answered the rents" within the meaning of the *Nullum Tempus Act*? In *A.-G. N.S.W.* v. *Love*, [1898] A.C. 679 at p. 686, it was held that: "If the Crown is not actually in possession, but that in the Crown's accounts some person is charged with the rent which they had not paid and still stand as a Crown debtor in the Crown books, and that condition of things has existed within the sixty years, the title by that condition of things, although the possession may have been for sixty years, was not adverse, because during that period something was payable to the Crown which had not been paid."

From time to time there would be rent unpaid by the South Essex Gun Club to the Crown but in the Crown's accounts that rent would be charged against the gun club until it was eventually paid and having been paid would later begin to accrue again. During the currency of that lease the Crown could not, in violation of its terms, grant any right of occupation to any other person.

The defendant purchased this fishery business and equipment and part of lot 15 [which included the land here in dispute] in December, 1937, from James E. and Harry McLellan. The sale of the equipment was under a conditional sales contract dated December 11, 1937. The equipment included the buildings on the land and in that contract they are described as "erected on Government lands adjacent to the fishery". The respondent must have known that those vendors were not then asserting any title to these lands.

On April 1, 1944, a building permit was issued to the defendant for the erection of a fish and storage building and on the same date a permit of occupation was granted to him to "occupy a site 40′ × 60′... situate a distance of thirty (30) rods westerly from the Main Drive and opposite Lot No. 15, according to the [McPhillips Plan]". That permit called for the payment of an annual fee and was subject to other terms therein stated. The fee was paid up to and including the year ending March 31, 1951. That permit specifically provided that the defendant accepted it on the terms therein contained and the defendant signed it. That permit provided that upon termination the defendant "shall, at the option of the Minister, remove or destroy without delay the improvements placed on the said lands and shall deliver up possession of the said lands to the Minister in a condition satisfactory to the Superintendent of the Park and should the permittee neglect or fail to do so within thirty days of the receipt of written notice from the Minister or his authorized representative, the Minister may accept such refusal or negligence of the permittee to remove such improvements as a forfeiture of all rights or claims to the improvements and the same may then be disposed of by the Minister in such a manner as he may consider advisable, and in the case of such action by the Minister the permittee shall have no right or claim for damages resulting therefrom."

In 1951 it came to the attention of officers of the National Parks Branch of the Department of Mines and Resources that the defendant was occupying land additional to that covered by the permit granted to him in 1944, including a second building. By a letter dated June 5, 1951, addressed to the defendant, that permit of occupation was cancelled as of

March 31, 1951, and a new licence of occupation of an area large enough to include the site of both the buildings together with an area sufficient for the storage of boats, nets and other equipment in season, was offered to the defendant, but the defendant refused it taking the position that he has taken in this action, namely, that he had acquired title by possession.

The acceptance by the respondent of the permit of occupation, dated April 1, 1944, and the payment of the annual fee thereunder must be construed as an acknowledgment by him to the Crown of the Crown's title to the lands therein described. It is unnecessary to consider what effect that acknowledgment and agreement to surrender would have had if as of that date the title of the Crown had been barred by the operation of the statute. I have already held that it was not and therefore the acknowlegdment was consistent with the fact.

The permit having been cancelled the Crown became entitled to possession of the lands described therein. There is no claim by the respondent in this action for relief from the forfeiture of the buildings thereon. Those buildings have a substantial value and it would be a severe hardship on the respondent if they were forfeited to the Crown. The Crown may still be willing to grant the respondent the more extensive permit which he earlier rejected, containing the permission to remove the buildings on the termination thereof....

Appeal allowed.

[The Crown is, of course, entitled to the benefit of the Statute of Limitations; see McQueen v. *The Queen* (1887), 16 S.C.R. 1.

Note the peculiar doctrine recognized only in Ontario under which a person in possession of Crown land for less than the limitation period nevertheless has standing to sue for a declaration that a patent of the land granted to another is void, whether for fraud or mistake or improvidence in granting it to someone other than the "squatter" who has cleared and cultivated the land. This doctrine is summarized by Masten J. in *Johnston* v. *Steacy*, decided in 1919, but reported in 59 O.L.R. 475, [1926] 4 D.L.R. 902, as follows: "A careful consideration of these cases has led me to the conclusion that as early as 1853 the Court of Chancery recognised the *locus standi* of complainants whose bill of complaint rested upon facts similar to those shewn in the present case. I understand the jurisdiction to be founded upon the deprivation of a right to present a claim to the Crown Lands Department where the plaintiff makes a *primâ facie* case shewing himself entitled to the benefit of the established custom in that Department of giving a preferential right to squatters. While this equity may perhaps be somewhat anomalous, it has been exercised for so long a time in the Province of Ontario that it has become a part of our law." The rule in the other provinces and in respect of federal Crown land does not recognize any such right in a squatter: see *Smith* v. *The King* (1908), 40 S.C.R. 258; *Farmer* v. *Livingstone* (1882), 8 S.C.R. 140.]

3. WHEN POSSESSION IS "ADVERSE"

PFLUG AND PFLUG v. COLLINS. Ontario High Court. [1952] O.R. 519, [1952] 3 D.L.R. 681

Land originally conveyed in 1929 to one C and his wife as tenants in common was sold by C to plaintiffs in 1941 under an instalment agreement and plaintiffs took possession. C's wife had died in 1935, survived by children. In 1947 plaintiffs agreed to sell the land to a third person and it was then discovered that an interest on devolution from the deceased wife belonged to her children. Plaintiffs paid the children off, allegedly on behalf of C, and thereafter sued C's estate (he having died) to recover the sums so paid. Defendant, C's administratrix, pleaded, *inter alia*, that the claims of the deceased wife's beneficiaries were statute-barred.

WELLS J.: ... The submission of the defendant, as I understand it, is that in 1947, when the true situation as to title was discovered by the plaintiffs, there had been a period of continuous possession, as against the children of the late Mary Closky, of more than 10 years and that the title of the children of Mary Closky had been extinguished by operation of the statute; in consequence, there was no necessity for obtaining any releases from them, that they had no title. As a result, any moneys paid over to them were paid over under a misapprehension as to the law governing the matter as to their interest in the property and, in consequence, there is now no liability for these moneys on the part of the administratrix of the Closky estate.

If, on the evidence, this defence were established, it would, I think, constitute a good answer to the plaintiffs' claim. It is clear from the evidence that when the moneys were paid they were paid to obtain a release of actual interests which the three children of Mary Closky had in the lands in question. That is the assumption on which the whole matter proceeded. The statute which governs the matter would appear to be s. 4 of the *Limitations Act*. R.S.O. 1937, c. 118 [R.S.O. 1950, c. 207, s. 4] which makes the period 10 years. It also appears by s. 5 that the rights of Mary Closky's children first accrued at the time of her death, and by s. 15 of the statute it is provided that at the determination of the period limited by the statute to any person for making an entry or distress, or bringing any action, the right and title of such person to the land for which such entry, distress, or action might have been brought within such period shall be extinguished. My attention was also drawn to s. 11 of the statute, which would seem to make it clear that Closky's possession as one tenant in common did not preserve the rights of his co-tenants....

This defence, of course, like any other defence, must be proved by those asserting it, and it may be pertinent to examine what the defendant has to establish to set up this defence effectively in answer to the plaintiffs' claim. She did not elect to adduce any evidence.

As Rinfret J. (as he than was) said in the case of *A.-G. Can.* v. *Cummings*, [1926] 1 D.L.R. 52, in giving the judgment of the Court: "It was for the respondents to show title. The Statute of Limitations is a defence, and the burden of proving such a possession as would bring it within the requisite statutory conditions fell upon the respondents."

Similarly, in the case of *Dom. Improvement & Dev. Co.* v. *Lally* (1911), 24 O.L.R. 115 at p. 118, speaking of the defendant, Garrow J. A. said: "The onus was of course wholly upon him to prove by satisfactory evidence such an occupation by him, to the exclusion of the plaintiffs and their predecessors, as would confer a title under the statute—an onus which, in my opinion, he has signally failed to satisfy."

As to the nature of the onus to be discharged, reference may be made to the decision of Osler J. A. in the case of *McIntyre* v. *Thompson* (1901), 1 O.L.R. 163 at pp. 166–7: "In the well-known case of *McConaghy* v. *Denmark* (1880), 4 S.C.R. 609, it was said by the Supreme Court that 'by a long unbroken chain of decisions extending over a period of upwards of forty years, it has been held by the Courts in Upper Canada that the possession which will be necessary to bar the title of the true owner must be an actual, constant, visible occupation by some person or persons ... to the exclusion of the true owner for the full period of twenty (now ten) years.' I agree with what is said by Street, J., in *Coffin* v. *North American Land Co.* (1891), 21 O.R. at p. 87, that since that decision the tendency has been more than ever in the direction of requiring satisfactory proof of a possession in all respects answering these conditions: *Harris* v. *Mudie* (1882), 7 A.R. 414; *Griffith* v. *Brown*, (1880) 5 A.R. 303. And in *Sherren* v. *Pearson* (1887), 14 S.C.R. 581, 585, it was again laid down by the Supreme Court that 'to enable the defendant to recover he must shew an actual possession, an occupation exclusive, continuous, open or visible and notorious for twenty (ten) years. It must not be equivocal, occasional, or for a special or temporary purpose'."

Further in this regard, reference may be made to the decision in *Harris* v. *Mudie* (1882), 7 O.A.R. 414.

Finally, summing the matter up, reference may be made to the judgment of the Divisional Court in the case of *Wright* v. *Olmstead* (1911), 3 O.W.N. 434 at p. 435, where Mulock C. J. (later C.J.O.) said: "To succeed, the plaintiff must shew: (a) actual possession for the statutory period by himself and those through whom he claims; (b) that such possession was with the intention of excluding from possession the owner or persons entitled to possession; and (c) discontinuance of possession for the statutory period by the defendant and all others, if any, entitled to possession. If he fails in any of these respects, he fails to establish a right to possession: *Marshall* v. *Smith*, [1895] 1 Ch. 641; *Littledale* v. *Liverpool College*, [1900] 1 Ch. 19 (C.A.)."

It would also appear to be clear that if the possession which is relied on under the statute is to extinguish the title of the owner, the possession which is relied on as establishing the statutory title must be continuous. This matter was discussed in the Nova Scotia case of *Handley* v. *Archibald* (1899), 30 S.C.R. 130, which dealt with a statute which, in respect of the matters under consideration, would seem to be in substantially the same form as our own statute. In the Supreme Court of Canada, the Chief Justice in commenting on the terms of 3 and 4 Wm. IV, c. 27 from which a great deal of our own statute was taken, had this to say, at p. 137:

"Whatever doubts there may have been having regard to the language of the Act, when the statute 3 & 4 Wm. 4 was first passed, it is now elementary law that the statute does not run against a party out of possession unless there is a person in possession: *Smith* v. *Lloyd*, 9 Ex. 562; *McDonnell* v. *Mc Kinty*, 10 Ir. L. R. 514; and further, if there has been a series of persons in possession for the statutory term between some of whom and their predecessors there has been no privity in such case the bar of the statute is complete, but if there has been any interval between the possession of such persons then inasmuch as during that interval the law refers the possession to the real owner having title, the benefit of the former possession of a precedent wrongdoer is lost to a trespasser who subsequently enters, in whose favour the statute consequently runs only from the date of his own entry. *The Trustees Agency Co.* v. *Short*, 13 App. Cas. 793. And this rule is not affected by the old common law principle that in case of disseisin there could be no remitter without actual entry inasmuch as the statute does not deal with feudal possession or seisin but with actual or constructive statutory possession as distinguished from seisin."

Reference may be also made to the decision of a Divisional Court in Ontario in the case of *Shunk* v. *Downey* (1909), 13 O.W.R. 398, where the judgment of the Court was given by Boyd C. That was a case where some wild, scrubby land was in question. Possession by those claiming title by virtue of the statute was intermittent, and in respect of this the Chancellor observed, at p. 401: "In the periodical yearly intervals recurring between the summer pasture and the getting of firewood in winter (in the early spring and the late fall), when the pedal possesion of the land would be vacant, the ownership and legal possession would revert to the true owner. This is putting it in the strongest way for the defendant, and treating the occupation of the land for wood and pasture purposes as adverse to the legal owner, or as interrupting his possession in point of law."

Later, he noted a similar decision in an Indian appeal in the Privy Council, saying:

"I would note that the same principle of decision which distinguishes Canadian authorities has been carried out in the Privy Council in an Indian appeal, *Radhamoni Debi* v. *Collector of Khulna*, L.R. 27 Ind. App. 136 (1900), of which it is enough to cite the head-note: 'To constitute a plaintiff's title by adverse possession, the possession required to be proved must be adequate in continuity, in publicity, and in extent, and is displaced by evidence of partial possession by the defendant.' The reasons are given by Lord Robertson, speaking for the Judicial Committee."

The Court of Appeal has also dealt with the matter in the case of *McDonald* v. *McDonald* (1890), 17 O.A.R. 192....

It would also seem to be clear that once a title is established under a statute and the right of a prior owner is extinguished, the title cannot be defeated by any subsequent acknowledgment by those who have acquired this statutory title. This point is dealt with by Davies J. in the case of *Hamilton* v. *The King* (1917), 35 D.L.R. 226 at p. 235, 54 S.C.R. 331 at p. 346:

"It seems clear under the decided cases of *Re Alison*, 11 Ch. D. 284, and *Sanders* v. *Sanders*, 19 Ch. D. 373, at p. 382, that where a statutory title has once been acquired under the Statute of Limitations it cannot be defeated by any subsequent acknowledgment or even by any subsequent payments of rent unless these continue for such a period as creates a new statutory title.

"The reasoning of the Judges in these two cases in appeal would indicate that the statutory title so gained was, as stated by Jessel, M.R., 'a complete title which extinguished the other'."

[The learned Judge then considered the evidence and concluded as follows:]

It seems to me that, interpreting the evidence as reasonably as one can in favour of Charles Closky, it has not been proved by the defendant that the possession of Charles Closky was of that continuous nature, to the exclusion of the children of Mary Closky which might give him a title as against them under the Statute of Limitations. This period was from February, 1935, down to October, 1941. On the basis of the authorities I have quoted, the type of possession enjoyed by Closky has not been shown to have been of the nature which would lay a foundation for a possessory title by reason of the statute. The period of occupation by the plaintiffs was only from November, 1941, and at the time the payments were made to the children of Mary Closky and releases obtained from them the 10 years required by the statute had not elapsed in so far as the possession of the plaintiffs was concerned, unless there could be added to their period of possession a period of possession by Closky sufficient to found a title under the statute. The evidence as to Closky's occupation and possession does not go this far, in my opinion. As a result, in the view I have taken of the evidence or lack of evidence, the defendant has not discharged the onus that is on her by showing that there was an actual possession for the statutory period against the children of Mary Closky by Charles Closky and those claiming under or through him. It has also not been shown that during the period prior to the sale to the plaintiffs all the children of Mary Closky were out of possession of the lands and premises.

Under these circumstances, therefore, I do not think the defence raised has been made out, and the plaintiffs must accordingly succeed....

Judgment for plaintiffs.

[The judgment of Wells J. was affirmed on appeal: [1953] 1 D.L.R. 841, [1953] O.W.N. 140 (C.A.). See also as to a contest between co-tenants, *Wade* v. *Wade* (1939), 14 M.P.R. 1 (N.B.); Cf. *Isaryk*, v. *Isaryk*, [1955] O.W.N. 487 referred to *supra*, at p. 388.

Is it possible for one tenant in common to establish a so-called "possessory" title in respect of the interest of another co-tenant and to the exclusion of the remaining co-tenants? See *Re Hipkiss*, [1956] O.W.N. 725.

Use of land by a lessee after the expiration of the lease will not extinguish the paper title if during the alleged running of the limitation period the land has been used concurrently with the lessee by the paper titleholder and his transferee: see *Dominion Atlantic Ry. Co.* v. *Halifax & South Western Ry. Co.*, [1947] S.C.R. 107, [1947] 1 D.L.R. 431.

Occupation under a servant of the paper titleholder (e.g. as a member of the servant's family) will not extinguish the paper title: see *National Trust Co.* v. *Lowthian*, [1943] O.W.N. 125.]

[C conveyed wild land in 1889 to K by absolute deed but as security only. In an action to redeem brought in 1910 K contended that C's right was statute-barred by reason of K's continued possession for the 20 year limitation period during which C made no payments of any kind. The only proof of possession by K was his payment of the taxes. *Held*, this was sufficient proof of possession in the circumstances and C's action failed: *Kirby* v. *Cowderoy* [1912] A.C. 599, 5 D.L.R. 675. See also *Bell and Maedel* v. *Bell and Bell* (1957), 9 D.L.R. 2d 767 (Ont.) where Ferguson J. said (at p. 770): "Payment of taxes by a person in possession is usually deemed to be evidence of adverse possession...." *Held*, on the evidence in the *Bell* case, payment of taxes was consistent with an alleged new agreement for remaining in possession with the titleholder's consent.]

[The common owner of two properties built a fence in 1913 between the respective houses on them, and in 1919 conveyed the westerly property to defendants' predecessor in title. The conveyance did not include all the land on the westerly side of the fence but left out a small triangular parcel. In 1934 plaintiffs purchased from the erstwhile common owner the easterly parcel, and by the conveyance obtained the paper title to the triangular parcel. Defendants' predecessor occupied this parcel along with the westerly land until the sale of such land to defendants in 1930. The latter then took possession of this whole area and were still in possession when action was brought in 1939. While the 10 year limitation period had not run from defendants' purchase, it was contended that the title of the common grantor to the triangular parcel had been extinguished prior to the grant to plaintiffs. However, there was evidence that when defendants purchased in 1930 they were told by their grantor-predecessor that he did not own the triangular parcel. The trial Judge held that this was relevant to the intent with which the parcel was used during the running of the limitation period from 1919 on, and he gave judgment for plaintiffs. *Held*, on appeal, the statement to defendants was immaterial in the circumstances and they were entitled to set up the Limitations Act: see *Taylor* v. *Townley*, [1942] 4 D.L.R. 478, [1942] O.W.N. 559 (C.A.). *Quaere*, whether this case does not discount the relevance of an intent to exclude the legal owner.]

MCGUGAN v. TURNER. Ontario High Court. [1948] O.R. 216

Action by executors of H for a declaration of their ownership of certain land. The land was part of a parcel which had been owned by H's father who had devised part to H and the other part to another son D, subject in both cases to a life estate in his widow. The father died in 1906 and his widow died in 1912. Neither H nor D lived on the land so devised to them but they delineated their portions in 1906 by blazed trees. It appeared, however, that this delineation and the acts of possession exercised in pursuance thereof was not in accordance with the descriptions in the conveyances made to the sons in 1906 by their father's executors. Defendants were successors in interest to D, and they contended that they held the title to some of the land now claimed by plaintiffs.

SMILY J.:... The defendants contend that any acts of ownership performed by either Hugh Turner or Daniel Turner and their successors in title, on the assumption that the lands were devised as contended by the plaintiffs, were performed in ignorance of the true and proper construction of the will of the father and of their respective rights and on an erroneous interpretation of such will, and therefore were not intended to, and do not, result in any alteration of the ownership as devised by such will, and that there has been no exclusive possession by either Hugh Turner or Daniel Turner, "in view of the facts the lands have been used in common by them both as pasturage".

As to the first contention, no authority was submitted on behalf of the defendants on the point, and I know of no principle which would support such contention. The matter is now governed by The Limitations Act, R.S.O. 1937, c. 118, and the relevant sections are 4 and 15. No exception is made in the statute, in the said sections or any other, of ignorance or mistake as to the true ownership. In fact it has been held that a common error by the owners in regard to the true line of division between their properties does not prevent the statute running where the statute does not require it to be shown that the possession was adverse and not with acquiescence or permission: see *Martin* v. *Weld et al.* (1860), 19 U.C.Q.B. 631 at 632. This, of course, applies to the present statute.

The defendants did not raise any question by reason of the lands not being enclosed, and, of course, it is well established that this is not necessary in such circumstances as are here present, where trees have been blazed and the boundaries have been defined: see *McGregor* v. *Keiller et al.* (1883), 9 O.R. 677.

In regard to the second contention of the defendants, that there has been no exclusive pos-sesssion by either of the brothers on the ground that the lands have been used in common by them both as pasturage, such use was by special agreement, each being allowed so many head of cattle. There was also an arrangement whereby a windmill and water-tank were built on the land between the two properties as divided by them, and this was said to be done in case it was later decided to fence the properties, or in case of dispute, and it would no doubt also serve in the event of a sale by one of the brothers of his portion. This arrangement and agreement, in my opinion, are a recognition by each of the brothers of ownership in the other of his particular portion and in effect amounts to a tenancy, or licence, in respect of the use by each brother of the other's portion, and as to any land which was used by Daniel Turner as a tenant of Hugh Turner the former would be estopped from disputing the latter's title.

In my opinion the acts of possession and ownership are sufficient to establish actual, exclusive, continuous, open, peaceable and undisputed possession of the land in question by the plaintiffs' predecessor in title, the late Hugh Turner, deceased....

It may be noted that the use made of these lands by Hugh Turner would appear to be a natural and ordinary use by an owner, as indicated by a similar use made by the defendants and their predecessors in title of their adjoining lands.

I am therefore of the opinion that the plaintiffs have established title by possession of the land in question....

Judgment for plaintiffs.

IREDALE v. LOUDON. Supreme Court of Canada. 1908. 40 S.C.R. 313

Appeal from a judgment of the Ontario Court of Appeal, 15 O. L. R. 286, reversing a judgment at trial, 14 O.L.R. 17, in favour of plaintiff. The latter was one of several co-owners of a two-storey building, and he occupied the second storey (consisting of a room) for business purposes. Access was by a stairway which led up from a landing inside the street door, and there was another door at the top of the stairway leading to the second storey room. In 1882 plaintiff sold his share in the property to his co-owners but he continued to use the room paying a mothly rent until 1890. Thereafter he remained in occupation without payment of rent, and in 1906 when defendant co-owners proposed to make alterations to the premises he sued, *inter alia*, to enjoin interference with his possession and use of the premises.

SIR CHARLES FITZPATRICK C. J.: I am in favour of allowing the appeal for the reasons given by Mr. Justice Duff.

DAVIES J.: I agree with the judgment of the trial judge in this case and think the appeal should be allowed and his judgment restored.

The questions to be determined are whether or not the evidence shewed the plaintiff to have had such an open and exclusive possession for such a length of time of the up-stairs flat of the building in dispute with the passage way leading exclusively to it as gave him a statutory title to this flat and passage way as against the defendants, and, if so, whether or not as against them he had a right to an injunction restraining them from carrying out their declared intention of pulling down the lower part of the house and so destroying the upper flat and stairway.

I am unable to draw any distinction between the possession of the plaintiff with respect to the upstairs rooms and the stairway....

I also agree on the legal aspect of the case with what I would gather to have been the conclusion of Mr. Justice Osler, though he expresses it in a guarded way, that the right of support by the lower story of the building which was essential to the continued existence of the plaintiff's acquired rights in the stairway and workshop was a proprietary right in his property rather than a positive easement.

I have read and carefully considered the numerous authorities cited by counsel having more or less a bearing upon the legal questions in dispute, and, while no case can be found exactly deciding that a title to a set of chambers or rooms or flat in a building not resting on the soil directly can be acquired or gained by possession under the Statute of Limitations, still there are so many dicta on the point by distinguished and learned judges that I have reached the conclusion that such a title to such a limited part of a building can be so acquired.

Of course the rights so acquired are subject to the conditions which limit all questions of rights by length of enjoyment only.

I did not understand it to be contended that a valid grant could not be made of an upper room or flat in a building which would give the grantee such a right as amounted to ownership of the space within the room or flat or part of the building granted with, as against the grantor, a right of support and a necessary right of passage to the premises.

It would seem clear from the authorities that such is the case, *Reilly* v. *Booth*, 44 Ch. D. 12.

Mr. McPherson did, however, as I understand his argument, contend that the statute did not operate to enable an estate to be acquired by possession in a part of a building not connected directly with the soil and that even if it did, the right to support was an easement not within the statute and could only be acquired by twenty years' possession, and not by twelve.

[The learned Judge then referred to the Statute of Limitations and continued as follows:]

Once that conclusion is reached, that an upper room or flat is land within the statute and capable of being acquired by possession for a period of twelve years, then it appears to me we are, *ex necessitate*, bound to hold that the right of support is a proprietary right passing with the premises acquired by possession, essential to its existence and inseparable from it. If it is not so but is on the contrary a positive easement within the thirty-fifth section, then it would not be acquired until twenty years had elapsed. The result would be that an exclusive right to the use of the rooms would have been acquired under the fourth section after twelve years' open and exclusive possession, but that such right would be made illusory and liable to be defeated at any time during the eight years between the twelve years and the twenty years by the owner, whose right to the rooms had been extinguished, pulling down the whole structure or otherwise withdrawing the support. I cannot think that a fair construction of the Act. The true construction of the two sections, I think, is to hold that the easements specially legislated for in the thirty-fifth section are positive and affirmative easements only. Otherwise we would have the strange anomaly created by two sections of the same statute, one section declaring that a title might be acquired to part of a building by twelve years of open exclusive possession, and the other that no title was acquired to that right of support which is essential to the former's existence, and that a subsequent owner whose title was extinguished to the house or part of the house above him could destroy it altogether by taking away that which had been its natural and necessary support during the whole period necessary to acquire the possessory title....

DUFF J.: It is, I think, too late to dispute the proposition that an upper room not resting directly upon the soil but supported entirely by the surrounding parts of a building might at common law be the subject of a feoffment and livery as a corporeal hereditament, that is to say, as land; Co. Litt, 48 b.; Sheppard's Touchstone 202; 1 Preston Estates 8, 506; *Yorkshire Fire & Life Ins. Co.* v. *Clayton*, 8 Q.B.D. 421; or that the exclusive use or possession of such a room may validly be granted for a limited or an unlimited time; *Reilly* v. *Booth*, 44 Ch. D. 12.

That such a room may be the subject of a tenancy at will or for a term is not of course to be questioned by anybody.

Now I cannot understand a tenancy of a corporeal hereditament under which the tenant does not get as against the landlord the exclusive possession of some defined or definable portion of land or of a building or other structure erected upon land. I am then, I must admit with great respect, unable to follow the argument that possession of an upper room under such a tenancy, does not involve a discontinuance of possession on part of the owner as well as such a possession by the tenant as may under the Statute of Limitations ripen into a possessory title. If you have a subject which is land and such a possession of that subject I think the ground is clear for the operation of the statute. This indeed seems to be involved in the enactments both of section 8, which provides that when a person is in possession of land as a tenant from year to year or other period without a lease in writing the right of the person entitled to the land subject to the tenancy shall be deemed to have first accrued for the purposes of the statute at the determination of the first of such periods, and of section 7, which contains a similar provision relating to land held under a tenancy at will. The legislature seems in these sections to have recognized expressly the possession of a tenant at will or from year to year as involving a discontinuance of possession within the meaning of the statute by the person entitled to the land subject to the tenancy, and I can find nothing in the statute which detracts from the force of this recognition.

The courts have had no difficulty—if we except the technical point suggested but rejected by Mellish L. J., in the case to which I am about to refer—in applying the statute to seams of coal, although unopened, held under a tenancy at will. In *Low Moore Co.* v. *Stanley Coal Co.* 34 L.T.N.S. 186, the Court of Appeal (Lord Cairns L. C., Lord Coleridge C.J. and Mellish L. J.) affirming the judgment of the Court of Exchequer (Bramwell, Pollock and Amphlett BB.) decided that a tenant at will of seven seams of coal who had entered upon the first two seams only, had for the purposes of the statute (by reason of his tenancy and his possession of the first two seams under it) possession of the remaining five seams, and that at the expiration of the statutory period he had acquired by virtue of that possession a possessory title. The scope of his tenancy was held for the purposes of the statute to define the scope of his possession. So here the plaintiff's tenancy is not disputed and once the subjects of that tenancy are determined the scope of his possession is for the same purposes fixed.

It is argued that here there can be no possession within the meaning of the statute, inasmuch as the existence of the plaintiff's shop and therefore his possession of it depends upon the physical support afforded by the subjacent parts of the structure. But that argument seems to prove far too much. The upper of two strata of soil, divided horizontally, depends for its maintenance upon the support of the lower, which may in turn depend upon the support of strata below. Can it be said that the upper stratum is, because of this physical dependence, incapable of a separate exclusive possession? I confess I cannot understand how that can be maintained; indeed the case I have just cited seems to be conclusive upon the point. The seams of coal in question there depended upon the support of the soil below, which remained in the possession of the owner; *Trustees, Executors and Agency Co.* v. *Short*, 13 App. Cas. 793; to the same extent as the maintenance of the plaintiff's shop depends upon the support it receives from the lower story....

But the plaintiff has failed to satisfy me that he has vested in him as the holder of a possessory title to the shop a right of support from the lower story. The Statute of Limitations, when the statutory conditions concerning possession are satisfied, bars the right of the owner of the paper title to make an entry or to bring an action for possession, and moreover extinguishes his title. The possession of the intruder is thus protected, but the statute does not profess to annex to a possessory title so acquired any incidental rights which rest only upon the implication of a grant or of what in law is the equivalent of a grant, and it is, I think, a settled rule that such rights cannot, as against a dispossessed owner, be derived from the statute. *Wilkes* v. *Greenway*, 6 Times L.R. 449.

Apart from such an implication has the owner of an upper story of a building any such right of support? I think he has none. So far as concerns this case the controversy whether such a right of support, when it exists, is properly described as an easement or as a right incident to the property in respect of which it is enjoyed is I think to quote Lord Blackburn in *Dalton* v. *Angus*, 6 App. Cas. 740, at page 809, "a question as to words rather than as to things." The substantial point to be determined here is whether it is a right which may arise from the natural situation of the property itself—(as the rights of a riparian proprietor in respect of the flow of a stream)—or one which must have its origin in a grant or the legal equivalent of a grant. That this last is so as regards the right of support for a building from the subjacent or adjacent soil is very clearly settled law, and I cannot resist the conclusion that the right in question here must stand upon the same footing. I venture with very great respect to say that I agree, in this, with the view expressed by Lord Selborne in *Dalton* v. *Angus*, at pages 793 and 794, and seemingly concurred in by Lord Watson (see p. 831).

It follows I think that the plaintiff is not entitled to prevent the defendants demolishing their part of the building merely because some part to which he has acquired a possessory title would thereby lose the support which it now receives; and I did not understand Mr. Tilley to argue that failing to establish a right of support he is on any other principle entitled to prevent the defendants destroying their part of the building.

The plaintiff is therefore not entitled to an injunction in the broad terms of the order granted by Mabee J., but he is I think entitled to an order restraining the defendants from interfering with so much of the structure as rests upon that part of the soil itself to which he had acquired a possessory title.

Appeal allowed.

[Idington and Maclennan JJ. dissented. On the question whether the so-called right of support was, in the circumstances, a proprietary interest other than an easement, see *Humphries* v. *Brogden* (1850), 12 Q.B. 739, 116 E.R. 1048; and *Howley Park Coal and Cannel Co.* v. *Londen & North Western Ry.*, [1913] A.C. 11, at p. 27.

In *Midland Railway Co.* v. *Wright*, [1901] 1 Ch. 738, a railway was the grantee of land under and through which it constructed a tunnel as part of the railway undertaking. Trustees under the will of the original vendor conveyed the land in 1859 to defendant's predecessor who took possession without notice of the previous sale, and he and his successors remained in possession of the surface from that time on. The surface occupiers authorized a telegraph company in 1859 to erect posts and pass telegraph wires over the land for an annual payment. The railway took over the telegraph company's works in 1868, and paid similarly for use of the surface until 1896. Thereafter action was brought to establish ownership of the surface and to prevent removal of the wires by defendant. *Held*, the action failed. Per Byrne J. (at p. 744): "It is sufficient for the purposes of the present case to say that I consider that the defendant and his predecessors in title have acquired by possession title to the surface of the land, with so much of what is beneath as is necessary for the enjoyment of it, subject to the right of the plaintiffs to the tunnel and to so much of the underlying and super-incumbent strata as is necessary for its due and proper enjoyment as and for a tunnel... I think the defendant has shewn title to the surface and to the space above."]

TURTA v. C.P.R. AND IMPERIAL OIL LTD. Alberta Appellate Division. [1953] 4 D.L.R. 87, 8 W.W.R. (N.S.) 609

Appeal from a judgment of Egbert J. (1952), 5 W.W.R. (N.S.) 529, declaring plaintiff's right to petroleum under certain land. The majority on appeal affirmed the trial judgment in favour of plaintiff, founding itself on the application of the Torrens system of land title registration in force in Alberta. It was thus unnecessary for the majority to consider any claim to the petroleum based on length of possession. However, this claim was considered by Clinton J. Ford J. A. who dissented from the majority view on the merits and held that plaintiff could not claim the petroleum under his certificate of title when it had been originally reserved but by error of the Registrar the reservation was omitted in a grant to the original transferee from the C.P.R.

The case is reproduced here only on the limitations point.

CLINTON J. FORD J. A. (dissenting):... The plaintiff claims to have acquired title to the petroleum by possession of the land continuously and exclusively for a period longer than 12 years, during which no entry or distress was made thereon, nor action brought to recover the land, and claims that by reason thereof any title of the Canadian Pacific Railway Co. thereto was extinguished by the *Real Property Limitation Act*, 1874 (Imp.), c. 57, which retained amongst others, s. 34 of the *Real Property Limitation Act*, 1833 (Imp.), c. 27, and was brought into force in the Province by s. 2 of Consolidated Ordinances, 1898; later under c. 90, R.S.A. 1922, and finally replaced by c. 8, Statutes of Alberta, 1935 (limiting the time to 10 years); now c. 133, R.S.A. 1942.

In view of what I have already held, it becomes necessary to consider this claim. There can be no doubt of the fact that the plaintiff has occupied the land as a farm continuously from the time of purchase of the respective halves until he transferred them to members of his family, and that the period of possession of the farm is longer than the period of limitation. If I understand the position taken by the plaintiff, it is that, if his title to the petroleum is not valid, he was, nevertheless, in possession under a colourable "title", with the result that the title of the Canadian Pacific Railway Co. to the petroleum is extinguished. The case of *Seddon* v. *Smith* (1877), 36 L.T. 168, was relied upon as well as other cases based upon it; also *Re Heier* (1952), 7 W.W.R. (N.S.) 385 at p. 389, to the effect that minerals are part of the land; and *Belize Estate & Produce Co.* v. *Quilter*, [1897] A.C. 367, for the law that a certificate of title of ownership under the statute is subject to the claim of a possessory title. It was also urged that if the plaintiff did not have actual possession of the minerals, he had constructive possession of them by virtue of possession of the surface under colour of title: *Wood* v. *LeBlanc* (1904), 34 S.C.R. 627.

It is to be observed that in the *Seddon* case the mines and minerals had not been excepted as was the petroleum in the case at bar. In my opinion, this is the real point of distinction. The exception and the reservation of mines and minerals create a separate estate in them as capable of tenure as that of the surface of the land.

In *M'Donnell* v. *M'Kinty* (1847), 10 Ir. L.R. 514 at p. 525, it was said by Blackburne C. J. in speaking of quarries excepted from title to the land: "The excepting of the quarries in the deed of 1738 severed them both as to estate and possession from the estate in possession of the lands; in both respects they became thereon separate and distinct; the grantor's estate and possession of the quarries remained unaffected; he retained them as he had them;

they were never out of him; *Cardigan* v. *Armytage*, 2 B. & Cress. 197 [107 E.R. 356]."

The case cited discussed the effect of an exception of a part of the thing granted (referring to Co. Litt, 47a.) and expresses the rule adopted by Blackburne C. J.

In *Farquharson* v. *Barnard Argue Roth Stearns Oil & Gas Co.* (1910), 22 O.L.R. 319 at p. 326, [aff'd 25 O.L.R. 93, which was aff'd by [1912] A.C. 864, 5 D.L.R. 297 (P.C.).] Boyd C. expressed a similar view, stating that the possession of the surface-owner is not adverse to or inconsistent with the possession in law of the subjacent proprietor, and refers to *Hodgkinson* v. *Fletcher* (1781), 3 Doug. K.B. 31, 99 E.R. 523.

I refer to the 5th edition of MacSwinney on Mines at p. 316, s. 1105, where it is stated: "Mere non-user by a mine-owner, no matter for how long a time, will not, however, give the surface owner a title to mines or quarries by prescription.... The Limitation Acts do not apply to the mere want of actual possession by the owner; but to cases where the owner has been out of possession, and some other person has been in possession."

One of the many cases cited as authority for the statement is *Trustees, Executors & Agency Co.* v. *Short* (1888), 13 App. Cas. 793 at p. 799, in which Lord Macnaghten says: "We entirely concur in the judgment of Blackburne, C. J., in *McDonnell* v. *McKinty*, 10 Ir. L.R. 514, and the principle on which it is founded."

Apart from authority, it would appear as if, in principle, that the owner of the land who excepts the mines and minerals on a transfer of the surface, should not be disentitled to them after the lapse of the prescribed time for acquisition of a title by possession by the transferee of the land. If so, the title to the minerals under a certificate, as now granted under the *Land Titles Act*, would appear to be lost after the present prescribed period of 10 years' possession by the surface owner has elapsed. This situation would result, since the possession, while it must be open, continuous and exclusive, need not be adverse: *Sinclair* v. *McLellan* (1919), 15 A.L.R. 86 at p. 89. The Statute of Limitation can hardly be construed to produce such a result, having regard to the purpose of excepting mines and minerals in the contract made by the parties.

See 22 Hals., 2nd ed., p. 573, para. 1252, "Effect of Non-user", where it is stated that "the grantor's title is not barred by the simple omission to exercise his right".

In my opinion, the argument as to possessory title in the plaintiff fails.

[The judgment of the majority in the Alberta Appellate Division was affirmed by a majority of the Supreme Court of Canada: [1954] S.C.R. 427, [1954] 3 D.L.R. 1. The Supreme Court held, *inter alia*, that plaintiff's action was one for recovery of land and was properly brought within the permitted 10 year period. Rand J. took a different view on the limitations question which he expressed as follows in the concluding part of his judgment: "The remaining question is whether the action is barred by the *Limitation of Actions Act*, R.S.A. 1942, c. 133. On the view which I have taken that the petroleum rights were acquired by Turta and the C.P.R. deprived of them, the possession, in the absence of physical workings and so far as such incorporeal rights can be the subject of possession, must be taken to be an incident of ownership. In the circumstances there has been no legal or physical disturbance of that possession; at the most, certain entries have been made on the certificate claiming rights which do not exist. The action is not, then, one to recover the land but to have those entries expunged and for a declaration of the plaintiff's interest. Since there has been no trespass and since the steps taken have, at the most, raised only a cloud upon the title, the question is whether an owner can be deprived of his land by the mere assertion on the register of unfounded claims. I know of no provision of law which, by the passage of time, raises any right based on that mode of protecting an interest; it would be a novel form of prescription which the law does not recognize. Its true interpretation is that of a continuing assertion against which proceedings of the nature here can be taken at any time, and no question of limitation arises."]

FINNEGAN v. DZUS. Ontario High Court. [1956] O.R. 69, 1 D.L.R. 2d 344

Action for a declaration of title to certain land and for possession. Plaintiff proved a title stemming from two uncles who were tenants in common. Defendants claimed by reason of vesting orders made in a partition action but plaintiff attacked the validity of the partition proceedings. The learned Judge reviewed this issue and concluded that the attack on the partition proceedings failed. However, he went on to deal with the position under the Limitations Act if it turned out he was wrong in his conclusion on the partition action.

Plaintiff's claim to part of the land in issue was based on the will of one uncle who devised to his brother for life, remainder to the plaintiff subject to a right in her mother to live on the land and to be supported therefrom for life. This uncle died in 1915, and the life tenant brother and plaintiff and her mother lived on the land until 1917 only when those claiming under the partition proceedings took and kept possession. The life tenant brother died in 1938. Plaintiff claimed through him certain other land which was the subject of a trust under which (as revised after Court proceedings) support for the settlor and for plaintiff's mother and for the survivor of them was to be provided out of the land and thereafter it was to be conveyed to plaintiff. The latter's mother died in the last week of 1943.

WELLS J.:... So far as the interest which the plaintiff took under the will of her uncle John Nisbet was concerned her right to the remainder arose in respect of the lands concerned in the partition action at the time of the death of her uncle James Nisbet, and in my opinion her interest would be extinguished by s. 6 (1) of the *Limitations Act*.

In respect of the plaintiff's interest which came to her through either the deed from her uncle James Nisbet to Hotte or the subsequent deed to Davis her right to an interest in these lands would be precisely as it would be in respect of the small parcel of 11 acres or 12.3 acres which I have not yet taken into consideration and I shall discuss her rights generally in respect of the larger portion of the lands and the smaller parcel together. In my view, however, it is not necessary to place, and I do not place, my judgment in respect of the lands sold in the partition action on the *Limitations Act*. I prefer to place it on the grounds I have previously mentioned, namely, that there was nothing improper in so far as this plaintiff is concerned in the way the actions were carried on, and on the ground that she is bound by the judgments in those actions and whatever title she had to the lands which were sold in the partition action was transferred by the Court to the purchasers on the judicial sale.

Now, in respect of the small parcel of 11 acres or 12.3 acres, while Sheehan undoubtedly went into possession of these lands at the time the vesting order of the 70-acre parcel was made to him, there is nothing to show in any of the proceedings proved before me that this smaller parcel was ever dealt with in the partition action and it would appear that Sheehan, in so far as this parcel was concerned, was a trespasser. Here again the plaintiff acquired title from two sources—as to a one-half interest, under the will of her uncle John Nisbet, the other, as I apprehend it, under the judgment and settlement effected by Sutherland J. from James Nisbet. For the reasons I have already expressed in respect of the other interests which she acquired from her uncle John Nisbet, her rights to recover the interest which she inherited from her uncle John Nisbet would now seem to me to have been extinguished by the operation of s. 6(1) of the *Limitations Act*, R.S.O. 1950, c. 207. That section was first passed by the Legislature in 1874 as c. 16, s. 3, following the enactment of s. 2 of the Imperial statute, 1874, c. 57, and in almost similar language....

In respect of the other half-interest, which she took by reason of the deed from her uncle James Nisbet to Hotte and its revision by the judgment of Sutherland J., the matter is not so clear and so free from difficulty. It may be that the plaintiff has not established any status at the present time to maintain her action in respect of this half-interest in the 11-acre parcel.

She has not obtained a conveyance from either Hotte or Davis, in one of whom the legal estate to the lands must have been vested, but disregarding this consideration, the plaintiff in my view is now precluded from asserting any estate in the half-interest which came to her from her uncle James Nisbet by reason of the application of s. 6 (1) of the *Limitations Act* which I have just quoted.

For reasons which were not explained when the deed was drawn rectifying the deed to Hotte and creating Davis a new trustee the 11-acre parcel was not included, but it was included in the original deed to Hotte and the failure of someone in carrying out the judgment to obey the order of the Court and to include it in the new deed to Davis is not such a failure as should be allowed to preclude this plaintiff from asserting her claim, if in fact she has one. All she got under the judgment of Sutherland J. was a right to a conveyance of the lands on the death of her uncle and her mother, whichever survived last.

It is argued very strenuously by Mr. Chitty that s. 6(1) has no application to this situation. As he stated in his argument: "The situation then as to the half-interest in the 12 acres under the settlement as declared by the judgment was that James had a life interest, on his death the remainder passed to the trustees of the settlement in trust to convey to the plaintiff on the death of Jane. The plaintiff's interest was not a remainder either on the death of James or of Jane, but a right to a conveyance on the death of the survivor. It is submitted, therefore, that whatever the plaintiff's estate was it was not a 'future estate or interest... expectant' on a prior estate within the wording of s. 6 (1) of the Limitations Act."

Some support is given to this view by the late Mr. E. D. Armour in his work on Real Property, 2nd ed., pp. 498 to 500. It would appear to me, however, that the view expressed by Lightwood on this section in his work on Possession of Land, 1894, pp. 212-3, substantially meets the objections raised by Mr. Armour. As he says: "Where the previous estate is extinguished by the operation of the statute, it appears to be doubtful whether the remainder is thereby accelerated so that a right of entry accrues to the remainderman, and the statute runs against him. (See Hayes' Conveyancing, I 269; 11 Jur. N.S., Part II., p. 151; Sol. Journ. p. 691.) Probably it would not be deemed to have determined for all purposes, but to be in effect transferred to the stranger in whose favour time has been running. In other words, he gains a possessory estate *pur autre vie.*"

This observation would seem to have some application to the present case for in respect of the lands, including the 11-acre parcel, James' rights would appear to have been extinguished by the operation of the statute some time in 1927 or 1928. James died in 1938 and Jane Murphy in 1943.

If the statute applies, as I think it does, then the plaintiff's estate or interest or right to a conveyance was extinguished in 1948. It is quite true that the interest that the present plaintiff took under the judgment of Sutherland J. was not a remainder in the true sense of the word, but I think it might properly be described as a future interest expectant on the execution of the prior trust for the maintenance of James Nisbet and Jane Murphy. All that this plaintiff had, as Mr. Chitty says, was a right to the execution of the trust in her favour by a conveyance to her by the trustee on the death of her uncle James and her mother Jane Murphy, and at the best it was an interest enforceable in a Court of equity if the trustee failed to complete the trust vested in him by the conveyance to the present plaintiff. Reference may be made also to the reasoning of the majority of the Court of Appeal in *Miller* v. *Collins*, [1896] 1 Ch. 573, particularly at p. 586.

Lewin on Trusts, 12th ed., p. 1109 states:

"Where there is a statutable bar at *law*, the same period was always, either by analogy or in obedience to the statute, adopted as a bar in *equity* in reference to equitable claims.

"The language of Lord Camden upon this subject has been admired as peculiarly energetic. 'As a Court of Equity' he said, 'has no legislative authority, it cannot properly define the time of bar by a *positive* rule to an hour, a minute, or a year: it is governed by circumstances. But *as often as Parliament has limited the time of actions and remedies to a certain period in legal proceedings, the Court of Chancery has adopted that rule, and applied it to similar cases in equity*; for when the legislature has fixed a time at *law*, it would be preposterous for *equity*, which by its own proper authority always maintained a limitation, to countenance *laches* beyond the period that *law* is confined to by Parliament; and therefore in all cases, *where the legal right has been barred by Parliament, the equitable right to the same thing has been concluded by the same bar*'."

And the learned author then goes on to discuss other authorities which I think emphasize this point of view at p. 1110, and finally at p. 1112 he says: "It results from the foregoing statements of the doctrine of the Court, that, as a general rule, where both *cestui que trust* and trustee are out of possession for the time prescribed by the statutes of limitation, the former suffers for the neglect of the latter and is barred."

In this case it is of course quite clear, as I have already stated, that in respect of the lands claimed by the plaintiff, and including this 11-acre parcel, neither the plaintiff, James Nisbet, her mother Jane Murphy through herself and finally by means of her statutory committee, or either of the trustees of James Nisbet, namely, Hotte or Davis, were in possession of any of these lands after the year 1917. Under these circumstances it would appear that the plaintiff's claim to this half-interest in the 11-acre parcel was, pursuant to s. 6 (1) of the *Limitations Act*, extinguished in the year 1948, 5 years after the death of her mother....

Action dismissed.

[T devised land to A for life, remainder to B. After T's death A and B joined in 1827 in a conveyance of the land to C. One D was in possession from 1832 during A's lifetime and remained in possession for a period sufficient to extinguish the title in fee simple of C if the limitation period ran from the time of the conveyance to him or from any earlier time. However, the limitation period had not run if calculated from the time of A's death to the institution of action by C. Result? See *Sladden* v. *Smith* (1858), 7 U.C.C.P. 74 (C.A.); and see ss. 5 and 6 of the Ontario Limitations Act, reproduced, *supra*, at pp. 617-618.

In *Stuart* v. *Taylor* (1914), 33 O.L.R. 20, 22 D.L.R. 282 (App. Div.), doubting *Sladden* v. *Smith*, *supra*, the material facts were as follows: T devised certain land to three of his sons, G, O and J, as tenants in common for life, there being an intestacy as to the remainder. T died in 1860, survived by seven children (including, G, O and J). The three life tenants took possession of the land which they divided and fenced into three portions. One D took possession of a southerly strip of this land and held it for some 40 years at the time of action brought. Of the three life tenants, O died first some 35 years before action, G died in 1911 and the last surviving life tenant, J, died in 1912. Among the questions raised in the case were (1) whether D's possession extinguished the interests of G, O and J and their successors, when G, O and J were not only life tenants under the will but reversioners in respect of the intestacy; and (2) whether D's possession extinguished the reversionary interests of the other four children, it being clear that these reversionary interests fell in with respect to the interest of each life tenant upon his death. How should the case be disposed of in the light of ss. 5(11) (12), 6(1) and 11 of the Ontario Limitations Act, *supra*?]

[In *Matheson* v. *Mitchell* (1918), 44 O.L.R. 619, aff'd 46 O.L.R. 546, 51 D.L.R. 477 (App. Div.), land had been devised in fee simple on condition subsequent and a breach of the condition had continued for more than 10 years before action brought by the testator's executor. *Held*, the limitation period ran from the time the condition was first broken and plaintiff was not entitled to say that he had "waived" the earlier breaches and was relying on recent breaches within the limitation period. *Quaere*, as to the result if there were merely intermittent breaches.]

[In *Thuresson* v. *Thuresson* (1901), 2 O.L.R. 637 (C.A.), rev'g 30 O.R. 504, T purchased land in 1870 and took title by a conveyance to F and M to such uses as T should by deed or will appoint and in default of and until such appointment to the use of F and M. After the purchase T put his mother in possession who with her two daughters remained in possession until her death in 1878 and thereafter the daughters continued in possession without payment of rent or acknowledgment of any kind. In 1892, T appointed the land to the use of B who next day reconveyed to T in fee simple. T died in 1894, having devised the land to plaintiffs who sued for its recovery in 1897. Plaintiffs relied on the deed of appointment as giving a new start to the Statute of Limitations but the trial Judge held that title had been extinguished in favour of the daughters before 1892. The Divisional Court reversed, holding in effect that while the limitation period may have run against F and M in respect of their fee, it did not run against the future interest reposed in T by way of a power of appointment, and this power (exercisable by T during his lifetime), when exercised, was effective to vest an estate in B and his assignees against which there had been no running of the limitation period. *Held*, on appeal, by a majority, since the limitation period had run against the fee of F and M there was nothing that could be revived by the exercise of the power, and hence plaintiffs' action was properly dismissed. Do you agree? Consider how far the case turned on the nature of a power of appointment and how far it turned on the express provisions of the governing limitations legislation.]

NOTE ON DISABILITIES

For a general discussion, see *Armour*, Real Property (1916, 2d ed.), pp. 504 ff.; *Weaver*, Limitations (1939), pp. 339 ff., which must be read subject to subsequent statutory changes.

Briefly, the disabilities generally applicable throughout the common law provinces are those of infancy and mental incompetency. Absence from the jurisdiction at the time a right of action accrues in respect of land still operates to extend the limitation period in Alberta, Nova Scotia, Prince Edward Island and Saskatchewan. Coverture remains a disability in the limitations legislation of British Columbia, Newfoundland and Nova Scotia. However, under the decision in *McDonald* v. *Rudderham* (1921), 54 N.S.R. 258, 56 D.L.R. 589 (C.A.) the enactment of Married Women's Property Acts has nullified the disability of coverture specified in limitations legislation. Imprisonment is not a disability in any common law province.

It should be noted that the disability provisions apply to extend the ordinary limitation period where the disability exists when the right of action accrues and not where it supervenes during the running of the period.

DOE v. JESSON. King's Bench. 1805. 6 East 80, 102 E.R. 1217

Action of ejectment. Thomas Jesson died in 1777, seised of certain land of which possession was taken by his brother who in turn gave possession to defendant. Deceased left a son John who was 10 years old at his death, and a daughter Frances who was about 6 years old when her father died. John put out to sea and was seen on his return from his first voyage about a year after his father's death. He went to sea again but was not heard of thereafter. Frances claimed through her brother in an action brought in 1804. The question was when the right of entry, against which the limitation period would run, accrued. There were continuing and successive disabilities of infancy of John and Frances, the latter coming of age in 1792.

The jury found a verdict for plaintiff and found also that John died abroad about 1785, 1786 or 1787 but not before. A motion was made to set aside the verdict and grant a new trial on the ground that Frances was at the most entitled to only 10 years for bringing her action after she came of age, even if she were not bound to make her entry within 10 years from the death of her brother.

LORD ELLENBOROUGH C. J.: The time allowed by the statute for making an entry might be indefinitely extended if the construction contended for by the plaintiff were to be admitted. There is no calculating how far it might be carried by parents and children dying under age, or continuing under other disabilities in succession. The brother John, through whom the lessor of the plaintiff, Frances, claims, being under the disability of nonage at the time of his father's death, when his title first accrued, and dying under that disability, it appears to me that the proviso in the second clause of the statute (where resort is to be had to it to extend the period for making an entry beyond the 20 years) required the lessor Frances, as heir to her brother, to make her entry within 10 years after his death: and that not having done so, this ejectment was brought too late. The word "death" in that clause must mean and refer to the death of the person to whom the right first accrued, and whose heir the claimant is: and the statute meant that the heir of every person, to which person a right of entry had accrued during any of the disabilities there stated, should have 10 years from the death of his ancestor, to whom the right first accrued during the period of disability, and who died under such a disability, (notwithstanding the 20 years from the first accruing of the title to the ancestor should have before expired). As to the period when the brother might be supposed to have died, according to the statute 19 Car. II, c. 6, with respect to leases dependent on lives, and also according to the statute of bigamy, 1 Jac. I, c. 11, the presumption of the duration of life, with respect to persons of whom no account can be given, ends at the expiration of seven years from the time when they were last known to be living. Therefore in the absence of all other evidence to shew that he was living at a later period there was fair ground for the jury to presume that he was dead at the end of seven years from the time when he went to sea on his second voyage, which seems to be the last account of him. That was about the year 1778, which would carry his death to about 1785.

LAWRENCE J.: Upon the death of the father Thomas Jesson, in 1777, the right descended to John, the son, then under age, who died under that disability. The lessor Frances is the heir of John; and the statute gives to the party to whom a right of entry accrues, and who is under a disability at the time, 10 years after the disability removed, notwithstanding the 20 years should have elapsed after his title first accrued; and to his heir the statute gives 10 years after the death of such party dying under the disability. Here more than 10 years had elapsed after the death of the brother before this ejectment was brought. It appears probable enough upon looking into the case of *Stawell* v. *Lord Zouch*, Plowd. 355, that the word death was introduced into the statute of James in order to obviate the difficulty which had arisen in that case upon the construction of the statute of fines, 4 H. VII, c. 24, for want of that word.

GROSE and LE BLANC, Justices, assenting.

Rule absolute.

4. EFFECT OF THE RUNNING OF THE LIMITATION PERIOD

GRAY v. RICHFORD AND MCCONNELL. Supreme Court of Canada. 1878. 2 S.C.R. 431

Appeal from a judgment of the Ontario Court of Appeal, 1 O.A.R. 112, making absolute a rule nisi for a new trial in an action of ejectment. Plaintiff claimed as devisee under the will of James Gray, and defendant R, besides denying plaintiff's title, claimed as lessee of M under a demise in 1870. Defendant M claimed title by length of possession and by deeds from John Gray to Adam Gray in 1862 and from Adam Gray to M in 1858, 1862 and 1868.

James Gray took possession of the land in 1830 and in 1847 his son Adam became his tenant at will. On his death in 1857 James Gray devised the land to his son John subject to an executory devise over to plaintiff on the death of John without leaving issue, an event which happened in 1874.

STRONG J.:... The defence of the Statute of Limitations has, in my judgment, entirely failed. Adam Gray went into possession as a tenant at will to his father in 1847, so that the Statute began to run in 1848, at the expiration of a year from the commencement of that tenancy. James Gray, the testator, died in 1857, having made the will already referred to. The Statute having begun to run in the lifetime of the testator, it is well settled, and beyond the reach of controversy, that the Plaintiff is not entitled to the protection accorded by the Statute to remainder-men, reversioners, and other owners of future estates, as he would have been if the Statute had only commenced to run after the testator's death. If, therefore, there had been nothing to interrupt the running of the Statute, a title under it would have been acquired by Adam Gray, or the Defendant, McConnell, in 1868. That there was such an interruption, however, seems very clear. In 1862, Adam Gray, being then in possession, took a conveyance from John Gray, the devisee in fee, subject to the gift over to the Plaintiff, under the will of James Gray.

The effect of this conveyance does not seem to have been pressed in the Court of Common Pleas, and in the Court of Appeal the learned Judges were equally divided on the question which arose upon it. It appears to me that from the date of this deed the Statute of Limitations was out of the question. I put the doctrine of estoppel aside, not because I do not entirely agree with Mr. Justice Moss and Mr. Justice Patterson in their well supported judgments on that point, but because I think the same conclusion is arrived at in a more simple way upon the Statute itself.

Mr. Justice Patterson points out that the aphorism that when the Statute once begins to run nothing stops it, has reference only to disabilities, and that it does not mean that if a man has been for nineteen years in tortious possession of an estate, and then gets a conveyance of the fee from the true owner, he can, after the lapse of a year, say, he is in with a good title under the Statute. The Statute of Limitations is, if I may be permitted to borrow from other systems of law terms more expressive than any which our own law is conversant with, a law of extinctive, not one of acquisitive prescription—in other words, the Statute operates to bar the right of the owner out of possession, not to confer title on the trespasser or disseisor in possession. From first to last the Statute of 4 Wm. 4 says not one word as to the acquisition of title by length of possession, though it does say that the title of the owner out of possession shall be extinguished, in which it differs from the Statute of James, which only barred the remedy by action, but its operation is by way of extinguishment of title only....

... In order that the Statute may operate against the owner out of possession, actual possession in fact in another is essential, in order that the rule of law which attributes a possession actually vacant to the person who has the legal title may be rendered inapplicable.

Then applying this view of the Statute to the facts before the Court on this Appeal, let me inquire who was the owner out of possession between the 31st of March, 1862, the date of the deed from John Gray to Adam Gray, and the 14th September, 1874, the day on which John Gray is proved to have died, to be affected by the Statute? Not John Gray, for he had conveyed to Adam, not the Plaintiff, for his possessory title had not accrued. There was, therefore, no one whom the Statute could affect. It had ceased to operate, for the possession was rightful from that date....

In short, the Statute has no application, except so long as the title and possession are separate; when the possession is in the rightful owner Statutes of Limitation are not required....

Appeal allowed.

[Taschereau and Fournier JJ. concurred. The concurring judgments of Ritchie J. and of Henry J. are omitted.

E, who purchased land under a deed to her in 1916, died intestate on August 1, 1928, survived by her husband, four children (defendants) and four grandchildren (plaintiffs) who were children of a son of E who predeceased her. On her death, her husband and her four children occupied the land. The husband died in 1937, leaving all his estate by will to defendants. Plaintiffs sued as heirs at law of E on March 1, 1944, claiming an interest in E's estate. Defendants pleaded, *inter alia*, the Statute of Limitations. One of defendants obtained administration of E's estate in 1938 and thereafter conveyed to himself and his co-defendants separate interests in the land. The deed to E had not been registered when she bought, but when this was discovered, it was registered on July 25, 1938 before administration was taken out. *Held*, by a majority, registration of the deed must be considered as an acknowledgment of E's title (before expiry of the limitation period) and gave a fresh start to the Statute of Limitations to the benefit of plaintiffs: see *Whitehead* v. *Whitehead*, [1946] 2 D.L.R. 737, [1946] O.W.N. 461 (C.A.), where Hogg J. A. dissented on this point because there was no evidence that the registration was done by defendants or on their instructions.]

[Ordinarily, extinction of another's title by length of possession is limited to the particular area of which possession has been enjoyed for the statutory period. The doctrine of adverse possession under "colour of title" has, however, permitted an occupant of part of another's land to enlarge his possessory claim constructively to include a larger area than that actually occupied where this area is delineated by the terms of a writing (e.g. a deed) which, while ostensibly giving title, is in truth ineffective although taken by the claimant in good faith. The doctrine was expounded in *Wood* v. *LeBlanc* (1904), 34 S.C.R. 627, at p. 635 by Davies J., where he said in part: "Now, in my judgment, the possession necessary under a colourable title to oust the title of the true owner must be just as open, actual, exclusive, continuous and notorious as when claimed without such colour, the only difference being that the actual possession of part is extended by construction to all the lands within the boundaries of the deed but only when and while there is that part occupation. And before it can be extended it must exist and is only extended by construction while it exists. It may be that a person with colourable title engaged in lumbering on land would be held while so engaged and in actual occupation of part to be in the constructive possession of all not actually adversely occupied even if that embraced some thousands of acres within the bounds of his deed. But it is clear to my mind that if and when such person withdraws from the possession of the part by ceasing to carry on the acts which gave him possession there he necessarily ceases to have constructive possession of the rest. His possession in other words must be an actual continuous possession, at least of part." See also *Allison* v. *David*, [1951] 1 D.L.R. 445 (N.S.); *Hudlin* v. *Ashley Colter Ltd.*, [1954] 2 D.L.R. 257, 33 M.P.R. 6 (N.B.C.A.).]

[Possession for the requisite limitation period will not be defeated by the subsequent registration of a deed from the former paper titleholder whose title has been extinguished by the adverse possession: see *Carson* v. *McMahon*, [1940] 4 D.L.R. 249, 15 M.P.R. 109 (N.B. C.A.). Contrast *McVity* v. *Tranouth*, [1908] A.C. 60, rev'g 36 S.C.R. 455, where T, holder in fee simple, conveyed to X who reconveyed to T and her husband as tenants in common. X registered the conveyance to him in 1891 but not the reconveyance. In 1895 X mortgaged to M who took without notice of the reconveyance and registered the mortgage deed. In 1902 T and her husband, who had been in possession since 1891, learned of X's fraud and when sued by M in 1903 asserted their possessory right. *Held*, M was entitled to succeed.]

[Where land subject to an easement or to a restrictive covenant is in possession of another for a period sufficient to extinguish the title of the fee simple holder, the possessor remains nonetheless subject to the easement or restrictive covenant because they are independent interests in third persons against which a limitation (prescriptive) period runs only when their enjoyment has been disturbed: see *Re Nisbet and Potts' Contract*, [1905] 1 Ch. 391, aff'd [1906] 1 Ch. 386 (C.A.). However, an adverse possessor is not as such liable on any covenant as if he were an assignee, unless estoppel can be invoked against him: see *Cheshire*, Modern Law of Real Property (1962, 9th ed.), pp. 436, 800.

While in a vendor and purchaser transaction a "possessory" title has been regarded as a good marketable title (see *In re Atkinson's and Horsell's Contract*, [1912] 2 Ch. 1 (C.A.); *Re Holmwood and Hall* (1927), 33 O.W.N. 146), what is the nature of the proof required to force such a title on the purchaser? See *Re Boustead and Warwick* (1887), 12 O.R. 488 and *Megarry and Wade*, Law of Real Property (1959, 2nd ed.), p. 980. But cf. *Ashe* v. *Hogan*, [1920] 1 Ir. R. 159.]

TAYLOR v. TWINBERROW. King's Bench. [1930] 2 K.B. 16

Appeal by defendant from an order for possession.

SCRUTTON L. J.:... The facts were as follows: In 1900 Mrs. Emma Ferguson, who was then the purchaser, granted a tenancy from year to year to Alfred Henry Taylor, father of H. W. Taylor, of a cottage and lands. A. H. Taylor allowed his brother-in-law, Twinberrow, to live in the cottage rent free from 1900, at first as his foreman then as a relative whom he was benefiting. In 1919 A. H. Taylor purchased the freehold from the executors of Emma Ferguson, and himself became the freeholder. In 1925 Mr. Twinberrow died, and his widow stayed on in the cottage rent free. In 1928 A. H. Taylor died, and his son H. W. Taylor under his will became freeholder of the cottage. The widow then claimed a title by adverse possession.

It was argued for her, as I understood the argument, that her husband was at first a tenant at will and that by virtue of s. 7 of the Real Property Limitation Act, 1833, time began to run against A. H. Taylor one year after the commencement of the tenancy, and therefore that in 1913 Twinberrow acquired a title against A.H. Taylor; that that title was the same title as Taylor had, a tenancy from year to year; that the merger of Taylor's title as tenant in his title as freeholder by purchase did not affect Twinberrow's title as tenant from year to year, which passed on his death to his widow; that there had never been any notice to determine that tenancy from year to year; and that consequently the widow remained in possession till a proper notice to terminate such a tenancy was given and expired.

The fallacy of this argument rests in my opinion in a misunderstanding of the legal effect of the expiry of the twelve years' adverse possession under s. 7 of the Act of 1833. It is treated as if it gave a title, whereas its effect is merely negative to destroy the power of the then tenant A. H. Taylor to claim as landlord against his sub-tenant in possession. It would not destroy the right of the freeholder, if Taylor's tenancy was determined, to eject the sub-tenant. The freeholder would not be in any way bound by the legal relations between tenant and sub-tenant after the expiry of the tenant's tenancy. That this is so appears to follow from the decision of the Court of Appeal in *Tichborne* v. *Weir* (1892), 67 L.T. 735. A freeholder in 1802 granted a lease to B.—a tenant—for eighty-nine years with a repairing covenant. B. equitably mortgaged the lease to G., who in 1836 entered into possession against B. and did nothing to acknowledge B.'s title for forty years, thereby as against B. obtaining a defence under the Statute of Limitations. G. and his subsequent assignee of his interest paid the rent named in B.'s lease to the freeholder, and in 1891, on the expiry of the term in the lease, delivered up the house to the freeholder, who sued the assignee on the repairing covenant. It was held by the Court of Appeal that the Statute of Limitations had not the operation of transferring to G. B. 's rights against and obligations to the landlord but only of extinguishing B.'s rights against G. "The statute," said Bowen L. J., "makes no transfer of any kind.... The most that can be said is that he [G.] acquired an absolute title to the land as against everybody but the landlord." (67 L.T. at p. 737). The result of this case is in my opinion correctly stated in Darby and Bosanquet's Statutes of Limitations, 2nd ed., p. 493, as follows: "It has been said that the effect of the statute is to execute a conveyance to the person in possession, and not only to extinguish the right of the former owner, but to transfer the legal fee simple. But the truer view is, that the operation of the statute in giving a title is merely negative; it extinguishes the right and title of the dispossessed owner, and leaves the occupant with a title gained by the fact of possession, and resting on the infirmity of the right of others to eject him"....

A further argument of the appellant was to this effect, that the decision in *Walter* v. *Yalden*, [1902] 2 K.B. 304, showed that a surrender by tenant to landlord did not defeat the rights of a sub-tenant who had acquired a right against his immediate landlord by virtue of the Statute of Limitations, and such a sub-tenant's right lasted as long as the original lease from landlord to tenant would have lasted but for the surrender, but that the statute did not begin to run against the landlord till that time. But, first, this decision shows that time did not begin against the landlord till 1919, the date of the merger, and had therefore not expired in 1929, when this action was brought; and secondly, while a surrender cannot affect the lawful title of an under-lessee, whose sub-lease must be properly determined by notice in a regular manner, because a surrender has only the same effect as an assignment (*Walter* v. *Yalden*; *Pleasant lessee of Hayton* v. *Benson* (1811) 14 East, 234), which would not destroy a sub-lease, there is no decision that merger resulting from the tenant's purchase of the landlord's reversion has any such effect. If the merger takes place the original lease is determined; there is no need to give six months' notice to terminate a tenancy from year to year. The new reversioner cannot give notice to himself as the old tenant; and, as has been seen, the sub-tenant has no term which requires such a notice to be given to him.

For these reasons the appeal fails and must be dismissed with costs....

Appeal dismissed.

[The concurring opinion of Lawrence L.J. is omitted.

T, a tenant under a lease from L, encroaches on land of a third person and enjoys it in conjunction with the demised premises for a period sufficient in other circumstances to extinguish the title of the fee simple holder. Subsequently, T purchases the fee in the demised premises only. Is he entitled to retain the encroachment? Would it make any difference if the encroachment was on land which was also owned by L? See *King* v. *Smith*, [1950] 1 All E.R. 553 (C.A.); and see the authorities cited in *Williams*, Canadian Law of Landlord and Tenant (1957, 3rd ed.), p. 541.

While as between a tenant and his landlord, the latter may be entitled to possession of any encroachment effected by the tenant, does it follow that the tenant or the landlord may assert either trespass or a possessory claim against the paper titleholder of the encroachment? See *Bruyea* v. *Rose* (1890), 19 O.R. 433.

In 1868 T orally let a farm to her son R at a yearly rent. R paid rent down to 1881 but thereafter remained in possession without payment of rent or acknowledgment of his mother's title. T died in 1899, and by her will she gave all her estate to her four children, directing that all money owing to her by any child, whether for rent or otherwise, should be taken into account in determining each child's share. *Held*, while R was entitled to hold the farm by reason of length of adverse possession, twelve years' rent should be deducted from his share of the estate: see *In re Jolly*, *Gathercole* v. *Norfolk*, [1900] 1 Ch. 292.]

[Land sold for unpaid taxes assessed against the paper titleholder had been occupied by another for a period prior to the tax sale sufficient to extinguish the paper title. *Held*, the effect of the applicable taxing legislation was to give the tax sale purchaser a good title and it was immaterial that he was in fact the previous paper titleholder: see *Soper* v. *Windsor* (1914), 32 O.L.R. 352, 22 D.L.R. 478 (App. Div.); *Stackhouse* v. *Wade* [1951] 1 D.L.R. 60, 26 M.P.R. 312 (N.B.C.A.). *Quaere*, whether legislation should be construed to defeat the possession of an occupier who has occupied for the limitation period prior to the tax sale deed. The tax sale may well interrupt the running of the limitation period if that period has not yet expired, but is not the situation different if the period has previously expired? See *Slaughter* v. *Taylor*, [1951] O.R. 821, [1951] 4 D.L.R. 697 (C.A.); cf. *Hovey* v. *Trafton*, [1952] 1 D.L.R. 63 (N.B.C.A.). In *McIntyre* v. *Haynes*, [1925] 2 D.L.R. 546, [1925] 1 W.W.R. 881, 35 B.C.R. 40 (C.A.), it was held that a tax sale did not interrupt the running of the limitation period, and where the period matured before the expiry of the redemption period and before the tax sale deed was given the occupier was entitled to resist the claim of the tax sale purchaser.

If, notwithstanding a tax sale, the previous owner remains in possession, the limitation period runs against the tax sale purchaser from the expiry of the redemption period: see *Smith* v. *Midland Ry.* (1883), 4 O.R. 494.]

INDEX

www.ingramcontent.com/pod-product-compliance
Lightning Source LLC
LaVergne TN
LVHW080153090826
844660LV00050B/1256

* 9 7 8 1 4 8 7 5 7 7 0 6 3 *